EVIDENCE

EVIDENCE
Text, Problems, and Cases

Fourth Edition

RONALD J. ALLEN
John Henry Wigmore Professor
Northwestern University School of Law

RICHARD B. KUHNS
Professor of Law
Washington University

ELEANOR SWIFT
Professor of Law
University of California at Berkeley School of Law

DAVID S. SCHWARTZ
Associate Professor of Law
University of Wisconsin Law School

PUBLISHERS

76 Ninth Avenue, New York, NY 10011
http://lawschool.aspenpublishers.com

Aspen Publishers
Attn: Permissions Department
76 Ninth Avenue, 7th Floor
New York, NY 10011-5201

Printed in the United States of America.

1 2 3 4 5 6 7 8 9 0

ISBN 0-7355-5622-9

Library of Congress Cataloging-in-Publication Data

Evidence : text, problems, and cases / Ronald J. Allen . . . [et al.]. — 4th ed.
   p. cm.
    Rev. ed. of: Evidence : text, problems, and cases / Ronald J. Allen,
Richard B. Kuhns, Eleanor Swift ; with the assistance of David S. Schwartz.
3rd ed. c2002.
    ISBN 0-7355-5622-9
    1. Evidence (Law) — United States I. Allen, Ronald J. (Ronald Jay),
1948- II. Allen, Ronald J. (Ronald Jay), 1948- Evidence.

KF8935.A83 2006
347.73′6 — dc22   2006005220

About Aspen Publishers

Aspen Publishers, headquartered in New York City, is a leading information provider for attorneys, business professionals, and law students. Written by preeminent authorities, our products consist of analytical and practical information covering both U.S. and international topics. We publish in the full range of formats, including updated manuals, books, periodicals, CDs, and online products.

Our proprietary content is complemented by 2,500 legal databases, containing over 11 million documents, available through our Loislaw division. Aspen Publishers also offers a wide range of topical legal and business databases linked to Loislaw's primary material. Our mission is to provide accurate, timely, and authoritative content in easily accessible formats, supported by unmatched customer care.

To order any Aspen Publishers title, go to *http://lawschool.aspenpublishers.com* or call 1-800-638-8437.

To reinstate your manual update service, call 1-800-638-8437.

For more information on Loislaw products, go to *www.loislaw.com* or call 1-800-364-2512.

For Customer Care issues, e-mail *CustomerCare@aspenpublishers.com*; call 1-800-234-1660; or fax 1-800-901-9075.

Aspen Publishers
a Wolters Kluwer business

SUMMARY
OF CONTENTS

Contents   ix
Preface   xlv
Acknowledgments   xlix
Introduction to the Study of Evidence   li
Special Notice on Citations   liii

Chapter One   The Case of People v. Johnson   1
Chapter Two   The Process of Proof: How Trials Are Structured   77
Chapter Three   Relevancy, Probative Value, and the Rule
                     403 Dangers   117
Chapter Four   Laying the Foundation for Proof   167
Chapter Five   The Character, Propensity, and Specific Acts Rules   227
Chapter Six   The Other Relevance Rules   321
Chapter Seven   The Impeachment and Rehabilitation of
                     Witnesses   351
Chapter Eight   The Hearsay Rule   413
Chapter Nine   Lay Opinions and Expert Witnesses   609
Chapter Ten   The Process of Proof in Civil and Criminal Cases:
                     Burdens of Proof, Judicial Summary and
                     Comment, and Presumptions   697
Chapter Eleven   Judicial Notice   765
Chapter Twelve   Privileges   787

Table of Cases   903
Table of Authorities   913
Index   925

SUMMARY
OF CONTENTS

Contents

Preface

Acknowledgments

Introduction to the Study of Evidence

Special Notice on Citations

Chapter One   The Case of People v. Johnson   1

Chapter Two   The Process of Proof: How Trials Are Structured

Chapter Three   Relevancy, Probative Value, and the Rule
                  of 403 Danger   71

Chapter Four   Laying the Foundation for Proof   161

Chapter Five   The Character, Propensity, and Specific Acts Rules   227

Chapter Six   The Other Relevance Rules   321

Chapter Seven   The Impeachment and Rehabilitation of
                  Witnesses   351

Chapter Eight   The Hearsay Rule   413

Chapter Nine   Lay Opinions and Expert Witness

Chapter Ten   The Process of Proof in Civil and Criminal Cases:
                  Burdens of Proof, Judicial Summaries and
                  Comment, and Presumptions   607

Chapter Eleven   Judicial Notice   765

Chapter Twelve   Privilege   781

Table of Cases   905

Table of Authorities

Index

CONTENTS

Preface   *xlv*
Acknowledgments   *xlix*
Introduction to the Study of Evidence   *li*
Special Notice on Citations   *liii*

CHAPTER ONE

THE CASE OF PEOPLE v. JOHNSON   1

A   The People of the State of California v. James Johnson   2
          Notes and Questions   75

CHAPTER TWO

THE PROCESS OF PROOF:
HOW TRIALS ARE STRUCTURED   77

A.   THE ADVERSARY SYSTEM   78
B.   THE ROLE OF THE TRIAL PARTICIPANTS   78
C.   THE STRUCTURE OF THE TRIAL   80
     1.   Pretrial Motions   80
     2.   Jury Selection   80
     3.   Preliminary Instructions   81
     4.   Opening Statements   81
     5.   Presentation of Evidence and the Burden of Production   82
          a.   The Order of the Parties' Presentation of Cases   82
          b.   The burden of Production   83

6.   Post-evidence Matters   84
7.   Closing Arguments   85
8.   Jury Instructions and the Burden of Persuasion   85
9.   Jury Deliberations and Verdict   86
10. Post-trial Motions   87

D. EXAMINATION OF WITNESSES AND FRE 611   88
1.   FRE 611   89
2.   Interpretation and Illustration of FRE 611(a) and (b)   89
     a. FRE 611(a): Breadth of the Court's Power   89
     b. Direct Examination   89
     c. FRE 611(b): The Scope of Cross-examination   90
     d. Redirect and Recross-examination   91
3.   Elaboration of FRE 611(a) and (b) and the
     Examination of Witnesses   91
     a. Direct Examination   91
     b. Cross-examination   92
          i.   Strategy and Goals of Cross-examination   93
          ii. Cross-examination Technique   93
     c. Direct Examination of "Adverse" and "Hostile"
         Witnesses   94
4.   Interpretation and Illustration of FRE 611(c): Leading
     Questions   95
5.   Elaboration of FRE 611(c) and Leading Questions   95
     a. What Is a Leading Question?   95
     b. Leading Questions: Tactical Considerations   97

E. OBJECTIONS AND PRESERVATION OF ERROR FOR
    APPEAL: FRE 103   97
1.   FRE 103   98
2.   Interpretation and Illustration of FRE 103(a) and (d):
     Objections, Offers of Proof, and Preservation of
     Evidentiary Issues for Appeal   98
3.   Elaboration of FRE 103(a)(1) and (2) and Objections   99
     a. Two Types of Objections   99
     b. Timing of Objections   101
     c. Stating the Objection   102
     d. Tactical Considerations   104
4.   Elaboration of FRE 103(a) and (d): Preservation of
     Error for Appellate Review   104
     a. Making the Record — in General   105
     b. Making the Record for Appeal of Evidentiary
         Rulings   106
     c. Standards of Appellate Review of Evidentiary
         Errors   106

F. REFLECTIONS ON NATURAL REASONING AND THE
    ADVERSARY SYSTEM   107
    1. The Adversary System Reconsidered   107
    2. Why Have Rules of Evidence?   109
    3. Natural Reasoning and the Trial Process   110
    4. The Behavior of Fact Finders   113
            Trial Objection Cheat Sheet   115

                            CHAPTER THREE
                        ─────────────────────

                    RELEVANCY, PROBATIVE VALUE,
                      AND THE RULE 403 DANGERS   117

A. RELEVANCY — THE BASIC CONCEPT   117
    1. FRE 401 and 402   118
    2. Interpretation and Illustration of FRE 401 and 402   118
        a. Relevant Evidence Is Offered to Prove a Fact of
            Consequence (Materiality)   119
        b. Relevant Evidence Must Make a Fact of Consequence
            More or Less Probable   121
            i.   Probability Is Determined from Knowledge
                  and Experience   121
            ii.   Relevancy Requires Reasonable Generalizations   122
            iii. FRE 401's Minimal Standard of "Any Tendency"   123
        c. Direct Versus Circumstantial Evidence   124
        d. Background Information   126
        e. Relevancy Is Not Sufficiency   126
    3. Elaboration of FRE 401 and 402   127
            Knapp v. State   127
            Notes and Questions   128
            Key Points   129
            Problems   129
    4. Reflection on the Requirement of Relevancy   132
B. PROBATIVE VALUE AND THE RULE 403 DANGERS   133
    1. FRE 403   134
    2. Interpretation and Illustration of FRE 403   134
        a. Probative Value   135
            i.   Strength of the Underlying Inferences   135
            ii.   Certainty of the Starting Point   136
            iii. Need   136
                  Note   137
        b. Rule 403 Dangers   137
            i.   Unfair Prejudice   138

			ii.	Confusion of the Issues	139
			iii.	Misleading the Jury	139
			iv.	Undue Delay, Waste of Time, and Needless Cumulative Evidence	140
		c.	Probative Value Substantially Outweighed by One of the FRE 403 Dangers		141
			i.	The Meaning of "Substantially Outweigh"	141
			ii.	The Effect of Limiting Instructions on the Balancing Process	142
				Notes and Questions	144
				Key Points	147
				Problems	147
	3.	Elaboration of FRE 403: Appellate Review of Judicial Discretion Under FRE 403			149
				United States v. Hitt	151
				Notes and Questions	154
				Old Chief v. United States	154
				Notes and Questions	158
				Problems	159
	4.	Reflection on Judicial Discretion to Admit and Exclude Evidence			160
C.	REFLECTION ON THE BASIC CONCEPT OF RELEVANCY				161

CHAPTER FOUR

LAYING THE FOUNDATION FOR PROOF   167

A.	LAYING THE FOUNDATION FOR WITNESSES			167
	1.	FRE 601		168
	2.	Interpretation and Illustration of FRE 601		168
	3.	Elaboration of FRE 601: Challenging a Witness's Mental Competency		169
			Key Points	171
	4.	FRE 602		171
	5.	Interpretation and Illustration of FRE 602		171
		a.	The Requirement of Personal Knowledge	171
		b.	The Requirement of Evidence Sufficient to Support a Finding	171
			Key Point	172
			Problems	173

B. THE AUTHENTICATION AND IDENTIFICATION OF
    EXHIBITS   173
    1. FRE 901   173
    2. Interpretation and Illustration of FRE 901   174
        a. What the Exhibit Is Claimed to Be   174
        b. The Requirement of Evidence Sufficient to
            Support a Finding   175
        c. FRE 901(b) Illustrates How to Produce Evidence
            Sufficient to Support a Finding   175
        d. Judicial Determinations of Sufficiency Under
            FRE 901(a)   176
        e. The Process of Laying the Foundation   177
    3. Elaboration of FRE 901: Real Evidence, Demonstrative
        and Computer-Generated Exhibits, Recordings and
        Written Documents   178
        a. Real Evidence   179
            i.   Identification Through a Readily Identifiable
                  Characteristic   179
            ii.   Identification Through Chain of Custody   180
            iii. Unchanged Condition Established Through
                  Chain of Custody   180
            iv.   Under FRE 901(a), the Complete Chain of
                  Custody Is Not Always Required   180
                  Key Points   182
                  Problems   183
        b. Demonstrative Exhibits   184
            i   Demonstrative Exhibits Must Assist the Trier
                  of Fact   184
            ii.   Application of FRE 403 to Demonstrative
                  Exhibits   184
        c. Demonstrations and Experiments in Court   185
        d. Recorded and Computer-Generated Reenactments,
            Animations, and Simulations of Events   185
                  Key Points   186
                  Problems   187
        e. Recordings   187
            i.   Satisfying the FRE 901 Foundation with
                  a Percipient Witness   187
            ii.   "Silent Witness" — Satisfying the FRE 901
                  Foundation Without a Percipient Witness   188
            iii. Application of FRE 403 to Recordings   189
                  Key Points   189
                  Problems   190
        f. Written Documents   191

			i.	Signature	191
			ii.	Contents and Other Circumstances	191
			iii.	Ancient Documents	192
			iv.	Electronic Writings	192
				Key Point	194
				Problems	194
		g.	FRE 901 Provides Flexibility in Application		195
	4.	FRE 902: Written Documents That Are Self-authenticating			195
		a.	FRE 902		195
		b.	Interpretation of FRE 902		196
			Key Point		198
			Problems		198
C.	THE BEST EVIDENCE RULE				198
	1.	FRE 1001, 1002, 1003, 1004, 1005, 1006, and 1007			198
	2.	Interpretation and Illustration of FRE 1001, 1002, 1003, 1004, 1005, 1006, and 1007			200
		a.	Summary of the Basic Principles of the Best Evidence Rule		200
			i.	FRE 1002	200
			ii.	FRE 1003	200
			iii.	FRE 1004	201
			iv.	FRE 1006	202
		b.	Policies Underlying the Best Evidence Rule		202
			Seiler v. Lucasfilm, LTD.		202
			Problems		205
	3.	Elaboration of FRE 1002 and 1006			205
		a.	When Is a Writing Offered to Prove Its Own Content Under FRE 1002?		205
			i.	The Content of the Writing, Recording, or Photograph Is a Fact of Independent Legal Significance	205
			ii.	The Writing Recording, or Photograph Is Used to Prove an Event	205
			iii.	Facts About the Writing Are Not Its "Content"	206
		b.	Types of Summaries and Rule 1006		207
			i.	Voluminous Documents Underlying a Summary Must Be Admissible, But Need Not Be Admitted at Trial	207
			ii.	Illustrative Aids	207
			iii.	Analytic Summaries	207
				Key Points	208
				Problems	208

	4.	FRE 1008		210
	5.	Interpretation and Illustration of FRE 1008		210
		Notes		212
		Key Points		213
		Problem		213
D.	JUDICIAL FACTFINDING UNDER FRE 104			213
	1.	FRE 104		214
	2.	Interpretation and Illustration of FRE 104		214
		a.	Questions of Admissibility Generally	214
		b.	Judicial Fact Finding under FRE 104(a)	215
		C.	The Process of Decision Under FRE 104(a)	216
			Note	216
			Key Points	217
			Problem	217
E.	FRE 104, CONDITIONAL ADMISSIBILITY, AND THE PROBLEM OF CONDITIONAL RELEVANCY			218
	1.	Interpretation and Illustration of FRE 104(b)		218
		a.	Conditional Admissibility	218
		b.	The Problem of Conditional Relevancy: The "Sufficiency" Standard of Proof in FRE 104(b)	219
	2.	Elaboration of FRE 104(b): The Rule in Practice		221
		Notes and Questions		222
		Key Points		224
		Problems		224

CHAPTER FIVE

THE CHARACTER, PROPENSITY, AND SPECIFIC ACTS RULES

		THE CHARACTER, PROPENSITY, AND SPECIFIC ACTS RULES		227
A.	THE RELEVANCE OF CHARACTER EVIDENCE TO PROVE CONDUCT ON A PARTICULAR OCCASION			227
B.	GENERAL PROHIBITION ON USE OF CHARACTER AND "PAST SPECIFIC ACTS" EVIDENCE TO PROVE CONDUCT ON A PARTICULAR OCCASION			230
	1.	FRE 404 and 405		230
	2.	Interpretation and Illustration of FRE 404(a) and (b)		230
	3.	Elaboration of the FRE 404(a) and 404(b) character and specific acts prohibitions		232
		a.	The Rationale for Restricting Evidence of a Person's Character	232
			i. Weakness of the Propensity Inference	232
			ii. Low Probative Value of the Evidence to Prove Character	233

		iii.	Diversion from Main Issues	233
		iv.	Bad Person Prejudice	233
	b.	Exceptions to the FRE 404(b) Prohibition Against the Use of Specific Acts		234
		Key Points		234
		Problems		235

C. THE ADMISSIBILITY OF SPECIFIC ACTS THAT ARE DEEMED RELEVANT WITHOUT A CHARACTER INFERENCE — 236

1. Interpretation and Illustration of the Second Sentence of FRE 404(b) — 236
2. Elaboration of the Second Sentence of FRE 404(b)` — 237
   a. The Permissible Uses of Specific Acts Evidence — 237
      i. Evidence that is essential to the narrative of the proponent's case — 238
      ii. Evidence showing relevant states of mind — 238
      iii. Evidence showing identity — 239
   b. Preliminary Factfinding with Respect to Whether the Person in Question Committed the Act — 239
   c. Probative Value and Prejudice Generally — 240
      Key Points — 241
      Problems — 241
3. Further Elaboration of the Second Sentence of FRE 404(b) — 244
   a. The problem of "res gestae" — 244
   b. The Problem of Specific Acts Evidence to Prove Intent — 245
   c. The Intent/Specific Acts Problem where Intent Is Not Disputed — 245
      i. The Argument for Exclusion — 246
      ii. The Impact of Old Chief — 246
   d. Past "Accidents" or "Coincidences" and the Anticoincidence Theory — 247
   e. Modus Operandi and the Character Inference — 249
      Key Points — 250
      Problems — 250

D. REFLECTION ON CHARACTER, PROPENSITY, AND SPECIFIC ACTS EVIDENCE — 251

1. The Distinction Between What FRE 404(b) Prohibits and Permits — 251
   RICHARD B. KUHNS, THE PROPENSITY TO MISUNDERSTAND THE CHARACTER OF SPECIFIC ACTS EVIDENCE — 253
2. Approaches to the Admissibility of Specific Acts Evidence — 254
3. Specific Acts Evidence: Limiting Instructions and Closing Argument — 256

E. HABIT AND ROUTINE PRACTICE   257
    1. FRE 406   257
    2. Interpretation and Illustration of FRE 406   257
        a. The Importance of Habit and Routine Practice
            Evidence   258
        b. Methods of Proving Habit and Routine Practice   258
        c. The Distinction Between Habit and Character   259
        d. Judicial Fact-finding on the Question of Habit   260
    3. Elaboration of FRE 406   260
        a. The Rationale for Permitting Habit and Routine
            Practice Evidence   260
        b. The Strategy for Distinguishing Between Habit and
            Character   261
        c. A Particular Application of the Character/Habit
            Distinction: Drinking "Habits"   262
        d. Evidence of Custom or Routine Practice of an
            Organization   262
                Key Points   264
                Problems   264
F. SIMILAR HAPPENINGS   266
    1. No Specific Federal Rule for Similar Happenings   267
    2. Similar Happenings, Character, and Habit Evidence Compared   267
    3. The Approach to the Admissibility of Similar Happenings   268
    4. The Application of FRE 403 to Similar Happenings
        Evidence in Practice   269
    5. Similar Happenings Offered to Show an Institutional
        Policy or Practice   270
    6. Evidence of Similar Nonhappenings   270
                Key Points   270
                Problems   271
G. EXCEPTIONS TO THE PROHIBITION ON USE OF
    CHARACTER TO PROVE CONDUCT ON A PARTICULAR
    OCCASION   273
    1. Interpretation and Illustration of FRE 404(a)(1)-(3)   273
        a. FRE 404(a)(1) and (2): A Criminal Defendant's Right
            to Open the Door to Character Evidence   273
        b. FRE 404(a)(1) and (2): The Prosecution's Right to
            Respond to a Defendant's Character Evidence   274
        c. FRE 404(a)(2): The Prosecution's Right to Use
            Character Evidence to Respond to Defense Attacks on
            the Victim's Conduct   274
        d. The FRE 404(a) Requirement of Pertinence   275
        e. FRE 404(a)(3): The Character of Witnesses   275
    3. Elaboration of the FRE 404(a)(1) and (2) Exceptions   276

a. The Relevance of Character Evidence in People v.
   Johnson   276

b. The Rationale for the FRE 404(a)(1) and (2)
   Exceptions   276

c. Evidence of Character in Civil Actions   279
   Key Points   280

4. Interpretation and Illustration of FRE 404(b) and 405(a):
   How Character is Proven
      Problems   281

5. Elaboration of the Permissible Methods of Proving a
   Person's Character to Show Action in Conformity with
   Character   283

a. The Prohibition Against the Use of Specific Acts   283

b. The Probative Value of Opinion and Reputation
   Evidence to Prove Character   283

c. Reputation Evidence Versus Opinion Evidence   284
   Key Points   285

d. The Cross-examination of Character Witnesses   285

   i. The Relevance of the Specific Acts Inquiries   285

   ii. The Prejudicial Impact of Specific Acts
      Questions   285

   iii. The Relationship Between the Character Trait
      and the Specific Acts Inquiries   286

   iv. The Character Witness's Likely Knowledge of the
      Specific Act   287

   v. The Cross-examiner's Reasonable Belief that the
      Act Occurred   287

   vi. Acts, Arrests, and Convictions   288

   vii. The Form of the Questions on Cross-examination   288

e. Limitations on the Use of Character Evidence in
   Practice   289

   i. The inherent weakness of good character
      evidence   289

   ii. The Potential Unfairness of FRE 405   289
      Key Points   290
      Problems   290

H. EVIDENCE OF A PERSON'S CHARACTER WHEN
CHARACTER IS AN ESSENTIAL ELEMENT OF A CLAIM
OR DEFENSE   291

1. Interpretation and Illustration of FRE 405(b)   292

2. Elaboration of FRE 405(b)   292

a. In general   292

b. Reputation versus character in defamation cases   293
   Key Point   294

		Problems	294
I.		EVIDENCE OF SEXUAL ASSAULT AND CHILD MOLESTATION	295
	1.	FRE 413-415	296
	2.	Interpretation and Illustration of FRE 413-415	296
		a. The Relationship Between FRE 413-415 and Other Rules of Evidence	296
		i. FRE 413-415 and FRE 404	296
		ii. FRE 413-415 and FRE 403	297
		iii. FRE 413-415 and Other Rules of Evidence	297
		b. FRE 413-415 and Preliminary Factfinding	298
		c. The Broad Definition of "Offense of Sexual Assault"	298
		d. The Meaning of "Without Consent" in FRE 413(d)(2) and (3)	298
	3.	Elaboration of FRE 413-415	299
		a. The Extent to Which FRE 413-415 Change the Law of Evidence	299
		i. Limiting Instructions and Closing Argument	299
		ii. Previously Inadmissible Character Evidence	299
		iii. The Application of FRE 403 to Previously Inadmissible Character Evidence	299
		iv. The Results of FRE 403 Balancing: Acquaintance Rape, Stranger Rape, Child Molestation, and Sexual Harassment	301
		b. The Underlying Rationale for the New Rules	302
		i. Unfair Prejudice	302
		ii. Probative Value and Recidivism	302
		iii. A Contextual Assessment of Probative Value	303
		c. The Significance of FRE 413-415 to Federal Litigation	304
		Key Points	305
		Problems	305
J.		EVIDENCE OF AN ALLEGED VICTIM'S PAST SEXUAL BEHAVIOR OR DISPOSITION IN SEX OFFENSE CASES	306
	1.	FRE 412	307
	2.	Interpretation and Illustration of FRE 412	307
		a. The Relevance of an Alleged Victim's Sexual Behavior or Disposition to Prove Conduct	308
		b. The Underlying Propensity Theory	308
		c. The Scope of FRE 412	309
		i. The Meaning of "Other Sexual Behavior" and "Sexual Predisposition"	309
		ii. The Applicability of FRE412 When the Issue Is the Victim's Behavior on a Particular Occasion	309

	iii.	The Applicability of FRE 412 in Other Contexts	310
	iv.	Hostile Work Environment Cases	310
	v.	The Admissibility of "Other Sexual Behavior" and "Sexual Predisposition" Evidence in Civil Cases	311
	vi.	The Admissibility of "Other Sexual Behavior" and "Sexual Predisposition" Evidence in Criminal Cases	311
	vii.	The Notice Requirement	312

3. Elaboration of FRE 412 — 312

a. The Rationale for a Rule Excluding Evidence of Prior Sexual Behavior and Sexual Predisposition — 312

b. FRE 412 and the Constitutional Rights to Present Evidence and to Confront and Cross-examine Witnesses — 313

    i. Chambers v. Mississippi — 313

    ii. Davis v. Alaska — 314

    iii. Olden v. Kentucky — 315

    iv. The Implications of Chambers, Davis, and Olden for Rape Shield Provisions — 316

c. Two Approaches to the Exclusion of Other Sexual Behavior and Sexual Predisposition Evidence — 316

d. Rape Shield Rules and the Defendant's Right to Testify — 317

e. FRE 412 and Discovery in Civil Cases — 317

    Key Points — 318

    Problems — 318

CHAPTER SIX

THE OTHER RELEVANCE RULES — 321

A. INADMISSIBLE TO PROVE "NEGLIGENCE," "CULPABLE CONDUCT," OR "LIABILITY" — 321

1. FRE 407 — 322

2. Interpretation and Illustration of FRE 407 — 322

a. The Exclusionary Mandate — 322

    i. The Inference of Negligence or Culpable Conduct — 322

    ii. Products Liability Actions — 322

    iii. Activities That May Be Subsequent Remedial Measures — 324

    iv. The Effectiveness of the Remedial Action — 324

    v. The Timing of the Remedial Action — 324

    vi. Remedial Action Taken Prior to Plaintiff's Injury and FRE 403 — 325

        b. Permissible Uses of Subsequent Remedial Measure Evidence   325

        c. The "If Controverted" Requirement   326

        d. The Relationship Between FRE 407 and FRE 403   326

   3. Elaboration of FRE 407   327

        a. The Rationale for FRE 407 and the Other Inadmissible to Prove Negligence or Culpable Conduct Rules   327

           i. Low Probative Value   327

           ii. Countervailing FRE 403 Factors   327

           iii. Not Discouraging Desirable Conduct   327

           iv. Not Punishing Desirable Conduct   328

        b. Subsequent Remedial Measures Taken by Third Persons   328

           Key Points   328

           Problems   328

   3. FRE 408   329

   4. Interpretation and Illustration of FRE 408   330

        a. The Exclusionary Mandate; Permissible Uses; FRE 403   330

        b. Conduct or Statements Made During Negotiations   331

        c. Compromise Negotiations and Discovery   332

        d. The Attempt to Resolve a Disputed Claim Requirement   332

        e. The Applicability of FRE 408 to Criminal Cases   333

        f. The Party's Own Offer to Compromise   334

        g. Compromises and Offers of Compromises by Third Persons   334

   5. Elaboration of FRE 408   335

   6. FRE 409   335

   7. Interpretation and Illustration of FRE 409   335

        a. The Exclusionary Mandate   335

        b. The Admissibility of Statements Made in Conjunction with Medical and Similar Payments   336

        c. The Question Whether FRE 409 Permits Evidence of Payment for Purposes Other than to Show Liability   336

        d. The Question What Constitutes a "Similar" Expense   336

   8. FRE 411   337

   9. Interpretation and Illustration of FRE 411   337

        a. The Exclusionary Mandate   337

        b. The Permissible Uses of Evidence of Liability Insurance   337

Key Points	338
Problems	338
Notes and Questions	340

B. REFLECTION ON THE "INADMISSIBLE TO PROVE
    NEGLIGENCE" RULES   342
C. WITHDRAWN GUILTY PLEAS, PLEAS OF NO CONTEST,
    AND OFFERS TO PLEAD GUILTY   343
    1. FRE 410   343
    2. Interpretation and Illustration of FRE 410   343
        a. Withdrawn Guilty Pleas   343
        b. Pleas of No Contest   344
        c. Statements Made in Conjunction with the Process
            of Making and Negotiating Pleas   344
        d. The Scope of FRE 410(4)   345
        e. The Exceptions to FRE 410(3) and (4)   346
        f. Waiver of FRE 410's Exclusionary Mandate   346
            Key Points   347
            Problems   347
D. "FIGHTING FIRE WITH FIRE" — THE DOCTRINE OF
    CURATIVE ADMISSIBILITY   348
            Key Points   349
            Problems   350

CHAPTER SEVEN

THE IMPEACHMENT AND REHABILITATION OF WITNESSES

THE IMPEACHMENT AND REHABILITATION OF WITNESSES	351

A. SOME BASIC CONCEPTS   351
    1. Impeachment: The Inferential Process   351
        a. The Testimonial Inferences   351
        b. Types of Impeachment Evidence   353
        c. Impeachment Evidence Versus Substantive Evidence   353
    2. Extrinsic Evidence and Impeachment   355
    3. Bolstering Credibility   356
B. IMPEACHMENT AND REHABILITATION WITH
    CHARACTER EVIDENCE   357
    1. FRE 608   358
    2. Interpretation and Illustration of FRE 608(a)   358
        a. Reputation and Opinion Evidence to Prove Character
            for Truthfulness   358
        b. The FRE 608(a)(2) Limitation on Evidence of
            Truthful Character   359

		Key Points	361
		Problems	361
3.		Interpretation and Illustration of FRE 608(b)(1)	362
	a.	The Prohibition Against the Use of Extrinsic Evidence	362
	b.	The 2003 Clarifying Amendment	362
	c.	The Limited Scope of Permissible Inquiry	363
	d.	No Fifth Amendment Waiver	363
4.		Elaboration of FRE 608(b)(1)	364
	a.	The Rationale for the Prohibition Against Extrinsic Evidence	364
	b.	The Scope of Permissible Questions	364
		i. The Meaning of Untruthfulness	364
		ii. Questions about Arrests, Charges, and Administrative or Judicial Findings	365
	c.	Questions About Specific Acts and FRE 403	366
	d.	The "Discretion of the Court" to Exclude Questions About Specific Acts	366
	e.	Good Faith Requirement; Practical Considerations	367
	f.	FRE 608(b)(1) Specific Acts Showing Good Character for Truthfulness	367
	g.	Cross-Examination	368
5.		Interpretation and Illustration of FRE 608(b)(2)	368
		Key Points	369
		Problems	369
6.		FRE 609	372
7.		Interpretation and Illustration of FRE 609(a) and (b)	373
	a.	The Two FRE 609(a)(1) Balancing Tests	373
		i. Probative Value	374
		ii. Unfair Prejudice	374
		iii. The Reverse FRE 403 Balancing Test for Criminal Defendants	374
		iv. The FRE 403 Balancing Test for Other Witnesses	375
		v. The Factual Circumstances of the Crime	375
	b.	The Automatic Admissibility of FRE 609(a)(2) Dishonesty and False Statement Convictions	375
		i. The Rule	375
		ii. The Meaning of "Dishonesty or False Statement"	376
		iii. The Significance of the Underlying Details of the Crime	377
	c.	The FRE 609(b) Reverse Balancing Test	378
8.		Elaboration of FRE 609(a)	379
	a.	The Rationale for Permitting Impeachment with FRE 609(a)(1) Convictions	379

		b.	Prior Convictions and Prejudice	380
		c.	Extrinsic Evidence	380
		d.	The Factual Details of the Conviction	381
		e.	Hearsay	381
		f.	Practical Considerations	382
			Key Points	384
			Problems	384

C. IMPEACHMENT AND REHABILITATION WITH A
WITNESS'S PRIOR STATEMENTS — 386

1. FRE 613 — 387
2. Interpretation and Illustration of FRE 613 — 387
   a. FRE 613(a) — 387
   b. FRE 613(b) — 388
3. Elaboration of FRE 613(b) — 388
   a. FRE 613(b)'s Departure from the Common Law — 388
   b. Extrinsic Evidence in Practice: Practical
      Considerations — 389
   c. Probative Value and FRE 403 Concerns — 390
      i. The Risk of Improper "Substantive" Use — 390
      ii. Loss of Memory and Inconsistency — 391
      iii. Inconsistent Statements About Collateral Matters — 391
          Key Points — 392
          Problems — 392
4. The Impeachment of Experts with Statements in
   Treatises — 393
5. Prior Consistent Statements — 394
   a. Admissibility for Truth Pursuant to FRE 801(d)(1)(B) — 394
   b. Admissibility to Rehabilitate Pursuant to
      FRE 401- 403? — 394
      i. Putting Inconsistent Statements in Context
         Following Impeachment with Prior Inconsistent
         Statement — 394
      ii. Rehabilitation with Consistent Statements in
          Other Contexts — 395
   c. Extrinsic Evidence — 396
      Key Points — 396
      Problems — 396

D. OTHER IMPEACHMENT TECHNIQUES — 398

1. Bias — 399
   a. Relevance — 399
   b. Extrinsic Evidence — 399
   c. Possible Limitations on Extrinsic Evidence of Bias — 400
   d. Bias Versus Character — 400

     Key Points   401
     Problems   401
  2. Mental or Sensory Incapacity   403
    a. Relevance   403
    b. Extrinsic Evidence   404
    c. Mental Incapacity as a Bar to Testimony 404
     Keys Points   405
     Problems   405
  3. Contradiction   405
    a. Relevance   405
    b. Extrinsic Evidence   406
    c. The "No Extrinsic Evidence to Impeach on a
      Collateral Matter" Doctrine   407
     i. What Is Not Collateral Generally   407
     ii. Evidence That Is Directly Relevant to the Issues
      in Litigation   407
     iii. Evidence That Impeaches a Witness Apart from
      Contradiction   407
     iv. Evidence That Logically Undermines a Witness's
      Story   408
     v. A Test for "Collateralness."   408
     Key Points   408
     Problems   409
E. REFLECTION ON THE IMPEACHMENT PROCESS 410

CHAPTER EIGHT

THE HEARSAY
RULE   413

A. THE GENERAL RULE OF EXCLUSION AND THE
  DEFINITION OF HEARSAY   413
  1. FRE 801 and 802   414
  2. Interpretation and Illustration of FRE 801 and 802 414
    a. The Relevancy of Sally's Statement   415
    b. Sally's Statement Bears Testimonial Dangers 415
    c. The Relevancy of Hearsay   417
    d. Hearsay Policy Differentiates Between Witnesses and
      Hearsay Declarants   418
     Key Points   421
     Problems   421
  3. Elaboration of FRE 801 and 802: Implications of the
    General Rule of Exclusion   421

		a.	Identifying What a Hearsay Statement Is Offered to Prove	421
		b.	Testimony by Witnesses About Their Own Out-of-Court Statements May Still Be Hearsay	423
		c.	Hearsay, Lay Opinions, and the Firsthand Knowledge Rule	423
		d.	Multiple Hearsay	424
			Key Points	425
			Problem	425
	4.	Interpretation and Illustration of FRE 801(c): Nonhearsay Statements with No Hearsay Dangers		425
		a.	Nonhearsay Uses	425
			i. Effect on the Listener	427
			ii. Legally Operative Facts	428
			iii. Identifying Nonhearsay Uses	429
		b.	Statements Relevant for Both Nonhearsay and Hearsay Uses	429
			Key Point	430
			Problems	430
	5.	Interpretation and Illustration of FRE 801(a)(2): Nonverbal Conduct		432
		a.	The Relevancy of Nonverbal Conduct	432
		b.	Application of FRE 801(a)(2)	433
			i. Assertive Conduct	433
			ii. Nonassertive Conduct	433
			ii. FRE 801(a)(2)'s Intent Test	434
	6.	Elaboration of FRE 801(a)(2): Justification for the Distinction Between Assertive and Nonassertive Conduct		434
		a.	Absence of Hearsay Danger	434
		b.	Necessity	435
		c.	Should Nonassertive Conduct Be Excluded from the Definition of Hearsay?	436
			i. The Difficulty of Accurate Classification	436
			ii. The Danger of Ambiguity	436
			iii. Is Cross-examination Important for Evaluating Nonassertive Conduct?	437
		d.	Disguised Assertions	437
			Key Points	438
			Problems	439
	7.	Utterances Relevant for the Truth of the Declarant's Unstated Beliefs		440
		a.	The Relevancy of Unstated Beliefs	440
		b.	Application of FRE 801(a)(1) and (c)	442

		i.	The Literal Approach	442
		ii.	The Common Law Approach	443
		iii.	FRE 801(a)-(c) Rejects the Common Law Approach	444
	8.		Elaboration of FRE 801: Courts Reject the Liberal Approach and Apply an "Intent Test"	445
		a.	Intent to Assert Unstated Beliefs	445
		b.	Does an "Intent" Test Identify High Sincerity Risk?	446
		i.	What Kind of Intent?	446
		ii.	Factual Uncertainty	447
		iii.	The Burden of Proving Intent	447
		c.	Some Courts Still Adhere to the Common Law Approach	448
			Key Points	448
			Notes and Questions	449
			Problems	449
	9.		Reflection on the Definition of Hearsay: Should FRE 801 Be Revised?	450
B.	A GENERAL APPROACH TO THE ADMISSION OF HEARSAY UNDER THE EXEMPTIONS AND EXCEPTIONS			452
	1.		Justification for the Exemptions and Exceptions	452
	2.		The Categorical Approach	453
	3.		The Process of Admission	453
	4.		The Foundational Requirements	453
	5.		Multiple Exemptions and Exceptions May Apply	454
	6.		The Confrontation Clause	455
C.	HEARSAY EXEMPTIONS			455
	1.		FRE 801(d)(1) and (2)	455
	2.		Interpretation and Illustration of FRE 801(d)(1): The Testifying, Witness Must Be "Subject to Cross-examination Concerning the Statement"	456
		a.	Preliminary Factfinding	456
		i.	The Declarant Is Testifying at Trial	456
		ii.	Examination Concerning the Statement	457
		iii.	Denial of, or Inability to Remember, the Prior Statement	457
		iv.	Inability to Remember the Underlying Events	457
		v.	Personal Knowledge Is Required	459
		b.	Other Justifications for the FRE 801(d)(1) Exemptions	459
	3.		Interpretation and Illustration of FRE 801(d)(1)(A): Prior Inconsistent Statements	459
		a.	Preliminary Factfinding	459

		i.	Inconsistency	460
		ii.	Inconsistency Due to Evasion	460
		iii.	Under Oath at a Trial, Hearing, or Other Proceeding	460
	b.		Justification for the FRE 801(d)(1)(A) Limitations	461
	c.		Prior Inconsistent Statements Not Within FRE 801(d)(1)(A)	461
4.			Interpretation and Illustration of FRE 801(d)(1)(B): Prior Consistent Statements	462
	a.		Preliminary Factfinding	462
		i.	A Charge of Recent Fabrication or Improper Influence or Motive	462
		ii.	To "Rebut" the Charge	462
	b.		Justification for the FRE 801(d)(1)(B) Limitation	463
	c.		Prior Consistent Statements Not Within FRE 801(d)(1)(B)	464
5.			Interpretation and Illustration of FRE 801(d)(1)(C): Prior Statements of Identification	464
	a.		Preliminary Fact-finding	464
		i.	Made After Perceiving a Person	464
		ii.	Identification of a Person	465
	b.		Justifications for the Admissibility of Prior Statements of Identification	465
	c.		Constitutional Concerns	466
			Key Points	467
			Problems	467
6.			Interpretation and Illustration of FRE 801(d)(2): Party Admissions in General	469
7.			Interpretation and Illustration of FRE 801(d)(2)(A): A Party's Own Statements	470
	a.		Preliminary Factfinding	470
	b.		Individual and Representative Capacity	471
	c.		Admissions, Personal Knowledge, and Lay Opinions	472
8.			Elaboration of FRE 801(d)(2)(A): Justification for the Admissibility of Party Admissions	472
	a.		The Opportunity to Explain	473
	b.		Fifth Amendment Concerns	473
	c.		Responsibility for One's Own Statements and Fairness	473
9.			Further Elaboration of FRE 801(d)(2)(A)	474
	a.		Preliminary Factfinding on the Identity of the Declarant	474
	b.		Admissibility of Party Admissions in Multiparty Cases: The Bruton Problem	475
10.			Interpretation and Illustration of FRE 801(d)(2)(B): Adoptive Admissions	476

		a.	Preliminary Factfinding	476
		b.	Justification for the Admissibility of Adoptive Admissions	477
		c.	Adoption by Silence	477
	11.	Interpretation and Illustration of FRE 801(d)(2)(C) and (D): Admissions by Agents, Servants, and Employees	478
		a.	Preliminary Factfinding	478
			i. Statements by Attorneys	479
			ii. Other Specifically Authorized Statements	479
			iii. Statements Made During the Relationship That Concern a Matter Within the Scope of an Agent's Employment	480
		b.	Justification for the Admissibility of Statements Under FRE 801(d)(2)(C) and (D): Necessity, Fairness, and Reliability	480
		c.	Personal Knowledge and Lay Opinions	481
		d.	Admissions by Government Employees	482
	12.	Interpretation and Illustration of FRE 801(d)(2)(E): Co-conspirators' Admissions	482
		a.	Preliminary Factfinding	482
			i. Proof of Co-membership	483
			ii. During the Course of the Conspiracy	483
			iii. In Furtherance of the Conspiracy	484
		b.	Justification for the Admissibility of Co-conspirators' Admissions	484
	13.	Elaboration of FRE 801(d)(2)(E): Applying FRE 104 to the Co-conspirator Exemption	485
		a.	Bourjaily v. United States	485
		b.	The Amendment to FRE 801(3)(2): The Requirement of Additional Evidence	486
		c.	Process for Admission of a Co-conspirator's Statement	486
			Key Points	487
			Problems	488
D.	HEARSAY EXCEPTIONS NOT REQUIRING THE UNAVAILABILITY OF THE DECLARANT			490
	1.	FRE 803		491
	2.	Interpretation and Illustration of FRE 803(1): Present Sense Impressions		493
		a.	Preliminary Factfinding	494
		b.	Justification for the Admissibility of Present Sense Impressions	494
	3.	Interpretation and Illustration of FRE 803(2): Excited Utterances		494
		a.	Preliminary Factfinding	495
		b.	Justification for the Admissibility of Excited Utterances	495

4. Elaboration of FRE 803(1) and (2): Effects of the
Categorical Approach 496
   a. The Categories Determine Admissibility 496
   b. The Categorical Terms Require Judicial Interpretation 497
      i. Time Lapse Between Event and Statement 497
      ii. Content of the Statement 498
   c. Use of the Statement Itself in Preliminary Fact-finding 499
   d. Proof of Personal Knowledge 500
      Key Points 501
      Problems 501
5. Interpretation and Illustration of FRE 803(3): State-of-
Mind Declarations 502
   a. Preliminary Factfinding 502
   b. Justification for the State-of-Mind Exception 503
   c. State-of-Mind Utterances Are Classified as Either
Direct or Circumstantial 504
6. Elaboration of FRE 803(3): Relevant Uses of State-of-
Mind Evidence 505
   a. Future and Past State of Mind of the Declarant 505
   b. Future Conduct of the Declarant 506
   c. Evidence of State of Mind Used to Prove Past Facts 506
   d. The *Hillmon* Case 507
      i. Walter's Future Conduct 508
      ii. Hillmon's Future Conduct 508
      iii. Recent Interpretations of *Hillmon* 509
      Key Points 509
      Problems 510
7. Interpretation and Illustration of FRE 803(4): Statement
for Medical Diagnosis or Treatment 512
   a. Preliminary Factfinding 512
   b. Justification for the Admissibility of Statements for
Medical Purposes 513
   c. Statements About the Cause or External Source Must
Be "Pertinent" 513
   d. Requiring Proof of Medical Purpose 514
   e. Statements Made for Diagnostic Evaluations for
Litigation 515
8. Elaboration of FRE 803(4): Patient's Statements as the
Basis for Expert Opinion 515
      Key Points 516
      Problems 516
9. Interpretation and Illustration of FRE 803(5): Past
Recollection Recorded 517

		a.	Preliminary Factfinding	517
			i. The Contents of the Statement	517
			ii. The Declarant Must be a Witness with Failed Memory	518
			iii. Made with Personal Knowledge and Fresh Memory	518
			iv. The Record Reflects the Witness's Knowledge Correctly	519
			v. The Record May Only Be Read to the Jury	519
		b.	Justification of the Admissibility of Past Recollection Recorded	519
	10.		Elaboration of FRE 803(5)	520
		a.	Past Recollection Recorded Can Be Created by Multiple Declarants	520
		b.	Multiple Hearsay Requires a Hearsay Exception or Exemption for Each Level	521
		c.	Present Recollection Refreshed	521
		d.	The Impact of FRE 612 on Refreshing Recollection	522
			Key Points	523
			Problems	523
	11.		Interpretation and Illustration of FRE 803(6): Business Records	524
		a.	Preliminary Factfinding	525
			i. The Broad Scope of What Constitutes a Business Record	525
			ii. Personal Knowledge and Near Contemporaneity Are Required	526
			iii. Made Pursuant to a "Business Duty"	526
			iv. Custodian or Other Qualified Witness	527
		b.	Justification for the Admissibility of Business Records	528
	12.		Elaboration of FRE 803(6)	528
		a.	Exclusion for Untrustworthiness	529
			i. Burden of Persuasion	529
			ii. Circumstances Indicating Lack of Trustworthiness	529
		b.	Opinions and Diagnoses	530
		c.	Records Containing Multiple Levels of Hearsay	531
			i. Sources of Information with No Business Duty	531
			ii. Use of Multiple Exceptions and Exemptions	532
		d.	Computer Documents and Electronic Data as Business Records	532
			Key Points	534
			Problems	534

13. Interpretation and Illustration of FRE 803(8): Public
     Records and Reports   535
     a. Preliminary Factfinding   536
         i.   Activities of the Office or Agency   536
         ii. Matters Observed and Reported Pursuant to a
              Duty Imposed by Law, Excluding Matters
              Observed by Police Officers and Other Law
              Enforcement Personnel in Criminal Cases   536
         iii. Factual Finds in Investigative Reports   537
         iv. Exclusion for Lack of Trustworthiness   538
     b. Justification for the Admissibility of Public Records   538
14. Elaboration of FRE 803(8)(B): The Meaning of "Other
     Law Enforcement Personnel"   539
     a. The Meaning of Law Enforcement Personnel   539
         i.   United States v. Oates   539
         ii. Prosecutorial Function   539
         iii. Routine and Regular Activities   540
     b. The Relationship Between FRE 803(8)(B) and (C) and
         Other Exceptions   540
15. Elaboration of FRE 803(8)(C): The Problem of
     Multiple Hearsay Sources Within Investigative Reports   541
     a. Are Otherwise Inadmissible Hearsay Sources
         Admissible for Their Truth?   542
     b. Administrative Findings   542
16. Other Exceptions for Records Under FRE 803   543
         Key Points   543
         Problems   544
17. Interpretation and Illustration of FRE 803(22): Judgment
     of Previous Conviction   545
     a. Preliminary Factfinding   545
     b. Justification for the Admissibility of Criminal
         Judgment   546
     c. The Admission of Misdemeanor Convictions for
         Impeachment   546
E. HEARSAY EXCEPTIONS REQUIRING THE
    UNAVAILABILITY OF THE DECLARANT   547
1. FRE 804   547
2. Interpretation and Illustration of FRE 804(a): Grounds for
    a Finding of Unavailability   548
    a. Preliminary Factfinding   548
    b. Preference for Former Testimony or Deposition   549
    c. Reasonable Means to Procure Attendance   549
    d. Unavailability Caused by the Proponent   550
        Problem   550

3. Interpretation and Illustration of FRE 804(b)(1): Former
   Testimony   551
   a. Preliminary Factfinding   551
      i.   Opportunity to Develop by Same Party or a
            Predecessor in Interest   551
      ii.   Opportunity and Similar Motive   551
      iii. No Opportunity   552
      iv.   No Requirement of "Offered on Same Issue"   552
   b. Justification for the Admissibility of Former Testimony   553
4. Elaboration of FRE 804(b)(1)   553
   a. The Opportunity to Develop Testimony   553
   b. Identity of Parties   554
   c. Former Testimony Offered Against a Party Who Was
      Not a Party to the Original Action   554
      i.   In a Civil Case, the Party in the Former
            Proceeding May Also Be a Predecessor in Interest   555
      ii.   What Is a Predecessor in Interest?   555
   d. Lack of Similar Motive Due to Difference in
      Procedural Context   556
   e. Method of Introducing Former Testimony   557
   f. Objections to the Contents of the Former Testimony   557
      Key Points   558
      Problems   558
5. Interpretation and Illustration of FRE 804(b)(2):
   Dying Declarations   559
   a. Preliminary Factfinding   559
   b. Justification for the Admissibility of Dying
      Declarations   560
      Key Point   560
6. Interpretation and Illustration of FRE 804(b)(3):
   Declarations Against Interest   561
   a. Preliminary Factfinding   561
      i.   Content Against Interest   561
      ii.   Ascertaining the Declarant's Knowledge   562
      iii. Distinct from Party Admission   562
   b. Justification for the Admissibility of Declarations
      Against Interest   562
7. Elaboration of FRE 804(b)(3)   563
   a. Doubts About the Underlying Rationale for the
      Exception   563
      i.   Mixed Motive Statements   563
      ii.   Statements Made with No Motive to Lie   563
   b. Requirement of Corroboration for Statements Against
      Penal Interest Offered to Exculpate the Accused   563

		c.	Statement That Inculpate Accomplices	564
		d.	Should the Corroboration Requirement Apply to Inculpatory Statements Too?	565
			Key Points	565
	8.		Interpretation and Illustration of FRE 804(b)(4): Statements of Personal or Family History	565
		a.	Preliminary Factfinding	566
			i. Personal Knowledge of One's Own Personal and Family History	566
			ii. Statements of Relations and Intimate Associates	566
			iii. Concerning Personal History	566
		b.	Justification for the Admissibility of Statements of Personal or Family History	566
			Key Points	567
			Problems	567
	9.		Interpretation and Illustration of FRE 804(b)(6): Forfeiture by Wrongdoing	569
		a.	Preliminary Factfinding	570
			i. The Declarant Was a Witness or a Potential Witness Against a Party	570
			ii. The Party Engaged in Wrongdoing that Did Procure the Unavailability of the Declarant	570
			iii. Intent to Procure the Declarant's Unavailability as a Witness	570
			iv. Content of Declarant's Statement	571
		b.	Justification for the Admissibility of Forfeiture by Wrongdoing Statements	571
		c.	Acquiescence in Wrongdoing	572
		d.	Application of FRE 403	572
		e.	Is a FRE 104(c) Hearing Required?	573
			Key Points	573
			Problem	573
F.	THE RESIDUAL EXCEPTION			574
	1.		FRE 807	574
	2.		Interpretation and Illustration of FRE 807	575
		a.	Preliminary Factfinding	575
		b.	Circumstantial Guarantees of Trustworthiness	576
			i. Reliability of Testimonial Qualities	576
			ii. Independent Corroboration	577
		c.	Equivalency	577
		d.	Near Miss	577
		e.	Offered to Prove a Material Fact	578
		f.	More Probative on the Point Than Other Reasonably Available Evidence	578

g.   Serve the General Purposes of the Rules and Interests
     of Justice   579
h.   Notice   579
3.   Elaboration of FRE 807: How Much Hearsay Is Admitted
     Under the Residual Exception?   579
          Key Points   580
          Problems   581

G.   HEARSAY AND THE CONFRONTATION CLAUSE   582
1.   Ohio v. Roberts   582
     a.   Firmly Rooted Hearsay Exceptions   583
     b.   Not Firmly Rooted Exceptions Require "Particularized
          Guarantees of Trustworthiness"   583
2.   Crawford v. Washington   584
          Notes and Questions   595
3.   The Definition of Testimonial Statements in the Aftermath
     of Crawford v. Washington   595
     a.   Formalized Testimonial Materials   596
     b.   Statements a Reasonable Person Would Realize
          Would Be Used in Investigation or Prosecution of a
          Crime   597
     c.   Categories of Nontestimonial Statements Mentioned
          in Crawford   598
4.   Testimonial Statements That Satisfy the Confrontation
     Right   598
     a.   The Declarant Testifies   599
     b.   Unavailability and Prior Opportunity for Cross-
          examination   599
          i.   Unavailability   599
          ii.   Prior Opportunity for Cross-examination   600
5.   Exceptions to the Requirement of Confrontation   600
     a.   Dying Declarations   600
     b.   "Forfeiture-by-Wrongdoing"   601
6.   Defendants' Right to Confrontation When Nontestimonial
     Statements Are Offered Against Them   601
          Notes and Questions   602
          Problems   603

H.   REFLECTION ON THE HEARSAY RULE   603
1.   The Traditional Goals of Hearsay Policy   603
2.   The Reliability Theory Does Not Work   604
3.   A Rule of Discretion   604
4.   Abolition   605
5.   Reformulating Hearsay Policy   605
     a.   Is there a Need for a Hearsay Rule in Modern Civil
          Litigation?   605

b.   Regulation Premised on the Excesses of the Adversary
     System   606
c.   Notice-based Admission in Civil Cases: Reliance on
     the Adversary System   606
d.   Why Hearsay Should Be Treated Differently in
     Criminal Cases   607
e.   Conclusion   607

CHAPTER NINE

LAY OPINIONS AND EXPERT WITNESSES   609

A. LAY OPINIONS   611
    1.   FRE 701   611
    2.   Interpretation and Illustration of FRE 701   611
         a.   Fact versus Opinion   612
         b.   Rationally Based on the Perception of the Witness   613
         c.   Helpful to a Clear Understanding of the Witness's
              Testimony or the Determination of a Fact in Issue   614
         d.   Not Based on Scientific, Technical, or Other
              Specialized Knowledge Within the Scope of
              Rule 702   617
    3.   Elaboration of FRE 701: Trial Court Discretion   618
              Key Points   620
              Problems   620
B. EXPERT WITNESSES   625
              Samuel Gross, Expert Evidence   625
              Carol Krafka et al., Judge and Attorney
              Experiences, Practices, and Concerns Regarding
              Expert Testimony in Federal Civil Trials   626
    1.   FRE 702   628
    2.   Interpretation and Illustration of FRE 702   628
         a.   Scientific, Technical, or Other Specialized
              Knowledge   628
         b.   Assist the Trier of Fact   628
         c.   A Witness Qualified as an Expert   629
         d.   FRE 403 and Litigation Incentives   630
         e.   Summary Witnesses   631
    3.   Elaboration of "Scientific Evidence" Under FRE 702:
         Frye and *Daubert*   631
         a.   From *Frye* to *Daubert*   631
              Daubert v. Merrell Dow Pharmaceuticals, Inc.   633
              Notes and Questions   641

4. Elaboration of Technical or Other Specialized Knowledge
under *Kumho Tire*   646
Kumho Tire Company, Ltd. v. Carmichael   646
Note   650
Key Points   650
Problems   650
5. Reflection on Scientific Evidence and the *Daubert* Case   654
6. FRE 705   660
7. Interpretation and Illustration of FRE 705   660
8. FRE 703   662
9. Interpretation and Illustration of FRE 703   662
10. Elaboration of FRE 703: Opinions Based on Otherwise
Inadmissible Evidence   664
Key Points   668
Problems   668
C. OPINIONS ON AN ULTIMATE ISSUE   670
1. FRE 704   670
2. Interpretation and Illustration of FRE 704(a)   670
3. Interpretation and Illustration of FRE 704(b)   672
Key Point   673
Problems   674
D. COURT APPOINTED EXPERTS   675
1. FRE 706   675
2. Interpretation and Illustration of FRE 706   676
E. VARIETIES OF SCIENTIFIC EVIDENCE AND EXPERT
TESTIMONY   678
1. DNA Profiling   678
David H. Kaye & George F. Sensabaugh Jr.,
Reference Guide on DNA Evidence   678
2. Some Recent Controversies   689
a. Psychological and Behavioral Sciences   689
b. Toxic Tort Causation   690
c. Traditional Law Enforcement Investigative Tools   692
Question   696

CHAPTER TEN

THE PROCESS OF PROOF IN CIVIL AND
CRIMINAL CASES: BURDENS OF PROOF, JUDICIAL
SUMMARY AND COMMENT, AND PRESUMPTIONS

     697

A. THE BURDENS OF PROOF IN CIVIL CASES   698
1. The Burden of Production   699

a. The Role of and Rationale for Production Burdens   699

b. The Relationship Between Production Burdens and
Persuasion Burdens   699

c. The Relationship Between the Burden of Production
and the Burden of Persuasion Illustrated   700

d. Procedural Mechanisms for Enforcing Burdens of
Production   702

e. The Allocation of Burdens of Production   702

     Key Points   703

2. The Burden of Persuasion   703

a. The Role of Rules Setting Forth Burdens of Persuasion   704

b. The Premises Underlying the Preponderance Rule   704

c. Higher Burdens of Persuasion   706

d. The Meaning of "Preponderance of the Evidence"
in Practice   707

e. The Relative Nature of the Burden of Persuasion   707

f. The Allocation of the Burden of Persuasion   707

     Schechter v. Klanfer   708

     Notes and Questions   710

     Key Points   712

B. THE BURDENS OF PROOF IN CRIMINAL CASES   713

1. The Burden of Persuasion: In re Winship's Mandate of
Proof Beyond a Reasonable Doubt   713

     Notes and Questions   714

     Key Point   716

2. The Scope of *Winship*: Explicit Shifts in the Burden of
Persuasion and Other Matters   716

a. The *Mullaney* Decision   716

b. The *Patterson* Decision   718

c. The Functional Equivalence of *Mullaney* and
Patterson   719

d. *Mullaney's* Departure from *Winship*   719

e. Evaluating *Mullaney* and *Patterson*: The Theory that
the Greater Includes the Lesser   720

f. Giving Content to *Winship*: Tests for Assessing the
Validity of Affirmative Defenses   721

     i. The Elements Test   721

     ii. The Political Compromise Test   721

     iii. The Proportionality Test   722

     iv. Justice Powell's Two-part Test   723

g. Affirmative Defenses After *Patterson*   723

     Martin v. Ohio   723

     Notes and Questions on *Martin*   730

		Key Points	731
		Notes and Questions on the Application of *Winship* In Other Contexts	731
		Key Points	735
	3.	The Burden of Production in Criminal Cases	735
		Notes and Questions	735
		Key Points	736
C.	JUDICIAL SUMMARY OF AND COMMENT ON THE EVIDENCE		737
	1.	The Advantages and Disadvantages of Permitting Summary and Comment	737
	2.	The Criteria for Evaluating Judicial Summary and Comment	739
		Notes and Questions	740
	3.	Standardized Comments	741
	4.	The Relationship Between Comments on the Evidence and the Burden of Persuasion	742
		Key Points	743
		Notes and Questions	743
D.	PRESUMPTIONS		744
	1.	Irrebuttable or Conclusive Presumptions Explained and Illustrated	745
		Key Points	746
		Problems	746
	2.	Mandatory Rebuttable Presumptions Explained and Illustrated	746
		a. Mandatory Production Burden Presumptions	747
		Notes and Questions	748
		Key Points	748
		b. Mandatory Persuasion Burden Presumptions	748
		Notes and Questions	749
		Key Points	750
		c. Decisionmaking with Respect to the Facts Giving Rise to Mandatory Presumptions	750
		Key Point	751
		Problems	751
	3.	Permissive or "Weak" Presumptions Explained and Illustrated	752
		Key Points	752
	4.	The Complexity of Presumptions	752
		Notes and Questions	753
	5.	The Federal Rules Approach to Presumptions	757
		a. The "Not Otherwise Provided for by Act of Congress" Exception	757

b. The Relationship Between FRE 301 Presumptions and
        Other Means of Allocating Burdens of Production and
        Persuasion   758
            Key Points   759
    6. Presumptions in Criminal Cases: The Impact of *Winship*   759
            Notes and Questions   760
            Key Points   762
            Problems   763

CHAPTER ELEVEN

JUDICIAL NOTICE   765

A. JUDICIAL NOTICE OF ADJUDICATIVE FACTS   765
    1. FRE 201   765
    2. Interpretation and Illustration of FRE 201(a) and (b)   766
        a. Types of Adjudicative Facts That Are Frequently
            Noticed   766
        b. The Scope of FRE 201(a): What Are Adjudicative
            Facts?   766
        c. The Scope of FRE 201(b): The Required State of
            Knowledge of Adjudicative Facts That May Be
            Judicially Noticed   767
    3. Elaboration of FRE 201(a) and (b)   768
        a. Further Illustration of 201(b) Standards   768
            In Re Thirtyacre   768
            Notes and Questions   769
        b. Sources of Information Under FRE 201   769
    4. Interpretation and Illustration of FRE 201(c), (d), and (e) 770
    5. Interpretation and Illustration of FRE 201(f) and (g)   771
        a. Judicial Notice of Adjudicative Facts in Civil Cases:
            Mini Directed Verdicts   771
        b. Judicial Notice of Adjudicative Facts in Criminal
            Cases: Judicial Comments   771
        c. Timing of Judicial Notice   772
            i.   Judicial Notice to Preserve Civil Verdicts   772
            ii. Judicial Notice to Preserve Criminal Verdicts   772
                 Key Points   773
                 Notes and Questions   774
                 Problems   774
B. JUDICIAL NOTICE AS PART OF JUDICIAL
    DECISIONMAKING   776
    1. Judicial Cognizance of Common Knowledge Without
        Formal Judicial Notice   776

		a.	The Jury's General Background Knowledge	776
		b.	Judges' Own Background Knowledge	777
	2.	Judicial Cognizance of Legislative Facts		778
			Notes and Questions	779
	3.	Judicial Notice of Substantive Law		780
			Key Point	780

C. CAN THE APPROPRIATE BOUNDS OF JUDICIAL
NOTICE BE SPECIFIED WITH ANY CLARITY?
REFLECTION ON JUDICIAL NOTICE: 780
   1. Judicial Use of Background Knowledge   780
       In Re Marriage of Tresnak   780
       Notes and Questions   783
       Problems   783

CHAPTER TWELVE

PRIVILEGES   787

A. THE LAW OF PRIVILEGE   787
   1. A General Introduction   787
   2. The Unique Operation of Privilege Rules   788
   3. Historical Background and Current Status of Privilege
      Rules   789
B. GENERAL STRUCTURE OF PRIVILEGES   792
   1. Holder of the Privilege   792
   2. Invocation   792
   3. Scope and Limits   794
   4. Waiver   795
   5. Exceptions   796
   6. Drawing Adverse Inferences from Invoking a Privilege   796
   7. Constitutional Limitations on Privilege   797
C. THE ATTORNEY-CLIENT PRIVILEGE   797
   1. Elements of the Privilege   797
      a. Communications with a Lawyer or Representative of a
         Lawyer   798
      b. Communications for the Purpose of Legal Service   800
      c. The Scope of Confidential Communications
         Included in Privilege   801
         Key Points   802
         Problems   803
         Note on the Attorney-Client Privilege, the Work-
         Product Doctrine, and the Ethical Duty of
         Confidentiality   804

			Notes and Questions	807
			Problems	808
	2.	The Corporate Client		808
			Upjohn Co. v. United States	810
			Key Points	817
			Notes and Questions	818
			Problems	820
	3.	The Government Client		821
	4.	Exceptions to the Privilege		822
		a.	Breach of Duty by a Lawyer or Client	822
		b.	Document Attested by a Lawyer	822
		c.	Identity of Client, Fee Information, and Related Matters	822
		d.	Communication in Furtherance of a Crime or Fraud	823
			Problems	825
	5.	Reflection on the Attorney-Client Privilege		826
			Ronald J. Allen et al., A Positive Theory of the Attorney-Client Privilege and the Work Product Doctrine	826
			Notes and Questions	840

D. THE MARITAL PRIVILEGES — 842

	1.	The Marital Communication Privilege		842
		a.	Elements of the Privilege and Its Justifications	842
		b.	Holder	843
		c.	Scope of the Privilege	843
			i. Valid Marriage	843
			ii. Confidentiality	844
			iii. What Is a "Communication"?	845
		d.	Exceptions	845
			Problems	846
	2.	The Marital Testimonial Privilege		847
		a.	Elements of the Privilege and Its Justifications	847
			Trammel v. United States	848
			Notes and Questions	852
		b.	Exceptions	854
			Key Points	855
			Problems	855

E. THE PHYSICIAN-PATIENT AND PSYCHOTHERAPIST-PATIENT PRIVILEGES — 855

	1.	The Physician-Patient Privilege		856
	2.	The Psychotherapist-Patient Privilege		857
		a.	Jaffee v. Redmond	857

		Jaffee v. Redmond	857
		Notes and Questions	868
	b.	Scope of the Privilege After Jaffe	869
		i. Who Is a Psychotherapist?	869
		ii. Communications	870
		iii. Waiver	870
	c.	Exceptions to the Privilege	871
		i. Constitutional Limits	871
		ii. Compelled Disclosures	872
		iii. Dangerous Patient	873
		iv. Crime-Fraud Exception	873
		Key Points	874
		Problems	874
F.	THE CLERGY-COMMUNICANT PRIVILEGE		875
1.	The Privilege and Its Justifications		876
2.	Scope of the Privilege		876
	a.	Definition of Clergy	877
	b.	Nature of the Communication	878
	c.	Expectation of Confidentiality	878
	d.	Exceptions	879
		Key Points	880
		Problems	880
G.	OTHER PRIVILEGES		881
1.	Other Professional-Client Relationships		881
2.	Parent-Child Privilege		882
3.	Communications Made in Settlement Negotiations		884
4.	Privileges Protecting Outside Sources of Information		886
	a.	Government Informant's Privilege	886
	b.	Journalist's Privilege	886
	c.	Scholar's (Academic Researcher's) Privilege	888
5.	Peer Review Privilege		889
6.	Self-evaluative Privilege		890
7.	Government Privileges — Executive Privilege		892
	a.	State Secrets Privilege	892
	b.	Presidential Communications Privilege	894
	c.	Official Information (Deliberative Process) Privilege	896
		Problems	900

Table of Cases	903
Table of Authorities	913
Index	925

PREFACE

In the fourth edition of this book, we focus the study of evidence law on the text of the Federal Rules of Evidence and the ideas and principles that underlie them. The book presents the rules in a systematic format that is used consistently throughout. This format provides students with the text of the rules, the basic interpretation and illustration of the rules' terms, an elaboration of principles and policies used to explain and interpret the rules, illustrations from recent case law, and a set of problems that calls for the application of each significant rule in its most basic as well as its most challenging contexts. New problems have been added to further our goal of offering problems within a wide range of difficulty. This edition also includes three on-going "saga" problems that build, in successive chapters, on a developing fact pattern. These unique problems demonstrate how the rules of evidence actually apply to individual items of evidence in "layers" as students' knowledge of those rules increases. And, throughout this edition, changes in the law and new cases have been added to update our presentation of the FRE.

We have not been content to present a mass of doctrines and cases. We have endeavored instead to show, through discursive text and problems, the relationship between the theories underlying the rules and the rules themselves. This emphasis on the underlying theories reflects our view that the study of any field of law should not consist primarily of ingesting enormous amounts of doctrinal "stew." Rather, the pursuit should be gaining an understanding of the conditions that give rise to the forms of regulation of decision making that are contained in the rules of evidence.

From its inception, another factor has heavily influenced this book. We believe that the field of evidence is in large measure a coherent whole rather than an amalgam of virtually unrelated parts. Unlike traditional works on evidence, we present an analytic theme in our text that attempts to show the underlying relationships between the various common law categories of evidence. This theme is relevancy and the assumptions about decision making that inhere in a system of proof based on relevancy. With this theme we explore all of the major Federal Rules of Evidence, requiring students to develop a systematic approach to the admission of evidence that begins with the relationship of evidentiary facts to the essential elements of the case.

Only with such a beginning can the exclusionary principles, and judicial interpretation and application of them, be understood.

Because evidence is primarily concerned with establishing facts for the purpose of resolving disputes, we are concerned that students have a sense of the nature of the process by which facts are established and of the roles played by each of the participants in the courtroom. Consequently, we begin in Chapter One with the study of a transcript from a real case. This introduces students to the process of analyzing evidence in terms of the essential elements of a legal dispute, as well as experiencing what is at stake in even run-of-the-mill trials. We believe that the transcript serves as an effective introduction to much of the course to follow. Although accurate fact finding is the dominant goal of trial, the rules of evidence also regulate with other variables in mind, such as efficiency and incentives to out-of-court behavior. Beginning with the transcript, which we return to throughout the text, allows these matters, to be highlighted. We have also based a series of problems on the transcript so that student investment in reading it pays off with a deeper understanding of the context within which isolated evidence issues arise and are resolved.

Chapter Two — The Process of Proof — provides additional background information on trial process and strategy that brings the evidence course alive. It describes how trials are structured, how witnesses are examined, and it begins our exploration of the relationship between inferential reasoning as used by the fact finder and the process of presenting proof at trial.

Chapter Three examines the single most important concept in the study of evidence — relevancy — and introduces students to the trial judge's "discretion" to exclude even relevant, and probative, evidence. Some judicial opinions, including the U.S. Supreme Court's majority opinion in Old Chief v. United States, give students a more concrete understanding of how the context of the whole "case" can influence the judge's exercise of discretion. Chapter Four contains the rules that establish the required "foundation" for many different types of evidence, including a newly organized discussion of FRE 104 and the problem of conditional relevance. The "best evidence rule" is also included in Chapter Four, a change from the third edition. Chapter Five focuses on the character and propensity rules. We start by introducing the primary rule of exclusion, the policies that justify exclusion, and the policing of the borderline between forbidden "character" and permitted "non-character" uses of specific acts. We then turn to instances in which character is a permissible topic of proof. Chapter Six contains the remaining relevancy rules.

Chapter Seven presents the doctrines of impeaching and rehabilitating witnesses, prior to the study of the hearsay rule. The attention paid to examining witnesses, we believe, paves the way for Chapter Eight's treatment of hearsay. Chapter Eight contains revised text on the problem of "implied assertions" that we think streamlines presentation without sacrificing complexity. The chapter concludes with a completely revised discussion of the confrontation clause, following the Supreme Court's decision in Crawford v. Washington. Discussion of the applicaton of Crawford, and important post-Crawford case law, concludes with reference back to the problems throughout the book that presented confrontation issues.

Chapter Nine, which focuses on the rules governing lay and expert witness opinion testimony, includes the principal Supreme Court cases and the amendments to the Federal Rules, effective in 2000. Chapter Ten presents a newly streamlined look at burdens of proof and the related doctrines of presumptions; Chapter Eleven adds the study of judicial notice; and the book concludes, as before, with an examination of rules of privilege in Chapter Twelve.

Despite the substantial amount of text, this book is not a treatise on the law of evidence. We have not attempted to cover "everything." Rather, we have put together materials that we believe will contribute to the effective teaching of the law of evidence. Our selection of materials has been driven by one criterion alone. We have selected materials that in our judgment are the most effective pedagogical tools.

We are indebted to many individuals who have assisted us in various ways in the creation of this book. Professor Allen would particularly like to thank his able research assistants Steven Bierly and Paul Whitten and his assistant, Joann Thompson. Professor Kuhns would like to thank Tara Zaffe. Professor Swift is very grateful to Will Pao, Jim Kerwin, Laura Trachtman, Michael Schaps, and Jennifer Dukart for their research assistance and enthusiasm for the law of evidence.

Ronald J. Allen
Richard B. Kuhns
Eleanor Swift
David S.Schwartz

March 2006

ACKNOWLEDGMENTS

The authors gratefully acknowledge permission to reprint excerpts from the following:

Allen, Ronald J., The Evolution of the Hearsay Rule to a Rule of Admission, 76 Minn. L. Rev. 797 (1992). Reprinted with permission.

Allen, Ronald J., et al., A Positive Theory of the Attorney-Client Privilege and the Work Product Doctrine, 19 J. Legal Stud. 359 (1990). Reprinted with permission.

Blakely, Newell H., Article IV: Relevancy and Its Limits, 30 Hous. L. Rev. 281 (1993). Reprinted with permission.

Chayes, Abram, The Role of the Judge in Public Law Litigation, 89 Harv. L. Rev. 1281 (1976). Reprinted with permission.

Gross, Samuel R., Expert Evidence, 1991 Wis. L. Rev. 1113 (1991). Copyright © 1991 by The Board of Regents of the University of Wisconsin System; Reprinted by permission of the Wisconsin Law Review.

Kuhns, Richard B., The Propensity to Misunderstand the Character of Specific Acts Evidence, 66 Iowa L. Rev. 777 (1981). Reprinted with permission.

McCormick, Charles Tilford, et al., McCormick on Evidence (John W. Strong, ed., 5th ed. 1999). Reprinted with permission of the West Group.

Park, Roger C., A Subject Matter Approach to Hearsay Reform, 86 Mich. L. Rev. 51 (1987). Reprinted with permission.

Pennington, Nancy, and Reid Hastie, Juror Decision-Making Models: The Generalization Gap, 89 Psychol. Bull. 246 (1981). Reprinted with permission.

Seigel, Michael L., Rationalizing Hearsay: A Proposal for a Best Evidence Hearsay Rule, 72 B.U. L. Rev. 893 (1992). Reprinted with permission. Copyright © 1992 by Boston University Law Review, Boston University. Forum of original publication. Boston University bears no responsibility for any errors which have occurred in reprinting, translation, or editing.

INTRODUCTION
TO THE STUDY
OF EVIDENCE

Evidence law is, in one sense, one of the most practical courses that you will take in law school. It is the study of rules in action, rules that are interpreted and applied in the often heated context of adversarial litigation over matters of life and death, personal rights (and obligations), property rights, human relationships, and even such matters as the structure of government and the meaning of the Constitution. As you read the text, the judicial opinions, and the problems in this book, you will be analyzing and evaluating the impact that evidence law has on the litigants and the outcomes of their cases. One of the most significant manifestations of evidence law is the rules of evidence. We concentrate in this book on the Federal Rules of Evidence. The Federal Rules were adopted by Congress in 1975, and since then close to 40 states have revised their rules of evidence, in many instances adopting the Federal Rules virtually verbatim. When you first read the Federal Rules of Evidence you many think them to be cold and sterile doctrines written in abstract conceptual terms, but you will soon find them imbued with the human drama of the courtroom. Behind the masks of the law there are real people who are called on to testify concerning matter of great personal and social import, as well as parties whose cases rest on that testimony.

The study of evidence, however, is not just the study of the rules of evidence. It is the study of the vast complex of ideas, principles, customs, and values underlying the process of litigation. The rules of evidence give form and content to this process — they determine the admissibility of evidence, define the roles of all the participants at trial (judge, jury, advocates, and witnesses), and structure the relationships among these various actors. They reflect our society's views on many issues, among them: (1) the appropriate means of resolving disputes; (2) the nature of knowledge, what it means to "know" something, and how knowledge is transmitted to others; (3) the dynamics of small group decision-making, and the confidence that we invest in the common person to reach wise and informed judgments that affect the lives of fellow citizens; (4) moral and ethical concerns, such as how difficult it should be for the prosecution to obtain a conviction in a criminal case, or whether certain individuals (spouses, children, friends) should have a privilege not to testify against those close to them; and (5) the relationship between the ideal of justice and the value of efficiency. The rules of evidence rest on and are a crystallization of these various, often conflicting, views. To understand the rules requires an understanding of the compromises they make between competing beliefs and interests; thus, to study the rules one must engage with the foundation of beliefs that underlies them.

The study of evidence will serve any lawyer well, no matter what specialization that person pursues. Obviously litigators must know and understand the rules of evidence in order to use them effectively. Do not overlook that while litigation is virtually always the worst-case scenario of any legal transaction, competent lawyers must always be prepared for it no matter what the nature of the relevant legal enterprise happens to be. If a contractual relationship fails or a merger is not consummated and litigation results, what will matter is how well the parties will be able to defend their respective positions. That will be determined in significant measure by the application of the rules of evidence in the trial itself, and by their implications throughout pretrial procedures, including negotiations leading to settlement.

To use the rules effectively, one must understand their meaning, source, and purpose. To do so requires that one see the rules in relationship to the assumptions, values, and concerns that give rise to them. Even if — indeed, especially if — one intends to become a litigator, it will not do to be content with a cursory grasp of the language of the various rules. One must be in a position to work with the rules, and to argue for one's position from the perspective of the purposes that underlie the relevant provisions.

For those who do not intend to become litigators, and who are reasonably sure that their legal transactions will never collapse into disputes, it is essential to see the rules as summaries of underlying social, philosophical, and moral beliefs and to look carefully at those beliefs. For such individuals, the value of the inquiry lies not in some future utility but instead in its enlightenment of our shared vision of how disputes should be resolved in a civilized society. With that enlightenment may come — indeed, we hope *will* come — disagreement. You may not like all that you see; and if you do not, you will be in a better position to work for change through the legislative and rule-making processes.

We attempt in these materials to facilitate an inquiry into the meaning and use of the rules of evidence as well as all that underlies them. At times we focus extensively — in fact, almost exclusively — on the rules themselves, while at other times we deal quite explicitly with the assumptions and values from which the rules are derived. On completion of this inquiry, you should have a thorough understanding of the rules of evidence, as well as considerable appreciation for the concerns that give rise to them.

SPECIAL NOTICE
ON CITATIONS

In general, some citations and footnotes have been omitted from quoted material without indication. Footnotes are numbered consecutively in each chapter; that is, the original footnote numbers in quoted material have not been retained. Where an editors' footnote appears within an excerpt of quoted material, it is marked " — EDS." In addition, throughout the text we quote from the Federal Rules of Evidence and from the Federal Rules' legislative history without giving specific citations. The Federal Rules quoted in the text include amendments through April 1, 1997. The advisory committee appointed by the Supreme Court to draft the rules accompanied each rule with an Advisory Committee Note. The Notes are set forth at 56 F.R.D. 183. The judiciary committees of both the House of Representatives and the Senate held hearings on the Federal Rules. The report of the House Committee is H.R. Rep. No. 650, 93d Cong., 1 Sess. (1973), appearing at 1974 U.S.C.C.A.N. 7075; and the report of the Senate is S. Rep. No. 1277, 93d Cong., 2d Sess. (1974), appearing at 1974 U.S.C.C.A.N. 7051. The Conference Committee report is H.R. Rep. No. 1597, 93d Cong., 2d Sess. (1974), and appears at 1974 U.S.C.C.A.N. 7098.

We have deleted *cert. denied* references throughout the book.

EVIDENCE

CHAPTER ONE

THE CASE OF PEOPLE v. JOHNSON

We start with an edited transcript of a real trial, People v. Johnson.[1] A trial transcript is a good place to start for a number of reasons. Most of you have not experienced litigation, and the transcript allows you to study a complete trial, to get a sense of its structure and dynamic, that is, a sense of how it is put together and how it unfolds. The transcript introduces you to the principal stages of trial process so that you can begin to appreciate the organization of a case, who is doing what to whom, and why. The transcript also introduces you to the Federal Rules of Evidence[2] and gives an overview of much that is to follow in succeeding chapters. We hope that you will get a sense of the rules of evidence in action, and an awareness of the distinction between the rules in real life and their theoretical justifications.

Another reason we begin with a transcript is to increase your understanding of the human element at work in the law of evidence. The Johnson case involves serious issues of real people in a dangerous environment with a lot at stake. The case concerns criminal charges of battery brought against an inmate at a California state prison. But Pelican Bay is not just any prison; rather, it was designed as a high-tech "state of the art" facility to house the state's most violence-prone inmates. The Security Housing Unit (SHU) at Pelican Bay was designed for control of prison gang members, not for rehabilitation. A class action lawsuit brought under the federal civil rights act alleged that the isolation conditions in the SHU amounted to cruel and unusual punishment. Prisoners housed in the general population areas of the prison also complained of the use of excessive force by guards and the denial of basic medical attention and access to legal counsel. In January of 1995, U.S. District Court Judge Thelton Henderson found that Pelican Bay staff routinely used unwarranted violence on inmates (based on 105 pages of documented violent incidents including assaults, beatings, and naked cagings in inclement weather, and an unusually high number of lethal

---

1. The names of all the participants have been changed to provide some anonymity to the parties involved. In addition, we have added footnotes, made very minor editorial changes, and eliminated essentially repetitious testimony.
2. The *Johnson* case was tried in California state court and was governed by the California Evidence Code. The California Code, enacted in 1965, was extremely influential in the drafting of the Federal Rules of Evidence seven years later and there are only a few substantive differences between the Code and the Rules. We refer to the applicable Federal Rules in the footnotes to the transcript.

shootings). He also found that Pelican Bay operated a medical and mental health care program that was significantly deficient. The judge ordered prison officials to stop housing mentally ill inmates in the SHU, but refused to hold that incarceration there constituted cruel and unusual punishment for all prisoners. Judge Henderson's opinion is reported as Madrid v. Gomez, 889 F. Supp. 1146 (N.D. Cal. 1995).

As you begin reading the transcript, remember that much has already occurred in the *Johnson* case. The parties have selected a jury and have participated in a preliminary hearing, mutual discovery, and motions in limine. These pretrial events shape issues of proof, as you will see. In addition, they shape the understanding of the participants: Judges are informed, and perhaps influenced, by what they learn in the pretrial stage; jurors are educated in the voir dire process; and the lawyers learn more about the respective strengths and weaknesses of their own case and that of their opponent. Indeed, this last point cannot be overemphasized. The single most important variable in success at litigation is preparation. If you take away one "rule" of evidence from this course, let it be "prepare, prepare, prepare." As you read the transcript, try to get an insight into how well these lawyers prepared.

A.   *THE PEOPLE OF THE STATE OF CALIFORNIA* v. *JAMES JOHNSON*

SUPERIOR COURT, DEL NORTE COUNTY, CALIFORNIA
    DATE: Monday, July 27, 1992, 1:45 P.M.

1   APPEARANCES

    For the People: William Cummings, II, ESQ., District Attorney
    For the Defendant: Mark Deemer, ESQ., Attorney at Law
    THE COURT: In the People versus Johnson let the record reflect that all jurors,
5   counsel and the defendant are present. I am going to read to you now the
        charge that has been filed against the defendant, again reminding you that the
        information is not evidence but is charged as follows:[3] "Superior Court of Del
        Norte, State of California. The People of the State of California, plaintiff,
        versus James Johnson, C-66125, defendant, No. 92-190-X. Information.
10   "The District Attorney of the County of Del Norte, State of California,
        hereby charges James Johnson (C-66125) with having committed, in the
        County of Del Norte, the crime of:
            "Count 1. Battery on a correctional officer, in violation of Section 4501.5
15   of the Penal Code, a felony.
            "On or about March 28, 1992, the defendant did willfully and unlawfully being a person confined in a State Prison of this state, commit a battery

---

    3.   The role of the judge includes informing the jury of the substantive law that will govern the jury's verdict. In California, an information is the pleading filed in Superior Court for the prosecution of a felony. Is there any reason why the judge read the information to the jury rather than simply reading the Code section that the defendant allegedly violated? Is there any reason why the judge did not try to translate the legalese into English?

1   upon the person of any individual who is not himself a person confined
           therein to wit, Officer Huston.
                    "Count 2. Battery on correctional officer, in violation of Section 4501.5
           of the Penal Code, a felony.
5   "On or about March 28th 1992, the defendant did willfully and unlaw-
           fully being a person confined in a State Prison of this state, commit a battery
           upon the person of any individual who is not himself a person confined
           therein to wit, Officer Van Berg.
                    "Dated June 23rd, 1992, William Cummings, II, District Attorney.
10   Signed Wm. Cummings for Richard Davis Deputy District Attorney."[4]
           MR. DEEMER: At this time there is a motion to exclude witnesses. I see two are
           in the courtroom.
           THE COURT: All persons who are present as witnesses in the matter will have to
           remain outside the courtroom and not discuss their testimony with any other
15   witnesses until the hearing is concluded.[5] Counsel are responsible for enfor-
           cing this order as to their own witnesses.
                    Now, before we get under way with the evidence there are also a few other
           things. One is an instruction that I will read to you that will cover how you are to
           handle certain things that may come up during the course of the trial. Because
20   you must determine the facts in this case solely from the evidence, you must be
           guided by the following principles.[6] One, you must not consider as evidence
           any statement or arguments of counsel, meaning the attorneys, except that if
           counsel agree or stipulate to any fact you must regard such fact as being con-
           clusively proved.
25   Second, you must not consider as evidence any off the record evidence
           that was rejected or any evidence that is stricken out by me.
                    Third, as to any question to which an objection is sustained, you must
           not speculate as to what the answer might have been or as to the reason for the
           objection.
30   And fourth, since a question is not evidence you must not suspect that any
           insinuation suggested by a question is true. In other words, you can consider
           the questions only as they supply meaning to the answer. Because, for instance,
           an answer of "yes" or an answer of "no" doesn't mean anything unless you know
           what the question was. But the question is not evidence. Only the evidence that
35   comes from the witness is evidence. So nothing that is said in a question should
           be assumed by you to be true or considered by you to be fact.
                    It may also happen during the course of the trial, in fact it has happened a
           couple times already, that you have seen we'll have what are called bench
           conferences, and this is where the attorneys come up here to the bench and
40   we discuss matters out of your hearing. The reason for this is from time to time

---

4.   Substantive law provides the essential elements that the prosecution will have to prove to obtain a
conviction. What are the essential elements of the crimes with which defendant Johnson is charged? *Battery*
is not defined in the information but an instruction on the elements of a battery is given at page 64 infra. In a
civil case, the essential elements of the plaintiff's case are derived from the common or statutory law that
governs the dispute.
5.   FRE 615 permits the court to exclude witnesses from the courtroom while another witness is
testifying to safeguard against the possibility of "contaminating" a witness. The objective is to preclude a
witness from altering or modifying testimony to explain or dovetail with the testimony of another witness.
6.   When you have finished reading the instructions, consider how well they communicate the
salient aspects of the role that the jurors are about to undertake. Note in particular that the judge provides
very little illumination concerning the legal standards relevant to this trial. Why do you suppose that is?

1   things come up in the course of the trial. Sometimes it has to do with objections
       to the admissibility of evidence. Sometimes it has to do with motions the attor-
       neys are making before the court or other matters that should be heard out of the
       presence of the jury. If it is going to be something lengthy we'll probably give you
5   a recess and have you step out of the court room. But if it is something very brief,
       to save the time of doing that, we come up here to the bench and we try and speak
       in tones of voice that are low enough and for that very reason you should try not
       to overhear what we are saying. If it would help you, certainly feel free to
       converse among yourselves as long as it is not about the case. If you would
10   like to stand up in place and stretch and generally make yourself comfortable,
       feel free to do that and we can get back to you shortly if that happens.[7]

       If there is anyone in the jury that feels they need a recess for any reason,
       please do not hesitate or feel embarrassed. If you need to use the rest room or
       whatever it is, I would rather take care of it, just take a few minutes and break
15   the proceedings and have you take care of it and then you won't be distracted
       and thinking about something else when you are listening to the evidence
       when we are here in court.

       Also, if any of you would like to take notes you may do so. Usually it's not
       necessary. I expect in this case where it's going to be a fairly short trial lasting a
20   couple days or so that you will probably be able to hold most everything in your
       memory. We do have the court reporter taking everything down on a word for
       word basis. So during your deliberations if you need to know exactly what some
       witness said that will be available to you and that testimony can be read back to
       you by the reporter. A few juries like to take notes and you may if you wish.
25   The one caution is you should be very careful that your note taking does not
       interfere with your ability to closely watch and observe the witnesses as they give
       their testimony because it oftentimes happens in trials and it may happen in this
       trial that one witness will testify to something and another will testify to exactly
       the opposite. Just in the words that they are saying you may not be able to figure
30   out which one you believe. It may be necessary for you to rely upon such things
       as facial expression or tone of voice or what we call body language, the general
       things that we use in our day to day life when we decide whether we believe what
       somebody is telling us or we don't. Don't let your note taking interfere with
       closely watching and scrutinizing and observing the witnesses as they testify.
35   Also, you should not on your own undertake any investigation of this
       matter.[8] You should not try to interview any witnesses, not try to visit the scene
       where anything may have happened. You should not consult any reference
       works and you should not try to perform any experiments. And that is because
       the evidence in this case, strictly the evidence that comes from the witnesses,
40   is all that should be considered in deciding what your verdict should be in this
       case. So do not try to gather evidence of facts or information from any other
       source except from the witnesses.

---

7.   A "bench conference" or a "sidebar" may be initiated by either side or by the judge when a point of
contention or procedure arises that requires resolution for the smooth functioning of the proceeding. Most
bench conferences are on the record — that is, they are recorded by the court reporter — but they occur
outside the jury's hearing, in order to keep the jury from overhearing what is discussed. Longer hearings on
the admissibility of evidence may also be held without the jury present. See FRE 104.

8.   Why shouldn't jurors learn more about the specific facts of the case by conducting their own
inquiry? Jurors bring their own background knowledge and general experience with them, and they use this
knowledge to interpret the testimony they hear. Wouldn't it be useful for them to read up on subjects that
are pertinent to the dispute as well?

1   I have already mentioned to you that you should be very careful not to —
when you encounter the attorneys or other people involved in this case during
the recesses be very careful not to fall into conversation with them.[9] We
mentioned that before lunch.

5   One final thing and that is that you should not consider as evidence the
fact that the defendant is here in physical custody of officers. You should not
take into consideration as evidence either for him or against him whether he is
confined in physical restraints or the clothing that he is wearing or that there
may be additional security here in the courtroom. Those are not facts that

10   should be considered in any way as showing whether the defendant is guilty or
not guilty. Disregard those matters and decide the case strictly on the evidence.

         All right. The final thing before we get under way with the evidence is
that the attorneys have the opportunity to make opening statements to the jury
and these are very brief outlines the attorneys could give you if they wish

15   showing what they expect the evidence in the case is going to prove. Sometimes it happens, of course, that the evidence comes out differently from what
they expect. The witness may remember something differently from what one
or the other of the attorneys may think the witness is going to testify to. But
generally speaking the attorneys can give a fair outline of what's going to

20   happen in the case and what they expect the issues are going to be. But, of
course, if there is any difference between what they say the evidence is going
to be and what it actually is, of course you follow the evidence.

         Since the prosecution has the burden of proof and presents evidence
first, the prosecutor makes the first opening statement. When he is finished

25   defense counsel has a choice. He can either make his opening statement at
that time or if he prefers he can wait until the prosecution presents their
evidence and then make his opening statement. Mr. Cummings?[10]

      MR. CUMMINGS: Thank you, Your Honor.[11] Ladies and gentlemen, we are
about to get under way and the purpose of my opening statement is basically to

30   give you some idea of where I believe our witnesses are going to take us in
testimony. Witnesses are the people who testify from the witness stand,
nowhere else. In other words, as the judge told you, what the attorneys
have to say is not evidence, and you notice neither side here have raised
their hands to tell the truth and nothing but the truth. So your testimony

35   comes from the witness stand.

         As the prosecutor in the case I expect to call three, probably four wit-
nesses. I may call more. I have an option of putting on rebuttal witnesses if I

---

9. Why should jurors not discuss the case with anyone else, including other jurors? Jurors are undergoing a learning process. Does learning occur most effectively when the learner sits passively, as this instruction directs these jurors to do? What are possible risks of discussion that offset its value in an educational process? Why is the court imposing this type of decision-making process on the jury?

10. What aspect of the jury's role did the judge focus on in the instructions? Do the instructions prepare the jury for its decision-making role? Has the judge adequately informed the jury about the role of the court or the adversaries?

11. The primary purposes of an opening statement are to state the facts that the advocate expects to produce at trial; to present these facts within the framework of a story or theme that is persuasive and that will be the basis for closing argument; and to personalize the client. Argument about what inferences should be drawn from the evidence is made in the closing arguments, not here. The opening statement is also used to introduce the jury to weaknesses in the case. Jury surveys have shown that opening statements are very important in jury decisionmaking, and that jurors often vote consistently with views they form during the opening. See the discussion in Chapter Two, Section F. Reflections on Natural Reasoning and the Adversary System.

1   want to. You will see that if it happens. Eye witnesses are going to start out with
        Officer Huston who has worked at Pelican Bay State Prison who is what we
        call a percipient witness, which means he saw, he was present when the
        incident happened in 1992 at one of the branches at Pelican Bay State Prison.
5   They call it B Facility. And I will have testimony about what B Facility means
        and what type of people are housed in B Facility.

        The defendant, Mr. Johnson, was in his cell with his cell mate, a person
        by the name of Butler and that for whatever reason they refused to give up some
        trays, food trays. That on that date, March the 28th, 1992, Butler and inmate
10   Johnson were in their cell. They had been fed in their cell, and, as I indicated
        before, for unknown reasons they weren't going to give up their trays.

        At that point in time several officers were summoned to go over to the
        cell and try to talk to them to give up their trays. And it's a mainline produc-
        tion, meaning they have to feed, get back the trays, and they have a lot of
15   people to take care of. Officer Huston will testify that basically there was a
        couple trays inside the cell and that he and other officers went into his cell
        along with some other people and talked to them about giving up the trays.

        Officer Huston will tell you — and I would suspect Officer Van Berg will
        tell you basically the same story — that Mr. Johnson had possession of the
20   trays, he was holding on to them, and that in the door of the cell, the actual
        cell door, there was a little food port door. You can slide one tray at a time
        through there. And you can't slide two through and you can't slide one with a
        lot of garbage piled on top, just enough to slide one tray back and forth.

        For whatever reason, inmate Johnson, the defendant in this case, was
25   standing in the cell with the trays in his hand and he had had some discussion
        with the officers about a package. He wanted some package. And he was not
        going to relinquish those two trays. So basically what happened in the case, as
        Officers Huston and Van Berg and Walker will testify, is that a sergeant sent
        some of them over to discuss the matter with inmate Johnson and to try to
30   persuade them basically verbally to give up the tray, "we have got to get on our
        route, our day's business."

        He asked at that point in time to see a sergeant. And the officers will
        testify that what they told Johnson at that point in time was, "We'll get you a
        sergeant; we'll have a sergeant drop by and talk to you, but we can't do it right
35   now. We have got our work to do. We have got to finish up what we are doing."

        At that point Johnson was going to give up the trays. He was not verbally
        abusive. He was not physically — didn't appear to be physically dangerous at
        that point. He was just standing there with his trays. So the officer — and he
        wasn't too far back from the cell door. So one of the officers, the Officer Smith,
40   signaled to the gentleman who controls — the sectional officer who controls
        the doors electronically or hydraulically but they are controlled from a dif-
        ferent location — go ahead and open up the cell door.

        So the cell door was opened a substantial distance, wide enough for some-
        body to charge out. And behind the door you have Johnson hanging on to the two
45   trays piled with garbage. And basically at that point with Walker in front, Van
        Berg, Smith was there and Huston was there, their testimony is going to be that
        Johnson dropped the trays, kind of lowered his head a little bit and charged Officer
        Walker who was kind of at the head of this line where he can get the job done.

        At that point in time the officers met him. The approximate location was
50   the doorway to the cell. Stopped him at the door as he tried to approach them

1 rapidly. He was swinging his fists, clenched right fist, that the officers basically
   pushed him back into the cell. The cells are not that large. Got him on top of a
   table and subdued him. One officer had handcuffs on one side of him and Mr.
   Johnson still was swinging, being combative. He was still trying to injure
5 people and they were trying to subdue him. So four or five officers at this
   point, trying to subdue him and get him cuffed up, handcuffed.

   During the course of that melee two officers were injured. One ended up
   with a broken bone — I think it was a bone chip in his thumb — and was off work
   a period of time, suffered some injuries. Another officer went down to Sutter
10 Coast Hospital with a shin injury, received a small laceration on his shin.

   These are the two counts of battery that I am going to ask you to consider.
   The people will put on a final witness, probably an officer by the name of
   Henderson who will testify about a 969B package. It's a package of documents
   from the prison certified to verify that that person was lawfully in custody at
15 Pelican Bay State Prison at the time. I do have to prove that he was in custody
   at the time. And it basically establishes the fact that he was in our prison
   system as well, which is another element that I have to prove.

   I would expect at this point in time that would be my case in chief.
   Depending on how and what the defense puts on, I may call rebuttal wit-
20 nesses, probably officers or actually two lieutenants, Foster and Kurtz. I will
   call those two as rebuttal. Thank you.

   MR. DEEMER: Reserve.[12]
   THE COURT: First witness.
   MR. CUMMINGS: Officer Huston I believe is outside.
25 THE COURT: Raise your right hand.

GEORGE HUSTON

called as a witness by the People, after having been sworn to tell the truth, the whole
truth and nothing but the truth, was examined and testified as follows:

   THE CLERK: Be seated and state your name and address for the record.
30 THE WITNESS: George Huston, Pelican Bay State Prison.

Direct Examination

   Q: BY MR. CUMMINGS: Thank you, Your Honor. Sir, what's your occupa-
        tion?[13]
   A: Correctional officer.
35 Q: How long have you been a correctional officer?

---

12.   Defense counsel is reserving his right to make his opening statement following the presentation
of the state's case. Should he have delayed, or should he have made his statement right now? Most defense
attorneys make their opening statement right after the plaintiff or prosecution in order to challenge that
version of the case and to make sure that the jury hears both sides. Otherwise, there is a risk that the jury is
already convinced by the time the defense begins.

13.   As you read the prosecutor's direct examinations, make a note of what testimony you think tends
to establish the essential elements of the prosecution's case against the defendant. For example, at what
point does Officer Huston provide testimony to show that the defendant's alleged battery was committed
against a person not confined in State Prison?

 1   A: Six years.
     Q: Where are you currently employed?
     A: Pelican Bay State Prison.
     Q: How long have you worked at Pelican Bay?
 5   A: Since November '89.
     Q: Was that basically the opening date for the prison?
     A: Yes.
     Q: So you are part of the original team that started out at the institution?
     A: Yes, sir.
10   Q: Sir, were you working in the capacity of a correctional officer on March the
          28th, 1992?
     A: Yes.
     Q: Did you have occasion to come into contact with an inmate by the name of
          Johnson seated at the other end of this table?
15   A: Yes.
     Q: Do you recognize him today?
     A: Yes, I do.
     Q: What facility was he housed in, do you know?
     A: Facility B.
20   Q: What is the significance of Facility B?
     A: It's a general population.
     Q: As opposed to what, sir?
     A: Security Housing Unit.
     Q: Is there a transition of inmates from one facility like SHU, Security Housing
25   Unit, to, say, general population?
     A: Yes.
     MR. DEEMER: Objection. I don't see the relevance.
     THE COURT: Sustained.
     Q. BY MR. CUMMINGS: Officer, what type of people — what type of inmates
30   are typically housed in Facility B?
     MR. DEEMER: Again, objection. I don't see the relevance.
     THE COURT: Approach the bench.

     (The following bench conference was had outside the presence of the jury.[14])

     THE COURT: Where is the relevance?
35   MR. CUMMINGS: The relevance is the fact that Facility B is a transition
          facility from Security Housing Unit to General Population and there are
          more incidents of violence and reported violence in general at Facility B
          than there is in the General Population. Conversely there is less out of SHU.
     MR. DEEMER: Less what?
40   MR. CUMMINGS: Less reported violence and there is actually less in SHU
          than there is in Facility B. Facility B is a transition facility where they take
          people who have been in SHU and kind of mainline them back into the way
          of General Population.

---

14.   Here, the bench conference was recorded by the court reporter. If the conference were held off
the record, the lawyers must remember to summarize what occurred for the record when the trial goes back
on the record. Failure to "perfect the record" may result in an inability to appeal any asserted error in the
trial judge's ruling.

1   THE COURT: How does that help the jury?
     MR. CUMMINGS: I think where you have an allegation of battery against the
          officers I think it's important that they understand that the facility which this
          person was housed is a facility where — it's a facility where people go, they are
5   in transition. I am not going to say in transition from what to what. The fact of
          the matter is that you have already given these preliminary rulings that you are
          going to allow Mr. Deemer to go into some issues of "Do you know Officer
          Walker's propensity" or "Do you know his reputation for violence among
          other inmates?"[15] I think when you have that kind of testimony coming
10   out, I think it is relevant on the issue that in Facility B we have people
          who are in fact more prone to violence and have proven to be more prone
          to violence and are in fact in transition trying to get back into the general
          mainstream of General Population.
     THE COURT: I will allow you to establish that this is a maximum security
15   section, but I think the implication that the jury is likely to get from this
          testimony if you are allowed to go forward with it is in fact he has just
          been in trial for something coming out of SHU. I don't think you should
          be allowed to do that because it gets into impermissible character evidence.[16]
          So if you want to describe physically what Facility B is and if you want to
20   describe what precautions are taken in Facility B, you can do that. But you
          can't go into what he may have done in prison unless it becomes otherwise
          relevant. At this point I don't think it is relevant so I am going to sustain the
          objection.

     (The following proceedings were had in open court.)

25   Q. BY MR. CUMMINGS: Officer Huston, would you tell me physically how
          Facility B is set up? Are they single-celled, are they double-celled cells?
     A: They are double-celled cells.
     Q: Are they arranged in what sort of a format?
     A·   One hundred twenty-eight inmates available per housing unit, eight housing
30   units.
     Q: This is still a Level IV maximum security prison setting; is that correct?
     A: Yes.
     Q: Sir, do you work or were you working on March the 28th, 1992, in B Facility?
     A: Yes, I was.

---

    15.   If an advocate knows that an evidentiary problem is likely to arise at trial, the advocate can
attempt to get a pretrial resolution of that issue. Motions to suppress illegally obtained evidence are
examples of this. A more general procedure involves filing a motion in limine. Motions in limine (meaning
at the threshold) can be used to get pretrial rulings on virtually any evidentiary question. Here, the defense
has obtained a ruling from the judge that he will admit reputation evidence about one of the officers.
Whether raising an evidentiary objection in a motion in limine is sufficient to preserve that objection for
appeal is discussed in Chapter Two.
    16.   Why is the judge going to admit reputation evidence with respect to Officer Walker, but not
character evidence with respect to the defendant? The answer to this question requires analysis of why
character evidence is relevant. The testimony regarding Walker's reputation for violence would be relevant
to show defendant's state of mind of fear of Walker, whereas the testimony about the defendant's violent
character would be relevant to show that he acted in conformity with his character and was the aggressor. As
you will see in Chapter Five, infra, under FRE 404 character evidence is normally not admitted to show that
a person committed an act in conformity with that character. This is one example of the general principle
that relevancy is a necessary but not a sufficient condition for admissibility.

1 Q: What was your position or what did you do in B Facility?[17]
   A: Yard officer.
   Q: What's a yard officer?
   A: Yard officer maintains safety and security on the yard, General Population
5   inmates. And in that first response, emergency response.
   Q: When you say "first response," what do you mean by "first response"?
   A: In an emergency I am designated to respond anywhere in the facility.
   Q: So if there was an incident in B Facility, it would be expected that you would
        respond; is that correct?[18]
10 A: Yes.
   Q: Are you aware of an incident involving inmate Johnson on March 28th of this
        year?
   A: It wasn't really an incident.
   Q: What was it?
15 A: It was a simple denial of a breakfast tray. When an inmate gets fed in the
        morning they are supposed to — after breakfast they gave up their breakfast
        trays and silverware. Floor officer on that day said that inmate Johnson and his
        cellie, cell mate Butler, were holding their breakfast trays.
   Q: And at some point in time somebody summoned you; is that correct?
20 A: Yes.
   Q: Who was that, do you know
   A: I don't remember on the day. There was several of us and we were told to go
        over and see if we could get the breakfast trays.
   Q: What did you expect to do that day, did you know?
25 A: Go over and simply, "Give us the trays."
   Q: Talk to them first?
   A: Yeah.
   Q: Is that what you did?
   A: I didn't myself. The officer that ordered him to give up the trays is the one that
30   ordered — gave him the direct order.
   Q: Which officer ordered him to give up the trays?
   A: Officer Smith.
   Q: Was the order to give up the trays once or more than once if you know?
   A: More than twice.
35 Q: Could you see from where you were at inmate Johnson inside his cell?
   A: Yes.
   Q: Physically tell us how he appeared at the time that he was ordered to give up
        and relinquish those two trays.
   A: Quiet. Did not say anything except he asked to see the sergeant.
40 Q: Did he indicate why he wanted to see a sergeant?
   A: No.
   Q: Did he have anything in his hands as you remember?

   17. Notice the form of the prosecutor's questions to Officer Huston concerning his work at B Facility
and the incident involving the defendant. The prosecutor is using "who, what, where, when, why, and how"
questions. A direct examination usually takes the form of short, nonsuggestive questions that, when asked
and answered in sequence, tell the witness's story efficiently.
   18. The prosecutor here, and three questions later, is using a common form of "leading question"
that explicitly suggests the answer that the advocate is looking for. The tag "isn't that correct" or "isn't it true
that" permits only a yes or no answer. Thus, the information that the jury hears is really supplied by the
lawyer's question; the witness's response simply confirms or denies it.

1 A: Not at that immediate moment. After the food port was opened, he picked up his trays and acted like he was going to give us the trays.

Q: You indicated the food port. Where is the food port located?

A: In the middle of the door about waist high.

5 Q: Can you describe it for us?

A: It's approximately probably a four-to-five-inch opening. Has a door on it, probably twelve inches wide.

Q: It's a hinged door?

A: Yes.

10 Q: And that door opens and shuts?

A: Yes, and it is locked when it's not used.

Q: It is locked when it's not used?

A: When it's not used.

Q: Normally a person can pass how many trays through a food port opening?

15 A: One.

Q: How many trays did inmate Johnson have in his hands?

A: He had two trays with disposable garbage on the top of them.

Q: Would those two trays with the garbage on top pass through the food port door?

20 A: No.

Q: How would a person normally pass the trays through, just slide them through?

A: Yes. Officer would unlock the food port and it's got another lock. When you pull down on it and at that time they pass the food tray through and the officer grabs it and takes it.

25 Q: At some point in time it became clear to you that inmate Johnson was not going to slide the trays through the food port door.

A: No. When he picked up the trays and brought them to the food port it was not subtle, I guess. He didn't say anything, he was calm, walked up to the door and held the tray.

30 Q: At that point in time did somebody order the door be opened?

A: Yes. Officer Smith.

Q: And is that an appropriate method to get back the trays?

A: Yes.

MR. DEEMER: Excuse me. A, lack of qualifications; B, lack of foundation; and,
35 C, it's leading.[19]

THE COURT: Are you asking for an expert opinion, Mr. Cummings?

Q. BY MR. CUMMINGS: Officer Huston, you stated that you have worked as a correctional officer at Pelican Bay for six years?

A: Yes.

40 Q: And during those six years, did you receive special education and training for your job?

A: Yes.

Q: What was that?

---

19. The objection's references to lack of qualifications and foundation amount to the same thing. Does this witness possess the knowledge to answer the question adequately? Essentially the witness is being asked to offer an opinion concerning the proper operation of the prison system. To do so, he should be qualified as an expert, who is a specially qualified person empowered under the Rules of Evidence to offer testimony because of special competence. See FRE 702. Opinions by nonexperts are admissible in somewhat limited, but very important, circumstances. See FRE 701.

1   A: There are training manuals, and training courses for correctional officers on-
          site and throughout the state that we attend.

     Q: And does this training include the handling of specific problems that inmates
          sometimes cause?

5   A: Yes it does.

     Q: And based on this training, do you have an opinion on the proper means to
          handle situations like inmate Johnson's, that is, on whether it is appropriate to
          open the cell door? Just tell us whether you have an opinion.

     A: Yes I do.

10   MR. CUMMINGS: I would offer Officer Huston's opinion now based on his
          special experiences and training at Pelican Bay.

     THE COURT: You may answer.

     Q. BY MR. CUMMINGS: Is opening the cell door an appropriate way to get
          back the food trays?

15   A: Yes, on the General Population side it is. If the inmates are General Popula-
          tion inmates so they are out of their cells a lot of the time and if they are, what
          we say, programmed and everything else and they seem calm and everything
          else, well, we — yeah, we get the trays that way, especially when they have
          more than two trays or have two trays with garbage on the top.

20   Q: I am going to draw a distinction here between the Secured Housing Unit, the
          SHU inmates, and the General Population inmates. Inmate Johnson was at
          that point a General Population inmate?

     A: Yes, he was.

     Q: And if this incident had occurred on the Secured Housing Unit side, the other

25   section of the prison, would the doors have been opened in this fashion?

     A: Absolutely not.

     Q: So the procedure is different from your experience whether a person is in
          General Population or is in the Secured Housing Unit?

     A: Yes, it is.

30   Q: For inmate Johnson, housing in General Population, this was an appropriate
          way to retrieve the trays, if necessary?

     A: Yeah.

     Q: Was the door opened?

     A: Yes, the door was opened.

35   Q: What happened when the door opened?

     A: Inmate Johnson — when the door was opened up inmate Johnson immedi-
          ately instantly dropped the food trays. He was standing just inside the door, up
          next to the door. Dropped the food trays immediately and bowed his head,
          brought up his fists and just tried to come through the door and hit Officer

40   Walker in the chest.

     Q: Where did Officer Walker make contact or where did Johnson make contact
          with Walker?

     A: In the door. In the doorway after the door was opened. Officer Walker was on
          the outside of the cell.

45   Q: Do you recall the other officers who were present?

     A: The other officers that I knew that were present were Officer Smith and
          Officer Walker and Officer Van Berg.

     Q: Were there other officers there that you don't recall by name?

     A: Yes, Officer White was there, but I didn't find that out until after the incident.

1   Q: When officers are retrieving food items, trays, et cetera, in General Population are they wearing protective gear?

A: No.

Q: What happened when Johnson charged the officers and made contact with
5   Walker?

A: Officer Walker immediately grabbed him and pushed him inside the cell and
inmate Johnson fell back up against the desk area, which is approximately
three feet inside the cell.

Q: What was inmate Johnson doing at that time?

10   A: Combative.

MR. DEEMER: One moment, Your Honor. I am going to object to that term.
It's conclusionary.[20]

THE COURT: Overruled.

Q. BY MR. CUMMINGS: Describe for me what you mean by "combative"?

15   A: Swinging his arms, not complying with orders, using his strength.

Q: What sort of orders were being given to Johnson at that time?

A: To cuff up.

Q: What's cuff up?

A: Handcuff.

20   Q: Standard procedure?

A: Yes.

Q: Was there a cell mate in the same cell?

A: Yes.

Q: Do you recall his name?

25   A: Inmate Butler.

Q: What did inmate Butler do, if anything?

A: Inmate Butler was immediately told to get down by Officer Smith in the cell.

Q: What does "get down" mean?

A: "Get down" means hit the floor in a prone position.

30   Q: Did he comply?

A: Yes, he did comply immediately.

Q: And he was secured, too?

A: Yes, Officer Smith restrained him.

Q: Why was inmate Johnson and inmate Butler secured, handcuffed? What's the
35   purpose?

A: Because if they are combative or not complying with orders; disciplinary
reasons, you know.

Q: Officer safety reasons?

A: Yes, officer safety and security.

40   Q: Inmate Butler basically did exactly what he was told to do?

A: Yes, he did.

Q: Was there kind of a wrestling or a pushing or a shoving or some sort of an
altercation inside the cell?

A: Yes. Inmate Johnson was not complying. He was swinging, he was kicking, he
45   was using his strength against us. In fact, after we got him pushed up against

---

20.   The objection that a question calls for a conclusion is just another way to say that it calls for an
opinion. Here the opinion would be a lay opinion, not an expert opinion. But is "combative" a fact or an
opinion? What is the difference? Even though the objection is overruled, note how the prosecutor develops
the record by having the witness explain what "combative" means.

1   the desk area, we couldn't get him handcuffed in the cell. So we brought him
       out of the cell, put him in the prone position outside the cell. He was in the
       prone position. He wouldn't give up his hands for restraint. I finally got one
       handcuff on the right wrist. Several orders — he wouldn't give up his left one.
5   He kept it underneath him. When I did get it out from underneath him, he
       brought — and husbanding his strength he wouldn't let me have his wrists. It
       took me a little while to get him restrained and in the left handcuff. He was
       resisting it.
       Q: Using both his hands and his feet?
10   A: Both hands and feet.
       Q: Was he saying anything during this period of time?
       A: No.
       Q: Sir, were you injured in that altercation?
       A: Yes, I was.
15   Q: Describe your injuries for us.
       MR. DEEMER: Excuse me. May we approach the Bench at this time?

(The following proceedings were had at the bench, outside the hearing of the jury.)

       MR. DEEMER: My understanding is that the witness is going to testify that he
       received a gash and yet he also testifies at the preliminary hearing — and
20   I assume his testimony isn't going to change today — that he doesn't know
       how he received the injury. So I think this testimony at this point becomes
       irrelevant.
       MR. CUMMINGS: I think that's an awkward summary. What he is going to
       testify to is he received the injuries as a result of this melee. He cannot testify
25   that inmate Johnson slugged him, kicked him or directly caused it. But for the
       melee he certainly would not have been injured in that fashion. Obviously
       this witness can testify to what he observed on his own body. He doesn't have
       to be a doctor or a nurse or anything else to testify what injuries he personally
       received on his own body, and that's all I am looking for, and whether or not
30   he went to the hospital or went home or returned to work.
       THE COURT: I would possibly preclude you or limit you in some fashion if you
       attempted to call a doctor.
       MR. CUMMINGS: I have no intention of it.
       THE COURT: He can testify to his own knowledge what he observed on his own
35   body. I am not going to preclude him from that.

(The following proceedings were had in open court.)

       Q. BY MR. CUMMINGS: Officer Huston, where were you injured?
       A: My left shin had a one-inch gash.
       Q: Did you ever seek medical attention for that?
40   A: Yes, they did a triage and then I was sent to Sutter Coast Hospital.
       Q: And you were treated at Sutter Coast?
       A: Yes.
       Q: How long did this whole thing take — or how little time did it take?
       A: Everything happened real fast. I couldn't give you a time on it. Everything was
45   instantaneous from the time the food trays were dropped and Mr. Johnson

1   trying to get through the door and I really couldn't give you — several — probably several seconds. When the adrenaline is flowing you have no idea how long it is.

  Q: Sir, when you are working as a yard officer as you were that day, do you carry a
5   side-handled baton?

  A: Yes, I do.

  Q: In this incident involving inmate Johnson did you have to — or did you have time to remove your side-handled baton?

  A: I did not. At that time I had no time to.

10 Q: I take it, then, you were not expecting trouble when the door was being opened.

  A: Absolutely not.

  Q: You were taken by surprise?

  A: Yes, I was.

15 MR. CUMMINGS: Thank you sir. Nothing further.

Cross-examination

  Q. BY MR. DEEMER: Officer Huston, who at that point unlocked the food port?

  A: Officer Smith.

20 Q: And then was anything done with the food port prior to the door being opened?

  A: You mean was there anything — it was opened prior to the door being —

  Q: But was it then closed again?

  A: I could not say whether it was or not.

25 Q: Now, did any of the other officers at the time you were all at the door — and I take it there is eight or ten officers at the door; is that correct?

  A: I have no idea if there was eight or ten. I am saying there was the four that I know of.

  Q: But there were more than four. There were some other officers —

30 A: I understand that there was, but I didn't have any identification and know who the officers are and how many others.

  Q: Hey, I am not trying to trip you. All I am trying to figure out is there were four officers there that you know including yourself?

  A: Yes.

35 Q: And there were some officers you didn't know?

  A: Yes.

  Q: You don't remember what the total number of the other officers were?

  A: No.

  Q: Could it have been as many as eight or ten?

40 A: I guess maybe, yes.

  Q: Now, did any of the officers just prior to the time the cell door was opened put on some gloves?

  A: I have no idea. I didn't put any on my myself, no.

  Q: Do you recall any officers putting on — pulling out the side-handled batons,
45   PRC 24 or something like that?

 1   A: No, I don't recall that.
     Q: Now, when the door was opened — first of all, there is absolutely nothing
          aggressive about the defendant up until the time the door is opened; is that
          correct?
 5   A: No, there wasn't anything aggressive about him until he dropped the trays.
     Q: Okay. And when the door is opened Walker is standing in front of him?
     A: Yes.
     Q: And at that point the defendant is standing there and he has got two trays in his
          hands and he just drops the trays like that; is that correct?
10   A: Instantly.
     Q: And brought his hands up toward his head?
     A: He brought them up, yeah.
     Q: How were they shaped when he brought them up towards his head?
     A: In a clenched fist.
15   Q: And at that point you observed Walker push him?
     A: I, at that point — he had struck Walker in the chest.
     Q: With what?
     A: With his fist.
     Q: And then Walker pushed him back?
20   A: And Walker pushed him back into the cell.
     Q: And then the melee ensues?
     A: Yes.
     Q: Now, you search inmates' cells frequently, don't you?
     A: In my job once in a while I do.
25   Q: And when you search an inmate's cell, whether he is in General Population or
          in SHU, the first thing you do is get the inmate out of the cell; is that correct?
     MR. CUMMINGS: Objection. Relevance.
     THE COURT: Overruled. You may answer.
     THE WITNESS: If you are going to search the cell, yes, you bring the inmate out
30   and — out of the cell.
     Q. BY MR. DEEMER: In your training except when you are forming some sort
          of what they call a cell extraction team, you are never supposed to be in the
          same room like a closed room, like a cell or a sally port or something like that
          with an inmate, are you?[21]
35   A: Not in a cell with an inmate. In a sally port, yeah, you are in with the General
          Population inmates.
     Q: Let's stick with a cell. The reason you don't go into a cell with an inmate is
          because you are afraid something might happen; is that correct?
     A: It's safety and security.
40   Q: So wouldn't the normal procedure of removing these trays have been to order
          the inmates to the cell port to cuff up and remove them from the cell?
     A: It depends on the circumstances.
     Q: All right. How long have you known Officer Walker?
     A: Approximately one and a half years.
45   Q: You weren't at Folsom with him?
     A: No.

---

21.   What is an extraction team? A sally port? Again, is the lawyer attending to the jury?

1 Q: If something is to be removed forcibly from an inmate or an inmate is to be forcibly moved, isn't the normal way to do it by means of a cell extraction team?

A: If he is to be forcibly removed from his cell?

5 Q: Either something is to be forcibly removed from him or he is to be forcibly moved from the cell. In either instance — and he is in the cell. Isn't the cell extraction team normally the way to do that?

A: If he fails to comply with cuffing up and stuff like that, yes, it could be done.

Q: Prior to opening the cell door you never asked the inmate to cuff up, did you?

10 A: No, not that I — not myself, no.

Q: Now, when you opened the door — or excuse me. When the door was opened, did you expect that the trays were going to be handed out to you?

A: Yes. Yes, I did think he was going to give the trays to the officer.

Q: Now, in connection with this case did you prepare some sort of a report?

15 A: Yes, I did a 115, CDC 115 report.

Q: And that's a rules violation report?

A: That's a rules violation report.

Q: And that's basically what is done for disciplinary purposes; is that correct?

A: Yes.

20 Q: Do you have a copy of that with you?

A: Yeah, yes, I do.

Q: Could you look at that? Have you got it there?

A: Yes.

Q: On the CDC 115 — and I am asking you to go down one, two, three lines, the
25 sentence that begins "The inmates were given repeated orders." Would you read that to yourself?

A: "The inmates were given — "

Q: Just read it to yourself. You don't have to read it to the jury.

A: Yes.

30 Q: All right. And in that report basically you state that Officer Smith instructed the control booth officer, quote, "to open the door to the cell in order for staff to enter and retrieve the trays." Is that correct?

A: What line are you reading there?

Q: One, two, three, four, five, six lines down. I think that is the fifth line down.
35 "Officer Smith instructed the control booth officer," quote, "to open the door." Do you see that there?

A: Yes.

Q: So Smith instructed — what you thought at least at that point in time was that staff was going to enter and retrieve the trays; is that correct?

40 A: Well, when you say "enter," if I am handing my hand through the door I am entering the cell.

Q: But earlier you testified that he was going to hand — you expected the trays to be handed out; is that correct?

A: Yes, hand them right at the door, yes.

45 Q: Now, on the next line down you indicate that Johnson rushed toward Correctional Officer Walker; is that correct?

A: Yes.

Q: Attempting to strike him with clenched fists; is that correct?

A: Yes.

1   Q: Doesn't say any place in there that he actually struck him with a clenched fist, does it?
    A: What line are we reading here? Yes.
    Q: It doesn't say that, does it?
5   A: No.
    Q: And it doesn't say anything in your report about an open food port, does it?
    A: No.
    Q: It doesn't say anything in your report about who opened the food port, does it?
    A: No.
10 Q: Sir, do you remember testifying at the preliminary hearing?
    A: Yes, I do.
    Q: Is it correct to state — you have had an opportunity to review your preliminary hearing transcript, haven't you?
    A: Yes, I did read it.
15 Q: By the way, did you discuss your testimony with some of the other officers?
    A: No.
    Q: And is it correct that based on your testimony from the preliminary hearing transcript you don't know how you received the gash in your leg?
    A: No, I don't.
20 Q: And, sir, in connection with injuries that you received on the job you get some sort of Workers' Comp; is that correct?
    MR. CUMMINGS: Objection. Relevance.[22]
    MR. DEEMER: Want me to make my offer of proof in front of the jury or the bench?
25 THE COURT: Overruled. You may answer.
    THE WITNESS: Yes. Yes, I do get workmen's compensation.
    Q. BY MR. DEEMER: And officers get a different level of Workers' Comp if they are injured by an inmate as opposed to some sort of accidental injury; isn't that correct?
30 A: Yes.
    Q: If you are injured by an inmate you get three-quarters of your base pay as Workers' Comp. If you just happened to have an ordinary injury on the job it's one-half; is that correct?
    A: No. If it's an assaultive by an inmate the first three days I get back on sick time.
35   So in other words, if I am out on sick time because of an injury from an inmate, well, then I don't lose those three days' sick time. It's taken off my books and it's covered. Doesn't come off my books.
    Q: But if you have been injured on an ordinary type accident, that would come off your books?
40 A: Yes, the first three days would be on-site injury. The first three days I would lose, okay, and then would be picked up by workmen's comp.
    Q: And there is also a difference in the Workers' Comp rate, too; isn't there?
    MR. CUMMINGS: Same objection. Relevance.
    THE COURT: Overruled.

---

22.   Relevance refers to whether an item of evidence tends to prove the proposition it is offered to prove, and whether that proposition is of significance — is material — to the litigation. Here, the objection is that Workers' Compensation payments have no significance — are not "material" — to the litigation. Relevancy is examined in Chapter Three.

1   *THE WITNESS:*   It's two-thirds pay whether it is one injury or not, whether it's a
        staff injury from an inmate or —
    MR. DEEMER: No further questions.

Redirect Examination[23]

5   *Q. BY MR. CUMMINGS:*   If a person is in General Population is it to the best of
        your knowledge appropriate for food trays to be retrieved in the fashion that
        they were retrieved in this case? In other words, open up the door a little bit.
    A: Yes.
10 Q: There was nothing wrong with that?
    A: No. I had a housing unit for a year and a half down there with General
        Population inmates. They are programmed inmates.
    Q: Tell us what "programmed" means.
    A: Program is they go to work, they are — disciplinaries are very few, they are
15   usually not staff assaultive. I don't know how to say this. They are calm
        inmates. They are programmed to prison life.
    Q: Now, that is very different from somebody who is in another portion of the
        institution that is, a SHU, Security Housing Unit, inmate; is that correct?
    A: Oh, yes, it's a lot different in Security Housing Unit.
20 Q: If hypothetically this same incident happened on the Secured Housing Unit
        side of Pelican Bay, which is not where it occurred, if it happened over there
        would it be appropriate for the correctional officers to order a door opened to
        retrieve the tray?
    A: No.
25 Q: Why not?
    A: Because they are assaultive to inmates or staff. They are highly disciplinary.
    Q: Is it safe to say that if they are in the other side, the Secured Housing Unit side,
        you are basically expecting trouble all the time?
    A: Yes.
30 Q: Are you expecting less trouble or hopefully none at all when they are in the
        General Population side?
    A: Yes, hopefully, yes.
    Q: What would you have done if inmate Johnson had been in the Secured
        Housing Unit? What would have been appropriate then?
35 A: I would have a vest on. I would have a partner with me before I went to the
        cell. When I picked up the breakfast tray I would open the food port. There
        would only be one inmate up to the food port and he would pass the tray in
        and I would not be standing in front of the food port.
    Q: You take additional precautions?
40 A: Oh, yes.
    Q: It's embarrassing to even ask you this, but are you in any way financially
        benefitted by getting injured on the job?

---

23. The two parties in this case constantly seesawed back and forth with redirect and recross-
examinations, trying to have the last word. This is quite boring for the jury, and usually develops no
new information. Much of this repetitive testimony has been edited out of this transcript.

 1   A: Heavens, no. I have got a scar to prove it, and I don't like my scar.
     Q: That scar came out of this incident?
     A: Yes, it did.
     MR. CUMMINGS: Thank you sir. Nothing further.
 5   MR. DEEMER: Nothing.
     THE COURT: Thank you. You are excused. You can either leave or stay, as you
            wish. Next witness.
     MR. CUMMINGS: Officer Van Berg.
     THE COURT: Come up to the front, please, and raise your right hand.

10   RICHARD VAN BERG

     called as a witness by the People, after having been sworn to tell the truth, the whole
     truth and nothing but the truth, was examined and testified as follows:

     THE CLERK: Be seated in the witness chair and state your name and business
            address for the record.
15   THE WITNESS: Richard Van Berg.

                            Direct Examination

     Q. BY MR. CUMMINGS: Your business address is fine. Pelican Bay State
            Prison?
     A: Right.
20   Q: Officer, what's your occupation?
     A: Correctional officer.
     Q: How long have you been so employed?
     A: Six years.
     Q: Where are you currently stationed?
25   A: Pardon?
     Q: What's your current assignment at the prison?
     A: B Facilities at Pelican Bay.
     Q: How long have you been at Pelican Bay?
     A: Two and a half years.
30   Q: You were there when the institution opened?
     A: Yes.
     Q: Sir, were you working as a correctional officer on March the 28th, 1992?
     A: Yes, I was.
     Q: Did you have occasion on that day to come into contact with an inmate by the
35   name of Johnson?
     A: Yes, I did.
     Q: Same individual seated at the end of counsel table?
     A: Yes, it is.
     Q: Do you recall where he was?
40   A: He was inside of his cell.
     Q: Was there a cell mate?

1   A: Yes, there was.
    Q: Do you recall his name?
    A: Not offhand.
    Q: What is your routine assignment in B Facility?
5   A: I am a search and escort officer.
    Q: Would you tell us what a search and escort officer does?
    A: Searches cells, escorts inmates, delivers 115 rules violations, assists the pro-
         gram sergeant. He has a variety of duties.
    Q: Were you involved in attempting to retrieve some trays from inmate Johnson
10   on that date?
    A: Yes, I was.
    Q: Were you assigned to that or was that your normal duty for that day? Did
         someone tell you to assist?
    A: I was ordered to go to A block and assist in receiving the trays.
15 Q: Had you had any prior contact with inmate Johnson?
    A: No.
    Q: Do you know inmate Johnson at all?
    A: No.
    Q: What other officers were in front of inmate Johnson's cell when you got there?
20 A: The only two that I recall were Officer Smith and Walker.
    Q: Were there other officers besides those two and you don't recall the names?
    A: Yes.
    Q: Did you hear Officer Smith make any orders or any commands of inmate
         Johnson?
25 A: Yes.
    Q: What did he order him to do?
    A: He ordered him to return the food trays to him through the food port on
         several occasions.
    Q: I take it two or more?
30 A: Yes.
    Q: Could you observe what inmate Johnson was doing from your position?
    A: From what I could see he was just standing at the door holding his food trays.
    Q: Door was closed at that point?
    A: Yes.
35 Q: I am referring to the full cell door now, not the food port door.
    A: Right. The food port was open.
    Q: Do you recall if the food port door was open?
    A: Yes.
    Q: Did you have a pretty good view of the person behind that door?
40 A: Fairly well, yeah.
    Q: You can tell whether or not they are swinging their arms or they look like they
         might be combative, I take it.
    A: Yes.
    Q: Did it appear to you that inmate Johnson was going to be combative?
45 A: No, he was just standing there holding those two trays and had once asked to
         speak to a sergeant.
    Q: And did you hear anybody reply what would happen as far as getting a sergeant
         to see him?

1   A: He was told that he could see a sergeant but first he had to return the food
         trays.
    Q: Did he say anything?
    A: No.
5   Q: Did he take one of the trays off the other tray and slide it on through the food
         door as ordered?
    A: No.
    Q: He just stood there with the two trays in his hand?
    A: Yes.
10 Q: At some point in time did Officer Smith order the door be opened?
    A: Yes.
    Q: Was the door open?
    A: Yes, it was.
    Q: Was it open wide enough so that inmate Johnson could charge through if he
15   wanted to?
    A: Yes.
    Q: Were you expecting that to happen?
    A: No.
    Q: Did inmate Johnson — was he verbally assaultive or verbally threatening at
20   all?
    A: No.
    Q: Was he physically assaultive? Did he appear to be physically dangerous at all?
    A: No, not at that point.
    Q: When the cell door opened what happened?
25 A: Inmate Johnson just dropped the food trays and rushed, you know, one sud-
         den step towards the door.
    Q: Did he do anything with his hands?
    A: I seen one hand come out through the cell door. I believe it was his right hand
         and it was in a clenched fist. Officer Walker was standing right up against the
30   door so when it opened he was attempting to assault Officer Walker.
    Q: Let me make this clear. Did inmate Johnson make forward motions towards
         Correctional Officer Walker?
    A: Yes.
    Q: Or did Officer Walker make motions towards Johnson?
35 A: No, inmate Johnson stepped towards Officer Walker.
    Q: So he moved forward?
    A: Yes.
    Q.   Did he appear to be attempting to fight or strike Walker?
    A: Yes
40 MR. DEEMER: One moment. That's leading.
    THE COURT: Overruled. You may answer.
    Q. BY MR. CUMMINGS: Did you see inmate Johnson strike Officer Walker?
    MR. DEEMER: Same objection.
    THE COURT: Overruled. You may answer.
45 THE WITNESS: Actual body contact, no.
    Q. BY MR. CUMMINGS: Is that because from your position you couldn't see it?
    A: Yes.
    Q: What did you see Officer Walker do when inmate Johnson moved toward
         him?

1 A: The two just came together, Officer Walker had ahold of inmate Johnson and they were going back inside the cell.

Q: Is that appropriate? Is that what a correctional officer should do in that situation is take command of him?

5 A: Yes.

Q: At some point in time did you come in contact with the other officers' hands on inmate Johnson?

A: Yes.

Q: Was that inside the cell or outside the cell?

10 A: That was outside the cell.

Q: And why did you get involved at that point?

A: I assisted Officers Walker and I believe Huston in trying to get inmate Johnson's arm behind him so we could place it in handcuffs.

Q: And at that point in time was inmate Johnson being combative?

15 A: Yes.

Q: Was he being resistive?

A: Yes, absolutely.

Q: Was he complying with the orders that were being given him at that point?

A: No.

20 Q: Were you injured, sir?

A: Yes, I was.

Q: Where?

A: My left thumb.

Q: How?

25 A: I'm not sure how it happened.

Q: In the course of that altercation you were injured, I take it.

A: Yes.

Q: Did you seek medical attention?

A: Yes, I did.

30 Q: Where did you go?

A: Sutter Coast Hospital.

Q: Did they tell you that something had happened to your hand?

A: Yes, I had a bone chip.

Q: One of the bones in your hand was chipped?

35 A: Yes, sir.[24]

MR. CUMMINGS: Thank you sir. Nothing further.

Cross-examination

Q. BY MR. DEEMER: I have been watching you around the court. Those cowboy boots aren't state issue, are they?

40 A: No.

Q: Sir, you wrote a report in this matter, didn't you?

A: Yes, I did.

---

24.   Does Officer Van Berg have personal knowledge of the bone chip in his thumb? He does have knowledge of what the hospital told him about his injury, but if he testified "They told me I had a bone chip," it would be hearsay under FRE 801 and would be inadmissible unless it fit within an exception under FRE 803 or 804.

1 Q: You have a copy of that report with you, don't you?
   A: Not with me, no.
   MR. DEEMER: If I could approach the witness, Your Honor.
   THE COURT: Yes.
5 Q. BY MR. DEEMER: You will have to pardon my underlining, but I would like
      to show you your report and see if it refreshes your recollection at all.[25]
   MR. CUMMINGS: I don't believe there has been a question posed that indi-
      cates he does not recall.
   MR. DEEMER: I would just appreciate it if he would review it.
10 THE WITNESS: Yes, I'm done with that.
   Q. BY MR. DEEMER: There is nothing in that report that gives any indication
      about a food port being opened, is there?
   A: No.
   Q: How high up is the food port from the floor?
15 A: I'm going to guess probably three and a half feet.
   Q: And the food port is up high enough so that, for example, if you want to move
      an inmate or have an inmate cuff up that he can basically back up to the food
      port and stick his hands sort of like that; is that correct?
   A: Yes.
20 Q: And so basically the food port is probably just a little bit lower than waist high
      for most people?
   A: Yeah, probably pretty close to waist high.
   Q: Now, who opened the food port?
   A: Officer Smith, I believe.
25 Q: And how did he open the food port?
   A: Take your key and take the padlock off the food port and then open it up.
   Q: And again your report doesn't make any mention about the defendant
      being — requested to pass food trays through the food port, was there?
   A: No.
30 Q: Now, as a practical matter while the defendant is standing in front of the door
      with these — he is standing with two trays in his hand; is that correct?
   A: Yes.
   Q: If the port is open the trays could just be slid right through; isn't that correct?
   A: One at a time, yes.
35 Q: And of course also if the doors — if the food tray door is open somebody could
      just reach in and grab a tray fairly easily, is that correct, if somebody handed it
      to them?
   A: If it was pushed out to you. I wouldn't advise anybody sticking their hands
      though there.
40 Q: Would it be fair to state that most of the inmates are afraid of Officer
      Walker?[26]
   A: That what?
   Q: That the inmates are afraid of Officer Walker?

   25. Is the report admitted into evidence? Should it be? Normally an advocate can "refresh the
memory" of a witness in any fashion that the judge will allow. If one party uses a document to refresh a
witness's memory, the opposing party will be permitted to inspect it, examine the witness on it, and in many
cases admit it into evidence. See FRE 612.
   26. How would the witness know this? What objections can be made to this question? Why was
none made?

1 A: No.
Q: And you don't know how you sustained the injury that you sustained?
A: No.
MR. DEEMER: No further questions.
5 MR. CUMMINGS: Officer Walker.

BRANDON WALKER

called as a witness by the People, after having been sworn to tell the truth, the whole truth and nothing but the truth, was examined and testified as follows:

THE CLERK: Be seated in the witness box and state your name and business
10   address for the record, and could you also spell your name, please?
THE WITNESS: Brandon Walker and I am at Pelican Bay State Prison.

Direct Examination

Q. BY MR. CUMMINGS: Thank you. Sir, what's your occupation?
A: Correctional officer.
15 Q: How long have you been a correctional officer?
A: Just over five years.
Q: What prison are you currently assigned to?
A: Pelican Bay State Prison.
Q: How long have you been at Pelican Bay?
20 A: Since April of '91.
Q: Where did you come from, what institution?
A: Folsom.
Q: Sir, were you a correctional officer on duty on March the 28th, 1992?
A: Yes, I was.
25 Q: Did you have occasion on that date to come into contact with inmate Johnson?
A: Yes.
Q: Do you recognize inmate Johnson today?
A: Yes, I do, sir. He is sitting over next to Mr. Deemer.
30 Q: Before March the 28th, 1992, the day of this incident, did you know inmate Johnson?
A: No, I did not.
Q: Had you had any prior contact to your knowledge with inmate Johnson at Pelican Bay?
35 A: Not to my knowledge.
Q: What about at Folsom?
A: Not to my knowledge.
Q: What's your assignment at Pelican Bay or what was your assignment on March the 28th?
40 A: B Facility, 7 block, floor.
Q: What's a floor officer do?

1   A: We do just cell searches. We have to take inmates to R and R for packages or
           for picture ID, we take them there. Basically it's an escort position.
     Q: Is feeding part of your normal duties?
     A: Oh, yes, sir.
5   Q: Actually takes up quite a bit of time?
     A: Well, for cell feeding it takes about an hour to feed both buildings. And then if
           we are feeding in the dining room it takes anywhere from an hour and a half to
           two hours.
     Q: When you say you worked normally 7 Block, is that the same block that
10   inmate Johnson is on?
     A: No, sir.
     Q: I believe he is in 8 Block; is that correct?
     A: That is correct.
     Q: Were you sent to inmate Johnson's cell that day?
15   A: Yes, I was.
     Q: Who sent you?
     A: Sergeant Kurtz.
     Q: What were you told?
     A: I was told that he had two food trays that he would not give up and we were to
20   go and relinquish those trays.
     Q: How did you expect to do that, do you know?
     A: Well, ideally it would have been to open the food port and have him hand us
           the trays.
     Q: When you arrived on March the 28th, what other officers were present outside
25   Johnson's cell?
     A: My partner. He came. The two yard officers, Smith and Huston, they came.
           And Officer Van Berg. So there were five of us.
     Q: Do you know whether any of those officers normally work 8 Block or were they
           all sent?
30   A: They were all sent from the yard.
     Q: When you arrived did you make — did you order inmate Johnson to give up
           the trays?
     A: No.
     Q: Did you hear somebody else do it?
35   A: Yes.
     Q: Who?
     A: Officer Smith.
     Q: How many times, roughly?
     A: Three or four. He had been sitting on his bed and then when he started telling
40   him to give up the trays then he stood up and stood at the door. So three, four
           times maybe.
     Q: Was inmate Johnson saying anything to any of the officers at that time?
     A: No, he indicated that he had a 602, which is an appeal form that the inmate
           fills out for a sergeant, and then he was requesting to see a sergeant at that
45   time.
     Q: Did you hear anybody respond to his request to see a sergeant?
     A: Yes, Officer Smith did.
     Q: What did he say?

1 A: He said that he would be permitted to see the sergeant but that we needed to have the food trays at that time.

   Q: Why couldn't you just stop the whole operation and get him a sergeant right away?

5 A: Because sergeants on the yard have got other duties and if we were to set precedents in calling a sergeant over every time there was a small problem, then sergeant — we wouldn't be able to operate with just one sergeant in the yard.

   Q: Somebody ordered the door to be opened?

10 A: Yes.

   Q: Who?

   A: Smith.

   Q: And when Officer Smith ordered the door be opened, you were the first one who would normally have contact with whoever was behind it?

15 A: Right, because of my position where the door was opening. As the door opened I was number one.

   Q: What were you expecting to happen?

   A: I was expecting to get the trays and then to leave.

   Q: I take it you had your own job to do that day?

20 A: Yes.

   Q: Did you carry on that day a side-handled baton?

   A: Every day, yes.

   Q: In this incident did you pull your side-handled baton?

   A: No, I did not.

25 Q: Did you use your side-handled baton in any fashion?

   A: No, sir.

   Q: If you are expecting trouble, officer, do you normally pull out your side-handled baton if you are anticipating it?

   A: If I am anticipating it, yes.

30 Q: Were you anticipating trouble on this day in this incident?

   A: No, I was not based on — he was not showing any signs of any kind of tension or anger or anything. He was merely standing with two trays with trash all over them.

   Q: That's what I want to go into next. Was he being verbally abusive to anybody?

35 A: Not at all.

   Q: Did he give you indications from his body language that he was going to be aggressive or going to be violent?

   A: None.

   Q: The door opened up. What happened next?

40 A: He dropped the food trays.

   Q: Then what happened?

   A: Then he lunged towards me.

   Q: Did he make contact with you?

   A: Yes, he did.

45 Q: What part of his anatomy struck what part of your anatomy?

   A: He attempted to strike me in the facial area with his fists, but as soon as he lunged towards me and basically, you know, grabbed my body, then I was able to turn him back around and push him back into the cell trying to put him on the floor.

 1 Q: Is that what you are trained to do?
    A: Yes.
    Q: Is that what you are supposed to do to take control of the situation?
    A: Yes.
 5 Q: And when you got your hands on him did he go backwards or what happened?
    A: No. We were kind of almost kind of like dancing. We were kind of wrestling
        standing up and trying to get him to go to the floor and the whole time he was
        still trying to punch me. You know, he was punching me in the side.
    Q: You two were basically face to face real close together?
10 A: Right, holding on to one another.
    Q: And you are doing your best to hold on to him and he is attempting to strike
        you?
    A: Yes.
    Q: And he is striking you?
15 A: Yes, he is. And kicking.
    Q: And kicking? Were there other officers behind you?
    A: Yes, there was.
    Q: Did several of them go into the cell also?
    A: Yes.
20 Q: At some point in time did you actually end up on the ground?
    A: Yes, I did.
    Q: Did somebody get a handcuff on him?
    A: Before he left the cell he had handcuffs.
    Q: One or both, do you remember?
25 A: He had both.
    Q: Before he left the cell?
    A: Uh-huh.
    Q: Was he resisting being handcuffed?
    A: Ever since — ever since he lunged towards me. See, when we are assaulted
30   out there it's our job to, you know, communicate as much as possible telling
        him what we want them to do. And in this case we were all telling him to get
        down and his cellie was possibly a problem. So one of the officers went in and
        told him to stay back and he resisted the whole time.
    Q: When you say "he," you are referring to Johnson.
35 A: Inmate Johnson, yes.
    Q: Were you injured to the point of having to receive any outside medical
        treatment?
    A: No, I was not.
    MR. CUMMINGS: Thank you sir. Nothing further.

40   *Cross-examination*

    Q. BY MR. DEEMER: Sir, you prepared a report in this matter, did you not?
    A: Yes, I did, sir.
    Q: And you got it with you?
    A: Yes.
45 Q: And you got an opportunity to review it today, haven't you?
    A: Yes.

1   Q: That report doesn't mention anything about food ports, does it?
    A: Well, or cell ports.
    Q: I am talking about your report, the one you signed.
    A: Yes, sir, I am looking at that right now. No, it does not indicate.
5   Q: And when the door gets open you say the defendant dropped the trays; is that
      correct?
    A: Yes, yes, he did.
    Q: About how far from the door is he when the trays dropped?
    A: An inch. Well, the trays — we have to count for the distance that composes the
10   trays was about maybe twelve inches plus a couple more. He was within a foot
      and a half.
    Q: And the door opens and the trays drop; is that correct?
    A: That is correct.
    Q: Do you recall seeing his head drop?
15   A: No, I don't recall that.
    Q: Do you recall what he did with his head?
    A: No, I don't.
    Q: You say Johnson's hands come up; is that correct?
    A: I'm sorry?
20   Q: Johnson's hands come up?
    A: His hands come up simultaneously as he is lunging toward me, yes.
    Q: And how far out the door does he get?
    A: Just about — he wasn't all the way out of the door.
    Q: You came here from Folsom; is that correct?
25   A: That is correct.
    Q: And regardless of what your beliefs are about what your behavior patterns are,
      isn't it fair to state that inmates are generally afraid of you?
    MR. CUMMINGS: Objection. Lack of foundation.
    THE COURT: Overruled. You may answer.
30   THE WITNESS: I don't know the fact that an inmate is afraid of me. Why would
      they be afraid of me?[27]
    Q. BY MR. DEEMER: Well, I will put it this way. Are you aware of the fact that
      inmates are afraid of you because you tend to be, say, a little bit more physical
      with them than they think you should be?
35   A: No, I don't think that's accurate.
    MR. DEEMER: I have no further questions.

Redirect Examination

    Q. BY MR. CUMMINGS: Sir, why did you transfer from Folsom to Pelican
      Bay?
40   A: The area.
    Q: I take it it was your choice?
    A: Oh, yes.
    Q: Do you know what a 602 is?
    A: Oh, yes.

---

27.   How would he know the answer to that question? Why was this allowed?

1 Q: What is it?
   A: It's an inmate appeal form.
   Q: Is that where the inmate typically could write down grievances regarding an
        officer?
5 A: Sure.
   Q: When an inmate grieves an officer on a 602 that's an actual document,
        correct?
   A: Yes, it is.
   Q: Are you made aware of that?
10 A: I am supposedly. If it pertains to me, yes.
   Q: And by CDC policies are you required to respond to that?
   A: Within five days.
   Q: To an actual written response?
   A: Yes.
15 Q: To your knowledge had you had any other contact with Johnson anywhere in
        the CDC system or outside the CDC system before March 28th of this year?
   A: Prior to the day that he refused to give up his food tray, I don't think I have ever
        met the man.
   MR. CUMMINGS: Thank you. Nothing further.

20   *Recross-examination*

   Q. BY MR. DEEMER: Emotionally exciting though, isn't it?
   MR. CUMMINGS: Objection. Relevance.
   THE COURT: Overruled. You may answer.
   Q. BY MR. DEEMER: It's emotionally exciting, though, isn't it, when you are
25   involved in an altercation?
   A: Well, is a victim emotionally excited?
   Q: Well, it's emotionally exciting when you win, isn't it?
   MR. CUMMINGS: Object as being argumentative.
   THE COURT: Sustained as argumentative.
30 Q. BY MR. DEEMER: When you get into one of these altercations with an
        inmate is it fair to say your adrenaline gets pumped up pretty good?
   A: Oh, absolutely. And then understand this, it's not my desire to go and get into
        a physical altercation because not only is that not my job, but I could get hurt.
        And so when I am asked by the department to go and do something that is
35   going to require possibly physically taking something away or restraining
        them, I have possibilities of getting hurt and that's not what my intentions are.
   Q: When you go to — when you went to the door you are not dressed the way you
        are now, are you?
   A: Oh, no.
40 Q: You got a jumpsuit on of some sort. Let me rephrase it. Some sort of utility
        type fatigues on; is that correct?
   A: I might have. If we are not on lock-down then I am not entitled to wear the
        jumpsuit-type clothing.
   Q: Do you recall whether you had a jumpsuit-type clothing on or fatigue
45   clothing?

1   A: I was not wearing fatigues, no.

      Q: What were you wearing that particular day?

      A: I don't recall.

      Q: But regardless of what you are wearing when you go in there, your name tag or

5   some sort of a name thing is on.

      A: Absolutely.

      Q: Your shirt?

      A: That's part of the uniform, yes.

      Q: And those cell doors, they got little holes in them, don't they?

10   A: Yes.

      Q: When you stand up close to the cell door you can look outside and you can see what's there?

      A: I'm sure I wouldn't have to stand even right up to the cell door. You can probably see me if I was standing in the day room with my name.

15 MR. DEEMER: No further questions.

    (Court was adjourned at 4:05 P.M., to be resumed at 9:00 A.M., Tuesday, the 28th day of July, 1992.)

CRESCENT CITY, CALIFORNIA
Tuesday, July 28, 1992, 9:00 A.M.

20 THE COURT: The record will reflect that all jurors, counsel and defendant are present. You may call your next witness.

    MR. CUMMINGS: Officer Smith.

STEPHEN SMITH

called as a witness by the People, after having been sworn to tell the truth, the whole
25 truth and nothing but the truth, was examined and testified as follows:

    THE CLERK: Please be seated and state your name and business address for the record.

    THE WITNESS: Stephen Smith, Pelican State Prison.

Direct Examination

30 Q. BY MR. CUMMINGS: Sir, what's your profession?

      A: Correctional officer.

      Q: How long have you been a correctional officer?

      A: Eight years.

      Q: What institutions have you worked at?

35   A: I worked at the Idaho State Prison for two years, San Quentin for three and a half years, and I have been in Pelican Bay for approximately three years.

      Q: Are you part of the start-up team up here?

      A: Yes, sir.

      Q: Sir, were you a correctional officer employed in that capacity on March the
40   28th, 1992?

      A: Yes, sir, I was.

1   Q: And did you have occasion to come into contact with inmate Johnson and
         actually Johnson's cell mate Butler on that date?
    A: Yes, I did.
    Q: Under what circumstances?
5   A: I was — I'm a yard officer. I was out on a yard and my supervisor asked me,
         wanted me to go over to A block and pick up a tray. Apparently Mr. Johnson
         didn't want to give up his food tray that morning out of his cell. So I went over
         to pick up the tray.
    Q: And where was inmate Johnson in the cell when you first saw him?
10 A: He was sitting on the end of the bunk, the lower bunk.
    Q: Where were the trays if you remember?
    A: The trays were approximately less than a foot inside the door sitting on the
         floor next to the wall.
    Q: How many were there?
15 A: There was two trays with a pile of garbage on them.
    Q: Would those trays pass through the food port door if they wanted to?
    A: If you took the tray, took the garbage off and everything one at a time they
         would.
    Q: If you were going to pass it through the food port door would you have to pass it
20   lengthwise or could you pass them crosswise?
    A: Lengthwise.
    Q: So I take it the food port door is somewhat narrow.
    A: I really can't tell you the exact width of it. I have never measured one, but it
         would be difficult to put a tray through sideways.
25 Q: What exactly did you order inmate Johnson to do?
    A: Well, if I may, I didn't order him at first. What I did is I walked up. He was
         sitting on the end of the bunk. He had a piece of paper in his hand. As I arrived
         at his cell I said, "How are you doing? What's up? Are you having a bad day?"
         Mr. Johnson at that time stood up. He said, "I need to see a sergeant, man." I
30   said, "Well, you can see a sergeant later on. Right now I am here to pick up
         those trays. Sergeant asked me to get them."
             At that time he walked over towards the door. He had some paperwork in
         his hand, a 602, a green piece of paper. Started to come towards the door and
         he never spoke again. He reached down, picked up the trays, both trays with a
35   pile of garbage. He had them both in his hand like in this manner. He had the
         piece of paper underneath holding all of that in his hands. He walked over to
         the door. And it's a normal procedure — as I walked up to the door I had
         already opened up the port —
    Q: The food port door?
40 A: Yes, sir. I had opened that up. It's a little slot about this wide, that high. I
         already opened that up as I arrived and he stood there in front of the door. He
         never spoke again, not another word.
    Q: Did you ask him anything else?
    A: Yes, I asked him at that time, "Can I have the trays?" He stood there looking at
45   me.
    Q: No response?
    A: No response, just stood there looking. I asked him a second time, "Are you
         going to give me the trays?"

1 Q: Let me show you this photograph that has been marked Exhibit 1 for identi-
      fication. Can you tell me what that is a photograph of?
   A: It's the port door.
   Q: Do you mean the food port door like the one in inmate Johnson's cell door?
5 A: Yes.
   Q: How do you know?
   A: It looks just like the food port doors in all the cells in B facility.
   Q: Is it a fair and accurate picture of the food port door?
   A: Yes.
10 MR. CUMMINGS: I move the admission of People's Exhibit 1.[28]
   MR. DEEMER: This photograph may be misleading, your Honor, because it
      does not show the width of the cell door. It does not show how wide the food
      port door is, to any scale.
   MR. CUMMINGS: There has already been testimony that the port door is
15   twelve inches wide, wide enough for the tray. The jury knows this, so the
      photograph is not misleading.
   THE COURT: I'll admit it in this situation since there has been testimony about
      its width already. Exhibit 1 is received in evidence.
   Q. BY MR. CUMMINGS: Now, Officer, if the door to this food port is open, and
20   you are standing in front of it, you can pass your trays through here just by
      sticking them through?
   A: One at a time. It was obvious that he had such a load in his hands that he could
      not pass them through the port.
   Q: Did it appear to you that inmate Johnson was acting aggressively towards the
25   correctional officers?
   A: Well, when we first arrived no, sir. He had a very docile attitude. He was not
      aggressive. That's why we went with the procedure we did. There was no
      vulgarities, which is the normal — you usually get, "Well, I want to see so
      and so; you are not doing this and that." There was no argumentativeness out
30   of him at all. When I explained to him, "You will see the sergeant after you
      give me the trays. I will tell the sergeant to come and talk to you," he got up,
      walked over in a very docile manner.
   Q: If an inmate had been acting violently, verbally abusive, kicking, spitting,
      screaming, would it then be appropriate to have the door opened?
35 A: No.
   Q: What is the difference?
   A: Well, if the inmate is violent, we just can't open the door up and have him
      attack us. So if he is already in his cell, we are not going to open the door up
      just to get, you know, a bunch of trouble.
40 Q: Do you know why inmate Johnson wanted to see a sergeant?

---

28. Generally speaking, to have an exhibit admitted into evidence the attorney must first have the
exhibit marked for identification by the court reporter. By marking an exhibit for identification and then by
referring to the identification number or letter when the exhibit is used, the attorney can ensure that the
record accurately reflects which exhibit is being discussed. The attorney must then introduce the necessary
foundational testimony to show that the exhibit is what the attorney claims it to be. Then the proponent
offers the exhibit into evidence ("Your Honor, we now offer Exhibit 1 into evidence"), and makes sure that
the trial court rules on its admissibility. The requirement of authentication is a prerequisite to the admissibility of evidence, and thus it is for the judge to decide whether the conditions of admissibility have been
satisfied under the terms of FRE 901(a). Authentication of all kinds of exhibits is discussed in Chapter Four.

1   A: I found out later. I didn't know then. But apparently he had a 602, something
         about some property. He wanted his property right now or something and I
         don't work the unit so I wasn't involved in that. I found out later.
    MR. DEEMER: Objection. Hearsay and not the best evidence. If there is going
5   to be testimony about the 602 report it should be admitted on its own.
    MR. CUMMINGS: The exact contents are not important here, Your Honor. He
         had a complaint. That's all we're testifying to.
    THE COURT: Testimony about the complaint in general is permitted. Detail
         about the contents is not important.
10 Q. BY MR. CUMMINGS: So, tell us in general what a 602 is.
    A: A 602 is an appeal process that the convicts use if there is a discrepancy, any
         type of discrepancy. They can utilize it if they don't get enough toothpaste, if
         they think they want some toothpaste. If an officer is disrespectful they can
         utilize a 602, which is an appeal process. We have four different levels on that.
15   It will come to you directly, which is an informal level, which you respond
         directly to that convict. If he has a complaint against me, I file or I give him a
         written answer on that. It is processed through the department. We have a
         system where it is logged in a log and then once — if he is not satisfied with my
         response, he sends it on up the line. There are four separate levels.
20 Q: So there is a whole appeal process for inmates to air their grievances?
    A: Yes, sir.
    Q: Is the point of that to cut down on friction between correctional officer staff?
    A: Absolutely. That is the main purpose of the 602 process is to alleviate any
         problems at a lower level.
25 MR. CUMMINGS: Thank you. Nothing further.

Cross-examination

    Q. BY MR. DEEMER: Sir, is it fair to state that some inmates at least have a
         certain fear of officers' use of force and violence, whether or not that is
         justified?
30 A: I'm sure they probably feel that way.
    Q: And is it also fair to state that if an officer starts into a cell with the presence of
         other officers that it would be reasonable for an inmate to assume that some
         sort of force and violence is going to be imposed upon him?
    MR. CUMMINGS: Objection. Lack of foundation.[29]
35 THE COURT: Overruled. You may answer.
    THE WITNESS: I don't think so. We are on a GP.
    Q. BY MR. DEEMER: You are what?
    A: It's a General Population and many times we go in the cells with the inmates
         there.
40 Q: But basically the more officers — talking of the type of situation we are talking
         about here. The more officers that are outside the door, the more likely it is for

---

29.   Under FRE 701, a lay witness's opinion must be rationally based on personal knowledge. Could
Officer Smith know what is reasonable for inmates to assume? As it turns out, he does have personal
knowledge on which to base his opinion and defense counsel probably regrets asking this question.

1   an inmate to believe that because of his refusal when that door is opened, what
          is going to happen?
    A: Whenever we have a problem we always send over a lot of officers. That is not
          an unusual thing. And we do not open the door up and rush in there and do
5   anything. In the three years that I have worked B Facility, I have never cell
          extracted anyone on second watch, not one time.
    MR. DEEMER: One moment. No further questions.
    MR. CUMMINGS: Nothing.
    THE COURT: Thank you. You are excused. You can leave or stay as you wish.
10   Next witness.
    MR. CUMMINGS: Yes. Ruth Taylor.
    THE COURT: Come up to the front and raise your right hand.

RUTH TAYLOR

called as a witness by the People, after having been sworn to tell the truth, the whole
15   truth and nothing but the truth, was examined and testified as follows:

    THE CLERK: Be seated in the witness chair and state your name and business
          address for the record and could you spell your name for us, please.
    THE WITNESS: Sure. My name is Ruth Taylor and my business address is
          Pelican Bay State Prison.
20   THE COURT: You may examine.

Direct Examination

Q. BY MR. CUMMINGS: Thank you, Your Honor. Miss Taylor, what's your
          occupation?
    A: I am a correctional case records specialist.
25   Q: Tell us what your job basically entails.
    A: Analyzing commitments, calculating release dates, normally case work for the
          inmates.
    Q: Keeping track of how many days they gain or they lose and when they are due
          out?
30   A: Yes, sir.
    Q: Do you have with you today the C File — and I will ask you in a minute what a
          C File is. But do you have the C File of inmate Johnson?
    A: Yes, I do.
    Q: What is a C File?
35   A: It's a collection of all of his records during the period that he was incarcerated
          with the Department of Corrections under that CDC number. It is main-
          tained by the Department of Corrections and contains all original records,
          except medical records, pertaining to that inmate's incarceration, including
          information on sentencing, classification actions, disciplinary hearings and
40   grievances, and parole. Information related to an inmate's movement in
          and out of the prison system is summarized on a sheet attached to the
          cover of the file.

1 Q: I am going — do you know what a 969B package is?
   A: Yes, I do. It is a collection of certified copies of documents from the C file,
        including abstracts of judgments and the chronological case history.
   Q: This has been marked People's Exhibit No. 2 for identification and would ask
5   you to identify that if you could, please.

        (Exhibit 2 was marked.)

   A: Yes.
   Q: Does it show abstracts, court abstracts?
   A: Yes, it does.
10 Q: What is an abstract?
   A: That is the document the courts provide committing an individual to the
        Department of Corrections.
   Q: Are those true copies, certified to be true copies of the ones in the original C
        File?
15 A: Yes, they are.
   Q: And to the best of your knowledge are they identical to the ones in the C File?
   A: Yes, they are.
   MR. CUMMINGS: Thank you, ma'am. Move People's 2 in.
   MR. DEEMER: Objection, yes, sir, to pages — well, considering the cover letter
20   page 1, would be pages 2 and 3, the chronological listings, in view of the fact
        there is great varieties of inadmissible hearsay.
   THE COURT: Any reason why those pages should not be included?
   MR. CUMMINGS: It will be stipulated that in any case he is a state inmate.
   MR. DEEMER: We'll stipulate he is an inmate.
25 THE COURT: Both sides are stipulating the defendant was a state inmate on the
        date of this alleged offense, which would have been March 28th, 1992?[30]
   MR. CUMMINGS: With that stipulation I will withdraw Exhibit 2.
   THE COURT: Ladies and gentlemen, you should regard the fact that the defen-
        dant was confined as an inmate in the state prison on March 28th, 1992 as
30   being conclusively true because of the stipulation without any further proof as
        to that fact.
   MR. CUMMINGS: Thank you. Nothing further.
   MR. DEEMER: I have no questions.
   THE COURT: You are excused. You may leave or stay as you wish.
35 MR. CUMMINGS: No further witnesses, Your Honor.
   THE COURT: People rest?
   MR. CUMMINGS: I am resting.[31]

    30. Parties can stipulate that certain facts are not subject to dispute for purposes of deciding their
case. Such an agreement relieves the party with the burden of proof from having to submit evidence on the
stipulated fact. And the opponent may be willing to stipulate to facts that are uncontrovertible or that might
require evidentiary proof that is even more harmful or embarrassing to their own case. Because stipulations
eliminate the need for proof, their enforcement can be justified on grounds of efficiency.
    There is recent authority that a court can require the prosecution in a criminal case to accept a
stipulation offered by the defendant, and thus to forego proof of the stipulated fact, when that proof is not
probative of any other fact or issue in the case. But a party may not be required to forego proof when this
would impair the presentation of the party's case or would be relevant to other issues. The effect of
stipulations on the application of FRE 403 is discussed in Chapter Three.
    31. The prosecution has now completed its case. The court will entertain various motions
from defense counsel; after that the defense will present whatever case it chooses to. Before reading the

1   (The following proceedings were had outside the presence of the jury.)

     THE COURT: Let the record reflect that the jury has left the court room. We still
     have left the attorneys and defendant.

     MR. DEEMER: Motion to dismiss at this time.[32] The information charge is
5   battery on Huston and a battery on Van Berg. Battery is described as the
     unlawful application of force upon the person of another. Van Berg does
     not know how he got injured. Huston does not know how he got injured.
     There is no testimony — no testimony from anybody that any of these injuries
     were inflicted by the defendant. There is no testimony about any of his feet
10   coming in contact. There is no testimony about what he had on in the way of
     shoes. There is no testimony of his fists coming in contact. And frankly I never
     felt there was enough evidence to even bring this case past the preliminary
     hearing stage. Judge Schott did.

     But we are at trial now and there is simply not enough evidence before
15   the jury from which the jury can conclude beyond a reasonable doubt that a
     battery has been committed upon these officers. They could have scraped
     themselves going through a door. Anything could have happened. And there
     is absolutely no evidence whatsoever of the defendant striking either Officer
     Van Berg or Officer Huston, and I don't think you can submit this case to the
20   jury at the present time. You are just asking them to totally speculate as to what
     took place.

     MR. CUMMINGS: Sometimes I wonder whether Mr. Deemer and I actually sat
     through the same trial and heard the same evidence. I find it somewhat
     amazing when he says there is no evidence of any direct striking. There is
25   no evidence and that is true of any direct striking. No one can testify truthfully
     that this right blow caused injury to my left hand or et cetera. However, what
     the testimony is very clear on and is clear from multiple witnesses is that the
     fracas continued, resistance continued. He was kicking. Multiple officers
     testified he was kicking. Multiple officers testified he was swinging over
30   and over again with a clenched fist.

     A couple of officers viewed it a little differently. One saw him duck down
     as to put his head down. A couple officers did not see it that way. It's just the
     perception of different officers perceiving the same incident slightly different,
     an honest recitation of what the facts were.

35   You have a person who is obviously of a stocky build, of a firm stature,
     and he is for some reason hell-bound that he is going to go ahead and do what
     he can to make his point for whatever reasons. Drops those trays and moves
     forward at a rapid motion. Multiple officers testified in an aggressive fashion.
     Defense attorney would have you believe that Walker walks in and subdues
40   him. That's not what the testimony was.

---

remainder of the transcript, think about how the prosecution has proved its case and about what you might
do were you defense counsel.

32.   At the close of the prosecution's case, the defense may move for judgment of acquittal based on
the insufficiency of the evidence to sustain a conviction. The test in California, which is fairly standard, is
whether there is "substantial evidence" — that is, evidence that is reasonable, credible, and of solid
value — such that a reasonable trier of fact could find the defendant "guilty beyond a reasonable
doubt" on each element of the offense. People v. Johnson, 26 Cal. 3d 557, 606 P.2d 738 (1980). The
same test is applied by an appellate court deciding an appeal that alleges insufficiency of the evidence.

1   Walker's testimony was that "he was on top of me pushing me back for a
        while; I was on top of him pushing him back for a while." He even said it was
        "kind of like dancing" at one point and basically the whole time the order is to
        "get down," none of which are being complied with. I mean what standard are
5   we going to put on correctional officers in a prison? Are we going to say,
        "Unless you can come in and say this person kicked me in my left thumb
        and because of that I know I was injured"? These officers know they were
        injured because inmate Johnson caused a nothing incident to grow into a
        significant injury with two injuries, both of which required some hospital
10   treatment. Submit it.
      THE COURT: The motion is denied. I agree that the case is weak, particularly
        with the two counts that are charged. Had there been a charge of an assault
        against Officer Walker it would be almost a slam dunk.[33] There is plenty of
        evidence to suggest to the jury that count. But that was not charged. As to the
15   two who were charged I think the jury can draw the inference because there
        was ample testimony of the defendant striking and kicking in the course of this
        struggle. They could draw the inference that it was kicks or blows from the
        defendant causing injury to Officers Huston and Van Berg. So the motion is
        denied.[34]
20   MR. CUMMINGS: Your Honor, People have a motion at this time basically to
        amend and conform the information to the facts as they were deduced during
        the trial. That would be Count 3, Penal Code Section 4501.5, the victim
        being Walker.
      MR. DEEMER: Your Honor, I think it's a little bit late for that motion. Number
25   one, the district attorney has rested. Prior to that he might have made the
        motion. Secondly, the real problem is there really isn't any testimony to
        support that allegation in the 995. Motions to attend — Mr. Cummings
        did the preliminary hearing in this matter and he is the one that did the
        charging, and I think that if that's the way he feels at this point in time,
30   that — I mean he has simply charged — there is just no way that he should
        be allowed to add Count 3 at this point in time or to amend it.
      THE COURT: Well, there is no showing of why that could not have been done
        in a timely fashion. Apparently the facts were out front in the beginning, at
        least at the time of the hearing. So the motion to amend is denied. Anything
35   further before we hear the defense case?
      MR. CUMMINGS: No, Your Honor.
      MR. DEEMER: No, Your Honor.
      THE COURT: Return the jury to the courtroom, please.

      (The jury was returned to the courtroom.)

40   THE COURT: The jury has returned to the courtroom. Both attorneys and
        defendant are present. It is the defense case, Mr. Deemer.

---

33.   So why wasn't the defendant charged with assault on Walker?
34.   Consider the prosecution and defense theories of what evidence is necessary to sustain a conviction for the crime of battery. Wouldn't there likely be case law on this point that should be helpful to the
court? Why didn't either lawyer refer to any? When you read the judge's final charge to the jury, notice
whether the court gives the jury any instructions that are helpful in answering the question "what is a
battery."

1   MR. DEEMER: Thank you. Ladies and gentlemen of the jury, it's my oppor-
       tunity at this time to outline to you basically where I expect the defense case is
       going to go. And again, you never know what witnesses are going to testify to
       sometimes so I may end up being surprised. But essentially what I believe took
5   place is this.[35] Is that the defendant was notified that a package had arrived —
       that he was aware of the fact somehow or other that a package had been sent to
       him by his family. A substantial period of time goes by.
              The first thing that happens is that apparently the wrong Johnson is taken
       down to get the package. To get the package the inmates in General Popula-
10   tion have to go to what they call R and R, which I understand stands for release
       and receiving or receiving and release or something of that sort. I wonder if
       there is some sort of analogy with R and R in the service.
              So apparently around the 12th of March the wrong Johnson goes down to
       R and R to get the package. The next day — and probably most of you remem-
15   ber this; it was the 13th of March — the electricity goes off and there was some
       delays. Now, the officer that's in charge of doing the R and R routine and
       escorting inmates out to get the package had to go on vacation. So he leaves a
       note in the sergeant's office or in the office in this unit, which the defendant
       watches this note written and gets stuck up on one of those little post-em slips
20   to go down and get the package.
              This officer goes on vacation and this drags on and drags on. The defen-
       dant says "I want to see a lieutenant or a sergeant I can get my package." That
       never happens. Finally on the 28th he withholds the tray, which I agree is
       disobedient. He is asked to give up the tray.
25   Now, essentially everything that you have heard up until the time that
       the defendant drops the trays is consistent with the defendant's recollection
       except one or two things. Number one, the defendant does not recall the tray
       slot being opened and is standing there waiting for the tray slot to be opened in
       order to slide the trays through the slot.
30   The second thing is that he has this recollection of Officer Walker pla-
       cing gloves on just before the doors open. And the third thing is that the
       defendant has been incarcerated as you have heard since around 1983 or
       '85 and he knows Officer Walker, knows who Officer Walker is. Officer
       Walker came up here from Folsom and he knows what Walker's reputation
35   is. At least among the inmates Officer Walker has a reputation for pounding
       on inmates.
              So there he is standing with the trays in his hand. Walker is on the other
       side. He can obviously identify him because it says Walker on the name tag.
       And the door opens and instead of the tray slot opening, the door opens and he
40   figures he is going to get pounded. He drops the trays, drops his head, puts his
       hands up over his head, and as the officers testified, the melee ensues.
              The defense testified that to his knowledge he never, ever came in con-
       tact with Officer Huston or Officer Van Berg, which is really curious because
       so far they have — and I doubt that it will come back to this, but neither of
45   them testify as to any contact by them between them and the defendant in
       terms of force. And the only officer he comes in contact with is this Officer

---

       35.   It is actually improper for a lawyer to express a belief as to what happened. Why might that be so?
Why, in any event, did the state not object at this point?

1   Walker until after he is escorted out of the cell, at which place some additional
       incidents take place. But it wasn't any of the officers that got battered at that
       time.
              There are two other inmate, possibly three other inmate witnesses. One
5   of them is the defendant's cell mate, whose recollection of the incident is
       somewhat different from the officers and who I believe in essence is going to
       testify that Officer Walker came in, just piled through the door and the
       defendant ended up getting beaten. The other inmate is an inmate who is
       in an adjacent cell who could see the crowd of what they believed is eight or
10   ten officers outside the door and see this incident take place. There is — one
       of these two inmates, I'm not sure which, was with the defendant I believe at
       some point in time prior to this incident and observed Walker engaging in
       some, shall we call it, aggressive conduct towards another inmate outside a
       kitchen area and then some comments made by either Walker or Walker and
15   Van Berg afterwards. And which goes to basically what he thinks is going to
       happen when the door opened.
              Now, what I got to have you understand is this, is that I'm not trying to
       establish that Walker is a bad guy or is an aggressive officer in this case. The
       key thing is this, if you have reason to believe that you are going to be assaulted
20   you can do something to defend yourself. And in essence I believe what the
       testimony is going to show is that the defendant had this belief that when this
       door opens he drops — I mean he is standing there totally not aggressive,
       dropped the trays, okay, ducks his head and does the most normal thing
       that all of us would do under those circumstances, puts his hands over his
25   head to avoid getting beat.[36] . . .

GEORGE BUTLER

called as a witness by the Defendant, after having been sworn to tell the truth, the
whole truth and nothing but the truth, was examined and testified as follows:

       THE CLERK: Could you state your name for the record, please.
30   THE WITNESS: George Butler.

Direct Examination

       Q. BY MR. DEEMER: Mr. Butler, you are an inmate out at Pelican Bay, right?
       A.   Yes.
       Q: And the jury is going to know this anyhow. You are out there because you are
35   convicted of a felony of some sort?[37]

       36.   What do you think of the style and effectiveness of this opening statement? Has defense counsel
personalized his client? Has he effectively summarized the facts concerning the defense of self-defense and
presented them as a memorable story or theme?
       37.   FRE 609 provides that felony convictions may be admitted to impeach the character for truth-
fulness of any testifying witness. Why would inmate Butler's commission of the crimes of robbery and
battery have anything to do with his truthfulness on the witness stand at this trial? The defense could make a
motion in limine seeking a ruling that Butler's convictions should not be admissible under Rule 609. If this
is not successful, the defense will often bring out the convictions on direct examination — as was done
here — to minimize the impact on the jury.

1	A:	Yes.
	Q:	What kind of felonies have you been convicted of?
	A:	Robbery.
	Q:	Anything else?
5	A:	Battery.
	Q:	And do you know Mr. Johnson?
	A:	Yes.
	Q:	How do you know him?
	A:	He was my cell mate.
10	Q:	How long was he your cell mate?
	A:	Three months.
	Q:	And where was he your cell mate?
	A:	In Pelican Bay B Facility, 8 Block.
	Q:	And do you remember an incident taking place with him on or about, say,
15		towards the end of March sometime?
	A:	Yes.
	Q:	Where did that incident take place?
	A:	In his cell.
	Q:	Do you recall — I take it you got fed in the cell that day; is that correct?
20	A:	Yes.
	Q:	Why were you fed in the cell?
	A:	Because we was on institutional lock-down.
	Q:	Institutional lock-down?
	A:	Yes.
25	Q:	What's that mean?
	A:	They was having problems out off the main facilities and for institutional security reasons they felt the best to feed us in our cells.
	Q:	And did you get fed in your cells that morning?
	A:	Yes.
30	Q:	Did somebody come around to pick up the trays?
	A:	Yes.
	Q:	Do you know whether or not the trays were turned over?
	A:	Yes.
	Q:	They were or weren't?
35	A:	No.
	Q:	And do you know why the trays weren't turned over?
	A:	Yes.
	Q:	Can you tell the court why — or the jury why?
	A:	Because we had a problem. We was having a problem with the cell in which
40		my cell mate felt the need to talk to the sergeant, you know, a higher, you know, correctional officer other than a floor officer.
	Q:	What was that problem?
	A:	My cell mate had a package up in R and R. They continuously played around with him and wouldn't give him his package and which is a known procedure
45		is go to the higher person in the chain of command. And he continuously asks the floor officer can he speak to a sergeant, which the floor officer continually denied and ignored him.
	Q:	How long had this problem been going on about a package?
	A:	About 30 days.

1 Q: Would you tell the jury what R and R is?
   A: It's receiving and release. It's where if you get mail packages it comes to there
        and they got to inspect and everything. They will call you up there when your
        property is ready to come get it.
5 Q: And do you know — do you know how Johnson got notified there was a
        package of some sort?
   A: Yes. In the beginning of the month they told him that he had a package up
        there, but they want to send it back home because that they didn't have a
        proper form on the top of the box. So they told him to send the address and
10   everything back to R and R. But about 20 days later he filled the 602 — that's a
        document that you form when you have a grievance with the correctional
        facility. And they wrote him back and said that they would talk to him about it.
        And they told him his package has been sitting up there for like 20, 30 days,
        and they say they would give it to him and he continuously asked the correc-
15   tional officers about it and they just ignored him.
   Q: How often are you allowed to get packages?
   MR. CUMMINGS: Objection. Relevance.
   THE COURT: Overruled.
   THE WITNESS: I believe every 90 days, 90 days to six months, I believe.
20 Q. BY MR. DEEMER: Ninety days to six months?
   A: Yes.
   Q: What kind of packages? These packages come from your family?
   A: Yes.
   A: What do they send you?
25 A: Shoes, sweat suits and thermals, you know, little food to eat.
   Q: Little what?
   A: Food, little cookies and chips, Kool-Aid.
   Q: And on the day this incident took place was it an officer that you asked to be
        taken back out initially?
30 A: Yes.
   Q: What was the next thing that happened?
   A: He asked us to get our trays up. And my cell mate said, "I would like to speak to
        a sergeant." And the officer said, "Give us the trays." The officer didn't say,
        "Well, I will go get a sergeant." He said, "Give me the trays." And then my
35   cellie said, "I want to talk to a sergeant." And the officer just closed the door to
        the cell and say, "You guys will be sorry for this," and walked off.
   Q: Then did some other officers appear?
   A: Yeah, about 20 minutes later we sitting in the cell and about like — it was
        about seven to twelve officers walked inside the building with their gloves and
40   everything on, you know, and came to the door and said, "Give us the trays."
        And my cellie, he walked up to the door, they cracked the door open and ran
        up in there.
   Q: How many times do you recall when the officers were there at the front of the
        door, how many times do you recall somebody asking for the tray to be given?
45 A: They only said it one time.
   Q: Do you recall whether the cell port was open or closed at that time?
   A: The door to the cell?
   Q: The port.
   A: It was closed.

1   Q: Did you ever see the cell port open?
    A: No.
    Q: And when the door was open what happened?
    A: They rushed in. They just rushed in.
5   Q: What did your cellie do?
    A: He was like — they had him held — like three or four held him. They rushed
         me and pushed me to the back of the wall and told me to get down.
    Q: Did you see what happened after that?
    A: No. Then they picked me up and they said, "Let's take him out." They had
10   him handcuffed and they was grabbing him by his arms and they said — I
         think he had a cut or something on the side. They said, "This must be a
         weapon." And the MTA was laughing about it. In the sally port they was
         banging him up against the wall, and he pushed my head against the wall
         and took us to the — outside in front of the program office.
15 Q: All right. Where was Johnson cuffed up to the best of your recollection?
    A: In the cell.
    Q: Now, do you know Officer Walker?
    A: Excuse me?
    Q: Do you know who Officer Walker is?
20 A: No. I believe he is a tall officer. I don't really —
    Q: And when you saw — have you ever — excuse me. When you saw the number
         of officers you saw outside the door, what did you think was going to happen?
    MR. CUMMINGS: Objection. Relevance. Calls for speculation.
    THE COURT: Overruled. You can answer.
25 THE WITNESS: I knew they was going to rush up in there.
    Q. BY MR. DEEMER: That was what was in your mind?
    A: Yes.
    MR. DEEMER: No further questions.

Cross-examination

30 Q. BY MR. CUMMINGS: Mr. Butler, how long had you lived with your cell
         mate, Mr. Johnson?
    A: I think about three months.
    Q: Are you pretty good friends with him?
    A: Yeah, he was all right.
35 Q: Do you know whether or not Mr. Johnson has any gang affiliation?
    A: No.
    MR. DEEMER: Objection. That's irrelevant. Highly prejudicial.
    THE COURT: The no answer will stand. However, it's not relevant.
    Q. BY MR. CUMMINGS: Sir, do you have any gang affiliation?
40 A: Yes.
    Q: What is it?
    A: I'm a Crip.
    MR. DEEMER: Well, again there is some case law just came down. Counsel
         knows that is clearly not admittable under these circumstances.
45 MR. CUMMINGS: I will do it here or I will do it at the side bar.

1   *THE COURT*:   Approach the bench.

(The following proceedings were had outside the presence of the jury.)

MR. CUMMINGS: I believe Lieutenant Stokes is the one who can testify to the fact that he has knowledge, I find out today, that Mr. Johnson is also a Crip. That is also typical to put fellow gang members of the same gang in the same
5   cells.
THE COURT: How is he going to confess that he is a Crip?
MR. CUMMINGS: Through intelligence gathering techniques. I'm not sure exactly how.
MR. DEEMER: You haven't provided me with any discovery on this.
10   *MR. CUMMINGS*:   I just found out today.
THE COURT: Intelligence gathering techniques other than hearsay?[38]
MR. CUMMINGS: Well, certainly if he asked the person and he admitted it, it would be an admission. I would have an exception to the hearsay.[39]
MR. DEEMER: But the problem is that whether or not they are gang members
15   at this stage of the proceedings is really totally irrelevant and highly prejudicial.
MR. CUMMINGS: No, it is not. It is not irrelevant because what a gang expert is I believe Lieutenant Stokes will testify that gang members testify in a fashion that is helpful to other gang members and that's also been common knowl-
20   edge of the jury.[40] And probably don't even need an expert for that.
MR. DEEMER: First of all, if you were to ask my client if he were a gang member he would simply deny it. Secondly, if you were a gang member based on what other gang members — based on what I know about and they had confidential information sufficient to establish that — based on
25   what I know about the handling of these matters, it wouldn't be a General Population. He would be in SHU.
MR. CUMMINGS: Pure speculation.
MR. DEEMER: It's not speculation because that is their policy and I mean —
MR. CUMMINGS: This gentleman has an admitted gang affiliation and he is
30   in GP.
THE COURT: If you can show that this defendant has admitted to some officer that he is a member of the same gang as this witness, you might be able to make it, other than by hearsay. But certainly if it's going to be the usual way that they determine they are gang members just by confidential informants,
35   they can make administrative decisions based on that, but that's not admissible in court. So you have established this defendant is a member of the gang and the defendant is —

---

38.   Lieutenant Stokes does not appear to have firsthand knowledge that inmate Johnson is a gang member, as would be required by FRE 602. Therefore, he would be relating hearsay if he stated that his "intelligence sources" had told him that Johnson was a Crip.

39.   As you will see in Chapter Eight, statements made by parties, in this case by inmate Johnson, are exempted from the general prohibition against hearsay under FRE 801. Thus if Johnson himself told Stokes that he was a Crip, Stokes could testify about this statement to the jury.

40.   Do you think the behavior of gang members is well known to the public? Why would it be well known to this particular jury?

1 *MR. DEEMER:*   If he proposes to go with somebody else — other than an admis-
sion, if it is based on some sort of confidential arrangement —
MR. CUMMINGS: That has already been ruled on. I am clear on the rule.
THE COURT: All right.

5 (The following proceedings were had in open court.)

Q. BY MR. CUMMINGS: Mr. Butler, you already indicated that you have been
or at least you are a member of the Crips; is that correct?
A: Yes.
Q: What is the Crips?
10 A: An organization in Los Angeles.
Q: What kind of organization?
A: A neighborhood protecting organization.
Q: Is "a gang" a fair term to apply to that or not?
A: No, that's not a fair term.
15 Q: Sir, when you were in your cell — do you recall what day this happened by the
way?
A: Saturday. It happened on Saturday.
Q: Do you know what month?
A: It was May or March the 28th.
20 Q: March the 28th is the date. And on March the 28th when this incident started
to happen where were you in your cell?
A: I was sitting at the desk.
Q: An officer earlier testified that you were sitting either — I think you testified
you were sitting either at the desk or on a bunk. Does that sound possible?
25 A: Yes, 'cause I was at the desk.
Q: So the officer would have been truthful about that; is that correct?
A: Yes.
Q: The officer, one of the officers also testified that when the incident actually
started that you stood up for a short period of time; is that correct?
30 A: Yes.
Q: So the officer would have been truthful about that; is that correct?
A: Yes.
Q: The officer, one of the officers testified that you were given a command the
same way that you said you had been to get down and the officer testified that
35 you complied fully. Is that what you did, exactly what you were told?
A: Yes.
Q: Is that accurate?
A: Yes.
Q: So the officer is being truthful about that; is that correct?
40 A: Yes.
Q: The officer testified the way they are trained in their procedures require them
to basically secure you or handcuff you until the incident is over and then
release you. Is that what happened?
A: To me, yes.
45 Q: To you, correct?
A: Yes.
Q: So the officer was truthful in that line of questioning; is that correct?

 1 A: Yes.
    Q: You indicated that you heard your cell mate request a package; is that correct?
    A: He requested to talk to the sergeant.
    Q: About a package.
 5 A: Yes.
    Q: And what was the response of the officers at that point?
    A: When they came to the door they had the gloves and everything on. They
         came up, they said "give us the trays." And my cellie says, "Can I talk to a
         sergeant" "Give us the trays." I bent and my cellie bent over to the doors. And
10   there was no talking until they rushed in there hollering "get down, get
         down."
    Q: Did your cell mate at some point in time drop the trays in his hands?
    A: He didn't have time to touch them. When he bent over, the door opened up.
    Q: Did he have the trays in his hand?
15 A: I don't believe so.
    Q: Is that because you were in the back of the cell and couldn't see everything?
    A: No, I was standing — the reason why I was standing up is because when they
         say "give us the trays" I was going to attempt to give them the trays. He was in
         front. So when he bent over I stood and that's when the door opened up.
20 Q: Did you see your cell mate raise either one of his two arms?
    A: No.
    Q: Did you see your cell mate make a fist?
    A: No.
    Q: Did you see your cell mate swing at any of the officers?
25 A: No.
    Q: Sir, from the position that you were in inside the cell did your roommate, your
         friend, Mr. Johnson, did he kind of duck his head down?
    A: He bent over to grab the trays, of course.
    Q: You are saying he did not have his trays in his hands; is that correct?
30 A: That's correct.
    Q: How many trays were on the floor in front of him?
    A: Two.
    Q: Was there some garbage piled up on top of them?
    A: No, food.
35 Q: Food or whatever. Was there a mound of something on top of them?
    A: No.
    Q: Can you put two food trays through the food port door in the cell door at the
         same time?
    A: Yes.
40 Q: You don't have to feed them out one at a time?
    A: No.
    Q: And if there is some garbage piled on top, some paperwork, wrappers, what-
         ever, some disposable garbage on top, can you feed them through that food
         port door?
45 A: Yes, you would have to compact it down a little bit.
    MR. CUMMINGS: Thank you sir. Nothing further.
    MR. DEEMER: No questions.
    THE COURT: You are excused. Thank you. Next witness.
    MR. DEEMER: Call inmate Green.

MICHAEL GREEN

called as a witness by the Defendant, after having been sworn to tell the truth, the whole truth and nothing but the truth, was examined and testified as follows:

1   *THE CLERK:*   Would you state your name for the record and spell it, please.
     THE WITNESS: Michael Green.

Direct Examination

     Q. BY MR. DEEMER: Mr. Green you are an inmate at Pelican Bay; is that
5   correct?
     A: Yes.
     Q: And you are in there because you have been convicted of a felony. The jury is going to know this anyhow so go ahead and tell them what the felony is.
     A: Murder.
10   Q: Any others?
     A: (No audible response.)
     Q: And do you know Johnson, Mr. Johnson?
     A: Yes.
     Q: Did you know him around the end of March 1992?
15   A: Yes.
     Q: Do you recall an incident taking place either — well, excuse me. Where did you live in relationship to where he lived?
     A: In the next cell.
     Q: Do you recall an incident taking place in connection with attempting to get a
20   food tray from him sometime?
     A: Yes.
     Q: Do you recall what date that was?
     A: No.
     Q: Do you recall what time of day it was?
25   A: The morning.
     Q: Do you have any recollection of what day of the week it was?
     A: No.
     Q: First of all, do you recall how many officers you could see outside his cell?
     A: About eight.
30   Q: And what did you observe those officers do?
     MR. CUMMINGS: Objection. Vague as to time.
     Q. BY MR. DEEMER: Well, when you first observed the officers, what did you observe the officers do?
     A: Come to Johnson's cell.
35   Q: In front of the cell, yes.
     A: They was talking to him.
     Q: Do you recall what they said?
     A: No, I was in the vent.
     Q: You were what?
40   A: I was listening in the vent.

1   Q: What did you hear?
   A: They had asked him to give him the tray.
   Q: And did he say anything?
   A: Yeah, he was going to give them the tray.
5   Q: Then how were the officers that were outside — did you take a look to see how they were dressed?
   A: They was in —
   Q: What were they wearing?
   A: Police uniforms.
10 Q: After he said something about giving the tray, then what happened?
   A: One of the police, they didn't care. They just went to get it anyway.
   Q: Now, do you know who Officer Walker is?
   A: Yeah, I know him.
   Q: Did you see him there that day?
15 A: Yeah, I seen him.
   Q: How long have you known him?
   A: Just since he has been over there.
   Q: In where, Pelican Bay?
   A: Yeah, since I have been in Pelican Bay.
20 Q: Did you ever know him at Folsom?
   A: I never been to Folsom.
   Q: Do you have a fear of Officer Walker?
   A: Yeah.
   Q: Why is that?
25 A: Because I hear he is, you know, a bad cop.[41]
   Q: When you say he is a "bad cop," you mean what?
   A: That he is no good, he sets inmates up and, you know, he don't go by the policy of Pelican Bay.
   Q: I am having a hard time understanding.
30 A: He doesn't go by the policy of Pelican Bay.
   Q: All right. And do you know — have you ever seen him rough anybody up?
   A: No.
   Q: What about Officer Van Berg, do you know him?
   A: Yeah.
35 Q: Do you know what his reputation is amongst the inmates?
   A: Same thing.
   Q: And do you recall any discussion between officers and inmate Johnson with respect to a sergeant?
   A: Yeah, he had asked — he had been trying to see the sergeant for his package
40   prior to the events several days and on that day and before all the doors came, but they kept denying him.
   Q: Then after the officers went into the cell, when they came back out again did you see anything?

---

41. In questioning inmate Green, is defense counsel seeking to prove that Officer Walker is, in truth, a "bad cop" who roughs up inmates? Or, is he seeking to prove that Walker has a bad reputation and that, whether true or not, this reputation causes inmates to fear him? The first purpose would be to prove that Walker was aggressive and acted consistently with his character, inadmissible under FRE 404. The second would be reputation evidence used to prove effect on Johnson's state of mind. Keep this distinction in mind as you read the testimony of inmate Johnson, and of Lieutenant Stokes later in the transcript.

1   A: Yeah, they had him handcuffed, pulling his hair. They had him bent over,
         pulling his — how they grab his hands.
    Q: Did they move him past your cell or in some other direction?
    A: Just go straight out.
5   MR. DEEMER: No further questions.

Cross-examination

    Q. BY MR. CUMMINGS: Mr. Green, you indicated that you have previously
         been convicted of a murder; is that true?
    A: Yeah.
10 Q: First or second degree?
    A: First.
    Q: You said that was your only felony conviction?
    A: Yeah, it is.
    Q: Did you go to trial or did you plead?
15 A: I went to trial.
    Q: At the same time you went to trial were you charged with Count 2, an assault
         with a deadly weapon on the person, use of a firearm.
    A: That's all in with the murder.
    Q: But you were convicted of that, too, weren't you?
20 A: Yeah, everything.
    Q: Were you convicted also of burglary at first degree?
    A: Yeah.
    Q: All at the same time?
    A: It's all during the same offense.
25 Q: What's your term you are serving, sir?
    A: Life sentence.
    Q: You indicated that you — let me go back a little bit. You indicated that you did
         hear the officers asking for trays; is that correct?
    A: Yes.
30 Q: And how many times did they ask?
    A: I can't remember.
    Q: Once, twice, three, four times?
    A: I don't remember.
    Q: Was it more than once?
35 A: I don't remember.
    Q: How good of a position are you in to hear when you got your ear up to that
         vent?
    A: All I got to do is jump up on the sink and put my ear to the vent and I can hear
         what goes on in the next cell.
40 Q: Pretty darn well?
    A: Pretty darn well.
    Q: You indicated that you personally expressed some concern, some fear regard-
         ing Officer Walker; is that true?
    A: Uh-huh.
45 Q: What are you basing it on?
    A: What am I basing it on?

1   Q: Yeah. You testified that you never saw him rough anybody up; is that correct?
    A: Right.
    Q: So this is stuff —
    A: But I had an experience with police that do that sort of thing.
5   Q: But you are not talking about Officer Walker, are you?
    A: No.
    Q: You are talking about some other policemen.
    A: Yeah.
    Q: You basically have a fear or a concern with a lot of cops, a lot of policemen
10   about getting roughed up, don't you?
    A: With anybody?
    Q: I think the answer to that probably is how would you answer that? Do you?
    A: I mean if I hear you use unprofessional cop, of course.
    Q: Are you personally scared, concerned for your own safety around probably
15   most cops?
    A: No, not most cops.
    Q: Around a certain percentage of them?
    A: Just the ones I know don't go by the procedure.
    Q: And had you ever been roughed up by Officer Van Berg?
20 A: No, but I seen him in action.
    Q: Do you know what Van Berg looks like?
    A: No, I know what he looks like.
    Q: Tall, short?
    A: Short.
25 MR. CUMMINGS: Thank you, sir. Nothing further.

Redirect Examination

    Q. BY MR. DEEMER: But it is common knowledge amongst black inmates that
         Officer Walker as — you people that Officer Walker is prone to beat on you; is
         that correct?
30 A: Uh-huh.
    MR. DEEMER: No further questions.
    MR. CUMMINGS: Nothing.
    THE COURT: Anything further of this witness?
    MR. DEEMER: No, sir.
35 THE COURT: You may step down. The next witness.
    MR. DEEMER: Call the defendant.

JAMES JOHNSON

called as a witness by the Defendant, after having been sworn to tell the truth, the
whole truth and nothing but the truth, was examined and testified as follows:

40 THE CLERK: Please state your full name for the record.
    THE WITNESS: James Johnson.

Direct Examination

1   *Q. BY MR. DEEMER:*   Mr. Johnson, you are an inmate at Pelican Bay State Prison?

A: Yes, sir.

Q: Are you — or obviously you are there because you have been convicted of a
5   felony.

A: Rape.

Q: How many times?

A: Once.

MR. CUMMINGS: Say that again.

10   THE DEFENDANT: Once.

Q. BY MR. DEEMER: And back sometime in February or March was there a problem concerning a package of some sort?

A: Yes, there was.

Q: And would you explain to the jury what that problem was?

15   A: Well, February my family and them send me a package. The package — I didn't know that the package was there in the institution until the institution sent me a little form and let me know that they had the package. But they say the package was improper to issue to me because the fact that the package didn't have a form on top of the package. So they wouldn't let me have the
20   package. But instead the officer that was working down there, I wrote a 602 out to the officer and he wrote me back and let me know I could come down there and we can settle the difference over the package. He stated this to the officer that was working on floor to bring me out. But instead of bringing me down there they brought this other Johnson down there in my place because they
25   didn't see fit to use the numbers which we go by, C numbers, D numbers and things like that in prison.

    Now, by them not doing that and just going by the last name there was a mistake made. So they sent the wrong guy down there. When I come back I talked to the floor officer and floor officer let me know that my package was
30   down there and he would make an effort to get me down there on time. That was on Friday. But on occasion they get me down there they couldn't get me down there because there was so much going on. Friday he wrote out a note and he stuck it on the window. I am right there in the office with him. He stuck it on the window and he stated on the note for the next officer to come on to
35   take me down on R and R.

    I am asking all the officers that's in the building that know about the note that he left in there, let me go down and get my package. Now, they tell me, "We can't let you go down there now; we got the lights went out on us; we can't let you go down there. So we try next Friday." And that next Friday continued
40   on and continued on and continued on until so many Fridays.

    Now, I started asking the floor officer to see a sergeant. They wouldn't let me see a sergeant, too. I asked them over and over again to let me see a sergeant and the sergeant never come see me. So I found out that my package had been setting down there 27 days after that. You know what I'm saying? So

1   now nobody is making no efforts to let me get my property. You know what I'm
        saying?
                So what I do is at that Friday they had an incident in the building,
        building eight. They had an incident where another convict cut another
5   convict with a razor. That put us on lock-down. We can't go nowhere. We
        can't do nothing. No moving or nothing.
                So now that Saturday before that incident happened I asked them about
        a sergeant and he told me no. So that Saturday came along. I asked the floor
        officer that morning about seeing the sergeant. He said no. I took the trays and
10   I hold the trays.
        MR. CUMMINGS: Objection, Your Honor, at this point. No question pending.
        Q. BY MR. DEEMER: So Saturday morning you held the trays, right?
        A: Uh-huh.
        Q: What time do you guys get fed?
15   A: We got fed around seven.
        Q: And does somebody come around to get the trays?
        A: Yeah.
        Q: Who comes around to get the trays?
        A: Floor officer.
20   Q: When you are being fed how does he get the trays?
        A: He come by and you can unlock the tray slot to receive trays.
        Q: And what did you tell him when he unlocked the tray slot?
        A: I told him I would like to see a sergeant. He said, "No, you ain't seeing no
              sergeants." So I say, "I am going to hold these trays until I see a sergeant."
25   Q: Then what did he do with the tray slot?
        A: He locked the tray slot back and he said I was in trouble and he walked to
              the next cell and picked up their trays and walked out the block. Then when
              he came back about 20 minutes, 30 minutes later, he came back with at least
              12 officers. When they come in the building, Walker is in front of all the
30   officers.
        Q: When they come up, where is Walker standing? Do they come up to the cell
              door?
        A: Yeah.
        Q: Who was in the lead?
35   A: Walker.
        Q: Do you know him?
        A: Yes, I do.
        Q: How long have you known him?
        A: I been knowing him ever since Folsom.
40   Q: Did you ever have contact with him there?
        A: I had contact with him and I know of other inmates that had contact with him,
              too.
        Q: And does that — did that cause some sort of apprehension to you?
        A: Yes, it does.
45   Q: Could you explain to the jury what apprehension your prior association and
              knowledge of Walker caused in you?
        A: The officer as he claimed to be is not — he is not a good officer at all. He give
              you this one side of him. He will give you this one side of him and then the

1   next time you see him is another side that came out in him and he is violent.
    He is a violent officer.[42]
Q: What did you think would happen to you when Walker showed up?
A: I thought — what I thought was going to happen did happen. When he
5   opened up that door and ran in on him, he assaulted me.
Q: Did the officers come up to the door of the cell?
A: Walker was the only officer. It wasn't no Smith, there wasn't no Huston. It
    wasn't no Van Berg. It wasn't none of them guys. Walker was the only guy that
    came and ordered — they say Smith ordered the officer open up the door.
10 Smith did not order officer to open up the door. It was Walker that ordered
    them to open up the door.
Q: Did anybody talk to you — before they opened the cell door did anybody talk
    to you about giving up the trays?
A: Walker asked me — he asked me and my cellie — we both in the cell. He says,
15 "Are you going to give up the trays?" I gets up off my bed and go and pick up
    the trays. As soon as I get ready to pick up the trays, the door come open and
    Walker run in on me.
Q: Was the cell port open at any time?
A: No.
20 Q: What do you do when Walker comes in on you?
A: There wasn't nothing I could do but cover myself up because I already knew
    what was coming.
Q: What happened?
A: Walker come up in there socking me with the gloves that he had on.
25 Q: And how long did that go on?
A: That went on for about a good two seconds.
Q: Then what happened?
A: Then all the rest of the officers came in, they come in the cell, and they was all
    like grabbing me over this way, grabbing me over that way. And then when
30 they did get me on the ground and gets me handcuffed, it wasn't I was resisting
    the officer. I wasn't resisting no officer at all.
MR. CUMMINGS: Objection.
Q. BY MR. DEEMER: At some point they got you on the ground?
A: Yes.
35 Q: They described you as resisting.
A: No, wasn't no resisting.
Q: What happened?
A: Once Walker ran into the cell on me and have me on the table, me off the
    table, put me on the floor, and handcuffed me right away. It can't be no more
40 than three seconds for them to do all that.
Q: Then what happened?
A: They took me out the building. Van Berg had my hair behind like this, pulling
    my hair. Took me out the section, took me right there on the side of the
    section right where the entrance is to coming into the building, and Van Berg
45 took my head and smashed it into the wall.

---

42. Again, consider what the defense is seeking to prove: that Officer Walker is in fact a violent
officer, or that inmate Johnson has reason to believe that he is, and therefore fears him?

1 Q: Did he say anything?
     A: He said he been wanting to do that for a long time.
     Q: Did he use any expression which you might think is impolite in front of a jury?
         Do you remember that?
5 A: (No audible response.)
     Q: It's all right if you don't. Did you ever have any contact with Officer Huston.
     A: I never had no contact with Officer Huston.
     Q: Other than Mr. Van Berg grabbing you by the head —
     A: I never had no contact with Officer Van Berg.
10 Q: Did you ever kick Officer Van Berg?
     A: No, I never touched him. I never touched Officer Huston neither.
     Q: You indicate that you had some other — you say you have known Walker for a
         long time.
     A: Yeah.
15 Q: How long had you known him at Folsom?
     A: It's New Folsom. He was there up until the time he came here, which was two
         years ago. And when he was there he had the same type of attitude that he got
         here.
     Q: While he has been up here have you ever observed him, either he or Van
20   Berg — have you ever observed him lay hands on an inmate?
     A: Yes, I have.
     Q: Where did that take place?
     A: In the kitchen.
     Q: What happened then?
25 A: He snatched a Hispanic guy up off the seat, took him out the kitchen, drug
         him by the hair out of the kitchen in the front by the sally port and jumped on
         the guy.
     Q: Then when they came back do you recall a statement being made?
     A: Yes, Van Berg said that the guy that he did like that had assaulted the staff, and
30   it wasn't like that.
     Q: Did that — how did that make you feel?
     A: At the time I looked at it like this: If they did him like that, who would be next?
         You know what I'm saying? And he showed — it shows in the action that
         anybody could have been next, you know? That's not no frequent thing.
35   It's not nothing that a person — a person has to be taught to treat somebody
         like that. And it had to have been in all this time to do this. This is not no "I'm
         going to do this today and tomorrow I am not going to do it." This is an
         everyday occasion when they can do this.
     Q: Did this cause you to fear Officer Walker?
40 A: Yes, it did.
     Q: Are there other inmates, for example, besides yourself and inmate Green who
         is here that have expressed to you their fear of Mr. Walker?
     A: There is plenty of guys that I ran across that have the same feeling.
     Q: Is that fear more in connection with — is that by black inmates or is that all
45   inmates?
     A: It's about all inmates, not just black inmates.
     MR. DEEMER: No further questions.

Cross-examination

1 *Q. BY MR. CUMMINGS:* Mr. Johnson, you indicated that you had been convicted, what, one time before of rape?

A: Yes.

Q: It sounds like you took real personal offense at the way Officer Walker treated
5 you; is that true?

A: No, it wasn't the way he treated me.

Q: What was it?

A: The things I knew about him.

Q: So it wasn't what he did, it's what you thought he was going to do.

10 A: It wasn't what I thought — it wasn't what I was thinking he was going to do. It's
what I knew he was going to do. Once I seen him in the front of the line, I
knew.

Q: In other words, Officer Walker didn't have to do anything. As you just said,
when you saw him in the front of that line in your mind you were sure to
15 yourself, I'm positive of that, you knew what was coming.

A: Yes.

Q: Now, given that state of mind, sir, your state of mind, you were going to protect
yourself?

A: No, I was not going to protect myself.

20 Q: Why not?

A: There wasn't no need to protect myself.

Q: There wasn't any need?

A: No, there was no need to protect myself.

Q: Let me see if I got this straight. You are positive in your own mind that Walker,
25 who you fear is at the head of the line, you see it doors go closed and you know
what's going to happen, don't you?

A: Yes.

Q: And you are not scared?

A: I'm not going to put up no defense towards him.

30 Q: So you didn't act in self defense.

A: I didn't act at all.[43]

Q: Do you respect the rights of other people?

A: Yes, I do.

Q: And you want them to respect your rights, too?

35 A: Yes, I do.

Q: You had indicated earlier that you were convicted one time of rape, Sir?

A: Yes, I was.

Q: Were you paroled out of the Department of Corrections?

A: Yes.

40 Q: Sometime in '84?

A: August 31st, '84.

---

43. Given this testimony, what story of the incident, from the defendant's point of view, should
defense counsel argue to the jury? This testimony contradicts the officers' testimony that they saw the
defendant raise his fist against Officer Walker. Would the raising of the fist be justified under the theory of
self-defense — a use of force reasonably necessary to prevent an injury that the defendant reasonably
believes to be imminent?

1   Q: That's exactly the right date, August 31st, 1984. And went home for a while?
    A: Yes.
    Q: Did you end up back in the criminal system?
    A: Yes.
5   Q: And was that as a result of a 1985 conviction again out of Long Beach, Count
         2, you were convicted of a rape by force or fear?
    A: Yes.
    Q: Also convicted of a burglary first degree?
    A: Yes.
10 Q: Sentenced to 23 years state prison?
    A: Yes.
    Q: Sir, do you have any gang affiliations?
    A: No.
    Q: Your testimony was that at the head of that cell door that Officer Walker was
15   there and you knew him.
    A: Yeah.
    Q: And at least you knew of him.
    A: Yes.
    Q: Smith wasn't there?
20 A: Smith was there, Smith was there, but Smith was not like Smith say he was on
         the side of the door. Smith was way behind. He was way behind Walker.
         Walker is the only one in front of this door. Walker is the only one. Ain't
         no — I can't even imagine at that time that this happened that any other
         officers could have been in front of Walker. It wasn't no other officer in
25   front of Walker. It was only Walker in front of the cell.
    Q: Now, the officers testified almost unanimously — and you heard them — that
         actually it was unanimously that you were acting aggressive once the cell door
         opened and you dropped the trays.
    A: No, I was not acting aggressively at all with no officers, period.
30 Q: Sir, have you ever acted aggressively?
    A: What do you mean?
    Q: Are you an aggressive person?
    A: I think everybody have aggression in them.
    Q: And I know you said for the defense attorney you weren't resisting, but tell us
35   what you were doing.
    A: I wasn't doing — it wasn't too much that I could do, period.
    Q: Officer Walker testified that he was the first one through, made contact with
         you — or actually you made contact with him close to the door. True or not
         true?
40 A: That's not true.
    Q: Where did contact get made?
    A: Contact got made when that door came open and Walker ran up in that cell
         on me. That's where contact got made, the only contact.
    Q: Multiple officers testified that they saw a clenched fist, probably your right fist,
45   come swinging at the front officer. True or not true?
    A: Not true.
    Q: Officers are lying about that?
    A: Officers are lying about that.

1 Q: Officers testified they saw you kicking. True or not true?
   A: Not true.
   Q: Officers lying about that?
   A: Officers are lying about that.
5 Q: All of them?
   A: All of them.
   Q: Officers testified that you were difficult to handcuff. True or not true?
   A: Not true.
   Q: Officers are lying about that, too?
10 A: Yes, sir.
   Q: Officers testified that you ended up going from inside the cell to the outside of
       the cell so that they could finish up what they had to do, which was get you
       cuffed up and secured.
   A: I was handcuffed on the outside of the cell, yes. That's where they brought me
15   out of the cell to the outside of the cell.
   Q: And you got handcuffed.
   A: Yes.
   Q: So the officers were telling the truth about that?
   A: They had to get me handcuffed.
20 Q: How well do you know Officer Walker?
   A: I know him — I know him quite — I think I know him well enough.
   Q: How many times did you come in contact?
   A: I come in contact with Officer Walker this time here and a time when he was
       in New Folsom.
25 Q: So one time three years ago or more and one time up here?
   A: Yes.
   Q: Two times three years apart?
   A: Yes. But I see him do other things besides how many times I know him.
   MR. CUMMINGS: Nothing further.
30 THE WITNESS: Him and Van Berg, too.

Redirect Examination

   Q. BY MR. DEEMER: Are you right-handed or left-handed?[44]
   A: I am left-handed.
   MR. DEEMER: No further questions.
35 MR. CUMMINGS: Nothing.

(There was a lunch recess taken from 12:00 P.M. to 1:38 P.M. of the same day.)

   THE COURT: The district attorney is now present and, Mr. Deemer, you have
       indicated you do not intend then to call any further witnesses?
   MR. DEEMER: No, sir.
40 THE COURT: Defense rests. Prosecution, any rebuttal evidence?
   MR. CUMMINGS: Yes, Your Honor. Lieutenant Stokes.

---

   44. Why is this question asked? More importantly, pay attention to whether any further reference is
made to the answer.

1   MR. DEEMER: Your Honor, while he is calling Lieutenant Stokes, could we
          have an offer of proof at the bench?
     THE COURT: Yes, approach the bench.

     (The following proceedings were had outside the presence of the jury.)

5   MR. CUMMINGS: I intend to call Stokes and ask him whether or not he is
          aware of the professional reputation of Correction Officer Walker.
     MR. DEEMER: The only thing you can ask him is whether or not — what his
          reputation is among the inmates. What his reputation is among the staff, I
          don't think is very relevant.
10   THE COURT: I am going to overrule the objection because although the
          inmates and the staff are not precisely the same, they are a part of the com-
          munity within the prison and are in communication with one another on a
          constant basis. So reputation is something that is back and forth and it is the
          kind of thing that would be known. And it's a question that goes solely to
15   reputation and not to prior incidents in the officers' personnel file. I think the
          whole Pitchess issue is side stepped anyway, so you can ask strictly about
          reputation.
     MR. CUMMINGS: Reputation both among the inmates and among the correc-
          tional staff?
20   THE COURT: Yes, if he knows. Of course, foundation first.
     MR. CUMMINGS: I just want to make it clear in the record that we are at the
          rebuttal stage at this point.
     THE COURT: Right, the defense has rested.[45]
     MR. CUMMINGS: Exactly.

25   (The following proceedings were had in open court.)

ROBERT STOKES

called as a witness by the People, after having been sworn to tell the truth, the whole
truth and nothing but the truth, was examined and testified as follows:

Rebuttal Examination

30   Q. BY MR. CUMMINGS: Thank you, Your Honor. Lieutenant, we know that
          you are currently employed as a lieutenant and you were employed as a
          lieutenant, a correctional lieutenant, on March the 28th, 1992, when you
          were at Pelican Bay State Prison, correct?
     A: Yes, sir.
35   Q: What were your duties on the 28th of March this year?

---

45.   Rebuttal evidence is put on by the prosecution after the defense has rested. It is restricted to
evidence made necessary by defendant's case — such as response to new evidence or to new grounds of
innocence — and should not include what the prosecutor should have proved in the case-in-chief.

1   A: I was the watch commander, second watch, six o'clock in the morning until
             two o'clock in the afternoon.
    Q: Lieutenant, as a watch commander are you responsible for any specific busi-
5   ness within the prison or as a whole on that shift?
    A: I am basically in charge of the overall security of the prison. And as the watch
             commander I coordinate any problems that one facility would have that
             would need assistance from another facility.
    Q: Are you directly responsible for B Facility when you are on duty?
10 A: No, sir, I am not.
    Q: Do you have occasion to work with or direct the work of different correctional
             officers?
    A: Yes, sir, I have.
    Q: Sir, do you know the reputation among the inmates of certain correctional
15   officers?
    A: Yes, I do.
    Q: Where does that information come from?
    A: That comes —
    Q: How is it you would know that?
20 A: Specifically, sir, are we talking about the staff, specific staff in B Facility?
    Q: Yes, specific staff. Do you have occasion in your job capacity to know what the
             reputation is of certain staff members among the inmates?
    A: Yes, sir, I would. Mainly through the appeal process.
    Q: Would you explain that?
25 A: The appeal process is a way of airing grievances by the inmates. It is generally
             recorded on a CDC 602.
    MR. DEEMER: Excuse me, Your Honor. If this is the basis of his knowledge, I
             don't think that he ought to be allowed to testify to that. Moreover, that is just
             hearsay statements of the inmates.
30 THE COURT: Approach the bench, counsel.

    (The following proceedings were had outside the presence of the jury.)

    THE COURT: Well, I'm not going to permit Bob go into specific instances to
             prove conduct on a particular occasion. But I will allow him to go as far as he
             has, i.e., to show that that's generally how he keeps his finger on the pulse of
35   what's going on in there. But that point we are going to have to get to the
             bottom-line question of what reputation is, if there is one.
    MR. CUMMINGS: That's fine. This is being preliminary and foundational.
             That's all.
    THE COURT: I will note for the record that since I handle several hundred
40   habeas corpus issues a year and almost all of that have to go through the 602
             process before they go to court and usually the 602s are attached, I read
             hundreds of 602s myself and I am aware that they give a pretty good overview
             of what's — what the scuttlebutt is inside the prison. So it seems to me that this
             is an appropriate place for his source of knowledge, but not specific instances,
45   as to reputation generally.
    MR. CUMMINGS: That's fine.

1   (The following proceedings were had in the presence of the jury.)

     Q. BY MR. CUMMINGS: Sir, in your capacity as a lieutenant in Pelican Bay
          State Prison have you had occasion to determine what you believe is the
          reputation of Officer Walker among the inmates?
5   A: Yes, sir, I have.
     Q: What would your opinion be as to what his reputation is among the inmates?
     A: Among — his reputation among inmates and of staff — and as he worked for
          me for 13 months — is he is an excellent officer; he is very fair and he is very
          understanding and he runs a very smooth block.[46]
10   Q: And what are you basing this on?
     A: My 13 months of supervision of B Facility.
     Q: And when you were supervising B Facility was Officer Walker one of the
          officers in your command?
     A: Yes, sir, he was.
15   Q: And that was for a period of 13 months?
     A: Approximately 11 months for Officer Walker. He left for two months and then
          came back.
     MR. CUMMINGS: Thank you, sir. Nothing further.

                                    Cross-examination

20   Q. BY MR. DEEMER: When was the last time you discussed Officer Walker's
          reputation amongst inmates?
     A: I'm sorry.
     Q: Have you ever discussed Officer Walker's reputation with inmates?
     A: No, sir, I have not.
25   Q: All right. And as a practical matter as a lieutenant you really don't have that
          much contact with inmates, do you?
     A: Not as much as you do as a sergeant over an officer.
     Q: And basically what you are really familiar with is reputation amongst the other
          correctional officers. Would that be fair to say?
30   A: No, I am familiar with his manner of doing his job for that time that he worked
          for me.
     Q: Are you aware of the fact that at least one lieutenant out there has refused to
          have Officer Walker on his or her watch because of problems?
     A: I'm not familiar with that, no, sir.
35   A: Do you know Lieutenant Rodriguez?
     Q: I know of Lieutenant Rodriguez, yes.
     Q: Does she have something to do with B Facility?
     A: I believe she works the evening watch from two o'clock in the afternoon till
          ten o'clock at night.
40   A: And you are aware of the fact that she has refused to work on the watch with
          Officer Walker?
     A: I am not aware of it, no, sir.
     A: No further questions.

     46.   Is it possible that this testimony about Officer Walker's reputation among inmates can be based
solely on the 602 forms? Do the 602 forms contain such positive assertions about officers?

1   MR. CUMMINGS: Nothing further.

THE COURT: May he be excused?

MR. DEEMER: Yes.

MR. CUMMINGS: Yes.

5   THE COURT: You can leave or stay as you wish. Any further evidence, prosecution?

MR. CUMMINGS: No, People would rest. People have rested.

THE COURT: Defense?

MR. DEEMER: I have one witness but she is not going to be able to be here,
10   Your Honor, so I have no choice but to rest at this time.

THE COURT: Both sides rest then?

MR. CUMMINGS: Yes.

THE COURT: What remains, ladies and gentlemen, is to put their jury instructions in their final form. That could not be done until this point, although
15   there has been some done to this point already. I am going to give you a recess for that purpose.

(The following proceedings were had in the presence of the jury.)

THE COURT: Let the record reflect that all jurors, counsel, and defendant are present. Ladies and gentlemen of the jury, you have heard all the evidence
20   and now it is my duty to instruct you on the law that applies to this case.

The law requires that I read the instructions to you, and you will have these instructions in written form in the jury room to refer to during your deliberations.

You must base your decision on the facts and the law. You have two duties
25   to perform. First, you must determine the facts from the evidence received in the trial and not from any other source. A fact is something proved directly or circumstantially by the evidence or by stipulation. A stipulation is an agreement between attorneys regarding the facts. Second, you must apply the law that I state to you, to the facts, as you determine them, and in this way arrive at
30   your verdict and any finding you are instructed to include in your verdict.

You must accept and follow the law as I state it to you, whether or not you agree with the law. If anything concerning the law said by the attorneys in their arguments or at any other time during the trial conflicts with my instructions on the law, you must follow my instructions.
35   You must not be influenced by pity for a defendant or by prejudice against him. You must not be biased against the defendant because he has been arrested for these offenses, charged with a crime, or brought to trial. None of these circumstances is evidence of guilt and you must not infer or assume from any or all of them that he is more likely to be guilty than
40   innocent. You must not be influenced by mere sentiment, conjecture, sympathy, passion, prejudice, public opinion, or public feeling. Both the People and the defendant have a right to expect that you will conscientiously consider and weigh the evidence, apply the law, and reach a just verdict regardless of the consequences.[47]

---

47.   Why does the judge give this instruction? Does it describe the normal way an individual absorbs information? If not, why is an artificial decision-making process being urged upon the jury?

Statements made by the attorneys during the trial are not evidence, although if the attorneys have stipulated or agreed to a fact, you must regard that fact as conclusively proved.

If an objection was sustained to a question do not guess what the answer might have been and do not speculate as to the reason for the objection.

Do not assume to be true any insinuation suggested by a question asked a witness. A question is not evidence and may be considered only as it enables you to understand the answer.

Do not consider for any purpose any offer of evidence that was rejected, or any evidence that was stricken by the court; treat it as though you had never heard it.[48]

Evidence consists of testimony of witnesses, writings, material objects, or anything presented to the senses and offered to prove the existence or non-existence of a fact.

Evidence is either direct or circumstantial. Direct evidence is evidence that directly proves a fact, without the necessity of an inference. It is evidence which by itself, if found to be true, establishes that fact.

Circumstantial evidence is evidence that, if found to be true, proves a fact from which an inference of the existence of another fact may be drawn.

An inference is a deduction of fact that may logically and reasonably be drawn from another fact or group of facts established by the evidence.

It is not necessary that facts be proved by direct evidence. They may be proved also by circumstantial evidence or by a combination of direct evidence and circumstantial evidence. Both direct evidence and circumstantial evidence are acceptable as a means of proof. Neither is entitled to any greater weight than the other.

However, a finding of guilt as to any crime may not be based on circumstantial evidence unless the proved circumstances are not only (1) consistent with the theory that the defendant is guilty of the crime, but (2) cannot be reconciled with any other rational conclusion. If the circumstantial evidence permits two reasonable interpretations, one of which points to the defendant's guilt and the other to his innocence, you must adopt that interpretation that points to the defendant's innocence, and reject that interpretation that points to guilt.

Further, each fact which is essential to complete a set of circumstances necessary to establish the defendant's guilt must be proved beyond a reasonable doubt. In other words, before an inference essential to establish guilt may be found to have been proved beyond a reasonable doubt, each fact or circumstance upon which such inference necessarily rests must be proved beyond a reasonable doubt.[49]

Every person who testifies under oath is a witness. You are the sole judges of the believability of a witness and the weight to be given the testimony of each witness.

---

48.   Such instructions are common in the course of a trial. Do you think jurors are influenced by rejected or stricken evidence, a judge's instruction notwithstanding?

49.   What, exactly, might this instruction mean? See the discussion of "circumstantial evidence" in Chapter Three.

1   In determining the believability of a witness you may consider anything
that has a tendency in reason to prove or disprove the truthfulness of the
testimony of the witness, including but not limited to any of the[50] following:

5   The extent of the opportunity or the ability of the witness to see or hear or
otherwise become aware of any matter about which the witness has testified;

The ability of the witness to remember or to communicate any matter
about which the witness has testified; The character and quality of that testimony;

10   The demeanor and manner of the witness while testifying; The existence
or nonexistence of a bias, interest, or other motive;

Evidence of the existence or nonexistence of any fact testified to by the
witness;

The attitude of the witness toward this action or toward the giving of
15   testimony;

A statement previously made by the witness that is consistent or inconsistent with the testimony of the witness or the witness's prior conviction of a
felony.

Discrepancies in the witness's testimony or between his or her testimony
20   and that of others, if there were any, do not necessarily mean that the witness
should be discredited. Failure of recollection is a common experience; and
innocent misrecollection is not uncommon. It is a fact, also, that two persons
witnessing an incident or a transaction often will see or hear it differently.
Whether a discrepancy pertains to a fact of importance or only to a trivial
25   detail should be considered in weighing its significance.

A witness who is willfully false in one material part of his or her testimony
is to be distrusted in others. You may reject the whole testimony of a witness
who willfully has testified falsely as to a material point, unless, from all the
evidence, you believe the probability of truth favors his or her testimony in
30   other particulars.

You are not bound to decide an issue of fact in accordance with the
testimony of a number of witnesses, which does not convince you, as against
the testimony of a lesser number or other evidence, which appeals to your
mind with more convincing force.

35   You may not disregard the testimony of the greater number of witnesses
merely from caprice, whim, or prejudice, or from a desire to favor one side
against the other. You must not decide an issue by the simple process of
counting the number of witnesses who have testified on the opposing side.
The final test is not in the relative number of witnesses, but in the convincing
40   force of the evidence.

The fact that a witness has been convicted of a felony, if such be a fact,
may be considered by you only for the purpose of determining the believability of that witness. The fact of such a conviction does not necessarily
destroy or impair a witness's believability. It is one of the circumstances
45   that you may take into consideration in weighing the testimony of such a
witness.

---

50. This instruction tracks the language of Cal. Evid. Code §780, which lists permissible topics
of impeachment. You will study the Federal Rules governing cross-examination and impeachment in
Chapter Seven.

1   A defendant in a criminal action is presumed to be innocent until the
       contrary is proved, and in case of a reasonable doubt whether his guilt is
       satisfactorily shown, he is entitled to a verdict of not guilty. This presumption
       places upon the People the burden of proving him guilty beyond a reasonable
5   doubt.

              Reasonable doubt is defined as follows. It is not a mere possible doubt
       because everything relating to human affairs and depending on moral evi-
       dence is open to some possible or imaginary doubt. It is that state of the case,
       which after the entire comparison and consideration of all the evidence,
10   leaves the mind of the jurors in that condition that they cannot say that
       they feel an abiding conviction or a moral certainty of the truth of the
       charge.[51]

              In the crimes charged in the information there must exist a union or joint
       operation of act or conduct and general criminal intent. To constitute general
15   criminal intent it is not necessary that there should exist an intent to violate
       the law. When a person intentionally does that which the law declares to be a
       crime, he is acting with general criminal intent, even though he may not
       know that his act or conduct is unlawful.

              Any person who, while confined in a state prison, commits a battery
20   upon a person who is not themselves confined in a state prison, is guilty of
       a felony.

              Every person who willfully and unlawfully uses any force or violence
       upon the person of another is guilty of battery.

              As used in the foregoing instruction, the words "force" and "violence"
25   are synonymous and mean any unlawful application of physical force against
       the person of another, even though it causes no pain or bodily harm or leaves
       no mark and even though only the feelings of such person are injured by the
       act. The slightest unlawful touching, if done in an insolent, rude, or angry
       manner, is sufficient.

30   It is not necessary that the touching be done in an actual anger or with
       actual malice; it is sufficient if it was unwarranted and unjustifiable.

              The touching essential to a battery may be a touching of the person, of
       the person's clothing, or of something attached to or closely connected with
       the person.

35   It is lawful for a person who is being assaulted to defend himself from
       attack if, as a reasonable person, he has grounds for believing and does believe
       that bodily injury is about to be inflicted upon him. In doing so such person
       may use all force and means which he believes to be reasonably necessary and
       which would appear to a reasonable person in the same or similar circum-
40   stances to be necessary to prevent the injury which appears to be imminent.[52]

              I have not intended by anything I have said or done, or by any questions
       that I have asked, or by any ruling I may have made, to intimate or suggest
       what you should find to be the facts, or that I believe or disbelieve any witness.

              The People and the defendant are entitled to the individual opinion
45   of each juror. Each of you must consider the evidence for the purpose of

---

51.   Does either advocate make use of this reasonable-doubt instruction in closing argument?
52.   Does either advocate make use of this self-defense instruction in closing argument? Which party
has the burden of proof on this issue? Does the judge ever make this clear?

1   reaching a verdict if you can do so. Each of you must decide the case for
    yourself, but should do so only after discussing the evidence and instructions
    with the other jurors.
        Do not hesitate to change an opinion if you are convinced it is wrong.
5   However, do not decide any question in a particular way because a majority of
    the jurors, or any of them, favor such a decision.
        Do not decide any issue in this case by chance, such as the drawing of lots
    or by any other chance determination.
        The attitude and conduct of jurors at all times are very important. It is
10 rarely helpful for a juror at the beginning of deliberations to express an
    emphatic opinion on the case or to announce a determination to stand for
    a certain verdict. When one does that at the outset, a sense of pride may be
    aroused, and one may hesitate to change a position even if shown it is wrong.
    Remember that you are not partisans or advocates in this matter. You are
15 impartial judges of the facts.
        In your deliberations do not discuss or consider the subject of penalty or
    punishment. That subject must not in any way affect your verdict.
        At this time the attorneys will give their closing summations, and like the
    opening summations they are not evidence. They are a chance for the attor-
20 neys to sum up for you what they claim the evidence has shown.[53] In doing
    that I assume they will discuss both the testimony that you have heard and also
    some of the instructions I have read to you. Of course, if you notice any
    difference between what they tell you the evidence is and what the instruc-
    tions were, you must decide what the evidence is and follow my instructions
25 that I have given to you.
        Since the prosecution has the burden of proof the prosecutor makes the
    first closing summation followed by defense counsel, and then in order that
    each side will have an opportunity to reply to the other, the prosecutor is
    allowed a rebuttal argument.
30 MR. CUMMINGS: Thank you, Your Honor. Ladies and gentlemen, this is my
    opportunity to sum up what I believe the evidence has been, which is just
    what the judge explained to you. If anything you hear from me differs from
    what your own recollection was, from what your recollection of what the
    witnesses swore to tell you the truth about on the witness stand, you should
35 go by your own recollection and you should go by your own notes. Neither
    counsel is trying intentionally to mislead you, and sometimes when we are
    explaining our case we are thinking a witness or two ahead and sometimes we
    don't get exactly all the details right.
        I told you in the beginning that I expected the case to be predominantly
40 Pelican Bay State Prison officers. It was. I told you that it was going to involve
    two batteries. In reality it involved three batteries. I will explain that in a little

---

53.   Closing argument is the final opportunity for the advocates to speak directly to the jury about the
case. Many closing arguments contain summations of the evidence, meaning a recitation of the key
witnesses and key testimony. But where the case is not long and complicated, and where not many witnesses
have testified, the jury may not need much help keeping things straight. Summing up the evidence should
be contrasted, then, with arguing the evidence, where the advocate seeks to persuade the jury about
contested facts and about why his or her client is entitled to prevail. Such arguments should be simple
enough to be clearly understood, and sound enough to withstand the jury's scrutiny. As you read the closing
arguments of the prosecution and the defense, consider whether these two standards have been met.

bit. It involves the credibility of numerous officers. This was a scenario which I believe the very first officer, Officer Huston, almost wanted to sum up as a great big nothing originally because that's really what it was, something that the inmate himself had some control over.

Inmates for whatever reason do things that you and I do not understand and we are never going to understand because we don't think that way and we are not in that environment. But for some reason inmate Johnson chose to draw the line that day over some package that he claimed that he wasn't getting, may or may not be true. Maybe it's 100 percent true for all I know. Entirely possible. However, in any case, as the officer explained to you in court and to Mr. Johnson in his cell, that wasn't the way to go about it.

Pelican Bay State Prison and the State of California cannot stop all things and run in and get this man, a sergeant, at that point in time and run and get his parcel for him. It's just not possible. They deal with a mainline system or a mainline production and it really is. You are feeding a tremendous number of inmates, got to get trays back, you have got to go on to the next one, you have got another job assignment. That's what these officers had to do.

What is interesting is that it appears that the major thrust of the evidence in this case is not, although the defendant denies doing it, is not so much that it didn't happen — he certainly acknowledges that it happened — but it was all their fault. Of course, it is never their fault. It is always somebody else's fault. But what we really have here and what the defense would like to paint the picture of is that Walker, Officer Walker, is on trial.[54] See, Officer Walker ought to be sitting over there where inmate Johnson is because what they are really trying to do is prosecute Officer Walker, and I urge you and the law urges you to stay focused on who is on trial. The person on trial in this case is inmate Johnson. There is no other. It is inmate Johnson that caused the fracas. It is inmate Johnson that drew the line. It is inmate Johnson who decided for whatever reason something was going to give that day and something did give and of course it had nothing to do with him.

So the People put on witnesses like Officer Huston, who when I asked him about "Would you describe for us what happened on March the 28th, 1992 as that incident," his response was something like "I mean, it wasn't really even an incident originally," and it wasn't an incident. It escalated into an incident and it is a serious matter where two officers were injured.

In this situation it is important to remember that basically none of the officers that were actually there came in and testified in court were assigned to Mr. Johnson's care. They were rovers.

They were yard officers. They were other block officers who were called by the sergeant and went to go and basically talk this guy out of his trays, do what was necessary to talk him out of his trays, get the trays back and get on with their own assignments, and that's exactly what they tried to do.

Classic situation where three officers tell you what they see and what they feel is exactly what happened, and I'm sure you all noticed there were some differences between Officer Huston's version, Officer Van Berg's version and Officer Walker's version. Those are the three primary ones that ended up in

54.   Here the prosecutor seems to be challenging the defense theory of the case, that Officer Walker was the first aggressor. This puts the defense on the defensive, as you will see.

1   the cell at least in one point in time and there were three different versions to a slight degree.[55]

One person has the inmate holding two trays. Don't be confused. It is not important whether he is holding two trays in two separate hands or two trays in
5   one hand. That's not important. What is important is that the officers are telling you the truth because the three stories do not come out exactly the same. These three officers or these four officers or these five officers did not get together and decide, "Okay, folks, this is what happened," because obviously you are not going to have some small discrepancies, and one of
10 the instructions in the jury instruction package that the judge just read to you and that you will see back in the jury room is that people who see and hear an event often see and hear it differently and report it differently. That does not mean they are not being truthful. Be more suspicious of the people that take the stand and tell you five people in a row exactly what happened almost
15 verbatim. Common sense tells you there is probably something wrong.

In this case they relayed that basically the officer that did most of the talking was Smith. Smith came in and told you what he said. He explained that he made a demand that basically started out as a request. It escalated into a demand or an order to return the trays, get the trays back. He made com-
20 ments like, "Are you having a bad day today, guy?" and stuff to that effect, something to try to spark the guy to just give up the trays. They have got their job to do. These are not correctional officers who are dealing with Johnson on a regular basis. There is no vendetta here. The only one who alleges any sort of vendetta is Johnson.

25 You heard Officer Walker say, "I don't know inmate Johnson." I don't recall any officer that was there that had any prior dealings with this particular inmate. Now, that doesn't mean that this inmate was necessarily lying to you when he says, "There is some sort of history here between Walker and myself." He may very well believe that for reasons you and I cannot understand. But in
30 his mind he may be telling the truth in his own mind. That happens unfortunately quite often.

So basically the way the story seemed to shake out remarkably consistently in his point of view was the person, inmate Johnson, gets up in the cell. He is holding them in front of him, he is roughly a little bit behind, foot, foot
35 and a half, whatever, behind the door. Smith again signals to the control booth officer to open the door.

As soon as the door is opened wide enough for a person to get through if he wanted to, trays are dropped instantly, denied by the defendant, but the officers were all pretty consistent. And immediately — and some officers saw
40 him duck his head, some officers didn't, and you would have to understand that they all had a different perspective. That's common sense. They all had a different perspective from where they were.

The ones closer are going to see a little bit better than the ones behind. One officer had to go off to the side and look through what is the equivalent of
45 a window so he could see whether or not Johnson had any weapons because he is concerned for the officers. He actually left and went off to one side.

---

55.   The prosecutor is able to summarize the testimony of several officers by emphasizing the consistency in their stories. Arguing the facts involves more than reciting testimony; it requires choosing those facts and inferences that together create the story that should win the case.

1   So you had a person who has just dropped the trays, who was not showing
        any sign of aggression before. He is not being violent and everybody agrees on
        this, no sign of aggression. If they were trying to make Johnson out to be a bad
        guy, they would make him out to be violent, they would make him out to be
5   verbally abusive, they would make him out to be throwing a fit, acting out
        some frustration or some anger. And they were all consistent in that there was
        no hint that this guy was going to go off and unfortunately these people do go
        off at times. Folks do blow up in prisons and that happened in this case.

               So he drops his trays and the officers were not exactly the same as to what
10   they saw, but it was remarkably similar to what the threat was. They saw
        inmate Johnson making a forward motion coming at the officer in front,
        Walker. Walker happened to be in front. He of course was going to be the
        one that came in contact with him first. It's the only logical conclusion.

               Walker basically does what he is trained to do, wrestles with the guy for a
15   while. He even says it is even like dancing a little bit, but basically gets him
        back into the cell, and the whole time he is saying, "Get down, get down,
        knock it off, stop the aggression," and that's for everybody's safety, including
        the inmates. Butler, the defendant's roommate, cell mate in his cell, does
        exactly what he is told and he basically complies with all instructions. He gets
20   cuffed up for a few minutes while they secure the situation and it's all over.

               Is that what happens with this gentleman? No, it is not. He continues to
        fight. Every officer was consistent to the extent that the aggression continued,
        the fighting continued, kicking and fists were going. And then the officer, I
        believe it was Van Berg who was trying to handcuff him, said, "I couldn't get
25   the second cuff on him." So they did what they had to do. They got him cuffed
        up. Perfectly reasonable, perfectly responsible to do when you are operating
        in a maximum-level prison. You are not operating out of the streets of Cres-
        cent City. You are not operating at Del Norte High School. You are operating
        in a maximum-security prison.

30   Every officer had a little bit different version, but every officer also had a
        little bit different role and a little bit different perspective as to where they
        were.

               I started out by saying that this is a credibility issue and you should think
        of it as a credibility issue and think about, as the judge explained to you in the
35   instructions, who has a motive in this case. Let's say a motive to lie. You can
        consider that. Who has a motive to be less than truthful with you?[56] Four
        correctional officers who come in here and swore to tell you the whole truth
        and they got their law enforcement career on the line. If they were caught
        lying they would lose their jobs. I am sure their whole usefulness to the
40   California correction system goes right out the window.

               Or the defendant? You heard the defendant is serving 20-plus years or
        about. Some of his witnesses, one of which is serving life for murder in the first
        degree who has nothing to lose with a few lies. Not a thing. We can't do
        anything to him and he knows that. And everybody basically admitted to
45   one degree or another that they are friends. One of the inmates admitted

---

    56.   How persuasive do you find the arguments that follow concerning the motives of the officers and
the inmates to lie? What could the defense argue in response? Which group do you think had the most
compelling reason to lie about the incident?

1   that he was a Crip. The defendant denied any Crip affiliation but they were
         roommates together. There is some degree of friendship among the whole
         group of them. I think that's fairly obvious.

             It is fair to look at who has the motive to tell you the truth, who has got the
5   motive to lie in that case. There is no motive on the part of the correctional
         officers, but coming here and telling you basically what happened as best they
         can recall. In this case one of the elements the People do have to prove — and
         I do have to prove that he was a state prisoner at the time of the incident. It's a
         small thing, but it has been proven. That was stipulated to. It just means that
10   both defense attorney and I agreed he was a state prisoner at the time the judge
         accepted the stipulation, and that is a fact that has been proven at this point in
         time. No further documentary evidence or anything else need be given.

             The verdict forms in this case are basically three separate pieces of paper.
         The first one is going to have Count 1 on it and it's going to say was guilty and
15   it will name — it will say battery and it will name Officer Huston being the
         victim of that battery. Officer Huston was the first gentleman who testified,
         who testified that as a result of this fracas, had it not been for this fracas with
         this fight, he would not have gotten a gash. He got a gash in his shin, went to
         Sutter Coast and got medical treatment. That's an injury. That's more than a
20   battery, okay? But certainly qualifies as a battery. But that's Count 1. I am
         asking you to return a verdict of guilty on Count 1.

             A separate piece of paper has Count 2. Again it's a battery and it's a
         battery of, in this case, officer Van Berg. Officer Van Berg was the second
         officer that testified. As a result of this fracas he cannot tell you exactly what
25   blow but that's not what their attention is focused on. Their attention is
         focused on quieting people down and breaking it up. As a direct result of
         this fracas and this fight he ended up with a bone chip knocked on his hand,
         basically a fracture of one of the bones in his hand, and ended up going to
         Sutter Coast and was treated medically for it. Those are two batteries.

30   Let's talk a little bit about how simple the section is, the section of the law
         is Penal Code section 4501.5, which is the battery section, it says, "Any
         person who while confined in a state prison," we have stipulated to that,
         he is confined in the state prison, "commits a battery on a person who is
         not themselves confined in a state prison," that would be staff, correctional
35   officers, civilian workers, "is guilty of a felony," period. It's one sentence. It's
         not a big complicated law. "Any person who while confined in the state prison
         commits a battery upon a person who is not themselves confined in a state
         prison is guilty of a felony."

             I told you earlier I would define battery for you, too, while I am at it.
40   Battery has a one-sentence definition. "Every person who willfully and unlaw-
         fully uses any force or violence upon the person of another is guilty of a
         battery," period. That's it.[57]

             I told you earlier there was a third battery in the case and legally there is a
         third battery in the case and I am not asking you to return a verdict of guilty on
45   that. It is not before you for your consideration. But a battery does not require
         injuries. Legally speaking you don't have to have people actually injured.

---

     57. Advocates often refer to the instructions during closing argument, particularly those that define
critical legal terms. Here, the prosecutor reads the definition of battery, but makes no argument that the
facts proved against the defendant satisfy the definition.

1   The relevant portion of that instruction says the slightest unlawful touching, if done in an insolent, rude or angry manner is sufficient for a battery. So
no injury need result. So you really could have another battery which was not
charged as far as the victim being Officer Walker because he was attacked

5   basically when the person charged the front door. That was not charged.
Thank you, ladies and gentlemen.

MR. DEEMER: I don't mean to sound like I am running away. When I opened
that door to get something I remember one time many years ago when I was a
deputy district attorney down in Compton with an attorney there who had

10   problems and one day after going to trial he said, "Your Honor," he says, "I am
going out to get the witness, going to solve my case and prove my client
innocent," and he walked out the door. We all sat around and sat around
and nothing happened. Sat around and nothing happened and finally they
sent the bailiff out to get him. He had completely forgotten about the trial and

15   he was sitting in his office talking to clients.[58]
            Mr. Cummings always makes a lot of fun about my chart and I admit I
use it on a regular basis. I am supposed to stop waving my hands so I wave the
stick instead. This is basically kind of a circumstantial evidence case and I
know that there is a lot of direct testimony about what people observed, but

20   unfortunately one of the things you have to do when you evaluate that testimony is to decide do people see what they really say they saw. That is, you have
to evaluate some circumstances that go around that testimony because there is
a lot of things that cause people to perceive — that may cause Johnson to
perceive things one way and the officers to perceive things a different way.[59]

25   What you got to do with this is figure out what's going on in this guy's mind,
what's he doing. And one of the things — basically three rules which you are
going to get in the jury instructions. First of all, the circumstances have to be
consistent with the theory. Not only consistent with the theory of defense guilt,
but it can't be reconciled with any other rational conclusion. Each fact neces-

30   sary to the set of circumstances has to be proved beyond a reasonable doubt.
            And of course the other thing which I also keep on the back of this — I
only billed the court once for this by the way — is the presumption of innocence. You got to remember that burden is on the district attorney, not on me.
I don't have any burden. James Johnson doesn't have any burden. And if there

35   is a reasonable doubt as to whether James is guilty or not, you got a moral
obligation and a legal obligation to come back with a not-guilty verdict. You
got to remember that. That's very important.
            So when you look at that — and part of this I will sort of backtrack over
Mr. Cummings's argument. You look at that and you talk about, first of all, the

40   motive to be truthful. All right. These officers don't have a motive to be
untruthful. Well, you know, there is something I found really interesting is
that when they got Lieutenant Stokes on the stand about how we really stress
making sure these officers write down every last important detail. What's the
important detail that wasn't in any of the reports by their own admission?

45   There isn't anybody that mentions anything about the cell port in the

58.   Jury attention is at its peak during the first minutes of argument. Does defense counsel accomplish anything with this opening gambit?
59.   Does defense counsel argue from the facts how inmate Johnson *did* perceive things?

1   reports but the witnesses were asked about it. Not a one. Not even Lieutenant
           Stokes.
                   All right. I think Lieutenant Stokes made it clear, his testimony made it
           clear that these reports start out at the lower level and get passed on up to the
5   upper level, and I think it's highly unlikely that he, in the kind of environment
           you are dealing with out there, that you are not going to get a certain amount
           of cover your derriere. And this isn't because they are trying to protect them-
           selves against the inmates.
                   I think what you are dealing with is a suggestion where they are kind
10   of — they got to make it look good and I think that's a normal course of events,
           make it look good to the higher-ups, that the lower-downs are doing the job
           right. In other words, the farther up the paperwork goes, you want to make sure
           there is no criticism that is going to float back down to the bottom. So there is a
           motive and there is a motive to ignore things.[60]
15   When I look at the circumstances in this case, the first thing that struck
           me is that the three officers all — and demeanor of a witness is something you
           can look at. The three officers that testified about the assaultive behavior all
           give the appearance — I'm sorry, I don't know how to express it — of being —
           give the appearance of being cowboys. There is just something about their
20   manner, their dress, their boots, everything. They are cowboys. And I suspect
           that they run that institution pretty much the same way. That's the first thing
           that bothers me.[61]
                   The second thing, a significant item is the cell port. The third thing is the
           defendant — by the way, the comment was made that the defendant's motive
25   is, "Well, I don't want to accept responsibility; it is always somebody else's
           fault." And again I think that same issue goes with the report-writing issue. I
           mean, I dare say that any of you that get in an auto accident and write a report
           to your insurance company are going to try to diminish your fault somewhat.
           There is very few of us that come around and say, "Yeah, I made a left turn in
30   front of the guy and smacked him and that's it."
                   The officers have the same motive. They want to make sure it's some-
           body else's fault and that's inevitable. That affects their appreciation —
           excuse me, their perception. But you go and you look at the circumstances
           and Johnson obviously wanted something done about his seeing a sergeant.
35   He listened to a great number of people, "Well, the sergeant can't see every-
           body," although this problem seems to have been one that had been floating
           around since the first part of the month. And Mr. Cummings says Johnson
           chose to draw the line. I agree. He drew the line, "I want something done; I
           want to see a sergeant."
40   And it's obvious from the testimony that if he just kept on drawing the
           line at some point in time he would have seen a sergeant. That doesn't mean
           Johnson made a choice to go out and start battering the officer or officers.[62]

---

    60.   Was this an effective argument about the officers' motive to be untruthful about the incident?
Did it respond to the prosecutor's argument about motive?
    61.   Does defense counsel weave in the other facts that might support the defendant's story that the
officers were the first aggressors?
    62.   This appears to be a response to the prosecutor's theme that inmate Johnson chose to have this
aggressive encounter with the officers. Defense counsel does present some of the facts that tell the story from

1   When you look at the circumstances surrounding this whole situation, John-
       son is calm, he is not abusive, and all the testimony is, depending on who
       perceived it correctly — and there is obviously some different perceptions —
       he is standing there. When the door opens he doesn't throw the tray at the
5   officers. He just drops it.[63]
              And the general testimony is that his head drops down and I gather
       whatever was going on with his fists, whether it was pushing towards the
       officer or whatever, there was no — I guess there is even some discrepancy
       amongst the officers' testimony as to whether there was, quote, an assault or an
10   attempt to assault the officer — or Officer Walker.[64] But, you know, I am
       accused of putting Officer Walker on trial and I apologize. But, you know,
       you are dealing with somebody that's in a maximum-level prison, level four,
       and I'm not concerned with really whether Walker is a bad guy or not as I told
       you originally. You know, there is a lot of testimony around here brought in by
15   the prosecution about Walker as a great officer, he is wonderful. I expect
       CDC staff to stick with each other on those kind of issues. You notice
       none of them go down the inmate population and say, "Hey, have you
       guys had problems with Walker," or, "What's your opinion about Walker
       in terms of how he uses force and violence?"
20   I think what's significant is that this inmate is terrified of him and at least
       two other inmates seem to think that — or one other inmate, rather, says, "You
       know, I have seen him engage in this kind of conduct before." You are kind of
       totally at the mercy of those cops out there. It's not like being out in the street.
              So he is standing here and he is waiting for the cell port door to be
25   opened. Now, possibly the cell port door was open.[65] I suspect the cell
       port door was closed. But even if it is open you notice nobody ever says,
       "Pass the food tray through the cell port." It's, "Give us the food tray, give
       us the food tray."
              You know, if this cell port is, say, basically at waist high or a little
30   below — some say it's a little below, it's twelve inches wide, six inches high
       and four inches deep — I can understand how in his perception even if the
       officers are right about the cell port door being open — and I question that —
       I can understand from his perception how standing there he would be aware
       of the cell port door opening.
35   What happened? The cell door opens and here is Walker. What goes
       through his mind? "I am going to get the you know what beat out of me." He
       drops the trays, ducks and the melee ensues. I really think that's an honest
       interpretation of what happen. And it's obvious that in any kind of a con-
       frontation like that the officers are going to see and believe in the fact that they
40   are going to assume that an assault has taken place and obviously the inmate is
       the one that's going to get blamed.[66]

Johnson's point of view. Notice, however, that on a few key points, he does not forcefully argue the truth of
Johnson's own testimony.
       63.   The defendant testified that he bent over to pick up the trays.
       64.   Defense counsel does not mention that the defendant testified that he was lefthanded, whereas
Officers Van Berg and Smith testified that it was Johnson's right fist that was thrust through the cell door at
Walker.
       65.   The defendant testified that the food port door was closed.
       66.   Could everybody be telling the truth? Perhaps the defendant did drop the trays, duck his head
from fear, and even raise his fist to protect himself, but perhaps his behavior was interpreted as aggressive by

1   I think what really happens is the officers may well have perceived this as a battery, but what happens is Mr. Johnson figures, "I am going to get the you know what kicked out of me," he drops the trays and down he goes. Now, regardless of how you see that initial confrontation, Mr. Cummings is right.

5   The issue involving a battery against Walker ain't on trial here today. The issue that's on trial is was there a battery against Van Berg and was there a battery against Huston.

You know what? If you sit back and think about the testimony I will bet your recollection is the same as mine. There wasn't one bit of testimony about

10   this defendant striking any other officer. In fact, none of the officers — neither of those two officers testified the defendant struck him. They didn't testify that way at the preliminary hearing. They didn't testify here that way.

I assume with all these other officers, "Oh, yeah, I saw him strike Van Berg," or, "I saw him strike somebody else with his foot" or something of this

15   sort. None of — nobody has testified about the defendant striking anybody other than Walker and that issue isn't on trial here. Huston and Van Berg both stated — and I'm going to just paraphrase their testimony to my notes — but I believe that there was a question to the effect of, you know, on Officer Huston's part, "Do you know how you received the gash specifically?" "No." And

20   on Van Berg's part, "Do you know how you got hurt?" "No."

I don't know if they banged their legs on the cell door. I don't know if they banged their legs when Van Berg was banging my client's head against the wall, if he banged his thumb by accident at the same time. I don't know what happened. And you don't know what happened. The problem is that you can't

25   speculate as to what happened because without that evidence that's presented before you in some way, shape or form that my client kicked them or hit them or did something like that, the DA doesn't have a case. And there is absolutely not one bit of evidence before the court as to Van Berg and as to Huston and I think you need to go look at that and go into that jury room and come back

30   with a verdict of not guilty.

This case has absolutely no business wasting your time and your money. This is not — the defendant is entitled to a not-guilty verdict. There is absolutely no contact where the defendant is exercising force. There is lots of force being exercised on the defendant. But there is absolutely not one shred of

35   evidence that the defendant exercised any force against Huston or Van Berg.[67] Thank you.

MR. CUMMINGS: I would suspect Mr. Deemer has been watching the Olympics on TV the last couple of nights and he has watched how some of the referees score those boxing matches where one makes contact, okay, that's a

40   point. That one didn't score, this one did score. Ladies and gentlemen, this whole argument regarding that not one bit of evidence did either one of these officers actually testify that a blow struck them causing that injury and the DA doesn't have a case is nonsense. It's ridiculous.

---

the equally fearful officers. Wouldn't this be an appropriate point in the argument for the defense counsel to remind the jury of the self-defense instruction, and to argue that it applies? Or even to relate this self-defense theory to the reasonable doubt instruction?

67.   Shouldn't the judge's instructions cover the question whether evidence of direct touching is required for battery? Do they? It is the advocate's responsibility to request instructions on issues of law that are raised by the facts. Then the advocate can read those instructions to the jury during closing.

1   There is nothing in the law that requires any officer to come in here or
anybody to tell you or anybody else that "It was his third right jab that caught
my thumb that jammed it against the floor that caused the injury." It's ridiculous. Think about it logically.

5   What the law is trying to prevent and punish is the acts and the resulting
injury. Because you have officers who are honest enough to come up here and
say, "We can't tell you exactly what blow it was, I can't tell you exactly even
when it happened because professionally what we are trying to do is subdue a
person, get him down, get him quiet, get him cuffed. We are trying to do it fast

10   for everybody's safety, officer safety, safety of this gentleman, safety of his
roommate, cell mate, everybody involved," and that's what they are supposed
to be doing. That's what the State of California pays them to do.

           So this idea that because they cannot truthfully tell you exactly what
blow caused the injury the People don't have a case is not true. Legally it's just

15   a fiction, a lie. It seems like Mr. Deemer and the defense is — what they are
really trying to say is that Walker had it in for — at least this guy believed that
Walker had it in for him. Remember the testimony from the defendant himself. Had two prior contacts. Walker recalls none but then again he probably
deals with thousands of people, or has in his career. It's had two prior contacts

20   with him, one at Folsom and one here. Based upon that and some other
perceptions that he has from other people he is scared to death of an officer
that he doesn't have regular contact with, scared to death.

           Ladies and gentlemen, that type of an argument, if that were legally
sufficient for a self-defense argument, which is what he is really saying, he

25   is really saying that it was perfectly appropriate for Johnson in this case to do
what he did. Now, the defense is trying to minimize, of course, what he did.
The defense would have you believe, "Well, you know, he was covering up his
head so of course he had to drop the trays; and because he didn't throw the
trays at the officer, which is one thing he could have done, then it couldn't

30   really be an assault."

           That's ridiculous. He chose to drop the trays, maybe duck, maybe not
duck. The evidence is 50/50 on that. But in any case it was real clear about
right fist coming up clenched and moving forward, him being the aggressor. I
even asked one officer is there any way — it's almost embarrassing asking

35   these questions. But is there any way that you could have mistaken him for
bowing down, the forward motion. He said no. Did he act aggressively? Was
he acting violently? At that point he was. That's all that mattered.[68]

           Because Johnson initiated that and the officers responded in a profes-
sional and appropriate fashion and because of that two of them were injured

40   and that's all we are asking you to return a verdict on are those two counts.
Nothing more. It is real important that people realize that the burden is on the
People and I do have to prove my case and I have to prove my case beyond a
reasonable doubt and just that, beyond a reasonable doubt.

           As the law says, it is not a mere possible doubt, because everything is open

45   to some doubt. In other words, you can have some doubt and you can still

---

68.   The theory of a self-defense claim is that the defendant has the right to respond with reasonable
force when he has reasonable fear of bodily injury. Thus, inmate Johnson's aggressive move, if it occurred,
could be viewed as a reasonable response to the aggression he feared from the assembled group of officers. Is
this ever explained to the jury?

1   convict Mr. Johnson of Counts 1, Counts 2. You can have some doubt. I could
     not and I cannot and no prosecutor can ever prove their case beyond any
     shadow of a doubt. This is not *Perry Mason*. Nor can we do it beyond any
     possible doubt. I can't do it. I don't believe anybody can because we are
5   dealing with human fears and human people and you are always going to
     have different perceptions. Always do.
         It's just gut level feelings, folks. Beyond a reasonable doubt, four correc-
     tional officers come in here and tell you what happened on March the 28th,
     1992, to the point where you believe beyond a reasonable doubt that what
10   they say happened really did happen; and if you can do that, you can find Mr.
     Johnson guilty of Count 1, guilty of Count 2. Thank you very much.
     THE COURT: You shall now retire and select one of your number to act as
     foreperson. He or she will preside over your deliberations. In order to reach
     verdicts all twelve jurors must agree to the decision, to the findings you have
15   been instructed to include in your verdict. As soon as all of you have agreed
     upon a verdict so that when polled each may state truthfully that the verdict
     expresses his or her decision, dated and signed by your foreperson and then
     return with them to this courtroom. Return any unsigned verdict forms.
         Count 1 has to do with Officer Huston. Count 2 is identical except it
20   applies to the allegation concerning Officer Van Berg. It is either guilty or not
     guilty, date and sign the verdict form.

     (The bailiff was sworn.) . . .

     (At 6:37 P.M. court was reconvened.)

     THE COURT: Let the record reflect the defendant and both attorneys and the
25   jury are present in court. Mr. Baker, has the jury reached a verdict?
     MR. BAKER: Yes, sir.
     THE COURT: Hand the verdict to the bailiff, please.
     THE CLERK: "Superior Court of the State of California, County of Del Norte,
     People of the State of California versus James Johnson. We the jury impa-
30   neled in the above-entitled matter find the defendant, James Johnson, guilty
     of battery on a correctional officer in violation of Section 4501.5 of the Penal
     Code, Officer Huston, Count 1.
         We the jury empaneled in the above-entitled matter find the defendant,
     James Johnson, guilty on Count 2, battery on correctional officer in violation
35   of Section 4501.5 of the Penal Code, Officer Van Berg.

NOTES AND QUESTIONS

1. Defendant Johnson appealed his conviction to the District Court of Appeals in
California. The appellate court stated that "[t]he only real dispute in appellant's case
was who provoked the incident." Was this the way the case was presented to the jury in
the closing arguments? Did the defense attorney even make an argument that the
correctional officers started the melee? Consider the evidence in the case that
would sustain such an argument, or the related argument that the various combatants

misinterpreted each other's conduct to be aggressive. Think about the stories you could tell to the jury that would raise a reasonable doubt about Johnson's guilt.

2. Would evidence of other incidents at Pelican Bay have affected the outcome in *Johnson*? Here is an excerpt from Judge Henderson's opinion in the Pelican Bay class action, Madrid v. Gomez, 889 F. Supp. 1146, 1162, 1199-1200 (N.D. Cal. 1995):

> . . . Castillo refused to return his food tray in protest against a correctional officer who had called him and other inmates derogatory names. After leaving the tray near the front of the cell, Castillo retreated to the back and covered himself with his mattress for protection, in anticipation of a cell extraction. . . . Castillo, who is small in stature, made no verbal threats or aggressive gestures. . . .
>
> To accomplish [his] removal, two rounds from a 38 millimeter gas gun were fired into the cell. A taser gun was also fired, striking Castillo in the chest and stomach. Then, without attempting to retrieve the tray, . . . some number of officers entered the cell. . . . Castillo testified that one of the officers then hit him on the top of the head with the butt of the gas gun, knocking him unconscious. When he regained consciousness, he was on the floor with his face down. An officer was stepping on his hands and hitting him on the calves with a baton. . . . When he regained consciousness again, he was dragged out of the cell face down; his head was bleeding, and a piece of his scalp had been detached or peeled back. . . . [H]e was taken to the infirmary and then the hospital. . . .

On the basis of this and other incidents, Judge Henderson concluded:

> We agree that the extent to which force is misused at Pelican Bay, combined with the flagrant and pervasive failures in defendants' systems for controlling the use of force . . . reveal an affirmative management strategy. . . . All together, [the evidence] paints a picture of a prison that all too often uses force, not only in good faith efforts to restore and maintain order, but also for the very purpose of inflicting punishment and pain.

Why do you think the defense lawyer in *Johnson* did not put the "management strategy" of Pelican Bay on trial? If the lawyer had tried, would the judge have permitted it? How many incidents would have to be tried in such a case? How would the prosecution have responded? How long would the *Johnson* case have taken to try if other incidents were explored at trial?

CHAPTER TWO

THE PROCESS OF PROOF: HOW TRIALS ARE STRUCTURED

As you begin your study of the law of evidence, it can be useful to put yourself in the role of the trial lawyer trying to present a case persuasively to the jury. This necessarily requires you to imagine at the same time how the trial process appears to the jurors. It is a bewildering mixture of the familiar and the unfamiliar. To begin with, most litigated events involve conventional human affairs. Although the prison setting in the *Johnson* case is outside the personal experience of most people, the crucial question for decision is simply how a fight came about, which reduces, as is typical, to the question of whom to believe — here, the inmate or the guards. Although the issues that typify litigation are usually within general experience, the decision-making methodology differs radically from the manner in which an ordinary citizen makes day-to-day decisions. The trial setting is unusual, perhaps on occasion mystifying, and often intimidating for jurors. Indeed, a theme running through the trial process that you may have already detected is the insulation of the jury from much of what happens during trial. Although, historically, juries were allowed to decide issues of law as well as fact — even as late as the end of the 19th century in the United States — the modern jury decides only factual issues. Therefore, virtually all legal discussion — including the proper substantive and procedural law to be applied to the case, and whether evidence should be admitted or excluded — occurs outside the hearing or presence of the jury. Relatively brief legal discussions in the midst of trial may be conducted in a sidebar conference, in which the lawyers and judge talk in low voices so as not to be heard by the jurors. Longer discussions are held either in the judge's chambers, or, if in the courtroom, at times when jurors are not present.

This theme of jury insulation also runs through the evidence course, because, to a large degree, the rules of evidence focus directly on the question of what evidence the jury will be allowed to hear. The policy implications of most evidence rules are therefore based on someone's answer to the question: What is the effect on the accurate resolution of disputes of allowing a jury to consider this type of information?

A.   THE ADVERSARY SYSTEM

The rules structuring litigation, including the rules of evidence, are derived from, and implement, the dominant theory of dispute resolution in this country, known as the adversary system. Adverse parties each present a self-serving version of the truth to a presumably disinterested fact finder, judge or jury, which hears the evidence the parties present and decides in a disinterested fashion what actually happened, and thus what verdict is appropriate. The adversarial process, in turn, is derived from a conception of the appropriate role of government in the resolution of disputes between private individuals and between the state and an individual. The government has the obligation to provide a fair and disinterested forum for the impartial resolution of disputes; and for the most part that is all the government has an obligation, or a right, to do. Even in criminal cases, the courts stand apart from the prosecution, treating the representatives of the sovereign as though they were representing a private party. The parties are responsible for investigating the case, preparing the case for trial, and in large measure controlling the presentation of evidence at trial. In this country, many believe that adversarial investigation and presentation of evidence is more likely to yield a verdict consistent with the truth than is a process more dominated by a tribunal.

    This conception of the role of the government in the resolution of disputes is not universally shared. In the "inquisitorial" systems of many Western European countries disputes are not "private" matters to the extent that they are in the United States, and the adjudicative tribunal often involves itself actively in investigation, and controls the trial process much more than the litigants do. Those who favor continental systems are inclined to the view that control by a disinterested tribunal will lead to less abuse and manipulation of the evidence, thus increasing the chances that judgments consistent with the truth will emerge. For a discussion of these and related matters, see Mirjan Damaska, The Faces of Justice and State Authority (1986); Mirjan Damaska, Evidentiary Barriers to Conviction and Two Models of Criminal Procedure, 121 U. Pa. L. Rev. 506 (1973); John Langbein, The German Advantage in Civil Procedure, 52 U. Chi. L. Rev. 823 (1985); Ronald J. Allen, Stefan Köck, Kurt Riechenberg, and D. Toby Rosen, The German Advantage in Civil Procedure: A Plea for More Details and Fewer Generalities in Comparative Scholarship, 82 Nw. U. L. Rev. 705 (1988); Mirjan Damsaka, Evidence Law Adrift (1997).

B.   THE ROLES OF THE TRIAL PARTICIPANTS

Although probably quite familiar to you from fictional and real-life courtroom dramas, the well-defined roles of participants in a trial are worth briefly reviewing: *Witnesses* are people with knowledge of out-of-court events who are called on to reveal that knowledge in court, under oath, in front of the judge, jury, and litigants.

    The jury (meaning each of its members) uses its senses to perceive information in the courtroom and its reasoning capacity to evaluate and make inferences about that information in order to reach a conclusion about which version of disputed events is (closer to?) the truth. Jurors are expected to come to conclusions about disputed facts in the case without bringing to bear any outside or firsthand knowledge of their own: Typically, they know nothing about the case beforehand, and (as in the *Johnson* case, page 4, supra) are instructed by the judge not to investigate the facts on their own. However, jurors are not expected to disregard their own generalized background knowledge and experience, and indeed it is assumed that they will use their knowledge and experience in reasoning and making inferences about the evidence before them. As is typical, the jury instructions in the *Johnson* case did not give the jury any guidance about what its reasoning process should be, other than to define "inference" and "circumstantial evidence," and to rule out certain "irrational" factors: emotions, the number of witnesses on a side, chance, or the drawing of lots. Pages 61-65, supra.

The advocates provide information to the jury through the use of witnesses, documents, and other exhibits.[1] Because the jury is passive, the role of the advocates is to investigate, interview, select, prepare, and present the sources of information that the advocates think will most advance their respective cases. This competitive process is at the heart of the adversary system of proof and it results in the presentation of competing and contradictory versions of events. The advocates also argue inferences and conclusions to the jury, but the jury is instructed that attorneys' statements are not evidence.

The judge controls the trial process by setting limits, primarily pursuant to the rules of evidence, on the advocates' proof in the interests of rationality of results, fairness between the parties, social and moral values, and efficiency. The judge has power to make all the trial participants conform to their roles in courtroom behavior and decorum. In addition, the judge may call witnesses and may question witnesses whether called by the court or not. See FRE 611 and 614. But the judge is not supposed to control the content or the overall presentation of the advocates' cases. Thus, a standard jury instruction states that neither side had to produce all witnesses who might have knowledge of the facts, or present all objects or documents that might be mentioned. Throughout this course you should ask whether the judge should have the power to keep knowledge about the disputed facts from the jury.

A note on bench trials. The rules of evidence have been created and shaped over time with the jury in mind as the fact finder. However, many trials are held without a jury. While the parties in most criminal cases and many civil claims for damages have a constitutional right to trial by jury, the parties sometimes waive that right and agree to a try the case to the judge without a jury. In addition, many civil cases — primarily, those seeking so-called "equitable" relief, such as injunctions — are tried before a judge without a jury. In such "bench trials," the judge acts not only as the decision maker on points of law and admission or exclusion of evidence, but also as the sole fact finder, weighing the evidence. A similar situation is presented by "evidentiary hearings": pretrial proceedings (such as a preliminary hearing in a criminal case) in which witnesses are called to testify. The rules of evidence typically apply in bench trials and evidentiary hearings, but because no jury is present, the application of the rules may be relaxed somewhat. The theory is that a judge, due to experience and professional training, can disregard inadmissible evidence far more easily and effectively than a jury. Therefore, erroneous admission or exclusion of evidence is thought to be less problematic; and the judge can couch findings in such a way as to claim that the decision would not be affected by a particular doubtful evidentiary ruling.

---

1. The judge in *Johnson* instructed the jury that "[e]vidence consists of testimony of witnesses, writings, material objects, or anything presented to the senses and offered to prove the existence or non-existence of a fact." Page 62, supra.

C.   THE STRUCTURE OF THE TRIAL

1.   Pretrial Motions

Trials usually begin with "motions *in limine*" (pronounced "in ***lim***-in-ay," meaning "at the threshold"). These are motions made by the parties to obtain rulings on anticipated evidentiary problems. Parties anticipating the introduction of problematic evidence by their adversaries make motions in limine to *exclude* that evidence, though motions in limine can be used to get a pretrial ruling on any evidentiary question. Motions in limine are often made in writing, with short supporting briefs, and argued outside the presence of the jury.

Tactical considerations will typically drive counsels' decisions on whether to file motions in limine. For example, a criminal defendant, such as Johnson, may want to testify only if the jury will not learn of his prior criminal convictions. In order to make an informed decision about whether to testify, the defendant could file a motion in limine asking that the prior convictions be excluded from evidence. This would eliminate uncertainty as to whether the defendant's prior felonies will come before the jury. If no motion in limine were made, defense counsel would have to wait until the prosecutor were to ask, while cross-examining the defendant, "Isn't it a fact, Mr. Johnson, that you were convicted of rape in 1981?" and then object. Even if the objection were sustained, the jury, having heard the question, might nevertheless believe the prosecutor had a good-faith basis for asserting that the defendant had such a conviction. But if defense counsel were to have made a successful motion in limine, the prosecutor would be instructed ahead of time by the judge not to ask such a question at all.

2.   Jury Selection

Following motions *in limine*, the jury selection process begins. Jury selection varies both in the process for selection and the number of jurors empanelled, depending on the type of case and the jurisdiction; anywhere from six to 12 jurors may be required. In federal court, 12 jurors sit in criminal trials and six in civil trials.

The jury selection process is founded on the belief that trials are more likely to result in an accurate verdict — assigning liability or blame only where warranted by the facts — by having cognitively competent, disinterested jurors. Consequently, the process allows parties to object to potential jurors who are incompetent, who have a financial or emotional interest in the case, or who cannot put aside any preconceptions about the case they may have in order to decide it based on the evidence produced at trial.

The primary means of selecting a jury is by questioning the jury "venire" — the group from whom the jury panel will be chosen — in order to uncover any ground for dismissing them. The questioning process, called "voir dire,"[2] may be conducted by the trial judge, the lawyers, or by means of a written questionnaire, or by a combination of any of the three. (The most common practice in federal court is for the judge to do

---

2.   "Voir" is pronounced "vwahr" and "dire" is usually pronounced "deer," although the prevailing pronunciation in the South is "dire" (as in "dire straits"). The term voir dire applies not only to jurors in jury selection, but also to trial witnesses, when the latter are asked questions outside the presence of the jury in order to determine whether some aspect of their testimony will be admitted into evidence in front of the jury.

the questioning, with the lawyers' participation limited to suggesting questions to ask.) Questions may be directed to individual jurors, or to the venire as a whole. The judge can dismiss potential jurors "for cause" (such as some type of bias for or against one of the parties) or practical reasons (such as inability to serve for the length of the trial). The lawyers can request dismissal for cause, or may make so-called "peremptory challenges." Because the lawyers are not required to give reasons for exercising peremptory challenges, they may be used, as a practical matter, for any reason at all, or no reason beyond a hunch or a whim. The only constraints on peremptory challenges are that each side is given only a limited number, and that they may not be used merely because of the race or sex of the potential juror. See Batson v. Kentucky, 476 U.S. 79 (1986) (race); J.E.B. v. Alabama ex rel. T.B., 511 U.S. 127 (1994) (sex).

Properly conducted, voir dire is a sensible way to begin a trial designed to elicit a rational verdict. Even if people are generally rational, competent actors, from time to time some are also unable to put aside interests and biases that may infect their decisions (as is true of judges as well, who are disqualified for similar reasons). Investing some time and effort in removing such people from the trial makes eminent good sense. Like much of the trial process, the laudable social goal is achieved through taking advantage of the self-interest of the parties, whose respective desires to wind up with the most favorable jury possible will, it is hoped, cancel out and result in a reasonably fair-minded panel of jurors.

3. Preliminary Instructions

Once the jury is empanelled and sworn, the judge will typically issue some preliminary jury instructions. Again, practice varies from court to court, and judge to judge: These instructions may be nothing more than admonitions not to talk about the case prior to jury deliberations; or may include certain generic guidelines about considering the evidence or credibility of witnesses; or, less typically, may even include instructions about the substantive law governing the case. In *Johnson*, the court read the jury a series of generic instructions as well as the "information," the written criminal pleading setting forth the charge, which stated the statutory elements of the alleged crime.

4. Opening Statements

Now, the lawyers take turns introducing their respective cases to the jury, in the order in which they will present evidence: The plaintiff (civil) or prosecution (criminal) proceeds first, then the defendant. An opening statement is neither evidence nor argument, but is supposed to be a compact narrative of what the lawyer believes in good faith the evidence will show. The "official" purpose is to provide the jury with a coherent overview of the case to make it easier for the jurors to assimilate the testimony they will soon hear, testimony that may necessarily tell the story in a fragmented, nonchronological fashion.

Argument is not allowed in an opening statement, and can result in an objection being sustained. Generally speaking, conclusions or inferences derived from the evidence, contentions about legal rules, and comments about witness credibility are considered "argument." For example, pointing out weaknesses in your adversary's case would clearly constitute objectionable argument. However, the line between a factual statement and an argument is not always clear, much like the distinction between factual news reporting and editorializing, and is equally hard to draw. A great deal falls into a gray area between "evidence" and "argument." Consider the facts of People v. Johnson: To say in an opening statement that "the defendant violently attacked Officer Walker" is closer to "argument" than is "the defendant punched Officer Walker with his fists," yet both could be considered statements of evidence. How much leeway the lawyers get depends heavily upon the discretion of the trial judge. A good practical method to assess the evidence/argument distinction is to ask whether a witness could say it on the stand — if so, then it is probably evidence.

Notwithstanding the rule against argument, the lawyers are advocates, and they will present the facts in the light most favorable to their cases. A well-presented opening statement can, without editorializing, offer a compelling argument for one side, and many trial advocates contend that juries begin to make up their minds on hearing the opening statements. (There is empirical research to support this view.)

Trial lawyers often describe the opening statement as the lawyer's "covenant with the jury." The representations about what "the evidence will show" are best viewed as promises, because the jury may resent or mistrust the lawyer whose claims in opening statement are not backed up by evidence admitted during trial. This means that it is risky in opening statement to stress evidence whose admissibility is in doubt.

5.   Presentation of Evidence and the Burden of Production

The evidence-presentation phase is obviously the core of the trial. The manner in which the parties introduce evidence is discussed below. (See infra, Section D.) This section deals with the order in which the parties present their cases and with the key, related issue of the burden of production.

a.   The Order of the Parties' Presentation of Cases

After opening statements, the plaintiff/prosecution presents its case-in-chief. This means calling a series of witnesses to the stand. Primarily through the direct examination of these witnesses,[3] the plaintiff/prosecution must present evidence sufficient to prove — that is, sufficient to support a finding by the jury to establish — each element of its cause of action (or of the crime charged). In the *Johnson* case, for example, the charge of battery (one of several charges against Johnson) required the prosecution to prove: (1) willful and unlawful (2) use of force or violence (3) upon the person of another.

After the plaintiff or prosecution "rests" its case, and any motion to dismiss is heard (and denied), defendant's case begins. Like the plaintiff, the defendant conducts direct examinations of witnesses, but the thrust of the defense case is to cast doubt on the plaintiff's evidence and to present evidence sufficient to prove each element of any affirmative defenses.

---

3.   Two important devices make it unnecessary, in many instances, to prove facts through testimony or other evidence at trial: These are known as "stipulation" (facts agreed by the parties) and "judicial notice" (see Fed. R. Evid. 201, discussed in Chapter Eleven, infra).

When the defense rests its case, the plaintiff/prosecution has an opportunity to call witnesses in a so-called "rebuttal" case. (The term "case-in-chief"is used to distinguish the plaintiff's main case from its rebuttal case.) The presentation of rebuttal evidence proceeds in the same way as in the case-in-chief, except that the scope of rebuttal evidence is limited. Rebuttal evidence must respond to either (a) matters raised as part of defendant's affirmative defenses; or (b) attacks during the defense case on the credibility of the plaintiff/prosecution's evidence. Normally, a plaintiff or prosecutor will not be allowed to repeat evidence presented in its case-in-chief, or to present evidence that should have been part of its case-in-chief. A defendant may be entitled to a "sur-rebuttal" (a rebuttal to the rebuttal), but this is unusual. The rebuttal case is necessarily much shorter than the case in chief.

b.   The burden of production

The "burden of production" (discussed in detail in Chapter Ten) means producing enough evidence so that a "reasonable" factfinder can make a finding for the plaintiff or prosecution on each element of the civil claim or criminal charge. The "factfinder," again, is the jury in jury trials (or the judge in bench trials). The "finding" involved is a finding of the facts necessary to establish those elements of the claim or charge, and it must meet the applicable "burden of persuasion" – "beyond a reasonable doubt" in criminal cases, and "more likely than not" (also known as "a preponderance of the evidence") in civil cases.

Thus, the plaintiff meets its burden of production in civil cases with evidence sufficient for a reasonable jury to find that the facts establishing each element of the plaintiff's claim are more likely than not true. In a tort case, for instance, the plaintiff has to present evidence sufficient for jury findings on duty, breach, causation and damages. In a criminal case, the prosecution meets its burden of production if it offers enough admissible evidence so that a reasonable jury can find that each element of the crime charged has been established "beyond a reasonable doubt." In the *Johnson* case, for example, this meant producing evidence sufficient for the jury to find beyond a reasonable doubt that, among other things, Johnson touched Huston or Van Berg.

(Note: In civil cases, defendants have the burden of production on their affirmative defenses. In criminal cases, however, the prosecution has the burden of production to *negate* any defenses, such as "self defense" in the *Johnson* case.)

A failure by the plaintiff or prosecutor to meet the burden of production on each element of a claim can result in a judgment as a matter of law for the defense on that claim. Motions for judgment as a matter of law can be made at several different points in the litigation process. In civil cases, motions for summary judgment (before trial), nonsuit/directed verdict/dismissal (after plaintiff's case-in-chief), directed verdict (after close of evidence) or JNOV (after verdict) all argue that the moving party wins the case on facts that are not genuinely disputed. (In federal civil cases, such motions made during or after trial are now all called motions for judgment as a matter of law. See Fed. R. Civ. P. 50.) In criminal cases, only the defendant can move for judgment as a matter of law, and may do so after the prosecution's case-in-chief, after close of evidence or after the verdict.

There is a basic similarity between all these motions seeking judgment as a matter of law on a factual record: In each, the court is supposed to refrain from usurping the jury's role. This means that the judge should not resolve conflicts in the evidence or questions of witness credibility. Moreover, if the party with the burden of production has produced enough evidence to support a finding by a reasonable jury, the court should not issue judgment based on the judge's own view of how the jury should decide the case. Put another way, the judge has to make all inferences in favor of the party opposing judgment as a matter of law.

The verbal formulae for judgment as a matter of law may sound different in summary judgment as compared to a post verdict motion, and in civil as compared to criminal cases, but they are all essentially the same: whether there is evidence sufficient for a reasonable jury to find for the prosecutor or plaintiff (or civil defendant on an affirmative defense). A defense counsel in a civil case might argue:

> Your honor, plaintiff's evidence is not sufficient to support a finding by a reasonable jury that its version of the facts is more likely than not true. Some of the necessary facts are just plain missing, and on others, the evidence is based on inferences that are just too weak. Plaintiff's case should not get to the jury; judgment should be granted as a matter of law.

For criminal cases, substitute "prosecution" for "plaintiff" and "beyond a reasonable doubt" for "more likely than not."

The burden of production, and the resultant prospect of losing a judgment as a matter of law, has important implications for the order in which a party will present its evidence. While evidence that arises during the defendant's case can ultimately be relied upon by the plaintiff or prosecution as proof of such elements, it is extremely unwise for a plaintiff or prosecutor to do so, because the defense can make its motion for judgment as a matter of law at the end of the plaintiff's (or prosecutor's) case in chief, without putting on any of its own witnesses. The defense in People v. Johnson, did just that, arguing that there was insufficient testimony to show that the alleged battery victims, Huston and Van Berg, were ever actually touched by the defendant Johnson.

6.   Post-evidence Matters

After the close of evidence, the court may take up certain legal matters with the lawyers outside the presence of the jury. The defendant may make a motion for "directed verdict" on the ground that "no reasonable jury" could find for the plaintiff because the evidence, as a matter of law, fails to establish one or more elements of the plaintiff's claims; or that the plaintiff has not raised sufficient evidence to dispute an affirmative defense. Similarly, the plaintiff could move for judgment as a matter of law on the ground that the defendant has not raised sufficient evidence to dispute its claims. (The prosecution cannot move for a directed verdict of guilt, because that would be deemed a violation of the criminal defendant's Sixth Amendment right to jury trial.)

At this stage the parties also argue over jury instructions. Most courts require the litigants to submit proposed jury instructions. These are to assist the court, which has the ultimate responsibility to decide how the jury will be instructed; indeed, the trial court can come up with its own instructions, and need not adopt what is proposed by the parties. Many of the instructions are standard (and may be contained in books or manuals of "pattern" jury instructions). The parties typically agree quickly upon generic instructions of the sort given in every case — an instruction on the burden of persuasion, for example. Arguments usually arise over how to instruct the jury on substantive law, particularly in areas where the law is developing or unsettled. If a party disagrees with an instruction the court decides to give, it may object and argue instructional error as a basis for appeal. For that reason, some trial judges, hoping to reduce grounds for appeal, may try to pressure or cajole the parties to agree on compromise instructions on controversial points.

In order to avoid keeping the jury waiting while the final jury instructions are physically typed up, the court may hold the jury instruction conference before the close of evidence; however, most judges like to wait until the evidence phase is near an end, because some important jury instruction questions will depend upon what evidence was actually presented. Once these legal issues are resolved, the jury is called back to the courtroom for one last phase of presentations — closing argument and jury instructions.

7. Closing Arguments

Unlike opening statements, in which argument and discussion of the law are prohibited, closing argument permits both. In closing argument, the lawyers "argue" the facts. Significantly, they may only discuss facts based on evidence admitted at trial. "Arguing the facts" is not merely summarizing the evidence; rather, lawyers in closing argument should analyze the evidence, identifying and arguing for the inferences and conclusions they believe should be drawn from it. A critical feature of closing argument should be to explain to the jury the chain of inferences that connect the evidentiary facts heard by the jury with the facts of consequence in the case. If you found the closing argument of defense counsel Deemer in the *Johnson* trial to have been unsatisfactory, an important reason for this may be that he failed to establish this inferential chain as to much of his key evidence. Throughout this book, we use diagrams to illustrate this chain of inferences, which you will see is necessary not only to argue the significance of evidence to a jury, but also to determine the application of such rules as relevance and hearsay.

An effective closing presents a coherent story of the events that proves one's case, while trying to show how the most likely interpretation of every point of conflict or ambiguity in the evidence supports that story. The lawyers should stress evidence corroborating key points of their cases as well as evidence that undermines the credibility of witnesses whose testimony contradicts key points.

Finally, it is also important to weave key jury instructions into the closing argument: In this way, the lawyers can show the jury how they believe the evidence maps onto the controlling substantive law — how they have proved the elements of their case and how the other side has failed to cast doubt on the proof or to prove its own case. This aspect of the closing links the facts of consequence with the essential elements required by the substantive law, a point that we illustrate diagrammatically throughout this book.

Courts vary in their practice of whether closing argument goes before or after jury instructions. The important point is that disagreement over jury instructions has been resolved before closing argument. That way, even if closing argument goes before the jury is actually instructed, the lawyers can refer to the jury instructions in their closing.

8. Jury Instructions and the Burden of Persuasion

Because jury instructions are a fertile source of "error" for the losing litigant to raise on appeal, most trial judges instruct the jury by simply reading word-for-word the written set of instructions. While extemporizing or ad-libbing might keep the jury's attention better than a droning verbatim recitation, trial judges typically opt for the prudent (if dull) approach of sticking to the script. (An exception to this might be the type of boilerplate instructions and admonitions given to the jury before opening statements.) Jury instructions can be quite lengthy and complex, and difficult if not impossible to remember on one hearing. Thus, courts in many jurisdictions provide the jury with a written copy of the instructions to take into the jury room for their deliberations; strangely, however, many courts do not allow that, and at most will offer only verbal repetition of instructions if it occurs to the jurors to request it.

An important concept explained to the jury in every case in the form of a jury instruction (and usually by the lawyers in closing argument as well) is the burden of persuasion. Earlier, we explained the burden of production as requiring a party to produce evidence sufficient to support a finding on a particular issue. The burden of persuasion specifies the degree of certainty that the jury must have in order to make a finding on a particular issue. This concept is further explained in Chapter Ten. In civil cases, the jury must find by a preponderance of the evidence that the plaintiff's claims are true. A preponderance of the evidence means greater than a 50 percent probability, or "more likely than not." In criminal cases, the burden of persuasion is guilt "beyond a reasonable doubt."

9.   Jury Deliberations and Verdict

After closing arguments and jury instructions, the jurors go into the jury room for their deliberation. Jurors are allowed to have all the exhibits — the documents and objects admitted into evidence — with them in the jury room. They can also request to have portions of testimony read back to them (and are usually instructed that they can do this). Such "read-backs" involve bringing the jurors back into the courtroom, with the lawyers present, to hear the court-reporter reading the testimony from the steno-graphic notes (typically in a monotone). Some courts allow jurors to take notes during trial, and to bring their notes with them into deliberations. While jurors may ask questions about the facts or the law during deliberations (by having the bailiff bring out a note to the judge), the answers are often very uninformative. Unless the parties agree on a response, the judge will be loath to create grounds for appeal with an informative but arguably erroneous response to a question.

Again, depending on the type of case, the jury verdict may or may not have to be unanimous. While unanimity is required in federal criminal cases, many jurisdictions permit nonunanimous verdicts in civil and even some criminal cases. Federal civil verdicts must be unanimous unless the parties agree otherwise. F.R. Civ. P. 48.

In criminal cases, a verdict takes the form of a decision — guilty or not guilty — on each crime charged. Civil verdicts present more possibilities. In some trials, the jury is asked only for a general verdict — "we find for the plaintiff," plus an amount of money damages, where that is the issue, or "we find for the defendant." In many cases, particularly where the legal issue has a more complex structure, the court may use a "special verdict" form or "jury interrogatories." Under these latter practices, the jury is asked for its answers to a series of questions from which a judgment can be derived. These questions might ask for separate jury findings on each element of a claim or a defense. Given that the burden of proof is on the plaintiff to prove each element of its case, a special verdict form or jury interrogatories may work to the defendant's advantage, because a "wrong" answer to any one of several questions may result in a defense judgment. On the other hand, if a general verdict is used in a legally complex case, the jury may not have followed the correct path to its final verdict. Such mistakes in the jury's reasoning process are not considered proper grounds for an appeal. Indeed, the evidence rules in most jurisdictions prohibit any inquiry into the jury's mental processes or deliberations. See, e.g., FRE 606(b). Once the jury has rendered its final verdict, and announced it in court, the jury is dismissed.

Some trials are "bifurcated" or even "trifurcated" — conducted in two or three separate phases, each one with its own set of jury instructions and closing arguments, and its own separate verdict. Examples of this are civil cases involving punitive damages and criminal cases involving the death penalty. In both these examples, the logically prior issue is liability or guilt — is the defendant liable at all? — whereas the issue of penalty, which may be based (at least in part) on other bad conduct separate from the tort or crime alleged in the case, calls for evidence irrelevant to liability or guilt but that might sway the jury against the defendant. These kinds of cases are thus "bifurcated" into a "liability" or "guilt" phase — whether the defendant committed the tort or crime — and a "penalty" phase. The penalty phase is not even reached if the jury returns a defense verdict in the liability phase.

10.   Post-trial motions

Once the jury has rendered its verdict and been dismissed, the jury trial proper is over. Significantly, the "verdict" is not the same as the "judgment" in a case. A verdict is the jury's ultimate decision. A judgment is a judicial act that concludes a case. After a jury trial, the trial judge eventually enters a judgment on a jury verdict. The judgment, usually a short document of a page or two signed by the trial judge, may do nothing more than restate the jury's verdict. In some cases, however, the judgment may include further issues that are not decided by a jury — such as injunctive relief, for example. It is the judgment, rather than the verdict itself, which has such legal effects as res judicata and that is subject to appellate review. Also, the judgment may differ from the jury verdict if, for example, the court grants a post-trial motion reversing the verdict.

Post-trial motions form an important aftermath of the trial. They do not occur right away, but within periods of a few weeks (set by statute or court rule) after the jury's verdict, but before the entry of judgment in the case. There are two types of post-trial motions: motion for judgment notwithstanding the verdict, and motion for new trial. The party that loses the case (or loses at least one ultimate issue) can bring either of these motions, and typically brings both together. In essence, a post-trial motion is an "appeal" from a jury verdict, only it is made to the trial judge rather than to an appellate court. And, indeed, an appeal from a jury verdict to a court of appeal requires that these motions have been made; technically, appellate review of a jury trial is actually review of a trial court decision denying a motion for new trial or for judgment notwithstanding the verdict.

A motion for judgment notwithstanding the verdict (also known by its Latin equivalent, "judgment *non obstante veredicto*," or "JNOV" for short) seeks judgment as a matter of law, on the ground that (again, considering the evidence in the light most favorable to the nonmoving party), the court can say that no reasonable jury could have reached this particular verdict. If the motion is granted, the court reverses the jury verdict and enters a directly contrary judgment: A defense verdict is overruled and judgment entered for the plaintiff, or vice versa.

A judgment notwithstanding the verdict allows the court, in effect, to delay the type of decision put to it in a directed verdict motion. A court might be inclined to direct a verdict in favor of the defendant, for example, due to the apparent insufficiency of the plaintiff's evidence. By deferring its ruling on this question until after the jury renders its verdict, however, the court allows the jury the opportunity to find against the plaintiff and thereby possibly avoids the need itself to make an outcome-dispositive ruling that would be subject to appellate review. In federal court, a motion for judgment notwithstanding the verdict can only be made if the moving party had previously moved for a directed verdict. (Fed. R. Civ. P. 50(b).)

The parties can move for a new trial on any of several grounds: erroneous jury instructions, excessiveness or inadequacy of a jury's damage award, irregularities in the trial or the jury deliberations, or — most significant for our purposes — erroneous admission or exclusion of evidence. These new trial motions argue that significant errors undermined the trial, which, therefore, must be done over.

The losing party can also move for new trial on the ground that the verdict is "against the weight of the evidence." This is a lower standard than that required to get a judgment as a matter of law. Put another way, while a JNOV argues, in essence that the nonmoving party has failed to meet its burden of production, a new trial motion typically argues that the nonmoving party failed to meet its burden of persuasion. In contrast to motions for judgment as a matter of law, the trial judge gets to weigh conflicting evidence and assess witness credibility in considering whether to grant a new trial. Again, granting a new trial motion results in trying the case over, rather than determining the outcome of the case.

D.   EXAMINATION OF WITNESSES AND FRE 611

The questioning (or "examination") of witnesses, and the witnesses' answers — their testimony — form the core of the trial, as seen above. Most evidence in most trials takes the form of testimony. Of course, documents, photographs, demonstrative and other tangible objects are introduced into evidence. However, as we will see in this course, the rules of evidence require presentation of testimony about documentary or tangible evidence to establish its admissibility and often to explain its significance. (Documentary and tangible evidence requires a witness to provide foundation testimony unless the parties agree to forego the formalities.) Therefore, witness testimony is generally the most crucial form of evidence.

The examination of witnesses in the evidence-presentation phases of the trial follows a pattern of taking turns. The party calling the witness conducts a direct examination. The opposing party cross-examines, with cross-examination being limited in scope to matters raised on direct examination. The party calling the witness may respond to points made on cross by conducting a redirect examination. Recross and further redirect examinations can be permitted.

The rules for presenting testimony, including the order of examinations, are not set out in the rules of evidence or any procedural code. Rather, they arise from an unwritten tradition of trial practice that has developed over the years. The only provision of the Federal Rules dealing directly with witness examinations is FRE 611, which seems to take largely for granted the established modes of presenting direct and cross-examinations, specifying only a few limitations and otherwise granting the trial judge broad discretion over "the mode and order" of examining witnesses.

1. FRE 611

RULE 611.   MODE AND ORDER OF INTERROGATION AND PRESENTATION

(a) Control by court. The court shall exercise reasonable control over the mode and order of interrogating witnesses and presenting evidence so as to (1) make the interrogation and presentation effective for the ascertainment of the truth, (2) avoid needless consumption of time, and (3) protect witnesses from harassment or undue embarrassment.

(b) Scope of cross-examination. Cross-examination should be limited to the subject matter of the direct examination and matters affecting the credibility of the witness. The court may, in the exercise of discretion, permit inquiry into additional matters as if on direct examination.

(c) Leading questions. Leading questions should not be used on the direct examination of a witness except as may be necessary to develop the witness' testimony. Ordinarily leading questions should be permitted on cross-examination. When a party calls a hostile witness, an adverse party, or a witness identified with an adverse party, interrogation may be by leading questions.

2. Interpretation and Illustration of FRE 611(a) and (b)

a. FRE 611(a): Breadth of the Court's Power

FRE 611(a) recognizes in broad terms the sweeping authority of the judge to control the examination of witnesses during the trial. Indeed, even the two express provisions purporting to limit the scope of cross-examination (subsection (b)) and the use of leading questions (subsection (c)) may be overridden in the discretion of the trial judge to serve the purposes outlined in Rule 611(a). This principle is reflected by the words "should" in Rule 611(b) and (c) and the Advisory Committee note to FRE 611(a), which states:

> Spelling out detailed rules to govern the mode and order of interrogating witnesses and presenting evidence is neither desirable nor feasible. The ultimate responsibility for the effective working of the adversary system rests with the judge. The rules set forth the objectives which he should seek to attain.

Thus, the following discussion of FRE 611 and witness examination is best understood not as a summary of binding rules, but rather as a description of the common trial practice that judges tend to follow out of long-standing tradition.

b. Direct Examination

Trials are usually won or lost on the strength of a party's case-in-chief rather than the weaknesses in the opponent's case. Direct examination — the questioning of witnesses you call in your case-in-chief — is the most straightforward and effective way to prove your case. Indeed, each party must plan to meet its burden of production with evidence developed through direct examination. It is simply not feasible — or strategically sound — to depend on eliciting needed evidence through cross-examination. Therefore, direct examination is extremely important, and probably the dominant feature of success at trial.

FRE 611 says nothing affirmatively about direct examination, but simply assumes that direct examination will be conducted. As we discuss below, FRE 611(b) states that direct examination should set a limit on the scope of cross-examination and in 611(c) provides that, with limited exceptions, leading questions should not be used on direct examination.

c.   FRE 611(b): The Scope of Cross-examination

Cross-examination is one of the defining features of the adversary system. "For two centuries, common law judges and lawyers have regarded the opportunity of cross-examination as an essential safeguard of the accuracy and completeness of testimony. They have insisted that the opportunity is a right, not a mere privilege."[4] Direct examination generally reflects some degree of cooperation between the examiner and the witness, and therefore raises the danger that the witness will be permitted, if not encouraged, to present a self-serving version of events. Cross-examination is an effective way to test the witness's credibility and show that there may be another side to the story. It also provides some of the more exciting moments in a trial.

FRE 611(b) establishes, as a guideline, that two general areas of inquiry are permissible for cross-examination. First, it is permissible to explore matters about which the witness has testified on direct examination. For example, in the *Johnson* case defense counsel's cross-examination of the correctional officers explored details of the altercation about which the witnesses testified on direct examination.

Second, it is always permissible to ask questions that may impeach the credibility of the witness even though there may have been no reference to these matters on direct examination. For example, the prosecutor in the *Johnson* case cross-examined Johnson's cellmate, George Butler, about Johnson's and Butler's gang affiliations even though this subject was not part of the direct examination (pages 43-45, supra). The purpose of these questions, as the sidebar conference makes clear, was to undermine Butler's credibility by showing his bias or prejudice in favor of Johnson. Similarly, in the *Johnson* case it was appropriate for the prosecutor to ask defense witnesses about prior convictions not mentioned on direct examination because proof of prior convictions is one of the traditional ways to impeach a witness's character for truthfulness.

The same principle applies to the rehabilitation of witnesses on cross-examination. Thus, if a direct examiner impeaches a hostile witness, it would be appropriate to rehabilitate the witness on cross-examination with questions about matters relating to credibility that were not covered on direct examination.

---

4.   John W. Strong, et al., McCormick on Evidence 34 (5th Ed. 1999). Wigmore suggested that the "abuses and puerilities often found associated with cross-examination" were outweighed by its value. "It may be that in more than one sense it takes the place in our system which torture occupied in the mediaeval system.... Nevertheless, it is beyond any doubt the greatest legal engine ever invented for the discovery of truth." 2 John Henry Wigmore, A Treatise on the System of Evidence in Trials at Common Law 1697 (1904). The latter phrase is oft-repeated. See, e.g., California v. Green, 399 U.S. 149, 158 (1970).

Unless the court exercises its discretion pursuant to the last sentence of FRE 611(b), it is improper to explore on cross-examination subjects that were not mentioned on direct examination and that do not affect the credibility of a witness. Consider, for example, the testimony in the *Johnson* case of Ruth Taylor, the records specialist (page 35, supra). Her direct examination testimony was limited to questions about Johnson's criminal record. Thus, even if Taylor had been an eyewitness to the jail cell incident, it would have been inappropriate, in the absence of special permission from the court, to question her about the incident on cross-examination. If the defendant wanted to explore the matter with Taylor, the proper course of action would be to call her as a witness during the presentation of the defense.

d. Redirect and Recross-examination

The direct examiner may conduct a redirect examination when cross-examination has been completed. The scope of redirect is limited to matters that were raised in cross-examination; this means that the direct examiner is usually not permitted to prove an essential element of the case that was overlooked, although judges vary widely in how strictly they will enforce this limitation.

Recross and further redirect examinations are sometimes allowed. Each such successive examination is smaller in scope since it is limited to responding to the immediately preceding redirect or recross-examination. Although the party calling the witness is theoretically entitled to the "last word," judges will not let this process go on ad nauseam. Such seesawing back and forth with redirect and recross, trying to have the last word, can irritate the judge and jury, and usually develops no new information. (This occurred frequently in the *Johnson* trial, but has been edited out of the transcript in Chapter One.)

3. Elaboration of FRE 611(a) and (b) and the Examination of Witnesses

a. Direct Examination

On direct examination, the goal is to let the witness provide pieces of narrative, in his or her own words, that build an overall "story" to the jury. It is important to help your witness appear as credible as possible, since the witness will be supporting your case. Furthermore, most of the evidence you will introduce at trial comes in through direct examination. Although you can also introduce evidence through cross-examination, the danger in relying on cross-examination (by definition, the questioning of witnesses called by your opponent) to introduce key evidence is that you have no control over what witnesses your opponent will call; if your opponent elects not to call a witness you were counting on to introduce some vital testimony, document, or other evidence, you may find you have failed to prove some essential element of your case.

Conducting an effective direct examination can be more challenging than you might think. Generally speaking, the witness will describe one or more incidents or factual occurrences, things the witness did or perceived. Your role as questioner is generally that of a skilled, sympathetic interviewer. Imagine that you know someone who has a very interesting story to tell, and that you would like someone else to hear the story. Although you could tell the story in your own words, you believe it would be much more effective coming from the person who had the experience firsthand. The witness should be allowed to testify in a narrative format, with the lawyer's questions keeping the story moving forward, keeping the witness from digressing, and helping to vary the pace so the witness's story does not become boring.

Questions for the most part should be open-ended: "What happened next?" "What did you see?" "Why did you do that?" Witnesses should be allowed to explain their actions. One way to remind a witness to concentrate on communicating with the jury is occasionally to begin a question with an admonition: "Tell the jury . . ." As the direct examiner, you also have to pace the testimony by asking several short questions and answers followed by a question with a longer narrative answer, followed by short questions again. Consider the kind of narrative that occurs when a lawyer fails to pace the testimony with questions, such as when defendant Johnson spoke at the outset of his direct examination. Was this an effective presentation of Johnson's story? Should witnesses be allowed to testify in that manner?

As a general rule, a witness you call in your case will be cooperative enough to meet with you in advance. (There is an important exception to this. See "c. Direct Examination of 'Adverse' and 'Hostile' Witnesses," below.) This means that you can and should "prepare" the witness by giving some idea of the subject matter you plan to cover. Many attorneys rehearse the direct examination, asking the planned questions and giving tips about how to answer them. The idea of this is not to put words in the witness's mouth but to help the witness tell the story effectively and avoid pitfalls that would unduly damage credibility. Preparing the witness, while essential, also poses an additional challenge. Having rehearsed the direct testimony with a cooperative witness and become thoroughly familiar with it, you must nevertheless appear to have a genuine interest in the questions being asked and to ensure as much as possible that the witness is not merely reciting a rehearsed text, but sincerely communicating to the jury.

b.   Cross-examination

FRE 611(b) embodies the "American" or "restrictive" rule of cross-examination, in contrast to the wide-open rule of cross-examination, used in the English trial system, which permits the opposing party to question witnesses about anything that is relevant to the case. The primary advantage of the American rule is that it allows the parties to control the development of their cases. For example, the plaintiff may wish to introduce a document into evidence early on in the trial and may need to call the defendant or somebody closely associated with the defendent to authenticate the document. Even if the witness has knowledge of other aspects of the case, the plaintiff, for reasons of strategy, may not want to go into those matters at this time or with this witness. If the plaintiff limits the direct examination to the question of authentication, application of the restrictive cross-examination rule will prevent the defendant on cross-examination from exploring the witness's knowledge about other aspects of the case.

The primary advantage of the English rule is that it avoids the necessity of determining what the scope of direct examination was. While the English rule also avoids the necessity of recalling witnesses who may have testimony to give regarding several issues in a case, FRE 611(b) reserves for the trial judge the discretion to accomplish the same efficiency by permitting questions about matters that are beyond the scope of direct examination, in which case the examination shall be conducted "as if on direct examination." This means, in effect, that the witness has become the cross-examiner's witness and that, therefore, "leading questions should not be used . . . except as may be necessary to develop the witness' testimony." FRE 611(c).

i. **Strategy and Goals of Cross-examination.**   An important strategic goal for you as a cross-examiner is to take advantage of the subtle opportunity to argue your case. Whole lines of questioning can develop themes that you can emphasize by repetition and then argue to the jury in closing. Leading questions, which can be asked on cross-examination, also provide an opportunity to make assertions that emphasize the inferences or interpretations you want the jury to draw from the evidence.

A second goal of cross-examination is to fill in gaps in your evidence or obtain favorable admissions. Sometimes an adverse witness is the only witness who can provide admissible testimony needed to establish an element of your claim or defense, or to tell part of the story you want to convey to the jury. In many instances, you may have to call such a witness yourself as an "adverse witness." In addition to filling in gaps, some witnesses called by your opponent may make (voluntarily or otherwise) admissions favorable to your side. Helpful testimony can be particularly strong when it comes from the mouth of the adversary or his witnesses.

Finally, you can use cross-examination questions to control damage by minimizing the effect of adverse testimony by one or both of two means. Without discrediting the witness, you can try to show how the witness's version of the facts is consistent with, or at least not inconsistent with, your theory of the case. Or you can discredit the witness by attacking his or her credibility, either on specific points or overall. Typically, a witness will not have been called by your opponent to testify unless that testimony helps the opponent's case. (If it does not, you may not need to bother with cross-examination.) There are several techniques for discrediting, or attacking the credibility of, a witness. These techniques, known collectively as "impeachment," are discussed in Chapter Seven.

ii. **Cross-examination Technique.**   The manner of conducting cross-examination is perhaps most easily understood by contrasting it with direct examination. Because direct examination seeks to develop the story through the witness's own words and to bolster the witness's credibility, the direct examiner wants the jury to focus on the witness. Factual information arising out of the testimony should therefore come from what the witness says, not the questioner. Questions should be shorter than the answers; and should generally be open-ended. The question "why" is often effective on direct.

On cross-examination, by contrast, the lawyer wants to provide (in effect) most of the information the jury hears, while attempting to limit what the witness actually says by asking leading questions. This usually means making an assertion of fact to which the witness can fully respond by simply agreeing with a "yes" or "no" answer. Skilled cross-examiners try to formulate precise, narrow questions that don't call for explanation, keeping open-ended questions to a minimum. In particular, "how" and "why" questions are generally avoided like the plague: Such questions are an open-ended invitation to the witness to give a self-serving explanation of the facts and argue inferences adverse to your case. After a "why"-type question, you may be standing there while the witness goes on at length and you have no basis to shut the witness off.

An old saw about cross-examination is not to ask "one question too many." This usually means that you shouldn't ask the witness to agree to a conclusion or inference that constitutes the point you will make in closing argument, even if you feel that the conclusion follows logically from a series of propositions that the witness has agreed to. The witness will invariably disagree and attempt to give a self-serving explanation, arguing his or her own case. It can be difficult to know when you have reached the stopping point where the next question is the "one too many." If words like "thus" and "therefore" seem to be part of the question, that is a red flag not to ask it.

c. Direct Examination of "Adverse" and "Hostile" Witnesses

FRE 611(c) sets forth two circumstances in which a direct examination may be conducted in the manner of a cross-examination, using leading questions and following the tactics of cross-examination: the direct examination of "adverse" and "hostile" witnesses.

"Adverse witness" is a term used in common legal parlance to refer to "an adverse party, or a witness identified with an adverse party" within the meaning of FRE 611(c). This concept includes not only the adverse party, but also his/her/its agents, employees, and people who, through legal or other ties, are strongly identified with the adverse party. It is not uncommon to call such an adverse witness in your case-in-chief. You would typically call an adverse witness where some item of evidence necessary to prove your case is uniquely within the knowledge of the adverse witness; or where there is reason to believe that the adverse witness will be so disliked or disbelieved by the jury that his testimony will necessarily help rather than hurt your case. An example would be calling the alleged sexual harasser to the stand to show the jury what a bad guy he is, with the goal of thereby supporting the plaintiff's credibility. If an adverse witness is necessary or strategically helpful to your case, you may not want to run the risk of waiting to cross-examine this witness. Your adversary may not call this witness; or may do so but keep the direct examination so circumscribed that you will not be able to cover the subjects you want on cross-examination. (See FRE 611(b), limiting scope of cross-examination.)

When questioning an adverse witness on direct examination, you are allowed to use leading questions and, as a tactical matter, should use all the techniques of cross-examination. Although using cross-examination techniques, you do not have a limitation on the scope of questioning as you do on an actual cross-examination. When you are finished, your adversary has the right to do a "friendly cross-examination," during which leading questions will normally be prohibited, as though that were a direct examination. See Advisory Committee Notes to FRE 611(c) (the word "Ordinarily" in "Ordinarily leading questions should be permitted on cross-examination" is designed to encourage judges to prohibit leading questions on "friendly cross-examination").

A "hostile witness" is one who is presumed friendly or neutral when called to the stand (i.e., a nonadverse witness), but who, during questioning, demonstrates an attitude sufficiently hostile to the questioner to raise an inference of opposition to the examiner's client or identification with the adverse party. The examining attorney then asks the court to declare the witness "hostile." If the court does so, the examiner can proceed with leading questions, and may want to use the other cross-examination techniques as well.

In addition to asking leading questions, the party calling an adverse or hostile witness may also impeach that witness — attack the witness's credibility using the techniques and rules discussed in Chapter Seven. According to FRE 607, "the credibility of a witness may be attacked by any party, including the party calling the witness." Indeed, the rule suggests that a party may impeach a witness on direct examination even if the witness is not formally adverse or hostile. FRE 607 abolishes the common law "voucher rule," according to which a party who called a witness was held to vouch for the credibility of that witnesses. See 3A John Henry Wigmore, Evidence §896, at 658-660 (James Chadbourne rev. 1970). Despite the unqualified language in FRE 607, some courts have held that it is impermissible to impeach one's own witness if the impeachment is a subterfuge to get otherwise inadmissible evidence before the jury. The admissibility of evidence for impeachment purposes, when that evidence is inadmissible as "substantive evidence," is discussed in Chapter Seven.

4.   Interpretation and Illustration of FRE 611(c): Leading Questions

Leading questions are questions that suggest the answer the examiner is seeking. A classic example of a leading question takes the form of a statement with a brief interrogative tag at the beginning or end, such as "You saw defendant Johnson lunge out of his cell with his fist, didn't you?" FRE 611(c) confirms — again, in the form of a guideline to the trial judge — the common practice that leading questions are normally prohibited on direct, but allowed on cross-examination. This rule thus accounts for the most obvious difference between the mode of conducting direct and cross-examination. ("Redirect" is treated the same as direct examination, and recross the same as cross-examination for purposes of the leading question rule.) The assumption underlying FRE 611(c) is that a witness is likely to be friendly or at least cooperative with the party calling the witness, and will not be equally cooperative with the cross-examiner. This presumed bias against the cross-examiner may make leading questions essential in order to get at the truth. If counsel were not permitted to ask a very specific "Isn't it true that . . . ?" question that calls for a yes or no answer, it might be impossible adequately to explore the details and nuances of the witness's knowledge and testimonial qualities. Conversely, because of the witness's presumed willingness to cooperate with the direct examiner, there is thought to be a risk that the suggestiveness in leading questions on direct examination may cause the witness to distort the truth in the direct examiner's favor.

5.   Elaboration of FRE 611(c) and Leading Questions

a.   *What Is a Leading Question?*

A leading question is best defined as one that suggests the answer the questioner wants the witness to give. This definition is probably overbroad; on some level, many if not most questions asked on direct suggest in some way what the questioner wants the witness to say. If they didn't, there would be no way to direct the witness's attention to the type of information the examiner is seeking. Therefore, many, perhaps most, questions that fit this definition will ultimately be allowed, because the judge (or opposing counsel) believes them to be nonleading or else to be "borderline" or close calls that do not merit the trouble of making or sustaining an objection. Ultimately, the "test" of a leading question may often come down to a matter of degree — how suggestive is the question? — that is heavily dependent on context. You have to develop an intuitive feel for when these "borderline" questions are leading or nonleading.

A common misconception is that questions calling for "yes or no" answers are leading; in actuality, some in that form are, some aren't. For example, "Do you live in Chicago?" is not leading.

Leading questions are often phrased as an assertion of fact, ending either with a tone of voice implying a question mark at the end, or with an actual verbal tag asking the witness to agree.

You were at home the night of the murder, isn't that correct [. . . isn't that true? . . . right? . . . weren't you?]?
Weren't you at home the night of the murder?
You were at home the night of the murder?
Isn't it a fact that you were at home the night of the murder?

In this form, the questions are clearly leading. But questions can be leading without taking this form. It is the suggestion of the desired answer that makes a question leading. A typical leading question occurs when the questioner suggests a fact to a witness who seems to have overlooked it. Consider the following piece of direct examination of Officer Huston from the *Johnson* trial (page 13, supra).

Q: Why was inmate Johnson and inmate Butler secured, handcuffed? What's the purpose?
A: Because if they are combative or not complying with orders; disciplinary reasons, you know?
Q: Officer safety reasons?
A: Yes, officer safety and security.

The prosecutor wanted the witness to give "safety" as the reason for handcuffing the inmates, but the witness said "discipline" instead. Imagine that defense counsel had made a timely objection after "Q: Officer safety reasons?" and that the objection was sustained (as it should be). The problem with the question is its leading form, not that the answer will put inadmissible matter before the jury. (This will be further explained when we deal with the subject of "objections.") Here, the prosecutor can then simply rephrase the question.

Q. BY MR. CUMMINGS: Okay, Officer Huston, was "officer safety" a further reason to handcuff the inmates?
MR. DEEMER: Objection. That's still leading.
THE COURT: Sustained.

This question is phrased more like a normal question than a statement, but it is really no different from the first time it was asked: It still suggests the desired answer.

Q. BY MR. CUMMINGS: [Huge sigh.] Did you have any reasons other than dis-
    ciplinary reasons for handcuffing the inmates?

This question may be borderline. It could technically be construed as leading because,
in the present context, the question suggests that Huston should say "yes." Whether a
question unduly suggests the desired answer may often depend on context. But the
judge would in all likelihood overrule a "leading" objection at this point; also the jury
will start to think that the objecting lawyer did not want the information to come out.

A: Yes.
Q: What other reason or reasons?
A: Officer safety.

To be sure, the "leading" objection did not keep the witness from supplementing his
answer in the manner suggested by the questioner — an attentive witness would know
what he's supposed to say from the first phrasing of the leading question. However, the
objections may serve to make the point to the jury that the ultimate answer was the
"lawyer's answer" more than the witness's, and — who knows? — the questioner might
have moved on without getting the answer after the first objection was sustained.

b. Leading Questions: Tactical Considerations

In practice, there will be considerable variation in how much leading you can "get
away with" in direct examination. If the opposing counsel does not object, the court is
unlikely to stop you on its own initiative. Even if objections are made, the trial judge
has virtually unreviewable discretion to allow leading questions. In the *Johnson* case,
the prosecutor got away with numerous leading questions that were truly objectionable
because the defense counsel didn't bother to object (perhaps because he was discour-
aged that the judge overruled his "leading" objection when he made one). See, e.g.,
pages 19-20, 27-28, supra.

There is a down side, however, to asking a lot of leading questions. Because the
focus on direct examination should be on the witness, rather than on the examiner,
leading questions can backfire as a direct examination technique. A witness who
delivers key testimony in response to leading questions on direct examination will
give the impression of saying whatever the lawyer wants, and can lose credibility.
And of course, conducting a direct examination in this way makes the examiner
vulnerable to objection: "Your honor, counsel is testifying rather than the witness."
On the other hand, if the witness is weak, equivocal, or otherwise has difficulties getting
his testimony out in his own words, it may on balance be better to lead than not — if
you can get away with it.

E. OBJECTIONS AND PRESERVATION OF ERROR FOR APPEAL: FRE 103

The substantive rules of evidence revolve most clearly around two features of the trial
process that remain to be considered: trial objections, and "making a record" that

preserves evidentiary issues for appellate review. These two subjects are closely inter-twined. Evidentiary rulings admitting evidence over objection will virtually never be the basis of appellate reversal without a clear, direct, and correct objection in the trial record. If evidence is excluded, the losing side must make sure that the substance of the evidence, and the theory of its admissibility, are apparent from the record in order to preserve the issue for appeal. FRE 103(a)(2). It is the job of the advocates to create a record that adequately reflects the objection, any response to it, and the judge's ruling. This is called "perfecting the record" and "preserving the issue for appeal." In this section we will first discuss the principles and mechanics of objections, and then turn to appellate review of the trial record.

1.   FRE 103

RULE 103.   RULINGS ON EVIDENCE

(a) Effect of erroneous ruling. Error may not be predicated upon a ruling which admits or excludes evidence unless a substantial right of the party is affected, and

(1) Objection. In case the ruling is one admitting evidence, a timely objection or motion to strike appears of record, stating the specific ground of objection, if the specific ground was not apparent from the context; or

(2) Offer of proof. In case the ruling is one excluding evidence, the substance of the evidence was made known to the court by offer or was apparent from the context within which questions were asked.

Once the court makes a definitive ruling on the record admitting or excluding evidence, either at or before trial, a party need not renew an objection or offer of proof to preserve a claim of error for appeal.

(b) Record of offer and ruling. The court may add any other or further statement which shows the character of the evidence, the form in which it was offered, the objection made, and the ruling thereon. It may direct the making of an offer in question and answer form.

(c) Hearing of jury. In jury cases, proceedings shall be conducted, to the extent practicable, so as to prevent inadmissible evidence from being suggested to the jury by any means, such as making statements or offers of proof or asking questions in the hearing of the jury.

(d) Plain error. Nothing in this rule precludes taking notice of plain errors affecting substantial rights although they were not brought to the attention of the court.

2.   Interpretation and Illustration of FRE 103(a) and (d): Objections, Offers of Proof, and Preservation of Evidentiary Issues for Appeal

An objection is the means by which a lawyer can interrupt the trial to oppose the introduction of evidence. Although objections are most frequently made to questions or answers during a witness's testimony, objections can be made to any type of evidence: real evidence, demonstrative evidence, or testimony. The purpose of an objection is twofold: (1) if the objection is sustained, to increase your chances of winning the trial by excluding harmful evidence from consideration by the trier of fact; (2) if the objection is overruled, to preserve for appeal your argument that the evidence should have been excluded, pursuant to FRE 103(a)(1).

When an objection is made, one of three things will usually happen. The court will "sustain" (agree with) the objection, "overrule" (disagree with) the objection, or ask counsel for further elaboration or argument, usually outside the hearing of the jury, such as at the sidebar. If the judge rules on the objection right away, the losing lawyer may feel it necessary to try to make further argument before the trial proceeds any further, and may ask to approach the bench to argue the point. Trial lawyers typically request such sidebar conferences when the judge's ruling will admit significantly prejudicial evidence, or will deprive the party of an opportunity to present evidence at the right moment in the trial.

Moreover, where an objection has been sustained, it may be necessary for the lawyer offering the evidence to approach the bench to make an offer of proof. FRE 103(a)(2) provides that in order to preserve an appeal of an erroneous ruling excluding evidence (an incorrectly sustained objection), the party must "[make] the substance of the evidence... known to the court" unless the substance "was apparent from the context in which the questions were asked." This procedure of advising the court of the substance of the excluded evidence is called an "offer of proof." Id. An offer of proof can take the form of a statement on the record by counsel summarizing what the excluded evidence would show (e.g., "Your honor, the witness would testify that Officer Smith told him that the prison was on lockdown because Officer Walker had beaten an inmate.").

FRE 103(a) provides that an evidentiary ruling will be a ground for reversal on appeal only if two conditions are met. The error must "affect a substantial right" of a party, meaning that the ruling made some difference in the outcome of the trial. Second, the party must have made a timely objection and, where the ruling excludes evidence, an "offer of proof" alerting the court to the substance of the excluded evidence. Failure to object will probably mean that the judge's ruling, or the adversary's behavior, cannot be grounds for reversal. There is an exception to this general rule. "Plain" error, referred to in FRE 103(d), means an error so serious, and so obvious, that it can be grounds for reversal even though no objection was made to it during trial. The trial judge should have noticed it, and it is highly probable that it affected the outcome. This doctrine was originally developed in criminal cases to protect defendants from the errors of appointed counsel. Under FRE 103(d) it applies in civil cases as well.

3. Elaboration of FRE 103(a)(1) and (2) and Objections

a. Two Types of Objections

There are two basic types of objections: an objection to the improper form of a question, and an objection to the admissibility of the answer.

An objection to admissibility of the answer is intended to exclude inadmissible evidence. Such objections are made when it appears that the question, even if properly phrased, calls for evidence barred by exclusionary rules of evidence or whose relevance or foundation has not been established. Most of the substantive law of evidence that you will study in this course concerns these questions of admissibility, and the grounds for ruling on the objections are for the most part found in the rules of evidence.

An objection to the form of the question is intended to regulate the mode of questioning and the behavior of the examiner. In contrast to objections going to admissibility, objections as to form are governed by traditional trial practice and the trial judge's inherent, discretionary authority rather than formal evidence rules.[5] Examples of objections to the form of the question include "leading," "argumenta-tive," see page 30, supra, or "calls for a narrative response." Other examples of objec-tions to the form of the question include "compound," "vague," "ambiguous," "mischaracterizes the testimony." (See "Trial Objection Cheat Sheet," page 115, infra.)

Questions objectionable as to form may be sustained even though the evidence they seek is ultimately admissible. Consider the beginning of Officer Van Berg's direct examination in People v. Johnson (page 20, supra):

Q: Did you have occasion on that day [March 28] to come into contact with an inmate by the name of Johnson?
A: Yes, I did.
Q: Same individual seated at the end of counsel table?
A: Yes.

The last question is leading, and would have been objectionable had the defendant's identity as the perpetrator been in dispute. It would be the form of the question that is objectionable, not the answer. The same information could be obtained through a proper nonleading question:

Q: Do you see that person in the courtroom today?
A: Yes.
Q: Where?
A: Seated next to the defense counsel.

A common mistake of inexperienced attorneys is to move on to the next question after an objection to the form of the question — such as "leading" — has been sustained.

Questions can violate more than one rule relating to form, and it is appropriate to mention multiple grounds for the objection.

Q: Did you see the defendant first lunge at Officer Walker and then eventually strike Officer Huston?
DEFENSE COUNSEL: Objection: leading, compound.
THE COURT: Sustained.

In addition to its leading form, the question is also compound because it asks the witness to describe two logically separable facts of importance to the case. The objec-tions can also be made one after the other, if the first one is overruled.

DEFENSE COUNSEL: Objection, compound.
THE COURT: Overruled.

---

5.   An arguable "source" of authority to rule on objections as to form is FRE 611(a), which directs the trial judge to "exercise reasonable control over the mode and order of interrogating witnesses and present-ing evidence[.]" Courts rarely cite FRE 611(a) for these or other purposes, however. In fact the rule adds little, if anything, to what is explicit or implicit in other rules. For example, FRE 403 provides authority to exclude cumulative evidence, and FRE 102 admonishes courts to construe the rules "to secure fairness in administration, elimination of unjustifiable expense and delay, and promotion of growth and development of the law of evidence to the end that the truth may be ascertained and proceedings justly determined."

DEFENSE COUNSEL: Leading.
THE COURT: Sustained.

It is also possible, of course, that a question can be framed in an objectionable form and seek arguably inadmissible matter. Consider the discussion of "Facility B" during the Huston direct examination in *Johnson*. Suppose the prosecutor, Cummings, had introduced this subject with the question:

Q: Isn't Facility B a transition facility for violent inmates coming out of SHU, before they are placed in general population?

This question is not only leading (an objection to form), but it also calls for arguably inadmissible character evidence to the effect that defendant Johnson is a violent person because he was housed in Facility B. This example also illustrates how a timely objection will not always be adequate to prevent the jury from hearing inadmissible matter — here, it was embedded in the prosecutor's leading question.

b. Timing of Objections

Making timely objections is probably the most difficult trial skill to learn. In a very short time — often no longer than the second or two before the witness answers the question — you have to determine whether the question is objectionable, on what basis, whether tactically the objection is worth making, and then actually say "objection," typically while getting to your feet. This is challenging to do. But failing to make a timely objection can result in a failure of both goals of objecting at all. A failure to object — and even an untimely objection — fails to keep the evidence from the jury, and normally waives the evidentiary error on appeal. There is a narrow exception to this so-called "contemporaneous-objection rule". Under FRE 103(d), an appellate court may correct "plain error" in spite of the absence of a contemporaneous objection. The plain error exception is used "sparingly," and only to correct "particularly egregious errors" that would result in a miscarriage of justice if not corrected. United States v. Young, 470 U.S. 1, 15 (1985).

A timely objection to the form of the question must be made before the question is answered. This point is easy to understand. In *Johnson*, the defense counsel was consistently late in objecting to the prosecutor's questions (see, e.g., page 22):

Q: Did he appear to you to be attempting to fight or strike Walker or any of the officers?
A: Yes.
MR. DEEMER: One moment. That's leading.

If the answer is given before the objection, judges will often allow the answer to stand, and will either overrule the objection or simply say, "the witness already answered" or "the answer stands." But there is also an expectation that the witness should not jump the gun with his answer. If the witness answers an objectionable question after the objecting lawyer has already started speaking or before the judge rules, the judge may strike the answer and caution the witness not to answer questions while objections are being made or ruled on.

A timely objection to the inadmissibility of an answer must be made as soon as the inadmissibility becomes apparent. This can be tricky. Typically, it will be apparent that a question is likely to call for an objectionable response: "Did they tell you that something had happened to your hand?" sounds like it calls for inadmissible hearsay, for example. Or suppose a supervising correctional officer were to testify that he sent the correctional officers to Johnson's cell to retrieve the trays, but that he did not go himself. If such a witness were asked whether Johnson hit or kicked Huston or Van Berg, the question would clearly call for speculation or lack the foundational requirement of first-hand knowledge. Where a clear potential for an inadmissible answer inheres in the question, the objection should be made before the answer is given. However, in contrast to objections to the form of the question, where the judge is unlikely to strike the answer, if you did not object fast enough to an inadmissible answer, you might still object belatedly and ask the judge to strike the answer.

Sometimes, the objectionable matter cannot be anticipated from the question. "Tell us what happened next" is generally an unobjectionable question, but the witness could say all kinds of things that are not admissible testimony. Consider, for example the lengthy narrative defendant Johnson gave in response to defense counsel's question "Would you explain to the jury what that problem [concerning the package] was?" The lengthy answer that followed contained some arguably objectionable hearsay and irrelevant matter. It is fair game to cut the witness off with an objection and motion to strike as soon as the objectionable character of the answer becomes clear; most judges will be more lenient about striking inadmissible portions of an answer in this situation, even if you did not jump in at the first possible moment. For example:

Q: Tell us what happened next.
A: Well, the Sergeant told me we were on lockdown because —
COUNSEL: Objection. Hearsay. Move to strike.
THE COURT: Sustained. The answer is stricken.

When inadmissible matter has gotten in front of the jury and you failed to object (presumably because you couldn't anticipate the objectionable matter from the question) the proper response is a motion to strike the offending testimony, and perhaps a request for the judge to admonish the jury to disregard it.

Q: Tell us what happened next.
A: Well, the Sergeant told me we were on lockdown because another inmate had gotten beat up by Officer Walker.
COUNSEL: [Snapping belatedly to attention.] I move to strike the last answer. It's inadmissible hearsay.
THE COURT: The last answer is stricken. The jury will disregard it.

c.   Stating the Objection

An objection is not preserved for appeal unless "a timely objection or motion to strike appears of record, stating the specific ground for the objection." FRE 103(a)(1).

In practice, you will encounter and even make both specific and general objections. A general objection is an expression of an objection without stating the grounds. Where the basis for the objection seems obvious, the lawyer may say nothing more than "objection" — or the judge may rule on it without waiting for the lawyer to specify the grounds. You may hear similarly "general" objections using some boilerplate phrase that does not specify the ground, such as "Objection to the form of the question," or one that is merely vague and conclusory, such as "irrelevant, incompetent, and immaterial." It may not hurt your case if you make a general objection that is sustained, because your goal of keeping the evidence out is accomplished, and you have no basis to appeal your own successful objection. If a general objection is overruled, however, it is likely to be deemed to waive the issue on appeal for failure to state the ground. Therefore, it is better practice to specify your grounds in the objection.

It is vital to state the correct basis for the objection. The judge is required to rule only on the stated ground of the objection. If you state an invalid basis for an otherwise proper objection, your objection could be overruled even if it could have been sustained on another ground. Judges do not usually cue an attorney as to the correct objection, or make the correct objection on their own. More likely, the judge will simply overrule an incorrect objection.

Specific objections need only communicate the basic reason for the objection. "Objection, hearsay" should probably be sufficient to preserve the point for appeal; it is not necessary to spell out your theory as to how the only relevant use of the out-of-court statement is for the hearsay purpose of proving the truth of the matter asserted. Indeed, most judges frown upon so-called "speaking objections" — making arguments in the course of stating an objection — and may even specifically warn the lawyers at the start of the trial to refrain from doing so. The general rule of decorum, then, is to state the ground for an objection as succinctly as possible; and if extended argument is needed, the objecting lawyer is expected to request a sidebar conference.

As you can see from the "Trial Objection Cheat Sheet," which follows on pages 115-116, there are certain commonly used words or phrases to make certain routine objections. But these are not magic words; anything that gets the point across succinctly will do. "Objection, calls for inadmissible character evidence" and "Objection, Rule 404" probably would both suffice to make the same point. In addition, laundry lists of common or boilerplate objections should not obscure the fact that an objection can be based on any rule or principle that would exclude the evidence. Some of these principles may not be adequately expressed in the common boilerplate terms.

Some experienced trial practitioners suggest trying to put objections into plain language rather than using legal buzz-words. Since the objection tends to signal the jury that you want to keep them from hearing something, that impression may only be reinforced when the objection is stated in legalese. Thus, it may be preferable to say "Objection — this witness has no way of knowing who wrote the document" rather than to say "Objection — lack of foundation." On the other hand, using plain language could run afoul of a judge's warning against "speaking objections." In addition, there may be occasions when you want to obscure your reasons from the jury. You have to use your judgment.

If offending matter has already been stated by the witness, the proper procedure is to make a motion to strike. You need to specify both the grounds for the motion (which are the same kinds of points as grounds for objections) and the portion of testimony you contend should be stricken. "I move to strike the witness's answer in its entirety. It's hearsay." or "Motion to strike as nonresponsive. I move to strike the witness's answer after the word 'yes.'" Having testimony stricken is, of course, a much less effective remedy than preventing it from coming into the record before the jury. As the old saying goes, "you can't unring a bell." However, it should be done to preserve the issue for appeal. Moreover, the remedy can have a practical consequence if the jury asks for a "read-back" of the trial transcript during jury deliberations: Stricken portions of testimony are omitted from the read-back.

d. Tactical Considerations

Many objectionable questions are asked with impunity because the opposing counsel decides an objection is not worth making. Again, an objection signals to the jurors that counsel wants to keep them from hearing some information. This could create an impression of having something to hide, and this downside of objecting has to be weighed against the damage to one's case if the evidence comes in. Other downsides to objecting can include irritating the judge or jury, or (if the objection is made during your opponent's cross-examination of your witness) possibly confusing the witness. Objections to the form of a question may simply cue your adversary to phrase a clearer, more effective question. Moreover, an objection can often underscore the damaging aspects of an objectionable question, and wisdom may on these occasions dictate silence in the hope that the jury will miss the point. Finally, objectionable questions sometimes will be helpful to your case either because the specific answer will be helpful or because the question will "open the door" to helpful testimony that might not otherwise be admissible.

On the other hand, there are tactical advantages to making objections. Jurors will expect the lawyers to make some objections, which gives you some leeway to do so without reaching an irritation threshold. Moreover, by sitting mute while your witness is being flogged with seemingly unfair questions, you may send a signal that you are being lazy, inattentive, or indifferent to your case. Finally, objections — particularly if sustained — can disrupt the rhythm or flow of your opponent's examination or leave your opponent stumped as to how to ask a proper question to get in some important piece of evidence.

Of course, these tactical considerations in favor of objections — particularly those regarding disruption of one's adversary's questioning — do not justify making objections in bad faith. To be sure, some trial attorneys will cross the line and make objections purely to rattle the opposing counsel; but one hopes that bad karma will be visited upon them. You should have a good faith, arguable basis for any objection you make.

4. Elaboration of FRE 103(a) and (d): Preservation of Error for Appellate Review

The appellate court reviewing the defendant's conviction in People v. Johnson ruled that the prosecutor committed prosecutorial misconduct by referring to Johnson's alleged gang membership when questioning inmates Butler and Johnson, and in closing argument to the jury. (See pages 43-45, 56, and 69, supra). The court held this to be misconduct because no evidence was ever produced that gave the prosecutor reasonable grounds for believing that Johnson was in fact a gang member. The court held the error was harmless, however, because

> the passing mention of gangs was a peripheral matter in appellant's case. The jury knew that the defense witnesses were inmates in a maximum security prison [and that] appellant was a rapist, Butler a robber, and Green a murderer. In these circumstances, it is not

reasonably probable that the jury's assessment of credibility would have been materially different if gangs had never been mentioned.

How are such issues concerning erroneous admission (or exclusion) of evidence raised and preserved for appellate review?

a. Making the Record — in General

When a judgment is rendered based on a jury or bench trial, any appeal is most likely to focus on the evidence "in the record." Appellate questions of substantive law will look at whether sufficient evidence supports the legally defined elements of the claims or defenses. Evidentiary questions will consider whether the appellant's rights were unduly harmed by excluding evidence that should have been admitted or admitting evidence that should have been excluded. Such determinations can't be made without, typically, a review of "the record" of the trial.

The phrase "the record" often is meant as a broad reference to the trial court's file on the case. It contains all the court papers filed by the parties' lawyers, transcripts of any trial or evidentiary hearing held by the court, and any evidence submitted in a trial, hearing, or motion. The trial "record" is a subset of the court's file, including the trial transcripts and exhibits. The key point is that the record serves as the universe of facts and trial court rulings within which an appellate court must operate in making its rulings on appeal. Appellate courts are not allowed to "go outside the record" by considering facts or legal arguments that have not been presented to the trial court.

At trial, therefore, it is vitally important for counsel to be attentive to the record to ensure that it is complete, both in terms of evidence and legal arguments and rulings. "Making the record" very often means nothing more or less than having what is said recorded (typically stenographically) and ultimately transcribed by the court reporter so that it becomes part of the official trial transcript. Sometimes, the judge, either inadvertently or by design, will conduct some important moments of legal argument or ruling during the trial without the court reporter present — an argument in chambers or a sidebar conference, for example, might go unrecorded, and therefore be "off the record." In such cases, it is the responsibility of the lawyer to put the matter "on the record" — that is, to summarize what occurred when the court reporter is back on duty and making the verbatim record. Otherwise the matter occurring off the record could be effectively insulated from appellate review. For example, the sidebar conference involving whether to admit evidence about "Facility B" in *Johnson* happened to be held on the record. Had it not been, an appellate court would have been no more able to review the issues raised in that discussion than you would have been as a reader of the transcript.

Likewise, lawyers have to be conscious of the record becoming garbled or confusing. There are a number of mistakes that inexperienced trial lawyers occasionally make that can be avoided by paying careful attention to what is occurring at trial. Think about the following issues: (a) overlapping — if a trial is being conducted with a court reporter, which is still typical today, the reporter cannot accurately record what happens when more than a single person talks at once. In such a circumstance, the careful attorney will be sure to go back and explain "for the record" what transpired; (b) spelling — names often cause problems because quite different spellings are often pronounced similarly (e.g., White, Whyte, Wite, Wyatt); (c) figures — when an attorney says "thirty-one-o-four," does this mean 3104, 31.04, 30,104, or what? Make sure it is clear; (d) gestures — make sure gestures are explained ("let the record show that the witness pointed at the defendant").

b. Making the Record for Appeal of Evidentiary Rulings

For purposes of appeal of evidentiary rulings, "making the record" means complying with FRE 103. The appealing party must have made ("on the record") a specific objection or an offer of proof, depending on whether the disputed item of evidence was admitted or excluded. See FRE 103(a)(1) and (2). This requirement of FRE 103(a) is a mainstay of the adversary system. The judge is not responsible for running an error-free trial. Rather, the burden is on the parties to protect their own interests through timely arguments aimed at redressing errors that significantly affect their interests. The advocates must therefore take the initiative to object to their opponents' improper use of evidence or other inappropriate courtroom behaviors. In addition, the advocates must make known the grounds for their objections, and the opponent is always given the opportunity to respond. Only then is the judge required to, and is in a better informed position to, make a ruling that affects the conduct of the trial This requirement raises the stakes of the lawyer's tactical decisions as to when or when not to object.

Motions in limine and FRE 103 interact in important ways. Formerly in many federal courts (and still in several state court systems), if a motion in limine to exclude evidence was denied, the advocate was required to renew the objection to the evidence at trial in order to preserve the issue for appeal. Effective December 1, 2000, however, FRE 103(a) was amended to provide that any "definitive ruling on the record admitting or excluding evidence, either at or before trial" is now sufficient "to preserve a claim of error for appeal." This amendment was specifically intended to apply to "so-called *in limine* rulings." Advisory Committee Notes to FRE 103.

c. Standards of Appellate Review of Evidentiary Errors

Analytically, appellate courts proceed through two steps in considering whether a trial judgment should be reversed for an erroneous evidentiary ruling. The first analytical step asks "was there error?" Most, but not all, evidence questions are reviewed on appeal under an "abuse of discretion" standard. This means the appellate court will not "substitute its judgment" for that of the trial court — that is, the appellate court will not redecide the issue as though it were the original decision maker. (The latter kind of appellate review is called "independent" or "de novo" review.) Under the abuse of discretion standard, to find error at all, the appellate court has to conclude that the trial court's decision was not merely wrong, but something close to an unreasonable decision.

Second, if there was error, was the error "harmless"? FRE 103(a) states that an appeal based on an erroneous ruling admitting or excluding evidence at trial cannot win a reversal unless the error affects a "substantial right" of the party. "Substantial right" has been construed by courts in most circumstances as invoking the "harmless error" standard. An error is harmless if it did not affect the outcome of the trial. Would the jury have reached the same result had the erroneously admitted evidence been excluded (or had the erroneously excluded evidence been admitted)? If so, the error is harmless. California Evidence Code §353, interpreted in the appeal of the *Johnson* case, similarly requires that the error resulted in a "miscarriage of justice." Both FRE

103 and the California Code thus require the appellate court to answer the same question — how likely is it that the error actually affected the outcome?

What degree of certainty must there be in evaluating the hypothetical state of affairs (the outcome of the trial had the error not been made)? Here, there is some variation among different courts. For example, the U.S. Court of Appeals for the Ninth Circuit formulated the "harmless error" standard as requiring the appellate court to affirm the trial court if the evidentiary error "more probably than not was harmless," or if there was a "fair assurance" that the error was harmless (e.g., United States v. Hitt, 981 F.2d 422 (9th Cir. 1992)). The Third Circuit phrased the standard differently: The trial court will be affirmed only if it is "highly probable" that the evidentiary error did not affect substantial rights (e.g., McQueeney v. Wilmington Trust Co., 779 F.2d 916 (3d Cir. 1985)). The California standard applied in the People v. Johnson appeal holds that a judgment should be reversed only if it is "reasonably probable" that the error affected the outcome.

The foregoing has assumed what might be thought of as "garden variety" — that is to say, nonconstitutional — error. Some erroneous evidentiary rulings are held to violate constitutional rights — for example, erroneous admission of hearsay might violate a criminal defendant's Sixth Amendment right to confront opposing witnesses. Where constitutional error occurs, the trial court judgment will be affirmed only if the error was "harmless beyond a reasonable doubt."

F.   REFLECTIONS ON NATURAL REASONING AND THE ADVERSARY SYSTEM

1.   The Adversary System Reconsidered

In the United States, the adversary system remains the dominant theory of litigation. The concept that disputes are for the most part private matters controlled by private individuals before relatively passive judges does not seem under serious reconsideration on a broad scale. Perhaps it should be, however, for at least two reasons. The first is that the adversary system is based on the assumption that each party will be effectively represented, which means among other things that the parties will have the resources necessary to fund the litigation. This assumption is often false and can lead to poor presentation of one side or the other (or both) of a dispute. Such wealth disparity can in turn lead to the dramatic effect of litigants with resources being systematically and on occasion decisively favored over their impecunious adversaries.

The second reason for reconsidering our commitment to the adversarial system is the possibility that the nature of cases being litigated is changing from the bipolar assumptions of the traditional model, which involves two private litigants disputing an essentially private matter, to a "public law model" that looks much different. Consider the following:

> The characteristic features of the public law model are very different from those of the traditional model. The party structure is sprawling and amorphous, subject to change over the course of the litigation. The traditional adversary relationship is suffused and intermixed with negotiating and mediating processes at every point. The judge is the dominant figure in organizing and guiding the case, and he draws for support not only on

the parties and their counsel, but on a wide range of outsiders — masters, experts, and oversight personnel. Most important, the trial judge has increasingly become the creator and manager of complex forms of ongoing relief, which have widespread effects on persons not before the court and require the judge's continuing involvement in administration and implementation. School desegregation, employment discrimination, and prisoners' or inmates' rights cases come readily to mind as avatars of this new form of litigation. But it would be mistaken to suppose that it is confined to these areas. Antitrust, securities fraud and other aspects of the conduct of corporate business, bankruptcy and reorganizations, union governance, consumer fraud, housing discrimination, electoral reapportionment, environmental management — cases in all these fields display in varying degrees the features of public law litigation. . . .

[As a consequence of this changing model of litigation] [t]he courts . . . continue to rely primarily on the litigants to produce and develop factual materials, but a number of factors make it impossible to leave the organization of the trial exclusively in their hands. With the diffusion of the party structure, fact issues are no longer sharply drawn in a confrontation between two adversaries, one asserting the affirmative and the other the negative. The litigation is often extraordinarily complex and extended in time, with a continuous and intricate interplay between factual and legal elements. It is hardly feasible and, absent a jury, unnecessary to set aside a contiguous block of time for a "trial stage" at which all significant factual issues will be presented. The scope of the fact investigation and the sheer volume of factual material that can be exhumed by the discovery process pose enormous problems of organization and assimilation. All these factors thrust the trial judge into an active role in shaping, organizing and facilitating the litigation. We may not yet have reached the investigative judge of the continental systems, but we have left the passive arbiter of the traditional model a long way behind.

Abram Chayes, The Role of the Judge in Public Law Litigation, 89 Harv. L. Rev. 1281, 1282-1283, 1284, 1297-1298, 1302 (1976).

These two matters, wealth disparity and the changing nature of litigation, cast some doubt on the foundations of the adversarial system of litigation, although they are by no means dispositive arguments against it. As you proceed with your studies, consider on the one hand whether full-blown adversarial litigation within the rules of evidence is too complex and burdensome for simple, straightforward cases involving at least one party with relatively scarce resources, and on the other hand whether the adversarial process and strict rules of evidence are too rigid and crude to deal with complex modern litigation. Think also of what possible alternatives there might be.

Yet another issue to consider emerges from the *Johnson* transcript. The rules of evidence are not rigidly adhered to at every turn in a trial; in many specific instances, they are either largely ignored or applied for the most part with a large dose of lenient discretion. On the other hand, at a few crucial places in the trial the rules of evidence seem to matter a great deal and lead to pointed arguments. In the *Johnson* trial, for example, this occurred where character evidence is disallowed in order to preclude inference of action in conformity therewith. See pages 8-9, supra. Why is that? Is that a healthy or a troubling sign? How typical do you think the transcript is in this respect?

As you will also see, each year more and more cases involve expert testimony of various kinds, which means that one or both of the litigants think that the case can be tried fairly only by employing specialized knowledge that is beyond the common knowledge and experience of the layperson. As your studies progress, ask how well the legal system takes advantage of the knowledge and expertise of other disciplines. For that matter, how well does it take advantage of the knowledge of the common citizen? That question leads to the next issue.

2. Why Have Rules of Evidence?

To resolve disputes about past events, we have to make judgments about what actually happened. This means finding facts, which in turn requires evidence of those facts. The law of evidence structures the process of proof at trial, but it does so with an interesting constraint. In many instances the individuals deciding the facts will be laypersons chosen at large from the community to serve on juries. They are amateurs at legal factfinding. Jurors are not, however, amateurs at factfinding in general. Every competent member of society from an early age begins to collect and perfect methods of factfinding that facilitate navigating the environment, and most of us do so with remarkable efficiency. In large measure, the law relies on these natural reasoning processes that its fact finders (juror or judge) possess. Indeed, the law could rely on them exclusively. It could permit the parties to present whatever evidence they like, the fact finders to make whatever investigation they like, and let the natural reasoning process of the fact finders lead them to whatever decision they believe to be appropriate. This would be a system of free proof rather than one constrained by a complex law of evidence.

Obviously, the legal system has not adopted a system of free proof, or else the previous sentence would have ended your course on evidence. It instead regulates the process of proof in various ways for various reasons. Some of these ways and their underlying reasons are perfectly understandable and uncontroversial. Others are more problematic. Consider the following justifications for regulating the proof process and reflect on how persuasive they are:

(1) *Efficiency*. Litigants pay only a small fraction of the cost of maintaining the judicial system. Judicial resources are provided free of charge to litigants, and they constitute a large subsidy to litigation. The litigants have virtually no incentive to preserve judicial resources; indeed they have every incentive to squander them in an effort to win their cases. A system of free proof allowing the litigants to do more or less what they liked would lead to a substantial wasting of judicial resources. Further, a rich litigant could simply wear down a more impecunious opponent through the endless presentation of trivia. For both reasons, trials are structured by judges to keep irrelevant, redundant, and unimportant issues out of the process in order to maximize the value of the resources available to decide disputes and in order to advance the likelihood that truth will determine outcomes. See FRE 403.

(2) *Policy*. Various policies extraneous to the system of litigation itself are affected by litigation. Consider two general examples. First, compelling witnesses to testify about certain kinds of communications they have had can have a destructive effect on human relationships, both professional and personal. Maintaining the privacy of these relationships are equally or more important than accurate adjudication, and thus litigation is structured to protect them through the provision of various privileges — such as attorney-client, psychotherapist-patient, or husband-wife — that exempt certain individuals from testifying in certain circumstances. See Article V of the Federal Rules of Evidence.

The second general example of extraneous policy considerations has to do with encouraging kinds of socially useful activity other those arising out of confidential communications. Suppose an accident occurs at a bridge, and the owner of the bridge does some repair to the bridge that reduces the probability of a similar accident occurring. The act of repair may indicate that the bridge was dangerous and thus be evidence of negligence on the owner's part. Admitting evidence of the act of repair at trial to prove negligence will create disincentives for future bridge owners to repair their bridges. In order to encourage the reduction of social risk, after-the-fact repairs are excluded at trial. See FRE 407. There are many similar examples. See FRE 408-410.

(3) *Accuracy.* Another argument for regulating the proof process is to help jurors avoid reaching erroneous results. One reason for the hearsay rule (Article 8 of the Federal Rules) is the belief that jurors cannot accurately appraise hearsay evidence. FRE 403 allows judges to keep "unfairly prejudicial" evidence from the jury, on the ground that admitting it risks leading jurors away from rationality. This argument, paradoxically, calls into question the very institution of jury decisionmaking. The argument is in essence that the proof process must be controlled in order to keep distracting, prejudicial, and difficult-to-appraise material away from the jury, because such material will lead the jurors to substitute emotion or caprice for rationality, thus increasing the risk of wrong results. Consider in the next section how the trial process both accommodates and attempts to modify how the law assumes jurors will reason and behave.

3.   Natural Reasoning and the Trial Process

As we previously indicated, the trial must look somewhat strange from the point of view of the jurors. Jurors typically sit passively through disjointed presentations of evidence, although there are now some experiments being done with allowing jurors to ask questions during the presentation of evidence that suggest jury questions may promote juror understanding of the facts and issues, and alleviate doubts about the trial evidence. Steven D. Penrod & Larry Heuer, Tweaking Commonsense: Assessing Aids to Jury Decision Making, 3 Psychol. Pub. Pol'y & L. 259 (1997); see also Franklin Strier, The Road to Reform: Judges on Juries and Attorneys, 30 Loy. L.A. L. Rev. 1249 (1997). Particularly because of the passivity of jurors, the judge's initial instructions to the jury and the parties' opening statements are crucial — they are the only sources of information that will create a context for the jury. Only after the close of the evidence does the judge typically give full instructions on the law, as occurred in *Johnson.* Often the instructions are not clear, although the ones in *Johnson* are for the most part fairly clear. Consider, though, the instruction on reasonable doubt, on page 83, supra:

> Reasonable doubt is defined as follows. It is not a mere possible doubt because everything relating to human affairs and depending on moral evidence is open to some possible or imaginary doubt. It is that state of the case, which after the entire comparison and consideration of all the evidence, leaves the mind of the jurors in that condition that they cannot say that they feel an abiding conviction or a moral certainty of the truth of the charge.

How helpful is that? Can it be made any clearer? This instruction is somewhat vague because the idea lying behind it is somewhat vague. In many cases, however, the instructions are vague because they are filled with incomprehensible legalese that simply leaves the jury baffled. The lack of helpfulness of many jury instructions, and the resultant lack of comprehension of them, is scandalous in a system dedicated to both lay decision-makers and rationality. Again, though, can you think of any reason why such a scandal continues to persist? Jury instructions are not just the means by which jurors are controlled by trial judges. They are also one of the important means by which appellate judges control trial judges. Jury instructions embody the substantive law that the trial judge applies to the trial, and appellate courts review jury instructions nondeferentially. Moreover, in contrast to evidentiary errors, instructional errors are almost never deemed "harmless" by appellate courts. What might be the implications of that point? In any event, you should ask yourself whether this ordering of events makes sense, and whether the jury should be better informed by the trial judge at an earlier time in the process.

Professor Phoebe Ellsworth has spent considerable time studying the deliberative process of jurors. Her work confirms prior work and anecdotal experience that, notwithstanding the difficulties, juries are quite good at factfinding. Her work also confirms earlier findings that jurors are less adept at dealing with the legal issues in cases. She recently summarized her findings in a way that vividly captures the difficulty of being a juror:

> There is no reason to believe that the jurors' misunderstanding of the law is a function of their mental capacities. It seems more plausible that the system is set up to promote misunderstanding. Factors blockading the serious jury trying to perform its task include: the convoluted, technical language; the dry and abstract presentation of the law following the vivid, concrete, and often lengthy presentation of evidence; the requirements that jurors interpret the evidence before they know what the verdict choices are; the fact that juries usually do not get copies of the instructions to take with them into the jury room; the lack of training in the law for jurors as part of their jury duty; the general failure to discover and correct jurors' preconceptions about the law; the failure to inform jurors that they are allowed to ask for help with the instructions; and the fact that those who do ask for help are often disappointed by a simple repetition of the incomprehensible paragraph. [Phoebe Ellsworth, Are 12 Heads Better Than 1?, 38 Law Quadrangle Notes 56, 64 (1995).]

The jurors' task involves finding facts and applying the law to those facts. We say we want the hallmark of trials to be rational deliberation, which includes accurate factfinding and an adequate understanding of the law, yet the structure of trials is somewhat, perhaps significantly, at odds with effective learning on the part of jurors. Why might that be so? How would power shift at trials if they were structured otherwise? Is much of what you have seen designed to keep control of a trial in the hands of the lawyers? The trial judge? Is that sensible?

We have so far concentrated on the manner in which jurors learn about the litigated events. After the presentation of evidence and closing argument of counsel, juries retire to deliberate and reach a verdict. The law's reach extends to this aspect of the process as well. Because certainty is never possible to achieve at trial, jurors are instructed as to the proper decision rule to apply in the face of the inevitable uncertainty with which they will have to grapple. This comes in the form of an instruction on burdens of persuasion. In civil cases, the normal burden of persuasion is proof by a preponderance of the evidence; in criminal cases it is proof beyond reasonable doubt. Jurors are told that the relevant burden of persuasion is to be applied to "every element" of the cause of action. These matters are discussed in detail in Chapter Eleven.

Coupling the burden of persuasion to "every element" seems unproblematic on its face, but there is a problem lurking in the shadows. This coupling recommends an unnatural decision-making process to jurors. If followed literally, jurors would be obligated to analyze the various combinations and permutations of elements, applying the appropriate burden of persuasion as they go. There are two difficulties. First, this procedure would quickly get impossibly complicated; second, people do not typically reason about conventional, everyday affairs in this fashion. The chart below shows how complicated and unconventional the recommended decision-making process is. Compiled by Professors Nancy Pennington and Reed Hastie, the chart displays the jury instructions for a relatively simple homicide case involving a defense of self-defense.

JUROR DECISIONMAKING
Decision Alternatives and Attributes: Murder Case

Decision alternative	Attribute				Decision rule
	1. Identity	2. Mental state	3. Circumstances	4. Actions	
Not guilty	Not the right person	NA	NA	No Killing	1 or 4
Self-defense (not guilty)	Right person	(a) Fear of life (b) Fear of great bodily harm	Under immediate attack	(a) Killing (b) Exhaust escape (c) In defense (d) Reasonable retaliation	1 and (2a or 2b) and 3 and 4a and (4b and 4c and 4d)
Manslaughter	Right person	(a) Heat of sudden passion (b) Diminished capacity	(a) Great provocation (b) Threat to life not immediate	(a) Did not exhaust escape (b) Became the attacker (c) Used excessive force	1 and (2a or 2b) and (3a and 3b) and (4a and 4b and 4c)
Second degree murder	Right person	Intent to inflict injury likely to result in death	Insufficient provocation	(a), (b), (c) Like manslaughter (d) Use deadly weapon (e) Deliberate, cruel act	1 and (2 or [3 and 4d] and 4e) and (4a or 4b or 4c)
First degree murder	Right person	(a) Intent to kill (b) Purpose formed (motive)	(a) Insufficient provocation (b) Interval between plan and killing	(a), (b), (c) Like manslaughter (d) Formed plan to kill (e) Killed in accordance with plan	1 and (2a and 2b) and (3a and 3b) and (4a or 4b or 4c) and 4d and 4e

Note: NA=not applicable
Source: Nancy Pennington & Reed Hastie, Juror Decision-Making Models: The Generalization Gap, 89 Psychol. Bull. 246, 251 (1981).

Had you come across something like this chart in a book on chemical analysis or medical diagnosis, it perhaps would not have appeared strange; but as a protocol for juror decisionmaking, it appears completely out of place. The chart, and the instructions it implements, implies that the focus at trial is on the discrete issues identified as "elements"; but as we have already commented, the jurors are not fully informed of those elements until just prior to retiring to deliberate. In the *Johnson* case, for example, battery was not defined until the court's closing instructions. The focus at trial is thus not on whether some formal element is true or false; it is on competing versions of reality — in the *Johnson* case, who started the fight and why? Even the lawyers in *Johnson* more or less ignore the elements in their closing arguments, focusing again on the two competing versions of reality. To be sure, the competing versions of reality involve differing elements. And once the jury has settled on "what happened," it must consult the judge's instructions to determine who wins, which is precisely the finding that emerges from the empirical work of Nancy Pennington and Reed Hastie.

That the process of deliberation involves mediating among the conflicting versions of what happened rather than a minute parsing of the individual elements of the causes of action is supported by another consideration. Any decision-making methodology to which a chart like the one above could be applied would have to involve issues with relatively clear answers. Chemical analysis provides a good example. Litmus paper turns blue or red when immersed in an acid or an alkaline solution; a solvent does or does not dissolve a substance. Trials rarely involve questions that can be answered so unequivocally. At the end of the day, the jury in the *Johnson* case will have to decide who started the fight and why, but in doing so the jurors will have to sift through a lot of ambiguous and conflicting testimony.

That the intellectual task at trial involves organizing the proffered evidence in light of competing versions of the plausible is unavoidable, given the structure of trials. Cases possess ambiguity because of the need to organize large amounts of data (evidentiary complexity), to resolve conflicting and inconsistent testimony (evidentiary tension), and to fill in intermediate premises unsupported by evidence presented at trial (evidentiary gap). The presentation of information at trial quite obviously must be incomplete in the typical case (neither Officer Huston nor Officer Van Berg could say how they received their injuries) and often inconsistent information will be presented (eyewitness testimony about Officer Walker's conduct differed considerably). Witnesses testify only to what they have observed, and rarely will one witness observe everything relevant to any particular litigated issue.

Even in a case with a single witness, what is observed must be richer than what is related, if for no other reason than that memory decays with time. In addition, rhetorical skills invariably are less developed than observational skills. Consider a simple example — a case involving assault where part of the proof is testimony that the defendant made "threatening" gestures toward the plaintiff. Testimony characterizing seemingly simple gestures is often a summary of richly textured human acts that may be observed with ease but related only with difficulty, which is precisely why lay opinions such as this are often allowed. To understand such testimony, the juror must reconstruct this richly textured event. And of course in doing so, the juror may have to account for testimony to the effect that the gesture was not made in a threatening way. As case complexity increases, it is implausible that a juror merely continues to add data to the data banks rather than organizing and simplifying the data, which after all is how individuals apparently cope with the complexity of everyday life. One remembers a trip to the store yesterday rather than walking to the garage, opening the door, entering the garage, opening the car door, searching for the proper key, identifying the ignition, and so on.

There is another interesting aspect of jury decisionmaking that is highlighted by the chart. The chart suggests an orderly, deductive approach to decisionmaking: Lay out the assumptions and deduce the correct results. At some point, jurors will indeed "deduce" their verdict in such a fashion, but probably only after all the hard work is done. The hard work involves figuring out what happened. In that effort, deduction, the law's prize tool in virtually all other areas, takes a back seat to induction. Consider again the closing arguments in the *Johnson* case. Neither side attempted to lay out a formal proof of guilt or innocence; instead, they used the testimony to stitch together a story that, they hoped, would seem plausible to the jurors, given their (the jurors') general knowledge and experience.

4.   The Behavior of Fact Finders

The advocates at trial attempt to persuade the fact finder by advancing plausible accounts of what happened, but what seems "plausible" to a person is determined by the sum of that person's knowledge and experience rather than by the outcome of formal logical manipulations. That this is so is evident from your own experience. Reflect for a moment on how you appraise the things that you see. You look for patterns in them, searching for common threads, especially ones that tie what you are observing to what you have previously observed, although always holding yourself open to the twin possibilities that something is unique in the event under observation or that you made a mistake previously in what you came to believe. You engage in various kinds of analogical reasoning, some involving cause and effect, some filling in unobserved aspects of what you are observing by reference to what you have come to believe is commonly associated with what you presently are viewing; you rely on generalizations formed out of prior experience, and so on. These are the tools that humans use to understand, navigate, and manipulate their environment, and not surprisingly they are the tools that jurors use to resolve the disputes of historical fact before them. At the end of the day, when a consensus has emerged out of bringing the combined experience of the jurors to bear on the evidence presented at trial, the jurors look to the verdict options to determine who wins and loses. And probably on occasion when they do so and see the implications of their positions, they reconsider. To this extent there is a relationship between the largely (but not exclusively) inductive processes that drive evidence comprehension and deliberation and the virtually exclusively deductive process that drives verdict selection.

The instructions on elements, in short, merely provide the verdict options. By contrast, few instructions are given on how to reason or deliberate, because jurors, as competent members of their community, are assumed to know how to do both, an assumption that is surely correct. Judges do typically give one instruction about jury reasoning, the one given in the *Johnson* case — "use your common sense." If more elaborate instructions are necessary, the argument becomes one for deciding cases in some other way.

One last point. At the beginning of the *Johnson* transcript, the judge instructed the jury on what "evidence" is. Think about the nature of "evidence": What exactly, is it? Before reading these pages, you most likely would have thought it a dumb question — "evidence," obviously, is the testimony and exhibits at trial. Is that now so obvious? The testimony and exhibits at trial are meaningless until interpreted by a human observer — judge or juror. Moreover, the interpretation given to any piece of evidence cannot be determined in advance, for it is a function of the background and experience of the fact finder. If "evidence" is what is presented at trial, how can it be that one fact finder thinks the "evidence" proves guilt and another innocence? Does everyone in this class agree that defendant Johnson was guilty of a battery, or do some believe he should have been acquitted? The point we want you to think about, though, is the dynamic nature of trials and "evidence." There is a relational aspect to "evidence"; it (the evidence) is what some human being thinks it is, and what that person thinks it is cannot be determined in advance by a set of rules. If it could, factfinding perhaps could make the transformation from being largely inductive to largely deductive; but if it could, jurors (and judges) would become superfluous. Another way of looking at this is that historical factfinding requires judgment in addition to logic — not in contrast to logic, but in addition to it.

The necessary reliance on judgment is one of the distinguishing features of peculiarly human institutions, which the law of evidence surely is for all of its pretense to analytical rigor. These are matters we would encourage you to reflect on as you proceed throughout the course. Nor are they just matters of academic interest. You are about to turn the page to begin your study of the concept of relevancy. Right at the heart of that concept lie many of the issues we have been addressing here.

TRIAL OBJECTION CHEAT SHEET

Note: this list of objections is not intended to be exhaustive. A comma separating objections suggests interchangeable phrasing; a semicolon suggests different but closely related objections.

OBJECTIONS TO THE FORM OF THE QUESTION:

Argumentative	Question contends that the witness must agree with a disputable inference, is framed as if it were closing argument to the jury, or seeks to pick a fight with the witness or embarrass the witness. This objection is often made (and sustained) inappropriately to questions that are proper, vigorous cross-examination, as in "Objection, your honor, tough question!"
Asked and answered	Question has previously been asked of the same witness by the same examiner. (Does not apply to question asked by the opposing counsel.) Technically, there is nothing wrong with repeating questions, but judges may sustain this objection if they feel testimony is cumulative, or the examination is too lengthy or out of control.
Assumes facts not in evidence	Question is phrased so that to answer it, the witness would have to adopt, by implication, an asserted fact that is in dispute but that has not been proved.
Calls for narrative	Question asks the witness to describe events very broadly or generally. Technically, there is nothing wrong with a "narrative" answer, and many questions can only be phrased in open-ended fashion to avoid leading; rather the danger is that the question will permit the witness to ramble and possibly interject inadmissible evidence. The objection might also be phrased as "too general."
Compound	Question asks the witness to testify about more than one separate fact.
Leading	Question suggests the desired answer to the witness; improper during direct examination of friendly or neutral witnesses, but okay on cross-examination or direct examination of adverse or hostile witnesses.
Misstates the evidence; mischaracterizes the testimony	Premise of the question distorts the evidence that has been presented, or misquotes the witness's testimony.
Unintelligible; vague; ambiguous; confusing	Question is not sufficiently clear to be answered. "Unintelligible" means garbled; "vague" means not sufficiently specific; "ambiguous" means susceptible of two or more different interpretations.

OBJECTIONS TO INADMISSIBILITY OF THE ANSWER (OR PROFFERED EXHIBIT):

Hearsay	Answer to question would call for (or evidentiary item contains) a statement other than one made by the witness while testifying at trial, offered to prove the truth of the matter asserted.
Irrelevant	Answer has no probative value relating to any fact of consequence to the case.
Lack of foundation	Insufficient factual basis has been established to show that the witness has requisite knowledge (personal sensory perception or experience, expert opinion, lay opinion, knowledge of character) to give admissible testimony; or to show that exhibit is what its proponent claims.
Lack of authenticity	Insufficient factual basis to show that exhibit is what its proponent claims.
Calls for speculation, speculative	Answer to question calls for the witness to speculate or guess about matters beyond witness's factual knowledge; this is a form of "foundation" objection.
Calls for opinion; calls for conclusion	Answer would violate the rule limiting lay (nonexpert) opinion to those opinions and inferences that are based on the witness's perception of an event and are helpful to the jury in understanding the facts.
Inadmissible character evidence	Violates FRE 404.
More prejudicial/ misleading/etc. than probative, Rule 403	Probative value substantially outweighed by one or more of the Rule 403 dangers.
Cumulative	Answer would repeat earlier testimony. This is not technically improper, but comes within judge's discretion under Rule 403. This objection is often stated as "Asked and answered."
Nonresponsive	Witness has given an "evasive" answer that does not fairly meet the substance of the question.
Beyond the scope of the question	Answer has exceeded the scope of the question (i.e., the witness has "volunteered" information that was not asked for); this assumes the answer has been given, and is therefore a basis for a motion to strike.
Beyond the scope of direct/cross-/redirect/ etc. examination	Question seeks testimony that is not responsive to immediately preceding examination. Testimony is supposed to respond to matters raised in the immediately preceding examination (i.e., cross responds to direct, redirect responds to cross, re-cross responds to redirect, etc.).
Not the best evidence	Answer would violate the best evidence rule, which requires use of original writing, recording, or photograph to prove its contents.

CHAPTER THREE

RELEVANCY, PROBATIVE VALUE, AND THE RULE 403 DANGERS

A. RELEVANCY — THE BASIC CONCEPT

Relevancy is the foundational principle for all modern systems of evidence law. Only *relevant* evidence helps the jury achieve rational outcomes, meaning outcomes based on the jurors' use of their reasoning capacity. The basic tenets of this principle were spelled out almost a century ago by James Bradley Thayer, upon whose creative shoulders Wigmore erected his Treatise on Evidence in Trials at Common Law:

> Observe . . . one or two fundamental conceptions. There is a principle — not so much a rule of evidence as a presupposition involved in the very conception of a rational system of evidence, as contrasted with the old formal and mechanical systems[1] — which forbids receiving anything irrelevant, not logically probative. How are we to know what these forbidden things are? Not by any rule of law. The law furnishes no test of relevancy. For this, it tacitly refers to logic and general experience — assuming that the principles of reasoning are known to its judges and ministers, just as a vast multitude of other things are assumed as already sufficiently known to them.
>
> There is another precept which should be laid down as preliminary, in stating the law of evidence; namely, that unless excluded by some rule or principle or law, all that is logically probative is admissible. This general admissibility, however, of what is logically probative is not, like the former principle, a necessary presupposition in a rational system of evidence; there are many exceptions to it. Yet, in order to [have] a clear conception of the law, it is important to notice this also as being a fundamental proposition. In an historical sense it has not been the fundamental thing, to which different exclusions

---

1. Continental legal systems had a formal system of required proof. For example, a conviction for a serious crime could only be had upon the presentation of two eyewitnesses or a confession. Circumstantial evidence would not do. But strong circumstantial evidence constituted a "half-proof" that legitimated the use of torture in order to extract a confession, and so on. For discussions, see John Langbein, *Torture and the Law of Proof: Europe and England in the Ancien Régime* (1977); L. Jonathan Cohen, Freedom of Proof, in *Facts in Law* (William L. Twining, ed., 1983); Mirjan Damaska, *The Death of Legal Torture*, 87 Yale L.J. 860 (1978). — EDS.

were exceptions. What has taken place, in fact, is the shutting out by the judges of one and another thing from time to time; and so, gradually, the recognition of this exclusion under a rule. These rules of exclusion have had their exceptions; and so the law has come into the shape of a set of primary rules of exclusion; and then a set of exceptions to these rules. . . .

In stating thus our two large, fundamental conceptions, we must not fall into the error of supposing that relevancy, logical connection, real or supposed, is the only test of admissibility; for so we should drop out of sight the chief part of the law of evidence. When we have said (1) that, without any exception, nothing which is not, or is not supposed to be, logically relevant is admissible; and (2) that, subject to many exceptions and qualifications, whatever is logically relevant is admissible; it is obvious that, in reality, there are tests of admissibility other than logical relevancy. Some things are rejected as being of too slight a significance, or as having too conjectural and remote a connection; others, as being dangerous, in their effect on the jury, and likely to be misused or overestimated by that body; others, as being impolitic, or unsafe on public grounds; others, on the bare ground of precedent. It is this sort of thing, as I said before — the rejection on one or another practical ground, of what is really probative — which is the characteristic thing in the law of evidence; stamping it as the child of the jury system. [James Bradley Thayer, A Preliminary Treatise on Evidence at the Common Law 264-266 (1898).]

1.   FRE 401 and 402

RULE 401. DEFINITION OF "RELEVANT EVIDENCE"

"Relevant evidence" means evidence having any tendency to make the existence of any fact that is of consequence to the determination of the action more probable or less probable than it would be without the evidence.

RULE 402. RELEVANT EVIDENCE GENERALLY ADMISSIBLE; IRRELEVANT EVIDENCE INADMISSIBLE

All relevant evidence is admissible, except as otherwise provided by the Constitution of the United States, by Act of Congress, by these rules, or by other rules prescribed by the Supreme Court pursuant to statutory authority. Evidence which is not relevant is not admissible.

2.   Interpretation and Illustration of FRE 401 and 402

Under FRE 401 and 402, judges will exclude all evidence that is *not relevant*. These rules might also appear to provide a system of free proof that requires the admission of all evidence that is relevant. In large measure this is so. However, as Thayer noted, some evidence was subject to rejection at common law for reasons that are currently spelled out in FRE 403, as discussed in Section B, infra. There are other specific rules of evidence (some of which were introduced in Chapter One, such as the opinion and hearsay rules) that provide for the exclusion of evidence on other grounds. The concept of relevancy begins the process of admitting evidence, but it does not end it.

In deciding whether an item of evidence is relevant under FRE 401, the judge must consider two issues: (1) Is the item offered to prove a fact that is "of consequence" to the case? (2) Does the evidence actually tend to prove (or disprove) that fact by making it more (or less) probable? The common law perceived these two issues as two separate concepts — *materiality* (meaning the connection to a fact of consequence in the case) and *relevancy* (meaning that the connection was logically probative). While the term *materiality* is not used in the Federal Rules (the Advisory Committee Note to FRE 401 rejects the term as "loosely used and ambiguous"), it is still common parlance among judges and trial lawyers and you should be familiar with it.

a. Relevant Evidence Is Offered to Prove a Fact of Consequence (Materiality)

In general, a proposition of fact is "of consequence" (i.e., material) in a legal dispute if it matters to the legal resolution of that dispute; that is, if it can be connected through inferential reasoning to one of the essential legal elements of the substantive law that governs the case. This relationship can be illustrated with a simple diagram:

Diagram 3-1

EF ————————→ FOC ————————→ EE

The arrow drawn from the EF (the evidentiary fact offered into evidence) to the FOC (the fact of consequence the EF is offered to prove) represents an inference that the jury can make. The EF is evidence presented to the jury in the courtroom; the FOC is a proposition of fact that is not presented but that the jury can decide to believe, on the basis of drawing an inference; the FOC connects to the EE (essential element) again through an inference.

Consider this example:

Diagram 3-2

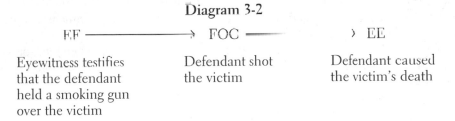

EF ————————→ FOC ——— 〉 EE

Eyewitness testifies   Defendant shot   Defendant caused
that the defendant   the victim   the victim's death
held a smoking gun
over the victim

If an eyewitness testifies that she saw the defendant holding a smoking gun over the victim, this is an evidentiary fact offered into evidence. From this testimony, the jury may make the inference that defendant did in fact shoot the victim. This is a fact of consequence, because from it the jury may infer the identity of the person who caused the victim's death, which is an essential element in the law of homicide.

The substantive law determines the essential elements in every case. In the *Johnson* case, for example, the essential elements of the crime with which Johnson was charged were (1) the unlawful use of force or violence (2) by a person incarcerated in state prison (3) against a person not incarcerated. The prosecution presented testimony from several eyewitnesses that Johnson was kicking and struggling with the correctional officers both inside and outside his cell. This testimony was relevant to prove that

Johnson used force and violence, as required by the first essential element listed above. Now consider the defense attorney's question to inmate Butler concerning the frequency with which prisoners at Pelican Bay are allowed to receive packages from home (page 42, line 16, supra). Does this information tend to prove a fact of consequence in the *Johnson* case? Can you identify any connection between it and one of the essential elements? If you cannot, then the information may be irrelevant — "immaterial," in common law parlance — and would be excluded under FRE 401 and 402.

The relevance of some evidentiary facts requires that several inferences be made prior to reaching a readily identifiable fact of consequence to the litigation. For example, the prosecution offered testimony that Officer Huston suffered a gash on his left shin (page 14, line 37, supra). The following diagram shows how this testimony can be used to prove that Johnson used force and violence against Huston, as required by the first and third essential elements in the Johnson case:

Diagram 3-3

EF ——————→ IF ——————→ FOC ——————→ EE

| Huston testifies that he had a gash on his shin after the struggle | Huston did have a gash on his shin after the struggle | Johnson's struggling caused the gash | Johnson used force and violence against Huston |

The first inference to the IF (inferred fact) is that Huston's testimony is true — he did have the gash *after* the struggle with Johnson. From this inferred fact, the fact of consequence can be identified.

Sometimes even longer chains of reasoning are required. For example, inmate Butler testified that the correctional officers were wearing their gloves when they approached Johnson's cell (page 42, line 39, supra). This evidentiary fact connects to the defense theory that the guards started the fight with Johnson. Wearing gloves generates the inference that a guard is prepared to have contact with an inmate, not just to collect a food tray; and if a guard is prepared to have contact, he intends to fight; and if he intends to fight, then he starts the fight; and if the guards start the fight, then Johnson's use of force and violence may be self-defense and not unlawful. This chain of inferences is shown in Diagram 3-4.

Diagram 3-4

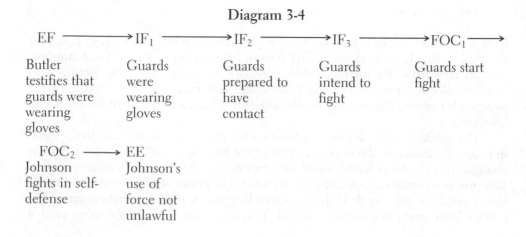

EF ——————→ IF$_1$ ——————→ IF$_2$ ——————→ IF$_3$ ——————→ FOC$_1$——→

| Butler testifies that guards were wearing gloves | Guards were wearing gloves | Guards prepared to have contact | Guards intend to fight | Guards start fight |

FOC$_2$ ——→ EE

| Johnson fights in self-defense | Johnson's use of force not unlawful |

Each arrow represents an inference in the chain starting from the evidentiary fact, leading to a series of inferred facts, which connect to what can easily be identified as facts of consequence, which then connect to an essential element in the case. Whether the chain of reasoning is long or short, what is important to remember is that the facts of consequence in a case cannot be determined without knowing the substantive law that governs the dispute. Black v. M & W Gear Co., 269 F.3d 1220, 1236 (10th Cir. 2001) (plaintiff's husband killed in a rollover of his tractor lawnmower manufactured by defendant; husband's alcohol consumption irrelevant because contributory negligence is not a defense in a product liability case).

b. Relevant Evidence Must Make a Fact of Consequence More or Less Probable

Once the proponent identifies the fact of consequence, the proponent must also be prepared to say why the evidence offered actually tends to prove (or disprove) this fact. Stated in the terms of FRE 401, the evidence offered must make the fact of consequence *more or less probable.*

i. Probability Is Determined from Knowledge and Experience. As the excerpt from Thayer points out, there are virtually no legal rules governing this test of relevancy. Thayer refers to a test of "logic and general experience." This is because the jury uses its generalized knowledge and experience as well as the various intellectual tools discussed on pages 113-115 of Chapter Two to draw inferences such as those diagramed above. The jurors have already developed their generalized knowledge, as described on page 114, and by Professors David A. Binder and Paul Bergman:

> All of us . . . have accumulated vast storehouses of commonly-held notions about how people and objects generally behave in our society. From this storehouse one formulates a generalization about typical behavior. The generalization, in turn, becomes the premise which enables me to link specific evidence with an element one hopes to prove. [David A. Binder & Paul Bergman, Fact Investigation 85 (1984).]

The Advisory Committee Note to FRE 402 calls these generalizations "principles evolved by experience or science, applied logically to the situation at hand." To test whether an evidentiary fact is logically probative of a fact of consequence, the judge examines the generalizations underlying each inference in the proponent's proposed chain of reasoning. For example, the inferential leap from "the guards wore gloves" to "the guards were prepared to fight" requires a generalization about the behavior of prison guards. Such a generalization might be articulated as follows: "Guards probably don't wear gloves to pick up food trays, but they would be likely to wear gloves when they prepare to come into contact with inmates." What do you think of this generalization? Does it support the necessary inference? Does it make the inferred fact more probable? Because such generalizations are only rough estimates of human behavior (and other kinds of occurrences), they cannot "prove" that an inference is true. Nevertheless, they do operate as part of a type of syllogistic reasoning: from major premise (the generalization) and minor premise (the evidentiary fact) to the conclusion (the inference to be drawn). This form of reasoning, based on generalizations from knowledge and experience, can also be diagrammed:

Diagram 3-5

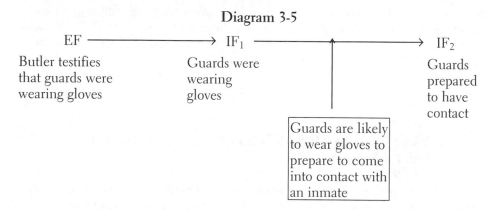

EF $\longrightarrow$ IF$_1$ $\longrightarrow$ IF$_2$

Butler testifies that guards were wearing gloves

Guards were wearing gloves

Guards prepared to have contact

Guards are likely to wear gloves to prepare to come into contact with an inmate

ii.   Relevancy Requires Reasonable Generalizations.   Judges will admit evidence as making a fact of consequence more or less probable when they think there are *reasonable* generalizations based on common knowledge and experience that will support each inference in the chain of reasoning. Phrased another way, the test of relevancy is "whether a reasonable person might believe the probability of the truth of the consequential fact to be different if that person knew of the proffered evidence." 2 Jack B. Weinstein & Margaret A. Berger, Weinstein's Federal Evidence §401.04[2](b) (Joseph M. McLaughlin, ed., Matthew Bender 2d ed. 2001). The judge thus estimates the probabilities of such generalizations in a subjective way, from the perspective of the reasonable juror.

What if the trial judge has doubt about whether a generalization is reasonable? In such a case, the judge can require the proponent of the evidentiary fact to produce evidentiary support for the generalization itself. In the *Johnson* case, for example, the judge might ask: "How would the jury know that guards wear gloves to prepare for contact with inmates?" The judge could require the defense to produce testimony about glove-wearing practices in Facility B at Pelican Bay. This would turn the underlying generalization into an evidentiary fact in the chain of reasoning:

Diagram 3-6

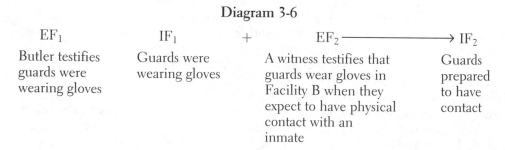

EF$_1$ IF$_1$ +   EF$_2$ $\longrightarrow$ IF$_2$

Butler testifies guards were wearing gloves

Guards were wearing gloves

A witness testifies that guards wear gloves in Facility B when they expect to have physical contact with an inmate

Guards prepared to have contact

A proponent will have to present proof of an underlying generalization if the judge requires it, or may do so simply to persuade the jury that the generalization has particularly strong probative force.

Judges do not require objective proof of most generalizations that sound reasonable, due to the lack of empirical knowledge about most of human behavior. Nevertheless, there are at least two obvious limits implicit in the "reasonable juror" test: The necessary generalizations cannot be known to the judge to be false ("people can see through brick walls")[2] and they cannot be speculation ("people with red hair seem to be more aggressive than people with black hair").[3] A relevance theory based on such generalizations should be rejected. Some generalizations express invidious stereotypes based on factors such as gender, race, ethnicity, religion, age, and sexual preference. Once articulated, many such generalizations probably fall within the "false" or "guesswork" categories of unacceptability, or lack any connection to the individual case. Jinro America Inc. v. Secure Investments, Inc., 2001 U.S.App.LEXIS 25987 *37 (9th Cir. 2001) (majority held syllogism "(a) Korean businesses generally are corrupt; (b) Jinro is a Korean business; (c) therefore, Jinro is corrupt" to be impermissible under FRE 403; concurrence held that generalizations about Korean businesses were irrelevant to prove Jinro's conduct). Of course, stereotypes and biases may also surface during confidential jury deliberations if the background facts necessary to trigger them are available. Some of these problematic stereotypes have been identified and addressed in the Federal Rules. For example, FRE 610 prohibits evidence of religious beliefs or opinions on the question of credibility, and FRE 412 limits the use of evidence of a victim's sexual behavior or predisposition in cases involving allegations of sexual misconduct. It is also assumed that a diverse jury will express a range of views during deliberation and will correct for such stereotypes.

iii. FRE 401's Minimal Standard of "Any Tendency."   FRE 401 defines relevant evidence as having *"any tendency* to make the existence of any fact . . . of consequence . . . more or less probable." (emphasis added). This is a minimal test of a logically probable inference from the offered item to a fact of consequence. The judge compares how probable the fact of consequence is with and without the offered evidentiary fact. For example, in determining the relevance of inmate Butler's testimony in the *Johnson* case that the guards wore gloves, it need only be the case that "guards who wear gloves are somewhat more likely to have anticipated contact with inmates than if they were not wearing gloves." The judge will find the offered fact relevant if it makes a fact of consequence somewhat more or less likely than it would be were the evidence not known. Professor Vaughn Ball analyzes the results of this comparison in the following way:

> If and only if the probability . . . is the same with and without the evidence, the evidence is irrelevant. . . . If these probabilities are different, the evidence is relevant. It seems to be recognized on all sides that the *size* of the change is of no importance in determining relevancy. The exclusion of evidence which makes a change, but a change too small to justify the time consumed in receiving the evidence, is dealt with by Rule 403. . . . [T]here are no degrees of relevancy. It seems everywhere conceded that the term *relevant* refers to

---

2.   Conversations in the cockpit of an airliner just before crashing were not relevant to the mental state and psychic damages of the passengers because the passengers could not hear the conversations. Pregeant v. Pan Am. World Airways, Inc., 762 F.2d 1245, 1249 (5th Cir. 1985) (error harmless). – EDS.

3.   Testimony by an expert that it was "possible" but "not probable" that the defendant's Nike sneaker was the source of an inculpatory footprint was excluded as "lacking probative value" under Rule 401. United States v. Ferreira, 821 F.2d 1, 5 (1st Cir. 1987). Whether this ruling was rightly decided under FRE 401 would depend on the nature of the generalization that the expert relied on to find a "possibility." – EDS.

the distinction between some probative force and no probative force...between some change in probability and no change. [Vaughn C. Ball, The Myth of Conditional Relevancy, 14 Ga. L. Rev. 435, 446 (1980).]

What if the judge rejects a proponent's generalization, based on the judge's own idiosyncratic view of the world? For example, a judge might think: "How can I be certain that guards wear gloves in anticipation of contact with inmates? I think that guards wear gloves to keep their hands clean." Excluding evidence that the guards wore gloves, based on the judge's personal views and beliefs of how the world works, or of how people behave, would distort the flow of information to the jury.

This raises the question of how certain the trial judge has to be that the evidentiary fact has the minimal relevant connection to the case. FRE 401 does not contain a specific standard of proof, unlike FRE 104, which you will read about later. The absence of a specifically higher standard, plus the policies underlying the minimal test of relevancy established in FRE 401, persuade us that the judge should find evidence to be relevant if the judge believes there is any probability that the relevant connection exists. Thus, even if there are alternative explanations of the glove-wearing practices of guards at Pelican Bay, if the proponent's underlying generalizations are reasonable, the evidence is relevant.

By so strongly favoring admissibility, FRE 401 reduces idiosyncratic exclusions of evidence. As stated in the Weinstein and Berger treatise, implicit in the Federal Rules is the concept that the relevance of evidence is determined by whether the evidence *could influence a reasonable juror or reasonable jury*, rather than whether the evidence does or would influence the trial judge. The minimal test of relevancy serves one of the most important goals of the Federal Rules of Evidence: to promote rational decision-making by promoting the jury's access to relevant evidence. For a synopsis of the philosophical, academic, and legal debates underlying "the strong federal policy favoring admissibility of, and reliance on, all helpful information...," you should read District Judge Jack B. Weinstein's opinion in United States v. Shonubi, 895 F. Supp. 460, 492 (E.D.N.Y. 1995), 103 F.3d 1085 (2d Cir. 1997) (sentence vacated).

c.   Direct Versus Circumstantial Evidence

The common law distinguished between two types of relevant evidence: direct and circumstantial. Direct evidence typically is defined as evidence that, if believed, establishes an essential element. For example, if the correctional officers had testified in the *Johnson* case that Johnson kicked Officers Huston and Van Berg, this testimony, if believed, would have been direct evidence that Johnson committed a battery against them. And the testimony of an eyewitness identifying a bank robber, if believed, would be direct evidence of the element of identity. In both examples, the fact of consequence is itself identical, or essentially identical, to the essential element, the difference being the legal terminology in which the essential element is phrased. Because no inferences other than those pertaining to the credibility of the eyewitness mediate between the evidentiary fact, the fact of consequence, and the essential element, this type of evidence is known as *direct* evidence.

In most cases, however, the connection between an evidentiary fact and an essential element is not so immediate and may require many intervening inferences. This type of evidence is known as *circumstantial.* Suppose a witness testifies that immediately after a bank was robbed, he saw the defendant (charged with the bank robbery) running a block away from the bank. This would be viewed as circumstantial evidence of the defendant's guilt on the ground that the testimony does not directly establish the essential element of identity. Additional inferences are necessary to explain the defendant's conduct in such a way as to connect the defendant to the robbery — he was attempting to flee to avoid being caught after the crime. And because there are numerous other explanations for the defendant's running, an inference of identity does not automatically follow.

Analytically, there is no difference between direct and circumstantial evidence because both require the jury to use inferential reasoning. Direct evidence establishes an essential element only if the jury believes the eyewitness, and this requires inferential reasoning about the eyewitness's ability to observe the event correctly, to remember it, and to describe it accurately. These standard issues of credibility must be resolved by the fact finder in order to evaluate any testimonial evidence, and they are the kinds of issues about which people use natural reasoning constantly in their everyday life. Generally speaking, then, what distinguishes circumstantial from direct evidence is the length of the inferential chain.

It is important to note that the labels "direct" and "circumstantial" do not reflect the evidence's probative force. Circumstantial evidence can often be more reliable than direct evidence. A fingerprint or blood spot found on a murder weapon, identified as the defendant's by fingerprint analysis or DNA testing, are examples of circumstantial evidence that can be very accurate, and are probably more reliable than many eyewitnesses, as will be discussed in Chapter Nine.

We would venture to say that *all* litigated cases rely on at least some circumstantial evidence, and many essential elements (intent, for example) are typically proved only in this way. Nevertheless, some jurisdictions still distinguish between circumstantial and direct evidence in instructing the jury as was done in the *Johnson* case — that each fact in a chain of circumstantial evidence necessary to proof of guilt must be proved beyond a reasonable doubt (page 62, supra). This instruction cannot possibly be applied to every intermediate inferred fact in a chain of reasoning, and giving it is very confusing to the jury. The ultimate inference of guilt in a criminal case will typically depend on a number of intermediate inferred facts, each proved by a number of individual items of evidence. Only rarely will any one such fact, of itself, be *necessary* to proof of guilt. As stated by the High Court of Australia:

> [I]t may sometimes be necessary or desirable to identify those intermediate facts which constitute indispensable links in a chain of reasoning towards an inference of guilt. Not every possible intermediate conclusion of fact will be of that character. If it is appropriate to identify an intermediate fact as indispensable it may well be appropriate to tell the jury that that fact must be found beyond reasonable doubt before the ultimate inference can be drawn. But where . . . the evidence consists of strands in a cable rather than links in a chain, it will not be appropriate to give such a warning. It should not be given in any event where it would be unnecessary or confusing to do so. It will generally be sufficient to tell the jury that the guilt of the accused must be established beyond reasonable doubt and, where it is helpful to do so, to tell them that they must entertain such a doubt where any other inference consistent with innocence is reasonably open on the evidence. . . .
>
> [T]he prosecution bears the burden of proving all the elements of the crime beyond reasonable doubt. That means that the essential ingredients of each element must be so proved. It does not mean that every fact — every piece of evidence — relied upon to prove an element by inference must itself be proved beyond reasonable doubt. . . . Indeed, the probative force of a mass of evidence may be cumulative, making it pointless to consider

the degree of probability of each item of evidence separately. [51 A. Crim. R. 181, 184-185 (1990).]

d. Background Information

In most cases, judges admit some testimony that may not seem to have any obvious connection to any fact of consequence in the case. Reasonable background information about the witness who is testifying is "always admissible . . . it allows the jury to make better informed judgments about the credibility of a witness and the reliability of that witness' observations." United States v. McVeigh, 153 F.3d 1166, 1201 (10th Cir. 1998). And when witnesses describe actions or events, they are often allowed to describe them in some detail, simply to help the jury relate to and understand what it did not and cannot see for itself. Inmate Butler's explanation of how inmates receive packages from home, referred to on page 42, supra, is an example of such detail. The Latin phrase *res gestae* — meaning "things done" — is often used to justify the admission of broader context to an important incident. Parties also use many kinds of exhibits that in and of themselves do not tend to prove any fact of consequence but that are nonetheless part of, or illustrate, the story to which the jury is listening.

The Advisory Committee Note to FRE 401 explicitly approves of the admission of this kind of contextual evidence, despite its lack of immediate consequence to the case:

> Evidence which is essentially background in nature can scarcely be said to involve disputed matter, yet it is universally offered and admitted as an aid to understanding. Charts, photographs, views of real estate, murder weapons, and many other items of evidence fall in this category.

e. Relevancy Is Not Sufficiency

The question of admissibility under FRE 401 is separate from the question whether an item of evidence is sufficient proof to justify sending a case to the jury. The question of admissibility goes to logical effect, and "any tendency" under FRE 401 requires only a minimum level of logical effect. The question of sufficiency goes to whether a reasonable person could be persuaded by the evidence to the level demanded by the applicable burden of persuasion, as will be discussed in Chapter Ten. Typically, a party's case will require many items of evidence to meet the burden of producing evidence sufficient to support a verdict. As the Advisory Committee Note to FRE 401 states, quoting McCormick's treatise, "A brick is not a wall. "

Moreover, most items of evidence will not trigger just one inference or just one underlying explanatory generalization. Evidence typically can be interpreted in several different ways, thus triggering competing and often contradictory inferences. For example, several competing explanations have probably already occurred to you as to why the guards were wearing gloves (if they were) in the *Johnson* case. These competing explanations may be made the subject of proof by the opponent, and may be argued to the jury during closing argument. It is usually for the jury, in its ultimate deliberations, to choose among them. To be admitted under FRE 401, an item of evidence needs only to make a fact of consequence *somewhat more or less likely than it would be were the evidence not known.*

3. Elaboration of FRE 401 and 402

The following case illustrates the low threshold of probative connection required by the concept of relevance, both at common law and under the Federal Rules.

KNAPP v. STATE[4]
168 Ind. 153, 79 N.E. 1076 (1907)

The appellant appeals from a judgment in the above-entitled cause, under which he stands convicted of murder in the first degree. Error is assigned on the overruling of a motion for new trial.

Appellant, as a witness in his own behalf, offered testimony tending to show a killing in self defense. He afterwards testified, presumably for the purpose of showing that he had reason to fear the deceased, that before the killing he had heard that the deceased, who was the marshal of Hagerstown, had clubbed and seriously injured an old man in arresting him, and that he died a short time afterwards. On appellant being asked, on cross-examination, who told him this, he answered: "Some people around Hagerstown there. I can't say as to who it was now." The state was permitted, on rebuttal, to prove by a physician, over the objection and exception of the defense, that the old man died of senility and alcoholism, and that there were no bruises or marks on his person. Counsel for appellant contend that it was error to admit this testimony; that the question was as to whether he had, in fact, heard the story, and not as to its truth or falsity. While it is laid down in the books that there must be an open and visible connection between the fact under inquiry and the evidence by which it is sought to be established, yet the connection thus required is in the logical processes only, for to require an actual connection between the two facts would be to exclude all presumptive evidence. Within settled rules, the competency of testimony depends largely upon its tendency to persuade the judgment. As said by Wharton: "Relevancy is that which conduces to the proof of a pertinent hypothesis." 1 Wharton, Ev. §20. In Stevenson v. Stuart, 11 Pa. 307, it was said: "The competency of a collateral fact to be used as the basis of legitimate argument is not to be determined by the conclusiveness of the inferences it may afford in reference to the litigated fact. It is enough if these may tend in a slight degree to elucidate the inquiry, or to assist, though remotely, to a determination probably founded in truth."

We are of opinion that the testimony referred to was competent. While appellant's counsel are correct in their assertion that the question was whether appellant had heard a story to the effect that the deceased had offered serious violence to the old man, yet it does not follow that the testimony complained of did not tend to negative the claim of appellant as to what he had heard. One of the first principles of human nature is the impulse to speak the truth. "This principle," says Dr. Reid, whom Professor Greenleaf quotes at length in his work on Evidence (volume 1 §7n), "has a powerful operation, even in the greatest of liars; for where they lie once they speak truth 100 times." Truth speaking preponderating, it follows that to show that there was no basis in fact for the statement appellant claims to have heard had a tendency to make it less probable that his

---

4. For an interesting discussion of the *Knapp* case and the appropriate manner of analyzing the questions it raises, see Richard D. Friedman, *Route Analysis of Credibility and Hearsay*, 96 Yale L.J. 667, 679 (1987). — EDS.

testimony on this point was true. Indeed, since this court has not, in cases where self-defense is asserted as a justification for homicide, confined the evidence concerning the deceased to character evidence, we do not perceive how, without the possibility of a gross perversion of right, the state could be denied the opportunity to meet in the manner indicated the evidence of the defendant as to what he had heard, where he, cunningly perhaps, denies that he can remember who gave him the information. The fact proved by the state tended to discredit appellant, since it showed that somewhere between the fact and the testimony there was a person who was not a truth speaker, and, appellant being unable to point to his informant, it must at least be said that the testimony complained of had a tendency to render his claim as to what he had heard less probable. . . .

Judgment affirmed.

NOTES AND QUESTIONS

1. Although the court in *Knapp* does not state the essential elements of the case under the substantive law, you can probably deduce those elements yourself from the *Johnson* case. What are they? How do the evidentiary facts testified to by the physician connect to a fact of consequence in the case? Can you draw a diagram of this connection? Are the tests of relevance stated in the court's opinion similar, if not identical, to FRE 401 and 402?

2. The court articulates the chain of reasoning that it relies on to establish the relevance of the physician's testimony. It requires a generalization about the truth-telling propensities of people. Is this generalization reasonable? Why does the court think so? Do you? There are numerous cases in which courts admit evidence of the possession of a firearm to prove that a defendant is guilty of distributing illegal drugs and vice versa — that is, they also admit evidence of drug trafficking to prove that a convicted felon knowingly possessed a firearm. In both types of cases, the courts are willing to assume the logical nexus between guns and drug traffic. "Guns are among the tools of the drug trade." United States v. Rhodes, 229 F.3d 659 (7th Cir. 2000). On what does the court base its assumption? On judicial experience? On the government's argument? On the testimony of an expert witness? Does it matter?

3. Notice the emphasis that the court gives to the defendant's inability to remember who told him about the incident involving the old man. What is the court's point? Consider this point again after reading Section B, infra on FRE 403.

4. The classic articles that have forged the concept of logical relevancy adopted by the Federal Rules of Evidence and described in this chapter are George F. James, Relevancy, Probability and the Law, 29 Calif. L. Rev. 689 (1941); Herman C. Trautman, Logical or Legal Relevancy — A Conflict in Theory, 5 Vand. L. Rev. 385 (1952). See also 2 Jack B. Weinstein & Margaret A. Berger, Weinstein's Federal Evidence §401 (Joseph M. McLaughlin ed., Matthew Bender 2d ed. 2001); 1A Wigmore on Evidence §37 (Peter Tillers rev. 1983).

The approach of the Federal Rules is typically contrasted with that of Wigmore, who argued that the law distinguished between "logical" and "legal" relevancy. 1 John Henry Wigmore, Evidence in Trials at Common Law §28, at 409-410 (3d ed. 1940): "[L]egal relevancy denotes . . . something more than a minimum of probative value." It is not altogether clear what this means. Presumably Wigmore was attempting to distinguish between evidence that had some very slight probative value and that which had considerably more persuasive force. The concept of "legal relevancy" does not appear in the Federal Rules, but it is a term that is still used by some practicing lawyers and judges. For our purposes, relevancy refers only to the minimal threshold test of FRE 401. But FRE 401 taken in combination with FRE 403, to be discussed in Section B, infra, may provide outcomes consistent with Wigmore's approach. If an item of evidence has only a barely perceptible logical effect, it is also likely either to be misleading or to lead to delay and waste of time, thus being excludable under FRE 403.

KEY POINTS

1. FRE 402 requires that evidence must be relevant to be admitted at trial, and that all relevant evidence is admissible unless otherwise provided.

2. FRE 401 requires that to be relevant, an evidentiary fact must connect by a process of inferential reasoning to a "fact of consequence" in the case. The essential elements of the substantive law that governs the case determine what facts are "of consequence."

3. FRE 401 requires that to be relevant, an evidentiary fact must make a fact of consequence "more or less probable." The judge decides this issue under the "any tendency" standard by examining the necessary inferences and the reasonableness of the generalizations underlying them.

PROBLEMS

3.1. Consider the following items of evidence from the *Johnson* case. Are they relevant under FRE 401? State the argument for the proponent of the evidence: What fact of consequence (and essential element) is the item offered to prove? Why does the item make this fact more or less probable? Then make the opponent's argument.

(a)   Several correctional officers testified that the reports that they wrote following the incident did not state that they opened the food port door before the cell door was opened electronically.

(b)   The prosecution asked inmate Butler whether he was a gang member and whether defendant Johnson was a gang member. Butler answered that he himself was a Crip and that he did not know if Johnson had any gang affiliation. (Page 43, lines 35-42, supra.)

(c)   The prosecution asked Officer Huston whether inmates in transition from SHU were housed in Facility B. Huston answered "Yes." (Page 8, line 26, supra.)

3.2. At 2:00 P.M. in the afternoon of September 15, 1998, Denise Driver stopped her school bus at its regular stop on Cedar Street. Several young school children between the ages of 8 and 12 left the bus and stood on the gravel shoulder along the side of Cedar Street. As the bus started forward, it hit one of the children, Paul Pedroso, age 10. Paul has been hospitalized since the accident.

Paul's parents have sued Driver and Driver's employer, the San Ramon School District, for negligence on Paul's behalf. They allege that Driver failed to keep a proper lookout and veered off the roadway onto the gravel shoulder where Paul was standing quietly, waiting for the bus to pass. Driver and the school district allege that Driver kept a proper lookout; that Paul was not standing quietly but was playing tag with several other children along the side of the road; and that when Paul ran out into the roadway unexpectedly, Driver had no opportunity to stop in time to avoid hitting him.

At trial in the case of Pedroso v. Driver, Denise Driver testifies in her own defense. Assume that she is a competent witness. During the direct examination of the driver, the following questions and answers occur.

1 Q: Are you still employed as a bus driver?
2 A: No, I quit after the accident.
3 Q: Why?
4 A: It is just like trying to haul a truck load of diamonds. (Voice breaks)
5   Every one of those kids were precious and I just did not have the
6   heart to go back.
7 Q: Would you like a glass of water?
8 A: No, I am okay.
9 Q: Is this document, marked Exhibit A for identification, a letter you
10   received from the school board after the accident?
11 A: Yes.
12 Q: Your Honor, I offer this document as Exhibit for admission:

Exhibit A

San Ramon School Board
2001 Main Street
San Ramon, CA 94901

Dear Ms. Driver,

The San Ramon School Board urges you to return to your work as a school bus driver as soon as you feel able to do so. You have always been a safe driver, and the tragic accident of a month ago does not change our high opinion of you.

/S/ Jean Smith
President, San Ramon School Board

During cross-examination of the driver by the plaintiffs' attorney, the following occurred:

13 Q: Isn't it true that you received a speeding ticket for driving the school bus
14   with the children in it, at 70 miles per hour in a 45 m.p.h. speed zone just a
15   month before the accident in this case occurred?
16 A: Yes.

As attorney for the defendant, what is your theory of relevance for the testimony at lines 4-6 and for Exhibit A? As attorney for the plaintiff, what is your theory of relevance for the question and answer in lines 13-16? For each item, state the connection between the EF and the EE.

3.3. In the case of United States v. Ray, Bernard Ray, the Chief Executive Officer of Rundown Corp., is charged with the federal crime of trading on inside information. The prosecution must prove that Ray intended to profit from the purchase or sale of securities by using "inside" information — information confidential within Rundown and not yet known to the public. Specifically, the prosecution alleges that Ray sold 100,000 shares of Rundown stock on March 16, 2004; that Ray made this sale based on his knowledge of "inside" information that Rundown was facing disastrous losses during the upcoming second quarter (April to June) of 2004; and that Ray intended to profit from this sale. In fact, Rundown Corp. did suffer disastrous financial losses between April and June of 2004, causing the company to file for bankruptcy in December of 2004.

These losses had been projected by Rundown Corp.'s outside auditing firm in March 2004. The chief outside auditor Arthur Andrews sent a confidential memorandum to the office of June Jacobs, the Chief Financial Officer of Rundown, by messenger on the morning of March 14. On the afternoon of March 14, chief auditor Andrews sent an e-mail to Jacobs advising her to inform Ray about these projections. Ray claims that he was not informed about the projected losses until the weekly meeting of Rundown's Executive Committee held on March 18. If called as a witness, Jacobs will assert her Fifth Amendment privilege to refuse to testify about these events. The government has a copy of the March 14 e-mail that it wants to enter into evidence to prove that Ray knew about the projected losses before March 16.

Is the e-mail relevant under the standard of Rule 401? Why?

3.4. In the case of State v. Blair, on September 14, 2005, Norma Waits, a 35-year-old woman, was brutally attacked in her apartment. There were no signs of forced entry. Norma's housekeeper found Norma unconscious the next morning and then called 911.

Norma was a successful and beloved singer for the local Opera Company. After an extensive investigation, police arrested Jimmy Blair, a 45-year-old prominent entertainment lawyer, and charged him with aggravated assault and battery and attempted murder. Norma does not remember the attack and cannot identify the attacker.

Jimmy and Norma had been dating since 2002. Their relationship began when they met at a fundraising gala for the Opera. Norma's friends reported that Jimmy was charming and supportive. None of them had suspected any trouble, though they did note that Norma had become more isolated in the two years preceding the attack. Norma's best friend stated that she had been unable to see much of Norma in 2005, despite repeated attempts to arrange activities. Additionally, Norma's career had begun to falter, and she took an extensive leave from the Opera, citing unspecified health problems. As the prosecution builds its case against Jimmy, many items of potentially admissible evidence are considered. For the following items, decide whether you think each item is relevant under Rules 401 and 402 and why. Identify the fact of consequence that the item might make more or less probable, and the generalizations needed to support any inferences. Is other evidence needed to determine relevance?

(1) A police witness would testify that on the morning after the attack, police found a suitcase in Norma's apartment half-packed with her belongings.

The police also found a plane ticket for a flight to Los Angeles on that day with Norma's name on it. The ticket was torn in half.

(2)   Exhibits include photographs of Norma showing severe bruising on parts of her body that would normally be covered by clothing. The photos are date stamped July 25, 2004. A police witness will testify that she found these photographs in a locked drawer in Norma's apartment, which she opened with a key found among Norma's personal effects.

(3)   A friend of Norma's says that a month before the attack, Norma told the friend that she planned to tell Jimmy that she was going to break up with him and leave the Bay Area soon. Norma also said that she was afraid Jimmy would be furious.

4. Reflection on the Requirement of Relevancy

The Federal Rules of Evidence have as their central goal the factually accurate resolution of disputes that are brought to federal court. This is not to say that other values do not affect the Rules, as explicitly stated in FRE 102, or that the search for truth does not accommodate other values. It is to say, however, that the dominant policy expressed in the Rules, in the Advisory Committee Notes, in judicial interpretations, and professional and academic commentary is the pursuit of factually accurate outcomes.

This policy rests on a belief that disinterested fact finders, such as jurors, have the capacity to reconstruct prior events by using their powers of reasoning — by drawing inferences from evidence presented to them in the courtroom, based on their own generalized knowledge and experience. To the extent that the evidence presented is accurate and complete and the jury's generalizations are accurate, this reasoning process can yield accurate outcomes. The accuracy of this reasoning process is advanced in no small measure by the requirement of relevancy discussed above.

The trial system, in short, pursues the search for truth from the perspective of a correspondence theory of knowledge. It assumes that things happen and that what happens is knowable by human beings. The system also assumes that accurate knowledge is produced through human reasoning — that persons (witnesses) can coherently communicate information about happenings to disinterested third parties (jurors) who then will draw accurate inferences based on that information. You can see that the role of witnesses and the role of the jury described on page 78, supra, are grounded in these assumptions.

Suppose, though, that you are convinced that there is a reality and that you can know it. Are you as convinced that your fellow human beings can know it, or do you have doubts about the rationality of the human species? Even if you are a disinterested observer of events, is anyone else? How often have you seen a person's perceptions of an event determined by ideology or wishful thinking? Consider the videotape of the Los Angeles police arrest of and use of force against Rodney King. Viewers' perceptions of that event could apparently differ dramatically. If that is not an uncommon occurrence, what are its implications for the social reconstruction of reality that occurs at trial based on the testimony of witnesses whose perception may be affected by factors that are not rational?

Moreover, how much faith do you have in disinterested third parties such as jurors drawing the appropriate inferences about what happened based on the evidentiary facts described to them by witnesses? How different was student opinion in your class about the credibility of witnesses in the transcript of the *Johnson* case in Chapter One? Do people use a uniform body of generalized knowledge and experience to evaluate such data? Or are you more impressed with the remarkable divergence of opinion that constantly seems to follow from the presentation of information to a group of individuals? Again, does that increase or decrease your faith in the rationality of the trial process?

Empirical research has also been done on the intellectual strategies that people use — alone and in groups — to come to conclusions about disputed facts. The landmark works in this field that may have the most compelling applications to jury decisionmaking are Michael J. Saks and Robert F. Kidd, Human Information Processing and Adjudication: Trial by Heuristics, 15 Law & Socy. Rev. 123 (1980-1981), and Amos Tversky and Daniel Kahneman, Judgment Under Uncertainty: Heuristics and Biases, 185 Science 1124 (1974). This literature offers practitioners the opportunity to understand jurors' decision-making strategies, and it offers law reformers the opportunity to improve the procedures and evidentiary policies underlying our system of trial.

Questions about the validity of the assumption of jury rationality are of great importance. The outcomes of jury factfinding are always uncertain. There is no methodology and no objective point of view within the system of trials to test whether the jury has correctly decided the ultimate facts.[5] To the extent that one has doubts about jury rationality, one should have serious reservations about continuing our current system of trial. On the other hand, to the extent one has greater faith in our capacity to understand and communicate our knowledge about the world in a rational manner, then one may feel somewhat more sanguine about the model of jury reasoning. And whatever degree of skepticism you possess, you must also consider what alternatives there are to our reliance on this model.

Additional perspectives on policies that underlie the Federal Rules of Evidence can be found in Kenneth W. Graham Jr., There'll Always Be an England: The Instrumental Ideology of Evidence, 85 Mich. L. Rev. 1204, 1219-1220, 1227-1234 (1987); Rosemary C. Hunter, Gender in Evidence, Masculine Norms vs. Feminist Reforms, 19 Harv. Women's L.J. 127 (1996); Kit Kinports, Evidence Engendered, 1991 U. Ill. L. Rev. 413; Michael L. Seigel, A Pragmatic Critique of Modern Evidence Scholarship, 88 Nw. U. L. Rev. 995, 998 (1994).

B. PROBATIVE VALUE AND THE RULE 403 DANGERS

FRE 403 affords the trial court authority to exclude evidence that is admittedly relevant under Rules 401 and 402, but that the judge believes might distract the jury from its role of rational decisionmaking. This authority also existed under the common

---

5. The results of DNA testing may come as close to "objective certainty" as our system can provide. Numerous persons convicted of rape or murder have been freed from incarceration on the basis of subsequent DNA testing (not available at the time of trial) of body samples, such as hair and semen, found on the victim. The testing virtually excludes the defendant as the source of the samples. In one such case, however, the prosecutor remains convinced that the released convict was guilty: "It really doesn't change my opinion that much . . . The case was a circumstantial-evidence case. There was a myriad of [sic] circumstances that pointed in his direction." *New York Times*, August 23, 2001.

law, referred to as *judicial discretion*. As you read FRE 403, you will see that the rule provides guides for the exercise of the court's discretionary power to exclude. The judge is not free to choose between admission and exclusion unrestrained by fixed principles. Rather, the judge has some flexibility in choice of outcome, but is restrained by standards articulated in the rule. Rule 403 does not allow a trial judge "to remove relevant evidence from the jury's universe solely because he finds the evidence unpersuasive; the ultimate arbiter of the persuasiveness of the proof must be the factfinder, not the lawgiver." Blake v. Pellegrino, 329 F.3d 43, 47 (1st Cir. 2003). Remember that the judge's power to exclude under FRE 403 means that the advocates cannot present all the relevant evidence they would like to offer to the jury, and the jury will not see and hear admittedly relevant information.

1.   FRE 403

RULE 403.   EXCLUSION OF RELEVANT EVIDENCE ON GROUNDS OF PREJUDICE, CONFUSION, OR WASTE OF TIME

Although relevant, evidence may be excluded if its probative value is substantially outweighed by the danger of unfair prejudice, confusion of the issues, or misleading the jury, or by considerations of undue delay, waste of time, or needless presentation of cumulative evidence.

2.   Interpretation and Illustration of FRE 403

When the opponent objects to the admission of evidence on any of the grounds stated in the rule, the judge must carefully evaluate the probative value of the offered item, estimate the "Rule 403 danger" that it poses, and then apply the terms of the balancing test that the rule sets forth. Relevant evidence is to be excluded only if its probative value is *substantially* outweighed by one of the rule's articulated dangers. The rule itself and its Advisory Committee Note give judges little guidance in interpreting the meaning of its terms. How is the judge to measure probative value? What is the difference between "confusion of the issues," "misleading the jury," and "unfair prejudice"? We will develop the meaning of these terms in some detail. We believe that careful analysis of the Rule 403 dangers can have a critical impact on the trial judge's ruling.

Consider an example of evidence raising Rule 403 dangers. James Johnson, the defendant, testified in the *Johnson* case that he observed Officer Walker attack another inmate, allegedly for no good reason: "He snatched a Hispanic guy up off the seat, took him out the kitchen, drug him by the hair out of the kitchen in the front by the sally port and jumped on the guy" (page 54, lines 25-27, supra). This testimony was offered to show that Johnson had good reason to fear Officer Walker when Walker came to his cell door. This testimony about Officer Walker's conduct on another occasion could also cause the jury to think about Walker, not about Johnson's state of mind. The jury could think that Walker is a bad person and hold this against the government; also, the jury could think that Walker has a propensity for violence and therefore would have attacked Johnson. As we explain at pages 138–139, infra, these are the two ways in which this evidence might be unfairly prejudicial to the government's case. Thus,

Johnson's testimony might be objected to by the prosecution under FRE 403,[6] and the judge must weigh the probative value of the evidence against these risks of unfair prejudice.

a.   Probative Value

To decide the merits of a Rule 403 objection, the judge must first analyze the persuasive effect that the item of evidence will be likely to have on the jury's thinking about the fact of consequence it is offered to prove. This is its *probative value*. Remember that evidence is relevant if it has "any" tendency to make the fact of consequence more or less probable; probative value measures the strength of the effect on the probabilities, even if only in general terms like "highly," "somewhat," or "minimally" probative. Defendant Johnson's testimony as to Officer Walker's conduct is clearly relevant to show that Johnson had reason to fear Walker, but what is its probative value? In United States v. Buchanan, 964 F. Supp. 533, 537 (D. Mass. 1997), the district court posed the issue as follows:

> In evaluating probative value I am obliged to consider first "how strong a tendency" the proffered evidence has to prove the issue of consequence in the litigation, . . . and second, the proponent's need for the evidence.

i.   Strength of the Underlying Inferences.   Most courts and commentators agree that the primary measure of probative value is the strength of the inferences that connect the evidentiary fact to the fact of consequence and then to an essential element in the case. This strength depends on the rough probabilities of the generalizations underlying those inferences. If, as Johnson said, he saw Officer Walker beat up another inmate with no provocation, then a generalization underlying the inference that Johnson feared Walker could be articulated as follows:

Diagram 3-7

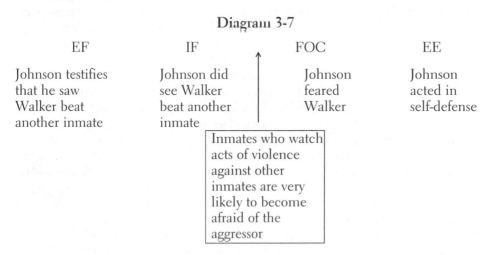

EF	IF	FOC	EE
Johnson testifies that he saw Walker beat another inmate	Johnson did see Walker beat another inmate	Johnson feared Walker	Johnson acted in self-defense

Inmates who watch acts of violence against other inmates are very likely to become afraid of the aggressor

---

6.   California Evidence Code §352, on which FRE 403 is based, contains essentially the same balancing test:

> The court in its discretion may exclude evidence if its probative value is substantially outweighed by the probability that its admission will (a) necessitate undue consumption of time or (b) create substantial danger of undue prejudice, of confusing the issues, or of misleading the jury.

The judge's rough estimate of the probability expressed in this generalization — here, the frequency with which inmates do become afraid, estimated as "very likely" — is the major component of the judge's estimate of the probative value of Johnson's testimony. There is no single "correct" way to articulate this generalization, and there is no precise or accurate way to estimate its degree of frequency. Human behavior rarely can be reliably predicted. Moreover, details of the offered evidence would affect how the generalization is framed, such as was the beating extremely violent? Additional evidentiary facts can also increase or decrease the probative value of the offered item. Were such beatings frequent or unusual? Was there already "bad blood" between Johnson and Walker, or between the Hispanic inmate and Walker? Some of these facts could be the subject of further testimony from Johnson, or from additional witnesses as well. The fact finder, if the evidence is admitted, will then make inferences from these facts, based on its own background knowledge and experience. You can see that the judge's estimate is just that — a rough attempt to place a value on an inference that a reasonable jury could make and that cannot be quantified with precision.

ii.   **Certainty of the Starting Point.**   The certainty of the starting point of the inferential chain can also affect probative value. If witnesses admit that they are themselves uncertain about what facts they actually perceived, or if a document contains ambiguous language, judges may discount the value that they attribute to the evidence for purposes of FRE 403. What about uncertainty in the starting point based on the judge's doubts about a witness's truthfulness? For example, should defendant Johnson be believed? Did he really see Officer Walker attack another inmate? Doubts about Johnson's credibility could reduce the probative value of the facts he testifies about. But courts *do not count the witness's credibility* when estimating probative value. Ballou v. Henri Studios, Inc., 656 F.2d 1147, 1154 (5th Cir. 1981). The prevailing view is that evaluating the credibility of witnesses is a matter uniquely within the competence of the jury, and that the judge's role is to estimate the probative value of testimony *if believed*. If judges were to use their discretionary power under FRE 403 to exclude the testimony of witnesses they do not find to be credible, then the jury's principal fact-finding function would be vastly diminished.

iii.   **Need.**   The Advisory Committee Note to FRE 403 mentions two other factors that a judge may take into account in applying the rule's balancing test. First, the Note advises that judges should balance "the probative value of and *need* for the evidence against the harm likely to result from its admission" (emphasis added). Then, the Note closes with the statement that the "availability of other means of proof" may also be weighed in the decision to exclude evidence on grounds of unfair prejudice. No explanation of these terms is given, nor is the judge advised how to take these factors into account. Case law reveals that there are many ways in which judges do take need into account. The centrality of the point to be proved, and the degree to which it is disputed by the opponent, can increase a party's need for evidence and would increase its probative value. In United States v. Davis, 154 F.3d 772 (8th Cir. 1998), tapes and transcripts of defendant Jarrett's threats made to government witnesses were offered to show Jarrett's consciousness of his own guilt on charges of possessing drugs and a firearm. Jarrett argued that the probative value of this evidence was lowered by lack of need — several other witnesses had already testified to the facts of Jarrett's possession. The court rejected this claim:

> We are hesitant to conclude that the testimony of other witnesses [about possession] made [the tapes and transcripts] unnecessary when [Jarrett has] repeatedly attacked the credibility of those other witnesses. [Id. at 780.]

The lack of alternative means of proving a fact of consequence can also raise the probative value of an item of evidence "in the relative sense, as being determined by supply and demand." Charles A. Wright and Kenneth W. Graham Jr., Federal Practice and Procedure: Evidence §5214 at 269. Alternatively, if there is already substantial evidence on the same point, there is less need for an additional item and its probative value is lower. Frank v. County of Hudson, 924 F. Supp. 620, 626 (D.N.J. 1996) (evidence of unrelated child sexual abuse by a defendant in a sexual harassment and discrimination case was excluded, although admissible under FRE 413-415, because four plaintiffs making similar accusations of defendant's workplace harassment "reduces the relative weight" of the proffered child abuse evidence); United States v. Haywood, 280 F.3d 715, 723 (6th Cir. 2002) (other evidence of the defendant's "intent to sell" crack cocaine reduced the prosecution's need to prove an unrelated act of possession of the drug). You can see that this fine-tuning of probative value requires that the judge be familiar with evidence that is already admitted and that is expected to be admitted at trial. The judge may also need to inquire about what other evidence is available to the parties. If the judge is not able to make this contextual judgment of probative value at the time a Rule 403 objection is made, the judge can defer decision until later in the trial when more evidentiary context has been provided, using the technique of conditional admissibility that will be discussed in Chapter Four, Section E, infra.

NOTE

Some commentators believe that the length of the inferential chain of reasoning reduces the probative value of an item of evidence. They reason that the more inferences that are necessary to make this connection, the more opportunity a jury has for making an error in its inferential reasoning process. (A doctrine related to this perceived risk, still persistent in some jurisdictions, is that an "inference upon an inference" is not allowable.) We do not agree with this general proposition, however. A higher number of inferential steps in a chain of reasoning does not automatically reduce probative value. Indeed, DNA evidence, for example, requires complicated chains of reasoning and can yield a high probability. While it is true that some chains of reasoning are longer and some are shorter, the important point is that some are stronger in the sense of being more convincing, while some are weaker in the sense of being not very persuasive. At issue is the strength of the connection between the evidentiary fact and the final inference rather than the number of steps that must be taken to get to that final conclusion. This is a function primarily of the strength of the generalizations underlying each step.

b. Rule 403 Dangers

The second step in resolving a Rule 403 objection is for the judge to estimate the danger that the item of evidence poses to the jury's rational decision-making process and to the judicial system's interest in efficient decisionmaking. FRE 403 identifies major sources of risk of error in the jury's reasoning process. Evidence that is unfairly prejudicial or confusing or that will mislead the jury can be excluded. In addition, if the production of evidence causes undue delay, is a waste of time, or is needlessly cumulative, it may be excluded as well. Whatever the kind of danger, the judge will attempt to make a realistic estimate of the danger posed. This will include the *nature of the danger, the likelihood that the jury will be negatively affected, and the probable degree of the harmful effect.* And if a single item of evidence raises more than one of these probative dangers, this may significantly increase the probable degree of harm

    i. Unfair Prejudice.   The term *unfair prejudice* refers to the danger that evidence might suggest an improper basis upon which the jury could decide the case. Evidence is *not* unfairly prejudicial simply because it is detrimental to a party's case.

> If all evidence adverse to a defendant was subject to exclusion under F.R.E. Rule 403, then no government evidence would ever be deemed admissible. The test...is not whether the evidence is detrimental, but whether it is so unfairly prejudicial as to substantially outweigh its probative value. [United States v. Weinstock, 153 F.3d 272, 278 (6th Cir. 1998).]

Case law has established that there are two principal risks of unfair prejudice within the scope of FRE 403. The first risk is that evidence about a party can trigger a response that has nothing to do with its logical connection to a fact of consequence. This response can turn the jury against that party (or in favor of that party) and improperly influence the jury's decisionmaking. The Advisory Committee Note to FRE 403 suggests that this improper reaction is "commonly, though not necessarily, an emotional one." Wigmore describes the danger as occurring when evidence would "be likely to stimulate an excessive emotion or to awaken a fixed prejudice . . . and thus dominate the mind of the tribunal and prevent a rational determination of the truth." John Henry Wigmore, Code of Evidence 355 (3d ed. 1942).

    For example, recall the testimony of defendant James Johnson concerning Officer Walker's attack on another inmate, discussed on page 134, supra. Walker's attack might trigger a response of anger or disgust that prejudices the jury against Walker. There is a risk that this prejudice could influence the outcome in the *Johnson* case in an unfair way, such as the jury viewing a verdict in favor of Johnson as a punishment of Walker. If a Rule 403 objection is made, the trial judge would have to estimate this danger of unfair prejudice by identifying the nature of the danger and its likely effect, United States v. Haywood, 280 F.2d 715, 723 (6th cir. 2002) ("[b]y branding Haywood as a criminal possessing crack cocaine, this evidence had 'the natural tendency to elicit the jury's opprobrium'), as well as the degree of probable effect."

    This type of unfair prejudice can also operate against corporate entities. In BE&K Construction Co. v. Will and Grundy Building Trades Council, AFL-CIO, 156 F.3d 756, 764 (7th Cir. 1998), defendant union offered a videotaped speech to show that it intended only lawful activity and not a secondary boycott. The court excluded the video as highly prejudicial because it included inflammatory statements such as "BE&K is a parasite on the life of the community."

    The second principal risk of unfair prejudice is if evidence could be used by the jury in a manner that violates a rule of evidence law. A single item of evidence can generate several different inferences and be used by the jury in more than one way. For example, Officer Walker's attack on the other inmate triggers the permissible inference that defendant Johnson feared Walker. It also triggers an impermissible inference about Officer Walker's propensity to use violence against inmates in general, and thus to use violence against Johnson. This is impermissible under FRE 404(b), which prohibits the use of prior specific acts, such as Walker's attack, to prove action in conformity with character, as we will see in Chapter Five. The risk that the jury will use Johnson's testimony for this improper purpose qualifies as a danger of unfair prejudice under FRE 403. Johnson's testimony thus has a proper relevant use — to prove that he feared Walker — as well as an improper use — to prove Walker's violent character. If the prosecution objects to Johnson's testimony, FRE 403 requires the judge to balance the testimony's permissible probative value against the danger that it will be used improperly. United States v. Pierce, 136 F.3d 770, 776 (11th Cir. 1998) (probative value of identification of defendant in a surveillance photo by his parole officer not substantially outweighed by risk of prejudice from the parole officer appearing as a witness, highlighting defendant's prior contact with the criminal justice system).

   ii.   Confusion of the Issues.   Evidence confuses the issues when it focuses the jury's attention too closely on a factual issue that is not central to the outcome of the case. Such issues are termed *collateral*, which usually means that their connection to the essential elements is trivial and may be based on complicated or attenuated theories of relevance. Typically, then, proof of collateral issues will require the use of multiple witnesses or will consume considerable time in court. If the jury gets involved and interested in deciding a collateral issue, it will spend less of its attention on the important questions. It is not that these collateral issues are irrelevant; rather, they are too distracting and tend to *confuse the issues* . For example, evidence of several other incidents of violence against inmates at Pelican Bay, offered by the defense to show that defendant Johnson was justified in being fearful of prison guards, would require testimony from several witnesses, and might be hotly disputed by the prosecution. The jury might confuse the issues and focus its attention on whether those other incidents occurred, instead of on whether Johnson committed the alleged acts of battery. Halvorsen v. Baird, 146 F.3d 680 (9th Cir. 1998) (evidence from six witnesses that each had been involuntarily detained in a detoxification center when they were not drunk was not permitted to bolster plaintiff's case that he had been treated similarly; risk of confusing jury by involving it in a dispute over whether these six individuals were drunk or not).
   Another risk of confusion in the *Johnson* case would be that the evidence of additional violent incidents might cause the jury to focus on an issue that is not a question that the jury is being asked to decide in the lawsuit — such as the prison's policy toward inmates at Pelican Bay. In contrast, in United States v. Crosby, 75 F.3d 1343, 1348 (9th Cir. 1996), the court held that the trial court erred in excluding as "confusing" evidence that the victim's own husband may have committed the assault for which the defendant was on trial. This evidence was not confusing, the appellate court said, because it "added no new issues to the case, as it dovetailed neatly with defendant's theory that someone else had committed the crime."

   iii.   Misleading the Jury.   Courts often refer to evidence as both "confusing and misleading" and make no effort to distinguish between the two dangers. The danger of being *misleading* , however, usually involves a risk that an item of evidence will cause the jury to draw a *mistaken* inference. In Jones. v. Ford Motor Co., 320 F.

Supp. 440 (E.D.Va. 2004), plaintiff alleged that a defect in the design of the Ford cruise control system caused her automobile to accelerate suddenly, resulting in her personal injuries. To prove that Ford was on notice of the defective condition, the plaintiff offered government reports from Canada and Japan about sudden acceleration problems with cruise control systems in General Motors cars. The district court excluded these reports under Rule 403 as potentially misleading, since the cruise control systems in Ford cars were not functionally similar and the jury could mistakenly equate them to the General Motors systems. Facts taken out of context or presented in a falsely suggestive manner can also trigger this danger.

Specific types of evidence can be viewed as misleading if the judge fears that the jury will give the evidence more weight than it deserves. For example, videotaped reenactments of accidents or other events have been called misleading because jurors may treat them as documentations of the actual event. Some kinds of scientific evidence and expert testimony are also believed to be overpersuasive. Many courts reject a criminal defendant's lie detector evidence on the grounds that the jury may over-value polygraph results as an indicator of truthfulness because of their scientific nature. United States v. Call, 129 F.3d 1402, 1406 (10th Cir. 1997). But a court should not exclude such testimony simply on the theory that scientific techniques by their very nature overwhelm the jury. United States v. West, 962 F.2d 1243, 1248 (7th Cir. 1992) (error to exclude psychiatrist's testimony on the ground that it would mislead the jury with confusing psychiatric terminology — "there was nothing more technical or confusing about [the doctor's] testimony here than the psychiatric testimony in most cases"); In re Paoli R.R. Yard PCB Litigation, 35 F.3d 717, 746 (3d Cir. 1994) ("[t]here must be something about the particular scientific technique such as its posture of mythic infallibility that makes it especially overwhelming").

The use of complex statistics and probabilistic evidence, such as DNA identification evidence, epidemiological studies in toxic tort cases and employer hiring practices in discrimination cases, is also challenging for the jury. Even where the probability data is empirically valid, there is still a risk that the translation of statistical probability into "real numbers" that the jury can understand may mislead or confuse the jury: "The apparent precision of statistical evidence often stands in marked contrast to the uncertainties of other testimony....The danger is that such evidence will overshadow equally probative but admittedly unscientific and anecdotal nonstatistical evidence." The Evolving Role of Statistical Assessments as Evidence in the Courts 150 (Report of the Panel on Statistical Assessments as Evidence in the Courts) (Stephen E. Fienberg, ed., 1989). "The danger ... is that statistics on the frequency with which certain blood type combinations occur in a population will be understood by the jury to be a quantification of the likelihood that the defendant, who shares that unique combination of blood characteristics, is guilty." State v. Joon Kyu Kim, 398 N.W.2d 544, 548 (Minn. 1987). Despite this risk of overpersuasion, the probative value of, and the need for, this kind of evidence is very high. State statutes provide for the use of blood testing and probability estimates in paternity cases, and many courts have approved the admission of probability testimony about DNA testing when it is properly presented and challenged. Other commentators believe that jurors tend to prefer anecdotal evidence and will ignore statistical evidence when it conflicts. Research on this juror response to statistical versus anecdotal evidence is not yet decisive.

iv.   Undue Delay, Waste of Time, and Needless Cumulative Evidence.   Each of these dangers illustrates a different aspect of the same underlying problem: The introduction of evidence always absorbs court time, incurs expense by the opposing parties and by the state-run judicial system, and expends the attention of the jury. The dangers of delay and waste of time are easily quantifiable. For example, if a continuance is required for production of evidence or to transport the jury to view the scene of the crime, the trial will be delayed. And if a trial judge has imposed strict time limits on the length of trials, requests for extension of time to present rebuttal evidence are decided under the FRE 403 balancing test: "As a general rule, evidence may not be excluded solely to avoid delay....Under Rule 403, the court should consider the probative value of the proffered evidence and balance it against the harm of delay." General Signal Corp. v. MCI Telecommunications Corp., 66 F.3d 1500, 1509-1510 (9th Cir. 1995). Courts have held that evidence may waste the jury's time if offered to prove stipulated, collateral, or background facts.

The danger underlying *needless presentation of cumulative evidence* is less quantifiable. It includes the expenditure of trial time on repetitive testimony, plus the risk of losing the attention of the jury. During the *Johnson* trial, Officer Smith described for the prosecution what happened between Officer Walker and defendant Johnson when Johnson's cell door was opened. Officers Huston, Van Berg, and Walker had already testified about this occurrence. Thus the defense might have objected, in the terms of FRE 403, that Officer Smith's testimony was a needless presentation of cumulative evidence and should be excluded. Here the judge must assess the degree to which the testimony actually is repetitive. Obrey v. Johnson, 400 F.3d 691 (9th Cir. 2005) (in an action alleging a pattern of discriminatory promotion practices, testimony from three witnesses who would have testified to their own experiences of discrimination was not cumulative or repetitive as it tended to support the pattern or practice theory). Also, there may be reasons why repetition is needed — such as the centrality of the fact of consequence being proved, the degree to which that fact is in dispute, and the probative value of the corroboration itself. It is unlikely that Officer Smith's testimony would be considered "needless" in the Johnson case, since Johnson's behavior was the central focus of the dispute and each side offered several witnesses to the events. Coles v. Jenkins, 1998 WL 964506 (W.D. Va. 1998) (court denied motion in limine to prevent defendant's use of three experts to testify regarding the dangerousness of a state highway, since each expert had a slightly different area of expertise).

c.   Probative Value Substantially Outweighed by One of the FRE 403 Dangers

The final step is for the trial judge to weigh the probative value of the offered item of evidence against the danger that this item poses under FRE 403. FRE 403 offers no criteria by which these concepts are to be calibrated. How does one determine when a danger *substantially outweighs* probative value?

i.   The Meaning of "Substantially Outweigh."   There does not appear to be a scale — a common measure — with which to compare probative value versus the degree of risk that Rule 403 dangers pose to the jury's reasoning process. If that is so, *a fortiori* there is no means of calibrating which weighs more. There is no "quantum effect on rationality" that can be assigned to an item of evidence. One way that judges might think about the balancing test is to predict an overall effect of an item of evidence on the jury: What is the likelihood that the "bad" aspect of the evidence will seriously dominate the mind of the jury, overwhelming the "good" aspect? If the likelihood seems high, admission of such evidence may lead to "bad" factfinding as the incremental "badness" of the evidence exerts itself, and exclusion under FRE 403 would be justified.

We might ask, however, why evidence should ever be admitted if its "bad" aspect appears to dominate over the "good" to even a small degree? Would not such evidence always taint the jury's factfinding? The rule's requirement that probative value be outweighed "substantially" appears to require that some risks of negative impact be tolerated. This is sensible because the judge's ability to predict such effects is so imprecise.

Another way to think about the requirement of substantiality is that it measures the judge's confidence level: Evidence should be excluded only when the judge is quite confident that the prejudicial aspects of the evidence outweigh its probative value. The requirement can be thought of, in other words, as providing a burden of proof to be applied under FRE 403 to the admission of evidence. The burden in FRE 403 favors wrongful decisions to admit evidence over wrongful decisions to exclude it. This is in keeping with the strong belief of the drafters of the Federal Rules of Evidence that the underlying principles of the rules — truth and justice — will best be furthered when more rather than less evidence is deemed admissible.

In practice, how do judges conduct the balancing test of FRE 403? One commentator suggests the following table to show how Rule 403 would properly operate:

Probative value of offered relevant evidence	Negative effect of Rule 403 listed factor	Whether trial court may exclude evidence
High	High, Mid, or Low	No
Mid	High	No (Perhaps Yes)[*]
	Mid or Low	No
Low	High	Yes
	Mid	No (Perhaps Yes)[*]
	Low	No

[*] If probative value were near the bottom of the "mid" range and the negative effect extremely high, or if probative value were extremely low and the negative effect near the top of the "mid" range, Rule 403 might allow exclusion.

[Newell Blakely, Article IV: Relevancy and Its Limits, 30 U. Hous. L. Rev. 281, 317 (1993).]

ii.   The Effect of Limiting Instructions on the Balancing Process.   The balancing of probative value versus a Rule 403 danger is also affected by FRE 105, which provides as follows:

> When evidence which is admissible as to one party or for one purpose but not admissible as to another party or for another purpose is admitted, the court, upon request, shall restrict the evidence to its proper scope and instruct the jury accordingly.

The Advisory Committee Note to FRE 403 states that "[i]n reaching a decision whether to exclude on grounds of unfair prejudice, consideration should be given to the probable effectiveness or lack of effectiveness of a limiting instruction."

This means that when an item of evidence has a proper relevant use to prove a fact of consequence but also creates the risk of an improper use — an impermissible inference or an unfairly prejudicial effect — the judge may give a limiting instruction that directs the jury to consider the evidence only for its proper use. In the example from the *Johnson* case, Johnson's testimony about Officer Walker's attack on another inmate could have been accompanied by a limiting instruction — that the jury was to consider this testimony only for its effect on Johnson's state of mind, and for no other purpose. If the judge believes that the jury will probably follow such an instruction, the judge may find that the risk of unfair prejudice is lowered and will admit the item. Other instructions can be given that could reduce the confusing or misleading risks of admitted evidence. The judge's belief that the jury can and will follow limiting instructions could decrease the judge's estimation of the risk of Rule 403 dangers.

It is not clear, however, that the jury can or will follow such an instruction. Social science researchers have attempted to investigate this issue. The findings from many empirical studies are summarized in Lieberman and Arndt, Understanding the Limits of Limiting Instructions, 6 Psychol. Pub. Pol'y & L. 677 (2000). Some of this research has concluded that the giving of an instruction may serve to emphasize the inadmissible evidence or improper inference, which may be more damaging than simply letting the matter go unnoticed. Other studies show that jurors follow limiting instructions selectively, and should be more likely to follow them when the judge offers an explanation as to why jurors should ignore certain uses of the evidence. The most common explanation for the failure of jurors to follow limiting instructions is that jurors react negatively to limits on their ability to perform "free behaviors" — especially when they are instructed to ignore uses of evidence that appear to them highly relevant. Overall, the effectiveness of limiting instructions may be hindered by the jury's lack of understanding of the policy behind a rule of exclusion and the jury's lack of comprehension of the instruction itself. See Peter Meijes Tiersma, Reforming the Language of Jury Instructions, 22 Hofstra L. Rev. 37 (1993). Lieberman and Arndt propose a number of strategies for mitigating the problem of ineffectiveness, including judicial instructions that "soft sell" the limits on the jury and emphasize issues of procedural fairness. 6 Psychol. Pub. Pol'y & L. at 704-705 (2000).

As a general rule, however, courts assume that instructions do effectively exclude improper evidence from the jury's consideration. The U.S. Supreme Court has offered the following rationale:

> The rule that juries are presumed to follow their instructions is a pragmatic one, rooted less in the absolute certitude that the presumption is true than in the belief that it represents a reasonable, practical accommodation of the interests of the state and the defendant in the criminal justice process. [Richardson v. Marsh, 481 U.S. 200, 211 (1987).]

And an experienced trial judge supports the giving of limiting instructions:

> While the videos might be used by the jury improperly, a limiting instruction to the jury, here given repeatedly, specifying the purpose for which they can use the videos is sufficient to ensure that there will be no unfair prejudice to the defendant....

There is always some danger that the jury will ignore the court's instructions about the limited way in which evidence should be considered. Juries in the product liability cases tried in this court have been responsible. The "runaway jury" concern is not substantiated. [Gonzalez v. Digital Equipment Corp., 8 F. Supp. 2d 194, 198 (E.D.N.Y. 1998) (Weinstein, J.).]

Judicial reliance on the use of limiting instructions to resolve FRE 403 problems will be demonstrated throughout this book. United States v. Candelaria-Silva, 162 F.3d 698 (1st Cir. 1998) (evidence of defendant's flight admitted as evidence of guilt of the crime charged; danger that jury would give it undue weight was cured by court's instruction that flight may not always reflect feelings of guilt, that many innocent people flee, and that flight alone is insufficient to sustain a conviction). In some circumstances, however, courts recognize that limiting instructions are not a "sure-fire panacea for the prejudice resulting from the needless admission of [prejudicial] evidence." United States v. Haywood, 280 F.3d 715, 724 (6th Cir. 2002). In United States v. Garcia-Rosa, 876 F.2d 209, 222 (1st Cir. 1989) the court held that the prejudicial effect of the evidence was so severe that it could not "be remedied merely through a limiting instruction . . . [and] [i]f limiting instructions could remedy all such errors, the government would easily be able to circumvent Rule . . . 403.").

Are limiting instructions the best resolution to Rule 403 problems? Some commentators urge that rather than reforming limiting instructions, they should be abolished, and that this will require trial judges to weigh probative value versus risk of unfair prejudice more carefully in making FRE 403 decisions.

NOTES AND QUESTIONS

1. Numerous cases in federal court apply Rule 403 to the prosecution's use of photographs, videotapes and other demonstrative evidence to portray the graphic effects of violent crime and accidents. The inflammatory nature of such exhibits calls for careful analysis of their probative value and limitations on their use.

In United States v. Yahweh, 792 F. Supp. 104 (S.D. Fla. 1992), the district judge admitted gruesome autopsy photographs from "arguably the most violent case ever tried in a federal court." The defendant objected to the use of these photographs, particularly in enlarged format, under FRE 403. To determine probative value, the judge carefully reviewed the relevance of each of the photographs and noted that the enlarged size was necessary to furnish the detail that corroborated witnesses' description of events prior to death. The judge required the medical examiners to select those photographs that illustrated their testimony and to explain the need for each photograph on the basis of content and size. In addition, the judge found that the display of the enlarged photographs enabled all jurors simultaneously to follow the witnesses' testimony. The judge also brought his own background knowledge and experience out into the open:

For twenty years, this court has stood by the jury box to observe as witnesses testified in front of the jury box concerning exhibits being published to the jury there. In this court's view, the larger 30" X 40" pictures were the right size to illustrate and clarify the witness' testimony; in fact, even the 16" x 20" size was inadequately small by comparison. [Id. at 108.]

On the issue of unfair prejudice, the judge determined that the blown-up photos did not distort the nature of the wounds, acknowledged the grisly nature of the pictures, and ordered that the most offensive ones be reduced in size to 16" x 20" for use in jury deliberations. The photographs were not, in the judge's opinion, flagrantly or deliberately gruesome depictions of the crime. The judge also "carefully observed the jurors and their reactions to the photos.... [T]he jurors showed no signs of being disturbed by the exhibits." Id. at 168. Finally, the judge commented on the nature of unfair prejudice cognizable under FRE 403:

> Relevant evidence is inherently prejudicial; but it is only unfair prejudice, substantially outweighing probative value, which permits exclusion of relevant matter under Rule 403. Unless trials are to be conducted on scenarios, on unreal facts tailored and sanitized for the occasion, the application of Rule 403 must be cautious and sparing.... It is not designed to permit the court to "even out" the weight of evidence, to mitigate a crime.... [Id. at 106.]

See also United States v. Sampson, 335 F.2d 166 (D.Mass. 2004) (photographs of injuries inflicted by the defendant on the deceased held relevant in the penalty phase of a capital murder case to prove necessary mental state and aggravating factors; court excluded many gruesome photos of victims' bodies in advanced stages of decomposition as inflammatory and misleading and refused to admit the bloody clothing of the victims).

2. In capital punishment cases, statements from victims and victims' families about the effect of the defendant's conduct are admitted in the sentencing phase of trial, after guilt has been determined. But in the prosecution of Timothy McVeigh for the 1998 bombing of the federal building in Oklahoma City, statements from victims about the horrific injuries they and others suffered were admitted during the guilt phase of trial. The appellate court acknowledged that "[t]he description of the destruction and carnage following the explosion is the most emotionally powerful of the evidence presented during the guilt phase." United States v. McVeigh, 153 F.3d 1166, 1202-1203 (10th Cir. 1998). Proof of how the crime occurred was, however, held to be probative of the elements of the crimes charged — use of a weapon of mass destruction and a malicious intent to kill. Id. Testimony concerning long-term effects of the bombing, however, such as loss of jobs, attendance at funerals, and the lasting emotional trauma of severe injury, were found to be "not particularly relevant" to the guilt phase and to have emotional content. Any error in the admission of such testimony was, however, held to be harmless. Id. at 1203-1204.

3. There are many cases involving various ways in which parties, and sometimes their lawyers, attempt to destroy, alter, or suppress evidence that is adverse to their position in a lawsuit. Instances of such "spoliation" take many forms — subornation of perjury, threats to and intimidation of witnesses, solicitation of murder of a witness, and alteration or destruction of documents. Evidence of spoliation conduct is generally admissible against the spoliator — giving rise to an inference that evidence was unfavorable to the spoliator's position or to an inference of the party's general consciousness of guilt or liability. See generally Kathleen Kedigh, Spoliation: To the Careless Go the Spoils, 67 U. Mo. (K.C.) L. Rev. 597 (1999) (describing the standards of proof of spoliation and the other remedies available, including discovery sanctions, exclusion of the spoliator's evidence, and a separate tort claim against the spoliator).

For our purposes, evidence of spoliation offered at trial raises recurring questions of relevance and of unfair prejudice under Rule 403. In a civil case involving circumstantial proof that the plaintiff attempted to suborn favorable perjured testimony from a witness, the Third Circuit stated the relevance theory as follows, citing analysis from Wigmore's treatise, existing case law and the text of FRE 401 itself:

> One who believes his own case to be weak is more likely to suborn perjury than one who thinks he has a strong case, and a party knows better than anyone else the truth about his own case. Thus, subornation of perjury by a party is strong evidence that the party's case is weak. Admittedly the conclusion is not inescapable: Parties may be mistaken about the merits or force of their own cases. But evidence need not lead inescapably towards a single conclusion to be relevant. . . . The evidence of subornation here does cast into doubt the merits of [plaintiff's] claim, even if it does not extinguish them. [McQueeney v. Wilmington Trust Co., 779 F.2d 916, 921 (3d Cir. 1985).]

Spoliation behavior is usually illegal and may involve threats of violence or worse. Thus, evidence of such behavior raises a risk of unfair prejudice, in the sense of generating an emotional response against the party as a "bad person," under Rule 403. The court in *McQueeney* reversed the trial court's decision to exclude evidence of the plaintiff's alleged attempt to suborn perjury with the following analysis of its probative value and potential for unfair prejudice:

> Intuition and the unanimity of the commentators and numerous courts that have considered it suggest not only that subornation of perjury is relevant but that it is powerful evidence indeed. . . . The court did not articulate any reasons for its finding of prejudice, and this does not appear to us to be the kind of evidence with obvious or overwhelming potential for unfair prejudice. In the absence of a showing of particularized danger of unfair prejudice, the evidence must be admitted. Were we to rule otherwise, evidence could be excluded on an unfounded fear of prejudice and we would effectively preclude all evidence of subornation of perjury. [Id. at 922-923.]

Consider whether in *McQueeney* the Third Circuit has, in effect, created a precedential ruling of law on the strong probative value and general lack of unfair prejudicial effect of spoliation evidence. We return to the topic of appellate rulings on Rule 403 questions on pages 151-153, infra.

4. In White v. Honeywell, Inc., 141 F.3d 1270 (8th Cir. 1998), the plaintiff filed an action against her employer, Honeywell, for racial harassment and discriminatory discharge under Title VII of the Civil Rights Act. Title VII protects a worker from discriminatory conduct that is so severe and pervasive as "to create an objectively hostile or abusive work environment." As part of her proof, the plaintiff offered a union representative to testify that when he confronted one of White's supervisors, Bill Megarry, with White's complaints about her treatment, Megarry said: "If the dumb n***** doesn't like it she can sign out." At trial, the judge excluded this testimony under Rule 403, stating on the record that it was "so prejudicial and so inflammatory" that it had to be excluded, even though it was of "heavy" relevance. Later the court also acknowledged "it is what is normally called a 'smoking gun' kind of statement" but it was a "very, very exacerbating kind of evidence," and that it was "very prejudicial," and that the decision was "close." White lost at trial and appealed the judgment, asserting, among other things, that exclusion of the Megarry statement was error. The appellate court reviewed a number of the legal

issues in the case as to which the statement was relevant and highly probative, and wrote as follows:

> In a case where race discrimination is the issue, the introduction of alleged racist remarks is not to be unexpected. The possibility that a jury might be so inflamed by the contents of the remark so as to decide the case based on passion, needs to be balanced against the fact that such remarks are potent evidence of attitude and environment. Having already heard the other racially pejorative appellations contained in the evidence, we doubt this additional statement would have been enough to have caused the jury to decide the case on an unfair basis. . . . Here, because such evidence is so highly probative, the potential unfair prejudicial effect, i.e., its tendency to further inflame the jury is not enough to substantially outweigh its probative value.

The appellate court treated the ruling of the district court as an abuse of discretion in weighing probative value versus unfair prejudice. Did the district court also commit an error of law? What effect does the language of the appellate court have on district courts in future Title VII cases?

KEY POINTS

1. An objection made under FRE 403 to an item of evidence requires the trial judge to determine whether admission of the evidence creates any Rule 403 danger to the jury's decision-making process and, if so, whether this danger will substantially outweigh the probative value of the evidence.

2. Probative value means the degree to which the evidence will alter the probabilities of a fact of consequence and an essential element in the case. This is determined primarily by the judge's estimate of the strength of the generalizations connecting the evidence to the disputed issue and by the proponent's need for the evidence.

3. The judge estimates the risk of harm from evidence that bears a Rule 403 danger by predicting the nature of the jury's reaction to the evidence, the degree of that reaction, and the likelihood that the harmful reaction will occur.

4. Because FRE 403's balancing test requires the danger to *substantially* outweigh the probative value, even a very significant risk of danger may not result in exclusion if there are no alternative or less dangerous means of proving the fact of consequence. The court will also use a limiting instruction to reduce the danger in order to admit the evidence.

PROBLEMS

3.5. Return to Problem 3.1, State v. Johnson, at page 129. Do any of the items of evidence present any of the Rule 403 dangers? Can you articulate the nature of the danger, the likelihood that the jury will be affected, and the probable degree of the harmful effect? How would you rule on a FRE 403 objection?

3.6. Return to Problem 3.2, Pedroso v. Driver, at page 129. Do any of the items of evidence present any of the Rule 403 dangers? Can you articulate the nature of the danger, the likelihood that the jury will be affected, and the probable degree of the harmful effect? How would you rule on a FRE 403 objection?

3.7. In Problem 3.2, what if the plaintiffs request that the jury be taken to the scene of the accident in order to view Cedar Street and the gravel shoulder? What arguments could be made in support of and in opposition to this request under FRE 401 and 403?

3.8. Return to Problem 3.3, United States v. Ray, at page 131. The prosecution offers the following evidence:

(a) In October 2000, Ray sold 25,000 shares of Rundown stock one week before a major and abrupt fall in Rundown's share price.

(b) In May 2003, Ray purchased 30,000 shares of Rundown 30 days before the company announced the profitable acquisition of a competitor, an event which caused the stock price to rise by 25 percent.

Will the defense prevail if it objects to this evidence under FRE 403?

3.9. Barbara Ruben has filed suit for legal malpractice against the attorney who represented her in an arbitration proceeding against a drug company for injurious side effects she suffered from one of its products. She alleges that but for the attorney's negligence she would have won her claim against the drug company and would have been awarded $1,000,000 in damages. Ruben cites four specific errors that she claims caused her to lose the arbitration. At trial, Ruben and the attorney will offer competing expert testimony on the two issues in the case: whether the attorney's conduct fell below the applicable standard of care and whether a reasonable fact finder would have arrived at a different result but for the attorney's negligence. The attorney plans to present testimony from the arbitrator who decided Ruben's claim against the drug company. He will testify that his adjudication of that claim would not have been any different had Ruben's attorney performed exactly as she claims he should have performed. Ruben will object under FRE 403. What result?

3.10. K and G were indicted for arson in the burning of a diner that they owned in Great Neck, New York. The report of the Fire Marshal's Office concludes that the diner fire had been intentionally set. The prosecution will prove that K and G owned two diners; that their diner in Westbury, Connecticut, operated at a profit; and that the diner in Great Neck sustained serious losses for several years. The prosecutor wants to introduce the following evidence: the fact that K and G had not paid property taxes on the Great Neck diner for several years, and tax liens had been recorded against it; testimony from a cook at the Westbury diner that K and G asked him whether he knew anyone who would be willing to "start a fire." Are these items admissible? Are they sufficient to send the case to the jury? What if K and G testify that they were about to make a profitable sale of the Great Neck diner?

3.11. Douglas is being prosecuted for burglary. The prosecutor offers W1 to testify that Douglas usually wore a black "New York Yankees" cap and jacket and W2, an expert on gangs, to testify that in Douglas's neighborhood such black clothing is likely to signify membership in a gang. The prosecutor argues that this is relevant circumstantial evidence that Douglas committed the burglary, since gang members are more likely to commit burglaries than people who are not members of gangs.

The defense attorney objects under Rules 401 and 403 to the testimony of W1 and W2 and argues that if the objection is overruled, the defense will have to call W3, another gang expert, to testify that wearing the cap and jacket does not show gang membership and that gang members are no more likely to commit burglary than anyone else. Defense counsel would also call W4, Douglas's brother, to testify that

Douglas is an avid Yankees fan. What arguments can be made for and against admission of the testimony of W1 and W2?

3.12. Cynthia Richards allegedly slipped and fell on a Halloween costume in the "seasonal" area of a Kmart store. She claims that Kmart was negligent in failing to adequately maintain its store. During discovery, a Kmart supervisor testified that the store had no particular schedule for patrolling the store for cleanup, but that all employees are expected to pick up clutter promptly. Ken Ceasar, a Kmart customer service employee on duty the night of Richards's fall, testified that he was in charge of watching the whole floor, walking the aisles, and picking up items that were not supposed to be on the floor "as soon as he discovered them." He had no particular memory of the night in question.

Kmart has filed a motion in limine to exclude a videotape made secretly in the store by an investigator for Richards. The videotape was made one year after the incident, during Halloween season. It is a genuine video, and has not been altered or edited in any way. It shows merchandise on two unidentified store aisles that had fallen to the floor, and it shows Mr. Ceasar ignoring the merchandise and stepping on it, rather than promptly removing it. Prepare arguments for Kmart and for Richards on this motion in limine.

3.13. Denise McCallum is charged with armed robbery for holding up a convenience store at gunpoint. The police found a .38 caliber, "snub-nosed" revolver in a trash can a block away from the convenience store, and the store clerk told police that the robber's gun "looked just like that one." Consider arguments for and against a FRE 403 objection to the admission of the following evidence offered by the prosecutor at trial:

(a)   Testimony of McCallum's roommate that two months before the robbery, she saw a snub-nosed .38 caliber revolver in McCallum's bedroom. Official statistics report that there are known to be at least 25,000 such handguns in the possession of individuals in the city.

(b)   Evidence that McCallum was unemployed for six months before the robbery.

3.   Elaboration of FRE 403: Appellate Review of Judicial Discretion Under FRE 403

Application of FRE 403 calls for the exercise of judicial discretion, meaning that the judge applies criteria and standards that are not mechanical but require the use of *judgment*. The trial court makes judgments that estimate the probability of inferences; that evaluate the nature, likelihood, and degree of dangers to jury decisionmaking; and that compare probative value to those dangers. On appeal, these judgments are reviewed under the abuse of discretion standard, which is a very deferential standard of appellate review. It means that appellate courts will tolerate trial court decisions that the appellate judges would not have made themselves. Reversal is justified only when the trial court "abuses" its discretion:

> Had any one of us been in a position to exercise the discretion committed to a trial judge . . . we would have no hesitancy in stating that the decision would have been otherwise; but as appellate judges we cannot find that the action of the district judge was so unreasonable and so arbitrary as to amount to a prejudicial abuse of the discretion

necessary to repose in trial judges during the conduct of a trial. [Napolitano v. Compania Sud Americana De Vapores, 421 F.2d 382, 384 (2d Cir. 1970).]

There are many reasons why appellate courts defer to the trial courts' judgments under FRE 403. Here are some of them:

(1) *Complexity and Uncertainty.* The Rule 403 balancing test requires complex fact-based judgments unique to each case. Judgments about probative value and the Rule 403 dangers are at best, as we have just discussed above, rough estimates and predictions of effect on the jury's decisionmaking. The estimates that are made in one case may have little bearing in the next. The ultimate standard of "substantially outweighs" also requires balancing where there is no calibration for the weighing process, and the standard is such that precision is not called for. What is "substantial" can vary greatly among judges: "the district court is engaged in a 'comparison of intangibles' and is thus 'afforded a special degree of deference.'" Estate of Moreland v. Dieter, 395 F.3d 747, 755 (7th Cir. 2005).

(2) *Competence.* The trial judge has more experience than appellate judges with making judgments of this kind. The trial judge is also closer to the evidence in the particular case, meaning that the judge has watched its presentation in the context of the entire trial and has observed its effect on the particular jury: "Only in an extreme case are appellate judges competent to second-guess the judgment of the person on the spot, the trial judge." Id.

(3) *Tolerance for Outcomes that Appear Inconsistent.* Under an abuse of discretion standard of review, appellate courts will affirm trial court outcomes that may appear to be inconsistent, even in cases that appear to be similar to the appellate court. That is what it means for the appellate court to "defer" to the trial court's judgment, even when it (or another trial court) might have decided the Rule 403 question differently. Largely because of the factors of competence, complexity, and uncertainty, appellate courts may not be able to know whether outcomes actually are inconsistent, and probably could not create sufficiently detailed precedent necessary to achieve uniform and consistent outcomes among trial courts. The contextual facts of Rule 403 decisions affect the weighing process too greatly.[7] The abuse of discretion standard of review is an acknowledgment of the limits of the knowledge of an outside reviewer.

Most appellate decisions affirm district courts' FRE 403 decisions, whether they admit or exclude the disputed evidence. The standard of review for abuse of discretion is often defined somewhat differently by the Circuit Courts of Appeal. Here is a clear statement of the applicable principles: "Under this standard, we will leave rulings about admissibility of evidence undisturbed unless we are 'left with the definite and firm conviction that the [district] court . . . committed a clear error of judgment in the conclusion it reached upon a weighing of the relevant factors or where it improperly applies the law or uses an erroneous legal standard.'" United States v. Lucas, 357 F.3d 599, 608 (6th Cir. 2004). Thus, there are some errors in applying Rule 403 that appellate courts will hold to be errors of law, such as not giving the terms of the

---

7.   In countering the prosecution's argument that one of its prior opinions conclusively established how a Rule 403 balancing should come out, the Ninth Circuit replied:

[The prior opinion] doesn't help the government because it did not purport to set a minimum level for probative value under Rule 403. Nor could it, as probative value must be weighed against offsetting factors, such as delay, which differ in every case. Moreover, probative value itself can only be determined in light of the evidence and arguments of a particular case. [United States v. Crosby, 75 F.3d 1343, 1348 (9th Cir. 1996).]

rule their legally correct meaning, Blake v. Pellegrino, 329 F.3d 43, 45 (1st Cir. 2003) ("When . . . the admission or exclusion of evidence involves a question of law, such as the proper interpretation of a provision contained in the Federal Rules . . . , we afford de novo review"), or violating a criminal defendant's constitutional right to put on witnesses in his defense, United States v. Turning Bear, 357 F.3d 730, 734 (8th Cir. 2004) (improper exclusion of opinion testimony about a witness's credibility under Rule 403 held to violate the defendant's Fifth and Sixth Amendment rights to present witnesses in his defense).

Some balancing decisions are held to be abuses of discretion when the results are "clear errors of judgment," plainly against the logic and effect of the facts in the case. McQueeney v. Wilmington Trust Co., 779 F.2d 916 (3rd Cir. 1985) (discussed at page 146, supra). And appellate courts also try to ensure that district courts will engage in the full consideration of all the Rule 403 factors. See, e.g., Securities and Exchange Commission v. Peters, 978 F.2d 1162, 1172 (10th Cir. 1992) (failure to adequately consider the possibility of a limiting instruction, contrary to suggestion in the Advisory Committee Note to FRE 403, considered to be significant in finding abuse of discretion); United States v. Cruz-Garcia, 344 F.3d 951, 956 n.2 (9th Cir. 2003) ("While district judges are not required to explain all of their evidentiary rulings, it makes our job easier when they do . . . we are better able to accord it the full deference to which it is due . . . [and] the court may discover that [its] explanation just doesn't make sense . . . [and] may change its view of the matter, avoiding error. . . .").

Sometimes appellate review of FRE 403 decisions does create precedent for district courts to follow. Consider the two cases discussed in Notes 3 and 4 at pages 146-147, supra. The two appellate opinions presented below will give you practice in evaluating probative value and Rule 403 dangers yourself, and in applying the rule's balancing test. You should ask yourself why the appellate court found an abuse of discretion, and whether its decision will have precedential effect.

UNITED STATES v. HITT
981 F.2d 422 (9th Cir. 1992)

KOZINSKI, Circuit Judge.

Dale Lee Hitt was convicted of possessing an unregistered machine gun in violation of 26 U.S.C. §5861(d). The government alleged he had altered a semiautomatic rifle so it would discharge more than one shot per trigger pull — the defining characteristic of a machine gun. 26 U.S.C. §5845(b). The rifle had indeed been modified in a way consistent with the government's theory, though Hitt's lawyer suggested it had been modified by its previous owner. Some internal parts usable for machine guns (but not themselves illegal) were found in a gun case in Hitt's room, but Hitt's lawyer suggested they too might have come from the rifle's previous owner.

The key question, though, was whether the rifle would in fact rapid-fire. The government and Hitt each had their own experts test-fire it: In the government's test, the rifle did fire more than one shot per trigger pull, but when Hitt's expert (witnessed by two police officers) tested it, it didn't. Hitt's expert suggested the gun may have fired automatically in the government's test because of a malfunction, perhaps because the internal parts were dirty, worn or defective. In response, the government introduced a photograph of the rifle which, it argued, showed the rifle was neither dirty, worn nor defective.

Unfortunately, the photograph showed nothing of the gun's interior. All the jury could see was the outside, and not very well at that, as the gun occupied only a small part of the 4"×6" photograph. The rest was taken up by about a dozen other weapons — nine other guns, including three that looked like assault rifles, and several knives — all belonging to Hitt's housemate. Hitt objected to admission of the photograph under Fed. R. Evid. 403, but the district court overruled his objection.

I

A. Under Fed. R. Evid. 402, "[a]ll relevant evidence is admissible," except as otherwise provided. We let jurors see and hear even marginally relevant evidence, because we trust them to weigh the evidence appropriately. Nonetheless, when the probative value of the evidence is "substantially outweighed by the danger of unfair prejudice . . . or misleading the jury," Fed. R. Evid. 403, the evidence must be kept out.

B. The photograph's probative value was exceedingly small. The defense theory was that the gun fired as an automatic because the *internal* parts were dirty, worn or defective. The prosecution understood this too: When the prosecutor cross-examined the defendant's expert, he asked whether there was "exceptional dirt *in*" the rifle, and whether there were "worn or dirty parts *in* that machine."

But the gun's external appearance reveals nothing at all about its internal state. Firearms are designed so the internal parts suffer most of the strain from the discharge. Wear, dirt and defects that affect the internal mechanism generally have no effect on the firearm's appearance; it's not uncommon for a gun that looks clean and in working order to misfire because of dirt or defects inside. Here there was absolutely no indication that the type of wear, dirt or defect Hitt's expert was talking about could be seen by inspecting the outside of the gun.

Moreover, even if the rifle's inside condition were somehow related to its outside appearance, it's virtually impossible to tell whether the gun is clean or dirty from the photograph, in which the rifle is seen from several feet away. The photograph might well have been excludible under Rule 402 as totally irrelevant, had a Rule 402 objection been made.

C. At the same time, the photograph was fraught with the twin dangers of unfairly prejudicing the defendant and misleading the jury. It showed a dozen nasty-looking weapons, which the jury must have assumed belonged to Hitt. The photograph looked like it was taken at Hitt's residence: The guns were laid out in an obviously residential room; the jury knew Hitt was arrested at home, the photograph was talked about in the same breath as two others identified at trial as having been taken in Hitt's bedroom. Moreover, there was no one else the jury could have suspected of owning the guns. Hitt's roommate, who in fact owned all the other weapons, wasn't even mentioned during Hitt's trial. Inferring that all the weapons were Hitt's wasn't just a plausible inference; it was the only plausible inference.

Once the jury was misled into thinking all the weapons were Hitt's, they might well have concluded Hitt was the sort of person who'd illegally own a machine gun, or was so dangerous he should be locked up regardless of whether or not he committed this offense. Rightly or wrongly, many people view weapons, especially guns, with fear and distrust. Like evidence of homosexuality, see, e.g., United States v. Gillespie, 852 F.2d 475, 478 (9th Cir. 1988); Cohn v. Papke, 655 F.2d 191, 194 (9th Cir. 1981), or of past crimes, see, e.g., United States v. Bland, 908 F.2d 471, 473 (9th Cir. 1990), photographs of firearms often have a visceral impact that far exceeds their probative value. See, e.g., United States v. Green, 648 F.2d 587, 595 (9th Cir. 1981) (per curiam). The prejudice is even greater when the picture is not of one gun but of many.

But the photograph could do more than arouse irrational fears and prejudices. It could also lead the jury to draw some perfectly logical — though mistaken — inferences. Hitt's main defense was that he had the bad luck of owning a rifle that was defective or dirty, or perhaps had been modified by its previous owner. A jury that thought Hitt owned almost a dozen guns could very reasonably have viewed this argument with skepticism. The jurors could have inferred that a gun enthusiast like Hitt would be able to tell if the gun had been modified by someone else, or be able to make the modifications himself. Or they could have thought that someone that interested in guns would naturally keep them clean and in good working order. Of course, the jury shouldn't have drawn these inferences, because none of the other guns were Hitt's. Yet the inferences were entirely plausible once the jury concluded Hitt owned the whole arsenal.

D. The district judge has wide latitude in making Rule 403 decisions. But this latitude isn't unlimited. Where the evidence is of very slight (if any) probative value, it's an abuse of discretion to admit it if there's even a modest likelihood of unfair prejudice or a small risk of misleading the jury.

The evidence here was not only highly prejudicial and at most marginally probative — it was also misleading. It's bad enough for the jury to be unduly swayed by something a defendant did; it's totally unacceptable for it to be prejudiced by something he seems to have done but in fact did not. Admitting the photograph, with nothing at all to keep the jury from being misled — no limiting instruction, no redaction — violated Rule 403.

II

Having determined there was error, we must next decide whether it was harmless. There is a conflict in our circuit about the standard of review for harmless error. Some cases require that we affirm only if we can say with "fair assurance" that the error was harmless. This standard seems to have the Supreme Court's blessing. See *Kotteakos v. United States*, 328 U.S. 750, 764-65, 90 L. Ed. 1557, 66 S. Ct. 1239 (1946). Other Ninth Circuit cases compel affirmation if it is "more probable than not" that the error was harmless. See, e.g., United States v. Lui, 941 F.2d 844, 848 (9th Cir. 1991).... [8]

We needn't resolve this conflict here, though, because the error wasn't harmless under either standard. This was a close case: An expert on one side claimed the gun fired more than one shot per trigger pull; an expert on the other (corroborated by two police officers) said it didn't. The photograph may well have made the difference between acquittal and conviction. We can't say it was more probable than not that

---

8.   This isn't just wordplay: A 55% likelihood that the error was harmless qualifies as "more probable than not," but it's hardly a "fair assurance" of harmlessness. Kotteakos defines "fair assurance" as absence of a "grave doubt," 328 U.S. at 765, and a 45% chance that the defendant would have been acquitted but for the error certainly seems like a "grave doubt." While we obviously don't deal in such precise probabilities, "more probable than not" and "fair assurance" can, in some cases, lead to conflicting results.

Hitt would have been convicted without the photograph. A *fortiori*, then, we can't say with "fair assurance" that he would have been convicted without it.

NOTES AND QUESTIONS

1. Judge Kozinski's opinion in *Hitt* relies on two empirical generalizations to estimate probative value and the danger of unfair prejudice. What are they? How does Judge Kozinski know they are valid? Were they the subject of proof at trial? Is there any justification offered for them?

2. Did the prosecution need to use the photograph in *Hitt* to rebut the suggestion that the interior of Hitt's rifle was dirty or worn? Was there alternative, less prejudicial evidence available? For example, where was the rifle itself? Who has the obligation to raise the issue of minimizing the misleading impact of the photograph?

3. Judge Kozinski also stated a general rule for conducting the balancing test under FRE 403: "Where the evidence is of very slight (if any) probative value, it's an abuse of discretion to admit it if there's even a modest likelihood of unfair prejudice or a small risk of misleading the jury." How does this language fit within the table reproduced on page 168, supra? Does it contradict the FRE 403 requirement that the danger "substantially" outweigh the probative value?

OLD CHIEF v. UNITED STATES
519 U.S. 172 (1997)

SOUTER, Justice.

[Petitioner Johnny Lynn Old Chief was arrested in 1993 after a fracas involving at least one gunshot. He was charged with assault with a dangerous weapon, using a firearm in relation to a crime of violence, and with violation of 18 U.S.C. §922(g)(1), which makes it unlawful for anyone "who has been convicted in any court of a crime punishable by imprisonment for a term exceeding one year" to "possess in or affecting commerce, any firearm."[9] In the indictment, Old Chief was charged with having been convicted of an earlier assault causing serious bodily injury. Before trial, he requested that the trial court order the government not to mention any detail regarding the prior conviction except to state that defendant had been convicted of a crime punishable by imprisonment exceeding one year. This was treated as an offer to stipulate and agree that the jury could be instructed that he had been convicted of such a crime as required under §922(g)(1). Old Chief contended that Rule 403 rendered the name and nature of his prior offense unfairly prejudicial, since the jury was likely to generalize his earlier bad act into bad character, and to use his character as increasing the probability that he did the bad act with which he was now charged. The government refused to join in any stipulation and insisted on its right to prove its case its own way. The district court agreed, ruling that if the government did not want to stipulate, it did not have to. At trial, the government introduced a document regarding

---

9.   "[A] crime punishable by imprisonment for a term exceeding one year" is defined to exclude "any Federal or State offenses pertaining to antitrust violations, unfair trade practices, restraints of trade, or other similar offenses relating to the regulation of business practices" and "any State offense classified . . . as a misdemeanor and punishable by a term of imprisonment of two years or less." 18 U.S.C. §921(a)(20).

Old Chief's prior conviction that showed that on December 18, 1988, he did knowingly and unlawfully assault Rory Dean Fenner, said assault resulting in serious bodily injury" for which Old Chief was sentenced to five years' imprisonment.

Justice Souter's opinion noted that the jury's potential use of this prior conviction for a propensity inference would violate FRE 404(b), and thus the admission of Old Chief's specific prior conviction raised a risk of unfair prejudice that must be analyzed under Rule 403.]

As for the analytical method to be used in Rule 403 balancing, two basic possibilities present themselves. An item of evidence might be viewed as an island, with estimates of its own probative value and unfairly prejudicial risk the sole reference points in deciding whether the danger substantially outweighs the value and whether the evidence ought to be excluded. Or the question of admissibility might be seen as inviting further comparisons to take account of the full evidentiary context of the case as the court understands it when the ruling must be made. This second approach would start out like the first but be ready to go further. On objection, the court would decide whether a particular item of evidence raised a danger of unfair prejudice. If it did, the judge would go on to evaluate the degrees of probative value and unfair prejudice not only for the item in question but for any actually available substitutes as well. If an alternative were found to have substantially the same or greater probative value but a lower danger of unfair prejudice, sound judicial discretion would discount the value of the item first offered and exclude it if its discounted probative value were substantially outweighed by unfairly prejudicial risk. As we will explain later on, the judge would have to make these calculations with an appreciation of the offering party's need for evidentiary richness and narrative integrity in presenting a case, and the mere fact that two pieces of evidence might go to the same point would not, of course, necessarily mean that only one of them might come in. It would only mean that a judge applying Rule 403 could reasonably apply some discount to the probative value of an item of evidence when faced with less risky alternative proof going to the same point. Even under this second approach, as we explain below, a defendant's Rule 403 objection offering to concede a point generally cannot prevail over the Government's choice to offer evidence showing guilt and all the circumstances surrounding the offense.[10] . . .

The first understanding of the Rule is open to a very telling objection. That reading would leave the party offering evidence with the option to structure a trial in whatever way would produce the maximum unfair prejudice consistent with relevance. He could choose the available alternative carrying the greatest threat of improper influence, despite the availability of less prejudicial but equally probative evidence. The worst he would have to fear would be a ruling sustaining a Rule 403 objection, and if that occurred, he could simply fall back to offering substitute evidence. This would be a strange rule. It would be very odd for the law of evidence to recognize the danger of unfair prejudice only to confer such a degree of autonomy on the party subject to temptation, and the Rules of Evidence are not so odd.

Rather, a reading of the companions to Rule 403, and of the commentaries that went with them to Congress, makes it clear that what counts as the Rule 403 "probative value" of an item of evidence, as distinct from its Rule 401 "relevance," may be

---

10. While our discussion has been general because of the general wording of Rule 403, our holding is limited to cases involving proof of felon status. On appellate review of a Rule 403 decision, a defendant must establish abuse of discretion, a standard that is not satisfied by a mere showing of some alternative means of proof that the prosecution in its broad discretion chose not to rely upon.

calculated by comparing evidentiary alternatives. The Committee Notes to Rule 401 explicitly say that a party's concession is pertinent to the court's discretion to exclude evidence on the point conceded.

... The Notes to Rule 403 then take up the point by stating that when a court considers "whether to exclude on grounds of unfair prejudice," the "availability of other means of proof may ... be an appropriate factor." ...

Old Chief's proffered admission would, in fact, have been not merely relevant but seemingly conclusive evidence of the element. The statutory language in which the prior-conviction requirement is couched shows no congressional concern with the specific name or nature of the prior offense beyond what is necessary to place it within the broad category of qualifying felonies, and Old Chief clearly meant to admit that his felony did qualify, by stipulating "that the Government has proven one of the essential elements of the offense." App. 7. As a consequence, although the name of the prior offense may have been technically relevant, it addressed no detail in the definition of the prior-conviction element that would not have been covered by the stipulation or admission. Logic, then, seems to side with Old Chief....

There is, however, one more question to be considered before deciding whether Old Chief's offer was to supply evidentiary value at least equivalent to what the Government's own evidence carried. In arguing that the stipulation or admission would not have carried equivalent value, the Government invokes the familiar, standard rule that the prosecution is entitled to prove its case by evidence of its own choice, or, more exactly, that a criminal defendant may not stipulate or admit his way out of the full evidentiary force of the case as the Government chooses to present it.

This is unquestionably true as a general matter. The "fair and legitimate weight" of conventional evidence showing individual thoughts and acts amounting to a crime reflects the fact that making a case with testimony and tangible things not only satisfies the formal definition of an offense, but tells a colorful story with descriptive richness. Unlike an abstract premise, whose force depends on going precisely to a particular step in a course of reasoning, a piece of evidence may address any number of separate elements, striking hard just because it shows so much at once; the account of a shooting that establishes capacity and causation may tell just as much about the triggerman's motive and intent. Evidence thus has force beyond any linear scheme or reasoning, and as its pieces come together a narrative gains momentum, with power not only to support conclusions but to sustain the willingness of jurors to draw the inferences, whatever they may be, necessary to reach an honest verdict. This persuasive power of the concrete and particular is often essential to the capacity of jurors to satisfy the obligations that the law places on them. Jury duty is usually unsought and sometimes resisted, and it may be as difficult for one juror suddenly to face the findings that can send another human being in prison, as it is for another to hold out conscientiously for acquittal. When a juror's duty does seem hard, the evidentiary account of what a defendant has thought and done can accomplish what no set of abstract statements ever could, not just to prove a fact but to establish its human significance, and so to implicate the law's moral underpinnings and a juror's obligation to sit in judgment. Thus, the prosecution may fairly seek to place its evidence before the jurors, as much to tell a story of guiltiness as to support an inference of guilt, to convince the jurors that a guilty verdict would be morally reasonable as much as to point to the discrete elements of a defendant's legal fault.

But there is something even more to the prosecution's interest in resisting efforts to replace the evidence of its choice with admissions and stipulations, for beyond the power of conventional evidence to support allegations and give life to the moral under-pinnings of law's claims, there lies the need for evidence in all its particularity to satisfy the jurors' expectations about what proper proof should be. Some such demands they bring with them to the courthouse, assuming, for example, that a charge of using a firearm to commit an offense will be proven by introducing a gun in evidence. A prosecutor who fails to produce one, or some good reason for his failure, has something to be concerned about. "If [jurors'] expectations are not satisfied, triers of fact may penalize the party who disappoints them by drawing a negative inference against that party." Saltzburg, A Special Aspect of Relevance: Countering Negative Inferences Associated with the Absence of Evidence, 66 Calif. L. Rev. 1011, 1019 (1978) (foot-notes omitted). Expectations may also arise in jurors' minds simply from the experi-ence of a trial itself. The use of witnesses to describe a train of events naturally related can raise the prospect of learning about every ingredient of that natural sequence the same way. If suddenly the prosecution presents some occurrence in the series differ-ently, as by announcing a stipulation or admission, the effect may be like saying, "never mind what's behind the door," and jurors may well wonder what they are being kept from knowing. A party seemingly responsible for cloaking something has reason for apprehension, and the prosecution with its burden of proof may prudently demur at a defense request to interrupt the flow of evidence telling the story in the usual way . . . .

In sum, the accepted rule that the prosecution is entitled to prove its case free from any defendant's option to stipulate the evidence away rests on good sense. A syllogism is not a story, and a naked proposition in a courtroom may be no match for the robust evidence that would be used to prove it. People who hear a story interrupted by gaps of abstraction may be puzzled at the missing chapters, and jurors asked to rest a momen-tous decision on the story's truth can feel put upon at being asked to take responsibility knowing that more could be said than they have heard. A convincing tale can be told with economy, but when economy becomes a break in the natural sequence of narra-tive evidence, an assurance that the missing link is really there is never more than second best.

This recognition that the prosecution with its burden of persuasion needs eviden-tiary depth to tell a continuous story has, however, virtually no application when the point at issue is a defendant's legal status, dependent on some judgment rendered wholly independently of the concrete events of later criminal behavior charged against him. As in this case, the choice of evidence for such an element is usually not between eventful narrative and abstract proposition, but between propositions of slightly varying abstraction, either a record saying that conviction for some crime occurred at a certain time or a statement for admitting the same thing without naming the particular offense. The issue of substituting one statement for the other normally arises only when the record of conviction would not be admissible for any purpose beyond proving status, so that excluding it would not deprive the prosecution of evidence with multiple utility; if, indeed, there were a justification for receiving evidence of the nature of prior acts on some issue other than status (i.e., to prove "motive, opportunity, intent, preparation, plan, knowledge, identity, or absence of mistake or accident," Fed Rule Evid. 404(b)), Rule 404(b) guarantees the opportunity to seek its admission. Nor can it be argued that the events behind the prior conviction are proper nourishment for the jurors' sense of obligation to vindicate the public interest. The issue is not whether concrete details of the prior crime should come to the jurors' attention but whether the name or general character of that crime is to be disclosed. Congress, however, has made it plain that distinctions among generic felonies do not count for this purpose; the fact of the qualifying conviction is alone what matters under the statute....The most the jury needs to know is that the conviction admitted by the defendant falls within the class of crimes that Congress thought should bar a convict from possessing a gun, and this point may be made readily in a defendant's admission and underscored in the court's jury instructions. Finally, the most obvious reason that the general presumption that the prosecution may choose its evidence is so remote from application here is that proof of the defendant's status goes to an element entirely outside the natural sequence of what the defendant is charged with thinking and doing to commit the current offense. Proving status without telling exactly why that status was imposed leaves no gap in the story of a defendant's subsequent criminality, and its demonstration by stipulation or admission neither displaces a chapter from a continuous sequence of conventional evidence nor comes across as an officious substitution, to confuse or offend or provoke reproach.

Given these peculiarities of the element of felony-convict status and of admissions and the like when used to prove it, there is no cognizable difference between the evidentiary significance of an admission and of the legitimately probative component of the official record the prosecution would prefer to place in evidence. For purposes of the Rule 403 weighing of the probative against the prejudicial, the functions of the competing evidence are distinguishable only by the risk inherent in the one and wholly absent from the other. In this case, as in any other in which the prior conviction is for an offense likely to support conviction on some improper ground, the only reasonable conclusion was that the risk of unfair prejudice did substantially outweigh the discounted probative value of the record of conviction, and it was an abuse of discretion to admit the record when an admission was available. What we have said shows why this will be the general rule when proof of convict status is at issue, just as the prosecutor's choice will generally survive a Rule 403 analysis when a defendant seeks to force the substitution of an admission for evidence creating a coherent narrative of his thoughts and actions in perpetrating the offense for which he is being tried.

The judgment is reversed, and the case is remanded to the Ninth Circuit for further proceedings consistent with this opinion.

NOTES AND QUESTIONS

1. Despite the *Old Chief* opinion, some prosecutors continued to offer evidence of the nature of a defendant's prior felony in cases filed under 18 U.S.C. §922(g)(1), and some district courts continued to admit such evidence over a defense offer to stipulate to the defendant's status as a felon. Appellate courts found error when the prior felony would generate the risk of unfair prejudice but in many cases found the error to be harmless due to the "overwhelming evidence" of the defendant's unlawful possession of a firearm. See, e.g., United States v. Harris, 130 F.3d 829, 830 (8th Cir. 1998) ("When evidence of a defendant's guilt is overwhelming, the Old Chief violation is harmless.") In *Harris*, four prior felonies were admitted to prove the defendant's status as a convicted felon, despite his offer to stipulate. A dissenting opinion by Judge Heaney argued that the government should not be entitled to the benefit of the harmless error rule when it violated the straightforward holding of *Old Chief*: "The government can provide no rational argument for failing to abide such a straightforward rule other than to impermissibly destroy a defendant's character and credibility as a witness." Id.

2. Also following *Old Chief*, parties have offered a wide variety of stipulations to avoid the admission of evidence that bears the danger of unfair prejudice. In the majority of cases, trial courts have rejected such stipulations and appellate courts have refused to extend *Old Chief* beyond its holding on the issue of "status" §922(g)(1). See, e.g., United States v. Hall, 152 F.3d 381, 401 (5th Cir. 1998) (defendant's offer to stipulate to the identity of a murder victim and the cause of death did not render irrelevant photographs of victim's body in a decomposed state after defendant had buried it); United States v. Crowder, 141 F.3d 1202 (D.C. Cir. 1998) (defendant's offer to stipulate to intent element in crime of possession of drugs with intent to distribute does not render government's evidence of a similar crime inadmissible to prove intent); United States v. McVeigh, 153 F.3d 1166, 1200 n.24 (10th Cir. 1998) (court rejected defendant's offer to stipulate that eight law enforcement officers were killed in the course of their duties in the bombing of the Oklahoma City federal building). But see United States v. Merino-Balderrama, 146 F.3d 758 (9th Cir. 1998) (in a prosecution for possession of child pornography videos, error to allow the jury to watch the videos where defendant offered to stipulate to their content but denied ever watching them and thus denied the requisite element of "knowing" what the the videos were. The court held that the videos were highly prejudical and that the box covers of the videos were equally probative on the issue of knowledge since they depicted child pornography and defendant admitted he had seen the covers).

3. In *Old Chief*, Justice Souter's opinion defines concepts of " evidentiary richness" and " narrative integrity" as factors that can increase the probative value of an item of evidence. Use of these factors in making and reviewing decisions under FRE 403 would not seem to be limited to §922(g)(1) cases. For example, in United States v. Vallejo, 237 F.3d 1008 (9th Cir. 2001), defendant Vallejo was charged with illegal importation of marijuana in a car he was driving from Mexico to the United States. Vallejo claimed that he did not know that the packages of marijuana were hidden inside the vehicle. The Ninth Circuit held that it was error for the district court to exclude Vallejo's evidence of the identity of the person who he claimed had hidden the drugs in the car, intending to smuggle them into the United States himself. The court made the point that the need to satisfy juror expectations added to the probative value of this evidence. The court wrote: " Vallejo . . . was not allowed to provide an answer for the jurors' question: 'If defendant did not know there were drugs in the car and did not place them there himself, who did?'" Id. at 1023.

PROBLEMS

3.14. D is charged with knowingly transmitting two images of child pornography through interstate commerce via computer. He denies making any such transmission and claims that many other people use his computer. To prevent the jury from viewing the two images, the defendant offers to stipulate that the two images constitute child pornography. Should the trial judge accept this stipulation or permit the jury to see the images?

3.15. Robin Lake was tried and convicted of possession of cocaine with the intent to sell. The cocaine was found in her car by CHIPS Officer Hammett in a search he conducted after he had stopped Lake and placed her under arrest. At trial, Hammet testified that Lake had appeared " extremely nervous" when he placed her under arrest and told her to open the car to retrieve her belongings. Lake's nervousness was repeatedly emphasized in the prosecutor's closing argument as indicating she did not want the drugs to be discovered.

Lake sought to explain her nervousness, and counter the inference of consciousness of guilt, by testifying that she had been in prison several years earlier for bank fraud conspiracy, that she had been sexually assaulted by male guards while she was an inmate, and that this was the cause of her nervousness when she learned she was under arrest. (In fact, Lake had been paid a $500,000 settlement by the federal government because of the attacks.) The district court excluded this testimony under FRE 403, holding that the defense " can certainly have her explain that she was nervous because she was afraid she was about to be arrested and she didn't want to be arrested. But that doesn't mean she gets to tell about all the intimate horrible details of prison . . . .we're not going to turn this into a demonstration that we've got a Mother Teresa here, who is a national TV star, who was sexually abused in prison. None of those things have anything to do with this case." Lake appeals her conviction and cites as one error the exclusion of her testimony. How should the appellate court rule on this claim of error?

4.   Reflection on Judicial Discretion to Admit and Exclude Evidence

The exercise of judicial discretion required by FRE 403 allows the trial court considerable freedom to admit or exclude evidence. As we have stated above, appellate courts treat lower court Rule 403 decisions with great deference, and appellate findings of abuse of discretion are infrequent. As you study the major rules of exclusion in this casebook, you will see that these rules — the character rule, the other relevance rules, the hearsay rule, the best evidence rule and the rules of privilege — do not grant such explicit discretion to the trial court. Rather, these exclusionary rules, and their exceptions, are so-called "bright line" rules. Some of these, such as the rule prohibiting the use of extrinsic evidence to prove specific acts that impeach a witness's truthfulness, are truly "bright line." Others control the admission/exclusion decision with doctrinal definitions and categories.

The categorical rules operate in two ways. The hearsay rule, for example, establishes categories that require judicial factfinding; the character rule establishes categories of permissible uses of specific acts that require the trial judge to identify particular noncharacter theories of relevance. Under both types of categorical rules, the trial judge's task is to determine whether the proffered item of evidence fits within a doctrinal category. This decision of whether the item "fits" usually is determinative of admission or exclusion. Thus, discretion — the estimation and balancing of probative value and dangers to jury decisionmaking — is not exercised under these categorical rules. This is not because the categorical terms are applied mechanically; they require very careful thinking by the trial judge. But it is a different kind of thinking, and it can be treated less deferentially by appellate courts if they treat the application of the categorical term as a question of law.

As you study these major exclusionary rules, you should consider the justifications for their bright-line or categorical nature as opposed to the discretionary standards of Rule 403. Think in terms of how best the exclusionary policy of the rule can be enforced; which type of rule best serves the goals of accurate outcomes, fairness to the parties, and an efficient judicial system; and which type of rule judges are most competent to decide and to review. You will also see that there are some fairly recent trends in judicial application of the major exclusionary rules that erode their bright-line nature. Trial courts are making estimates of probative value and using this factor to decide whether admission under the categorical rule is justified. Appellate court deference to this non-rule-based exercise of discretion in admission/exclusion decisions, combined with the harmless error doctrine, leaves these decisions unreviewed.

More will be said about these categorical rules, and their erosion through the introduction of discretionary thinking, in Chapters Five and Eight, infra.

C. REFLECTION ON THE BASIC CONCEPT OF RELEVANCY

The essence of the Federal Rules' approach to relevancy is that evidence is relevant if it has the capacity to influence a disinterested person on a fact of consequence. What the infinitive *to influence* means in this context is somewhat vague, though. We know when we have a sense of being "convinced" or "persuaded" or of being placed in "doubt" by an argument or by evidence. But must an analysis of the influence of evidence stop at such an ephemeral point? Some have argued that it must. See, e.g., Henry M. Hart, Jr. and John T. McNaughton, Evidence and Inference in the Law, 87 Daedalus 40, 44 (Fall 1958):

> The adjudicative facts of interest to the law, being historical facts, will rarely be triable by the experimental methods of the natural sciences.... For the most part the law must settle disputed questions of adjudicative fact by reliance upon the ambiguous implications of non-fungible "traces" — traces on human brains and on pieces of paper and traces in the form of unique arrangements of physical objects.

Perhaps Hart and McNaughton are correct that the law must be satisfied with evidence in the form of "traces on human brains." But must the implications of these traces be ambiguous? There has been great interest recently in efforts to articulate in a more rigorous fashion what it means for evidence to have persuasive force. These efforts have centered primarily on the implications of a theorem of mathematics known as Bayes' Theorem, which provides a rigorous method for combining a person's assessment of the probability of an event with new evidence concerning that event to arrive at a new assessment of the probability of the event. For what follows we are indebted to Professor Richard Lempert's work on Bayes' Theorem, which can be found in Richard Lempert, Modeling Relevance, 75 Mich. L. Rev. 1021 (1977). That work was heavily influenced by Professor John Kaplan's article, Decision Theory and the Factfinding Process, 20 Stan. L. Rev. 1065 (1968), which in turn was heavily influenced by Vaughn C. Ball, The Moment of Truth: Probability Theory and Standards of Proof, 14 Vand. L. Rev. 807 (1961). Some commentators have proposed alternatives to Bayes' Theorem, see Jonathan L. Cohen, The Probable and the Provable (1977), while others have critiqued its application to jury reasoning, among them William L. Twining and Alex Stein, Evidence and Proof, The International Library of Essays in Law and Legal Theory (1992); Ronald J. Allen, Factual Ambiguity and a Theory of Evidence, 88 Nw. U. L. Rev. 604 (1994); Paul Bergman and Al Moore, Mistrial by Likelihood

Ratio: Bayesian Analysis Meets the F-Word, 13 Cardozo L. Rev. 589 (1991); Craig R. Callen, Notes on a Grand Illusion: Some Limits on the Use of Bayesian Theory in Evidence Law, 57 Ind. L.J. 1 (1982); Richard D. Friedman, Infinite Strands, Infinitesimally Thin: Storytelling, Bayesianism, Hearsay, and Other Evidence, 14 Cardozo L. Rev. 79 (1992); David Kaye, Naked Statistical Evidence, 89 Yale L.J. 601 (1980); Nancy Pennington and Reid Hastie, A Cognitive Theory of Juror Decision Making: The Story Model, 13 Cardozo L. Rev. 519 (1991); Bernard Robertson and G. A. Vignaux, Probability — The Logic of the Law, 13 Oxford J. of Legal Studies 457 (1993).

English mathematician Thomas Bayes (1702-1761) demonstrated that the following formula is derivable from the axioms of conventional probability. In the formula,

O_G	=	odds of guilt or liability
$O_{G/E}$	=	odds of guilt or liability given the new evidence (E)
$P_{E/G}$	=	probability of obtaining the evidence in question if the person is guilty or liable
$P_{E/\text{not } G}$	=	probability of obtaining the evidence in question if the individual is not guilty or liable

The formula is:

$$O_{G/E} = \frac{P_{E/G}}{P_{E/\text{not } G}} \times O_G$$

This formula expresses that the odds of guilt or liability after evidence is received are determined by the relationship between the probability of obtaining the evidence if the person is guilty or liable and the probability of obtaining the evidence if the person is not guilty or liable. In other words, to go from a prior assessment of the odds of liability to an assessment in light of the new evidence requires that the prior assessment be modified by the likelihood that the evidence would have been presented at trial if the person is liable as compared to the likelihood that it would have been presented if the person is not liable.

Do not let the discussion of probability theory obscure an important insight here. What makes evidence "relevant" is its capacity to influence the fact finder. That, in turn, is a function of the probability of receiving the evidence if the person is liable as compared to the probability of receiving the evidence if the person is not liable. Take a simple example. Suppose that in a burglary case, the prosecution wished to introduce evidence that the defendant does not like the Chicago Bears. If the defendant is guilty, the probability of receiving this evidence is a function of the proportion of burglars who are Chicago Bears fans, which we shall assume is .95 (at least in Chicago). The probability of receiving the evidence if the defendant is not guilty is a function of the proportion of nonburglars who are Chicago Bears fans, and there is no reason to think that proportion would differ from the proportion of burglars who are fans of the Bears. Thus the ratio of these probabilities (.95/.95) is 1.0, and 1.0 multiplied by the prior odds of guilt will result in no change in those odds. Therefore, this evidence is irrelevant because it has no impact on the assessment of the odds of guilt.

We do not suggest that this way of viewing relevance has any value other than perhaps explaining how some rational people may evaluate evidence. Even as an explanatory effort, however, it has serious limitations. The formula requires that the decision-maker have a preliminary assessment of the odds of guilt or liability *before* the receipt of an item of evidence that is subjected to Bayesian analysis, and it is unclear what that should be in our system of trials (especially criminal trials). Davis v. State, 476 N.E.2d 127, 138 (2d Dist. Ct. App. Ind. 1985) (in applying Bayes' Theorem, expert witnesses, who testified to the probabilities of parentage derived from blood test evidence, properly employed a neutral prior probability (50/50) instead of a prior probability variable based upon circumstantial, nontest evidence of the defendants' parentage). In addition, the probabilities associated with most evidence will virtually always defy quantification. More troublesome still, Bayes' Theorem requires that the decision-maker evaluate each bit of evidence as it is introduced, rather than permitting the decision-maker to hear all the evidence and deliberate on all of it at the conclusion of the trial process. At trial, by contrast, jurors are explicitly told not to form any conclusions until all the evidence is in. The reason for this is the belief that once opinions are formed they are hard to change. Individuals will rationalize new evidence they hear to make it consistent with their preconceptions. To the extent this is true, the party first producing evidence would have a great advantage at trial, since presumably that evidence will tend to establish that party's case. And, while it may be correct that if the likelihood ratio is 1 after the correct questions about the probabilities of obtaining evidence are asked, it is not clear that correct answers to those questions can be obtained in litigation. Care must be taken in thinking about relevancy and Bayes' Theorem.

Consider evidence that a defendant (charged with bank robbery) was running from the scene of the bank robbery that took place close to a train station. Fleeing might mean that the defendant robbed the bank and is trying to escape. It also might mean that she is trying to catch a train. Assume that it could be established as an empirically valid proposition that 70 percent of the people running from the crime are running because of guilt. The probability of obtaining the evidence of running if the defendant is guilty is .7; the probability of obtaining the evidence if defendant is innocent is .3. So far, the prosecution would be able to show the relevance of the evidence of running. Now suppose that defendant establishes that 70 percent of the people near a train station who are running are doing so to catch a train. Now, is the probability of obtaining the evidence of running if defendant is innocent also .7? If so, is the likelihood ratio under Bayes' Theorem 1? The trouble with relying on this ratio in litigation is that these are not the only two explanations of people running that will occur to the jury, and these other explanations could change the ratio. Many other evidentiary facts in the case, such as how fast or slow the defendant is running, or what she is wearing, will also affect the probabilities of each explanation of what the running means. And, of course, there are very few statements about the probabilities of human behavior that can be established with such precision. In most cases, the likelihood ratio cannot be established definitively and the judge will admit the evidence, leaving it up to the jury to interpret or explain it.

Bayes' Theorem, in short, is an interesting way of thinking about the idea of relevance, even if it is not completely compatible with the trial process. It also provides a useful way to think about the grounds of exclusion under the Federal Rules. Unfair prejudice, confusion, or misleading of the jury exists whenever the jury forms a likelihood ratio that is quite different from what the "true" likelihood ratio is. This can occur whenever the jury misevaluates either component of the ratio for whatever reason.

There is another way to think about the grounds for exclusion that also involves some simple mathematics and that permits taking into account a fact finder's preferences. "Unfair prejudice" describes the situation where the preferences of the fact finder are affected for reasons essentially unrelated to the persuasive power of the evidence to establish facts of consequence in the case. Assume that the defendant in the burglary case has been arrested for other offenses in the past and assume further that a prior record has no empirical relationship with the probability that a person has committed a subsequent crime. Suppose evidence of the prior record is admitted at trial. One effect of that evidence may be to reduce the fact finder's concern with accuracy. Given that the defendant has had previous brushes with the law, the fact finder may then think that even if the defendant did not commit the crime charged she undoubtedly committed others, and consequently it would do no great wrong to convict her even if she is innocent of this particular charge. Given the defendant's background, in other words, the "disutility" (i.e., cost) of a wrongful conviction is not what it would be with a person who has never been in trouble with the law.

A fact finder's appraisal of the disutility of one type of error as compared to another can be articulated algebraically. We are indebted to John Kaplan, Decision Theory and the Factfinding Process, 20 Stan. L. Rev. 1065 (1968) for much of what follows. In the formula,

D_g = the disutility of acquitting a guilty person or returning a wrongful verdict for a defendant in a civil case

D_i = the disutility of convicting an innocent person or of returning a wrongful verdict for a plaintiff in a civil case

P = the probability necessary to return a verdict of guilty or liability in a civil case

A rational decision-maker presumably decides issues in such a way as to minimize the disutilities associated with the decision. When the relevant facts are known, that is a simple matter, but in the context of trials the facts are not known with certainty. Therefore, a way must be found to take account of that uncertainty. This can be done through the concept of "expected disutility," which is the disutility associated with a decision multiplied by the probability that the decision is factually accurate. Suppose that there is a disutility of 10 (whatever the units of "disutility" may be) associated with convicting an innocent person and a disutility of 1 associated with acquitting a guilty person. How should a decision-maker decide when faced with imperfect knowledge? The formula below provides some guidance:

$$P > \frac{1}{1 + \frac{D_g}{D_i}}$$

Plug the figures suggested above into the formula. If $D_g = 1$ and $D_i = 10$, then:

$$P > \frac{1}{1 + \frac{1}{10}} = .91$$

In a criminal case, then, if it is 10 times worse to convict an innocent person than to acquit a guilty person, a jury should vote for conviction only when guilt has been established to a probability of at least .91. Compare this to civil cases. The normal view in civil cases is that the disutility of a wrongful verdict for a defendant is equal to that of a wrongful verdict for a plaintiff. Thus $D_g = D_i$ and the formula reduces to $P > .5$, which is the normal burden of proof in civil cases.

Suppose that in a certain case there is no disutility in convicting an innocent man. Suppose that a heinous crime has outraged a community and someone — it really does not matter much who — must be punished in order to expiate the anger and fear of the citizens. In such a case, as the value of D_i nears zero, the denominator of the fraction becomes a very large number. Therefore, in order to convict there need only be a probability $P > 1/$ [a very large number], which equals a very *small* probability. Anyone will do, in short, so long as someone is sacrificed to the community's needs.

Now consider the other side of the coin, where it is the sense of a community that a person has already been punished enough for her digressions. For example, consider the case of the president of a small-town bank who has embezzled funds and been caught. The person has lost her job and has been disgraced publicly. When brought to trial, the jurors may feel that no more punishment is due. In the formula, D_g (the disutility of acquitting a guilty person) falls to zero. Consequently, the denominator of the fraction approaches 1, and thus the probability needed to convict, P, becomes 1.0. This cannot occur, and the individual is acquitted.

Obviously, these examples and this way of thinking about preferences and prejudice only roughly mirror what occurs in the real world, yet they provide some insights into the decision-making process. The effective advocate will not only provide a compelling factual story, but in addition will, to the extent permitted (and much greater latitude will be given in criminal cases), attempt to demonstrate why the costs of a verdict for that advocate's adversary are too high. To the extent a party is able to do this, the scales have been tilted in that party's favor.

Whether or not this discussion has been enlightening about the reality of the trial process, it is at least instructive about one meaning of the word *prejudice* in FRE 403. "Prejudicial" information is that which would tend to make the fact finder balance the disutilities of wrongful decisions inconsistently with the requirements of law. In other words, it would be prejudicial in a civil case to provide information that would tend to influence the jury to think it five times worse to return a wrongful plaintiff's verdict than a wrongful defendant's verdict. Similarly, because in criminal cases the law requires proof beyond a reasonable doubt, it would be prejudicial to admit evidence that would cause the fact finder in a criminal case to think it equally bad to acquit a guilty person as to convict an innocent person.

Note, however, that while this discussion may be enlightening about prejudice, it says very little about when prejudice "substantially outweighs" probative value, which is the standard under FRE 403, and we have little to add to our previous discussion of that issue. To briefly reiterate, there are three variables: the nature of the inappropriate effect (an effect that cannot be logically justified); the strength of the judge's conviction that the evidence will have that inappropriate effect on the jury; and the magnitude of the illogical or harmful effect. A judge will not know for certain that a jury will be inappropriately influenced by evidence; the judge can only appraise the likelihood that the evidence will have that effect. Moreover, it seems reasonable to think that some evidence will be more powerful than other evidence in its harmful impact on the jury.

We suggest that "substantiality" is some mix of these two variables. The trial judge could be convinced beyond a reasonable doubt that the evidence would have a serious harmful effect. Alternatively, the judge could conclude that there is some small possibility that the evidence would have some slight improper effect, thus moving the jury away from an accurate outcome. For most judges, "substantiality" probably lies somewhere between these two extremes.

CHAPTER FOUR

LAYING THE FOUNDATION FOR PROOF

There is a universal principle of evidence law that no evidence is admissible until it is first shown to be what its proponent claims that it is. This universal requirement is sometimes called *laying the foundation* for proof. Remember that in the *Johnson* case the judge instructed the jury that "[e]vidence consists of testimony of witnesses, writings, material objects, or anything presented to the senses and offered to prove the existence or non-existence of a fact" (page 62, line 12, supra). In this chapter, you will study the rules that establish what foundation is required to secure the admission into evidence for these various types. Section A discusses the necessary foundation for introducing testimony from witnesses (FRE 601-606). Section B presents the various foundational requirements for exhibits, including real, demonstrative, documentary, and electronic evidence (FRE 901 and 902). Section C concerns the cluster of rules commonly known as "the best evidence rule" (FRE 1001-1008). Sections D and E focus on FRE 104, the rule allocating factfinding on preliminary foundational questions between judge and jury.

The foundational requirements differ for each type of evidence, but in all cases the proponent must present foundational facts that are adequate under the rules presented in this chapter. Failure to do so may give rise to an objection from the opponent and then to exclusion by the court. Thus the effect of these foundational requirements is to give the judge additional control — beyond FRE 401, 402, and 403 — over what evidence the advocates may present to the jury and to increase the information available to the jury for its decision-making process. Satisfaction of the foundational requirements does not guarantee admission either. Other exclusionary rules, to be studied in subsequent chapters, may still apply.

A. LAYING THE FOUNDATION FOR WITNESSES

Witnesses are produced at trial to present information to the trier of fact. Our system of proof assumes that the trier can evaluate the credibility of witnesses and can reconstruct events based on the information they present in court. The foundational requirements for witnesses are set forth in FRE 601 (competency), FRE 602 (personal knowledge), FRE 603 (oath or affirmation to testify truthfully), and FRE 605 and 606 (incompetency of judge and jurors to testify in the case before them). These rules, in effect, define what a "witness" is. The Advisory Committee Notes to each of these rules contain useful discussion of the principles underlying each foundational requirement. The rules regulating the admission of lay and expert opinion testimony of witnesses are contained in Article VII of the Federal Rules and will be discussed in Chapter Nine.

1. FRE 601

RULE 601. GENERAL RULE OF COMPETENCY

Every person is competent to be a witness except as otherwise provided in these rules. However, in civil actions and proceedings, with respect to an element of a claim or defense as to which State law supplies the rule of decision, the competency of a witness shall be determined in accordance with State law.

2. Interpretation and Illustration of FRE 601

FRE 601 states a bold general assumption: that every person is competent to testify as a witness. The boldness of this assumption is best understood against the historical background of the strict regulations imposed at common law, and later in most states by statute. These were rules of competency that kept certain categories of persons off the witness stand entirely. Spouses were incompetent to testify for or against a spouse. Persons interested in the suit, including parties, could not testify. Atheists were categorically held to be incompetent, as were felons, young children, and the mentally ill. All of these categories were, as you can see, aimed at persons who judges and legislators thought were not trustworthy. It was assumed that they either possessed a motive for coloring the facts in favor of their interest, or suffered defects of character, youth, or mental capacity that created risks of untrustworthiness. In addition, the opponent could challenge a witness on grounds of individual incompetence. The party presenting the witness would then have to demonstrate that the witness did possess what are commonly called the four testimonial qualities — the ability to observe events, to remember them, to relate them accurately, and to understand the duty to tell the truth.

The first sentence of FRE 601 abolishes all categorical grounds of incompetence, subject only to the limit that where state law furnishes the rule of decision in federal court, a state-created category of incompetency will be applied. FRE 605 and 606 do prohibit the presiding trial judge and members of the sitting jury from testifying in the case at issue. These prohibitions are established not because of doubts about the trustworthiness of such witnesses, but because of the procedural complications and the potentially unfair prejudicial effect such testimony would be likely to have on the (other) jurors.

In general, however, the Advisory Committee Note to FRE 601 makes clear that, apart from the judge and the jury, people who witnessed relevant events cannot be prevented from testifying solely because of their status or their interest in the case. Note, however, that the fact of a witness's status (a felony conviction or a spousal or familial relationship to a party) or a witness's interest in the outcome of a case might still affect that witness's truthfulness. Thus such facts are relevant, and are usually admissible, to impeach the credibility of the testifying witness, as you will see in Chapter Seven. The Federal Rules of Evidence permit the jury to decide whether such status or interest affects a witness's credibility, whereas the categorical incompetencies of statutes and the common law would have withheld that witness from the jury entirely.

3. Elaboration of FRE 601: Challenging a Witness's Mental Competency

The Advisory Committee Note to FRE 601 states that "[n]o mental or moral qualifications for testifying as a witness are specified." FRE 603, which you should read, abolishes the moral qualification of taking a religious oath in favor of acknowledgment of the secular obligation to testify truthfully. Thus it is correct to say that there are no moral, and certainly no religious, qualifications to be a witness. But can it be correct that "every person" is competent to testify, no matter what that person's physical or mental condition? Is there no longer any authority under FRE 601 for a federal judge to decide that an individual witness's testimonial abilities are so impaired — either temporarily or permanently — that the witness should not testify? For example, in the *Johnson* case, the defense considered calling another inmate, Grant, to testify about a prior incident involving Officer Walker. Grant had recently been found mentally incompetent to stand trial because he was unable to understand the nature of the proceedings against him or to aid in his own defense. Because of this mental condition, the defense conceded that Grant "rambled all over the place" and had a very short attention span. The court held as follows:

> Well, competent to stand trial and competent to take an oath are not the same. And if anything I would say standing trial involved a good many more considerations. If Grant appears to be reasonably rational as the questioning proceeds, he can testify. If his testimony comes out as gibberish, of course, we can terminate the testimony. [Transcript, People v. Johnson]

The court in *Johnson* had power under Cal. Evid. Code §701 to disqualify a witness "incapable of expressing himself concerning the matter so as to be understood . . . or . . . incapable of understanding the duty of a witness to tell the truth."

Since the authority to disqualify is not mentioned in FRE 601, the federal circuit courts of appeal have taken two primary approaches to challenges to the competency of a witness like Grant. In United States v. Ramirez, 871 F.2d 582, 584 (6th Cir. 1989), the Court held that FRE 601 could not be used to evaluate the ability of persons to testify:

> The authority of the court to control the admissibility of the testimony of persons so impaired in some manner that they cannot give meaningful testimony is to be found outside of Rule 601. For example, the judge always has the authority under Rule 403 to balance the probative value of testimony against its prejudicial effect. Similarly, under Rule 603, the inability of a witness to take or comprehend an oath or affirmation will allow the judge to exclude that person's testimony. An argument can also be constructed that a person might be impaired to the point that he would not be able to satisfy the "personal knowledge" requirement of Rule 602.

Other courts have asserted that, under FRE 601, the trial court retains the discretion it had under common law to decide whether an individual witness is competent to testify. See, e.g., United States v. Devin, 918 F.2d 280, 291-292 (1st Cir. 1990). Under either view, the trial court may need to hold a hearing on the competency issue at which the witness in question would be placed under oath and examined out of the presence of the jury. Presumably, other testimony, such as that from treating physicians, could also be taken. The judge has ample authority to hold such a hearing under FRE 104(c) and would decide the preliminary question of incompetence under FRE 104(a) by a preponderance of the evidence. In Section D of this chapter, we will discuss this fact-finding process in greater detail.

Appellate courts seldom overturn a trial court's finding that a witness is competent to testify, emphasizing that most disabling factors should be treated as matters affecting credibility for the jury to resolve, not as matters of competence. For example, in United States v. Cassidy, 2002 U.S. App. LEXIS 18298 (4th Cir. 2002) the appellate court stated the following:

> At various times during his testimony, the witness spoke very slowly and nodded and chuckled inappropriately to the jury. The court excused the jury and instructed the witness to stop acting in this manner. During voir dire examination the behavior of the witness became even more bizarre. He had trouble recalling certain events, contradicted himself repeatedly, and seemed to be disoriented. At one point he could not tell the court for several minutes what day of the week it was....The court decided to deny the motion to strike...[and] noted that the erratic behavior of the witness would weigh heavily against his credibility in the eyes of the jury....The district court did not clearly abuse its discretion in admitting the testimony....Where there is doubt, we will respect the district court's finding that sufficient credibility existed to permit the jury to 'hear the testimony for what it is worth.'"

Also, appellate courts may reverse the trial court's exclusion of the testimony of a witness who had been found insane and incompetent to stand trial if there is evidence in the record that the witness had sufficient memory, understood the oath, and could communicate what he saw. United States v. Lightly, 677 F.2d 1027, 1028 (4th Cir. 1982).

Child witnesses can raise troublesome issues of competence with regard to their ability to remember events and to relate them accurately and truthfully. A federal statute establishes a presumption of competency for children who are victims of crimes of abuse and who have witnessed crimes against others. 18 U.S.C. §3509(c). A competency examination may be held only if compelling reasons exist and only upon motion by the opposing party and an offer of proof of incompetency. United States v. Walker, 261 F.Supp.2d 1154, 1155 (D.N.D. 2003) (defendant's request for a competency hearing on his claim that the child witness was "merely repeating a well-drilled narration of the alleged incident without understanding it" rejected under the statute as supported by no evidence or offer of proof of any coaching.) Such examination is conducted primarily by the court away from the jury, with attorneys but not parties present. The questions focus on the child's "ability to understand and answer simple questions." 18 U.S.C. §3509(c)(8) (1996). In United States v. Allen J., 127 F.3d 1292, 1296 (10th Cir. 1997), the court held that the child witness's failure to respond to the trial judge's questions, her wrong answers to some of counsel's questions, and her nonsensical answers to others raised questions of credibility, not competence.

KEY POINTS

1. FRE 601 establishes that all persons are competent to testify. In most cases, facts that bear on competency are treated as affecting the weight of the witness's testimony but do not disqualify the witness.

2. Particular challenges to the competency of individual witnesses may be resolved as a matter of the trial court's Rule 601 discretion, or under FRE 602, FRE 603, and FRE 403.

4. FRE 602

RULE 602.   LACK OF PERSONAL KNOWLEDGE

A witness may not testify to a matter unless evidence is introduced sufficient to support a finding that the witness has personal knowledge of the matter. Evidence to prove personal knowledge may, but need not, consist of the witness' own testimony. This rule is subject to the provisions of rule 703, relating to opinion testimony by expert witnesses.

5.   Interpretation and Illustration of FRE 602

FRE 602 mandates that before a witness may testify about a matter, the witness must be shown to have personal knowledge of that matter by evidence "sufficient to support a finding." The requirement that witnesses must "know" the matters about which they testify as a result of their own sensory perception is essential to our system of proof: Witnesses perceive real world events and describe these events to the jury, and the jury perceives the witnesses and evaluates whether or not to rely on them.

a.   The Requirement of Personal Knowledge

The most common kind of personal knowledge is visual perception, making the witness an eyewitness or *percipient witness* who was present at an event or occurrence. For example, the prosecutor in the *Johnson* case referred to the correctional officers as percipient witnesses because they were present at the incident and perceived it (page 6, line 3, supra). However, knowledge can be based on any of the senses. Inmate Green, for example, testified to what he heard at the vent between his cell and defendant Johnson's (page 48, line 1, supra). FRE 701, the rule regulating the admission of opinion testimony from lay witnesses, also contains a personal knowledge requirement. If a witness's testimony is *not* based on personal knowledge, then it is probably based either on speculation or on what someone else has said to the witness, which makes it disguised hearsay, as will be discussed in Chapter Eight.

b.   The Requirement of Evidence Sufficient to Support a Finding

As FRE 602 makes explicit, the proponent of a witness must produce evidentiary facts that the judge finds are "sufficient to support a finding" of personal knowledge; that is, a jury could *reasonably find* that it is more probable than not that the witness has personal knowledge. Note that this is the same standard applied to preliminary questions of fact under FRE 104(b) and under FRE 901 as well, as you will see in Sections E and B of this chapter. Under all of these evidence rules, the trial court screens the proponent's evidence by applying the same "sufficiency" standard of proof. If a "sufficient" showing of personal knowledge is still disputed by the opponent, then final resolution of the question is given to the jury as part of its decision-making role.

To satisfy the sufficiency standard, usually all the proponent needs to do is to ask whether the witness did in fact see or hear the matters that are about to be described to the jury. FRE 602 provides that the witness's own testimony — "I saw that" — will suffice. Additional corroboration that the witness did in fact perceive the matter is admissible, but would not be necessary to satisfy the sufficiency standard. A jury could reasonably believe the witness's testimony, and the judge may not evaluate credibility. The Supreme Court articulated this standard in the context of a discussion of FRE 104(b):

> In determining whether the Government has introduced sufficient evidence to meet Rule 104(b), the trial court *neither weighs credibility nor makes a finding* that the Government has proved the conditional fact by a preponderance of the evidence. The court simply examines all the evidence in the case and decides whether the jury *could reasonably find* the conditional fact . . . by a preponderance of the evidence. [Huddleston v. United States, 485 U.S. 681, 690 (1988) (emphasis added).]

And commentators have described the "sufficiency" standard similarly:

> The concept of sufficiency does not concern the question whether the trier actually will make such a finding, that is, [it does not concern] ordinary questions of credibility or the persuasive effect that evidence will actually have on the mind of the particular jury or judge as trier of fact. It does not ordinarily matter, therefore, that the testimony of the fact may be contradicted or impeached. . . .
>
> Sufficiency is not primarily concerned with credibility nor with the choice among competing permissible inferences; . . . all conflicts in the evidence are resolved against the party who challenges the sufficiency of the evidence, including conflicts and contradictions within a witness's or a party's own testimony. . . . The proponent is entitled to the most favorable of competing rational inferences and to have inferences drawn from the most favorable findings. [Fleming James Jr., Geoffrey Hazard Jr., and John Leubsdorf, Civil Procedure §7.19 at 436, 441 (5th ed. 2001).]

In civil cases, motions for summary judgment are often decided on the basis of affidavits, which must state facts on personal knowledge. Fed. R. Civ. P. 56(e). If the foundation for the affiant's knowledge is not set forth in the affidavit with some particularity, it may not be sufficient to raise a genuine issue of material fact. Sheppard v. Union Pac.R.R.Co., 2005 U.S.Dist. LEXIS 1987 (E.D.Mo. 2005).

KEY POINT

FRE 602 requires that all witnesses (other than experts testifying to their opinions) must have personal knowledge of the matters about which they testify. The proponent of a witness must present evidence sufficient to support a finding of the witness's personal knowledge, typically by having the witness testify that the witness saw, heard, or otherwise perceived those matters.

PROBLEMS

4.1. Review the testimony by Officers Huston and Van Berg in the *Johnson* case concerning the injuries they claimed they received in the struggle with Johnson (pages 14 and 23, supra.) Did the officers speak from personal knowledge? Would you object to any of their testimony if you were the defense? Could you lay a proper foundation under Rule 602 if you were the prosecutor?

4.2. You are the lawyer for the plaintiffs in Problem 3.2 at page 129. Write out the questions you would ask to lay the foundation for the following evidence:

(a) An elderly retired neighbor who lives near the bus stop where Paul was injured and who says he can offer eyewitness testimony that Paul was standing on the gravel shoulder when he was hit.

(b) A co-worker of Denise Driver who could testify that after the accident Driver said to her, "I shouldn't have been in such a hurry."

4.3. The plaintiff's deceased husband suffered from asbestos-related diseases as a result of his occupational exposure to asbestos. At issue is whether the decedent was exposed to products manufactured by defendant OCF. In his deposition, the decedent identified an OCF product as an asbestos material with which he knew he had worked. But he also testified that his memory was adversely affected by the morphine he was taking: "It throws me out of gear. It's killing my brain. I'm screwed up. Sometimes my memory goes to heck, sometimes it doesn't." OCF claims that the deposition shows that the decedent was confused, inconsistent, and not certain about his knowledge of the OCF product. Do you think the court should strike the decedent's deposition testimony pursuant to FRE 601 or FRE 602?

B. THE AUTHENTICATION AND IDENTIFICATION OF EXHIBITS

In addition to witnesses, information is conveyed to the jury through the use of exhibits. The term *exhibits* encompasses a wide array of items — real and demonstrative evidence; written documents of all kinds; audio, video, and photographic recordings; and electronic and digital data compilations. The foundational requirement for exhibits is set forth explicitly in FRE 901.

1. FRE 901

RULE 901. REQUIREMENT OF AUTHENTICATION OR IDENTIFICATION

(a) General provision. The requirement of authentication or identification as a condition precedent to admissibility is satisfied by evidence sufficient to support a finding that the matter in question is what its proponent claims.

(b) Illustrations. By way of illustration only, and not by way of limitation, the following are examples of authentication or identification conforming with the requirements of this rule:

(1) Testimony of witness with knowledge. Testimony that a matter is what it is claimed to be.

(2) Nonexpert opinion on handwriting. Nonexpert opinion as to the genuineness of handwriting, based upon familiarity not acquired for purposes of the litigation.

(3) Comparison by trier or expert witness. Comparison by the trier of fact or by expert witnesses with specimens which have been authenticated.

(4) Distinctive characteristics and the like. Appearance, contents, substance, internal patterns, or other distinctive characteristics, taken in conjunction with circumstances.

(5) Voice identification. Identification of a voice, whether heard firsthand or through mechanical or electronic transmission or recording, by opinion based upon hearing the voice at any time under circumstances connecting it with the alleged speaker.

(6) Telephone conversations. Telephone conversations, by evidence that a call was made to the number assigned at the time by the telephone company to a particular person or business, if (A) in the case of a person, circumstances, including self-identification, show the person answering to be the one called, or (B) in the case of a business, the call was made to a place of business and the conversation related to business reasonably transacted over the telephone.

(7) Public records or reports. Evidence that a writing authorized by law to be recorded or filed and in fact recorded or filed in a public office, or a purported public record, report, statement, or data compilation, in any form, is from the public office where items of this nature are kept.

(8) Ancient documents or data compilation. Evidence that a document or data compilation, in any form, (A) is in such condition as to create no suspicion concerning its authenticity, (B) was in a place where it, if authentic, would likely be, and (C) has been in existence 20 years or more at the time it is offered.

(9) Process or system. Evidence describing a process or system used to produce a result and showing that the process or system produces an accurate result.

(10) Methods provided by statute or rule. Any method of authentication or identification provided by Act of Congress or by other rules prescribed by the Supreme Court pursuant to statutory authority.

2.   Interpretation and Illustration of FRE 901

There are two parts to FRE 901. FRE 901(a) establishes the basic foundation and the evidentiary standard that the proponent of an exhibit must satisfy. FRE 901(b) sets forth illustrations of the kinds of foundation facts that the drafters of the Federal Rules decided should satisfy that standard.

FRE 901(a) requires the proponent of an exhibit to do two things: (1) to state what the proponent *claims* the exhibit to be; and (2) to produce evidence "sufficient to support a finding" that it is what the proponent claims. While it is difficult to grasp these concepts in the abstract, some general comments about the application of FRE 901 will serve as a framework for specific examples and problems discussed below.

a.   What the Exhibit Is Claimed to Be

As you learned in Chapter Three, the proponent of any item of evidence must have in mind a theory as to why that item is relevant to prove facts that are of consequence in a case. Relevance thus requires the proponent of an exhibit to articulate a connection between the exhibit and the parties or the litigated events in the case. This *connection* is typically what the proponent *claims* the exhibit to be for purposes of FRE 901, and what courts require the proponent to prove in order to identify or authenticate it. The Rule 901 foundation, therefore, follows from the articulation of why tangible objects, photos, recordings, or written documents are relevant.

Consider as an example a rental agreement between Harry, a landlord, and Jane, a tenant. Jane has filed suit against the landlord for failure to make promised improvements and offers the rental agreement as an exhibit. The rental agreement states that the owner of the property must make specific improvements. Harry, the defendant, claims that no written agreement was ever signed, that Jane has a month-to-month tenancy, and that there is no obligation to make improvements. Jane therefore seeks to introduce the rental agreement into evidence to prove that the defendant does have this obligation. On this theory of relevance, Jane *claims* that the exhibit is an agreement *signed by the defendant landlord*.

The Advisory Committee Note to Rule 901(a) states that the facts necessary to authenticate an item are a "special" aspect of relevancy: "[A] telephone conversation may be irrelevant because on an unrelated topic or because the speaker is not identified. The latter aspect is the one here involved." By analogy, whether Jane's exhibit is signed by the defendant identifies it as a fact specific to the case against the landlord and would satisfy FRE 901. Additional facts that make the rental agreement relevant, for example that it covered the time period during which repairs should have been made, may also require proof, as will be discussed in Section E of this chapter.

b. The Requirement of Evidence Sufficient to Support a Finding

Under FRE 901(a), Jane would need to produce evidence sufficient to support a finding that the rental agreement is what she claims it to be — the agreement signed by Harry, the defendant landlord. Imagine if the attorney for Jane simply handed the rental agreement to the jury. How would the jury know what it is? The attorney cannot just tell the jury what it is (you know from the instructions to the jury in the *Johnson* case that what an attorney says to the jury is not evidence). Of course, the jury might infer simply from looking at the document that it was signed by the defendant if the name on the document is the same as the defendant's. But what if the name was a very common one? Or just initials? The jury would not be able to make this inference with a very high degree of certainty. United States v. Skipper, 74 F.3d 608, 612 (5th Cir. 1996) (mere similarity in name between a criminal defendant and the person named in the record of a prior conviction alone does not satisfy the identification requirement of Rule 901). So while the signed document on its own might satisfy FRE 401 (having some tendency to show that the defendant signed the document), FRE 901(a) requires more. It requires the proponent to satisfy a higher standard of probability — *evidence sufficient to support a finding* — that it was the defendant landlord who actually signed the document. How can this be done?

c. FRE 901(b) Illustrates How to Produce Evidence Sufficient to Support a Finding

FRE 901(b) now comes into play. It sets forth various options for satisfying the FRE 901(a) requirement. Jane's foundational evidence might come from the testimony of someone who saw the landlord sign the agreement — a person with personal knowledge under FRE 901(b)(1). If there is no person with personal knowledge of the fact at issue, then circumstantial evidence can be offered, such as the testimony of someone who can recognize the landlord's signature (FRE 901(b)(2)); or from a comparison between the landlord's signature on another document and on the rental agreement itself (FRE 901(b)(3)). Whatever method is used, the added requirement of satisfying FRE 901 affects the parties, the jury, and the judge. Jane, the party proponent, has the added burden of locating the proper witness and presenting that witness at trial. The jury will get the added benefit of learning additional foundation facts in order to make its decision about the connection of the rental agreement to the tenant's case. For example, if Jane is able to satisfy FRE 901(b)(1), the jury could draw the inferences shown in Diagram 4-1:

DIAGRAM 4-1

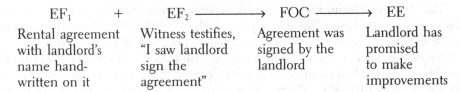

EF_1 + EF_2 ⟶   FOC ⟶   EE

Rental agreement	Witness testifies,	Agreement was	Landlord has
with landlord's	"I saw landlord	signed by the	promised
name hand-	sign the	landlord	to make
written on it	agreement"		improvements

The judge will have the added power to exclude the tenant's exhibit if the FRE 901(a) requirement is not satisfied. You can see the utility of the FRE 901(b) illustrations. If the proponent's foundation falls squarely within one, the trial judge will routinely decide that the FRE 901(a) burden is satisfied. But often the evidence is more ambiguous.

For example, what if Jane testifies that she mailed the agreement to Harry's business address and received the agreement by return mail with a signature added? This foundation might satisfy FRE 901(b)(4), since the contents of the document (the name) and the circumstances (mailing it to Harry and receiving it by return mail) indicate that the landlord signed it. But would Jane's testimony satisfy the FRE 901(a) standard of "evidence sufficient to support a finding"?

d. Judicial Determinations of Sufficiency Under FRE 901(a)

As stated in the previous discussions of FRE 602, pages 171-172, supra, evidence "sufficient to support a finding" means evidence upon which the judge thinks a jury *could* reasonably find a fact to be more likely true than not. The judge will not assess credibility in making this determination. Thus in the hypothetical just discussed, the judge will assume that Jane's testimony about mailing the rental agreement is true. The judge's determination of "sufficiency" will depend primarily on the judge's assessment of the strength of the generalizations underlying the inference that it was the defendant who signed the agreement and sent it back to the tenant by return mail. The judge's task of making this rough estimate of underlying probabilities involves the same thought process as estimating probative value under FRE 403. How likely is it that landlords will receive rental agreements that have been mailed to them, will sign them, and will return them by mail immediately? *Could* a jury reasonably believe that it is more likely than not? Additional evidence — such as that Harry opens all of his own mail — would increase the probability that Harry did sign it.

As will be discussed on page 222 of this chapter, when the judge applies a "sufficiency" standard to screen preliminary questions such as whether Harry the landlord signed the rental agreement, these questions can be disputed in a number of ways. The proponent of the evidence is not required to rule out all possibilities inconsistent with authenticity, or to prove beyond any doubt that the item is what it is claimed to be. Harry could still testify that he did not sign the agreement, that the signature is not genuine, or that he was out of town on the day the agreement was received and mailed. All of this evidence would be heard by the judge, perhaps outside the presence of the jury pursuant to FRE 104(c). So long as the judge determines, as a preliminary matter, that a jury *could* reasonably find the preliminary question in the tenant's favor, the judge will find that FRE 901(a) has been satisfied and will admit the rental agreement into evidence. Admission of the agreement does not end the matter, however. Harry can submit all of his conflicting evidence to the jury, because the question of whether Harry signed the agreement must still be decided by the jury as part of its ultimate deliberations in the case. "[I]t is the jury who will ultimately determine the authenticity of the evidence, not the court." United States v. Goichman, 547 F.2d 778, 784 (3d Cir. 1976). After all, if the signature is not Harry's, he has probably made no promise to make improvements.

The judge will exclude the agreement from the jury's consideration if, on hearing the evidence from both parties, the judge concludes that no jury could *reasonably* find that Harry signed it. If such is the case, Jane has not fulfilled the FRE 901(a) burden. The judge will not submit an exhibit to the jury that the jury could not *reasonably* believe to be authentic. United States v. Schultz, 917 F. Supp. 1320, 1339 (N.D. Iowa 1996) (documents from defendant's alleged gambling operations held inadmissible under Rule 901(a) because no government witness testified that the documents were actually seized from a specific location controlled by defendant; rather, testimony was only that the documents were "consistent with" the types of documents seized there).

e.   The Process of Laying the Foundation

An exhibit is typically received into evidence after being given a number or letter designation to show which party submitted the exhibit and its sequence in the trial. In most trials, the mechanics of marking and numbering exhibits occurs before the trial itself, outside the presence of the jury, by agreement between the parties. An exhibit will be numbered "for identification" only, prior to its admission into evidence. At trial, the proponent shows the exhibit first to the opposing attorney and then to the witness who is going to testify about it. The proponent then questions the witness about the exhibit, presumably eliciting foundational facts sufficient to satisfy the FRE 901(a) requirements.

In the tenant's case against the landlord, for example, the tenant might produce a witness for purposes of proving the requisite foundation.[1]

Q: Please tell the jury your name and occupation.
A: My name is Joseph Jones and I am not employed.

---

1. An extremely helpful text which contains numerous examples of foundational testimony is Edward J. Imwinkelried, Evidentiary Foundations (5th ed. 2002).

Q: Do you know the defendant Harry Hunt in this case?
A: Yes, he is my uncle.
Q: Did you previously work in the defendant's office?
A: Yes, I worked there two summers ago.
Q: I am handing you a piece of paper marked plaintiff's Exhibit 7 for identification. Do you recognize it?
A: Yes
Q: What is it?
A: It is a rental agreement from my uncle's office.
Q: How do you know that?
A: It is printed with his business logo, and it states that it is a rental agreement between himself and Jane Smith, Tenant.
Q: Do you recall seeing this particular agreement before?
A: Yes.
Q: Could you tell us how you remember it?
A: It was the first day I was working for my uncle two years ago. He asked me to deliver some rental agreements to his tenants after he signed them. He had a stack of them. This one was on top.
Q: What happened next?
A: He signed the whole stack of them, and then gave them to me to deliver. As I said, this one was on top and I took it to the apartment at the address shown here. I really liked the apartment, which is why I remember it.
Q: So to the best of your recollection, you saw the defendant sign Exhibit 7 two years ago?
A: Right.
Q: Your honor, I now offer plaintiff's Exhibit 7 for identification into evidence as plaintiff's Exhibit number 7.

After the foundation is laid, the proponent asks the judge to admit the exhibit "into evidence." The opponent may object, either because the foundation is not adequate under FRE 901(a) or on grounds of some other exclusionary rule, such as hearsay or FRE 403. The judge will rule on the objection, or the parties may present further testimony from the testifying witness or from other witnesses first. If other witnesses are necessary, the judge may conditionally admit the exhibit *subject to* additional evidence being produced, using the technique of conditional admission to be discussed in Section E, infra. If the judge overrules the objection and admits the exhibit, it retains its number and is recorded by the court clerk as an official part of the record. It may then be inspected by the jury. Exhibits remain in the custody of the clerk during trial; they are taken into the jury room during deliberations and are part of the record on appeal.

3.   Elaboration of FRE 901: Real Evidence, Demonstrative and Computer-Generated Exhibits, Recordings and Written Documents

The foundational requirements established by FRE 901 are described in the rule's title as requirements of "authentication" or "identification." These are not doctrinal terms that have a single, well-defined meaning. "Identification" usually refers to *who* authored a writing, or *whose* voice was heard speaking; "authentication" usually refers to the genuineness of the connection between *what* the exhibit is and the specific facts of the case. Also, two of the FRE 901(b) illustrations add an element of accuracy or genuineness — the requirement of FRE 901(b)(2) that nonexpert familiarity with handwriting be acquired apart from the litigation, and the requirement of FRE 901(b)(9) that the information contained in the exhibit be accurate. The standard of FRE 901(a) is flexible, and the FRE 901(b) illustrations are not exhaustive. The starting point is always to ask: Why is this exhibit relevant? What does the proponent claim it to be, based on its connection to the parties or to the litigated events in this case? The kinds of foundations that have traditionally satisfied Rule 901 are discussed below and serve as examples and analogies for the authentication of exhibits of all types.

a.   Real Evidence

Real evidence refers to tangible items that played some role in the litigated event and from which the jury may draw inferences. Examples are the weapons used in a crime or a home appliance that is alleged to be defective. The item's connection to the specific events in dispute makes it relevant, and that connection is "what the proponent claims" for purposes of satisfying FRE 901.

Thus the foundation for real evidence typically consists of a witness who can identify the item's physical involvement in the case. Consider a murder trial where the prosecution wishes to introduce a knife under the relevance theory that it is the murder weapon. Not just any knife will do. Under FRE 901(a), the prosecution must claim that this knife has a connection to the specific events or parties in the case. A typical claim would be either that the knife was found at the crime scene or that it belongs to the defendant.

Suppose that several months have elapsed between the finding of the knife at the crime scene and its introduction as an exhibit at trial. How does the witness who found the knife, and who is called on to identify the knife in court, know that it is the one he found?

i.   Identification Through a Readily Identifiable Characteristic.   One typical method of identification is that the witness may recognize the knife — typically because it has a readily identifiable characteristic. The witness's personal knowledge satisfies FRE 901(b)(1). The identifier could be a unique design or initials on the handle, as shown in Diagram 4-2:

DIAGRAM 4-2

EF_1	+	EF_2 $\longrightarrow$	FOC
A knife marked as Exhibit A has the initials "KRS" on its handle		Police officer testifies, "I can identify the knife marked Exhibit A as the knife I found at the crime scene because I recognize the initials 'KRS' on the handle"	The knife marked Exhibit A was found at the crime scene

Or the identifier could be a label, a number, or a tag affixed to the knife when it was discovered. In United States v. Abreu, 952 F.2d 1458, 1467-1468 (1st Cir. 1992), a drug agent testified that he recognized a shotgun as the one he seized at defendant's apartment by identifying the evidence tag placed on the gun at the time of seizure and by his signature on the tag. This would satisfy FRE 901(b)(4). Sometimes a fingerprint on a weapon is used as the identifying characteristic. In *Abreu*, the foundation for identifying defendant's palmprint on the shotgun was incomplete under FRE 901(b)(3) because there was no testimony that the inked palmprint specimen used for comparison was the defendant's.

ii.   Identification Through Chain of Custody.   Chain of custody is the second typical method of identification, most often used when an exhibit is generic and has no readily identifiable characteristic. For example, the links in the chain of custody of the knife would consist of the people who handled the knife between the time of its discovery at the crime scene and its appearance in the courtroom. A complete chain of custody under FRE 901(b)(4) would require the testimony of *all* such people plus testimony to show that the exhibit was stored in a secure place when it was not being handled.

iii.   Unchanged Condition Established Through Chain of Custody.   The chain of custody can also establish that the item has not been tampered with and that it is in the same condition as it was when it was discovered. This showing may be required if the condition of the item is as important as its identity and if it is an item that might be adulterated or tampered with. For example, the knife found at the crime scene might have fingerprints on it, or a substance seized from a defendant might be an illegal drug. The complete chain of custody would show that these conditions existed when the items were found, when they were tested, and perhaps even when they were presented in court. If the knife is tested for fingerprints — or if a chemical test is conducted on drugs seized from a defendant — the laboratory technician becomes part of the chain of custody. There needs to be evidence that the knife or the drug that reached the laboratory was the same knife or drug found at the crime scene or seized from the defendant, and that it had not been tampered with since. In United States v. Williams, 85 Fed.Appx. 341 (4th Cir. 2004) a police officer testified that he seized suspected drugs from the defendant, that he placed the drugs in the Property Section at the police department, that he later submitted the drugs to the State Lab for testing, and that, after the lab completed the analysis, he returned the drugs to the Property Section. He also testified that the drugs appeared to be the same as when he first recovered them.

iv.   Under FRE 901(a), the Complete Chain of Custody Is Not Always Required.   Cases decided under FRE 901(a) make it clear that the complete chain of custody need not always be proved to satisfy the sufficiency standard. Even where gaps exist in the chain of custody of substances that require testing, courts have held that a jury *could* reasonably find that the exhibit in question was adequately identified and still in an unchanged condition. For example, in United States v. Shaw, 920 F.2d 1225, 1229 (5th Cir. 1991), amphetamine seized from the defendant's motel room was properly admitted despite gaps in the chain of custody. The evidence custodian could not recall who delivered the drug to the Department of

Public Safety (DPS) for analysis or whether it was placed in the DPS night deposit box, and access to the drug was available to numerous DPS chemists. "A break in the chain of custody will not necessarily lead to the exclusion of the evidence.... Rather, 'the ultimate question is whether the authentication testimony is sufficiently complete so as to convince the court that it is improbable that the original item had been exchanged with another or otherwise tampered with.'" United States v. Grant, 967 F.2d 81, 82 (2d Cir. 1992) (quoting United States v. Howard-Arias, 679 F.2d 363, 366 (4th Cir. 1982)).

At trial, the opponent may again dispute the identity of the exhibit and its possible changed condition and try to persuade the jury that it has no probative value in the case. In United States v. Ladd, 885 F.2d 954, 956-957 (1st Cir. 1989), blood and urine samples were drawn from the body of the deceased to determine the presence of cocaine and heroin. The samples were sent to the state laboratory and to a private laboratory (CSL) for analysis. At the state lab, the procedures were sloppy enough to cause concern about authenticity, but the appellate court held that that concern went to the weight, not to the admissibility of the lab results. In the private lab, however, a defect in the identification of the samples required exclusion:

> As to the reports from the State Lab, the facts brook little dispute. The only witness who testified concerning the procedures employed at the facility was John Sloane, a state chemist. Sloane testified that the laboratory's usual custom and praxis were followed. His testimony supported a finding that the samples of Massey's bodily fluids, once delivered, were stored in a loosely tied bag in a refrigerator in the laboratory; that the bag (if not the individual jars) was numbered and labelled; that the samples were removed for internal testing and eventually replaced; that the laboratory's procedures were followed on these occasions; and that the tested samples comprised Massey's blood and urine, respectively. This evidence, we think, was sufficient to sanction admissibility of the State Lab's reports.
>
> To be sure, defense counsel's attack on the laboratory's protocol, and on the storage and handling of the specimens, was robust. He showed that access was easy and cross-checking minimal. He probed skillfully at weaknesses in the safeguards employed, casting doubt on the samples' security and on the effectiveness of the state's preventatives. Fundamentally, however, this cross-examination went to the weight of the evidence, not to its admissibility.
>
> In the last analysis, the prosecution's chain-of-custody evidence must be adequate — not infallible. Here, some links in the chain were rusty, but none were missing. Without question, the defense succeeded in showing a certain sloppiness, regrettable in a forensic laboratory. Yet the net effect of any such disarray on the authenticity of the evidence depended on what inferences a reasonable factfinder might choose to draw from it. Where, as in this case, a trier chooses among plausible (albeit competing) inferences, appellate courts should not intrude....
>
> The tests conducted by the private laboratory, CSL, do not fare nearly as well. When a blood sample is received by the State Lab, it is assigned an identification number. Massey's blood sample was numbered T87-1938-BBO. When the decision was made to forward the sanguineous specimen to CSL for more critical testing, a messenger called for it. According to CSL's records, the sample it received was numbered T87-1936-BBO. The last-digit discrepancy ("1938" versus "1936") was never explained. It was later struck over — the "6" altered to look like an "8" — but the record is silent as to when, where, how or why this emendation occurred. The record is likewise inscrutable as to the identity of the reviser.

Perhaps most puzzling, the prosecution made almost no effort to clear up the discrepancy. It chose not to present the testimony of the State Lab staffer who released the sample, the courier, or the CSL staffer who logged it in. Similarly, the prosecution offered no evidence to show whether the allegedly miswritten number (T87-1936-BBO) was assigned to some other specimen still in house, or to account for that designation. In short, there was no competent proof to indicate that the sample extracted from Massey's corpse was the one which CSL tested. An important step in the custodial pavane was omitted.

The conclusion is, we think, inescapable. As to CSL's findings, the linkage was not merely rusty — it had parted. Due to the missing link, the CSL test results should not have been admitted into evidence.

A claim of tampering must be supported by specific evidence, as it was in *Ladd*, to defeat the government's proof of chain of custody. In United States v. Bokshoven, 258 F.Supp.2d 397, 401 (E.D.Pa. 2003), the defendant was charged with smuggling heroin into the country by secreting a foam mat, soaked with the drug, in the lining of his suitcase. The government offered a mat it claimed had come from defendant's suitcase into evidence. The defendant challenged the sufficiency of the government's chain of custody of the mat claimed to be from his suitcase by offering evidence that many similar instances of using foam rubber to smuggle heroin had been discovered, and the mats seized, within recent months. The court held that this was "insufficient to overcome the presumption of regularity" in the government's handling of contraband. Even when evidence of tampering is shown, it may not defeat admissibility. In United States v. Demarey, 1996 U.S.App. LEXIS 10101 (6th Cir. 1996), fraudulent vouchers submitted by the defendant to a V.A. hospital for reimbursement had markings and notations on them when offered at trial. The markings had not been present when the defendant had submitted the vouchers for payment, and no explanation was offered for how they got onto the vouchers. Because the markings did not cover the amounts or the signature, the court held that they did not alter any material part of the voucher and did not raise any genuine issue of authenticity. Of course, the defendant's challenges can be presented to the jury as affecting the "weight" of the government's evidence of authenticity.

Once an item of real evidence has been authenticated, it is still potentially subject to the judge's discretion to exclude pursuant to FRE 403. However, it is customary for judges to treat real evidence as being highly probative and thus of considerable assistance to the jury, sometimes with little analysis of what the jury would learn for purposes of deciding a fact of consequence in the case. Thus, the admission of even gruesome objects has been upheld if they played a part in the litigated events.

KEY POINTS

1. Real evidence is a tangible exhibit that played some role in the events that are in dispute at trial.

2. Real evidence is usually identified pursuant to FRE 901(b)(1) by testimony from a witness who recognizes the exhibit because of its readily identifiable characteristic, or by testimony concerning its chain of custody pursuant to FRE 901(b)(4). FRE 901(a) requires the judge to decide whether the proffered testimony is evidence sufficient to support a finding of the exhibit's identity. For some real evidence such as drugs or blood samples, it is also necessary to establish the exhibit's unchanged condition.

3. Real evidence may be subject to exclusion under FRE 403.

PROBLEMS

4.4. Darren is charged with possessing an unregistered sawed-off shotgun in violation of federal law. "Possession" is defined as the control of, or ability to control, the weapon. At trial, an agent of the Bureau of Alcohol, Tobacco, and Firearms will testify as follows: She conducted a lawful search of the home of Rhonda Adams; she found Darren asleep in the master bedroom; she searched the master bedroom and found a black attaché case under the bed in which Darren was sleeping; she opened the case, and it contained a sawed-off shotgun. Now the prosecution wants to offer a sawed-off shotgun into evidence as Exhibit 2. The prosecutor claims that Exhibit 2 is the gun found in the black attaché case in the room where Darren was sleeping. First, the ATF agent will identify Exhibit 2 as being a Korean-made Shinn A Sipja 12-gauge shotgun with a sawed-off barrel and cutback stock. What additional questions would the prosecution ask the agent to satisfy FRE 901(a)? Try to use both the readily identifiable characteristic and the chain of custody methods of identifying real evidence.

4.5. Jim Zeal and Stephani Goldstein were in a sailboat, the *Rastafari*, when it was stopped and boarded by the U.S. Coast Guard on the high seas, some 300 nautical miles southeast of Miami, Florida. The boarding officers searched the vessel and discovered a large quantity of a green leafy substance. Subsequently, Zeal and Goldstein were charged with conspiracy to import marijuana into the United States.

(a) At trial nine months later, the prosecution offers into evidence 11 nautical charts with navigational markings on them indicating a planned route between Kingston, Jamaica, which the government offers to show was a standard port of call for drug runners, and Miami. The prosecution asserts that the Coast Guard had seized the charts from the boat and that they are relevant to prove the conspiracy of illegal importation. To establish the authenticity of the charts, the prosecution calls Coast Guard Ensign Smythe, who testifies that he recognizes the charts as the ones he seized from the boat, and then deposited in the safe aboard the Coast Guard cutter, because of drawings of Bob Marley on each one. Is this testimony sufficient under FRE 901(b)(1)?

(b) The prosecutor also wants to establish that the leafy green substance found on board the *Rastafari* is marijuana. The prosecutor plans to show Exhibit C, a bag containing a leafy green substance, to a government chemist who testifies that, based on her in-court inspection, the substance in the bag is marijuana. But first, the prosecution offers Ensign Smythe to testify that he seized a bag of a leafy green substance from the ship and placed it in the Coast Guard safe along with the charts, and that while Exhibit C "could be" that bag, he does not know whether it is. Does this testimony satisfy FRE 901? What if FBI Agent Owens testifies that he found both the bag and the charts in the same box in the FBI evidence room and brought them to the courthouse. Would that be sufficient?

4.6. Defendant Ingram is charged with being a felon who knowingly possessed two bullets in violation of federal law. The prosecution offers two bullets into evidence that it claims are those bullets. The chain of custody is as follows: The detective who seized the bullets from defendant's apartment did not look at the headstamps on the bullets when he placed them into a small envelope within a larger envelope. When the bullets were logged into the ballistics unit, one "B" headstamp was noted on the log. Later, the clasp on the small envelope was discovered to be broken and a detective replaced it with tape. An ATF agent later noticed an "X" marked on the projectile portion of each bullet. And another detective logged the bullets out of the ballistics unit for six days. Based on these facts, the defendant objected to the admission of the bullets on the grounds that the chain of custody "was so broken that no jury could find that the bullets offered by the prosecution were the bullets possessed by Mr. Ingram." What result?

b. Demonstrative Exhibits

Demonstrative exhibits reproduce or depict persons, objects (such as items of real evidence that are not brought into court) or scenes that are connected to the litigated events in the case. Examples are models, diagrams, drawings, or photographs. These exhibits are offered to illustrate or explain the testimony of witnesses, including experts, and to present complex and voluminous documents. They can also be referred to by counsel during opening and closing arguments. In theory at least, demonstrative exhibits do not have independent probative value on the substantive issues in a case. They are relevant because they assist the jury in understanding testimonial, documentary, and real evidence. *Illustrative evidence* refers to illustrative aids that are not admitted into evidence, as discussed at pages XX, infra.

Demonstrative exhibits are authenticated by testimony from the witness whose testimony they illustrate. This witness has knowledge of the nature of the exhibit's content and the connection of that content to the case. For example, the prosecution might offer a photograph of the knife in Diagram 4-2 that was allegedly found at the crime scene. A witness who saw the real knife (or whatever was the subject of the demonstrative evidence) might testify, "I recognize the knife in the photograph because of the initials 'KRS' on the handle. This is a photograph of the knife I found at the crime scene." If a drawing, or a model, of the knife were proffered, the witness would testify in a similar manner.

i.   Demonstrative Exhibits Must Assist the Trier of Fact.   The proponent must also be prepared to show that the exhibit is a "fair,"or "accurate," or "true" depiction of what the proponent claims that it portrays. Although this additional requirement is not part of the literal FRE 901 burden, courts enforce it to make sure a demonstrative exhibit will *assist* the trier of fact by increasing its understanding of the relevant events. This normally will be assumed with real evidence. It would be highly unusual, for example, for a trial court to exclude from evidence a murder weapon on the ground that the jury does not need to observe the weapon for purposes of its deliberations, even if such a conclusion might be correct.

In the *Johnson* case, Officer Smith testified to the foundation for Exhibit 1, a photograph of a food port door in Facility B (page 33, lines 1-9, supra). He affirmed that Exhibit 1 was a "fair and accurate picture" of the door. Notice that Smith could say this even though he did not take the photograph himself. In McEachron v. Glans, 1999 U.S. Dist. LEXIS 21926 (N.D.N.Y. 1999), the court noted that a witness authenticating a photograph or videotape does not need to be the photographer but must recognize and identify the object depicted and testify that the photo fairly and correctly represents it. Photos, drawings, diagrams, or models can be described as "fair" depictions of what they represent by the person who made them or by a person who saw the real thing. Claims that a demonstrative exhibit is misleading or prejudicial would be decided under FRE 403.

ii.   Application of FRE 403 to Demonstrative Exhibits.   Some demonstrative exhibits are generally admitted as a matter of course, such as photographs of the scene of a crime or accident. But sometimes their admission raises Rule 403 dangers such as unfair prejudice and risk of misleading the jury. Photographs of gruesome injuries at a crime scene or autopsy may generate the danger of unfair prejudice; complex charts and graphs may present a danger of misleading the jury; and even photographs may be misleading (and have lower probative value) if they portray a scene in a different condition than when the relevant incident occurred. The judge decides the FRE 403 objection in typical fashion, by estimating the exhibit's probative value and weighing that against the pertinent danger. Recall the district court's decision admitting autopsy photographs in United States v. Yahweh, described on pages 144-145, supra.

c.   Demonstrations and Experiments in Court

Sometimes a witness's testimony about an out-of-court event can be illustrated through a demonstration or experiment in court. Such in-court demonstrations are tested for relevancy under FRE 401. United States v. Howard, 51 Fed. Appx. 118, 120 (4th Cir. 2002) (in-court experiment with a "Dickey John" machine, which measures the moisture level of corn, showed that "spraying . . . water on the exterior of a sample of corn could raise the moisture reading of the corn sample . . . [which made] defendants' explanation for the high moisture readings of the disputed bushels [of corn] at least slightly more probable"). They are also tested under FRE 403 because of their potential for misleading or confusing the jury. The proponent of the demonstration must lay a proper foundation establishing the similarity of circumstances and conditions between the out-of-court event and the in-court presentation. The conditions need not be identical, but they must be sufficiently similar to provide a fair comparison. In United States v. Gaskell, 985 F.2d 1056, 1060-1061, (11th Cir. 1993), a demonstration by an expert witness as to the amount of force needed to cause a seven-month-old infant's fatal injuries was held inadmissible. Shaking the rubber doll was not substantially similar due to stiffness of the doll's neck, differences in the weight of head, and absence of testimony concerning the number of oscillations required to produce the infant's injuries.

d.   Recorded and Computer-Generated Reenactments, Animations, and Simulations of Events

A variety of filmed or computer-generated recordings can be used in trials to portray out-of-court events for the jury, typically in personal injury and criminal cases. *Reenactments* involve the use of human models; *animations* typically consist of computer-generated drawings that depict people or objects in motion. Both are used to illustrate what witnesses have already testified to, and they are subject to the same requirement of being "fair and accurate" representations as a single drawing. They must accurately reflect the testimony and the physical evidence and the reasonable inferences that may be drawn from them.

Computer-generated *simulations* are more complex in that they are produced by inputting information into a computer program that determines how an event "must have happened" and then provides a visual image of that conclusion. A simulation adds information beyond the testimony of percipient witnesses, both in terms of the data inputs into the computer and the programming that analyzes and then graphically portrays the output. State v. Tollardo, 77 P.3d 1023, 1027 (N.M.Ct. App 2003) (a simulation is a "computer-generated exhibit created when information is fed into a computer that is programmed to analyze the data and draw a conclusion from it"). The most complete foundation for simulated accident reconstruction will involve the sufficiency of the input data, the reliability of the underlying technical or scientific principles, the accuracy of the computer's operating system, and the accuracy of the mathematical formulae programmed into the computer.[2] Extensive pretrial discovery is typically required to permit the opponent to challenge the exhibit effectively and to cross-examine the witnesses presenting it.

Of course, the use of reenactments, animations, and simulations is subject to objection under FRE 403. The principal risks are that the presentation inevitably simplifies the real-world events and that much data pertinent to accident reconstruction are supplied by outside sources who are unknown. Cautionary instructions are typically given concerning the limited purpose of an animation, the limited facts it is based on, and the jury's role in ultimately deciding those facts. Hinkle v. City of Clarksburg, 81 F.3d 416, 425 (4th Cir. 1996) (approving a limiting instruction that states: "This animation is not meant to be a recreation of the events, but rather it consists of a computer picture to help you understand [the expert's] opinion . . . the video is not meant to be an exact recreation of what happened during the shooting, but rather it represents [the expert's] evaluation of the evidence presented"). Nevertheless, there is concern among courts that jurors will be misled or overly influenced by such animated exhibits. In Racz v. R. T. Merryman Trucking, Inc., 1994 WL 124857, at *5 (E.D. Pa. Apr. 4, 1994), the court excluded the defendant's computer-generated reconstruction of an accident made by an accident reconstruction expert. The reconstruction was based on that expert's evaluation of testimony about the accident:

> Relying upon the old adage, "seeing is believing," we conclude that the jury may give undue weight to an animated reconstruction of the accident. . . . The apparent decision of the accident reconstructionist to discount the testimony of a witness who reported seeing the trailer portion of the truck encroach into the decedent's lane of travel is magnified and given enhanced credibility when such decision becomes part of the data upon which an animated visual representation is based. It would be an inordinately difficult task for the plaintiff to counter, by cross-examination or otherwise, the impression that a computerized depiction of the accident is necessarily more accurate than an oral description of how the accident occurred. Because the expert's conclusion would be graphically depicted in a moving and animated form, the viewing of the computer simulation might more readily lead the jury to accept the data and premises underlying the defendant's expert's opinion, and, therefore, to give more weight to such opinion than it might if the jury were forced to evaluate the expert's conclusions in the light of the testimony of all of the witnesses, as generally occurs in such cases.

KEY POINTS

1. Demonstrative exhibits reproduce the likeness of some tangible object, person, or scene and are helpful to the jury's understanding of other testimonial, documentary, or real evidence. More complex forms of demonstrative exhibits include in-court demonstrations and experiments and out-of-court reenactments, animations, and simulations.

2.   Gregory P. Joseph, A Simplified Approach to Computer-Generated Evidence and Animations, 43 N.Y.L. Sch. L. Rev. 875 (1999-2000) contains checklists for most types of and uses for simulations.

2. Demonstrative exhibits are usually identified pursuant to FRE 901(b)(1) by testimony from a witness as to what their contents are, the witness's basis for being able to identify them, and the witness's opinion that they are a fair and accurate reproduction.

3. Demonstrative evidence may be subject to exclusion under FRE 403.

PROBLEMS

4.7. In the *Hitt* case, page 151 supra, assume that Hitt's rifle has been admitted as Exhibit H. How would the prosecution authenticate the photograph that included Hitt's rifle? Who do you think the foundation witness would be?

4.8. In the *Johnson* case, if the prosecutor asked Officer Huston to look at a model of the food port door that was constructed before the trial, what questions would the prosecutor ask to lay the foundation to admit the model into evidence as an exhibit? Suppose that the prosecutor wants to show that two food trays cannot fit through the model food port door. What other exhibits would be needed for this demonstration? What questions would the prosecutor ask to lay the foundation for the demonstration? What other considerations should enter into the judge's decision whether to admit the model or permit the demonstration?

e. Recordings

Audio, video, and photographic recordings of events that occurred outside the courtroom are a cross between demonstrative evidence and eyewitness testimony. Although they may be offered together with the testimony of a witness who perceived the events, the recordings themselves are an independent record of them, imprinted not in human memory but on tape or film or some other medium by mechanical, electronic, or other processes. The recording reveals what the equipment "saw" or "heard," perhaps with less risk of human fallibility than an eyewitness. Consider, for example, if the fight in the *Johnson* case had been recorded by an automatic video camera. Even though there were many eyewitnesses to the melee, the film record would be an independent version of the event that could be used as substantive evidence (just as was the famous video of the use of force by Los Angeles police against Rodney King). Indeed, wouldn't the "memory" of the video recording be more reliable than either the guards' or the inmates' versions? Such a recording, if properly authenticated, would be admissible as substantive proof that the out-of-court events occurred.

i. Satisfying the FRE 901 Foundation with a Percipient Witness. When a camera or other device records what a witness is also seeing, that "percipient witness" can authenticate the recording. The foundation is similar to that for demonstrative evidence under FRE 901(b)(1). The witness would identify the events in the recording, state the basis for the witness's ability to identify the events, and affirm that the recording is a "fair," or "accurate," or "true" record of the events perceived. For example, a government informant who participated in taped conversations could authenticate both the recording and the transcripts of the tape by testifying that they were correct to the best of his knowledge. United States v. Wright, 932 F.2d 868, 880 (10th Cir. 1991). This is indeed a very simple foundation! At common law, courts took a much stricter attitude to ensure the accuracy of tape and film recordings, requiring proof of the equipment operator's qualifications, the working condition of the equipment, and the absence of material alterations, typically through a complete chain of custody of the recording itself from the time it was made until presentation in the courtroom. The following commentary explains why courts now permit a simplified foundation:

> First, there are now electronic techniques for determining whether a tape has been altered. . . . Secondly and more importantly, the courts have gone back to fundamentals and [have] begun to treat the question of a tape recording's authenticity as a simple question . . . under Federal Rule 104(b). . . . Has the proponent presented sufficient evidence to support a rational finding of fact that the tape recording is authentic? Given that test, many modern courts are no longer insisting on the traditional, strict foundation. . . . If a witness testifies that he or she heard a conversation and that the tape accurately reproduces the conversation, there is a permissive inference of the tape's genuineness. [Edward J. Imwinkelried, Evidentiary Foundations 84-85 (4th ed. 1998).][3]

ii. "Silent Witness" — Satisfying the FRE 901 Foundation Without a Percipient Witness.   Sometimes a recording device records what no human witness has seen or heard, or what no human can see — like the X-ray taken of Officer Van Berg's broken thumb chip. When a recording thus functions as a "silent witness," a percipient witness does not exist and cannot testify to the simplified foundation. Instead, "recordings made by . . . equipment that operate[s] automatically . . . may satisfy the requirements of the [FRE] . . . so long as a witness testifies to the type of equipment or camera used, its general reliability, the quality of the recorded product, the process by which it was focused, or the general reliability of the entire system." United States v. Stephens, 202 F.Supp.2d 1361, 1368 (N.D.Ga. 2002). For example, in United States v. Pageau, 526 F. Supp. 1221, 1224 (N.D.N.Y. 1981) a sound and video recording of an assault by prison guards on an inmate was admitted based on a foundation as to the accuracy of the recording process, despite lack of testimony from any percipient witness that it was a fair and accurate representation of the events. By now, of course, courts trust the science that underlies most recording processes and do not require proof of the basic scientific theories. But the operation of a particular automatic camera or a hospital's X-ray taken of a particular patient does require some foundational testimony to satisfy FRE 901(b)(9) — evidence that the process or system produced an accurate result.

Courts do differ, however, in the degree to which they require the complete foundation set forth above. Courts can read FRE 901(a) narrowly to require proof only of the identity of what was recorded and perhaps a minimal chain of custody, but not the recording's accuracy. In an opinion where the crux of the case against the defendant was 32 audio and videotapes, for example, the court declined to require the strict traditional foundation for each tape. It found sufficient the operator's testimony that the taping equipment was "routinely checked" to make sure it was working properly, and that after recording the tapes, he turned them over either to an FBI agent or to a state police officer. The FBI agent then described the chain of custody of the tapes. United States v. Sivils, 960 F.2d 587, 597 (6th Cir. 1992). This trend is consistent with one of the major thrusts of the Federal Rules, which was to liberalize the admission of

---

3.   Some federal circuits have raised the burden in criminal cases and have held that the prosecution must provide "clear and convincing evidence" that a tape recording is a "true, accurate, and authentic recording of a conversation, at a given time, between the parties involved." United States v. Welch, 945 F.2d 1378, 1383 (7th Cir. 1991). Accord, United States v. Morrison, 153 F.3d 34, 56 (2d Cir. 1998).

evidence. Other courts insist on a more complete showing of how a recording was made, of its chain of custody, and of its unchanged condition in order to show accuracy, often relying on FRE 403 as well as FRE 901. In United States v. Thompson, 130 F.3d 676, 683 (5th Cir. 1997), the recording of a jail inmate soliciting the murder of the judge who had sentenced him was admitted pursuant to the testimony of an FBI agent that he made the original recording; that he tested the recording equipment both before and after the tape was made; that he placed the recording device in the jail library and turned it on; that he returned several times to observe the conversation between the two inmates as it took place; and that when they left the library, he retrieved the tape and turned it over to the FBI clerk responsible for maintaining evidence.

Recordings can also be authenticated by their content alone. In Gonzalez v. Digital Equip. Corp., 8 F. Supp. 2d 194, 197 (E.D.N.Y. 1998), videos created by IBM and Apple to demonstrate product safety features and solutions to problems arising from computer keyboard usage were authenticated as to their source pursuant to FRE 901(b)(4) by their internal labels, the manner of their production, and the information that they contained.

iii. Application of FRE 403 to Recordings. Sometimes the admission of recordings can raise dangers under FRE 403. Video recordings and reenactments that portray gruesome events such as personal injuries, autopsies of crime victims, or the details of tort or crime sites, are frequently objected to as unfairly prejudicial. Because of the immediacy of their visual impact, they have added capacity to generate emotional responses and may arouse the jury's hostility or sympathy for one side, thus influencing the outcome in an unfair way. Video recordings and computer-generated animations and simulations may also convey an impression of objective reality to the jury. Courts have recognized the danger that such evidence is misleading if its contents do not correspond closely enough to the actual conditions and context of the events that are at issue at trial. In another sense of the term, an exhibit might be misleading if the jury will not be able to estimate its probative worth accurately, typically because it may overestimate the item's value due to the immediacy of the apparent reality it portrays. A related probative danger is confusion of the issues, which could occur if the jury's attention is distracted by the dramatic power of an exhibit from a careful evaluation of the issues in dispute.

In each case, the trial court will weigh these dangers against the probative value of the recording pursuant to the balancing test of FRE 403, and the appellate court will reverse only for abuse of discretion. Gov't of the Virgin Islands v. Albert, 241 F.3d 344 (3d Cir. 2001) (gruesome 45-minute video of crime victim shown to jury; thoughtful concurring opinion stated "to hold that admitting this evidence was not an abuse of the trial judge's discretion is equivalent to ruling that admitting unduly inflammatory evidence can never be cause for reversal; if this evidence was not unduly inflammatory, then nothing is.").

KEY POINTS

1. Recordings of events may be authenticated pursuant to FRE 901 if a percipient witness can testify that the recording is a fair and accurate record of the real-world event.

2. If the recording functions as a "silent witness" because there is *no* percipient witness to the event, FRE 901 may require proof of the recording process and of the chain of custody of the recording itself.

3. Recordings may be subject to exclusion under FRE 403.

PROBLEMS

4.9. Sarah Sparrow's 20-year-old son, in jail for car theft, contacted the FBI and described in detail his mother's participation in three unsolved bank robberies. After the son's release, the FBI asked him to tape record conversations with his mother about the robberies. The son was given a tape recorder and produced six tapes for the FBI. Both his voice, and his mother's voice speaking about her role in the robberies, can be clearly heard. Sarah Sparrow was charged with three counts of armed bank robbery. Sparrow files a motion in limine to object to the use of the tapes at trial on grounds that they lack foundation, that they are inherently unreliable due to her son's involvement with the FBI, and that they are more prejudicial than probative. What is the government's response to each objection? Draft questions for the son that would satisfy the percipient witness foundation.

4.10. During his trial on federal charges of drug sales, the defendant challenges the authenticity of Exhibit 8, a tape recording offered against him, claiming that the tape was altered to incriminate him. X, a confidential informant employed by the federal Drug Enforcement Administration (DEA), testified that he recorded four conversations, during which drug sales were made, that he had with the defendant between July 17 and July 19, 2004; that he used a microrecording device to make these recordings; that Exhibit 8 is the microcassette upon which the conversations were recorded; that he turned the cassette and recorder over to his DEA contact without altering the tape in any way; that he has not seen the cassette and recorder since; and that he recognizes his own voice and the voice of the defendant. Is this testimony sufficient to establish the authenticity of Exhibit 8 under either the percipient witness or "silent witness" foundation? Why?

4.11. Able, Bold, and Curry (the protesters) participated in an anti-war protest in Freedom National Historic Park on July 4, 2004. The protest started peacefully but got out of control, and Park Rangers moved in to restore order. The three protesters were arrested and found guilty of "refusing to obey the lawful order of a Park Ranger."

At the trial, a Park Ranger, Officer Miller, testified that he made a two-hour video tape of the entire protest with a hand-held video camera. He further testified that he was familiar with the camera that he used; that it had operated correctly on the day in question; and that following the protest, he removed the videocassette from the camera and labeled it with his name and the date and gave it to the video technician at the Park Ranger office. However, the tape that the government produced at trial was only 15 minutes long. This tape, admitted as Exhibit 5, was not in the cassette that had been labeled by Officer Miller. There was no witness who could testify as to how it was created or about what happened to Miller's video after it was delivered to the Park Ranger technician. Miller testified, "I picked up this tape at the Park Ranger station before bringing it to court" and "to the best of my recollection, this edited tape shows pretty much what I saw at the last 15 minutes of the protest on July 4th."

The video portrays rowdy scenes of a protest in Freedom Park. In these scenes, Able, Bold, and Curry can be seen throwing garbage at park statues. Many other demonstrators are wearing "death" masks. The Park Rangers can be heard ordering groups of demonstrators to "back off," to "disperse," and finally to "lie down on the ground," and Able, Bold, and Curry are visible in the video. They remained standing both during and after the giving of these orders.

Assume all proper objections were made under the FRE that we have studied so far. Did the trial judge commit error in admitting the video into evidence?

f. Written Documents

Typically, a written document is relevant because its contents are connected to the litigated events of a case by the identity of its author or by knowledge of its organizational source. The law of evidence, however, does not treat the signature or recital of authorship on the face of a document, without more, as sufficient proof of authenticity. FRE 901(b) includes several illustrations of how to lay a foundation that is sufficient to authenticate a written document.

i. **Signature.** Proof of the genuineness of a signature is sufficient to identify the author of a writing. Observation of the act of signing a document, as exemplified by the testimony of the landlord's nephew in our hypothetical case between the tenant and the landlord (page 178, supra), will satisfy FRE 901(b)(1). Identification of a signature based on familiarity with handwriting will satisfy FRE 901(b)(2), and under FRE 901(b)(3) either the jury or an expert may compare the signature on the exhibit itself with a specimen that has been authenticated pursuant to FRE 901. United States v. Saddley, 393 F.3d 669 (6th Cir. 2005) (under FRE 901(b)(3) a lay person can identify and compare signatures). For example, in N.L.R.B. v. General Wood Preserving Co., 905 F.2d 803, 810 (4th Cir. 1990), 17 signatures were authenticated by employees who identified them as their own; six others were authenticated by witnesses who had observed the six named employees sign the documents; and five others were authenticated by comparing them with specimens bearing authenticated signatures.

ii. **Contents and Other Circumstances.** FRE 901(b)(4) is an extremely broad and flexible standard that permits proof of authorship or source through many types of evidence. For example, the author may be identified by a document's contents, United States v. Jones, 107 F.3d 1147, 1149 (6th Cir. 1997) (defendant's signature on a greeting card sent to the father of her son-in-law could be authenticated by the father, even though he was unfamiliar with her handwriting, because it contained references to her daughter and granddaughter, and was signed with defendant's name), and/or by the circumstances in which it was found, United States v. Gonzalez-Maldonado, 115 F.3d 9, 20 (1st Cir. 1997) (notebook found in a person's briefcase in that person's room, along with an identification card, is sufficiently authenticated as belonging to that person by such circumstantial evidence).

Records of a business or other institution can be authenticated as to source under FRE 901(b)(4) through proof of matching letterhead, comparison with matching forms, testimony about the routine practices of the institution in generating such records, and through testimony of a custodian about how the business's filing or data retrieval system operates and that the document was retrieved from a certain file or in a certain way. If a computerized data retrieval process or system is used, further testimony may be required to satisfy the requirement of FRE 901(b)(9) that the computerized process must produce an accurate result. How much information will be required about input, processing, and output depends on the nature of the data, the potential for manipulation, and its verifiability. United States v. Whitaker, 127 F.3d 595, 601 (7th Cir. 1997) (computer records used by defendant to keep track of drug transactions were authenticated by testimony of an FBI agent describing how he retrieved them from defendant's computer by installing Microsoft Money on the computer and printing out the documents).

FRE 901(b)(7) provides for the authentication of certain types of public records or reports. Proof that they "are from the public office where items of this nature are kept" can be provided by testimony from the custodian, such as Ruth Taylor in the *Johnson* case, or by a certificate of authenticity from the public office. Or, a witness may simply testify that the record is from the appropriate public office. For example, an immigration agent's testimony that he retrieved documents from the defendant's INS file in Denver and that he was familiar with the record-keeping practices of the INS was held sufficient in United States v. Hernandez-Herrera, 952 F.2d 342, 344 (10th Cir. 1991).

iii.   Ancient Documents.

iii.   **Ancient Documents.**   If a writing is more than 20 years old and is in a place where it would likely be if it were authentic, the document will be admitted as "genuine" pursuant to FRE 901(b)(8) as an ancient document. In Threadgill v. Armstrong World Industries, Inc., 928 F.2d 1366, 1376 (3d Cir. 1991), correspondence dating from the 1930s that showed corporate knowledge of the dangers of asbestos had first been stored in a company vault, then moved to a personal office in 1969, and finally returned to the corporation's Director of Environmental Affairs in 1974. The court held that the manner of retaining the documents was what might have been expected.

The third requirement of this rule — that the document be in such condition as to create no suspicion concerning its authenticity — has been interpreted narrowly by some courts dealing with German documents generated during World War II that implicate current U.S. citizens in Nazi war crimes. That is, suspicions that go to the accuracy of the contents of the document, or to its completeness, do not count. The only issue that the proponent must address is whether the documents are the type of document they are claimed to be, typically by their storage location and by the expert testimony of historians who specialize in Nazi-era German history and Nazi policies and practices. "[W]hether the contents of the document [an identity card] correctly identify the defendant goes to its weight and is a matter for the trier of fact." United States v. Demjanjuk, 367 F.3d 623, 631 (6th Cir. 2004). These German documents, like many ancient documents, are admitted to prove the truth of the matters they record; thus, they are hearsay. An extremely broad "ancient documents" exception to the rule excluding hearsay, FRE 803(16), provides for the admission of a "document in existence twenty years or more the authenticity of which is established."

iv.   Electronic Writings.

iv.   **Electronic Writings.**   Due to the enormous growth in electronic commerce in recent years, the recording, communication, and preservation of digital information pervades our society. Understandably, then, electronic writings (also known as "e-evidence") are increasingly used in both civil and criminal litigation. Most common are computer-generated data files, e-mails and Internet postings. The authentication of such electronic writings can be hotly contested when authorship is in dispute. There are no subsections of FRE 901(b) that address these new electronic technologies, but FRE 901 provides flexibility in applying its standard of sufficiency. Courts have developed analogies to traditional writings in admitting e-mails, chat group discussions, and Web postings.

E-mails can be authenticated by their authorship. The electronic signature that they bear may not be sufficient, however, because of the risk of manipulation of e-mail headers. Additional data such as the address that an e-mail bears, the use of the "reply" function to generate the address of the original sender, the content of the information included in the e-mail, and other circumstances can suffice. United States v. Siddiqui, 235 F.3d 1318, 1322 (11th Cir. 2000); Mark D. Robins, Evidence at the Electronic Frontier: Introducing E-Mail at Trial in Commercial Litigation, 29 Rutgers Computer & Tech. L.J. 219, 228 (2003) ("Other factors that courts frequently consider in authenticating writings and other items will similarly apply to e-mail messages.") Authorship of identity-protected postings on chat groups can be determined by content and circumstances. In United States v. Simpson, 152 F.3d 1241 (10th Cir. 1998), the government sought to prove the content of chat room conversations concerning the defendant's possession of child pornography between a police officer and the defendant, both of whom were using assumed names. Simpson contended that the government could not prove that the statements attributed to him were in his handwriting, his writing style, or his voice pursuant to FRE 901(b)(2)-(5). The court noted the need for flexibility in its approach to authenticating this evidence:

> The specific examples of authentication referred to by Simpson are merely illustrative, however, and are not intended as an exclusive enumeration of allowable methods of authentication.
> The evidence introduced at trial clearly satisfies [the FRE 901(a)] standard. In the printout of the chat room discussion, the individual using the identity "Stavron" gave Detective Rehman his name as B. Simpson and his correct street address. . . . The discussion and subsequent e-mail exchanges indicated an e-mail address which belonged to Simpson. . . . And the pages found near the computer in Simpson's home and introduced as evidence as Plaintiff's Exhibit 6 contain a notation of the name, street address, e-mail address, and telephone number that Detective Rehman gave to the individual in the chat room. . . . Based on this evidence, the exhibit was properly authenticated and admitted as evidence. [Id. at 1249.]

Courts are skeptical about attributing documents obtained from a website to the organization or individual who maintains the site. "Anyone can put anything on the Internet . . . the Court holds no illusions that hackers can[not] adulterate the content on any web-site from any location at any time." St. Clair v. Johnny's Oyster & Shrimp, Inc., 76 F.Supp.2d 773, 775 (S.D.Tex. 1999). Web postings, therefore, require proof of the process by which they were generated. In re Homestore.Com, Securities Litigation, 347 S.Supp.2d 769, 782-83 (C.D.Calif. 2004) ("To be authenticated, some statement or affidavit from someone with knowledge is required; for example, Homestore's web master or someone else with personal knowledge would be sufficient.") Information retrieved from government websites, however, has been treated as self-authenticating, subject only to proof that the webpage does exist at the governmental web location. United States EEOC v. E.I. DuPont de Nemours & Co., 2004 U.S.Dist.LEXIS 20753 (D.La. 2004). Issues of completeness of electronic records are treated as a matter of evidentiary weight, rather than authentication and admissibility, as long as the complete records are available. United States v. Tank, 200 F.3d 627, 629 (9th Cir. 2000) (chat group member had created computer text files containing all the "recorded" online discussions among group members, with some deletions; completeness went to weight, not admissibility, and defendant himself could have recovered deleted material from the hard drive to show whether any material alterations had been made).

KEY POINTS

1. Written documents are usually identified pursuant to FRE 901 by testimony that identifies the author or the source of the document, typically using the signature, the contents, the location of the document, or other circumstances.

2. Writings created by new electronic technologies are identified and authenticated by analogies to Rule 901(b) illustrations.

PROBLEMS

4.12. Return to Problem 3.4, State v. Blair, at page 131. Police found a postcard in Norma's apartment postmarked September 12, 2005. In handwriting it says "See you at 9:00 p.m. on the 14th." It is signed "Jimmy." The government claims that Jimmy Blair wrote this postcard. Why is it relevant? What options are there to authenticate it?

4.13. In a hearing where the judge served as fact finder to certify the election of Union as the collective bargaining agent with Employer, the trial judge counted 13 signature cards allegedly signed by employees of Employer voting for Union as the bargaining agent. Authentication was based on the judge's own comparison of the signatures on the cards with signatures on the respective employees' W-4 forms. The Union offered a lay witness to compare the signatures, but the judge held this to be unnecessary. The W-4 forms had not been authenticated or offered into evidence. What errors, if any, did the trial judge commit?

4.14. Return to Problem 3.2, Pedroso v. Driver, at page 129. Has Exhibit A been adequately authenticated under FRE 901 on the basis of Driver's testimony? Why?

4.15. Return to Problem 3.3, United States v. Ray, at page 131. For each item of evidence or alleged fact below, identify the various possibilities for laying a proper foundation under FRE 901. Note that there may be more than one approach for each item of evidence. Also, think about this from the standpoint of investigating the case: What evidence would you want to gather before trial in order to introduce the evidence at trial. Once at trial, what different witnesses could you call, and what questions would you ask?

(a)   Exhibit 1: A copy of Andrews' confidential written memo to Rundown CFO June Jacobs dated March 14, 2004.
(b)   Exhibit 2: A copy of Chief Auditor Andrews' email to Jacobs, also dated March 14, 2004.
(c)   Ray's sale of 100,000 shares on March 16, 2004.

4.16. Corporation UGI is being sued for the toxic waste clean-up costs of a site owned and operated by MGC, one of UGI's wholly owned subsidiaries. In order to establish the absolute control that UGI exercised over MGC, the government offers an article from the *Philadelphia Daily Stockholder*, which it obtained from UGI's files. The article is an in-depth analysis of UGI's tight control over its subsidiaries, including MGC. The article is dated February 26, 1980. Can the government authenticate the article using FRE 901? What other problems with its admissibility might there be?

g. FRE 901 Provides Flexibility in Application

You can see from these FRE 901(b) illustrations that what it means to identify or authenticate particular types of evidence varies widely. There is no one "correct" foundation that must be satisfied in each case, or for each particular type. Courts apply the standard of Rule 901(a) flexibly and do not always require that a particular subsection of Rule 901(b) be satisfied. The treatises on evidence law are full of fascinating case law examples of the kinds of foundations that have been laid to authenticate exhibits — particularly those that are susceptible to tampering and change of condition. Over time, courts do tend to distill the elements of an adequate foundation into criteria that they apply routinely. But in drafting the ultimate criterion of FRE 901(a) so loosely — that a matter is what the proponent claims it to be — the drafters of the Federal Rules have permitted flexibility in the application of the authentication requirement. Remember, however, that the starting point of your analysis of the requisite foundation should always be relevancy.

4. FRE 902: Written Documents That Are Self-authenticating

a. FRE 902

RULE 902. SELF-AUTHENTICATION

Extrinsic evidence of authenticity as a condition precedent to admissibility is not required with respect to the following:

(1) Domestic public documents under seal. A document bearing a seal purporting to be that of the United States, or of any State, district, Commonwealth, territory, or insular possession thereof, or the Panama Canal Zone, or the Trust Territory of the Pacific Islands, or of a political subdivision, department, officer, or agency thereof, and a signature purporting to be an attestation or execution.

(2) Domestic public documents not under seal. A document purporting to bear the signature in the official capacity of an officer or employee of any entity included in paragraph (1) hereof, having no seal, if a public officer having a seal and having official duties in the district or political subdivision of the officer or employee certifies under seal that the signer has the official capacity and that the signature is genuine.

(3) Foreign public documents. A document purporting to be executed or attested in an official capacity by a person authorized by the laws of a foreign country to make the execution or attestation, and accompanied by a final certification as to the genuineness of the signature and official position (A) of the executing or attesting person, or (B) of any foreign official whose certificate of genuineness of signature and official position relates to the execution or attestation or is in a chain of certificates of genuineness of signature and official position relating to the execution or attestation. A final certification may be made by a secretary of embassy or legation, consul general, consul, vice consul, or consular agent of the United States, or a diplomatic or consular official of the foreign country assigned or accredited to the United States. If reasonable opportunity has been given to all parties to investigate the authenticity and accuracy of official documents, the court may, for good cause shown, order that they be treated as presumptively authentic without final certification or permit them to be evidenced by an attested summary with or without final certification.

(4) Certified copies of public records. A copy of an official record or report or entry therein, or of a document authorized by law to be recorded or filed and actually recorded

or filed in a public office, including data compilations in any form, certified as correct by the custodian or other person authorized to make the certification, by certificate complying with paragraph (1), (2), or (3) of this rule or complying with any Act of Congress or rule prescribed by the Supreme Court pursuant to statutory authority.

(5) Official publications. Books, pamphlets, or other publications purporting to be issued by public authority.

(6) Newspapers and periodicals. Printed materials purporting to be newspapers or periodicals.

(7) Trade inscriptions and the like. Inscriptions, signs, tags, or labels purporting to have been affixed in the course of business and indicating ownership, control, or origin.

(8) Acknowledged documents. Documents accompanied by a certificate of acknowledgment executed in the manner provided by law by a notary public or other officer authorized by law to take acknowledgments.

(9) Commercial paper and related documents. Commercial paper, signatures thereon, and documents relating thereto to the extent provided by general commercial law.

(10) Presumptions under Acts of Congress. Any signature, document, or other matter declared by Act of Congress to be presumptively or prima facie genuine or authentic.

(11) Certified domestic records of regularly conducted activity. The original or a duplicate of a domestic record of regularly conducted activity that would be admissible under Rule 803(6) if accompanied by a written declaration of its custodian or other qualified person, in a manner complying with any Act of Congress or rule prescribed by the Supreme Court pursuant to statutory authority, certifying that the record — (A) was made at or near the time of the occurrence of the matters set forth by, or from information transmitted by, a person with knowledge of those matters; (B) was kept in the course of the regularly conducted activity; and (C) was made by the regularly conducted activity as a regular practice.

A party intending to offer a record into evidence under this paragraph must provide written notice of that intention to all adverse parties, and must make the record and declaration available for inspection sufficiently in advance of their offer into evidence to provide an adverse party with a fair opportunity to challenge them.

(12) Certified foreign records of regularly conducted activity. In a civil case, the original or a duplicate of a foreign record of regularly conducted activity that would be admissible under Rule 803(6) if accompanied by a written declaration by its custodian or other qualified person certifying that the record — (A) was made at or near the time of the occurrence of the matters set forth by, or from information transmitted by, a person with knowledge of those matters; (B) was kept in the course of the regularly conducted activity; and (C) was made by the regularly conducted activity as a regular practice.

The declaration must be signed in a manner that, if falsely made, would subject the maker to criminal penalty under the laws of the country where the declaration is signed. A party intending to offer a record into evidence under this paragraph must provide written notice of that intention to all adverse parties, and must make the record and declaration available for inspection sufficiently in advance of their offer into evidence to provide an adverse party with a fair opportunity to challenge them.

b.   Interpretation of FRE 902

FRE 902 defines those documents that, on the basis of their appearance or self-evident content alone, are so likely to be authentic that the proponent need produce no extrinsic evidence to prove it.

Certain kinds of public documents and public records have been produced by a formal process that triggers a generalization that the document itself, and the signatures on it, are very likely to be genuine. The formalities, such as a seal or a statement of certification as required by FRE 902(1)-(4) and (8), indicate that someone has paid attention to genuineness. The 969B package, offered into the *Johnson* case as Exhibit 2, contained certified copies of the original documents in Johnson's C File (page 36, line 18, supra). It was thus probably a self-authenticating public record under the California equivalent to FRE 902(4). A passport has been held to be a public document, which must be accompanied by official certifications to be self-authenticating under FRE 902(2) or (3). United States v. Pluta, 176 F.3d 43, 49 (2d Cir. 1999).

Other kinds of writings, just from looking at them, trigger a generalization that they are genuine because they are very difficult to forge. For example, it may more reliably be inferred that the writings defined in FRE 902(5)-(7) and (9) are from the source they appear to be from. However, it must be acknowledged that this justification for the rule has been weakened: "[M]odern technological developments [computers, scanners, publishing software, and internet access] make it easier to produce...a counterfeit." Wright & Gold, Federal Practice and Procedure: Evidence §7140 (2000). Pursuant to FRE 902(7), trade inscriptions and the like are usually treated as establishing the authenticity of the item to which they are affixed, as well as their own genuineness. There is split authority as to whether writings such as an owner's manual, or electronic writings such as e-mail messages, that bear a company's trademark should also be considered self-authenticating. Whitted v. General Motors Corp, 245 F.3d 1200 (7th Cir. 1995) (trade inscription on cover of owner's manual does not authenticate the contents of the manual).

FRE 902(11) and (12) became effective in December 2000 and are referred to in FRE 803(6), discussed at page 527, infra. They are intended to simplify the authentication of business records and to substitute a written declaration for the production at trial of a custodian or other witness knowledgeable about the factors specifically listed. One unanswered question is whether the written declaration must include detailed information to support the factor that, for example, the record was made "as a regular practice," or whether the declaration can simply recite that conclusion. Most reported cases refer to verbatim recitation of the required factors; however, the court in Rambus, Inc v. Infineon Techs. Ag, 348 F.Supp.2d 698 (E.D.Va. 2004) found that the specific facts stated in the declarations were insufficient to satisfy the requirements of FRE 803(6). Notice of a party's intent to use Rules 902(11) and (12), together with the records themselves, must be provided to the opponent for verification and potential challenge. If only conclusory statements are made in written declarations, then the burden falls on the opponent to take discovery on the underlying specific facts.

As stated in the Advisory Committee Note to FRE 902, admission of a document pursuant to Rule 902 is not dispositive of authenticity. The opponent can offer proof that the document is a phony or bears a forged signature. Self-authentication also does not resolve questions as to the source or accuracy of information that is reported in self-authenticated documents. United States v. Bisbee, 245 F.3d 1001, 1007 (8th Cir. 2001) (evidence tending to contradict the facts reported in certified documents does not render them inadmissible). Objections can also still be made that inadmissible hearsay statements or expert opinions are included in, for example, newspapers or periodicals.

KEY POINT

FRE 902 provides that some written documents can be authenticated by their appearance alone, without the testimony of a foundation witness. The opponent may still dispute the authenticity of these "self-authenticating" documents.

PROBLEMS

4.17. To prove that two persons are not U.S. citizens and have been illegally smuggled into the United States, the government offers their alleged passports from Poland. To authenticate the documents, an INS supervisory inspector, with extensive experience in conducting inspections to exclude persons from the United States, testifies that he recognizes the passports as genuine Polish passports. When asked the basis for his opinion, he states: "They're identified as such right on the document." Sufficient?

In the same case, the INS inspector offers Volume Two of INS policies which, on its title page, states that it is issued by the Department of Homeland Security and bears a facsimile of the official seal of the Department. When asked how he recognizes the exhibit as the genuine volume he answers "Look at the title page." Sufficient? What is the difference between the passports and Volume Two?

4.18. Return to Problem 4.16 at page 194. Does Rule 902 provide alternative means for authenticating the newspaper?

C.   THE BEST EVIDENCE RULE

The best evidence rule — really a cluster of rules — imposes additional foundational requirements on the proponent of writings, recordings, and photographs. The theory of the rule is simple: When a writing, recording, or photograph is offered to prove its content, the chances are good that the original will be more trustworthy than a copy. Therefore, the best evidence rule creates a requirement for the production of originals. The requirement may be excused, and other "secondary" evidence of the contents may be admitted if the absence of the original is explained or justified.

1.   FRE 1001, 1002, 1003, 1004, 1005, 1006, and 1007

RULE 1001.   DEFINITIONS

For purposes of this article the following definitions are applicable:
(1) Writings and recordings. "Writings" and "recordings" consist of letters, words, or numbers, or their equivalent, set down by handwriting, typewriting, printing, photostating, photographing, magnetic impulse, mechanical or electronic recording, or other form of data compilation.
(2) Photographs. "Photographs" include still photographs, X-ray films, videotapes, and motion pictures.

(3) Original. An "original" of a writing or recording is the writing or recording itself or any counterpart intended to have the same effect by a person executing or issuing it. An "original" of a photograph includes the negative or any print therefrom. If data are stored in a computer or similar device, any printout or other output readable by sight, shown to reflect the data accurately, is an "original".

(4) Duplicate. A "duplicate" is a counterpart produced by the same impression as the original, or from the same matrix, or by means of photography, including enlargements and miniatures, or by mechanical or electronic re-recording, or by chemical reproduction, or by other equivalent techniques which accurately reproduces the original.

RULE 1002. REQUIREMENT OF ORIGINAL

To prove the content of a writing, recording, or photograph, the original writing, recording, or photograph is required, except as otherwise provided in these rules or by Act of Congress.

RULE 1003. ADMISSIBILITY OF DUPLICATES

A duplicate is admissible to the same extent as an original unless (1) a genuine question is raised as to the authenticity of the original or (2) in the circumstances it would be unfair to admit the duplicate in lieu of the original.

RULE 1004. ADMISSIBILITY OF OTHER EVIDENCE OF CONTENTS

The original is not required, and other evidence of the contents of a writing, recording, or photograph is admissible if — (1) Originals lost or destroyed. All originals are lost or have been destroyed, unless the proponent lost or destroyed them in bad faith; or (2) Original not obtainable. No original can be obtained by any available judicial process or procedure; or (3) Original in possession of opponent. At a time when an original was under the control of the party against whom offered, that party was put on notice, by the pleadings or otherwise, that the contents would be a subject of proof at the hearing, and that party does not produce the original at the hearing; or (4) Collateral matters. The writing, recording, or photograph is not closely related to a controlling issue.

RULE 1005. PUBLIC RECORDS

The contents of an official record, or of a document authorized to be recorded or filed and actually recorded or filed, including data compilations in any form, if otherwise admissible, may be proved by copy, certified as correct in accordance with rule 902 or testified to be correct by a witness who has compared it with the original. If a copy which complies with the foregoing cannot be obtained by the exercise of reasonable diligence, then other evidence of the contents may be given.

RULE 1006. SUMMARIES

The contents of voluminous writings, recordings, or photographs which cannot conveniently be examined in court may be presented in the form of a chart, summary, or calculation. The originals, or duplicates, shall be made available for examination or copying, or both, by other parties at reasonable time and place. The court may order that they be produced in court.

RULE 1007. TESTIMONY OR WRITTEN ADMISSION OF PARTY

Contents of writings, recordings, or photographs may be proved by the testimony or deposition of the party against whom offered or by that party's written admission, without accounting for the nonproduction of the original.

2. Interpretation and Illustration of FRE 1001, 1002, 1003, 1004, 1005, 1006 and 1007

a. *Summary of the Basic Principles of the Best Evidence Rule*

i.   FRE 1002.   FRE 1002 provides the basic principle of the best evidence rule: An original is required when a proponent seeks to prove the content of a writing, recording, or photograph. FRE 1002 applies broadly, insofar as *writings* and *recordings* are defined very broadly under FRE 1001(1) to include any form of data compilation. However, the scope of FRE 1002 does not extend beyond writings, recordings, and photographs. There is no explicitly articulated "best evidence principle" enacted in the Federal Rules that requires the proponent to offer the best evidence of whatever it is that he or she wishes to prove. Generally speaking, a party may prove its case by any admissible evidence, regardless of whether anything "better" (i.e., more persuasive or reliable) is available. Of course, the advocate may be motivated to use the most highly probative evidence in order to persuade the jury, but evidence law gives the judge little control over the advocate's choice.

What constitutes an *original* that will satisfy FRE 1002 is also defined broadly by FRE 1001(3): any "counterpart intended to have the same effect by a person executing or issuing it," such as carbon copies when a document is executed in quadruplicate; any negative or print of a photograph; and any printout of data stored in a computer if such output is shown to reflect the data accurately. The key issue in applying Rule 1002 is the determination of when the "content" of these kinds of items is being proved, discussed at pages 205-206, infra.

ii.   FRE 1003.   FRE 1003 provides that duplicates may be furnished instead of an original in most circumstances. FRE 1001(4) broadly defines *duplicate* to include photocopies, which are commonly used. CD versions of audio recordings originally made on a digital memory chip can be admitted as duplicates. Enhanced copies of recordings also qualify as duplicates. In United States v. Seifert, 351 F.Supp.2d 926, 928 (D.Minn. 2005), the court admitted a digitally enhanced copy of a surveillance videotape as a duplicate pursuant to FRE 1001(4), finding that the copy was a "fair and accurate depiction of the original. . . . The enhancements more readily reveal, but remain true to, the recorded events." The technician testified to all of the steps used to enhance the image, including changing the tape from analog to digital, correcting the images to real time, enlarging the objects of interest to fill the screen, and adjusting brightness and contrast. Concerns about whether a recording is of such poor quality that it cannot be understood by the jury are determined under Rule 403, once the recording has been authenticated.

FRE 1003 provides that a duplicate may not be used if the opponent presents evidence that disputes the authenticity of the original, or if other aspects of the original or duplicate — incompleteness, erasures, defects — make it unfair for the proponent to use the duplicate. In Ruberto v. Commissioner, 774 F.2d 61 (2d Cir. 1985), for example, photocopies of cancelled checks were excluded as duplicates because the copies of the backs of the checks, where the endorsement would be visible, could not be matched to the copies of the fronts of the checks. But in United States v. Sinclair, 74 F.3d 753, 760-761 (7th Cir. 1996), the court upheld admission of photocopies of the defendant's allegedly false expense account reports submitted to his employer, although the copies did not reproduce the reverse side of the originals. The court found that the omitted portions would not have affected the usefulness of the copies since all they would have shown were itemizations of less than $200 out of thousands of dollars of claimed expenses.

iii. **FRE 1004.** FRE 1004 provides the standard catalog of common law exceptions that justify or explain why a proponent should not be required to produce an original. Loss or destruction of the original, pursuant to FRE 1004(1), may be proved by testimony from a person with knowledge, or by circumstantial evidence that the proponent has made a reasonable, diligent, and unsuccessful search for the original. The party need not explain with absolute certainty what happened to the original, but has the burden to prove that its loss or destruction was not in bad faith, as discussed on page 212, infra. Negligent destruction of documents has been held insufficient to establish bad faith. Cross v. United States, 149 F.3d 1190, 1998 WL 255054 *5 (10th Cir. 1998) (the purposeful destruction or withholding of original documents and the fabrication of secondary evidence will support a finding of bad faith under Fed. R. Evid 1004(1)).

If originals are not lost but are in the possession of others, the court may require the proponent to show that they cannot be obtained by reasonable, diligent, and unsuccessful use of judicial process or other inquiry pursuant to FRE 1004(2). United States v. Crisp., 190 F.R.D. 546, 553 (E.D. Ca. 1999) (government's mere allegation that taxpayers failed to produce business records that were returned to them held to be insufficient). If the originals are in the possession of the opponent, then, pursuant to the requirements of FRE 1004(3), secondary evidence of their contents may be offered if the opponent fails to produce them at trial. If the opponent has described the contents of a writing in testimony or in a written admission, FRE 1007 permits the use of this testimony or admission against that party to prove such contents, without accounting for the absence of the original.

It is important to note that Rule 1004 permits the proponent to use any "other evidence" of the content of the original. No preference is given to any particular type of secondary evidence once the original is not available. A common form of secondary evidence is the oral testimony of a witness who once perceived the original and claims to remember it. United States v. Shores, 93 Fed. Appx.868 (6th Cir. 2004) (police testimony describing photograph in defendant's bedroom admissible under FRE 1004(3) because photograph was still in defendant's possession). All types of copies are also equally acceptable. For example, in United States v. Ross, 33 F.2d 1507 (11th Cir. 1994), transcripts of tape recorded telephone conversations in Spain were admissible as secondary evidence where the recordings had been destroyed in a routine procedure by Spanish police. Official records are an exception to this principle of equal acceptability. FRE 1005 establishes a priority for proof of such official records: a certified copy or a copy that a witness can testify is correct is preferred over other types of secondary evidence. Only if such copies cannot be obtained with "reasonable diligence" may other evidence of contents be given.

iv.   FRE 1006.   FRE 1006 permits the proponent of voluminous writings, recordings, and photographs to present the contents of these items in the form of a summary, chart, or calculation. These voluminous materials must themselves be shown to be admissible. Peat, Inc. v. Vanguard Research, Inc., 378 F.3d 1154, 1160 (11th Cir. 2004) ("Rule 1006 is not a back-door vehicle for the introduction of evidence which is otherwise inadmissible.") The trial judge has substantial discretion to decide whether the underlying originals are too voluminous to be conveniently examined in court. In United States v. Briscoe, 896 F.2d 1476 (7th Cir. 1990), the court admitted cover sheets summarizing transcripts of recorded conversations because in-court examination of the transcripts was inconvenient, although not impossible.

The proponent is obligated to produce the originals in time to permit the opponent to examine and copy them, obviously to check the summary for any errors or inconsistencies, and for purposes of cross-examination. Courts are strict in enforcing this requirement. United States v. Modena, 302 F.3d 626, 633 (6th Cir. 2002) (willingness to provide underlying documents, if requested prior to trial, is inadequate; opponent has absolute right to production of underlying material, and party seeking to use summary must state when and where material may be reviewed even absent a discovery request). If the originals are no longer available, Rule 1006 would not apply, but a summary might be admissible under FRE 1004 as secondary evidence.

b.   The Policies Underlying the Best Evidence Rule

The following opinion of the Ninth Circuit Court of Appeals concerns a party's attempt to offer secondary evidence of detailed drawings when that party's good faith loss of the originals had not been proved. The opinion discusses the policies that justify requiring production of originals in general, as well as when non-production is not excused.

SEILER v. LUCASFILM, LTD.
808 F.2d 1316 (9th Cir. 1986), cert. denied, 484 U.S. 826 (1987)

FARRIS, Circuit Judge.
Lee Seiler, a graphic artist and creator of science fiction creatures, alleged copyright infringement by George Lucas and others who created and produced the science fiction movie *The Empire Strikes Back*. Seiler claimed that creatures known as "Imperial Walkers" which appeared in *The Empire Strikes Back* infringed Seiler's copyright on his own creatures called "Garthian Striders." *The Empire Strikes Back* appeared in 1980; Seiler did not obtain his copyright until 1981. . . .

FACTS

Seiler contends that he created and published in 1976 and 1977 [drawings of] science fiction creatures called Garthian Striders. In 1980, George Lucas released *The*

Empire Strikes Back, a motion picture that contains a battle sequence depicting giant machines called Imperial Walkers. In 1981 Seiler obtained a copyright on his Striders, depositing with the Copyright Office "reconstructions" of the originals as they had appeared in 1976 and 1977.

Seiler contends that Lucas' Walkers were copied from Seiler's Striders which were allegedly published in 1976 and 1977. Lucas responds that Seiler did not obtain his copyright until one year after the release of *The Empire Strikes Back* and that Seiler can produce no documents that antedate *The Empire Strikes Back.*

Because Seiler proposed to exhibit his Striders in a blow-up comparison to Lucas' Walkers at opening statement, the district judge held an evidentiary hearing on the admissibility of the "reconstructions" of Seiler's Striders. Applying the "best evidence rule," Fed. R. Evid. 1001-1008, the district court found at the end of a seven-day hearing that Seiler lost or destroyed the originals in bad faith under Rule 1004(1) and that consequently no secondary evidence, such as the post–*Empire Strikes Back* reconstructions, was admissible. In its opinion the court found specifically that Seiler testified falsely, purposefully destroyed or withheld in bad faith the originals, and fabricated and misrepresented the nature of his reconstructions. The district court granted summary judgment to Lucas after the evidentiary hearing.

On appeal, Seiler contends (1) that the best evidence rule does not apply to his works, [and] (2) that if the best evidence rule does apply, Rule 1008 requires a jury determination of the existence and authenticity of his originals.... [4]

DISCUSSION

1. APPLICATION OF THE BEST EVIDENCE RULE

...We hold that Seiler's drawings were "writings" within the meaning of Rule 1001(1); they consist not of "letters, words, or numbers" but of "their equivalent." To hold otherwise would frustrate the policies underlying the rule and introduce undesirable inconsistencies into the application of the rule....

In the days before liberal rules of discovery and modern techniques of electronic copying, the rule guarded against incomplete or fraudulent proof. By requiring the possessor of the original to produce it, the rule prevented the introduction of altered copies and the withholding of originals. The purpose of the rule was thus long thought to be one of fraud prevention, but Wigmore pointed out that the rule operated even in cases where fraud was not at issue, such as where secondary evidence is not admitted even though its proponent acts in utmost good faith. Wigmore also noted that if prevention of fraud were the foundation of the rule, it should apply to objects as well as writings, which it does not....

The modern justification for the rule has expanded from prevention of fraud to a recognition that writings occupy a central position in the law. When the contents of a writing are at issue, oral testimony as to the terms of the writing is subject to a greater risk of error than oral testimony as to events or other situations. The human memory is not often capable of reciting the precise terms of a writing, and when the terms are in dispute only the writing itself, or a true copy, provides reliable evidence. To summarize ... the importance of the precise terms of writings in the world of legal relations, the fallibility of

4. The Court's decision on the Rule 1008 issue is discussed at pages 211-213, infra.-EDS.

the human memory as reliable evidence of the terms, and the hazards of inaccurate or incomplete duplication are the concerns addressed by the best evidence rule....

. . . The contents of Seiler's work are at issue. There can be no proof of "substantial similarity" and thus of copyright infringement unless Seiler's works are juxtaposed with Lucas' and their contents compared. Since the contents are material and must be proved, Seiler must either produce the original or show that it is unavailable through no fault of his own. Rule 1004(1). This he could not do.

The facts of this case implicate the very concerns that justify the best evidence rule. Seiler alleges infringement by *The Empire Strikes Back*, but he can produce no documentary evidence of any originals existing before the release of the movie. His secondary evidence does not consist of true copies or exact duplicates but of "reconstructions" made after *The Empire Strikes Back*. In short, Seiler claims that the movie infringed his originals, yet he has no proof of those originals.

The dangers of fraud in this situation are clear. The rule would ensure that proof of the infringement claim consists of the works alleged to be infringed. Otherwise, "reconstructions" which might have no resemblance to the purported original would suffice as proof for infringement of the original. Furthermore, application of the rule here defers to the rule's special concern for the contents of writings. Seiler's claim depends on the content of the originals, and the rule would exclude reconstituted proof of the originals' content. Under the circumstances here, no "reconstruction" can substitute for the original.

Seiler argues that the best evidence rule does not apply to his work, in that it is artwork rather than "writings, recordings, or photographs." He contends that the rule both historically and currently embraces only words or numbers. Neither party has cited us to cases which discuss the applicability of the rule to drawings.

To recognize Seiler's works as writings does not, as Seiler argues, run counter to the rule's preoccupation with the centrality of the written word in the world of legal relations. Just as a contract objectively manifests the subjective intent of the makers, so Seiler's drawings are objective manifestations of the creative mind. The copyright laws give legal protection to the objective manifestations of an artist's ideas, just as the law of contract protects through its multifarious principles the meeting of minds evidenced in the contract. Comparing Seiler's drawings with Lucas' drawings is no different in principle than evaluating a contract and the intent behind it. Seiler's "reconstructions" are "writings" that affect legal relations; their copyrightability attests to that.

A creative literary work, which is artwork, and a photograph whose contents are sought to be proved, as in copyright, defamation, or invasion of privacy, are both covered by the best evidence rule. We would be inconsistent to apply the rule to artwork which is literary or photographic but not to artwork of other forms. Furthermore, blueprints, engineering drawings, architectural designs may all lack words or numbers yet still be capable of copyright and susceptible to fraudulent alteration. In short, Seiler's argument would have us restrict the definitions of Rule 1001(1) to "words" and "numbers" but ignore "or their equivalent." We will not do so in the circumstances of this case.

Our holding is also supported by the policy served by the best evidence rule in protecting against faulty memory. Seiler's reconstructions were made four to seven years after the alleged originals; his memory as to specifications and dimensions may have dimmed significantly. Furthermore, reconstructions made after the release of *The Empire Strikes Back* may be tainted, even if unintentionally, by exposure to the movie. Our holding guards against these problems.

PROBLEM

4.19. What if Seiler had not published drawings but had built models of Garthian Striders in 1976 and 1977, and had obtained a copyright based on a reconstruction of those models in 1981? Would the result be different? Do the policies of the best evidence rule apply equally to models?

3. Elaboration of FRE 1002 and 1006

a. When Is a Writing Offered to Prove Its Own Content Under FRE 1002?

The best evidence rule requires an original only when the proponent is offering a writing, recording, or photograph as relevant *to prove its own content*. When the precise terms of the writing are at issue, accuracy is important and the original would be required. This happens in two principal ways.

i. The Content of the Writing, Recording, or Photograph Is a Fact of Independent Legal Significance. The content of a writing, recording, or photograph may be a fact of independent legal significance in the case under the applicable substantive law. For example, writings may themselves constitute a crime or tort. In an obscenity prosecution, the content of an allegedly obscene film must be proved as an essential element of the case. United States v. Levine, 546 F.2d 658 (5th Cir. 1977). Similarly, in a libel suit, the allegedly libelous writing is offered to prove that its own contents are libelous. When there are disputes over terms of written agreements (such as contracts, wills, and trusts), and either the substantive law requires the agreement to be proved by the writing or the party chooses to rely on the writing to prove the terms, the best evidence rule applies. For example, in our landlord-tenant hypothetical on page 176, supra, the tenant, Jane, would have had to produce the original written rental agreement in order to prove the landlord's obligation to make improvements. In still other cases, the contents of a document are at issue because they prove notice. Tracinda Corp. v. DaimlerChrysler AG, 2005 U.S.Dist. LEXIS 5096 (D.Del.) (contents of newspaper article at issue when used to prove defendants were aware of the matters reported).

In all of these examples, the writings and recordings are "non-hearsay" statements, relevant as legally operative facts or for their effect on the listener (or viewer), as will be discussed on pages 427-429 of Chapter Eight, infra. As such, their exact content must be proved and Rule 1002 applies.

ii. The Writing, Recording, or Photograph Is Used to Prove an Event. Writings can record many different kinds of events — a business ledger, for example, records what items the salesperson sold and what price was paid. What people have said, for example in testimony they gave at trial, may also be viewed as an event that might be recorded by a stenographer or by a tape recording. When the proponent is trying to prove the event using a percipient witness, there is no requirement that a documentary record of the event be produced instead. Oral testimony is being used to prove the *event*, not the *content of a writing*. R&R Associates, Inc. v. Visual Scene, Inc., 726 F.2d 36, 38 (1st Cir.1984) (testimony as to cost of items admissible; "no evidentiary rule . . . prohibits a witness from testifying to a fact simply because the fact can be supported by written documentation").

However, sometimes the proponent has chosen to use a writing, recording, or photograph to prove that an event occurred. For example, in the *Johnson* case, the fight in Johnson's cell was the out-of-court event at issue. It may be proved, as it was in the trial, by oral testimony. But if the prosecutor chose to use a writing (such as Officer Walker's report) or a recording (such as a videotape) to prove what happened, he would be using it to prove its contents and the original would be required. In United States v. Howard, 953 F.2d 610 (11th Cir. 1992), a federal agent could testify about a conversation that he overheard, even though it was also tape recorded. The testimony was offered to prove the contents of the conversation, not the contents of the tape. As you will see in Chapter Eight, a writing that is offered as a record to prove an event will probably be treated as hearsay, and a hearsay exception must be found as well.

iii.   Facts About the Writing Are Not Its "Contents."

In some cases, a writing may be referred to, but it is a fact about the writing, not the precise terms of its contents, that the proponent is trying to prove. In these cases, FRE 1002 does not apply. In The Travelers Ins. Co. v. United States, 46 Fed. Cl. 458 (Ct. Fed. Cl. 2000), a tax refund case, the government introduced five memoranda as business records of the plaintiff, Travelers. These memoranda mentioned two disputed facts about some mortgage notes that had been issued by Travelers — the notes' corporate nature and their date of issuance. Travelers claimed that the original mortgage notes should be offered instead of the memoranda and objected on the basis of FRE 1002. The court upheld the admission of the memoranda, stating:

> Plaintiff is correct that Rule 1002 does not render these documents inadmissible. The rule . . . prevent[s] the introduction of evidence designed to prove the *terms* of the document, where often small changes in words may be of significance. . . . It does not, however, prevent the introduction in evidence of facts about the document, or facts that exist independently of the document that are not given legal consequence by the terms of the document. Here, the two contentions for which plaintiff wishes to use the memoranda are facts about the mortgage notes and facts that exist independent of the obligations themselves. The corporate nature of the mortgage notes does not depend on the terms of the notes; it is a fact independent of the mortgage notes. The date of issuance of the mortgage notes is a fact independent of the notes as well. [Id. at 463, emphasis added]

As another example, bank robberies come within the jurisdiction of the federal courts if the bank deposits are insured by the Federal Deposit Insurance Corporation (FDIC). Testimony of a witness that the deposits "are insured" has been held sufficient; production of the original insurance policy is not required. United States v. Sliker, 751 F.2d 477, 483 (2d Cir. 1984) (the proof required is the fact of insurance, not the content of the insurance policy.)

Testimony *about* a writing, or about an event that happens to be recorded in a writing, can be difficult to distinguish from testimony about the content of a writing. Uncertainty often is resolved by treating a document's contents as "collateral" to the proceeding, and thus excused from the requirement that an original be produced under FRE 1004(4). Jackson v. Crews, 873 F.2d 1105 (8th Cir. 1989) (defendant not using testimony about printed flyer to prove its contents; but if he had been, contents were collateral).

b. Types of Summaries and Rule 1006

i. Voluminous Documents Underlying a Summary Must Be Admissible, But Need Not Be Admitted at Trial.   A summary of voluminous documents admitted pursuant to FRE 1006 is itself evidence and obviates the need to introduce the original material into evidence. Therefore, courts have held that when a summary or chart is offered as a Rule 1006 exhibit, the proponent must establish that the documents underlying it are admissible in evidence. United States v. Bray, 139 F.3d 1104, 1109 (6th Cir. 1998) (a chart or summary based on inadmissible hearsay, or on documents that are irrelevant, unfairly prejudicial, or nonauthenticated, would not be admitted). In United States v. Samaniego, 187 F.3d 1222, 1223-1226 (10th Cir. 1999), the circuit court held that the district court had made an error of law by not requiring the government to prove that the telephone records underlying the proffered summary were admissible as business records under FRE 803(6). The government had to lay the required foundation or forego the use of the summary. Note that the summary itself is prepared for trial and need not conform to the business record requirements of Rule 803(6). Badgett v. Rent-Way, Inc., 350 F.Supp.2d 642 (W.D.Pa. 2004).

It is not required, however, that the underlying voluminous materials are *actually* admitted at trial because the rule provides that the summary may substitute for those materials:

> [G]iven Rule 1006's provision that the underlying documents need not themselves be in evidence, however, it is plain that a summary admitted under Rule 1006 is itself the evidence that the trier of fact should consider. . . . Once a Rule 1006 summary is admitted, it may go to the jury room, like any other exhibit. [United States v. Bray, 139 F.3d at 1109.]

ii. Illustrative Aids.   To be distinguished from Rule 1006 summaries are summaries and charts that are used simply as "illustrative" or "pedagogical" aids to summarize and display the testimony of a witness or documentary evidence that has already been admitted at trial. Id. at 111-112 (describing pedagogic devices, or illustrative aids such as chalkboard outlines, flip charts, or drawings). Such devices are not within the terms of FRE 1006. Their use is controlled by the trial judge pursuant to FRE 611(a).There is authority that these aids should not be admitted into evidence as exhibits and should not be taken into the jury room. United States v. Buck, 324 F.3d 786 (5th Cir. 2003). Even though FRE 901 may not fully apply if an aid is not treated as an exhibit, a foundation for the accuracy of illustrative evidence, similar to that for other forms of demonstrative exhibits, must be laid pursuant to FRE 611(a) and FRE 403. Many courts endorse the use of illustrative aids as a trial management technique "so long as an appropriate limiting instruction informs the jury that the chart itself is not evidence but is only an aid in evaluating the evidence." United States v. DeBoer, 966 F.2d 1066, 1069 (6th Cir. 1992).

iii. Analytic Summaries.   A third type of summary or chart combines the characteristics of a Rule 1006 exhibit and a Rule 611(a) illustrative aid. That is, these summaries are not merely illustrative. Instead, they contain an analysis, made by the person who created the summary, of data that has already been admitted into evidence. Circuit courts are split on whether this type of analytic summary should be admitted into evidence as an exhibit under Rule 1006, in addition to the underlying data. Either way, the jury is instructed that "the summary is not independent evidence of its subject matter, . . . [that it] is only as valid and reliable as the underlying evidence it summarizes," and that the jury is the ultimate judge of its accuracy. United States v. Bray, 139 F.3d at 1112. Courts should be scrupulous in determining that these summaries accurately portray the evidence already admitted, particularly if, as exhibits, they will be in the jury room during deliberations. United States v. Taylor, 210 F.3d 311, 315 (5th Cir. 2000) (reversible error to admit an "organizational chart" of a drug conspiracy that portrayed photographs of the alleged participants, with arrows showing the alleged flow of drugs among them; the arrows did not accurately reflect the underlying testimony). And if the analytic summary reflects assumptions or inferences about the evidence, there must be evidentiary support in the record for these assumptions or inferences. United States v. Hart, 295 F.3d 451 (5th Cir. 2002) (government witness who prepared an analytic summary could not state her assumption that "all" of defendants' debts had to be reported in a Farm and Home Plan disclosure form, since no evidence supporting this assumption had been offered at trial).

So long as they are accurate, however, such summaries may present only one party's side of the case. United States v. Sawyer, 85 F.3d 713, 739 (1st Cir. 1996) (not error to admit summaries that did not depict full range of defendant's expenditures; defendant had opportunity on cross-examination to place the summaries within the context of his total financial activity and to explore any misleading impressions that he claims the summaries created; defendant could also offer his own contrary evidence including his own summary).

KEY POINTS

1. FRE 1002 requires the proponent of a writing, recording, or photograph to produce the original item when the proponent is trying to prove the content of the item. This requirement applies when the content of the item has independent legal significance or when the item is the record of an event and the proponent has chosen it as the means of proving the event.

2. FRE 1003 permits the proponent to produce a duplicate instead of the original in most circumstances.

3. FRE 1004 permits the proponent to produce secondary evidence of the original if the absence of the original can be explained or justified. No particular type of secondary evidence is preferred. Only FRE 1005 states a preference for certified or compared copies of public records.

4. FRE 1006 permits the use of summaries of voluminous writings, recordings, and photographs without the admission of the originals into evidence. The originals or duplicates must, however, be available to the opponent. A summary admitted under Rule 1006 is itself substantive evidence.

PROBLEMS

4.20 Return to Problem 4.15, United States v. Ray, at page 194. Does FRE 1002 apply to the government's offer of Exhibits 1 and 2? Why? Do Exhibits 1 and 2 satisfy FRE 1002? Could the government prove Ray's stock sale on March 16, 2004, by calling

Ray's stock broker as a witness and asking her whether she sold Ray's 100,000 shares of Rundown stock at his direction March 16th? Would this violate FRE 1002?

4.21. Workman, a dentist, was indicted for his participation in a scheme to conceal his income and assets from the Internal Revenue Service. In 1991, before the indictment was issued, Workman was interviewed by Donna Jackson, a lawyer representing Workman's wife in their divorce proceedings. The conversation, in which Workman made statements about concealing assets, was tape recorded. Ms. Jackson also took notes. Ms. Jackson's secretary, who was not present at the interview, typed a transcription of the conversation based on the tape recording. Assume that the tape, the notes, the transcript, Jackson, and her secretary are still available. What are the several ways in which the prosecution could present the content of the 1991 conversation at Workman's trial? Would any of the best evidence rules apply?

The prosecution now learns that Ms. Jackson erased the tape in the ordinary course of business, lost her notes, and does not remember the contents of the conversation. Can the transcript be admitted into evidence?

4.22. In a wrongful death case alleging that the defendant driver was intoxicated when his car crossed a median strip in a divided highway, causing a head-on collision with the plaintiff's intestate, the plaintiff offers testimony from the state police officer who was first on the scene of the accident. The officer would testify that when he approached the defendant's car, he saw several empty bottles of Budweiser beer on the front seat. Must the plaintiff produce the original labels and bottles?

4.23. Return to Problem 4.5 at page 183. To prove that Jim Zeal and Stephani Goldstein were conspiring to import marijuana from outside of the U.S., the prosecution offers the testimony of Ensign Chandler who also boarded the *Rastafari*. Chandler will testify that he discovered a global positioning system (GPS) in the boat; that a GPS device uses global positioning satellites to track and record the location of any device and therefore the location of an object, such as the boat, to which the device is attached; and that the backtrack feature on the GPS graphed the *Rastafari*'s journey from Kingston, Jamaica, to the point at which it was seized by the Coast Guard. Chandler will have to admit that he did not seize the GPS or obtain any record of the data he observed as a display on its screen. The defendants object on the grounds that Chandler's testimony violates the best evidence rule. What result?

4.24. In a libel suit, the plaintiff alleges that the defendant sent a typewritten letter to plaintiff's employer with defendant's signature on it, stating that plaintiff was a liar and thief. The plaintiff offers a photocopy of the letter into evidence, properly authenticated by the employer's assistant who made the photocopy from the original letter as soon as it was received. The defendant claims that the signature is not his and objects pursuant to FRE 1002 and 1003 that the copy is inadequate for handwriting analysis of the signature since he always used a special ink. What result? What if the assistant testifies that he made a thorough search for the original that proved fruitless? Would this make the copy admissible? Or could the plaintiff testify as to the contents of the letter and forget about the photocopy?

4.25. In a murder-for-hire prosecution, the government introduces the tape recording of a conversation between the defendant and the alleged hired assassin. The conversation on the tape is at times very difficult to hear. The government also offers a transcript of the tape recording for the jury to read as it listens to the tape. The agent who made the transcript testifies that she listened to the tape several times, updated the transcript repeatedly, and reported the conversation as she heard it. Nothing indicates that the agent intentionally mistranscribed the recorded conversation, but the defendant objects on grounds of authentication and best evidence. Are there any other objections that the defense can make? How should the government respond? How should the court rule? And if the court admits the tape, what specific instruction might the court give to the jury?

4.26. In the prosecution of Jenkins for conspiracy to distribute cocaine, the government offers several charts summarizing the data collected on the government's "pen register," an electronic device that identifies all the telephone numbers of all of the calls made and received on Jenkins's telephone. The charts are authenticated by the agent who made them from the original electronic data. All of this data was produced to Jenkins. Defendant Jenkins objects on two grounds: (1) lack of access to the actual pen register; (2) the charts include only the calls to and from numbers identified with co-conspirators and are misleading because they do not include innocent calls, such as to the pizza parlor or dry cleaners. What result?

4.   FRE 1008

RULE 1008.   FUNCTIONS OF COURT AND JURY

When the admissibility of other evidence of contents of writings, recordings, or photographs under these rules depends upon the fulfillment of a condition of fact, the question whether the condition has been fulfilled is ordinarily for the court to determine in accordance with the provisions of rule 104. However, when an issue is raised (a) whether the asserted writing ever existed, or (b) whether another writing, recording, or photograph produced at the trial is the original, or (c) whether other evidence of contents correctly reflects the contents, the issue is for the trier of fact to determine as in the case of other issues of fact.

5.   Interpretation and Illustration of FRE 1008

FRE 1008 makes a specific allocation of fact finding between judge and jury in the application of the best evidence rules. The judge's general authority to make the preliminary determinations that are necessary to apply all of the rules of evidence is established in FRE 104. We discuss this general authority under Rule 104 in detail, in Section D, infra. Reading Section D will aid in understanding Rule 1008.

The reference in FRE 1008 to FRE 104 is a reference to judicial factfinding under FRE 104(a). As the first sentence of Rule 1008 indicates, preliminary facts necessary to the application of FRE 1001-1007 are questions for the judge to decide under Rule 104(a) *unless* subsection (a), (b) or (c) applies. Here are some of the preliminary issues that may arise under these rules:

(1)   whether an offered writing, recording or photograph is an "original" under Rule 1001 (3) (unless subsection (a) or (b) applies) ;

(2)   whether a given writing, recording or photograph qualifies as a duplicate and is thus presumptively admissible under Rules 1001(4) and 1003;

(3)   whether a genuine question is raised as to the authenticity of the original for purposes of Rule 1003;

(4)   whether it would be unfair to admit a duplicate in lieu of an original as provided for in Rule 1003;

(5) whether an original is lost or destroyed, and whether a diligent search has been conducted for the original under Rule 1004(1);

(6) whether the proponent lost or destroyed evidence in bad faith;

(7) whether an original can be obtained by any available judicial process under Rule 1004(2);

(8) whether an adverse party has possession or control over the original and, if so, whether proper notice was given to that party under Rule 1004(3);

(9) whether evidence goes to a collateral matter or to a controlling issue.[5]

If these issues raise questions of disputed fact, the judge is to decide them, pursuant to FRE 104(a), by a preponderance of the evidence, as we discuss in Section D, infra.

However, the second sentence of Rule 1008 provides that three specific factual issues are for the "trier of fact to determine." This means that the judge should not decide the question by a preponderance of the evidence, but should determine only whether there is sufficient evidence to support a jury finding on the matter. If there is, the question should be given to the jury to decide. The Advisory Committee Note to Rule 1008 explains this policy:

> [Q]uestions may arise which go beyond the mere administration of the rule preferring the original and into the merits of the controversy. For example, plaintiff offers secondary evidence of the contents of an alleged contract, after first introducing evidence of loss of the original, and defendant counters with evidence that no such contract was ever executed. If the judge decides that the contract was never executed and excludes the secondary evidence, the case is at an end without ever going to the jury on a central issue. . . . The latter portion of the instant rule is designed to ensure treatment of these situations as raising jury questions. The decision is not one for uncontrolled discretion of the jury but is subject to the control exercised generally by the judge over jury determinations. See Rule 104(b).

In the opinion in Seiler v. Lucasfilm, Ltd., supra, the appellate court held that the district court had correctly concluded that the best evidence rule did apply to Seiler's drawings. Therefore, Seiler had to produce his original drawings unless excused pursuant to FRE 1004(1). In making his claim that secondary evidence of the drawings should be admitted, Seiler also claimed that he had raised an issue under the second sentence of Rule 1008. The appellate court wrote as follows:

> As we hold that the district court correctly concluded that the best evidence rule applies to Seiler's drawings, Seiler was required to produce his original drawings unless excused by the exceptions set forth in Rule 1004. The pertinent subsection is 1004(1). . . .
>
> In the instant case, prior to opening statement, Seiler indicated he planned to show to the jury reconstructions of his "Garthian Striders" during the opening statement. The trial judge would not allow items to be shown to the jury until they were admitted in evidence. Seiler's counsel reiterated that he needed to show the reconstructions to the jury during his opening statement. Hence, the court excused the jury and held a seven-day hearing on their admissibility. At the conclusion of the hearing, the trial judge found that the reconstructions were inadmissible under the best evidence rule as

---

5. This list is based on a similar list set forth in Stephen Saltzburg, Michael M. Martin and Daniel J. Capra, 3 Federal Rules of Evidence Manual 2096-2097 (7th ed. 1998).

the originals were lost or destroyed in bad faith. This finding is amply supported by the record.

Seiler argues on appeal that regardless of Rule 1004(1), Rule 1008 requires a trial because a key issue would be whether the reconstructions correctly reflect the content of the originals. . . . [6] Seiler's position confuses admissibility of the reconstructions with the weight, if any, the trier of fact should give them, after the judge has ruled that they are admissible. Rule 1008 states, in essence, that when the admissibility of evidence other than the original depends upon the fulfillment of a condition of fact, the trial judge generally makes the determination of that condition of fact. The notes of the Advisory Committee are consistent with this interpretation in stating: "Most preliminary questions of fact in connection with applying the rule preferring the original as evidence of contents are for the judge. . . . [T]hus the question of . . . fulfillment of other conditions specified in Rule 1004 . . . is for the judge." In the instant case, the condition of fact which Seiler needed to prove was that the originals were not lost or destroyed in bad faith. Had he been able to prove this, his reconstructions would have been admissible and then their accuracy would have been a question for the jury. In sum, since admissibility of the reconstructions was dependent upon a finding that the originals were not lost or destroyed in bad faith, the trial judge properly held the hearing to determine their admissibility. . . .

Affirmed.

NOTES

1. In the *Seiler* case, the district judge decided under FRE 1004 and FRE 104(a) that Seiler had destroyed all originals of his drawings in bad faith, obviously taking Seiler's credibility into account. This ruling meant that Seiler's non-production of his original drawings was not excused, and therefore no secondary evidence of their contents (his reconstructions) was going to be admitted. Seiler, however, contended that the judge was required to give to the jury the question under FRE 1008(c) of whether "other evidence of contents" (his reconstructions) correctly reflected the contents of his original drawings, and thus had to admit his reconstructions. The jury, not the judge, would then have evaluated Seiler's credibility. The appellate court held, however, that the Rule 1008(c) did not come into play until the district court had decided the Rule 1004(1) issue first. In a similar case, Lowry's Reports, Inc. v. Legg Mason, Inc., 271 F.Supp.2d 737, 756 (N.D.Md. 2003), the court acknowledged that the jury, not the court, "determines whether the original existed and whether other evidence accurately reflects its terms. . . . Nevertheless, the court must first determine whether there is sufficient evidence of good-faith loss or destruction. . . ."

2. Note that the defendant, Lucasfilm, Ltd., did not take the position that the asserted original drawings never existed, as the appellate court acknowledges in footnote 6, supra. Nor did Lucasfilm produce a competing original, or offer its own evidence of the originals other than Seiler's reconstruction. Lucasfilm simply asserted its right under FRE 1002 to insist that Seiler produce either his original drawings or prove

---

6.   Lucas conceded the originals existed and Seiler conceded the items he sought to introduce were not the originals. Hence, as subsections (a) and (b) are not in issue, Seiler is arguing that 1008(c) requires that the case be submitted to the jury.

a valid excuse for non-production under FRE 1004(1). Since Seiler could not do this, his secondary evidence of his drawings was inadmissible and there was no Rule 1008(c) issue for the jury to decide. Simply put, the 1004(a) question was decided first and was dispositive without the judge deciding any of the questions reserved for the jury under FRE 1008(c).

3. If the district judge had decided that Seiler's loss of his original drawings was in good faith, the judge would not then be permitted to refuse admission to Seiler's reproductions because the court did not believe that the reconstructions genuinely reflected Seiler's originals. It would be for the jury to resolve this Rule 1008(c) issue.

KEY POINTS

1. FRE 1008 provides that most preliminary questions of fact under the best evidence rules are for the judge pursuant to FRE 104(a), and the judge will admit or exclude the offered evidence accordingly.

2. If the opponent raises an issue as to the existence of or the true content of the original, then that issue must go to the jury under FRE 104(b), and the judge must admit the evidence to permit the jury to decide the issue.

PROBLEM

4.27. Flanagan sues Zeppelin Electric Products, Inc., alleging that an oral agreement was made whereby Flanagan would remove gravel from Zeppelin's lot for consideration of $65 per hour. Flanagan and his crew toiled away until the gravel was completely removed. Zeppelin refused to pay Flanagan's bill, disputing the actual number of hours worked. At trial Flanagan offers into evidence a summary of data that he says he transcribed each week from tally sheets recorded at the worksite, indicating the number of hours worked by each employee. He claims that the tally sheets were discarded or lost. Defense counsel objects on the ground that the summary violates the best evidence rule and claims that the so-called tally sheets probably never existed. What result under FRE 1004, 1006, and 1008? What fact questions would the judge instruct the jury to decide?

D. JUDICIAL FACTFINDING UNDER FRE 104

FRE 104 establishes the power of the judge to decide preliminary questions concerning the admissibility of evidence and the process by which these questions are to be decided. It is an important rule, and you will want to reread this section as you encounter it throughout the course. We discuss it here because you have now become familiar with several rules of evidence that illustrate the different kinds of decisions that judges make under Rule 104. In particular, we focus here on judicial factfinding pursuant to Rule 104(a).

1.   FRE 104

RULE 104.   PRELIMINARY QUESTIONS

(a) Questions of admissibility generally. Preliminary questions concerning the quali-fication of a person to be a witness, the existence of a privilege, or the admissibility of evidence shall be determined by the court, subject to the provisions of subdivision (b). In making its determination it is not bound by the rules of evidence except those with respect to privileges.

(b) Relevancy conditioned on fact. When the relevancy of evidence depends upon the fulfillment of a condition of fact, the court shall admit it upon, or subject to, the intro-duction of evidence sufficient to support a finding of the fulfillment of the condition.

(c) Hearing of jury. Hearings on the admissibility of confessions shall in all cases be conducted out of the hearing of the jury. Hearings on other preliminary matters shall be so conducted when the interests of justice require, or when an accused is a witness and so requests.

(d) Testimony by accused. The accused does not, by testifying upon a preliminary matter, become subject to cross-examination as to other issues in the case.

(e) Weight and credibility. This rule does not limit the right of a party to introduce before the jury evidence relevant to weight or credibility.

2   Interpretation and Illustration of FRE 104(a)

a.   *Questions of Admissibility Generally*

The trial judge's decision to admit or exclude an item of evidence always requires the judge to answer one or more preliminary questions necessary to the application of the rules of evidence. There are at least three kinds of preliminary questions: questions of law, questions of fact, and questions that require the exercise of discretion. FRE 104(a) provides that, in general, all of these preliminary questions are to be decided by the court.

For example, application of the best evidence rules discussed in Section C required the trial court in the *Seiler* case to determine whether Seiler's original "draw-ings" fell within the scope of Rule 1002. This was a question of law. In addition, the court had to decide under Rule 1004(1) whether Seiler had lost or destroyed the originals in bad faith. This required the court to find the facts about Seiler's conduct and then to apply the legal standard of "bad faith" to those facts. As another example, FRE 403 presents several questions of law for a court, such as what is the meaning of the term *unfair prejudice*; that is, what dangers to jury reasoning does that term include? Rule 403 also requires judicial discretion: estimating the probative value of an item of evidence; evaluating the degree of danger to jury reasoning; and deter-mining whether the danger "substantially" predominates over probative value.

As you study the Federal Rules of Evidence throughout this course, you should be able to identify, usually from the text of the rules themselves, whether the judge is deciding questions of law or fact, or is exercising discretion, in applying each rule. This is not an abstract exercise. As an advocate, you must be prepared to make your offers of proof and arguments to help the judge perform each kind of decision-making task.

There is one exception to FRE 104's delegation of decisionmaking to the judge, and that is FRE 104(b). The power of the court to decide preliminary questions of fact is "subject to the provisions of subdivision (b)." We shall discuss FRE 104(b) in detail in Section E, infra. For now it is sufficient for you to understand two things about FRE

104(b). First, this language means that FRE 104(b), rather than FRE 104(a), would apply to fact finding on preliminary facts that are critical to the relevance of offered items of evidence. Second, FRE 104(b), like FRE 602 and FRE 901, applies the "sufficiency" standard, meaning that the judge decides only whether "evidence sufficient to support a finding" on the preliminary fact question has been introduced.

b. Judicial Fact Finding under FRE 104(a)

The application of many evidence rules requires determination of preliminary questions of fact, most of which are not critical to the relevance of the offered item and are therefore for the judge to decide pursuant to Rule 104(a). Under the best evidence rules, if a party asserts that *a testator's original will existed but was destroyed in a fire*, that is a question of fact that must be decided in order to determine, under FRE 1004(1), whether non-production of the original is excused. Another example that may be familiar to you is the evidence rule that creates a "privilege" for communications between attorney and client, meaning that such communications are not admissible at trial. Application of the privilege, in order to secure exclusion of the communication, requires determination of the preliminary fact question that the communication was *made during the attorney-client relationship*.

FRE 104(a) states the general principle that preliminary questions of fact shall be determined by the court, but it does not contain an explicit standard of proof. The Supreme Court has held that judges are to decide preliminary questions of fact under FRE 104(a) "*by a preponderance of the evidence*" *in both civil and criminal cases*. Bourjaily v. United States, 483 U.S. 171, 175 (1987).

> Evidence is placed before the jury when it satisfies the technical requirements of the evidentiary Rules, which embody certain legal and policy determinations. The inquiry . . . is not whether the proponent of the evidence wins or loses his case on the merits, but whether the evidentiary Rules have been satisfied. Thus, the evidentiary standard is unrelated to the burden of proof on the substantive issues, be it a criminal case . . . or a civil case. . . . The preponderance standard ensures that before admitting evidence, the court will have found it more likely than not that the technical issues and policy concerns addressed by the Federal Rules of Evidence have been afforded the consideration. [Id.]

Thus Rule 104(a) imposes a persuasion burden on preliminary fact questions. Typically the proponent, the party asserting that application of an evidence rule permits admission of an item, must bear this burden. The proponent must produce evidence that actually persuades the judge that the preliminary fact is more probable than not. And, if the opponent is using an evidence rule to exclude an item — such as the application of the attorney-client privilege — the opponent then bears the burden of satisfying the application of the exclusionary rule.

The persuasion burden under Rule 104(a) means that the judge must be persuaded that it is more likely than not that the preliminary fact is true — in our examples, that the testator's original will was destroyed by fire, or that the client's attorney-client communication was made during the relationship. In making this decision, the judge is the fact finder and takes the credibility of witnesses into account. And, pursuant to Rule 104(a), the judge is not bound by the rules of evidence, except for privileges. This means that the judge may take otherwise inadmissible evidence, such as hearsay, into account. As we shall see in Chapter Eight, this also means that the judge may take the contents of the proffered item itself into account, even though it has not yet been admitted. If the judge is not persuaded on the preliminary question of fact, the judge will not apply the rule in favor of the party seeking application of the rule; in our two examples, the judge would not admit secondary evidence because nonproduction of the original will would not be excused; and the judge would not exclude the attorney-client communication.

c. The Process of Decision Under FRE 104(a)

There are well-accepted procedures that govern judicial decisions of preliminary fact questions under FRE 104(a), although the rule does not state many specifics. When the parties are in dispute over a preliminary question of fact, both sides may present evidence to the judge on the factual issue. This may take place in front of the jury or outside the presence of the jury to protect it from hearing inadmissible evidence. Rule 104(c) leaves the question whether to hold such a hearing to the discretion of the judge, except with regard to the voluntariness of a confession.

The jury is not instructed to redecide the preliminary question; nor could it, since the jury may not be exposed to any inadmissible evidence that the judge used in the Rule 104(a) decision. Nor is the jury ever told what preliminary facts the judge has found. In United States v. Tracy, 12 F.3d 1186 (2d Cir. 1993), for example, the court held that the trial judge erred in telling the jury that, since the fact of conspiracy had been proved to his satisfaction, the statements of alleged co-conspirators were admissible under an exception to the hearsay rule. When the judge is persuaded about a Rule 104(a) preliminary fact and admits an offered item, the opponent may still challenge the admitted item's weight and credibility, and may introduce evidence that reduces its probative value, as provided by FRE 104(e). Such evidence may also challenge the existence of the preliminary fact, but the jury is not instructed to re-decide the preliminary question.

You can see that decisionmaking on preliminary questions necessary to the admission of evidence could absorb a great deal of trial time and energy. Even if the jury is excluded from FRE 104(c) hearings, the jury's time is wasted. There are two principal devices for resolving these issues before trial. In civil cases, many judges require that disputes over the admissibility of evidence be resolved through pretrial discovery and agreements reached at pretrial conferences. In both civil and criminal cases, motions in limine can be filed to seek determinations of admissibility and exclusion of particular evidence before trial. But sometimes preliminary issues catch both parties and the judge by surprise, and considerable trial time can be spent deciding them.

NOTE

The classic treatment of the policies underlying the division of authority between judge and jury on most preliminary questions is John M. Maguire and Charles S. Epstein, Preliminary Questions of Fact in Determining the Admissibility of Evidence, 40 Harv. L. Rev. 392 (1927). These authors conclude that authority over preliminary questions is justifiably allocated to judges, as FRE 104(a) does, for several reasons: (1) to reduce the complexity of jury trials (by not instructing juries on preliminary fact questions); (2) to expedite the trial process by eliminating these questions from trial; (3) to increase the predictability of the outcomes of admissibility decisions (because different juries might decide preliminary fact questions differently); (4) to preserve issues in a clear and coherent fashion for appeal (because rulings by judges under FRE 104(a) are on the record and can be appealed); and (5) to promote the substantive concerns underlying the various exclusionary policies of the rules of evidence (by giving to the judge the authority to decide whether or not those exclusionary policies apply). Each of these reasons makes some sense, although none provides, alone or with any or all of the others, obvious boundaries between the judge and the jury. The most powerful justification is that allocating most preliminary questions of fact to the judge furthers the substantive concerns that underlie the exclusionary rules of evidence.

Many exclusionary rules — for example, the rules concerning character and hearsay — implement the rule-drafters' policy decision that some types of evidence may inhibit, or even taint, the jury's rational decisionmaking. When evidence is excluded because it may reduce the rationality of jury decisionmaking, there is a persuasive reason to give the exclusion decision to the judge exclusively. This is what Rule 104(a) accomplishes. It ensures that the decision of preliminary fact questions under most evidence rules is for the judge. The jury does have a fact-finding role in the situations covered by Rule 104(b), as will be discussed in Section E, infra.

Additional readings on preliminary factfinding in general and the policies underlying Rule 104 and its application are Norman M. Garland and Jay A. Schmitz, Of Judges and Juries: A Proposed Revision of Federal Rule of Evidence 104, 23 U.C. Davis L. Rev. 77 (1989); John Kaplan, Of Mabrus and Zorgs — An Essay in Honor of David Louisell, 66 Cal. L. Rev. 987 (1978); Stephen A. Saltzburg, Standards of Proof and Preliminary Questions of Fact, 27 Stan. L. Rev. 271 (1975).

KEY POINTS

1. Most preliminary questions of fact raised by the application of the rules of evidence to decide the admissibility of an offered item are for the judge to decide pursuant to FRE 104(a).

2. Both parties may present evidence on FRE 104(a) preliminary questions of fact, and the judge must be persuaded by a preponderance of the evidence by the party asserting the application of the rule.

3. In deciding preliminary questions pursuant to FRE 104(a), the judge may consider evidence that would not be admissible under the rules of evidence, but may not consider privileged evidence.

4. After the judge decides the preliminary question under FRE 104(a), the judge either admits or excludes the item. The judge does not inform the jury about the decision on the preliminary question.

5. The opponent may attempt to reduce the item's probative value, if the item of evidence is admitted, with evidence that the preliminary fact is not true, but the jury does not redecide the preliminary question.

PROBLEM

4.28. In deciding whether the transcript in Problem 4.21 at page 209 and the photocopy in Problem 4.24 at page 209 are admissible, what preliminary fact questions would the judge have to decide?

E.   FRE 104, CONDITIONAL ADMISSIBILITY, AND THE PROBLEM OF CONDITIONAL RELEVANCY

Determining the relevancy of an offered item of evidence pursuant to FRE 401 and 402 sometimes raises a question about one or more related issues of fact. For example, in the *Johnson* case on page 43 line 43, defense counsel objected to the testimony of Johnson's cell mate, Butler, that Butler himself belonged to a gang, the Crips. The objection was made on grounds of relevance because there was a related issue of fact that was missing — whether defendant Johnson was also a member of the Crips. Without some evidence that Johnson also belonged to the same gang, Butler's testimony about his own gang membership could not be connected to the prosecution's relevance theory that Butler had a specific motive to lie to help Johnson, his fellow gang member.

Most offered items of evidence require additional contextual facts to link them to the dispute. And all items of evidence require the use of generalized propositions of fact that support the inferences necessary to reach a fact of consequence. These generalizations could be made a matter of proof if the judge is skeptical about whether they are reasonable. For example, generalized knowledge about the guards' glove-wearing practices in Facility B might have been necessary to establish the relevance of inmate Butler's offered testimony that the guards were wearing gloves on page 42, line 39.

1.   Interpretation and Illustration of FRE 104(b)

FRE 104(b) speaks to this issue of related facts being necessary to relevancy in two ways:

> (b) Relevancy conditioned on fact. When the relevancy of evidence depends upon the fulfillment of a condition of fact, the court shall admit it upon, or subject to, the introduction of evidence sufficient to support a finding of the fulfillment of the condition.

First, Rule 104(b) explicitly approves the "conditional admissibility" of offered items when additional facts or generalizations are necessary to establish their relevance. Second, the rule appears to establish the "sufficiency" standard of proof for the determination of those additional facts or generalizations. We shall discuss both meanings of the rule.

a.   Conditional Admissibility

The missing "conditions of fact" in the *Johnson* trial could have been made the subject of additional testimony. Lieutenant Stokes was supposed to testify about Johnson's gang membership; the guards' glove-wearing practices could have been the subject of testimony from a Pelican Bay guard. But none of this additional testimony could be given until inmate Butler, who was testifying about the *offered items* (that he was a Crip and that the guards were wearing gloves), was off the witness stand. So how could the judge rule on whether the offered items were relevant and admissible while Butler was still testifying?

This problem can be resolved by *conditional admissibility*, a process by which an item of evidence can be admitted provisionally, subject to the proponent's subsequent production of additional evidence. The judge can admit inmate Butler's offered testimony of his own gang membership "conditioned upon" Lieutenant Stokes's testimony about Johnson's gang membership. The judge could admit Butler's testimony that the guards wore gloves "conditioned upon" later testimony about the glove-wearing practices of guards in Facility B. FRE 104(b) permits this practice by allowing admission "subject to" proof of the necessary additional facts. If the additional evidence is not subsequently produced, the judge could strike inmate Butler's testimony from the record and instruct the jury not to consider it. In fact, Butler's testimony that he was a Crip should have been struck from the record because the prosecution offered no evidence that defendant Johnson was also a Crip. However, the defense never requested that this testimony be struck.

Of course, the opponent to the offered item may be convinced that the plaintiff has no evidence of the "condition of fact" and is concerned that the jury will not later disregard the item that has been admitted "conditionally" despite the judges instruction to do so. In such a case, the opponent would state this concern to the trial judge. If the judge believes that the risk that the proponent will not prove the condition of fact is substantial, the judge may not conditionally admit the offered items and can require the proponent to produce the additional evidence first. Normally, however, the judge will let each party present the evidence in the order in which each sees fit.

There are other situations in which evidence is admitted "conditioned upon" subsequent proof. For example, when judges balance probative value versus a danger under FRE 403, the full probative value of the evidence, its full measure of danger, or the proponent's need for it, may not be apparent until additional evidence is taken in the case. Here, admission of the offered item conditioned upon subsequent proof that enhances probative value or reduces a Rule 403 danger is extremely useful.

The device of conditional admissibility thus includes admitting evidence provisionally and controlling the order of proof if necessary. If the proponent of the conditionally admitted item fails to connect it with proof of the condition of fact, the evidence should be excluded and the jury instructed to disregard that item. United States v. Anderson, 933 F.2d 1261 (5th Cir. 1991) (reversal of arson conviction required when trial court failed to exclude evidence of four previous fires, admitted conditionally, once the government failed to prove that the four previous fires were arson and that defendant was involved).

b. The Problem of Conditional Relevancy: The "Sufficiency" Standard of Proof in FRE 104(b)

The text of FRE 104(b) also seems to require proof of "conditions of fact" that are necessary to relevance by "evidence sufficient to support a finding." This appears to be a higher standard than the "any tendency" standard stated in FRE 401. And so, this language has led to the identification of a special evidence doctrine that suggests there is a *special class of identifiable cases of "conditional relevancy"* where the relevancy of an offered item of evidence depends on the existence of some other fact. For this class of cases, the other fact then has to be proved under the "sufficiency" standard. However, as we have stated above, most offered items require additional facts to link them to the case at hand, and all offered items of course require generalizations to support their relevance. Thus the question arises as to whether Rule 104(b) can or should be applied by courts to a *special class* of disputes about relevance.

As an example of such a dispute, consider the case of MDU Resources Group v. W.R. Grace & Co., 14 F.3d 1274 (8th Cir. 1994), in which one page of a five-page document concerning the dangers of asbestos was offered by the plaintiff to prove that defendant Grace, the manufacturer of asbestos fireproofing material, knew or should have known of the dangers of asbestos and was liable to plaintiff for failure to warn. Grace had sold asbestos fireproofing material to the plaintiff in September 1968. Thus, it was argued, the document was relevant to prove Grace's knowledge of the dangers *only if it was received by Grace prior to September 1968.*[7]

Assume that the proponent of the document, the plaintiff, presents evidence that the document was found in the bottom of a file drawer belonging to a Grace official, in a stack of unrelated and undated papers. If there was no indication on the document itself as to when it was received by Grace, should it be found to be relevant? Under the minimal "any tendency" standard of Rule 401, perhaps so. Knowing that the document was in Grace's files makes it more likely that Grace knew of the document by September 1968 than if the document were not in the files. Thus the document could be admitted into evidence against Grace. But if the trial court treats the date of receipt under Rule 104(b) as a "condition of fact" upon which the relevancy of the document depends, the "evidence sufficient to support a finding" standard established in that Rule would be applied.

We are familiar with this "sufficiency" standard from our study of Rules 602 and 901 earlier in this chapter. Under Rule 602, the preliminary fact question is whether a witness has personal knowledge of the matter about which the witness is testifying. Under Rule 901, the preliminary fact question is the identification or authentication of an offered exhibit. The Advisory Committee Notes to both rules make it clear that they are special applications of Rule 104(b). Evidence "sufficient to support a finding" under Rules 104(b), 602 and 901 means the same thing — evidence from which a jury *could* reasonably find the preliminary fact to be more probable than not. This is a production burden — if the judge finds that the proponent has produced evidence from which a jury *could* find the preliminary fact, the judge must apply the evidence rule in the proponent's favor.

Perhaps this higher standard would not be satisfied by the mere presence of the proffered document in Grace's files. It would not be unreasonable for a court to find that a reasonable jury *could not be persuaded* that it was more probable than not that the document was received by Grace prior to September 1968. There is no underlying generalization about *when* Grace received the document that seems to rise to that degree of probability. Therefore, if the Rule 104(b) "sufficiency" standard were applied, the document would be excluded as irrelevant unless the plaintiff presented more evidence on the question of Grace's receipt. This seems to contravene both the letter and the spirit of minimal relevance standard of Rule 401.

In a seminal article critiquing the application of the sufficiency standard to "conditional relevance" issues as a special evidence doctrine, Professor Ball contends that evidence is relevant unless the probability of the conditional event — thus the probability stated in the underlying generalization about the date of Grace's receipt of the

---

7. This case is discussed at length in a very helpful article analyzing the debate over Rule 104(b) and suggesting a possible justification for the rule. Callen, Rationality and Relevancy: Conditional Relevancy and Constrained Resources, 2003 Mich.St.L.Rev. 1243.

document — is zero. Vaughn C. Ball, The Myth of Conditional Relevancy, 14 Ga. L. Rev. 435, 445-454 (1980). And Professor Ronald J. Allen extended Ball's thesis in The Myth of Conditional Relevancy, 25 Loyola L.A. L. Rev. 871 (1992), by demonstrating that there is no analytical distinction between relevancy and conditional relevancy.

Remember, relevancy does not mean sufficiency; "any tendency" does not mean more probable than not. FRE 104(b), however, would appear to require the judge to apply the higher threshold of "evidence sufficient to support a finding." Several other commentators have pointed out that if the judge applies the higher FRE 104(b) standard, this will result in exclusion of evidence that would be admitted under the lower standard of FRE 401 and that the jury would find useful. Richard Friedman, Conditional Probative Value: Neoclassicism Without Myth, 93 Mich. L. Rev. 439, 449 (1994); Dale A. Nance, Conditional Relevance Reinterpreted, 70 B.U. L. Rev. 447, 459-462 (1990). If no "conditional relevance" issue is raised by the parties, the court would typically treat the relevance of offered items of evidence as a Rule 401 question. If the issue is raised, typically by objection, a fact necessary to relevance may become a 104(b) question, at least if the objecting lawyer persuades the judge that Rule 104(b) applies and the judge thinks that the necessary fact is sufficiently important and disputed. Because there is no *analytic* difference between questions of relevance and questions of conditional relevance, there is no way to define a *special class of identifiable cases* in which Rule 104(b) should apply. The text of the rule does not provide any limits on its use.

In even the simplest trials, much evidence makes sense only in conjunction with other evidence, and at almost every step of the way it would be plausible, in an arid and coldly logical sense, to say that the proof at hand can only make a difference if some other point is proved or accepted on the basis of common experience in the world. Yet stopping a trial to entertain such arguments, decide which point should be proved first, obtain a commitment to prove some other point, assess the sufficiency of proof, and even instruct the jury, would confound trials, confuse everyone, and hamstring lawyers and judges. [Christopher B. Mueller and Laird C. Kirkpatrick, Evidence §1.13 (2d ed. 1999).]

2.   Elaboration of FRE 104(b): The Rule in Practice

In actual practice, however, there are very few reported cases in which preliminary questions of fact are identified and formally decided under FRE 104(b). Most of them raise questions of *notice*, e.g., United States v. Ansaldi, 372 F.3d 118, 130-131 (2d Cir. 2004) (admissibility of an FDA paper that described how GBL converted to GBH, the date-rape drug, upon ingestion depended on evidence sufficient to support a finding that defendant was aware of the contents of the paper) and Cagle v. State, 6 S.W.3d 801, 803 (Ct. App. Ark 1999) (fact that murder victim had methamphetamine in his system at the time of death was properly excluded since there was no evidence to show under the state equivalent of Rule 104(b) that defendant knew this and was justifiably afraid); *identification*, e.g., United States v. Koontz, 143 F.3d 408, 412 (8th Cir. 1998) (fact of whether an authentic booking report pertained to a specific person was a question for the jury, and the trial court's duty was to determine whether there was evidence in the record sufficient to support such a finding); and *basis for lay or expert testimony*, e.g., State v. Hale, 2004 Wash.App. LEXIS 2963 (Wash.Ct.App. 2004) (admission of lay opinion that to "tax" a person meant to take that person's property without their knowing it depended on evidence sufficient to support a finding that the word "tax" was actually spoken) and Fuentes v. Thomas, 2000 WL 1114892 (D. Kan. 2000) (evidence presented at trial to link doctor's opinion to circumstances of the victim's death would be tested under Rule 104(b)). Under the Supreme Court opinion in Huddelston v. United States, 485 U.S. 681 (1988), Rule 104(b) also applies to the determination of the occurrence of a specific act pursuant to FRE 404(b) as discussed on page 239 of Chapter Five, infra.

If the judge does treat a preliminary fact question as a Rule 104(b) condition of fact, typically the proponent of the offered item presents evidence or makes an offer of proof as to how the "sufficiency" standard will be satisfied. Judges may permit both sides to present evidence and may hold a hearing outside the presence of the jury pursuant to Rule 104(c). All of the evidence for and against the question must be admissible into evidence. In screening the sufficiency of this evidence, the judge may not take witnesses' credibility into account, as discussed on page 172, supra. If the judge finds that there is evidence sufficient to support a finding of the preliminary fact, then the judge will admit the offered item and may instruct the jury that the jury itself first must decide the preliminary question, and must decide it favorably, before using the offered item of evidence in its decisionmaking. The opponent may contest the preliminary question at trial and argue to the jury that the offered item is irrelevant unless the preliminary question is established.

In the *Grace* case, the plaintiff had submitted evidence that the document about asbestos risks had been found in a folder maintained by Grace with dated documents, all of which had dates of 1968 or earlier. Four of the five pages of the document itself were dated 1966. On this basis, together with some other facts, the appellate court held that the plaintiff had offered evidence sufficient to support a finding under Rule 104(b) that Grace had received the proffered document before September 1968:

> Once the plaintiff established these facts, the District Court should have made a preliminary determination that facts sufficient to prove the relevancy of the document had been established. It should then have submitted the document to the jury with an instruction that, if it found that Grace received the document before September of 1968, the jury could consider it as evidence that Grace was aware of the hazards of asbestos.... If the jury did not find that the document was received before September of 1968, then the document would be irrelevant to the question of liability. Grace can still argue that the document was not received before September of 1968, but any such argument would be for the jury to consider in determining... relevancy... [Id. at 1281-1282.]

NOTES AND QUESTIONS

1. Prior to the Federal Rules of Evidence, judges usually assumed the authority to decide all preliminary questions of fact themselves, pursuant to the preponderance of the evidence standard of FRE 104(a) or even a higher "clear and convincing" standard of proof for some questions. The lower standard of FRE 104(b) protects, at least to some degree, the authority of the jury over factfinding. If preliminary questions raised by FRE 602 (personal knowledge) and FRE 901 (authentication and identification) were to be decided by the judge under the preponderance standard of FRE 104(a), "the functioning of the jury as a trier of fact would be greatly restricted and in some cases virtually destroyed. These are appropriate questions for juries." Advisory Committee

Notes to FRE 104. This policy is consistent with the overarching goal of the Federal Rules: to promote rational decisionmaking through the admission of relevant evidence.

On the other hand, if jurors were required to decide *all* preliminary questions of fact necessary to the administration of the rules of evidence under the standards of FRE 104(b), the jury would be overwhelmed. It would spend too much of its time on the preliminary factfinding that would be necessary just to decide what evidence it could then use to decide the case. Every trial would contain numerous "minitrials" on admissibility questions, and there would be serious concern as to whether the jury would be able to focus on its real job of deciding the essential elements of the dispute. Therefore, as we note on page 215, supra, FRE 104(a) gives most preliminary questions to the judge exclusively and reduces the role of the jury as gatekeeper.

As you study the substantive rules of evidence law throughout this course, you should be able to identify the preliminary questions of fact that must be decided in order for each particular rule to be applied. You should also be able to classify them under FRE 104(a) and FRE 104(b), relying both on the literal terms of the rule and on the policies underlying the allocation of authority between the judge and the jury.

2. The problems of deciding when to apply FRE 104(b) to "conditional facts" necessary to relevance, and the conflict between that Rule's "sufficiency" standard and the minimal standard of FRE 401, still remain. It would not be difficult to eliminate these problems, however. FRE 104(b) could be amended as follows to retain the technique of conditional admissibility — admitting evidence "subject to" additional proof of factual propositions or generalizations that will make it relevant — without deviating from the relevancy standard of FRE 401:

> (b) Relevancy. The court shall admit evidence over a relevancy objection upon, or subject to, a finding that the evidence could rationally influence a reasonable person's assessment of any fact that is of consequence to the determination of the action. [Ronald J. Allen, The Myth of Conditional Relevancy, 25 Loyola L.A. L. Rev. 871, 883-884 (1992).]

Professor Richard Friedman suggests a similar revision of FRE 104(b) that focuses on "probative value conditional on further evidence" — where an evidentiary fact's probative value is not sufficient to overcome an FRE 403 objection, for example, the court should admit the offered evidence subject to the introduction of additional evidence that increases probative value sufficiently. Friedman, 93 Mich. L. Rev. at 472. Professor Dale Nance's proposed revision of FRE 104(b) focuses explicitly on "conditional admissibility" — it would permit the admission of any type of potentially inadmissible evidence subject to subsequent presentation of whatever additional evidence is necessary to overcome objections to its admissibility. Nance, 70 B.U. L. Rev. at 453.

3. It has been argued that FRE 104(b) is a valuable tool that "reflects the [jury's] need to refrain from considering information when the benefits of doing so do not justify the costs that would result." Callen, Rationality and Relevancy: Conditional Relevancy and Constrained Resources, 2003 Mich.St.L.Rev.1243, 1248. More specifically, Professor Callen contends that Rule 104(b) "limits parties' ability to offer evidence that might not warrant the jury's efforts to evaluate it" by requiring evidence sufficient to support a finding on preliminary conditions of fact "when that evidence (i) significantly lowers the cost of evaluating the proffered evidence or adds to its benefits and (ii) would be likely to be available if the inference that the proffering party wishes to

prove were true." Id. at 1301. Professor Callen admits, however, that the rule as drafted seems "open-ended" and he relies on predictable and limited judicial application to confine its reach.

4. It is also the role of FRE 403 to exclude items of evidence that are really not worth the jury's time and effort to consider them. Without the "condition of fact" that may be necessary to establish an item's relevance, the item's probative value is low even though it may be "minimally" relevant. As you think about the examples we have given in the text above, and the Problems set out below, consider whether the offered items would be excluded under FRE 403, unless proof of the condition of fact were forthcoming, without any reliance on FRE 104(b).

KEY POINTS

1. Is a "condition of fact" necessary to establish the relevance of an offered item of evidence is in serious dispute, FRE 104(b) provides that the court may admit the offered item "conditional upon" later proof of the necessary fact.

2. The FRE 104(b) standard is higher than the FRE 401 "any tendency" standard. In some cases, courts require the proponent to satisfy the higher standard of "evidence sufficient to support a finding" in proving a "condition of fact" deemed necessary to the relevance of an offered item of evidence.

3. Both parties may present evidence on FRE 104(b) "condition of fact" questions, and the judge must determine whether there is evidence sufficient to support a finding that the preliminary fact is true. In making this decision, the judge may consider only evidence that would be admissible to the jury.

4. After the judge determines the sufficiency of the evidence on the preliminary question under FRE 104(b), as under FRE 602 and 901, the judge either admits or excludes the offered item. The judge does not inform the jury about his or her determination of sufficiency.

5. The opponent may present evidence relevant to disprove the preliminary fact to the jury. The jury will decide the preliminary fact as part of its ultimate decision-making. The judge may instruct the jury that it must decide the preliminary fact question before it can consider the offered item of evidence to which it pertains.

PROBLEMS

4.29. Return to Problem 4.15, United States v. Ray, at page 194. Exhibits 1 and 2 have been admitted into evidence. Exhibit 3 is an exact copy of Exhibit 1. It bears the handwritten initials "BR" on the upper left corner. Government investigators have obtained the following information from interviewing Beth Barker:

I have been employed as Bernard Ray's executive secretary since 1998. I followed the following practice in handling Mr. Ray's mail, including hand delivered documents. Each work day, Monday through Friday, I place incoming mail and other delivered documents in the "in" box on Mr. Ray's desk three times each day, at around 10 a.m., around 1:30 p.m. and around 4:00 p.m. At 8:30 a.m. each morning, I take all of the documents in Mr. Ray's "out" box, check to make sure that Mr. Ray has initialed them, and then place them in Mr. Ray's files. Mr. Ray always reads and initials his mail and other documents and puts them in his "out" box. In response to a request from federal investigators, on September 1 of 2005 I found Exhibit 3 in Mr. Ray's files in a folder labeled "Correspondence – Andrews." I recognize the initials "BR" as Mr. Ray's handwriting.

The prosecution offers Exhibit 3 into evidence to prove that Ray read Exhibit 3, bearing Bernard Ray's initials on it, prior to his sale of stock on March 16, 2004. Is there a "conditional relevance" objection to admitting the memo? Is there an argument that the existence of the memo, without more, is sufficient to meet this conditional relevance objection? Would the testimony of Barker be sufficient to meet this conditional relevance objection? What should the trial court do?

4.30. David Falco was fatally shot by police during the execution of a search warrant at his residence. When they entered, Falco got a gun and ran down a hallway toward the officers. The officers claim that Falco was raising the weapon. One of the officers shot Falco three times. Falco's family sues that officer, the police department, and the city for wrongful death. Plaintiffs offer the opinions of their expert, Dr. Okoye, based on an adequate investigation, (1) that Falco's hands were raised upward in a probable "surrender" position when he was shot in the forearm, shoulder, and back, and (2) that if he was holding a gun in his right hand, he would have dropped it when he was shot in the right forearm. The trial court will admit opinion (2) only after evidence is presented at trial that Falco carried the gun in his right hand. How should the court justify its ruling? What level of proof that Falco carried the gun in his right hand should the court require?

4.31. Defendant Cox is charged with the murder of David Lee. Cox's close friend Hamley was in jail at the time of Lee's murder, charged with molesting Lee's child. In fact, four days before Lee's murder, Hamley was charged at a court hearing with three additional felonies based on David Lee's testimony. The court refused to reduce Hamley's bond despite testimony from Hamley's mother. Cox was not present at that hearing, although he spent almost every day at the Hamley house during this time. At Cox's murder trial, the state offers a deputy prosecutor to testify about what happened at the Hamley court hearing, on the theory that Cox murdered Lee as an act of retaliation against Lee because Hamley was still imprisoned. Cox objects to this testimony on the ground that the state has not proved beyond a reasonable doubt that Cox knew what happened at the court hearing. What should the trial court do?

4.32. Robert Grant is charged with two counts of selling crack cocaine. The evidence against him is based on the testimony of DEA Agent Mary Gray, who was working undercover. An informant, now deceased, told Agent Gray that she could get crack from "Bobby" but did not tell her "Bobby's" last name. Agent Gray can testify that on August 15, 1999, she met with the person known to her as "Bobby" and the informant; that Bobby sold her 30 grams of crack cocaine for $2000; that they discussed arrangements for another sale; and that Bobby gave Gray his pager number. Gray will also testify that on August 22, 1999, she paged Bobby and asked to buy two ounces of crack cocaine. Bobby agreed, and on the next day sold the Agent approximately 50 grams of crack for $3000.

However, 18 months have passed between these two drug sales and the upcoming trial in February, 2001. Agent Gray cannot positively identify Robert Grant as "Bobby;" no lineup identification was ever made. There is some evidence linking Grant to the pager number used by "Bobby," but there is also evidence that many other people had access to this pager.

The government plans to offer into evidence as Exhibit 10 a tape recording of a later conversation concerning a large drug sale. Gray will testify that on November 5, 1999, she paged Bobby, he called back, she recognized his voice, she then recorded their telephone conversation during which Bobby agreed to sell a larger amount (1 kilo) of crack cocaine, and that Exhibit 10 is that recording. Gray will admit that this sale never took place. Is Exhibit 10 relevant? Has it been authenticated? Should the court apply the technique of "conditional admissibility"?

What if DEA Agent Randy Jones, who processed Robert Grant at the federal lock-up after Grant's arrest in April 2000, will testify that the voice of "Bobby" on the tape is Robert Grant's? Is the tape now relevant to prove that "Bobby" is Robert Grant? Has a fact of conditional relevance been proved under FRE 104(b)?

CHAPTER FIVE

The Character, Propensity, and Specific Acts Rules

The law of evidence would be very simple if it were the case that "all relevant evidence is admissible," but FRE 402 goes on to say "*except* as otherwise provided . . . by these rules." The exceptions and qualifications to the general rule admitting relevant evidence are the focus of many of the Federal Rules of Evidence. FRE 403, as you have seen, allows the trial judge to exclude relevant evidence on a discretionary, case-by-case basis. In contrast, FRE 404-415, sometimes called "the relevance rules," establish certain categorical exclusions of otherwise relevant evidence. In this chapter, we will focus on the most important of these rules: the exclusion of otherwise relevant character evidence and of so-called "past specific acts." FRE 404-406 and 412-415.

As we begin our examination of these rules, you should keep in mind that the exclusionary provisions may not be a complete bar to the admissibility of a particular piece of evidence. Rather, they prohibit the proponent from offering the evidence only in a particular context or for a particular purpose. For example, FRE 404(b) limits the use of specific acts to prove character but authorizes their use for other purposes, such as to prove motive or intent. Thus, in order to apply the rules properly, you must ask the question that should always be your first question: What is the proponent of the evidence trying to prove? In other words, what is the proponent's theory of relevance? Only after you answer this question will you be able to apply the rules.

A. THE RELEVANCE OF CHARACTER EVIDENCE TO PROVE CONDUCT ON A PARTICULAR OCCASION

Imagine a simple tort case in which a pedestrian is hit by a car and injured. The plaintiff pedestrian claims that she was walking in a clearly marked crosswalk when the defendant driver negligently drove his SUV into her. The defendant claims that the plaintiff was contributorily negligent because she darted out into the middle of the street and was not in the crosswalk. What sort of evidence would the attorneys want to put before the jury to corroborate the testimony of their clients?

Suppose counsel for the plaintiff has the following evidence —

1) Witness 1, who has seen the defendant drive on many occasions, to testify that the defendant is a careless driver who often fails to stop for pedestrians in crosswalks;
2) Witness 2, a public records custodian, together with Exhibits 1 through 5, public records establishing that the defendant has had several car accidents and traffic infractions in the past;
3) Witness 3, a shopkeeper whose storefront overlooks the crosswalk, to testify that he sees the plaintiff cross the street nearly every day, and that she invariably uses the crosswalk

— and the defendant offers

4) Witness 4, a friend of the defendant, to testify that the defendant has remade himself into a very safe driver in the past two years.

All of this evidence meets the basic test of relevance under FRE 401, tending to make a fact of consequence (was the driver negligent? was the pedestrian contributorily negligent?) more likely or less likely. While this evidence may not be compelling by itself, you can see that a rational jury could find it useful to consider. As a matter of common sense, it is easy to see how each item of evidence is logically connected to the issues that the parties have to prove in the case. Yet, for reasons that will be explained in this chapter, only the testimony of Witness 3 is likely to be admitted; the rest should be excluded as improper character evidence under FRE 404.

A few definitions will be helpful in analyzing the material presented in this chapter.

1. *Propensity* means a tendency of a person or thing to behave in a certain way. A common thread in this chapter is the "propensity inference" — an argument that evidence about propensity is relevant to show how a person or thing behaved or operated on a specific occasion that is the subject of the litigation. All four of the examples of evidence in the Pedestrian v. Driver hypothetical is of this nature.

2. *Character* (FRE 404) is a type of propensity, probably the most common and familiar. Neither the Federal Rules nor their common law counterparts, however, define the terms *character* or *character trait*. This absence of a definition can occasionally raise difficulties. For a working definition, *character* in evidence law is a trait of a person to act a certain way, and evidence of a person's character is relevant — but, as we shall see, generally inadmissible — to show that he committed a particular act consistent with his character trait on a specific occasion that is the subject of the litigation. As will be seen, evidence that the defendant is a "negligent" or "careless" driver is character evidence.

3. *Past specific acts*, also known as "other crimes, wrongs or acts" (FRE 404(b)) are instances of a person's past conduct that are not the subject of *this case*. That is, they are not the conduct giving rise to alleged civil or criminal liability in the litigation before the court — they may be in the future, they may have been in the past, but not *now*. Yet such past specific acts may nevertheless be *relevant* to the current case. In the Pedestrian v. Driver hypothetical, the driver's past accidents and traffic infractions are examples of "past specific acts" or "other . . . acts." Defendant Driver should not be held

liable in this case for any traffic mishaps other than hitting Plaintiff Pedestrian. Yet those infractions and accidents other than hitting Plaintiff Pedestrian are relevant to the case, because they give rise to an inference that Driver may have driven negligently on the occasion in question when he collided with Plaintiff Pedestrian. Similarly, the many specific (although perhaps countless) times Pedestrian walked in the crosswalk prior to the accident are not themselves the subject of the litigation. What matters is whether Pedestrian walked inside the crosswalk when she was hit by Driver. But the prior instances may give rise to an inference that she stayed inside the crosswalk on the occasion in question.

4. *Habit* (FRE 406) refers to a propensity that the law of evidence distinguishes from character. While character evidence is generally excluded, evidence of habit is admissible. Generally speaking, propensities toward conduct that is more consistent, routine, and repetitive tend to be categorized as "habit," while conduct that is less so tends to be called "character." It might also be said that "habits" tend to be somewhat more morally neutral while behavior that is more morally loaded tends to be categorized as "character." The testimony of Witness 3 in the Pedestrian v. Driver hypothetical would probably be admitted as habit evidence.

In preparing a case for trial, it is natural for litigants to search out evidence of character and past specific acts. In terms of sheer volume, most evidence introduced in trials (civil or criminal) is circumstantial evidence, and evidence of character and past specific acts is a very commonplace, easily found, and intuitive form of circumstantial evidence. The personalities of all of us are often conceived of as a set of "character traits," and our lives are a constant stream of actions. Who we are and what we do are closely intertwined. In a typical litigated case, where it is disputed whether a (civil or criminal) defendant acted in a certain way, what could be more natural than to look at the kind of person the defendant is, and what he has done before, in order to determine whether he committed the acts alleged in the litigation? If a person is charged with fraud, it would be useful to know whether he is "honest." If he is alleged to have committed an assault, it seems relevant to know whether he is "violent." The "character" inference is a commonsense form of reasoning which holds that a person with a dishonest character is more likely than an honest person to have committed the fraud in question; or that a violent person is more likely than a nonviolent one to initiate a physical assault. (See Diagram 5-1, infra.) Thus, use of character evidence is tempting for litigants.

It is crucial to see how past specific acts fit into the character inference. How do we know what someone's character is? How do we know whether a person is "careless" or "dishonest" or "violent"? And how would we prove that in court? Perhaps the most intuitive answer is to look at the person's conduct. As summed up by the adage "handsome is as handsome does," character traits are ultimately generalizations drawn from specific instances of conduct. Thus, "past specific acts" are the intuitively obvious source of character evidence and in practice are often relevant to prove character, which in turn is relevant as circumstantial evidence of how a person may have acted on a particular (disputed) occasion. This chain of reasoning, illustrated in Diagram 5-2, infra, is precisely what the Federal Rules prohibit. As we will see, while evidence of character may *sometimes* be used to prove or disprove conduct on a specific occasion, FRE 404(b) does not allow past specific acts to show character to prove conduct on a specific occasion.

B.   GENERAL PROHIBITION ON USE OF CHARACTER AND "PAST SPECIFIC ACTS" EVIDENCE TO PROVE CONDUCT ON A PARTICULAR OCCASION

1.   FRE 404 and 405

(The Advisory Committee has proposed a clarifying amendment to FRE 404(a) that will probably become effective on December 1, 2006. The language added by that amendment appears in italics, and the language deleted by the amendment appears in brackets.)

RULE 404.   CHARACTER EVIDENCE NOT ADMISSIBLE TO PROVE CONDUCT; EXCEPTIONS; OTHER CRIMES

(a) Character evidence generally. Evidence of a person's character is not admissible for the purpose of proving action in conformity therewith on a particular occasion, except: (1) Character of accused. [Evidence] *In a criminal case, evidence* of a pertinent trait of character offered by an accused, or by the prosecution to rebut the same, or if evidence of a trait of character of the alleged victim of the crime is offered by an accused and admitted under Rule 404(a)(2), evidence of the same trait of character of the accused offered by the prosecution; (2) Character of victim. [Evidence] *In a criminal case, and subject to the limitations of Rule 412,* evidence of a pertinent trait of character of the alleged victim of the crime offered by an accused, or by the prosecution to rebut the same, or evidence of a character trait of peacefulness of the alleged victim offered by the prosecution in a homicide case to rebut evidence that the alleged victim was the first aggressor; (3) Character of witness. Evidence of the character of a witness, as provided in rules 607, 608, and 609.

(b) Other crimes, wrongs, or acts. Evidence of other crimes, wrongs, or acts is not admissible to prove the character of a person in order to show action in conformity therewith. It may, however, be admissible for other purposes, such as proof of motive, opportunity, intent, preparation, plan, knowledge, identity, or absence of mistake or accident, provided that upon request by the accused, the prosecution in a criminal case shall provide reasonable notice in advance of trial, or during trial if the court excuses pretrial notice on good cause shown, of the general nature of any such evidence it intends to introduce at trial.

RULE 405.   METHODS OF PROVING CHARACTER

(a) Reputation or opinion. In all cases in which evidence of character or a trait of character of a person is admissible, proof may be made by testimony as to reputation or by testimony in the form of an opinion. On cross-examination, inquiry is allowable into relevant specific instances of conduct.

(b) Specific instances of conduct. In cases in which character or a trait of character of a person is an essential element of a charge, claim, or defense, proof may also be made of specific instances of that person's conduct.

2.   Interpretation and Illustration of FRE 404(a) and (b)

Our initial focus is on two parts of FRE 404:

(a) Character evidence generally. Evidence of a person's character is not admissible for the purpose of proving action in conformity therewith on a particular occasion. . .

(b) Other crimes, wrongs, or acts. Evidence of other crimes, wrongs, or acts is not admissible to prove the character of a person in order to show action in conformity therewith....

The text of FRE 404(a) begins by prohibiting the use of evidence of a person's character to prove action in conformity therewith. This general prohibition, which is substantially a restatement of the common law, provides the backdrop against which the more specific and detailed rules admitting and excluding various forms of character evidence must be understood. The basic prohibitions of FRE 404(a) and 404(b) (putting aside, for the moment, the qualifications and exceptions stated in the rule) are broad and straightforward. Under FRE 404(a), evidence of character is not permitted to show conduct on a particular occasion. This bars the basic inference shown in Diagram 5-1:

Diagram 5-1

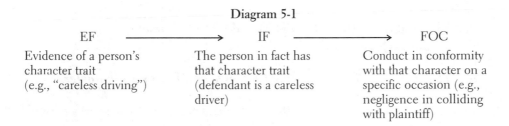

EF	IF	FOC
Evidence of a person's character trait (e.g., "careless driving")	The person in fact has that character trait (defendant is a careless driver)	Conduct in conformity with that character on a specific occasion (e.g., negligence in colliding with plaintiff)

FRE 404(b) elaborates further on this principle by making clear that past specific acts cannot be admitted to show conduct on a particular occasion by means of the prohibited character inference. As a matter of logic, evidence of past conduct similar to the acts that allegedly give rise to liability — for instance, evidence of past driving infractions and accidents to show that it is more likely that the driver was negligent in the incident in question — is usually relevant precisely because we make the character inference. Driver's past driving conduct shows him to be a certain type of driver, the kind who is more likely to do that type of thing — negligent driving — on further occasions. FRE 404(b) thus prohibits the chain of inferences shown in Diagram 5-2:

Diagram 5-2

EF	to prove	IF	to show	FOC
Past specific acts (e.g., past traffic infractions and accidents)		The character of a person (e.g., a character trait for negligent driving)		Conduct in conformity with that character trait on the occasion in question (negligence in hitting pedestrian)

(Note: The words "prove" and "show" in FRE 404 are used interchangeably.) FRE 404(b)'s prohibition of a particular mode of proving character to show action in conformity with that character trait may seem unnecessary given the general prohibition in FRE 404(a). But there are two good reasons for spelling it out. First, there are limited exceptions (set out in FRE 404(a)(1),(2) and (3)) in which character evidence may be offered to prove conduct on a specific occasion. FRE 404(b) makes clear that even when these exceptions apply, the means of proving character cannot be past specific acts.

Second, as suggested above, past specific acts are a common and intuitively obvious form of evidence that litigants are naturally inclined to look for. Absent the express prohibition in FRE 404(b), it might not be sufficiently clear to courts and litigants that the specific acts evidence is in many instances relevant only because it proves character in order to show conduct in conformity with character, i.e., that the relevance of this evidence depends on the prohibited character inference. FRE 404(b) stands as a reminder that past specific acts evidence is objectionable on this ground. (Whether and in what circumstances these objections will ultimately be sustained remains to be seen, infra.)

3.   Elaboration of the FRE 404(a) and 404(b) character and specific acts prohibitions

a.   *The Rationale for Restricting Evidence of a Person's Character*

There are good reasons for restricting the use of character evidence to show a person's action in conformity with that character:

i.   Weakness of the Propensity Inference.   First, the probative value of character evidence to show action in conformity with character will seldom, if ever, be very great. A person who is generally honest will at least occasionally be less than fully honest; a person whom we may fairly describe as having a violent character will on many occasions react to adverse situations in a peaceful manner. Moreover, on the occasion giving rise to the litigation, there may have been particular stresses on the individual or some other unusual circumstances that increased the likelihood of acting "out of character."

In the *Johnson* case, for example, evidence of Walker's reputation for violence is relevant to show that he was violent at the time of the alleged jail cell altercation. Yet the evidence does not suggest that Walker was violent in a majority of his encounters with inmates. If that were the case, it is unlikely that he would have retained his job. Rather, the defendant's evidence suggests only that Walker happened to be violent somewhat more often than the other correctional officers. Alternatively, consider the prosecution's evidence about Walker's *good* character. Walker may have been a generally peaceful person, but the stress of the incident with Johnson could have caused Walker to act "out of character." Even if one fully credits the defense evidence and discounts the prosecution evidence (or vice versa), the evidence tells the fact finder very little about the likelihood that Walker behaved violently at the one specific time that is the focus of the litigation. In short, the inference in Diagram 5-1 from a general character trait like violence, peacefulness, honesty, or dishonesty (IF) to action in conformity with that character trait on a specific occasion (FOC) is likely to be quite weak. For discussions of empirical evidence suggesting the low probative value of character evidence, see David P. Leonard, The Use of Character to Prove

Conduct: Rationality and Catharsis in Evidence Law, 58 U. Colo. L. Rev. 1, 26-31 (1987); Miguel A. Mendez, Essay: The Law of Evidence and the Search for Stable Personality, 45 Emory L.J. 221 (1996).

ii. Low Probative Value of the Evidence to Prove Character. Furthermore, the inference from the evidence offered (e.g., the testimony about Walker's reputation for violence) to what a person's character actually is (EF to IF) may itself be weak. As will be seen below, when character evidence is permitted, it must take the form of the witness's opinion about a person's character or that person's character "reputation" in the community. Such evidence often comes across as too vague and general to be convincing. How convinced were you by the inmates' testimony about Walker's reputation for violence in the *Johnson* case?

Evidence of past specific acts — for instance, specific instances in which Walker beat an inmate, if such evidence existed — may be much more powerful than general opinions, but even that evidence may not be very probative of a person's character. While a person's character is undoubtedly reflected in his conduct, how much conduct do we need to observe before we can make reliable "character" judgments? Would two instances of Walker assaulting inmates suffice to prove that he had a "character" to be violent toward inmates? What if those incidents were "out of character" for him?

iii. Diversion from Main Issues. If the character evidence is disputed, there is a risk of digressing into a "minitrial" on character and diverting the fact finder's attention from the main issues in the case. In *Johnson*, for example, there was conflicting testimony about Walker's reputation for violence or nonviolence. Moreover, the risk of confusion of issues would be heightened if character was to be proven by past specific acts. If, for instance, the defense in *Johnson* wanted to introduce evidence that Walker had previously assaulted two inmates, we can easily see the potential for minitrials on those incidents. Were those prior assaults similar in relevant respects to Johnson's situation? Did Walker provoke the assault or simply defend himself? How many facts are disputed about the prior assaults, and how many witnesses are there to those events?

iv. Bad Person Prejudice. Character evidence may also be unfairly prejudicial, particularly if it is evidence of the character of a party to the lawsuit. Inherent in the concept of character — or at least in the attributes that most people and most courts think of as character — is a moral quality or sense of rightness or wrongness. Consider, for example, the meaning of the words we use to describe what we refer to as character traits, e.g., *honesty, dishonesty, peacefulness,* and *violence.* Evidence that a litigant possesses one of these traits may arouse an emotional response and dispose the jury to decide in favor of that person if it is a positive character trait or against the person if it is a negative one.

This danger is intensified when a negative character inference might be drawn from past specific acts. Consider, for example, a murder case in which the prosecutor offers evidence that the defendant has committed an unrelated murder on a prior occasion. One way that this evidence is relevant is to show that the defendant has a generally violent character — and more specifically, a character trait to commit murder — and thus may have committed the murder on the occasion in question.

At the same time, the prejudicial impact of the evidence may be substantial. The jury is likely to have little sympathy for a one-time murderer even if it has a reasonable doubt about the defendant's guilt on the current charge. The jurors may also make unfounded assumptions about the likelihood that someone who has committed murder in the past will do so again. The risk is probably especially great that a jury, on hearing about a criminal defendant's bad character, may be willing to ignore a reasonable doubt and convict a person who may not (in the jurors' view) have been sufficiently punished in the past and who may commit crimes in the future. But as Justice Cardozo famously said, "the law has set its face against the endeavor to fasten guilt upon [a criminal defendant] by proof of character or experience predisposing to an act of crime." People v. Zackowitz, 254 N.Y. 192, 172 N.E. 466 (1930).

As you can see from the foregoing points, character evidence raises classic FRE 403 issues, in which probative value must be weighed against FRE 403 dangers of consumption of time, confusion of issues and unfair prejudice. FRE 404 can be understood as reflecting a judgment that the FRE 403 dangers inherent in character evidence will so often substantially outweigh the probative value that it makes sense to exclude it as a general rule rather than to permit case-by-case decisions on whether to admit it. And while character evidence admissible under the FRE 404(a) exceptions can be proven by opinion or reputation testimony, it cannot be proven by past specific acts. Although specific acts may be slightly more probative of character than vague, general reputation or opinion evidence, the FRE 403-type dangers of minitrials and unfair prejudice are probably much greater. Therefore, you can see the reason underlying 404(b)'s categorical prohibition of specific acts to prove character to prove conduct on a particular occasion.

b.   Exceptions to the FRE 404(b) Prohibition Against the Use of Specific Acts

Despite the unqualified nature of the prohibition against specific acts evidence in FRE 404(b), there are limited instances in which it is permissible to use evidence of a person's specific acts to prove that person's character to show action in conformity with character. FRE 608(b) and 609, which we will consider in Chapter Seven, explicitly authorize the use of specific acts for this purpose. The revised Federal Rules dealing with the admissibility of sexual misconduct evidence, FRE 413-415, also contemplate the use of specific acts to prove character to show action in conformity with character.

There are also a number of purposes for which specific acts are admissible because they are not offered pursuant to the prohibited chain of inferential reasoning set out in Diagram 5-2. (See sections C and H, infra.)

KEY POINTS

1. Evidence of a person's character is relevant to show the person's action in conformity with character on a particular occasion.

2. The Federal Rules prohibit the use of character evidence to show action in conformity with character except in the situations set forth in FRE 404(a) (discussed in section G, infra).

3. The Federal Rules do not define "character" or "character trait." Typically, character traits are qualities or aspects of a person that tend to be reflected in occasional, rather than routine, conduct and tend to have moral overtones (e.g., honesty or dishonesty) and, therefore, inherent prejudice.

4. Past specific acts, or instances of conduct other than the ones that form the subject matter of the litigation, are often relevant to prove character in order to show conduct in conformity on a specific occasion. However, they are excluded from evidence for this purpose by FRE 404(b).

PROBLEMS

5.1. Return to Problem 3.3, United States v. Ray, at page 131. The prosecution offers evidence that (a) in October 2000, Ray sold 25,000 shares of Rundown stock one week before a major and abrupt fall in Rundown's share price; and (b) in May 2003, Ray purchased 30,000 shares of Rundown 30 days before the company announced the profitable acquisition of a competitor, an event which caused the stock price to rise by 25 percent. For what purposes is this evidence relevant? Is it objectionable?

5.2. Return to Problem 3.4, State v. Blair, at page 131. The prosecution offers the following evidence. For what purposes is this evidence relevant? Is it objectionable?

(a)   That in 2003, Blair pleaded guilty to a charge of simple assault after making an unprovoked attack with his fists on a man in a bar.

(b)   Testimony from Blair's then-girlfriend that on two occasions in 2000 she called 911 because Blair had beaten her. She received medical treatment on both occasions, though she did not press charges against Blair.

(c)   That Blair was arrested for battering Norma in September 2003. Norma received medical treatment for her injuries, but no charges were filed against Blair.

5.3. Return to the case of United States v. Hitt, at p. 151. Recall that the prosecution offered a photograph of the defendant posing with several guns that were not his. Suppose that the guns did in fact belong to Hitt. With that assumption, what arguments could be made for the relevance of the photograph? Can any objection be made under FRE 404(b)? Can you think of any additional arguments in support of an FRE 403 objection?

5.4. Joseph Zachary has been convicted of first degree murder for the premeditated killing of Marty Coppola. According to the evidence presented to the jury, Zachary got into a heated argument with Coppola at a bar. He went back to his apartment where he retrieved a 9 mm pistol, returned to the bar and shot Coppola. To prove premeditation, the prosecution argued that Zachary returned to the bar intending to kill Coppola. The defense argued for first degree manslaughter based on (1) Zachary's testimony that he did not intend to use the gun on Coppola and (2) corroborated testimony that Zachary pulled the gun only after Coppola tried to punch him in the face. The prosecution, over defense counsel's objection, introduced evidence that Zachary also owned a .38 caliber magnum revolver and a .45 caliber pistol in addition to the murder weapon. No evidence was offered about how or why Zachary chose the 9 mm pistol. In admitting the evidence of the other guns, the trial judge agreed with the prosecutor's argument that the evidence "shows the defendant had a murderous propensity."

Assuming that all arguments have been properly preserved for appeal, what arguments should the defense make to the appellate court that the evidence concerning the other guns should have been excluded from the trial? How should the prosecutor respond?

C. THE ADMISSIBILITY OF SPECIFIC ACTS THAT ARE DEEMED RELEVANT WITHOUT A CHARACTER INFERENCE

The basic provision of rule 404(a) prohibits a certain kind of propensity inference — specifically, a "character" inference, one that asks the fact finder to infer that a person acted a certain way on the occasion in question because it was his "character" to act that way. The basic provision of FRE 404(b) emphasizes this prohibition with respect to evidence of past specific acts. But nothing in these rules prohibits the use of past specific acts that are relevant for some purpose other than to prove character to prove, in turn, conduct on a particular occasion. In other words, past specific acts that are relevant without making the full character inference illustrated in Diagram 5-2, supra, are not excluded by the first sentence of FRE 404(b).

Because, as seen above, past specific acts are an important and common type of evidence, the drafters of the rules did not leave this point about their admissibility for noncharacter purposes to implication, but chose instead to spell it out in the second sentence of FRE 404(b).There are a variety of labels for the type of evidence considered here: specific acts evidence, prior bad acts, bad conduct evidence, uncharged misconduct, and so forth. We tend to use the term *past specific acts*. Regardless of the terminology, the issues are the same.

1.   Interpretation and Illustration of the Second Sentence of FRE 404(b)

FRE 404(b) provides in part:

> (b) Other crimes, wrongs, or acts. Evidence of other crimes, wrongs, or acts . . . may, however, be admissible for other purposes, such as proof of motive, opportunity, intent, preparation, plan, knowledge, identity, or absence of mistake or accident, provided that upon request by the accused, the prosecution in a criminal case shall provide reasonable notice in advance of trial, or during trial if the court excuses pretrial notice on good cause shown, of the general nature of any such evidence it intends to introduce at trial.

We have seen that, pursuant to the first sentence of FRE 404(b), a person's specific acts are not admissible to prove the person's character in order to show action in conformity with character. Specific acts may be admissible, however, pursuant to the second sentence of FRE 404(b) to prove a fact of consequence that is not called "character" or a "character trait." While specific acts offered for some noncharacter purpose are often prior bad acts of a criminal defendant offered by the prosecution, nothing in the rules of evidence limits the noncharacter use of specific acts to acts that are somehow "bad" or to acts of a criminal defendant.

In order to admit evidence pursuant to the second sentence of FRE 404(b), the proponent must satisfy three requirements. First, the proponent must articulate some noncharacter purpose for which the specific acts evidence is relevant. Second, the proponent must introduce evidence that the person who allegedly committed the act in fact did commit the act. Third, the proponent must be prepared to respond to a likely FRE 403 objection to the evidence.

Assume, for example, a case in which the defendant is charged with shooting a police officer, and the prosecution wants to introduce evidence that the defendant robbed a bank shortly before the shooting. The prosecution would first have to articulate a noncharacter purpose for introducing evidence of the defendant's involvement in the bank robbery. In this case, the prosecution would maintain that the bank robbery evidence is offered, not to show that the defendant more likely shot the police officer in conformity with a general character for dishonesty or lawlessness, but rather to establish a motive for the shooting: Because the defendant had recently robbed a bank, the defendant had a particular fear of capture and, therefore, a motive for shooting the police officer. Second, the prosecution would have to have evidence — perhaps, for example, a videotape of the robbery or eyewitness testimony — suggesting that the defendant was indeed the bank robber. Finally, the prosecution would have to be prepared to respond to an objection that the probative value of the bank robbery evidence (to prove that the defendant had a motive for the shooting and, therefore, that the defendant did shoot the officer) is substantially outweighed by the FRE 403 exclusionary factors.

If the proponent of the evidence is the prosecutor, there is a fourth requirement — that the prosecution respond to a criminal defendant's demand for notice. According to the Advisory Committee Note on this notice requirement (added by a 1991 amendment), its purpose is "to reduce surprise and promote early resolution on the issue of admissibility." The rule states no absolute time limits and no particular form that the request and response must take.

2. Elaboration of the Second Sentence of FRE 404(b)

a. The Permissible Uses of Specific Acts Evidence

FRE 404(b) prohibits the use of specific acts evidence only when offered to prove character to prove conduct in conformity on a specific occasion. Any relevant purpose of specific acts evidence that falls outside that chain of inferences (described in Diagram 5-2) falls outside the prohibition of FRE 404(b) and is potentially admissible. Technically, it should have been unnecessary to set out any permissible noncharacter purposes in FRE 404, but the second sentence of FRE 404(b) happens to list the traditional purposes for which the common law permitted the use of specific acts. However, the phrase "such as" in FRE 404(b) expressly makes clear that the list is not exhaustive. To secure admission pursuant to the second sentence of FRE 404(b), it is not necessary to identify one of the listed purposes. It is sufficient for the proponent of specific acts evidence to convince the court that the evidence is offered for some purpose other than proving a person's character to prove conduct in conformity with character on a specific occasion

Recall that the "past specific acts" we are discussing are acts that appear to be unrelated to the litigated events, although in many cases they might themselves have been the basis for civil or criminal liability. The eight examples listed in the second sentence of FRE 404(b) — motive, opportunity, intent, preparation, plan, knowledge, identity, or absence of mistake or accident — can be grouped into three broad and overlapping categories that might be help you to discern patterns in the kinds of specific acts evidence deemed to avoid the FRE 404(b) first sentence exclusion.

i.   Evidence that is essential to the narrative of the proponent's case.

Sometimes the events giving rise to civil or criminal liability are an inextricable, *essential* part of a larger story involving other actions by a party. These other actions are in turn relevant to an essential element, tending to prove who did the act or what the act was. The prosecution in a homicide case might want to present evidence that the defendant stole a gun in a burglary a week before the homicide to explain how he came into possession of the gun used in the crime — an example of *opportunity* or *preparation*. In the same homicide case, the prosecution might offer evidence that the defendant was involved with the victim in a drug deal that went bad, in order to establish the defendant's *motive* to kill the victim. Or, under a different set of facts, a homicide might be part of a broader *plan* or scheme to further a drug-dealing conspiracy — if the victim were a potential witness against the conspirators, or a competing drug dealer — in which case the prosecution might offer specific acts evidence in the form of evidence of the (uncharged) drug dealing conspiracy.

"Motive," "opportunity," "plan," and "preparation" are all terms that capture the idea of these various narrative elements. As we saw in the *Old Chief* case, litigants have an acknowledged strong interest in presenting evidence that tells the jury a story that is coherent and has "narrative richness" — that doesn't leave the jury wondering "how" and "why." In addition, these kinds of facts are relevant in other ways, typically as circumstantial evidence tending to show *identity* — who committed the crime or conduct that is the subject of the litigation — or the fact that the crime or conduct occurred, where those facts are in dispute.

It could be said that the examples given above are not properly considered "past specific acts" at all, in the sense we that have been using the term. Why not? Because, at least in some cases, they arguably are indeed part of a single, cohesive chain of events giving rise to liability. Even if this is so, they nevertheless are frequently lumped into the "past specific acts" category to the extent that they theoretically could have been the subject of additional civil claims or criminal charges.

ii.   Evidence showing relevant states of mind.

States of mind are at issue in many litigated cases: Mental states may be an element of the criminal charge or the civil claim, and the defendant can put his state of mind at issue by asserting mistake, accident, or lack of knowledge. In such cases, past specific acts can be admissible for the noncharacter purpose of proving *knowledge*, *intent* or *absence of mistake or accident*. The same evidence that showed "preparation" or "motive" in the homicide example above, may also be relevant to show an intent to kill or the kind of premeditation that must typically be shown in a murder case. Past specific acts might also show the requisite knowledge. For instance, in a prosecution for conspiracy to distribute narcotics, the prosecution might offer a prior conviction for dealing cocaine to show the defendant's knowledge that the substance he transported was in fact cocaine.

This last example also illustrates what is meant by *absence of mistake or accident*. Past specific acts may be relevant to rebut a defendant's assertion that he is not liable or guilty because he was mistaken about crucial facts or that the conduct was unintentional. In the cocaine dealing example, if the defendant claims he did not know the white powder was cocaine, his past conviction for dealing powder cocaine would be relevant to undermine that claim. Past specific acts are also occasionally offered to rebut a claim of "accident" under the so-called doctrine of chances. For instance, in a case where an alleged sexual harasser claims that he mistakenly believed the plaintiff welcomed his sexual advances, it might be relevant to show that he had harassed several other women in the workplace on previous occasions, claiming "mistake" each time. The theory is that such accidents are unlikely to recur with the same person so frequently, implying that intentional conduct must be involved.

iii. Evidence showing identity. In cases where the defense theory is that the wrongful conduct was perpetrated by some other known or unknown person, past specific acts can be relevant as circumstantial evidence that the defendant is indeed the perpetrator. To be sure, "other conduct" offered for any of the other noncharacter purposes above is ultimately relevant to "identify" the defendant as the culprit. *Identity* is probably listed separately as a way of including the "modus operandi" theory: Where other conduct is so distinctive and nearly identical in its attributes or methods to the litigated conduct as to suggest by itself that the same perpetrator did the past and present acts, it can be admitted as showing identity.

b. Preliminary Factfinding with Respect to Whether the Person in Question Committed the Act

The probative value of specific acts evidence for any of the noncharacter purposes covered by FRE 404(b) (second sentence) depends in part on the strength of the proof that the person committed the act and, if culpability is important to the relevance of the evidence, that the person did so culpably. What standard should the trial judge use in determining whether to admit the specific acts evidence? In Huddleston v. United States, 485 U.S. 681 (1988), the Supreme Court resolved a conflict in the federal circuits by holding that the question of the person's culpable involvement was one of conditional relevance governed by FRE 104(b). Thus, under the Federal Rules, the proponent of the evidence can satisfy the preliminary fact requirement by introducing "evidence sufficient to support a finding" by a preponderance of the evidence that the person was culpably involved in the act. This standard of proof is relatively low, as we discussed at pages 219-220, supra.

Despite *Huddleston*, some state courts continue to apply an FRE 104(a)-type standard in assessing a person's involvement in prior acts. In these states, as a condition of admissibility, the proponent of the evidence must *persuade the trial judge* that (a) the person allegedly responsible for the act did in fact commit the act and (b) the person did so culpably (if culpability in the commission of the act is important to its relevance, as it usually is). Although both West Virginia and Colorado have evidence rules that are identical to FRE 104(a) and (b), both states' courts have held that the question of the defendant's culpable involvement in a prior bad act was one for the court to determine by a preponderance of the evidence pursuant to FRE 104(a). State v. McGinnis, 455 S.E.2d 516 (W. Va. 1995); People v. Garner, 806 P.2d 366 (Colo. 1991). Cf. Harrell v. State, 884 S.W.2d 154, 160-161 (Tex. Crim. App. 1994) (other crimes evidence admissible only if court finds pursuant to Tex. R. Crim. Evid. 104(b) evidence sufficient to support a finding *beyond a reasonable doubt* that person was culpably involved in the act).

The principal reason for using the higher FRE 104(a) preliminary fact standard would be to protect criminal defendants from the unfair prejudice that inheres in the admission of a defendant's bad acts. As you read the remaining materials in this section, consider whether it is appropriate to adjust preliminary fact rules to deal with unfair prejudice or whether it is preferable to deal with unfair prejudice by relying exclusively on a rule like FRE 403, which specifically sets forth a balancing test for assessing probative value and unfair prejudice.

c. *Probative Value and Prejudice Generally*

Finding a relevant "noncharacter" purpose for specific acts evidence under the second sentence of FRE 404(b) and satisfying the preliminary fact standard does not mean that the evidence is automatically admissible. The term "may" in FRE 404(b) makes it clear that admissibility is subject to compliance with the other rules of evidence, the most important of which in the context of specific acts evidence is FRE 403. Past specific acts evidence offered under the second sentence of FRE 404(b) nearly always raises a potential FRE 403 objection. This is because in virtually every (perhaps every) instance in which past specific acts are offered for one of the FRE 404(b) (second sentence) purposes, there will still be the risk that the jury will consider the past conduct for the impermissible purpose of proving character to prove conduct in conformity with character on a specific occasion. Thus, for example, if the prosecutor in a homicide case offers evidence of the defendant's burglary-theft of a gun to show preparation and opportunity, the jury may nevertheless use the evidence to determine that the defendant has a character to commit crimes and is therefore more likely to have committed the homicide — or is just a bad person who should be punished on that basis. In other words, past specific acts evidence that fits within FRE 404(b) (second sentence) is likely to be relevant for two purposes — one admissible, the other not. Thus, a classic FRE 403 objection is presented, based on the argument that the prejudice flowing from the impermissible purpose substantially outweighs the probative value of the permissible purpose.

Factors for the court to consider in making the FRE 403 balancing decision include

(1) how probative the noncharacter purpose is of some contested issue in the case;

(2) how probative the specific act is to prove the noncharacter purpose (e.g., whether there is a sufficiently close temporal proximity between the specific act and the crime charged; whether there is a "substantial similarity" between the past act and the crime charged, see United States v. Haywood, 280 F.3d 715 (6th Cir. 2002));

(3) how probative the evidence is to establish that the act occurred (e.g., whether there is a dispute about the nature of the act or the defendant's involvement in it);

(4) how much of a risk of unfair prejudice would result from introduction of the evidence (e.g., how heinous is the specific act); and

(5) how effective a limiting instruction is likely to be in reducing the risk of unfair prejudice.

In sum, when the prosecution offers specific acts evidence against a criminal defendant, there inevitably will be the risk of "bad person" prejudice: Jurors may be willing to ignore a reasonable doubt because they regard the defendant as a bad person who perhaps has not been sufficiently punished for prior misdeeds and who may commit similar bad acts in the future. In addition, there is a risk that the jury may use the act in an improper character-propensity sense as evidence that the defendant committed the crime charged. Keep in mind, though, that FRE 403 is a rule favoring admissibility (probative value must be "substantially outweighed" by the countervailing factors) and that there is a long tradition of admitting prejudicial specific acts evidence for noncharacter purposes. On the basis of our anecdotal impressions and review of reported cases (admittedly unscientific data, since reported cases may not be representative of the many unreported day-to-day decisions by trial courts), it appears that in practice, FRE 403 is seldom a barrier to the admissibility of specific acts evidence.

KEY POINTS

1. FRE 404(b) prohibits the use of specific acts *only* to prove character to show action in conformity with character.

2. Admissibility of specific acts for noncharacter purposes requires the proponent to do three things: (a) convince the judge that there is a legitimate noncharacter purpose for the evidence; (b) satisfy the preliminary fact standard with respect to the culpable involvement of the person who allegedly committed the act; and (c) respond to an FRE 403 objection.

3. The list of purposes in FRE 404(b) for which specific acts evidence may be admissible is not exhaustive. Specific acts evidence may be admissible for *any* noncharacter purpose.

4. Under the Federal Rules, the question of whether a person was culpably involved in the specific acts is an FRE 104(b) preliminary fact question. The proponent can satisfy the standard by offering evidence sufficient to support a finding by a preponderance of the evidence that the person was culpably involved in the act.

5. FRE 403 may sometimes require exclusion of specific acts evidence offered for noncharacter purposes.

PROBLEMS

5.5. Consider whether the specific acts evidence should be admissible in the following cases:

(a) Jill's home was burglarized, and there was no evidence of a forced entry. In the case against the defendant, the prosecution offers evidence that a week before the burglary, the defendant stole Jill's purse containing her key ring.

(b) The defendant is charged with growing marijuana. She claims that her friends are responsible and that she thought the plants were weeds. The prosecution offers eyewitness testimony from a neighbor that he had seen the defendant harvest marijuana on her property the year previously.

(c)   The defendant is charged with killing X, who was about to testify as an eyewitness in a major drug conspiracy trial. The prosecution offers evidence of the defendant's participation in the conspiracy.

5.6. Jerry Kozinski is being tried for burglary of an office building. A "Z" was found spray-painted on the front door of the burglarized building the same morning the burglary was discovered. The prosecution offers the following evidence. Is it admissible?

(a)   Evidence that Kozinski had pleaded guilty to a residential burglary two years ago in which a "Z" was found spray painted on the front door of the burglarized house.
(b)   Records from Blockbuster Video showing that Kozinski had rented "The Mark of Zorro" (in which the protagonist leaves behind a letter "Z" at the scenes of his exploits) eight times in the past three years.

5.7. Return to Problem 3.3, United States v. Ray, at page 131. The prosecution offers evidence that (a) in October 2000, Ray sold 25,000 shares of Rundown stock one week before a major and abrupt fall in Rundown's share price; and (b) in May 2003, Ray purchased 30,000 shares of Rundown 30 days before the company announced the profitable acquisition of a competitor, an event which caused the stock price to rise by 25 percent. Assume that the defense counsel's earlier FRE 403 objection to this evidence (see Problem 3.7 at page 148)) has been overruled. Can the defense object to this evidence under FRE 404? Does that objection suggest any additional arguments for an FRE 403 objection? How should the prosecutor respond?

5.8. Return to Problem 3.4, State v. Blair, at page 131. The prosecution offers the following evidence. What arguments can be made for and against admission?

(a)   That in 2003, Blair pleaded guilty to a charge of simple assault after making an unprovoked attack with his fists on a man in a bar.
(b)   That Blair was arrested in 2000 on two occasions when his then-girlfriend called 911 because Blair had beaten her. She received medical treatment on both occasions, though she did not press charges against Blair.
(c)   That Blair was arrested for battering Norma in September 2003. Norma received medical treatment for her injuries, but no charges were filed against Blair.

5.9. Greg Simpson is charged with armed robbery and burglary. According to the testimony of Fred Able, a knife-wielding man wearing jeans, a T-shirt, and a ski mask broke into his home by coming through an unlocked window. The intruder, who had a slight limp and appeared to be over six feet tall, demanded Able's money and threatened to kill him if he called the police. The prosecution offers the testimony of Pam Wellington that one week before the incident at Able's house, a man who she identifies as Simpson came to her door, said his car had broken down, and asked to use the telephone. He was wearing jeans and a T-shirt. Before Wellington could respond, Simpson pushed his way into the house, pulled out a knife and demanded Wellington's money and jewelry. As Wellington began to comply, her dog attacked Simpson and bit him in the leg. Simpson fled through the front door. Simpson is six feet tall. Both crimes occurred at approximately 11:00 A.M. in the same neighborhood. Simpson objects to Wellington's testimony on the grounds that the evidence (a) is impermissible character evidence, (b) should be excluded because of FRE 403, and (c) should be excluded because he was acquitted of burglary and attempted robbery in the Wellington incident. How should the court rule?

5.10. Garvin is charged with illegal possession of a firearm, which was discovered in a Cadillac parked outside Garvin's house. Garvin frequently used the Cadillac, which belonged to his aunt. The prosecution wishes to introduce evidence that Garvin had previously been arrested for robbery, that the police were at his house to execute a warrant to search for proceeds of robbery, that they discovered the key to the Cadillac during the search, and that Garvin's aunt then identified herself as the owner of the Cadillac and consented to its search. How much of this evidence should be admissible? For what purpose?

5.11. Hernandez is charged with smuggling illegal aliens. He was a passenger in a vehicle traveling behind the van in which the illegal aliens were discovered. The driver of the van has testified that driver of the car in which Hernandez was riding was involved in the smuggling. The prosecution's theory is that Hernandez was there to look out for border patrol officers. Hernandez claims that he was an innocent passenger. Over his objection the prosecution introduced evidence that Hernandez was arrested for smuggling aliens four years ago and that he was convicted of smuggling aliens 10 years ago. During the closing argument the prosecutor made the following statements to the jury about Hernandez's prior smuggling activity:

> Where do you start? I submit to you that you start by looking at the past. This is what this evidence is all about, the — well, you can use it for a limited purpose. It is what we call Rule 404(b) evidence. . . .
>
> Basically, that evidence was presented so that you can see, was this some kind of mistake? Was somebody there at the wrong place at the wrong time? Was it innocent behavior out there that was being exhibited by the defendant, Hernandez, when he just happened to be a passenger in a car following an alien load? Is that all innocent behavior?
>
> How do you know that he's not just some innocent passenger? Basically because you've seen the progression. You've seen the progression of how to accomplish this. And you look at it in the context of 404(b) material. Look at it in the context of intent. Look at it in the context of lack of mistake.

Has the prosecutor identified a legitimate purpose for the evidence? Even if the answer is yes, should the evidence have been admitted?

5.12. Defendant Flynn is charged with homicide with malice aforethought. Proof of malice may be satisfied if the prosecution establishes that a defendant was aware of a serious risk of death or serious bodily injury but did not care. If a defendant was voluntarily intoxicated at the time of the homicide, such unawareness is irrelevant if the defendant would have been aware of the risk had the defendant been sober.

The following facts are not disputed: The accident occurred on September 20, 2004, at approximately 6:20 P.M. Flynn spent the afternoon on the day of the collision drinking beer with friends. Then Flynn drove his car south on a four-lane highway (speed limit 50 miles per hour) at 6:00 P.M. at speeds estimated at 70-100 miles per hour. Flynn several times crossed a median divider and directed his southbound car into the northbound lanes to avoid congestion in the southbound lanes. At some point,

Flynn lost control of his car, slid into the northbound lanes, and struck a car coming toward him. The driver of that oncoming car was killed.

Flynn will claim that he drank only a few beers with his friends. However, testimony will show that immediately after the accident his blood alcohol level was measured at .26. Admissible expert testimony will inform the jury that a person's driving ability is impaired at a blood alcohol level of .08.

The prosecution wishes to introduce the following evidence:

(a) that Flynn had three prior drunk driving convictions entered against him in the 10 years prior to the accident;

(b) that after the third conviction in 1998 Flynn's driver's license was suspended for one year;

(c) testimony from the expert that a blood alcohol level of .26 would usually require drinking 15 beers;

(d) testimony from a bar patron that Flynn drank "at least a dozen beers" between 3:00 and 5:30 P.M. on the day of the accident.

What arguments can be made for and against admission of this evidence, and how should the court rule?

3.   Further Elaboration of the Second Sentence of FRE 404(b)

Our description of three categories of specific acts evidence admissible under the second sentence of FRE 404(b) — narrative completeness, states of mind, and identity — was not intended to suggest that any past specific act that can be shoehorned into one of these descriptors should be deemed admissible. On the contrary, we believe that lax application of the 404(b) (second sentence) categories poses a real risk of undermining the policies behind the basic 404(b) prohibition of past specific acts to prove character to prove conduct on a particular occasion. In the sections that follow, we consider specific applications of the second sentence of FRE 404(b) that may well be in some tension with the prohibitory language of the first sentence of FRE 404(b).

a.   The problem of "res gestae"

While evidence of past acts to show "motive" or "opportunity" might supply elements that fill out the story of the case, they are also independently relevant: For example, a person with a motive is more likely to have done the act in question than someone with no motive. However, parties sometimes argue for admission of evidence that is not technically relevant on the ground that it purportedly involves the "same transaction" as the conduct at issue in the case, or helps to "complete the story" of the case. Such evidence is often called *res gestae*, a Latinism that may give the argument to admit such evidence more weight than it deserves. For example, it is all too easy for a prosecutor to argue that prior criminal acts of a defendant are part of the "larger narrative" the prosecution wants to tell. Consider People v. Zackowitz, 254. N.Y. 192, 172 N.E. 466 (1930), which forms the basis of problem 5.4 at page 235, supra. The prosecution did in fact argue that the past acts evidence was relevant background narrative (using the term *res gestae*). But why was that particular part of the narrative at all helpful, let alone necessary to understanding the "story" of the crime? Judge Cardozo, writing for the court, plainly believed it was not.

Courts have taken different views on how carefully to limit marginally relevant or irrelevant past acts evidence that is offered only to "complete the story." Compare United States v. Bowie, 232 F.3d 923, 929 (D.C. Cir. 2000) ("there is no general 'complete the story' or 'explain the circumstances' exception to Rule 404(b) in this Circuit"), with United States v. Brooks, 670 F.2d 625, 628–29 (5th Cir.1982) (admitting evidence that marijuana was found in defendant's car as "arising out of the same transaction or series of transactions as the charged offense" of possession of cocaine with intent to distribute). In our view, courts should not admit such evidence unless it is necessary to a coherent and intelligible description of the conduct giving rise to civil or criminal liability.

b. The Problem of Specific Acts Evidence to Prove Intent

FRE 404(b) identifies "intent" as one of the permissible noncharacter uses of past specific acts evidence. Some courts have formulated the admissibility of past specific acts evidence to prove intent this way: "Where a defendant claims that his conduct has an innocent explanation, prior act evidence is generally admissible to prove that the defendant acted with the state of mind necessary to commit the offense charged." United States v. Zackson, 12 F.3d 1178, 1182 (2d Cir. 1993). In *Zackson*, for example, the prosecution introduced evidence that the defendant had previously participated in a marijuana-selling conspiracy to rebut his contention that he did not willingly participate in a cocaine-dealing conspiracy.

How does the prior marijuana selling prove intent without making a character inference? The relevance of the prior marijuana conspiracy is to prove that the defendant has a propensity to engage intentionally in drug-selling activities, offered to show that he so intended on the occasion of the charged cocaine conspiracy. It appears to us that this use of past specific acts requires the very type of character inference prohibited by the first sentence of FRE 404(b).

Perhaps one could view "intent" as something other than "conduct," so that the use of past specific acts to prove *intent* on a particular occasion is different from the prohibited use of past specific acts to prove *conduct* on a particular occasion. Or perhaps the law of evidence could be seen as making an "intent exception" to the prohibition of specific acts to prove character to prove conduct on a specific occasion as a pragmatic concession to the need for circumstantial evidence to prove states of mind. Whatever the justification, many courts and commentators seem willing to gloss over the difficulty that use of past specific acts to prove intent violates the prohibition in the first sentence of FRE 404(b).

c. The Intent/Specific Acts Problem where Intent Is Not Disputed

The danger of allowing past specific acts to prove character to prove intent is particularly troubling in the following scenario. Suppose the defendant is charged with knowing sale of heroin. Prosecution witnesses will include the alleged purchaser and individuals who can identify the substance as contraband and establish a chain of custody. The defense will be that the police arrested the wrong person and that the defendant had nothing to do with the heroin transaction to which the prosecution's evidence relates. The prosecution offers evidence that the defendant knowingly sold heroin two years ago on the ground that this prior sale is evidence of the defendant's knowledge, which is one of the elements of the offense. The defendant objects that the evidence should be excluded according to FRE 403. In support of the objection, the defendant offers (a) to stipulate that whoever sold the heroin did so with the requisite knowledge and (b) to accept a jury instruction explaining the stipulation to the jury.

i.   **The Argument for Exclusion.**   As we pointed out in our initial discussion of FRE 403 at pages, supra, the need for evidence is one of the factors to consider in making the FRE 403 determination. Even without the stipulation and jury instruction, there may be little need for the prior act evidence in the heroin sale case as long as the defendant does nothing to suggest lack of knowledge. It seems likely that the jury would infer knowledge from the facts of possession and sale and from the failure to deny knowledge. Thus, even if one believes there is a strong inferential link between the prior knowing sale and present knowledge, the evidence, in context, appears to have low probative value. (Do you think the prosecutors would consider dropping the drug sale case if they did not have evidence of previous drug selling?) The stipulation and jury instruction further decrease the need for the evidence.

Against this low probative value, one must assess the FRE 403 risk of unfair prejudice. If the evidence were admitted, there is the risk that the jury would consider it in two improper ways: First, the jury might infer that because the defendant sold heroin once before, the defendant is the kind of person who has a character trait for selling heroin and, therefore, probably sold it on this occasion. This particular chain of inferences, however, is clearly prohibited by the first sentence of FRE 404(b). Second, there is the risk of "bad person" prejudice: The jurors may be willing to forego a reasonable doubt in order to convict and remove from the streets someone who is involved with drugs. The lack of need for the evidence coupled with the possibility of misuse of the evidence by the jurors creates a strong argument to exclude the prior heroin sale evidence on FRE 403 grounds.

Early leading cases on this issue held that the past specific act evidence should be excluded where the defendant offered to stipulate. See United States v. Colon, 880 F.2d 650, 660 (2d Cir. 1989); United States v. Jenkins, 7 F.3d 803, 806-07 (8th Cir. 1993); United States v. Crowder, 87 F.3d 1405, 1410 (D.C. Cir. 1996), *vacated and remanded*, 519 U.S. 1087 (1997), *reversed on remand*, 141 F.3d 1202 (D.C. Cir. 1998) (en banc).

ii.   **The Impact of Old Chief.**   Recall that in Old Chief v. United States, page 154, supra, the Supreme Court acknowledged that the FRE 403 balancing process must include the "assessment of evidentiary alternatives." The Court then held that the defendant's stipulation precluded the prosecution from introducing evidence of the defendant's prior conviction when the conviction was relevant only to show the defendant's legal status as a former felon. At the same time, the Court observed that the probative value of evidence includes its "descriptive richness," its contribution to the "narrative integrity" of a party's case, and its ability to convince a jury of what is "morally reasonable." With respect to FRE 404(b) issues, the Court stated in dictum:

The issue of substituting one statement [i.e., the stipulation] for the other [i.e., the evidentiary proof] normally arises only when the record of conviction would not be admissible for any purpose beyond proving status, so that excluding it would not deprive the prosecution of evidence with multiple utility; if, indeed, there were a justification for receiving evidence of the nature of prior acts on some issue other than status (i.e., to prove "motive, opportunity, intent, preparation, plan, knowledge, identity, or absence of mistake or accident," Fed. Rule Evid. 404(b)), Rule 404(b) guarantees *the opportunity to seek* admission. [519 U.S. at 190 (emphasis added).]

What impact should *Old Chief* have on our sale-of-heroin hypothetical? Superficially, *Old Chief* seems to state two general rules about when prosecutors are free to decline defense stipulations that would eliminate prosecution evidence: a general rule that prosecutors may decline such stipulations, and a narrow exception in the circumstances of a defendant's "status." Yet, the central focus of *Old Chief* is less about "stipulations" than about the FRE 403 balancing process. In the above drug-dealing hypothetical, there seems to be no greater need to prove intent than to prove a defendant's status as a felon: Because it is not disputed, intent is reduced to something of a technicality and is not part of the narrative of the prosecution's case. It seems clear to us that under the FRE 403 balancing process, the past acts of drug dealing to prove (undisputed) intent should usually be excluded.

In fact, most courts have taken the opposite view, holding that *Old Chief* generally supports the admissibility of such evidence. United States v. Bilderbeck, 163 F.3d 971, 977-978 (6th Cir. 1999); United States v. Williams, 238 F.3d 871, 876 (7th Cir. 2001). At least two courts of appeals have held that *Old Chief* overrules or at least greatly restricts prior circuit precedent allowing defendants to rely on stipulations to avoid the prejudicial impact of prior crimes offered to show intent or knowledge. United States v. Hill, 249 F.3d 707 (8th Cir. 2001); United States v. Crowder, 141 F.3d 1202 (D.C. Cir. 1998) (en banc). We view these cases as mistakenly decided, to the extent that they seem to construe *Old Chief* as a sort of restriction on the need for a careful FRE 403 balancing in situations where defendants offer to stipulate to a technical issue to preclude prejudicial past acts evidence.

d. Past "Accidents" or "Coincidences" and the Anticoincidence Theory

What does FRE 404(b) have to say in cases where the defendant disputes intent — by claiming mistake or accident — and the prosecution (or plaintiff) wants to offer evidence of prior similar purported "accidents"? Another application of FRE 404(b) (second sentence) that carries the potential for misuse is the so-called *anticoincidence theory of relevance*, also known as "the doctrine of chances." Used to refute a defense of "mistake or accident," the anticoincidence theory is based on the generalization that if the specific acts are sufficiently numerous and similar to the crime charged, "coincidence" or "randomness" is unlikely to explain their occurrence. Instead, it is more likely that there is some unifying causal explanation — for example, a single person's intentional, repetitive action — for the occurrence of such numerous and similar events. As one court colorfully put it, "The man who wins the lottery once is envied; the one who wins it twice is investigated." United States v. York, 933 F.2d 1343, 1350 (7th Cir. 1991); see Mark Cammack, Using the Doctrine of Chances to Prove Actus Reus in Child Abuse and Acquaintance Rape: People v. Ewoldt Reconsidered, 29 U.C. Davis L. Rev. 355 (1996); Edward J. Imwinkelried, The Use of Evidence of an

Accused's Uncharged Misconduct to Prove Mens Rea: The Doctrines that Threaten to Engulf the Character Evidence Prohibition, 130 Mil. L. Rev. 41, 54-75 (1990).

Consider the following hypothetical: Adam White is charged with aggravated battery on his three-year-old son, Jeremy, who suffered a facial bruise and a broken left arm. White claims that the injuries occurred when Jeremy accidentally fell down a flight of stairs. The prosecution offers to prove that on three prior occasions when Jeremy was in the custody of his father he suffered broken bones, and that on two occasions White brought Jeremy's younger sister, Ruth, to the hospital emergency room with severe head injuries.

Defense counsel objects that the past specific acts are offered to prove that White has a character trait for physically abusing his children and is therefore barred under FRE 404(b). The prosecutor responds that the evidence is offered for the noncharacter purpose of proving "absence of mistake or accident" pursuant to FRE 404(b) (second sentence) under the anticoincidence theory. Defense counsel then objects that there is not evidence sufficient to support a finding, as required under *Huddleston* and FRE 104(b), that any of the prior incidents are (as the prosecution claims) intentional batteries by White rather than accidents or batteries committed by someone else.

Viewing each incident in isolation, the defense argument seems to have merit: There is not evidence sufficient to support a finding of the defendant's culpable involvement with respect to any single incident. But how likely is it that mere coincidental occurrence of similar "accidents" can explain all of the injuries? Instead, it may be rational to infer that intentional acts account for at least some of the injuries. Moreover, the defendant is the only identifiable person present at the time the incidents occurred. Thus, it seems reasonable to believe — perhaps even highly probable — that the defendant was culpably involved in one or more of the incidents, even though we do not know which one(s). Is the evidence sufficient to support a finding by a reasonable trier of fact under FRE 104(b) that the defendant was probably culpably involved in one or more of the past incidents as well as the present one? However that question is answered, it seems appropriate in this type of situation to focus attention for preliminary factfinding on the acts in the aggregate rather than on each individual incident viewed separately.

Finally, defense counsel could object under FRE 403 that, even if there is evidence sufficient to support a finding that the *prior* acts were intentionally committed by White, that is insufficiently probative that the *current* incident was nonaccidental to overcome the FRE 403 dangers of undue prejudice and confusion of issues.

As you can see, the doctrine of chances allows past specific acts to prove intent where there may not be evidence sufficient to support a finding that any single past specific act was itself intentional. To be relevant, "anticoincidence" evidence has to support the inferences both that at least some of the past "accidents" were not in fact accidents and that the number of past nonaccidents suffices to refute the defense of accident on the occasion giving rise to the current claim or charge.

This reasoning process poses an obvious danger of creating a significant "doctrine of chances" loophole in FRE 404(b)'s specific acts prohibition. First, as Professor Imwinkelried has pointed out, one can always conceptualize the inference from specific act to character to action in conformity with character in terms of the doctrine of chances. Imwinkelried, supra, at 54-67. For example, evidence of a murder defendant's prior violent acts — which would be objectionable as evidence of the defendant's violent character to show action in conformity with that character — can be portrayed as "doctrine of chances" evidence. The prosecutor could focus on the objective improbability that the prior acts and the act in question would have occurred randomly and suggest that, therefore, the defendant must be culpably responsible for them as well as the act that is the subject of the current prosecution.

A second, closely related problem: How do we know when we have enough past purported "accidents" to refute the current claim of accident or coincidence? Prosecutors have often argued — sometimes successfully — that one prior incident is enough. Compare United States v. York, 933 F.2d 1343, 1350 (7th Cir. 1991) (upholding admission of evidence of prior unsolved murder of defendant's wife to rebut claim that death of defendant's business partner was accidental), with Wynn v. State, 718 A.2d 588 (Md. 1998) (reversing admission of prior incident of allegedly knowing possession of stolen goods offered to rebut defense that current possession of stolen goods was not knowing). But if one or two or even a few prior incidents are deemed enough to satisfy the anticoincidence theory — at least for occurrences more commonplace than winning the lottery — much of FRE 404(b)'s basic prohibition could be eroded, at least in cases where a party claims mistake or accident.

On closer examination, the doctrine of chances looks a lot like a version of the character inference prohibited by the first sentence of FRE 404(b). If it is justified, it is in cases where the statistical inference is strong enough to make the evidence more probative than garden-variety evidence of past specific acts. The question is: "How frequently does a typical, innocent person suffer this type of loss? . . . Once the inquiry focuses on relative frequency, it is evident that sometimes even just one uncharged incident will be admissible to trigger the doctrine of chances." Imwinkelreid, supra, at 53-54; see also Westfield Ins. Co. v. Harris, 134 F.3d 608, 615 (4th Cir. 1998) (evidence that defendant made at least seven prior fire insurance claims probative of whether fire in question was deliberately set or an accident).

A final concern is this: Are unaided intuitions of jurors sufficient to make what is arguably a complex statistical inference? You have undoubtedly encountered instances in which statisticians have estimated the likelihood that a certain eventuality "could have occurred by chance." Indeed, in criminal cases, forensic evidence is often expressed in terms of statistical probabilities. An argument could be made that, in many — if not all — cases, courts should require expert statistical evidence to establish how many incidents are sufficient to trigger the doctrine of chances.

e. Modus Operandi and the Character Inference

A "modus operandi" is a pattern of behavior sufficiently distinctive or idiosyncratic to support the inference that the same person who committed the prior act must also have committed the one in question in the current case. It is thus relevant where the defendant denies committing the act in the case before the court. Because a high degree of distinctiveness and similarity is required to establish modus operandi, the doctrine will necessarily apply only in limited circumstances. See United States v. Thomas, 321 F.3d 627, 635 (7th Cir. 2003).

Courts have traditionally accepted past specific acts evidence under a "modus operandi" theory under FRE 404(b) and its common law analogues for the noncharacter purpose of proving "identity." Yet, as suggested above in the case of "intent," it is difficult to see how modus operandi evidence is relevant to prove identity without making a character inference. The proponent asks the fact finder to infer that the defendant has a propensity to act in a certain distinctive way, as shown by past instances, and therefore acted in that way on the occasion in question. The only justification to treat modus operandi evidence differently from other character evidence is that, because of the high standard of uniqueness and similarity of the behavior, it is more probative than generic character evidence. In this respect, modus operandi may be simply a special case of the doctrine of chances.

KEY POINTS

1. FRE 404(b) (second sentence) permits use of past specific acts to prove "intent" even though, arguably, the relevance of such evidence depends on making the same sort of character inference usually prohibited by the first sentence of FRE 404(b).

2. Where "intent" or "knowledge" is an element of the criminal charge or civil claim but is not disputed by the defendant, the use of past specific acts to prove intent should arguably be excluded under FRE 403. However, at least in drug prosecutions, most courts have held that *Old Chief* usually supports admission of such evidence.

3. The "doctrine of chances" allows admission of prior incidents as to which the defendant denies culpable involvement in order to rebut a defense of "mistake or accident" under the "anticoincidence" theory — the argument that it is extremely unlikely that the past and current incidents could have occurred randomly without the defendant's intentional involvement.

PROBLEMS

5.13. Felix Unger is charged with arson for allegedly intentionally setting fire to the Odd Cuppa Joe Diner. Unger contends that the fire, which destroyed the diner, was an accident. The prosecution offers the following evidence. Is it admissible?

(a) Evidence that two other businesses owned by Unger burned down, one 20 years ago and one 10 years ago, and that he claimed the fires were accidental.
(b) Evidence that Unger pleaded guilty to arson in connection with the fire 10 years ago.

5.14. Patty Wurst is being tried for bank robbery. She asserts the defense of duress based on the contention that her codefendants, members of a religious cult, kidnapped her and threatened to kill her if she did not participate in the robbery. In rebuttal, the prosecution offers evidence that Wurst had robbed a convenience store a year before her alleged kidnapping. Is the evidence admissible?

5.15. Return to problem 5.4 at page 235. Assume that the trial court admitted evidence of the other guns, not to show Zachary's "murderous prosperity," but to "complete the story of the crime." Based on all that you have read, how should Zachary's appeal be argued by the defense and prosecution? How should the appeal be decided?

5.16. (a) In her trial for possession of one kilogram of cocaine with intent to sell, Ann has pled not guilty. The prosecution offers the testimony by a police officer that three weeks prior to the charged crime, Ann sold cocaine to Brenda. The defense objects, and the following colloquy takes place at the side bar:

DEFENSE: It's improper character evidence, your honor.
PROSECUTOR: No, it's admissible on the issue of intent.
DEFENSE: We haven't put intent in issue here, Your Honor, so at best the testimony is premature. And there wasn't even a conviction, so it can't get in.

What should be the ruling of the trial court on these arguments, and why?

(b) During the defense case-in-chief, Ann testifies that she didn't know that the one kilogram of material found in the trunk of her car was cocaine. On cross-examination, the prosecutor asks, "Isn't it true, Ann, that you were involved in drugs 11 years ago, which led to a conviction for selling heroin?" Ann's truthful answer would be "Yes." The defense again invokes the rule against character evidence, but the prosecutor claims, "It goes to knowledge, intent and plan, Your Honor." What should be the ruling of the trial court on this argument, and why?

5.17. Martha Woods is charged with the murder of her eight-month-old preadoptive foster son, Paul. Paul was placed with Ms. Woods when he was five months old. Up to that time he had been a normal, healthy baby. On five occasions during the first month that he was with Ms. Woods, Paul suffered instances of gasping for breath and turning blue from lack of oxygen. On the first four occasions, he responded to mouth-to-mouth resuscitation. On the last occasion he went into a coma and died a week later.

On each occasion Paul was in Ms. Woods's custody and only she had access to him. On each occasion Paul was taken to the hospital, and on the first four occasions he was released after several days in apparently good health. A pathologist testified as an expert witness for the prosecution that Paul's death was not an accident. The witness said he was 75 percent certain that Paul's death was homicide caused by smothering, and he attributed the 25 percent doubt to the possibility of some disease currently unknown to medical science.

The government offers to prove Ms. Woods has had custody of or access to nine children who suffered a minimum of 20 episodes of cyanosis (a blue coloring due to lack of oxygen). Three of the children were her own; two were adopted; two were relatives; and two were children of friends. Seven of the nine children died.

Should the evidence be admitted?

D.   REFLECTION ON CHARACTER, PROPENSITY, AND SPECIFIC ACTS EVIDENCE

1.   The Distinction Between What FRE 404(b) Prohibits and Permits

The term *propensity* as applied to the actions of an individual means a tendency or an inclination to behave in a particular manner. There is no dispute that this concept provides an apt description of the inferential process at work when character evidence is offered to show action in conformity with character. When we describe a person as being honest or as having a character trait of honesty, we mean that the person tends to behave honestly. Proof of a character trait for honesty permits the fact finder to draw a "propensity inference" about conduct on a particular occasion. In other words, the generalization underlying the inference from character to action in conformity with character is that people have a propensity to act in conformity with their character traits. See Diagram 5-1 at page 231, supra.

Courts and commentators frequently refer to the prohibition against use of specific acts evidence in the first sentence of FRE 404(b) as a prohibition against the use of "propensity evidence" or a prohibition against making "propensity inferences" or using specific acts for "propensity purposes." Almost all of the permissible uses of specific acts evidence, however, also require the fact finder to make propensity inferences that are very similar to the propensity inference that the first sentence of FRE 404(b) prohibits. Thus, despite the common association of the term *propensity* with the first sentence of FRE 404(b), the concept of propensity is not helpful in determining what FRE 404(b) prohibits and what it permits.

Consider the following two hypotheticals: (1) D_1 is charged with assault and defends on the ground of self-defense. The prosecution offers to prove that on three different occasions the defendant engaged in unprovoked violence against various individuals unrelated to the victim. (2) D_2 is charged with murder by use of a shotgun and defends on the ground that the killing was an accident. The prosecution offers to prove that on three different occasions the defendant intentionally fired a shotgun at the victim.

Most courts would exclude the evidence in the first hypothetical on the ground that it consists of specific acts offered to prove a character trait for violence in order to show action in conformity with that trait. These same courts would admit the evidence in the second hypothetical on the ground that it shows intent or malice or absence of accident.

The suggested results in the hypotheticals may be desirable because of the greater probative value of the evidence in the second hypothetical. However, one cannot justify the results in terms of the concept of propensity, for the two hypotheticals require the fact finder to make similar propensity inferences: From proof of each defendant's prior conduct, the proponent of the evidence wants the fact finder to infer first that each defendant has a tendency or inclination or propensity to behave in a particular manner — to act violently toward individuals (D_1) or to engage in intentional acts of violence against a particular person (D_2). The proponent then wants the fact finder to make the further inference that each defendant acted in conformity with that tendency or inclination or propensity on the occasion of the alleged crime.

Even in cases in which evidence of prior crimes is offered to show identity or modus operandi, the relevance of the evidence requires the fact finder to make a propensity inference similar to the inference in the preceding hypotheticals. Consider, for example, Problem 5.9 at page 242, supra, where the prosecution is seeking to prove that the defendant committed robbery and burglary by showing that the circumstances surrounding her burglary and attempted robbery of another person were similar to the circumstances of the charged crime. The unusual characteristics of the crime that we know the defendant committed (if they are unusual enough) act as a signature that identifies the defendant as the perpetrator of the charged crime.

One way to view the relationship between the two crimes is that the first crime suggests that the defendant has a propensity to behave in a certain unusual manner. The proponent of the evidence wants the fact finder to infer that the defendant acted in conformity with that propensity on the occasion of the alleged crime. Alternatively, relying on the doctrine of chances, one might characterize the similar crime evidence as relevant to the defendant's guilt not because of the defendant's propensity but because it is unlikely that two individuals would commit separate crimes in the same unique manner. This latter characterization, however, does not alter the fact that the relevance of the evidence to prove the defendant's guilt requires the fact finder to make a propensity inference. The unarticulated but necessary assumption is that criminals generally have a propensity not to commit crimes in the same unusual manner in which somebody else has committed a crime. Proof that the defendant committed the prior crime places the defendant outside the category of people who share this propensity and, at the same time, identifies the defendant as a person having the propensity to commit crimes in the particular, unusual manner.

FRE 404(b) does not use the term *propensity* to distinguish between the prohibited and permissible uses of specific acts evidence. Rather, FRE 404(b) uses the term *character*. The Federal Rules, however, do not attempt to define *character*. On the question of whether the concept of character is helpful in distinguishing between what FRE 404(b) prohibits and permits consider the following:

RICHARD B. KUHNS, THE PROPENSITY TO MISUNDERSTAND THE CHARACTER OF SPECIFIC ACTS EVIDENCE

66 Iowa L. Rev. 777, 794-796 (1981)

[I]n giving content to the prohibition against the use of some specific acts evidence, one cannot simply equate character evidence with propensity evidence. All character evidence offered to show action in conformity with character is propensity evidence, but not all propensity evidence is character evidence. The question, therefore, necessarily arises whether one can give some additional independent content to the term character or character trait.

There would appear to be only two substantially overlapping factors that may be helpful in distinguishing character evidence from other bad acts propensity evidence. First, case law and scholarly commentaries dealing with specific acts evidence suggest that the character label is used when the evidence has an indirect bearing on an issue and, therefore, a relatively low probative value. For example, evidence of a defendant's previous assaults on third persons offered to prove that the defendant was the first aggressor would probably be regarded as impermissible character evidence. Evidence of previous assaults by the defendant on the murder victim, however, might not be regarded as character evidence. Second, simply as a matter of common usage, describing a particular propensity as a character trait may seem more appropriate in some instances than in others. Thus, an individual's propensity for violence demonstrated by assaults on various third persons might readily be described as a character trait for violence. In contrast, violence directed only against a particular individual arguably does not manifest a propensity that is commonly thought of as a "character trait."

This general sense of what constitutes character is an inadequate basis for distinguishing between permissible and impermissible uses of specific acts evidence for propensity purposes. First, it is simply too imprecise for meaningful application on a case-by-case basis. For example, even if one concludes that in a murder prosecution evidence of the defendant's assaults on random third persons would be regarded as inadmissible character evidence but that previous assaults on only the victim would be viewed as non-character and, therefore, potentially admissible evidence, how should the following evidence be classified: previous assaults against only those third persons who, like the murder victim, are (a) all redheads, (b) all members of the same family, (c) all between the ages of four and six, (d) all between the ages of 20 and 25? Perhaps it would be appropriate to view the fact that the various victims happened to be between the ages of 20 and 25 to be fortuitous and, therefore, to place the character label on this evidence. It is less clear, however, which, if any, of the other proofs of specifically directed violence should be regarded as manifesting a character trait.

Second, and more importantly, the general sense of what constitutes a character trait is not sufficiently related to the factors which justify excluding some specific acts evidence. The prohibition against use of specific acts to prove character to show action in conformity with character encompasses one of these factors: Specific act character evidence tends to have a relatively low probative value. There is no necessary relationship, however, between some independently derived notion of what constitutes a character trait and problems of prejudice, time consumption, and distraction of the fact finder from the central issues of the case. The time consumption and distraction concerns arise whenever the prior acts are numerous or there is a dispute about the nature of the act or a party's participation in it. These potential problems are in no way dependent upon whether the acts tend to show something that might be labeled a character trait.

Similarly, the potential for prejudice from specific acts evidence is not related to the question whether the evidence is offered to prove character or to show some other fact. Potential prejudice exists whenever there is a danger that the fact finder will be influenced not simply by the probative value of the evidence but also by its conclusion that a party is a bad person and, therefore, particularly deserving of punishment. Any bad act, of course, has the potential for influencing the fact finder's decision in such a manner, and thus in one sense any specific bad act is evidence of a general character for badness. Yet, it is clear from the established precedent for permitting bad acts to be used in a propensity sense to prove such issues as motive, intent, or identity that this general way in which bad acts tend to show character is not sufficient to place the acts within the character evidence prohibition.

The primary determinants in applying the character prohibition appear to be the probative value of the specific acts evidence and whether the relevant propensity can, as a matter of common usage, readily be labeled as a character trait. Prejudice, however, is not a function of either of these factors. The degree of prejudice associated with any specific act evidence is a function of how the fact finder is likely to respond to the badness of the act. Consider, for example, two prosecutions for heroin possession. In one case the defendant claims he did not know the substance was heroin. In the other the defendant claims that the heroin was in the sole possession of his companion. To rebut the first defendant's claimed absence of knowledge, the prosecutor offers to prove that the defendant had previously sold heroin to schoolchildren. To establish the second defendant's possession the prosecutor offers to prove that on two previous occasions the defendant had possessed heroin. The latter evidence is more likely than the former to fall within the character evidence prohibition, but in the eyes of the fact finder the sale of heroin to schoolchildren is likely to be more prejudicial. . . .

2.   Approaches to the Admissibility of Specific Acts Evidence

The first sentence of FRE 404(b) stands at least as a symbolic recognition of the substantial FRE 403 problems that can inhere in specific acts evidence, particularly when offered against a criminal defendant. That sentence, however, may be little more than a symbol. Typically, all a prosecutor will have to do to ensure admissibility of specific acts evidence is convince the court that (a) the evidence satisfies the minimal FRE 401 standard for relevance, (b) the evidence shows something — anything — other than a character trait, a term that the rules do not define, (c) any question of the defendant's culpable involvement in the act satisfies the minimal FRE 104(b) preliminary fact test, and (d) the evidence does not run afoul of the FRE 403 balancing test, a test that favors admissibility. These are quite limited restrictions on admissibility. In fact, prejudicial — albeit also sometimes quite probative — specific acts evidence is frequently admissible.

If you believe that FRE 404(b) should have a greater exclusionary impact, what changes in FRE 404(b) would you recommend to accomplish this objective? Consider the following possibilities, for each of which there is precedent:

(a) strengthen the notice requirement, for example, by requiring the prosecution on its own initiative to provide the notice and requiring the prosecution to set forth a specific noncharacter purpose for which the evidence is offered (See FRE 412 (c) infra);
(b) require the judge to decide either by a preponderance of the evidence or by some higher standard that the defendant was culpably involved in the specific act as a condition of admissibility (State v. Moore, 440 So. 2d 134 (La. 1983));
(c) limit the purposes for which specific acts evidence is admissible, which was a common approach to specific acts evidence prior to the adoption and influence of the Federal Rules (State v. Johnson, 183 N.W.2d 194 (Iowa 1971) (general rule of exclusion with exceptions for evidence of motive, intent, absence of mistake or accident, common scheme, and identity));
(d) impose a time limitation so that only evidence of relatively recent specific acts will be admissible (FRE 608(a) and (b) infra);
(e) apply a reverse FRE 403 balancing test to specific acts evidence so that the evidence will be admissible only if the probative value outweighs or substantially outweighs the countervailing FRE 403 concerns (FRE 412(b)(2), infra, and FRE 609(a) and (b), infra).

None of the alternatives is ideal. A rigorously enforced notice requirement may result in the exclusion of relevant evidence because of an inadvertent, harmless mistake, and if one is serious about confining specific acts evidence to predesignated categories or a certain time frame, there will inevitably be situations in which highly probative evidence does not fit the parameters of admissibility. A high standard of proof for preliminary facts may have the same effect. Moreover, if there is uncertainty about a defendant's culpable involvement in a bad act, that uncertainty reduces the prejudicial impact of the evidence as well as its probative value. To the extent that the jury has doubts about whether the defendant committed the bad act, the jury is less likely to regard the defendant as a bad person. Perhaps the best of the alternatives is some form of reverse FRE 403 balancing test. However, if one is concerned that judges may be too insensitive to the prejudicial impact of specific acts evidence, a less discretionary rule of exclusion may be warranted. See page 307, infra, where we discuss the alternative approaches to exclusion of an alleged rape victim's prior sexual behavior.

On the other hand, perhaps you have come to the conclusion that the current rules do not tend to result in the inappropriate admission of specific acts evidence. If so — and perhaps even if not — consider what value is served by retaining the FRE 404(b) ban on the admission of specific acts to prove character to show action in conformity with character. Since the only thing that distinguishes specific acts character evidence from permissible specific acts evidence is the relatively low probative value of the former, is it not likely that evidence currently excluded by FRE 404(b) would also be excluded by a proper application of the FRE 403 balancing test? Moreover, if there are instances in which a proper balancing of probative value and prejudice would result in the admission of evidence currently excluded by FRE 404(b), would not the abolition of the character evidence ban be a positive development?

As you will see in Section E, infra, recent amendments to the Federal Rules have abolished the character evidence ban for evidence of a defendant's prior sexual misconduct in cases involving charges of sexual assault or child molestation. As you examine these materials, consider whether FRE 413-415 are a first, healthy step in the right direction; an unwise departure from the character evidence ban; or perhaps an appropriate limited response to a particular problem.

3.   Specific Acts Evidence: Limiting Instructions and Closing Argument

Although our primary concern, like that of the Federal Rules, has been with questions of admissibility, rules of admissibility have consequences that go beyond the question of whether the jury will get to hear particular evidence. You are already familiar with one of those consequences — the right of a person against whom evidence is admitted to a limiting instruction when evidence is admitted for only a limited purpose. A second consequence is that the rules of admissibility have traditionally been thought of as regulating the appropriate scope of closing argument. For example, if evidence is admitted against a criminal defendant for the limited purpose of showing motive, the prosecutor cannot argue that the evidence shows the defendant's character or general propensity for criminal conduct. Given this traditional understanding of the relationship between the rules of admissibility and closing argument, abolition of the FRE 404(b) character evidence ban would permit parties to make character/propensity arguments to the jury. Is this a good reason to retain the FRE 404(b) character evidence ban? Or should we perhaps have different rules for admissibility and for closing argument?

From the perspective of trying to reduce "bad person" prejudice, it is certainly desirable to prohibit the prosecutor from specifically calling the defendant's bad character to the attention of the jury. Moreover, there is no sound reason for not honoring a defendant's request to admonish the jury not to let "bad person" prejudice affect its decision. To accomplish these objectives, however, one does not need to distinguish between character and noncharacter uses of specific acts evidence in making admissibility decisions. Instead, one could simply apply FRE 403 in deciding whether to admit all specific acts evidence, prohibit the prosecutor from referring to the defendant as a bad person or a person of bad character, and on the defendant's request instruct the jurors that they should not ignore a reasonable doubt because they consider the defendant a bad person.

One benefit of this approach to specific acts evidence is that it eliminates the need for an instruction telling the jury that it may not use the evidence to prove character to show action in conformity with character but that it may use the evidence for some other purpose (e.g., to show motive). Typically the permissible purpose, like the prohibited purpose, requires the fact finder to make a propensity inference. Moreover, the permissible and the prohibited propensity inferences are virtually indistinguishable except in two inconsequential ways. First, by definition the generalization underlying the prohibited inference relies on the concept of character and thereby emphasizes the risk of unfair prejudice. Second, because of the generality of propensities that we think of as character traits, the prohibited propensity inference is likely to be less probative than the permissible propensity inference. One can deal with the first difference by a direct, simple instruction about unfair prejudice. As for the second difference, while low probative value may be a reason to exclude evidence pursuant to FRE 403 or perhaps to give a cautionary instruction about the danger of overestimating probative value, there is no need to tell the jury to ignore admitted evidence simply because it has low probative value.

A second possible benefit of distinguishing between rules governing admissibility and rules governing closing argument would be the development of a broader prohibition against prejudicial references to bad character in closing argument. FRE 404(b) prohibits only the inference from character to action in conformity with character. It does not, for example, limit the ability of the prosecutor to characterize a defendant as a bad or violent person on the basis of the evidence suggesting that the defendant committed the crime charged; courts frequently permit such argument. Samuel R. Gross, Make-Believe: The Rules Excluding Evidence of Character and Liability Insurance, 49 Hastings L.J. 843 (1998).

E. HABIT AND ROUTINE PRACTICE

Although the Federal Rules, like the common law, severely limit the circumstances in which a party may introduce character evidence to show action in conformity with character, both the Federal Rules and the common law permit the use of evidence of a person's habit to show action in conformity with that habit on a particular occasion. Similarly, they both permit evidence of business custom or the routine practice of an organization to show action in conformity with that custom or practice.

1. FRE 406

RULE 406. HABIT; ROUTINE PRACTICE

Evidence of the habit of a person or of the routine practice of an organization, whether corroborated or not and regardless of the presence of eyewitnesses, is relevant to prove that the conduct of the person or organization on a particular occasion was in conformity with the habit or routine practice.

2. Interpretation and Illustration of FRE 406

Whereas most of the Federal Rules address the issue of exclusion or admissibility, FRE 406 is written as though it merely announces that a certain category of evidence is relevant. This is undoubtedly a flaw in the drafting of the rule, since its purpose is to clarify that habit and routine practice are not just relevant, but admissible. Even then, FRE 406 seems technically unnecessary: Since FRE 402 makes all relevant evidence admissible unless it is subject to an exclusionary rule, and since nothing in the Federal Rules excludes evidence of "habit" (as distinct from "character"), there is no reason to suppose that relevant habit evidence would not be admissible. Nonetheless, FRE 406 serves two important functions.

First, FRE 406 places no special restrictions on admitting habit evidence. Although most jurisdictions today do not limit the use of habit and routine practice evidence, many older cases – including some federal cases — required eyewitnesses or other corroboration to admit the evidence. FRE 406 makes clear that these former restrictions no longer apply.

Second, FRE 406 provides a useful clarification that habit evidence is not subject to the strictures of FRE 404-405 even though habit evidence closely resembles character evidence in its form and logic. Like traits of "character," "habits" are tendencies or propensities of persons to behave in certain predictable ways. Like character evidence, the relevance of habit evidence depends on what we have called a "propensity inference" — the inference that a person is more likely to have acted in a certain way on a particular occasion if it was his propensity (character or habit) to act in such a way.

Organizations may also have behavioral propensities, but, as will be explained later in this section, FRE 406 implies that inadmissible character traits are understood by evidence law to be traits of individual persons, rather than collective groups of persons.

a.   The Importance of Habit and Routine Practice Evidence

Habit or routine practice evidence can be very useful circumstantial proof of action on a particular occasion. For example, to show that Alice was in the crosswalk of an intersection when she was hit by the defendant's car, Alice may introduce evidence of her habit for using the crosswalk at that intersection. To establish this habit Harry may testify, "I have seen Alice cross the street at this intersection hundreds of times, and every time she has used the crosswalk."

Moreover, evidence of routine practice of an organization may sometimes be the only way to prove action on a particular occasion. Consider, for example, how an insurance company could prove that it had sent out a cancellation notice. It seems unlikely that any employee would have a specific memory of mailing the notice in question. The insurance company, however, will probably be able to rely on its routine practice to prove that the notice was sent: The company could introduce a copy of the cancellation notice along with the following testimony of one of the company employees: "This copy came from our filing cabinet. It is the routine practice of the company to put such copies in the file only when originals are prepared, signed, and placed in the outgoing mail box. Every day at 3:00 P.M., a designated employee takes mail from our outgoing mailbox and deposits it with the U.S. mail."

Routine practice evidence may also be admissible to help establish an organization's liability. Vining ex rel. Vining v. Enterprise Financial Group, 148 F.3d 1206 (10th Cir. 1998) (evidence of abusive pattern of insurance policy rescissions); United States ex rel. Koch v. Koch Industries, 1999 U.S. Dist. LEXIS 16632 (N.D. Okla. Sept. 28, 1999) (company-wide, management-directed scheme to mismeasure the volume of oil it produced on virtually all leases). The sorts of organizations to which FRE 406 applies must be cohesive enterprises rather than loose associations. See United States v. Rangel-Arreola, 991 F.2d 1519, 1523 (10th Cir. 1993).

b.   Methods of Proving Habit and Routine Practice

FRE 406 does not deal with the types of evidence that a proponent may use to prove habit or routine practice in order to prove conduct on a particular occasion, but that would be unnecessary. The FRE 404(b) prohibition on specific acts evidence to prove "character" does not apply to the use of specific acts to prove "habit," which by definition is distinct from character. Typically proponents use evidence of the type described in the foregoing illustrations: The habit witness is likely either to mention a number of specific acts or to offer a summary or "opinion" based on a large number of observations that are not individually described. If the court characterizes the summary as opinion testimony rather than specific act testimony, that characterization should cause no problem as long as the opinion meets the helpfulness and firsthand knowledge requirements of FRE 701, the lay opinion rule. A routine practice witness may describe specific instances or, as in the illustration, describe generally what the practice is.

Although reputation evidence is one of the traditional methods of proving a character trait, a proponent should not be able to use reputation evidence to prove habit or routine practice. Reputation evidence offered for this purpose would be hearsay, and while there is a hearsay exception for reputation evidence offered to prove character, FRE 803(21), there is no exception for reputation evidence offered to prove habit or routine practice.

c. The Distinction Between Habit and Character

Federal Rules 404-406 restrict the use of character evidence but not habit evidence to show conduct on a particular occasion, and as suggested above, habit evidence closely resembles character evidence and relies on the same kind of "propensity" inference in order to be relevant. Thus, the classification of a person's propensity as "habit" rather than "character" is frequently dispositive of its admissibility.

The Federal Rules define neither "character" nor "habit." However, both common usage and the case law suggest that the term *habit* refers to a propensity that is much more specific and routine than a character trait. For example, getting up every morning at 6:00 A.M. is an activity that as a matter of common usage we would refer to as a habit, whereas being violent (which typically is not something that occurs in a regularized, routine manner) is something we would call a character trait. Similarly, as we suggested, a court would probably regard testimony about Alice's crossing the same intersection in the crosswalk as habit evidence. Charmley v. Lewis, 302 Or. 324, 729 P.2d 567 (1986). Courts, however, would consider testimony that Alice acted carefully and cautiously generally as evidence of a character trait. Should evidence that a person "regularly stayed within crosswalks when crossing the street" be regarded as character evidence or habit evidence? Cf. Kovacs v. Chesapeake & Ohio Ry., 134 Mich. App. 514, 351 N.W.2d 581 (1984) (testimony that person approached railroad crossings in prudent, careful manner admissible as evidence of habit).

Although courts rely almost exclusively on the extent to which activity is specific and routine in deciding whether to call it habit evidence, there is another factor that tends to distinguish habit from character. As the preceding crosswalk and 6:00 A.M. rising examples suggest, activity that we think of as constituting a habit tends to be morally neutral, at least compared to character traits, which have a more salient moral connotation: being violent is bad; being careful is good.

The same factors that distinguish habit from character — regularity, specificity, and moral neutrality — inhere in what the common law referred to as business custom and what FRE 406 refers to as "routine practice of an organization." Indeed, according to the Advisory Committee Note to FRE 406, this phrase refers to "behavior on the part of a group" that is "equivalent" to the behavior of an individual that we characterize as habit.

d.   Judicial Factfinding on the Question of Habit

The immediately preceding discussion has dealt with whether a particular activity is a habit or a character trait. A closely related but distinct issue, which can arise both with proffered habit evidence and with proffered routine practice evidence, is whether the evidence establishes the existence of the habit or routine practice in the particular case. Reconsider, for example, the illustration in which Harry offered to testify about Alice's habit of using the crosswalk at a particular intersection. The first question that one must ask is whether the activity is the type that can qualify as a habit rather than a character trait. In other words, is crossing a particular intersection in the crosswalk, if sufficiently regularized, a habit as opposed to a character trait? Assuming that the answer is affirmative, one must then consider whether the witness's testimony can establish that Alice's activity is sufficiently regularized to be her habit. If Harry had seen Alice cross the intersection many times, always using the crosswalk, the answer to this second question would also be affirmative. On the other hand, if Harry offered to testify (1) that Alice used the crosswalk only 60 percent of the time or (2) that he had seen Alice cross at the intersection only three times, a court would exclude the evidence on the ground that it does not show Alice's habit. In the first alternative, Alice's activity is not sufficiently regularized or routine; in the second alternative, Harry's knowledge of Alice's activity is insufficient to determine whether the activity is regularized and routine. Consider what the result should be if Harry offered to testify that on all of the hundreds of times he had seen Alice use the crosswalk he was crossing the street with her. Should this evidence be admissible to prove Alice's habit to show that she was using the crosswalk on the occasion in question, when she was alone?

In situations in which it is arguably a close question (1) whether the type of activity could fit within the habit or routine practice category or (2) whether in the particular case the evidence is sufficient to establish the habit or routine practice, courts tend to exercise fairly tight control over the admissibility of the evidence. Courts rarely articulate the precise bases for their conclusions, however. Consider, for example, a situation in which a court has excluded proffered habit evidence on the ground that the witness has not observed the activity enough times to establish whether the habit in fact exists. The court may have decided by a preponderance of the evidence pursuant to FRE 104(a) that the evidence did not establish a habit. Alternatively, the court, applying FRE 403, may have concluded that the relatively low probative value of the evidence (in light of the few instances to which the witness could testify) did not warrant taking the time to litigate the matter. It may not be clear which of these theories the court relied on. Indeed, the court may not specifically have considered these two theoretically distinct justifications for its exclusionary decision.

3.   Elaboration of FRE 406

a.   The Rationale for Permitting Habit and Routine Practice Evidence

The factors that tend to distinguish habit and routine practice from character — the relatively more routine and specific nature of the activity and the absence of moral connotation — suggest the rationales for permitting evidence of the former and severely restricting evidence of the latter. First, because of the regularized, specific nature of habit and routine practice evidence, it is likely to be much more probative of action on a particular occasion than is character evidence. In other words, the generalization that people have a propensity to act in conformity with their habits is likely to be true more of the time than the generalization that people act in conformity with their character traits. Second, to the extent that habit or routine practice evidence is morally neutral, it does not have the potential for prejudice that inheres in character evidence. Gamerdinger v. Schaefer, 603 N.W.2d 590, 594 (Iowa 1999). In addition given the difficulty of recalling a specific instance of routine, repetitive behavior, habit or routine practice may be the only evidence available for an individual, or particularly an organization to prove a particular instance of conduct.

b.   The Strategy for Distinguishing Between Habit and Character

Legal authority distinguishing habit from character is less clear than one would like. The Advisory Committee Note to FRE 406 is vague, if not inconsistent, on this point. The Note begins by quoting McCormick's Handbook on the Law of Evidence that habit is "more specific" than character and is defined as a "person's regular practice of meeting a particular kind of situation with a specific type of conduct, such as the habit of going down a particular stairway two stairs at a time, . . . or of alighting from railway cars while they are moving." But the Note follows this serviceable definition by citing language from a case suggesting that habit means activities of "invariable regularity that are perhaps not 'volitional.'" Advisory Committee Note to FRE 406 (quoting Levin v. United States, 338 F.2d 265 (D.C. Cir. 1964)):

While the *Levin* definition seems unduly narrow, the McCormick passage does not tell us much about any qualitative difference between character and habit; nor does it provide us with much of a basis for labeling activity that falls between the fairly extreme examples of generality and specificity. For example, what about evidence that a person (a) is a careful driver, (b) always or usually stops at stop signs, (c) always or usually stops at a particular stop sign? The case law indicates that the first and probably the second pieces of evidence would be character evidence and that the last piece of evidence would be habit evidence. Jones v. Southern Pacific Railroad Co., 962 F.2d 447, 448 (5th Cir. 1992) (nine various safety violations over 29-year period not evidence of habit); Weil v. Seltzer, 873 F.2d 1453 (D.C. Cir. 1989) (passing off steroids as antihistamines not habit; habit is something that occurs with "invariable regularity"); Simplex Inc. v. Diversified Energy Systems, Inc., 847 F.2d 1290 (7th Cir. 1988) (supplier's conduct in making late deliveries on other contracts not a habit); Charmley v. Lewis, 302 Or. 324, 729 P.2d 567 (1986) (frequently crossing same intersection within unmarked crosswalk is habit evidence). These results, however, are by no means obvious from McCormick's description. For an excellent discussion of the difficulties in distinguishing between character and habit, see 1A John Henry Wigmore, Evidence in Trials at Common Law 1624-1630 (Peter Tillers rev. 1983).

Given the difficulty in articulating *a priori* criteria for distinguishing between habit and character, the advocate who wishes to convince a judge that evidence should fall into one category or the other should follow a twofold strategy. First, of course, it will be important to look at the existing case law and to draw analogies to and distinctions from situations in which courts have designated evidence as habit or character. Second, one should try to relate the desired classification to the evidentiary justifications for having different rules for habit evidence and character evidence in the first place. For example, if the specificity of the conduct, the consistency of the behavior, and its contextual similarity to the conduct at issue suggest relatively high probative value, argue that these specific factors warrant placing the evidence in the habit category. Similarly, to the extent that there is a risk of unfair prejudice, argue that risk of prejudice is one of the hallmarks of character evidence and that the evidence in question therefore should fall in the character category. Focusing on probative value and prejudice has the benefit of promoting rational evidentiary decisionmaking, though to be sure, this focus will not always provide easy answers to the question whether one is dealing with habit or character. The reality seems to be that the distinction between habit and character is a difference of degree rather than a clear categorical distinction.

c.   A Particular Application of the Character/Habit Distinction: Drinking "Habits"

The occasional difficulties in distinguishing character from habit are well illustrated by the special, but frequently recurring, situation of evidence of a person's alcohol consumption practices offered as circumstantial evidence of intoxication on a specific occasion. Consider a case in which the defendant is charged with vehicular homicide following a hit-and-run accident on a Friday evening and the prosecution wants to establish that the defendant was drunk at the time of the accident. Assume that the prosecutor is prepared to introduce eyewitness testimony about the defendant's propensity to drink and drive. Regardless of whether one regards a drinking problem as an illness, presenting such evidence to the jury is likely to be prejudicial in the sense that jurors may tend to ignore a reasonable doubt because of their lack of sympathy for a person who drinks and drives. Thus, in this respect, for evidentiary purposes a tendency to drink too much — or at least a tendency to drink too much and then drive — is like a character trait. On the other hand, if the evidence of drinking were quite specific — for example, drinking six or seven shots of whiskey between 5:00 P.M. and 6:00 P.M. every Friday after work for the last 50 Fridays — the activity is as regular and routine as much of the evidence that gets the label *habit*.

Ultimately, admissibility of the prosecution's evidence in our vehicular homicide prosecution will turn on comparing the precise nature of the evidence with the existing case law. As the Advisory Committee's Note to FRE 406 points out, "evidence of intemperate 'habits' is generally excluded when offered as proof of drunkenness in accident cases." A number of courts, however, admit evidence of a person's drinking propensities that tend to be specific and routine. Loughan v. Firestone Tire & Rubber Co., 749 F.2d 1519, 1522-1523 (11th Cir. 1985) ("uniform pattern of behavior" over six years that included drinking on job, usually drinking in early morning hours, and carrying beer cooler in truck); State v. Kately, 270 N.J. Super. 356, 637 A.2d 214 (1993) (admitting testimony that defendant had been drinking in field across from defendant's home every night each week for about a year, that defendant would consume from one to two six-packs of beer, and that defendant was drunk four or five nights a week).

d.   Evidence of Custom or Routine Practice of an Organization

Do organizations have character traits? An argument can be made that, as far as the law of evidence is concerned, they do not: The character evidence prohibitions set out in FRE 404 apply to evidence of the character "of a person." While corporations and other organizations may be treated as a "person" for certain legal issues, FRE 406 distinguishes between the conduct of "a person" and that of "an organization." Reading FRE 404 and 406 together, and giving the same terms the same meaning, thus suggests that "a person" in FRE 404 does not include organizations. Nevertheless, the handful of reported decisions that seem to touch on this issue have not clearly or consistently decided this question. See also Advisory Committee Note to FRE 406 (suggesting that organizational routine practice is "equivalent" to individual habit).

If a court assumes that organizations do not have character traits, then there is no risk of slipping across the "line" that theoretically distinguishes habit from character, and these courts may not look to precisely the same criteria for proving the custom or practice of an organization as they do for proving the habit of an individual. While courts may insist upon a showing that an organizational practice is routine and repetitive, they might not insist that the conduct be morally neutral or even so commonly repeated as to happen on a daily basis. Thus, for example, some courts would allow evidence that a police department has a custom or routine practice of using unlawfully excessive force, or a business corporation may be shown to have a practice of defrauding customers or discriminating against racial minorities in hiring, for the purpose of proving the organization's conduct on a specific occasion.

As with habit, an objection can be made to evidence of the custom or routine practice of an organization on the ground that the proffered specific acts of the organization are insufficient to establish the custom or practice, or that the witness offering an opinion of the organizational practice lacks sufficient firsthand knowledge of the claimed practice. In addition, the opponent can object to organizational practice evidence under FRE 403 by arguing that, for example, past bad acts of the organization have low probative value for proving a routine practice, but high prejudicial effect. However, in one important respect, the objections to organizational practice evidence may differ from the objections that can be made to individual habit evidence. The opponent can object to evidence offered to show the habit of a person by arguing that the propensity is in fact not a habit, but rather a character trait. In contrast, there may be no "character" objection to evidence of organizational practice. Note, however, that even where past specific acts of an organization may be deemed insufficiently routine to fit within FRE 406, the evidence may still be deemed admissible as "past similar happenings," discussed in Section F, infra.

The kinds of organizations contemplated in FRE 406 are made up of human beings, and in many cases, the custom or practice of the organization will necessarily be shown by evidence of specific acts of individuals who work for or otherwise constitute the organization. Likewise, when FRE 406 speaks of using "routine practice" to prove the "conduct of ... [an] organization on a particular occasion," the rule glosses over the reality that organizations act through their individual agents or employees. This reality should occasionally raise the red flag of an objectionable character inference if the proponent of the evidence is trying to use purported organizational practice to prove the conduct of an individual.

In a comparatively straightforward case of routine organizational practice, consider again the problem of an insurance company proving it sent out a cancellation notice based on an inference from its routine practice of mailing such notices. The inference from the routine practice is that the notice "was sent by the company." Clearly, some unidentified person or persons did the sending, but the law of evidence seems to gloss over this on the theory that the identity of the employee(s) who did the sending is not so important, and the conduct is legally attributable to the organization anyway.

A somewhat more problematic example might arise where the routine practice of the organization involves misconduct. Numerous instances of police brutality or employment discrimination might be offered to show a "pattern and practice" of such misconduct as circumstantial evidence that the plaintiff suffered such a wrong on a particular occasion. If the numbers are sufficient to establish the "routine practice" of the organization, it should be permissible for the jury to infer conduct on a particular occasion so long as the proponent seeks to prove the organization's conduct, as opposed the conduct of a particular person. Courts may be more likely to balk at attempts to use FRE 406 to show "guilt by association," that is, an inference that an individual member behaved a certain way because such behavior was typical of an organization with which he was involved. United States v. Angelilli, 660 F.2d 23, 40-41 (2d Cir. 1981) (practices of criminal conspiracy could not be offered to support the inference that alleged member of conspiracy committed the relevant criminal act).

KEY POINTS

1. FRE 406 places no specific limitations on the use of habit or routine practice evidence to show action on a particular occasion.

2. The admissibility of habit or routine practice evidence is likely to turn on the resolution of two closely related but distinct questions: Is the activity in question a habit (or routine practice), or is it a character trait? Is the evidence in the particular case sufficient to establish the existence of the habit or routine practice?

PROBLEMS

5.18. Return to Problem 3.2 at page 129, supra. Leaving aside any problem of hearsay, is Driver's Exhibit A admissible to show her habit of good driving?

5.19. Defendant Lefty Frizzell is charged with shoplifting some tools from Deuce Hardware. At trial, he testifies that he bought the items but was not given a sales receipt. In rebuttal, the prosecution offers testimony of the store manager that it was the standard practice of the cashiers to give sales receipts for every purchase. Is the testimony admissible over the defense's objection that this is inadmissible character evidence?

5.20. Defendant Harry Lately is being sued for negligence for speeding through a yellow light and colliding with the plaintiff's car on Lately's way to work. The plaintiff offers the testimony of Lately's supervisor that Lately was "frequently late to work and always seemed to be in a rush." Is the testimony admissible over the defense's objection that this is inadmissible character evidence?

5.21. Return to Problem 3.3, United States v. Ray, at page 131. The prosecution offers Beth Barker as a witness. On direct examination, Barker is prepared to testify:

I have been employed as Bernard Ray's executive secretary since 1998. I followed the following practice in handling Mr. Ray's mail, including hand delivered documents and intra-office memos. I would place incoming mail and other delivered documents in the "in" box on Mr. Ray's desk three times each day, at around 10 A.M., around 1:30 P.M. and around 4:00 P.M. At 8:30 A.M. each morning, I take all of the documents in Mr. Ray's "out" box, check to make sure that Mr. Ray has initialed them, and then place them in Mr. Ray's files. Mr. Ray always reads and initials his mail and other documents and puts them in his "out" box. In response to a request from federal investigators, on September 1, 2005, I found Exhibit 3 in Mr. Ray's files. Exhibit 3 is a March 14, 2004 memo from auditor Arthur Andrews to Rundown CFO June Jacobs. It has Mr. Ray's initials in the top left corner.

Any objections? What additional questions might the prosecution have to ask in order to secure admission of this testimony?

5.22. You are preparing to prosecute Petro R. for aggravated manslaughter involving a fatal hit-and-run accident. There is no dispute that Mr. R. was driving his car on a Sunday evening and that he hit another car that was waiting to make a turn, killing the driver. Your theory of the case is that Mr. R. was drunk at the time of the accident and that his intoxication supports the aggravated manslaughter charge, which requires "extreme indifference to human life." Mr. R. was never tested for drunkenness because he had left the scene.

You have a witness, Bernie Zurella, the bartender at Rova Farms, a social club catering to people of Russian extraction. Zurella is prepared to testify as follows:

> For the past five years Mr. R. has come into the club virtually every weekend; usually both Saturday and Sunday nights. He always stays about an hour, drinks vodka steadily, becomes loud and noisy, and leaves. I really cannot remember whether he was actually at the club on the night of the accident.

Will you be able to use this testimony?

5.23. The plaintiff has sued the defendant manufacturer for injuries sustained when a can of refrigerant exploded. The plaintiff claims that the explosion was caused by a defect in the product, and the manufacturer claims that the explosion resulted from the plaintiff's use of a heating coil to heat the refrigerant before pouring it, contrary to the instructions on the can. Should the court admit the manufacturer's evidence that it was the plaintiff's habit to use an immersion heating coil to heat cans of refrigerant? What additional information, if any, would you want to know to decide the admissibility issue?

5.24. How should the court rule in the following cases:

(a) A bank teller seeks to withdraw a guilty plea to theft on the ground that it was involuntary. To prove that the teller entered the plea with full awareness of his rights and the consequences of the guilty plea, the state offers to prove the trial judge's habit of providing defendants with this information before accepting a plea. The proffered evidence consists of the judge's testimony about her own practices and three transcripts from unrelated cases in which the judge informed defendants of their rights and the consequences of a guilty plea.

(b) In a medical malpractice suit against a drug manufacturer, the defendant claims that it is not liable because its sales representative fully informed the treating doctor of the dangers associated with the drug. The defendant offers the testimony of the sales representative that he had a habit of discussing the dangers of the drug in question with physicians, that the discussion included information about a particular study detailing the dangers, and that the presentations to physicians would "go virtually the same way with every physician."

(c) In a medical malpractice suit against a doctor, the plaintiff alleges that she was not adequately informed about the risks of the surgery she underwent. To establish the doctor's practice of not providing adequate information for an informed consent, the plaintiff offers the testimony of three other patients of the defendant. They will all testify that they had the same procedure as the plaintiff and that the information they received about the surgery was virtually identical to the information the plaintiff claims to have received. Should this evidence be admissible? Would your answer change if there were only two such witnesses? Seven witnesses? Ten?

F.   SIMILAR HAPPENINGS

In thinking about "past specific acts" or occurrences other than those giving rise to the civil claim or criminal charge, there remains one further category aside from those covered by FRE 404, 405, and 406. This category is typically referred to as "similar happenings," and it entails prior conduct by persons or occurrences involving inanimate objects that are offered for some purpose other than to prove character, habit, or routine practice. Evidence of similar happenings (or nonhappenings) falls into three broad categories:

(1) **Organizational propensity.** Past similar conduct of, or occurrences within, an organization, offered to show that the organization has a "propensity" toward certain acts or occurrences to prove the organization's conduct (strictly speaking, the conduct of one or more agents or employees of the organization) on a specific occasion. Organizational "propensity" is some factor attributable to the organization, rather than to chance (typically a formal or informal policy), that would tend to cause the acts or occurrences.

   Examples include evidence of numerous instances of race discrimination against others to show a company-wide practice offered as circumstantial proof that the company discriminated against the plaintiff; evidence of other contracts between the plaintiff and the defendant offered to prove the terms of the current contract between the plaintiff and the defendant; evidence of prior safety violations of a company to raise an inference of negligent behavior on the occasion giving rise to the plaintiff's injury; past fraudulent transactions by a company to show fraud against the plaintiff on a particular occasion.

(2) **Organizational liability.** Past similar conduct of, or occurrences within, an organization, offered to establish an element of liability, such as "notice" or "pattern or practice" liability, or to establish a standard of care.

   Examples include prior safety violations of a company to show that the company "knew or should have known" about potentially tortious conditions; repeated acts of police misconduct to show an institutional "policy, pattern or practice," the latter being an element of municipal liability for torts of employees; evidence of a routine custom of vehicle safety inspections to show a standard of care that was breached in a case where no safety inspection was made prior to the accident in question.

(3) **Characteristics of objects.** Past similar behavior or operation of, or occurrences involving, an inanimate object.

   Examples include evidence that an instrumentality has caused other similar injuries in the past (e.g., that people have injured themselves falling on the same set of stairs, or that an allegedly defective product or machine has malfunctioned in the past); or evidence that similar objects have had other characteristics similar to an object at issue in the case (such as evidence that similar real properties have a value comparable to the value claimed in a property dispute).

1. No Specific Federal Rule for Similar Happenings

There is no specific Federal Rule dealing with similar happenings. Indeed, you might wonder why it is even considered a particular category of evidence at all. Yet courts and commentators do, in fact, usually treat evidence of similar happenings or nonhappenings as a distinct category of evidence, see, e.g., 1 McCormick on Evidence §196-200 at 691-710 (John W. Strong, ed. 5th ed. 1999), probably for two reasons. First, similar happenings evidence bears close resemblance to the kinds of "past specific acts" evidence that is strictly regulated by FRE 404-406. Second, the reasoning process that makes "similar happenings" evidence relevant often relies on a propensity inference similar to that involved in character evidence. Thus, the same kinds of recurring FRE 403 dangers that undoubtedly underlie FRE 404 may arguably exist for similar happenings. Perhaps for this reason, many older cases reflect a fairly strict judicial control — as a matter of case law applying FRE 403 and its common law analogues — over similar happenings evidence. Modern cases have liberalized admission of similar happenings evidence and tend to treat it as a classic instance of FRE 403. The bottom line is that similar happenings evidence is governed only by FRE 401-403.

2. Similar Happenings, Character, and Habit Evidence Compared

If you take another look at the examples of the three categories of similar happenings evidence, you can see some obvious points of comparison with the kinds of "propensity" evidence we have studied so far in this chapter. Category (1) resembles character evidence prohibited by FRE 404(b), in that past similar happenings are being offered to show organizational propensity to prove the conduct of the organization on a specific occasion. The reason FRE 404(b) does not apply is that the propensity in question is not that of a person, but a thing. Even though most organizations consist of groups of people, so long as the propensity is being attributed to an organization, courts will usually not consider it to be "character" evidence. Similarly, category (3) evidence is offered to show the propensity of a thing (like a machine or a piece of property). This too falls outside the scope of FRE 404 since character (as that term is understood by most courts) is an attribute of individual people, not inanimate objects.

Category (1) of similar happenings evidence probably overlaps with routine practice evidence under FRE 406, which allows proof of the routine practice of an organization in order to prove conduct on a specific occasion. But there will undoubtedly be instances in which a court will find evidence of organizational behavior to be insufficiently routine or morally neutral to qualify as FRE 406 evidence. For instance, a company may often defraud customers, but perhaps not so often as to make it a "routine." Again, such evidence is analogous to evidence of an organization's "character," but the law of evidence recognizes character traits only of individual persons. Therefore, specific acts to prove the (quasi) "character" of an organization to prove the organization's conduct on a specific occasion comes within the "similar happenings" rather than the "character" rubric. Ultimately, it is somewhat academic whether such evidence is deemed to fall within FRE 406 or the "similar happenings" category: either way, the admission or exclusion is likely to depend on an application of FRE 403 factors.

Category (2) resembles evidence covered by FRE 405(b): the past similar happenings are offered to prove something other than conduct of the organization on a particular occasion. The organization's "propensity" — its pattern or practice, for instance — is a fact of consequence or essential element by itself.

Where the proponent offers evidence of an "institutional propensity," the opponent of the evidence should be alert to the possibility that the evidence is really a disguised effort to prove the character of an individual. The use of past specific acts to show organizational propensity makes sense if the acts tend to show a causal mechanism by which some factor intrinsic to the organization — a formal or informal policy, for example — supports the inference that the individual acts or occurrences are not based on random factors. (The relevance of such similar acts evidence may be, in effect, a kind of "doctrine of chances" theory raising similar dangers of misuse.)

If, as is often the case, the purported "similar happenings" are really the actions of a person offered to show how that person behaved on a particular occasion, the admissibility of the proffered evidence will necessarily involve a consideration of FRE 404-406. Consider a products liability case in which the plaintiff sustained injuries after a can of refrigerant exploded. The defendant claims the can exploded because, contrary to the instructions on the can, the plaintiff used an immersion heating coil to heat the refrigerant. To substantiate this claim, the defendant offers evidence that on other occasions the plaintiff used a heating coil to heat cans of refrigerant. If the court regards the evidence as showing the plaintiff's character trait for carelessness, it is inadmissible under FRE 404. On the other hand, (1) if the court finds that the evidence falls within some noncharacter FRE 404(b) purpose or (2) if the court regards the evidence as sufficient to establish a habit, the evidence is potentially admissible. Either way, however, what on the surface appears to have been a past similar happening involving the can of refrigerant turns out to be a question of individual human behavior.

3.   The Approach to the Admissibility of Similar Happenings Evidence

Don't be too caught up in the notion of "similarity" with all similar happenings evidence. Assuming the proponent of similar happenings evidence offers witnesses with firsthand knowledge of these events, the only rules that a judge will probably have to consider are FRE 401-403. Since no rule makes similarity a special condition of admissibility, it is not an FRE 104 preliminary fact for the judge to consider. Rather, the judge's task is to determine only whether the evidence is relevant and if so whether the probative value is substantially outweighed by the countervailing FRE 403 factors. As with any evidence, the probative value of similar happenings evidence depends on the purpose for which the evidence is offered. The probative value may or may not depend heavily on similarity of the proffered happenings. For example, in a civil rights suit alleging municipal liability based on a "pattern and practice" of excessive force by police, it may be that the only relevant "similarity" of the incidents is that they were all committed by members of the defendant's police force. On the other hand, in a products liability case, courts may require a showing of similarity of past injury incidents to establish that the other users all used the product as directed and thereby eliminate possible causes of injury other than product defect.

Similarity in this category of evidence really refers to the presence or absence of extraneous factors that will make the past happenings more or less probative for the case at hand. This probative value is balanced against the FRE 403 dangers: waste of time, confusion of issues, and unfair prejudice caused by risk of improper inferences. Although FRE 403 is the governing rule, many courts considering "similar happenings" evidence render decisions without making explicit reference to FRE 403 and instead discuss admissibility in terms of the similarity of the prior incidents. See First Security Bank v. Union Pac. R. Co., 152 F.3d 877 (8th Cir. 1998).

4. The Application of FRE 403 to Similar Happenings Evidence in Practice

Since the FRE 403 balancing test favors admissibility, one's initial instinct may be that courts should be liberal in admitting similar happenings evidence when the only barrier to admissibility is FRE 403. The case law is consistent with this instinct when similar happenings evidence is offered to show *notice* of a possible defect (e.g., prior fuel tank explosions offered to show defendant had notice of dangerous placement of fuel tank). Four Corners Helicopters, Inc. v. Turbomeca, 979 F.2d 1434 (10th Cir. 1992). When the issue is notice, the probative value of the evidence depends primarily on whether the defendant was or should have been aware of the other incidents and not on how similar they are to the incident that gave rise to the litigation. But see First Security Bank v. Union Pac. R. Co., 152 F.3d 877 (8th Cir. 1998) (substantial similarity required even when evidence offered to show notice).

By contrast, when the probative value of the evidence depends on the degree of similarity among the happenings, courts are likely to require a high degree of similarity as a condition of admissibility. Most federal courts speak of a requirement of "substantial similarity." First Security Bank v. Union Pac. R. Co., supra; Wheeler v. John Deere Co., 862 F.2d 1404, 1407 (10th Cir. 1988). For example, if the plaintiff offers incidents of uncontrollable skidding by cars with Acme tires to prove Acme tires caused the plaintiff's car to skid uncontrollably, the evidence is not likely to be admissible unless the plaintiff can introduce evidence of similarity in the type of road, weather conditions, and other factors that tend to eliminate alternative causal explanations for the skidding incidents. Brooks v. Chrysler Corp., 786 F.2d 1191 (D.C. Cir. 1986) (excluding other automobile accidents because of insufficient showing of substantial similarity). Perhaps one can justify this careful screening by courts on the ground that the probative value of similar incidents standing alone is sufficiently low that it is substantially outweighed by the FRE 403 efficiency and confusion factors.

In making the FRE 403 determination, one should look not merely at the time that it will take initially to introduce the evidence but also at the total time that it will take to deal with the evidence. Once the proponent introduces the evidence, the other party is likely to feel compelled to respond with evidence suggesting that the events did not occur at all or that there are not relevant similarities among the events — a process that may be quite time consuming. Thus, unless the proponent is prepared to demonstrate at the outset that the evidence has more than minimal probative value, an FRE 403 decision to exclude similar happenings evidence may often be warranted.

5.   Similar Happenings Offered to Show an Institutional Policy or Practice

One of the most important uses of similar happenings is to show an institutional policy or practice. For example, in a prisoners' class action challenging the practices of violence at Pelican Bay Prison, the setting that gave rise to the *Johnson* case in Chapter One, the plaintiffs relied on testimony and records describing numerous incidents of excessive force against inmates to establish their claim that state prison officials were aware of the problem at Pelican Bay and, in fact, "implicitly sanctioned the misuse of force and acted with knowing willingness that harm occur." Madrid v. Gomez, 889 F. Supp. 1146, 1199-1200 (N.D. Cal. 1995). See also Austin v. Hopper, 15 F. Supp. 2d 1210 (M.D. Ala. 1998). In that lawsuit, the institutional practice was itself the focal point of the suit: liability followed directly from the establishment by the plaintiffs of the institutional practice, without having to draw further inferences about conduct on a specific occasion.

In civil rights cases brought by individuals against a municipal police force for police brutality, evidence of other incidents of excessive force is legally necessary in order for plaintiffs to win a judgment against a city, county, or other "municipality": "[A] plaintiff must prove a specific pattern of conduct or series of incidents violative of constitutional rights in order to sustain the existence of a municipal policy or custom." Sherrod v. Berry, 827 F.2d 195, 206 (7th Cir. 1987); see Monell v. New York City Dept. of Social Servs., 436 U.S. 658 (1978).

6.   Evidence of Similar Nonhappenings

"Similar happenings" evidence is also understood to include evidence of nonhappenings offered to prove lack of notice or that an event did not occur or did not occur in the manner or for the reason alleged (e.g., evidence of the absence of people falling down a staircase to rebut the plaintiff's claim that the staircase was dangerous). See generally Annot., Admissibility, in Negligence Action, of Absence of Other Accidents or Injuries, 10 A.L.R. 5th 371 (1993). In this type of case a court is likely to require evidence that the conditions were similar during the time of the nonhappenings. In addition, the court is likely to require a significant number of nonhappenings. Whereas evidence that two or three people fell down a staircase may be quite probative to show that the staircase was dangerous, evidence that two or three people managed to use the staircase without falling is not very probative of the proposition that the staircase is safe. Those two or three people may fortuitously have avoided the dangerous spot. Evidence that several hundred people used the staircase without falling under conditions similar to the conditions that existed when the plaintiff fell, however, is quite probative of the proposition that the staircase was not dangerous at the time of the plaintiff's fall.

KEY POINTS

1. Evidence of similar happenings or nonhappenings is offered to show such matters as (a) the behavioral propensity of an organization or an object, (analogous to the "character" of a person) to show the behavior of the organization (or its agents or employees) on a specific occasion, (b) the institutional policy of an organization where

that is a fact of consequence or essential element, or (c) the behavior or characteristics of an inanimate object.

2. There is no specific Federal Rule governing the use of similar happenings. As a practical matter in most cases the controlling rules are likely to be FRE 401-403.

3. Because similar happenings evidence involves either no propensity inference at all, or else a propensity inference about organizations or things rather than individual persons, it is not considered to be evidence of "character" or "habit" and is therefore not governed by FRE 404-406.

4. Except when similar happenings evidence is offered to show notice, courts tend to require a showing of similarity as a condition of admissibility.

PROBLEMS

5.25. Henry purchased Acme Household Cleanser and used it for the first time to clean his kitchen. He suffered severe burns where the cleanser came into contact with his skin. Henry sues Acme Corp., the manufacturer, for strict product liability, alleging $50,000 in damages. Henry offers testimony that during the five years before the incident seven people were severely burned by Acme Household Cleanser and that four of these instances were reported to Acme. Should any of this evidence be admissible?

5.26. Paul Preston has sued National Motor Corporation ("NMC") for personal injuries arising out of an auto accident in which his "Bounder" sports utility vehicle rolled over while making a tight turn on a highway entrance ramp. Preston claims that a design defect in the Bounder makes it prone to rollover accidents. Preston offers evidence showing 50 incidents of rollovers by Bounders on entrance or exit ramps while traveling at or below the speed limit. On what basis could the defense object? Should the evidence be admitted?

5.27. The plaintiff William Lane has brought a damages action against the Los Angeles Police Department for violating his civil rights by using a potentially lethal "chokehold" in making arrests under circumstances where deadly force is not warranted. Lane offers evidence of 20 incidents in which the chokehold was applied to persons other than himself. Lawyers for the LAPD argue that the evidence is inadmissible character evidence to prove that Lane was choked on a specific occasion and that the other incidents are too dissimilar from one another to be probative and too sporadic to constitute a routine practice under FRE 406. Lane argues that the evidence is offered to prove that the LAPD had a "custom, policy, pattern or practice" of unwarranted use of the chokehold. Should the evidence be admitted?

5.28. Layla Calhoun's estate has brought a wrongful death action against the R&D Railroad. Calhoun was killed instantly when her car collided with a train at a railroad crossing. The crossing is a busy one with more than 10 trains passing by every day. Calhoun was traveling east and the train was traveling north. The crossing had warning signs and lights but no crossing gates. The plaintiff's expert, a traffic engineer, will testify that the crossing was abnormally dangerous, primarily because of the absence of a crossing gate. The plaintiff would like to introduce the following evidence:

a)   a report about the crossing prepared by the traffic engineer for litigation in a different case eight years ago; the report reaches essentially the same conclusion that the engineer is going to testify to now;

b)   evidence of five other accidents occurring at the same intersection;
c)   the opinion of a former head of the National Transportation Safety Board that the defendant has "corporate indifference" to safety issues.

How much of this evidence should be admissible? For what purpose(s)? With respect to the evidence in (b), what additional information may be important to your answer? For example, should it matter whether the accidents occurred at the same time of day or whether the trains and the automobiles were coming from the same direction as the train and automobile involved in this suit?

5.29. Fred Johnson is suing Farming Partners for breach of an oral contract for the sale of tomatoes grown by Johnson. Johnson claims that the contract was for the sale of tomatoes outright at a quoted price. Farming Partners claims that the agreement was for it to take the tomatoes on consignment. To establish Farming Partners' routine business practice, Johnson offers the testimony of two other tomato farmers that they entered into oral contracts with Farming Partners for the sale of tomatoes, that the contracts were for outright sales, and that Farming Partners breached the contracts by maintaining the position that they had accepted the tomatoes only on a consignment basis. Is this evidence admissible?

5.30. Peter French has brought a sex discrimination suit against his former employer, Acme Mortgage Co. French had worked as a loan originator, whose job it was to procure applications for mortgage loans. He claims that Jane Brown, a loan processor, engaged in sexually provocative behavior and that she refused to process the loan applications he secured unless he would have sex with her. French has a document, purportedly signed by his and Brown's supervisor recommending that French be fired. The document says, "French has complained to me about Brown's sexual harassment. The situation has become intolerable. I know French's complaints are true, but in the current market it's easier to replace an originator than a processor. I recommend we fire French." Shortly after the date on the document, French was fired.

Acme claims never to have seen the document prior to the litigation. Moreover, Acme personnel will testify that they were unaware of any sexual harassment complaints about Brown and that French was fired for inadequate job performance.

Acme wishes to introduce into evidence:

(a) a written contract between French and a former employer, Don Wilson, that contains terms extremely favorable to French along with the testimony of Wilson that his signature is a forgery, that there was no such agreement, that he saw the document for the first time after French had brought a breach of contract suit against him, and that French ultimately lost the law suit;

(b) evidence that French was unsuccessful in two suits against other former employers.

How much of this evidence should be admissible?

5.31. Ed Naples has brought an action against Acme Lawn Tool Company for breach of an oral employment contract. Acme fired Naples six months after he had been hired as Vice President for Sales. Naples claims the contract was for a fixed term of one year; Acme claims that it was an "at will" contract. Acme offers the testimony of several members of the Acme Board of Directors that all officers of the company are employed on an at-will basis. Should this evidence be admitted? What, if any, additional information would be helpful to your decision?

5.32. Pamela King has sued the Whoopie Amusement Park for personal injuries she sustained riding on Whoopie's roller coaster. According to Pamela's testimony, "A tree limb hit me in the face when I was riding on the roller coaster." The force of the blow broke her glasses and pieces of the lens were lodged in her eye. As part of its defense Whoopie offers the testimony of the amusement park manager (a) that during the entire summer up to the time of the plaintiff's injury nobody had complained about low-hanging branches along the path of the roller coaster and (b) that on the day the plaintiff was injured over 1,000 other persons rode the roller coaster without incident. For what purposes is the defendant's evidence relevant? Should it be admitted?

5.33. Return to Problem 3.2 at page 129. Should Driver be permitted to testify on direct examination that she has never had a driving accident?

G.   EXCEPTIONS TO THE PROHIBITION ON USE OF CHARACTER TO PROVE CONDUCT ON A PARTICULAR OCCASION

1.   Interpretation and Illustration of FRE 404(a)(1)-(3)

(The Advisory Committee has proposed a clarifying amendment to FRE 404(a) that will probably become effective on December 1, 2006. The language added by that amendment appears in italics, and the language deleted by the amendment appears in brackets.)
FRE 404(a) provides:

(a) Character evidence generally. Evidence of a person's character is not admissible for the purpose of proving action in conformity therewith on a particular occasion, except: (1) Character of accused. [Evidence] *In a criminal case, evidence* of a pertinent trait of character offered by an accused, or by the prosecution to rebut the same, or *if evidence of a trait of character of the alleged victim of the crime is offered by an accused and admitted under Rule 404(a)(2), evidence of the same trait of character of the accused offered by the prosecution;* (2) Character of victim. [Evidence] *In a criminal case, and subject to the limitations of Rule 412, evidence* of a pertinent trait of character of the alleged victim of the crime offered by an accused, or by the prosecution to rebut the same, or evidence of a character trait of peacefulness of the alleged victim offered by the prosecution in a homicide case to rebut evidence that the alleged victim was the first aggressor; (3) Character of witness. Evidence of the character of a witness, as provided in rules 607, 608, and 609.

a.   FRE 404(a)(1) and (2): A Criminal Defendant's Right to Open the Door to Character Evidence

A criminal defendant is free to introduce evidence of the defendant's own character (FRE 404(a)(1)) or the victim's character (FRE 404(a)(2)). This is often called "opening the door" to the character issue. For example, in the *Johnson* case the defendant could have introduced evidence of his own peaceful character for the purpose of showing action in conformity with that character trait at the time of the altercation with the prison guards (i.e., for the purpose of showing that he was behaving peacefully and was not the aggressor). FRE 404(a)(1). Similarly, Johnson could have introduced evidence that one or more of the prison guards who were victims had a violent character in order to suggest that they were the aggressors in the incident. FRE 404(a)(2). In fact, Johnson did introduce evidence of prison guard Walker's character for violence (see e.g. page 48, 52-53). As we discuss in Section 3, infra, however, it is not clear that Johnson introduced the evidence to suggest that Walker was the first aggressor.

b.   FRE 404(a)(1) and (2): The Prosecution's Right to Respond to a Defendant's Character Evidence

When a defendant elects to open the character evidence door, the prosecution in its rebuttal case may introduce character evidence to rebut the defendant's evidence. For example, if an assault defendant introduces evidence of the defendant's own good character for peacefulness, the prosecution can respond with evidence that the defendant has a character trait for violence in order to show that the defendant was the aggressor. FRE 404(a)(1). Similarly, if an assault defendant introduces evidence of the victim's character for violence in order to suggest that the victim was the aggressor, the prosecution may respond with evidence of the victim's character for peacefulness. FRE 404(a)(2). In the *Johnson* case, some of the prosecution's rebuttal focused on Officer Walker's good character (page 60, supra). One thing the prosecution may have been attempting to do was to prove Walker's good character so that the jury could infer that Walker did not act improperly at the time of the altercation with Johnson.

Note that when defendants open the door to a victim's bad character, they also open the door to their own bad character. See the latter portion of FRE 404(a)(1). Thus in the preceding hypothetical where the assault defendant introduced evidence of the victim's character for violence, the prosecutor could respond not only with evidence of the victim's character for peacefulness but also with evidence of the defendant's character for violence.

Whenever the prosecution is rebutting the defendant's character evidence, the prosecution's evidence must be about the same character trait addressed by the defendant's evidence. This limitation is implicit in the term *rebut*, and FRE 404(a)(1) makes the limitation explicit when the prosecution responds to evidence of the victim's bad character with evidence of the defendant's "same" bad character. Thus in the foregoing hypotheticals, the prosecutor could not respond to the defendant's evidence about the victim's violence or the defendant's peacefulness with evidence of the victim's honesty or the defendant's dishonesty. This prosecution evidence would not *rebut* the defendant's evidence because a person can be both violent and honest or peaceful and dishonest.

c.   FRE 404(a)(2): The Prosecution's Right to Use Character Evidence to Respond to Defense Attacks on the Victim's Conduct

FRE 404(a)(2) also provides that the prosecution may introduce evidence of a homicide victim's character for peacefulness, if the defendant has suggested that the victim was the first aggressor. Assume, for example, that Johnson had killed Officer

Walker and was being prosecuted for homicide. Assume further that Johnson or other defense witnesses testified that Walker was the first aggressor and that Johnson had acted in self-defense. This defense testimony is not character evidence. The defendant is not trying to show Walker's general character for violence. Rather, the defendant is offering evidence of specific actions of Walker that constitute an element of the self-defense claim. The prosecutor, however, can respond to this testimony with evidence of Walker's good character for peacefulness. This character evidence is admissible because Johnson introduced evidence that Walker had been the first aggressor; it is not dependent upon Johnson's opening the door to his own or Walker's character. However, since *Johnson* was not actually a homicide case, the prosecution could not open the door to Walker's peaceful character to show action in conformity with character.

Even if *Johnson* had been a homicide case, the prosecution could not have opened the door to defendant Johnson's character for violence. The prosecution can never introduce evidence of the defendant's character unless the defendant has first introduced character evidence. The possibility that the prosecution might improperly open the door to Johnson's character was the focus of a sidebar early on in the *Johnson* case. When the prosecution sought, over objection, to inquire into the nature of the facility where the defendant was housed, the court indicated that the prosecution witnesses could describe Facility B but could not directly state that the inmates in that facility tended to be violent (pages 8-9, supra). If the jurors heard such testimony about the inmates, they might infer that Johnson, one of the inmates, was a violent person and therefore probably had acted violently at the time of the alleged attack on the guards.

d. The FRE 404(a) Requirement of Pertinence

According to FRE 404(a)(1) and (2) the defendant's and the prosecution's character evidence must tend to establish a "pertinent" character trait. For example, in the *Johnson* case it would have been permissible for the defendant to introduce evidence of his own character for peacefulness or evidence of a prison guard victim's character for violence to show that the guard, not Johnson, was the aggressor. Similarly, it would be permissible for a defendant charged with perjury to introduce evidence of the defendant's character for honesty to show that the defendant did not intentionally lie on the particular occasion in question. In the *Johnson* case, however, it would not have been permissible for the defendant to have introduced evidence of a prison guard's character for dishonesty to show that the guard was the aggressor; and it would not be permissible to introduce evidence of a perjury defendant's character for peacefulness to show that the defendant did not commit the perjury.

e. FRE 404(a)(3): The Character of Witnesses

FRE 404(a)(3) is a cross-reference to the rules that permit the impeachment and rehabilitation of witnesses with evidence of their character for truthfulness. The relevance of any witness's testimony depends upon the assumption that the witness is testifying truthfully. Thus parties are permitted to introduce evidence that either undermines or supports a witness's truthfulness. One way to do this is to show the witness's character for truthfulness. From evidence that a witness has a bad (or good) character for truthfulness, one can infer that the witness is acting in conformity with that character trait by being untruthful (or truthful) on the witness stand. We will consider the rules that govern evidence of a witness's character for truthfulness in Chapter Seven. For now, it is sufficient for you to know that FRE 404(a)(3) is a cross-reference to those rules.

3. Elaboration of the FRE 404(a)(1) and (2) Exceptions

a. *The Relevance of Character Evidence in People v. Johnson*

The evidence of Walker's character in the *Johnson* case is relevant for two distinct purposes. Diagrams 5-3 and 5-4 illustrate these two purposes.

As Diagram 5-3 indicates, reputation evidence of Walker's character is relevant to show that Walker acted in conformity with that character on March 28, 1992 (i.e., to show that he may have been the aggressor against Johnson). The evidence, however, may not be admissible for this purpose under FRE 404(a)(2), which permits the defendant to open the door to a pertinent character trait of "the victim of the crime." Although Walker was one of the correctional officers present at the scene, the defendant was charged with battery against only Officers Huston and Van Berg (pages 2-3, supra). Thus, in a formal sense, Walker was not the victim of any crime. What arguments can you make that the evidence of Walker's character should none-theless be admissible to prove that Walker was the first aggressor?

Diagram 5-4 illustrates an alternative theory of relevance. Because the reputation evidence of Walker's violent character was introduced in conjunction with evidence that the defendant knew of the reputation, the evidence is relevant to a claim of self-defense. One element of self-defense is that any aggressive action by a defendant must be the result of a reasonable fear of bodily harm. Johnson's awareness of Walker's reputation for violence suggests the reasonableness of Johnson's actions. Similarly, the prosecution testimony that Walker was not known among the inmates as a violent person is evidence from which one may infer that Johnson had no reason to fear Walker.

This second theory of relevance does not involve using character evidence to show action in conformity with character. Therefore, it is not within the scope of FRE 404; rather, admissibility of the evidence for this purpose depends solely on the application of the basic relevance concepts embodied in FRE 401-403. The fact of consequence is what Johnson was thinking when Johnson acted, not whether Walker acted in con-formity with Walker's character. Indeed, for the purpose of showing what Johnson was thinking, it does not matter whether Walker really was a violent or peaceful person. What is important is whether the defendant had a reasonable (even if incorrect) belief that Walker was violent.

We suggest that you reread pages 40, 52-53, 55-57, and 71-73, supra, in Chapter One. Did the judge and the attorneys adequately distinguish these two theories of relevance?

b. *The Rationale for the FRE 404(a)(1) and (2) Exceptions*

As we have seen, there are substantial concerns justifying the FRE 404(a) prohibi-tion against the use of character evidence to show a person's action in conformity with

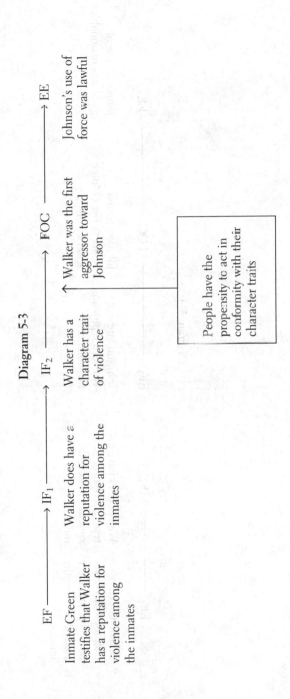

Diagram 5-3

Diagram 5-4

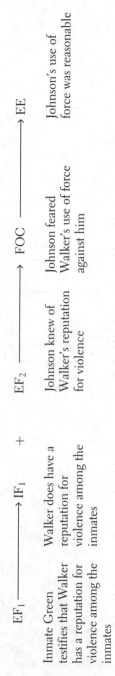

EF₁ ⟶ IF₁   +   EF₂ ⟶ FOC ⟶ EE

EF₁

Inmate Green testifies that Walker has a reputation for violence among the inmates

IF₁

Walker does have a reputation for violence among the inmates

EF₂

Johnson knew of Walker's reputation for violence

FOC

Johnson feared Walker's use of force against him

EE

Johnson's use of force was reasonable

character. One might ask why, then, there are any exceptions to the FRE 404(a) general rule of exclusion. Consider whether the following reasons provide a sufficient answer for the existence of FRE 404(a)(1) and (2).

First, as we suggested in subsection B.3.a, above, the problem of unfair prejudice is likely to be greatest with respect to evidence of a criminal defendant's bad character. This type of evidence, however, will never be admissible unless the defendant chooses to open the door to the character evidence inquiry. Second, despite the low probative value of character evidence to show action on a particular occasion and despite the risk of unfair prejudice to the prosecution (e.g., the jury may be willing acquit a guilty defendant who assaulted a person with a bad character), a criminal defendant should not have to face the consequences of conviction without having had every opportunity to establish a reasonable doubt. Proof of the defendant's good character or the victim's bad character may establish such a doubt.

Third, any risk of unfair prejudice to the defendant from evidence of a victim's good character seems relatively remote. The concern here is that jurors, on hearing of the victim's good character, would be willing to convict a defendant about whose guilt they had a reasonable doubt but who they believe nonetheless may have committed a crime against a good person. Moreover, the defendant has the right to keep the victim–character evidence door closed except in homicide cases where the defendant claims that the victim was the first aggressor. In these relatively rare instances, the defendant and the victim may have been the only persons present at the time of the killing. The unavailability of the victim to contradict the defendant's evidence arguably justifies allowing the prosecution to resort to character evidence to establish its case.

Perhaps the most controversial aspect of these rules is the recent amendment to FRE 404(a)(1), which permits the prosecution to introduce evidence of the defendant's bad character after the defendant opened the door only to the victim's character. Reconsider the assault hypothetical in which the defendant introduces evidence of the victim's character for violence to suggest that the victim was the first aggressor. On the one hand, evidence of the victim's bad character is implicitly a statement of the defendant's good character: The evidence of the victim's violence is relevant to suggest that the victim was the first aggressor only if the fact finder understands the evidence as suggesting that the victim is more violent than the defendant. In other words, to the extent that character evidence about aggressiveness is relevant to the question of who is the first aggressor, it is relevant in a relative sense; to say that the victim is violent is inevitably to say that the defendant — in comparison to the victim — is peaceful. Thus, the amendment to FRE 404(a)(1) merely recognizes that opening the door to the victim's bad character is one way of opening the door to the defendant's good character. On the other hand, as we have suggested, evidence of the defendant's bad character raises substantial unfair prejudice concerns. Thus, as a practical matter, the impact of the amendment to FRE 404(a)(1) may be to increase the opportunity for admitting prejudicial evidence or, perhaps more likely, to deter defendants from attacking the character of victims in the first place. As you consider the material in this chapter, think about how important it is for defendants to be able to introduce character evidence.

d.   Evidence of Character in Civil Actions

FRE 404(a), which expressly prohibits the use of character evidence to show action in conformity with a person's character in civil actions, is substantially a restatement of the common law. A minority common law rule, followed in a handful of federal cases, permits defendants in civil actions to open the door to character evidence in civil actions based on culpable conduct proscribed by the criminal law. (For example, a civil assault and battery defendant could introduce evidence of a character for peacefulness.) However, the pending revision to the Federal Rules clarifies that character evidence cannot be admitted in federal civil cases under FRE 404(a)(1) or (2).

KEY POINTS

1. The Federal Rules allow a criminal defendant to open the door to the use of character evidence to show action in conformity with character in the situations set forth in FRE 404(a)(1) and (2):

(a)   a criminal defendant may open the door to the defendant's own character, in which case the prosecution in rebuttal may offer evidence of the defendant's character;

(b)   a criminal defendant may open the door to the victim's character, in which case the prosecution in rebuttal may offer evidence of the victim's character or the defendant's character;

(c)   in a homicide case the prosecution may open the door to the victim's character for peacefulness in order to rebut a claim that the victim was the first aggressor.

2. Any party may introduce character evidence for impeachment and rehabilitation purposes to the extent allowed by FRE 607-609.

3. When the use of character evidence is permissible, the character evidence must relate to a pertinent character trait.

4. Except in the context of impeaching and rehabilitating witnesses, FRE 404 prohibits the use of character to show action in conformity with character in civil cases.

4.   Interpretation and Illustration of FRE 404(b) and 405(a): How Character is Proven

FRE 404(b) provides in part:

(b) Other Crimes, Wrongs, or Acts. Evidence of other crimes, wrongs, or acts is not admissible to prove the character of a person in order to show action in conformity therewith. . . .

FRE 405(a) provides:

(a) Reputation or opinion. In all cases in which evidence of character or a trait of character of a person is admissible, proof may be made by testimony as to reputation or by testimony in the form of an opinion. On cross-examination, inquiry is allowable into relevant specific instances of conduct.

When character evidence is admissible under one of the FRE 404(a) exceptions, in what form can the evidence be offered? There are three possibilities. First, a witness might offer specific instances of conduct of the person whose character is in question. One's character, after all, is known to others by how one behaves. Second, a witness could offer to testify that in the witness's opinion the person in question has the particular character trait. Finally, a witness could offer to testify that the person has a reputation in the community for having the kind of character trait that is relevant to the litigation. An individual's reputation is what people say about the individual, and when reputation evidence is offered to prove character, it is the truth of the reputation that is important. Thus reputation evidence is hearsay — evidence of what people out of court say about the individual offered to prove the truth of what they say. FRE 803(21) provides an exception to the hearsay rule for evidence of reputation offered to show an individual's character.

FRE 404(b)'s prohibition on the use of specific acts to prove a person's character for the purpose of showing action in conformity with that character trait expressly applies to the FRE 404(a) exceptions. Therefore, even where character evidence is admissible under FRE 404(a)(1) or (2), it may not be proven by past specific acts. For example, during the prosecution's rebuttal in the *Johnson* case, the trial judge made it clear that Lieutenant Stokes could not testify about specific acts for the purpose of proving Walker's good character (page 59, supra).

FRE 405(a) provides that reputation evidence and opinion evidence are permissible means of proving character *whenever* a party offers admissible character evidence to show action in conformity with that character. Assume, for example, that in *Johnson* the defense and the prosecution were interested in proving Walker's character for violence or peacefulness for the purpose of showing whether he was the first aggressor. See Diagram 5-3 at page 277, supra. The following evidence could be used for this purpose: Inmate Green, a defense witness, testified on direct examination that Walker had a reputation for being a "bad cop" (page 48, supra); on redirect examination Green testified that Walker was known among the inmates — that is, had a reputation among the inmates — for violence; and during the prosecution's rebuttal case, Lieutenant Stokes testified Walker had the reputation as a good correctional officer (page 60, supra). Pursuant to FRE 405(a) it also would have been permissible for these witnesses to offer their opinions about Walker's violence or peacefulness.

For ease of reference, we will refer to witnesses who give reputation or opinion testimony about a person's character pursuant to FRE 405(a) as "character witnesses." The last sentence of FRE 405(a) permits the opposing party to ask character witnesses specific acts questions on cross-examination. We deal with this part of the rule in section 5e, infra.

PROBLEMS

5.34. In the *Johnson* case, assume that one of the charges was assaulting Officer Walker. For what purposes, if any, should the following evidence be admissible?

(a) Officer Huston's testimony for the prosecution that on several previous occasions Johnson had assaulted other prisoners and prison guards;

(b)   Inmate Green's testimony for the defense that Officer Walker has a reputation for violence;

(c)   Officer Walker's testimony for the prosecution in rebuttal that Johnson has a reputation for violence.

5.35. The defendant has been charged with perjury before a federal grand jury. As part of its case-in-chief the prosecutor offers the following evidence:

(a) W_1's testimony that he knows of at least five occasions on which the defendant has lied.

(b) W_2's testimony that the defendant has a reputation in the community for dishonesty.

As part of the defense, the defendant offers the following evidence:

(c) W_3's testimony that the defendant has a reputation in the community for honesty. Which pieces of evidence are objectionable?

5.36. Mayer is charged with assault with a deadly weapon and claims self-defense. In his defense, Mayer offers testimony that (a) two weeks before the alleged assault the victim had threatened him with a knife, (b) the victim had a reputation for carrying weapons, and (c) on the morning of the trial the victim threatened to kill Mayer's sister. For what purposes is this evidence relevant? Is it admissible?

5.37. Clarence Hill is being prosecuted for the attempted murder of Ted Ellsworth in a jurisdiction that views mere words as potentially adequate provocation, which would be a defense to the attempted murder charge.

Clarence and several eyewitnesses testify as follows: They and Ted Ellsworth were all in a local tavern, and Hill and Ellsworth were at opposite ends of the bar. Ellsworth taunted Hill with racial slurs and derogatory references to Hill's wife. Hill became enraged and shot Ellsworth.

The prosecutor is convinced that these witnesses are lying and wants to introduce the testimony of Ruth Watson that Ellsworth has a reputation in the community for peacefulness, compassion, and absence of racial prejudice. Ellsworth is not available to testify. Is Ruth Watson's testimony admissible?

5.38. On the night of October 7, Elton Haywood called the police to report a prowler in his backyard and then went outside with a shotgun to search for the prowler. When the police arrived, they mistook Haywood for the prowler, and despite — or perhaps because of — Haywood's loud, persistent protestations, they handcuffed him. Eventually the police took Haywood to the Dry-U-Out Detoxification Facility, where he spent the night locked in a cell with a urine-soaked floor. Haywood has filed a civil rights and false imprisonment suit against the facility and several of its employees. Although Haywood has had a drinking problem in the past, he claims that he had had nothing to drink on the night of the incident and that he was wrongfully detained. The defendants offer expert opinion testimony that Haywood is an alcoholic and that a common characteristic of alcoholics is to deny that they have been drinking when they plainly have. Is the evidence admissible?

5.   Elaboration of the Permissible Methods of Proving a Person's Character to Show Action in Conformity with Character

a.   The Prohibition Against the Use of Specific Acts

The FRE 404(b) prohibition against the use of specific acts to prove character to show action in conformity with character may seem counterintuitive. The people that we know — or that we think we know — the best are likely to be people that we know by their deeds. Thus, it would seem that specific acts evidence would often be the most probative form of character evidence. Nonetheless, as discussed above, there are substantial FRE 403-type countervailing concerns that justify excluding specific acts to prove character to show action in conformity with character. These include: bad person prejudice stemming from evidence of prior *bad* acts; confusion of issues and undue consumption of time if there are factual disputes surrounding the alleged prior conduct; and the relatively low probative value of the character inference generally.

As discussed above, there are limited instances in which it is permissible to use evidence of a person's specific acts to prove that person's character to show action in conformity with character. FRE 608(b) and 609 contemplate use of specific acts to prove the character of a witness for truthfulness or untruthfulness, and FRE 413-415 contemplate the use of specific acts to prove character to show action in conformity with character in certain cases of sexual misconduct.

b.   The Probative Value of Opinion and Reputation Evidence to Prove Character

The probative value of opinion or reputation evidence to prove a person's character will depend in part on how long, how well, and in what contexts the witness has known (opinion) or has known about (reputation) the person whose character the evidence is offered to prove. The common law (which did not permit opinion evidence at all in most jurisdictions) required that a reputation witness testify to the person's reputation in the community. In theory, this focus on the community as a whole was designed to ensure that evidence be fairly reflective of the views about the person in question. As a practical matter today, however, there will not be many instances in which an individual has a reputation throughout the entire community in which the person lives. Indeed, in our complex, urbanized society, it is not clear what the entire community would be. Courts wisely recognize this fact and permit reputation testimony to be based on what a witness has heard in some relevant community — perhaps the neighborhood where the person lives or the place where the person works. Consider, for example, the *Johnson* case, where defense counsel objected on relevance grounds to evidence of Walker's good reputation among the prison staff. According to the defense, the evidence should have been limited to Walker's reputation among the inmates, but the judge disagreed:

> I am going to overrule the objection because although the inmates and the staff are not precisely the same, they are a part of the community within the prison and are in communication with one another on a constant basis. So reputation is something that is back and forth and it is the kind of thing that would be known. [Page 58, supra.]

Even if there is no difficulty in defining the relevant community, there may be a question whether the witness knows or knows about the individual well enough to testify in the form of opinion or reputation. The Federal Rules do not deal specifically with the foundation requirement for character witnesses. FRE 403, however, provides latitude for trial judges to exclude testimony that is marginally probative because the witness does not have much of a basis for knowing or knowing about the person in question. United States v. Watson, 669 F.2d 1274 (11th Cir. 1982) (not error to exclude testimony of character witness who knew individual for brief period of time, which did not coincide with relevant events at trial).

Character witnesses are likely to be friendly, cooperative witnesses on direct examination. Thus, if the witness in fact has a sufficient basis for offering character evidence, there should seldom be any difficulty in eliciting the appropriate foundational information and in getting responses in the form of reputation or opinion testimony to questions about pertinent character traits. Michelson v. United States, 335 U.S. 469, 471 (1948), where a bribery defendant opened the door to his own character, provides a good, albeit somewhat sparse, example of a direct examination of a character witness:

Q: Do you know the defendant Michelson?
A: Yes.
Q: How long do you know Mr. Michelson?
A: About 30 years.
Q: Do you know other people that know him?
A: Yes.
Q: Have you had occasion to discuss his reputation for honesty and truthfulness and for being a law-abiding citizen?
A: It is very good.
Q: Have you talked to others?
A: Yes.
Q: And what is his reputation?
A: Very good.

For an elaboration of the common law foundation requirements for reputation and opinion testimony, see Mason Ladd, Techniques and Theory of Character Testimony, 24 Iowa L. Rev. 498 (1939).

c. *Reputation Evidence Versus Opinion Evidence*

Opinions are generalizations from more specific facts, and an opinion about a person's character will naturally be a generalization based on the witness's perception of that person's behavior. In situations other than character testimony, when a witness testifies in the form of opinion, it is permissible — indeed, desirable — to inquire into the underlying basis for the opinion on both direct and cross-examination. Because of this standard practice, the use of opinion evidence to prove character creates the possibility that the opinion witness could testify about various specific acts that provide the basis for the opinion. The common law's reluctance to permit litigation over specific acts is precisely the reason that the majority common law rule prohibited opinion testimony, along with specific acts testimony, to prove character to show action in conformity with character.

Nonetheless, witnesses who are called to testify about an individual's character are likely to have rather strong personal feelings about the individual who is the subject of their testimony. If they testify in terms of reputation, the real gist of what they are thinking and of what motivates their testimony may well be their *opinion* about the defendant's character. Recognizing this possibility, the drafters of the Federal Rules took the position that these character witnesses should be permitted to offer their opinions directly. Thus FRE 405(a) permits both reputation and opinion testimony in all instances in which character evidence is admissible. At the same time, however, the Advisory Committee Note to FRE 405 makes it clear that the use of opinion testimony to prove character to show action in conformity with character should "be confined to the nature and extent of observation and acquaintance upon which the opinion is based." Opinion testimony should not be allowed to evolve into testimony about specific acts on which the opinion may be based.

KEY POINTS

1. FRE 404(b) prohibits the use of specific acts to prove a defendant's character for the purpose of showing action in conformity with character, except in the limited situations governed by FRE 413-415, FRE 608(b), and FRE 609, which we will consider later.

2. FRE 405(a) permits the proponent to offer both reputation and opinion testimony in the limited situations in which FRE 404(a) allows the use of character evidence to show a person's action in conformity with character.

3. If a character witness offers opinion testimony, it is not permissible to explore on direct examination the specific acts that may be the basis for the witness's opinion.

d. The Cross-examination of Character Witnesses

Although a character witness cannot testify about specific acts on direct examination, the cross-examiner is allowed to question the character witness about specific acts relevant to character, pursuant to the last sentence of FRE 405(a). Assume, for example, that John Smith is charged with murder and that as part of the defense Mary Martin testifies, pursuant to FRE 404(a)(1), that John has a good reputation in the community for peacefulness. The prosecutor, when cross-examining Mary, can ask about various violent acts that John supposedly committed.

i. The Relevance of the Specific Acts Inquiries. The permissible relevant purpose for asking specific acts questions in the preceding example is *not* to prove John's character for violence. Indeed, FRE 404(b) prohibits questions about specific acts to prove John's character. Rather, the permissible relevant purpose of the prosecutor's questions is to test Mary's credibility as a reputation witness: If she denies having heard of the acts of violence, one can infer that she does not have a very good sense of what John's reputation is; and if she has heard of the acts, one may doubt the truth of her testimony (or question her conception of what a reputation for peacefulness means). United States v. Adair, 951 F.2d 316, 319 (11th Cir. 1992); United States v. Alvarez, 860 F.2d 801, 826-827 (7th Cir. 1988).

Because the specific act questions are admissible only to impeach the character witness and not to prove the character of the person who is the subject of the testimony, the party calling the character witness is entitled to a limiting instruction pursuant to FRE 105. For example, in our John and Mary hypothetical, the judge might say, "Ladies and gentlemen of the jury, I instruct you that the questions the prosecutor asked Ms. Martin about various acts of violence allegedly engaged in by Mr. Smith were asked for the sole purpose of assessing Ms. Martin's knowledge of Mr. Smith's reputation. You must not consider them as evidence of Mr. Smith's character."

ii.   **The Prejudicial Impact of Specific Acts Questions.**   To the extent that jurors are unwilling or unable to follow a limiting instruction regarding specific acts questions posed pursuant to FRE 405(a), there is a two-fold risk of prejudice. In the preceding hypothetical, for example, the jurors may infer from the questions to Mary about John's violent acts that John is a violent person and may have acted in conformity with that violent character trait by murdering the victim of the charged crime, as the prosecution has alleged. This use of the evidence would violate FRE 404(b), thereby raising the FRE 403 danger of unfair prejudice in the sense that the jury may use the evidence in a logically relevant but legally impermissible manner. In addition, the jurors may be willing to ignore a reasonable doubt if they regard John as a bad, dangerous person. This possibility raises the FRE 403 danger of unfair prejudice in the sense that the jurors may base their decision on an emotional and legally improper ground.

The most prejudicial specific acts questions, as the preceding hypothetical demonstrates, are those that relate directly to the character trait about which the character witness testified. These questions, however, are also likely to be the most probative for the legitimate purpose of testing a character witness's knowledge of the defendant's character for peacefulness. Since FRE 405(a) specifically authorizes these questions, and since high prejudice is likely always to be a concomitant of high probative value with FRE 405(a) specific acts questions, courts regularly permit the cross-examiner to ask character witnesses questions that are in fact extremely prejudicial.

iii.   **The Relationship Between the Character Trait and the Specific Acts Inquiries.**   Specific act inquiries made pursuant to FRE 405(a) must be "relevant" to the character trait about which the character witness testified on direct examination. One aspect of this relevance requirement is that the specific acts must relate to the character trait in question. For example, in our hypothetical involving Mary's testimony about John's reputation for peacefulness, it would be appropriate to ask Mary about John's specific acts of violence but not about acts of dishonesty. United States v. Westerbrook, 896 F.2d 330, 335 (8th Cir. 1990) (character witness testified as to defendant's honesty; improper to ask character witness about defendant's conviction for possessing controlled substance).

One might argue that, in a minimal FRE 401 sense, any bad act is relevant to a bad character trait, and any good act is relevant to a good character trait. Moreover, since the purpose of the inquiry is to test the character witness's knowledge of the principal witness's character, the key to relevance arguably should be the likely notoriety of the act rather than its relationship to the character trait about which the witness testified. Nonetheless, courts are likely to require that FRE 405(a) specific acts questions to character witnesses relate to the character trait about which the witness has testified — a result that one can probably justify under FRE 403, if not FRE 401.

iv. The Character Witness's Likely Knowledge of the Specific Act. A second restriction on the use of specific acts evidence to impeach a character witness is also a matter of relevance — or at least probative value for the purpose of FRE 403 balancing. The questions should be limited to acts about which the witness is likely to have known or to have heard. United States v. Alvarez, 860 F.2d 801, 827 (7th Cir. 1989). For example, if Mary on direct examination testified that she had known John well for five years and was familiar with his reputation during that time, it may not be reasonable to expect that she would have heard about an isolated act of violence that occurred 15 years ago. Even if she had heard about the act, it may not be reasonable to expect a single 15-year-old act of violence to affect her view of John's reputation for peacefulness during the past five years. But see *Alvarez*, supra (trial court did not abuse its discretion by permitting inquiry about specific act occurring 10 years before character witness giving reputation testimony knew the defendant). Cf. Michelson v. United States, 335 U.S. 469 (1948) (where two character witnesses testified to knowing defendant 30 years and a third character witness testified to knowing defendant half that long, not error to allow questions about matters that occurred 20 and 27 years ago).

Assessing whether a character witness is likely to have heard of any particular act will involve consideration of several factors. For example, in our Mary and John hypothetical, how well and how long has Mary known or known about John? Is John's act likely to have been the subject of discussion because of the nature of the act? Is John the kind of person whose activities are likely to be known to people situated similarly to Mary? Questions that are only marginally probative for legitimate impeachment purposes may be excluded because of their low probative value and high degree of unfair prejudice.

v. The Cross-examiner's Reasonable Belief that the Act Occurred. A third limitation on the use of specific acts questions (not specifically mentioned in FRE 405(a)) relates to the cross-examiner's belief that the specific acts occurred. If the prosecutor had no knowledge about whether John, in our hypothetical, had committed any violent acts, it should be permissible to ask Mary in a non-suggestive manner, "Do you know of any violent acts that John has committed?" However, any but the most general inquiry about specific acts is likely to suggest to the jury that the cross-examiner believes that the act occurred. When such an implication inheres in the question, the cross-examiner must have a reasonable basis for believing that the act occurred. United States v. Adair, 951 F.2d 316, 319 (11th Cir. 1992); United States v Alvarez, supra.

Some courts have suggested that the better practice is to require the cross-examiner to demonstrate the factual basis to the judge, outside the presence of the jury, before asking the questions. United States v. Reese, 568 F.2d 1246 (6th Cir. 1977). In *Alvarez*, supra, the court followed this practice, and the prosecutor responded with an affidavit from an FBI officer stating that defendant had confessed to the act in question.

In discussing this limitation on the cross-examination of character witnesses, the Supreme Court in Michelson v. United States, supra, noted that as a matter of logical relevance the requirement should be that the cross-examiner of the reputation witness have a reasonable belief that there were *rumors about the act*, regardless of whether it in fact occurred. Nonetheless, the Court approved the existing rule requiring the cross-examiner to demonstrate to the judge the reasonable basis for believing that the *act in fact occurred*:

But before this relevant and proper inquiry [here, a question to the defendant's character witness about the defendant's arrest] can be made, counsel must demonstrate privately to the court an irrelevant and possibly unprovable fact — the reality of the arrest. From this permissible inquiry about reports of arrest, the jury is pretty certain to infer that defendant had in fact been arrested and to draw its own conclusions as to character from that fact. The [requirement of a reasonable basis] thus limits legally relevant inquiries to those based on legally irrelevant facts in order that the legally irrelevant conclusion which the jury probably will draw from the relevant questions will not be based on unsupported or untrue innuendo. It illustrates Judge Hand's suggestion that the system may work best when explained least. Yet, despite its theoretical paradoxes and deficiencies, we approve the procedure as calculated in practice to hold the inquiry within decent bounds. [335 U.S. at 481 n.18.]

vi.   Acts, Arrests, and Convictions.   Like *Michelson*, decisions under the Federal Rules permit prosecutors to ask defense character witnesses not only about defendants' prior *acts* but also about their prior *arrests*. United States v. Wellons, 32 F.3d 117 (4th Cir. 1994); United States v. Jordan, 722 F.2d 353, 358 (7th Cir. 1983). An arrest, however, is "conduct" by the police, not the defendant.

As a matter of logical relevance, asking about the arrest rather than the conduct leading to it is not inappropriate. The purpose of the question is to test what the character witness knows or has heard about the defendant, and in some instances there may have been as much or more publicity about the arrest than the underlying acts. On the other hand, if there is reason to believe that the defendant did not engage in the conduct leading to the arrest, the question may be particularly prejudicial. There is always the risk that the jury may use a specific act question improperly to infer that the defendant has a bad character. If the defendant has engaged in the conduct suggested by the question, the jury at least gets an accurate assessment of the kind of person the defendant is. Evidence of the defendant's arrests creates not only this risk but also the risk that the jury will regard the arrest, perhaps incorrectly, as evidence that the defendant actually engaged in the illegal activity. Nonetheless, inquiry about arrests may be appropriate. United States v. Grady, 665 F.2d 831, 834-835 (8th Cir. 1981) (permitting inquiry about arrests on charges that were later dismissed).

Sometimes specific act questions to a defendant's character witness refer to the defendant's prior convictions. United States v. Collins, 779 F.2d 1520 (11th Cir. 1986). Like an arrest, a defendant's prior conviction is logically relevant — without regard to the truth of the underlying facts — to test the character witness's awareness of the defendant's background or reputation. Permitting questions about convictions, however, may be even more prejudicial than permitting questions about arrests. While there may be little likelihood that the defendant did not commit the acts leading to a conviction, the very certainty of those facts, as validated by the conviction, may make it especially difficult for the jury to disregard the improper inference that the defendant is a bad person.

vii.   The Form of the Questions on Cross-examination.   The common law, which in most jurisdictions permitted a criminal defendant to use only reputation evidence when opening the door to character, was quite exacting about the proper form of specific acts questions on cross-examination. Since the direct examination testimony was limited to what the witness had *heard* people say about the defendant, asking on cross-examination whether the witness *knew* about some bad act was objectionable. The proper form for the specific acts questions on cross-examination was,

"Have you heard . . . ?" not "Did you know . . . ?" By contrast, if the jurisdiction happened to permit opinion testimony on direct examination, a witness offering an opinion about the defendant's character presumably would be basing that opinion in whole or in part on personal knowledge. Thus it would be proper to ask on cross-examination whether the opinion witness knew about specific acts.

If there were ever sound reasons for insisting on the proper form of cross-examination questions about specific acts, those reasons have been seriously eroded by the allowance of opinion as well as reputation testimony on direct examination. The Advisory Committee Note to FRE 405 asserts that the distinctions in the form of the cross-examination questions "are of slight if any practical significance" and that the second sentence of FRE 405(a) "eliminates them as a factor in formulating questions." United States v. Scholl, 166 F.3d 964, 974 (9th Cir. 1999) (no merit to argument that "Did you know . . . ?" rather than "Have you heard . . . ?" was improper in cross-examining character witness).

e. Limitations on the Use of Character Evidence in Practice

i. The inherent weakness of good character evidence. The most common use of character evidence to show action in conformity with character pursuant to FRE 404(a)(1) and (2) is a criminal defendant's opening the door with evidence of the defendant's own *good* character. Nonetheless, for reasons that are probably apparent, the occasions on which criminal defendants elect to open the door to the character evidence inquiry are relatively rare. In most cases, reputation and opinion evidence about a defendant's good character is not likely to be highly persuasive. The ban on using specific acts to prove character means that the opinion or reputation witness cannot provide persuasive or illustrative examples to support the opinion or reputation testimony. As a result, that testimony will necessarily take the form of (often bland) generalities. In sharp contrast, the cross-examiner of such character witnesses can go into specific bad acts under FRE 405(b). Depending on what the prior bad acts look like, they are potentially very persuasive and effective in undermining the positive character testimony.

Consider, then, who is likely to benefit from a rule that permits criminal defendants to open the door to character evidence. Or to put the issue somewhat differently, consider what kinds of people you would like to be able to call as character witnesses if you were a criminal defendant. To the extent that criminal defendants may benefit from the use of character evidence, is the benefit likely to be derived from the content of the character testimony or from the character (and/or reputation) of the character witnesses? If the character of the character witnesses is likely to make the biggest difference, is it desirable to have a rule that, in effect, benefits people primarily because of whom they know?

ii. The Potential Unfairness of FRE 405. We have already noted that courts may exclude on FRE 401-403 grounds questions about acts that do not relate to the character trait in issue and that are sufficiently remote from the time frame about which the character witness testified. As we pointed out above, however, FRE 403 is not often applied to exclude Rule 405 specific acts questions. As a result, FRE 405 appears to give a significant unfair advantage to the cross-examiner. For example, in our preceding murder hypothetical, the defendant, John, is limited to the use of relatively bland reputation or opinion evidence of his peaceful character. The prosecutor, by contrast, can ask Mary, the character witness, about all sorts of violent acts in which John may have engaged. Granted, in theory the purpose of the prosecutor's questions is not to prove the defendant's character but only to impeach the credibility of the character witnesses. And granted, the defendant is entitled to a limiting instruction from the judge. How likely is it, though, that the jury will be able to confine its consideration of the violent acts to the theoretically legitimate impeachment purpose?

Is it sufficient to answer that the process is not unfair because the defendant has the choice initially to decide whether to open the door to character evidence? If you are defense counsel and if you feel compelled to call character witnesses, what can you do to blunt the effect of the prosecutor's cross-examination of your character witnesses?

KEY POINTS

1. Whenever a character witness testifies in the form of reputation or opinion about a person's character, FRE 405(a) permits the opposing party to ask the witness on cross-examination about specific acts committed by the person who is the subject of the character testimony. Courts also permit questions about the person's arrests or convictions.

2. The specific acts (or arrests or convictions) must relate to the character trait about which the witness has testified.

3. The purpose of the specific acts question is to impeach the testimony of the character witness, not to show the character of the person about whom the witness has testified.

PROBLEMS

5.39. Return to Problem 5.35 at page 282, where the defendant has been charged with committing perjury before a federal grand jury. Assume that there is no objection to W_3's testimony that the defendant has a reputation in the community for honesty. On cross-examination of W_3 the prosecutor asks:

(a) "Did you know that the defendant was convicted of perjury five years ago?"
(b) "Did you know that last year the defendant was arrested and charged with obtaining money by false pretenses?
(c) "Have you heard that the defendant was investigated for filing a false income tax return ten years ago?"
(d) "Have you heard that the defendant was convicted of assault last year?"

In rebuttal, the prosecution offers the following evidence:

(e) W_4's testimony that in her opinion the defendant is a very dishonest person.
(f) W_4's testimony that this opinion is based on her having observed the defendant lie and cheat on several previous occasions.

Which pieces of evidence are objectionable?

5.40. Dick Davis is charged with the murder of Ralph Green and claims self-defense. After the prosecution has presented its case, Davis offers the following evidence:

(a) W_1 to testify that he and Davis are Elks, that he knows Davis well from weekly meetings, and that Davis has an excellent reputation for honesty among the Elks.

(b) W_2 to testify that Ralph Green has a reputation in the community for violence.

(c) W_3 to testify that two years ago Ralph Green was convicted of aggravated assault, a felony.

(d) W_4 to testify that she told the defendant of three different times that she had seen the victim make unprovoked attacks on other people.

In rebuttal, the prosecution offers the following evidence:

(e) W_5 to testify that Ralph Green has a reputation in the community for peacefulness.

(f) W_6 to testify that Davis has a reputation in the community for violence.

Which evidence is objectionable?

5.41. Return to Problem 3.3, United States v. Ray, at page 131. Is the following evidence admissible? Might the answer change depending on the order in which the evidence is offered?

(a) For the prosecution: Testimony from a partner in the brokerage firm that handled Bernard Ray's stock transactions: "Bernard Ray is an unusually shrewd and well-informed investor. He personally directs each and every trade of shares in his account."

(b) For the defense: Testimony from June Jacobs, Rundown's CFO: "Bernard Ray, although a great salesman and inspirational leader to the company, is extremely unsophisticated about finance and securities markets. He delegated all financial matters to others in both the running of the company and in decisionmaking regarding his personal investments."

(c) For the defense: Five instances since the year 2000 in which major trades of securities (other than Rundown stock) were made at the discretion of one of Bernard Ray's brokers.

(d) For the prosecution: evidence that Ray has a PhD in economics.

H. EVIDENCE OF A PERSON'S CHARACTER WHEN CHARACTER IS AN ESSENTIAL ELEMENT OF A CLAIM OR DEFENSE

Consider an action in which Martha sues George for libel because George has circulated a leaflet claiming that Martha was dishonest. An element of Martha's claim is that the allegedly libelous statement is false. Since the statement that Martha is dishonest is a statement about her character, Martha's actual character for dishonesty is an essential element of her claim.

Nothing in FRE 404 or in any other Federal Rule specifically prohibits or restricts the use of character evidence when character *is an essential element of a claim or a defense*. FRE 405, however, addresses the type of character evidence that one can use in this type of situation.

1.   Interpretation and Illustration of FRE 405(b)

FRE 405(b) provides:

> (b) Specific instances of conduct. In cases in which character or a trait of character of a person is an essential element of a charge, claim, or defense proof may also be made of specific instances of that person's conduct.

Occasionally the substantive law makes a person's character an essential element of a claim or a defense, as the element of falsity (or in some jurisdictions, the defense of truth) does in a defamation action when an allegedly defamatory statement is a statement about a person's character. For example, the fitness or character of a person is a factor to consider in deciding whether to award child custody to that person. A claim that a hospital was negligent in hiring a careless physician makes the physician's carelessness — that is, character for lack of care — an element that the plaintiff must establish in order to recover. Similarly, a negligent entrustment claim that the defendant was negligent in permitting a careless, unqualified employee to drive the plaintiff's vehicle makes the employee's character for lack of care an element that the plaintiff must prove in order to prevail. In wrongful death cases, the plaintiff's damages may depend in part on the character of the decedent, thereby making the decedent's character an essential element of proof.

FRE 405(b), in conjunction with FRE 405(a), makes it clear that all three forms of character evidence — reputation, opinion, and specific acts — are potentially admissible when character is an essential element of a claim or defense. For example, in our libel hypothetical in which George wants to establish the truth of the statement that Martha is a dishonest person, George could call witnesses to testify (1) that Martha had a reputation for dishonesty in the community, (2) that in the witnesses' opinion Martha was dishonest, and (3) that Martha had engaged in specifically described dishonest acts.

The only limitation on the use of any of these types of evidence to prove character when character is an essential element of a claim or defense is FRE 403. In particular with respect to specific acts, courts should balance the probative value of the acts in proving the character trait at issue against (1) the risk that the evidence may engender an emotional response from the jury and (2) the time and effort it would take to litigate the details of what the person may or may not have done.

2.   Elaboration of FRE 405(b)

a.   In general

When the substantive law makes the character of a person an essential element of a claim or a defense, the party with the initial burden of producing evidence will have to introduce character evidence in order to avoid a directed verdict. By contrast, when character evidence is offered to show action in conformity with character, it is, as the Advisory Committee notes, "circumstantial" evidence of a person's conduct, and it is *never essential* that character evidence be offered for this purpose. Consider, for example, a prosecution for a crime involving "dishonest" acts — such as embezzlement or perjury — where the defense offers evidence of the defendant's good character for honesty. The substantive criminal law does not make the defendant's character for dishonesty or honesty an element of the crime or any defense; the defendant may be guilty or innocent of the charged embezzlement or perjury regardless of whether the defendant happens to be a generally dishonest or a generally honest person. Evidence of the defendant's character for honesty, however, is relevant in that it generates one possible, though not essential, inference that the defendant did not act dishonestly by embezzling or committing perjury.

It may be worth noting that FRE 405(b)'s express permission of the use of past specific acts to prove character when character is an essential element is not inconsistent with, or an exception to, the specific acts prohibition in FRE 404(b). Again, FRE 404 prohibits using character evidence *only* to prove conduct in conformity with that character trait on a specific occasion. Note how, here, character is not being offered to show that someone acted a certain way on a particular occasion. Proof of character in the foregoing examples is an end in itself — it is proof of the essential element or fact of consequence — rather than circumstantial proof of some further conduct. Looked at another way, the use of character in FRE 405(b) does not fall within the chain of inferences described in Diagrams 5-1 and 5-2 at page 231, supra, and does not fall within the specific acts prohibition of 404(b) at all. So even if 405(b) did not expressly mention that specific acts are permitted — indeed, even if it had not been written at all — it would still be the case that character as an essential element would be subject to proof by any relevant means. FRE 405(b) is thus another "reminder" to courts (like FRE 404(b) (second sentence) and FRE 406) not to apply the character and specific acts prohibitions beyond their confined boundaries.

b. Reputation versus character in defamation cases

In our discussion of FRE 404(a), we noted that evidence of a person's reputation is one way to prove a person's character. It is important to keep in mind, particularly in the context of defamation actions, the difference between "character" and "reputation." *Character* is an integral part of a person. *Reputation*, by contrast, is what people say about a person. In defamation actions, a plaintiff's reputation — regardless of whether it happens to coincide with the plaintiff's actual character — is always relevant, because the substantive law makes injury to reputation the basis for assessing damages. Consider, for example, the previous hypothetical in which George circulated a pamphlet stating that Martha was dishonest. Her damages, if she prevails on the substantive claim, will be based on how much George's statement damaged her reputation, not on what kind of a person she is or was. Character becomes an essential element in a defamation action, as we illustrated previously with the George and Martha example, only if (1) the defendant claims that the allegedly defamatory statement is true and (2) the statement is one about the plaintiff's character.

The interesting question, not addressed in the Federal Rules, is whether one should be able to use specific acts to prove a character trait for the purpose of establishing reputation. On the one hand, evidence of character is certainly relevant to prove reputation: If we know, for example, that a person is honest, it is more likely (than if we knew nothing about the person's character) that the person has a reputation for honesty. On the other hand, the same considerations that militate against using specific acts to prove character to infer action in conformity with character also exist when specific acts are offered to prove character for the purpose of inferring what a person's reputation is. There may be time-consuming distracting litigation about a variety of specific acts, and proof of the specific acts may be extremely prejudicial.

KEY POINT

1. When character is an essential element of a claim or a defense, FRE 405(b) permits proof of character with specific acts evidence. (In addition, it is always permissible to prove character with reputation or opinion evidence pursuant to FRE 405(a).)

PROBLEMS

5.42. Paul Vincent has sued Office Barn for injuries he sustained from being physically abused by store security guard Arnold Stallone, who mistakenly believed Vincent had been shoplifting. The claim is negligent supervision and/or hiring, and the plaintiff must prove (1) that Stallone had a propensity for violence and (2) that Office Barn knew or should have known of the propensity and was therefore negligent in hiring him as a security guard and in failing to supervise him adequately. Vincent offers the following testimony. Is it admissible?

(a) W_1 to testify that he has known Stallone for 10 years, and in his opinion, Stallone is a violent person.
(b) W_2 to testify that Stallone beat him up with no provocation in a bar one year before Stallone began working at Office Barn.
(c) W_3 to testify that Stallone had been arrested four times, and convicted twice, for assault prior to working for Office Barn.

Office Barn offers the following testimony. Is it admissible?

(d) W_4 to testify that she has lived in the same neighborhood as Stallone for five years and that he has a reputation as a peaceful person.

5.43. Return to Problem 3.2 at page 131. Is the evidence of Driver's speeding ticket likely to be admissible? For what purpose(s)?
5.44. Paul Plant, a candidate for public office, has sued Diane Daniels for defamation for circulating a pamphlet stating that Paul is a violent person with a bad temper and that on May 23 Paul stole a pistol from a local sporting goods store. Paul testifies that both statements are untrue.

(a)   Paul calls Edgar James, who offers to testify that since the publication of the pamphlet Paul has had a reputation in the community for violence and for dishonesty.

    (b)   Diane calls Zelda Young, who offers to testify that she observed Paul engaged in a fistfight at a local tavern last year.

    (c)   Diane calls Florence Newman, who offers to testify that before the alleged defamation Paul had a reputation in the community for being violent and for being dishonest.

    (d)   Diane calls Winston Hampton, who offers to testify that on two occasions last year when he was with Paul, Paul stole merchandise from a local department store.

Assuming that proper objections are made, which pieces of evidence should be admissible?

5.45. The defendant is charged with the sale of heroin. He claims that he was entrapped by the entreaties of the purchaser, a supposed friend who was in fact an undercover narcotics officer. According to the substantive law, the defense of entrapment is not available if the defendant was predisposed to commit the crime. To show predisposition the prosecution offers evidence (a) that the defendant has the reputation in the community as a drug dealer and (b) that on five specific occasions the defendant has sold drugs to schoolchildren. Should the defendant's objections to these pieces of evidence be sustained?

I. EVIDENCE OF SEXUAL ASSAULT AND CHILD MOLESTATION

As part of the Violent Crime Control and Enforcement Act of 1994, Congress enacted three rules, FRE 413-415, that relate to the admissibility of sexual misconduct evidence in cases involving charges of sexual assault and child molestation. The obvious purpose of the rules is to make sexual misconduct evidence more freely admissible. In our discussion of these rules, the terms *sexual assault* and *sexual misconduct* include both sexual assault and child molestation.

Evidence commentators have been particularly critical of FRE 413-415, which were enacted directly by Congress and not subject to the typical rule-making process. Charles Alan Wright and Kenneth W. Graham Jr., Federal Practice and Procedure §5411-5417B (Supp. 2001); Edward J. Imwinkelried, A Small Contribution to the Debate over the Proposed Legislation Abolishing the Character Evidence Prohibition in Sex Offense Prosecutions, 44 Syracuse L. Rev. 1125 (1993); Perspectives on the Proposed Federal Rules of Evidence 413-415, 22 Ford. Urban L.J. 265 (1995).

Because most criminal sexual assault cases arise in state courts, a significant potential impact of FRE 413-415 is as a model for state evidence codes. Approximately three-quarters of the states have evidence rules based on the Federal Rules. States, however, have not rushed to adopt these new rules. But see Ariz. R. Evid. 404(c); Cal. Evid. Code §1108 (West 1995); Mo. Ann. Stat. §566.025 (Vernon Supp. 2001).

1.   FRE 413-415

RULE 413.   EVIDENCE OF SIMILAR CRIMES IN SEXUAL ASSAULT CASES

(a) In a criminal case in which the defendant is accused of an offense of sexual assault, evidence of the defendant's commission of another offense or offenses of sexual assault is admissible, and may be considered for its bearing on any matter to which it is relevant.

(b) In a case in which the Government intends to offer evidence under this rule, the attorney for the Government shall disclose the evidence to the defendant, including statements of witnesses or a summary of the substance of any testimony that is expected to be offered, at least fifteen days before the scheduled date of trial or at such later time as the court may allow for good cause.

(c) This rule shall not be construed to limit the admission or consideration of evidence under any other rule.

(d) For purposes of this rule and Rule 415, "offense of sexual assault" means a crime under Federal law or the law of a State (as defined in section 513 of title 18 United States Code) that involved — (1) any conduct proscribed by chapter 109A of title 18, United States Code [which contains several sexual abuse crimes]; (2) contact, without consent, between any part of the defendant's body or an object and the genitals or anus of another person; (3) contact, without consent, between the genitals or anus of the defendant and any part of another person's body; (4) deriving sexual pleasure or gratification from the infliction of death, bodily injury, or physical pain on another person; or (5) an attempt or conspiracy to engage in conduct described in paragraph (1)-(4).

RULE 414.   EVIDENCE OF SIMILAR CRIMES IN CHILD MOLESTATION CASES

[This rule is similar in structure and content to FRE 413, but it applies to offenses of child molestation rather than sexual assault. Section (d) defines "child" as "a person below the age of fourteen" and removes the "without consent" phrase that occurs in subdivisions (2) and (3) of FRE 413.]

RULE 414.   EVIDENCE OF SIMILAR ACTS IN CIVIL CASES CONCERNING SEXUAL ASSAULT OR CHILD MOLESTATION

[This rule makes FRE 413 and FRE 414, including the notice requirement, applicable to civil cases in which a claim is based on a party's alleged sexual assault or child molestation.]

2.   Interpretation and Illustration of FRE 413-415

a.   *The Relationship Between FRE 413-415 and Other Rules of Evidence*

i.   FRE 413-415 and FRE 404.   The purpose of FRE 413-415 is to liberalize the admissibility of character evidence in sexual assault and child molestation cases, by removing the two primary objections that would otherwise be available under FRE 404. First, the prosecution is permitted to open the door to use of character evidence in such cases, a right otherwise reserved to criminal defendants under FRE 404(a). Second, the prosecution may offer past specific acts of sexual assault or child molestation as evidence that the defendant committed the current offense, notwithstanding the FRE

404(b) ban on past specific acts to prove character to show action in conformity on a particular occasion. United States v. Enjady, 134 F.3d 1427, 1431 (10th Cir. 1998) (Congress intended "to lower the obstacles to admissibility of propensity evidence in a defined class of cases"). This liberalization of the pre-existing rules is consistent with the language of FRE 413-415: sexual assault evidence "*is admissible* and may be considered for its bearing on *any matter* to which it is relevant" (emphasis added). In addition, this understanding of FRE 413-415 is suggested by their legislative history (David J. Karp, Evidence of Propensity and Probability in Sex Offense Cases and Other Cases, 70 Chi. Kent L. Rev. 15, 15 n.* (1995); Dale A. Nance, Forward: Do We Really Want to Know the Defendant?, 70 Chi.-Kent L. Rev., 3, 8 (1994)) and by the Justice Department, which lobbied for the enactment of the rules (Karp, supra at 19).

Consider, for example, a case in which the defendant is charged with attempted rape and the prosecution offers to prove that on two occasions within the past five years the defendant had sexually assaulted two women. Assume that the two women were unrelated to the victim of the attempted rape and that there were no unusual similar features among the three incidents. Are the two prior incidents relevant to identify the defendant as the perpetrator of the crime charged? Perhaps, but only because the evidence shows a general tendency to engage in sexual assaults. That sounds like a description of character evidence. If so, then the evidence, before the adoption of FRE 413, would have been inadmissible pursuant to both FRE 404(a) and the first sentence of FRE 404(b). FRE 413 removes the FRE 404 impediments to the admissibility of relevant sexual assault evidence.

ii. FRE 413-415 and FRE 403.   When FRE 413-415 were first enacted, there was some concern that these rules made no explicit reference to existing exclusionary rules and no indication of the extent to which judges may have discretion to exclude sexual misconduct evidence under FRE 403.[1] However, every appellate case dealing with this issue has concluded that sexual misconduct evidence is subject to FRE 403 balancing. United States v. Guardia, 135 F.2d 1326 (10th Cir. 1998). In fact, some of these cases have suggested that if FRE 403 were not available to exclude prejudicial evidence of sexual misconduct, admitting such evidence would violate a defendant's due process right to a fair trial. United States v. Castillo, 140 F.3d 874 (10th Cir. 1998) (FRE 414); United States v. Enjady, 134 F.3d 1427 (10th Cir. 1998) (FRE 413). Thus in the attempted rape hypothetical, the defendant could argue that the prior sexual assaults should be excluded on FRE 403 grounds.

iii. FRE 413-415 and Other Rules of Evidence.   Can the FRE 413-415 language that prior sexual assault evidence is admissible be construed as an exception to other exclusionary rules of evidence, such as the hearsay rule? The argument strikes us as unsound. "Congressional proponents of the legislation creating Rule 413 intended that 'the general standards of the rules of evidence will continue to apply, including the

---

1.   Typically when the Federal Rules address the potential admissibility of evidence, they use the term "may." See, e.g., FRE 404(b) (specific acts evidence "may, however, be admissible for other purposes"). *May* indicates that admissibility is subject to other exclusionary provisions, including a court's power to exclude probative evidence pursuant to FRE 403. By contrast, FRE 413-415 state that sexual misconduct evidence "is admissible," thereby giving rise to the argument — wrong, in our view, and properly rejected by the courts — that judges may have less discretion to exclude or that exclusionary rules may not be applicable to such evidence. It is worth noting that, in the one instance where the drafters of the Federal Rules clearly intended for admissibility to be mandatory, the rule states that the evidence "*shall be* admitted." FRE 609(a)(2) (emphasis added), discussed in Chapter Seven.

restriction on hearsay evidence and the court's authority under rule 403 to exclude evidence whose probative value is substantially outweighed by its prejudicial effect.'" 2 Weinstein's Federal Evidence 413-11 (2d ed. 2005). In light of the uniform view that FRE 403 can be invoked to exclude sexual assault evidence, it seems likely that courts will conclude that other established rules — for example, the hearsay rule — are also applicable to evidence offered pursuant to FRE 413-415. Thus in the attempted rape hypothetical, it is unlikely that a court would permit the prior sexual assaults to be proven by out-of-court hearsay statements that would not otherwise be admissible.

b.   FRE 413-415 and Preliminary Factfinding

As is the case with specific acts evidence admissible pursuant to the second sentence of FRE 404(b), there is no requirement that the sexual assault resulted in a conviction or even a criminal charge. If there is a question about the nature of the defendant's involvement in an alleged sexual assault, a court should resolve this issue in the same manner that it resolves the issue when there is a question about a defendant's culpable involvement in other types of specific acts. Under the Federal Rules, as a result of the Supreme Court's decision in *Huddleston*, discussed at pages 239, supra, there must be "evidence sufficient to support a finding" (FRE 104(b)) that the defendant was culpably involved in the act. United States v. Mann, 193 F.3d 1172 (10th Cir. 1999). For example, in the preceding rape hypothetical, assume that the defendant offers the testimony of a friend who provides the defendant with an alibi for the times of the noncharged sexual assaults; assume further that the prosecution's proof of those specific acts consists of the alleged victims' testimony and that there is a history of personal animosity between the alleged victims and the defendant. Even though the judge may disbelieve the alleged victims, there is sufficient "evidence to support a finding" under FRE 104(b) that the assaults occurred, because the judge is not permitted to take credibility into account. Thus the prosecution would have satisfied the preliminary fact requirement.

c.   The Broad Definition of "Offense of Sexual Assault"

The definition of what constitutes an "offense of sexual assault" is potentially very broad. Any acts having the characteristics described in §§(d)(2) through (d)(5) are apparently included as long as some state has enacted a criminal statute that embraces that conduct. Assume, for example, in our rape hypothetical that the prosecution seeks to introduce evidence that the defendant has engaged in consensual sexual activity that involves pain or injury. If any state happens to encompass that sexual activity within its criminal law, the prosecution's evidence arguably falls within the scope of the rule as admissible even if the activity is not a federal crime or a crime in the state where the defendant is being prosecuted.

d.   The Meaning of "Without Consent" in FRE 413(d)(2) and (3)

Nothing in FRE 413 indicates whether the term *consent* in section (d) means legal or actual consent. Consider a situation in which a defendant is charged with the rape and the victim is an adult. Prior sexual contact with other adults against their will (i.e., without *actual* consent) is without question a type of sexual assault that falls within the scope of FRE 413. What about prior sexual contact with a minor that was with the minor's actual consent but not legal consent because of the minor's age? Should this type of evidence be admissible? Should it matter whether the defendant was aware of the minor's age?

3. Elaboration of FRE 413-415

a. *The Extent to Which FRE 413-415 Change the Law of Evidence*

i. Limiting Instructions and Closing Argument. Prior to the adoption of FRE 413-415, admissible sexual misconduct evidence was subject to the FRE 404(b) restriction that it could not be used to prove the defendant's character for the purpose of showing action in conformity with character. Thus when sexual misconduct evidence was admitted for some noncharacter purpose, the defendant was entitled to a limiting instruction, and the prosecutor could not argue to the jury that the specific acts showed the defendant's character or general propensity for engaging in sexual assaults. Now, pursuant to FRE 413-415, all admissible sexual misconduct evidence "may be considered for its bearing on any matter to which it is relevant." Presumably there is no right to a limiting instruction and no restriction on the prosecutor's making a character/propensity argument to the jury. But see pages 256-257, supra (suggesting that such a limitation on closing argument would be desirable).

ii. Previously Inadmissible Character Evidence. As a practical matter, FRE 413-415's intended effect of overriding the FRE 404 restrictions on character evidence in sexual assault and child molestation cases may not have a significant impact on *admissibility decisions*. The FRE 404(b) restrictions on admissibility have been limited, insofar as many courts have been quite liberal in admitting specific acts evidence in sexual misconduct cases. Indeed, in these types of cases some courts, including federal courts prior to the adoption of FRE 413-415, United States v. Yellow, 18 F.3d 1438 (8th Cir. 1994), have often admitted the kind of propensity evidence that they would probably exclude if the case were not a sexual misconduct prosecution. Robert N. Block, Comment, Defining Standards for Determining the Admissibility of Evidence of Other Sex Offenses, 25 UCLA L. Rev. 261 (1977).

On the other hand, even courts that readily admit sexual disposition might have formerly limited that evidence to sexual conduct with the same victim. FRE 413-415 expresses no preference for prior conduct toward the same victim as opposed to sexual conduct involving third parties. Moreover, the trend prior to the adoption of FRE 413-415 had not been uniformly in favor of broader admissibility for prior sexual assault evidence. 1 McCormick on Evidence supra at 669 n.52 (citing case that overruled prior, more liberal standard of admissibility); Lannan v. State, 600 N.E.2d 1334 (Ind. 1992).

iii. The Application of FRE 403 to Previously Inadmissible Character Evidence. The clear intent of FRE 413-415 is to make previously inadmissible evidence admissible. How, if at all, is a judge to take into account this mandate for more liberal admissibility in making the FRE 403 determination with respect to a particular piece of evidence?

Perhaps not surprisingly, the cases take a variety of approaches to this issue. At one extreme is Frank v. County of Hudson, 924 F. Supp. 620 (D.N.J. 1996), where the court stated, "Child sexual abuse deservedly carries a unique stigma in our society; such highly prejudicial evidence should therefore carry a very high degree of probative value if it is to be admitted." Id. at 626-627. The analysis in *Frank* suggests that FRE 403 is likely to require exclusion of sexual misconduct evidence not falling within one of the traditional noncharacter purposes for admitting specific acts evidence. That may or may not be desirable as a matter of policy. As a matter of law, it is wrong because it makes FRE 413-415 a nullity.

At the other extreme, some courts have been willing to admit evidence of very old, seemingly isolated, and sometimes dissimilar instances of sexual misconduct. For example, in United States v. Meacham, 115 F.3d 1488 (10th Cir. 1997), where the defendant was charged with transporting a minor in interstate commerce with the intent that she engage in sexual activity, the court held that it was proper to admit two similar incidents of child molestation that occurred over 30 years earlier. There was no evidence of more recent incidents with third persons to indicate a continuing pattern of conduct. See also United States v. Gabe, 237 F.3d 954 (8th Cir. 2001) (20-year-old incident of child molestation admissible); United States v. Eagle, 137 F.3d 1011 (8th Cir. 1998) (upholding admission of evidence of prior statutory rape of defendant's current common law wife in prosecution for child molestation); United States v. Larson, 112 F.3d 600 (2d Cir. 1997) (16- to 20-year-old similar incidents of child molestation admissible; 21- to 23-year-old similar incidents excluded).

For two cases in which the court of appeals first held that the admission of specific acts evidence pursuant to FRE 404(b) was prejudicial error and then later held that the same evidence was properly admissible pursuant to FRE 414, see United States v. Sumner, 204 F.3d 1182 (8th Cir. 2000), and United States v. LeCompte, 131 F.3d 767 (8th Cir. 1997). Prior to LeCompte's second trial, the district court granted his motion in limine to exclude the sexual misconduct evidence and the government appealed. In reversing the district court, the Eighth Circuit observed:

> [T]he danger of unfair prejudice noted by the District Court was that presented by the "unique stigma" of child sexual abuse, on account of which LeCompte might be convicted not for the charged offense, but for his sexual abuse of T.T. This danger is one that all propensity evidence in such trials presents. It is for this reason that the evidence was previously excluded, and it is precisely such holdings that Congress intended to overrule. [Id. at 770]

Do you agree?

For another view of the relationship between FRE 413-415 and FRE 403, see United States v. Guarda, 135 F.3d 1326 (10th Cir. 1998):

> All of the rules in Article IV of the Federal Rules of Evidence, not just Rule 404, are "concrete applications [of rules 402 and 403] evolved for particular situations." Fed. R. Evid. 403 advisory committee's note. The fact that Congress created Rule 413 can only mean that Congress intended to partially repeal the "concrete application" found in 404(b) for a subset of cases in which Congress found 404(b)'s rigid rule to be inappropriate. That conclusion is not surprising, given the fact that propensity evidence has a unique

probative value in sexual assault trials and that such trials often suffer from a lack of any relevant evidence beyond the testimony of the alleged victim and the defendant. . . .

While Rule 413 removes the per se exclusion of character evidence, courts should continue to consider the traditional reasons for the prohibition of character evidence as "risks of prejudice" weighing against admission. For example, a court should, in each 413 case, take into account the chance that "a jury will convict for crimes other than those charged — or that, uncertain of guilt, it will convict anyway because a bad person deserves punishment." [T]he government urges us to approve a lenient 403 balancing test. We agree that Rule 413, like all other rules of admissibility, favors the introduction of evidence. Rule 413, however, contains no language that supports an especially lenient application of Rule 403. Furthermore, courts apply Rule 403 in undiluted form to Rules 404(a)(1)-(3), the other exceptions to the ban on propensity evidence. Those rules allow a criminal defendant to use character evidence of himself, his victim, or in limited circumstances, of other witnesses, in order to "prove action in conformity therewith." Fed. R. Evid. 404(a)(1-3). Like Rule 413, these rules carve out exceptions to Rule 404(a) and reflect a legislative judgment that certain types of propensity evidence should be admitted. Courts have never found, however, that because the drafters made exceptions to the general rule of 404(a), they tempered 403 as well.

Similarly, under Rule 404(b), evidence of a person's prior acts can be used for other purposes other than proving character. Despite Rule 404(b)'s legislative judgment in favor of admission, Rule 403 applies with all its vigor to Rule 404(b) evidence.

When balancing Rule 413 evidence under 403, then, the district court should not alter its normal process of weighing the probative value of the evidence against the danger of unfair prejudice. In Rule 413 cases, the risk of prejudice will be present to varying degrees. Propensity evidence, however, has indisputable probative value. That value in a given case will depend on innumerable considerations, including the similarity of the prior acts to the acts charged, the closeness in time of the prior acts to the charged acts, see id., the frequency of the prior acts, the presence or lack of intervening events, and the need for evidence beyond the testimony of the defendant and alleged victim. Because of the sensitive nature of the balancing test in these cases, it will be particularly important for a district court to fully evaluate the proffered Rule 413 evidence and make a clear record of the reasoning behind its findings. [135 F.3d at 1330-1331.]

iv. The Results of FRE 403 Balancing: Acquaintance Rape, Stranger Rape, Child Molestation, and Sexual Harassment. Despite — or perhaps because of — the variety of approaches to FRE 403, the results in particular cases may sometimes have more to do with the nature of the case than with what the court articulates about the relationship between FRE 403 and FRE 413-415. Although in the past courts have been divided on the admissibility of sexual assault evidence in child molestation cases, David P. Bryden and Roger C. Park, "Other Crimes" Evidence in Sex Offense Cases, 78 Minn. L. Rev. 529, 531 n.12 (1992), the trend seems to be strongly in favor admitting such evidence under FRE 414. United States v. Gabe and United States v. LeCompte, supra; Christina E. Wells and Erin Elliott Motley, Reinforcing the Myth of the Crazed Rapist: A Feminist Critique of Recent Rape Legislation, 81 B.U. L. Rev. 127, 177-178 (2001). In rape cases, on the other hand, courts traditionally appear to have been less willing to admit prior sexual assault evidence in acquaintance rape cases than in stranger rape cases, see Bryden and Park, supra at 531 n.11, and this tendency may be continuing. Both in acquaintance rape cases (FRE 413) and in sexual harassment actions involving acquaintances (FRE 415), courts have seemed particularly sensitive to unfair prejudice concerns and have not been reluctant to exclude sexual misconduct evidence. United States v. Acevedo, 117 F.3d 1429 (table of unpublished decisions),

No. 96-2149, 1997 U.S. App. LEXIS 17578 (10th Cir. July 14, 1997); Cleveland v. KFC Nat'l Management Co., 948 F. Supp. 62 (N.D. Ga. 1996). For a discussion of these and other similar cases, see Wells and Motley, supra; Jane Harris Aiken, Sexual Character Evidence in civil Actions: Refining the Propensity Rule, 1997 Wis. L. Rev. 1221.

The apparent willingness to exclude sexual assault evidence in cases involving alleged sexual misconduct by an acquaintance may be undermining one of the objectives of FRE 413 and FRE 415. Bryden and Park, supra at 576-582, note that in acquaintance rape cases in which defendants claim consent, there may be a relatively greater need for sexual assault evidence. There is not as likely to be physical evidence to establish that a rape occurred. Thus, the defendant's prior sexual misconduct may be particularly important in resolving the inevitable credibility conflict between the defendant and alleged victim. Karen Andrews, The Admissibility of Other-Crimes Evidence in Acquaintance-Rape Prosecutions, 17 S. Ill. U. L.J. 341 (1993); Sara Beale, Prior Similar Acts in Prosecutions for Rape and Child Sex Abuse, 4 Crim. L.F. 307 (1993).

b.   The Underlying Rationale for the New Rules

Regardless of how much or how little the new rules in practice will liberalize the use of sexual misconduct evidence, their underlying premises must be (1) that sexual misconduct evidence has relatively high probative value to show action on a particular occasion and (2) that the probative value of this type of evidence is not likely to be outweighed by its prejudicial impact. Both of these propositions may be true, but neither is free from doubt. Because of the controversy surrounding FRE 413-415, we include references here to some of the legal and social science literature that has examined these two basic propositions.

i.   Unfair Prejudice.   The prejudicial impact of any specific acts evidence — that is, the extent to which it may make the jury willing to ignore a reasonable doubt and convict a bad, perhaps dangerous person — is a function of how bad or dangerous the specific acts are in the minds of the fact finder. We suspect many of you and many jurors share the view that child molestation and sexual assault are among the most serious and heinous crimes. To the extent that this assessment is correct, the only justification for creating an exception to the prohibition against the prosecution's opening the door to proof of the defendant's character and doing so even with specific acts evidence is the relatively high probative value of such evidence.

ii.   Probative Value and Recidivism.   The already liberal admissibility of sexual misconduct evidence in some jurisdictions suggests that at least some courts regard sexual assault evidence as more probative than other types of character evidence. Moreover, some — perhaps many — of you may believe intuitively that prior sexual misconduct evidence is particularly probative propensity evidence. The important empirical question is whether this intuition is in fact true with respect to sexual misconduct against third persons. Repeated abuse of the same person — particularly a spouse or son or daughter — may be quite common. Evidence of repeated sexual violence against the same person, however, is likely to be considered noncharacter evidence and, therefore, potentially admissible in any event pursuant to the second sentence of FRE 404(b).

Studies of recidivism indicate that the recidivism rate for sexual offenders is not consistently higher than for other serious crime offenders. Roger Park, however, has argued that the important recidivism factor should be how often sex offenders commit other sex crimes in comparison to how often other offenders commit crimes similar to the ones of which they were convicted. Roger C. Park, Character at the Crossroads, 49 Hast. L.J. 717, 756-754 (1998). By this standard, the propensity of rapists to be recidivists is relatively high. Id.at 762. Moreover, sex crimes are known to be underreported, and recidivism statistics rely on arrest and conviction rates. A. Nicholas Groth, Robert E. Longo, and J. Bradley McFadin, Undetected Recidivism among Rapists and Child Molesters, 28 Crime & Delinquency 450 (1982). Forty-five percent of all rapes in the United States are never reported, and studies show that only 5 to 10 percent of acquaintance rape cases are reported. Karen Andrews, The Admissibility of Other-Crimes Evidence in Acquaintance-Rape Prosecutions, 17 S. Ill. U. L.J. 341, 342-343 (1993). Moreover, there is evidence that police do not pursue an arrest if they do not believe the victim. Gary D. LaFree, Rape and Criminal Justice: The Social Construction of Sexual Assault 59-60, 66-69, 207-226 (1989); Julie Horney and Cassia Spohn, Rape Law Reform and Instrumental Change in Six Urban Jurisdictions, 25 Law and Soc. Rev. 117 (1991).

iii. A Contextual Assessment of Probative Value. Consider the likely impact of one's political and social values in assessing the probative value of sexual assault evidence. If one regards sexual assaults as largely analogous to all other violent crimes, then there is no reason for character evidence rules to differ across those crimes. The generally low probative value of character evidence to show action in conformity with character and the potential for unfair prejudice to criminal defendants would militate against using the action-in-conformity with character inference in all cases.

On the other hand, if one considers sexual assaults as one manifestation of a male-dominated social structure that tends to discriminate against and oppress women — especially women of color and poor women — in a variety of ways, it is reasonable to expect that prosecutors, judges, and fact finders may approach sexual assault cases with some of the biases that inhere in that societal oppression. Special rules of admissibility to compensate for those biases may be appropriate. Bryden and Park, supra at 583.

Recent legal literature suggests that this type of discriminatory bias does exist. Empirical research based on Uniform Crime Reports and real and mock jury trials reveals that men are more likely to rape women of color and poor women, but are less likely to be convicted when they do so. If the perpetrators are convicted, they serve less jail time when these women are their victims. One explanation is that judges and juries are more likely to see these women as sexually available and therefore not capable of being assaulted. Gary D. LaFree, Rape and Criminal Justice: The Social Construction of Sexual Assault 219-220 (1989); G. Chezia Carraway, Violence Against Women of Color, 43 Stan. L. Rev. 1301 (1991); Kimberle Crenshaw, Mapping the Margins: Intersectionality, Identity Politics, and Violence Against Women of Color, 43 Stan. L. Rev. 1241 (1991); Dorothy E. Roberts, Rape, Violence, and Women's Autonomy, 69 Chi.-Kent L. Rev. 359 (1993). In addition, traditional and still currently powerful stereotypes blame the woman for acquaintance rape or even deny that the activity is rape when the woman is seen as contributing to her predicament. Lois Pineau, Date

Rape: A Feminist Analysis, 8 Law and Philosophy 217 (1989). See also Andrews, supra; David P. Bryden and Sonja Lengnick, Rape in the Criminal Justice System, 87 J. Crim. L. & Criminology 1194 (1997); Karen M. Kramer, Note, Rule by Myth: The Social and Legal Dynamics Governing Alcohol-Related Acquaintance Rapes, 47 Stan. L. Rev. 115 (1994); citations at page 331, infra. These attitudes make jurors willing to discount, if not disbelieve, victims' stories, and since there often will be no evidence of physical injury in an acquaintance rape situation, the victim's credibility will usually be critical to a successful prosecution. To the extent that jurors share these stereotypical attitudes the likelihood of a conviction is small; and if juries are unlikely to convict, prosecutors are unlikely to bring cases. Admitting evidence of a defendant's prior sexual assaults may challenge the jurors' stereotypes and in turn make prosecutors more willing to pursue acquaintance rape cases. Allowing evidence of a defendant's prior sexual assault record also may increase convictions in cases where poor women and women of color are the victims.

Perhaps this bias and stereotyping explains the pre-FRE 413-415 state of the law described at page 301-302, supra. As we noted there, many courts have tended to be relatively liberal in admitting evidence of a defendant's prior sexual conduct in child molestation cases and in cases involving sexual assaults by strangers. This same liberal view of admissibility, however, has not extended to cases involving sexual assault by an acquaintance. We can think of no basis for believing that a sexual assault defendant's prior sexual conduct is likely to be less probative in acquaintance assault situations than in stranger assault situations.

Does this contextual perspective on relevance provide a sufficient basis for the new rules, which will encourage the admission of sexual assault evidence in acquaintance rape situations? Would it be desirable to limit FRE 413-415 to situations in which the defendant and victim are acquaintances? Consider the following critique of FRE 413-415: Some feminists have argued that the new rules merely re-enforce societal stereotypes of rapists as vicious predators and revive the idea that women who make accusations of rape need to have a corroborating witness (in these cases, women who have been prior victims). Aviva Orenstein, No Bad Men!: A Feminist Analysis of Character Evidence in Rape Trials, 49 Hastings L.J. 663 (1998); Wells and Motley, supra. Does this analysis change your views about the desirability of FRE 413-415?

c.   The Significance of FRE 413-415 to Federal Litigation

The controversy surrounding the adoption of FRE 413-415 focused almost exclusively on the role of FRE 413 and FRE 414 in criminal prosecutions. As we noted at the outset of Section E, however, sexual assault and child molestation are predominantly state crimes. Thus, although most of the limited number of FRE 413-415 cases to date are criminal cases, there will probably be relatively few opportunities for federal courts to apply FRE 413 and FRE 414. By contrast, FRE 415 — the civil case counterpart to FRE 413 and FRE 414 — may become the primary vehicle for giving content to the federal sexual misconduct rules. 23 Wright and Graham, supra at §5411B (Supp. 2001). For example, plaintiffs with sexual harassment claims (including federal civil rights suits) based on unlawful sexual touching may seek to introduce evidence of the defendants' prior sexual misconduct pursuant to FRE 415. Cleveland v. KFC

Nat'l Mgmt. Co., 948 F. Supp. 62 (N.D. Ga. 1996); Jane Harris Aiken, Sexual Character Evidence in Civil Actions, 1997 Wis. L. Rev. 1221.

KEY POINTS

1. FRE 413-415 permit the use of specific acts to prove a person's character or propensity for engaging in sexual assault to prove action on a particular occasion.

2. Evidence potentially admissible under FRE 413-415 may be excluded pursuant to FRE 403.

PROBLEMS

5.46. Defendant has been charged with "intentionally having sexual contact with a minor with the intent to become sexually aroused or gratified." During its case in chief the prosecution introduced evidence that the defendant lured a three-year-old girl into his home, fondled her, and gave her a piece of candy. Defendant testified in his own behalf and denied the incident. On rebuttal, the prosecution offers the testimony of a 12-year-old girl that, a week before the alleged incident with the three-year-old girl, the defendant offered the witness $20 if she would come into his home and expose herself. Should the evidence be admitted?

5.47. Alex Abrams is charged with attempted sexual assault and battery. Brenda Bailey, the alleged victim, testifies that she was at a bar where she met a man whom she identifies as the defendant Abrams; that he followed her to her car as she left the bar after midnight; that he grabbed her from behind, pinned her to the ground, and attempted to assault her sexually; and that her screams brought other patrons from the bar and her assailant ran away. Abrams testifies that Bailey has misidentified him; that it was a dark night; and that he had been at the bar earlier but left before midnight and was at home when the alleged attack occurred.

The prosecution seeks to admit the following evidence. Testimony from two women that seven years ago and five years ago, respectively, they were sexually assaulted by Abrams after he followed them out of a bar. Should this evidence be admitted prior to the adoption of FRE 413-415? After their adoption?

Would the result be different if the sexual assaults were more recent? If they had occurred during the daytime at the women's homes?

5.48. Carl Corbin is charged with rape. Doris Davis, the alleged victim, testifies that she met Corbin in a bar; that they talked for a while and she agreed to accompany him to another bar for drinks and dancing; that after spending a few hours at this second bar she accepted his offer of a ride back to her car; that along the way he stopped at a park and said he wanted to have sex with her; that she said no and told him she was afraid she would get pregnant; and that he forcibly raped her. Corbin testifies that Davis consented to have sexual relations with him after a fun evening.

The prosecution seeks to admit the following evidence: Testimony from a woman that she had dated Corbin for a brief period of time three years ago; that he wanted to have sexual relations with her; that she told him no but he then forced her to have sex; and that she never reported the incident to anyone. Should this evidence be admitted prior to the adoption of FRE 413-415? After their adoption?

Would the result be different if the woman would testify that she met Corbin in a bar; that after a few drinks and dancing he offered to drive her home; that he stopped at the same park where he had stopped with Davis; and that he forced her have sex after she said no?

5.49. Agatha Lewis has brought an action for damages against Brian Bellows, who, she alleges, transmitted AIDS to her. Agatha establishes with blood test evidence that she did not have the AIDS virus 18 months ago, that she now has the virus, and that Brian has the virus. Agatha testifies that she is not an intravenous drug user, that she has not had a blood transfusion, and that the only person with whom she has had intimate sexual contact subsequent to the negative AIDS test is Brian. She further testifies that she met Brian at a party; that they went to his apartment after the party and had sexual intercourse; that she had sexual intercourse with him two or three additional times in the next two weeks; and that she had no further contact with him. In his defense, Brian admits that he met Agatha at a party. He claims that he gave her a ride to her apartment after the party and that he did not on that night or on any other occasion have sexual intercourse with Agatha. In rebuttal Agatha offers the testimony of three women that during the past year they met Brian at parties and had brief sexual affairs with him. Should this evidence be admitted prior to the adoption of FRE 413-415? After their adoption?

5.50. Steve Sanders, a 21-year-old college junior, is charged with the rape of Betty Brown, a classmate. According to the prosecution, the rape occurred during their first (and only) date. Sanders admits having had intercourse, but he claims that Brown consented. The prosecution offers the following pieces of evidence:

(a)   the testimony of Ann Williams, a 16-year-old high school student, that she recently had consensual sexual intercourse with Sanders;

(b)   the testimony of Ellie Wilson, another student, that on her first date with Sanders he was extremely aggressive and ripped some of her clothing before she could stop him;

(c)   a wallet belonging to Mary Miller that was seized from Sanders's room and Mary Miller's testimony that one month ago a masked man raped her in the laundry room of the dormitory and stole her wallet (Sanders claims that he found the wallet on a street corner the night before it was seized from his room, and that he was studying in the library at the time of the rape).

How should the court rule prior to the adoption of FRE 413-415? After their adoption?

J.   EVIDENCE OF AN ALLEGED VICTIM'S PAST SEXUAL BEHAVIOR OR DISPOSITION IN SEX OFFENSE CASES

Until fairly recently, many courts were quite liberal in permitting rape and other sex crime defendants to introduce evidence of the alleged victim's sexual history when the defendant claimed that the victim had consented. The most common form of prior sexual history evidence was reputation testimony, but a number of jurisdictions also permitted specific acts evidence. Starting in the 1970s, states began to enact "rape shield" legislation to curb the admissibility of some of this evidence. FRE 412, which was most recently amended in 1994, was also the product of specific legislative action. Congress added FRE 412 to the Federal Rules in 1978. For a discussion of the background and legislative history of Rule 412, see 23 Charles Alan Wright and Kenneth W. Graham Jr., Federal Practice and Procedure §5381 at 483-491 (1980), §5381.1 at 190-199 (Supp. 2001).

1. FRE 412

RULE 412. SEX OFFENSE CASES; RELEVANCE OF ALLEGED VICTIM'S PAST SEXUAL BEHAVIOR OR ALLEGED SEXUAL DISPOSITION

(a) Evidence generally inadmissible. The following evidence is not admissible in any civil or criminal proceeding involving alleged sexual misconduct except as provided in subdivisions (b) and (c):

(1) Evidence offered to prove that any alleged victim engaged in other sexual behavior.

(2) Evidence offered to prove any alleged victim's sexual predisposition.

(b) Exceptions.

(1) In a criminal case, the following evidence is admissible, if otherwise admissible under these rules: (A) evidence of specific instances of sexual behavior by the alleged victim offered to prove that a person other than the accused was the source of semen, injury or other physical evidence; (B) evidence of specific instances of sexual behavior by the alleged victim with respect to the person accused of the sexual misconduct offered by the accused to prove consent or by the prosecution; and (C) evidence the exclusion of which would violate the constitutional rights of the defendant.

(2) In a civil case, evidence offered to prove the sexual behavior or sexual predisposition of any alleged victim is admissible if it is otherwise admissible under these rules and its probative value substantially outweighs the danger of harm to any victim and of unfair prejudice to any party. Evidence of an alleged victim's reputation is admissible only if it has been placed in controversy by the alleged victim.

(c) Procedure to determine admissibility.

(1) A party intending to offer evidence under subdivision (b) must (A) file a written motion at least 14 days before trial specifically describing the evidence and stating the purpose for which it is offered unless the court, for good cause requires a different time for filing or permits filing during trial; and (B) serve the motion on all parties and notify the alleged victim or, when appropriate, the alleged victim's guardian or representative.

(2) Before admitting evidence under this rule the court must conduct a hearing in camera and afford the victim and parties a right to attend and be heard. The motion, related papers, and the record of the hearing must be sealed and remain under seal unless the court orders otherwise.

2. Interpretation and Illustration of FRE 412

FRE 412 has a two-fold rationale. First, the combination of relatively low probative value and significant countervailing FRE 403 concerns warrants, at least in criminal cases, a flat rule of exclusion rather than individual case-by-case balancing to determine admissibility. Second, independent of FRE 403 concerns, substantive policy considerations justify the exclusion of relevant evidence. Thus FRE 412 excludes some evidence of an alleged sexual assault victim's sexual conduct in order to protect the alleged victim from harassment and embarrassment and to avoid deterring such a person from testifying about the sexual assault.

a. The Relevance of an Alleged Victim's Sexual Behavior or Disposition to Prove Conduct

Some people adamantly maintain that evidence of a sexual assault victim's prior sexual history is irrelevant to the issue of consent. FRE 412 (b)(1)(B), however, explicitly permits proof of sexual behavior between the defendant and the alleged victim to prove the victim's consent. Moreover, there is no explicit limitation on the use of prior sexual conduct to prove consent in civil cases. Is such conduct relevant under the minimal test of FRE 401? Consider an alleged victim whose only prior consensual intercourse was in the context of a marriage relationship. What generalizations can you frame that say something about the likelihood that such a victim consented or did not consent to sexual intercourse with a stranger? With an acquaintance? If the defendant's defense of consent is based on evidence that is arguably ambiguous as to whether the victim consented, is evidence of the alleged victim's prior consensual sexual conduct with third persons probative of consent? Again, can you think of a generalization that permits one to make the inference from the evidentiary fact (prior sexual conduct) to the fact of consequence (consent)? We suggest that in both examples the relevance of the evidence depends on being able to frame generalizations about the alleged victim's propensities regarding sexual conduct.

b. The Underlying Propensity Theory

The concept of relevance with which we have been dealing explicitly and implicitly throughout the course rests on the premise that individuals have propensities to behave in particular ways and that we can arrive at reasonable conclusions about historical facts by taking these propensities into account. For example, at the most basic level, when a person says that event X occurred, we regard the person's statement as relevant, at least in a minimal FRE 401 sense, to establish that X occurred because we assume, on the basis of our common experience, that individuals generally have a propensity to tell the truth. Similarly, a premise underlying the character evidence rules is that individuals have propensities to behave in characteristic ways and that if we know something about the individuals' conduct on some occasions, we can make reasonable — although sometimes admittedly quite weak — inferences about their conduct on other occasions. Given this pervasive reliance on the premise that we can infer something about an individual's conduct on some occasions if we know how the individual behaved on other occasions, and given the very low FRE 401 threshold requirement for "relevance," courts have not been willing to reject all evidence of an alleged victim's prior sexual behavior as irrelevant to the issue of consent.

Indeed, before rape shield legislation such as FRE 412, the rape defendant's right to introduce reputation evidence about the victim's prior sexual conduct was regarded as an application of the general principle, codified in FRE 404(a)(2), that a defendant can introduce reputation (and under FRE 405(a), opinion) testimony to prove the victim's character to show action in conformity with that character trait by the victim. In other words, just as a homicide defendant claiming self-defense could introduce evidence of the victim's reputation for violence to suggest that the victim was the first aggressor, it was regarded as appropriate for the rape defendant claiming consent to introduce evidence of the victim's reputation for promiscuity or lack of chastity to suggest that the victim consented to the intercourse.

The theoretical justification for introducing evidence of specific instances of the victim's consensual sexual intercourse was more varied. Some courts claimed that the evidence was admissible to show the victim's "intent." Other courts admitted the evidence to "impeach" the credibility of the rape victim without bothering to explain what relationship existed between consensual sexual intercourse and general truth-telling. Still other courts frankly admitted that the specific acts evidence was being used in a propensity sense or that it was being used to show character. These latter courts took the position that there was an exception to the propensity-character rule for evidence of prior sexual conduct, an exception that one might analogize to the use of a criminal defendant's prior sexual misconduct in sexual assault prosecutions.

c. The Scope of FRE 412

FRE 412 excludes most evidence of an alleged victim's prior sexual behavior and sexual predisposition, even when it is relevant under the above-described propensity theory. We will deal with the reasons for this rejection of past practice in the next section. Here we want to focus on the actual application of FRE 412.

i. The Meaning of "Other Sexual Behavior" and "Sexual Predisposition." The exclusionary provisions in FRE 412(a) come into play only with respect to evidence of "other sexual behavior" and "sexual predisposition." The rule does not define either of these phrases, but the Advisory Committee's Note provides some examples. *Sexual behavior* "connotes all activities that involve actual physical conduct . . . or that imply sexual intercourse or conduct" — for example, "use of contraceptives," "birth of an illegitimate child," or "venereal disease." It also includes "activities of the mind, such as fantasies or dreams." *Sexual predisposition* includes "evidence that does not directly refer to sexual activities or thoughts but that the proponent believes may have a sexual connotation for the factfinder" — for example, evidence "relating to the alleged victim's mode of dress, speech, or lifestyle."

ii. The Applicability of FRE 412 When the Issue Is the Victim's Behavior on a Particular Occasion. If a defendant offers evidence for the purpose of showing the alleged victim's sexual conduct on a particular occasion, the theory of relevance presumably will be that the evidence shows something about the sexual predisposition (i.e., propensity) of the individual and that from this predisposition one can infer how the victim behaved on a particular occasion. Thus all evidence (whether in the form of reputation, opinion, or specific act) offered to show conduct on a particular occasion would be evidence of "sexual predisposition." If evidence of dressing in a provocative manner, telling lewd jokes, or soliciting sex were offered for this purpose, it would not be necessary to determine whether the evidence constituted "other sexual behavior." Such evidence, when offered to show the alleged victim's sexual conduct on a particular occasion, either is evidence of "sexual predisposition" or is irrelevant.

Such character evidence offered by a criminal defendant falls within the terms of FRE 404(a)(2) — opening the door to a "pertinent" character trait of the victim. However, as the Advisory Committee has explained, the pending amendment to FRE 404(a)(2) makes clear that character evidence relating to the victim's sexual predisposition offered to show conduct on a particular occasion "is governed by the more stringent provisions of Rule 412."

iii. The Applicability of FRE 412 in Other Contexts. The definitions of "other sexual behavior" and "sexual predisposition" become important when evidence of an alleged victim's prior activity is offered for some purpose other than to show sexual conduct on a particular occasion. Assume, for example, that a defendant is charged with rape and claims that the alleged victim has falsely accused him. To suggest a motive for the false accusation the defendant offers to testify that he had threatened to reveal to the alleged victim's spouse that the alleged victim had a secret job as a nude dancer and had solicited sex from him.

Do these activities constitute "sexual behavior"? Perhaps the answer is yes with respect to soliciting sex, for the Advisory Committee's Note indicates that sexual behavior includes "activities of the mind, such as fantasies or dreams." Nude dancing, on the other hand, seems to fall more readily into the Advisory Committee's description of "sexual predisposition" — activity that "may have a sexual connotation for the fact finder . . . [such as] mode of dress . . . or lifestyle." It is not clear, however, that evidence is governed by FRE 412 merely because it may suggest a sexual predisposition to the fact finder. If the activity in question is not "sexual behavior," it falls within the scope of FRE 412 only if it is "offered to prove any alleged victim's sexual predisposition." Does the language "To prove . . . sexual predisposition" apply only to evidence offered to show action in conformity with that predisposition, or does it apply to evidence that may suggest to the fact finder a sexual predisposition but that is offered for some other purpose? In our hypothetical, the defendant would argue that the evidence of nude dancing (and soliciting sex, if that activity is not "sexual behavior") is being offered to prove the alleged victim's motive for lying, not her sexual predisposition.

If nude dancing and soliciting sex fall within the FRE 412(a) general exclusionary rule for "other sexual behavior" or "sexual predisposition," the evidence is inadmissible unless it falls within one of the FRE 412(b) exceptions. If these activities do not fall within either of the prohibited categories of evidence, the only limits on the admissibility of the evidence are FRE 401-403.

iv. Hostile Work Environment Cases. There is at least one line of cases holding that FRE 412 applies to evidence suggesting a sexual predisposition even when the evidence is offered to prove something other than the alleged victim's action in conformity with the predisposition. In sex discrimination suits based on a hostile work environment, defendants frequently claim that the plaintiffs welcomed or created the environment that they claim is discriminatory. To establish this defense they have offered to show that the plaintiffs have behaved provocatively, used vulgar, sex-charged language, and engaged in other behavior that is similar to the activity about which they are complaining. Courts have held that FRE 412 applies to this evidence. Socks-Brunot v. Hirschvogel Inc., 184 F.R.D. 113 (S.D. Ohio 1999); Sheffield v. Hilltop Sand & Gravel Co., 895 F. Supp. 105, 108-109 (E.D. Va. 1995). According to *Socks-Brunot*:

> Evidence tending to prove both prior sexual conduct of the plaintiff and workplace conversations of the plaintiff is covered by Rule 412. Generally, evidence admissible for one purpose but inadmissible for another may be heard by a jury, pursuant to Federal Rule of Evidence 105. The general rule is inapplicable with regard to evidence covered by Rule 412. [184 F.R.D. at 119]

But cf. Morales-Evans v. Administrative Office of the Courts, 102 F. Supp. 2d 577, 581 n.7 (D.N.J. 2000) (evidence of prior sexual relationship with supervisor considered only "to provide context" for supervisor's allegedly inappropriate remark; "not... considered as evidence of sexual predisposition or behavior...; therefore this consideration does not run afoul of Rule 412").

v. The Admissibility of "Other Sexual Behavior" and "Sexual Predisposition" Evidence in Civil Cases. In hostile work environment and other civil cases the balancing test in FRE 412(b)(2) governs admissibility of evidence of an alleged victim's sexual behavior and predisposition. *This test differs from the FRE 403 balancing test in two respects.* First, it is a reverse FRE 403 test. In contrast to FRE 403, which favors admissibility, FRE 412(b)(2), by requiring that the probative value must substantially outweigh countervailing factors, favors exclusion. Wolak v. Spucci, 217 F.3d 157, 163 (2d Cir. 2000).

Second, one should probably interpret "unfair prejudice" in FRE 403 as referring only to prejudice against a party to the litigation. The Advisory Committee Note to FRE 403 states that "'[u]nfair prejudice'... means an undue tendency to suggest decision on an improper basis, commonly, though not necessarily, an emotional one." By contrast, FRE 412(b)(2) specifically refers to prejudice against a party *and* harm to the alleged victim. Consider, for example, an alleged rape victim's civil suit against a defendant who claims that the plaintiff consented to the intercourse. If the defendant offers evidence of prior consensual intercourse with the plaintiff, the court must weigh the probative value of this evidence against both the risk that the evidence may make the jury unfavorably disposed toward the plaintiff (FRE 403-type prejudice) and the harm to the victim (e.g., embarrassment, invasion of privacy) from the presentation of evidence about the victim's prior sexual activity.

vi. The Admissibility of "Other Sexual Behavior" and "Sexual Predisposition" Evidence in Criminal Cases. For criminal cases FRE 412(b)(1) delineates only three exceptions to the general rule of exclusion. The first two exceptions are quite narrow: evidence of (a) the victim's sexual behavior with third persons to suggest that they may be the source of semen or injury and (b) the victim's sexual behavior with the defendant to suggest consent. As a result, these exceptions may not encompass all of the situations in which, in fairness, a court should permit a criminal defendant to introduce evidence of an alleged victim's sexual behavior or predisposition. The rule acknowledges this possibility by providing in the third exception for admission in those cases in which "exclusion... would violate the constitutional rights of the defendant." This language is a reference (1) to the due process doctrine that a criminal defendant has the constitutional right to present a defense and (2) to the Sixth Amendment confrontation clause right to confront and cross-examine witnesses. While these rights do not allow criminal defendants to present evidence and cross-examine witnesses in complete disregard of the rules of evidence, the Supreme Court has held that rules of evidence cannot unduly restrict these rights. There was, of course, no need to include the third exception in the rule. The Constitution is the supreme law of the land. If the defendant has a constitutional right to introduce the evidence, no non-constitutional rule can justify exclusion.

If the defendant's evidence falls within one of the first two exceptions, it is not automatically admissible. Rather, the evidence must be "otherwise admissible under these rules." Consider, for example, a rape case in which the defendant claims that the alleged victim consented to the sexual intercourse. To prove consent, the defendant offers to testify that on one occasion three years ago he had consensual sex with the victim. This evidence falls within the FRE 412(b)(1)(B) exception, but the court retains discretion to exclude the evidence on FRE 403 grounds.

vii.   The Notice Requirement.   The notice and hearing requirement in FRE 412(c) is more demanding than any other notice requirement in the Federal Rules. Cf. FRE 404(b), FRE 413-415. Any notice requirement has the potential for increasing the thoughtfulness of the decision-making process simply because it gives the parties time to prepare their arguments. A stringent notice requirement may have the additional impact of deterring litigants from pressing weak claims.

3.   Elaboration of FRE 412

a.   *The Rationale for a Rule Excluding Evidence of Prior Sexual Behavior and Sexual Predisposition*

There are substantial reasons to be concerned about the liberal admissibility of an alleged sexual assault victim's sexual history. The ability to introduce evidence of the victim's sexual history gives the defendant the opportunity to try to make the victim and the victim's character the focal point of the litigation. The prospect of a degrading and humiliating examination by defense counsel may discourage many victims from cooperating with prosecutors, or even reporting sexual assaults in the first place. One cannot, however, attribute the humiliation and degradation of rape victims solely — or perhaps even primarily — to liberal rules of admissibility for prior sexual conduct. Disbelief of, disrespect for, and insensitivity toward rape victims has existed throughout the criminal justice system. Susan Brownmiller, Against Our Will: Men, Women and Rape 408-420 (1976); Colleen A. Ward, Attitudes Toward Rape: Feminist and Social Psychological Perspectives (1995); Morrison Torrey, When Will We Be Believed? Rape Myths and the Idea of a Fair Trial in Rape Prosecutions, 24 U.C. Davis L. Rev. 1013 (1991).

In cases that are tried, there may be disputes about whether the victim in fact engaged in any of the conduct that the defendant wishes to attribute to the victim. In addition, there are the risks that the jury may overestimate the probative value of the prior sexual history evidence on the question of consent or be prejudiced against the victim because of the sexual conduct. There is evidence that juries may too readily acquit defendants because they disbelieve a female victim or believe that "she got what she deserved." Harry Kalven and Hans Zeisel, The American Jury 249-254 (1966); David P. Bryden and Sonja Lengnick, Rape in the Criminal Justice System, 87 J. Crim. L. and Criminology 1194 (1997); Aviva Orenstein, No Bad Men!: A Feminist Analysis of Character Evidence in Rape Trials, 49 Hastings L.J. 663 (1998); Beverly J. Ross, Does Diversity in Legal Scholarship Make a Difference?: A Look at the Laws of Rape, 100 Dick. L. Rev. 795 (1966); Torrey, supra. Because of prevailing racism, class biases, and sexual stereotypes, this phenomenon is particularly likely to occur when the victim is a woman of color or a poor woman or when she was acquainted with the man who raped her. Gary D. LaFree, Rape and Criminal Justice: The Social Construction of Sexual Assault 219-220; G. Chezia Carraway, Violence Against Women of Color, 43 Stan. L. Rev. 1301 (1991); Kimberle Crenshaw, Mapping the Margins: Intersectionality, Identity Politics, and Violence Against Women of Color, 43 Stan. L. Rev. 1241 (1993); Lois Pineau, Date Rape: A Feminist Analysis, 8 Law & Philosophy 217 (1989);

Dorothy E. Roberts, Rape, Violence, and Women's Autonomy, 69 Chi.-Kent L. Rev. 359 (1993).

Finally, there is the problem that prior sexual history will frequently be of no more than marginal relevance to the question of whether the victim consented on the occasion in question. Indeed, as we noted earlier, one of the principal reasons that the rules of evidence severely restrict the use of character to show action in conformity with character is that the strength of the inference from character to action on a particular occasion is almost invariably weak. We can think of no reason to believe that the inference from prior consensual intercourse — especially if the activity is with third persons — to consent with the defendant is a particularly strong propensity inference.

In theory, FRE 403 and its common law counterparts might have been adequate devices for taking into account these concerns that warrant caution in the use of evidence of a rape victim's prior sexual conduct. However, the policy of protecting a rape victim from humiliation is not, strictly speaking, the sort of concern that readily fits among the FRE 403 dangers. Moreover, in practice, many individuals perceived — correctly, we believe — that courts were often too willing to admit marginally probative, highly prejudicial evidence of the victim's prior sexual activity in rape and other sexual assault prosecutions. The response to this perception has been the adoption of "rape shield" rules or statutes such as FRE 412 that specifically address and limit the situations in which evidence of a victim's prior sexual conduct may be admitted.

Since rape shield provisions are now common, it is difficult to assess how liberal judges would have been in admitting evidence of victims' past sexual behavior and sexual predisposition in the absence of such rules. Some might argue that recent increased public awareness and concern with sexual assault crimes, e.g., the enactment of FRE 413-415, make rape shield provisions less necessary today than when they were first enacted. Others firmly believe, as we suggested earlier, that attitudes stereotyping women as sexual objects and as provoking sexual contact in innocent situations will find their way into the jury box. From this perspective, rape shield provisions continue to be vitally important both as devices for contributing to accurate factfinding and as symbolic affirmations of the independence and individuality of women.

b.   FRE 412 and the Constitutional Rights to Present Evidence and to Confront and Cross-examine Witnesses

As we noted earlier, the Supreme Court has relied on both the due process clause and the Sixth Amendment confrontation clause to hold that criminal defendants sometimes have the constitutional right to present exculpatory evidence that would violate some nonconstitutional evidence rule. We explore here the development and application of these constitutional rights.

i.   Chambers v. Mississippi, 410 U.S. 284 (1973).   The leading Supreme Court case dealing with the due process prong of the constitutionally required evidence doctrine is Chambers v. Mississippi. Chambers was charged with murdering a police officer, and there was conflicting testimony about whether Chambers or McDonald was the murderer. McDonald had made a sworn statement to Chambers's attorneys in which he admitted the killing, but before the trial McDonald repudiated his confession. At trial Chambers called McDonald as a witness and elicited the confession. On cross-examination the prosecution established that McDonald had repudiated the confession. The court would not permit Chambers to try to undermine the credibility of his own witness by challenging McDonald about the repudiation. Chambers then sought to introduce the testimony of three witnesses that at different times, all before the sworn statement, McDonald had confessed to them that he killed the police officer. The trial court excluded this evidence because it was hearsay. In reversing Chambers's conviction the Court stated:

> The hearsay statements that were involved in this case were originally made and subsequently offered at trial under circumstances that provided considerable assurance of their reliability. . . .
>
> Few rights are more fundamental than that of an accused to present witnesses in his own defense. . . .
>
> We conclude that the exclusion of this critical evidence, coupled with the State's refusal to permit Chambers to cross-examine McDonald, denied him a trial in accord with traditional and fundamental standards of due process. In reaching this judgment, we establish no new principles of constitutional law. Nor does our holding signal any diminution in the respect traditionally accorded to the States in the establishment and implementation of their own criminal trial rules and procedures. Rather, we hold quite simply that under the facts and circumstances of this case the ruling of the trial court deprived Chambers of a fair trial. [Id. at 300, 302-303.]

   ii.   Davis v. Alaska, 415 U.S. 308 (1974).   A similar rationale underlies Davis v. Alaska, the Supreme Court's leading confrontation clause case upholding the defendant's constitutional right to cross-examine witnesses in a manner that violates state evidentiary rules. Davis was charged with stealing a safe from an Anchorage bar. The prosecution's case consisted primarily of (1) scientific evidence suggesting that particles found in the defendant's car could have come from the safe and (2) the testimony of Richard Green that shortly after the theft he observed the defendant and his car at the place where the safe was eventually discovered. The defendant sought to introduce evidence that Green, who lived near the place where the safe was found, was at the time on probation for burglary as a result of an adjudication of delinquency. This evidence, the defense argued, was relevant to show Green's bias — that is, his interest in deflecting suspicion to someone other than himself because of a fear that his probation might be revoked. Relying on a state rule mandating the confidentiality of juvenile adjudications, the trial court ruled that the defense could make no reference to the adjudication or the probation. The Supreme Court reversed:

> The Sixth Amendment to the Constitution guarantees the right of an accused in a criminal case "to be confronted with the witnesses against him." This right is secured for defendants in state as well as federal criminal proceedings. . . . Confrontation means more than being allowed to confront the witness physically. 'Our cases construing the [confrontation] clause hold that a primary interest secured by it is the right of cross-examination.' . . .
>
> We cannot accept the Alaska Supreme Court's conclusion that the cross-examination that was permitted defense counsel was adequate to develop the issue of bias properly to the jury. While counsel was permitted to ask Green *whether* he was biased, counsel was unable to make a record from which to argue *why* Green might have been biased. . . . [I]t seems clear to us that . . . defense counsel should have been permitted to expose to the jury the facts from which jurors, as the sole triers of fact and credibility, could appropriately draw inferences relating to the reliability of the witness. Petitioner was thus denied the right of effective cross-examination. . . .

The claim is made that the State has an important interest in protecting the anonymity of juvenile offenders.... The State argues that exposure of a juvenile's record of delinquency would likely cause impairment of rehabilitative goals of the juvenile correctional procedures. This exposure, it is argued, might encourage the juvenile offender to commit further acts of delinquency, or cause the juvenile offender to lose employment opportunities....

We do not and need not challenge the State's interest as a matter of its own policy in the administration of criminal justice to seek to preserve the anonymity of a juvenile offender.... Here, however, ... [s]erious damage to the strength of the State's case would have been a real possibility had petitioner been allowed to pursue this line of inquiry. In this setting we conclude that the right of confrontation is paramount. [Id. at 315, 318-319 (emphasis in original).]

iii. Olden v. Kentucky, 488 U.S. 227 (1988).

In Olden v. Kentucky, the Supreme Court considered the applicability of *Davis* to a case in which the trial judge had excluded evidence of the alleged victim's prior sexual conduct. Starla Matthews, the alleged victim, testified that the defendant, in the presence of his friend Harris, kidnapped, raped, and sodomized her. Then, at her request, the defendant and Harris drove her to a location near the home of Bill Russell. The defendant claimed that Matthews had consented to their sexual activity.

Although Matthews and Russell were both married to and living with other people at the time of the incident, they were apparently involved in an extramarital relationship. By the time of trial the two were living together, having separated from their respective spouses. Petitioner's theory of the case was that Matthews concocted the rape story to protect her relationship with Russell, who would have grown suspicious upon seeing her disembark from Harris' car. In order to demonstrate Matthews' motive to lie, it was crucial, petitioner contended, that he be allowed to introduce evidence of Matthews' and Russell's current cohabitation. Over petitioner's vehement objections, the trial court nonetheless granted the prosecutor's motion in limine [to] keep all evidence of Matthews' and Russell's living arrangement from the jury. Moreover, when the defense attempted to cross-examine Matthews about her living arrangements, after she claimed during direct examination that she was living with her mother, the trial court sustained the prosecutor's objection. [Id. at 229-230.]

The jury acquitted Harris of all involvement in the incidents and convicted the defendant of only sodomy. The Kentucky Court of Appeals affirmed.

By way of explanation, the court stated: "[T]here were the undisputed facts of race; Matthews was white and Russell was black. For the trial court to have admitted into evidence testimony that Matthews and Russell were living together at the time of the trial may have created extreme prejudice against Matthews." [Id. at 230-231.]

The Supreme Court reversed:

While a trial court may, of course, impose reasonable limits on defense counsel's inquiry into the potential bias of a prosecution witness, to take account of such factors as "harassment, prejudice, confusion of the issues, the witness' safety, or interrogation that [would be] repetitive or only marginally relevant," ... the limitation here was beyond reason. Speculation as to the effect of jurors' racial biases cannot justify exclusion of cross-examination with such strong potential to demonstrate the falsity of Matthews' testimony. [Id. at 232.]

iv. The Implications of *Chambers, Davis,* and *Olden* for Rape Shield Provisions.   One principle that the Court stressed in *Chambers, Davis,* and *Olden* is the general right of the states to regulate their own procedures (including evidence rules). Nonetheless, those procedures must sometimes give way to a defendant's constitutional rights even when the procedures have laudatory goals. Thus the defendant's right to present a reasonable defense took precedence over the state's hearsay policy in *Chambers*, the state's confidentiality rule for juvenile records in *Davis*, and the state's interest in keeping prejudicial information from the jury in *Olden*. Similarly, in some cases the defendant's right to present a defense may override an evidentiary rape shield rule, despite its laudatory purpose and general reasonableness.

A second common principle in the cases is that the importance of the evidence is what triggers the defendant's constitutional right. The Court referred to the evidence as "critical" in *Chambers*. In *Davis* the Court stated that evidence made a "serious challenge" to the state's case a "real possibility," and in *Olden* the Court emphasized that the evidence had a "strong potential" for demonstrating that a key prosecution witness was lying.

Given the abstract nature of these principles — local control over rules of evidence and the defendant's right to present evidence — and the very fact-specific way in which they may clash with each other, it should not be surprising that the contours of the constitutionally required evidence doctrine are imprecise. Indeed, because the facts are important, we encourage you to read *Chambers, Davis,* and *Olden* in their entirety. Nonetheless, there are two generalizations that one can fairly make about the case law involving constitutional challenges to the exclusion of evidence of a victim's prior sexual conduct or sexual predisposition. First, the vast majority of the challenges are unsuccessful. Ex Parte Dennis, 730 So. 2d 138 (Ala. 1999) (collecting cases). Second, probably the most common type of successful constitutional challenge occurs in cases like *Olden*, in which the defendant seeks to introduce the evidence to impeach the alleged victim by showing bias. United States v. Platero, 72 F.3d 806 (10th Cir. 1995); Commonwealth v. Black, 337 Pa. Super. 548, 487 A.2d 396 (1985). Courts, however, have admitted evidence of an alleged victim's prior sexual conduct for other purposes. Commonwealth v. Wall, 606 A.2d 449 (Pa. Super. 1992) (defendant has constitutional right to present evidence showing alleged victim has sufficient knowledge to have fabricated charges); State v. Jacques, 558 A.2d 706 (Me. 1989) (same); People v. Slovinski, 166 Mich. App. 158, 420 N.W.2d 145 (1988) (constitutional right to present evidence that alleged victim was prostitute when defendant claims that incident giving rise to charge was act of prostitution); Cox v. State, 102 Nev. 253, 721 P.2d 358 (1986) (in response to prosecution evidence that alleged victim was born-again Christian who worked as a high school secretary, defendant has constitutional right to show alleged victim applied for "escort's license"); State v. LaClair, 121 N.H. 743, 433 A.2d 1326 (1981) (constitutional right to introduce alleged victim's inconsistent statement about prior sexual activity).

c. Two Approaches to the Exclusion of Other Sexual Behavior and Sexual Predisposition Evidence

FRE 412 presents an interesting example of two quite different approaches to the problem of regulating the admissibility of sexual behavior and sexual predisposition evidence. In civil cases, where there is no established doctrine of constitutionally required evidence, Congress chose to rely exclusively on a balancing test that favors exclusion. By contrast, in criminal cases, where the constitutionally required evidence doctrine provides what is in effect a safety valve for an overly strict exclusionary rule, Congress created only two specific, very narrow exceptions to a general rule of exclusion.

Do you think it is desirable to have an evidentiary rule that tends to force courts to resolve issues of admissibility in terms of constitutional law? In any event, are the criteria for determining whether evidence is constitutionally required likely to be applied consistently from case to case?

Particularly in light of your analysis and discussion of the following problems, consider whether it would be preferable to have a general balancing test for both criminal and civil cases. If your answer is no, are there any additional exceptions that you would add to FRE 412(b)(2)?

d. Rape Shield Rules and the Defendant's Right to Testify

When a criminal defendant seeks to testify about a rape victim's prior sexual conduct, there may be a conflict between the jurisdiction's rape shield rule and the constitutional right to testify, a right closely related to the due process and confrontation clause rights that we have been discussing. The Seventh Circuit dealt with such a situation in Stephens v. Miller, 13 F.3d 998 (7th Cir. 1994) (en banc), a case that generated seven opinions. We urge you to read *Stephens* and to consider (1) whether the court resolved the constitutional issue properly and (2) what implications *Stephens* may have for the questions we raised at the end of subsection c, supra.

e. FRE 412 and Discovery in Civil Cases

The prohibition in FRE 412 raises recurring issues in certain civil cases, particularly sexual harassment cases, about the scope of pretrial discovery into, for example, the sexual behavior or predisposition of a plaintiff alleging sexual harassment. It is a black-letter principle of civil procedure that the scope of discovery is broader than the scope of evidentiary admissibility at trial. The Federal Rules of Civil Procedure require parties to respond fully to discovery requests that are "reasonably calculated to lead to the discovery of admissible evidence." Fed. R. Civ. P. 26. The prospect of compelled disclosure of private or embarrassing information in discovery raises many of the same problems — deterring plaintiffs from filing meritorious claims or witnesses from coming forward — addressed by FRE 412, but FRE 412 deals expressly only with admission of evidence at trial, not disclosure in pretrial discovery. For a compelling instance of invasive discovery into female plaintiffs' sexual histories in a sexual harassment case, see Jenson v. Eveleth Taconite Co., 130 F. 3d 1287 (8th Cir. 1997); Clara Bingham and Laura Leedy Gansler, Class Action: The Story of Lois Jenson and the Landmark Case That Changed Sexual Harassment Law (2002).

Courts have held, in the context of objections to discovery requests or motions for protective orders, that discovery requests into a plaintiff's sexual behavior are governed by Fed. R. Civ. P. 26(c). However, because that provision expressly incorporates the ultimate admissibility of evidence as a benchmark, it is clear that FRE 412 should be taken into account in deciding discovery motions on these issues. See Sanchez v. Zabihi, 166 F.R.D. 500, 510-02 (D.N.M. 1996). Indeed, the Advisory Committee

Note to proposed FRE 412 states that "in order not to undermine the rationale of Rule 412, however, courts should enter appropriate orders pursuant to Fed. R. Civ. P. 26(c) to protect the victim against unwarranted inquiries and to ensure confidentiality. Courts should presumptively issue protective orders barring discovery unless the party seeking discovery makes a showing that the evidence sought to be discovered would be relevant[.]" Arguably, the party seeking discovery should also show that the evidence would not be barred by FRE 412.

KEY POINTS

1. FRE 412 severely limits the extent to which a party can introduce evidence of an alleged victim's sexual predisposition or sexual behavior in both criminal and civil cases.

2. FRE 412(a) and (b)(1) prohibit a criminal defendant from introducing such evidence unless it is (1) specific instances of sexual behavior with a third person offered to show the source of semen, injury, or other physical evidence; (2) specific instances of sexual behavior with the defendant offered to show consent; or (3) constitutionally required evidence.

3. Constitutionally required evidence refers to the due process and confrontation clause rights to present evidence developed in cases like *Chambers*, *Davis*, and *Olden* and to the closely related right of a criminal defendant to testify.

4. In civil cases, evidence of an alleged victim's sexual predisposition or behavior is admissible only if it satisfies the FRE 412(b)(2) reverse FRE 403 balancing test that takes into account both prejudice to a party and harm to the alleged victim.

PROBLEMS

5.51. Return to Problem 5.48 at page 305. To prove that Davis in fact consented to sexual intercourse, the defense seeks to admit the following evidence:

(a) testimony from Corbin that he and Davis had consensual sexual relations on several prior occasions;

(b) testimony from three men that they had met Davis at bars and had consensual sex with her;

(c) testimony that Davis has a reputation in the community for promiscuity;

(d) testimony from Sue Smith, a friend of Corbin, that at the first bar on the night in question Davis told Smith that she was attracted to Corbin and would like to have sexual relations with him.

Should this evidence be admitted prior to the adoption of FRE 412? After its adoption, assuming the defense has complied with the procedural requirements of FRE 412(c)?

5.52. In Problem 5.51 assume that Corbin claims that he did not have the requisite mental state for rape because he reasonably (although perhaps mistakenly) believed that Davis had consented to sexual intercourse. Should any of the evidence be admissible to support his claim prior to the adoption of FRE 412? After its adoption?

5.53. The defendant, a successful banker with no known history of sexual misconduct, is accused of sexually assaulting the teenage daughter of his next door neighbor. He claims that she is falsely accusing him because he threatened to reveal to her parents that she and the defendant's son were having a sexual affair. FRE 412 is applicable. Should the court sustain the prosecution's objection to the defendant's evidence about the alleged victim's sexual affair?

5.54. Dawkins, age 23, has been charged with forcibly raping M.M., a 15-year-old girl. Dawkins claims that he believed M.M. was 18 and that she consented. M.M. will testify about the rape. The medical evidence is inconclusive on the question of whether there had been forcible rape. The prosecution wants to offer evidence that two years ago Dawkins forcibly raped his 12-year-old niece and claimed that she had consented. Dawkins wants to offer evidence that last year M.M. charged Craig Wilson with rape. Assume, alternately, (a) that Wilson is unavailable to testify, (b) that, if permitted, Wilson will testify and deny the rape, and (c) that, if permitted, Wilson and other witnesses will present compelling evidence that the rape charge against Wilson was false. FRE 412-414 are applicable. How should the court rule?

5.55. Frances Meyer, a police officer, has brought sex discrimination hostile work environment action against the police chief, the mayor, and the town of Pleasantville. Her claim includes allegations that pornographic magazines and wall posters were continually on display at the police station despite her objections; that the police chief would regularly relate in her presence the plots of pornographic movies; that he pinched her buttocks; that he continually told her she was "really missing something" by not having sex with him; and that he used lewd language in her presence. The defense is based on the theory that Meyer welcomed or encouraged this type of behavior. For this purpose the defense offers evidence that Meyer herself told lewd jokes at the police station; that she regularly watched pornographic movies at home; that she was having a very public affair with a married man; that she would talk at the police station about her sexual fantasies; and that on several occasions she had gone to a strip club. FRE 412 is applicable. Should some or all of the defense evidence be admissible?

5.56. Bryan, a 25-year-old super star basketball player, is charged with felony sexual assault on a 19-year-old woman, Mary, who worked at the front desk in a resort hotel where Bryan was staying. Bryan admits having sex with Mary in his hotel room but asserts it was consensual. Mary asserts that Bryan forced her to have sexual relations and that she said "no" several times. There are no other witnesses to these events.

Mary received a medical examination approximately 15 hours after the encounter with Bryan. The exam revealed some internal injuries that the prosecution claims are consistent with the use of force during sexual relations, although the report of a prosecution expert states that the injuries could also be consistent with consensual sex. Bryan's T-shirt was found to have a small stain of Mary's blood on it. Are the following items of evidence admissible?

(1) In its case in chief, the prosecution offers the testimony of three women as follows: W_1 says that 10 years ago, she and Bryan were "making out" when he tore her blouse off and fondled her; W_2 says that in college she and Bryan were dating and having consensual sex but that several times he was very aggressive and intimidated her into having sexual relations when she didn't want to; W_3 says that she met Bryan in a hotel a year ago, flirted with him, and then went to his hotel room where he forced her to have sex.

(2) The defense will ask several witnesses about Mary's sexual activities in the three days before her hospital examination. Their answers will reveal several

sexual encounters, possibly including one (based on DNA evidence) after the events with Bryan and before Mary's hospital exam.

(3) For the defense, hospital records showing that Mary was treated for an intentional overdose of a prescribed antidepressant medication one month before the encounter with Bryan, which the defense claims was an "attention-seeking" suicide attempt. (The court would first have to hold that Mary waived her right to keep her medical records private.)

CHAPTER SIX

THE OTHER RELEVANCE RULES

At the outset of Chapter Five we noted that the Federal Rules — like the common law — have a variety of rules, sometimes referred to as "relevance rules," which exclude concededly relevant evidence. In Chapter Five our concern was the relevance rules regulating character evidence. Here our primary focus will be on relevance rules that make evidence inadmissible to prove fault or liability, but that permit such evidence for other purposes. FRE 407-409, 411. We conclude the chapter with a consideration of FRE 410, which makes inadmissible certain evidence relating to guilty pleas, and with a discussion of a subject for which there is no specific Federal Rule — the doctrine of curative admissibility.

A. INADMISSIBLE TO PROVE "NEGLIGENCE," "CULPABLE CONDUCT," OR "LIABILITY"

The Federal Rules preclude evidence of subsequent remedial measures (FRE 407), compromises and offers of compromise (FRE 408), payment of medical and other similar expenses (FRE 409), and liability insurance (FRE 411) to prove fault or liability. Keep in mind that these rules you are about to examine here in Section A do not exclude evidence altogether. Rather, they prohibit the proponent from offering the evidence only to prove liability or fault. For example, FRE 408, which prohibits offer of compromise evidence for this purpose, acknowledges that offers of compromise may be admissible for other purposes, such as showing the bias of a witness. Thus, as was true with the character evidence rules we examined in Chapter Five — and as you will see is true with the impeachment and hearsay rules we examine in Chapters Seven and Eight — your analysis of admissibility must always begin with the question of relevance: *What* is the proponent of the evidence trying to prove; *what* is the proponent's theory of relevance? Only after you answer this question will you be able to apply a relevance rule.

If the answer to the relevance inquiry is that there is both a permissible and an impermissible purpose for which the proponent may wish to offer the evidence, the ultimate admissibility of the evidence will depend on the application of FRE 403: Is the probative value of the evidence for the permissible purpose substantially outweighed by the risk that the jury may consider the evidence for the impermissible purpose? If the answer is no (i.e., if the answer is that the evidence is admissible), the party against whom the evidence is admitted will be entitled to a limiting instruction pursuant to FRE 105.

1.   FRE 407

FRE 407. SUBSEQUENT REMEDIAL MEASURES

When, after an injury or harm allegedly caused by an event, measures are taken that, if taken previously, would have made the injury or harm less likely to occur, evidence of the subsequent measures is not admissible to prove negligence, culpable conduct, a defect in a product, a defect in a product's design, or a need for a warning or instruction. This rule does not require the exclusion of evidence of subsequent measures when offered for another purpose, such as proving ownership, control, or feasibility of precautionary measures, if controverted, or impeachment.

2.   Interpretation and Illustration of FRE 407

a.   The Exclusionary Mandate

   i.   The Inference of Negligence or Culpable Conduct.   When a person takes steps to alter a condition or object that caused an injury so as to make future injury less likely, one possible inference to draw from the remedial action is that the person who made the alteration believed that the object or condition before the alteration posed an unreasonable risk of injury. If we know that the person responsible for the object or condition has this belief, it is more likely that the object or condition did create an unreasonable risk of injury than if we knew nothing about the person's belief. Indeed, pursuant to this theory of relevance, when a party to an action takes subsequent remedial action, it is the equivalent of an admission of negligence or culpable conduct. Diagram 6-1 illustrates this reasoning.

   ii.   Products Liability Actions.   Prior to a 1997 amendment, FRE 407's exclusionary provision extended only to evidence offered to prove "negligence or culpable conduct," and it was unclear whether this language applied to subsequent remedial measure evidence in products liability actions. Compare Prentiss & Carlisle v. Koehring-Waterous, 972 F.2d 6 (1st Cir. 1992) (evidence not admissible) with Bizzle v. McKesson Corp., 961 F.2d 719 (8th Cir. 1992) (evidence admissible; proof of defect is not proof of negligence or culpable conduct). Now FRE 407 makes it clear that its exclusionary mandate extends to subsequent remedial measure evidence offered to prove product defects.
   As a matter of consistency and logical relevance, the extension of FRE 407 to products liability actions is appropriate. Typically, there is a notion of fault or culpability associated with the concept of defect. Defective products are ones that are more

Diagram 6-1

EF $\longrightarrow$ IF$_1$ $\longrightarrow$ IF$_2$ $\longrightarrow$ FOC $\longrightarrow$ EE

EF	IF$_1$	IF$_2$	FOC	EE
Eyewitness testifies that, after an accident in which a toy rifle discharged, the manufacturer designed a safety catch for the toy	Manufacturer did design a safety catch for a toy rifle after an accident	Manufacturer believed that the toy rifle created an unreasonable risk of injury without the safety catch	The toy rifle did create an unreasonable risk of injury without the safety catch	The manufacturer was negligent in producing the toy rifle without the safety catch

dangerous or less fit for their intended use than one might reasonably expect them to be; such products exist because designers, manufacturers or other persons made decisions about the products that were less reasonable than they could have been; and failing to measure up to the standard of reasonableness is acting culpably.

Given this understanding of "defect," the subsequent remedial measure evidence is relevant in a products liability case in precisely the same way that it is relevant in a negligence action: From the remedial measure we infer that the individual taking the remedial action believes that the product was not as safe as it might reasonably have been, and from this belief we infer that the product indeed was not as safe as it might reasonably have been. See Diagram 6-1. Indeed, if there is no notion of culpability associated with defect, subsequent remedial measure evidence is simply not relevant to prove defect. (Regardless of whether the underlying action is for negligence or strict liability, the evidence may be relevant and admissible for some other purpose — for example, to show that a different design was feasible. See subsection b, infra.)

iii.   Activities That May Be Subsequent Remedial Measures.   A subsequent remedial measure is any action that a person takes after an event to reduce the likelihood of an event's reoccurrence. It may include, for example, sending a memorandum to employees urging them to observe safety regulations, First Security Bank v. Union Pac. R. Co., 152 F.3d 877 (8th Cir. 1998) (admonishing employees about location of rail cars in relation to crossing); altering the design of a product, Flaminio v. Honda Motor Co. 733 F.2d 463 (7th Cir. 1984) (motorcycle design); repairing or altering the condition of property, Knight v. Otis Elevator Co, 596 F.2d 84 (3d Cir. 1979) (placing "guards" around elevator buttons); disciplining or firing an individual whose alleged negligence was responsible for an accident, Specht v. Jensen, 863 F.2d 700 (10th Cir. 1988) (disciplining police officers for violation of Fourth Amendment); Hull v. Chevron U.S.A., Inc. 812 F.2d 584 (10th Cir. 1987) (firing forklift operator following accident); sending a recall notice, Chase v. General Motors Corp., 856 F.2d 17 (4th Cir. 1988) (recall of cars manufactured before design change); changing rules or regulations, Ford v. Schmidt, 577 F.2d 408 (7th Cir. 1978) (change in prison regulations); or posting warning signs, In re Joint Asbestos Litigation, 995 F.2d 343 (2d Cir. 1993) (posting warning sign on asbestos product).

iv.   The Effectiveness of the Remedial Action.   Courts rarely focus on the question whether a remedial measure "if taken previously, would [in fact] have made the injury or harm less likely to occur." For example, courts readily accept that firing an employee can be a subsequent remedial measure within the meaning of FRE 407 without examining whether the action is likely to reduce the chance of future accidents. There is, however, precedent for the proposition that FRE 407 does not apply to investigations, which are not "remedial measures" but only "initial steps toward ascertaining whether any remedial measures are called for." Fasanaro v. Mooney Aircraft Corp., 687 F. Supp. 482, 487 (N.D. Cal. 1988). Compare Rocky Mountain Helicopters, Inc. v. Bell Helicopters, 805 F.2d 907, 918 (10th Cir. 1986) (investigative reports not subsequent remedial measures) with Maddox v. Los Angeles, 792 F.2d 1408,1417 (9th Cir. 1986) ("investigation and measures taken were remedial measures").

v.   The Timing of the Remedial Action.   For evidence of a remedial measure to be inadmissible under FRE 407, it must occur "after an injury or harm caused by an event." The purpose of this language, according to the Advisory Committee Note, is to make it clear that "the rule applies only to changes made after the occurrence that produced the damages giving rise to the action." Thus, if the defendant changed a product design after the plaintiff was injured, FRE 407 would apply to prevent the plaintiff from introducing evidence of the design change to show defect. On the other hand, if the defendant took the remedial action subsequent to the injuries of several other people but prior to the plaintiff's injury, FRE 407 would not preclude admissibility of the design change. Trull v. Volkswagon, Inc., 187 F.3d 88 (1st Cir. 1999); Chase v. General Motors Corp., 856 F.2d 17 (4th Cir. 1988).

vi. Remedial Action Taken Prior to Plaintiff's Injury and FRE 403. To what extent should FRE 403 be a basis for excluding remedial action evidence to show culpable conduct or defect when the remedial action was taken prior to the plaintiff's injury? Consider Bogosian v. Mercedes-Benz, Inc., 104 F.3d 472 (1st Cir. 1997), where the plaintiff was injured when the vehicle she had parked rolled backward and ran over her left ankle. She offered evidence that subsequent to the manufacture of her car, but before the accident, Mercedes-Benz began installing in its vehicles a park ignition interlock system, which prevents a driver from removing the ignition keys if the automatic transmission is not securely in the park position. After noting that FRE 407 did not bar such evidence to prove defect and that there was no other issue, such as feasibility, for which the evidence was relevant, the court upheld the trial judge's FRE 403 exclusionary decision. To have admitted the evidence would have "risked the danger that 'jurors too readily equate subsequent design modifications with admissions of prior defective design.'" Id. at 481.

Why is this a danger? Is the court implying that jurors would inevitably overestimate the probative value of such evidence as an admission of design defect? Is the holding in any event consistent with the drafters' intent to limit the FRE 407 exclusionary rule to remedial measures occurring after the event giving rise to the litigation? Other courts have not been so reluctant to admit pre-"event" remedial measures. In re Air Crash Disaster, 86 F.3d 498, 531 (6th Cir. 1996); Chase v. General Motors Corp., supra at 22.

On the other hand, why should it matter in the first place whether the remedial action is taken after the plaintiff's injury or after some third person's earlier injury? Are not the reasons for exclusion virtually the same in either case? See Kelly v. Crown Equip. Co., 970 F.2d 1273 (3d Cir. 1992).

b. Permissible Uses of Subsequent Remedial Measure Evidence

FRE 407 makes it clear that subsequent remedial measure evidence may be admissible for other purposes. As is the case with FRE 404(b), the list of permissible other purposes is not exclusive. Subject to FRE 403 and other exclusionary rules, subsequent remedial measure evidence may be admissible for *any* purpose other than to show negligence or culpable conduct.

The purposes listed in the second sentence of FRE 407 are the permissible purposes for which subsequent remedial measure evidence is most likely to be relevant. For example, the fact that the defendant repaired a staircase suggests that the defendant was the owner of the building containing the staircase or at least that the defendant, rather than somebody else, had control over the staircase and was responsible for keeping it in good order. Cf. Lee v. E.I. Dupont, 249 F.3d 362 (5th Cir. 2001) (subsequent design change to scaffold admissible against defendant to show that defendant rather than plaintiff's employer was responsible for maintaining the scaffold). If a defendant testifies that the staircase was in good condition at the time of the accident, the fact that the defendant had repaired or authorized the repair of the staircase is relevant to impeach the defendant's credibility: Making or authorizing the repair seems inconsistent with the witness's testimony that the staircase was safe at the time of the accident. Cf. Anderson v. Malloy, 700 F.2d 1208 (8th Cir. 1983) (in rape victim's negligence action against motel operator, defendant testified that safety chains and peep holes on doors would only provide false sense of security and that everything necessary for security had been done; plaintiff permitted to show subsequent installation of safety chains and peep holes both to show feasibility and to impeach defendant). Finally, as we suggested previously, taking subsequent remedial action rebuts a defendant's claim that it was not feasible to maintain the staircase in a safer condition. Cf. Dixon v. International Harvester Co., 754 F.2d 573 (10th Cir. 1985) (defendant claimed additional protective metal on logging vehicle not feasible because it would impair vision; evidence of subsequent installation of protective metal on similar vehicles admissible).

c.   The "If Controverted" Requirement

Despite the somewhat ambiguous placement of the "if controverted" phrase in the second sentence of FRE 407, both the Advisory Committee Note to FRE 407 (in its second paragraph) and the existing case law, Hull v. Chevron U.S.A., Inc., 812 F.2d 584 (10th Cir. 1987), indicate that the "if controverted" requirement applies to *all* of the permissible uses of subsequent remedial measure evidence. Thus, one should read the "if controverted" phrase as governing the offer of subsequent remedial measure evidence not only to prove feasibility but also to prove other purposes "such as . . . ownership [or] control." By the terms of the rule, the "if controverted" phrase does not apply to evidence offered for impeachment. There is no need for it to do so. Impeachment evidence is evidence offered to undermine the credibility of a witness, and every witness's credibility is regarded as a matter that can be controverted.

Even if the "if controverted" phrase did not appear in FRE 407, FRE 403 should be a basis for excluding evidence of a subsequent remedial measure offered to prove an issue that is not controverted. But cf. pages 245-247, supra (discussion of *Old Chief*, FRE 403, and evidence of specific bad acts).

d.   The Relationship Between FRE 407 and FRE 403

When a party offers subsequent remedial measure evidence for a legitimate, contested purpose, the question of admissibility in theory should turn on the applicability of FRE 403: Is the probative value of the evidence for the legitimate purpose (e.g., feasibility) substantially outweighed by the possibility that the jurors may use the evidence for the impermissible purpose of inferring negligence or other culpable conduct? In fact, if subsequent remedial measure evidence is relevant to prove some contested issue other than negligence, culpable conduct, defect, or need for a warning, the result almost invariably is that the evidence is admissible. Christopher B. Mueller and Laird C. Kirkpatrick, Federal Evidence §130 (2d ed. 1994). The party against whom the evidence is admitted, of course, is entitled to a limiting instruction.

3.   Elaboration of FRE 407

a.   The Rationale for FRE 407 and the Other Inadmissible to Prove Negligence or Culpable Conduct Rules

There is a four-fold rationale for FRE 407 and for the other rules — FRE 408 (offers of compromise), 409 (medical expenses), and 411 (liability insurance) — that exclude evidence to prove negligence or culpable conduct.

i.   Low Probative Value.   First, the evidence has relatively low probative value for the prohibited purpose. For example, a defendant may take subsequent remedial action out of an abundance of caution even though there was no negligence or design defect. Similarly, a party may offer to compromise a claim in order to avoid litigation costs, not because the party is at fault.

ii.   Countervailing FRE 403 Factors.   Second, countervailing FRE 403 considerations may warrant exclusion. These considerations include a concern that admission of the evidence to prove negligence or fault may tend to mislead the jury or confuse the issues. Jurors may reasonably expect that the evidence they hear has a bearing on what they are supposed to decide. Thus, if they hear evidence that in fact has very low probative value, they may be misled into thinking that the evidence is more probative than it really is. Moreover, if the jurors happen to have only a vague understanding of their task, they may confuse the issues and focus on an improper issue. Consider, for example, a case in which a defendant has made a design change following an accident and the plaintiff wants to introduce evidence of that design change. If the defendant claims that it was not feasible to have a different design, the evidence would be admissible — not to show negligence or fault but to show that a design change was feasible. Assume, however, that the defendant does not claim lack of feasibility. Now the only way in which the design change is relevant is as an admission of fault or liability. The evidence has such low probative value for that purpose, however, that if jurors hear the evidence, they may become confused and use the evidence to decide an issue for which the evidence is more probative — in this case feasibility. In other words, the jurors may decide for the plaintiff on the ground that a design change could have been made without regard to whether they believe the defendant was culpable. Similarly, if evidence of liability insurance is admitted, jurors may infer, again incorrectly, that it is proper for them to place the loss on the insured rather than on the party who was at fault.

iii.   Not Discouraging Desirable Conduct.   Third, the rules excluding evidence to prove liability or fault traditionally have been justified on the ground that we do not want to discourage individuals from engaging in socially desirable conduct. In this respect, these rules are similar to some rules of privilege. We exclude evidence of confidential communications between lawyers and clients in part because we do not want to discourage clients from being candid when they consult lawyers for legal advice. Similarly, we exclude evidence of subsequent remedial measures, offers of compromise, payment of medical expenses, and maintaining liability insurance to prove fault in part because we do not want to discourage individuals from engaging in these types of socially desirable conduct.

Consider whether these traditional justifications provide a sufficient basis for excluding relevant evidence. At least with careful instructions about the proper uses of the evidence, is it likely that jurors will overestimate the probative value of the evidence or become confused about the issues? To what extent do you think individuals take into account — or even know — the rules of evidence in making decisions about subsequent remedial measures, offers of compromise, or payments of medical expenses? (The answer may depend to a substantial extent on whether the individual has sought the advice of counsel before engaging in the activity.)

iv.   **Not Punishing Desirable Conduct.**   A fourth but less frequently articulated rationale for these exclusionary rules is that, regardless of deterrence, prejudice, or confusion, we do not want to "punish" or disadvantage individuals for doing good things. This rationale is most frequently associated with the exclusionary rule for payment of medical expenses, sometimes referred to as the "good Samaritan" rule. We suggest, however, that the rationale is equally applicable to — and perhaps more compelling than the deterrence rationale for — the limitations on the use of remedial measure, compromise, and liability insurance evidence.

b.   *Subsequent Remedial Measures Taken by Third Persons*

Consider whether FRE 407 should apply to evidence of remedial measures taken by persons other than the party against whom the evidence is offered. In In re Air Crash Disaster, supra, Northwest Airlines and McDonnell Douglas were both defendants. To prove McDonnell Douglas's culpability, Northwest sought to introduce remedial measures that it had undertaken on its McDonnell Douglas–manufactured aircraft following the accident that gave rise to the litigation. The *Air Crash Disaster* court concluded that FRE 407 mandates exclusion of the evidence, but other courts have reached the opposite conclusion. For an elaboration, see Note 1, at pages 340-341, infra.

KEY POINTS

1. FRE 407 makes evidence of subsequent remedial measures inadmissible to prove negligence, culpable conduct, defect, or need for a warning or instruction.
2. FRE 407's exclusionary mandate applies only to remedial action taken after the event that is the subject of the litigation.
3. Subject to FRE 403, subsequent remedial measure evidence may be admissible for other purposes, the most likely of which are those listed in FRE 407: to show ownership, control, or feasibility or to impeach the credibility of a witness. The evidence should be admissible for these other purposes only if they are contested issues in the case.

PROBLEMS

6.1. Return to Problem 3.2 at page 129. Assume that six months ago the San Ramon School District adopted a policy requiring all of its bus drivers to take a special driver education course each year. Will the plaintiff be able to admit evidence of this policy adoption?

6.2. Lisa Evans is suing the Jones Manufacturing Co. for the wrongful death of her husband, Edward. Edward suffered a severed torso when a coworker turned on an industrial baling machine, manufactured by the defendant, when Edward was inside the hopper attempting to clear a jam. Lisa wishes to introduce evidence that after Edward's death

(a) Jones Manufacturing Co. fired the individual responsible for designing safety features on the baler; and
(b) Edward's employer, Loman Industries, modified the baler by installing an access door to the hopper and by making the baler inoperable when the access doors were open.

Should Jones's objection to these pieces of evidence be sustained?

6.3. Eugene Wright is suing the Loop Ladder Co. for personal injuries that he received when a ladder on which he had been standing fell to the ground with him on it. Eugene claims that a plastic tip on the ladder was too weak and that it broke, causing the ladder to fall. The defendant claims that the plastic tip broke from the impact of the fall or at some later time. An expert witness testifies for the defendant that the tip was adequate for its purpose. Plaintiff offers evidence that shortly after his accident, the Loop Ladder Company substituted a strengthened plastic cap on all of its ladders. Should this evidence be admitted? Would it make any difference in your analysis if the expert were a Loop employee who had authorized the change in the plastic tip?

6.4. Return to Problem 5.25 at page 271. Consider the admissibility of the following evidence against Acme:

(a) testimony that following the incident involving Henry, Acme hired outside consultants to prepare a report on the safety of its cleanser;
(b) the consultants' post-accident report analyzing the toxicity of the cleanser;
(c) testimony that following the report Acme reduced the toxicity of its cleanser formula.

Would any of your answers change if an Acme executive had testified, "There is nothing safer than Acme Cleanser"?

3. FRE 408

The Advisory Committee has proposed amendments to FRE 408 that will probably become effective on December 1, 2006. We reproduce first the current version of the rule followed by the proposed amended rule.

RULE 408. COMPROMISE AND OFFERS OF COMPROMISE

Evidence of (1) furnishing or offering or promising to furnish, or (2) accepting or offering or promising to accept, a valuable consideration in compromising or attempting to compromise a claim which was disputed as to either validity or amount, is not admissible to prove liability for or invalidity of the claim or its amount. Evidence of conduct or statements made in compromise negotiations is likewise not admissible. This rule does not require the exclusion of any evidence otherwise discoverable merely because it is presented in the course of compromise negotiations. This rule also does not require exclusion when the evidence is offered for another purpose, such as proving bias or prejudice of a witness, negativing a contention of undue delay, or proving an effort to obstruct a criminal investigation or prosecution.

RULE 408. COMPROMISE AND OFFERS TO COMPROMISE [WITH PROPOSED AMENDMENTS]

(a) **Prohibited uses.** Evidence of the following is not admissible on behalf of any party, when offered to prove liability for, invalidity of, or amount of a claim that was disputed as to validity or amount, or to impeach through a prior inconsistent statement or contradiction:

(1) furnishing or offering or promising to furnish or accepting or offering or promising to accept a valuable consideration in compromising or attempting to compromise the claim; and

(2) conduct or statements made in compromise negotiations regarding the claim, except when offered in a criminal case and the negotiations related to a claim by a public office or agency in the exercise of regulatory, investigative, or enforcement authority.

(b) **Other Purposes.** This rule does not require exclusion if the evidence is offered for purposes not prohibited by subdivision (a). Examples of permissible purposes include proving a witness's bias or prejudice; negating a contention of undue delay; and proving an effort to obstruct a criminal investigation or prosecution.

Except where noted, the following discussion applies to both versions of FRE 408.

4.   Interpretation and Illustration of FRE 408

a.   *The Exclusionary Mandate; Permissible Uses; FRE 403*

One plausible inference to draw from offers of compromise is that the offerors — like people who take subsequent remedial action — believe they were at fault in the incident giving rise to a claim against them. If they have this belief, one can then make the further inference that they were in fact at fault. In short, one way in which compromising or offering to compromise a claim is relevant is as a tacit admission of fault or liability.

As is the case with subsequent remedial measure evidence, there are other possible explanations for wanting to compromise a claim. For example, some individuals who adamantly believe they are not at fault may be willing to settle a claim because the potential litigation costs are significantly greater than the amount of settlement.

The FRE 408 mandate excluding compromise evidence to prove the validity or amount of a claim and the list of permissible uses for compromise evidence are the equivalent of the two sentences in FRE 407. To encourage settlements, FRE 408 excludes evidence of compromises and of offers to compromise on the questions of liability for or the amount of claims. At the same time, the rule makes it clear that such evidence may be admissible for other purposes. The list of other purposes, which is not exclusive, includes the purposes for which offers of compromise are most likely to be relevant. For example, to show the bias of a witness who testifies for the plaintiff, the defendant may want to establish that the settlement of that witness's claim against the plaintiff includes a provision for the plaintiff to pay to the witness a portion of any judgment obtained against the defendant. Brocklesby v. United States, 767 F.2d 1288 (9th Cir. 1985). A municipality's settlement of a police brutality action may be admissible to show that the municipality knew of and condoned the officer's conduct. Spell v. McDaniel, 824 F.2d 1380 (4th Cir. 1987). Proof of negotiations and offers to compromise may indicate that a party was acting in good faith to resolve a claim and thus rebut a charge of undue delay. Californian & Hawaiian Sugar Co. v. Kansas City Terminal Warehouse Co., 602 F. Supp. 183 (W.D. Mo. 1985). Cf. Athey v. Farmers Ins. Exch. 234 F.3d 357 (8th Cir. 2000) (compromise negotiations admissible to show bad faith in negotiating). Offers of compromise during an income tax audit may be admissible to show the taxpayer's knowledge and to rebut a claim of good faith in a tax evasion prosecution. United States v. Hauert, 40 F.3d 197 (7th Cir. 1994).

The proposed amendment to FRE 408 adds a prohibition against using compromise evidence to impeach a witness "through a prior inconsistent statement or contradiction." Such use of compromise evidence, according to the Advisory Committee, "would tend to swallow the exclusionary rule and would impair the public policy of promoting settlements." Some courts have reached this same conclusion without the benefit of the amendment. EEOC v. Gear Petroleum, Inc., 948 F.2d 1542 (10th Cir. 1991). Do you think the proposed amendment is desirable, or should the admissibility of compromise evidence for these impeachment purposes be governed by FRE 403?

The final sentence of FRE 408 does not contain "if controverted" language. Nonetheless, in order to have sufficient probative value to overcome an FRE 403 objection, the purpose for which the evidence is offered should be a contested issue in the case; if it is a contested issue, the evidence is likely to be admissible despite the risk that the jury may use the evidence for the impermissible purpose of showing the validity or amount of a claim. But see Ramada Development Co. v. Rauch, 644 F.2d 1097, 1107 (5th Cir. 1981) (settlement offered to show notice excluded because there are other ways "less in conflict with the policy behind the rule" to prove notice).

b. Conduct or Statements Made During Negotiations

FRE 408 excludes not only compromises and offers of compromise but also — at least in civil actions — conduct or statements made during compromise negotiations. (On the applicability of FRE 408 to criminal prosecutions, see subsection e, infra.) This is a significant departure from the common law rule, which excluded only statements of offer and acceptance. Consider, for example, a situation in which Amy and John are involved in an automobile accident. Amy threatens to sue, asserting that John was at fault and must pay for the damage to Amy's car. John offers one of the following responses:

(1) "Let's settle this matter ourselves so we don't have to pay fat fees to lawyers. I'll give you $500 and we'll call everything even."
(2) "There's no need to deal with lawyers, who'll demand a fat fee. This was my fault. I'll give you $500 and we'll call everything even."

Assume that Amy rejects the settlement offer and sues John. Both the common law and FRE 408 would preclude use of the offers of compromise against John to prove liability. The common law, but not FRE 408, would permit Amy to use John's acknowledgment of fault in the second statement to prove liability.

c. Compromise Negotiations and Discovery

The third sentence of the current FRE 408 makes it clear that a party cannot insulate from discovery documents and information that would otherwise be discoverable merely by making reference to or relying on such evidence in the compromise negotiations — a result that courts probably would reach even without this sentence in the rule. Assume, for example, that in the preceding hypothetical an insurance investigator with John's insurance company obtained a statement from Bob, an eyewitness, who confirmed that John had been at fault in the accident. If that statement were discoverable by Amy, John could not insulate it from discovery by making reference to it during their compromise negotiations. The proposed amendment to FRE 408 eliminates this provision on the ground that it merely restates existing law and is, therefore, superfluous.

d. The Attempt to Resolve a Disputed Claim Requirement

Offers of compromise and statements of fault are inadmissible pursuant to FRE 408 only if made during compromise negotiations over a disputed claim. If there is no disputed claim or if the statement of fault occurs outside the context of compromise negotiations, the statement of fault will be admissible. For example, in the preceding hypothetical if John made the offer and statement of fault before Amy made any claim, the statement would be admissible. Big O Tire Dealers, Inc. v. Goodyear Tire & Rubber Co., 561 F.2d 1365, 1372-1373 (10th Cir. 1977) (statements admissible as "business communications"; "discussions had not crystallized to the point of threatened litigation"). If John conceded full liability and was not attempting to reach a compromise, his statements also would be admissible. Perzinski v. Chevron Chem. Co., 503 F.2d 654 (7th Cir. 1974) (salesperson's statement that company would "take care of" plaintiff admissible).

In applying FRE 408, the trial judge must usually decide some preliminary questions of fact. What type of information is likely to be important to the preliminary question whether there is a disputed claim and a legitimate attempt to compromise that claim? Reconsider whether John's initial two statements, which we characterized as having been made after Amy threatened to sue, would be admissible under the following circumstances:

(a) There had been no threat to sue.

(b) The threat had been a spontaneous outburst at the time of the accident.

(c) The possible suit had been mentioned in the context of a polite but restrained conversation between Amy and John about various options available to them.

(d) The value of Amy's claim did not exceed $500. (Does it matter whether John or a reasonable person would probably have been aware of this fact?)

To what extent are the foregoing factors relevant to the judge's decision whether Amy and John were engaged in compromise negotiations over a disputed claim?

The answer to the foregoing question, of course, depends in part on how courts interpret "compromising . . . a claim which was disputed," and the courts of appeals provide varying answers. For example, compare Blu-J, Inc. v. Kemper C.P.A. Group, 916 F.2d 637, 642 (11th Cir. 1990) (FRE 408 exclusionary rule applies to "statements or conduct . . . intended to be part of the negotiations toward compromise") with Big O Tire Dealers v. Goodyear Tire & Rubber Co., supra at 1373 (FRE 408 exclusionary rule applies only after discussions "crystalize to the point of threatening litigation").

e. The Applicability of FRE 408 to Criminal Cases

If a person admits some wrongdoing in the course of negotiations to settle a civil claim, may the prosecution use the statement against the wrongdoer in a subsequent criminal prosecution? There is a split among the circuits on this question. Those courts holding that FRE 408 has no applicability to criminal cases rely on the "plain language" of FRE 408, that is, the terms "claim," "validity," and "amount," all of which suggest civil litigation. In addition, they maintain that the need for evidence in criminal prosecutions outweighs the value of promoting settlements in civil cases. Courts holding FRE 408 applicable to criminal as well as civil cases rely on the underlying purpose of the rule to promote compromise. They also note that portions of the last sentence of FRE 408 (the references to undue delay and obstructing justice) seem superfluous if FRE 408 does not apply to criminal cases. Compare United States v. Logan, 250 F.3d 350, 367 (6th Cir. 2000) (FRE 408 inapplicable to criminal cases) with United States v. Bailey, 327 F.3d 1131, 1144-46 (10th Cir. 2003) (FRE 408 applicable in criminal prosecutions).

The proposed amendment to FRE 408 takes a middle course. The proposed rule prohibits the use of actual compromises and offers and acceptances in criminal prosecutions, but it creates a limited exception to the general prohibition against the use of *conduct or statements made during compromise negotiations*. The exception — that is, the right to use in criminal prosecutions conduct and statements made during civil compromise negotiations — exists when "the negotiations related to a claim by a public office or agency in the exercise of regulatory, investigative, or enforcement authority." To illustrate a factual scenario that fits the scope of this exception, the Advisory Committee cited United States v. Prewitt, 34 F.3d 436, 439 (7th Cir. 1994). *Prewitt* was a mail fraud prosecution in which the court upheld the admissibility of statements of fault made during the compromise of a civil securities enforcement action. According to the Advisory Committee, "Where an individual makes a statement in the presence of government agents, its subsequent admission in a criminal case should not be unexpected."

The Advisory Committee suggested two possible ways to prevent the use in criminal prosecutions of statements of fault made during civil compromise negotiations. First, during civil negotiations, a person "can seek to protect against subsequent disclosure through negotiation and agreement with the civil regulator, or an attorney for the government." Second, "statements made in compromise negotiations of a claim by a government agency may be excluded in criminal cases where circumstances so warrant under Rule 403." As a possible example of such circumstances, the Advisory

Committee suggested a civil enforcement proceeding in which an individual was not represented by counsel.

How can a person ensure that an agreement with a civil regulator will be binding in a subsequent prosecution? In any event, is a person unrepresented by counsel likely to have the sophistication to seek such an agreement? And if the person is represented by counsel, how likely is it that an agreement will be necessary? Unless the civil authority demands an admission as part of the settlement, counsel can and should caution the client against making admissions of fault. With respect to FRE 403, how does the question of whether a person was or was not represented by counsel relate to FRE 403 concerns about an admission of fault?

f. A Party's Own Offer of Compromise

In Pierce v. F.R. Tripler & Co., 955 F.2d 820, 828 (2d Cir. 1992), the court held that FRE 408 applies to a party's effort to introduce its own offer of compromise. *Pierce* was an age discrimination suit in which the defendant, to show mitigation of damages, sought to introduce its offer of a job to the plaintiff. Although the purpose of the offer was to contest the amount of a claim, the defendant had argued that the policies underlying FRE 408 were inapplicable when a party sought to introduce evidence of its own offer compromise. For a case reaching the opposite result, see Bulaich v. AT&T Info. Sys., 778 P.2d 1031, 1036-37 (Wash. 1989) (applying Wash. R. Evid. 408; "when the settlement offeror is the same party attempting to gain admission of the settlement letter into evidence, the threat of admissibility should not be a deterrent to the articulation of the settlement proposal").

The "on behalf of any party" language in the proposed amendment to FRE 408 is intended to codify the result in *Pierce*. The Advisory Committee offered two reasons for the amendment. First, the offeror's revealing its own offer could "reveal the fact that the adversary entered into settlement negotiations," which would undermine the policy of FRE 408. Second, "proof of statements and offers made in settlement would often have to be made through the testimony of attorneys, leading to the risks and costs of disqualification.

g.   Compromises and Offers of Compromises by Third Persons

Consider a case in which the plaintiff sues the defendant, a restaurant, for food poisoning. The plaintiff claims that the restaurant was responsible for mishandling the food. The defendant seeks to introduce evidence that it had made a claim against its food supplier for $300,000, and that the supplier had settled the claim for $250,000. The defendant argues that the settlement evidence is an admission by the supplier that the supplier provided the restaurant with adulterated food, and that the adulteration — not the defendant's alleged mishandling of the food — was responsible for the food poisoning.

Just as we suggested that evidence of a third person's subsequent remedial measure does not implicate the policies underlying FRE 407 (see page 328, supra, and pages 340-341, infra), evidence of a third person's offer of compromise does not implicate the policies underlying FRE 408. The negotiations and settlement have nothing to do with the party against whom the evidence is offered, and it will be adequate protection for the third person to exclude the evidence if and when the third person becomes a party. Nonetheless, a literal reading of FRE 408, which applies to "compromising or attempting to compromise *a* claim" (emphasis added) may indicate that the exclusionary mandate applies to *any* offers and settlements, including those made by third persons. What impact, if any, should the proposed amendment to FRE 408 have on this issue? The "not admissible on behalf of any party" phrase may seem to support a claim that offers and settlements may not be offered by any party regardless of who made them. Unfortunately, nothing in the Advisory Committee Note addresses the admissibility of third person compromise evidence.

5. Elaboration of FRE 408

Consider whether FRE 408's expansion of the common law rule is desirable. The primary motives for compromising a claim will frequently be a desire to avoid the costs of litigation or the risk of losing (or foregoing) a good deal more than the person loses (or foregoes) in compromising the claim. Thus the probative value of an offer to compromise as an admission of fault or liability will often be quite low. As a result, the cost — in terms of foregoing relevant evidence — of applying the common law rule is not likely to be great. By contrast, FRE 408's extension of the exclusionary provision to clear-cut statements of fault shields highly probative evidence from the fact finder.

On the other hand, the effect of the common law rule was largely to penalize individuals who, unaware of the rules of evidence, would attempt to negotiate settlements themselves rather than deal through lawyers, who presumably would know to couch any faultlike statements in hypothetical terms. Putting compromise offerors without lawyers in the same position as compromise offerors with lawyers, even at the expense of some relevant evidence, may be desirable.

6. FRE 409

RULE 409. PAYMENT OF MEDICAL AND SIMILAR EXPENSES

Evidence of furnishing or offering or promising to pay medical, hospital, or similar expenses occasioned by an injury is not admissible to prove liability for the injury.

7. Interpretation and Illustration of FRE 409

a. *The Exclusionary Mandate*

Just as evidence of a subsequent repair or evidence of offering to pay a certain sum to settle a claim may be relevant to prove liability on the theory that it is an implied admission fault, paying or offering to pay another person's medical expenses may be an implied admission of fault: The payment raises an inference that the payor may feel legally responsible for the payment, and if the payor has that belief, it may be correct.

For reasons that the Advisory Committee states are "parallel those underlying Rules 407 and 408," FRE 409 excludes such evidence to prove liability. For example, if a driver hits a pedestrian and offers to pay the pedestrian's medical expenses, neither the offer nor the payment is admissible to prove the driver's liability. Similarly, if an insurance company pays a person's medical expenses before any trial or settlement, evidence of the payment is not subsequently admissible to prove the insurance company's liability. See Galarnyk v. Hostmart Mgmt., 2003 U.S. App. LEXIS (7th Cir. 2003) (plaintiff "fell in the bathroom of [a motel], converting gravitational energy to kinetic energy with such effectiveness that he punched a hole in the wall;" offers by defendant and defendant's insurance carrier to pay medical expenses not admissible to show liability).

b. The Admissibility of Statements Made in Conjunction with Medical and Similar Payments

In one significant respect FRE 409 differs from FRE 408: Statements made in conjunction with the payments — including statements of fault — are *not* excluded. According to the Advisory Committee:

> This difference in treatment arises from fundamental differences in nature. Communication is essential if compromises are to be effected, and consequently broad protection of statements is needed. This is not so in cases of payments [governed by FRE 409], where factual statements may be expected to be incidental in nature.

c. The Question Whether FRE 409 Permits Evidence of Payment for Purposes Other than to Show Liability

Although FRE 409, unlike FRE 407, 408, and 411, does not include an illustrative list of possible permissible uses for evidence of medical and similar payments, the common law counterpart to FRE 409 permitted evidence for other purposes. For example, in a dispute over where the plaintiff's injury occurred, a court admitted evidence of the defendant's payment of medical expenses to prove that the injury occurred on defendant's premises. Great Atlantic & Pacific Tea Co. v. Custin, 214 Ind. 54, 13 N.E.2d 542 (1938). There is no indication in the legislative history that the drafters of FRE 409 intended to depart from the common law in this respect, and there is precedent under the Federal Rules for admitting payments to prove something other than liability. Savoie v. Otto Candies, Inc., 692 F.2d 363 (5th Cir. 1982) (maintenance payments to prove status as seaman).

d. The Question What Constitutes a "Similar" Expense

FRE 409 is rarely invoked, perhaps because there are not enough good Samaritans among us. If there were, an issue that would undoubtedly arise in applying FRE 409 is what constitutes "similar expenses." For example, should evidence of paying to have an automobile repaired or paying subsistence income while an individual is recuperating from injury be excluded? How should the judge decide this preliminary question, and how should the proponent try to persuade the judge? See Great Coastal Express, Inc. v. Atlanta Mut. Cos., 790 So. 2d 966 (Ala. Civ. App. 2000) (state equivalent of FRE 409 not a bar to evidence that defendant paid for some of clean up following fuel leak; evidence admissible to infer defendant's negligence).

8. FRE 411

RULE 411. LIABILITY INSURANCE

Evidence that a person was or was not insured against liability is not admissible upon the issue whether the person acted negligently or otherwise wrongfully. This rule does not require the exclusion of evidence of insurance against liability when offered for another purpose, such as proof of agency, ownership, or control, or bias or prejudice of a witness.

9. Interpretation and Illustration of FRE 411

a. The Exclusionary Mandate

This rule is similar in purpose, structure, and application to FRE 407-409. With respect to liability insurance, however, the probative value of the forbidden inference is particularly weak: The underlying premise of the forbidden inference is that people with liability insurance are likely to be less careful than people without insurance, who will be individually responsible for the injuries they cause. Moreover, liability insurance is so pervasive that it is doubtful that individuals take into account the rules of evidence in deciding whether to obtain or to forego obtaining liability insurance.

If evidence of liability insurance were admissible on the question of fault, there would be a substantial risk of unfair prejudice. Jurors might be inclined to impose damages because of insurance or to forego or minimize damages out of sympathy for the uninsured. On the other hand, given the pervasiveness of liability insurance, if an uninsured party is not able to present evidence of absence of insurance, there is a risk that the jury may assume the party is insured and impose damages on the basis of this incorrect assumption.

b. The Permissible Uses of Evidence of Liability Insurance

Like FRE 407-409, FRE 411 excludes evidence of liability insurance only to prove negligence or wrongful conduct. The second sentence of FRE 411 lists the most common permissible uses of evidence of liability insurance. Like the lists of permissible purposes in FRE 407 and FRE 408, the FRE 411 list is not exclusive. When there is a permissible purpose, the admissibility of the evidence should depend on the application of FRE 403, and FRE 403 should require at a minimum that the issue for which the evidence is offered is a contested issue in the case.

Liability insurance offered for some legitimate, contested purpose is usually admitted. Morton v. Zidell Explorations, Inc., 695 F.2d 347 (9th Cir. 1982) (proof of purchasing insurance to rebut claim that contract not in effect); Hunziker v. Scheidemantle, 543 F.2d 489 (3d Cir. 1976) (proof of insurance covering alleged agent to prove agency); Newell v. Harold Shaffer Leasing Co., 489 F.2d 103 (5th Cir. 1974) (maintaining insurance introduced to show ownership or control). If, as is frequently the case, an insurance investigator testifies about the results of an investigation, evidence that the investigator represents a company that insures one of the parties will probably be admissible both as part of the general background information about the witness and as an indication of the possible bias of the witness. Conde v. Starlight I, Inc., 103 F.3d 210 (1st Cir. 1997). In addition, during the jury selection process, it is appropriate in many jurisdictions to ask the prospective jurors if they or any friends or relatives work for insurance companies. The theoretically legitimate reason for such questions is to identify jurors who may have a particular bias because of their own or their relatives' association with an insurance company. A likely impact of the questions, however, is to suggest to jurors that one or both parties is insured, and the jury may then be influenced in its decision on the basis of the assumptions it has made about insurance.

KEY POINTS

1. Under FRE 408, 409, and 411, evidence of compromises, offers of compromise, payment or offers to pay medical and similar expenses, and liability insurance is not admissible to prove liability.

2. Subject to FRE 403, such evidence may be admissible for other purposes. The permissible purposes listed in FRE 408 and FRE 411, like the permissible purposes listed in FRE 407, are the most common purposes for which evidence governed by those rules is likely to be admissible, but the lists are not exclusive.

3. When evidence is offered for a theoretically legitimate permissible purpose, FRE 403 should require exclusion if the issue is not a contested one.

PROBLEMS

6.5. Return to Problem 3.2 at page 129.

(a) Paul's mother offers to testify that shortly after the accident she received a note from Driver with $200. The note, which the plaintiff would like to introduce into evidence, says: "I'm so sorry about Paul's accident. I'm not a rich person but I hope this will help with some of the expenses."

(b) Plaintiff wishes to introduce evidence that after the law suit was filed, the school district offered to settle the suit for $25,000.

(c) In cross-examining the school district's accident reconstruction expert, plaintiff wishes to show that the witness has a professional relationship with the School District's liability insurance carrier.

Should any of this evidence be admitted?

6.6. Dave Defendant, while sitting in Evidence class, was preoccupied with his plans for the semester break. His hot coffee spilled on Paula Plaintiff, who was sitting next to him. Paula suffered a serious burn in the area where the coffee spilled. She sued Dave for negligence and Espresso-to-Go, where Dave purchased the coffee, for a defectively designed take-out cup, alleging $50,000 in damages. Paula offers to testify as follows on direct examination:

Q: Paula, what happened immediately after the spill?
A: Dave said he would pay for my ruined clothes.

Q: Did you ever talk to Dave about the case again?

A: Yes. After I filed this suit, Dave saw me in the hall one day and said he was sorry I had been hurt because he had been so clumsy and that he'd like to talk more but he was late for class. Then the next day he said he didn't think my case was worth $50,000, but that he'd like to pay all my bills and give me money for a "bar trip" after graduation.

What objections should defense counsel make to this testimony?

6.7. Assume that Paula settles with Dave and proceeds to trial against Espresso-to-Go.

(a) Paula calls Dave to testify about the incident and to describe the severity of Paula's burns. Are the following questions by defense counsel on cross-examination objectionable: "Isn't it true that you were sued by Paula for your own negligence? And isn't it true that you and Paula reached a compromise of that claim for a mere $500? And isn't it true that Paula really dropped the suit against you in exchange for your testimony here today?"

(b) Can Paula introduce evidence of Espresso-to-Go's substantial liability insurance policy? Would your answer change if, at trial, the owner of Espresso-to-Go had mentioned during testimony (1) that its products were so low risk that the company did not carry much insurance or (2) that he could not afford to lose the lawsuit because he needed everything to care for his ailing mother?

6.8. Paul Preston has sued Daniel Dripps for damages for assault and battery after Dripps attacked Preston at their daughters' hockey game. In a mediation session to discuss settlement, Preston's lawyer says that Preston would settle for payment of his medical expenses plus $5,000 if Dripps would admit he was wrong and apologize. Dripps says, "Well, I am sorry — I was in the wrong." He counter-offers to offer an apology and pay the medical expenses and no more. Preston says he doubts Dripps's sincerity about the apology. To demonstrate Dripps's sincerity, Dripps's attorney shows Preston's attorney an entry from Dripps's diary the day of the fight saying that he was at fault and was sorry. Negotiations break down over the $5,000. The day after the mediation, Preston's counsel sends out a document request demanding production of the diary, which the plaintiff had not known about prior to the mediation. Eventually, the case goes to trial. Is the following evidence offered by Preston admissible?

(1) Dripps's statement at the mediation that he was sorry and is in the wrong;
(2) Dripps's willingness to cover Preston's medical expenses;
(3) The entry from Dripps's diary admitting fault;
(4) Evidence that Dripps's homeowners' insurance company denied coverage for the alleged assault and battery on the ground that the policy did not cover intentional wrongful acts. (Preston argues that it shows that the insurance company found Dripps to have acted wrongfully and intentionally.)

Would any of your answers be different if this were a criminal prosecution of Dripps for battery?

6.9. Pam Palmer has sued Dick Davis for injuries she received in an automobile accident involving her car and the cars of Davis and Walter Williams. According to the plaintiff's complaint she was headed west on a two-lane road when Davis, who was heading east, crossed the road into her lane of traffic and hit her. Davis claims that he had been taking necessary evasive action in an unsuccessful effort to avoid hitting another car that had suddenly pulled in front of him from a side street. The driver of the third car was Walter Williams.

Williams has testified for the plaintiff that Davis was responsible for the accident. According to Williams, he had been traveling east at a normal rate of speed when Davis, who was speeding, suddenly approached from the rear. In an unsuccessful effort to avoid hitting Williams, Davis veered to the left, clipping the rear end of Williams's car and hitting the plaintiff's car as well.

Davis offers to show that he had filed suit against Williams for damage to his automobile and that Williams had paid Davis $500 to settle the suit, in which Davis had asked for $2000. Should this evidence be admitted over plaintiff's objection?

6.10. Roland Nast has filed an age discrimination suit against the Jones Hardware Co. for failing to promote him to a manager position and giving the job instead to a much younger employee.

   (a)   Although Nast had a reputation for being a bit hotheaded and argumenta-
         tive, Jim Jones, president of Jones Hardware, maintained during settlement
         negotiations that Nast's attitude and personality had nothing to do with his
         not getting the manager job. Instead, according to Jones, the problem was
         Nast's tardiness record. At trial, however, Jones testified that Nast's attitude
         and personality were primary factors in the decision not to promote him to a
         manager position. Can Nast introduce Jones's settlement negotiation state-
         ments?
   (b)   To rebut the claim of discrimination, Jones Hardware offers evidence that
         after Nast filed his complaint Jones Hardware offered Nast a position at a
         different branch store. This newly offered position had the same salary as the
         manager salary. Should the evidence be admitted?

NOTES AND QUESTIONS

1. In the typical case to which the exclusionary provisions of FRE 407-409 and FRE 411 apply, it is a party to the action who has made the implicit admission of fault by taking subsequent remedial action, offering to compromise a claim, offering to pay medical expenses, or procuring liability insurance. Occasionally, however, the admission of fault will be that of a third person. See, for example, Problem 6.2(b) at page 329, supra, where the decedent's employer, not a party to the lawsuit, took remedial action to make an industrial baling machine safer. Although a literal reading of FRE 407 suggests that the evidence should not be admissible to prove the defective condition of the baling machine, the underlying rationale for the exclusionary mandate does not apply. Using the evidence against the defendant manufacturer to prove a defect will not discourage the employer or other third persons from taking remedial action. Rather, it furthers the policy of the rule to exclude the evidence only when the person taking the remedial action is a party or is taking the action on behalf of the party. See also Problem 6.9, page 339, supra. It would not frustrate the policy of FRE 408 to use Williams's compromise with Davis to show that Williams (and not Davis) was responsible for the injuries that resulted from the accident; it would be sufficient to promote the policy of

FRE 408 to exclude the evidence for this purpose when Williams is a party and the evidence is offered against Williams.

Although the decisions are not uniform, there is precedent, at least with respect to FRE 407, for the proposition that the exclusionary mandate does not apply in these situations. Diehl v. Blaw-Knox, 360 F.3d 426, 430 (3d Cir. 2004) (following plaintiff's injury, employer modified piece of road-widening equipment that injured plaintiff; evidence of modification admissible against manufacturer of equipment); Mehojah v. Drummond, 56 F.3d 1213 (10th Cir. 1995) (suit against ranch by couple whose automobile struck cattle on highway; FRE 407 not applicable to subsequent installation of fence by owner of land leased to ranch); Pau v. Yosemite Park & Curry Co., 928 F.2d 880 (9th Cir. 1991) (suit against bike rental company following fatal accident on National Park trail; evidence that Park Service posted sign prohibiting bikes following the accident not precluded by FRE 407). See generally David P. Leonard, Selected Rules of Limited Admissibility, The New Wigmore §2.6.3 (1996). In Middleton v. Harris Press & Shear, Inc., 796 F.2d 747 (5th Cir. 1986), the case upon which the baling machine problem is based, the court held that the FRE 407 exclusionary provision was inapplicable. The court, however, relied on FRE 403 to uphold exclusion of the remedial action evidence on the ground that the evidence may confuse the jury and divert their attention from question of defect at the time of the accident. See also Gray v. Hoffman-La-Rouche, Inc., 2003 U.S. App. LEXIS 24321 (10th Cir.) (relying on FRE 403 to exclude evidence of subsequent remedial measure by third person).

2. If a person makes a direct out-of-court verbal acknowledgment of fault, that statement would be regarded as hearsay to prove the truth of the proposition that the person was at fault. Should an admission implied from conduct, such as a remedial measure or the payment of medical expenses, also be regarded as hearsay?

This question, of course, is purely academic for statements excluded by FRE 407-409 or FRE 411. The question may be important though for situations like those described in Problems 6.2(b) and 6.9 at pages 329 and 339, supra. You should make a note to yourself to return to these problems after you have studied Section A of Chapter 8.

3. Each rule that prohibits evidence to prove negligence or liability articulates the prohibition differently: FRE 407 excludes evidence "to prove negligence, culpable conduct, a defect . . . or a need for a warning or instruction"; FRE 408 excludes evidence "to prove liability for or invalidity of the claim or its amount"; FRE 409 excludes evidence "to prove liability for the injury"; and FRE 411 excludes evidence "upon the issue whether [a] person acted negligently or otherwise wrongfully." Similarly, the illustrations of possible permissible uses of the evidence vary from rule to rule. Compare, for example, FRE 407 (evidence of subsequent remedial measures may be admissible "for another purpose, such as proving ownership, control, or feasibility of precautionary measures, if controverted, or impeachment") with FRE 411 (evidence of liability insurance may be admissible "for another purpose, such as proof of agency, ownership, or control, or bias or prejudice of a witness"). And compare FRE 407, 408, and 411, all of which contain lists of permissible purposes, with FRE 409, which has no such list.

There is no indication in the legislative history that these differences in language were intended to convey different notions about what is prohibited or potentially admissible. In part the differences in the lists of permissible uses is probably a function of the fact that the most common alternative uses will vary from rule to rule. Beyond this, the explanation for the different terminology in the various rules is probably that different committees drafted each rule and that no committee made a serious effort to see that language was consistently used from rule to rule. In any event, the differences in language demonstrate at the very least a lack of attention to detail. Lack of care in drafting even on inconsequential matters inevitably raises the question about care in drafting generally. Does it also raise a question about how much reliance one should place on the particular language in any rule?

B.   REFLECTION ON THE "INADMISSIBLE TO PROVE NEGLIGENCE" RULES

Consider whether it makes sense for the Federal Rules to retain the exclusionary mandates set forth in FRE 407-409 and FRE 411. Commentators have pointed out, particularly with respect to FRE 407, the subsequent remedial measure rule, that it is common for proponents to be able to articulate some alternative, nonculpable-conduct theory for admitting the evidence. See, e.g., David. P. Leonard, Selected Rules of Limited Admissibility, The New Wigmore §2.8 (1996). To the extent that one can readily find some alternative permissible theory for the use of evidence that is subject to these rules, one can with good reason question the desirability of the rule in its present form: If courts tend to resolve the FRE 403 balance between the permissible and impermissible use in favor of admissibility (which is usually the case), and if one doubts the efficacy of limiting instructions, the relevance rule in fact would seem not to be serving its designed purpose. Alternatively, if the FRE 403 balance were usually to come out in favor of exclusion, the relevance rule would be stated in a deceptively (and thus perhaps undesirably) narrow manner: Despite the limited nature of the express exclusionary mandate, FRE 403 concerns could make the mandate quite broad.

Regardless of whether most decisions involving FRE 407-409 and FRE 411 result in admission or exclusion of the evidence, it may be that judges are simply applying the FRE 403 balancing test wisely on a case-by-case basis. Or perhaps the inherent difficulty of balancing and the breadth of judicial discretion lead to arbitrary and inconsistent results from case to case. Unfortunately we do not now have enough reliable information to assess the need for these relevance rules. Perhaps answers will emerge as we gain more experience and sophistication in studying the actual operation of the rules of evidence. But how can we gain that information? In the meantime, these potential problems should not be ignored. The task of the rule drafter should be to try to come up with the best possible rule in light of the best possible guess (based on logic, empiricism, and intuition) as to how various alternative formulations of the rule are likely to work in practice.

Consider the alternatives:

If there were no specific rules like FRE 407-409 and FRE 411, the task of balancing probative value against countervailing FRE 403 concerns would often be difficult. For example, is an offer to settle a $1000 claim for $300 sufficiently probative of liability and possible bias that it warrants exploring in detail the nature of the offer, the context in which it was made, and the various possible motivations for the offer? Similarly, is introducing evidence of a subsequent remedial action sufficiently probative as an admission of fault and as evidence of feasibility or control to justify exploring the possible motivations that the defendant had for taking such action?

With rules like FRE 407-409 and FRE 411, the judge still must engage in a balancing process that weighs probative value against countervailing efficiency and inaccuracy concerns. In addition, the judge must separate the permissible from the impermissible purpose for which the evidence is offered, balance the probative value of the evidence for its legitimate purpose against the prejudicial impact resulting from the possible use of the evidence for its prohibited purpose, and consider the efficacy of a limiting instruction. What, if anything, does one gain from this more complex balancing process? Should law reform efforts move in the direction of expanding or contracting the exclusionary mandates of the "not admissible to prove liability" relevance rules?

C. WITHDRAWN GUILTY PLEAS, PLEAS OF NO CONTEST, AND OFFERS TO PLEAD GUILTY

1. FRE 410

RULE 410. INADMISSIBILITY OF PLEAS, PLEA DISCUSSIONS, AND RELATED STATEMENTS

Except as otherwise provided in this rule, evidence of the following is not, in any civil or criminal proceeding, admissible against the defendant who made the plea or was a participant in the plea discussions:

(1) a plea of guilty which was later withdrawn;
(2) a plea of nolo contendere;
(3) any statement made in the course of any proceedings under Rule 11 of the Federal Rules of Criminal Procedure or comparable state procedure regarding either of the foregoing pleas; or
(4) any statement made in the course of plea discussions with an attorney for the prosecuting authority which do not result in a plea of guilty or which result in a plea of guilty later withdrawn.

However, such a statement is admissible (i) in any proceedings wherein another statement made in the course of the same plea or plea discussions has been introduced and the statement ought in fairness be considered contemporaneously with it, or (ii) in a criminal proceeding for perjury or false statement if the statement was made by the defendant under oath, on the record and in the presence of counsel.

2. Interpretation and Illustration of FRE 410

a. Withdrawn Guilty Pleas

Once a defendant has pleaded guilty, the defendant may withdraw the plea only with the permission of the court. The standards for permitting withdrawal of a plea typically are not articulated with any degree of specificity, but there must be "cause" or some good reason to permit the withdrawal. A court is likely to permit withdrawal of a plea if there is reason to believe that the plea is inaccurate because the defendant is innocent or if it appears that the defendant's rights were violated in the process of procuring the plea. To the extent that the concern is with the violation of the defendant's rights, exclusion may be necessary in order to make the remedy for the violation meaningful. If the prosecutor could respond to a withdrawn plea by using that plea against the defendant in a subsequent proceeding, the value of withdrawal as a remedy would often be substantially undermined. To the extent that the concern is with the reliability of a plea, the fact that a judge has already determined that the plea is unreliable casts doubt on the plea's probative value. Moreover, full relitigation of the reliability issue could be time consuming and could, as a practical matter, force the defendant to take the witness stand. If one can reasonably anticipate that the admission of marginally probative evidence will induce a defendant who would prefer not to testify to waive the Fifth Amendment right to remain silent, it is arguably appropriate to exclude the evidence in the first instance.

b. Pleas of No Contest

Only some jurisdictions permit pleas of no contest, and where they are permitted the court usually must approve the pleas. Pleas of no contest are by their nature compromises. They constitute an acquiescence to a criminal conviction without an admission of guilt or a determination of guilt after an adjudicatory trial. Their compromise nature makes uncertain their probative value to prove that the person committed the acts charged. Moreover, to use a no-contest plea for this purpose would tend to undermine the initial value of the plea as a device to encourage settlement. Olsen v. Correiro, 189 F.3d 52 (1st Cir. 1999).

c. Statements Made in Conjunction with the Process of Making and Negotiating Pleas

Federal Rule of Criminal Procedure 11, to which FRE 410(3) refers, governs plea bargaining and the judicial acceptance or rejection of guilty pleas. By specifically excluding (a) statements made in Rule 11 plea bargaining proceedings and (b) statements made in the course of plea bargaining with prosecutors, FRE 410(3) and (4) operate in the criminal negotiating process as the counterpart to FRE 408's prohibition against using evidence of attempts to settle or compromise civil claims.

As a matter of general principle, and perhaps even as a matter of practical reality, one may question the soundness of such a rule. An offer to plead guilty, at least if the plea is to a relatively serious charge, may have more probative value than the offer to settle — even for a substantial amount of money — a civil claim. Moreover, the offers to plead guilty that are excluded by FRE 410 usually occur in the context of plea negotiations, and there are several reasons why settling or compromising criminal charges may be regarded as undesirable and, therefore, something to be deterred. First, the possibility of pleading guilty to a charge that is substantially less severe than the crime initially charged may have the undesirable effect of pressuring an innocent individual to plead guilty in order to avoid the risk of possible conviction on the more serious charge. Second, the possibility of a plea to a lesser charge may have the arguably undesirable effect of undermining a legislatively dictated mandatory sentence for the crime initially charged or of limiting the range of the judge's sentencing discretion. Finally, a consequence of encouraging or even condoning plea bargaining is the possibility of unfairness or at least the appearance of unfairness from what are or seem to be inconsistent and arbitrary plea bargaining decisions from case to case by prosecutors. This, in turn, may lead to cynicism about or disrespect for the criminal law and perhaps undermine the force of criminal prohibitions and sanctions as general deterrents.

Despite these concerns, the Supreme Court has acknowledged that plea bargaining is an acceptable method for disposing of criminal cases, Santobello v. New York, 404 U.S. 257 (1971), and the reality is that plea bargaining is pervasive in the criminal justice system. Depending on the jurisdiction, anywhere from 70 percent to 95 percent of all criminal charges are disposed of by guilty pleas, and many of these pleas are the result of plea negotiations. Moreover, the criminal justice system does not have the resources to process the current and ever increasing volume of cases without heavy reliance on guilty pleas. Thus, as a practical matter, plea bargaining is a fact of life. In light of this reality, it may be at least as important to encourage guilty pleas as it is to encourage settlement of civil cases. Just as excluding statements made in conjunction with offers to settle civil suits may facilitate the negotiating process, excluding statements made during plea negotiations may facilitate obtaining guilty pleas.

d. The Scope of FRE 410(4)

There are two important limitations on the scope of the rule excluding statements covered by FRE 410(4). First, the statements must be made "in the course of plea discussions." For example, if a defendant is merely seeking leniency in the charging decision without suggesting any possibility of pleading guilty, a court may conclude that the conversation is not a plea discussion. Similarly, seeking dismissal of charges against third persons may be outside the scope of plea negotiations, United States v. Doe, 655 F.2d 920 (9th Cir. 1980), as are statements made following the completion of plea negotiations, United States v. Perry, 643 F.2d 38 (2d Cir. 1981). Second, the defendant's statements must be made "to an attorney for the prosecuting authority." For example, statements to police officers, who have no formal authority to plea bargain in any event, do not fall within the FRE 410(4) exclusion. United States v. Stern, 313 F. Supp.2d 155, 167-168 (S.D.N.Y. 2003); United States v. Brumley, 217 F.3d 905 (7th Cir. 1997). Statements made to police officers as part of the plea negotiation, however, may be covered by the rule if the police are acting as agents of the prosecutor. United States v. Millard, 139 F.3d 1200 (8th Cir. 1998).

Even if the statements are made to a prosecuting attorney, they may not be protected. There is a split of authority on the question of whether proffer sessions that explore possible cooperation with the government but that do not include discussions of a guilty plea fall within the FRE 410 exclusionary mandate. Compare United States v. Morgan, 91 F.3d 1193, 1195-96 (8th Cir. 1996) (statements not protected) with United States v. Frank, 173 F.R.D. 59, 69 (W.D.N.Y. 1997) (statements protected). See United States v. Stein, 2005 U.S. Dist. LEXIS 11141 (E.D. Pa.) (collecting cases).

There is substantial precedent for approaching the question whether FRE 410 is applicable from the perspective of the defendant. Statements will not be admissible if the defendant (or the defendant's attorney speaking as an agent) had a subjective belief that plea negotiations with a prosecuting authority were taking place and if that belief was objectively reasonable. United States v. Sayakhom, 186 F.3d 928 (9th Cir. 1999); United States v. Bridges, 46 F. Supp. 2d 462 (E.D. Va. 1999) (collecting cases).

e.   The Exceptions to FRE 410(3) and (4)

The two enumerated exceptions to FRE 410(3) and (4) will rarely be of consequence. The first exception merely acknowledges the rule of completeness encompassed in FRE 106. For example, if a defendant introduces part of a statement made in conjunction with plea negotiations, the prosecution can introduce other statements that provide a context or explanation for the statement introduced by the defendant. The second exception in effect permits the prosecution to bring perjury charges against a defendant who lies under oath during plea negotiations. Perjury prosecutions are relatively rare, however; and in any event, plea negotiations are seldom under oath.

f.   Waiver of FRE 410's Exclusionary Mandate

In United States v. Mezzanatto, 513 U.S. 196 (1995), the Supreme Court held that a defendant may waive the FRE 410(4) exclusionary mandate, at least with regard to the impeachment use of statements made in the process of plea negotiations. In *Mezzanatto*, the prosecutor, at the outset of plea discussions with the defendant and his counsel, insisted on the right to be able to use Mezzanatto's statements against him for impeachment purposes in the event of a trial. Mezzanatto agreed to this waiver, and during the plea discussions he made some incriminating statements. The prosecutor, however, terminated the plea negotiations at least in part because of some false statements that Mezzanatto had made. The case proceeded to trial. Mezzanatto testified, and over his objection the prosecution introduced into evidence some of Mezzanatto's plea bargain statements to impeach his testimony. In his opinion for the Court, Justice Thomas rejected the defendant's claims that waiver was inconsistent with the purpose of FRE 410 and that the possibility of waiver provided potential for prosecutorial overreaching.

In dictum Justice Thomas suggested that the waiver would be valid even if it were not limited to the impeachment use of the statements. Only Chief Justice Rehnquist and Justice Scalia expressed agreement with this dictum. Nonetheless, some courts have upheld waivers that allow prosecutors to use FRE 410 evidence in their cases-in-chief. United States v. Burch, 156 F.3d 1315 (D.C. Cir. 1998); United States v. Krilich, 159 F.3d 1020 (7th Cir. 1998). Cf. United States v. Velez, 354 F.3d 190, 196 (2d Cir. 2004) (government may "introduce defendant's proffer statements to rebut contrary evidence or arguments presented by the defense, whether or not defendant testifies").

Consider the potential impact of the Court's decision. It seems likely that at least some defendants will be unwilling to enter into plea negotiations if prosecutors demand waivers. Of course, prosecutors could choose to forego the demand in some or all of those cases. If a demand for waiver becomes the standard prosecutorial policy, however, there may well be a net decrease in the number of defendants willing to enter into plea negotiations. On the other hand, perhaps the opportunity to obtain waivers will make prosecutors more willing than they were previously to enter into plea negotiations.

KEY POINTS

1. FRE 410(1) and (2) provide that a defendant's withdrawn guilty pleas and pleas of nolo contendere are not admissible against the defendant.

2. FRE 410(3) and (4) provide that a defendant's statements made in the course of judicial plea acceptance proceedings and in the course of plea bargaining are also not admissible against the defendant. According to the language of FRE 410, statements qualify for exclusion only if they are made (a) to a prosecuting attorney (b) during plea discussions.

3. In determining whether the "plea discussions" and "attorney for the prosecuting authority" requirements are satisfied, many courts consider the matter from the defendant's perspective. The statements will be excluded if the defendants have a subjective belief that they are engaging in plea discussions with a prosecuting attorney and if that belief is objectively reasonable.

4. Defendants may waive the right not to have plea bargaining statements used against them, at least for impeachment purposes.

PROBLEMS

6.11. Attorney Yvonne Gruber heard a rumor that her client, Dawn Carson, was about to be indicted for income tax evasion. On behalf of Carson, Gruber spoke with an assistant U.S. Attorney about the possibility of a plea bargain. In response to a question, Gruber acknowledged that her client would be willing to plead guilty to a relatively minor charge. There were no further discussions, and Carson was eventually indicted for income tax evasion. Can the prosecution use Gruber's statement about Carson's willingness to plead guilty? Would your answer be different if Gruber had contacted the IRS and had the conversation with an IRS agent?

6.12. In the course of plea negotiations with an assistant U.S. Attorney, Tom Mason, after acknowledging that he sold heroin on three specific occasions, entered into a cooperation agreement. According to the agreement, Mason would not be prosecuted if he helped the police develop evidence against his supplier. Mason reneged on the agreement and is now being prosecuted for sale of heroin. During its case in chief the prosecution offers Mason's statement about selling heroin. Should Mason's objection be sustained? Does you answer depend upon whether the cooperation agreement contained a waiver of Mason's FRE 410 rights?

6.13. Return to Problem 3.2 at page 129. Assume that Driver was charged with reckless driving, a misdemeanor, as a result of the accident with Paul. Driver is grief stricken and has no interest in fighting the charge. Moreover, she is worried that if she seriously contests the ticket and is found guilty, the penalty may be stiffer than if she pleads guilty. If Driver pleads guilty, however, the plea can be used against her in a civil suit. The jurisdiction does not permit nolo pleas. What advice can you give her?

6.14. How literally should one read FRE 410's ban on the use of nolo contendere pleas? Consider the following:

(a)   After serving five years of a life sentence for murder, Morris's conviction was reversed because the investigating police officers failed to disclose an audio-taped interview with a key prosecution witness. Rather than proceeding with a new trial, Morris pled nolo contendere to manslaughter and, pursuant to the plea agreement, received a sentence of time served. Now Morris is suing the city and the investigating officers for violating his civil rights. A major part of his damage claim is for wrongful imprisonment. Morris has filed a motion in limine seeking to exclude any direct or indirect mention of his nolo plea. What result?

(b) Dr. Mildred Evans is the sole shareholder, sole officer, and sole director of ME, a professional corporation. ME entered into a partnership agreement with HealthScam to provide in-home medical care and supplies. After two years the partnership dissolved and Dr. Evans became an employee of HealthScam for a five-year term. HealthScam retained the right to terminate Evans, but if the termination was without cause, Evans's full salary would become immediately due. Before the partnership dissolved, the government had begun a criminal investigation of its activities. As a result of the investigation, HealthScam pleaded guilty to several felonies; and pursuant to Evans's authorization, ME entered a plea of nolo contendere to one count of mail fraud. Claiming that the statement accompanying ME's plea contained false information damaging to HealthScam, HealthScam terminated Evans's employment. Evans is suing HealthScam for her full five-year salary. The issue is whether her firing was for cause. HealthScam seeks to introduce the nolo plea and the agreement accompanying it. What result?

D.   "FIGHTING FIRE WITH FIRE" — THE DOCTRINE OF CURATIVE ADMISSIBILITY

The doctrine of curative admissibility — sometimes referred to as "fighting fire with fire" — permits a party to introduce normally inadmissible evidence in response to the opposing party's introduction of or attempt to introduce inadmissible evidence. Consider, for example, a case in which the plaintiff has sued a local restaurant for food poisoning that allegedly resulted from unsanitary conditions in the kitchen. During the direct examination of the restaurant owner, defense counsel asks the owner to tell the jury about special awards for cleanliness that the restaurant has received over the last five years. The plaintiff could object on the ground that this question calls for inadmissible character or propensity evidence. Having an objection sustained and even having the jury admonished to disregard the question, however, may be of little benefit to the defendant. At least some jurors are likely to assume that awards were received and to draw the improper propensity inference. Indeed, plaintiff's counsel may reasonably believe that the best way to minimize this possibility is not to object at all. In this type of situation, regardless of whether the plaintiff objected to the question, it arguably would be appropriate to permit the plaintiff, in rebuttal, to introduce evidence of citations the restaurant has received from the health department for unsanitary conditions. Although this evidence normally would also be objectionable on character-propensity grounds, allowing it to come in will provide some antidote to the defense counsel's improper evidence. Maintaining a "balance of errors" or permitting the plaintiff "to fight (the defendant's) fire with fire" may contribute to accurate factfinding. Moreover, this remedy is considerably more efficient than the alternatives of declaring a mistrial or reversing a judgment on appeal.

In other situations, the propriety of permitting a party to "fight fire with fire" is less clear. Consider, for example, a defendant who foregoes an adequate opportunity to object to excludable hearsay evidence. Should this failure to object be sufficient to permit the defendant to introduce, over the plaintiff's objection, excludable hearsay evidence? What would be the impact on trials and on litigation strategy if the curative admissibility doctrine were applied this broadly?

Most, but not all, jurisdictions recognize some version of the curative admissibility doctrine, and although there is no Federal Rule of Evidence dealing with the subject, federal courts have invoked the doctrine. All American Life and Casualty Co. v. Oceanic Trade Alliance Council International, Inc., 756 F.2d 474, 479 (6th Cir. 1985); Croce v. Bromley Corp., 623 F.2d 1084 (5th Cir. 1980). *Croce* was a wrongful death action brought by the widow and son of popular singer Jim Croce ("Bad, Bad Leroy Brown"), who died in a fatal plane crash. Despite repeated warnings from the trial judge, the defendants presented to the jury information suggesting the pilot's good reputation for safety. In response, it was permissible for the plaintiffs to introduce evidence of the pilot's past conduct for the limited purpose of preventing the jury from drawing the inference from the defendants' evidence that there were no such incidents.

1 McCormick on Evidence §57 at 254-256 (John W. Strong, ed., 5th ed. 1999) provides the following summary of the "fighting fire with fire" doctrine:

> Because of the many variable factors affecting the solution in a particular case, the diverse situations do not lend themselves easily to neat generalizations. However, the published decisions do identify two key factors, the prejudicial nature of the evidence and whether the opponent made a timely objection.... The following generalizations, having some support in the decisions, are submitted as reasonable:
>
> (1) If the inadmissible evidence sought to be answered is irrelevant and not prejudice-arousing, the judge, to save time and to avoid distraction from the issues, should refuse to hear answering evidence; but if he does hear it, under the prevailing view the party opening the door has no standing to complain....
>
> (2) Suppose...that the evidence, though inadmissible, is relevant to the issues and hence presumably damaging to the adversary's case, or though irrelevant is materially prejudicial and the adversary has seasonably objected or moved to strike. Here the adversary should be entitled to give answering evidence as of right. By objecting he did his best to save the court from mistake. His remedy by assigning appellate error to the ruling is inadequate. He needs a fair opportunity to win his case at the trial by refuting the damaging evidence....
>
> (3) If the first inadmissible evidence is relevant, or though irrelevant is prejudicial, but the adversary has failed to object or to move to strike out where an objection might have avoided the harm, the allowance of answering evidence should rest in the judge's discretion. The judge ought to weigh the probable impact of the first evidence, the time and distraction incident to answering it, and the likely effectiveness of a curative instruction to the jury to disregard it. However, here several courts have indicated that introduction of the answering evidence is a matter of right....
>
> (4) In any event, if the inadmissible evidence or even the inquiry eliciting it is so prejudice-arousing that an objection or motion to strike would not have erased the harm, the adversary should be entitled to answer it as of right.

KEY POINTS

1. There is no Federal Rule dealing with the doctrine of curative admissibility. Nonetheless, in limited situations courts will permit parties to introduce otherwise inadmissible evidence to respond to an opponent's inadmissible evidence.

2. The doctrine of curative admissibility is likely to apply only in situations in which a timely objection to the opponent's inadmissible evidence is unlikely to correct the unfairness of presenting or suggesting that evidence to the jury.

PROBLEMS

6.15. Return to Problem 3.2 at page 129. If the defense had made no reference to Exhibit A and if the defense evidence had been limited to the circumstances of the accident and Paul's injuries, would the cross-examination of Driver about her speeding ticket have been proper?

Assume, as in the Problem, that Driver offers Exhibit A into Evidence. Now should the plaintiff be permitted to cross-examine Driver about her speeding ticket? Does your answer depend upon whether there was an objection to Exhibit A and, if so, whether it was sustained or overruled?

6.16. Ralph Eastman is being tried for possession of cocaine. After the prosecution has presented its case, Eastman takes the witness stand and on direct examination testifies as follows:

Q: Mr. Eastman, do you live alone?
A: No, I share an apartment with Ed Higgins.
Q: Do you both have access to the entire apartment?
A: Yes.
Q: Does the cocaine that is the subject of this prosecution belong to you?
A: No.
Q: Did you ever have this cocaine in your possession?
A: No.
Q: Were you aware that the cocaine was in your apartment?
A: No.
Q: Have you ever in your life possessed cocaine?
A: No, never. I have never messed with any drugs.

After the defense presents the rest of its evidence, the prosecutor, in rebuttal, offers the testimony of Jack Evans that on one occasion last year at a party he snorted cocaine with Ralph Eastman and that when they were college roommates five years ago they smoked marijuana regularly. Defense counsel objects to the admission of the evidence. What result?

CHAPTER SEVEN

THE IMPEACHMENT AND
REHABILITATION
OF WITNESSES

Our concern in this chapter is with the theory and methods of impeaching and rehabilitating the credibility of witnesses. Some trials and much courtroom drama turn on the question of credibility. The rules of evidence considered here establish the framework within which the opposing parties may present evidence of witnesses' credibility to the jury.

A. SOME BASIC CONCEPTS

1. Impeachment: The Inferential Process

a. The Testimonial Inferences

The strength and accuracy of any witness's testimony is dependent upon certain testimonial abilities: A witness must be able to observe events, to remember them, and to relate them honestly and accurately. The jury must make inferences about these abilities — the ability to be honest, to narrate accurately, to perceive, and to remember — in order to credit the truth of what an in-court witness says (or, as you will see in Chapter Eight, what a hearsay declarant says if the hearsay evidence is admissible pursuant to a hearsay exception). For example, when a witness offers to testify, "The defendant's car ran the red light," the jury must infer that the witness is trying to communicate that the defendant was driving a car that did not stop at a red light, that the witness honestly believes this assertion, and that the witness's belief is based on the witness's accurate perception and memory about what happened.

Diagram 7-1 illustrates these inferences. If any of the inferences in the diagram is false, the evidence is not relevant to prove that the defendant did not stop at the red light. To help ensure that they are not false, the law requires witnesses to testify from firsthand knowledge (FRE 602) and to affirm that they will testify truthfully (FRE 603). For several reasons, however, the law does not generally require the proponent of evidence to make any other special showing regarding the accuracy of these inferences as a condition of admissibility. First, although there are obvious exceptions, our common experience tells us that people tend to be honest and accurate in most situations.

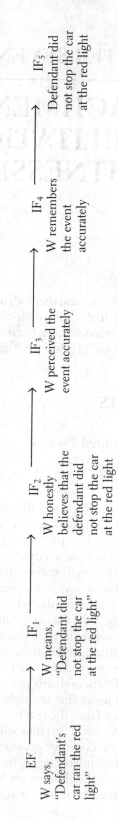

Diagram 7-1

(Consider the chaos in which we would live if the foregoing statement were not generally true.) Second, typically witnesses will testify to general background information about their residences and occupations, which will provide some minimal personal information for the jury to consider in assessing the strength of the inferences. Third, in the Anglo-American legal system, the task of assessing the accuracy of these inferences traditionally has been one for the jury rather than the judge. Finally, opposing counsel will have the opportunity to try to raise doubts about the strength of these inferences.

b. Types of Impeachment Evidence

Impeachment is the process of trying to raise doubts about the inferences illustrated in the Diagram 7-1. It is, in other words, an attempt to show that a witness may have inadvertently narrated the events incorrectly, been insincere (i.e., lied), misperceived the events about which the witness testified, or forgotten some or all of what happened. To the extent that the fact finder believes the impeaching evidence, the fact finder should conclude that what the witness said is less likely to be accurate than if there had been no impeaching evidence.

If the witness has offered an opinion or conclusion about some matter, there is a further impeachment concern. Consider, for example, a witness's testimony that the defendant was drunk. Even if the witness is sincere, is using the term "drunk" in a commonly understood sense, correctly perceived the events, and recalls them accurately, the witness may have misevaluated the defendant's symptoms and used erroneous generalizations for either of two reasons. First, the witness may not be a very good judge of drunkenness. For example, the witness may have associated loud, boisterous talk with drunkenness without realizing that the defendant always speaks in a loud, boisterous manner. Second the defendant's symptoms, although indicative of drunkenness, may in fact have had some other source. The impeaching party may suggest both of these possibilities to the fact finder, and the fact finder may then tend to disregard the witness's opinion.

There are a variety of ways to discredit a witness:

(1) Evidence that a witness has a character trait for untruthfulness suggests that the witness may be untruthful on the witness stand.
(2) Showing that the witness has a bias or interest in the case suggests a motive for being untruthful.
(3) Attacks on other testimonial qualities such as the witness's narrative or perceptive abilities may also undermine a witness's credibility. Such attacks may focus on general abilities (e.g., color-blindness) or on the specific exercise of those abilities on the occasion relevant to the case (e.g., witness not wearing glasses at time event observed).
(4) Proof of a witness's inconsistent statements suggests that the fact finder should be skeptical about the accuracy of the witness's testimony.
(5) Testimony from other sources that contradicts the witness may reduce the witness's believability.

c. Impeachment Evidence Versus Substantive Evidence

Evidence offered to impeach the credibility of a witness — like all other evidence that is admitted — must be relevant to prove or disprove some fact that is of consequence to the litigation. If it were not, the impeachment evidence would be inadmissible pursuant to FRE 402. The difference between evidence offered for "impeachment" purposes and evidence offered for "substantive" purposes is in the relevance theory that leads to the ultimate destination — that is, to the proof or disproof of some fact of consequence.

The evidentiary facts that we deal with in this chapter are those that relate to essential elements of a case because they may influence the jury's evaluation of witnesses (and hearsay declarants) as reliable sources of knowledge. Sometimes evidence that tends to impeach the credibility of witnesses will be relevant and admissible as substantive evidence of an essential element. When this is the case, there is no need to consider whether the evidence is admissible to impeach a witness, for as we illustrate at pages 410-411, infra, the impeachment use of the evidence inevitably requires an inferential chain of reasoning that is more circuitous than the chain of reasoning required to make the evidence relevant substantively. Often, however, impeachment evidence is inadmissible for a substantive purpose. Here are three examples to illustrate these points:

(1) In the case of a bank robbery, the teller who handed money over to the robber may testify that the defendant was not the robber. Other witnesses, customers in the bank, may identify the defendant as the robber. A police officer may establish that the teller is the sister of the defendant. The testimony of the customers implicitly impeaches the credibility of the teller (and vice versa), but each witness's testimony is independently admissible on the substantive question of the robber's identity. The testimony of the police officer is not independently admissible; its only relevance is to impeach the credibility of the teller by showing bias.

(2) In the running the red light hypothetical, the defendant wishes to impeach the plaintiff's witness with the witness's earlier statement, not made under oath, that the light was green when the defendant entered the intersection. Because of the hearsay rule, the prior statement is inadmissible as substantive evidence that the light was green. FRE 801(d)(1)(A). The defendant, however, may use the prior statement, without regard to its truth, to infer that the witness's direct examination testimony is not accurate. Knowing that the witness has made inconsistent statements about the same subject, regardless of which statement is true, casts some doubt on the witness's credibility. On one of the two occasions the witness may have been lying; at the very least, the inconsistency shows that the witness is not particularly careful about narrating the events of the accident.

(3) Della Dean is charged with perjury and testifies in her own defense. To impeach Della's testimony, the prosecution offers evidence that Della was convicted of perjury two years ago. It would be impermissible under FRE 404 to introduce evidence of past perjury to prove that Della committed perjury on the occasion charged in the current indictment. Since Della has testified as a witness, however, it will be permissible to introduce her prior conviction in order to impeach her credibility. FRE 609(a). The inferential process is as follows: Because Della has committed perjury, she is a generally untruthful person, who may be lying on the witness stand.

In short, to admit evidence for the purpose of impeaching the credibility of a witness is to admit evidence that, but for its impeachment value, would not be admissible — either because it would be irrelevant, as in the first hypothetical, or because some exclusionary rule (e.g., the hearsay rule or FRE 404(b)) would prohibit its substantive use, as in the latter two hypotheticals.

When evidence is admissible only to impeach the credibility of a witness, the limited admissibility has three significant consequences. First, the proponent of the impeachment evidence in resisting a directed verdict or summary judgment motion cannot rely on that evidence to satisfy a burden of production. Second, the proponent in closing argument cannot rely on the impeachment evidence as substantive proof of disputed facts. Third, whenever the evidence is relevant but inadmissible for some nonimpeachment purpose, the party against whom the evidence is offered can make an FRE 403 objection and, if the evidence is admitted, is entitled to a limiting instruction. Consider, for example, the hypothetical in which the defendant introduced evidence that a plaintiff's witness had made an inconsistent statement about whether the defendant ran the red light:

- The defendant could not rely on the substance of the inconsistent statement to support the production burden on the question of contributory negligence.
- If the case went to the jury, the defendant could argue that the inconsistency suggested the witness was mistaken or lying about the color of the light, but the defendant could not argue that the statement was a truthful assertion that the light was green for the defendant.
- The plaintiff would be entitled to an instruction that the jury could use the statement only to assess the witness's credibility, not as substantive evidence of the color of the light.

Do you think jurors are likely to be able to understand or follow a limiting instruction? If not, would it be desirable either (1) to exclude the evidence altogether on FRE 403 grounds or (2) to forego the limiting instruction? See Section E, infra.

2. Extrinsic Evidence and Impeachment

One can impeach a witness (1) by examination (usually cross-examination) of the witness and (2) by introduction of extrinsic evidence. *Extrinsic evidence* means any evidence other than that developed through direct or cross-examination of the witness. It may be an exhibit, such as a record of a prior conviction, or the testimony of another witness that impeaches the first witness by showing, for example, bias or an inconsistent statement that the first witness denied making.

If the cross-examiner were not allowed to use extrinsic evidence to impeach a witness, the witness could deny the facts relevant to the impeachment, and the impeaching party would be at a loss to correct the witness's misstatement. It would seem unfair to prohibit the use of extrinsic evidence to prove, for example, a witness's bias or inconsistent statement. On the other hand, excessive reliance on extrinsic impeachment evidence may substantially prolong trials and deflect emphasis from the critical substantive issues. Consider, for example, a prosecutor's effort to impeach a criminal defendant's character witness, W_1, by calling W_2 to testify to W_1's bias, followed by the criminal defendant calling W_3 to testify about W_2's bad character for truthfulness, followed by the prosecutor calling W_4 to testify about W_3's inconsistent statements, and so on. At some point — probably well before W_4 is called as a witness — FRE 403 concerns should require that this potentially endless chain of extrinsic impeachment evidence be broken.

As we discuss various impeachment techniques, we will consider the extent to which courts are likely to permit extrinsic evidence.

3.   Bolstering Credibility

FRE 608(a) prohibits introducing reputation or opinion evidence of a witness's good character for truthfulness unless the witness's character for truthfulness has been attacked. This prohibition is a specific application of the general common law rule that prevented a party from bolstering a witness's credibility until after there had been an attempt to impeach the witness's credibility. For example, if X testified for the plaintiff that the defendant's car ran through a red light and if there had been no effort to impeach X's credibility, the plaintiff could not introduce evidence of X's character for truthfulness or X's prior consistent statements. The Federal Rules contain no *general* prohibition against bolstering a witness's credibility prior to any impeachment. When a party attempts to introduce preimpeachment bolstering evidence not specifically excluded by FRE 608(a), admissibility under the Federal Rules should turn on the application of FRE 403. Nonetheless, federal courts continue to articulate the general common law prohibition against *all* bolstering prior to impeachment. United States v. Bolick, 917 F.2d 135, 137-140 (4th Cir. 1990) (citing no Federal Rule); United States v. Hilton, 772 F.2d 783, 787 (11th Cir. 1985) (citing FRE 608(a) even though preimpeachment bolstering did not involve reputation or opinion evidence); Raysor v. Port Authority of New York and New Jersey, 768 F.2d 34, 40 (2d Cir. 1985) (citing no Federal Rule). Preimpeachment bolstering may be appropriate, however, if an opening statement calls a witness's credibility into question. United States v. Cruz, 805 F.2d 1464 (11th Cir. 1986).

Although most reported cases dealing with preimpeachment bolstering involve attempts to show that a witness is being sincere or truthful, sincerity is only one of several testimonial qualities. As we noted in Section 1 at pages 351-353, supra, the value of a witness's testimony depends not only on the witness's sincerity but also on the witness's perceptions, memory and ability to narrate events accurately. If the jurisdiction has a general preimpeachment bolstering prohibition, it should apply to attempts to bolster these other testimonial qualities as well. United States v. Awkard, 597 F.2d 667 (9th Cir. 1979) ("party calling a witness should not be permitted to inquire in any way into the witness's ability to recall, or methods of pretrial memory refreshment, until such questions have been raised by the adversary").

In most cases of attempted preimpeachment bolstering, a reasoned application of FRE 403 will probably bring about the same exclusionary result as the common law rule. In the absence of impeachment, jurors are not likely to disbelieve a witness. In such a case, the independent bolstering evidence will have little independent probative value, and, therefore, it is not worth the court's time to hear the evidence.

There are, however, two potential problems with the common law rule. First, the line between improper bolstering and permissible examination may not always be clear. At one extreme, it would undoubtedly be regarded as bolstering to ask a witness about the witness's own prior consistent statements, the witness's character for truthfulness, or the witness's acts reflecting truthfulness. At the other extreme, questions that merely complete the narrative or emphasize the strength of witness's testimony are not typically characterized as "bolstering" evidence. For example, it is permissible for an eyewitness to testify that the witness got a good look at the defendant or that the line of vision was not obstructed. Blackburn v. Foltz, 828 F.2d 1177, 1185 (6th Cir. 1987). But how far should a direct examiner be allowed to go to suggest that an eyewitness's testimony is probably reliable? See Passman v. Blackburn, 652 F.2d 559, 568 (5th Cir. 1981) (defendant claimed that prosecutor's direct examination designed to establish that witness had acute vision was improper bolstering; court characterized evidence as going to the strength of the identification). Instead of trying to discern a line between ordinary examination and bolstering, it would be preferable to deal with this type of issue as one of relevance and FRE 403 balancing.

Second, impeachment is not the only thing that can raise doubts about a witness's credibility. For example, the physical appearance or nervousness of a witness may cause the jury to question the witness's truthfulness; jurors may doubt a story because it sounds improbable; or the contradictory eye-witness accounts of two witnesses may implicitly impeach one or both of them. In at least some of these situations, evidence that would be regarded as bolstering under the common law probably should be admissible, despite the absence of any effort to impeach the witness. In such a case, the proponent of the bolstering evidence should argue that FRE 608(a)(2) applies only to reputation or opinion evidence, that the Federal Rules have not adopted the *general* common law anti-bolstering rule, and that admissibility of bolstering evidence (other than reputation or opinion evidence) should be governed by FRE 401-403.

B. IMPEACHMENT AND REHABILITATION WITH CHARACTER EVIDENCE

In Chapter Five we considered evidentiary restrictions on the substantive use of character evidence. We noted that one of the FRE 404(a) exceptions to the general prohibition against using character evidence to show action in conformity with character was the use of character evidence for impeachment and rehabilitation. FRE 404(a)(3). It is to this subject that we now turn. We are concerned here with using evidence of a witness's character for truthfulness to infer action in conformity with that character trait on a particular occasion (i.e., to infer that the witness is either lying or telling the truth on the witness stand). FRE 608 refers to a witness's "character for truthfulness or untruthfulness." Unless the context suggests a contrary meaning, our use of the term *truthfulness* includes both truthfulness and untruthfulness.

The rules governing impeachment and rehabilitation with character evidence, as well as the rules governing other forms of impeachment and rehabilitation evidence, apply to *all* witnesses and to *all* kinds of cases. With some minor exceptions that we will discuss in due course, it makes no difference whether the witness happens to be a party. A party may use character evidence to impeach a witness in civil as well as criminal trials, and criminal defendants do not have the option to keep the door closed to inquiries about any witness's character for truthfulness.

Because the rules governing the use of character evidence for impeachment purposes (FRE 404(a)(3), 608, and 609) are different from the rules governing character evidence for substantive purposes (FRE 404(a)(1) and (2), 404(b), and 405) and because both sets of rules are intricate, the general subject of character evidence may seem confusing. The best way to eliminate the confusion is to focus initially on what should always be the first question: How is the evidence relevant? Once you answer this question, it should be relatively easy to apply the proper rules.

1. FRE 608

RULE 608. EVIDENCE OF CHARACTER AND CONDUCT OF WITNESS

(a) Opinion and Reputation Evidence of Character. The credibility of a witness may be attacked or supported by evidence in the form of opinion or reputation, but subject to these limitations: (1) the evidence may refer only to character for truthfulness or untruthfulness, and (2) evidence of truthful character is admissible only after the character of the witness for truthfulness has been attacked by opinion or reputation evidence or otherwise.

(b) Specific instances of conduct. Specific instances of conduct of a witness, for the purpose of attacking or supporting the witness' character for truthfulness, other than the conviction of crime as provided in rule 609, may not be proved by extrinsic evidence. They may, however, in the discretion of the court, if probative of truthfulness or untruthfulness, be inquired into on cross-examination of the witness (1) concerning the witness' character for truthfulness or untruthfulness, or (2) concerning the character for truthfulness or untruthfulness of another witness as to which character the witness being cross-examined has testified.

The giving of testimony, whether by an accused or by any other witness does not operate as a waiver of the accused's or the witness' privilege against self-incrimination when examined with respect to matters which relate only to character for truthfulness.

(Our initial discussion focuses on FRE 608(a). We discuss the remainder of the rule later in this section.)

2. Interpretation and Illustration of FRE 608(a)

a. *Reputation and Opinion Evidence to Prove Character for Truthfulness*

One method to impeach or to rehabilitate a witness is with reputation or opinion evidence offered to prove the witness's character for truthfulness in order to suggest that the witness is lying or telling the truth on the witness stand. Occasionally witnesses will testify that they are being truthful, thereby in effect offering opinion testimony about their own truthfulness. The usual method of impeaching or rehabilitating witnesses pursuant to FRE 608(a), however, is with extrinsic evidence — that is, opinion or reputation testimony offered by one witness about another witness's character for truthfulness. For example, in the *Johnson* case the defendant could have called witnesses to testify that Officer Huston (or any other prosecution witness) had a bad reputation for truthfulness.

FRE 608(a) permits both reputation and opinion evidence of character for truthfulness. The process of eliciting reputation or opinion testimony from a character witness pursuant to FRE 608(a) is identical to the process described in Chapter Five, where we dealt with the use of reputation and opinion evidence for substantive purposes. For a review of the foundation requirement and a discussion of why opinion witnesses should not be permitted to set forth the factual bases for their opinions, see pages 284-285, supra.

FRE 608(a)(1) limits the use of reputation or opinion evidence to "character for truthfulness or untruthfulness." This limitation repudiates the position of a few jurisdictions, which have permitted parties to impeach witnesses with evidence of general bad character or bad moral character. According to the Advisory Committee Note:

> In accordance with the bulk of judicial authority, the inquiry is strictly limited to character for veracity, rather than allowing evidence as to character generally. The result is to sharpen relevancy, to reduce surprise, waste of time, and confusion, and to make the lot of the witness somewhat less unattractive.

b. The FRE 608(a)(2) Limitation on Evidence of Truthful Character

According to FRE 608(a)(2) reputation or opinion testimony regarding a witness's good character for truthfulness is not admissible until the witness's character has been "attacked." It is not entirely clear, though, what kind of impeachment constitutes an attack on character for truthfulness. As FRE 608(a)(2) specifies, reputation or opinion evidence of bad character for truthfulness will suffice, but what does "or otherwise" in the last sentence of FRE 608(a)(2) mean? Courts traditionally have regarded impeachment by showing prior convictions, FRE 609, or bad acts that did not result in convictions, FRE 608(b), as an attack on a witness's character. Thus rehabilitation with reputation or opinion evidence would be appropriate. For example, since the prosecution in the *Johnson* case impeached the credibility of both inmate Michael Green and the defendant with evidence of prior convictions (page 49, lines 7, 21; page 55, line 1, supra), it would have been permissible for the defendant to call witnesses who would offer their opinions that Green and Johnson were truthful individuals.

On the other hand, courts have regarded proof of a witness's bias as not being an attack on the witness's character. United States v. Lindemann, 85 F.3d 1232 (7th Cir. 1996). For example, in the *Johnson* case, if the prosecution could have established that Johnson and his cellmate belonged to the same gang (page 43, line 35; and page 44, line 31, supra), this evidence would show the cellmate's possible bias but not the cellmate's bad character for truthfulness. Similarly, proof in a civil case that a witness for the plaintiff had recently gone through an acrimonious, contested divorce with the defendant suggests that the witness may be biased against the defendant but not that the witness is a generally untruthful person. Thus FRE 608(a)(2) would not permit Johnson or the defendant in the civil action to rehabilitate the impeached witness by offering opinion or reputation evidence of that witness's good character for truthfulness.

Sometimes there will be disagreement about how to categorize the impeaching evidence. Consider, for example, United States v. Medical Therapy Sciences, Inc., 583 F.2d 36, 41 (2d Cir. 1978), which involved a nursing home operator charged with

Medicare fraud. The defendant impeached a former employee and key prosecution witness with evidence, inter alia, that the witness had embezzled money and stolen patients from the defendant in an effort to set up a rival company. Responding to the defendant's argument that this evidence showed only bias, the appellate court stated that the trial judge could reasonably have considered the evidence as attacking the witness's character for truthfulness:

> [E]vidence of bias can take many forms. Some types of bias, for example bias stemming from a relationship with a party, do not necessarily involve any issue relating to the moral character of the witness, but suggest only that the witness' testimony may perhaps unwittingly be slanted for reasons unrelated to general propensity for untruthfulness. As such, character evidence is not relevant to meet such an attack. On the other hand, alleged partiality based on hostility or self-interest may assume greater significance if it is sought to be proven by conduct rising to the level of corruption. The commentators agree that "[e]vidence of corrupt conduct on the part of a witness should be regarded as an attack on his truthfulness warranting supportive evidence . . . ." [Id. at 41.]

Thus it was proper to permit the prosecution to rehabilitate the witness with character evidence pursuant to FRE 608(a).

When parties use other impeachment devices — for example, prior inconsistent statements or demonstrations of contradiction, courts are divided on the propriety of allowing the proponent of the witness to use reputation or opinion evidence to rehabilitate the witness. Compare United States v. Thomas, 768 F.2d 611, 618 (5th Cir. 1985) (impeachment by showing contradiction does not permit rehabilitation with FRE 608(a) character witness), with Beard v. Mitchell, 604 F.2d 485, 503 (7th Cir. 1979) (impeachment by showing prior inconsistent statement permits rehabilitation with FRE 608(a) character witness), and United States v. Medical Therapy Sciences, Inc., supra at 41 n.6 (impeachment with contradiction permits rehabilitation with FRE 608(a) character witness). The resolution of these cases, like the resolution in *Medical Therapy Sciences*, should turn on whether the impeaching evidence tends to impugn the witness's character for truthfulness.

The Advisory Committee Note to FRE 608 expresses approval of the settled precedent but offers no specific guidance with respect to the areas of uncertainty:

> [E]vidence of misconduct, including conviction of a crime, and of corruption . . . fall within this category [of attacks on character for truthfulness]. Evidence of bias or interest does not . . . . Whether evidence in the form of contradiction is an attack upon the character of the witness must depend upon the circumstances.

Why should proof of bias not be considered an attack on the character of the witness? Recall in the *Johnson* case that defense counsel on cross-examination of Officer Huston suggested Huston's alleged injury in the altercation with Johnson was fabricated because of the workers' compensation rules (page 18, line 20, supra). This inquiry suggests a particular bias or motive to lie. Does it also impugn Huston's character for truthfulness, so that the prosecution could have responded with FRE 608(a) character witnesses to testify about Huston's reputation for truthfulness? See if you can articulate a difference between character and bias that justifies different treatment under FRE 608(a). For the advocate, what "circumstances" are relevant to determining whether impeachment by proof of bias, an inconsistent statement, or a contradiction warrants rehabilitation with reputation or opinion evidence about the witness's good character for truthfulness?

KEY POINTS

1. FRE 608(a) permits a party to impeach the credibility of a witness by offering extrinsic evidence in the form of opinion or reputation testimony about the witness's character for truthfulness. The evidence must focus on truthfulness, not general moral character.

2. FRE 608(a) permits reputation or opinion evidence offered to prove a witness's good character for truthfulness only after the opposing party has attacked the witness's character for truthfulness.

PROBLEMS

7.1. Darby is being prosecuted for the armed robbery of a liquor store proprietor. During the presentation of the prosecution's case the proprietor made a positive identification of Darby as the robber. As part of the defense, Darby calls Sue Williams to testify that the proprietor has a reputation in the community for lying. Is the evidence admissible?

7.2. In the same case, another defense witness offers to testify that the proprietor has a reputation in the community for not remembering faces and for misidentifying people. Is the evidence admissible? Would your answer be different if the witness offered to testify that on the basis of her experience with the proprietor she is of the view that the proprietor has difficulty remembering faces and often misidentifies people?

7.3. Harper was arrested for sale of cocaine and accepted the government's offer to cooperate in obtaining evidence against his supplier. Harper identified Ellsworth as the supplier, and Ellsworth was eventually charged with sale of cocaine. At Ellsworth's trial, Agent Fowler, who was in charged of the investigation, testified that Harper had delivered what was in fact cocaine to him, and Harper testified that he had obtained the cocaine from Ellsworth. During the cross-examination of Harper, defense counsel elicited information about Harper's cooperation with the police. During the cross-examination of Agent Fowler, defense counsel elicited that Harper had three independent sources for cocaine. On redirect of Agent Fowler, the prosecutor asks:

(a) Do you believe Mr. Harper received the cocaine involved in this case from a source other than the defendant, Ellsworth?

(b) In your opinion is Mr. Harper's testimony in this case truthful?

(c) In your opinion is Mr. Harper a truthful person?

How should the court rule on Ellsworth's objections to these questions? Would any of your answers be different if defense counsel had referred to Harper as liar in the opening statement? If defense counsel had elicited from Harper on cross-examination that two years ago he was convicted of embezzlement?

7.4. Dan Dickson is charged with perjury and testifies in his own behalf. The prosecutor's cross-examination fails to shake Dickson's story or cast doubt on his credibility. Dickson then offers the testimony of Willa Wilson that Dickson has a good reputation in the community for truthfulness. Is Wilson's testimony admissible?

3. Interpretation and Illustration of FRE 608(b)(1)

FRE 608(b) provides in part:

(b) Specific instances of conduct. Specific instances of conduct of a witness, for the purpose of attacking or supporting the witness' character for truthfulness, other than conviction of crime as provided in rule 609, may not be proved by extrinsic evidence. They may, however, in the discretion of the court, if probative of truthfulness or untruthfulness, be inquired into on cross-examination of the witness (1) concerning the witness' character for truthfulness or untruthfulness . . . .

The giving of testimony, whether by an accused or by any other witness does not operate as a waiver of the accused's or the witness' privilege against self-incrimination when examined with respect to matters which relate only to character for truthfulness.

a. The Prohibition Against the Use of Extrinsic Evidence

The Federal Rules in the first sentence of FRE 608(b), like the common law, prohibit the use of extrinsic evidence of a witness's specific acts to prove character for truthfulness to show dishonesty or honesty on the witness stand. FRE 608(b) and a majority of states, however, do permit inquiry into a witness's own acts during the examination of that witness. The prohibition against the use of extrinsic evidence means that the examiner is bound by the answer of the witness; the impeaching party cannot introduce extrinsic evidence to contradict the witness. For example, in the *Johnson* case, defense counsel could have asked Officer Huston if he lied on his job application form. If Huston denied lying, however, defense counsel could not prove the lie by introducing the job application form, which would be extrinsic evidence, and then proving with other extrinsic evidence that the information contained on the form was false.

b. The 2003 Clarifying Amendment

A 2003 amendment to FRE 608(b) substituted the phrase "character for truthfulness" for the term "credibility" in the first sentence. This change makes it clear that the extrinsic evidence ban applies only to specific acts offered to show character for truthfulness and not to specific acts offered for other impeachment purposes, such as to show bias or contradiction. The admissibility of extrinsic evidence for noncharacter impeachment purposes is governed by FRE 403. Even before the amendment, most courts had interpreted the extrinsic evidence ban as applying only to specific acts offered to show character for truthfulness. See, e.g., United States v. Castillo, 181

F.3d 1129 (9th Cir. 1999).[1] Some courts, however, had interpreted the term "credibility" more broadly. United States v. Miller, 159 F.3d 1106, 1112 (7th Cir. 1998) (applying FRE 608(b) to exclude extrinsic evidence offered to contradict a witness).

c. The Limited Scope of Permissible Inquiry

FRE 608(b), like the rule in the majority of common law courts, is consistent with FRE 608(a) in that the specific acts must relate to character for truthfulness. This rule is considerably narrower than the rules in some state jurisdictions, which permit inquiry into acts relevant to prove a generally bad moral character. The result in these latter jurisdictions is that almost any bad act is relevant; and if the act is relevant, courts have almost invariably permitted the inquiry.

In explaining its limitation of the inquiry to acts relating to truthfulness, the Advisory Committee Note states:

> Effective cross-examination demands that some allowance be made for going into matters of this kind, but the possibilities of abuse are substantial. Consequently, safeguards are erected in the form of specific requirements that the instances inquired into be probative of truthfulness or its opposite.

The term *safeguards* in the preceding passage is plural because FRE 608(b), as originally drafted and as promulgated by the Supreme Court, also contained the requirement that the acts be "not remote in time." That language was deleted and the "in the discretion of the court" language was inserted by Congress. According to the House Judiciary Committee:

> The Committee amended the Rule to emphasize the discretionary power of the court in permitting such testimony and deleted the reference to remoteness in time as being unnecessary and confusing (remoteness from time of trial or remoteness from the incident involved?).

Despite the deletion of the time limitation, the time factor is obviously relevant in assessing probative value, and the concern with remoteness should be remoteness from the time of trial. Since the theory of relevance is that the witness's character for truthfulness indicates that the witness may be lying or truthful on the witness stand, quite obviously the concern is with the witness's current — that is, at the time of trial — character. In considering the time factor, it should be appropriate to reason by analogy to FRE 609, which, as you will see shortly, imposes specific time restrictions on prior convictions that can be used to impeach a witness.

d. No Fifth Amendment Waiver

Because of the centrality of cross-examination to our adversary system, the giving of testimony by a witness is regarded as a waiver or forfeiture of the witness's Fifth

---

1. We believe that the term of "credibility" in FRE 608(a) should also be interpreted narrowly to mean "character for truthfulness." Opinion evidence of a witness's sensory or mental incapacity has traditionally been admissible to impeach a witness's *credibility*, even though courts have not labeled such evidence as showing a *character* trait or *character for truthfulness*. FRE 608(a) should not be interpreted to limit this practice. See pages 403-405, infra.

Amendment right against self-incrimination, at least with respect to the subject matter of the witness's direct examination testimony. The last sentence of FRE 608(b) makes it clear that testifying is not a waiver of the privilege with respect to questions that are permissible only to undermine the witness's credibility. Consider, for example, our hypothetical question about whether Officer Huston had lied on his job application form. If making false statements on the form were a crime, Officer Huston could rely on the Fifth Amendment to refuse to answer.

4.   Elaboration of FRE 608(b)(1)

a.   *The Rationale for the Prohibition Against Extrinsic Evidence*

Not permitting the examiner to challenge the witness's answer with extrinsic evidence of bad character for truthfulness may sometimes appear unfair. For example, in our hypothetical in which Officer Huston denies that he lied on his job application form, assume that defense counsel is prepared to authenticate the job application form and to call 10 witnesses who will testify that the facts stated in the application are false. What could be better impeaching evidence than this extrinsic proof that the witness had lied not only on the job application form but also on the witness stand?

Perhaps the answer is that there could not be a more relevant or more effective impeachment. The effectiveness of the impeachment, however, depends on the certainty with which the impeaching party can establish the lie. It may be, for example, that the job application form is a forgery, that the statements on the job application are reasonably subject to more than one interpretation, or that the witnesses who would testify that Officer Huston lied on the application are themselves dishonest. If the impeaching party is allowed to introduce the extrinsic evidence, the party whose witness was impeached should have an opportunity to counter that evidence. And if that opportunity exists, a substantial amount of time and energy could be devoted to litigating the truth or falsity of facts whose only value is to impeach the credibility of a witness. Moreover, there would be the potential for this type of minitrial with every witness. Thus, while it may be true that catching the witness in a lie on the stand would be extremely effective impeachment, FRE 608(b), out of concern with the time and distraction that could result from litigating collateral matters, prohibits the impeaching party from introducing extrinsic evidence to prove the lie.

Consider the adequacy of this justification for the absolute ban on extrinsic evidence. Some extrinsic evidence may be very probative of untruthfulness and bear few dangers of a protracted minitrial. Some commentators believe that it would be preferable to rely exclusively on FRE 403 and to make admissibility decisions on a case-by-case basis. Kevin C. McMunigal and Calvin William Sharpe, Reforming Extrinsic Impeachment, 33 Conn. L. Rev. 363 (2001). What would be the advantages and disadvantages of a more discretionary rule?

b.   *The Scope of Permissible Questions*

i.   The Meaning of Untruthfulness.   Although the Advisory Committee Note to FRE 608(b) makes it clear that the terms *truthfulness* and *untruthfulness* are intended to limit the types of specific acts about which one may inquire, there is not uniform agreement about the scope of the limitation. At the extremes, courts tend to find that perjury or other instances of making false statements suggest untruthfulness, United States v. Jensen, 41 F.3d 946 (5th Cir. 1994) (submission of false tax return and false loan documents to obtain loan), and that acts of violence (e.g., murder, destruction of property) do not suggest untruthfulness. United States v. Geston, 299 F.3d 1130, 1137 (9th Cir. 2002) (violent conduct while under influence of alcohol not probative of untruthfulness). Cf. United States v. Wilson, 344 F.2d 1208 (10th Cir. 2001) (drug crimes not probative of truth or untruth). There is, however, a large gray area where courts sometimes reach seemingly inconsistent results. Compare, e.g., United States v. Wilson, 985 F.2d 348, 352 (7th Cir. 1993) (bribery probative of untruthfulness) with United States v. Rosa, 891 F.2d 1063, 1069 (3d Cir. 1989) (bribery "not the kind of conduct which bears on truthfulness or untruthfulness"). Consider, for example, whether activities such as failing to make a required report, knowingly purchasing stolen property, or engaging in theft should be considered acts that show a character trait for untruthfulness. (With respect to theft, the answer may turn on the specifics of the individual crime. Forcibly taking property from another arguably does not suggest untruthfulness, whereas obtaining money by false pretenses arguably is an act of untruthfulness.)

   ii. Questions about Arrests, Charges, and Administrative or Judicial Findings. Sometimes an impeaching party will have evidence that a witness was arrested or charged with some offense relating to untruthfulness or that an administrative or judicial body has found that a witness behaved in a manner indicating untruthfulness. For example, the witness may have been arrested for or charged with falsifying loan documents; the witness may have been disbarred for deceitful conduct; or a judge in an earlier proceeding may have implicitly or explicitly found that the witness had lied. In these situations FRE 608(b) permits the impeaching party to ask about the underlying conduct — whether the witness in fact falsified documents, engaged in deceitful conduct, or lied in an earlier proceeding. But what about asking whether the witness was *arrested* or *charged* with falsifying documents, whether the witness was *disbarred* for the deceitful conduct, or whether a *judge found* that the witness had lied?

   A witness' arrest or a factual finding about the witness is not a specific instance of the *witness's* conduct. Rather, as we pointed out in Chapter Five at page 288, supra, an arrest or a finding is activity engaged in by the arresting officer or the fact finder. Moreover, as we point out in Chapter Eight at pages 437-438, infra, this type of evidence is hearsay. The witness is not being asked directly whether the witness engaged in the conduct. Instead, the witness is being asked whether somebody else — the arresting officer (or person who authorized the arrest) or the fact finder — *said* that the witness engaged in the conduct. And, of course, that statement of the police officer or the fact finder is relevant to impeach the witness only if one believes the truth of what the officer or fact finder said.

   Despite the hearsay nature of questions about arrests, charges, and findings, there is precedent for permitting these types of questions. United States v. Whitmore, 359 F.3d 609 (D.C. Cir. 2004) (judge's finding that witness had lied); United States v. Whitehead, 618 F.2d 523 (4th Cir. 1980) (question about suspension from bar for activities involving misrepresentation and deceit); United States v. Scott, 74 F.3d 175,177 (9th Cir. 1996) (question about prior arrest). Even when a court concludes that such a question is improper, the rationale may not be hearsay. United

States v. Lopez, 944 F.2d 33, 38 (1st Cir. 1991) (no "abuse of discretion" in prohibiting FRE 608(b) cross-examination question about judicial finding that witness lied). The explanation for this precedent may be that counsel failed to make hearsay objections. See United States v. Whitmore, supra.

c.   Questions About Specific Acts and FRE 403

For a number of reasons, FRE 403 concerns may militate against even *asking* a witness about specific acts of untruthfulness. First, in some instances the witness's conduct, even if relevant to show untruthfulness, may have low probative value. Compare Ad-Vantage Telephone Directory Consultants, Inc. v. GTE Directories Corp, 37 F.3d 1460 (11th Cir. 1994) (accountant's 1969 sanction for ethical violation inadmissible on FRE 403 grounds because of remoteness in time) with United States v. Munoz, 233 F.3d 1117, 1135 (9th Cir. 2000) (14 to 16 year old incident not too remote). Second, if the witness acknowledges an act of untruthfulness, there is a risk of unfair prejudice. This risk is particularly great if the witness happens to be a party: The jury may be willing to decide against the party because the jury regards the witness as a bad person. United States v. DeGeratto, 876 F.2d 576, 582-583 (7th Cir. 1989) (emphasizing prejudicial nature of cross-examination about defendant's involvement in prostitution without discussing how such evidence was probative of truthfulness). Third, if there are numerous inquiries about the specific acts of truthfulness, there are likely to be concerns with time-consumption and confusion of the issues. Fourth, even if the witness honestly denies having committed a dishonest act, there is a risk that the jury may be more swayed by the suggestiveness of the question than by the answer. United States v. Dring, 930 F.2d 687, 692 (9th Cir. 1991) (quoting McCormick on Evidence for proposition that a "'slashing cross-examination may carry strong accusations of misconduct and bad character, which the witness's denial will not remove from the jury's mind'"). Finally, if the witness is a party and if the question relates to conduct similar to the conduct that is the subject of the litigation, there is a risk that the jury will consider the evidence, contrary to the dictate of FRE 404(b), as evidence that the defendant engaged in the conduct that is the subject of the litigation. United States v. Pintar, 630 F.2d 1270, 1285-1286 (8th Cir. 1980) (prosecution unduly emphasized illegal kickbacks that were not part of the charge and not admissible pursuant to FRE 404(b) in cross-examination of defendant).

Despite the FRE 403 grounds for objecting to FRE 608(b) questions, courts typically are quite liberal in permitting inquiry about specific acts to prove character for impeachment purposes. According to the Advisory Committee, "Effective cross-examination demands that some allowance be made for going into matters of this kind . . ."

d.   The "Discretion of the Court" to Exclude Questions About
Specific Acts

Consider the meaning of the "in the discretion of the court" language, which was added to FRE 608(b) by the House Judiciary Committee. Even without that language, it is clear that a court could rely on FRE 403 to exclude questions about marginally probative, unfairly prejudicial specific acts. Thus there is no need to provide explicitly for judicial discretion with respect to FRE 608(b). It seems likely that the phrase is nothing more than a reminder, albeit an unnecessary one, to the court and litigants that

FRE 403 may be a basis for exclusion. See United States v. Mateo-Sanchez, 864 F.2d 232, 236 (1st Cir. 1988) (emphasizing court's broad discretion). See David P. Leonard, Appellate Review of Evidentiary Rulings, 70 N.C. L. Rev. 1155 (1992), a particularly thoughtful analysis of the role of appellate courts in reviewing trial judges' FRE 608(b) decisions.

e.   Good Faith Requirement; Practical Considerations

Because of the suggestiveness that is likely to inhere in a question about a specific act relating to truthfulness, courts have held that the examiner must have a good-faith basis for believing that the act occurred. United States v. DeGeratto, 876 F.3d 576, 584 (7th Cir. 1989). Such a requirement is probably satisfied, for example, by knowledge that the witness had been arrested for the activity that is the subject of the question or by hearsay information obtained during the investigation of the case. For a discussion of this requirement in the context of impeaching character witnesses, see pages 287-288, supra, and page 369, infra.

A litigant who suspects that the opponent may ask a question without a factual basis for the inquiry should request a hearing on that issue outside the presence of the jury. Similarly, if a litigant suspects that the opponent may ask about some act falling outside the truthfulness limitation in FRE 608(b), the litigant should consider filing a motion in limine seeking a ruling on the issue. Unless the litigant knows that the opponent is aware of the potential impeaching evidence, however, filing such a motion may have the undesirable effect of alerting the opponent to the evidence.

f.   FRE 608(b)(1) Specific Acts Showing Good Character for Truthfulness

The primary focus of the case law and the literature dealing with FRE 608(b) is on questions relating to untruthfulness. Nonetheless, FRE 608(b) specifically permits questions that are probative of "*truthfulness or* untruthfulness" (emphasis added), and there is precedent for permitting litigants to question witnesses about good acts that tend to show the witness's truthful character. Unlike FRE 608(a), FRE 608(b) does not provide that evidence showing a truthful character is permissible only after the opposing party has attacked the witness's character. Nonetheless, as we suggested earlier, courts may rely on FRE 403 to prohibit preimpeachment efforts to bolster a witness's credibility.

The likely reason courts and commentators devote little attention to FRE 608(b)(1) good acts is that such evidence is obviously self-serving and, therefore, seldom worth objecting to or even attempting to introduce. While it may be important to try to rehabilitate a witness by putting in perspective or emphasizing the positive aspects of apparently bad acts that were the subject of impeaching questions, there is not likely to be much value in getting the witness to relate various other acts suggesting truthfulness. All of us, after all, probably engage in enough activity appearing to demonstrate truthfulness that such evidence would seem at best mundane. Moreover, there is the risk that the introduction of such evidence could have the opposite of its desired effect: If the lawyer feels it necessary to rely on such mundane evidence to convince the fact finder of the witness's truthfulness, perhaps there is reason to doubt the witness's truthfulness.

The first sentence of FRE 608(b), which prohibits extrinsic evidence, applies to specific acts relating to both truthfulness and untruthfulness. United States v. Melia, 691 F.2d 672, 674-675 (4th Cir. 1982) (improper to rehabilitate witness with extrinsic evidence that witness helped to solve various crimes). A witness responding to questions that put the witness in a favorable light, however, is likely to be cooperative. Thus there is virtually no risk that an examiner inquiring about good acts will receive an unfavorable answer.

g. Cross-Examination

Although most FRE 608(b)(1) questions about acts probative of untruthfulness will occur on cross-examination, there are two reasons why courts should probably not interpret the term cross-examination literally. First, as noted in the preceding section, FRE 608(b)(1) appears to contemplate questions to a witness that are probative of both the witness's truthfulness and the witness's untruthfulness. The same party, however, will not have an interest in asking both types of questions. Rather, one party — usually the party seeking to bolster the witness's credibility with questions about acts relating to truthfulness — will be able to pursue such an inquiry only on direct or, more probably, redirect examination. Second, and more important, FRE 607 permits the party who calls a witness to impeach the witness's credibility. Thus if a witness gives testimony that is unfavorable to the party who called the witness, that party may impeach the witness's credibility. For example, on direct examination the party calling the witness could show the witness's bias, inconsistent statement, or prior conviction (FRE 609). There is no conceivable reason why all of these impeachment devices, but not impeachment with questions about specific acts relating to untruthfulness, should be available to the direct examiner. Cf. Robinson v. Watts Detective Agency, Inc., 685 F.2d 729 (1st. Cir. 1982); United States v. Dixon, 547 F.2d 1079, 1082 n.2 (9th Cir. 1976) (both holding that in light of FRE 607, similar "cross-examination" language in a former version of FRE 609 should not be read literally and that it was permissible to prove prior convictions to impeach a witness on direct examination).

5. Interpretation and Illustration of FRE 608(b)(2)

FRE 608(b) provides in part:

> (b) Specific Instances of Conduct. Specific instances of the conduct of a witness, for the purpose of attacking or supporting the witness' character for truthfulness, other than conviction of crime as provided in rule 609, . . . may . . . , if probative of truthfulness or untruthfulness, be inquired into on cross-examination of the witness . . . (2) concerning the character for truthfulness or untruthfulness of another witness as to which character the witness being cross-examined has testified.

FRE 608(b)(2) addresses an issue we have considered previously: the cross-examination of reputation or opinion witnesses to test their knowledge of the reputation or the basis for the opinion about which they testify.

Once a character witness has given reputation or opinion testimony pursuant to FRE 608(a), the opposing party — in addition to impeaching the character witness with questions about the character witness's own acts of untruthfulness (FRE 608(b)(1)) — may impeach the character witness in the same manner in which a party may impeach character witnesses who give reputation or opinion testimony pursuant to FRE 404(a)(1) and (2): The impeaching party may ask the character witness if the character witness is aware of relevant specific acts committed by the person whose character was the subject of the witness's testimony. For example, if, as we hypothesized earlier about the *Johnson* case, the defense had called witnesses to testify that in their opinion Johnson was a truthful person, it would have been appropriate to ask these witnesses on cross-examination both about their own acts of untruthfulness (FRE 608(b)(1)) and about their knowledge of acts of dishonesty in which Johnson had engaged (FRE 608(b)(2)). It would not have been appropriate, however, to ask them if they knew about Johnson's previous rapes. As FRE 608(b) makes clear, the specific acts must relate to the character trait about which the FRE 608(a) character witness testified — truthfulness — and rapes are not (very) probative of truthfulness.

This FRE 608(b)(2) impeachment process is identical to the process for impeaching character witnesses that we described in Chapter Five. In effect, FRE 608(b)(2) is a specific, somewhat awkwardly worded application to FRE 608(a) character witnesses of the general principle set forth in the second sentence of FRE 405(a): "On cross-examination [of a character witness who offers reputation or opinion testimony], inquiry is allowable into relevant specific instances of conduct." As is the case in the context of relying on FRE 405(a) to impeach FRE 404(a) character witnesses, (1) the cross-examiner must have a good-faith basis for asking the questions, United States v. Reese, 568 F.2d 1246, 1249 (6th Cir. 1977), and (2) the legitimate purpose of the inquiry is to impeach the credibility of the character witness, *not* to prove the character of the principal witness, about whom the question is asked. Indeed, using the character witness's testimony about the principal witness's specific act to prove the principal witness's truthfulness would violate the FRE 608(b) prohibition against using extrinsic evidence to prove the principal witness's character.

KEY POINTS

1. FRE 608(b)(1) permits the impeachment and rehabilitation of witnesses with questions about the witnesses' own specific acts that show character for truthfulness. The examiner is bound by the witness's answer to such questions and may not introduce extrinsic evidence to challenge the answer.

2. FRE 608(b)(1) specific acts questions must relate to character for truthfulness, and they are subject to exclusion on FRE 403 grounds.

3. When an FRE 608(a) character witness offers opinion or reputation testimony about another witness's character for truthfulness, FRE 608(b)(2) permits the opposing party to ask the character witness about specific acts probative of truthfulness that the other witness may have committed. The purpose of the questions is to test the basis for the character witness's reputation or opinion testimony.

PROBLEMS

7.5. Defendant is charged with the sale of heroin. Two alleged purchasers and the arresting officer will be prosecution witnesses. There is evidence that one alleged purchaser in recent years has threatened and intimidated individuals who could offer incriminating evidence against him for his own drug trafficking activity and that the other alleged purchaser lied under oath in a civil action 13 years ago. The arresting officer, according to the defendant, stole $1,400 from the defendant at the time of the arrest. The officer denies the charge. The government has filed a motion in limine asking the court to preclude the defendant from asking about these incidents during cross-examination of the witnesses. How should the court rule?

7.6. Sam Browning is charged with murder. He plans to testify in his own behalf and to call Walt Williams to testify that Browning has a good reputation for peacefulness. The prosecutor has a good-faith basis for believing that three years ago Browning was involved in a bribery scheme; that he beat his wife (although no charges have ever been filed); and that last year Williams filed a false income tax return.

(a)   Can the prosecutor ask Browning about the bribery incident? The beating?
(b)   Can the prosecutor ask Williams if he has heard that Browning was involved in a bribery scheme three years ago? That Browning beat his wife three years ago?
(c)   Can the prosecutor ask Williams if he intentionally filed a false income tax return last year?

7.7. Ed Duke is being prosecuted for murdering Harry Howe, owner of Harry's Hash House. Harry was found dead on the floor of his Hash House and the till was open and empty. At trial Fred Finley testifies for the prosecution that the day before the murder Ed Duke said he was going to get Harry.

(a)   On cross-examination of Finley, defense counsel asks Finley whether he has ever been arrested for possession of marijuana.
(b)   Alex Adams offers to testify that several years ago he was an alter boy at the local church, that Finley was a chorister, and that several times Alex saw Finley steal church property such as cups and other religious objects.
(c)   Jane Jackson, a neighbor of Finley's parents, offers to testify that she has know Finley for Finley's entire life and that in her opinion he is untruthful.
(d)   In rebuttal, the prosecution calls Mark Mayer, who offers to testify that he lives in the same neighborhood as Fred Finley and that he knows Finley's reputation in the neighborhood for truth and veracity is good.
(e)   On cross-examination of Mayer, defense counsel asks if Mayer has heard that Finley was convicted of perjury two years ago.

Should objections to any of this evidence be sustained?

7.8. Davenport, a former police officer, is charged with obstructing justice by revealing the name of an undercover informant to the subject of an investigation. The prosecution has developed the following information about Davenport:

(a)   Prior to the criminal charge, the police department had fired Davenport after an administrative hearing, which resulted in findings that Davenport had committed a number of offenses including the alleged obstruction of justice.

(b)   Three years ago Davenport was suspended by the police department for 30 days for misappropriating departmental gasoline. Davenport took the gasoline for personal use and signed another officer's name in the gas log.

(c)   Two years ago Davenport was found to have taken a subway pass from a young man and ripped it up. Davenport denied taking the pass, but another officer found the pass, and Internal Affairs determined that Davenport had been lying.

(d)   Last year Alma Jones complained to the police department about Davenport's conduct when he arrested her for speeding. She claims that he was verbally abusive, that he threw her on the hood of the car and put a gun to her head, and that he offered to give her only a warning if she would have sex with him.

Assume Davenport will testify in his defense and deny the obstruction charge. To what extent and how can the prosecution use the above information in cross-examining Davenport? Please prepare specific questions for the prosecutor to ask.

7.9. Williams is charged with being a convicted felon in possession of a firearm. The only evidence of his possession was the testimony of Detective David Martin. Martin testified that while giving chase, he saw Williams throw a black object. After arresting Williams, Martin returned to the area and found a gun that showed signs of being thrown against a wall. Williams claims that he had no gun and that it was planted by Martin.

Can Williams cross-examine Martin about (a) a Superior Court judge's finding that Martin lied on the stand during a trial, (b) Martin's driver's license being suspended for driving while intoxicated and the fact that Martin never reported the information to his superiors, and (c) Martin's failure to comply with a court order to pay child support?

Consider whether the court should permit Williams to call the following witnesses:

(a)   Johnny Caravella to testify about a news story he wrote five years ago that identified Detective Martin as the subject of many police harassment complaints in the neighborhood. The sources for the story were unnamed people who lived in Martin's neighborhood.

(b)   Defense attorney Alice Weaver to testify that Martin has a reputation in the "court community" for being untruthful. Weaver's testimony is based on the opinions of three other defense lawyers she knows and her own experience with cases in which Martin has been a witness.

(c)   Chris Brown, an acquaintance of Martin, to testify that Martin wrongfully arrested him for drug possession, that a friend's belongings went missing when Martin arrested the friend, and that in his (Brown's) opinion Martin is very dishonest. Until six years ago Brown lived in Martin's neighborhood and saw Martin almost daily. Brown continues to see Martin regularly when he returns to the neighborhood to visit his mother.

7.10. The defendant is being tried for sexually molesting his seven-year-old stepdaughter. The stepdaughter is one of the prosecution witnesses. Consider whether any of the following evidence should be admissible:

(a) After the prosecution has presented its case, the defendant calls several witnesses to testify that the stepdaughter is manipulative and often lies.

(b) During the cross-examination of one of these witnesses, the prosecution asks whether the witness is aware of the fact that the stepdaughter recently admitted breaking an expensive antique even though she could easily have blamed her brother for the incident.

(c) During cross-examination of the defendant, the prosecutor inquires about whether the defendant molested his former wife's daughter. (The prosecutor knows that there was a complaint filed against the defendant with respect to that incident, that the charges were dropped, and that the defendant was divorced shortly thereafter.)

(d) During cross-examination of the defendant, the prosecutor also inquires about whether the defendant misrepresented his college class standing in campaign speeches made three years ago during an unsuccessful campaign for a legislative seat.

(e) As part of its rebuttal, the prosecution calls a clinical psychologist who had examined the stepdaughter. The psychologist offers to testify that (i) she never had trouble with the stepdaughter saying things that were untrue and (ii) psychological research shows that less than 1 percent of child sexual abuse claims are false.

7.11. Doris Delorme has been charged with possession of heroin with intent to sell. The heroin was discovered in a small private airplane in which Doris and Wally Winter, an alleged co-conspirator, were riding. Wally initially testified that Doris was part of their conspiracy and that Doris knew the heroin was on the airplane. The prosecutor then offered to elicit from Wally that he had pleaded guilty pursuant to a plea agreement that included a commitment to testify truthfully against Doris and, if requested, to take lie detector tests. What objection can Doris make to this evidence? What objection could Doris make if the prosecutor offered the evidence only after Doris had established that she had just obtained a divorce from Wally's brother and that Wally was convicted of perjury three years ago?

6.   FRE 609

The Advisory Committee has proposed amendments to FRE 609(a) that will probably become effective on December 1, 2006. The language that the amendments add appears in italics; the language that the amendments delete is in brackets.

RULE 609. IMPEACHMENT BY EVIDENCE OF CONVICTION OF CRIME

(a) General Rule. For the purpose of attacking the *character for truthfulness* [credibility] of a witness,

(1) evidence that a witness other than an accused has been convicted of a crime shall be admitted, subject to Rule 403, if the crime was punishable by death or imprisonment in excess of one year under the law under which the witness was convicted, and the evidence that an accused has been convicted of such a crime shall be admitted if the court determines that the probative value of admitting this evidence outweighs its prejudicial effects to the accused; and

(2) evidence that any witness has been convicted of a crime shall be admitted [if it involved dishonesty or false statement], regardless of punishment, *if it readily can be determined that establishing the elements of the crime required proof or admission of an act of dishonesty or false statement by the witness.*

(b) Time limit. Evidence of a conviction under this rule is not admissible if a period of more than ten years has elapsed since the date of the conviction or of the release of the witness from the confinement imposed for that conviction, whichever is the later date, unless the court determines, in the interests of justice, that the probative value of the conviction supported by specific facts and circumstances substantially outweighs its prejudicial effect.

[Section (c) restricts the use of convictions that have been the subject of pardon or annulment; section (d) restricts the use of juvenile adjudications; and section (e) provides that the pendency of an appeal does not make evidence of a conviction inadmissible.]

7.   Interpretation and Illustration of FRE 609(a) and (b)

FRE 609(a) permits impeachment with two types of convictions: (1) convictions for serious crimes (i.e., those punishable by imprisonment for more than one year, which is the federal definition of a felony), and (2) convictions, regardless of potential punishment, for crimes of dishonesty and false statement. The theory of relevance underlying the use of both types of prior convictions is similar to the theory of relevance underlying inquiries about specific instances of conduct pursuant to FRE 608(b)(1): The witness's specific acts that are the basis for the conviction show a general character trait or disposition inconsistent with truth-telling from that one can infer that the witness may not be telling the truth on the witness stand. The proposed amendment to the first sentence of FRE 609(a) makes this point clear by substituting the phrase "character for truthfulness" for the term "credibility." And, as the Advisory Committee Note to the proposed amendment points out, this language also makes it clear that the limitations of FRE 609 do not apply when prior convictions are offered for some purpose other than to prove the witness's character for truthfulness, such as to show contradiction.

An essential feature of FRE 609 is that, unlike FRE 608(b), it contains no prohibition against the use of extrinsic evidence. Thus, if a witness denies a conviction, it is permissible to establish the conviction with extrinsic evidence — for example, with a record of the conviction.

a.   The Two FRE 609(a)(1) Balancing Tests

If a conviction falls within FRE 609(a)(1) — that is, if it is a felony that is *not* a crime of dishonesty or false statement (e.g., if it is murder) — its admissibility to impeach a witness is subject to a balancing test. The balancing test for all witnesses *except* criminal defendants is FRE 403. For criminal defendants who are witnesses, FRE 609(a)(1) mandates a reverse-FRE 403 test: The probative value must outweigh the prejudice to the defendant. Whereas FRE 403, by requiring that the probative value must be substantially outweighed by the countervailing factors, favors admissibility, and in effect puts the burden on the party arguing for exclusion to justify that result, the reverse FRE 403 test in FRE 609 favors exclusion and in effect puts the burden on the prosecution to justify admissibility.

Consider, for example, a situation in which a witness has been released from imprisonment for murder six years ago. In deciding whether to admit evidence of the murder conviction to impeach the witness, the judge must first assess the probative value of the conviction. Then the judge must assess the prejudicial impact of the evidence and apply the appropriate balancing test. All of the issues that you studied in Chapter Three concerning the application of FRE 403 apply to the trial judge's decision.

i.   **Probative Value.**   The evidentiary fact that the conviction is offered to prove is the truthfulness of the witness at the time of the witness's testimony. Thus, the probative value assessment should include consideration of (1) the age of the conviction, (2) how probative murder is to show bad moral character or general disposition for law-breaking, which in turn shows a disposition for untruthfulness, and (3) the witness's intervening behavior. Six years may seem like a long time, and murder may not seem very probative of untruthfulness. On the other hand, six years is only slightly more than half of the time period prescribed in FRE 609(b), and in the absence of mitigating circumstances relating to the murder, it may be reasonable to infer that a person who is willing to commit such a serious crime has little regard for the law, including the requirement to testify truthfully. Moreover, a crime that in isolation may not seem very probative of truthfulness may be more probative if it is part of a continuing pattern of untruthfulness. Thus, conduct reflecting on truthfulness during the time between release from imprisonment and giving testimony should be an important part of the probative value determination. United States v. Gilbert, 668 F.2d 94, 97 (2d Cir. 1981), (conviction admissible; age of conviction and subsequent history did not suggest abandonment of earlier ways).

ii.   **Unfair Prejudice.**   Against the probative value assessment the judge must balance the potential for unfair prejudice. Here there are two primary concerns: First, to what extent will the jury consider the witness to be a bad person and, therefore, be disposed against the witness? For example, if the witness is the defendant, there is a risk that jury may ignore the reasonable doubt standard because it regards the defendant as a bad or dangerous person. Even if the witness is not a party, there is a risk that prejudice against the witness may spill over and affect the jury's attitude about the party who called the witness.

Second, to what extent is there a risk that the jury may use the conviction not only in its proper propensity sense to prove that the witness may be untruthful on the witness stand but also in an improper propensity sense? For example, if the witness is a defendant charged with a crime of violence, there is a risk that the jury, in violation of the prohibition in the first sentence of FRE 404(b), may use the murder conviction as evidence of the defendant's character for violence, for the purpose of inferring that defendant behaved violently in committing the crime charged.

iii.   **The Reverse FRE 403 Balancing Test for Criminal Defendants.**   The probative value of the murder conviction to prove untruthfulness remains the same regardless of whether the witness is a party to the action. The prejudice, however, is likely to be greatest when the witness is a criminal defendant. Even if the jury regards a nonparty witness as a bad person, it seems less likely that the jury would respond by thinking ill of and, as a result, punishing the party that called the witness. And the risk that a jury may utilize a prior conviction in an improper propensity sense exists only if some conduct of the witness is the subject of the current litigation. That, of course, will always be the case with criminal defendants who testify in their own behalf.

Because the risk of prejudice to criminal defendants is particularly high and because the probative value versus prejudice balancing process is inherently imprecise, FRE 609(a)(1) employs a reverse FRE 403 balancing test for witnesses who are criminal defendants. As a result, it is somewhat more likely, at least in theory, that the murder conviction — and other FRE 609(a)(1) convictions — will be admissible against witnesses who are not criminal defendants than against criminal defendants.

iv.   The FRE 403 Balancing Test for Other Witnesses.   FRE 609(a) does not give civil parties who are witnesses the benefit of the reverse FRE 403 balancing test. Rather, FRE 609(a) treats them in same manner as it treats nonparty witnesses. Their prior convictions will be admissible unless the probative impeachment value of the convictions is substantially outweighed by the FRE 403 countervailing factors.

The subject matter of civil litigation often does not involve the same type of morally culpable conduct that is typically the subject of criminal prosecutions. As a result, the risk of prejudice from using prior convictions for impermissible propensity purposes may be less in civil cases generally than in criminal prosecutions. Moreover, civil litigants as a class are not as likely to have prior convictions as are criminal defendants. On the other hand, some civil claims — for example, fraud or sexual assault — involve allegations of criminal conduct; and as we suggested in subsection iii, supra, the risk of bad person prejudice is likely to be greater with party witnesses than with nonparty witnesses. Do you think civil party witnesses should receive the same reverse balancing test that criminal defendants receive?

v.   The Factual Circumstances of the Crime.   When courts balance probative value of a conviction against unfair prejudice and other countervailing factors, they frequently discuss the conviction in only general terms. For example, a court is likely to consider that the conviction was for murder or selling drugs without examining the details of the murder or drug sale. United States v. Alexander, 48 F.3d 1477, 1488 (9th Cir. 1995) (not mentioning details of witness's conduct but citing as factors to consider "(1) the impeachment value of the prior crime; (2) the point in time of the conviction and the [witness's] subsequent history; (3) the similarity between the past crime and the crime charged; (4) the importance of the [witness's] testimony; and (5) the centrality of the [witness's] testimony.") Some courts, however, consider the underlying circumstances of the crime. Rodriguez v. Woodall, 2005 U.S. Dist. LEXIS 13790 (N.D. Ill.) (in admitting prior drug conviction, court took into account, inter alia, facts that defendant disregarded his oath as a police officer and abused the authority of his office).

The question whether courts should consider the underlying facts of a conviction has received the most attention in the context of deciding whether a conviction involves "dishonesty or false statement" within the meaning of FRE 609(a)(2). We discuss the issue further in that context at pages 377-378, infra.

b.   The Automatic Admissibility of FRE 609(a)(2) Dishonesty and False Statement Convictions

i.   The Rule.   Dishonesty and false statement convictions, as the language of FRE 609(a)(2) makes clear, are automatically admissible without regard to balancing and without regard to the seriousness of the crime. In short, if the conviction is for a crime of dishonesty or false statement, it is unnecessary to consider what the potential penalty for the crime is or any potential prejudicial impact of the conviction. As long as the conviction falls within the time limitation set forth in FRE 609(b), a court has no discretion to exclude it. For example, if a witness had been convicted of a misdemeanor offense of making a false statement on some type of application form, the impeaching party could admit the conviction to impeach the witness even if the conviction were nine years old and thus arguably not very probative of the witness's truth-telling on the witness stand now, nine years later. Even if the witness were a criminal defendant charged with the identical crime the evidence would be admissible.

ii.   The Meaning of "Dishonesty or False Statement."

ii.   The Meaning of "Dishonesty or False Statement."   Because of the automatic admissibility for crimes of dishonesty and false statement, the contours of this category of crimes are extremely important. To the extent that one equates "dishonesty" with "illegality," all crimes are crimes of dishonesty. Clearly, however, the term *dishonesty* in FRE 609(a)(2) should not be interpreted that broadly, for limitations in FRE 609(a)(1) would then be meaningless.

The Advisory Committee Note to FRE 609 equates "dishonesty or false statement" with the common law classification *crimen falsi*. The Senate Judiciary Committee Report and the Conference Report on the Federal Rules contain the following identical elaboration:

> [It means] crimes such as perjury or subornation of perjury, false statement, criminal fraud, embezzlement or false pretenses, or any other offense, in the nature of *crimen falsi* the commission of which involves some element of untruthfulness, deceit or falsification bearing on the accused's propensity to testify truthfully.

Despite the ambiguity in this description, it is fair to say that most federal courts have interpreted the phrase *dishonesty and false statement* relatively narrowly and that the case law tends to limit the phrase closely to the crimes named as examples in the preceding excerpt. Walker v. Horn, 385 F.3d 321, 334 (3d Cir. 2004) (robbery is not crime of dishonesty or false statement); United States v. Mejia-Alarcon, 995 F.2d 982 (10th Cir. 1993), (conviction for unauthorized use of food stamps not within FRE 609(a)(2)); United States v. Morrow, 977 F.2d 222 (6th Cir. 1992) (counterfeiting is crime of "dishonesty or false statement"); United States v. Karmer, 923 F.2d 1557 (11th Cir. 1991) (misdemeanor theft not usually within FRE 609(a)(2)); Wagner v. Firestone Tire & Rubber Co., 890 F.2d 652 (3d Cir. 1989) (forgery is crime of "dishonesty or false statement"). Indeed, in 1990 when the Advisory Committee proposed the current version of FRE 609, which left the "dishonesty or false statement" provision unchanged, the Committee stated, "[T]he Conference Report provides sufficient guidance to trial courts and . . . no amendment is necessary, notwithstanding some decisions that take an unduly broad view of 'dishonest,' admitting convictions such as for bank robbery or bank larceny." There are gray areas, however, and the case law is not entirely consistent. Compare, e.g., United States v. Wilson, 985 F.2d 348 (7th Cir. 1993) (failure to file income tax return is crime of "dishonesty or false statement") with Cree v. Hatcher, 969 F.2d 34 (3d Cir. 1993), (failure to file income tax return not within FRE 609(a)(2)). See generally Stuart P. Green, Deceit and Classification of Crimes: Federal Rule of Evidence 609(a)(2) and the Origins of Crimen Falsi, 90 J. Crim. L. & Criminology 1087 (2000).

iii. The Significance of the Underlying Details of the Crime.   In determining whether a conviction fits within FRE 609(a)(2), some courts look to the underlying criminal act, United States v. Barnes, 622 F.2d 107 (5th Cir. 1980), and others focus exclusively on the statutorily defined elements of the crime, Cree v. Hatcher, supra. Which approach do you think is preferable? Consider the following:

> To allow (or require) courts to look to the facts of a prior conviction in determining whether the crime involved dishonesty or false statement is likely to create both administrative burdens and legal uncertainty....
>
> A second reason for rejecting the fact-based inquiry approach is that it is at odds with the overall structure of the impeachment rules. By allowing (or requiring) courts to inquire into the underlying facts of the conviction, Rule 609(a)(1) is likely to be swallowed up by Rule 609(a)(2). Rule 609(a)(2) will become the rule rather than exception, even though the probative versus prejudicial weighing approach of the former rule is more representative of the Federal Rules approach generally.
>
> A third reason...rests on an understanding of criminal law and procedure.... [C]riminal offenses are defined by their elements, not by the facts of their commission. To admit conviction evidence is to tell the jury nothing more than that the elements of the crime of which the witness was convicted were proven beyond a reasonable doubt. Undoubtedly, a large majority of criminal acts do involve some form of deception. A rapist or kidnapper may use deception to lure a victim to a remote location. A perpetrator bent on violating the antitrust laws may use duplicity in doing so. But, in each case, the fact that deception was used will never have been found beyond a reasonable doubt. To allow a court to look to underlying facts in determining whether to admit a prior conviction as a crime of deceit is thus to invite a circumvention of the reasonable doubt standard itself. [Stuart P. Green, Deceit and the Classification of Crimes: Federal Rule of Evidence 609(a)(2) and the Origins of Crimen Falsi, 90 J. Crim. L. & Criminology, 1087, 1122 (2000).]

The proposed amendment to FRE 609(a)(2), page 373, supra, addresses at least the first two of these concerns:

Administrative Burden. The proposed amendment explicitly permits inquiry beyond the statutory elements to determine whether the crime involves dishonesty or false statement. At the same time, however, the "readily can be determined" language is designed to limit that inquiry and thus minimize the administrative burden in applying FRE 609(a)(2). The Advisory Committee notes that the amendment "does not contemplate a 'mini-trial' in which the court plumbs the record of the previous proceeding to determine whether the crime was in the nature of *crimin falsi*."

FRE 609(a)(2) Swallowing FRE 609(a)(1). According to the Advisory Committee, the new language mandates the admissibility of a conviction "only when the conviction *required* the proof of (or in the case of a guilty plea, the admission of) an act of dishonesty or false statement. Evidence of all other convictions is inadmissible under this subsection, irrespective of whether the witness exhibited dishonesty or made a false statement in the process of the commission of the crime...." (Emphasis added) Murder, for example, could not be included within FRE 609(a)(2) "even if the witness acted deceitfully in the course of committing the crime." Thus the amendment should alleviate the concern that FRE 609(a)(2) may swallow FRE 609(a)(1).

Circumventing the Reasonable Doubt Standard. Whether a crime involves dishonesty or false statement is obviously significant in assessing its probative value. The fact of dishonesty or false statement, however, is not critical to the *relevance* of the conviction. (If it were, 609(a)(1) convictions would be irrelevant!) Thus the question whether the conviction involves dishonesty or false statement is an FRE 104(a) preliminary fact, and typically the standard of proof for FRE 104(a) preliminary facts in criminal (as well as civil) cases is a preponderance of the evidence. That standard presumably is applicable to the preliminary fact of whether the conviction involved dishonesty or false statement, regardless of whether the judge is looking at (1) only the elements of the offense or (2) the apparent factual circumstances of the crime. If the judge considers only the elements of the offense, the conviction itself is an assurance that the reasonable doubt standard has been satisfied with respect to dishonesty or false statement. By contrast, if the judge considers factual circumstances not essential to the judgment, there is no assurance that anyone has found the facts indicating dishonesty or false statement beyond a reasonable doubt. Should such a prior beyond-a-reasonable-doubt finding be a prerequisite to admissibility under FRE 609(a)(2)?

The proposed amendment to FRE 609(a)(2) does not explicitly address the burden of proof issue. Both the language of the proposal and the Advisory Committee Note, however, indicate that the dishonesty or false statement facts must have been either admitted or found to exist beyond a reasonable doubt. According to the proposed amendment, FRE 609(a)(2) applies only to crimes that "*required* proof or admission of an act of dishonesty or false statement." (Emphasis added). And the Advisory Committee's examples of what may satisfy the "readily apparent" language of the proposed amendment suggest that, in the absence of the witness's admission, the reasonable doubt standard must be satisfied:

> Where the deceitful nature of the crime is not apparent from the statute and the face of the judgment — as, for example, where the conviction simply records a finding of guilt for a statutory offense that does not reference deceit expressly — a proponent may offer information such as *an indictment, a statement of admitted facts, or jury instructions to show that the factfinder had to find, or the defendant had to admit, an act of dishonesty or false statement in order for the witness to have been convicted.* (Emphasis added)

c.   The FRE 609(b) Reverse Balancing Test

All prior convictions falling within the scope of FRE 609(a) — including dishonesty and false statement convictions — are subject to the reverse FRE 403 balancing test in FRE 609(b) if they fall outside the 10-year time period specified in that subsection. The 10-year time period runs from the date of conviction or release from imprisonment, whichever is later. Thus, for example, a 12-year-old perjury conviction for which the witness served a three-year sentence would be automatically admissible despite the age of the conviction. If the witness had been imprisoned for only one year, however, FRE 609(b) would apply, and the conviction would be admissible only if its probative value substantially outweighed its prejudice — a test that, by virtue of the term *substantially*, is even more stringent than the reverse FRE 403 test in FRE 609(a). Indeed, although courts have not developed specific standards to distinguish FRE 609(b) balancing from FRE 609(a) balancing, they have indicated that FRE 609(b) convictions should rarely be admissible. United States v. Bensimon, 172 F.3d 1121, 1126-1127 (9th Cir. 1999); United States v. Pope, 132 F.3d 684, 687 (11th Cir. 1998).

8. Elaboration of FRE 609(a)

a. *The Rationale for Permitting Impeachment with FRE 609(a)(1) Convictions*

FRE 609(a) — like the rules in most states — permits a trial judge to balance probative value and prejudice in deciding whether to admit evidence of felonies, regardless of whether the underlying conduct could reasonably be described as having a bearing on the witness's character for truthfulness. The rule is thus far broader than FRE 608(b).

The common law origin of the prior conviction impeachment device probably accounts in part for its breadth and its uniform acceptance:

> At common law a person's conviction of treason, any felony, or a misdemeanor involving dishonesty (*crimen falsi*), or the obstruction of justice, rendered the convicted person *altogether incompetent as a witness*. These were said to be "infamous" crimes. By statutes or rules virtually universal in the common law world, this primitive absolutism has been abandoned; the disqualification for conviction of crime has been abrogated, and by specific provision or by decision it has been reduced to a mere ground for impeaching credibility. [1 John W. Strong, McCormick on Evidence §42, at 156-157 (5th ed. 1999) (emphasis added).]

In addition, the rule is justified by the belief that prior convictions, even if they are based on activity that does not relate very directly to truthfulness, may be especially relevant to the question of the witness's general credibility. Neither courts nor commentators, however, attempt to explain the apparent contradiction in the notion that convictions for acts only remotely related to truthfulness (e.g., aggravated assaults) may be especially probative of truthfulness. Consider to what extent the following explanation accounts for the apparent contradiction: A person of generally bad moral character is more likely to lie than a person of generally good moral character. Indeed, compelling proof of bad moral character may be particularly probative of untruthfulness. All of us, however, from time to time engage in "bad" acts that tend to suggest bad moral character; and since few, if any, of us are likely to consider ourselves to be of bad moral character, it must follow that a single bad act — or even a series of bad acts — is not necessarily very probative of general moral character. Thus, in the absence of a conviction, most jurisdictions prohibit inquiry into these acts unless they are likely to have more than very marginal value to the question whether the witness is lying — that is, unless they relate fairly directly to that issue by suggesting a character trait of untruthfulness as opposed to general bad moral character. On the other hand, because the criminal law tends to proscribe only the most reprehensible activity, convictions — especially when they are for serious crimes — are likely to be particularly probative of bad moral character and, therefore, untruthfulness.

From a cynical perspective one might further justify use of prior convictions to impeach on the ground that criminal defendants are disproportionately likely both to have records of prior convictions and to lie in the hope of obtaining acquittals. Thus the threat of impeachment with prior convictions may deter criminal defendants from testifying and, as a result, reduce the amount of false testimony presented in a criminal trial. This last rationale, however, seems inconsistent with the rationale underlying the final paragraph of FRE 608, which permits a witness to invoke the right against self-incrimination with respect to questions that "relate only to credibility." As the Advisory Committee's Note to FRE 608 explains, that provision exists at least in part to prevent the impeachment rules from unduly burdening a criminal defendant's right to testify.

b. Prior Convictions and Prejudice

Most prior convictions admissible under FRE 609(a) are likely to be more prejudicial than most nonconviction bad act evidence admissible under FRE 608(b). This is so because the substantive law tends to criminalize the most reprehensible behavior, because police and prosecutors tend to focus their limited resources on the most serious offenders, and because the fact of conviction represents the community's judgment of moral condemnation. As a result, there is a relatively high risk that juries may be predisposed against witnesses who are shown to have prior convictions. Whenever the witness is a party or somebody closely associated with the party, jurors' attitudes about the witness may improperly affect their decision.

In assessing probative value and prejudice pursuant to FRE 609(a)(1) and FRE 609(b), it is important to keep in mind the significance of the similarity between the prior conviction evidence and the current criminal charge. When the witness is a criminal defendant (or some other person whose alleged actions are the basis for the current litigation), similarity between the current criminal allegations and the facts underlying the impeachment evidence enhances the *prejudice*, not the probative value of the prior conviction. The only permissible inference to draw from the conviction is that the witness is an untruthful person and therefore may be lying on the witness stand. There is always the risk, however, that the jury will draw the inference prohibited by FRE 404 — that because the witness behaved illegally on the occasion of the conviction, the witness is likely to have behaved improperly on the occasion that is the subject of the litigation. This possibility is greatest when the prior behavior represented by the conviction is similar to the alleged activity that gave rise to the litigation. Consider, for example, our defendant-witness who has a six-year-old murder conviction. If the defendant is currently charged with murder, there is a risk that the jury will consider the prior conviction as evidence of the defendant's violence to infer that the defendant was probably violent at the time of the alleged murder. For an excellent discussion of this point, see United States v. Footman, 33 F. Supp. 2d 60 (D. Mass. 1998) (denying government's motion to impeach defendant with prior rape conviction in case involving charges of interstate transportation of minors for prostitution). By contrast, if the defendant with the six-year-old murder conviction is currently charged with possession of heroin, there is relatively less risk of prejudice. Most jurors are probably less likely to believe that there is a link — or least as strong a link — between prior violence and current drug possession than they are to believe that there is a link between prior violence and current violence. Of course, regardless of the current charge, the jurors may consider the defendant/murderer to be a particularly bad, violent person and allow this form of prejudice to affect their decisionmaking.

c. Extrinsic Evidence

Convictions are the result of a plea or a fact-finder's beyond-a-reasonable-doubt finding of guilt. They provide highly probative evidence that the underlying bad acts occurred, and the fact of a conviction can be easily established with a public record. Thus the concern with time-consuming litigation about collateral matters that arguably justifies the FRE 608(b) prohibition against extrinsic evidence, see page 364, supra, does not apply to convictions offered pursuant to FRE 609, which may be proven with extrinsic evidence. In practice, however, there is seldom any need for such extrinsic evidence. Because a party can so easily establish a conviction, it is unlikely that a witness will deny the conviction in the first place. Indeed, as we discuss at page 382, infra, if a prior conviction will be admissible to impeach a witness, the party calling the witness may have the witness acknowledge the conviction on direct examination.

d. The Factual Details of the Conviction

Just as courts have an interest in avoiding lengthy inquiry into alleged bad acts that have not resulted in convictions, courts also have an interest in not spending a great deal of time exploring the facts underlying a witness's conviction. Moreover, eliciting the factual details underlying a conviction is likely to increase its prejudicial impact. Thus courts typically will permit the impeaching party to mention the name of the crime, when and where it occurred, what sentence was imposed, and nothing more. United States v. Burston, 159 F.3d 1328, 1336 (11th Cir. 1998) (party entitled to elicit name and number of convictions); United States v. Smith, 131 F.3d 685, 687 (7th Cir. 1997) (accord; *Old Chief* not a bar to mentioning name of convictions admissible pursuant to FRE 609); United States v. Pandozzi, 887 F.2d 1526, 1534-1535 (1st Cir. 1989) (impeachment with sexual assault conviction; proper to elicit that crime was sexual assault and to prohibit reference to fact that victim was a child). Some decisions, however, go further in permitting the impeaching party to elicit some details of the crime. United States v. Wesley, 990 F.2d 360 (8th Cir. 1990) (when defendant impeached with illegal firearm possession conviction, not an abuse of discretion to elicit for impeachment purposes that weapon was a shotgun; fact that weapon was shotgun, however, also held to be admissible pursuant to FRE 404(b)). If a court looks to the details of a crime to determine that it is an FRE 609(a)(2) crime of dishonesty or false statement, see pages 377-378, supra, or to determine that the conviction is admissible pursuant to the appropriate FRE 609(a)(1) balancing test, it would seem that the impeaching party should be able to elicit the details that are essential to the admissibility decision. Cf. Wilson v. City of Chicago, 6 F.3d 1233, 1236-1237 (7th Cir. 1993) (details not admissible unless they bear directly on credibility) (dictum). While proof of the details may make the impeachment evidence more prejudicial, proof of the conviction without the details creates some prejudice without giving the jury the benefit of the facts that warrant admissibility in the first place.

Some courts prohibit the impeached witness from offering any explanation for the conviction. A number of courts, however, will permit the witness, particularly if the witness is also a party, to testify briefly about any mitigating or extenuating circumstances. If a witness tries to explain away the crime, however, the impeaching party may be able to elicit otherwise inadmissible details of the crime. United States v. Amachia, 825 F.2d 177 (8th Cir. 1987).

e. Hearsay

Regardless of whether the prior conviction is elicited from the witness or proved extrinsically with the record of conviction, the evidence is hearsay. The theory underlying FRE 609 is that the witness committed the acts that constitute the elements of the crime for which the witness was convicted and that proof of these acts suggests something important about the witness's credibility. In other words, the conviction is a manifestation of the jury's or the judge's assertion in an earlier proceeding that the witness committed the acts essential for the conviction, and it is the truth of this assertion that is critical to the relevance of the evidence.

The Federal Rules, as well as a number of other jurisdictions, have a judgments exception to the hearsay rule. Typically, however, the judgments exception is narrower than the rule authorizing impeachment with prior convictions. For example, FRE 803(22) extends the judgments exception only to convictions for crimes punishable by imprisonment for more than one year, whereas FRE 609(a)(2) authorizes the use of dishonesty and false statement convictions regardless of the potential penalty. If courts have even noticed this conflict between FRE 609(a) and FRE 803(22), they have not been bothered by it. Quite properly, in our view, courts considering the admissibility of misdemeanor convictions for impeachment under FRE 609(a)(2) have relied on that rule, which deals specifically with that issue, and have ignored the limitations in the more general FRE 803(22).

f.   Practical Considerations

Frequently parties will file motions in limine seeking an advance ruling on whether prior convictions will be admissible against them. Obtaining such a ruling may be important to a criminal defendant for two reasons. First, there is substantial empirical evidence suggesting that the admission of a criminal defendant's prior convictions contributes to the likelihood of a guilty verdict. Harry Kalven Jr. and Hans Zeisel, The American Jury 159-160 (1966); Anthony N. Doob and Hershi M. Kirshenbaum, Some Empirical Evidence on the Effect of Sec. 12 of the Canada Evidence Act Upon the Accused, 15 Crim. L.Q. 88, 91-95 (1972-1973); Note, To Take the Stand or Not to Take the Stand: The Dilemma of the Defendant with a Criminal Record, 4 Colum. J.L. & Soc. Probs. 215, 218-219 (1968). See generally Robert D. Dodson, What Went Wrong with Federal Rule of Evidence 609: A Look at How Jurors Really Misuse Prior Conviction Evidence, 48 Drake L. Rev. 1 (1999). Indeed, some states have prohibited or severely restricted prosecutors from impeaching criminal defendants with prior convictions. See Robert D. Dodson, supra, at 14-22.

Second, particularly for defendant-witnesses, it is likely to be tactically important for the witness to mention admissible prior convictions on direct examination. If the jury learns of the convictions for the first time on cross-examination, there is the risk that the jury will be prejudiced against the defendant for not "coming clean" on direct examination. The direct examiner, however, obviously has no interest in calling to the jury's attention convictions that would not otherwise be admissible.

In the *Johnson* case, defense counsel brought out on direct examination the prior convictions of the defendant, his cellmate, Butler, and inmate Green. Unfortunately, however, the direct examination was not complete with respect to Green's prior convictions. Thus the prosecution was still able to benefit from the implication that the witness was not fully forthcoming on direct examination (page 49, lines 7-27, supra).

Judges will frequently rule on motions in limine regarding the admissibility of convictions before a defendant has to decide whether to testify. There is apparently no obligation to make such a ruling, however. In Luce v. United States, 469 U.S. 38 (1984), the Supreme Court held that a defendant who chose not to testify after the trial judge refused to rule on his motion in limine could not seek reversal on the ground that the convictions should not have been admissible. To preserve that claim, the Court held, the defendant must testify.

The *Luce* Court relied primarily on two factors. First, there was a concern that with a contrary holding defendants who had no genuine interest in testifying might file motions in limine in the hope of creating reversible error in the event that the court ruled the convictions to be admissible. Second, Luce made his motion before trial and did not accompany it with any indication of how he planned to impeach prosecution witnesses or what the testimony of defense witnesses (including himself) would be. In this context, the Supreme Court quite reasonably took the position that the trial judge may not have had enough information to engage in the balancing process required by FRE 609.

Consider what should happen if the defendant receives an unfavorable ruling on a motion in limine before testifying. Can the defendant acknowledge the conviction on direct examination in order to remove any inference of hiding unfavorable information and at the same time preserve the admissibility issue for appeal? Despite the fact that this situation does not implicate the two concerns that were central to *Luce*, the Supreme Court in Ohler v. United States, 529 U.S. 753 (2000), held 5-4 that a defendant who acknowledges prior convictions on direct examination after a ruling that they will be admissible pursuant to FRE 609 cannot claim on appeal that the admissibility decision was erroneous. For a case refusing to follow *Ohler* and reaching the opposite result, see State v. Daly, 623 N.W.2d 799 (Iowa 2001). Which decision do you think is better — *Ohler* or *Daly*? (Of the state courts that have addressed these issues, most agree with *Luce* but are evenly divided on *Ohler*.)

Even after *Ohler* and *Luce*, a defendant who contemplates the possibility of testifying should probably pursue a motion in limine to exclude prior convictions. If the judge rules on the motion, the defendant at least will have a better sense of the consequences of testifying.

For defense counsel who pursue such motions, there are several important considerations. First, and most important, while there may be legitimate tactical reasons for withholding some information from the court and the prosecution, a defense counsel who is serious about wanting a ruling on the motion should provide the trial court with as much information as possible to make the decision. For example, the defense should indicate what the impeachment of prosecution witnesses is likely to entail, what the defense testimony will probably be, and why the defendant's testimony is important for a fair trial. Providing the judge with this information removes one of the principal concerns expressed by *Luce*.

Second, if the court does not grant the motion before trial, defense counsel should renew the motion at the close of the prosecution case and, if necessary, again immediately before the defendant will have to decide whether to take the stand. At each renewal of the motion defense counsel should refine the argument for exclusion of the convictions in light of the evidence that has been presented and the anticipated evidence. At some point along the way it is likely that the court will have sufficient information to make a reasoned FRE 609 ruling. And if the judge has all of the relevant information, there is no reason why the judge should not rule on the motion. Indeed, in this type of situation the defendant might argue that — particularly in light of the *Luce* and *Ohler* — it is an abuse of discretion and an unreasonable burden on the defendant's right to testify for the judge to refuse to make the ruling.

Third, if the trial judge is reluctant to make a definitive FRE 609 balancing decision without knowing what the evidence in the case actually is, defense counsel should seek a conditional ruling: For example, as long as the evidence presented by the defendant is limited to the representations accompanying this motion, the defendant's prior convictions are not admissible.

KEY POINTS

1. FRE 609(a)(2) provides that dishonesty and false statement convictions falling within the 10-year time limit described in FRE 609(b) are automatically admissible to impeach all witnesses (including criminal defendants) without regard to penalty or balancing.

2. FRE 609(a)(1) provides that other convictions falling within the 10-year time limit are admissible only if they are punishable by more than a year's imprisonment and if they satisfy the appropriate balancing test.

3. The balancing test for all witnesses except criminal defendants is FRE 403 (admissible unless probative value substantially outweighed by countervailing factors); the balancing test for criminal defendants who are witnesses is a reverse FRE 403 test (probative value must outweigh the prejudicial impact on defendant).

4. The 10-year time limitation in FRE 609(b) runs from the date of conviction or the date of release from imprisonment, whichever is more recent.

5. In federal courts, a defendant who acknowledges prior convictions on direct examination following an *in limine* ruling that the convictions will be admissible cannot challenge the *in limine* ruling on appeal. State courts are split on this issue.

PROBLEMS

7.12. Ellen Jamison is being prosecuted for perjury, and she testifies in her own defense. Eight years ago Ellen was convicted of perjury, and last year she was convicted of felonious assault against her husband. Can the prosecutor introduce evidence of these convictions?

7.13. James Burton is being prosecuted for illegal weapons possession. The weapon, a pistol, was found during a legal search of the house where James was living. The house is owned by James's mother, Teresa, and she has testified that the pistol belonged to a former boarder. Fifteen years ago Teresa was convicted of making a false statement under oath and third degree larceny. The convictions were the result of her having made false statements on an application for food stamps. Can the prosecutor introduce evidence of these convictions?

7.14. In the *Johnson* trial, which occurred in 1992, the following convictions were used to impeach the credibility of defense witnesses:

    (a)   robbery and battery (years not specified) by George Butler, the defendant's cellmate;

(b)   first degree murder, assault with a deadly weapon, and first degree burglary (years not specified) by Michael Green, another inmate;

(c)   rape (paroled in 1984) and first degree burglary (1985) by the defendant, Johnson.

Which of these convictions would be most likely and least likely to be admitted pursuant to FRE 609?

7.15. Mary Davenport is charged with possession of cocaine discovered during a legal search of the vehicle she was driving. In her defense she establishes that she had borrowed the car from a friend, and she testifies she had no idea that the cocaine was present. On cross-examination can the prosecution introduce evidence that nine years ago she was convicted of attempted possession of a controlled substance? Would your answer be different if, on direct examination, Mary not only denied knowledge of the cocaine in the car but also testified, "With the education my father gave me not to get involved in drugs, I never did"? Why?

7.16. Tom Jackson has filed a federal civil rights against Larry Oster, a prison guard, for injuries sustained in what Jackson claims was an unprovoked assault. Jackson is currently in prison for life with no possibility of parole as a result of his conviction eight years ago for aiding and abetting his brother in the murder of a police officer. Jackson has filed a motion *in limine* asking the court to exclude any reference to the conviction. Oster has filed a motion *in limine* asking the court to rule that for impeachment purposes the defendant can introduce evidence that the conviction was for murdering a police officer and that Jackson is serving a life sentence without possibility of parole. How should the court rule?

7.17. Houghton has been charged with bank robbery, using a firearm during the robbery, and possession of a firearm after having been convicted of a felony. Houghton was convicted of murder 15 years ago and paroled three years ago. He is willing to stipulate that he has been "convicted of a felony," and he plans to testify that he was not the robber. In a motion *in limine* he asks the court to exclude any evidence of or reference to the prior conviction except for the stipulation. How should the court rule?

7.18. Dawn Drabble is charged with robbery. In cross-examining a prosecution witness, Dawn wishes to show that the witness was convicted of felonious assault eight years ago. Later, Dawn testifies in her own defense, and the prosecution offers to show that she was convicted of felonious assault eight years ago. Are the convictions admissible?

7.19. Alex Dean is being prosecuted for murder. He has testified that he was with a friend at the time of the alleged killing. On cross-examination the prosecutor asked Alex if he had falsely stated that he had no criminal record on a job application filed with the Acme Parts Co. three years ago. Alex responded that he had applied for a job with Acme and that he had not lied on the job application form. The prosecutor now offers into evidence (1) Alex's job application form in which he responded "No" to the question whether he had ever been convicted of a crime and (2) a public record of Alex's conviction for armed robbery seven years ago. Alex has objected to the admissibility of both documents. What result?

7.20. Jane and Ed Farley are charged with embezzlement, and they both plan to testify. Dan Evans will testify for them as a character witness. Jane Farley was convicted of filing a false income tax return 15 years ago, and Ed Farley was convicted of felonious theft five years ago. Dan Evans was convicted of misdemeanor battery two years ago.

Pursuant to FRE 608(b) the prosecutor plans to ask the following questions on cross-examination:

(a)   To Jane Farley: Isn't it true that you filed a false income tax return 15 years ago?

(b)   To Ed Farley: Isn't it true that five years ago you made false representations to induce individuals to invest in a get-rich-quick scheme? (As the prosecutor knows, this was the underlying basis for theft charge.)

(c)   To Dan Evans: Isn't it true that two years ago you pretended to be a friend to Joe Newhouse and lured him to a deserted building where you knew he would be beaten? (As the prosecutor knows, this was the basis for the battery charge; Evans was convicted as an aider and abettor.)

Are any of these questions objectionable?

C.   IMPEACHMENT AND REHABILITATION WITH A WITNESS'S PRIOR STATEMENTS

A witness's prior statement — that is, a statement made at another time and place prior to the witness's current testimony — falls within the core definition of inadmissible hearsay if the statement is offered to prove its truth. FRE 801 (a)-(c); FRE 802. Prior inconsistent statements, however, are also relevant and traditionally have been admissible for the nonhearsay purpose of impeaching the witness's credibility. Proof of an inconsistency, regardless of which statement is true, suggests that the witness may have lied in making one of the statements or that the witness for some other reason — for example, faulty memory or lack of interest in the subject matter — has on one occasion not reported accurately what happened. Such proof allows the impeaching party to argue to the jury that the witness is not reliable.

Similarly, proof that a witness has made statements consistent with the witness's current testimony suggests, apart from the truth of the prior statements, that the witness is careful and thoughtful in speaking about the matter to which the statements relate. Thus, except to the extent that there is reason to believe the witness is deliberately telling consistent lies, knowing about the consistency gives us more reason to credit and rely on the witness's testimony than we would have without evidence of the consistency.

Sometimes a witness's prior statement will be admissible for its truth because it falls within an exception to the hearsay rule or an explicit exemption from the definition of hearsay. For example, a plaintiff's statement to a physician for diagnosis or treatment would be admissible pursuant to the physical condition exception to the hearsay rule. FRE 803(4). Similarly, a prior statement offered against a party to an action would be admissible for its truth as an admission under FRE 801(d)(2)(A). In addition, the Federal Rules and other modern codifications of evidence create a hearsay exemption for some prior statements. FRE 801(d)(1), which we discuss in Chapter Eight, exempts from the definition of hearsay — that is, allows to be used for their truth — prior inconsistent statements made under oath in a proceeding, prior consistent statements offered to rebut a charge of recent fabrication or undue influence, and prior statements of identification.

If a witness's prior statement is admissible for its truth, there is no need to consider whether it may *also* be admissible for the nonhearsay purpose of impeaching or rehabilitating the witness. Relying on the truth of the prior statement will inevitably do more to discredit or credit the trial testimony than relying merely on the fact of inconsistency or consistency. Our focus here is on the nonhearsay use of prior inconsistent and consistent statements that are not independently admissible for their truth.

1. FRE 613

RULE 613. PRIOR STATEMENTS OF A WITNESS

(a) Examining witness concerning prior statement. In examining a witness concerning a prior statement made by the witness, whether written or not, the statement need not be shown nor its contents disclosed to the witness at that time, but on request the same shall be shown or disclosed to opposing counsel.

(b) Extrinsic evidence of prior inconsistent statement of witness. Extrinsic evidence of a prior inconsistent statement by a witness is not admissible unless the witness is afforded an opportunity to explain or deny the same and the opposite party is afforded an opportunity to interrogate the witness thereon, or the interests of justice otherwise require. This provision does not apply to admissions of a party-opponent as defined in rule 801(d)(2).

2. Interpretation and Illustration of FRE 613

FRE 613 establishes the procedure by which an examiner may introduce evidence of a witness's prior inconsistent statement for the purpose of impeaching the witness's credibility. Typically the examiner will confront the witness with a prior inconsistent statement during cross-examination.

a. FRE 613(a)

FRE 613(a) makes it clear that the examiner need not disclose the contents of a prior inconsistent statement to the witness before asking whether the witness made the statement. This provision formally abolishes the rule derived from the Queen Caroline's Case, 2 Br. & B. 284, 129 Eng. Rep. 976 (1820), which required, at least with respect to written statements, that the witness be shown the statement prior to any questioning about the statement. The rationale for the rule of the *Queen's Case* stems from a concern that the witness may honestly have forgotten what is or appears to be an inconsistent statement. If such a witness were not shown the statement prior to questioning, a clever cross-examiner might be able to get the witness to deny having made the statement, thereby giving the false impression that the witness was a liar. On the other hand, showing the statement to the witness before questioning gives the dishonest witness the opportunity to concoct a false story that minimizes the impact of the inconsistency. For this reason many commentators have criticized the *Queen's Case* rule, which the Advisory Committee Note to FRE 613(a) characterizes as a "useless impediment to cross-examination."

FRE 613(a) provides that opposing counsel has the right, upon request, to learn of the statement. According to the Advisory Committee Note, this provision "is designed to protect against unwarranted insinuations that a statement has been made when the fact is to the contrary." Assume, for example, that defense counsel had reason to believe that one of plaintiff's eyewitnesses to an automobile accident had made a statement inconsistent with the witness's trial testimony about who was at fault. Counsel could interrogate the witness about whether the witness had ever made such a statement without first revealing its contents to the witness. Upon request, however, defense counsel would have to reveal the inconsistent statement to plaintiff's counsel.

b.   FRE 613(b)

FRE 613(b) also acknowledges that extrinsic evidence of inconsistent statements may be admissible, but it provides that in most instances there is a twofold condition for the admissibility of extrinsic evidence. The witness must have an opportunity to explain the statement, and the opposing party must have an opportunity to explore the inconsistency with the witness. To fulfill these requirements the party offering the prior inconsistent statement must generally do so when the witness is still testifying or must make sure that the witness is available for recall. United States v. Moore, 149 F.3d 773, 781-782 (8th Cir. 1998).

Requiring that the witness have the opportunity to explain the statement gives the fact finder a reasonable basis for evaluating the alleged inconsistency. For example, the witness may have a plausible explanation for why an apparently inconsistent statement is not in fact inconsistent, or the witness may deny having made the statement, in which case the fact finder will have to assess the relative weight of the extrinsic evidence and the witness's denial.

The "interests of justice" exception exists because there may be situations in which it is not possible to give the witness an opportunity to explain the apparent inconsistency. Consider, for example, a situation in which the impeaching party becomes aware of the prior inconsistent statement only after the witness has been dismissed and is no longer available. In such a case it may further the search for truth to permit extrinsic evidence of the inconsistent statement without any opportunity for the witness's explanation rather than to exclude the impeaching evidence altogether.

The final sentence of FRE 613(b) provides another exception to the usual requirement that the witness have an opportunity to explain or deny the statement: The requirement is inapplicable to inconsistent statements by a party falling within FRE 801(d)(2). That rule provides that a party's prior statements may be admissible for their truth regardless of whether the party testifies. Thus there is no need to restrict admissibility under FRE 613 when the party happens to be a witness.

3.   Elaboration of FRE 613(b)

a.   FRE 613(b)'s Departure from the Common Law

The common law imposed a rigorous foundation requirement as a condition for introducing extrinsic evidence of an inconsistent statement. The impeaching party could not introduce extrinsic evidence of a witness's statement without first indicating the precise time and place of the statement and the person to whom it was made and then asking the witness whether the witness had made the statement. This foundation requirement served at least three purposes. First, it ensured that the witness would not have to bear the inconvenience of being recalled later in the trial to explain the apparent inconsistency. Second, since witnesses occasionally will not be available to be recalled, the requirement ensured that the witness would have an opportunity to explain or account for the apparent inconsistency. Finally, since there is no need for extrinsic evidence if the witness fully concedes the inconsistency, the foundation requirement contributed to the efficient resolution of disputes.

Despite these benefits of the common law rule, the drafters of the Federal Rules made clear their intent to have a more flexible foundation requirement. According to the Advisory Committee Note to FRE 613(b):

> The traditional insistence that the attention of the witness be directed to the statement on cross-examination is relaxed in favor of simply providing the witness an opportunity to explain and the opposite party an opportunity to examine on the statement, with no specification of any particular time or sequence.

As a result of this liberalization of the common law foundation requirement, it is possible that an impeaching party may introduce extrinsic evidence of an inconsistent statement without ever having mentioned the statement to the witness. Consider, for example, a situation in which the witness suggests on direct examination that the defendant was speeding. Now suppose that the opposing counsel has information that the witness had said the defendant was not speeding. Under FRE 613, opposing counsel on cross-examination may do nothing more than get the witness to reconfirm the direct examination testimony. Then, later in the trial during the presentation of the defense case, counsel may attempt to introduce extrinsic evidence of the inconsistent statement. As long as the witness has not been dismissed and is subject to recall (or perhaps as long as witness is available and can be called anew by the opposing party), extrinsic evidence of the statement may be admissible. Indeed, the Advisory Committee Note to FRE 613(b) specifically contemplates this possibility in a hypothetical that it offers to justify the departure from the common law: "[S]everal collusive witnesses can be examined before disclosure of a joint prior inconsistent statement." In the situation hypothesized by the Advisory Committee, there is a sound reason for departing from the common law foundation requirement. Disclosure of the joint statement to the first witness would alert the other witnesses to the statement and as a result perhaps make cross-examination of them less effective. Outside of the probably infrequent joint statement context, however, there may be few situations in which legitimate tactical considerations of the impeaching party outweigh the benefits of the common law foundation requirement.

b. Extrinsic Evidence in Practice: Practical Considerations

Because of the benefits of the common law foundation requirement, it is probably not surprising that some courts have been unwilling to give an expansive reading to FRE 613(b). Some trial judges have prohibited litigants from introducing extrinsic evidence of prior inconsistent statements that they made no effort to explore with the witness on cross-examination, and appellate courts have upheld these decisions on the ground that the trial judges were appropriately exercising discretion to control manner and order of proof. FRE 611(a). United States v. Sutton, 41 F.3d 1257, 1260 (8th Cir. 1994). As a result, the impeaching party in these cases lost the opportunity to show the inconsistent statement. To avoid this situation, counsel should not rely on a literal reading of FRE 613(b). Instead, unless counsel feels that there is a compelling tactical reason not to do so, the safe course of action is to lay the traditional common law foundation and to confront the witness with the inconsistent statement on cross-examination. Indeed, many cross-examiners regularly use the elements of that foundation as part of their impeachment technique.

If the impeaching party lays the common law foundation and the witness denies making the inconsistent statement, the door should be open to proof of the statement with extrinsic evidence. If the party admits the statement, it is less clear whether extrinsic evidence of the statement will be admissible. Some courts take the position that the witness's acknowledgment of the statement removes any need for the extrinsic evidence, while other courts permit extrinsic evidence. The appropriate course of action, in our view, is not to have a flat rule of inadmissibility or admissibility but rather to view the issue as one governed by FRE 401-403. If the witness unequivocally acknowledges the inconsistency, there is no reason to waste the court's time with cumulative, extrinsic evidence. As a matter of FRE 403 (if not FRE 401), the extrinsic evidence should be inadmissible. On the other hand, if the witness tries to minimize the apparent inconsistency and suggests that there is less of an actual inconsistency than the extrinsic evidence indicates, the extrinsic evidence should probably be admissible so that the fact finder can evaluate the significance of the inconsistency.

c. Probative Value and FRE 403 Concerns

Since everyone occasionally makes inconsistent statements, proof of an apparently trivial inconsistency does little, if anything, to impeach a witness's credibility. If the inconsistency relates to the subject matter of the lawsuit, however, it provides a reason to be wary generally of the witness's testimony. The inconsistency, regardless of which statement is true, suggests either that the witness is willing intentionally to lie about the subject matter of the litigation or at least that the witness has been careless and inaccurate in reporting information important to the resolution of the litigation.

i. The Risk of Improper "Substantive" Use.

When an inconsistent statement relates to an issue in the lawsuit, there is, of course, the possibility that the jury will consider the statement not merely for its impeachment value but also for its truth. The risk of improper use is a danger of unfair prejudice within the scope of FRE 403. This risk of unfair prejudice, however, will seldom, if ever, be a basis for exclusion of the evidence. Inconsistent statements about the issues in the lawsuit are likely to be more probative for impeachment purposes than inconsistent statements about unrelated matters. Thus the most prejudicial inconsistent statements are also the most probative for their impeachment value. As you know, the FRE 403 balancing test favors admissibility. Thus the FRE 403 unfair prejudice argument is not likely to succeed unless the objecting party can show some way in which the statement at issue is likely to be uniquely prejudicial in comparison to other inconsistent statements. For a rare example of a case holding that prior inconsistent statements should have been excluded because their impeachment value was outweighed by the risk that the jury would use the statements for their truth, see United States v. Logan, 121 F.3d 1172 (8th Cir.

1997). Cf. United States v. Young, 248 F.3d 260, 268 (4th Cir. 2001) (probative value of witness's ambiguous responses to questions (e.g., "uhm-hmm") outweighed by risk that jury would consider truth of matters asserted in questions).

ii.   Loss of Memory and Inconsistency.   There is at least one type of situation in which an FRE 403 unfair prejudice argument should have a reasonable chance of succeeding. If a witness who testifies to a lack of memory about an event has made a prior statement about the event, some courts view the claimed current loss of memory and the prior statement as inconsistent with each other. When it is reasonable to regard the loss of memory as feigned and, therefore, tantamount to a denial of the earlier statement, the characterization of the statements as inconsistent is reasonable. To the extent that the claimed loss of current memory seems plausible, however, there is no inconsistency between the witness's testimony and the prior statement. Thus the prior statement has relatively low probative value for its legitimate impeachment use, but there is no reduction in the likelihood that the jury will consider the prior statement for its truth.

iii.   Inconsistent Statements About Collateral Matters.   Sometimes a witness's alleged inconsistent statement will be about a collateral matter   a matter that is wholly unrelated to the issues in the case. If an inconsistent statement is about a collateral matter, its probative value may be so low that on at least some occasions the FRE 403 efficiency concerns should require its exclusion. Consider, for example, a situation in which George sees an automobile accident as he is leaving a movie theater. A month later, in an interview with an insurance investigator, George states that he had been going to the theater every night the week of the accident because there was a Bogart festival. He further relates that he had seen *Casablanca* on the night of the accident. (Which Bogart movie George saw may be technically irrelevant to the issues in the case, but it is not unusual for a witness to include such details as part of a narrative of events.) At the trial George's testimony is consistent with his earlier statement in every respect except that he says he had seen *Key Largo* on the night of the accident. Assume that there is no dispute about what night the accident occurred and that it was the night that *Key Largo* was shown. Assume further that everyone concedes that there was not an accident on the night *Casablanca* was shown. Despite the facts that the inconsistency is collateral to the issues in the case and that it seems plausible that a person might have conflicting memories about which of two Bogart movies was showing on a particular night during the Bogart festival, one might want to permit the impeaching party to examine George about the inconsistency. The very low probative value of the evidence, however, may not warrant the consumption of time required to call an additional witness to offer extrinsic evidence of the inconsistency. Indeed, this is the result mandated by a common law rule that prohibited extrinsic evidence of an inconsistent statement about a collateral matter. Moreover, some federal courts have specifically adopted this rule. United States v. Grooms, 978 F.2d 425 (8th Cir. 1992); United States v. Tarantino, 846 F.2d 1384, 1409-1410 (D.C. Cir. 1998) (reciting the FRE 403 discretionary balancing test as authority).

Despite the cases approving the "collateralness" doctrine, the admissibility of extrinsic evidence of inconsistent statements under the Federal Rules should not turn on whether the statements are collateral in some common law sense. Rather, the important question for admissibility should be whether the probative value of the inconsistent statement for its impeachment value is substantially outweighed by countervailing FRE 403 factors. See United States v. Higa, 55 F.3d 448, 452 (9th Cir. 1995) (court has discretion to admit prior inconsistent statements on collateral matters). Indeed, a rigid application of the common law collateralness doctrine may not always be warranted. The impeachment theory relies on the fact of inconsistency rather than the truth of the prior inconsistent statement to discredit the witness. Thus even an inconsistency that does not relate to an issue in the case may have relatively high probative value to impeach the witness if the inconsistency does not seem innocuous or easy to rationalize. Moreover, the concern that the jury may improperly consider an inconsistent statement for its truth is not a concern when the substance of the statement has no bearing on the issues in the case. Thus a proper application of FRE 403 could result in permitting extrinsic evidence of statements that the common law would exclude.

Application of the common law "no extrinsic evidence to impeach on a collateral matter" rule or achieving the same result by applying FRE 403 to exclude extrinsic evidence of the inconsistent statement means, in effect, that the cross-examiner may ask the witness about the statement but that the cross-examiner is bound by the witness's answer.

KEY POINTS

1. Prior inconsistent statements may be admissible for the nonhearsay purpose of impeaching the credibility of a witness.

2. FRE 613(b) provides that normally a party may not introduce extrinsic evidence of a prior inconsistent statement unless the witness has an opportunity to explain or deny the statement and opposing counsel has an opportunity to question the witness about the statement.

3. Although FRE 613(b) liberalizes the common law foundation requirement for extrinsic evidence of inconsistent statements, some federal courts prohibit extrinsic evidence if the impeaching party does not call the statement to the witness's attention.

PROBLEMS

7.21. Return to Problem 3.2 at page 129. Assume that Jake O'Leary, an eyewitness, testifies for the defense that Driver did not veer off the roadway onto the gravel shoulder. Plaintiffs' counsel has a written statement from Pam Peters, Jake's former girl friend, that the evening after the accident Jake said, "That bus driver should have been more careful." Can plaintiffs' attorney ask O'Leary about the statement on cross-examination? If the question is permitted and Jake denies having made the statement, can plaintiff's attorney call Pam to testify that Jake made the statement?

7.22. Ed Macy is charged with felonious assault. He claims not to have been the assailant and will present an alibi defense. During his incarceration prior to trial, Macy's cellmate told him that Wally Wilder had confessed to committing the assault. At trial, Macy calls Wilder as a defense witness, and Wilder denies any involvement in the assault. Can Macy (a) ask Wilder about Wilder's alleged confession to the cellmate or (b) call the cellmate to testify about Wilder's alleged confession?

7.23. Danny Dickson has been charged with murdering a fellow prison inmate. Three inmates testified for the prosecution that Danny committed the murder, and none of them was cross-examined. Later in the trial Danny offered the testimony of two other inmates to the effect that the prosecution witnesses had told them that Danny had not committed the murder. The prosecution objects to this evidence. What result?

7.24. Return again to Problem 3.2 at page 129. Plaintiffs' counsel has located Wanda White, another school bus driver, who had dinner with Driver shortly after the accident. According to White, Driver said that she was going to quit her job because she hated "having to deal with those little brats every day." Can plaintiff's attorney call White to testify to this statement? Does your answer depend upon (a) whether Driver testifies as set forth at page 130, line 4? (b) whether plaintiff's counsel first asks Driver about the statement on cross-examination?

7.25. Review the direct and cross-examination of Officer Huston in the *Johnson* case (page 7, line 32, supra). What was the relevance of defense counsel's questions on cross-examination about whether the incident report prepared by Officer Huston made any reference to an open food port? Would that inquiry be appropriate under the Federal Rules? Would it be appropriate under the Federal Rules to introduce the incident report to show that it contained nothing about the food port?

4. The Impeachment of Experts with Statements in Treatises

Before the adoption of the Federal Rules some jurisdictions recognized a hearsay exception for learned treatises. The exception, however, did not receive broad acceptance, and where it existed courts tended to interpret it narrowly. Nonetheless, statements in learned treatises were frequently admissible for the nonhearsay purpose of impeaching or rehabilitating the credibility of an expert witness. Analytically, the process of using treatises in this manner is analogous to the use of prior statements for nonhearsay purposes: Initially, the witness had to acknowledge either reliance on the treatise or, in some jurisdictions, that the treatise was authoritative. This acknowledgment, in effect, constituted an adoption of the statements in the treatise. If statements in the treatise happened to be inconsistent with the witness's testimony, they were then admissible for the nonhearsay purpose of impeaching the witness's credibility.

The expert, of course, could attempt to account for the apparent inconsistency in the treatise. Such an explanation might involve reading additional statements from the treatise for the purpose of putting the supposedly inconsistent statement in proper context or explaining why it was not appropriate to rely on that part of the treatise.

FRE 803(18) contains a relatively broad hearsay exception for learned treatises. The Advisory Committee acknowledged that in part the rationale for this hearsay exception is that it "avoids the unreality of admitting evidence for the purpose of impeachment only, with an instruction to the jury not to consider it otherwise." The hearsay exception, however, does more than merely eliminate the need for a limiting instruction. FRE 803(18) does not require that any particular expert rely on or acknowledge the treatise as authoritative, nor does it require that the statements in the treatise be inconsistent with any expert's testimony. Thus, as other portions of the Advisory Committee Note make clear, the purpose of the exception is to permit affirmative use of statements in learned treatises apart from whatever impeachment value they may have.

If a statement in a treatise is admissible for its truth, there is no need to consider its possible admissibility for impeachment purposes. If the statement is not admissible for its truth, then one must turn to the prior statement analogy to find a possible non-hearsay basis for admission.

5.   Prior Consistent Statements

As we noted at page 386, supra, prior consistent statements may be relevant for two distinct purposes: to prove the truth of their contents, in which case they implicate hearsay concerns, and to rehabilitate or bolster a witness's credibility by demonstrating that the witness has spoken consistently about a matter. At common law, prior consistent statements were not admissible for their truth. They were admissible to rehabilitate the credibility of a witness, but only if they rebutted an express or implied charge of recent fabrication or improper influence. When prior consistent statements were admissible at common law, the party against whom the evidence was introduced was entitled to an instruction that the prior statements could not be used for their truth.

a.   Admissibility for Truth Pursuant to FRE 801(d)(1)(B)

FRE 801(d)(1)(B) exempts from the definition of hearsay a witness's statement that is "consistent with the declarant's testimony and is offered to rebut an express or implied charge against the declarant of recent fabrication or improper influence or motive." As we discuss in Chapter Eight at pages 462-464, infra, this rule makes admissible for their truth prior consistent statements that previously were admissible only for the nonhearsay purpose of showing consistency; and as we also discuss there, the Supreme Court in Tome v. United States, 513 U.S. 150 (1995), has interpreted FRE 801(d)(1)(B) narrowly: Only prior consistent statements made prior to the time that a motive to fabricate or an improper influence arose fall within the scope of the rule. Thus there are many prior consistent statements that cannot be admitted under this hearsay exemption.

b.   Admissibility to Rehabilitate Pursuant to FRE 401-403?

Neither the Federal Rules nor *Tome* explicitly addresses the question whether prior consistent statements that do not satisfy the *Tome*-FRE 801(d)(1)(B) criteria may nonetheless be admissible, not for their truth but for the *nonhearsay* purpose of rehabilitating a witness. If the answer is yes, the party against whom the evidence is admitted would be entitled to a limiting instruction, as was the case at common law when prior consistent statements were admitted only for their rehabilitation value.

   i.   Putting Inconsistent Statements in Context Following Impeachment with Prior Inconsistent Statement.   When a witness has been impeached with prior inconsistent statements, the uniform view is that contemporaneous prior consistent statements not satisfying the criteria of FRE 801(d)(1)(B) may be admissible to clarify or explain the alleged inconsistency. For example, in United States v. Denton, 246 F.3d 784 (6th Cir. 2001), after the defendant impeached a prosecution witness with specific portions of a prior statement that he claimed were inconsistent with the witness's testimony, the prosecutor was permitted to show portions of the prior statement that were consistent with the testimony. Accord, United States v. Payne, 944 F.2d 1458, 1470-1471 (9th Cir. 1991). This view is consistent with both the principle of completeness in FRE 106 and the FRE 613(b) requirement that a witness have an opportunity to explain or deny an inconsistent statement.

ii.   Rehabilitation with Consistent Statements in Other Contexts.   In other contexts courts are divided on the question whether FRE 801(d)(1)(B) regulates the use of prior consistent statements offered to rehabilitate witnesses. According to one view, FRE 801(d)(1)(B) governs the use of prior consistent statements for both hearsay and rehabilitation purposes; if the statement is not admissible for its truth, it is not admissible to rehabilitate. United States v. Miller, 874 F.2d 1255, 1273 (9th Cir. 1989); United States v. Quinto, 582 F.2d 224 (2d Cir. 1978). This view holds that the primary objective of FRE 801(d)(1)(B) is to eliminate the need for a limiting instruction when prior consistent statements are admissible. To state the matter somewhat differently, the objective is to make all consistent statements admissible for their truth, and the tacit premise is that the common law limitations on the use of prior consistent statements for rehabilitation remain operative. Thus there will never be an occasion to admit a prior consistent statement and tell the jury it may not consider the statement for its truth.

The contrary view is that FRE 801(d)(1)(B) is nothing more than a hearsay exemption. United States v. Ellis, 121 F.3d 908 (4th Cir. 1997). Since there is no rule restricting the use of prior consistent statements for nonhearsay purposes, the admissibility of prior consistent statements to rehabilitate should be governed by FRE 401-403. Thus there may be times when it is appropriate to introduce — with a limiting instruction, if requested — a prior consistent statement that does not fall within the scope of FRE 801(d)(1)(B).

Here are three examples of consistent statements that are relevant to rehabilitate a witness on nonhearsay theories of relevance and that would not be admissible for their truth pursuant to FRE 801(d)(1)(B):

(1) Plaintiff brings an action for negligence as a result of having been exposed to a potentially fatal chemical. Plaintiff's key witness, a former employee of the defendant, testifies that she caused the exposure. Assume that the defendant establishes that the witness had been fired immediately after the incident, thereby giving the witness a motive to fabricate testimony damaging to the defendant. Assume further that the witness's son was exposed to the chemical at the same time and that the witness made a prior consistent statement two weeks after the firing while admitting the son, who had just developed symptoms of the exposure, to the hospital. Here, one might reasonably conclude that prior consistent statement made after the motive to fabricate arose rehabilitates the witness because the motive to be truthful about the son's exposure outweighs the motive to fabricate.

(2) If a witness denies making a prior inconsistent statement or denies that it was inconsistent, proof of a prior statement consistent with the witness's trial testimony suggests that the alleged prior inconsistent statement may not have been made or that in context it may not have been as inconsistent as the impeaching party claims it is.

(3) When a party has attacked a witness's character for truthfulness, proof of a prior consistent statement may suggest that the witness's testimony is not behavior in conformity with the supposed dishonest character trait (or it may suggest that the witness is being consistently dishonest).

Do you think the prior consistent statements in the foregoing examples should be admissible? If so, should they be admissible for their truth or only for the limited purpose of rehabilitating the witness? If the former, how would you amend FRE 801(d)(1)(B)? If the latter, do you think jurors are likely to be able to distinguish between the hearsay and nonhearsay uses of consistent statements?

c. Extrinsic Evidence

If a prior consistent statement is admissible, there is no specific prohibition against or limitation on proof of the statement by extrinsic evidence. Typically, however, a party will be eliciting the statement from the witness who made it, and the witness is likely to be friendly to the examiner. Thus there will seldom be any need for extrinsic evidence.

KEY POINTS

1. Prior consistent statements offered to rebut an express or implied charge of recent fabrication or improper influence are admissible for their truth pursuant to FRE 801(d)(1)(B) as long as the statements were made before the motive to fabricate arose. (Such statements were admissible at common law only for the nonhearsay purpose of rehabilitating a witness.)

2. Prior consistent statements made in conjunction with allegedly inconsistent statements are admissible to put allegedly inconsistent statements in context even if the consistent statements do not satisfy FRE 801(d)(1)(B).

3. In other contexts, there is a split of authority on the question whether the Federal Rules permit the nonhearsay rehabilitation use of prior consistent statements not falling within FRE 801(d)(1)(B).

PROBLEMS

7.26. Return to Problem 3.2 at page 129. Assume the following occurred on direct examination of Driver after the direct examination set forth at page 130:

Q: Did you drive the bus onto the gravel shoulder?
A: No.
Q: In the days following the accident did you discuss it with anyone?
A: Yes, with my friend Wanda.
Q: And what did you talk about.
A: I told her that I'd been very careful, that I hadn't driven the bus onto the gravel shoulder, and that I felt so sad for those dear little children that I thought I was going to have to quit my job.

Is any of this evidence objectionable? Would your answer be different if this were redirect and if evidence of the "little brats" statement (see Problem 7.24 at page

393) had been elicited on cross-examination? In answering this last question, does it matter whether the discussion with Wanda referred to in Problem 7.24 and the discussion with Wanda referred to here were (a) part of the same conversation or (b) conversations occurring on different days?

7.27. Pam Peters has brought an action for personal injuries against the Ace Department Store for injuries that she claims to have sustained when she fell on some ice in the parking lot on January 23. Peters first consulted an attorney in March, and the suit was filed in April. The trial is taking place the following December. On direct examination Peters testified about the accident, the severe bruises that she suffered, and the continuing backaches and headaches that she has had continually from the day of the injury. During cross-examination defense counsel elicited the fact that Peters did not mention the fall or her alleged injuries when she visited her doctor for a routine checkup on March 1. Later in the trial the defendant offered the testimony of two women who have monthly bridge games with Peters to the effect that Peters said nothing about the fall or any injuries at their bridge games on January 30 and on February 28. Plaintiff objects to the admissibility of this evidence.

In rebuttal, the plaintiff offers the testimony of Ed Peters, Pam Peters's husband, that she told him about the accident on January 23 and that she has frequently mentioned headaches and backaches — at least two or three times a week ever since January 23. The defendant has objected to Ed Peters's testimony.

Should either plaintiff's or the defendant's objection be sustained?

7.28. Return to Problem 3.3 at page 131. On direct examination, Beth Barker testifies for the prosecution that she definitely remembers placing the March 14, 2004, auditor's memo in Ray's "in box" on the afternoon of March 14 and removing it the next day from his "out box," and that Ray's initials were on the memo.

(a) Consider the following cross-examination of Ms. Barker:

Q. Ms. Barker, on July 10, 2005, you made a statement in my office that was recorded by my assistant, did you not?

A   Yes

Q. And at that session in my office I asked you some questions about a March 14, 2004, auditor's memo, did I not?

A. Yes.

Q. Isn't it true that I asked you the following questions and you gave the following answers: [reading from the transcript prepared by the assistant]

Q. Ms. Barker, of all the memos you deal with, do you specifically recall the March 14 memorandum from Rundown's auditors?

A. No, I can't say that I recall that specific memo?

Should the prosecutor's objection to defense counsel's reading from the transcript be sustained?

(b) Defense counsel next offers into evidence Exhibit B, an authenticated written statement of Beth Barker dated December 19, 2004, which states (in pertinent part):

> I, Beth Barker, declare
>> I have removed hundreds of documents from Bernard Ray's "in box" in the years I worked as his secretary.
>> I do not have a specific recollection of the March 14, 2004, auditor's memo.
>> I declare under penalty of perjury that the foregoing is true and correct to the best of my knowledge.
>
> [signed] Beth Barker

Should the prosecutor's objection to the admission of Exhibit B be sustained?

(c)   On cross-examination, defense counsel asks Barker the following:

Q.   Ms. Barker, on August 12, 2005, were you arrested for embezzling $250 from a petty cash fund while you were employed at Rundown?
A.   Yes.
Q.   And when did the alleged embezzlement occur?
A.   I don't remember?
Q.   Was it before August 1st?
A.   I don't remember.
Q.   Ms. Barker, isn't it a fact that you made up this story about seeing the signed memo in Bernard Ray's mail box in order to get a deal with the prosecutor on your embezzlement charge?
A.   No, that's not true
DEFENSE COUNSEL: I have no further questions.

On redirect, the prosecutor offers into evidence an authenticated written statement of Beth Barker dated June, 30, 2005, stating that "I recall removing the March 14, 2004, auditor's memo from Mr. Ray's "out box" on March 15, 2004. It had Mr. Ray's initials on it, and I filed it." There is a dispute as to whether the alleged embezzlement occurred before or after June 30.

Should the June 30 statement be admitted over defense counsel's objection?

D.   OTHER IMPEACHMENT TECHNIQUES

Recall that at the outset of the impeachment discussion we described impeachment as the process of attempting to raise doubts about the testimonial abilities of witnesses — that is, to show that the witness is lying, careless with words, imperceptive, or forgetful. The Federal Rules specifically address only two permissible methods for raising these doubts: attacking a witness's character and showing a witness's prior inconsistent statement. The process of impeachment, however, is not so limited. The common law permitted the impeachment of witnesses with evidence of unorthodox religious beliefs, bias, mental or sensory incapacity, and contradiction.

FRE 610 prohibits relying on the content of a witness's religious beliefs to assess credibility: "Evidence of the beliefs or opinions of a witness on matters of religion is not admissible for the purpose of showing that by reason of their nature, the witness' credibility is impaired or enhanced." For impeachment techniques that the Federal

Rules do not specifically address, courts rely — or at least should rely — on FRE 401-403 to determine the admissibility of evidence.

1.   Bias

a.   Relevance

Modern courts and commentators frequently attach the label "bias" to what Wigmore identified as three methods of showing a witness's "emotional incapacity." According to Wigmore:

> Three different *kinds of emotion* constituting untrustworthy partiality may be broadly distinguished — bias, interest, and corruption: *Bias*, in common acceptance, covers all varieties of hostility or prejudice against the opponent *personally* or of favor to the proponent personally. [E.g., intimate family relationship with one of the parties.] *Interest* signifies the specific inclination which is apt to be produced by the relation between the witness and the *cause at issue* in the litigation. [E.g., the expectation of favorable treatment from the prosecutor or sentencing judge in return for the testimony.] *Corruption* is here to be understood as the *conscious false intent* which is inferrible from giving or taking a bribe or from expressions of a general unscrupulousness for the case at hand. [E.g., an attempt to bribe another witness or the receipt of money for *testimony*.] The kinds of evidence available are two:
>
> [1]   the *circumstances of the witness' situation*, making it "a priori" probable that he has some partiality of emotion for one party's cause;
> [2]   the *conduct of the witness* himself, indicating the presence of such partiality, the inference here being from the expression of the feeling to the feeling itself.

[3A John Henry Wigmore, Evidence §947, at 782 (James Chadbourn rev. 1970) (emphasis original).]

Proof of any of these types of bias can be particularly effective in discrediting a witness because it is highly probative of insincerity. Compare, for example, the likely impact of a prior inconsistent statement or an FRE 608(b) bad act with proof of a witness's close relationship with or expected favorable treatment from one of the parties. All of us make inconsistent statements at least occasionally, and having a bad character for truthfulness may mean nothing more than that the person is untruthful a bit more often than most people. Neither of these forms of impeachment suggests any particular reason to believe that the witness is being untruthful on the particular occasion of the witness's current testimony. By contrast, the types of bias described by Wigmore suggest a specific, concrete motive for fabricating testimony or at least being less than fully candid.

b.   Extrinsic Evidence

All common law courts permitted proof of a witness's bias both by examination of the witness and also by the introduction of extrinsic evidence, and in United States v. Abel, 469 U.S. 45 (1984), the Supreme Court upheld the proof of bias with extrinsic evidence under the Federal Rules. The evidence in *Abel* consisted of testimony from a prosecution witness that a defense witness and the defendant were both members of the same secret prison gang that required its members to commit perjury, theft, and murder on each member's behalf. Which type of bias, under Wigmore's analysis, does this suggest? Remember that the prosecution in the

Johnson case tried to prove that defendant Johnson and his cellmate, Butler, belonged to the same gang outside of prison.

c.   Possible Limitations on Extrinsic Evidence of Bias

Despite *Abel*, the right to introduce extrinsic evidence of bias is not automatic under the Federal Rules. There are at least two possible limitations on the use of such evidence. First, some federal courts hold that when the evidence of bias is a witness's prior statement, extrinsic evidence of the statement is not admissible unless the witness first has had an opportunity to explain or deny the statement. United States v. Betts, 16 F.3d 748, 764 (7th Cir. 1994) ("The weight of authority supports the proposition that when a party seeks to prove bias through extrinsic evidence of a witness' prior statement, he must first give the witness the opportunity to explain or deny that statement, even though Rule 613(b) is not strictly applicable."). This rule, in effect, is the foundation requirement for prior inconsistent statements applied to statements evincing bias regardless of whether they are inconsistent with the witness's testimony.

Second, there is always the possibility of a successful FRE 403 objection. Typically evidence of bias is highly probative, but if the witness fully admits the bias or if the evidence in fact suggests little about the witness's possible bias, a court should probably sustain an FRE 403 objection to extrinsic evidence. United States v. Adams, 799 F.2d 665, 671 (11th Cir. 1986) (extrinsic evidence of bias excluded because bias adequately shown through cross-examination). Evidence of bias may also raise the FRE 403 issue of unfair prejudice. Consider, for example, United States v. Abel, supra:

> Respondent argues that even if the evidence of membership in the prison gang were relevant to show [witness Mills's] bias, the District Court erred in permitting a full description of the gang and its odious tenets . . . .
>
> Respondent specifically contends that the District Court should not have permitted Ehle's precise description of the gang as a lying and murderous group. Respondent suggests that the District Court should have cut off the testimony after the prosecutor had elicited that Mills knew respondent and both may have belonged to an organization together. This argument ignores the fact that the type of organization in which a witness and a party share membership may be relevant to show bias . . . . The attributes of the Aryan Brotherhood — a secret prison sect sworn to perjury and self-protection — bore directly not only on the fact of bias but also on the source and strength of Mills' bias. The tenets of this group showed that Mills had a powerful motive to slant his testimony towards respondent, or even commit perjury outright.
>
> A district court is accorded a wide discretion in determining the admissibility of evidence under the Federal Rules. Assessing the probative value of common membership in any particular group, and weighing any factors counseling against admissibility is a matter first for the district court's sound judgment under Rules 401 and 403 . . . . [469 U.S. at 53-54.]

d.   Bias Versus Character

A troublesome issue that sometimes arises — particularly with the type of evidence that Wigmore refers to as "corruption" — is whether the evidence should fit within the "bias" category or the "character" category. For example, is proof that the witness attempted to bribe another witness evidence of corruption-bias, or is it evidence of character, or both? Is the evidence of gang membership in *Abel* character evidence or evidence of bias or both? The issue is important because extrinsic evidence of the witness's conduct is admissible to prove bias but not to prove character under FRE 608(b).

The issue is difficult to resolve in part because the term *character* is not defined and is probably not definable in any very helpful sense. Similarly, the contours of *corruption*, which the Advisory Committee's Note to FRE 608 equates with "character" and distinguishes from "bias" and "interest," are not clear. Moreover, it is not clear to what extent one should regard the concepts of character and bias as mutually exclusive or as potentially overlapping. In *Abel* the Court noted that the evidence of gang membership may show a bad character for truthfulness as well as bias. The Court suggested but did not decide that the FRE 608(b) prohibition against extrinsic evidence to prove character should not apply when the evidence is relevant and otherwise admissible to show bias.

To the extent that it is reasonable to infer from the corrupt act that the witness has some particular concern about or interest in the outcome of the present litigation, the evidence has relatively high probative value on the question whether the witness's testimony is tainted because of this interest. Thus it seems appropriate to attach the bias label to the evidence in order to permit exploration of the matter with extrinsic evidence. On the other hand, if the *only* reasonable inference to draw from the corrupt act is that the individual has a general lack of integrity or disregard for the truth, the probative value of the evidence to suggest untruthfulness on one specific occasion on the witness stand is relatively low. This evidence should receive the "character" label in order to prevent the possibility of time-consuming and distracting exploration of the matter with extrinsic evidence. In short, as Wigmore observed, "The only distinction that is here legitimate is between conduct indicating a corrupt moral character in general and conduct indicating a specific corrupt intention for the case at hand." 3A John Henry Wigmore, Evidence §963, at 808-810 (James Chadbourn rev. 1970).

Would it be desirable to abandon the distinction between "character" and "bias" and always to treat the question whether extrinsic acts evidence can be introduced as an FRE 403 issue? Reconsider pages 254-256, 364, supra, which raise the same question with respect to the character evidence prohibition in FRE 404(b) and the extrinsic evidence prohibition in FRE 608(b).

KEY POINTS

1. Showing a witness's bias is relevant to impeach the witness's credibility, because the bias suggests a particular reason or motive for the witness to lie or at least be less than completely candid.

2. There is no Federal Rule of Evidence dealing with bias. FRE 401-403 govern admissibility of evidence of bias.

3. Extrinsic evidence of bias is admissible, but some courts impose, as a condition of introducing extrinsic evidence of a prior statement showing bias, a foundation requirement that is similar to the foundation requirement for prior inconsistent statements.

PROBLEMS

7.29. Return to Problem 3.2 at page 129. Assume that plaintiff called Nancy Patterson, an accident reconstruction expert, who testified that in her opinion the bus veered on the roadway and was on the gravel shoulder when it hit Paul. Defense counsel has learned that Patterson is receiving a $5,000 fee, that she has testified 10 times on behalf of plaintiffs and only once on behalf of defendants, and that her husband's sister is married to Paul's uncle. Plaintiff's counsel has filed a motion *in limine* requesting that the court not permit any mention of these matters on the grounds that they are irrelevant and prejudicial. The motion is accompanied by affidavits from Patterson and other accident reconstruction experts stating that a $5,000 fee is in the low to normal range for the work that she has done and an affidavit from Patterson stating that she has not seen or heard from her husband's sister in over five years.

How should the court rule on the motion?

If the court denies the motion, can plaintiffs' counsel call other experts to testify that the fee is in the low to normal range?

7.30. Joan Dominick is being prosecuted for selling and conspiring to sell controlled substances. According to the prosecution's case, the conspiracy has lasted for a number of years and has involved three closely knit families. Joan acknowledges that some members of her family were involved in the conspiracy, and she admits being acquainted with the other alleged coconspirators. However, she claims that she was not involved in any illegal activity. The principal witness against Joan is Sean Matthews, an acknowledged member of the conspiracy, who has pleaded guilty and entered into a cooperation agreement with the government. According to Sean, Joan supplied him with large quantities of drugs on a number of occasions. On cross-examination, Joan wants to inquire about (a) the extent of Sean's involvement in the conspiracy, (b) his plea, and his cooperation agreement, (c) an occasion five years ago when she rejected his sexual advances and he became angry, and (d) a 10-year-old drug scam in which Sean lost $30,000 and claimed (incorrectly, according to Joan) that Joan was responsible for defrauding him. How much of this inquiry should the court permit?

7.31. Stella Starlet is a rising movie star, rock singer, and television personality. She has sued Frances Fisher, her former manager and agent, for fraud and breach of contract. Stella's services were in great demand, and according to the complaint Fisher would negotiate contracts only with individuals willing to pay a substantial sum, above the negotiated contract amount, in cash directly to Frances. One of Stella's key witnesses is Ken Olsen, a former employee of Fisher. Olsen testified in detail about Fisher's demanding and receiving sums to book Stella that were never accounted for. The following cross-examination of Olsen took place without objection:

Q: Do you know Stella Starlet personally?
A: Yes.
Q: You're quite fond of her, aren't you?
A: Well, I like her and respect her.
Q: You feel indebted to her, don't you?
A: Indebted? No.
Q: Isn't it true that in the two months prior to this trial she has taken you to dinner at expensive restaurants on at least seven occasions?
A: No, she has never done that.
Q: And isn't it true that last month she bought you diamond cuff links and a new set of expensive golf clubs?
A: No.
Q: Two weeks ago when you were having lunch with your friend Tom Thompson at the River Edge Cafe, didn't you tell Thompson that Stella had taken you to dinner seven times in the last two months and that she had bought you diamond cuff links and new golf clubs?

A: No.

As part of its defense, the defendant calls Tom Thompson to testify that two weeks ago at the River Edge Cafe, Ken Olsen was bragging that he had had dinner with Stella Starlet on seven occasions in the last two months and that she recently bought him diamond cuff links and new golf clubs. Should this evidence be admitted over plaintiff's objection?

7.32. Joyce Addison has filed a racial discrimination in employment suit against State University, which recently fired her. On cross-examination of Joyce can the university ask about allegations of racial discrimination that she made against two previous university employers?

7.33. Clarence Green, an inmate, has filed a federal civil rights action against Bull Brackton, a prison guard who shot and severely wounded Green. Green claims that the shooting was an unprovoked attack, and Brackton claims that he shot Green in self-defense. Elmer Novak, another prison guard, testifies for the defense that he observed the entire incident, that Green attacked Brackton, and that Brackton shot Green to avoid the infliction of serious bodily injury by Green. Green is black; Brackton and Novak are white. Consider whether the following evidence should be admitted over the opposing party's objection: On cross-examination of Novak, plaintiff's counsel asks

(a)   whether Novak is a member of the John Birch Society;
(b)   whether Novak had referred to Green with an insulting racial epithet;
(c)   whether Novak physically assaulted a black youth following a minor automobile accident involving the youth and Novak.

(Assume that the plaintiff has a reasonable factual basis for asking each of the preceding questions. Assume further that if the objections are overruled the witness will respond affirmatively to the first question and negatively to the last two questions.) On redirect examination, defense counsel seeks to establish

(d)   that Novak is an active member of the Christian Church of Holiness, whose membership is 40 percent black.

As part of its rebuttal, the plaintiff calls a black youth to testify

(e)   that last month, when he accidentally backed his car into Novak's car in a parking lot, Novak became enraged, used racial epithets, and beat him.

In rebuttal the plaintiff also offers the following testimony of Al Jensen, Green's cellmate:

(f)   that he has heard Novak hurl racial slurs at Green on a number of occasions;
(g)   that he personally has witnessed two occasions on which Novak and Brackton together made unprovoked attacks on black inmates.

2.   Mental or Sensory Incapacity

a.   Relevance

Any sensory or mental deficiency that inhibits a witness's ability to perceive events accurately at the time they occur or to remember and to narrate accurately what happened at the time of trial is relevant to cast doubt on the witness's credibility. Thus, for example, it is relevant to prove that a witness suffers from faulty memory, some form of mental illness that contributes to a witness's inability to distinguish fact from fantasy, intoxication at the time of the event to which the testimony relates or while on the witness stand, or color-blindness if accuracy with respect to color is important. Indeed, any fact relating to the witness's general testimonial capacities for narration, perception, and memory or about the exercise of these capacities on the occasion in question is relevant to impeach the witness. Subject to a court's discretion to control the mode of cross-examination (FRE 611(a)) and to FRE 403, it is permissible to inquire about these matters during the examination of the witness whose sensory or mental condition is at issue. United States v. Pryce, 938 F.2d 1343, 1345 (D.C. Cir. 1991) (prejudicial error to limit questions about witness's hallucinations to the time frame of the events about which witness testified); United States v. DiPaola, 804 F.2d 225, 229-230 (2d Cir. 1986) (permissible to exclude questions about witness's drinking problem in the absence of any showing that witness was under the influence at the time of the events or when giving testimony); Roberts v. Hollocher, 664 F.2d 200, 203 (8th Cir. 1981) (questions about Roberts's drug use permissible because they were "relevant to Roberts' physical state at the time of the alleged incidents and to his ability to accurately recall those incidents").

b.   Extrinsic Evidence

In addition to making inquiry on cross-examination, parties may introduce extrinsic evidence of a witness's mental or sensory incapacity. Courts traditionally have regarded such evidence as showing something different from a moral incapacity or character trait. Thus the restrictions on the proof of character are not applicable. As a result, for example, courts have permitted extrinsic evidence of such matters as strange, seemingly irrational acts of a witness, expert testimony from a psychiatrist about a witness's mental capacity, and courtroom experiments to demonstrate a witness's poor memory or eyesight.

It is appropriate to decide on a case-by-case basis how extensive a cross-examination to permit and how much, if any, extrinsic evidence to introduce about a witness's sensory or mental incapacity. The Federal Rules take this approach. In the absence of any exclusionary rule, admissibility decisions should turn on the application of FRE 401-403 and, if expert testimony is offered, FRE 702-706.

c.   Mental Incapacity as a Bar to Testimony

In considering an individual's mental incapacity it is important not to confuse mental incapacity as a subject matter for impeachment with mental incapacity as a complete bar to testimony. Early in the development of the common law, courts barred individuals regarded as mentally deranged or defective from testifying. As we discussed in Chapter Four, FRE 601 now presumes that every person is competent to be a witness, including a person with mental illness. If an individual's mental condition prevents the individual from understanding the oath or the obligation to testify truthfully, however, that would be a legitimate reason for refusing to let the individual testify.

KEY POINTS

1. Courts regard a witness's sensory or mental incapacity as something different from a character trait. Thus impeachment on these grounds is not limited by FRE 404 or FRE 608. Indeed, there is no Federal Rule dealing specifically with this form of impeachment.

2. FRE 401-403 and, if expert testimony is involved, FRE 702-706 govern proof of a witness's sensory or mental incapacity.

PROBLEMS

7.34. Al Drummond has been charged with possession and sale of cocaine. The key government witness is Jimmy Jones, an informant and, according to the government, a former co-conspirator in drug trafficking with Drummond. Jones had already pleaded guilty and been sentenced for his involvement in the drug incident for which Drummond is on trial. On cross-examination of Jones, defense counsel (with a factual basis for each question) asks:

(a) "Isn't it true that you are a heroin addict?"
(b) "Isn't it true that you are under the influence of heroin right now on the witness stand?"
(c) "Isn't it true that last week you sold two ounces of heroin to James Edwards?"

Are any of these questions objectionable? If objections are not made or are overruled, can the defendant later introduce extrinsic evidence to prove that Jones is an addict? was under the influence of heroin on the witness stand? sold heroin last week to James Edwards?

The defense calls as a witness Dr. Helen James, who is qualified as an expert on mental disorders. She offers to testify that she recently diagnosed Jimmy Jones as suffering from AKSS syndrome, a severe mental disorder. Should plaintiff's objection to this evidence be sustained?

7.35. Return to Problem 5.38 at page 282. If the court rules that the evidence is not admissible substantively, may the defendant nonetheless introduce the expert testimony to impeach Haywood's credibility?

3. Contradiction

a. Relevance

The last traditional method of impeaching a witness's credibility is by means of contradiction — that is, introducing evidence that contradicts something the witness has said. For example, if the witness said that she was wearing a yellow dress when she saw the automobile accident, it would contradict her testimony to establish that she was wearing a blue dress on that occasion; and if one can establish that a witness is incorrect about one thing, it is arguably appropriate to infer that the witness may be wrong about other things, including perhaps the substantively important aspects of the witness's testimony.

As Wigmore observed:

> The peculiar feature of [the] probative fact of error on a particular point [i.e., contradiction] is its *deficiency with respect to definiteness* and its *wide range with respect to possible significance*. Looking back over the various [impeachment devices] already considered, it will be seen that the evidence in those classes of cases was aimed clearly and specifically at a particular defect; it showed either that or nothing. Former perjury would indicate probably a deficient sense of moral duty to speak truth; relationship to the party, a probable inclination to distort the facts, consciously or unconsciously . . . .
>
> [Evidence of contradiction] is not offered as definitely showing any specific defect of any of these kinds, and yet it may justify an inference of the existence of any one or more of them. We know simply that an erroneous statement has been made on one point, and we infer that the witness is capable of making an erroneous statement on other points. We are not asked, and we do not attempt to specify, the particular defect which was the source of the proved error and which might therefore be the source of another error. The source might be a mental defect as to powers of observation or recollection; it might be a lack of veracity character; it might be bias or corruption . . . . The inference is only that since, for this proved error, there was *some unspecified defect* which became a source of error, the same defect may equally exist as the source of some other error, otherwise not apparent. [3A John Henry Wigmore, Evidence §1000, at 957-958 (James Chadbourn rev. 1970) (emphasis original).]

All of us, of course, from time to time make erroneous statements that can be contradicted. Thus, at least in the absence of showing many contradictions by the same witness, see id. §1000, at 958, proof of contradictions about matters unrelated to the issues being litigated — for example, that the witness in the preceding example was wearing a blue dress instead of a yellow dress — are often of only marginal probative value to impeach the witness's credibility.

b.   Extrinsic Evidence

FRE 401-403 govern the admissibility of evidence of contradiction, and as is the case with evidence of sensory or mental defects, courts applying FRE 403 may permit cross-examination but exclude extrinsic evidence to prove the contradiction if the contradiction appears to have little probative value to impeach the witness. For example, in our blue dress hypothetical, a court may permit some cross-examination about the color of the witness's dress, but if the witness does not admit being wrong about the color of her dress, the court may not permit the impeaching party to establish the contradiction with extrinsic evidence by calling other witnesses to testify that the dress was in fact blue. The color of the witness's dress is not relevant to any issue in the case; and although it is not uncommon for witnesses to include irrelevant details in their testimony, contradicting such matters is typically not very probative of how reliable the witness's testimony is on relevant, disputed facts. Thus under FRE 403, it will seldom if ever be worth the time and risk of confusing the jury to prove these contradictions with extrinsic evidence. As we observed earlier, all of us occasionally make statements that are subject to contradiction, and as the Wigmore excerpt points out it is seldom clear precisely what testimonial deficiency a contradiction shows.

c. The "No Extrinsic Evidence to Impeach on a Collateral Matter" Doctrine

At common law the admissibility of extrinsic evidence to contradict a witness was governed by the general principle that one may not introduce extrinsic evidence to impeach on a collateral matter. This is the same principle that we mentioned earlier in discussing extrinsic evidence of prior inconsistent statements. Pages 391-392, supra. For example, in the blue dress hypothetical, the collateralness doctrine would require exclusion of extrinsic evidence contradicting the witness's testimony that she had been wearing a yellow dress and also extrinsic evidence of a prior inconsistent statement in which she stated that she had been wearing a blue dress at the time of the accident. The color of the dress is collateral in that it has no bearing on an issue in the case.

We offer an examination of the collateralness doctrine here for two reasons. First, although the Federal Rules do not mention the collateralness doctrine, some federal courts have adopted and apply it both in the contradiction context, United States v. Bitterman, 320 F.3d 723, 726-727 (7th Cir. 2003), and in the inconsistent statement context, United States v. Grooms, 978 F.2d 425 (8th Cir. 1992). Second, mastering the collateralness doctrine requires focusing on the inferential process involved in the use of evidence that contracts a witness, and this focus is critical to a reasoned, persuasive argument about admissibility in FRE 403 terms.

i. What Is Not Collateral Generally.   Whether extrinsic evidence is collateral and therefore inadmissible pursuant to the collateralness doctrine is not always intuitively obvious. Prior editions of McCormick's hornbook suggested that "the inquiry is best answered by determining what facts are not within the term." McCormick then identified three such types of facts:

(1) facts relevant to the substantive issues in the case,
(2) facts relevant, apart from the contradiction, to impeach the credibility of a witness, if extrinsic evidence is generally admissible for the noncontradiction impeachment purpose; and
(3) facts recited by the witness that, if untrue, logically undermine the witness's story.

See, e.g., McCormick's Handbook on the Law of Evidence §47, at 110-112 (Edward W. Cleary, 3d. ed. 1984).

ii. Evidence That Is Directly Relevant to the Issues in Litigation.   Evidence that is directly relevant to substantive issues can be introduced for its substantive value apart from any impeachment value that it may have. In effect, the impeachment value of the evidence is secondary. As we stated earlier, if evidence is independently admissible, there is no need to consider whether it is also admissible for impeachment purposes.

iii. Evidence That Impeaches a Witness Apart from Contradiction.   The collateralness doctrine should not prohibit the use of extrinsic evidence that both contradicts the witness and also impeaches credibility in some other way, as long as it is clear that extrinsic evidence would be admissible for that independent impeachment purpose (e.g., to prove bias or a prior conviction). On the other hand, if a specific impeachment rule prohibits extrinsic evidence as FRE 608(b) does, it would undermine that prohibition to admit extrinsic evidence on the theory that the evidence contradicts the witness. Consider for example, the impact of a contrary rule with respect to FRE 608(b). In every case in which the witness denied committing a bad act, the proponent of the extrinsic evidence could argue that extrinsic evidence of the bad act was being offered not to prove character for untruthfulness but to show a contradiction. If that argument were accepted, the prohibition against extrinsic evidence in FRE 608(b) would become meaningless.

iv.   Evidence That Logically Undermines a Witness's Story.   Contradictions that logically undermine the witness's story are also considered noncollateral. To illustrate this third category, consider a personal injury action in which Sadie testifies for the plaintiff and explains that she happened to see the accident as she was walking home from the grocery store where she had gone to purchase milk for her children. Proof that Sadie bought beer instead of milk would contradict her story, but such proof would not logically undermine her testimony. What she bought is collateral. Thus on cross-examination counsel could question Sadie about what she bought, but the counsel would have to accept her answers; extrinsic evidence would be inadmissible. On the other hand, evidence that Sadie had not been in the area of the grocery store at all suggests that she may not have seen the critical events to which she testified. Just as there would be no general prohibition against extrinsic evidence that Sadie was almost blind, there should be no prohibition against the use of extrinsic evidence suggesting that Sadie might not physically have been in a position to observe what she claimed to have seen. In short, proof that Sadie had not been near the grocery store on the day of the accident tends logically to undermine her story about the accident. Thus it should not be regarded as collateral, and extrinsic evidence of her absence from the store should be admissible.

v.   A Test for "Collateralness."   There is a commonly stated test for collateralness that, if properly understood and applied, is consistent with all we have said so far: Could the fact have been proven with extrinsic evidence for any purpose except to show a (mere) contradiction? If the answer is yes, if, in other words, there is some relevant, permissible use for extrinsic evidence above and beyond its value as showing a mere contradiction, it is not collateral. On the other hand, if the only permissible purpose for offering the evidence is to prove a contradiction, the extrinsic evidence is collateral. Thus, for example, in our preceding illustrations it would not be collateral to prove by extrinsic evidence (a) a prior conviction that the witness denied, (b) facts constituting bias that the witness denied, (c) substantively relevant events that the witness denied, or (d) Sadie's absence from the grocery store. It would be collateral to prove (a) that the witness was wearing a blue dress instead of a yellow dress, (b) that the witness falsely denied committing a dishonest act, or (c) that Sadie bought beer.

KEY POINTS

1. Proving a contradiction is relevant to cast doubt on the credibility of a witness. FRE 401 and 403 should govern the admissibility of evidence for this purpose since there is no Federal Rule dealing specifically with contradiction.

2. Rather than invoking FRE 401-403, some federal courts rely on the common law prohibition against the use of extrinsic evidence to impeach on a collateral matter

to exclude extrinsic evidence that contradicts a witness on a collateral matter. Extrinsic evidence is collateral pursuant to this common law doctrine if the fact that the evidence establishes cannot be proven with extrinsic evidence for any purpose other than to show the contradiction.

3. In most cases proper application of FRE 403 would probably lead to the same result as the common law prohibition against extrinsic evidence to contradict on a collateral matter.

PROBLEMS

7.36. Dan Duncan is charged with possession of cocaine with intent to distribute. After the prosecution has completed its case, Duncan testifies that he works with disabled children and would not smuggle drugs for a million dollars; and he portrays himself as an anti-drug counselor who teaches kids to stay away from drugs. In its rebuttal case, can the prosecution offer witnesses to testify that (a) Duncan has been arrested for possessing cocaine and (b) Duncan sold them cocaine?

7.37. Return to Problem 3.2 at page 129. Assume that Eddie Keller, a 13 year old who had been on the bus with Paul, testifies for the plaintiff that Driver veered onto the gravel shoulder and hit Paul. Plaintiff's counsel then asks Eddie what happened next and he replies, "I don't know. I was scared. I went straight home and stayed in my room until supper." Defense counsel has learned from Jim Tobin, one of Eddie's classmates, that Eddie did not go straight home. Instead, he went to the local playground where he found Jim and beat him up in order to settle an argument that had developed earlier in the day. Can defense counsel ask Eddie about the incident with Jim? If there is no objection and Eddie denies the incident, can defense counsel call Jim to testify that Eddie beat him up?

7.38. See Problem 7.37. After beating up Jim, Eddie went to the corner drug store, where he was caught trying to steal comic books and candy. Can defense counsel ask Eddie about this incident? If there is no objection and Eddie denies the attempted theft, can defense counsel call Mark Manning, the druggist, to testify about what happened?

7.39. Defendant is charged with a liquor store robbery that occurred Sunday shortly after noon. To establish an alibi, W_1 testifies for Defendant as follows: "On Sunday morning at 12:15 P.M., as I was walking out of church, I observed Defendant across the street." (Other testimony establishes that the church and the liquor store are at opposite ends of the city.) W_2 offers to testify for the prosecution that on Sunday morning at about 12:15 P.M. he saw W_1 walking out of an all-night bar. Defendant objects to this evidence on the ground that its admission would violate (a) FRE 608(b)'s prohibition against extrinsic evidence of specific instances of conduct, (b) the general prohibition against the use of extrinsic evidence to impeach on a collateral matter, and (c) FRE 403. How should the court rule?

7.40. Daniels is charged with selling cocaine to an undercover police officer. Daniels testified on direct examination that he did not sell the drugs. He further testified that at the time of the alleged sale he had been playing dice with several other people, one of whom periodically left the game and returned with cash. Daniels suggested that the companion was the seller and that the undercover officer identified the wrong person. On cross-examination, the prosecutor asked if Daniels had actually seen the companion sell the cocaine. Daniels responded negatively. The prosecutor then asked Daniels if he was familiar with cocaine, and Daniels responded that he had never seen cocaine.

The prosecutor knows that Daniels tested positively for cocaine use three times in the last two years. Can the prosecutor inquire about these matters on cross-examination or introduce extrinsic evidence of the tests?

E.　REFLECTION ON THE IMPEACHMENT PROCESS

In our initial discussion of the difference in the inferential process between using evidence for impeachment purposes and using evidence for substantive purposes, we used two examples of situations in which evidence is relevant for both substantive and impeachment purposes but potentially admissible only for the latter purpose. See page 354, supra. One involved a witness's inconsistent statement not under oath about the color of a traffic light at the time of an automobile accident. On direct examination the witness testified that the light was red. The inconsistent statement was that the light was green. The other example involved a prior conviction for perjury by a defendant-witness who was charged with perjury. In both examples the permissible impeachment use of the evidence involves an inferential chain of reasoning that arrives at an essential element in the case by a route that is more circuitous than the chain of reasoning required to make the evidence relevant for its prohibited substantive purpose: This circuitous route requires the fact finder to make an inference that what the witness says is not reliable.

The Inconsistent Statement Case. Because of the hearsay rule the witness's inconsistent statement is not admissible as a direct assertion that can be relied on to prove that the light was green. The statement is admissible, however, because its inconsistency suggests fabrication or lack of care in making the statement that the light was red. Thus the witness may have been unreliable in claiming that light was red. And, if it was not red, it must have been some other color — green, or perhaps yellow.

The Perjury Case. Because of FRE 404(b) the witness-defendant's prior perjury conviction is not admissible as evidence of the defendant's character for untruthfulness to prove directly that the defendant lied at the time of the alleged perjury. The conviction is admissible, however, to suggest that the defendant is an untruthful person who may be lying on the witness stand. Thus the defendant may have been unreliable in denying the alleged perjury. This leaves as the alternative the proposition that the defendant committed the perjury as charged.

What basis is there in human experience to warrant permitting the jury to take the circuitous route but not the direct route to the ultimate relevance of the evidence? Even if there is a theoretically reasonable answer to the preceding question, do you believe that trial judges are capable of instructing juries in the nuances of the inferential process or, if they are, that juries are capable of comprehending and acting on those nuances?

If the distinction between the impeachment use and the substantive use of the prior inconsistent statement or the prior perjury is not one that judges and juries are likely to be able to appreciate and understand, there is a fundamental problem with our current approach to "impeachment" evidence. Moreover, it is a problem that, at least in practice, is not adequately addressed by the balancing process of FRE 403: In the overwhelming number of cases in which there is more than very marginal impeachment value to evidence that is inadmissible substantively, it will be admitted with limiting instructions. For example, in the perjury hypothetical, the defendant is entitled to an instruction that the prior perjury conviction is admissible only to impeach the credibility of the defendant as a witness and that it is not proper to infer that because the defendant committed perjury once before it is more likely that the defendant committed perjury on the occasion in question. If we are serious about the "substantive" prohibitions, we should not be so ready to admit for impeachment purposes evidence that in theory is inadmissible for substantive purposes; or if we want to admit evidence for impeachment purposes that theoretically is not admissible substantively, we need to rethink the desirability of the substantive prohibitions.

Our own view is that it is nonsensical to expect juries to make the extremely subtle distinctions between the impeachment and substantive uses of evidence. Moreover, we seriously doubt that many judges are sensitive to the distinction. Rather, we believe, they are likely, without thinking clearly about what they are saying, glibly to instruct juries that a particular piece of evidence may be considered only for its impeachment value.

One possibility for bringing some rationality to this process would be to retain the current distinctions between impeachment and substantive uses of evidence only for the purpose of deciding whether or at what point evidence will be admissible. In other words, specific acts would still be inadmissible as part of a prosecutor's case-in-chief to prove character to show action in conformity with character, and unsworn prior statements would initially be inadmissible for their truth. However, if this type of evidence gains enough added relevance from its impeachment value that it should be admissible for that purpose, it should be admissible for whatever probative value it has for any matter of consequence in the litigation.

The primary benefit of this proposal is that it would eliminate often confusing and difficult-to-follow limiting instructions. Unless further modified, however, the proposal would have another impact that some may consider undesirable. If there were no distinction between the substantive and impeachment uses of the evidence, lawyers in their closing arguments would be able to argue to the jury that they should consider the evidence for its substantive as well as impeachment uses. Thus, for example, in our perjury hypothetical the prosecutor would be free to argue that the prior perjury conviction shows that the defendant is the kind of person who commits perjury and the defendant, therefore, probably committed perjury on the occasion in question.

If permitting such argument in the prior conviction context or in other contexts is undesirable, what is the appropriate solution? Should we retain limiting instructions and the concept of limited admissibility in some select contexts? Should we abolish limiting instructions and retain the concept of limited admissibility both for the purpose of regulating the time of admissibility and for the purpose of regulating what counsel can argue? Or should we retain the status quo? Reconsider Chapter Five, Section D, at pages 254-257, supra.

CHAPTER EIGHT

THE HEARSAY RULE

The general rule excluding hearsay is one of the hallmarks of the Anglo-American law of evidence. It establishes as a general proposition that when statements are made by people outside of court, those statements are not admissible when offered to prove the truth of the matters asserted therein. But recall the excerpt from Thayer's Treatise quoted in Chapter Three: "[T]he law has come into the shape of a set of primary rules of exclusion; and then a set of exceptions to these rules. . . ." James Bradley Thayer, A Preliminary Treatise on Evidence at Common Law 26 (1898). The hearsay rule illustrates this principle. FRE 802 is the primary rule of exclusion. It is, however, subject to 29 exceptions and 8 exemptions pursuant to which many kinds of hearsay statements are admitted.

We will examine the exemptions in Section C and the exceptions in Sections D, E, and F of this chapter. Initially, however, it is important to understand what hearsay is, how it is defined, and what justifies its exclusion from the fact-finding process of trial. Remember that the classification of evidence as hearsay or not hearsay is not necessarily determinative of admissibility. Evidence of an out-of-court statement that is not hearsay may be inadmissible for some other reason (e.g., privilege), and evidence that is hearsay may be admissible under one of the exemptions or exceptions. Your desire ultimately to admit or exclude a particular out-of-court statement should not influence your initial analysis of whether that statement falls within the definition of the exclusionary rule.

A. THE GENERAL RULE OF EXCLUSION AND THE DEFINITION OF HEARSAY

Exclusion of hearsay requires a test that judges apply to individual items of evidence. Under FRE 801(c), hearsay is a statement offered "to prove the truth of the matter asserted." This brief definition of hearsay is deceptively simple. Its application will require an understanding of the reasons for the hearsay prohibition — reasons that are captured only imperfectly in any brief doctrinal definition.

1.   FRE 801 and 802

RULE 801. DEFINITIONS

The following definitions apply under this article:

(a) Statement. A "statement" is (1) an oral or written assertion or (2) nonverbal conduct of a person, if it is intended by the person as an assertion.

(b) Declarant. A "declarant" is a person who makes a statement.

(c) Hearsay. "Hearsay" is a statement, other than one made by the declarant while testifying at the trial or hearing, offered in evidence to prove the truth of the matter asserted.

(d) Statements which are not hearsay. A statement is not hearsay if — (1) Prior statement by witness. The declarant testifies at the trial or hearing and is subject to cross-examination concerning the statement, and the statement is (A) inconsistent with the declarant's testimony, and was given under oath subject to the penalty of perjury at a trial, hearing, or other proceeding, or in a deposition, or (B) consistent with the declarant's testimony and is offered to rebut an express or implied charge against the declarant of recent fabrication or improper influence or motive, or (C) one of identification of a person made after perceiving the person; or (2) Admission by party-opponent. The statement is offered against a party and is (A) the party's own statement in either an individual or a representative capacity or (B) a statement of which the party has manifested an adoption or belief in its truth, or (C) a statement by a person authorized by the party to make a statement concerning the subject, or (D) a statement by the party's agent or servant concerning a matter within the scope of the agency or employment, made during the existence of the relationship, or (E) a statement by a coconspirator of a party during the course and in furtherance of the conspiracy. The contents of the statement shall be considered but are not alone sufficient to establish the declarant's authority under subdivision (C), the agency or employment relationship and scope thereof under subdivision (D), or the existence of the conspiracy and the participation therein of the declarant and the party against whom the statement is offered under subdivision (E).

RULE 802. HEARSAY RULE

Hearsay is not admissible except as provided by these rules or by other rules prescribed by the Supreme Court pursuant to statutory authority or by Act of Congress.

(Our initial discussion focuses on FRE 801(a)-(c) and 802. We discuss FRE 801(d) in Section C.)

2.   Interpretation and Illustration of FRE 801 and 802

To appreciate the significance of the general rule of exclusion, consider that a friend of yours, Sally, tells you that she saw a gray SUV run through a red light and hit a pedestrian. Would you believe Sally? Would you rely on her information? If you know that Sally is a trustworthy person, and that she usually is a careful observer of things and has a good memory, you would probably have little reason to doubt what she says. You would view Sally as a reliable source of information about the accident. We learn many useful things about people, events and conditions from what others tell us.

Sally's knowledge about the accident would be particularly useful in a lawsuit brought by the pedestrian against the driver of the SUV. There are at least two ways in which the pedestrian could present Sally's knowledge to the jury. First, Sally herself could be called as a witness. In response to a question about what she saw, she would testify, "On June 1, I observed the gray SUV run a red light and hit a pedestrian."

Second, perhaps Sally made this same statement to her friend George on the day after the accident. George could then be called as a witness and would testify in response to a question about what Sally saw: "On June 2, Sally told me that on June 1 she had seen a gray SUV run a red light and hit a pedestrian." Sally's own testimony would be welcome in any courtroom in America. But George's testimony would be excluded by the hearsay rule. Why? Apply the terms of FRE 801(a)-(c): George's testimony describes (1) a *statement* (an "oral assertion"); (2) the statement is made by a *declarant* (Sally is a "person who made the statement"); (3) the statement was made by Sally *other than while testifying at the trial*; and (4) the statement is being offered by the pedestrian *to prove the truth of the matter asserted* (that the gray SUV ran the red light). Thus Sally's statement is *hearsay* and George's testimony about that statement would be inadmissible under FRE 802.

Notice that the term *hearsay* applies to Sally's statement because she is the out-of-court declarant; the hearsay rule operates to exclude evidence of that statement no matter how it is presented in court — through testimony such as George's, through a letter Sally wrote to George, through a tape recording of Sally speaking to George, and even through Sally's own testimony about her own out-of-court statement. And, by the way, there is no traditionally recognized hearsay exception that would admit Sally's out-of-court statement.

a. The Relevancy of Sally's Statement

Why should Sally's statement of belief about the gray SUV be admitted if Sally says it in court as a witness, but be excluded if George reports her statement to the jury? The answer to this question, which involves an explication of hearsay policy, begins with relevancy. Under FRE 401, Sally's statement is offered to prove that it is more likely that the SUV did run the red light and hit a pedestrian. We know from our study of impeachment in Chapter Seven that inferences about Sally's qualities of narration, sincerity, perception, and memory are necessary to connect her statement to the fact of consequence. These inferences about Sally's testimonial qualities, and the generalizations that underlie them, are shown in Diagram 8-1.

You can see, following this theory of relevancy, that Sally's eyewitness statement is important evidence for the pedestrian's case against the driver of the SUV. You can also see that if any of the diagrammed inferences about Sally's testimonial qualities are wrong, Sally's statement loses its relevance to the case. To the extent that there are doubts about the inferences, the evidence of Sally's statement loses probative value. Notice that the final inference — from the accuracy of Sally's belief to the conclusion about the event itself — is an inference that does not rest on a generalization about one of Sally's testimonial qualities. Rather, it expresses the assumption underlying the model of rational factfinding, that people's beliefs about the world can and do correspond to reality.

b. Sally's Statement Bears Testimonial Dangers

It is possible that, contrary to the generalizations articulated in Diagram 8-1, Sally did not speak accurately and honestly, or did not perceive accurately or remember accurately the event involving the SUV. If this is so, then relying on her belief about this event generates risks of error. We refer to these risks as *testimonial dangers*, or *hearsay dangers* when an out-of-court statement is being considered.

Diagram 8-1

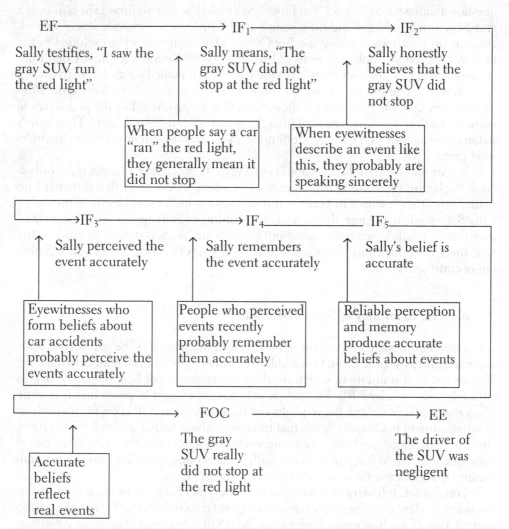

If Sally has mistakenly used the wrong words (a *narration* danger), then the SUV that she saw may be green, not gray. A narration problem may exist if speakers use words with which they are unfamiliar, or if they speak carelessly or inadvertently omit a critical word. A different problem arises if the speaker's words are subject to more than one interpretation (an *ambiguity* danger). An ambiguity problem exists if it is unclear from the context what the speaker is intending to assert. For example, if a person says, "Jon had a great catch," is the reference to fishing or baseball? Frequently, but not always, the answer will be clear from the context within which the statement is made. Thus narration problems arise when the speaker mistakenly chooses the wrong words; ambiguity problems arise when the hearer or reader misinterprets what the speaker is thinking and communicating. In either case, although the speaker such as Sally may be sincere, the inference from her words to what she means to say — IF$_1$ in the Diagram 8-1 — may be incorrect.

If Sally is trying to deceive the listener (a *sincerity* danger), her words will misrepresent what she really believes. If Sally is lying, then the inference from

Sally's words to her belief about the SUV that we (or the jury) as listeners attribute to Sally — IF$_2$ in the diagram — will not correspond to what she actually knows about the accident.

Other possibly wrong inferences about Sally's eyewitness statement involve the congruity between what Sally honestly believes she saw and what actually happened. Relevance requires that her belief be an accurate reflection of the event — that the Honda did fail to stop at the red light. This will not be the case if Sally did not observe the incident accurately (a *perception* danger). Perception as used here includes impressions received from any of the sensory organs. The identification of an odor or the hearing of another's words would present perception issues. A memory problem arises if at the time she makes the statement Sally has forgotten details about the event she perceived; for example, that the gray car was a truck not a SUV (a *memory* danger). If there are perception or memory problems with Sally's statement, then the inferences of perception (IF$_3$) or memory (IF$_4$) will be incorrect and the ultimate inference that Sally's belief accurately reflects what the SUV did (the FOC) will also be incorrect.

To summarize: If we could know with absolute certainty that Sally was lying or using the wrong words or that she misperceived or had forgotten what happened, Sally's eyewitness statement would not be relevant to prove that the gray SUV failed to stop at the red light. We do not know and cannot know these things for sure. Although we know there are always risks, we assume, on the basis of our common experience, that people generally tend to be truthful and accurate in their statements. Thus Sally's statement that the gray SUV ran the red light would be relevant to the pedestrian's lawsuit, even though we (or the jury) may ultimately decide that the SUV did *not* fail to stop.

c. The Relevancy of Hearsay

The very same inferences about Sally's testimonial qualities are necessary if Sally is presented to the jury as a hearsay declarant. This can be illustrated with the example of George testifying about Sally's out-of-court statement to the jury. The inferential chain of reasoning shown in Diagram 8-2, an abbreviated version of Diagram 8-1, would be necessary to the relevancy of George's testimony.

Diagram 8-2

EF ——————→	Four testimonial ——————→	IF$_1$ ———————
George testifies that Sally told him, "I saw a gray SUV run the red light"	inferences regarding George's narration, sincerity, perception, and memory	George's belief about what Sally said is accurate

↳ IF$_2$ ——————→	Four testimonial ——————→	IF$_3$ ———————
"Sally really did say, "I saw a gray SUV run the red light"	inferences regarding Sally's narration, sincerity, perception, and memory	Sally's belief about the gray SUV is accurate

↳ FOC ——————→	EE
A gray SUV really did not stop at the red light	The driver of the SUV was negligent

As you can see, inferences about Sally's testimonial qualities are necessary to the relevancy of George's testimony; they are the same in form and in basic content as they were in Diagram 8-1. Essentially, then, the content of the jury's inferential reasoning process about the probative value of both of Sally's statements is the same. Moreover, the same risk of error arises from the same four testimonial or hearsay dangers.

The relevance of hearsay has also been illustrated with a "testimonial triangle,"[1] which collapses the four inferences into two legs of a triangle:

Diagram 8-3

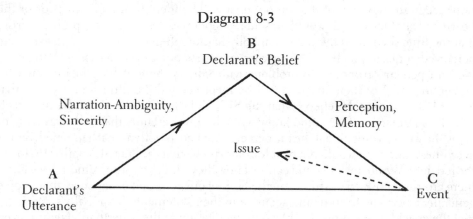

The triangle starts with the declarant's words — spoken or written outside of court — which are usually presented to the jury through testimony or an exhibit. The left leg of the triangle from A to B represents the inference from the declarant's words to the declarant's state of mind of "belief," an inference that requires reliance on the declarant's sincerity and narrative ability. The right leg from B to C represents the inference from the declarant's state of mind of belief to the existence of an event that caused that belief. This inference requires reliance on the declarant's perception and memory, and on our general assumption that accurate beliefs correspond to real events. Thus, the relevance of Sally's statement requires a complete trip around the testimonial triangle, and requires that we make the inferences about all four of Sally's testimonial qualities. Once again, this is the same structure of inferential reasoning that the jury would make if Sally were presented to testify as a witness. Why then does the hearsay rule differentiate so sharply between Sally's statement as a witness and her statement as a hearsay declarant?

d.   Hearsay Policy Differentiates Between Witnesses and Hearsay Declarants

The most common answer to this question focuses on three factors that differentiate witnesses (like Sally speaking in court) from declarants (like Sally speaking out of court). First, the witness in the courtroom is always under oath, thereby theoretically minimizing the likelihood of insincerity, whereas a declarant's out-of-court statement

1. The testimonial triangle concept was first popularized for the academic legal community by Professor Laurence Tribe in his article Triangulating Hearsay, 87 Harv. L. Rev. 957 (1974) and in Richard O. Lempert and Stephen A. Saltzburg, A Modern Approach to Evidence (1977). For a much earlier version of the triangle, see Charles Kay Ogden and Ivor Armstrong Richards, The Meaning of Meaning 10-12 (1927).

may or may not be made under oath. Moreover, the solemnity and formality of the court proceedings may cause the witness to be particularly careful about properly narrating the event.

Second, the jury is able to observe the demeanor of the in-court witness. Observing how the witness responds and reacts to questions, particularly on cross-examination, may give the jurors a somewhat better sense of the witness's sincerity, narrative ability, perception, and memory than they would get from having the content of the statement related to them by some third person. While demeanor evidence is often criticized as an ineffective indicator of outright insincerity, its use in evaluating other aspects of witness and party behavior has been noted. The opportunity for the trier of fact to assess the credibility of witnesses in person is a principal reason for the deference that appellate courts afford to factual findings at the trial level. See, e.g., Olin Guy Wellborn III, Demeanor, 76 Cornell L. Rev. 1075, 1077 (1991).

Third, and most important, the in-court witness is subject to cross-examination, which the opponent may use to elicit facts from the witness that are relevant to all four of the witness's testimonial qualities. We have seen in Chapter Seven how the topics of impeachment can all be addressed through cross-examination of a witness. The witness's answers, and the behavior of the witness in responding to questions, may clarify ambiguity, reveal mistakes in narration, reveal weaknesses in perception or memory, and provide information about the witness's character for truthfulness, the witness's bias, or the witness's motive to misrepresent the facts of the case. In addition, fear of cross-examination may motivate witnesses to be truthful and accurate in their testimony.

Some witnesses, of course, may beat the system and lie with persuasion and impunity. But to recognize that possibility is to recognize only that our adjudicatory system is not perfect. It is a truism, and many trial lawyers believe, that in the context of our adversary system, cross-examination is "beyond any doubt the greatest legal engine ever invented for the discovery of truth." 5 John Henry Wigmore, Evidence in Trials at Common Law 32 (James Chadbourn ed. 1974). The gist of the problem with hearsay is succinctly stated by the District of Columbia Circuit:

> The problem with hearsay is that it deprives the defendant of the opportunity to cross-examine the person who uttered the statement at issue. Here, the government presented allegations of prior drug dealing, and the defendant was unable to cross-examine the person who made them. At the time of the testimony, that person — the less-than-reputable convict, Thomas Rose — was sitting in a federal correctional institution. Meanwhile in court, telling Rose's story, was the clean-cut FBI agent, Neil Darnell. Thus, Evans had no opportunity to "test[] the recollection and sift[] the conscience" of his accuser... Cross-examination may be the "greatest legal engine ever invented for the discovery of truth,"... but it is not of much use if there is no one to whom it can be applied. [United States v. Evans, 216 F.3d 80, 84 (D.C. Cir. 2000).]

We must point out that while cross-examination of a hearsay declarant is usually not possible, it is not the only way to expose potential hearsay dangers. It may be possible, for example, to show with other witnesses or exhibits that a hearsay declarant has made inconsistent statements, is biased against one of the parties, or has an untruthful character. FRE 806 explicitly permits impeachment of hearsay declarants: "When a hearsay statement...has been admitted in evidence, the credibility of the declarant may be attacked...by any evidence which would be admissible for those purposes if declarant had testified as witness." Furthermore, the touted benefits of cross-examination may not always contribute to accurate factfinding. Cross-examination leads to the exposure of a witness's deliberate falsehood much less frequently in real life than in courtroom dramas. Thus cross-examination may yield only the jury's intuitive sense about a witness's general credibility. If so, it is worth considering whether this intuitive sense is likely to be accurate. Some individuals, because of their personalities or their fear of being the center of attention in a public trial, may appear to be less than forthright witnesses, when in fact they are only shy or nervous. Stereotypes can also affect the jury's perception of who is, or is not, a reliable witness.

Nevertheless, it is more difficult and burdensome for the opponent to obtain and present impeaching facts about hearsay declarants. Cross-examination of a live witness does operate as an efficient means of providing relevant information about a witness's testimonial qualities to the jury. The example in the *Evans* case also shows that a proponent could use hearsay as a strategic choice to keep a less-than-convincing declarant off the witness stand. For all these reasons, the opponent's lack of ability to cross-examine a hearsay declarant is the primary reason for excluding hearsay evidence.

Hearsay policy may be summarized as follows: A witness's oath, demeanor, and cross-examination are thought to reduce testimonial dangers and to make in-court testimony *more reliable*. Cross-examination also increases the likelihood that testimonial dangers — sincerity, narration-ambiguity, perception, or memory problems — will be exposed and evaluated by the jury. And it generates information that helps the jury decide whether to rely on a witness's statement. Therefore, because of these differences between a witness's in-court testimony and declarant's out-of-court statement, hearsay is viewed as less reliable and more difficult for the jury to evaluate. It is excluded in the interest of increasing the accuracy of jury decisionmaking. And we remind you that whenever the relevance of an out-of-court statement requires inferences about all four testimonial qualities of the declarant, or the complete trip around the triangle, then hearsay policy is implicated.

Another argument for excluding hearsay might be that the witness who is reporting the hearsay statement to the jury while on the stand (like George) may have misunderstood what the hearsay declarant (Sally) said, or might even have fabricated the existence of the declarant's statement. However, all testimony bears some risks of misperception and fabrication. We rely on cross-examination to test the sincerity and hearing ability of all witnesses, including George.

Of course, the hearsay rule could operate as a rule of preference. If a hearsay declarant like Sally is *available* to testify as a witness, it may be preferable to have her testify at the trial. Therefore, it could be preferable to require the proponent of the hearsay declarant (the pedestrian) to produce that person as a witness instead. The opposing party (the SUV driver) might understandably be reluctant to call Sally as a witness if her hearsay has already been admitted, because Sally might simply reaffirm and reinforce the substance of the hearsay. But what if the hearsay declarant is not available to testify? Sally may be ill or out of the country. If we still want to exclude her hearsay statement, we are not talking about a rule of preference but about whether the jury will hear Sally's information at all. If Sally is unavailable, how critical is it to provide the opportunity for the opponent to cross-examine her? Should we exclude relevant evidence for the sake of whatever benefit cross-examination might have brought?

It is still much too soon for you to be formulating any definitive judgments about the issues suggested in the preceding paragraph. You should, however, keep those issues in mind as you continue to study the definition of hearsay.

KEY POINTS

1. Hearsay is a person's statement (a) that is made at a time other than while the person is testifying at the hearing in which the statement is offered and (b) that is offered to prove the truth of the matter asserted in the statement.

2. A hearsay statement may be oral or it may be written.

3. Hearsay policy is to exclude hearsay because there is no oath, no observation of demeanor, and no opportunity to cross-examine the hearsay declarant to determine if there are sincerity, narration-ambiguity, perception, or memory problems (the testimonial or hearsay dangers).

4. If an out-of-court statement is offered to prove the sincere belief of the declarant in the matter asserted, and then to prove the accuracy of that belief about an event, then all four testimonial qualities of the declarant are involved in the relevancy of the statement and hearsay policy is implicated.

PROBLEMS

8.1. Return to Problem 3.2, Pedroso v. Driver, at page 129. The defendants object to the admission of Exhibit A on grounds that it is hearsay. Is it? If the defendant denies (on line 16) that she received a speeding ticket, the plaintiffs will offer the ticket into evidence. Defendants will object that it is hearsay. Is it?

8.2. Return to Problem 3.3, United States v. Ray, at page 131. June Jacobs' assistant would testify for the prosecution that on the afternoon of March 14, 2004, Jacobs told the assistant that she had just gotten some bad news and that she was going to Ray's office to tell him. Would this testimony be hearsay?

8.3 Return to Problem 3.4, State v. Blair, at page 131. The prosecutor seeks to admit the following statements made by Norma Waits. Who would testify to authenticate these statements? Are they hearsay? Do you think they should be excluded?

(a) A friend of Norma's says that a month before the attack, Norma told the friend, "Last week I told Jimmy that I was going to break up with him and leave the Bay Area soon. Jimmy was furious."

(b) In 2003, Norma's mother visited her apartment. Norma was upset and crying. Norma said to her mother that Jimmy had lost his temper and hit her earlier that day, and that when she tried to leave her apartment, he threw a vase at her. The mother saw the shattered vase on the floor.

(c) Inside the locked drawer in which police found photographs of Norma showing severe bruising and date-stamped July 25, 2004, a diary written by Norma was also found. In it she wrote that in early July 2004, Jimmy beat her after an argument.

3. Elaboration of FRE 801 and 802: Implications of the General Rule of Exclusion

a. Identifying What a Hearsay Statement Is Offered to Prove

The truth-of-the-matter-asserted test of FRE 801(c) requires the identification of the "matter" that an out-of-court statement is offered to prove. Looking at the testimonial triangle in Diagram 8-3 on page 420, supra, the event at point C — that the SUV failed to stop at the red light — is the fact of consequence that, for purposes of FRE 801(c), the declarant's utterance is offered to prove. This fact must then be connected to an essential element in a lawsuit. The line running from point C to "Issue" represents any further inferences that may be necessary to reach the essential element in the case. In this hypothetical, the only remaining inferential task after reaching point C is to decide whether failing to stop at the red light violated the requisite standard of care and therefore satisfies the essential element of negligence.

In many cases, however, after reaching point C, several additional inferences will be necessary for the utterance to be relevant to an essential element in the case. For example, George might testify that Sally said to him, "I had the green light and was just about to cross Main Street when I saw the gray SUV coming toward me down Main Street. It passed in front of me and hit a pedestrian who was also crossing Main Street with the green light." For this evidence to be relevant, the complete trip around the testimonial triangle is necessary to prove that Sally's statements — that she and the pedestrian had the green light — are true. Then, further inferences can be made: first, that if Sally and the pedestrian did have the green light, the red light must have been showing for oncoming traffic on Main Street; second, that the SUV therefore had the red light; third, that the SUV therefore failed to stop at this red light as illustrated in Diagram 8-4.

Are Sally's statements to George hearsay? Clearly they are *statements* made by a *declarant other than while testifying at the trial.* Applying FRE 801(c), are they *offered to prove the truth of the matter asserted*? You might answer "no," because it seems that her statements are offered to prove that the driver of the SUV failed to stop at the red light and Sally's statement did not assert this. But this is not a correct analysis. The truth-of-the-matter-asserted test should be applied to the last inference that depends on Sally's testimonial qualities. This is FOC_1 — that Sally did have the green light. Sally's statement *is* being offered to prove the truth of this assertion. Only if FOC_1 is true can the conclusion about the driver being negligent be drawn. The truth of FOC_1 rests on generalizations about all four of Sally's testimonial qualities; thus hearsay policy is

Diagram 8-4

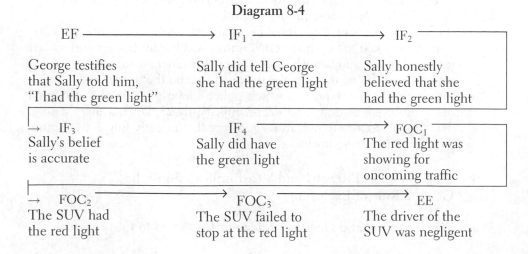

EF $\longrightarrow$ IF_1 $\longrightarrow$ IF_2

George testifies   Sally did tell George   Sally honestly
that Sally told him,   she had the green light   believed that she
"I had the green light"   had the green light

$\rightarrow$ IF_3 IF_4 $\longrightarrow$ FOC_1
Sally's belief   Sally did have   The red light was
is accurate   the green light   showing for
                                                     oncoming traffic

$\rightarrow$ FOC_2 $\longrightarrow$ FOC_3 $\longrightarrow$ EE
The SUV had   The SUV failed to   The driver of the
the red light   stop at the red light   SUV was negligent

implicated. The further inferences that connect Sally's statements to the essential element in the case *do not relate to her beliefs and do not require any further reliance on her narrative ability, sincerity, perception, or memory.* Thus they do not implicate hearsay policy. Do not be misled into applying FRE 801(c) to the final conclusions — that the light for the SUV was red, that the SUV failed to stop at the red light, or that the SUV driver was negligent. Sally's statements are hearsay. They are offered to prove the truth of the matters they assert, which is another way to articulate the test of FRE 801(c).

This same analysis must be made each time you apply the truth-of-the-matter-asserted test of FRE 801(c). If an inference that the matters contained in the declarant's assertions are true is required for relevance, then the assertions are "offered to prove" those matters, even if those matters are just a necessary step in the chain of reasoning that continues to some further conclusion.

b. Testimony by Witnesses About Their Own Out-of-Court Statements May Still Be Hearsay

FRE 801(b) defines a "declarant" as a person who makes a statement. This term generally is used to refer to people when they are making statements *outside of court*, and we have used it that way in the preceding sections. When people make statements to the jury in court, under oath, and subject to cross-examination, they are, obviously, functioning as witnesses. When witnesses testify in court about statements that they themselves made *outside of court*, those out-of-court statements may still be defined as hearsay by FRE 801(c) because they are "other than one made by the declarant while testifying at the trial or hearing." For example, in the case of the gray SUV, suppose that Sally testifies as a witness that "right after the accident, I remember telling George that the gray SUV ran the red light." Sally is testifying about her own hearsay statement. In this circumstance the hearsay declarant (Sally) is in fact in the courtroom and can be cross-examined. Some commentators have therefore argued that if witnesses report their own out of court statements, their evidence should not be regarded as hearsay. See, e.g., Edmund M. Morgan, Hearsay Dangers and the Application of the Hearsay Concept, 62 Harv. L. Rev. 177, 192-193 (1957). Others disagree, contending that cross-examination is less valuable when it is conducted long after the statement was made. And, if a witness's prior statements were not hearsay, witnesses could refer to and rely on their own prior prepared statements in their testimony. This is undesirable since the witness was not subject to cross-examination or to the scrutiny of the jury when preparing those statements. The various positions in the debate over the hearsay status of prior statements of witnesses are described in the Advisory Committee Note to FRE 801(d)(1). Under FRE 801(c), prior statements of witnesses are defined as hearsay unless specifically exempted. See FRE 801(d)(1), which we will examine in Section C infra.

c. Hearsay, Lay Opinions, and the Firsthand Knowledge Rule

You have previously encountered the lay opinion rule (FRE 701) and the firsthand knowledge rule (FRE 602) in Chapter Four. Here we address briefly the relationship between those rules and the hearsay rule.

Consider a situation in which Ellen, a bystander, is prepared to testify in the suit between the pedestrian and the driver of the gray SUV. Ellen might testify that "The gray SUV ignored the red light and hit the pedestrian in the crosswalk." There are three possible bases for Ellen's belief: First, she may have observed the entire incident; second, Sally may have told her what happened; or third, on the basis of her observation of the position of the car and the pedestrian after the accident, she could have concluded that the defendant's SUV must have run the red light. If the second variation were true, Ellen would in effect be relating a hearsay statement. She has no firsthand knowledge of the event herself. In the third variation, Ellen's testimony that the defendant ignored the red light would be a lay opinion, based on her firsthand knowledge of the position of the car and the person who was hit. If she testified about the facts she did observe, instead of just stating her conclusion, the jury might be just as capable as she is to draw the appropriate inference.

If the opponent is unsure about the basis for Ellen's testimony, the initial objection can always be "lack of firsthand knowledge." The objecting attorney should immediately ask the judge to permit inquiry, outside the presence of the jury, into the basis for Ellen's testimony. The opponent should ask "how do you know that the defendant ignored a red light?" If this inquiry reveals that Ellen is in fact relating hearsay ("Sally told me what happened"), the objecting attorney can then change the objection to hearsay. If the inquiry reveals that Ellen is expressing an opinion that is not based on her observation of the accident itself, then the objection would be lack of firsthand knowledge or a lay opinion objection. What is important, as a practical matter, is for the attorney to make some objection that will get the judge's attention and permit inquiry, preferably without the jury listening, into the basis for the witness's knowledge. Once the basis of knowledge is established, it should be relatively easy for the parties to address the question of why the evidence should or should not be admissible.

d. Multiple Hearsay

On some occasions evidence will contain multiple hearsay. Consider, for example, the pedestrian's attempt to prove that the gray SUV went through a red light by offering a properly authenticated police report that states "George reports that 'Sally told me that the gray SUV ran the red light.'" Here we have multiple hearsay. We care about the sincerity, narration, perception, and memory of the police officer who wrote the report, as well as both Sally and George, and none of them is on the witness stand subject to cross-examination when making their statements.

If the plaintiff called George as a witness to testify from memory about what Sally said, we would have single hearsay. If the plaintiff called the police officer as a witness to testify about what George said, we would still have double hearsay. Sally is a declarant because the letter continues to be offered for the truth of what Sally said. In addition, George is still a declarant as well. In multiple hearsay situations, the evidence will be inadmissible unless there is a hearsay exception or exemption for each layer of hearsay. FRE 805 provides that "[h]earsay included within hearsay is not excluded under the hearsay rule if each part of the combined statements conforms with an exception to the hearsay rule provided in these rules."

KEY POINTS

1. If a statement made outside of court is offered to prove the truth of what it asserts, it is defined as hearsay even though the declarant is the witness who is testifying about the statement.

2. A hearsay objection is appropriate after determining that a witness does not have firsthand knowledge of the events testified to, but is relying on what others have said.

3. Some hearsay statements include additional hearsay within them. In such cases of multiple hearsay, each hearsay component must be admissible through an exception or exemption.

PROBLEMS

8.4. In the pedestrian's suit against the driver of the gray SUV for personal injuries suffered when she was hit by a car while crossing Main Street, the pedestrian calls the police officer who arrived at the scene shortly after the accident.

(a)   The officer testifies that one unidentified bystander said to the officer that he saw that the red signal light controlling Main Street was working just a few minutes after the accident. Hearsay?

(b)   The police officer testifies that after interviewing all the available witnesses, including the pedestrian and the driver, she filed an accident report stating that the driver of the SUV failed to stop at the red stop light. The original report is offered into evidence. Hearsay?

(c)   The report also states that the pedestrian told the officer that, after the accident, the driver said to the pedestrian, "It's all my fault." Hearsay?

8.5 John and Mary Smith had a son, Brent, who was born on August 20, 1976. John and Mary were killed in a plane crash, and their son, if he survived them, was entitled to inherit their entire estates. In a probate proceeding in December 2000, an individual offers to testify as follows to establish his right to inherit the assets of John and Mary Smith: "My name is Brent Smith. I was born on August 20, 1976. I am 24 years old. I am the son of John and Mary Smith." Is any of this testimony objectionable as hearsay?

4.   Interpretation and Illustration of FRE 801(c): Nonhearsay Statements with No Hearsay Dangers

Not all out-of-court statements are hearsay. A critical aspect of the definition of hearsay is that, under the proponent's relevance theory, the statements are offered to prove the *truth* of the matters they assert. Many out-of-court statements are not offered for this relevance theory; they are offered for a *nonhearsay* use.

a.   Nonhearsay Uses

In our hypothetical concerning the gray SUV and the pedestrian, consider the following testimony of Sally about an event she witnessed: "In the morning, just before the accident, when I was getting gasoline at the service station, I heard Mike, a mechanic, say to the defendant who was driving a gray SUV, 'Your brakes are in bad shape. It would be dangerous for you to drive that SUV.'" Is Mike's statement hearsay? It is a statement made by a declarant who is not testifying at trial, but is it offered for the relevance theory of proving the truth of the matter Mike is asserting? The proponent of Sally's testimony, the plaintiff, might well argue as follows:

> Your honor, we are not offering this evidence to prove the truth of the matter asserted by the mechanic — that the brakes were in fact bad. Rather, we are offering the evidence to prove only that the mechanic spoke those words. This is relevant to show that the defendant had notice of the dangerous condition of his brakes before he got into his car and drove through the red light. One of the things that we must prove in order to prove one of our claims of negligence is that the defendant either knew or should have known about the dangerous condition of his brakes. This out-of-court statement is relevant to show that he did have such knowledge.

The trial judge should overrule the hearsay objection. Sally's testimony tends to prove that Mike's statement was made, and Mike's statement is relevant for what is called the "nonhearsay" use of "notice." It tends to prove that the driver heard these words and knew his brakes were bad, a fact of consequence in the case. In terms of FRE 801(c), the proponent is not offering Mike's statement to prove that the matters asserted are true. In terms of the inferential process in Diagram 8-1, the proponent is not offering Mike's statement to prove that his beliefs about the condition of the brakes are accurate in order to prove that the brakes were bad. Indeed, it is not being offered to prove anything about the declarant's belief. This can be illustrated with the following testimonial triangle:

Diagram 8-5

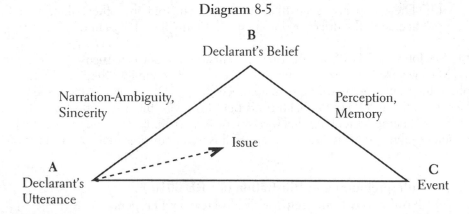

The line from the declarant's utterance at point A to the Issue represents the inference required to use Mike's statement to prove the fact of consequence — that the driver of the SUV had notice that his brakes were bad. The relevance of the evidence does *not* depend on making the inference from A to B or from B to C. Relevancy does not depend on what belief was in the mind of the declarant, or on whether that belief was accurate and corresponded to some event in the real world. Stated another way, relevance does not depend on Mike's memory, perception, sincerity, or narration. Therefore, hearsay policy is not implicated. There is no need to be concerned about the lack of oath, demeanor, and cross-examination of Mike.

   i.   Effect on the Listener.   In sum, the proponent of Mike's statement is offering it for the relevant nonhearsay use of showing its *effect on the listener*. Given the warning, the driver of the SUV had notice and therefore had the opportunity to respond. How the warning affected him — his conduct in responding to it — is relevant to whether he breached a requisite duty of care, which is an essential element of a negligence case. None of the inferences required for relevance depends on Mike's testimonial qualities, as shown in Diagram 8-6.

Diagram 8-6

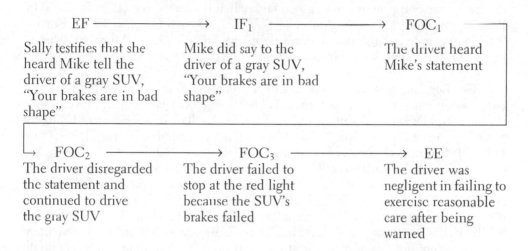

EF ⟶	IF$_1$ ⟶	FOC$_1$
Sally testifies that she heard Mike tell the driver of a gray SUV, "Your brakes are in bad shape"	Mike did say to the driver of a gray SUV, "Your brakes are in bad shape"	The driver heard Mike's statement

FOC$_2$ ⟶	FOC$_3$ ⟶	EE
The driver disregarded the statement and continued to drive the gray SUV	The driver failed to stop at the red light because the SUV's brakes failed	The driver was negligent in failing to exercise reasonable care after being warned

Of course, we do care about IF$_1$ — whether Mike spoke any words at all (is Sally lying?), whether Sally heard the words correctly, and whether, at the time she testifies, Sally remembers accurately what was said. But Sally is a witness, making her statement in court, under oath, and can be cross-examined on all these points. In his own defense, the driver of the SUV may claim that he did not hear Mike's statement, or that it was reasonable for him to disregard what the mechanic said. For example, Mike may have "winked" when he made the statement, or Mike frequently gave such warnings as a joke. But the proponent's theory of relevance — that the driver was *unreasonable* in disregarding Mike's warning — depends on Mike's *apparent* sincerity, not on Mike's *actual* sincerity. Therefore, we also care about whether Mike's words were spoken loudly enough for the driver to hear, and whether the words were spoken in apparent seriousness or in a joking manner. The proponent can deal with these concerns through the direct examination of Sally. Mike is no more likely to remember what he said, and how loudly he spoke, than Sally is. Indeed, anybody who heard the warning can testify about the loudness of the warning and the apparent sincerity with which it was given.

   Out-of-court statements offered to prove their *effect on the listener* are relevant in many different kinds of cases. Liability under the substantive law of torts and crimes often turns on the reasonableness of a listener's response to *warnings, notices, instructions, and threats*. In a civil rights action for an unwarranted shooting by police officers, brought against the officers and their supervisors, prior complaints charging abuse by one of the officers were not hearsay because they were offered to show the failure of the supervisors to respond to the prior complaints. Gutierrez-Rodriguez v. Cartagena, 882

F.2d 553, 575 (1st Cir. 1989). The effect of a statement can also be to create a specific state of mind, such as *knowledge, duress, good faith, provocation, or reasonable apprehension of bodily harm*. This state of mind may be an essential element in a civil or a criminal case. For example, whether a police officer acted with "probable cause" in making an arrest may be determined by what the officer was told the arrested person was doing. Reports of "homosexual violence" among prison inmates to prison officials are relevant to prove the officials' "deliberate indifference" — the state of mind required in a civil rights suit. Roland v. Johnson, 933 F.2d 1009 (6th Cir. 1991). And letters and reports received by an insurance company indicating that negligent maintenance caused a ship's sinking were not hearsay; they were offered to prove that the insurance company was not in bad faith when it rejected the claim for the ship. Pace v. Insurance Co. of N. Am., 838 F.2d 572, 583 n.8 (1st Cir. 1988). Finally, statements made to a listener can provide *motive* for conduct, and thus are relevant to explain the listener's subsequent behavior.

    ii.   Legally Operative Facts.   Another relevant nonhearsay use for an out-of-court statement is when the statement is itself a *legally operative fact*. For example, suppose Paul says to Sarah outside of court, "I offer to sell you my five-year old horse for $500." To prove the age of the horse, Paul's statement to Sarah is hearsay. In an action to establish that there was an offer for the sale of the horse, Sarah — or Paul or anyone else who heard the words — could testify to what Paul said. Under the substantive law of contracts, the words are themselves the event to be proved — the offer. McNaboe v. NVF Co., 2000 U.S. Dist. LEXIS 4418, *39 (D. Del. 2000) ("The words the offerors . . . uttered in making the offer are admissibile as nonhearsay as they are utterances to which the law attaches duties and liabilities."). Anyone who heard Paul's statement can testify that it was made, just as any eyewitness to an automobile accident could testify to the event that the gray SUV ran a red light. In the words of the Seventh Circuit:

> [This kind of utterance echos] the linguist's distinction between performative and illocutionary utterances. The latter narrate, describe, or otherwise convey information, and so are judged by their truth value (information is useful only if true—indeed is *information* only if it is true); the former—illustrated by a promise, offer, or demand—commit the speaker to a course of action. Performative utterances are not within the scope of the hearsay rule, because they do not make any truth claims. [United States v. Montana, 199 F.3d 947, 949 (7th Cir. 1999).]

    Such utterances do not make truth claims because none of the inferences required for relevance depend on Paul's testimonial qualities. No memory or perception danger exists because Paul is not relating some fact that he has observed. Moreover, under the objective theory of contracts, there is no sincerity or narration-ambiguity danger, for we do not have to make any inference that Paul is sincere. The proponent's theory of relevance is that Paul said the words in an *apparent* manner such that the offeree might reasonably be expected to take it seriously; this would be a valid offer. And whether the words were spoken in an *apparently* serious manner is something about which anyone who heard the words can testify and be fully cross-examined. Paul's subjective intent or understanding may be relevant to the issue of mutual mistake, which Paul may raise as a defense. But mistake only becomes an issue once there has been an offer and an acceptance. Thus to prove the offer, Paul's statement is nonhearsay. Its relevance can be illustrated on the testimonial triangle as the line from A to the Issue: From the fact that Paul spoke the words, we infer an essential element in a contract case.

Many different kinds of statements are *legally operative facts* because principles of substantive law give them *immediate legal significance*. For example, in litigation over whether a group insurance policy is excluded from ERISA coverage, the policy itself is admissible as nonhearsay, "excluded from the definition of hearsay . . . because it is a legally operative document that defines the rights and liabilities of the parties." Stuart v. Unum Life Ins. Co., 217 F.3d 1145, 1153 (9th Cir. 2000). Some statements are acts done with words that give rise to civil obligations or consequences — acknowledging debts, words of defamation or slander. And some words are criminal acts — perjury, extortionate threats, offers to sell drugs, statements forming a conspiracy. For example, in a bank fraud case, the defendant testified about what he had said to government investigators. This was not hearsay, but rather offered to show that he did not make the false statement as charged: "Where the content of discussions which actually occurred is a primary issue, a party is entitled to adduce evidence of those discussions at trial." United States v. Ballis, 28 F.3d 1399 (5th Cir. 1994). Sometimes verbal statements have immediate legal significance when they also accompany nonverbal acts. If information about the context within which such statements were made is necessary, it can be supplied by anyone who was there. Cross-examination of the declarant is not necessary to supply it.

    iii. Identifying Nonhearsay Uses.   A proponent's stock response to a hearsay objection in court is "not offered for its truth, your Honor." That response will not satisfy a thoughtful judge or a well-trained opponent. The proponent should be able to articulate the nonhearsay theory of relevance; for example, that the statement is offered to prove an effect on the listener (regardless of its truth) and that this effect on the listener is a fact of consequence in the case. The proponent should also be able to explain *why* exclusion of the statement is not appropriate; that is, why hearsay policy is *not* implicated. The critical step in this process is to show that the evidence is relevant without reliance on the declarant's testimonial qualities — that is, without a trip around the testimonial triangle.

    Some texts and study aids provide a laundry list of nonhearsay uses for out-of-court statements. Such lists typically include the two nonhearsay uses already identified — statements relevant for their effect on the listener and statements that are legally operative facts (also called "verbal acts"). The lists also include *prior inconsistent statements* offered to impeach witnesses, as discussed in Chapter Seven at pages 386-392, supra, and statements offered as *circumstantial evidence of the declarant's state of mind*, discussed on pages 504-505, infra. Christopher B. Mueller and Laird C. Kirkpatrick, Evidence §8.20-21 at 829-834 (2d ed. 1999), includes in the list of nonhearsay words that operate as identifying characteristics of an object (a license plate, a trade insignia) and words that have a performative aspect that dominates the assertive aspect (the ability to speak French, or to speak at all). These written or spoken words generate inferences that have nothing to do with their "truth" value; thus they might be called "*logically operative facts*." While these lists may help you to identify some common nonhearsay uses for out-of-court statements, the key to understanding nonhearsay is to focus on the inferences necessary to the relevance of the out-of-court statement. The list is no substitute for the analysis that underlies it.

b.   Statements Relevant for Both Nonhearsay and Hearsay Uses

Sally's testimony about what Mike the mechanic said to the driver of the gray SUV could also be relevant to prove that the brakes on the Honda were in fact bad. If offered for this purpose, the evidence is clearly hearsay because relevance now depends on the mechanic's sincerity, narration, perception, and memory. Assume that no hearsay exception applies to the mechanic's utterance.

The fact that the mechanic's statement would be excluded as hearsay for the purpose of proving that the brakes were bad creates a situation that frequently arises: A particular piece of evidence is admissible for one purpose (to prove notice) but inadmissible for another (to prove the brakes were bad). The question of admissibility is thus one of discretionary balancing for the trial judge under FRE 403. In this situation, the risk of unfair prejudice is that the jury, even after being given limiting instructions, will use the evidence for its improper hearsay purpose (here, to prove bad brakes). Is the probative value of the evidence for the admissible purpose (here, notice) substantially outweighed by the danger of unfair prejudice? We have seen in the discussion of FRE 403 in Chapter Three that probative value is affected by whether there are alternative means to prove notice. If there are not, the probative value of Mike's warning will be very high. And in many cases, other evidence to prove the truth of the content of the statement being offered to show notice — that the SUV's brakes were bad — will already have been admitted. This diminishes the risk of unfair prejudice. The Rule 403 decision is made within these contextual facts of the specific case.

KEY POINT

When an out-of-court statement is offered to prove its effect on the listener, or some legally operative fact, or some other matter where relevance does not depend on inferences about the accuracy of declarant's belief about an event, the statement is not hearsay. It is not offered for the truth of the matter it asserts.

PROBLEMS

As you examine the following problems, consider why the out-of-court statements are relevant and whether they are hearsay or nonhearsay. We have discussed three ways of articulating the hearsay test, and you should try to apply each one. Ignore the possibility that the statement may fall within a hearsay exception and focus solely on the question of whether the evidence is hearsay.

8.6. Sondra Evers is suing Jones's Deli for personal injuries sustained when she slipped and fell on a pool of spilled ketchup near the food takeout counter. Sondra claims that the ketchup had been on the floor long enough for Jones's employees to have known about it. Sondra calls Bertha Barlow, who offers to testify as follows: "About half an hour before Ms. Evers had her accident, I was walking past the takeout counter when I overheard someone exclaim loudly "There's ketchup on the floor!" Should this testimony be excluded as hearsay? What if Bertha also testifies that she saw a Jones's Deli clerk near the takeout counter when she heard the statement?

8.7. In a libel suit, plaintiff alleges that the defendant sent a signed, typewritten letter to plaintiff's employer stating that plaintiff was a liar and thief. Plaintiff offers a photocopy of the letter into evidence, properly authenticated by the person who made the photocopy from the original. Defendant objects that the letter is hearsay. What result? Defendant then calls plaintiff's former employer who will testify that plaintiff lied on the job and stole from the company. Plaintiff objects that this testimony is hearsay. What result? Finally, defendant calls Allan Brown to testify "Plaintiff has a reputation in the community for lying and stealing on the job." Is this testimony hearsay?

8.8. In a racketeering prosecution pursuant to the RICO statutes, a witness for the prosecution appears visibly nervous, speaks haltingly, and changes his testimony several times, but finally does identify one of the defendants as the person who paid him to deposit cash in phony bank accounts. At the close of the witness's testimony, the prosecutor asks whether the defendants have threatened him. The witness responds that two of the defendants called him at his home a week before the trial and made threats on his life if he testified. Hearsay?

8.9. The Federal Election Commission (FEC) has brought an enforcement action against the Christian Coalition for violating federal campaign finance laws during congressional elections in 1990, 1992, and 1994. Federal law prohibits corporations and labor unions from using their general treasury funds to make direct contributions to candidates; but they can make expenditures related to federal elections so long as these expenditures are for communications that do not expressly advocate the election or defeat of a clearly identified candidate. The Christian Coalition is a corporation and in 1992 it paid for its Executive Director to speak at a conference in Montana. In this videotaped speech, the Executive Director said that Montana's Democratic Congressman Pat Williams "is one of your top targets in the entire nation," and, "We're going to see Pat Williams sent bags-packing back to Montana in November of this year." The FEC asserts that this violates federal law. The Christian Coalition objects that the videotape of the speech is hearsay. What result?

8.10. In a prosecution of Joe Jamal for bank robbery, FBI Agent Guerrero testifies that a confidential FBI informant identified Jamal as a suspect. Defense counsel objects that the testimony is hearsay, offered to prove the truth of the matter asserted. The government claims that the testimony is offered to explain the Agent's investigatory procedures and to show why he developed a photo identification display for witnesses that included Jamal's photograph. What ruling?

8.11. K-T Corp. entered into an exclusive licensing agreement to market copyrighted computer software with the owner of the copyright. After several years, K-T filed suit against the owner alleging that the owner breached the licensing agreement by marketing very similar software through another company. During the testimony of the owner, K-T seeks to introduce a copy of the licensing agreement. The owner objects that this is hearsay. What result?

8.12. Return to Problem 3.2, Pedroso v. Driver, at page 129. Max testifies for defendants that he always rode the same school bus with Paul Pedroso and Paul's friend Tom, and that Paul and Tom used to play tag after getting off the bus together. Max testifies that on the day of the accident, he heard Tom say "Paul, you're *it*" as the two boys left the bus. Plaintiffs object to this testimony as hearsay. What result?

8.13. Return to Problem 3.3, United States v. Ray, at page 131. To prove that Ray was responsible for the sale of his 100,000 shares of Rundown stock, the prosecution offers the letter signed by Ray to his broker directing the broker to make the sale. Hearsay? To prove that Ray gave this order on March 16, 2004, the prosecution points to the handwritten date of "March 16, 2004" on the letter. Hearsay?

8.14. Brian Andronico is charged with conspiracy to distribute counterfeit currency. An undercover agent, Pamela Mertz, purchased counterfeit money from various conspiracy members six times in 2001. Mertz testified that she made purchases from a man driving a car with the license plate "ICE 2000." The prosecution can prove that the license plate "ICE 2000" is registered to Andronico. Should Mertz's testimony be admitted?

8.15. To prove consciousness as a basis for pain and suffering after an accident, plaintiff offers a witness to testify as follows: "Within 30 seconds of the accident I was at the plaintiff's side. She was lying on the ground, and I shouted to a passerby, 'Get help; she's unconscious.' At that moment the plaintiff said, 'I'm not unconscious.'" Is the evidence hearsay?

5.   Interpretation and Illustration of FRE 801(a)(2): Nonverbal Conduct

a.   The Relevancy of Nonverbal Conduct

Thus far all of our examples of hearsay have involved oral or written utterances, but in some instances hearsay is completely nonverbal. Consider, for example, the following testimony offered by a police officer in a battery prosecution: "When I arrived at the bar that was the scene of the fight, I asked who threw the first punch. One of the women who was present pointed at Jim Harris, the defendant, who was wearing a red shirt." This testimony is relevant because, as shown by her nonverbal conduct, the woman appears to believe that Harris threw the first punch. Consider Diagram 8-7:

Diagram 8-7

EF $\longrightarrow$	IF$_1$ $\longrightarrow$	IF$_2$
Police officer testifies, "I asked, 'Who threw the first punch' and I saw the woman point at the defendant"	The woman did point at the defendant	The woman's pointing means that she thinks that the defendant threw the first punch

$\longrightarrow$ IF$_3$ $\longrightarrow$	IF$_4$ $\longrightarrow$	IF$_5$
The woman honestly believes that the defendant threw the first punch	The woman perceived the event accurately	The woman remembered the event accurately

$\longrightarrow$ IF$_6$ $\longrightarrow$	FOC $\longrightarrow$	EE
The woman's belief was accurate	The defendant did throw the first punch	The defendent committed a battery

This theory of relevance depends on inferences about the testimonial qualities of the police officer, who is a witness, and of the woman. The inference from the woman's conduct (IF$_1$) to her belief (IF$_3$) (from A to B on the testimonial triangle) and the inference from her belief to the occurrence of the event at issue (FOC) (from B to C on the testimonial triangle) show that all of the hearsay dangers are present. The woman may have been falsely representing her belief to get Jim Harris in trouble (a sincerity risk); the arm movement may have been an involuntary tic that was not intended to express the intent that it appears to express (an ambiguity risk); the woman may not have seen clearly who threw the first punch (a perception risk); and she may have forgotten who threw the first punch by the time the officer asked (a memory risk). Indeed, in terms of the inferential process involved in using this evidence to prove that Harris threw the first punch, there is no pertinent difference between the intentional pointing and a verbal response that identifies Harris (e.g., "It was Jim Harris" or "It was the man in the red shirt").

b. Application of FRE 801(a)(2)

FRE 801(a) defines a "statement" as "(1) an oral or written assertion or (2) *nonverbal conduct of a person, if it is intended by the person as an assertion.*" (Emphasis added.) Applying this definition to our hypothetical raises a preliminary question of fact: Did the woman intend her nonverbal conduct (pointing) to be an assertion that Jim threw the first punch? What facts would you contend are relevant to the question of her intent? If the woman did so intend, her act of pointing, commonly called *assertive conduct*, will be found to be a "statement" and will be excluded as hearsay. If she did not so intend, her act is commonly called *nonassertive conduct*, and it may be admitted because it is not a "statement" and therefore not hearsay.

i. Assertive Conduct. Sometimes conduct is intentionally used by the actor as a substitute for words. That is, the actor wants to communicate a belief and uses conduct to do so. By raising your hand in class, for example, you communicate "I want to speak." Or by shaking your head from side to side when asked a question, you communicate that your answer is "no." Both of these actions would usually be intended by the actor to be assertions of what the actor is thinking. If they are so intended, then in the words of the Advisory Committee Note, such conduct "is clearly the equivalent of words, assertive in nature, and [is] to be regarded as a statement." The act of pointing, mentioned in the Note, would typically be found to be intended as the equivalent of words, and thus would be hearsay.

ii. Nonassertive Conduct. Sometimes conduct is not intended by the actor as an assertion. In our hypothetical about the fight in the bar, what if the woman did not point at Jim Harris but instead carefully maneuvered Jim to the back door of the bar and gave him a push out the door. If the police officer saw her do this and arrested Jim Harris, would the officer's testimony as to what the woman did be relevant in the battery prosecution? Would it be hearsay? It can be inferred from her conduct that the woman believed Jim started the fight, that her belief was accurate, and that Jim did in fact start the fight. Thus her conduct is relevant. But unlike the act of pointing, the act of carefully pushing Jim out of the back door may not be intended by the woman to assert her belief in Jim's guilt. She may be trying to protect Jim, and the last thing she wants is for the police officer to arrest him. If she does not intend to communicate her belief, then her conduct is nonassertive and, under the definition of FRE 801(a)(2), would not be a "statement" and therefore would not be hearsay.

However, you can see that the relevance of the woman's conduct, even if it is nonassertive, depends on inferences about all of her testimonial qualities. If any of these inferences is false, the woman's conduct is not relevant to prove Jim started the fight. For example, the woman may actually think Jim did not start the fight but wants the police to think he did (a sincerity risk); or she may want him to leave the bar for other reasons, such as that he has illegal drugs in his possession (an ambiguity risk). There are also potential perception and memory dangers: the woman may have confused Jim with another man wearing a red shirt who actually threw the first punch, or she may have forgotten what she actually saw. These are the same risks we have previously identified with regard to the woman pointing at Jim; and if the woman shouted "Jim Harris" in response to the officer's question, the same risks would be present.

iii.   **FRE 801(a)(2)'s Intent Test.**   FRE 801(a)(2) creates a doctrinal test for determining whether any particular item of nonverbal conduct evidence is or is not hearsay. Nonverbal conduct intended as an assertion, is hearsay; nonverbal conduct not intended as an assertion is not hearsay. This test thus involves a preliminary question of fact: Was the actor's nonverbal conduct intended as an assertion? This preliminary question will be decided on the basis of the *nature of the conduct* and the *circumstances surrounding it* as presented by both parties. There will be some close cases, and there may be situations in which conduct that is normally nonassertive is in fact intended to be assertive. For example, if the woman pushing Jim Harris out the back door made a lot of noise and called attention to her conduct, these contextual facts could generate the inference that she was intending to communicate her belief in Jim's guilt to the police officer.

FRE 104 governs the preliminary factfinding that is necessary to the judge's application of FRE 801(a)(2)'s intent test. Should the question of "intent" be governed by FRE 104(a) or (b)? As you know from Chapter Four, preliminary questions of fact are for the judge under FRE 104(a), unless they are necessary to the relevance of the offered evidence. In the hypotheticals that we have just discussed, the woman's intent to use her conduct to assert Jim's guilt is not necessary to the relevance of that conduct. The relevance of her conduct does depend on *her belief* about who started the fight; but that she *intends to assert that belief* is not necessary to relevance. Under FRE 104(a), the judge must be persuaded by a preponderance of the evidence on the question of intent. The Advisory Committee Note to FRE 801 states that "the rule is so worded as to place the burden upon the party claiming that the intention existed; ambiguous and doubtful cases will be resolved against him and in favor of admissibility." To what language in FRE 801 do you think the Advisory Committee is referring?

6.   Elaboration of FRE 801(a)(2): Justification for the Distinction Between Assertive and Nonassertive Conduct

Since the relevance of both the woman pointing and the woman pushing Jim out the back door depends on the accuracy of her belief and requires a complete trip around the testimonial triangle, both kinds of conduct implicate hearsay policy. Yet only the assertive conduct of the woman pointing is defined as hearsay; the nonassertive conduct of pushing Jim is not hearsay under FRE 801(a)(2)'s definition. Why?

a.   *Absence of Hearsay Danger*

The Advisory Committee's Note to FRE 801(a) suggests that nonassertive conduct should not be defined as hearsay because of the probable absence of any sincerity danger. If an actor has a belief about a disputed fact — that Jim Harris threw the first punch — but is not intending to assert or to communicate that belief, then the actor cannot be "lying" about it. It is the view of the Advisory Committee that a person can be insincere — can tell a lie — only if the person is intending to communicate a particular fact that would be the subject of the lie. Without the intent to assert that fact, there is no opportunity to fabricate it. Is this a common sense generalization? Do you agree with it? Is the absence of sincerity risk a sufficient reason to admit the woman's pushing Jim as not hearsay?

Surprisingly and unaccountably, the Advisory Committee Note to FRE 801(a) asserts that the testimonial qualities other than sincerity also do not present a high risk: "Admittedly [nonassertive conduct] is untested with respect to the perception, memory, and narration (or their equivalents) of the actor, but the *Advisory Committee is of the view that these dangers are minimal in the absence of an intent to assert...*" (emphasis added). On what empirical data does the Advisory Committee base this conclusion? There seems to be nothing inherent in nonassertive conduct that tends to reduce or eliminate the other hearsay dangers. Can you think of anything about the woman's conduct in pushing Jim out the back door that reduces the danger of ambiguity (she was worried about illegal drugs) or perception (she confused Jim with another man in a red shirt)? The Note indicates that the actor's motivation to be accurate and the need to rely on the actor's own conduct can reduce the degree of perception and memory dangers. But these factors are not built into FRE 801(a), and the woman's conduct in pushing Jim could be admitted as not hearsay without any reduction in the perception or memory danger involved.

Thus you should ask yourself whether the probable absence of just one hearsay danger (sincerity) is sufficient justification for removing nonassertive conduct from the definition of hearsay altogether. When we study the hearsay exceptions, we will see that the probable absence of one or more of the hearsay dangers is a principal justification for many of them.

b. Necessity

In general, excluding relevant evidence because of some hearsay dangers may be too great a price to pay when it is very burdensome or perhaps even impossible to obtain other, "better" evidence on the same point. Thus "necessity" is a reason for many of the exceptions to the hearsay rule. The concern about nonassertive conduct is that it is so pervasive and so often relied on as a matter of course in our everyday lives that we would be giving up too much relevant evidence by classifying such conduct as hearsay. For example, if we look out the window and see people wearing heavy overcoats, we assume it is cold outside; if a northbound vehicle proceeds through an intersection with a traffic light, we assume the driver thinks that the light is green for that vehicle; if we see people on the street begin to put up their umbrellas, we assume they believe it has begun to rain; if a shopkeeper repairs a loose board in the threshold to a shop after someone has tripped on it, we assume the shopkeeper thinks the loose board was dangerous. In these situations, the individual actors have beliefs about events or conditions that motivate their conduct; but they are probably not *intending to assert* the belief that it is cold, that the light is green, that it is raining, or that the loose board is dangerous.[2] Their conduct would not be defined as hearsay under FRE 801(a).

2. In Chapter Six, page 341, supra, we noted that subsequent remedial measures might be relevant to prove the belief of the actor that the situation remedied was dangerous. Now you can see why such

Another variation of the necessity argument for treating nonassertive conduct as not hearsay is that attorneys are not immediately sensitive to the hearsay characteristics of such evidence. If a rule treating nonassertive conduct as hearsay would be only sporadically applied, the rule arguably ought not to exist at all.

c. Should Nonassertive Conduct Be Excluded from the Definition of Hearsay?

Whether the foregoing reasons are sufficient to exclude nonassertive conduct from the hearsay prohibition has long been the subject of academic debate.[3]

i. The Difficulty of Accurate Classification.   One concern relates to the task of classifying conduct as assertive or nonassertive. The judicial task of determining under FRE 801(a) whether conduct is intended as an assertion is not easy, and inevitably entails the risk that the wrong decision will be made, either because the actor has cleverly disguised an assertion (e.g., the woman is trying to communicate that Jim is guilty by pushing him out the door when she knows he is not), because insufficient evidence of intent is available, or because the court misapplies the concept of intent to assert. Even if judges reach the correct result most of the time, considerable time and effort is spent arguing and deciding the question of intent.

ii. The Danger of Ambiguity.   A second, and perhaps more substantial, concern is that significant hearsay dangers are still attached to such conduct. The nonassertiveness of conduct, if a correct decision is made on the intent issue, eliminates the danger of insincerity. The lack of intent to assert, however, inevitably increases the ambiguity danger. Conduct that the actor does not intend to use as an assertion of belief may be difficult to interpret, and the fact finder may attribute a belief to the actor that the actor does not in fact hold. We have seen that the woman may have other reasons for pushing Jim out the back door. Similarly, a driver going through the intersection is unlikely to be intending to assert that the light is green but it may also be wrong to infer that the driver believes that the light is green. The driver may know that the light is red but because of some emergency the driver feels compelled to ignore the red light. A substantial ambiguity problem means the conduct has low probative value to prove the specific belief for which it is offered. At some point the conduct may be so ambiguous, and the probative value so low, that a court could rely on FRE 403 to exclude the evidence.

Moreover, if the driver of the northbound car is colorblind, the driver may have incorrectly perceived the color of the stop light. As noted previously, there is nothing about all nonassertive conduct that tends to minimize perception or memory problems.

---

conduct is unlikely to be classified as hearsay — it is unlikely that such actors are intending by their conduct to assert "dangerousness." But do not forget that the relevance of remedial measures to prove liability or fault still requires a complete trip around the testimonial triangle.

3.   See, e.g., Judson F. Falknor, The "Hear-Say" Rule as a "See-Do" Rule: Evidence of Conduct, 33 Rocky Mt. L. Rev. 133 (1964); Judson F. Falknor, Silence as Hearsay, 89 U. Pa. L. Rev. 192 (1940); Ted Finman, Implied Assertions as Hearsay: Some Criticisms of the Uniform Rules of Evidence, 14 Stan. L. Rev. 682 (1962); John M. Maguire, The Hearsay System: Around and Though the Thicket, 14 Vand. L. Rev. 741 (1961); Edmund M. Morgan, Hearsay and Non Hearsay, 48 Harv. L. Rev. 1138 (1935); Eustace Seligman, An Exception to the Hearsay Rule, 26 Harv. L. Rev. 146 (1912).

iii. Is Cross-examination Important for Evaluating Nonassertive Conduct?

Remember that the principal impact of the rule excluding hearsay is to require the presentation of witnesses, subject to oath, demeanor, and cross-examination. If testimony about the woman pointing is hearsay, the proponent *must produce that woman as a witness* (unless her conduct falls within a hearsay exception or exemption). If testimony about her pushing Jim out the back door is not hearsay, she *need not be called as a witness*. How important would cross-examination be in either case? Cross-examination might uncover some risk of insincerity. And, specific information about the woman's belief would obviously reduce the ambiguity risk. Furthermore, it is generally thought that cross-examination is most effective in exposing perception and memory problems, neither of which is minimized by the fact that out-of-court conduct is nonassertive.

Therefore, the usefulness of cross-examination of the actor may argue for defining nonassertive conduct as hearsay, which would require the proponent to bring the actor to court to testify. On the other hand, numerous hearsay exceptions permit admission of statements (without cross-examination of the declarant) that may also contain serious perception or memory problems. The ambiguity danger can be pointed out by the attorney for the opponent in closing argument to suggest that the nonassertive conduct is not probative. This is not as good as knowing for sure what belief motivated the conduct, but at least the attorney's argument can provide other plausible explanations for conduct with which the jury can grapple.

There is a middle ground between defining all nonassertive conduct as hearsay, thus excluding it wholesale, and FRE 801(a)(2)'s position of allowing it to be admitted wholesale. It would be possible to define hearsay as including both assertive and nonassertive conduct, to create a hearsay exception for nonassertive conduct, and to condition the applicability of that exception on the unavailability of the actor. Or the exception could be conditioned on a case-by-case showing of the kind of motivation or reliance by the actor that minimizes perception and memory dangers. Do you think such alternatives would be preferable to the Federal Rules' approach?

d. Disguised Assertions

Sometimes evidence that appears to be nonassertive conduct is in fact relevant only because of underlying assertive behavior of particular persons. The easiest example is when a judgment of conviction for a crime is used to prove that the defendant did do the illegal act. The conviction is relevant because it is evidence that 12 jurors voted or one judge decided that the defendant did do the act. Such conduct clearly is *intended to assert that belief*. Because the jury's vote may not appear on the face of the judgment of conviction itself, it is what we call a *disguised* assertion. Convictions are uniformly classified as hearsay. Once again, locating the hidden declarant (the jury) who is making a disguised assertion (the verdict of guilt) depends on your identification of the inference of belief that is necessary for the relevance of the offered item of evidence.

Now consider evidence that Greta was arrested (not convicted) for robbery. Is the arrest hearsay, if used to prove that Greta actually committed the illegal act? The answer depends on whether the arrest is assertive or nonassertive conduct of the hidden declarants, the officers who arrested Greta. There are several ways to analyze this problem. The officers may have been making the arrest because they observed

Greta in the act and thus believed that she did commit the robbery. If so, we think it is appropriate to regard their conduct as their intended assertion of that belief. Alternatively, the officers may have been executing a warrant or acting in response to a victim's accusation. They have no firsthand knowledge of Greta's behavior and may not be intending to assert their own belief about her criminal activity. But even if this is the case, the officers are making the arrest only because another hidden declarant — probably the individual who signed the complaint or the officer who signed the affidavit accompanying a warrant application — did make a specific assertion of belief that Greta robbed the bank. The apparently nonassertive arrest is occurring only because of, and is relevant only because of, this disguised assertion of belief in Greta's guilt — the factual proposition that the evidence is being offered to prove. The evidence, therefore, should be regarded as hearsay.

Consider also testimony that John's driver's license was revoked, which is offered to prove that John engaged in unsafe driving. It may well be that the hidden declarant, the person who generated the paperwork that officially revoked John's license, was acting in a bureaucratic manner and was not intending to assert anything about how John drove. Nonetheless, the revocation is occurring only because somebody — presumably the judge who found John guilty of a traffic offense — asserted that John had engaged in some illegal driving activity.

Our characterization of the arrest and revocation evidence as assertive is either a minority position or a refinement that most discussions of nonassertive activity do not bother to make. McCormick classifies the revocation evidence as nonassertive. See Charles T. McCormick, The Borderland of Hearsay, 39 Yale L.J. 489, 491 (1930). He also classifies as nonassertive conduct the payment by underwriters of the amount of an insurance policy offered to prove that a ship was lost. Id. at 490, 496 n.17. See also Ted Finman, Implied Assertions as Hearsay: Some Criticisms of the Uniform Rules of Evidence, 14 Stan. L. Rev. 682, 683 n.4 (1962) (citing conduct that leads to the institutionalization of a patient as nonassertive). Morgan, on the other hand, characterizes the institutionalization evidence and the revocation evidence as assertive. Edmund M. Morgan, Hearsay Dangers and the Application of the Hearsay Concept, 62 Harv. L. Rev. 177, 190 (1948). What do you think?

KEY POINTS

1. Evidence of nonverbal conduct is sometimes offered to prove the accuracy of the beliefs of the actor about events. If the actor is intending to communicate that belief through conduct, then the evidence is defined as hearsay. The actor's testimonial qualities of sincerity, perception, and memory are involved in the relevancy of the conduct.

2. If the actor is not intending to communicate belief, then the evidence is defined as not hearsay and is admitted to prove the truth of that belief, even though the actor's testimonial qualities of perception and memory are still involved.

3. The question of the actor's intent is a preliminary question of fact for the judge to decide pursuant to FRE 104(a). The burden to persuade the judge on the question of intent is on the opponent who is objecting to the admission of the actor's conduct as hearsay.

PROBLEMS

8.16. Ed Stephens is being prosecuted for bank robbery. Eyewitnesses claim that the robber wore a loud Hawaiian shirt. The prosecution offers the following testimony of Officer Emily James:

> The day after the robbery, I was following leads on various possible suspects. I went to the Stephens's home, and found only Mrs. Stephens there. I asked her if she would give me the shirt that her husband wore the previous day. She handed me a Hawaiian shirt, which is marked as Exhibit A. I also watched her as she entered the bedroom and I saw her conceal a leather bag under the bed. After she gave me the shirt, I conducted a search for the leather bag and found that it was full of money, which is marked as Exhibit B.

Defense counsel has objected to this entire testimony, and to Exhibits A and B on grounds of hearsay. What result?

8.17. Ralph Benson and Jerry Jackson owned a small yacht that they kept docked on Leech Lake, Minnesota. On the morning of June 15, Ralph, his wife, and two children set off across the lake in the yacht. A storm suddenly arose on the lake, and nobody has seen the Benson family or the yacht since that morning. Jackson sued the company that insured the yacht against damage or loss due to bad weather. The insurance company relies on a clause in the policy that permits recovery only if the yacht was navigable at the time of the loss. To prove that the yacht was navigable, Jerry Jackson offers to testify, "On the morning of June 15, I observed Ralph Benson carefully look around the yacht, place his wife and children on board, and set off across the lake." Counsel for the insurance company objects to this testimony on the ground that it is hearsay.

8.18. Return to Problem 8.6. at page 430, Sondra Evers's case against Jones's Deli.

(a) On cross-examination of Karen Larson, the manager of the delicatessen, Evers's attorney establishes that Jones's Deli operates a 24-hour surveillance camera that was positioned so that it would have shown the floor area by the food takeout counter. Evers's attorney then asks: "Isn't it true that you destroyed the surveillance tapes for the day in question?" Larson would answer "Yes," but the defense attorney objects on grounds of hearsay. What result? If the videotapes were available, would they be hearsay?

(b) Plaintiff Evers offers a videotape prepared at the request of her attorney showing her activities at her home, as relevant to prove the serious effect of the fall on her physical condition.

(c) For the defendant, Karen Larson would testify: "I am the manager of Jones's Deli and I was at the store from 8:00 A.M. until 5:30 P.M. on the day Ms. Evers fell. On that day I received no complaints about any spilled ketchup on the floor." Is this testimony relevant? What additional facts might the proponent need to present? Should the testimony be excluded on grounds of hearsay?

8.19. Ben Jacobsen, a 50-year-old former railroad firefighter, is charged with homicide for fatally shooting a man who had been sleeping in a box car in an infrequently used area of the switching yard. The crime occurred at approximately

11:00 A.M. on Tuesday, July 23. Jacobsen claims that he is not guilty and suggests that two teenage boys committed the crime. He calls to the stand Harry Winters, a railroad employee, who offers to testify as follows: "Shortly after 11:00 A.M. on Tuesday, July 23, I observed two teenage boys near the box car. They were running away from it." Is this evidence hearsay?

8.20. Plaintiff is suing a police officer for false arrest. The officer arrested Plaintiff for driving while under the influence of intoxicating liquor. At trial, Plaintiff submits properly authenticated proof that she had been acquitted by a jury of the charge in question. Hearsay?

8.21. Return to Problem 8.10 at page 431, supra. What if Agent Guerrero had not testified as to the specific contents of the confidential informant's statement but did testify that "in the course of my investigation leading to defendant Jamal's arrest, I had contact with a confidential informant." Hearsay?

8.22. To prove that Darcey had been using drugs, testimony of one of Darcey's friends is offered: "Last December 31, I visited Darcey at the State Drug Rehabilitation Center, where he is a patient." Hearsay?

8.23. In the prosecution of Donna Draper for conspiracy to import heroin, an illegal substance, the prosecution offered the testimony of Sergeant Edward Conley concerning a nine-year-old German shepherd named Bosco. Sergeant Conley testified that Bosco was trained to detect narcotics by smell. Sergeant Conley further testified that he took Bosco to a bank in Cranston, Rhode Island, on March 23, 1999. Bosco "searched" several areas of the bank, such as the vault and teller stations, and did not react. Conley then took Bosco to a room in which a bag containing $9,000 was located, and, when he instructed Bosco to search for drugs, the dog "showed a strong, positive aggressive alert, shaking the bag, ripping it apart, grabbing the money in his mouth, and ripping the money." Other evidence establishes that the currency to which Bosco reacted had been brought to the bank by Draper in order to purchase cashier's checks. Should this evidence be excluded on the ground that it is hearsay? On any other ground?

8.24. Return to Problem 4.23 at page 209. Is Ensign Chandler's testimony about the display on the GPS screen hearsay?

7. Utterances Relevant for the Truth of the Declarant's Unstated Beliefs

Verbal conduct, that is, oral or written words of a declarant, often expresses the belief of a declarant explicitly. But sometimes, the beliefs of the declarant that generate verbal conduct are not stated. They must be inferred from the words that are spoken or written. Is verbal conduct hearsay when offered to prove the truth of the unstated (inferred) beliefs? To answer this question we must first address the relevancy of such utterances.

a.   The Relevancy of Unstated Beliefs

Here are some examples of utterances that can be relevant only if they are offered to prove beliefs that the declarant holds but does not state explicitly. In our hypothetical case brought by the pedestrian against the driver of the gray SUV, suppose that Sally says to George "That SUV driver must be drunk" just after the pedestrian is struck. And suppose that the pedestrian is *not* trying to prove that the driver was drunk. The relevance of Sally's statement would depend on the inference that Sally has an unstated belief that the driver of the gray SUV was driving in a careless or wrongful manner when his car hit the pedestrian. The pedestrian would offer Sally's statement to prove this *unstated belief is true*. The fact of consequence is that the driver was driving carelessly or wrongfully. Under this theory, the relevance of the statement depends on all of Sally's testimonial qualities, thus requiring a complete trip around the testimonial triangle, as Diagram 8-8 illustrates:

Diagram 8-8

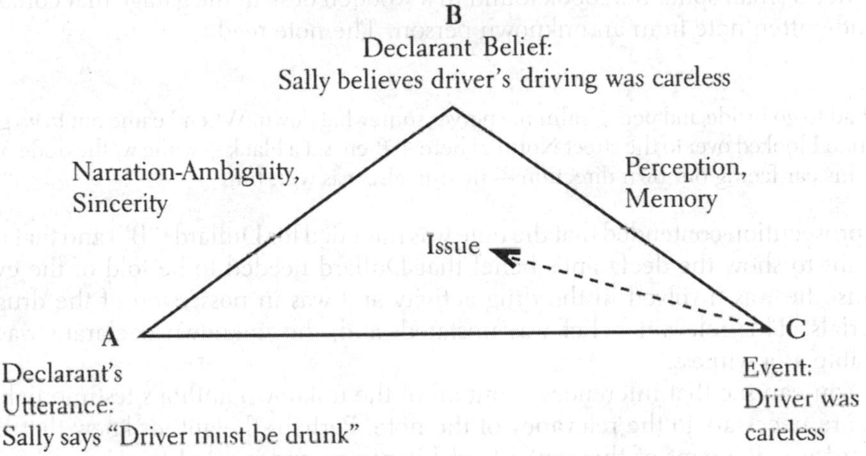

B
Declarant Belief:
Sally believes driver's driving was careless

Narration-Ambiguity,
Sincerity

Perception,
Memory

Issue

A
Declarant's
Utterance:
Sally says "Driver must be drunk"

C
Event:
Driver was
careless

Further inferences to reach the issue in the pedestrian's case will involve deciding what kind of wrongful driving Sally perceived. Other facts about the incident will show that Sally was probably referring to the driver's failure to stop at the red light.

In the hypothetical about Jim Harris's prosecution for battery, suppose that the woman said to Jim "get out of here quick" just after the police officer asked who had thrown the first punch. Or, a man said, "Jim Harris ought to confess." These statements might be relevant to the prosecution's case, but not to prove that Jim ought to get out or confess. The relevance of the statements would depend on an inference that the woman and the man held the belief that Jim had thrown the first punch. Again, this belief is unstated, but the prosecution would be offering the two statements to prove that this unstated belief is true. And again, this theory of relevance requires reliance on all of the testimonial qualities of the woman and man.

It may occur to you ask why the pedestrian would want to use Sally's out-of-court statement when questioning Sally at trial would reveal with more certainty what she believed about the accident. The same is true for the woman and man in the bar. Why not call them as witnesses and ask them whether they saw Jim throw the first punch? The answer is that sometimes declarants cannot be called as witnesses — they are unavailable, unwilling, or forgetful. Their out-of-court statements are the best source of their knowledge and beliefs, even if those beliefs are unstated.

One final example will help to make this point. In State v. Dullard, 668 N.W. 2d 585 (Iowa 2003), the Iowa Supreme Court addressed the question of whether the trial court had erroneously admitted a note, written by an unknown person, against the defendant Brent Dullard. On a tip, police had conducted a legal search of the house and garage that Dullard shared with his mother. In the garage, police found materials that are potential precursors of methamphetamine (ephedrine and ether) plus items commonly used in the manufacture of methamphetamine. Dullard was charged with possession of the precursor materials with intent to manufacture methamphetamine, a controlled substance.

Under Iowa law, Dullard and his mother had joint possession of the garage where all of the substances were found. Their joint possession required proof of Dullard's "actual knowledge or circumstances from which a jury could infer knowledge" in order to establish his possession of the precursors. This led the prosecution to offer into evidence a small spiral notebook found in a wooden desk in the garage that contained a handwritten note from an unknown person. The note read:

> B-
> I had to go inside and pee + calm my nerves somewhat down. When I came out to go get Brian I looked over to the street North of here + there sat a black + white w/ the dude out of his car facing our own direction — no one else was with him

The prosecution contended that the note was intended for Dullard ("B") and that it was relevant to show the declarant's belief that Dullard needed to be told of the events because he was involved in the drug activity and was in possession of the drug lab materials. This relevant belief was unstated; and, the unknown declarant was not available as a witness.

You can see that inferences about all of the unknown author's testimonial qualities are necessary to the relevancy of the note. Perhaps the author knew that Brent Dullard was ignorant of the contents of his garage and wanted to misrepresent his involvement (a sincerity risk); perhaps the author mistakenly wrote "B" and intended the note for "E" (a narration risk); perhaps the author had misperceived or forgotten about Brent's actual conduct and was mistaken about Brent's involvement (perception and memory risks). Even if all of these risks, or some of them, seem small to you, their existence implicates hearsay policy. If you were the attorney for Dullard, you would certainly want the opportunity to cross-examine the author of the note.

b.   Application of FRE 801(a)(1) and (c)

Courts and commentators have struggled for two centuries with the problem of how the rule against hearsay should classify the kinds of utterances that we have been discussing. The Iowa Supreme Court posed the question of whether this implied, unstated belief — which it also called an "implied assertion" using the terminology of the common law — is a hearsay statement under the definition contained in the Iowa rule of evidence identical to FRE 801(a) and (c).

i.   The Literal Approach.   FRE 801(a)(1) defines a "statement" as "an oral or written assertion." FRE 801(c) defines hearsay as a "statement...[of a declarant] offered in evidence to prove the truth of the matter asserted." Taking these terms literally, the declarant's written assertions in the note in *Dullard* were not offered to prove the truth of the matters or propositions that they assert. Those matters or propositions — that the police were watching or that the author of the note was nervous or worried and upset — were not relevant to prove that it was Dullard who had knowledge and control of the substances in the garage. Instead, the Court wrote, "the handwritten note is offered solely to show the declarant's belief, implied from the words and the message conveyed" that Dullard, the alleged recipient, had knowledge and thus possession of the drug lab materials. 668 N.W.2d at 591.

Under a literal approach to FRE 801(a) and (c), since that relevant belief was not stated as an assertion in the note, the note could not be a statement that was offered to prove the truth of the matter it asserted. The same result would be reached if these definitions were applied to Sally's statement that the "driver must be drunk" and to the statements that Jim Harris should "get out quick" or "ought to confess" in the hypotheticals we have just discussed. These utterances would not be hearsay because they are not offered to prove the truth of the matters they explicitly and literally assert.

ii.   **The Common Law Approach.**   At common law, courts used the phrase *implied assertions* to identify those utterances that were relevant not for the stated beliefs but for the implied beliefs of the declarant. The Iowa Supreme Court in *Dullard* treated the note as containing an "implied assertion" of the author's belief that Dullard had knowledge and possession of the drug lab materials. The Court described the common law approach:

> The starting point for the common law approach to implied assertions inevitably begins with the celebrated and durable case of *Wright v. Tatham*, 112 Eng. Rep. 488 (Ex. Ch. 1837). The case involved an action to set aside a will based on the incompetency of the testator. . . . At trial, the proponents of the will offered several letters written to the testator by various individuals concerning a variety of business and social subjects. . . . The purpose of the letters was to show the absent declarants must have believed the testator was able to engage in intelligent discourse on the various topics discussed in the letters. . . . This belief, therefore, constituted evidence of the testator's competency.
>
> In the course of holding that the statements contained in the letters were hearsay, the court in *Wright*, through the scholarship of Baron Parkes' opinion, utilized the now-famous example of a sea captain, who, after carefully inspecting his ship, embarked on an ocean voyage with his family, an action offered as proof of the seaworthiness of the ship. . . . Baron Parke used the illustration to show that such nonverbal conduct would nevertheless constitute hearsay because its value as evidence depended on the belief of the actor. . . . This illustration was important in the court's analysis because the main problem sought to be avoided by the rule against hearsay — an inability to cross-examine the declarant — is the same whether or not the assertion is implied from a verbal statement or implied from nonverbal conduct. Thus, assertions that are relevant only as implying a statement or opinion of the absent declarant on the matter at issue constitute hearsay in the same way the actual statement or opinion of the absent declarant would be inadmissible hearsay. [668 N.W.2d at 591]

Wright became the general rule at common law. Utterances not offered for the truth of the literal matters they asserted, but for the truth of the implied assertions of belief that made them relevant, were classified as hearsay.

If the goal of a definition of hearsay is to identify those out-of-court utterances that require evaluation of all of the declarant's testimonial qualities — where the trip around the complete testimonial triangle is required — then Baron Parkes's analogy makes sense. All of the examples of utterances relevant to prove unstated beliefs that we have discussed so far (which Baron Parkes would call implied assertions) require inferences about all of the declarants' testimonial qualities. Under hearsay policy, this justifies requiring oath, demeanor, and cross-examination. Professor Roger Park labeled this risk analysis a "declarant-oriented" test for hearsay; a test that "focuses on whether the use of the utterance will require reliance on the credibility of the out-of-court declarant." Roger C. Park, McCormick on Evidence and the Concept of Hearsay: A Critical Analysis Followed by Suggestions to Law Teachers, 65 Minn. L. Rev. 423, 424 (1981).

   iii.   FRE 801(a)-(c) Rejects the Common Law Approach.   The Advisory Committee Note to FRE 801(a) states that certain utterances are removed from the definition of hearsay, even though their relevance depends on the testimonial qualities of the declarant. This rejection of the "declarant-oriented" common law approach is briefly stated and sparingly justified as follows:

> [S]ituations giving rise to [nonassertive] . . . conduct are such as virtually to eliminate questions of sincerity. Similar considerations govern nonassertive verbal conduct and verbal conduct which is assertive but offered as a basis for inferring something other than the matter asserted, also excluded from the definition of hearsay by the language of subdivision (c).

The Note draws an analogy between nonassertive conduct, defined as not hearsay by FRE 801(a)(2), and two kinds of verbal utterances. The first sentence states that evidence of an actor's nonassertive conduct involves no sincerity danger. Why? Because the actor has no intent to use his conduct to communicate his belief. Think back to the earlier examples of nonassertive conduct admitted as not hearsay under FRE 801(a)(2). Without the intent to communicate, there is no opportunity for the actor to lie, that is, to decide to communicate false information through conduct. In the next sentence, the Note implies that the risk of insincerity is also nonexistent for "nonassertive verbal conduct and verbal conduct which is assertive but offered as a basis for inferring something other than the matter asserted" and that therefore such utterances should also be defined as not hearsay.

   "Nonassertive verbal conduct" may refer to hortatory declarations, instructions and commands. The exclamation "Jim, get out quick" would be an example of this type of utterance. Assertive verbal conduct "offered as the basis for inferring something other than the matter asserted" may refer to assertions like the note in *Dullard* — utterances relevant for unstated beliefs that still bear hearsay dangers. The Note does not explain or give examples of either kind of statement, however, so its meaning is somewhat ambiguous. Furthermore, "nonassertive verbal conduct" is an oxymoron, for virtually all conscious utterances are efforts to assert something.

   Nonetheless, there is agreement among courts and most commentators that when utterances are offered as relevant to prove the declarant's unstated beliefs, the Advisory Committee rejects the common law approach to the definition of hearsay. The key to determining whether utterances relevant for unstated beliefs are hearsay is to focus on the declarants' intent. If the declarants are not intending to assert their relevant but unstated beliefs, there would seem to be less opportunity for them to decide to lie — that is, to speak in a way that makes a false communication about those beliefs. The lack of intent may therefore reduce the risk of insincerity, as the Advisory Committee's analogy to nonassertive conduct suggests. While perception and memory dangers may not be reduced, this is true of nonassertive conduct as well, as we have seen. Thus the Advisory Committee seems to have decided that since nonassertive conduct that is not intended as an assertion of unstated belief is not hearsay, utterances like the note in Dullard that are similarly not intended as assertions of unstated belief should also be not hearsay. Some courts and commentators had previously taken this position.[4]

8. Elaboration of FRE 801: Courts Reject the Literal Approach and Apply an "Intent" Test

Words may be spoken or written with the *intent* to communicate something different from, or in addition to, what the words themselves formally articulate. People use language in many different ways to communicate. If the woman telling Jim to "get out quick" is intending to communicate her unstated belief that Jim threw the first punch by using this form of speech, it follows that she could choose to "lie" by communicating false information about Jim. When a speaker intends to communicate an unstated belief, there is enhanced danger of insincerity.

The truth-of-the-matter-asserted test of FRE 801(c) does not pick up this insincerity danger *if the test is applied literally*. Literal application tests for sincerity danger on only one criterion: Is the statement offered to prove the truth of its literal content, which the speaker or writer clearly did intend to assert? However, if the speaker or writer actually intends to communicate something *different from* or *more than* what is literally said, the literal truth-of-the-matter-asserted test may admit utterances that bear significant sincerity danger, as well as perception and memory dangers.

a. Intent to Assert Unstated Beliefs

For this reason, many courts and commentators have rejected a literal approach to the definition of hearsay. They recognize that there are some utterances with high sincerity risk that quite clearly should be classified as hearsay, even though these utterances are being offered to prove something different from what they literally assert. Courts have read "matter asserted" broadly enough to include matters that are *intentionally* implied, as well as expressed. In these cases, the hearsay danger of insincerity flows from the declarant's intent. In Park v. Huff, 493 F.2d 923, 927 (5th Cir.), *rev'd on other grounds*, 506 F.2d 849 (5th Cir. 1974) (en banc), the court said that a declarant's statements implying that the defendant was financing a murder conspiracy are hearsay when there is a "possibility that the declarant intended to leave a particular impression." The court in United States v. Zenni, 492 F. Supp. 464, 468-469 and n.21 (E.D. Ky. 1980) held that utterances offered for the truth of "implied assertions" are removed from the definition of hearsay only if the declarant *did not intend* to make the implied assertion about the fact sought to be proved. The court stated that while FRE 801(a)

> does not seem to require a preliminary determination by the trial court whether verbal conduct is intended as an assertion, it is submitted that such a determination would be required in the example given . . . [an airport inspector using a metal detector saying "go

---

4. See Ted Finman, Implied Assertions as Hearsay: Some Critisms of the Uniform Rules of Evidence, 14 Stan. L. Rev. 682, 684 n.8 (1962) (in discussing applicability of similar Uniform Rule of Evidence to hypothetical based on *Wright*, author concludes that letter writing evidence would be "statement" but would not be hearsay because not offered to prove truth of contents of letters).

on through" to a passenger to prove the passenger did not have a gun.] If an assertion were intended the evidence would be excluded. [Id.]

This intent test is a judicial creation. FRE 801(a)(1), defining verbal assertions as "statements," does not contain an intent test, in contrast to FRE 801(a)(2). Nonetheless, in somewhat backhanded language, the Advisory Committee Note to FRE 801(a) does emphasize that an intent to assert is critical to identifying hearsay: "The key to the definition is that nothing is an assertion unless intended to be one." Conversely, it would seem that if there is intent to assert, there is hearsay. Many evidence commentators agree:

> A number of scholars have advocated using the declarant's intent, or some objective manifestation of it, in determining what the declarant's statement asserts. Some version of an intent test seems necessary to keep the assertion definition [the literal truth-of-the-matter-asserted test] from being wholly arbitrary. [Roger C. Park, "I Didn't Tell Them Anything About You": Implied Assertions as Hearsay Under the Federal Rules of Evidence, 74 Minn. L. Rev. 783, 800 (1990).]

b.   Does an "Intent" Test Identify High Sincerity Risk?

A general principle that would identify utterances with high sincerity risk might be stated as follows: *When an out-of-court utterance is relevant to prove something different from or more than the truth of the declarant's literal utterance, the evidence is hearsay if the declarant is intending to communicate the truth of the unstated proposition that is critical to the relevance of the evidence.*

i.   What Kind of Intent?   One problem with such a test is that it is not clear what the meaning of "intent" is. When people speak, they have many beliefs in mind all at the same time. How central to the declarant's consciousness or thinking does a matter have to be for it to qualify as an "intended" communication? What kind of intent is necessary — how immediate, direct, or specific it should it be?

Consider Jill's statement to a friend of hers to whom she has been complaining about one of her co-workers, Mary. Jill says: "Well, at least I never stole from the company!" It seems clear from the context of the conversation that Jill has the specific intent to communicate to her friend the specific unstated proposition that Mary *did* steal from her employer. Jill has chosen a somewhat unusual way of expressing that proposition, but this does not diminish any of the hearsay dangers, including the danger of insincerity. Since she is intending to make an implicit communication, Jill has the opportunity to imply deliberately and falsely that Mary steals. The same analysis would seem to apply to the man's statement "Jim Harris ought to confess" in our hypothetical about who started the fight in the bar.

But while Jill's intent, and the man's intent, may be reasonably clear, in many cases it may be quite difficult to determine whether specific intent exists to communicate an unstated proposition. Consider the following:

> During the search of [co-defendant] Mayfield's apartment, the telephone rang, and a police officer answered it. An unidentified female voice asked to speak with "Keith." The officer replied that Keith was busy. The caller then asked if Keith "still had any stuff." The

officer asked the caller what she meant, and the caller responded "a fifty." The officer said "yeah." [United States v. Long, 905 F.2d 1572, 1579 (D.C. Cir. 1990).]

The defendant, Keith Long, was charged with possession of cocaine with intent to distribute. The caller's questions were clearly based on her belief that Keith was a drug-seller and had sold her drugs in the past. But what was the declarant intending to communicate? It may be that the declarant was simply intending to express her desire for drugs and not trying to assert the proposition "Keith is a drug-seller." Nonetheless, the declarant, at some level of consciousness, is basing her conduct on her knowledge that Keith has sold to her in the past and that her questions will communicate this fact. The declarant's out-of-court utterance was admitted at trial and Long was convicted. On appeal, Long argued that "the questions plainly revealed assumptions that are the functional equivalent of direct assertions. . . . [T]he caller, through her questions, in effect asserted that 'Keith ha[d] crack and s[old] it out of Mayfield's apartment.'" Id. The appellate court disagreed that "intent" was involved:

> With our inquiry focused on the *intent* of the caller, we have little trouble disposing of Long's theory about implied assertions. Long has not provided any evidence to suggest that the caller, through her questions, intended to assert that he was involved in drug dealing. The caller may indeed have conveyed messages about Long through her questions, but any such messages were merely incidental and not intentional. [Id. at 1580.]

Do you agree with the court's conclusion? Is the caller's statement more like Jill's "at least I never stole from the company" or like the statement of the note writer in *Dullard*?

ii. Factual Uncertainty. Another problem with an intent test may be "factual uncertainty" about whether the declarant has the specific intent to communicate an unstated belief. Factual uncertainty may exist because there is too much conflicting evidence of intent, or because there is an absence of evidence. Out-of-court utterances are typically described to the jury by someone who overheard them. Testimony from this witness about the immediate context in which the utterance was made may be the only information available to the jury. If the utterance was written, the document, and the witness authenticating it, may provide even less information pertinent to intent. 3 Stephen A. Saltzburg, Michael M. Martin and Daniel J. Capra, Federal Rules of Evidence Manual 1473 (7th ed. 1998), suggests that factual difficulties in applying an "actual intent" test can be adequately handled by an objective, rather than subjective, test of intent: "The question should be whether a reasonable person making a statement such as the declarant made would have intended to communicate the implied assertion that the proponent is offering for its truth."

iii. The Burden of Proving Intent. If an intent test is used, the question of the declarant's intent is a preliminary question that must be decided in order to apply FRE 801. This preliminary question is for the judge under FRE 104(a). Which party should bear the burden of persuading the judge as to whether the declarant has or does not have the requisite intent? The traditional legal device for dealing with uncertainty about factual issues is allocating the burden of proof. By assigning the burden of proving intent, or lack thereof, the risk of erroneous decisions can be assigned to one party instead of the other to further evidentiary policy.

As we noted earlier on page 434, the Advisory Committee Note to FRE 801(a)(2) dealing with nonverbal conduct states that the person claiming that the conduct was intended as an assertion should have the burden of proof on the intent issue. That is, the burden is on the party seeking exclusion of the conduct as hearsay. Both consistency and the general thrust of the Federal Rules in favor of admissibility suggest that the burden of proving intent should also be on the opponent of the evidence. On the other hand, if it will be quite difficult to prove intent in these cases, or if there is more ambiguity about what intent means, placing the burden on the opponent of the evidence may result in the admission of more evidence with substantial sincerity dangers. Most proposed intent tests do place the burden to prove intent on the opponent of the evidence. "As with conduct, the burden should be placed on the non-offering party to show that the declarant had the intent to communicate the implied assertion." 3 Stephen A. Saltzburg, Michael M. Martin, and Daniel J. Capra, Federal Rules of Evidence Manual at 1473.

c. Some Courts Still Adhere to the Common Law Approach.

The Iowa Supreme Court in *Dullard* rejected both the literal approach and an intent test, and adopted the common law's "declarant-oriented" approach to the definition of hearsay. The Court held that the note written by the unknown declarant was hearsay, even if its author did not intend to assert that Brent Dullard had knowledge of and possession of the substances in his garage.

> Absent unusual circumstances, the unknown declarant likely would not have thought about communicating the implied belief at issue...we are not convinced that the absence of intent necessarily makes the underlying belief more reliable, especially when the belief is derived from verbal conduct as opposed to nonverbal conduct.... The distinction drawn between intended and unintended conduct or speech only implicates the danger of sincerity...other "hearsay dangers remain viable, giving rise to the need for cross-examination. Moreover, even the danger of insincerity may...be present...where the reliability of the direct assertion...is insincere.... Implied assertions can be no more reliable than the predicate expressed assertion. [668 N.W.2d at 594-595]

Some federal circuit courts also seem to have applied the common law approach by excluding statements that are relevant only for the declarant's unstated belief without making any finding that the declarant intended to assert that belief. See Weinstein & Berger, Weinstein's Federal Evidence §801.10[2][c], at 801-10 to 801-12 nn. 13, 15 (McLaughlin ed., 2d ed. 2003); Callen, Hearsay and Informal Reasoning, 47 Vand. L.Rev. 43, 47-48 n. 18 (1994). Nevertheless, it is fair to say that the prevailing judicial practice is to admit as not hearsay statements relevant for unstated beliefs when the declarant did not intend to assert those beliefs, and to apply an intent test to exclude those statements that appear to bear significant sincerity danger due to opportunity to fabricate.

KEY POINTS

1. The Advisory Committee Note to FRE 801 construes FRE 801(a) and (c) as excluding oral and written utterances that are offered to prove a declarant's unstated

beliefs from the definition of hearsay. Such utterances are not offered to prove the truth of the literal matters they assert.

2. The relevancy of these utterances still depends on the declarants' testimonial qualities. However, when the declarant is not intending to communicate the unstated belief, the sincerity danger may be minimal, and the utterance is analogous to non-assertive conduct.

3. In the majority of jurisdictions, if a court finds that the declarant specifically intends to communicate an unstated belief, it will usually exclude the utterance as hearsay.

4. Intent to communicate may be difficult to prove either because of factual uncertainty or because of ambiguity in the meaning of intent.

NOTES AND QUESTIONS

1. Ever since Wright v. Tatham, there has been a continued practical and academic debate about whether these utterances — also called "implied assertions" — should be classified as hearsay or as not hearsay, and about the most effective doctrinal test for accomplishing this. An informative contribution to this debate is the Symposium on Hearsay and Implied Assertions: How Would (or Should) the Supreme Court Decide the *Kearley* Case?, 16 Miss. C. L. Rev. 1 (1995). Other articles include Craig R. Callen, Hearsay and Informal Reasoning, 47 Vand. L. Rev. 43 (1994); Paul S. Milich, Re-examining Hearsay Under the Federal Rules: Some Method for the Madness, 39 Kan. L. Rev. 893 (1991); Roger C. Park, "I Didn't Tell Them Anything About You": Implied Assertions as Hearsay Under the Federal Rules of Evidence, 74 Minn. L. Rev. 783 (1990); David E. Seidelson, Implied Assertions and Federal Rule of Evidence 801: A Quandry for Federal Courts, 24 Duq. L. Rev. 741 (1986); Olin Guy Wellborn III, The Definition of Hearsay in the Federal Rules of Evidence, 61 Tex. L. Rev. 49 (1982).

2. In 1992, a case before the Law Lords in the English House of Lords reaffirmed the common law approach to implied assertions set forth in Wright v. Tatham. Regina v. Kearley, 2 App. Cas. 228 (1992). However, some ten years later, section 115 of the Criminal Justice Act of 2003 rejected this approach. The key text is that the definition of hearsay includes only those statements where "the purpose of, or one of the purposes, of the person making the statement appears to the court to have been (a) to cause another person to believe the matter, or (b) to cause another person to act . . . on the basis that the matter is as stated." Would the note in *Dullard* be hearsay under this test?

PROBLEMS

8.25. Fred and John have just been arrested by the police for a robbery. Fred says to John: "Don't worry, I didn't tell them anything about you." Hearsay if offered to prove John participated in the robbery?

8.26. Return to Problem 8.6 at page 430, supra. To prove that there was ketchup on the floor where she fell, Sondra Evers presents Joel as a witness who will testify that shortly before Sondra's fall he heard another customer say, "Watch out for that ketchup!" Joel was standing in an aisle and did not see what the customer was looking at. Is it hearsay?

8.27. In the prosecution of Betty Wilson for maintaining a house where betting occurs, a police officer offers to testify that as she was executing a warrant for the search of the house in question, she answered the telephone, and heard the voice at the other end of the line say, "This is D.T.; put $25 on Rosebud in the fifth." Wilson's attorney objects that the evidence is hearsay. How should the court rule?

8.28. Victim was alone with Fred and Stanley when he was shot. To prove Fred shot the victim, the prosecution offers the following:

(a)   The victim's statement immediately thereafter: "Help me, Stanley, I've got a bullet in me."
(b)   The victim's statement at the hospital: "Whatever you do, don't let Fred in here. He wants to hurt me."

8.29. Delia is charged with transporting stolen cars in interstate commerce. A police officer testifies at Delia's trial that when Delia and two companions, E and F, were stopped, Delia was driving the stolen car, and that E said that the car belonged to E's brother, which was false. Hearsay? E and F are charged with conspiring with Delia to transport stolen cars in interstate commerce. F testifies at Delia's trial that when she met with E after their arrest, E said, "It would be better for you and me to take the blame than Delia — she couldn't stand it, she just couldn't." Hearsay?

8.30. Roger Sullivan has been charged with burglary of a 7-11 store. One customer in the store testifies that just before the burglary, he heard the cashier say "Hello, Roger, how's it going?" After the burglary, as the customers were being interviewed by the police, the same customer heard the cashier say "It was Roger Sullivan who came in here and waved his gun at me, that idiot." Is any of the customer's testimony objectionable hearsay?

8.31. Return to Problem 3.4, State v. Blair, at page 131 supra. In Norma's private diary, on a page dated the day before the attack on her, Norma has written:

Jimmy has really hurt me this time. He is getting more violent when I tell him I want to leave. I don't want anyone to read this and I am going to burn this diary when I leave for L.A.

Hearsay?

9.   Reflection on the Definition of Hearsay: Should FRE 801 Be Revised?

The goal of a definition of hearsay is at least twofold. It should advance hearsay policy by identifying evidence that should be subject to the hearsay prohibition of FRE 802. It should also provide rules that are as clear and as simple as possible for judges to apply quickly in the charged atmosphere of an ongoing trial. Thus it may be undesirable to burden the definition of hearsay with an intent test, both in terms of time and fact-finding competence. If so, must intent be ignored and the identification of hearsay remain focused solely on the literal content of the words uttered to see whether the evidence was offered to prove the truth of those words? We have seen that the literal truth-of-the-matter-asserted test results in the admission of both conduct and utterances that bear significant hearsay dangers. At least insofar as the definitional test is concerned, the Advisory Committee seems to have been fixated on sincerity. Nonassertive conduct, admitted through FRE 801(a), may bear reduced sincerity risk but still carries substantial perception and memory danger. Utterances relevant to prove unstated beliefs about events, admitted through FRE 801(c), carry similar perception and memory danger. They can also involve significant sincerity risks if some kind of intent test is not used to exclude those utterances bearing the highest sincerity risks.

An alternative is, of course, the "declarant-oriented" approach to defining hearsay adopted in Wright v. Tatham and discussed on page 444, supra. This approach would define all of these problematic utterances as hearsay without the necessity of any "intent" test at all. The result would be wholesale exclusion of utterances whenever relevance depends on the complete trip around the testimonial triangle. For an example of a declarant-oriented definition of hearsay for verbal utterances, see Tex. R. Crim. Evid. 801(c) and Tex. R. Civ. Evid. 801(c). In these rules, Texas has adopted a definition of "matter asserted" that focuses on the use of utterances to prove the beliefs of the declarant. "Matter asserted" includes "any matter explicitly asserted, and any matter implied by a statement, if the probative value of the statement as offered flows from declarant's belief in the matter." Professor Michael Graham proposes a similar definition that focuses on the presence of a necessary inference of sincerity:

> "Hearsay" is a statement offered in evidence, other than one made by the declarant while testifying at the trial or hearing, to the extent relevance depends upon (1) the truth of the matter asserted or (2) the declarant's belief in the truth or falsity of the matter asserted. [Michael Graham, "Stickperson Hearsay": A Simplified Approach to Understanding the Rule Against Hearsay, 1982 U. Ill. L. Rev. 887, 921 (1982).]

In practice, judges probably apply the truth-of-the-matter asserted language of FRE 801(c) in a literalistic fashion, until they are confronted with an out-of-court utterance where the declarant's specific intent to communicate an unstated belief is clear. Then they craft some kind of intent test to exclude it. Is such muddling through acceptable? Professor Roger Park contends that judges are doing fine with the current rule:

> A review of the published caselaw does not reveal any obvious signs of injustice. . . . The cases generally involve utterances classed as [not hearsay] that raise no real insincerity dangers affecting the purpose for which they are being used. . . . [F]ederal courts are reaching fair results in resolving implied assertion problems under the existing assertion definition. [Park, 74 Minn. L. Rev. at 836-838.]

It would be possible to abandon the categorical thinking that underlies the truth of the matter asserted test, the intent test, and the declarant-oriented test. If, as the Advisory Committee suggests, the lack of sincerity danger justifies treating utterances as not hearsay, then the definition could focus on the more functional question whether the utterance is one that, from its content or context, appears to raise few sincerity risks. Professor Paul Milich suggests a specific test that would shift the focus away from "intent" to a more functional appraisal of the risk of insincerity:

> If it appears from the circumstances and the language used that the declarant probably would not have used that particular locution to lie about the fact in question, then the reduced risk of insincerity frees the evidence from the definition of assertion and the federal definition of hearsay. [Paul S. Milich, Re-examining Hearsay Under the Federal Rules: Some Method for the Madness, 39 Kan. L. Rev. 893, 909 (1991).]

A shift in the definition toward an explicit appraisal of sincerity risk on a case-by-case basis affords the trial judge more discretion in applying the basic hearsay rule of exclusion. Lack of sincerity danger would be a stand-in for greater probative value, and out-of-court utterances would escape the definition because trial judges evaluate them as more probative. If appellate courts defer to this evaluation, then there could be less appellate review than is currently afforded under any of the more categorical "truth of the matter asserted," "intent" and "declarant-oriented" definitions. We have discussed here only a fraction of the academic ink that has been spilled on the question of the definition of hearsay. As we stated at the beginning of this chapter, a brief doctrinal definition can only imperfectly capture all of the reasons for the hearsay prohibition. Any test of hearsay that focuses solely on identifying sincerity danger reflects a choice to ignore perception and memory dangers. This reflects a compromise with other values at stake in our system of trial, including the efficiency of trials, confidence in jury fact-finding, the role of the trial judge and the nature of appellate review. Different defini-tions reflect a difference in thinking about where the compromise should be drawn. After you have studied the exemptions and exceptions to the general rule of exclusion, we will again examine some of the current and diverse thinking on the meaning, function, and future of the entire hearsay rule.

B.   A GENERAL APPROACH TO THE ADMISSION OF HEARSAY UNDER THE EXEMPTIONS AND EXCEPTIONS

Many out-of-court statements are admitted into evidence to prove the truth of the matters they assert. FRE 801(d) *exempts* eight types of out-of-court statements from the definition of hearsay, and FRE 803, 804, and 807 create 29 explicit *exceptions* to FRE 802's rule of exclusion. In terms of the process by which judges admit these various statements, there is no difference between an FRE 801(d) hearsay exemption and an FRE 803, FRE 804, or FRE 807 hearsay exception. We treat them separately in the sections of this chapter only as a matter of organizational convenience.

1.   Justification for the Exemptions and Exceptions.

There are differences, however, in the justifications for admitting the various types of hearsay statements. The drafters of the Federal Rules created the new status of *exemption* to admit hearsay statements whose principal rationale for admission is the possibility for cross-examining the declarant. Under FRE 801(d)(1), which admits some prior statements of a witness, there is an opportunity for delayed cross-examina-tion of the declarant-witness at the trial or hearing at which the prior statement is offered. In the case of admissions of a party opponent, under FRE 801(d)(2)(A), the party can take the stand and be subjected to direct and cross-examination. One must be careful not to press the cross-examination rationale for the exemptions too far. Only some prior statements of a witness fall within Rule 801(d)(1). And, a party may not be able to take the witness stand and explain fully any prior statement made by a loosely affiliated person admitted against the party under FRE 801(d)(2).

Most hearsay *exceptions* admitted under FRE 803, 804 and 807 are justified by the presence of circumstances that tend to minimize one or more of the hearsay dangers. Thus these statements may be more "trustworthy" than other hearsay and there is, in theory, less reason for concern about the absence of cross-examination.

We analyze these justifications in more detail in each of the following sections in this chapter, and you should ask yourself how persuasive you think they are. After you have spent considerable time and effort on identifying hearsay and on understanding how and why hearsay policy operates to exclude it, it may come as something of a shock to see how freely a lot of hearsay is admitted through the exemptions and exceptions.

2. The Categorical Approach

FRE 801(d), FRE 803, and FRE 804 all apply a categorical approach to the admission of hearsay. FRE 807 applies a noncategorical "trustworthiness" approach, which will be discussed separately in Section F. By "categorical approach" we mean that the rules establish specific categories of out-of-court statements that can be admitted for their truth. These categories are sometimes defined by who the declarant is, sometimes by the content of the statement, and sometimes by the circumstances in which the statement was made. You should read through these rules now to get a general sense of what these categories are like.

3. The Process of Admission

The process of admission under FRE 801(d), FRE 803, and FRE 804 goes something like this: A proponent typically offers to prove a declarant's out-of-court statement through the testimony of a witness who overheard it or through an exhibit that contains it, such as a document in which the statement is written or a tape or some other recording of it. The opponent typically objects on grounds of hearsay. In order to rule on this objection, the judge must decide whether the statement is hearsay under FRE 801(a)-(c). If it is, then the judge decides whether it fits within the categorical terms of a specific exemption or exception. The burden is on the proponent of the statement to produce foundational evidence — typically evidence of who the declarant is, what the content of the statement is, or the out-of-court circumstances in which the hearsay statement was made — that satisfies the categorical terms of the specific exemption or exception aimed for. From the text of a categorical hearsay exemption or exception, you can analyze the doctrinal terms of the category that it establishes. These doctrinal terms will tell you what foundational evidence needs to be produced if the proponent is to secure the admission of a hearsay statement.

4. The Foundational Requirements

We call this foundational evidence *foundation facts*. You saw in Chapter Four that the proponent of an exhibit must produce foundation facts that satisfy the standard for authentication and identification set by FRE 901(a). In the same way, under FRE

801(d), FRE 803, and FRE 804, the proponent must produce foundation facts that satisfy the standards set by the categorical subsections of those rules. Typically this will mean that the proponent must produce a witness who can testify about these foundation facts. We call this witness a *foundation witness*.

Take as one example a witness, Joe, who testifies in court and identifies Sam, the defendant, as the perpetrator of a crime or tort. At a lineup held at a police station just a few days after the crime or accident, Joe made a statement that the perpetrator was Peter, not Sam. Sam, the defendant, would obviously want to offer this prior statement into evidence to prove that he was *not* the perpetrator. Can Joe's prior statement be admitted for the truth of the matter it asserts? Yes, if it fits within a categorical exemption or exception. By reading FRE 801(d)(1)(A), you will see that the foundational requirements for it are as follows:

- the statement was made by a declarant who is now testifying in court as a witness;
- the declarant is subject to cross-examination concerning the statement;
- the contents of the statement are inconsistent with testimony given at trial;
- the statement was made under oath subject to the penalty of perjury; and
- the statement was made at a trial, hearing, other proceeding, or in a deposition.

Focusing for now just on the fourth requirement, the proponent will have to produce foundational evidence as to whether the statement was made under oath. A foundation witness who can present foundation facts about the oath might be Joe himself; it might be the police officer at the lineup; or, it could be anyone else who observed Joe and who could say, "Joe took the oath and made the statement." After hearing this foundational testimony, the judge will decide whether the categorical requirement has been satisfied. This is a preliminary question that is necessary to the application of an evidence rule. FRE 104 governs such questions, as you know. Applying the policies underlying Rule 104 you should be able to determine whether the judge applies Rule 104(a) or (b). As a general principle, FRE 104(a) applies unless the facts listed above as foundational requirements are necessary to the out-of-court statement's relevancy. Are they? You can see that they are not. Joe's prior statement would be relevant to prove that Sam was *not* the perpetrator whether or not it was under oath. Thus the judge would have to be persuaded by a preponderance of the evidence, pursuant to FRE 104(a), that the foundational requirement was satisfied. This is the proponent's burden, and it is the key to the admission of hearsay. We will have more to say about this judicial decision-making process as we discuss Rules 801(d), 803, and 804 in greater detail.

5.   Multiple Exemptions and Exceptions May Apply

As you study the hearsay exemptions and exceptions, keep in mind that an out-of-court statement may sometimes be admissible pursuant to more than one of them. For example, the deposition testimony given by a party who is now testifying as a witness could be admissible against the party as an admission under FRE 801(d)(2)(A) or as a prior inconsistent statement under oath under FRE 801 (d)(1)(A); a statement may be both a present sense impression under FRE 803(1) and an excited utterance under FRE 803(2); a document may qualify for admission as a public record under FRE 803(8) and as a business record under FRE 803(6). When this is the case, it is sufficient to overcome a hearsay objection to show that the evidence falls within one exemption or exception. Similarly, except in one context that we will consider later, the fact that evidence does *not* quite fit within a particular exemption or exception does not prevent its admission under a different one.

6.   The Confrontation Clause

There is one more introductory point to be made. In criminal prosecutions, defendants have a right "to be confronted with the Witnesses against them," which is protected by the Sixth Amendment to the U.S. Constitution. This right has been recently construed by the Supreme Court to mean that so-called *testimonial* hearsay statements may not be used by the prosecution in criminal trials. Crawford v. Washington, 541 U.S. 36 (2004). We will discuss the meaning given to the term *testimonial* and the complexities of applying the testimonial standard in Section G of this chapter. *Crawford* affects some, but not all, of the hearsay exceptions, and there are also exceptions to its prohibition, including that the declarant is testifying as a witness at the trial or that the defendant has had a previous opportunity to cross-examine the declarant, who is now unavailable. We raise the confrontation issue now because some of the hearsay statements that you will find to be admissible under a hearsay exemption or exception must still be tested under the interpretation of the Confrontation Clause in *Crawford* as well. We raise the *Crawford* issue explicitly at a few points in Sections C, D, E and F.

C.   HEARSAY EXEMPTIONS

FRE 801(d) exempts certain types of out-of-court statements from the definition of hearsay. These statements are admissible to prove the truth of the matters they assert, assuming that they are otherwise unobjectionable. FRE 801(d)(1) exempts certain kinds of statements previously made out of court by a testifying witness. FRE 801(d)(2) exempts out-of-court statements made by a party or by persons affiliated with a party, so long as the statements are offered *against* that party. Reading the Advisory Committee Notes to FRE 801(d) will give you some idea of the controversy surrounding the hearsay status of these two broad categories of out-of-court statements.

1.   FRE 801(d)(1) and (2)

RULE 801. DEFINITIONS

(d) Statements which are not hearsay. A statement is not hearsay if —
　　　(1) Prior statement by witness. The declarant testifies at the trial or hearing and is subject to cross-examination concerning the statement, and the statement is (A) inconsistent with the declarant's testimony, and was given under oath subject to the penalty of perjury at a trial, hearing, or other proceeding, or in a deposition, or (B) consistent with the declarant's testimony and is offered to rebut an express or implied charge

against the declarant of recent fabrication or improper influence or motive, or (C) one
of identification of a person made after perceiving the person;

(2) Admission by party-opponent. The statement is offered against a party and is
(A) the party's own statement, in either an individual or a representative capacity or (B)
a statement of which the party has manifested an adoption or belief in its truth, or (C) a
statement by a person authorized by the party to make a statement concerning the
subject, or (D) a statement by the party's agent or servant concerning a matter within
the scope of the agency or employment, made during the existence of the relationship,
or (E) a statement by a co-conspirator of a party during the course and in furtherance of
the conspiracy. The contents of the statement shall be considered but are not alone
sufficient to establish the declarant's authority under subdivision (C), the agency or
employment relationship and scope thereof under subdivision (D), or the existence of
the conspiracy and the participation therein of the declarant and the party against
whom the statement is offered under subdivision (E).

2. Interpretation and Illustration of FRE 801(d)(1): The Testifying Witness Must Be "Subject to Cross-examination Concerning the Statement"

FRE 801(d)(1) admits statements made outside of court by a person who is
testifying as a witness at trial. With the declarant-witness in court, subject to cross-
examination, you might think that *all* of that witness's out-of-court statements should
be admitted as exempt from the hearsay rule of exclusion. This is not the case, however,
as the rule admits only three categories of prior statements. There are two basic requirements that apply to all three categories:

- the out-of-court declarant is testifying at trial; and
- the declarant is subject to cross-examination concerning the statement.

Consider the example presented on page 454, supra: Joe is an eyewitness to a crime or
accident and he testifies in a criminal or civil case brought against Sam, the alleged
wrongdoer. At trial, Joe identifies Sam as the wrongdoer. Suppose that Joe had been
brought to a police lineup that included Sam in it just a few days after the incident.
After viewing the lineup Joe identified Peter, not Sam, as the perpetrator. Sam would
like to offer evidence of this prior statement in his own defense. Would it be admissible
under FRE 801(d)(1)(A), or (B), or (C)? First the judge would determine whether Joe
was the "declarant" and "is subject to cross-examination (by Sam's opponent) concerning the statement"; then the judge would determine whether Joe's prior statement
fits within the specific categories of (A), (B), or (C).

a. Preliminary Factfinding

i. The Declarant Is Testifying at Trial. The first foundational requirement is
that the person testifying — Joe — be identified as the same person — Joe — who made
the out-of-court statement. United States v. Carmichael, 232 F.3d 510, 520 (6th Cir.
2000) (defendant's offer of his own out-of-court statement to corroborate his defense
not admissible under FRE 801(d)(1)(B) because defendant did not testify). The proponent of Joe's hearsay statement can fulfill this requirement through Joe's own
acknowledgment that he made the out-of-court statement, or through the testimony
of another witness who can say that the witness Joe was the out-of-court speaker.

ii.   Examination Concerning the Statement.   Then the judge must determine that Joe is *subject to cross-examination concerning* the statement. The opponent's opportunity to cross-examine the declarant-witness is, as we have said, the principal justification for admitting Rule 801(d)(1) statements. Although the rule speaks in terms of *cross-examination* only, it has been construed to mean redirect examination as well. What this means is that either party may introduce a prior statement of a witness. If the proponent presents the witness's prior statement during direct, the witness must then be subject to cross-examination about it by the opponent. However, if the witness is presented with the prior statement for the first time by the cross-examiner, then it is the direct-examiner (the original proponent of the witness) who must now have the opportunity to *re-examine* the witness on redirect. Prior statements can also be admitted after the witness has testified, through the testimony of a third person. The declarant-witness must still be available in court or subject to recall by the opposing party to satisfy the requirement of cross-examination *concerning* the statement, if the witness was not asked about it during the original cross-examination.

Remember that the declarant-witness's prior statement is now being offered for its truth. Thus the opponent of the statement will want to cross-examine the declarant-witness *concerning* the statement in order to expose reasons why it should not be relied on by the jury. If the declarant-witness remembers both making the prior statement and the events that are the subject of the statement, the cross-examiner can elicit information pertinent to evaluating the declarant-witness's testimonial qualities at the time the statement was made. If the declarant-witness denies the truth of the prior statement, or attempts to explain it, the jury will decide what weight to give it. If the witness adopts as true the contents of a prior inconsistent statement, there is then no hearsay problem because the adopted inconsistency corrects and becomes a part of the witness's in-court testimony. United States v. Lopez-Lopez, 282 F.3d 1, 17 (1st Cir. 2000) (witness adopted prior statement that he had observed defendant for "only two or three seconds" as opposed to his trial testimony of "four or five" seconds; "adoption bypasses ... the entire hearsay problem"). But "adoption" of a prior *consistent* statement does not eliminate the hearsay problem.

iii.   Denial of, or Inability to Remember, the Prior Statement.   What if the witness denies making or cannot remember making the prior statement? If the prior statement is an authenticated writing or recording, there may be little doubt that it was made. If the prior statement was not recorded, then it will be the subject of testimony from someone who was present at the time — the police officer, for example, who was with Joe at the police lineup when Joe identified Peter and not Sam. At trial, if Joe denies making the prior inconsistent identification, should Joe still be considered to be a witness *subject to cross-examination concerning the statement*? How would you cross-examine him? There is likely to be nothing more than a swearing contest between two witnesses, such as Joe and the police officer, about whether the statement was made.

iv.   Inability to Remember the Underlying Events.   It may also happen that the witness cannot remember the underlying event that is the subject of the statement. If this seems far-fetched to you, consider United States v. Owens, 484 U.S. 554 (1988), in which a battery victim's prior statement identifying defendant Owens as his assailant was admitted under FRE 801(d)(1)(C). At trial, the victim had no memory of seeing the assailant; he could remember the attack, and making the prior identification of

Owens at the hospital, but he could not recall how he knew it was Owens who attacked him. How would you cross-examine this victim about his perception or memory of the assailant? Should the victim be considered to be a witness *subject to cross-examination concerning the statement*, in fulfillment of FRE 801(d)(1)?

In Owens, the Supreme Court rejected both a confrontation clause and a Rule 801(d)(1) challenge to the admission of the prior statement of identification. With respect to the adequacy of cross-examination under FRE 801(d)(1) the Court said:

> Ordinarily a witness is regarded as "subject to cross-examination" when he is placed on the stand, under oath, and responds willingly to questions. Just as with the constitutional prohibition, limitations on the scope of examination by the trial court or assertions of privilege by the witness may undermine the process to such a degree that meaningful cross-examination within the intent of the rule no longer exists.[5] But that effect is not produced by the witness's assertion of memory loss — which . . . is often the very result sought to be produced by cross-examination, and can be effective in destroying the force of the prior statement. Rule 801(d)(1)(C), which specifies that cross-examination need only "concer[n] the statement," does not on its face require more. [Id. at 561-562.]

Owens thus imposes a minimal requirement of what it means to cross-examine a witness *concerning* a prior statement. It does not matter that the witness denies making, or cannot remember, either the prior statement or the underlying event, or perhaps even both. In a case involving a child's prior statement identifying her uncle as having sexually abused her, the court admitted the hearsay identification despite the fact that the child could no longer remember the abuse, the abuser, or making the statement. Vaska v. State, 74 P.3d 225, 229 (Ct.App.Alaska 2002) ("courts that have interpreted *Owens* have, at least in dicta, reached an interpretation consistent with ours").

The Court in *Owens* emphasized that the Advisory Committee Note to FRE 801(d)(1)(C) expresses a preference for admitting prior statements of identification because of the problem of fading memories. But lower courts following *Owens* have also applied this minimalist position to statements governed by FRE 801(d)(1)(A). If the witness claims not to remember the underlying event, or answers questions about it evasively, courts sometimes regard the witness's prior statement about the event as inconsistent with the current testimony. See page 460, infra. In United States v. Milton, 8 F.3d 39 (D.C. Cir. 1993), the court held that a witness who claimed to have forgotten both the underlying events and the making of the prior inconsistent statement was nevertheless subject to cross-examination concerning it:

> When a witness has forgotten the basis for and the giving of testimony under oath in an earlier proceeding and that testimony is then introduced into evidence, defense questioning, though impaired, is not futile for the reasons given in Owens. It is still possible to bring out on cross-examination the "witness' bias, his lack of care and attentiveness . . . and even (what is often a prime objective of cross-examination) the very fact that he has a bad memory." And that is precisely what took place in this case. Defense counsel elicited testimony from Jones that tended to discredit her grand jury testimony. She admitted that when she appeared before the grand jury she was addicted to drugs, was suffering from withdrawal and was on the verge of a nervous breakdown. [Id. at 46-47.]

5.   The Court is acknowledging that there are other kinds of limitations on cross-examination that may arise. Sometimes the trial court will improperly foreclose a line of questioning, or the witness may assert a privilege or refuse to respond. These possibilities may make an individual not subject to cross-examination for purposes of FRE 801(d)(1)(C). The Supreme Court has discussed this problem in a

In *United States v. Keeter*, 130 F.3d 297 (7th Cir. 1997), the defendant claimed that the witness was feigning a loss of memory of both the litigated event and the prior statement, and thus could not be cross-examined. The Seventh Circuit, relying on *Owens*, held that the "Supreme Court's point was that the confrontation clause (and the rule) are satisfied when the witness must look the accused in the eye in court; shortcomings in the declarant's memory may be made known to the jury." *Id.* at 302.

   v.   Personal Knowledge Is Required.   The Ninth Circuit opinion in *Owens*, 789 F.2d 750 (9th Cir. 1986) also discussed the requirement of personal knowledge. Courts and commentators are agreed that the requirement applies to statements admitted under FRE 801(d)(1). Thus in *Owens*, where the witness-declarant could not remember seeing his assailant at the time of the attack, the defendant Owens argued that personal knowledge had not been shown. The appellate court concluded that it could not say that the district court had actually decided whether there was "evidence sufficient to support a finding" of personal knowledge, the standard required by FRE 602. *Id.* at 754-755. As we shall discuss later, some courts have applied FRE 104(a) to the personal knowledge requirement for hearsay declarants. This requires a higher threshold of proof to be met by proponents, and requires a decision by the judge under the preponderance of the evidence standard. Particularly in cases of failed memory, such a decision may be difficult to make.

b.   Other Justifications for the FRE 801(d)(1) Exemptions

   In addition to the witness-declarant being currently under oath and subject to some form of cross-examination, prior statements may be more reliable than in-court testimony. The witness's memory, for example, will have been fresher when making the prior statement. And, as we have seen in Chapter Seven, before the creation of the Rule 801(d)(1) exemptions, some prior statements were admissible for the nonhearsay purpose of impeaching (if inconsistent) or rehabilitating (if consistent) the credibility of the witness. If prior statements are going to be admitted to impeach or rehabilitate the witness, it is arguably appropriate to admit them for their truth as well, rather than to trust that the jury will understand and apply a limiting instruction.

3.   Interpretation and Illustration of FRE 801(d)(1)(A): Prior Inconsistent Statements

a.   Preliminary Factfinding

The foundational requirements for FRE 801(d)(1)(A) are:

* the contents of the statement are inconsistent with testimony given at trial;
* the statement was made under oath subject to the penalty of perjury; and
* the statement was made at a trial, hearing, other proceeding, or in a deposition.

---

series of options interpreting the Sixth Amendment's confrontation clause, which we discuss in Chapter Seven. See *Davis v. Alaska*, 415 U.S. 308 (1974); *Douglas v. Alabama*, 380 U.S. 415 (1965). — EDS.

i. Inconsistency. In the example of Joe's prior identification of Peter, the foundational requirement of its inconsistency with his in-court identification of Sam is determined by comparing the contents of the two statements. Generally, the inconsistency will appear from the contents alone, particularly when the statements are diametrically opposed such that the truth of one implies the falsity of the other. But inconsistency is not limited to such opposition; "any substantive divergence between two statements" will permit use of the prior statement. United States v. Jasin, 215 F.Supp. 2d 552, 591 (E.D.Pa. 2002) (citing Weinsten's Federal Evidence §801.21(2)(b)). Sometimes there may be doubt about the fact of inconsistency, if the allegedly inconsistent statement is ambiguous (if Joe also said that the perpetrator *might* be Sam), or if the witness claims to be able to explain away an apparent inconsistency (if Joe said he got the numbers in the lineup confused and really meant to identify Sam).

The judge should make an FRE 104(a) determination of inconsistency — under the higher standard of preponderance of the evidence — as a condition of admitting the statement for its truth. The relevancy of the prior statement is to prove the truth of its own content; relevancy is not dependent on whether the statement is actually inconsistent with the witness's trial testimony. The Rule 104(a) standard would also apply to the foundational requirements of oath and hearing.

ii. Inconsistency Due to Evasion. Some courts have found inconsistency when a witness claims a loss of memory of relevant events while testifying at trial, but had previously testified in detail about them before a grand jury. Inconsistency "may be found in evasive answers . . . silence, or changes in position," United States v. Dennis, 625 F.2d 782, 795 (8th Cir. 1980), or in a manifest reluctance to testify at trial, United States v. Thompson, 708 F.2d 1294, 1302 (8th Cir. 1983). In United States v. Bigham, 812 F.2d 943, 947 (5th Cir. 1987), the court noted the Advisory Committee's stated policy to admit prior inconsistent statements for their truth in order to protect against a turncoat grand jury witness who deliberately changes stories at trial. The court reasoned that this policy should also apply when the trial court concludes that the witness is feigning loss of memory and the loss is "not genuine." United States v. Keeter, 130 F.3d at 302 (affidavit and grand jury testimony admitted under FRE 801(d)(1)(A) when the witness, in fear that the government could not protect him from the defendant's retaliation, claimed inability to remember anything but his name; he could not recall meeting with the defendant, providing facts in his affidavit, or even appearing before the grand jury). The Seventh Circuit has held, however, that admission of a prior statement may be inconsistent with a claimed loss of memory even when the lack of memory is not found to be attributable to recalcitrance or other improper motives. United States v. Gajo, 290 F.3d 922, 932 (7th Cir. 2002) (claim of inability to remember what defendant said in English inconsistent with detailed testimony to the grand jury about what defendant had said).

iii. Under Oath at a Trial, Hearing, or Other Proceeding. The circumstances in which the inconsistent statement was made are also part of the FRE 801(d)(1)(A) foundation. The proponent must show that the statement was made under oath, that the person administering the oath had legal authority to do so, that the penalty of perjury attached, and that the statement was made in a trial, hearing, deposition or other proceeding. These foundation facts are relatively easy to prove, although you can see that Joe's prior inconsistent statement that it was Peter who committed the crime or tort, made at the lineup, would not satisfy the requirement of being made at a hearing. But is a lineup an *other proceeding* that would satisfy the rule's requirement? Typically, statements made in the course of interviews and lineups are held not to be within the meaning of other proceedings. The formality of trials, hearings, and depositions is thought to be conducive to reliability and truthfulness; the informality of most other interrogations is not. In United States v. Perez, 870 F.2d 1222 (7th Cir. 1989), the transcript of defense counsel's pretrial interview with an adverse government witness was not admissible under FRE 801(d)(1)(A). The statement was under oath and recorded by a court reporter. But it did not meet the requirements of a deposition under the Federal Rules of Criminal Procedure. The government was not present and the court did not authorize the interview.

b. Justification for the FRE 801(d)(1)(A) Limitations

The Advisory Committee originally proposed that *all* prior inconsistent statements could be used for their truth, as is true in California under Evidence Code §1235. Because such statements are closer in time to the events they relate to, and the declarant-witness is testifying before the jury, hearsay dangers are diminished. The House of Representatives, however, decided that admissibility should be limited to statements made under oath and *subject to cross-examination at the time they were made.* The final version of FRE 801(d)(1)(A) represents a compromise between these two positions: A witness's inconsistent statement may be used for its truth only if made at a trial, hearing, other proceeding, or in a deposition, but without the requirement of cross-examination. In many of these settings, the opportunity for cross-examination will have been available. But in a grand jury proceeding, while witnesses are placed under oath, the proceedings are secret and are held without the presence of the defendant. Thus there is no opportunity for cross-examination. The compromise permits admission of statements made to grand juries under FRE 801(d)(1)(A), used most commonly when government witnesses change their stories at trial or claim not to remember the facts about the defendant's culpability to which they testified previously.

Most hearings or other proceedings are likely to be transcribed, so the fact that the prior statement was made at all will be easier to prove. Both sides to the debate over FRE 801(d)(1)(A), reported in the Advisory Committee Note, also used arguments about the reliability of prior inconsistent statements. The requirements of oath and of being made at a hearing were intended to increase the trustworthiness of the statement. Speaking under oath may reduce sincerity danger; speaking at a formal hearing may positively impact the declarant's narration and sincerity. As we have said before, admitting hearsay for such reasons of increased trustworthiness is typical under the hearsay exceptions.

c. Prior Inconsistent Statements Not Within FRE 801(d)(1)(A)

At common law, any prior inconsistent statement could be admitted, but only as nonhearsay to impeach the testifying witness, not for its truth. Today, an allegedly inconsistent statement that does not fit within FRE 801(d)(1)(A) may still be admitted just to show that the witness has said inconsistent things and should not be relied on. The use of prior inconsistent statements for this impeachment purpose is discussed in Chapter Seven.

4.   Interpretation and Illustration of FRE 801(d)(1)(B): Prior Consistent Statements

a.   Preliminary Factfinding

In our previous example, Joe might have told the police the license plate number of the car involved in the crime or tort and then testified to this same number at trial. The statement to the police could be admissible for its truth as a prior consistent statement if the requirements of FRE(d)(1)(B) are satisfied. These requirements are:

> the contents of the statement are consistent with testimony given at trial; and the statement is offered to rebut a charge of recent fabrication or improper influence or motive.

The consistency of Joe's two statements would be apparent. If there are doubts about consistency, the preliminary question would be decided similarly to the question of inconsistency, discussed above.

    i.   A Charge of Recent Fabrication or Improper Influence or Motive.   It seems obvious that parties would find it advantageous to present their witnesses' prior consistent statements to the jury for their truth. But FRE 801(d)(1)(B) applies only if the credibility of the testifying witness has been attacked in the particular way spelled out in the rule. Proof of such attack will be apparent to the judge from the opponent's cross-examination of the witness or from the admission of other impeaching evidence, and prior consistent statements should not be admitted for their truth until such an attack has actually occurred. The kinds of impeachment techniques that qualify as charges of *recent fabrication or improper influence or motive* are analyzed in Chapter Seven. A common example of a motive to fabricate arises in criminal cases where confederates of the defendant negotiate a plea bargain and then testify against the defendant. The defense will seek to impeach such witnesses with the suggestion that they have received favorable treatment from the government in exchange for testimony inculpating the defendant. United States v. Campbell, 2000 U.S. App. LEXIS 27403, *12 (6th Cir. 2000) (defense counsel's cross-examination of the witness accused her of falsely implicating the defendant in order to qualify for a sentence reduction under the terms of her plea agreement).

    ii.   To "Rebut" the Charge.   In Tome v. United States, 513 U.S. 150 (1995), the question was raised whether the consistent statement could *rebut* the charge of improper influence or motive, as required by Rule 801(d)(1)(B), only if it was made *prior* to the date at which the improper influence or motive allegedly arose. In *Tome*, a child witness testified in court about acts of sexual assault by her father. After cross-examination, several of her prior statements making the same accusations were then admitted under FRE 801(d)(1)(B) to rebut the implicit charge that the child's in-court testimony was fabricated and was motivated by a desire to live with her mother. These out-of-court accusations had been made, however, *after* the child's motive to fabricate arose; that is, *after* primary custody had been awarded to the father. The Supreme Court majority held that the prior accusations did not, therefore, fall within the meaning of *rebut* under subsection (B). The majority reasoned first that the term meant rebutting a specific charge, not just bolstering credibility:

> [T]he question is whether A.T.'s out-of-court statements rebutted the alleged link between her desire to be with her mother and her testimony, not whether they suggested that A.T.'s in-court testimony was true. The Rule speaks of a party rebutting an alleged motive, not bolstering the veracity of the story told. [Id. at 157-158.]

The majority noted that this same common law meaning of "to rebut" had been adopted by the Advisory Committee in its Note to FRE 801(d)(1)(B), limiting the scope of subsection (B) to statements made *before* the motive to fabricate arose. Only pre-motive statements could *rebut* an improper motive because their consistency would show that the in-court testimony was not tainted by that motive. Four dissenting justices read the term *rebut* as raising a relevance issue rather than a rigid pre-motive timing requirement. In their view, not only pre-motive but some post-motive consistent statements might be relevant to rebut a charge of recent fabrication or improper influence or motive, and should be admitted under the rule.

Cases decided since *Tome* raise the question as to when a motive to fabricate arises. When several persons are complicit in a crime, each may seek to cooperate with the government in order to receive more lenient treatment. Typically, cooperation involves giving incriminating testimony against others. Does the motive to fabricate arise at the time of arrest? United States v. Trujillo, 376 F.3d 593, 611 (6th Cir. 2004) (it is not believable that "a day or two after [declarant-witnesses] were stopped with more than fifty kilograms of marijuana in their car and were subsequently arrested, they did not have a motive to lie, regarding the source of the marijuana, to get lenient treatment"). Or, not until discussions begin about what benefits, if any, are to be received in exchange for cooperation? Several Circuit Courts have refused to hold that a motive to fabricate always attaches upon arrest and require the trial court to make a finding about motive on the specific facts.

> [S]tatements made after arrest are not automatically and necessarily contaminated by a motive to fabricate in order to curry favor with the government. Indeed, we recognize that a variety of motives may drive a person's decision to disgorge the details of a crime he has committed . . .
>
> But given the complexity of the human psyche, we agree with the Fourth, Seventh, and Eighth Circuits that whether a witness had a motive to fabricate when prior consistent statements were made is plainly a question of fact to be resolved by the trial court based precisely on the particular circumstances of an individual case. Quite simply, the trial court is in the best position to make that determination and its determination deserves great deference. [United States v. Prieto, 232 F.3d 816, 820-821 (11th Cir. 2000).]

Do you think factfinding about the motives of the human psyche is possible? Would a bright line legal rule about when a motive to fabricate will be held to have arisen be preferable?

b. Justification for the FRE 801(d)(1)(B) Limitation

At common law, it was clear that only consistent statements made *before* the motive to fabricate arose were admissible. Broader admissibility, it was thought, would create a risk of admitting manufactured consistent statements, and could unfairly surprise the opponent. The majority in *Tome* adopted this common law justification and relied heavily on the intent of the Advisory Committee as expressed in its Note to Rule 801(d)(1)(B) in doing so.

c.   Prior Consistent Statements Not Within FRE 801(d)(1)(B)

Consistent statements that do not fall within FRE 801(d)(1)(B) may still be relevant to bolster credibility on other grounds. They are, however, not admissible for their truth. In Chapter Seven, we discussed whether or not prior consistent statements not within FRE 801(d)(1)(B) are admissible not for their truth but for the nonhearsay purpose of bolstering the witness.

5.   Interpretation and Illustration of FRE 801(d)(1)(C): Prior Statements of Identification

a.   Preliminary Factfinding

In our lineup example, now assume that Joe identified Sam at the lineup as the perpetrator of the crime or tort and also identified Sam when testifying in court. Statements identifying a person are admitted under FRE 801(d)(1)(C) without any necessary predicate testimony from the declarant-witness that is consistent or inconsistent with the out-of-court identification. The foundational requirements are:

- the statement is one of identification of a person; and
- the statement was made after the declarant perceived that person.

You can see that these foundation requirements are minimal. Joe's identification of either Sam or Peter at the lineup clearly qualifies. Indeed, the statement may be made in contexts other than lineups, and no oath is required. Thus FRE 801(d)(1)(C) adds to what may be admitted under (A) and (B). A prior identification that is *consistent* with in-court testimony (Joe's identification of Sam) can be admitted without proof of an express or implied charge of recent fabrication or improper influence or motive. In fact, the prosecution can ask Joe about his lineup identification of Sam even before Joe makes an in-court identification, and even if Joe has forgotten the underlying event and cannot make an in-court identification at all. If a pretrial identification is *inconsistent* with in-court testimony (Joe's identification of Peter), it can be admitted even if not admissible under FRE 801(d)(1)(A) because not made under oath or at a hearing. The jury as fact finder determines the accuracy of an out-of-court identification. The inability or hesitancy of a witness to make an in-court identification, recantation of a prior identification, or discrepancies in the descriptions given of the person identified, are all "customary grist for the jury mill." Manson v. Braithwaite, 432 U.S. 98, 116 (1977).

   i.   Made After Perceiving a Person.   According to the Advisory Committee Note, FRE 801(d)(1)(C) was intended to include statements of identification made at traditional lineups and show ups. The declarant would be reperceiving the person whom the declarant had seen previously committing a crime or participating in some other disputed event. But the language used in the rule is not limited to *reperceptions at lineups*. Subsection (C) has been interpreted very broadly to include statements that identify a person seen after the disputed event in a chance encounter; that identify the photograph of the person; and that identify a police artist sketch of the person. It has also been held to permit the admission of hearsay statements that identify people (for example in surveillance photos) who are known to the declarant, but when the declarant did not perceive the underlying disputed event.

The Third Circuit has held that a statement to police, made on the day after a series of home invasions in a neighborhood, that the witness "had seen three of the defendants in the area of the crime during the time the homes were invaded" was admissible under FRE 802(d)(1)(C). United States v. Lopez, 271 F.3d 472, 485 (3rd Cir. 2001). This statement was made without reperception of the defendants, and was acknowledged by the court to be simply "a person coming forward after a crime is committed and saying he saw particular persons at a certain place and time." This "Lopez rule" was rejected and, in our view, soundly criticized as contrary to the meaning of "identification" as used in Rule 801(d)(1)(C), which requires designation of a particular person (or photo) as being the same as the person previously perceived, and as allowing admission of out-of-court accusations of crimes as substantive evidence with no particular indicia of reliability. United States v. Kaquatosh, 242 F. Supp. 2d 562, 566-567 (E.D.Wis. 2003).

A similar split in authority exists as to whether a physical description of a person given by the declarant to the police, also without any reperception of the person, fits within FRE 801(d)(1)(C). United States v. Brink, 39 F.3d 419 (3d Cir. 1994) (admitting bank teller's statement to police, on the day following a bank robbery, that the robber had dark-colored eyes); Puryear v. State, 810 So.2d 901 (Fla. 2002) (excluding robbery victim's statement to police that assailant was a black male, missing every other tooth, and had body odor). Statements of accusation and description are frequently admitted under the hearsay exceptions for spontaneous and excited statements under FRE 803(1) and (2), which we discuss on pages 493-500, infra. If they are admitted instead under FRE 801(d)(1)(C), it is without any of the requirements of spontaneity and stress that those exceptions impose, although the declarant must testify as a witness and be subject to cross-examination. Whether such statements are "testimonial" and whether they are subject to exclusion in criminal trials under the Confrontation Clause as interpreted by *Crawford v. Washington* is discussed in Section G, infra.

ii. Identification of a Person. As drafted, subsection (C) appears to be limited to statements about the physical characteristics of persons. Why should identifications of persons but not, for example, automobiles be admissible? If that seems too far an extension of the exemption, what about descriptions of the clothing worn by the person? The answer to how narrowly or broadly to construe the language of subsection (C) lies in the justification for the admission of prior statements identifying people. In gray areas, one should be able to state the reasons for the exemption and argue by analogy for exclusion or admission of a particular piece of evidence.

b. Justifications for the Admissibility of Prior Statements of Identification

Remember that the basic justification for the FRE 801(d)(1) exemptions is the opportunity to cross-examine the witness-declarant. But since *all* prior statements are not admitted, why are prior statements of identification included within the exemption?

Subsection (C) is justified by the *need* for prior identification testimony. Although it applies to both civil and criminal actions, this exemption is of primary benefit to prosecutors in criminal proceedings. The Advisory Committee Note describes identifications made in court as "unsatisfactory and inconclusive . . . as compared with those made at an earlier time under less suggestive conditions." In some cases, the prosecutor's use of the prior statement of identification for its truth may be essential to avoid a directed verdict of acquittal. Some witnesses may have genuinely lost the ability to make an in-court identification, as occurred in the *Owens* case discussed at page 458, supra. In this situation, neither a prior inconsistent nor a prior consistent statement would be admissible without subsection (C). There is also a risk that a prosecution witness may testify falsely at trial because of intimidation or threats to self or family members. The categorical approach to admission, however, does not permit such a case-by-case assessment of need. If the out-of-court statement satisfies the categorical requirements, it is admissible. Would a case-by-case evaluation of need be a good idea?

It is not clear that the reliability of the declarant's testimonial qualities are enhanced by the subsection (C) foundational requirements. The out-of-court statement may be more reliable because it was made closer in time to the event in which the person identified participated. On the other hand, an oath is not required, the setting may be quite informal, and no circumstance decreases the risk of improper motive for making the identification. Moreover, when the statement is made in the context of a police-arranged lineup, neither the witness nor even the police officers who arranged for the identification may have been aware of possible subtle suggestive factors that could have influenced it. Studies have demonstrated that individuals' memories fade quickly. For an excellent summary of the psychological data bearing on the reliability of eyewitness identification testimony, see Brian L. Cutler and Steven D. Penrod, Mistaken Identifications: The Eyewitness, Psychology, and the Law (1995). Thus the argument for the admission of prior identifications is strongest with respect to identifications made soon after the perception of the person identified. Would it be desirable to amend subsection (C) to provide that the statement of identification must be made "soon" or "shortly" after the witness perceived the person identified?

We asked above whether items of clothing or objects should be included within subsection (C). The necessity justification just articulated is most compelling for identification of persons. In addition, the requirements of subsections (A) and (B) have been interpreted quite narrowly, evincing judicial concern that *all* prior statements of testifying witnesses not be admitted wholesale, which is what would happen if subsection (C) were broadened. The words *identification of a person* should, given this concern, be regarded as a serious substantive limitation on the scope of FRE 801(d)(1)(C).

c.   *Constitutional Concerns*

In addition to the hearsay issue, there is a substantial body of case law that focuses on whether a prior identification violated a criminal defendant's constitutional right to counsel or due process of law. See, e.g., Gilbert v. California, 388 U.S. 263 (1967) (criminal defendant has right to counsel at postindictment confrontation between witness and defendant; denial of right to counsel requires exclusion of pretrial identification evidence); Manson v. Brathwaite, 432 U.S. 98 (1977) (due process requires exclusion of unnecessarily suggestive pretrial identification if identification is likely to be unreliable).

KEY POINTS

1. The prior out-of-court statement of a testifying witness may be admitted for the truth of the matter it asserts if it is (A) inconsistent with the witness's testimony, (B) consistent with the witness's testimony and rebuts a charge of recent fabrication or improper influence or motive, or (C) a statement of identification of a person, made after perceiving that person.

2. The judge must be persuaded, pursuant to FRE 104(a), that the foundational requirements are satisfied prior to admitting the statements.

3. The witness must be subject to cross-examination concerning the statement by answering questions willingly; the witness need not necessarily remember the underlying event or making the prior statement.

PROBLEMS

8.32. Esther Kingsley and Robert Roby were riding in a car that crossed the median strip on a two-lane highway and collided with a pickup truck driven by William Burditt. Esther was killed in the crash and the executor of her estate is suing Robert for wrongful death, alleging that he was driving the car and that his negligence caused the accident. Robert claims that Esther was driving and that the accident was her fault.

(a) Several hours after the accident, William Burditt told a state trooper that "a man was driving." Two days later Burditt told a friend "the woman was not driving the car." Called by the plaintiff executor to testify at trial, Burditt testifies "I have a picture in my mind that the woman was behind the wheel. It seems when we hit, she was on the driver's side." Can the plaintiff use Burditt's prior statements to prove that Robert was driving? To impeach Burditt's credibility? If there is no other evidence that Robert was driving, will the judge grant a directed verdict against the plaintiff?

(b) What if Burditt's deposition had been taken by plaintiff and Burditt said "a man was driving" — admissible? For what purpose?

(c) What if there was no deposition but Burditt had previously submitted a sworn affidavit that said "a man was driving" in support of plaintiff's motion for summary judgment against Robert? Admissible? For what purpose?

(d) Assume that the statements in (a) are admitted to impeach Burditt. Plaintiff also asks Burditt: "Isn't it true that Robert paid you for the extensive damage done to your truck in the collision, just a week before this trial?" Burditt answers "Yes." Relevant? Admissible?

(e) Assume that the evidence in (d) is admitted. Robert then offers the testimony of Burditt's coworker that, on the day before the trial started, Burditt said: "You know, I think that it was the woman driving." Relevant? Admissible?

(f)   Assume that two *men* — Edwin and Robert — were in the car that collided with Burditt's truck. Edwin was killed in the crash and his estate sues Robert for wrongful death, claiming that Robert was driving. Robert says that Edwin was driving. Plaintiff offers testimony that Burditt said to a state trooper, just after the accident, "that man there was driving" and then pointed at Robert. Admissible? For what purpose?

(g)   Same facts as (f). What if, several days after the accident, Burditt said to a friend, "It was the man with black hair and the blue jacket who was driving." (Robert has black hair and was wearing a blue jacket on the day of the accident.)

8.33 Return to Problem 3.3 at page 131, United States v. Ray. On direct examination, Beth Barker testifies for the prosecution that she remembers placing the March 14, 2004 auditor's memo in Ray's in box on March 14, 2004, and removing it the next day from his out box, and that Ray's initials were on the memo. On cross-examination, defense counsel asks the following:

(a)   Q.   Ms. Barker, you testified at a preliminary hearing in this case, did you not?
      A.   Yes.
      Q.   And I asked you some questions at that time, do you recall that?
      A.   Yes.
      Q.   Isn't it true that I asked you the following questions, and you gave the following answers: [reading from transcript]
           "Q.   Ms Barker, of all the hundreds of pieces of mail and memos that you have placed in Mr. Ray's in box, do you specifically remember the March 14, 2004 memo from Rundown's auditor?
            A.   Well, no, not specifically."

Is Barker's answer from the preliminary hearing transcript admissible over the prosecutor's hearsay objection?

(b)   Defense counsel next offers Exhibit B into evidence, an authenticated written statement of Beth Barker dated December 19, 2004, which states (in pertinent part):

I, Beth Barker, declare:

I have removed hundreds of documents from Bernard Ray's in box in the years I worked as his secretary. I do not have a specific recollection of the March 14, 2004 auditor's memo.

I declare under penalty of perjury that the foregoing is true and correct to the best of my knowledge.

[signed] Beth Barker

Is this written statement admissible over the prosecutor's hearsay objection?

(c)   On cross examination, defense counsel asks Barker the following questions:

> Q.   Ms. Barker, on August 12, 2005, you were arrested for embezzling $250
> from a petty cash fund, while employed at Rundown?
> A.   Yes.
> Q.   And that alleged embezzlement occurred on August 5, isn't that so?
> A.   I believe so.
> Q.   Ms. Barker, isn't it a fact that you made up this story about removing the
> March 14, 2004, auditor's memo, with Mr. Ray's initials on it, from Mr.
> Ray's out box on March 15 in order to get a deal from the prosecutor on
> your embezzlement charge?
> A.   No, that's not true.
> DEFENSE COUNSEL: I have no further questions.

On redirect, the prosecutor offers in evidence an authenticated written statement of Beth Barker dated June 30, 2005, stating that "I recall removing the March 14, 2004 auditor's memo from Mr. Ray's out box on March 15, 2004. It had Mr. Ray's initials on it, and I filed it." Is the statement admissible over defense counsel's hearsay objection?

8.34. Ed Larson is being prosecuted for armed robbery of a bank. Terry Davis, an alleged accomplice, pleaded guilty to the same charge and is currently serving a 20-year sentence. Davis admitted that he was involved in the robbery, but he claimed that he could not remember whether he had a partner or, if he did have one, who the partner might have been. He also claimed not to remember ever having made a statement to anyone about having a partner. To prove that Larson committed the robbery with Davis the prosecutor offers (a) a transcript of Davis's grand jury testimony describing Larson's participation in the robbery and (b) the testimony of a police officer to the effect that following Davis's arrest several days after the robbery, he confessed to the crime and named Larson as his accomplice. The defendant has objected to both pieces of evidence. What result?

8.35. Larry Emerson is being tried for arson. The government's key witness, Alice Hastings, testified under a grant of immunity that she had cooperated with Larry in planning the arson, but then had withdrawn from the scheme. On cross-examination, defense counsel inquired about promises made to Hastings in return for her testimony and suggested that she was testifying against Emerson in order to shift responsibility for the crime from herself. The government then calls a police officer who was present at Hastings's arrest to testify that Hastings voluntarily began talking to the police; that she did not ask any questions about what benefits she might obtain; that another officer informed Hastings that her cooperation would be brought to the attention of the District Attorney; and that before any other statements about cooperation were made, Hastings identified Larry Emerson as the arsonist. Is this testimony admissible under FRE 801(d)(1)(B)?

6.   Interpretation and Illustration of FRE 801(d)(2): Party Admissions in General

Each subsection of FRE 801(d)(2) defines a specific type of out-of-court statement made by a declarant who is either a party in the case or has a particular type of affiliation with a party. The foundational requirements of subsections (A)-(E) focus primarily on the relationship between the party and the declarant. The single common requirement for all the subsections is that the proponent must offer the declarant's statement *against* the opposing party. It is the proponent's choice whether or not to use an opposing party's own statements, or statements of affiliates, to prove the case *against* that party at trial.

Before we discuss each FRE 801(d)(2) subsection in detail, you should read through them all again briefly:

> (d) Statements which are not hearsay. A statement is not hearsay if —
> (2) Admission by party-opponent. The statement is offered against a party and is (A) the party's own statement, in either an individual or a representative capacity or (B) a statement of which the party has manifested an adoption or belief in its truth, or (C) a statement by a person authorized by the party to make a statement concerning the subject, or (D) a statement by the party's agent or servant concerning a matter within the scope of the agency or employment, made during the existence of the relationship, or (E) a statement by a coconspirator of a party during the course and in furtherance of the conspiracy. The contents of the statement shall be considered but are not alone sufficient to establish the declarant's authority under subdivision (C), the agency or employment relationship and scope thereof under subdivision (D), or the existence of the conspiracy and the participation of the declarant and the party against whom the statement is offered under subdivision (E).

We will use the following example to illustrate subsections (A)-(E):

> Suppose that Day and Moore are partners in a business. They are being tried jointly for preparing and filing a false partnership income tax return in 1999. The government's evidence tends to show that Day and Moore diverted income from the partnership to themselves by cashing checks made out to the partnership. The government claims that Day and Moore did not account for the proceeds in either the partnership or their own income tax returns. At trial, Moore testifies in his own defense and denies all knowledge of and participation in such a scheme. The government then seeks to introduce against both Day and Moore a properly authenticated tape recording of a statement that Moore made, unbeknownst to Day, in an interview with an Internal Revenue Service agent who was investigating the 1999 partnership return. Moore's recorded statement implicates both Day and Moore in the income diversion and tax evasion scheme. It was not made under oath, however, and would not be admissible as a prior inconsistent statement under FRE 801(d)(1)(A).

Would Moore's recorded statement be admissible against Moore under FRE 801(d)(2)(A)? Would it be admissible against Day? Would the statement be admissible against Day under FRE 801(d)(2)(B), (C), (D), or (E)? If you can fit the statement under (A) against Moore, or under (B), (C), (D), or (E) against Day, then although it is offered for the truth of the matter it asserts — that Moore and Day both participated in the illegal scheme to file a false tax return — it will be exempt from the definition of hearsay and will be admissible as substantive evidence for its truth.

7. Interpretation and Illustration of FRE 801(d)(2)(A): A Party's Own Statements

a. *Preliminary Factfinding*

The foundational requirements for a party admission are:

- the statement is made by a party; and
- the statement is offered against that party.

This is perhaps the simplest foundation of all the hearsay exemptions and exceptions. Moore's recorded statement easily satisfies it, so long as it is offered against Moore himself. *Any* out-of-court statement made in *any* context by *any* party (whether plaintiff or defendant) to *any* action (whether civil or criminal) may be admissible, unless otherwise objectionable, if offered *against* that party. In Jewell v. CSX Transportation, Inc., 135 F.3d 361, 364-365 (6th Cir. 1998), the statement of a six-year-old plaintiff, made after she had suffered brain damage when the car in which she was riding was hit by a train, was admitted to prove that the car's driver had not been keeping a proper lookout. The court stated that "[t]rustworthiness is not a separate requirement for admission under FRE 801(d)(2)(A)." Id. at 365.

The party's statement must of course be relevant and not subject to exclusion under other rules of evidence. Guilty pleas, depositions, personal documents, and prepared charts, as well as conversational oral statements, have all been admitted for their truth under FRE 801(d)(2)(A). Trull v. Volkswagen of America, Inc., 187 F.3d 88, 98 (1st Cir. 1999) (plaintiffs' diagram from a prior lawsuit, showing a different version of the collision in question, was admitted against them in their suit against the manufacturer of their van). If a party's nonverbal conduct is hearsay under FRE 801(a) because it is intended as an assertion, it is a statement for the purposes of this or any other hearsay exception or exemption. A nod of assent in response to an incriminating question, for example, would be admissible as an admission against a defendant in a subsequent prosecution.

If a proponent offers a Rule 801(d)(2)(A) statement *against* a party at trial, the proponent must think that the statement is adverse to the interest of that party. For this reason, party admissions are sometimes referred to as "admissions against interest." We strongly urge you to avoid the phrase "admission against interest." First, the foundational requirements for the admissions exemption *do not require that the statement be "against interest" when it is made, nor that the person making the statement think that it is.* Sometimes a party's statement attains its "against interest" significance long after it is made. Second, as you will see, there is a completely distinct exception to the hearsay rule for "declarations against interest." Getting used to referring to admissions simply as admissions should help to avoid confusion between declarations against interest and admissions.

b. *Individual and Representative Capacity*

FRE 801(d)(2)(A) controls the admission of statements made by an individual person that are offered against that same individual person at trial. But a person can speak, and can be a party, either as an individual or as a representative — a trustee, executor, or guardian — of some other entity or individual. The rule provides for the admission of statements against the individual person even if those statements were made when the individual was speaking as a representative outside of court. In re Special Federal Grand Jury Empanelled Oct. 31, 1985 Impounded, 819 F.2d 56, 59 (3d Cir. 1987) (statements made to a grand jury solely in the declarant's capacity as an agent for a corporation could be admissible against him as an individual). And statements made outside of court by a person, whether as an individual or as a representative, will be admissible against that person if he appears as a party solely in a representative capacity. Estate of Shafer v. Commissioner, 749 F.2d 1216, 1219 (6th Cir. 1984) (letter written by son of a decedent admissible against him as coexecutor of his father's estate, whether it was written by the son as an individual or in his capacity as executor). When an entity such as a corporation is a party, the statements of its representatives can be admitted against the entity under FRE 801(d)(2)(C) or (D), but not pursuant to FRE 801(d)(2)(A), as we will discuss at pages 479-480, infra.

c.   Admissions, Personal Knowledge, and Lay Opinions

In two respects the admissions exemption operates differently from other hearsay exceptions. First, there is *no* requirement that a party admission be based on first-hand knowledge. This is in contrast to all other hearsay exceptions and Rule 801(d)(1) statements. The Advisory Committee Note to FRE 801(d)(2)(a) states that admissions of a party-opponent are free from "the restrictive influences of the opinion rule and the rule requiring first hand knowledge. . . ." McCormick offers the following justification for dispensing with the personal knowledge requirement for a party's own admissions:

> [T]he vast majority of admissions that become relevant in litigation concern some matter of substantial importance to declarants upon which they would likely have informed themselves, and as a result, such admissions possess greater reliability than the general run of hearsay, even when not based on firsthand observation. Moreover, the possibility is substantial that the declarant may have significant information that the opponent cannot prove. [McCormick on Evidence Vol. 2 §255, at 140 (John W. Strong, ed., 5th ed. 1999).]

Do you find this justification convincing? Is there some other justification for dispensing with the requirement? Would the proponent of the admission find it easy to prove what a party opponent knows without using the party's out-of-court statements?

Second, courts have tended to be liberal in admitting statements of opinion if the evidence is an admission. Since the party against whom an admission is offered can take the witness stand and explain the basis for the opinion, declining to exclude the lay opinion rule in this context seems reasonable. Combining freedom from the personal knowledge requirement and the lay opinion rule means that a party's admissions may be based on hearsay statements of others, or the party's inferences from circumstances. Should the lay opinion rule be applied to statements falling within hearsay exceptions? Since these declarants must have personal knowledge of the contents of their statements, the only "lay opinion" objection to these statements would be the use of conclusory language. If a witness offers opinions and conclusions on the stand, it is possible to elicit more factual specificity. By contrast, there is no guarantee that the hearsay declarant will be available to testify about the facts underlying the opinion. Thus sustaining a lay opinion objection to otherwise admissible hearsay may deprive the jury completely of relevant information.

8.   Elaboration of FRE 801(d)(2)(A): Justifications for the Admissibility of Party Admissions

As you can see from the breadth of Rule 801(d)(2)(A), the justification for its admissibility cannot rest on a claim of enhanced reliability. There are no limitations in the rule concerning the content of the out-of-court statement or the circumstances in which it was made. We emphasize again that it need not have been "against interest" when made. Instead, all five of the subsections of FRE 801(d)(2) are justified by considerations relating to the adversarial system of trial and to values of freedom of choice and personal responsibility in our larger society. These considerations operate most powerfully as justifications for the admissibility of a party's own statements under subsection (A). As we will see in succeeding sections of this chapter, these justifications become less powerful as the relationship between the party and the declarant becomes weaker. Then circumstances that may increase the need for or the reliability of the out-of-court statement are added to the foundational requirements of each subsection.

a. The Opportunity to Explain

The traditional rationale for permitting statements of a party to be used against that party for their truth is straightforward and related directly to the adversarial rationale for the hearsay rule: Hearsay is excluded primarily because the opponent lacks the opportunity to expose weaknesses in the declarant's narration, sincerity, perception, and memory through cross-examination. In civil cases, however, a party to an action cannot reasonably complain about the lack of an opportunity for self-cross-examination, for there is a viable alternative. The party can take the stand on direct examination and have a full opportunity to explain any difficulties with the party's own sincerity, narration, perception, or memory when the statement was made. In short, it seems absurd for a party who is directly affected by the outcome in the case, and who is sitting in the courtroom, to complain about not being able to cross-examine herself.

b. Fifth Amendment Concerns

In criminal cases, while it is true that the criminal defendant has the same right as any other litigant to testify, it is also true that the criminal defendant has the Fifth Amendment right to refuse to testify. Admitting a criminal defendant's statements under FRE 801(d)(2)(A) may put some pressure on the defendant to abandon that right.

Perhaps a sufficient answer to this concern is to note that any number of factors may make a defendant feel pressured to testify, and only some of these factors raise constitutional problems. At one extreme, a direct threat of punishment for refusing to testify would be regarded as a violation of the Fifth Amendment right not to testify. A defendant, however, may feel pressure to testify simply because of the nature or strength of the prosecutor's case, and this type of pressure does not raise constitutional problems. In any event, it is well settled that the FRE 801(d)(2)(A) exemption applies to criminal defendants as well as to all other parties to actions.

c. Responsibility for One's Own Statements and Fairness

Professors Lempert, Gross, and Liebman offer a moral responsibility rationale for the admissions exception:

> The law recognizes in the hearsay rule the fact that people do not always speak the truth, but recognizing this does not mean that parties before the court will be assumed to have failed in their moral duty to tell the truth or be relieved of the responsibility for their actions if they have failed. [Richard O. Lempert, Samuel R. Gross, and James Liebman, A Modern Approach to Evidence 537 (3d ed. 2000).]

Consider whether this is a viable theory. Even if one concedes that there are general and generally accepted moral norms of personal accountability and honesty, do they extend to mandating that a litigant's statements be used to work a legal deprivation against the litigant? Why should somebody who perhaps quite unwillingly becomes a litigant be required to shoulder this particular responsibility?

One answer might be based on the norms of fairness in a free society. People who choose to speak usually do so in their own self-interest. The party's own out-of-court statement presumably served that party's interest when it was made. Moreover, others may have taken action in reliance on the statement. There is a common law notion of fairness, enforced as a principle of estoppel, that operates to prevent people from switching positions they have taken cost-free. With benefits come burdens. A party is not irrevocably bound by a prior out-of-court statement if the party later wants to claim that it was inaccurate. But the party at least has to account for it when it is offered against him in court. This is a minimal burden.

Adversarial fairness is also a justification for admitting party admissions. The proponent may want to use as evidence what the opponent knows about the facts that are in dispute. But the civil party may not want to call the opponent to the witness stand during the case-in-chief. The civil plaintiff, for example, cannot prepare the defendant as a witness, thus what the defendant might say is unknown and could be harmful. And, of course, the prosecutor *cannot* call the criminal defendant to the stand because of the Fifth Amendment. Offering the opponent's hearsay statements thus may be the fairest way — and in a criminal case the only way, thus adding the element of necessity — for the proponent to prove what the opposing party knows.

9.   Further Elaboration of FRE 801(d)(2)(A)

a.   Preliminary Factfinding on the Identity of the Declarant

The foundational requirements for all hearsay exceptions and exemptions are preliminary questions of fact subject to FRE 104, and are typically for the judge to decide pursuant to FRE 104(a). These requirements are imposed by hearsay policy; they do not establish the relevance of the out-of-court statement. But consider a case in which relevancy and hearsay policy are determined by the same question of fact. Suppose that it is alleged that the defendant started a fight with a coworker. The defendant denies starting the fight. What if the coworker had previously received an unsigned letter expressing great animosity toward the coworker? The coworker claims that the defendant wrote this letter and that the animosity is relevant to prove that defendant started the fight. The defendant denies sending the letter. Since the letter is hearsay, the coworker offers it under FRE 801(d)(2)(A) against the defendant. Should FRE 104(a) or (b) control the judge's factfinding on whether the defendant wrote the letter?

In this case, this same fact is necessary both to the relevance (and authentication) of the letter under FRE 401 and to the admissibility of the hearsay statement under FRE 801(d)(2)(A). FRE 104(b) governs the relevance question; FRE 104(a) governs the hearsay policy question. Which should control? The difference between them would be that under FRE 104(b), the judge would have to admit the letter with less foundational evidence — only evidence sufficient to support a finding — that the defendant wrote it. Under FRE 104(a), the judge should admit the letter only if the judge is actually persuaded by a preponderance of the evidence that the defendant wrote it.

In this example, the letter *can only be relevant and harmful* to the defendant if the defendant in fact wrote it. If the defendant did not write the letter, the animosity it expresses *could not* rationally be used in a way that is harmful to the defendant. Therefore, since the Federal Rules of Evidence favor greater admissibility of relevant evidence, it would seem that the question should be decided under Rule 104(b) as a matter of relevance policy. It would be much easier for the coworker to meet the FRE 104(b) standard and to get the letter admitted than if FRE 104(a) were to apply. Of course, the defendant can still deny being the author and the jury will ultimately decide the question. The crucial point is that if the jury finds that it was not written by the defendant, we are fairly confident that the jury can disregard the letter as irrelevant

What if a second letter contained facts that would be harmful to the defendant even if he were not the author? For example, the letter might state that many people, including the defendant, hate the coworker. It has been argued that when the contents of the out-of-court statement could be relevant and harmful to a party, *even if not made by that party but by another person*, the judge should decide whether it was the defendant's own statement under FRE 104(a) as a matter of hearsay policy. Norman M. Garland and Jay A. Schmitz, Of Judges and Juries: A Proposed Revision of Federal Rule of Evidence 104, 23 U.C. Davis L. Rev. 77, 112-115 (1989). If the defendant's authorship of the second letter is left to the jury to decide under FRE 104(b), there would be a risk that the jury *could* rationally use its contents against the defendant even though the jury decided that the defendant was not the author. This would violate FRE 801(d)(2)(A) and hearsay policy. If instead the judge applies FRE 104(a), and was persuaded under the preponderance standard that the second letter was from the defendant, there would be more foundational proof, thus more certainty, that the defendant is the author. Thus the jury will be more likely to get the authorship issue right, and hearsay policy will be better served if it then uses the contents of the letter against the defendant. The first hypothetical letter written to the coworker does not require application of the higher standard of FRE 104(a) because its contents have no relevance for the coworker's case against the defendant unless it was authored by the defendant.

b.   *Admissibility of Party Admissions in Multiparty Cases: The Bruton Problem*

In some cases, there are multiple plaintiffs or defendants. One party's party admission is not admissible against anyone other than the party who made the statement. In Bruton v. United States, 391 U.S. 123 (1968), Bruton and Evans were tried jointly for armed robbery. Evans did not testify but was in court. The prosecution introduced into evidence an earlier confession by Evans that implicated both Evans and Bruton. Since the confession was admissible as a party admission only against Evans, the trial court instructed the jury that it could consider the confession as evidence only against Evans. Because Evans did not testify in his own defense, Bruton could not cross-examine him. The Supreme Court, relying in part on the probable inability of the jury to limit its consideration of the confession to Evans, held that introduction of the confession had violated Bruton's confrontation right. Thus whenever one declarant-defendant's confession implicates another codefendant, *Bruton* may preclude admission unless the declarant-defendant can be cross-examined.

Another way to accommodate the *Bruton* problem is to sever the trials of the codefendants. This, however, is an expensive remedy and prosecutors have sought other solutions. If all specific references to the codefendant are redacted from the declarant-defendant's statement, it may then be offered only against the declarant-defendant. In Richardson v. Marsh, 481 U.S. 200 (1987) the declarant-defendant's confession, as read to the jury, omitted any reference to Marsh or indeed to the presence of anyone else when the charged crime was planned. The jury was also instructed not to use the confession in considering Marsh's guilt or innocence. The Supreme Court held that confessions redacted in this manner did not fall within the *Bruton* rule and were admissible in a joint trial. Confessions redacted by substituting a single codefendant's name with blank spaces or symbols have been held to be incriminating of the codefendant and inadmissible under *Bruton*. Gray v. Maryland, 523 U.S. 185 (1998). Substitution of names with neutral pronouns such as "other guys" or "persons" has been held not to incriminate specific codefendants when there are several of them, and therefore not to violate *Bruton*. United States v. Molina, 407 F.3d 511 (1st Cir. 2005).

10. Interpretation and Illustration of FRE 801(d)(2)(B): Adoptive Admissions

a. Preliminary Factfinding

The foundational requirements for an adoptive admission are:

- a statement has been made;
- the party has done something to manifest adoption of it or to show belief in its truth; and
- the statement is offered against the party.

Under FRE 801(d)(2)(B), there is no limitation on who may make the statement that is subsequently offered against a party. It is thus not an exemption based on a relationship between the declarant and the party. Rather, it is based on the party's own conduct.

In the false partnership tax return example, for the government to use subsection (B) to secure the admission of Moore's recorded statement for its truth against Day, it would first have to prove that Day had heard Moore's statement or knew of it, and that he adopted it or showed that he believed it to be true. If the recording had been played to Day and he nodded "yes," or said, "That's right," the government could argue that these words satisfied the foundational requirements of subsection (B).

A party may manifest adoption of a statement in any number of ways, including through words, conduct, or silence. United States v. Jinadu, 98 F.3d 239 (6th Cir. 1996) (defendant answered "yes" during interrogation to question "you know that's China White heroin"); United States v. Pulido-Jacobo, 377 F.3d 1124, 1132 (10th Cir.

2004) (to prove truth of contents of a document, mere possession does not constitute adoption but "surrounding circumstances can tie the possessor and the document together in a meaningful way," e.g., by accepting the document and acting upon it); United States v. Joshi, 896 F.2d 1303, 1311 (11th Cir. 1990) (party nodded head after statement by another, and made a sound of agreement); Wagstaff v. Protective Apparel Corp., 760 F.2d 1074, 1078 (10th Cir. 1985) (party used for its own advantage a written statement prepared by another); Pillsbury Co. v. Cleaver-Brooks Div. of Aqua-Chem, Inc., 646 F.2d 1216, 1218 (8th Cir. 1981) (party signed statement prepared by another); United States v. Weaver, 565 F.2d 129, 135 (8th Cir. 1977) (party repeated statement of another). If ambiguous, the meaning of a party's behavior is ultimately for the jury to assess, but it has been held that the proponent must present evidence that the party heard, understood, and acquiesced in the statement. United States v. Datz, 61 M.J. 37, 42 (Ct.App.A.F.2005) (questions put to defendant during interrogation were so ambiguous that government did not demonstrate that defendant understood and acquiesced in them). Courts appear to conflict as to whether these preliminary questions are decided pursuant to FRE 104(a) or 104(b).

b.   Justification for the Admissibility of Adoptive Admissions

If a party has adopted or manifested belief in the truth of an uncross-examined statement made by another, an inference can be drawn that the party knows that the contents of the statement are accurate, or thinks that the person speaking is reliable and knowledgeable. The party can still dispute these inferences, and the statement's accuracy, at trial. The party can explain why the statement was unreliable and why, at the time, the party did not repudiate the statement. If the party in fact knew nothing about what the statement asserted, then the party went along with it presumably to get some advantage, or induce some reliance. This makes it fair to admit the statement against the party at trial.

c.   Adoption by Silence

A common type of adoptive admission is the admission by silence. Consider, for example, the situation in United States v. Ward, 377 F.3d 671 (7th Cir. 2004), in which defendant Ward was convicted of bank robbery. Prior to trial, when Ward was released on bond, he asked his sister to give him a bag he had asked her to hold for him following the robbery. The sister said that the bag was being safeguarded by two family friends. When Ward and his sister visited the friends and asked for the bag, the friends could not locate it. Ward became upset, and his sister said to the friends that the bag was "the money they got when they robbed the bank." Ward said nothing. At Ward's trial, the sister's statement and Ward's silence,[6] were admitted against him under FRE 801(d)(2)(B). On appeal, the court held that

---

6.   If the accusation had been made by a police officer after Ward had been arrested and informed of his *Miranda* rights, the evidence would not be admissible. See Doyle v. Ohio, 426 U.S. 610 (1976) (postarrest silence following *Miranda* warnings "insolubly ambiguous;" impeachment use of such silence violates due process). It is not unconstitutional, however, to impeach a criminal defendant by asking about the defendant's prearrest failure to come forward with exculpatory evidence, Jenkins v. Anderson, 447 U.S. 231 (1980), or by asking about postarrest silence when the record does not indicate the *Miranda* warnings had been given, Fletcher v. Weir, 455 U.S. 603 (1982).

the sister's "accusation" was "the type of statement that a party normally would respond to if innocent." Id. at 676.

A problem with using nonresponsiveness or silence as the basis for an inference of a subsection (B) admission is the ambiguity of the party's conduct. What does it mean if someone fails to respond to a statement? To a letter? Or to the calculation of a bill? Ward may not have heard his sister's statement; her statement might have been a joke or a bluff; or due to surrounding circumstances, Jim might not want to say anything or might not have the usual motive to deny the statement.

These ambiguities are resolved by preliminary factfinding on the question of whether the party's conduct "manifests" adoption or belief. "[T]he burden is on the proponent to convince the judge [under FRE 104(a)] that in the circumstances...a failure to respond is so unnatural that it supports the inference that the party acquiesced in the statement." Weston-Smith v. Cooley Dickinson Hospital, Inc., 282 F.3d 60, 67 (1st Cir. 2002). The judge considers the nature of the statement, the audience, and the surrounding circumstances. For example, in *Weston-Smith*, failure to respond to an accusatory statement made at a social occasion, when the party did not have information necessary to assess the accusation's truthfulness, was held not to be an adoptive admission. Id. at 68. The court's decision calls for an evaluation of probable human behavior. The party who opposes the admissibility of the statement can of course offer evidence on the preliminary fact questions as part of the judge's fact-finding process. This evidence may be re-submitted to the jury to reduce the probative value of the statement, if it is admitted.

What if Ward had testified at his trial that he did not even hear his sister's statement? If he did not hear it, his silence could not "manifest" either adoption or belief, but the accusatory contents of the sister's statement could still be harmful to the case against him. While there is substantial case law that this preliminary question should be decided under FRE 104(b), under the analysis set forth on page 217, supra, the judge should use FRE 104(a) to decide whether there is a preponderance of the evidence that Ward actually heard his sister's statement. This preliminary fact is solely a matter of hearsay policy, not of relevancy, because evidence of the sister's statement is relevant and harmful to Ward whether or not Ward heard it.

11.   Interpretation and Illustration of FRE 801(d)(2)(C) and (D): Admissions by Agents, Servants, and Employees

a.   Preliminary Factfinding

The foundational requirements for authorized admissions under subsection (C) are:

- the statement concerns a subject;
- the statement was made by someone whom a party authorized to make a statement concerning that subject; and
- the statement is offered against that party.

In the example of the false partnership tax return, Moore's recorded statement could only be admitted against Day under subsection (C) if the government had evidence showing that Day had given Moore authority to make the recorded statement on Day's behalf. FRE 801(d)(2) also states that the contents of the statement itself may be used to prove the issue of authority (if Moore stated on the tape that Day had asked him to speak with the government about their scheme, for example) but that other independent evidence of authority is also required. The foundational requirements for admissions by agents, servants, and employees under subsection (D) focus on the existence of the agency or employee relationship and do not require any showing of authority:

- the declarant is an agent or servant (employee) of the party;
- the statement was made during this relationship;
- the statement concerns a matter within the scope of the agency or employment; and
- the statement is offered against the party.

Under subsection (D), Moore's statement might be admitted against Day if a principal-agent (or employer-employee) relationship existed between them. Partners are treated as agents of the partnership; but are partners agents of each other? This may depend on the nature of their partnership. An agency relationship is typically defined by the principal having "the right to control the manner and method in which the work is carried out by the alleged agent." Chemtool, Inc. v. Lubrication Technologies, Inc., 148 F.3d 742, 745 (7th Cir. 1998). In addition, the proponent would need to prove that the statement was made during the relationship and that it concerned a matter within Moore's duties as an agent of Day. The contents of the statement itself may be used to prove the fact of agency and the scope thereof, but the *statement alone is not sufficient* under FRE 801(d)(2). Gomez v. Rodriguez, 344 F.3d 103, 117 (1st Cir. 2003) (statement by mayor's wife that she was interviewing employment applicants for him and applying "political" criteria, held inadmissible as statement of an agent, since no independent evidence in the record supported the existence of the agency relationship).

i. Statements by Attorneys.   Many of the cases involving authorized admissions that are offered under subsection (C) concern statements made by attorneys on behalf of their clients. Statements of facts made in litigation documents — pleadings, answers to interrogatories, responses to requests for documents, briefs — and in opening and closing statements at trial may all be found to be within the scope of the attorney's authority even though there is no specific grant of authority to make the particular statement. The nature of the relationship and the specific task undertaken by the attorney or other agent who represents a party imply authority to speak on the party's behalf. Whether or not such authority exists is a preliminary question for the judge to decide under FRE 104(a).

ii. Other Specifically Authorized Statements.   Some agents would ordinarily be viewed as having authority from a party to make statements that are necessary to the performance of their duties; for example, minutes taken by the secretary at a school board would be admissible as authorized statements under FRE 801(d)(2)(C) if offered against the board. Other employees of a party may be given specific authority to speak on a one-time basis, or to speak on a topic not within their normal relationship with the party. Subsection (C) may also apply to authorized statements made by persons in relationships with the party that are not within the definition of agency, such as employer-independent contractor, or parent-child.

iii. Statements Made During the Relationship That Concern a Matter Within the Scope of an Agent's Employment.

Subsection (D) does not require that the declarant have specific authority to speak. Nor does it require that the statement be made *within the scope of the agent's duties*. Rather, subsection (D) focuses on subject matter: The statement must *concern* a matter within the scope of employment, that is, must match the subject matter of the employee's job description. And it must be made during the agency relationship's existence. Typical cases involve agents speaking about their own job performance or about events that happened on the job that would be of legitimate concern to the speaker. For example, statements by superiors to company employees concerning the employee's standing in the company may be within subsection (D), depending on the superior's job, duties, and role in relation to the employee. In Carter v. University of Toledo, 349 F.3d 269, 271-272 (6th Cir. 2002), the plaintiff, an African-American professor, sued the defendant for failure to renew her contract because of her race. The plaintiff sought to testify that the University's Vice-Provost had said to her that the Dean who had refused the renewal was "trying to whitewash the college of education" and "was trying to get rid of black professors." The appellate court held that while the Vice-Provost was not a "direct decision-maker" concerning the plaintiff's employment, he did have "oversight of the affirmative action process at the University" and thus his statements concerned a matter within his authority. Statements are excluded as not concerning a matter within the scope of the agency when the declarant is like a bystander eyewitness who describes an event perceived at work that has no relation to the job or the concerns of the speaker. Wilkinson v. Carnival Cruise Lines, 920 F.2d 1560 (11th Cir. 1991) (statement by cabin steward about previous problems with sliding glass door in ship's swimming pool area did not concern a matter within scope of steward's employment since his job involved no responsibilities in the engineering department or for the swimming pool). Since the contents of the hearsay statement alone are not sufficient to prove the scope of authority, the proponent must present corroborating evidence. Mercado v. City of Orlando, 407 F.3d 1152, 1156 (11th Cir. 2005).

The proponent of a statement under subsection (D) must also provide evidence that the statement was made *during* the existence of the principal-agent relationship. This does not mean that the statement must be made "on the job" or during the performance of duties. Rule 801(d)(2)(D) abandons the common law requirement that agents must be *acting* within the scope of their authority when they make the statement. The exemption thus includes statements made away from the workplace to third parties uninvolved in the speaker's work. Kraus v. Sobel Corrugated Containers, Inc., 915 F.2d 227, 230-231 (6th Cir. 1990) (statement praising job performance of plaintiff shortly before her termination, made by a department manager during holiday dinner at the home of the plaintiff, would be admissible against the defendant in an age discrimination case).

b. Justification for the Admissibility of Statements Under FRE 801(d)(2)(C) and (D): Necessity, Fairness, and Reliability

Under both subsections (C) and (D), there is no guarantee that the declarant will be available to testify at trial. Thus the principal rationale for admitting statements under subsections (A) and (B) — that the party can choose to explain the statement —

may not apply. If the declarant is out of the country or otherwise unavailable, and the party had little or no knowledge of the statement when made, the justification that cross-examination is unnecessary because the party can explain the declarant's statement seems particularly weak.

Instead, other values justify these exemptions (and other exceptions) to the hearsay rule: necessity, fairness, and reliability. Necessity stems from the fact that individuals, corporations, and other institutional entities conduct their affairs through authorized representatives, agents and employees. These persons constitute a primary source of information about corporate activities. Such information is necessary to impose liability on corporate and institutional entities. And, as a matter of substantive law, individual and corporate or institutional parties are legally responsible for the activities of their authorized representatives, employees, and agents. It is probably essential for the proper functioning of this liability scheme for these declarants' statements to be admissible against principals and employers. Permitting the use of hearsay statements by these representatives, agents and employees can also be justified on grounds of fairness. If proponents cannot use this hearsay, they would either have to call the declarants as hostile witnesses or forego the information altogether if the declarant has disappeared. Parties gain advantages by being able to conduct their business affairs through their representatives, agents, and employees. Moreover, third parties rely on statements of these people when doing business with the principal. The advantages obtained and the reliance incurred make it seem fair to place some burden of accountability for such out-of-court statements onto the principal. United States v. Agne, 214 F.3d 47, 55 (1st Cir. 2000) (statements admissible against the president of a corporation under FRE 801(d)(2)(D), because evidence showed that the declarant, an employee of an affiliated company, was directly responsible to the president). When an agent's hearsay is admitted under subsection (D), the principal is not irrevocably bound by it but does bear the burden of contesting its reliability, if the principal does not want the jury to use it. While it may be difficult for the party to obtain the information necessary to explore weaknesses in the declarant's statement, the party is probably better able to do so, and to do so more efficiently, than the proponent of the statement.

In addition, the foundational requirements of FRE 801(d)(2)(C) and (D) generate some inferences about the reliability of the declarants' testimonial qualities. To state the strongest case, if a statement is authorized, it may be reasonable to infer that the principal selected a trustworthy and reliable spokesperson. Second, if a statement is authorized or is about a matter central to the activities of the agent, the declarant may have a solid basis for making the statement, and if central, the statement may be made carefully and accurately. Third, if the declarant is an agent at the time of the statement, it may be inferred that the declarant is loyal to the interests of the principal and would not lie to injure the principal.

c. Personal Knowledge and Lay Opinions

Many courts dispense with the personal knowledge requirement and the lay opinion rule under FRE 801(C) and (D) as well as (A) and (B). It is thus possible to admit a representative's or agent's conclusory statement that is based only on hearsay and rumor. This puts the principal under a heavy burden of disproving the reliability of the statement. Abandoning the personal knowledge requirement for a party's own admissions under subsection (A) may be justified because parties can impeach their own out-of-court statements by establishing their own lack of firsthand knowledge. But the principal may not be so easily able to show lack of firsthand knowledge in an employee's statement, particularly in a far-flung corporate context and particularly if the employee is not available. Again, necessity and fairness must justify abandoning the personal knowledge requirement. Abandoning the requirement means that more hearsay will be admitted and that corporate parties will bear the burden of impeaching its reliability or will suffer the risk of being unable to do so. Do you think that this result strikes the proper balance of necessity and fairness?

d. Admissions by Government Employees

When can statements made by government employees be offered against the government in civil or criminal cases? Some courts adhere to the traditional common law position that the answer is never, based on the rationale that no individual can bind the sovereign. Some courts have followed this principle. United States v. Evans, 1990 WL 32581 (6th Cir. 1990), (excluding testimony about an out-of-court statement made by the assistant U.S. Attorney on the case to the effect that Evans did not have the requisite intent to be guilty of the crime charged); United States v. Yildiz, 355 F.3d 80, 82 (2d Cir. 2004) (out-of-court statements of a government informant are not admissible in a criminal trial under FRE 801(d)(2)(D)). Courts have admitted statements of prosecutors made in court and in pleadings. United States v. Bakshinian, 65 F. Supp. 2d 1104, 1106 (C.D. Cal. 1999) (prosecutors have the power to bind the sovereign and are not disinterested in the outcome).

In civil cases, government manuals, sworn affidavits submitted to a judge, and depositions have been admitted under subsection (D). And in C & H Commercial Contractors v. United States, 35 Fed. Cl. 246, 256 (1996), a highly relevant memorandum by a government contracting officer that recited damaging representations made by government officials to a private contractor was admitted under subsection (D) without hesitation.

12. Interpretation and Illustration of FRE 801(d)(2)(E): Co-conspirators' Admissions

a. Preliminary Factfinding

The foundational requirements for co-conspirators' admissions are:

- the declarant and the party against whom the statement is offered were both members of the same conspiracy;
- the statement was made during the course of the conspiracy; and
- the statement was made in furtherance of the conspiracy.

The typical co-conspirator statement is offered by the government against a criminal defendant to prove that defendant's criminal conduct. The recorded statement by Moore in the false partnership tax return hypothetical would not be admissible against Day under subsection (E), even if the government had evidence that Moore and Day were co-conspirators. Statements made to tax investigators, after the tax return has been filed, would not be considered to be made *during* or in *furtherance of* a conspiracy.

Consider also the following example, which is a typical situation in which the government seeks to use subsection (E):

A government informer has infiltrated a drug-selling ring. He speaks and works only with a few people involved in the ring, and never sees or talks to the boss. The people he deals with, however, make many statements about the boss, such as "he gets the best stuff" or "he sold this for $100 per gram." These out-of-court statements, if true, are evidence of the boss's drug-selling activities.

If the boss is charged with selling drugs and with conspiracy to sell drugs, may the informant testify about the out-of-court statements made about the boss's conduct by the various "small fry" in the drug ring?

i. Proof of Co-membership. First, the proponent of a co-conspirator's statement under FRE 801(d)(2)(E) must prove that a conspiracy exists and that both the declarant (the "small fry") and the party (the boss) are members of it. Membership in a conspiracy requires a meeting of the minds to join an enterprise with others with the aim of accomplishing a specific purpose, sometimes phrased as "specific intent to further a common objective [which is usually, although not always, unlawful], and knowing and voluntary participation." The conspirators do not have to have contact with, or ever know, all of the other conspirators, but "[n]o one can join a conspiracy without knowledge of its existence . . . [and] the aim to forward or assist" it. United States v. Garcia-Torres, 280 F.3d 1,4 (1st Cir. 2002). There does not have to be a formal charge of conspiracy for the co-conspirators' admissions exception to apply. Indeed, the exception is not limited to use in criminal prosecutions. As a practical matter, however, the exception is most frequently invoked by prosecutors in criminal cases. Our discussion here reflects this common usage.

ii. During the Course of the Conspiracy. Statements made to the government informant in the drug ring example will satisfy this requirement if the conspiracy was ongoing when they were made. Statements made prior to a defendant's joining the conspiracy may not be used to prove the defendant's participation, but may be admissible to show the nature of the illegal enterprise and its preparations. United States v. Segura-Gallegos, 41 F.3d 1266 (9th Cir. 1994). And statements about events that occurred prior to the defendant's joining a conspiracy are admissible so long as these events were part of a "single, overarching" conspiracy and not multiple, independent conspiracies. United States v. Handlin, 366 F.3d 584, 591 (7th Cir. 2004). A defendant must affirmatively withdraw from a conspiracy for statements of co-conspirators no longer to be admissible against him. United States v. Robinson, 390 F.3d 853, 882 (6th Cir. 2004) (arrest or incarceration does not qualify as affirmative withdrawal).

The principal issue with respect to the *during* requirement is whether it extends to statements made in the so-called concealment phase of the conspiracy, after the objectives of the conspiracy have been either met or thwarted, usually by discovery and arrest. United States v. Osorio-Soto, 1998 U.S. App. LEXIS 1950 (10th Cir. 1998) (government seizure of the illegal drug ended the conspiracy because it was no longer possible to achieve its objectives). If statements made after an arrest cast blame on others, perhaps the declarant is lying in order to shift the blame away from himself or herself. During the concealment phase, there is a greater likelihood that each co-conspirator will be primarily concerned with self-protection. The majority position is that statements made during this conceal-ment phase are not within the scope of the exemption, as was true regarding Moore's recorded statement to the tax investigator. But see United States v. Gajo, 290 F.3d 922, 928 (7th Cir. 2002) ("concealment is . . . one of the main criminal objectives of an arson-for profit scheme because it facilitates the primary objective of fraudulently acquiring insurance proceeds"); United States v. Urrego-Linares, 879 F.2d 1234, 1240 (4th Cir. 1989) (statements by co-conspirator on a monitored telephone call to the defendant who had already been arrested held to be made in the course of the conspiracy).

   iii.   In Furtherance of the Conspiracy.   Statements that further the common objectives of the conspiracy, or set in motion transactions that are part of it, will satisfy the "in furtherance" requirement. Statements naming the drug ring boss in order to secure a sale, or to confirm lines of command, seem to further the goals of the illegal enterprise. "Idle chatter" and statements among conspirators that merely narrate past events have been held not to satisfy the requirement. United States v. Cornett, 195 F.3d 776, 783 (5th Cir. 1999). But statements that inform new conspirators, or keep co-conspirators informed, of significant events and problems have been held admis-sible. United States v. Jefferson, 215 F.3d 820, 823 (8th Cir. 2000) (conversations among three alleged co-conspirators concerning their botched attempt to murder their target by arson, and the resulting deaths of five others, admitted as in furtherance). Statements to customers, and to outsiders from whom the co-conspirator seeks help, may or may not further the conspiracy. In United States v. Urbanik, 801 F.2d 692 (4th Cir. 1986), casual conversation about weightlifting followed a drug purchase, during which the seller described the defendant to the buyer both as an excellent weightlifter and as the supplier of drugs. This was held not admissible against defendant because it was not in furtherance of the conspiracy. In United States v. Lee, 374 F.3d 637 (8th Cir. 2004) a co-conspirator's confession of murder to his brother (not a co-conspirator) to enlist his aid in selling weapons stolen from the murder victim was admitted as in furtherance of the conspiracy to use ill-gotten proceeds to fund a white supremacist group.

   ### b.   Justification for the Admissibility of Co-conspirators' Admissions

One largely artificial rationale for the co-conspirators' admissions exemption is that each co-conspirator authorizes (or is deemed to have authorized) the statements of other co-conspirators. A more practical rationale is necessity: Conspiracies tend to be secret enterprises. The criminal activities, particularly of the leadership, are very diffi-cult to prove. Some of the best evidence — and perhaps essential evidence if a prose-cutor is to prove a defendant's guilt beyond a reasonable doubt — will be statements about the conduct of other co-conspirators. Thus it is arguably appropriate to burden a person who chooses to engage in a conspiracy (particularly as an organizer or leader) with the risk that false or inaccurate co-conspirators' statements will be used against that person.

   There is also a somewhat weak reliability rationale for the exception: To the extent that the *during* and *in furtherance of the conspiracy* requirements are taken seriously, co-conspirators' declarations may tend to be trustworthy because they advance the interest of the speaker in the success of the criminal enterprise.

13. Elaboration of FRE 801(d)(2)(E): Applying FRE 104 to the Co-conspirator Exemption

Since it is the co-conspirator relationship that justifies the admission of co-conspirator hearsay, much attention has been paid to the process of proving this relationship. Prior to the adoption of the Federal Rules, most federal courts required the prosecution to produce only "*prima facie* proof" that the defendant and the hearsay declarant were co-conspirators. Once this standard was satisfied, the co-conspirator's statement would be admitted, assuming all other requirements were also fulfilled. But the jurors were also instructed to decide whether the defendant and declarant were co-conspirators before they could use the statement for its truth. The court was not allowed to "bootstrap" — that is, to use the content of the hearsay statement to determine whether the foundational requirements were fulfilled.

a. *Bourjaily v. United States*

In 1987, the Supreme Court in Bourjaily v. United States, 483 U.S. 171 (1987), held that all of the preliminary facts necessary to admit hearsay under FRE 801(d)(2)(E), including the co-conspirator relationship, are FRE 104(a) questions for the judge to decide by a preponderance of the evidence. The judge will *not* instruct the jury to decide the relationship issue as a necessary precondition to using the statement for its truth. This conclusion seems to be quite sound. The foundational question of co-membership in a conspiracy is a hearsay policy issue, not a relevance issue. Thus *Bourjaily*'s adoption of the FRE 104(a) test for deciding this question seems desirable.

Bourjaily also held that it is appropriate for the judge to consider the content of the hearsay statement itself in deciding whether the foundational requirements have been satisfied:

> Rule 104(a) provides: "In making its [preliminary fact] determination [the court] is not bound by the rules of evidence except those with respect to privileges." Similarly, Rule 1101(d)(1) states that the Rules of Evidence (other than with respect to privileges) shall not apply to "[t]he determination of questions of fact preliminary to admissibility of evidence when the issue is to be determined by the court under rule 104." The question thus presented is whether any aspect of ... [the] bootstrapping rule remains viable after the enactment of the Federal Rules of Evidence.... The Rule on its face allows the trial judge to consider any evidence whatsoever, bound only by the rules of privilege....
>
> It is sufficient for today to hold that a court, in making a preliminary factual determination under Rule 801(d)(2)(E), may examine the hearsay statements sought to be admitted. As we have held in other cases concerning admissibility determinations, "the judge should receive the evidence and give it such weight as his judgment and experience counsel." [Id. at 178-181.]

Bourjaily's resolution of the bootstrap issue is also reasonable and consistent with the terms of FRE 104(a). But since there may be reasons to distrust the reliability of alleged co-conspirators' statements, it may well be that it would be unwise to rely on *nothing* but the statement at issue to establish the foundational requirement of the party's membership in the conspiracy.

b.   The Amendment to FRE 801(d)(2): The Requirement of Additional Evidence

The Supreme Court promulgated an amendment, effective in December 1997, that added the following language to FRE 801(d)(2):

> The contents of the statement may be considered but are not alone sufficient to establish the declarant's authority under subparagraph (C), the agency or employment relationship and scope thereof under subparagraph (D), or the existence of the conspiracy and the participation therein of the declarant and the party against whom the statement is offered under subparagraph (E).

This language does not specify what kind of additional proof is needed, nor how much. Most courts post-*Bourjaily* had required some additional evidence from a source *independent* of the co-conspirator's hearsay statement to corroborate the defendant's membership in the conspiracy. The Advisory Committee Note to the amendment, however, appears to contemplate that evidence of the identity of the speaker and the context in which statement was made, as well as corroboration, might suffice. As we have noted previously, the requirement of additional evidence also applies to the key foundational issues under subsections (C) and (D) as well.

Prior to this amendment, courts found the requirement of independent evidence to be satisfied by behavior of the defendant that established a connection to the conspiracy: the defendant's own statements or statements of others that the defendant adopts; presence at locations where the co-conspirator said the defendant would be; attempts to silence the victim of the conspiracy; frequent phone contact with co-conspirators; or presence at drug deliveries. "Mere association" was held to be insufficient evidence of membership, but repeated meetings that coincide with large-scale drug deliveries were held sufficient. United States v. Ammar, 714 F.2d 238, 250 (3d Cir. 1983).

Reported cases since the amendment have continued to enforce the requirement of evidence corroborating the defendant's participation in the conspiracy's activities. United States v. Capelton, 350 F.3d 231 (1st Cir. 2003) (defendant possessed marked bills from drug transaction and was on the scene during the transaction); United States v. Stotts, 323 F.3d 520 (7th Cir. 2003) (defendant accompanied brother, who actually sold the drugs, to and from the sale, gestured for the buyer to follow him in her car, and nodded in agreement for her to inspect the drugs before paying); Qualley v. Clo-Tex Internat'l, Inc., 212 F.3d 1123, 1131 (8th Cir. 2000) (reversing the trial court, the appellate court held that independent evidence linking the defendant to the conspiracy to defraud the plaintiff was insufficient, even with the hearsay statements themselves, to satisfy the preponderance of the evidence burden).

c.   Process for Admission of a Co-conspirator's Statement

Some Circuit Courts of Appeal have established a requirement that the district court make an explicit finding, on the record, of the predicate facts necessary to the admission of co-conspirator hearsay pursuant to Rule 801(d)(2)(E). This finding may be made after both sides have presented their proof, but before the case is submitted to the jury. To present an effective story to the jury and to minimize the need to call the same witnesses twice, the prosecutor frequently offers co-conspirators' admissions *before* presenting the evidence to establish that all the conditions of the exception have been satisfied. When this occurs, the requisite finding cannot be made prior to the admission decision.

It is well settled, however, that the court has discretion to use the tool of conditional admissibility with respect to FRE 104(a), even though this section of the rule does not contain the "subject to" language of Rule 104(b). "A court may conditionally admit a challenged statement subject to later proof to satisfy the co-conspirator rule and defer a final ruling on admissibility until after hearing the relevant evidence." United States v. Roach, 164 F.3d 403, 409 (8th Cir. 1998). Should the judge give any instruction to the jury when conditionally admitting the co-conspirator's statement? The judge could say something like, "I am provisionally admitting these hearsay statements pursuant to what is called the co-conspirator admission provision. If the prosecutor does not introduce sufficient independent evidence of the existence of a conspiracy, I may ask you later to disregard these hearsay statements." Would this be a good idea? What are the risks?

Once a judge has conditionally admitted a co-conspirator's statements, the judge may be reluctant to find that the FRE 104(a) preliminary fact standard has not been satisfied. Such a finding would require the judge either to instruct the jury to disregard the co-conspirator's statement or to declare a mistrial. The instruction to disregard is not a realistic solution in many cases. Can the jury be expected to be able to obey it? And because the prosecutor will have presented all — or at least a substantial part — of the state's case before it becomes clear that the foundational requirements cannot be satisfied, the mistrial alternative will frequently be quite expensive. For these reasons, it may be wise for the judge to insist on proof of the foundational facts before proof of the co-conspirator's statement. United States v. Saneaux, 365 F.Supp.2d 493, 502 (S.D.N.Y. 2005) (paucity of government's proof that statements were "in furtherance" at motion in limine held to preclude conditional admission; government should place before the jury all evidence it relies on to satisfy the required foundation before jury may hear the recorded co-conspirator statements).

KEY POINTS

1. Under FRE 801(d)(2)(A), any statement made out of court by a party may be used against that party to prove the truth of the matter it asserts, so long as it is relevant and not otherwise objectionable.

2. FRE 801(d)(2) also provides a hearsay exemption for: (B) statements adopted by a party, or statements in which a party manifests belief; (C) statements authorized by the party; (D) certain statements made by an agent or employee of the party during the relationship and concerning matters within the scope of the agent's employment; and (E) certain statements made by a co-conspirator of the party during the conspiracy and in furtherance of it.

3. The judge must be persuaded, pursuant to FRE 104(a), that the foundational requirements for each of these exemptions are satisfied. The judge may use the statement itself in deciding the preliminary questions, but other evidence is necessary to find authority, agency and a co-conspirator relationship.

4. The primary justification for the FRE 801(d)(2) exemptions is that the party cannot fairly complain about the loss of cross-examination of the declarant because the

party can explain the unreliability in the statement, or because it is necessary and fair to impose on the party the risk and burden of not being able to do so.

PROBLEMS

8.36. Return to Problem 3.3, United States v. Ray, at page 131. The prosecution offers the following evidence. Defense counsel objects to each piece of evidence as hearsay. How should the court rule?

(a)   A Rundown V.P. to testify: "On March 15, 2004, Bernard Ray said to me that he had just read a memo from his auditor, Andrews, and Rundown stock was going to take a beating."

(b)   A senior VP at Andrews's accounting firm to testify: "On March 16, 2004, I spoke with Bernard Ray at our club. I said, 'Bernard, I hear that Rundown is going to project big losses in a few days. I assume you've already dumped most of your holdings.' Then Bernard said, 'Don't worry about me — I'm all set.'"

(c)   The prosecution offers an authenticated copy of the March 14, 2004 auditor's memo to prove that Rundown in fact projected losses for the second quarter of 2004.

8.37. Daniel Mahlandt has sued the Wild Canid Survival & Research Center, Inc. and its director of education, Kenneth Poos, for injuries sustained when Daniel was allegedly bitten by a wolf named Sophie. Sophie was owned by the Center but lived temporarily at the Poos home. She was enclosed in the yard by a five-foot chain link fence and was chained to the fence with a six-foot-long chain. Daniel, who was three-and-a-half years old at the time of the alleged biting, was found bleeding and hysterical inside the yard with Sophie. There were no eyewitnesses as to how Daniel got into the yard or whether Sophie bit him. One witness testified that she heard a child's screams and observed Daniel on the ground with Sophie straddling him. Sophie's face was near Daniel's, and Sophie was wailing. Kenneth Poos's son found Daniel and carried him into the house.

Kenneth Poos will testify that Sophie had been hand raised by humans since birth, has been very gentle, and that he takes her to various schools and institutions as part of his educational program for the Center. A defense witness, an expert on animal behavior, will testify that when a wolf licks a child's face, that is a sign of care; that a wolf's wail is a sign of compassion; and that Daniel's particular injuries were not consistent with a wolf attack.

Mr. Poos arrived at his home shortly after the incident. After seeing that Daniel was taken to a hospital, Mr. Poos talked to his son about what happened and then went to the Center to report the incident to the Center's president. The president was not in, so Mr. Poos left the following note on his door: "Please call me at home. Sophie bit a child that came into our backyard. All has been taken care of. I need to convey to you what happened. KP." Several weeks later there was a meeting of the Board of Directors of the Center. Mr. Poos was not present. The minutes of that meeting state that there was a "great deal of discussion about the incident of Sophie biting the child and its legal aspects." Plaintiff has offered into evidence against both Mr. Poos and against the Center (a) the note written by Mr. Poos and (b) the foregoing passage from the minutes of the board meeting. Both defendants have objected on hearsay grounds to the admission of both pieces of evidence. With respect to each defendant, what result?

8.38. Return to Problem 3.2, Pedroso v. Driver, on page 129. Paul's mother testifies for plaintiffs that Paul's teacher told her, several weeks after the accident, that Driver's supervisor had told the teacher that, in his opinion, Driver was not keeping a proper lookout before the accident. Defendants object on grounds of hearsay. Admissible?

8.39. Seven members of the Gangster Disciples (GD), a street gang (6,000 members) that operated a massive drug distribution business in the Chicago area, are being prosecuted for drug, weapons, and money-laundering offenses. The leader of the GD is known to be Larry Hoover, who for years ran the gang from inside of various prisons. His female partner owned a legitimate business called Save the Children Promotions. In an authorized IRS search of the Save the Children offices, agents found a document in a folder marked "L.H./S1." The document was a list describing the hierarchical and territorial organization of the entire GD operation. In some taped conversations, Hoover had mentioned his desire to develop such a document to keep track of gang members and their payments to GD. All seven defendants are mentioned in the list. On what basis can they object to admission of the list against them at trial? What result?

8.40. While in jail awaiting trial for three murders, Hobbs placed a telephone call to a former jailhouse friend, Mel Gray. The conversation was recorded, pursuant to jail policy. Hobbs and Gray discussed the recent conviction of Hobbs' alleged accomplice in the murders; Hobbs complained that the accomplice's lawyer "got the whole joint twisted." Gray then read Hobbs a newspaper article reporting that the accomplice had blamed the murders on Hobbs and that the accomplice testified that he had shot the victims only because he was afraid of Hobbs. Hobbs did not respond to Gray's reading of the article. Can the prosecution use the tape of this phone call against Hobbs at his trial under FRE 801(d)(2)(B) or (E)?

8.41. David Droz was convicted of conspiracy during 2004 to distribute cocaine. DEA officials had kept Droz under surveillance and recorded his phone calls. At trial, the prosecution secured the admission of three conversations between Droz and Pete Hidalgo, an alleged co-conspirator. The three conversations include (1) a phone call from Hidalgo to Droz on July 25, 2004, setting up a meeting at which Droz agreed to give Hidalgo $15,000 to purchase cocaine; (2) Hidalgo's statements to a state trooper who stopped his car on July 27 that the cash he was carrying was the proceeds from the sale of a car; the trooper then seized the cash; and (3) a phone message to Droz left by Hidalgo on July 27 that Droz's $15,000 had been seized and they needed a plan to get the money back. Was admission of any of these statements error?

8.42. In the prosecution of a wealthy show horse owner for insurance fraud, the government seeks to prove that the owner conspired to have one of his horses, Charisma, killed in order to collect insurances proceeds. The person who was hired to kill Charisma, Burns, was hired by Marty, the owner's horse trainer, and told that "the owner wanted it done on December 15 because he was in Asia, and because Charisma was scheduled to travel from New York to Florida on December 16." Marty paid Burns to do the job. Can the government use Burns's testimony about Marty's statements against the owner? Suppose that the government has independent proof that the owner was indeed in Asia on December 15, and that Charisma was scheduled to travel to

Florida on December 16? What result? Suppose that the government can also prove that, after Charisma's death, the owner intentionally lied to the insurance company about who was allowed to ride Charisma, in order to avoid one of the insurance policy's exceptions?

D. HEARSAY EXCEPTIONS NOT REQUIRING THE UNAVAILABILITY OF THE DECLARANT

FRE 803 excepts 23 different types of hearsay statements from the general rule of exclusion. There is no requirement in this rule that the declarant be unavailable to testify as a witness. Thus the justifications for admitting this much hearsay are especially important for your overall evaluation of the hearsay rule in practice. Some of the FRE 803 exceptions are legacies of almost 300 years of common law development and are rarely used in modern federal litigation. We will focus primarily on the exceptions that are most used today.

The premise of all FRE 803 exceptions is that these types of statements are reliable enough to be used in the jury's fact-finding even without cross-examination of the declarant by the opponent. In the words of the Advisory Committee Note, these kinds of statements "possess circumstantial guarantees of trustworthiness sufficient to justify nonproduction of the declarant in person at the trial even though he may be available." This means that something about the hearsay statement — its content, its source, the circumstances in which it was made — reveals something "trustworthy" about the declarant's testimonial qualities. This is the "reliability approach" to the admission of hearsay that we already saw at work in FRE 801(a) and (c) and in the FRE 801(d) exemptions as well.

The Rule 803 exceptions are categorical. They each define a specific type of out-of-court statement that may be admitted for the truth of the matter it asserts, and they each establish foundational requirements that the proponent must satisfy pursuant to the process described above in Section B. In this section, we now examine the categorical foundational requirements of the FRE 803 exceptions, and the reliability rationale underlying the more important ones. Remember that other rules may operate to exclude a hearsay statement even if it fits within a Rule 803 exception — relevancy, authentication, best evidence, the relevancy rules such as the character prohibitions, privilege, and, of course, FRE 403, may all have to be applied as well.

Two other general points apply to all Rule 803 (and Rule 804) exceptions. Because the declarant's statement is offered for its truth, the declarant is a source of knowledge for the jury, analogous to a witness testifying at trial. Therefore the fundamental requirement that witnesses must speak from personal knowledge applies as well to hearsay declarants under FRE 803 and FRE 804. The Advisory Committee Note to Rule 803 makes this clear:

> In a hearsay situation, the declarant is, of course, a witness, and neither this rule nor Rule 804 dispenses with the requirement of firsthand knowledge. It may appear from his statement or be inferable from circumstances. See Rule 602.

In addition, the opponent to an item of hearsay can attack the credibility of hearsay declarants in most of the ways that witnesses can be attacked. Rule 806 makes this clear:

When a hearsay statement, or a statement defined in Rule 801(d)(2)(C), (D), or (E), has been admitted in evidence, the credibility of the declarant may be attacked, and if attacked may be supported, by any evidence which would be admissible for those purposes if declarant had testified as a witness. Evidence of a statement or conduct by the declarant at any time, inconsistent with the declarant's hearsay statement, is not subject to any requirement that the declarant may have been afforded an opportunity to deny or explain. If the party against whom a hearsay statement has been admitted calls the declarant as a witness, the party is entitled to examine the declarant on the statement as if under cross-examination.

It is more difficult, of course, to impeach a hearsay declarant without the tool of cross-examination. Issues regarding impeachment under FRE 806 are discussed in Margaret Meriwether Cordray, Evidence Rule 806 and the Problem of Impeaching the Non-testifying Declarant, 56 Ohio St. L.J. 495 (1995).

1.   FRE 803

RULE 803. HEARSAY EXCEPTIONS; AVAILABILITY OF DECLARANT IMMATERIAL

The following are not excluded by the hearsay rule, even though the declarant is available as a witness:

(1) Present sense impression. A statement describing or explaining an event or condition made while the declarant was perceiving the event or condition, or immediately thereafter.

(2) Excited utterance. A statement relating to a startling event or condition made while the declarant was under the stress of excitement caused by the event or condition.

(3) Then existing mental, emotional, or physical condition. A statement of the declarant's then existing state of mind, emotion, sensation, or physical condition (such as intent, plan, motive, design, mental feeling, pain, and bodily health), but not including a statement of memory or belief to prove the fact remembered or believed unless it relates to the execution, revocation, identification, or terms of declarant's will.

(4) Statements for purposes of medical diagnosis or treatment. Statements made for purposes of medical diagnosis or treatment and describing medical history, or past or present symptoms, pain, or sensations, or the inception or general character of the cause or external source thereof insofar as reasonably pertinent to diagnosis or treatment.

(5) Recorded recollection. A memorandum or record concerning a matter about which a witness once had knowledge but now has insufficient recollection to enable the witness to testify fully and accurately, shown to have been made or adopted by the witness when the matter was fresh in the witness' memory and to reflect that knowledge correctly. If admitted, the memorandum or record may be read into evidence but may not itself be received as an exhibit unless offered by an adverse party.

(6) Records of regularly conducted activity. A memorandum, report, record, or data compilation, in any form, of acts, events, conditions, opinions, or diagnoses, made at or near the time by, or from information transmitted by, a person with knowledge, if kept in the course of a regularly conducted business activity, and if it was the regular practice of that business activity to make the memorandum, report, record, or data compilation, all as shown by the testimony of the custodian or other qualified witness, or by certification that

complies with Rule 902(11), Rule 902(12), or a statute permitting certification, unless the source of information or the method or circumstances of preparation indicate lack of trustworthiness. The term "business" as used in this paragraph includes business, institution, association, profession, occupation, and calling of every kind, whether or not conducted for profit.

(7) Absence of entry in records kept in accordance with the provisions of paragraph (6). Evidence that a matter is not included in the memoranda, reports, records, or data compilations, in any form, kept in accordance with the provisions of paragraph (6), to prove the nonoccurrence or nonexistence of the matter, if the matter was of a kind of which a memorandum, report, record, or data compilation was regularly made and preserved, unless the sources of information or other circumstances indicate lack of trustworthiness.

(8) Public records and reports. Records, reports, statements, or data compilations, in any form, of public offices or agencies, setting forth (A) the activities of the office or agency, or (B) matters observed pursuant to duty imposed by law as to which matters there was a duty to report, excluding, however, in criminal cases matters observed by police officers and other law enforcement personnel, or (C) in civil actions and proceedings and against the Government in criminal cases, factual findings resulting from an investigation made pursuant to authority granted by law, unless the sources of information or other circumstances indicate lack of trustworthiness.

(9) Records of vital statistics. Records or data compilations, in any form, of births, fetal deaths, deaths, or marriages, if the report thereof was made to a public office pursuant to requirements of law.

(10) Absence of public record or entry. To prove the absence of a record, report, statement, or data compilation, in any form, or the nonoccurrence or nonexistence of a matter of which a record, report, statement, or data compilation, in any form, was regularly made and preserved by a public office or agency, evidence in the form of a certification in accordance with rule 902, or testimony, that diligent search failed to disclose the record, report, statement, or data compilation, or entry.

(11) Records of religious organizations. Statements of births, marriages, divorces, deaths, legitimacy, ancestry, relationship by blood or marriage, or other similar facts of personal or family history, contained in a regularly kept record of a religious organization.

(12) Marriage, baptismal, and similar certificates. Statements of fact contained in a certificate that the maker performed a marriage or other ceremony or administered a sacrament, made by a clergyman, public official, or other person authorized by the rules or practices of a religious organization or by law to perform the act certified, and purporting to have been issued at the time of the act or within a reasonable time thereafter.

(13) Family records. Statements of fact concerning personal or family history contained in family Bibles, genealogies, charts, engravings on rings, inscriptions on family portraits, engravings on urns, crypts, or tombstones, or the like.

(14) Records of documents affecting an interest in property. The record of a document purporting to establish or affect an interest in property, as proof of the content of the original recorded document and its execution and delivery by each person by whom it purports to have been executed, if the record is a record of a public office and an applicable statute authorizes the recording of documents of that kind in that office.

(15) Statements in documents affecting an interest in property. A statement contained in a document purporting to establish or affect an interest in property if the matter stated was relevant to the purpose of the document, unless dealings with the property since the document was made have been inconsistent with the truth of the statement or the purport of the document.

(16) Statements in ancient documents. Statements in a document in existence twenty years or more the authenticity of which is established.

(17) Market reports, commercial publications. Market quotations, tabulations, lists, directories, or other published compilations, generally used and relied upon by the public or by persons in particular occupations.

(18) Learned treatises. To the extent called to the attention of an expert witness upon cross-examination or relied upon by the expert witness in direct examination, statements contained in published treatises, periodicals, or pamphlets on a subject of history, medicine, or other science or art, established as a reliable authority by the testimony or admission of the witness or by other expert testimony or by judicial notice. If admitted, the statements may be read into evidence but may not be received as exhibits.

(19) Reputation concerning personal or family history. Reputation among members of a person's family by blood, adoption, or marriage, or among a person's associates, or in the community, concerning a person's birth, adoption, marriage, divorce, death, legitimacy, relationship by blood, adoption, or marriage, ancestry, or other similar fact of personal or family history.

(20) Reputation concerning boundaries or general history. Reputation in a community, arising before the controversy, as to boundaries of or customs affecting lands in the community, and reputation as to events of general history important to the community or State or nation in which located.

(21) Reputation as to character. Reputation of a person's character among associates or in the community.

(22) Judgment of previous conviction. Evidence of a final judgment, entered after a trial or upon a plea of guilty (but not upon a plea of nolo contendere), adjudging a person guilty of a crime punishable by death or imprisonment in excess of one year, to prove any fact essential to sustain the judgment, but not including, when offered by the Government in a criminal prosecution for purposes other than impeachment, judgments against persons other than the accused. The pendency of an appeal may be shown but does not affect admissibility.

(23) Judgment as to personal, family, or general history, or boundaries. Judgments as proof of matters of personal, family or general history, or boundaries, essential to the judgment, if the same would be provable by evidence of reputation.

(Our initial discussion focuses on FRE 803(1) and (2). We discuss the significant subsections of FRE 803 later in this section.)

2. Interpretation and Illustration of FRE 803(1): Present Sense Impressions

There are two exceptions that provide for the admission of two different kinds of spontaneous hearsay statements — present sense impressions and excited utterances. The categorical requirements for each are somewhat different. FRE 803(1) provides:

(1) Present sense impression. A statement describing or explaining an event or condition made while the declarant was perceiving the event or condition, or immediately thereafter.

a. Preliminary Factfinding

The foundational requirements for present sense impressions are:

- the occurrence of an event or condition;
- the contents of the statement describe or explain the event or condition; and
- the declarant made the statement while perceiving the event or condition, or immediately thereafter.

Think back to the first illustration of an out-of-court statement that we used in this chapter. We found that Sally's statement "the gray SUV ran the red light and hit a pedestrian" would be hearsay, if reported by George at trial. But Sally's statement might have been made to George either while Sally was seeing the SUV, or within seconds or minutes of seeing it. Thus it might be admissible hearsay, if it qualifies as a present sense impression. The pedestrian, the proponent of the statement, must present evidence to show that it falls within the categorical terms of FRE 803(1). These are preliminary questions for the judge to determine pursuant to FRE 104(a). The court should be convinced by a preponderance of the evidence that there was an event occurring just before Sally's statement was made, and that Sally's statement describes it.

Many present sense impressions are presented in court through the testimony of witnesses who also perceived the event or condition themselves. If George saw the accident, he would be the foundation witness who could provide evidence showing that the event occurred and that Sally made the statement contemporaneously with it. The judge can determine whether the statement describes or explains the event or condition from the contents of the statement itself.

b. Justification for the Admissibility of Present Sense Impressions

The primary justification for admitting present sense impressions is that the contemporaneity of the statement and the event it is offered to prove tends to ensure the declarant's sincerity. This rationale falls squarely within the reliability theory advanced for admitting trustworthy hearsay. It is based on the generalization that contemporaneity between statement and event means that the statement is spontaneous rather than premeditated. If the statement is spontaneous, there is no time to develop the intent to fabricate. If there is no time or opportunity to fabricate, the statement is sincere. Additionally, the contemporaneity of the statement and the event virtually eliminates any memory problem.

3. Interpretation and Illustration of FRE 803(2): Excited Utterances

FRE 803(2) provides:

> (2) Excited utterance. A statement relating to a startling event or condition made while the declarant was under the stress of excitement caused by the event or condition.

a. Preliminary Factfinding

The foundational requirements for excited utterances are:

- the occurrence of a startling event or condition;
- contents of the statement relate to a startling event or condition;
- the statement was made by the declarant while under stress of excitement; and
- the stress of excitement was caused by the startling event or condition.

Sally's statement to George might also be an excited utterance. Again, the proponent must present evidence to satisfy the foundational requirements, and the judge will decide the preliminary questions pursuant to FRE 104(a). The judge may conclude that an SUV running through a red light and hitting a pedestrian is a *startling* event. Again, George would be the foundation witness to testify that the event occurred and that Sally was under stress of excitement when she made the statement. How might George describe Sally's behavior to prove that she was *under the stress of excitement*? George might also establish that Sally's stress was caused by the startling event, if he said, "She was perfectly calm before the accident." In Boucher v. Grant, 74 F. Supp. 2d 444, 450 (D.N.J. 1999), the court held that declarant Grant's hearsay statement was admissible under the following analysis:

> An automobile accident and a contemporaneous statement by an individual involved in that accident concerning its cause undoubtedly satisfy the first three elements of the excited utterance hearsay exception. The question becomes, then, whether the hearsay statements meet the last condition of admissibility, namely, spontaneity. . . .
> Boucher testified that his exchange with Grant occurred "within a minute" of the accident. . . . Grant himself testified that as a result of the crash, he was "scared . . . shaken up." . . . The brief lapse of time coupled with Grant's mental state cannot give rise to a finding of conscious reflection. Therefore, I conclude that the statement was made while Grant was still in an excited state and before he could reflect and fabricate.

Many factors such as the age of the declarant, the nature of the event, the lapse of time between the event and the statement, whether the statement was made in response to questions and the declarant's physical and mental condition are relevant to the question of whether the defendant was under the stress of excitement from the startling event at the time the statement was made.

b. Justification for the Admissibility of Excited Utterances

The justification for the exception is similar to the argument that present sense impressions are reliable. A statement made under the stress of a startling event or condition is likely to be spontaneous, and a person under stress is not likely to develop the intent to fabricate. If there is no opportunity to fabricate, the statement is likely to be sincere. Notice, however, that there is no foundational requirement of "contemporaneity" between the event and the statement. Stress of excitement is the substitute for contemporaneity. A longer time lag will not defeat application of the FRE 803(2) exception if the declarant remains under stress. So long as stress is operative, there is assumed to be no opportunity to plan to make a false statement and thus the statement is likely to be sincere. United States v. Obayagbona, 627 F. Supp. 329, 328 (E.D.N.Y. 1985) (the declarant must be sufficiently startled "to render inoperative the normal reflective thought process"). Since the duration of the declarant's stress of excitement is likely to be relatively short, memory danger may also be lessened.

However, as commentators have long recognized, the stress that decreases the sincerity danger may increase perception dangers and memory dangers, and perhaps even narration dangers as well. Consider the effects of seeing someone hit by a car — how carefully and accurately are you able to perceive and recount the details of such an event? These risks are discussed in Robert M. Hutchins and Donald Slesinger, Some Observations on the Law of Evidence: Spontaneous Exclamations, 28 Colum. L. Rev. 432 (1928); Fredric D. Woocher, Note, Did Your Eyes Deceive You? Expert Psychological Testimony on the Unreliability of Eyewitness Identification, 29 Stan. L. Rev. 969, 975-988 (1977). Nonetheless, the exception is well established in the Federal Rules and in most jurisdictions.

Compare the concern for contemporaneity or spontaneity under FRE 803(1) and (2) with the lack of such requirements for statements identifying a person admitted under FRE 801(d)(1)(C). We noted on page 465 that application of this exemption to statements not made after reperception of a person further undermines the potential reliability of such statements.

4. Elaboration of FRE 803(1) and (2): Effects of the Categorical Approach

a. The Categories Determine Admissibility

Do you agree that the probability of Sally's sincerity in making her statement about the gray SUV is increased by the fact that her statement was made contemporaneously with seeing the SUV, or by the fact that it was made under stress of a startling event? Analyzing this question requires you to think in terms of generalizations about large groups of out-of-court declarants who share either the FRE 803(1) or the FRE 803(2) characteristic in common. How can we be sure that everyone within this large group does have enhanced sincerity? The answer is, we cannot be sure. Even more troubling, how do we know that Sally has good eyesight and could perceive the SUV from the distance at which she was standing, or could perceive that the light was red? The answer is, we do not know. The only facts about Sally's testimonial qualities that FRE 803(1) and (2) require to be presented to the jury are the facts about spontaneity that satisfy the categorical requirements of the exceptions.

The effects of this categorical approach are twofold. First, if a statement clearly fits within the broad categorical generalizations of the specific exception, it must be admitted (unless there is some other objection to its admissibility unrelated to hearsay). "If a declaration comes within a category defined as an exception, the declaration is admissible without any preliminary credibility finding by the judge . . ." United States v. DiMaria, 727 F.2d 265, 272 (2d Cir. 1984). Except for the three specific exceptions, (FRE 803(6), 803(8), and 804(b)(3)), there is no explicit judicial discretion to exclude a particular statement that fits within a categorical exception because the judge doubts the sincerity, perception, memory, or narration of the hearsay declarant. United States v. Perkins, 1999 WL 506980 (6th Cir. 1999) (declarant, a police informant, had the opportunity to deliberately mislead the police in reporting the contents of a series of phone calls made over an extended period of time with defendant; nevertheless, declarant's statements fit within present sense impression exception). Second, if a judge thinks that a hearsay statement seems to be particularly trustworthy but it is neither contemporaneous with an event (it was made an hour later) nor made under the stress of excitement (it was made calmly), the judge has no explicit discretion under FRE 803(1) or (2) to admit it. The categorical requirements of each exception determine admissibility. Only FRE 807 permits the admission of hearsay based on judicial determinations that it is trustworthy.

b. The Categorical Terms Require Judicial Interpretation

Although there is no explicit discretion in most of the hearsay exceptions, judges do have some leeway when they interpret and apply the categorical terms of the exceptions to particular statements. How long a time lag is permitted by the term "immediately thereafter" in FRE 803(1)? Just what is "stress of excitement" in FRE 803(2), and how long does it last? There are no clear-cut answers to these questions in some cases. You will see in many of the Rule 803 and Rule 804 exceptions that there is considerable room for judicial interpretation. Since the categorical requirements are determinative of admissibility, judicial interpretation of these requirements is crucial to the administration of hearsay policy. These requirements are intended to ensure the trustworthiness of one or more of the declarant's testimonial qualities. It follows that judges should interpret and apply the doctrinal terms with the awareness that different interpretations can either increase or decrease the apparent trustworthiness of admitted hearsay statements.

i. Time Lapse Between Event and Statement. Not all seemingly contemporaneous statements are really spontaneous. They might have been thought up in advance, if the declarant had any foreknowledge that the relevant event might occur. And a time lapse of more than a few minutes may be plenty of time to think up something self-serving to say. Particularly if a statement is obviously self-serving, one may doubt its spontaneity and, therefore, its sincerity. Rigorous application of the contemporaneity requirement of FRE 803(1) would reduce this problem. Many courts have interpreted "immediately thereafter" in FRE 803(1) to mean within a matter of seconds, or as soon as is possible. United States v. Campbell, 782 F.Supp. 1258 (N.D.Ill. 1991) (911 call concerning a convenience store shooting made almost immediately after perpetrator had fled). Some courts, however, have stretched the interpretation of that doctrinal phrase to admit apparently spontaneous statements made 10 to 15 minutes after the event they describe or explain. See, e.g., United States v. Obayagbona, 627 F. Supp. 329 (E.D.N.Y. 1985) (statement made by undercover police officer about a drug transaction, made 14 minutes afterward, "was as spontaneous as possible" since it could not be made until after the arrest). A time lapse of one hour, however, has been held not sufficiently contemporaneous. Katona v. Federal Express Corp., 1998 WL 126059 (S.D.N.Y. 1998); and if the time lapse is unknown, courts may be cautious. United States v. Manfre, 368 F.3d 832, 840 (8th Cir. 2004) ("too much time had passed" between event and declarant's statement, "[a]t the very least, . . . an intervening walk or drive" before the statement was made; "we decline to expand [the exception] to cover a declarant's relatively recent memories").

FRE 803(2) places no specific time restraint on the scope of the exception. The temporal gap is therefore not dispositive, but is a relevant consideration in determining whether the statement is made while the declarant is still under stress. Other relevant factors include "the characteristics of the event; the subject matter of the statement; whether the statement was made in response to an inquiry; and the declarant's age, motive to lie and physical and mental condition." United States v. Alexander, 331 F.3d 116, 123 (D.C.Cir. 2003). Compare United States v. Winters, 33 F.2d 720 (6th Cir. 1994) (victim's speculations, made to police officers two days after being shot, about who might have wanted to hurt him were excluded as "the product of conscious reflection") with United States v. Tabaja, 91 Fed.Appx. 405 (6th Cir. 2004) (aunt of child kidnapped by his father and taken out of the country told police about a phone conversation she had with defendant about the kidnapping; aunt's excited emotional state could persist for eleven hour time gap due to the "devastating nature of the event"). In cases where the event is less startling, courts tend to require a shorter time lapse between event and statement.

Statements of young children about incidents of sexual abuse are frequently made hours or even days after the alleged incident occurred. Some courts admit these statements under FRE 803(2) citing various justifications — "first real opportunity" to speak to an adult or caregiver, or fear and guilt causing child to delay reporting, or lack of capacity to fabricate — while other courts are suspicious of such lengthy delays. Reed v. Thalacker, 198 F.3d 1058, 1062 (8th Cir. 1999) ("distorted recollection . . . can occur through deliberate coaching, inadvertent suggestion, confusion of fact and fantasy, or a simple defect in memory"). For a teenager, a time lapse of three hours has been held to be too long to reduce the risk of deliberate fabrication, particularly when the declarant had not appeared to be stressed in the interim. Stress can be rekindled by events that remind the declarant of the startling event or that generate additional anguish. United States v. Lossiah, 129 Fed.Appx. 434 (10th Cir. 2005) (child under age of 12 saw defendant at her school and "ran to tell" her teacher "Don't let him check me out . . . he raped me;" alleged attack had occurred two months before, but caused child to be fearful when she saw defendant at school).

Cases involving domestic violence may also justify courts in extending the period of time during which the declarant is under stress: "trauma and anxiety prompted by a spousal assault — which form the predicate for calling something an excited utterance — do not suddenly dissipate when the assailant leaves the scene." United States v. Green, 125 Fed.Appx. 659, 662(6th Cir. 2005); United States v. Cruz, 156 F.3d 22, 30 (1st Cir. 1998) (beating lasted until 4 a.m., declarant unable to escape the apartment for some time, "likely that [she] continued to suffer from the trauma" when she fled to the women's shelter and made her statement at 8 a.m.). Excited utterances about criminal activity made to 911 operators and police present challenging issues under Crawford v. Washington's holding that the Confrontation Clause applies to "testimonial" statements. See Section G, infra.

ii.   Content of the Statement.   The FRE 803(1) requirement that the declaration be one *describing or explaining an event or condition* is intended to be a limitation that is consistent with the exception's underlying rationale. United States v. Ferber, 966 F.Supp. 90 (D.Mass.1997) (handwritten notes reciting what someone said at a meeting fall within the exception). The Advisory Committee Note explains that the language of FRE 803(2) — *relating to a startling event* — "affords a broader scope of subject matter coverage." But the Advisory Committee does not elaborate on the meaning of the terms *describing, explaining,* and *relating,* and it is not intuitively obvious how broadly or narrowly they should be defined. The Note does cite two cases that apparently, in the view of the Advisory Committee, would fall within the meaning of *relating to* but not *describing or explaining*:

> See Sanitary Grocery Co. v. Snead, 67 App. D.C. 129, 90 F.2d 374 (1937), slip-and-fall case sustaining admissibility of clerk's statement, "That has been on the floor for a couple of hours," and Murphy Auto Parts Co. v. Ball, 101 U.S. App. D.C. 416, 249 F.2d 508 (1957), upholding admission, on issue of driver's agency, of his statement that he had to call on a customer and was in a hurry to get home.

Why do these statements relate to but not describe or explain an event or condition? The first statement refers to a past historical fact, and does not express a *present* description of the floor. The second refers to the driver's purpose in driving his truck, and does not describe the event or condition — the accident — that was the subject of his statement. Why should statements encompassing this broader range of facts be admissible under FRE 803(2) but not FRE 803(1)? United States v. Alarcon-Simi, 300 F.3d 1172, 1176 (9th Cir. 2002) (defendant sought admission of his own exculpatory statement just after the "traumatic incident" of being arrested for fraudulent check-cashing; defendant's statement that "he didn't know about [it]" held inadmissible as not relating to what "occurred *at the time of his arrest*" but to earlier events).

c. Use of the Statement Itself in Preliminary Factfinding

In general, the judge's preliminary factfinding necessary to apply the categorical terms of the Rule 801(d) exemptions and the Rule 803 exceptions is governed by FRE 104(a). May the judge rely on the content of the hearsay statement itself to establish the existence of the preliminary facts? This is the same "bootstrapping" issue that we discussed in the context of the Rule 801(d)(2)(E) co-conspirators' exemption, and that analysis is equally applicable here. FRE 104(a) permits the judge to use inadmissible evidence, and thus would permit use of the statement itself.

This issue frequently arises with regard to present sense impressions and excited utterances when the proponent wants to use the content of these statements to prove that an event (or a startling event) actually occurred. Other witnesses, including the foundation witness who testifies about the present sense impression or excited utterance, may be able to give testimony that the event occurred. But often, such independent evidence will not be available. For example, if Sally was speaking to George on her car phone when she said "a gray SUV just ran the red light and hit a pedestrian," George cannot provide independent evidence that the event described by Sally actually occurred. Statements admitted under FRE 803(1) and (2) can also be in writing, so there may be no other person present to verify either the event or when the written statement was made. The contents of the statement itself may be used by the judge to decide that an event occurred, when it occurred, and what kind of an event it was. United States v. Brown, 254 F.3d 454, 457 (3rd Cir. 2001) (statement by two declarants that "a man was waving a gun and threatening to shoot somebody" showed a startling event).

May the statement alone satisfy the Rule 104(a) burden of proving that an event occurred? Yes, according to the Advisory Committee Note. "[A]n excited utterance may of itself be sufficient to establish the occurrence of the startling event." Id. at 459. As a practical matter, there will usually be ample independent evidence that a startling event occurred. The nature of the event is likely to attract attention; and even if there are no eyewitnesses to the event other than the declarant, the declarant's nervousness or injuries or quivering voice would constitute at least some independent evidence of an exciting event. Id. at 459 (police officer described unidentified declarants as "very excited, very nervous, hopping around.") While acknowledging that the statement itself may be sufficient to establish the exciting event, the Advisory Committee Note states that "[w]hen declarant is an unidentified bystander, the cases indicate hesitancy in upholding the statement alone as sufficient, . . . a result which would under appropriate circumstances be consistent with the rule." Courts are no longer hesitant. United States v. Brown, supra; United States v. Montero-Camargo, 177 F.3d 1113, 1123 (9th Cir. 1999) ("trustworthiness of the statement is bolstered by the declarant's status as a mere bystander with no apparent motivation for providing false information."); Miller v. Crown Amusements, Inc., 821 F.Supp. 703 (S.D.Ga. 1993) (unidentified 911 caller).

d. Proof of Personal Knowledge

The proponent of a present sense impression or excited utterance must show that "the declarant had personally perceived the event or condition about which the statement is made." United States v. Mitchell, 145 F.3d 572, 575 (3d Cir. 1998). The content of the statement, and the circumstances surrounding the making of it, may be sufficient, even when the declarant is unidentified. In Miller v. Keating, 754 F.2d 507 (3d Cir. 1985), an unidentified bystander ran up to the parties involved in an automobile collision and exclaimed that one car (the defendant's) had cut into the line of traffic, thus causing the accident. The appellate court reversed the trial court's admission of this statement:

> When there is no evidence of personal perception, apart from the declaration itself, courts have hesitated to allow the excited utterance to stand alone as evidence of the declarant's opportunity to observe. . . . In some cases, however, the substance of the statement itself does contain words revealing perception. A statement such as, "I saw that blue truck run down the lady on the corner," might stand alone to show perception if the trial judge finds, from the particular circumstances, that he is satisfied by a preponderance that the declarant spoke from personal perception. . . .
>
> The circumstances external to the statement itself not only fail to demonstrate that the declarant was in a position to have seen what happened, they also fail to show that the declarant was excited when he spoke. No one so testified, and the trial judge made no finding of excitement. Thus, this last prong of the test for admissibility is also unsatisfied. [Id. at 511-512.]

Notice that in *Miller v. Keating*, the court treated the issue of personal knowledge as an FRE 104(a) issue for the judge. Most other opinions on this point agree. Miller v. Crown Amusements, Inc., supra, 821 F.Supp. at 705-706 ("the Court finds by a preponderance of the evidence that the declarant observed the accident. The caller specifically stated, '[W]e *noticed* [the truck sideswipe a person]' thus indicating actual perception.")

KEY POINTS

1. Generalizations about the lack of sincerity and memory dangers provide the justification for the present sense impression and excited utterance exceptions, but statements falling within these exceptions remain untested with regard to perception and narration dangers.

2. The rigor with which courts interpret and apply the terms defining the time lapse between the event or condition and the statement itself affects the degree of sincerity danger in both exceptions.

3. The judge may use the statement itself to determine whether and when the event or condition occurred pursuant to FRE 104(a), and in some cases may require no independent evidence.

PROBLEMS

8.43. Defendant Scott is charged with being a felon in possession of a firearm. Evidence will show that Scott fled from a routine traffic stop. He was chased for 150 yards by Officer Taylor, who radioed for backup assistance. Responding within five minutes to Scott's call, Officer Firdon arrived on the scene and observed Taylor apprehending and handcuffing Scott. Firdon describes Taylor as "panting, out of breath, and excited." Taylor informed Firdon that he had seen Scott throw a firearm about 70 yards from the scene of the arrest. When Firdon recovered a .38 revolver from that area, Taylor said, "That looks like the one he threw." At the time of Scott's trial, Taylor has moved out of state. May Firdon testify to Taylor's two statements to prove Scott's possession of a firearm?

8.44. Return to Problem 3.2, Pedroso v. Driver, at page 129. A teacher at Paul's school testifies for plaintiffs that Ann, who was on the school bus with Paul, was playing during recess in the schoolyard several days after the accident. Ann suddenly started to cry and exclaimed, "That's the bus driver who hit Paul on the side of the road" just as Denise Driver was walking by. Admissible?

8.45. Defendant Louis D'Onofrio is charged with illegal possession of a firearm as a convicted felon and two counts of brandishing a deadly weapon, one occurring on January 24 and one on January 26.

   (a) A 911 call was made by Mrs. D'Onofrio from her home at 2:15 A.M. on January 26. She told the operator that her husband, Louis, was drunk and threatening to shoot her. The operator could hear Louis yelling loudly. The operator asked whether her husband had a weapon. Mrs. D'Onofrio said that he had a gun and had pointed it at her. Can the tape recording of this conversation be admitted at defendant's trial?

   (b) Police officers arrived at the D'Onofrio home at 2:30 A.M. Mrs. D'Onofrio consented to their search for the gun. Mrs. D'Onofrio was upset and crying. She stated that she and Louis had been arguing on the evening of January 24; that he held the gun and threatened to kill her during the argument; that when she returned from work on January 25, Louis had the gun and killed the family cat; that he spent the evening of January 25 drinking and that she had called 911 at 2:15 A.M. when he began to make more threats. Can the officers testify about these statements at defendant's trial?

8.46. Defendant Jack Jordan is charged with arson as a result of a fire that destroyed his clothing store and the apartments above it. The prosecution claims that Jack employed his brother Mark and friend Thomas Telford to commit the deed and gave them a key to the store, which had not been broken into. The fire was ablaze by 11:00 P.M. and, apparently, Telford remained at the scene. He was told by tenants exiting the building that there might be other people trapped inside. At 2:00 A.M., Telford knocked on the window of his friend Larry's apartment, appeared "all hyped up" and "nervous" according to Larry, and told Larry that "Mark and I lit a building for Jack." Can Larry testify as to Telford's statement in Jack Jordan's trial?

8.47. John Dart is charged with endangering the life of the three-year-old daughter of his girlfriend, Karen. Karen and her children, three-year-old Brenda and seven-year-old Stephanie, had moved in with Dart in April of 2000. In November of 2000, Brenda was found unconscious at home, taken to the hospital, and diagnosed as having suffered a subdural hematoma. Dart claims that he saw her fall from the headboard of a bed onto the floor. The prosecution claims that Dart beat the child. At trial, the prosecution offers the testimony of Dorothy Bobbitt, a friend of Karen's, who lived about eight blocks from Dart's home. Bobbitt would testify as follows:

> On August 29, 2000, Stephanie came to my house, knocking on the door and trying to tear it off its hinges. She was hollering and screaming and crying, waving her arms and just crying. She wouldn't calm down. She just kept saying "He's going to kill her. He's going to kill her." I kept saying "Who? Who?" She couldn't talk. I went to get her some Kool-Aid real quick. My husband was trying to help me get her calmed down. He got a blanket because all she had on was a t-shirt and socks. She said "Dorothy, you've got to do something." And I kept saying "Who." And finally she said "John." And I said 'Who, your mom?" And she said "No, Brenda." And that's when she told me he had picked Brenda up by the face and that he had hit her up against the wall, and was being mean, and just all kinds of stuff. I really can't recall all she said, just some things stick in my mind.

Stephanie will not testify at trial. What objections can Dart make to the admission of Bobbitt's testimony? What result?

5.   Interpretation and Illustration of FRE 803(3): State-of-Mind Declarations

FRE 803(3) states:

> (3) Then existing mental, emotional, or physical condition. A statement of the declarant's then existing state of mind, emotion, sensation, or physical condition (such as intent, plan, motive, design, mental feeling, pain, and bodily health), but not including a statement of memory or belief to prove the fact remembered or believed unless it relates to the execution, revocation, identification, or terms of declarant's will.

a.   Preliminary Factfinding

The foundational requirements for statements of state of mind are:

- the contents of the statement express the declarant's state of mind that is currently existing at the time of the statement;

- state of mind may include emotion, sensation, physical condition, intent, plan, motive, design, mental feeling, pain, and bodily health; and
- a state of mind of memory or belief may not be used to prove the fact remembered or believed unless it relates to the declarant's will.

As with all exceptions that depend on content as a categorical requirement, the judge can determine content from proof of the statement itself. Thus the statements "I like Harold the best of all my children" or "I am miserably unhappy at work" fall within the FRE 803(3) exception, and will be admissible for their truth, if those current feelings are relevant. No other foundational facts concerning the declarant or the circumstances within which the statement was made are required.

Notice that Rule 803(3) defines *state of mind* broadly to include any sensation present in the mind of declarant, including emotion, intent and pain. The state of mind of a party, or of any person who becomes involved in litigated events, may be relevant at trial: For example, a criminal defendant's state of mind of "love" or "hate" can be relevant to show motive for the crime; a civil defendant's state of mind of "knowledge" can be relevant to prove notice; and in any type of case, a witness's state of mind of "bias" or "malice" toward one of the parties can be relevant to impeach the witness's credibility.

But the scope of the FRE 803(3) exception is specifically limited. Statements of memory or belief may be used to prove a declarant's then-existing relevant state of mind, but may not be admitted to prove the fact remembered or believed, unless that fact relates to the declarant's will. Thus the statement of belief "I think my brakes are bad," or the statement of memory "My brakes squeaked yesterday," may be used to prove the declarant's current state of mind of knowledge (notice), *but not the fact that the brakes are bad*. In contrast, the statement "I want Harold to inherit all of my estate so I have left it all to him in my will" is admissible to prove the state of mind of the declarant *as well as the terms of the declarant's will*.

b.   Justification for the State-of-Mind Exception

A statement relevant to prove the declarant's current state of mind requires inferences about the declarant's sincerity and narration. The fact of consequence is what is going on inside the mind of the declarant, and the declarant's statement must sincerely and accurately express what that is. The declarant is not perceiving anything outside the declarant's own mind, so there is no traditional risk of misperception. And, since the statement expresses the *then existing* mental state, there is no memory problem. Thus the primary rationale for the state-of-mind exception is that there are no perception or memory dangers. Under the reliability rationale of the Rule 803 exceptions, the absence of these dangers provides circumstantial guarantees of trustworthiness, and thus diminishes the importance of cross-examining the declarant.

There is, however, a weakness in the trustworthiness justification for the state-of-mind exception. Although it has been said that statements that express a present state of mind are likely to be spontaneous and therefore sincere, there is no independent requirement of proving spontaneity and there is no limit to the circumstances in which such statements can be made. The statement "I love my spouse" may be spontaneous, or it may be calculated to mislead if the declarant has a reason to want to create the false impression of affection. There are no definitive means of proving that the declarant really has the mental state that is being spoken about. Thus the sincerity risks in FRE 803(3) statements are substantial. If the statement is not spontaneous, then the declarant has the opportunity to fabricate. In United States v. DiMaria, 727 F.2d 265, 271-272 (2d Cir. 1984), the defendant's statement during his arrest "I only came here to get some cheap cigarettes" was offered by the defense to rebut a presumption of guilty knowledge raised by defendant's possession of cigarettes that were in fact stolen. The prosecution contended that this statement should not be admitted under FRE 803(3) as "an absolutely classic false exculpatory statement." The court acknowledged that a declaration of a mental state by an accused can readily be trumped up, but held that since it fell within FRE 803(3) "its truth or falsity was for the jury to determine." Some courts, however, have added a requirement that the declarant "must not have had time to reflect and to fabricate or misrepresent the state of mind being expressed." United States v. Secor, 73 Fed.Appx. 554, 566-567 (4th Cir. 2003). These cases usually involve exculpatory statements made by criminal defendants either long after the crime committed, when their states of mind are no longer relevant, or after they suspect they are under investigation and have a clear motive to represent themselves as innocent.

Necessity may justify the admission of state-of-mind statements despite their sincerity risks. Mental states are such a pervasive part of our substantive law that it would be unwise to bar from admissibility one of the primary sources for evidence about mental states. This rationale, however, is not always compelling. The state-of-mind exception is not limited to situations in which a person's mental state is an ultimate issue in litigation, where the declarant's statement might indeed be the only (or best) available evidence. Moreover, we are frequently able to infer mental states from the conduct of individuals, and we may rely on people's actions even more than people's words in assessing mental states.

Statements of memory or belief used to prove facts concerning the declarant's will do require reliance on the declarant's memory and perception, as well as sincerity and narrative ability. Making a will is an external event that the declarant has perceived, and remembers. Admission of these statements is justified by the likelihood that persons will speak carefully about their wills and the necessity that arises from the unavailability of the declarant.

c. State-of-Mind Utterances Are Classified as Either Direct or Circumstantial

Some utterances directly assert the declarant's mental state. For example, to prove that a witness has a motive to lie in favor of plaintiff, the defendant could offer evidence that the witness once said, "I can't stand the defendant." This is a direct statement of the witness's feelings and state of mind. But what if the witness said, "The defendant is a vile person who has done me great harm"? This statement is not a direct assertion of a mental state, but it probably reflects a state of mind of intense dislike. Because the mental state is not directly asserted, courts and commentators call this type of statement "circumstantial evidence" of the witness's state of mind.

Utterances that are circumstantial evidence of the declarant's state of mind are not offered to prove the truth of the literal matters they assert. The witness's statement is not offered to prove that the defendant is vile, or that the defendant has done great harm to the witness. Thus some courts and commentators have taken the position that utterances that are circumstantial evidence of state of mind are nonhearsay. People v. Morales, 684 N.Y.S.2d 853, 855 (Sup. Ct. 1999) (statement "I should have killed him, this guy had no business insulting my wife like that" admitted as not hearsay to prove defendant's then-existing belief that what victim had said to defendant's wife was grossly insulting and provoking, which was relevant to his state of mind defense). But unlike the categories of nonhearsay that we discussed at pages 427-429, supra — *effect on listener* and *legally operative facts* — the relevancy of state-of-mind utterances *does* involve potential sincerity and narration risks. If the witness in our hypothetical is lying or joking, and does not sincerely believe that the defendant is vile and has done wrong, then the witness's statement is not relevant to prove a motive to lie in favor of plaintiff. Therefore, utterances that are circumstantial evidence of state of mind are not a true nonhearsay category.

Rather, these utterances seem more like statements offered to prove the declarant's *unstated belief* about the declarant's own state of mind, similar to statements discussed at pages 440-442, supra. Statements of "unstated states of mind" do not involve perception or memory risks, but they do not *necessarily* bear diminished narration and sincerity dangers if they are intending to communicate the mental state. This is also true, of course, for direct assertions of state of mind. FRE 803(3) provides such a broad hearsay exception for statements of a declarant's then-existing state of mind that labeling them as direct or circumstantial, hearsay or nonhearsay, is purely academic in terms of admissibility under the Federal Rules.

6.   Elaboration of FRE 803(3): Relevant Uses of State-of-Mind Evidence

a.   *Future and Past State of Mind of the Declarant*

For a declarant's statement of state of mind to be relevant, the currently existing state of mind need not be an ultimate issue in the case. Evidence of a person's existing state of mind may be just one step in the inferential process to establish some fact of consequence. Frequently, inferences both forward and backward in time are made from statements of currently existing mental states. For example, consider a case in which a criminal defendant wishes to establish that some third person had a motive for killing the victim, in order to suggest that the third person was in fact the killer. The third person's statement, "I hate the victim," made a week before the killing, is admissible under FRE 803(3) to prove that one week before the killing the third person hated the victim. From hatred at that time we infer a future state of mind — there was probably still hatred a week later, when the killing occurred. The inference is based on the generalization that strong emotional feelings about an individual are not likely to change over a relatively short period of time. Hatred a week later is relevant to show a motive to harm the victim, and from motive we infer the possibility that the third person killed the victim.

Just as state of mind can be used to prove future state of mind, it can also be used to prove a past state of mind without relying on the declarant's perception or memory. Consider in the preceding murder case that the third person said two days after the murder, "The thought of the victim fills me with rage." The present state of mind of "rage" would be relevant to prove that declarant was probably also angry at the victim two days earlier, again because of a generalization about the stability of such states of mind. If angry two days earlier, the declarant may have had a motive to kill the victim at that time. Statements made months after the time at which the declarant's state of mind was relevant have been held too remote to be probative. United States v. Reyes, 239 F.3d 722, 743 (5th Cir. 2001).

b.   Future Conduct of the Declarant

Mary's statement on Monday "I plan to leave on my vacation to Hawaii on Tuesday" may be relevant to prove that she in fact left on Tuesday, and that she went to Hawaii. We first must infer the truth of the matter she asserts — that on Monday, Mary sincerely planned to leave on Tuesday for her vacation in Hawaii. Then, from this state of mind, we can infer that she probably had the same intent on Tuesday and, then, that she carried it out and did go to Hawaii.

The generalizations underlying the inference from Mary's state of mind to her future conduct concern the behavior of people; for example, that people with intentions or plans of the type that Mary had are not likely to change (in one day), or that people generally do the things (like go on vacations) that they intend or plan to do. The probability of each inference from intent to future conduct will vary depending on the nature of the intended activity and the time lag involved. In some situations the inferences may be so speculative that a person's stated intent may have very low probative value. Intent may be stated so far in advance, or may be so contingent, that there is little probative force to the generalization that people act in conformity with intent. What is important is that the inferences from Mary's state of mind to her conduct do not require any further evaluation of Mary's testimonial qualities. Thus FRE 803(3) could be used to admit Mary's statement of intent to show that she had that same intent at some future time, and that she acted on it. United States ex rel. Remtech, Inc. v. National Union Fire Ins. Co., 2000 WL 1171139 (9th Cir. 2000) (contractor's statement that a subcontractor would be "off the project" admissible to establish an intent or plan to terminate the subcontractor).

c.   Evidence of State of Mind Used to Prove Past Facts

FRE 803(3) provides that statements of memory or belief to prove the fact remembered or believed may not be admitted through the state-of-mind exception (unless they concern wills). It is common that past facts are asserted in the context of state-of-mind evidence; but proof of the truth of the past facts is not an acceptable use of FRE 803(3). To show the bias of Emily, who is testifying as a witness against John, evidence might be offered that Emily said outside of court, "I am angry at John because he stole all of my money last year." The statement about the theft is a statement of memory or belief. FRE 803(3) could not be used if the statement is offered to prove that John did steal the money, the fact remembered or believed. Why? The past fact of theft is an event outside Emily's mind. Her accurate perception and memory would be necessary to the statement's relevance. Since the justification for the FRE 803(3) exception is that perception and memory risks are nonexistent, the exception cannot be used when those risks are present. The same is true if Emily, the declarant, said "I believe that John stole all my money last year." All statements about past facts contain an implicit "I think" or "I believe." Admitting such statements as expressing a state of mind of "belief" would swallow the hearsay prohibition. United States v. Mandel, 437 F. Supp. 262 (D. Md. 1977) (admission of statements that refer to a relevant present state of mind but also past conduct of declarant and others would threaten continued existence of hearsay rule).

It is possible that if the past fact of theft is not relevant to the litigation, then the declarant's entire statement might be admissible simply to prove the relevant fact — Emily's anger at John. Theft would be a good reason to feel angry and it makes her statement all the more probative of her relevant state of mind of bias against John. Indeed, the past fact of theft need not even be true; if Emily believes it, however, her state of mind of anger is more probable. FRE 403 might be the basis for objection if the statement about the theft raises dangers of unfair prejudice against a party or confusion of the issues.

d. The Hillmon Case

Prior to the Federal Rules of Evidence, some courts applied the state-of-mind exception more broadly (and some courts still do). One of the leading state-of-mind cases, Mutual Life Insurance Co. of New York v. Hillmon, 145 U.S. 285 (1892), presents a challenging interpretation of the exception. *Hillmon* was an action by Sallie Hillmon to recover the proceeds of life insurance policies on the life of her husband John Hillmon, who, she alleged, died in Crooked Creek, Colorado, on March 17, 1879. The principal issue in the case was whether a body found in Crooked Creek was Hillmon's. The plaintiff contended that it was. The defendant insurance companies tried to establish that Hillmon was not dead. They alleged that a man named Walters had traveled to Crooked Creek with Hillmon and that the body was Walters's, not Hillmon's. Their evidence included the contents of a letter Walters had written to his sister, stating that he intended to go to Colorado. The sister testified that she received the letter around March 4, 1879, that the letter was in Walters's handwriting, that she had searched for the letter but could not find it, and that she remembered the contents of the letter. She then orally related the contents:

> Dear sister and all: I now in my usual style drop you a few lines to let you know that I expect to leave Wichita on or about March the 5th, with a certain Mr. Hillmon, a sheeptrader, for Colorado or parts unknown to me. I expect to see the country now. News are of no interest to you, as you are not acquainted here. I will close with compliments to all inquiring friends. Love to all. I am truly your brother, Fred. Adolph Walters. [Id. at 288.]

The trial court sustained a hearsay objection and excluded proof of this and a similar letter from Walters, and the jury found in favor of Sallie Hillmon. In reversing this judgment, the Supreme Court explained why proof of the letters was admissible:

> The letters in question were competent, not as narratives of facts communicated to the writer by others, nor yet as proof that he actually went away from Wichita, but as evidence that, shortly before the time when other evidence tended to show that he went away, he had the intention of going, *and of going with Hillmon*, which made it more probable both that he did go *and that he went with Hillmon*, than if there had been no proof of such intention. In view of the mass of conflicting testimony introduced upon the question whether it was the body of Walters that was found in Hillmon's camp, this evidence might properly influence the jury in determining that question. [Id. at 295-296 (emphasis added).]

i.   Walters's Future Conduct.   It is correct that Walters's statement in his letter is relevant to prove his own intent to leave Wichita and to go to Colorado. The Court held as much in the same paragraph. The Court's "nor yet" language may appear confusing, but we believe that it simply refers to steps in the logical chain of inferences: One must first infer from Walters's expression of intent to leave that he actually intended to leave (i.e., that the words are a sincere expression of his intent). Until one makes that first inference, it is not (yet) possible to infer from the letter that Walters did leave Wichita. And, as we have previously discussed, a declarant's statement of intent to do an act in the future fits within the FRE 803(3) exception, and may generate the further inference that the declarant actually did do that act without involving any additional hearsay dangers. So far so good; Walters's statement would be admissible to prove his own intent and his own future conduct.

ii.   Hillmon's Future Conduct.   Some courts, in apparent reliance on the italicized portions of the above quotation, have interpreted *Hillmon* to stand for the proposition that Walters's letters could also be used to show Hillmon's future conduct — that Hillmon went to Crooked Creek with Walters. As a result, these courts have used a declarant's statement about what a third person plans to do to prove what that third person in fact did, and they have justified admission of these statements under the state-of-mind exception. See United States v. Pheaster, 544 F.2d 353 (9th Cir. 1976) (statement of intent to meet Angelo to get drugs admissible to show that declarant did meet Angelo); People v. Alcalde, 148 P.2d 627 (Calif. 1944) (victim's statement of intent to go out with Frank admissible to prove that Frank went out with victim and thus had the opportunity to commit murder).

Such use of this exception is problematic, however, because the relevance of Walters's assertion that Hillmon planned to go to Crooked Creek is necessarily dependent on Walters's accurate perception and memory. Walters could know that Hillmon planned to go to Crooked Creek only if Walters had properly perceived and remembered some past fact — something that Hillmon (or perhaps some third person) said or did to indicate that Hillmon was going to Crooked Creek and wanted to travel with Walters. Thus all hearsay dangers are potentially present. Except regarding wills, however, the traditional state-of-mind exception applied (and FRE 803(3) today applies) only to declarations that do not have perception and memory problems. If Walters's letter directly expressed the fact on which his knowledge of Hillmon's intent was based (e.g., Hillmon had invited Walters to go with him), such an additional statement would not be admissible under the state-of-mind exception. It would be a statement of memory or belief, offered to prove the fact believed. United States v. Cohen, 631 F.2d 1223 (5th Cir. 1980) (the exception "does not permit a declarant to relate . . . why he held the particular state of mind, or what he might have believed that would have induced the state of mind").

In Walters's letter, past facts about Hillmon's conduct are implied, not expressed, by Walters's plan to travel "with Hillmon." Still, using Walters's own state of mind for the purpose of proving the state of mind of another person (Hillmon's intent to travel) or the future conduct of another person (Hillmon did travel to Crooked Creek) depends on an inference about Walters's perception and memory of some past fact about that other person. Otherwise, Walters's belief about what the other person will do would be irrelevant speculation. Permitting the state-of-mind exception to admit statements for purposes that so clearly depend on the declarant's perception and memory of past facts would undermine the policies of the rule.

iii.   Recent Interpretations of Hillmon.

A number of federal courts have held that FRE 803(3) does not support the use of a declarant's state-of-mind declaration to prove the conduct of a third person. The House Judiciary Committee approved the Rule 803(3) exception under the explicit assumption that the rule would limit the *Hillmon* doctrine to use of the declarant's state of mind to prove only the declarant's own future conduct. Other courts, however, have admitted declarants' statements of intent to meet a third person against that third person, to prove that the declarant and that person did meet. United States v. Johnson, 354 F.Supp. 2d 939, 962 (N.D. Iowa 2005) (discussing collected cases). Most of these decisions have required independent corroboration of the third person's conduct. See, e.g., United States v. Sperling, 726 F.2d. 69, 73-74 (2d Cir. 1984) (declarant's statement that she would meet with her drug source at noon that day was admissible to prove Sperling's participation in a drug conspiracy where agents observed Sperling meet with the declarant at noon). See Joseph A. Devall, Jr., Comment, 78 Tul.L.Rev. 911 (2004) for a survey of the split in state court authority on whether the state of mind exception permits statements of intent to prove the conduct of third persons.

Another possible interpretation of the Court's language in *Hillmon* is that it would be appropriate to infer that Walters planned to take the trip *only* if Hillmon would accompany him. It would be an intent conditioned on the occurrence of a future event, Hillmon's independent decision to accompany Walters, that may or may not occur. Since Walters was not in Wichita, this interpretation of Walters's intent permits the further inference, without reliance on Walters's perception or memory, that Hillmon did decide to go to Crooked Creek. It would be reasonable to infer that Walters left Wichita, acting on his intent to leave only in the company of Hillmon, and therefore that Hillmon left too. Treating Walters's statement as admissible hearsay, expressing only his own state of mind with no reliance on his perception or memory, depends on inferring from his letter that his plan was to take the trip *only* if Hillmon were going too. What do you think?

How should the problem of using state-of-mind statements against third persons be resolved? Keep in mind that concern with the inference from Walters's own intent (or belief) to Walters's own future conduct is *not* a hearsay problem. Rather, it is a problem of relevance that can be resolved by applying FRE 401 and FRE 403. If we are willing to invest trial judges with discretion to evaluate the strength of the inference from a declarant's intent forwards to future conduct, should we also be willing to commit to the trial judge's discretion the evaluation of the inference from intent (or belief) backward to a third person's conduct that caused the intent (or belief)? To do so would mean abandoning the hearsay rule as we know it in favor of judicial discretion. Keep this question in mind as you continue to study the Rule 803 exceptions. We return to it at the end of this chapter.

KEY POINTS

1. Statements expressing a declarant's current state of mind, both directly and circumstantially, are admissible under FRE 803(3) to prove that state of mind, if it is relevant in the case. Although sincerity and narration dangers are present, there are no perception and memory dangers.

2. State-of-mind evidence may not be admitted under FRE 803(3) if its relevancy is to prove an historical event or condition, typically the fact that caused the state of

mind. If statements of state of mind were used to prove past facts, or to prove the conduct of third persons, perception and memory dangers would be involved. Some courts do permit statements of a declarant's intent to be used to prove the future conduct of a third person, as well as the declarant's conduct, if there is corroboration.

3. Statements of past state of mind and past fact relating to the declarant's will may, however, be admitted under FRE 803(3).

PROBLEMS

8.48. Brenda White has been sued for negligence by the driver of an automobile that was hit by Brenda's car when Brenda was allegedly driving 100 MPH on a freeway between her home in the country and Central City. Is the following testimony admissible?

   (a) W_1 testifies that on the morning of the accident, Brenda White said, "I love to drive my car at 100 MPH."
   (b) W_2 testifies that on the morning of the accident, Brenda White said, "I intend to speed all the way to Central City."
   (c)   A bystander testifies that two miles before the accident a hitchhiker said, "I believe that blue car just sped right by me going 100 MPH."
   (d)   A bystander testifies that, at the scene of the accident, a hitchhiker said, "I remember that blue car sped right by me going 100 MPH."

8.49. The United States has filed an interpleader action to determine the true owner of the boxing championship belts awarded to boxer Roberto Duran. Duran claims they were stolen from his house by his brother-in-law in 1993. The FBI recovered the belts in 2003 from businessman Louis Baez, who claimed that the belts were not stolen. To prove theft, Duran and a number of witnesses would testify that in 2000, the brother-in-law apologized to Duran for stealing the belts. Admissible? Would the statement of apology alone be admissible?

8.50. In a personal injury case, Defendant Acme Co. denies that its employee, Grover Greer, was acting within the scope of his employment when the Acme truck he was driving collided with plaintiff. Plaintiff claims that Greer was making an Acme delivery to James Pepper. Defendant claims that Greer was doing an unauthorized errand of his own and was not taking the most direct route to Pepper's home, and thus Acme is not liable. Plaintiff offers the following evidence:

   (a)   As he got into his truck to make the delivery, Greer said, "I need to make a speedy delivery to Pepper. I think that the route I am about to take is a faster way to Pepper's house."
   (b)   Ten minutes after the accident Greer said calmly, "This road is usually the faster route to Pepper's house."
   (c)   Fifteen minutes after the accident Greer said calmly, "I thought this road would be a faster way to get to Pepper's house."
   (d)   Immediately after the accident, Greer jumped out of his truck, ran over to plaintiff, and said, "I'm sorry, I'm sorry. It was my fault. I was making a delivery for my boss and I was in a hurry."

8.51. Lyons Partnership owns all of the intellectual property rights to the character "Barney," the well-stuffed Tyrannosaurus Rex with a green chest and stomach, green spots on its back, and yellow "toeballs." Barney is readily recognizable to young children, who repeatedly parrot his song "I Love You." The *"Barney and Friends"* TV show is viewed weekly by 14 million children, and over 50 million copies of Barney-related videos have been sold. The live appearances of the Barney character, played by adults in costume, is completely controlled by Lyons, and Lyons does not license Barney costumes.

Lyons commenced an action against Nelson Costumes, alleging trademark infringement arising out of rental of a costume, "Duffy the Dragon," to the public. Lyons had to prove, under the Lanham Act, that it has a valid, protectable trademark and that the defendant is infringing its mark by creating consumer confusion. Proof of *actual confusion* is often paramount to the success of such a claim. Lyons offered three types of evidence of confusion at trial, all of which the district court excluded as "unreliable hearsay." Was this error? The evidence offered was as follows:

(a) Testimony from parents that when they rented the Duffy costume for their children's birthday parties, they were confused because the costume looked just like Barney.

(b) Testimony from a principal of an elementary school that when she wore the Duffy costume at a school rally, the children shouted, "Barney, Barney, Barney."

(c) Newspaper clippings from all over the country in which the persons pictured in photos were wearing the Duffy costume but the newspaper labeled them as "Barney."

8.52. In an antitrust action by small retailers of beer against Beer World, a super-market-style beer distributorship, the plaintiff-retailers must prove damages caused by loss of business to Beer World on account of Beer World's illegally low prices. Several retailers plan to testify that they were told by customers, some identified and some not identified, that the customers "are buying beer from Beer World because of lower prices." As counsel for the retailers, for what purpose would this testimony be admissible? As counsel for Beer World, what objections would you make to this testimony?

8.53. Return to Problem 3.2, Pedroso v. Driver, at page 129. Joan testifies for defendants that she also rode the same school bus as Paul and Tom, and that Paul and Tom always got off at the same stop. On the day of the accident, Tom said to Joan, "Paul and I are going to play tag when we get off the bus today." Admissible?

8.54. Oscar Small is charged with the kidnapping and murder of Spenser Reed, who has disappeared. The prosecution claims Small is engaged in extensive cocaine trafficking; that Small hired Reed to do house cleaning for him; that Reed stole cocaine from Small's house; and that Small found this out and retaliated by snatching Reed off the street, forcing Reed into his car, and murdering him. Small explains the presence of Reed's fingerprints in the car by claiming that Reed came over to his house, they took a friendly drive together, and Reed then left. The prosecutor calls several friends of Reed to testify as follows. Is their testimony admissible?

(a) W_1: "On the Saturday he disappeared, Reed looked very nervous. He said to me, 'I'm afraid of seeing Small.'"

   (b)   W₂: "A week before he disappeared, Reed said, "I don't ever want to see Small again.""

   (c)   W₃: "A few days before he disappeared. Reed said to me, 'I'm afraid of Small because he got really violent with me when he found out about the cocaine I took.'"

   (d)   W₄: "A few days before he disappeared, Reed said to me, 'I think Small is going to kill me.'"

8.55. Frank Jackson is charged with the murder of Steve Smart, whose body was found in a public park on Sunday, April 4.

   (a)   The prosecution offers the following testimony of Barbara Berry: "When I spoke to Steve on Saturday, April 3, he said, 'I'm meeting Frank Jackson later tonight.'"

   (b)   Instead of (a), the prosecution offers the following testimony of Carl Cole: "I spoke with Steve on the afternoon of April 3. He said he had to work at home all weekend to finish a report that was due Monday and that he was stuck in his apartment working unless Frank Jackson was available to meet him for a few hours."

7. Interpretation and Illustration of FRE 803(4): Statements for Medical Diagnosis or Treatment

FRE 803(4) states:

> (4) Statements for purposes of medical diagnosis or treatment. Statements made for purposes of medical diagnosis or treatment and describing medical history, or past or present symptoms, pain, or sensations, or the inception or general character of the cause or external source thereof insofar as reasonably pertinent to diagnosis or treatment.

a. Preliminary Factfinding

The foundational requirements for FRE 803(4) statements are:

- the statement must describe medical history, past or present symptoms, pain, sensations, or the inception or the general cause or external sources of symptoms;
- a statement about the cause or source must be reasonably pertinent to diagnosis or treatment; and
- the statement must be made for the purpose of medical diagnosis or treatment.

There is some overlap between this exception and statements of mental state admitted under FRE 803(3). A patient's description of currently existing sensation ("I feel dizzy") could fall within both. But FRE 803(4) also admits statements to prove current symptoms that exist outside the mind of the declarant ("The thermometer says I have a temperature of 102") and to prove past symptoms as well ("I had a runny nose yesterday, and I coughed a lot"). The relevance of these statements depends upon the accuracy of the declarant's perception and memory, as well as sincerity and narration; thus a complete trip around the testimonial triangle is required. The well-established test is that the declarant's motive in making the statement must be consistent with the purposes of promoting treatment.

FRE 803(4) does not specify that the declarant be the patient, relating the declarant's own medical history and symptoms. Family, friends, nurses and other medical personnel may convey information for purposes of medical treatment that will be admitted under FRE 803(4). Wilson v. Zapata OffShore Co., 939 F.2d 260 (5th Cir. 1991) (statement by plaintiff's sister to a physician for purposes of evaluating plaintiff's complaints was admissible). Even an unidentified declarant speaking to an ambulance crew may qualify under the exception if the court is persuaded that the declarant spoke for purposes of securing medical care for the patient. Bucci v. Essex Ins. Co., 393 F.3d 285, 299 (1st Cir. 2005). And if the patient is speaking to an intermediary — a child to a parent, for example, so that the parent can relate the symptoms to a doctor — the terms of the exception could still apply so long as the purpose of seeking medical help exists.

There is also recent case law that the rule covers statements made to psychotherapists, social workers, and other health care personnel, not just physicians and nurses. "[A]dmissibility . . . is based, not on the person to whom made, but on the purpose for which they are made, which gives rise to the presumption of reliability." Williams v. Virgin Islands, 271 F.Supp.2d 696, 704-705 (D.V.I. 2003). However, FRE 803(4) has been interpreted to apply only to statements by persons *seeking* care, not *giving* care. Thus statements made by doctors to patients, or by consulting physicians to treating physicians, are not within the FRE 803(4) exception. Field v. Trigg County Hosp., Inc., 386 F.3d 729, 735-736 (6th Cir. 2004).

b.   Justification for the Admissibility of Statements for Medical Purposes

The justification for this exception rests on the declarant's "selfish motive to be truthful" in making the statement. The assumption is that a person seeking medical diagnosis and treatment is highly motivated to speak carefully and honestly about symptoms and conditions in order to receive the proper medical care. Thus even though the declaration may not be spontaneous, and even though there may be perception and memory risks when past conditions and causes are related, the statement bears less danger of insincerity and inaccuracy.

c.   Statements About the Cause or External Source Must Be "Pertinent"

It is common for persons seeking medical treatment to describe how their injury occurred ("I was hit from behind while sitting in my car, and my neck aches terribly"). FRE 803(4) explicitly includes such hearsay statements to prove the truth of the matters they assert (the declarant was hit from behind in her car) if they are "reasonably pertinent to diagnosis or treatment." But sometimes, patients' statements make more specific attributions of causation, naming specific persons or entities that caused them harm. Should these statements also be admitted by FRE 803(4)?

In general, pertinence is determined from testimony of the medical professional as to the type of information "reasonably relied on by a physician in treatment or diagnosis." If the declarant's statements are not medically pertinent, there is some reason to suspect the declarant's motivation in speaking and thus to suspect lack of sincerity. Thus a statement such as "I was hit from behind by a red Mustang, with license plate number 445HCN, while I was sitting in my car" is not likely to fall within Rule 803(4).

The issue of pertinence frequently arises in cases of child abuse and molestation when the victim names the abuser to the health care professional. In United States v. Tome, 61 F.3d 1446 (10th Cir. 1995), the child declarant's statements identifying her father as the abuser were held to fall within the "pertinence" requirement. Quoting its own precedent, the court reasoned that

> [a]ll victims of domestic sexual abuse suffer emotional and psychological injuries, the exact nature and extent of which depend on the identity of the abuser. The physician generally must know who the abuser was in order to render proper treatment because the physician's treatment will necessarily differ when the abuser is a member of the victim's family or household. In the domestic sexual abuse case, for example, the treating physician may recommend special therapy or counseling and instruct the victim to remove herself from the dangerous environment by leaving the home and seeking shelter elsewhere. [Id. at 1450.]

Most courts agree that the identity of the abuser is pertinent in domestic abuse cases, and the definition of who is a member of the family or household is quite broad. United States v. Pacheco, 154 F.3d 1236, 1240-1241 (10th Cir. 1998) (defendant was not victim's natural father but had an intermittent relationship with victim's mother, and both victim and her mother stayed in his family home several months each year).

Statements made by victims of domestic violence have also been admitted when the name of the abuser is stated to a treating physician. United States v. Yazzie, 38 Fed. Appx. 407, 412 (9th Cir. 2002) (as in sexual abuse cases, the physician in domestic violence cases "must be attentive to treating the victim's emotional and psychological injuries, . . . which often depend on the identity of the abuser"). Other past facts about causation of physical and mental problems are also subject to the dual test of "motivation" and "pertinence." Willingham v. Crooke, 412 F.3d 553, 561-562 (4th Cir. 2005) (plaintiff's description of her arrest, including a gun being pointed at her, was admissible for diagnosis and treatment of her emotional trauma and physical injuries): McCollum v. McDaniel, 32 Fed.Appx. 49, 55 (4th Cir. 2002) (statement that injuries were caused by "assault" were admissible as statements relating to cause more than to fault).

d.   Requiring Proof of Medical Purpose

Courts are likely to assume that adults, and even teenagers, understand the purpose for which they are asked to give information to medical personnel. With young children being examined for sexual abuse, however, this assumption may not be justified. In the Eighth Circuit, identifications of abusers by child abuse victims are admissible only "where the physician makes clear to the victim that the inquiry into the identity of the abuser is important to diagnosis and treatment, and the victim manifests such an understanding." Olsen v. Class, 164 F.3d 1096, 1098 (8th Cir. 1999). Professor Robert Mosteller has also argued that evidence that the child victim's frame of mind is that of a patient seeking medical treatment is essential: "If a selfish treatment interest is indeed required to sustain admissibility. . . . courts should not simply invent such an interest from the facts and circumstances of the cases . . . [C]ourts should require a concrete indication that the declarant subjectively appreciates that the statement has potential treatment consequences." Robert P. Mosteller, Child Sexual Abuse and Statements for the Purpose of Medical Diagnosis or Treatment, 67 N.C. L. Rev. 257, 284-285 (1989). The Ninth and Tenth Circuits, however, have rejected the Eighth Circuit's requirement of such a specific showing. Absent some indication that the child declarants did not understand that they were seeking medical treatment, the declarants' self-interest in being truthful will be assumed. United States v. Edward J., 224 F.3d 1216, 1219 (10th Cir. 2000). Which approach do you think is preferable? Can a motive to be truthful when speaking with a physician always be assumed, even among adults?

e. Statements Made for Diagnostic Evaluations for Litigation

The sincerity rationale, of course, may not apply when a statement of physical condition is made for the purpose of diagnosis in preparation for litigation. The treatment motive that tends to ensure sincerity is lacking. Moreover, the possibility of receiving a high damage award is an incentive to exaggerate present and past symptoms or suffering. For this reason, the common law physical condition exception did not apply to declarations made for the purpose of diagnosis in preparation for litigation. FRE 803(4), however, specifically abandons this common law limitation. Most courts have held that admission of statements made to physicians only for the purpose of providing expert testimony is now permitted by the rule.

8. Elaboration of FRE 803(4): Patients' Statements as the Basis for Expert Opinion

FRE 803(4)'s admission of statements made to testifying experts may not be justified by the reliability of such statements, but it is understandable when one considers this exception in conjunction with the rules regulating expert opinion testimony. When a person's physical condition is at issue, there frequently will be an expert witness to testify about the nature of the condition. Moreover, the expert is likely to have reached conclusions about the person's physical condition at least in part on the basis of what the person said outside of court about present and past symptoms. At common law, such self-serving hearsay statements of physical condition were not presented to the jury; expert witnesses had to base their opinions solely on admissible evidence. This required the patient to testify about the physical condition at issue and then the treating physicians to testify (and be cross-examined) about the patient's treatment. The expert would then be asked to offer an opinion in response to a hypothetical question that incorporated the information already described in court.

Well aware of the problems with hypothetical questions, the drafters of the Federal Rules consciously sought to avoid them in providing for the presentation of expert information. See FRE 702, 703, and 705, discussed in Chapter Nine. A medical expert who has been consulted for diagnosis in preparation for litigation is almost certainly going to rely on the patient's statements about past and present symptoms. As long as the statements are of a type reasonably relied on by medical experts, the expert will want to recite these statements when explaining the diagnosis. Having made this commitment to facilitate the testimony of experts, the drafters of the Federal Rules further chose to take full advantage of the information that medical experts can supply. FRE 803(4) establishes this priority by making statements of physical condition fully admissible.

KEY POINTS

1. Statements describing medical history and symptoms are admissible under FRE 803(4) even though they involve inferences about all four of the declarant's testimonial qualities. The context of speaking for the purpose of medical treatment reduces the sincerity danger, and people may take care in perceiving and reporting their medical symptoms.

2. The statements may be made by the patient or by anyone who is seeking care by providing medical information about the patient.

3. If the statement contains information about the cause or source of the medical condition, there must be evidence that such information is reasonably pertinent to treatment or diagnosis. Such evidence is typically supplied by the physician seeking the information.

4. Statements made for purposes of medical diagnosis only, including a diagnosis undertaken in preparation for litigation, are included within the FRE 803(4) exception.

PROBLEMS

8.56. Consider whether the following declarations would be admissible in a personal injury action if made to the declarant's spouse, to the declarant's physician for treatment, or to a physician consulted for the purpose of giving expert testimony at trial:

    (a)   "I have a severe headache."
    (b)   "Yesterday, I had a severe headache."
    (c)   "I was hit in the head with a baseball bat."
    (d)   "John Jones hit me in the head with a baseball bat."

8.57. Return to Problem 3.2, Pedroso v. Driver, at page 129. Paul's treating physician testifies for defendants that, while he was examining Paul's injuries, Paul awoke and said "It's all my fault." Admissible?

8.58 Return to Problem 3.4, State v. Blair, at page 131. Norma's doctor would testify that during a routine medical examination in 2004, Norma explained some bruising on her ribs. She told the doctor that her boyfriend had hit her in the middle of an argument. The doctor then recommended a local counseling program for victims of domestic violence to her. Would the doctor's testimony be admissible? What if it is mandatory under state law for a doctor to report, to local law enforcement, injuries that are resonably suspected to be related to domestic violence?

8.59. Jenkins, a federal prison inmate, is charged with committing an assault resulting in serious bodily injury to another inmate. At trial, an emergency room physician who treated the victim testified on direct that "there was reportedly — and I got this second- or third-hand as I often do in the ER — a loss of consciousness in the ambulance." Admissible?

8.60. Defendant is charged with sexually abusing his nine-year-old stepson. When the alleged child victim was being examined by Dr. Wolfe, he denied that defendant was abusing him. Victim's mother then asked to speak to Dr. Wolfe and told the doctor that defendant had "brainwashed" the victim and that the victim had been abused by defendant. At defendant's trial, may Dr. Wolfe testify as to what the mother said?

9. Interpretation and Illustration of FRE 803(5): Past Recollection Recorded

FRE 803(5) states:

> (5) Recorded recollection. A memorandum or record concerning a matter about which a witness once had knowledge but now has insufficient recollection to enable the witness to testify fully and accurately, shown to have been made or adopted by the witness when the matter was fresh in the witness' memory and to reflect that knowledge correctly. If admitted, the memorandum or record may be read into evidence but may not itself be received as an exhibit unless offered by an adverse party.

a. Preliminary Factfinding

The foundational requirements for the past recollection recorded exception are:

* the declarant is testifying as a witness;
* the statement is in the form of a memorandum or record;
* the statement concerns a matter about which the witness cannot remember sufficiently to testify fully and accurately;
* the witness once had personal knowledge of the matter;
* the statement was made or adopted when the matter was fresh in the witness's memory; and
* the statement correctly reflects the witness's knowledge.

Written or recorded memoranda or notes about events are often a substitute for failed memory in our everyday lives. Try to remember something you once knew but now are unable to remember — say, whether a particular case was assigned in your Torts class during your first year of law school. You kept notes of all your first year law school assignments. Could these notes fulfill the foundational requirements of FRE 803(5)? Or, when people pack their household belongings for a cross-country move, they often keep detailed lists of objects placed in particular moving boxes. What questions would you ask to elicit the required foundation for admission of such a list under FRE 803(5)?

i. The Contents of the Statement.   FRE 803(5) places no limit on the subject matter or contents of a statement admitted as a past recollection recorded. The notes and lists discussed above could qualify. So could any form of record of any sort of event that later becomes relevant in litigation. United States v. Cash, 394 F.3d 560 (7th Cir. 2005) (record of a threatening phone call from a veteran made by a Veterans'

Administration representative). If the record is made as part of the functioning of a business or of a public or governmental institution, other exceptions for business and public records may also be available and the more onerous foundational requirements of FRE 803(5) would not need to be satisfied.

ii.   The Declarant Must Be a Witness with Failed Memory.   FRE 803(5) is unique in the Rule 803 exceptions in that it requires the presence of the declarant in court, as a witness. In this respect, therefore, the exception is analogous to the Rule 801(d)(1) exemptions for prior statements of a witness. Under FRE 803(5), however, it is categorically required that the witness *not* have sufficient memory of the underlying events that are the subject of the out-of-court statement, and that statement must be in written or recorded form. Collins v. Kibort, 143 F.3d 331 (7th Cir. 1998) (in an employment discrimination case, excerpts from plaintiff's diary concerning episodes with his employer were improperly admitted under FRE 803(5) because plaintiff did not testify that he could not remember the events). Thus in one sense the witness is both available (on the witness stand) and unavailable (no adequate current memory of the events recorded).

iii.   Made with Personal Knowledge and Fresh Memory.   There is an explicit requirement of a showing that the witness had personal knowledge of the matters when the memoranda or recording was made, and that it was made when that knowledge was "fresh" in the witness's memory. Typically if the witness remembers making the written recollection, the witness will be able to testify about the circumstances in which it was created. In *United States v. Cash*, the VA representative testified that she documents phone conversations while speaking with all of the veterans who call her because she gets another call as soon as she hangs up, and she includes exact questions and quotations from the veteran. 394 F.3d at 561. If the witness cannot remember making the written record, then the record's own contents, or the testimony of someone who saw the record being made, or other circumstantial evidence, would be used to satisfy the requirement of personal knowledge and fresh memory.

Notice that the record can either be *made* or *adopted* by the witness. Thus if the witness did not actually write or record the statement, but read over and adopted the written statements made by another, the requirement can be satisfied. United States v. Wimberly, 60 F.2d 281, 285 (7th Cir. 1995), (10-year-old sexual abuse victim was interviewed shortly after the alleged incident, then "read the document, reviewed it for errors, made corrections, initialed those corrections, and signed the attestation clause"). That the contents of the record reflected what the witness knew from firsthand knowledge would still have to be shown.

Courts have not adopted a bright-line rule to determine whether the witness's memory was "fresh" when the record was made. United States v. Green, 258 F.3d 683, 689 (7th Cir. 2001) ("the trial court may consider the lapse of time along with other circumstances that may be relevant in determining [whether] the witness had an accurate memory," citing cases where a three-year and 15-month delay were held not excessive under the circumstances). Additional evidence, such as lack of motive to misrepresent, clarity of statement, richness of detail, making changes and corrections, can show that the witness's recollection was still vital. Time lapses between a witness's making a statement and later adopting its recorded version may also be lengthy, creating risks that inaccuracies in the record would not be spotted. United States v. Lewis, 954 F.2d 1386, 1394 (7th Cir. 1992) (trial court is in the best position to gauge the significance of these difficulties, and this is why arbitrary time limitations are inappropriate).

iv. **The Record Reflects the Witness's Knowledge Correctly.** Some evidence that the statement is correct — that is, both sincerely and accurately recorded — is required. But if the witness cannot adequately remember the events recorded, it may be impossible for the witness to testify truthfully that the record is a correct reflection of what the witness knew when the record was made. What may often happen is that the witness-declarant simply answers "yes" to the question "Is this statement accurate?" and the basis for the witness's ability to so testify is not probed. There are several ways, however, to lay an adequate foundation on the requirement of "correctness." Sometimes the record itself contains information relevant to its accuracy. For example, the lists of items packed in moving boxes could contain a statement that the witness double-checked the contents of each box. Erasures and corrections in the list may indicate care about accuracy. Or a written statement signed by a suspect in criminal custody could contain the language, "This is an accurate statement to the best of my recollection." And, the witness may present circumstantial evidence as to why the statement is *likely to* have been accurate at the time that it was made. You as a law student could testify that you know you would have recorded your Torts assignments because you were motivated to be accurate. As we have stated before, these foundational requirements are FRE 104(a) questions for the judge to decide.

v. **The Record May Only Be Read to the Jury.** FRE 803(5) limits the use of a past recollection recorded statement. It may be read to the jury, but may not be received as an exhibit. Thus it may not be handed around by the jury or taken into the jury room for deliberations. Perhaps it is thought that jurors might put undue weight on a past recollection recorded merely because it is recorded and has status as an exhibit. When testimony in a deposition is admitted into evidence, it is typically treated in the same manner: The contents of the deposition are read to the jury, but the deposition is not itself admitted as an exhibit, or at least is not allowed into the jury room, unlike other admissible documents or records. If for some tactical reason of advantage the opponent wishes to have the FRE 803(5) record before the jury as a document, the opponent may offer it as an exhibit.

b. Justification for the Admissibility of Past Recollection Recorded

The absence of adequate memory creates the need for the admission of statements that record a witness's past recollection. In addition, the Rule 803(5) foundational requirements tend to indicate the record's increased trustworthiness. The fact that the record was made when the matter was fresh in the witness's mind may minimize any memory problem. Similarly, the requirement that the record be shown to be a correct reflection of the witness's knowledge provides information concerning the witness's sincerity in making the statement and accuracy and care in recording it. The foundational requirements do not address the accuracy of the witness's perception of the matter reported in the statement, but the witness's current availability for general cross-examination may furnish information pertinent to perception ability and opportunity. The degree to which these requirements are effective in increasing the trustworthiness of past recollection recorded, however, depends on the strictness with which trial courts apply them. For example, if the trial judge does not probe the basis for a witness's testimony that a written memo is "correct," we cannot be sure that sincerity and narration dangers are decreased.

10.   Elaboration of FRE 803(5)

a.   Past Recollection Recorded Can Be Created by Multiple Declarants

Sometimes one person observes events occurring outside of court and tells them to a second person who then makes a record based on what was said. When that occurs, there are two levels of hearsay contained in one document. For example, John might do the packing of his household goods and then call out what he puts into each box while a second person, Bob, makes the list. There are two declarants in this situation: the observer, John, who has observed the event (what item is packed where), and the recorder, Bob, who transfers information obtained from the observer into the record. If the observer does not check and adopt these lists, then the observer cannot later say in court that the lists correctly reflect what the observer saw. Therefore, the observer alone cannot provide a complete Rule 803(5) foundation. There are many other possible examples of this scenario. Employers may make oral statements that are recorded and transcribed by secretarial staff; people make statements at group meetings where one of the group members takes notes.

FRE 803(5) does not specifically address the effect of multiple person involvement in making the record. The Advisory Committee Note to FRE 803(5) states, "Multiple person involvement in the process of observing and recording . . . is entirely consistent with the exception." McCormick addresses the multiple person involvement issue as follows:

> A . . . type of cooperative report is involved when one person orally reports facts to another person, who writes them down. A store clerk or timekeeper, for example, may report information to a bookkeeper. In this situation, courts have held the written statement admissible if the person reporting the facts testifies to the correctness of the oral report (although at the time of the testimony, the detailed facts cannot be remembered) and the recorder of that statement testifies to faithfully transcribing that oral report. [McCormick on Evidence Vol. 2 §283, at 247 (John W. Strong, ed., 5th ed. 1999).]

The proponent of the cooperative report can satisfy all of the FRE 803(5) requirements only if both out-of-court declarants — the original observer of the information and the later recorder of the information — testify about the observing and recording process. This also gives the opposing party the opportunity to cross-examine both the observer and the recorder about their part in the creation of the record. Thus if the proponent relies solely on Rule 803(5) to admit a record produced by multiple declarants, each declarant in the hearsay chain must be presented as a witness. United States v. Green, 258 F.3d at 689 ("both the witness and the one transcribing the statement must testify"). This can be a cumbersome process for the proponent, and some of the declarants may not be available.

b. Multiple Hearsay Requires a Hearsay Exception or Exemption for Each Level

There are other strategies to admit a cooperative report created by multiple declarants. FRE 805 provides as follows:

> Hearsay included within hearsay is not excluded under the hearsay rule if each part of the combined statements conforms with an exception to the hearsay rule provided in these rules.

This means that whenever multiple layers of hearsay and multiple declarants are identified, *each declarant's hearsay statement must fall within either an FRE 801(d) exemption or a FRE 803, 804, or 807 exception.* The burden is on the proponent of multiple hearsay to satisfy the foundational requirements of all of the rules being used. Any combination of exceptions, exemptions, and nonhearsay statements is permitted. For example, suppose several friends help John pack up his household goods, and each one tells the recorder what is in each box. The recorder later compiles a list based on their hearsay statements. All of the friends are not available to testify, but their statements are probably present sense impressions within FRE 803(1). The combination of this exception for the friends and the past recollection recorded exception for the recorder who will testify in court will satisfy FRE 805 and overcome any multiple hearsay objection. Other combinations are also possible, if a record is made of an excited utterance or an admission by a party opponent, for example.

If the recorder is not available, or has no memory of the accuracy of the particular recording, another exception might apply to the recorder, such as FRE 803(1) or the exception for business records, FRE 803(6). It is important in applying the past recollection recorded exception that the recorder be truly recording, as opposed to interpreting or editing, what the witness was saying and has now forgotten. The absence of interpretation ensures that the witness's memory, not the recorder's consciously altered version of that memory, is what is recorded.

c. Present Recollection Refreshed

The past recollection recorded exception should not be confused with the process of refreshing memory (sometimes referred to as "refreshing recollection" or "present recollection refreshed"). When a witness initially cannot recall something, it may be possible to refresh the witness's memory by presenting that witness with a document or something else that the examiner thinks, or that the witness suggests, may jog the witness's memory. John, for example, might remember actually packing the objects that he placed in a particular box if he looks briefly at a packing list. Use of this list to "refresh" would be permissible because, under the Federal Rules of Evidence, there are no substantive limits on the type of item that may be used to refresh recollection. The view of most courts is more akin to that of Baker v. State:

> Although the use of a memorandum of some sort will continue quantitatively to dominate the field of refreshing recollection, we are better able to grasp the process conceptually if we appreciate that the use of a memorandum as a memory aid is not a legal phenomenon unto itself but only an instance of a far broader phenomenon. In a more conventional

mode, the process might proceed, "Your Honor, I am about to show the witness a written report, ask him to read it and then inquire if he can now testify from his own memory thus refreshed." In a far less conventional mode, the process could as well proceed, "Your Honor, I am pleased to present to the court Miss Rosa Ponselle who will now sing 'Celeste Aida' for the witness, for that is what was playing on the night the burglar came through the window."[7] Whether by conventional or unconventional means, precisely the same end is sought. One is looking for the effective elixir to revitalize dimming memory and make it live again in the service of the search for truth. [35 Md. App. 593, 604-605, 371 A.2d 699, 705-706 (1977).]

If some physical object, like a document, is used to refresh memory, it will first be marked as an exhibit for the purpose of identifying it in the transcript. Use of the object to refresh memory, however, is *not using the document as evidence*. Rather, the object is only a device to try to jog the witness's memory. If the witness's memory is refreshed, the witness will then proceed to testify on the basis of current (revived) recollection, and there will be no need for further reference to the object that revived the witness's memory. In the case of John's refreshed memory, it will be for the court to decide whether John can actually remember packing the objects or whether he is simply testifying from the packing list. If John is testifying from the list, then it must itself be admissible into evidence under a hearsay exception. Any exception would suffice, including FRE 803(5). Indeed, a standard (but not absolutely required) way to satisfy the FRE 803(5) foundational requirement of insufficient current memory is to show the witness the record, ask if it refreshes the witness's memory, and offer it if the memory is not refreshed. United States v. Weller, 238 F.3d 1215, (10th Cir. 2001) (not error for trial court to prohibit witness's use of an appraisal list of objects to refresh recollection where the judge believed that the list would be the source of direct testimony).

If the object is a writing that refreshes the witness's memory, the opposing party is entitled to inspect the document and to introduce into evidence "those portions which relate to the testimony of the witness." FRE 612. If the writing has refreshed the witness's memory, however, it will probably contain information that corroborates what the witness has said. Thus it is unlikely that the opposing party would want to introduce it into evidence. If the object does not revive the witness's memory, there will be no further occasion to refer to the object, unless the object happens to have some independent relevance to the lawsuit.

d.   The Impact of FRE 612 on Refreshing Recollection

With a friendly witness, the process of refreshing memory is likely to take place outside the courtroom while discussing and rehearsing the direct and anticipated cross-examination. If during this or any other preparation for courtroom or deposition testimony the witness uses a writing to refresh memory, the opposing party may be entitled to inspect the writing. This is because FRE 612 provides as follows:

RULE 612.   WRITING USED TO REFRESH MEMORY

Except as otherwise provided in criminal proceedings by section 3500 of title 18, United States Code, if a witness uses a writing to refresh memory for the purpose of testifying, either —

---

7.   Do you think Rosa Ponselle ever sang "Celeste Aida" — except perhaps in the shower? — EDS.

(1) while testifying, or
(2) before testifying, if the court in its discretion determines it is necessary in the interests of justice,

an adverse party is entitled to have the writing produced at the hearing, to inspect it, to cross-examine the witness thereon, and to introduce in evidence those portions which relate to the testimony of the witness. If it is claimed that the writing contains matters not related to the subject matter of the testimony the court shall examine the writing in camera, excise any portions not so related, and order delivery of the remainder to the party entitled thereto. Any portion withheld over objections shall be preserved and made available to the appellate court in the event of an appeal. If a writing is not produced or delivered pursuant to order under this rule, the court shall make any order justice requires, except that in criminal cases when the prosecution elects not to comply, the order shall be one striking the testimony or, if the court in its discretion determines that the interests of justice so require, declaring a mistrial.

FRE 612 may be the most important rule for you to remember after this class. It is not merely a rule of admissibility; it is also a rule of discovery. And one of the things it means is that any documents that a person looks at in preparing for a deposition may be discoverable by the opposing party — including perhaps documents that would otherwise be protected by the work-product doctrine or some privilege. Since many of you are likely to become involved in the process of taking depositions long before you are responsible for a trial, we urge you to find a special place in your memory for FRE 612.

KEY POINTS

1. Recorded statements concerning any relevant matters may be admissible for their truth under FRE 803(5) if the declarant testifies as a witness and is not able to fully recollect those matters, and if the foundation regarding the freshness and correctness of the statement is satisfied.

2. FRE 805 provides that each part of a multiple hearsay statement must conform to a hearsay exception or exemption.

3. If a statement is the product of reporting and recording by two or more out-of-court declarants, then all declarants must testify if FRE 803(5) is the sole hearsay exception relied on to admit the statement. FRE 803(5) can be used in combination with other exemptions and exceptions to admit statements containing multiple levels of hearsay.

PROBLEMS

8.61. Plaintiff Rhoda Bolt, a CPA and Chief Auditor for Aquatic Marine Corp. (AMC), has filed suit against AMC for sexual harassment and wrongful discharge due to AMC's creation of a hostile work environment. She alleges that the harassment, consisting of overtly sexual and demeaning comments and behavior from other employees, began in July 2000; that the atmosphere in the Auditing Department was overtly hostile to her; that this affected her ability to perform her job; and that she was wrongfully discharged in 2004.

(a) At trial, Plaintiff will offer notes that she wrote outlining many specific incidents of harassment that she cannot entirely recall. She testifies that she is not sure when she began taking notes on the incidents, but that it was some time in 2001; that she made the notes at home, usually but not always on the same day as the incident reported; and that the only reason she made the notes was to accurately record what happened and when. The notes terminate in 2004 when she was discharged by AMC. Are Bolt's notes admissible to prove a hostile work environment?

(b)   Defendant AMC will offer the personal notes made by Leveritt Darnell, Chief Financial Officer of AMC and Bolt's supervisor. Darnell testifies that after Bolt made several complaints about the problems and hostile work environment in the Auditing Department, he became concerned about Bolt's job performance. He says he wrote these notes for his own reference for a period of several months in 2004, before he discharged Bolt. The notes describe Darnell's perception of Bolt's current failures as Chief Auditor, and also mention incidents as early as 2001. They were not shown to Bolt nor to anyone else, but were placed by Darnell into his file on Bolt. Are Darnell's notes admissible if Darnell has insufficient memory to testify fully and accurately?

(c)   Defendant AMC will also offer a memorandum evaluating Bolt's job performance drafted by Darnell, written approximately five months after Bolt was terminated. Darnell based the memorandum on his own notes and on interviews with employees in the Auditing Department. He admits that this document was written to "express management's perspective" in the face of an impending EEOC investigation of Bolt's complaint. Is this memorandum admissible if Darnell has insufficient memory to testify fully and accurately?

8.62. While Andrew was crossing an intersection, he was hit by an automobile, which fled the scene of the accident. Sadie, Andrew's companion, rushed to his side, and asked, "Are you okay?" Andrew, who was still conscious, responded, "I don't know, but I got the license number of the car that hit me. It was 879-ACY. Write it down so we won't forget." Sadie had nothing to write on, so she kept repeating the license number to herself. When she got home, a few hours later, she wrote down the number. Andrew has brought an action for personal injuries against Roland Bowers, who is the registered owner of a green Plymouth with the license number 879-ACY. Neither Andrew nor Sadie remembers the license number now. Is Sadie's record of it admissible under any hearsay exceptions? Which ones?

11.   Interpretation and Illustration of FRE 803(6): Business Records

FRE 803(6) provides:

(6) Records of regularly conducted activity. A memorandum, report, record, or data compilation, in any form, of acts, events, conditions, opinions, or diagnoses, made at or near the time by, or from information transmitted by, a person with knowledge, if kept in the course of a regularly conducted business activity, and if it was the regular practice of that business activity to make the memorandum, report, record, or data compilation, all as shown by the testimony of the custodian or other qualified witness, or by certification that complies with Rule 902(11), Rule 902(12), or a statute permitting certification, unless the source of information or the method or circumstances of preparation indicate lack of

trustworthiness. The term "business" as used in this paragraph includes business, institution, association, profession, occupation, and calling of every kind, whether or not conducted for profit.

a. Preliminary Factfinding

The foundation requirements for business records are:

- the statement is in written or recorded form;
- the record concerns acts, events, conditions, opinions, or diagnoses;
- the record was made at or near the time of the matter recorded;
- the source of the information had personal knowledge of the matter;
- the record was kept in the course of regular business activity; and
- it was the regular practice of the business activity to make the record.

In addition to these requirements, FRE 803(6) also contains two unique features. It requires the proponent to produce a "custodian or other qualified witness" to testify about the foundational requirements or to present a written declaration certifying such foundation facts pursuant to FRE 902(11) or (12). It also contains a clause that permits the judge to exclude a business record that otherwise fits the exception, if "the source of information or the method or circumstances of preparation show lack of trustworthiness."

i. The Broad Scope of What Constitutes a Business Record.

No business or other organized entity can survive in today's world without keeping records of its activities. And there is very little litigation that does not use some type of business records as evidence. The exception for business records, originally a product of legislation as described in the Advisory Committee Note, was designed to liberalize the common law restrictions on the use of such records to prove the truth of the matters they assert. FRE 803(6) therefore defines "business" very broadly. What about the records of groups that do not seem to be businesses, such as the expense records of a Scout Troop, or records of expenses kept by students working on a student law journal or other student organization? When record-keeping activity assumes a public role, or provides a function within a formally organized institution, the terms of the exception probably apply.

You might wonder what kinds of records would *not* fall within its terms. Probably your notes as a student do not, nor would casual records you keep of your household expenses. But there are cases in which a person's own records of expenses, or income, kept for business reasons such as balancing bank accounts, maintaining a budget or preparing tax returns can qualify under FRE 803(6) so long as they are "systematically checked and regularly and continually maintained." Keogh v. IRS, 713 F.2d 496, 499 (9th Cir. 1983). The receipts that you receive when you have a car bumper replaced, or the bills that you, as a consumer, receive in the mail from the telephone company and various credit card companies, are business records generated by the body shop or the telephone company or the credit card company, but they are your own personal, not your business, records. Courts do not treat people as being in the business of being a consumer.

The term *record* also defines a broad range of documents — memoranda, reports, records, or data compilations. The distinguishing feature of the business record is that information has been stored somewhere outside of the human mind and can be recalled in some form other than oral testimony. The permissible contents of a business record are likewise broad, and include acts, events, conditions, opinions, or diagnoses — so long as they are topics that are regularly recorded as part of the regular business activity of the author.

    ii. Personal Knowledge and Near Contemporaneity Are Required.   The original source of the business record is like the observer discussed in regard to FRE 803(5). This original source must have personal knowledge of a matter and must start the process of making a record of that matter. The source may make the record alone, or may transmit information to a series of other people who record the information in various formats. FRE 803(6) also requires that the original source start this process of record-keeping at or near the time that the source observed the matter. An example will help to illustrate these requirements. In a suit for breach of contract, the purchaser claims that goods purchased from the seller were delivered in a damaged condition To prove damaged condition, the purchaser offers a document entitled "Damage Report." It identifies the shipment of goods as coming from the seller and describes the damaged condition of the items. Joan, the purchaser's employee who wrote the report, has left the company and cannot testify. Since the report is offered to prove the truth of the matters it asserts — that the boxes were labeled as coming from seller, and that the goods were damaged — it is hearsay. To fit within the business record exception, the proponent must prove that Joan had personal knowledge of the matters described and that she wrote the report or transmitted her knowledge close in time to her observation of the shipment. The judge must be persuaded, under FRE 104(a), by a preponderance of the evidence that these requirements are fulfilled.

    It is important to identify the activity with which the record should be contemporaneous. In In Re WorldCom, Inc. Securities Litigation, 2005 U.S.Dist. LEXIS 2215 *24-25 (S.D.N.Y. 2005), the consolidated securities class action arising out of the collapse of WorldCom, one of the defendants filed a motion in limine to exclude the Restatement of WorldCom's 2000 and 2001 financial statements, issued in 2004. The Restatement reveals an overstatement of WorldCom's net income by $74 billion in those two years. It was produced by a WorldCom's successor corporation, MCI, and audited by KPMG, Inc. In response to the claim that the Restatement was not contemporaneous with the financial events of 2000-2001, the court held that a financial statement is never created contemporaneously with the underlying business records; ". . . it is filed months after the end of the fiscal year . . . a restatement is the result of a process of review . . . that reflects the accounting work done [by the reviewer] 'at or near the time' that the report was created."

    iii. Made Pursuant to a "Business Duty."   Unlike the past recollection recorded exception, FRE 803(6) does not require testimony as to the accuracy of the contents of the record. United States v. Scholl, 166 F.3d 964, 978 (9th Cir. 1999) (estimates made by a casino floor walker of a particular gambler's winnings and losses need not be proven to be accurate before they are admitted). Trustworthiness is inferred from the two foundational requirements that contain the word *regular*. The record must be shown to be kept in the course of *regular* business activity, meaning an activity within the customary business purposes of the enterprise. Compare United States v. Skeddle, 981 F. Supp. 1069, 1072 (N.D. Ohio 1997) (customary for an accounting firm employee to take notes at client meetings, place them in the client files, and refer to them at a later time; therefore, notes were kept as part of the regular course of business) with AgriBioTech, Inc. v. Thomas, 2005 U.S.Dist. LEXIS 6465 (D.Nev.2005) (document entitled "Trott conference" appears to be notes of a meeting but no evidence offered that employee regularly took notes at meetings, or that it was his practice to make such notes, or that he was under any business duty to report his notes of the events of the meeting). That the declarant had a *business duty* to keep the record is a term often used to describe a regular business activity. In addition, the exception requires a showing that it was a *regular* practice to make the record, meaning that making such a record, or records like it, happens systematically or repeatedly. Compare Kassel v. Gannet Co., 875 F.2d 935, 944-945 (1st Cir. 1989) (exception does not extend to activity that is "casual or isolated" but some degree of discontinuity or selectivity is permissible) with Monotype Corp. PLC v. International Typeface Corp., 43 F.3d 443 (9th Cir. 1994) (e-mail from employee to a superior properly excluded as "far less of a systematic activity than a monthly printout" admitted in a prior case). In the *WorldCom* case described above, it was held that Generally Accepted Accounting Principles (GAAP) impose on businesses the duty to issue restated financial statements when the originals contain errors, and that it is the regular practice of *all* companies to file a restatement as a matter of course when required to do so.

iv. Custodian or Other Qualified Witness. Whether the proponent of a business record produces the custodian of the record or some other "qualified" witness, courts have interpreted this language in FRE 803(6) to require that the witness be able to explain the record-keeping procedures of the business organization. Personal knowledge of the specific records at issue is not required:

> Rule 803(6) does not require that the custodian personally gather, input, and compile the information memorialized in a business record. The custodian . . . need not be in control of or have individual knowledge of the particular corporate records, but need only be familiar with the company's recordkeeping practices. [Guillermety v. Secretary of Education, 341 F.Supp 2d 682, 690 (E.D.Mich. 2003)]

The foundation witness need not be an employee of the business, so long as there is a showing of familiarity with the record-keeping system. Compare United States v. Bell, 1999 WL 220119 (6th Cir. 1999) (highway patrol investigator familiar with data assembled in the records of the National Insurance Crime Bureau) with United States v. Dakota, 197 F.3d. 821 (6th Cir. 1999) (federal agent who seized records from office and analyzed them had no knowledge of the record-keeping procedures of the business entity).

FRE 803(6), together with FRE 902(11) and (12), now permit the foundation for business records to be provided by a written declaration, rather than a live testifying witness. While the foundational requirements remain the same, it appears from some cases that the declarations speak in wholly conclusory terms: "[T]he records were made and kept in the course of business by an employee who had personal knowledge of the facts recorded. . . . [t]his is sufficient." Spurlock v. Commissioner, T.C. Memo 2003-124 (U.S. Tax Ct.). In such a case, neither the opponent nor the jury is provided with any detailed, context-specific information with which to evaluate the reliability of the record. The notice requirement is intended to give the opponent the opportunity to take discovery to test the adequacy of the foundation in the declaration, but this results in increasing the costs of the opponent's pretrial discovery. United States v. Klinzing, 315 F.3d 803 (7th Cir. 2003) (defendant had right to depose record keepers or call them to the stand for cross-examination).

b. Justification for the Admissibility of Business Records

Like many other exceptions, the business records exception is justified on the grounds of necessity and reliability. The necessity is twofold. First, there is frequently multiple person involvement in the production of a business record. It would be time-consuming and inconvenient to call to the witness stand each individual who had a part in generating the record. And many individuals responsible for making records may be unidentifiable or no longer associated with the business for which the record was made. Thus the "necessity" for the business records exception is sometimes described as the need to bring the rules of evidence into conformity with modern business practices. Second, even if the people who were responsible for making the record were on the witness stand, they might not have any present memory of matters contained in the record. When this is the case, which is likely with respect to routine matters recorded in the ordinary course of business, all they can testify about is their routine practice in making such a record. The record itself is the only accurate source of the substantive information.

The reliability rationale for the business records exception is based on several factors. The requirement that the record be made at or near the time of the matter recorded minimizes any memory problem; a person who makes a record in the regular course of business has an incentive to be honest and accurate in order to advance in the business; the fact that the record is kept in the regular course of business suggests that it may be relied on or checked for accuracy, which provides an added guarantee of trustworthiness and an incentive for the record maker to be accurate in the first place; the routine nature of many records that are made and kept in the regular course of business suggests that there is not likely to be an incentive to lie about routine matters; and finally, the regularity of the record-making process often gives the record maker some expertise in record-making that tends to ensure accuracy.

You should now reconsider the examples on page 525, supra, which illustrate the kinds of personal records that may not qualify as business records. The justification for this disparate treatment must be that the arguments of necessity and the generalizations of reliability are much stronger for records kept by an ongoing, organized, or institutional entity. Do you agree?

12. Elaboration of FRE 803(6)

Not all records that are made and kept in the regular course of business are reliable. Consider, for example, records that are created for self-serving purposes, such as for promotion and public relations, or in preparation for litigation. You might think differently about the reliability of a discussion of the toxicity of a household cleaner contained in a company's annual testing report, as opposed to a discussion in a report prepared to defend against a lawsuit. Or consider the difference between job site accident reports filed by the injured employee or by an official public investigator.

a. *Exclusion for Untrustworthiness*

FRE 803(6) permits the judge to exclude a business record if "the source of information or the method or circumstances of preparation indicate lack of trustworthiness." This exclusionary clause is based on a concern articulated by the Supreme Court in Palmer v. Hoffman, 318 U.S. 109 (1943). The plaintiff, who was injured in a railroad grade crossing accident, claimed that the railroad was negligent in that the engineer failed to ring a bell, blow a whistle, or have a light burning in the front of the train. The defendant offered into evidence as a business record an accident report made by the engineer, who died before the trial. The Supreme Court, interpreting the then-existing federal business record statute, upheld exclusion of the record as not made "in the regular course of business."

> It is not a record made for the systematic conduct of the business as a business. An accident report may affect the business in the sense that it affords information on which the management may act. It is not, however, typical of entries made systematically or as a matter of routine to record events or occurrences, to reflect transactions with others, or to provide internal controls. . . .
>
> In short, it is manifest that in this case those reports are not for the systematic conduct of the enterprise as a railroad business. Unlike payrolls, accounts receivable, accounts payable, bills of lading and the like, these reports are calculated for use essentially in the court, not in the business. Their primary utility is in litigating, not in railroading. [Id. at 113-114.]

The approach of Palmer v. Hoffman is to interpret narrowly what constitutes regular business conduct or business duty in order to eliminate, almost on a categorical basis, documents prepared with a self-interested business or personal motivation. In our hypothetical, the Damage Report prepared by Joan about the damaged shipment might be viewed as self-interested; yet it was a regular practice of the company to prepare such reports, and it served a regular business interest to do so. The approach of FRE 803(6) is to permit the judge to deal with untrustworthiness on a case-by-case basis. Which approach do you think is preferable?

i. Burden of Persuasion. Which party should have the burden — the proponent to prove trustworthiness, or the opponent to prove lack of trustworthiness? From the structure of the "unless" clause and the policy of the Advisory Committee to relax admission standards for business records, courts have determined that the opponent to the business record has the burden of persuading the judge that a record lacks trustworthiness. Thus the seller of the damaged goods will attack Joan's self-interest (on behalf of her employer) in writing the Damage Report, and may question her method of preparing it. (Did she carefully inspect each item in the shipment?) Of course, the proponent of the record must be prepared to respond to the opponent's attack with facts that show trustworthiness.

ii. Circumstances Indicating Lack of Trustworthiness. The greatest concern about trustworthiness focuses on sincerity dangers, such as the motivation of the preparer. The significance of the record for the business is central; records specifically prepared for litigation are viewed as infused with a motive to distort the truth. Certain Underwriters at Lloyd's, London v. Sinkovich, 232 F.3d. 200, 205 (4th Cir. 2000) (report of an insurance investigator hired by plaintiff Underwriters was inadmissible as prepared in anticipation of litigation, even though the investigator regularly prepared such reports in the regular course of his business; the primary motive was to prepare for litigation). Where accident reports are prepared pursuant to a statutory duty, or a regular business routine, they may be found not oriented toward litigation. Other motives may also affect trustworthiness. Opponents charged that the Restatement prepared in the *WorldCom* case was unreliable because the preparers were motivated to maximize the restatement adjustments for tax purposes. The court held that this possible motive did not justify exclusion of the Restatement as untrustworthy, since it was required to comply with GAAP; was under intense scrutiny from the courts, the SEC, and the parties; and was created by scores of people, making any plan of manipulation exceedingly difficult. In re WorldCom, Inc. Securities Litigation, 2005 U.S. Dist. LEXIS 2215 *26-27 (S.D.N.Y.) Where the original source of the information or the method of preparation of the record is unclear or unknown, or when a record on its face is irregular or contains serious mistakes or inconsistencies, courts may find untrustworthiness. SEC v. Hughes Capital Corp., 124 F.3d 449, 455 (3d Cir. 1997) (no error in refusing to admit as untrustworthy photocopies of check stubs that had been altered when the person responsible could not remember what information he had changed).

b.   Opinions and Diagnoses

FRE 803(6) states that opinions and diagnoses contained within business records are admissible, while some states do not extend the exception so far. Calif. Evid. Code §1271, for example, covers only records of "an act, condition, or event." In re World-Com, Inc. Securities Litigation, 2005 U.S. Dist. LEXIS 2215 at *26 (a Restatement of financial statements "reflects accounting judgments to the same extent that any financial statement does"; it cannot be suggested that financial statements are not business records).

The difficulty with admitting opinions and diagnoses is that there will not necessarily be an opportunity to cross-examine the person who made these statements. The opponent will be less able to explore the underlying factual bases for the opinion or diagnosis and, in the case of expert opinions, to explore the purported expert's degree of expertise. In some cases, information about the expert or about the factual support for the opinion may be available from the foundation witness or may be contained in the document itself. To the extent that such information is not available, the party against whom the evidence is offered can argue for exclusion on several possible grounds such as the source has not been qualified as an expert (FRE 702); bases for the expert opinion cannot be disclosed (FRE 705); the probative value of the evidence is substantially outweighed by the time that it will take to present the evidence and the risk that, in the absence of critical evaluation, the jury will be misled and will give undue weight to the opinion (FRE 403). These concerns are particularly significant "if the opinion involves difficult matters of interpretation and a central dispute in the case, such as causation." McCormick on Evidence Vol. 2. §293, at 266 (John W. Strong, ed., 5th ed. 1999). Van der AA v. Commissioner, 2005 U.S. Tax Ct. LEXIS 21 (U.S. Tax Ct. 2005) (the business record rule does not override the rules governing opinion testimony; court would not admit valuation report into evidence without the availability of the author for cross-examination).

c. Records Containing Multiple Levels of Hearsay

If several people contribute to the creation of a business record, then there are multiple levels of hearsay in the document. Under FRE 805, each level must fit within a hearsay exception or exemption. If only FRE 803(6) is used to admit the entire document, then *all* declarants must be shown to satisfy *all* of its foundational requirements. For example, in the case of the Damage Report just discussed, Joan may have inspected the damaged goods and written notes about them; then her assistant, Linda, may have entered the contents of the notes onto a company Damage Form; and Eileen, the manager of the division, may have actually written the Damage Report based on the Damage Form. Each of these declarants perceived something as part of their regular business duty: Joan perceived the damaged goods, Linda perceived the notes, and Eileen perceived the Damage Form. If the information is transmitted along this business chain with near contemporaneity, then its final incarnation as the Damage Report may fall within FRE 803(6). The actual maker of the record, Eileen, does not have to have personal knowledge of the damaged goods. Rather, it is sufficient, according to the language of the rule, that the record was "made at or near the time *by, or from information transmitted by, a person with knowledge.*" (Emphasis added.) The custodian or other foundation witness would be required to testify (or submit a declaration) about the process by which the information was transmitted and the record was created.

Records containing multiple levels of hearsay are created in a wide variety of situations: A recording secretary may take notes on what happened at a board meeting and give those notes to a stenographer to transcribe; a doctor may orally recite the doctor's observations about a patient, which are then recorded by a medical assistant; an employee of a seller may report shipping information to an employee of a purchaser, who then records it. At each level, there is of course some risk that the declarants may fabricate, misunderstand, or incorrectly remember the events reported or recorded. It is the belief that, in general, routinely prepared records are accurate that justifies admission of the documents.

i. Sources of Information with No Business Duty. What if the original source of the information recorded in a business record is not acting in the regular course of business — that is, has no business duty? Consider, for example, a slight variation in the preceding hypothetical concerning the Damage Report. Suppose that the defense of the seller of the damaged goods is that the goods were damaged *after* delivery to the purchaser. Also suppose that Joan's Damage Report contains the following statement: "Just after delivery, Bystander reported to me that he had seen the seller's delivery truck in a rear-end collision on the highway an hour previously." If the Damage Report is offered to prove that the rear-end collision caused the damage to the delivered goods *before* delivery, there is now an additional hearsay step in the record — from Bystander to Joan. It is the truth of Bystander's statement that the record is offered to prove. Bystander has no business duty to ensure the accuracy of Joan's record. Thus the rationale for the business records exception is not applicable to Bystander's statement to Joan. Yet the record was made "from information transmitted by ... a person [Bystander] with knowledge." FRE 803(6), if read literally, would appear to make the record admissible.

According to the Advisory Committee Note, however, the intent was to exclude, without regard to the trustworthiness clause, statements from persons with no business duty to transmit information to the record keeper:

Sources of information presented no substantial problem with ordinary business records. All participants, including the observer or participant furnishing the information to be recorded, were acting routinely, under a duty of accuracy, with employer reliance on the result, or in short "in the regular course of business." If, however, the supplier of the information does not act in the regular course, an essential link is broken; the assurance of accuracy does not extend to the information itself, and the fact that it may be recorded with scrupulous accuracy is of no avail. An illustration is the police report incorporating information obtained from a bystander: the officer qualifies as acting in the regular course but the informant does not. The leading case, Johnson v. Lutz, 253 N.Y. 124, 170 N.E. 517 (1930), held that a report thus prepared was inadmissible.

In light of the legislative background to FRE 803(6), the rule has been interpreted consistently with the Advisory Committee's comments: Any declarant to whom the business records exception applies must transmit knowledge in the course of a regular business activity — that is, have a business duty to make the out-of-court statement. If not, Rule 803(6) may not be used to admit the recorded statement. United States v. Patrick, 959 F.2d 991 (D.C. Cir. 1992) (no business duty to supply name and address when purchasing a television, thus receipt with defendant's name and address on it was not an admissible business record). If information is provided by outside persons not acting within a business duty, the exception may still apply if it is the business's standard practice to verify or otherwise assure the accuracy of the information transmitted. United States v. Sokolow, 91 F.3d 396, 403 (3d Cir. 1996) (proof of claim forms submitted by insurance claimants were verified and audited before being incorporated into the insurance adjuster's records).

   ii.   Use of Multiple Exceptions and Exemptions.   The source of information in a business record may be a declarant whose statement falls within another hearsay exception or exemption. If Bystander's statement to Joan had been, "I just saw that truck in a rear-end collision," it might have been admissible under FRE 803(1), the present sense impression exception. If so, combining that exception for Bystander's statement with the business records exception for the other hearsay steps would make the entire record admissible, assuming that Joan has a business duty to report that a Bystander's statement was made to her. What if a doctor's record describing a patient's symptoms includes the patient's statement, "My arm is broken because I was assaulted by Paul"? The patient's statements about the general cause of injury may fit within FRE 803(4), the exception for statements made for medical treatment. Naming the assailant, however, is not likely to be pertinent to diagnosis or treatment. Therefore, FRE 803(4) would probably not be available to admit the name of the alleged attacker. There is also an additional concern. Since the information about who is responsible for the patient's injury is arguably not pertinent to treatment, there is concern that the doctor will not be motivated to be as careful in listening to, remembering, and recording such information, even if it is regularly done. To the extent that this concern reasonably exists, it becomes a basis for arguing that the business records exception is not applicable because "the source of information or the method or circumstances of preparation indicate lack of trustworthiness."

   ### d.   Computer Documents and Electronic Data as Business Records

   FRE 803(6) also permits reliance on computer, electronic and Web site documents. See the Advisory Committee Note to FRE 803:

> The form which the "record" may assume under the rule is described broadly.... The expression "data compilation" is used as broadly descriptive of any means of storing information other than the conventional words and figures in written or documentary form. It includes, but is by no means limited to, electronic computer storage.

Some computer documents, such as accounting records, represent the storage and sorting of declarations of fact that are entered by persons into the system. The process by which the data were input and used must be pursuant to a business duty in accordance with regular business practice. Some courts have also insisted on evidence concerning procedures for input control, including tests to insure accuracy and reliability. United States v. Scholle, 553 F.2d 1109 (8th Cir. 1997). Other computer documents, such as telephone records, are automatically generated by the computerized system without any human input of underlying data. These records may not be hearsay at all because there is no human declarant making a statement, but the accuracy of the process by which they are produced is still necessary for authentication under FRE 901(b)(9).

Many businesses and government offices publish internal information about their activities on Web sites. Every digital data entry is a record of such information, and provided that all of the requirements for business (or public) records are satisfied, each printout of this information would satisfy FRE 803(6) or FRE 803(8). For both computer and Web documents, if the data was collected and entered into the computer or onto the Web site in the regular course of business, then printing out a document for purposes of litigation does not trigger the untrustworthiness concerns of Palmer v. Hoffman. Of course, if the data were not simply downloaded for a printout but were selected, edited or corrected, then the reliability of the record can be questioned. Potamkin Cadillac Corp. v. B.R.I. Coverage Corp., 38 F.3d 627, 631, 633 (2d Cir. 1994).

E-mail documents may also qualify as business records if it can be shown that it was the regular practice of employees to write and maintain such e-mails. An exchange of e-mails between people in different companies may also be admissible under FRE 803(6) if adequate declarations as to business duty are provided by both businesses. DirecTV v. Murray, 307 F.Supp.2d 764 (D.S.C. 2004). In United States v. Ferber, 966 F. Supp. 90 (D. Mass. 1997), the government sought the admission of an e-mail sent from the employee of an investment banking firm to his superior, recounting an inculpatory conversation that the employee had had with the defendant. The defendant's statements were, of course, FRE 801(d)(2)(A) admissions, but the employee's recounting of the conversation in an e-mail was claimed to be a business record. The employee testified that it was his regular practice to send such e-mails to coworkers after important telephone conversations with clients. The court refused to admit the e-mail, however, finding that there was no evidence that Merrill Lynch, the employer, required such records to be maintained:

> [I]n order for a document to be admitted as a business record, there must be some evidence of a business duty to make and regularly maintain records of this type.... Were it otherwise, virtually any document found in the files of a business which pertained in any way to the functioning of that business would be admitted willy-nilly as a business record. This is not the law." [Id. at 98-99.]

Do you think this is too narrow a view of the use of e-mail to generate business records? What was the court's concern in *Ferber*?

KEY POINTS

1. FRE 803(6) requires testimony from a foundational witness (or a written declaration) to provide evidence of the foundation requirements for the exception. Once these requirements are satisfied, to obtain exclusion the opponent bears the burden of submitting evidence to show the record's lack of trustworthiness, arising from the record's sources of information or the method or circumstances of its preparation.

2. Each link in the chain of supplying and recording the information contained in the business record must have personal knowledge of the underlying event or have perception of the information transmitted about it, and must be acting in the course of a regular business activity in passing the information on or recording it. If information is supplied by or recorded by a declarant with no business duty, the information must be either verified or the FRE 803(6) exception alone cannot be used to admit the record. Any other hearsay exemption or exception may be used for that declarant, however, and the record may be admitted using a combination of exceptions and exemptions.

PROBLEMS

8.63. Return to Problem 8.61, at page 523. The notes and the memorandum written by Leveritt Darnell are offered as business records because Darnell is unavailable to testify. Who might serve as the foundation witness for these notes? What questions should be asked to satisfy FRE 803(6)? Will they be admitted?

8.64. Plaintiff is suing Chem-Clean manufacturing company for personal injuries resulting from his use of a Chem-Clean household cleaning product. Plaintiff was taken to the hospital emergency room. Plaintiff's medical records contain the following notation made by the emergency room physician: "Burn appears to be second degree. Covers area approximately 6 inches in diameter. Burn caused by Chem-Clean cleaning product, according to the patient." Can Plaintiff obtain the admission of this entire record without the testimony of the physician? Using what hearsay exceptions? What if plaintiff were suing Clean-rite company instead, and alleged that he had been using a Clean-rite product. Could Clean-rite obtain the admission of the entire medical record? Using what exceptions?

8.65. Mary is suing Pam for personal injuries resulting from an automobile accident. As part of her case, Mary calls Frank Williams, a bystander who observed the accident. He testifies that Pam ran a red light and collided with Mary. As part of her defense, Pam offers a properly authenticated police report, which contains the following statement: "Bystander Frank Williams stated that Mary ran red light." Should Mary's hearsay objection to this evidence be sustained?

8.66. Nutra Pet Products markets its wares by placing demonstrators in pet specialty stores. The demonstrators set up tables, display Nutra products, and answer customer questions. From May 2001-May 2003, 330,000 demonstrations took place. Nutra's main competitor, AIMS, Inc., became concerned that the Nutra demonstrators were making disparaging comments about AIMS dog food, and has sued Nutra for deceptive trade practices, namely a practice of making false statements about AIMS products. AIMS had a long-standing practice of conducting an annual "mystery tour" during which 25 mid-level employees visited retail pet stores throughout the country as "mystery shoppers" (i.e. their identity as AIMS employees concealed) to expose them to marketplace conditions. In 2003 the mystery tour focused on stores in which Nutra demonstrations were taking place. The AIMS employees were instructed to engage Nutra demonstrators in conversation, then leave the store and make an immediate record of what happened on a standardized form. In its lawsuit, AIMS plans to submit a number of the standardized forms that report statements made by Nutra demonstrators, such as that AIMS products contain carcinogens, sugar, animal fat from road kill, and other ingredients harmful to dogs. An AIMS employee will testify about the process by which the forms were made and kept by AIMS. Are the forms admissible as business records?

8.67. Joseph Reyes is charged with multiple counts of racketeering, murder, assault, firearms, and narcotics violations, as well as conspiracy charges, for the role he played as the head of a large drug distribution organization. At the time of these crimes, Reyes was confined in a state prison where he was visited by Ralph Vargas and others to receive instructions. Vargas became a cooperating witness and testified about his meetings with Reyes in prison and the orders he received to commit murders. To corroborate this testimony, the government offers the visitor logbook from the prison, which indicated that Vargas and other gang members visited Reyes on several occasions, including on days close in time to several murders. The coordinator of inmate records at the prison, who has overall responsibility for storing and maintaining the logbooks, testified that visitors must sign the logbooks in the prison lobby when they enter the building and that they are required to show identification to the lobby officer. The coordinator testified that she observed her own visitors sign the books; that she had no personal knowledge whether all visitors showed identification or whether the lobby officer checked the identification against the log entry, but that these were procedures that were supposed to be followed. The logbooks themselves reflect irregularities such as missing names, missing addresses, and different names in the same handwriting. Reyes also contends that visitors of inmates have an incentive to provide misinformation to avoid monitoring of their contacts.

What arguments would you make on behalf of Reyes to exclude the logbooks under FRE 803(6)? As the government, how would you respond? What result?

13. Interpretation and Illustration of FRE 803(8): Public Records and Reports

Every jurisdiction permits certain public records and reports to be admitted into evidence for their truth. The exception for public records has common law origins, but there are also many statutes governing the admissibility of particular kinds of public records. FRE 803(8) provides for the admission of three types of records:

> (8) Public records and reports. Records, reports, statements, or data compilations, in any form, of public offices or agencies, setting forth (A) the activities of the office or agency, or (B) matters observed pursuant to duty imposed by law as to which matters there was a duty to report, excluding, however, in criminal cases matters observed by police officers and other law enforcement personnel, or (C) in civil actions and proceedings and against the Government in criminal cases, factual findings resulting from an investigation made pursuant to authority granted by law, unless the sources of information or other circumstances indicate lack of trustworthiness.

a.   Preliminary Factfinding

- The basic foundation requirements for public records under FRE 803(8) are:
- the statement is in the form of a record or report from a public office or agency; and
- the contents of the record involve
  - the activities of that office or agency;
  - matters observed and reported pursuant to a duty imposed by law, but not matters observed by police or law enforcement in criminal cases; or
  - factual findings resulting from an investigation authorized by law, but not against the defendant in a criminal case.

A person with knowledge of the contents of the proffered public record is not required to lay this foundation and some public records, if identified and authenticated, can satisfy the foundational requirements with their contents alone. Like FRE 803(6), this exception also includes a general exclusionary clause that permits the judge to exclude public records if the sources of information or other circumstances indicate lack of trustworthiness.

   i.   Activities of the Office or Agency.   Subsection A is generally interpreted to admit records pertaining to a public agency's own internal "housekeeping" functions such as its own personnel records and budgetary information. It also includes records of official activities of the agency that are necessary to the performance of its public duties independent of any specific investigation or litigation, such as a county's registry of applicants for a firefighter position, or the record of an automobile's title history. In the *Johnson* case, the "C" file on defendant Johnson contained records of Johnson's movements into and out of the California Department of Corrections, which reflected the official tasks of the CDC — housing and transporting prisoners.

   ii.   Matters Observed and Reported Pursuant to a Duty Imposed by Law, Excluding Matters Observed by Police Officers and Other Law Enforcement Personnel in Criminal Cases.   Records that report what public employees have observed pursuant to their public duties are admitted under subsection (B) upon a minimal foundation. Consider the differences between these public reports and the business record exception of FRE 803(6). The foundation for business records requires evidence of near contemporaneity and regularity — circumstances that increase the trustworthiness of the records. These indicia of reliability are not required by FRE 803(8)(B).

   Observing and reporting matters under a "duty imposed by law" rarely requires independent proof of the pertinent law. Duty is presumed from the legal purpose of the public agency itself and the scope of employment of the public employee. Such public records span many fields, and may include weather reports, records of border crossings, accident scene measurements and descriptions, or damage reports. Many public records and reports are the product of multiple levels of hearsay, when one public employee observes and reports observations to a colleague or subordinate who is also a public employee, and who then records them. As long as each link in the chain bears a public duty, FRE 803(8)(B) encompasses the entire report.

The exclusionary terms of subsection (B) apply to criminal cases and operate against the admission of reports of matters observed by "police officers and other law enforcement personnel." Reports authored by police officers are readily identifiable. We will discuss at pages 539-540, infra, how broadly courts interpret the term "other law enforcement personnel." Despite the broad language of the rule, it is generally held that *criminal defendants may offer FRE 803(8)(B) records against the government.* United States v. Insaulgarat, 378 F.3d 456, 466 (5th Cir. 2004) (acknowledging that substantial authority supports use of subsection (B) statements by criminal defendants but adhering to Fifth Circuit precedent that applies the rule according to its terms). Judicial revision in most Circuits makes subsection (B) equivalent in scope to subsection (C).

iii.   Factual Findings in Investigative Reports.   A wide range of government investigative reports have been admitted in civil cases pursuant to subsection (C): findings of official misconduct, accident reports of police or incident reports by specialized agencies, safety and diagnostic studies relating to public health issues, and reports and studies on housing and employment discrimination. Such reports are powerful evidentiary tools, both because of the allegedly neutral weight of government investigation behind them and because of the persuasive impact of their findings and conclusions.

In 1988, the U.S. Supreme Court ended over 10 years of debate among the circuit courts as to whether evaluative opinions and conclusions contained in public investigative reports should be admitted as "factual findings" under subsection (C). In Beech Aircraft Corp. v. Rainey, 488 U.S. 153, 170 (1988), the court held: "As long as the conclusion is based on a factual investigation and satisfies the Rule's trustworthiness requirement, it should be admissible along with other portions of the report." *Beech* involved the crash of a Navy training aircraft that caused the death of two pilots onboard. The surviving spouses brought suit against the manufacturer of the aircraft, Beech Aircraft Corp., based on an alleged defect in the aircraft's fuel control system that may have caused a loss in engine power. The defendant relied on a report prepared by an investigating officer authorized by the Judge Advocate General's (JAG) Office of the Navy. This report concluded that "[t]he most probable cause of the accident was the pilots [sic] failure to maintain proper interval." Id. at 159. The Supreme Court upheld the trial court's decision to admit this evaluative conclusion. Its broad interpretation of the "factual finding" language rested on the language of the rule itself, the legislative history of the rule, the Advisory Committee's Note, the analytic difficulty of drawing a line between "fact" and "opinion," and the opportunity for exclusion of opinions and conclusions that lack trustworthiness under the general exclusionary clause of FRE 803(8). In addition, the Court stated that broad admissibility was consistent with "the Federal Rules' general approach of relaxing traditional barriers to 'opinion' testimony." Id. at 169.

The scope of "factual finding" is not unlimited, however. It has been held that preliminary or interim evaluative opinions of agency staff, interim reports, and preliminary memoranda do not satisfy this requirement of FRE 803(8)(C). Smith v. Isuzu Motors Ltd., 137 F.3d 859 (5th Cir. 1998). And an FBI report that is nothing more than a transcript of statements from informants is not a "factual finding." United States v. Ortiz, 125 F.3d 630, 632 (8th Cir. 1997). It is clear from its language that FRE 803(8)(C) permits use of factual findings only in civil cases and against the government in criminal cases. The prohibition against use against criminal defendants is grounded on concern that multiple, potentially inadmissible hearsay sources in such reports could run afoul of the Sixth Amendment confrontation clause that protects a criminal accused's right to confront and cross-examine witnesses. That this was the concern of the Advisory Committee is suggested by the Committee's continual reference to FRE 803(8)(C) as covering "evaluative reports," a term that suggests reliance on or evaluation of information supplied by third persons.

iv. Exclusion for Lack of Trustworthiness. Despite the awkward drafting of the rule, commentators agree that the exclusionary clause can be applied to all three subsections of FRE 803(8), although most cases involve concern about factual findings under subsection (C). And, like FRE 803(6), the burden is on the opponent to persuade the judge as to the record's lack of trustworthiness. United States v. Loyola-Dorminguez, 125 F.3d 1315, 1318 (9th Cir. 1997) (documents that fall under the public records exception are presumed trustworthy, placing the burden of establishing untrustworthiness on the opponent). The proponent must also be prepared to respond by citing factors that show trustworthiness. As stated in the Advisory Committee Note, factors of trustworthiness include the timeliness of the report; the skill, expertise, and motivation of the investigator; and the procedures followed in preparation of the record. Desrosiers v. Flight International of Florida, Inc., 156 F.3d 952, 962 (9th Cir. 1998) (JAG report containing opinions regarding the cause of an air crash was partially redacted as untrustworthy because the author was not shown to be an expert, had not attended accident reconstruction school, had no formal training in investigation of aircraft accidents, and had not previously written such reports). The identity and completeness of the sources of underlying information are also important, and it has been held that the exception should be applied "in a common sense manner... in determining whether the hearsay document... has sufficient independent indicia of reliability to justify its admission." Hickson Corp. v. Norfolk Southern Railway Co., 124 Fed. Appx. 336, 345 (6th Cir. 2005).

b. Justification for the Admissibility of Public Records

The rationale for the public records exception — at least with respect to routine matters — is virtually identical to the rationale for the business records exception: The inconvenience of calling public officials to testify and the likelihood that public officials may not recall the information in the records create the need for the exception. United States v. Midwest Fireworks Mfg. Co., 248 F.3d 563, 567 (6th Cir. 2001) (the public records exception "is a practical necessity [for]... government officers 'who have made in the course of their duties thousands of similar written hearsay statements'"). The public official's duty and the likelihood that public access to the records will reveal inaccuracies tend to ensure the records' reliability. As with all hearsay exceptions, there must be a sufficient showing of personal knowledge in subsection (A) and (B) records. There are no specific foundational requirements, however, that the record be made at or near the time of the event or that it be a regular practice of the public agency to make the record. Opinions and conclusions admitted under subsection (C) may, as we shall see, rest on information outside the investigator's own firsthand knowledge. "It is the methodology of factual investigation which provides a threshold safeguard against untrustworthiness." Ariza v. City of New York, 139 F.3d 132, 133 (2d Cir. 1998).

14.   Elaboration of FRE 803(8)(B): The Meaning of "Other Law Enforcement Personnel"

a.   The Meaning of Law Enforcement Personnel

i.   United States v. Oates.   In United States v. Oates, 560 F.2d 45 (2d Cir. 1977), an early and, at the time, influential opinion, the court reviewed the admission at trial of two public records — the handwritten worksheet and the official report of a Customs Service chemist. These documents recorded the testing procedure and test results on a white powder seized from one of the defendants, found to be heroin. The examining chemist did not testify due to illness, and there were inconsistencies between the two documents regarding the chain of custody. On appeal from appellant's conviction for possession of heroin with intent to distribute, the Second Circuit held that the reports were hearsay and were "factual findings" under FRE 803(8)(C), thus inadmissible against a criminal defendant. The court also considered whether the documents were admissible under FRE 803(8)(B):

> Though with less confidence, we believe that the chemist's documents might also fail to achieve status as public records under FRE 803(8)(B)   [T]he reports in this case conceivably could . . . be susceptible of the characterization that they are "reports . . . setting forth . . . (B) matters observed pursuant to a duty imposed by law as to which matters there was a duty to report." If this characterization is justified, the difficult question would be whether the chemists making the observations could be regarded as "other law enforcement personnel." We think this phraseology must be read broadly enough to make its prohibitions against the use of government-generated reports in criminal cases coterminous with the analogous prohibitions contained in FRE 803(8)(C). . . . We would thus construe "other law enforcement personnel" to include, at the least, any officer or employee of a governmental agency which has law enforcement responsibilities. Applying such a standard to the case at bar, we easily conclude that full-time chemists of the United States Customs Service are "law enforcement personnel." [The court then elaborated on the extensive role Customs Service chemists play in the development of evidence for criminal prosecutions.]
>
> Our conclusion that the chemist's report and worksheet do not satisfy the standards of FRE 803(8) comports perfectly with what we discern to be clear legislative intent not only to exclude such documents from the scope of FRE 803(8) but from the scope of FRE 803(6) as well. . . . The Advisory Committee, in unequivocal language, offers the specter of collision with the confrontation clause as the explanation for the presence of FRE 803(8)(C) in its proposed (and, since FRE 803(8)(C) was unaltered during the legislative process, final) form. [560 F.2d at 67-68]

ii.   Prosecutorial Function.   Since Oates was decided, many courts have interpreted the "law enforcement personnel" terminology more narrowly. In light of Congress's concern that it might violate a defendant's confrontation right to use a police report *instead of the live testimony of a police officer*, particularly when the report contained the police officer's eyewitness account of criminal conduct, these courts include only individuals whose functions are similar to police officers within the exclusionary language of (B). This includes public employees who perform a "prosecutorial" or investigative function in specific cases, such as customs inspectors and border patrol agents, as opposed to those who perform administrative duties in a regulatory scheme, make administrative decisions, or seek compliance with fines and citations. In a case that seemingly controverts the holding in Oates, the court in United States v. Rosa, 11 F.3d 315 (2d Cir. 1993), upheld admission of the factual observations contained in autopsy reports from the medical examiner's office because the employees of the office had no responsibilities for enforcing the law. The conclusions in the report as to the manner and cause of death, however, were excluded under FRE 803(8)(C). Does drawing this distinction make sense? Courts have held the following kinds of records to be admissible under subsection (B) because the authors were not law enforcement personnel: records of fire code violations, computerized printouts of currency records of the Federal Reserve Board (including that certain currency was not in circulation), records of drivers' license tests, and even tickets for moving and parking violations.

In criminal cases, the focus on admissibility of many types of public records now includes the question of whether such reports and records are "testimonial" statements under the interpretation of the Confrontation Clause set forth in Crawford v. Washington. See Section G., infra.

iii. Routine and Regular Activities. Since *Oates*, it is now well established that routine, bureaucratic and nonadversarial reports made by law enforcement personnel, and even by police officers, need not be excluded in criminal cases. Thus courts have not applied the exclusionary terms of subsection (B) in cases involving: records of serial numbers of weapons received in Northern Ireland; reports of the time and date of crimes, but not the facts and circumstances involved; a log of all 911 calls; stolen vehicle reports; and records relating to the regular maintenance checks of a breathalyzer unit. All of these records were considered reliable because they were routine and not made in an adversarial setting, whereas in United States v. Orozco, 590 F.2d 789 (9th Cir. 1979) observations made in adversarial settings such as crime scenes or interrogations were said to be less reliable because of the nature of the confrontation between police and defendant. Again, even for routine reports, the question remains whether the statements made therein are "testimonial" under *Crawford*.

b. The Relationship Between FRE 803(8)(B) and (C) and Other Exceptions

The court in *Oates* also considered whether the two chemist's reports could have been admitted as business records pursuant to FRE 803(6):

> [T]he government argues . . . that the chemist's report and worksheet in the case at bar fall clearly within the literal terms of . . . FRE 803(6). . . . [W]e assume for purpose of argument here, that . . . the chemist's report and worksheet might fall within the literal language of FRE 803(6). . . . This would not be the first time that a court has encountered a situation pitting some literal language of a statute against a legislative intent that flies in the face of that literal language. Our function as an interpretive body is, of course, to construe legislative enactments in such a way that the intent of the legislature is carried out. . . .
>
> [P]olice and valuative reports not satisfying the standards of FRE 803(8)(B) and (C) may not qualify for admission under FRE 803(6) or any of the other exceptions to the hearsay rule. . . . [560 F.2d at 73-77]

Under *Oates*, if a document is inadmissible under FRE 803(8) because of the specific exclusionary terms in subsections (B) and (C), it would be a subversion of the legislative intent to permit the document to be used as an FRE 803(6) business record. The justifications for admitting business and public records are, after all, very similar. In addition, it should not be permissible to circumvent the specific limitations on the scope of FRE 803(8) by resorting to the residual exception FRE 807. Some Courts of Appeals have differed with *Oates* and admitted lab reports identifying illegal substances as FRE 803(6) business records even without the testimony of the person who prepared the report. United States v. Roulette, 75 F.3d 418, 421 (8th Cir. 1996).

We do not believe, however, that the *Oates* dictum prohibiting resort to *all* other exceptions is sound. FRE 803(5), for example, requires the attendance of the author as a witness. If the police or law enforcement officer does testify and is available for cross-examination, a court should not forbid the use of FRE 803(5) by the government in criminal cases merely because the recorded recollection also happens to be in a public record falling within FRE 803(8)(B) or (C). United States v. Sawyer, 607 F.2d 1190 (7th Cir. 1979) (document falling within exclusionary provision of FRE 803(8)(B) admissible under FRE 803(5)). But see United States v. Pena-Gutierrez, 222 F.3d 1080, 1086 (9th Cir. 1999) (error to admit a law enforcement report under FRE 803(5)).

Some records of a governmental entity may contain information that is neither a "matter observed" nor a "factual finding." When that is the case, the report is not covered by FRE 803(8)(B) or (C) at all and, therefore, cannot fall within the exclusionary terms of FRE 803(8)(B) or (C). Thus it would not be a subversion of those limitations to resort to FRE 803(6) or to any other hearsay exception.

15. Elaboration of FRE 803(8)(C): The Problem of Multiple Hearsay Sources Within Investigative Reports

Many investigations that result in factual findings are based on hearsay information. Factual findings might be based on interviews of witnesses conducted by the investigator or on research evaluating both public and private records. In the *Beech* case, for example, the investigator relied on eyewitness accounts of the plane crash and reports analyzing the condition of the aircraft after the crash. Subsection (C) clearly contemplates that the investigator may use those sources, evaluate them, and then reject them or rely on them in making factual findings. Thus unlike business records under FRE 803(6) and public records under FRE 803(8)(B), where all sources must be operating under a business or public duty in order to conform to the requirement of the exceptions, *sources relied on under FRE 803(8)(C) need not be operating under any sort of public duty in relaying information to the investigator.* Hickson Corp. v. Norfolk Southern Railway Co., 124 Fed. Appx. 336, 345 (6th Cir. 2005) ("it is not necessary ... that the person who prepares the report have first-hand knowledge of the event ... [although] the 'independent indicia of reliability' is diminished"). Some of these hearsay sources may fall within their own exception or exemption to the rule of exclusion — for example, excited utterances, statements of parties, or business records. This would satisfy FRE 805 and would also provide some circumstantial guarantees of trustworthiness. If the underlying hearsay sources are not admissible, one safeguard is the public agency's ability to evaluate such sources before it decides to rely on them. If the original source has personal knowledge and no reason to misrepresent the information to the public official, under the circumstances, then the public report may be admitted. In re Air Disaster at Lockerbie Scotland on December 21, 1988, 37 F.3d

804 (2d Cir. 1994) (investigation of air crash relied in part on computerized records of passenger baggage based on hearsay reports from passengers' and crew members' friends and relatives).

Another safeguard is the court's ability to exclude the public report under the lack of trustworthiness clause in FRE 803(8). Courts have used this clause to exclude records of findings that are based on hearsay sources that are unidentified or that the court finds to be unreliable. Hickman v. Norfolk Southern Railway Co., 124 Fed. Appx. at 346 (unknown source reporting a toxic leak, transmitted by multiple levels of hearsay through state agencies and resulting in an erroneous time of occurrence, lacked "the necessary indicia of reliability"); Miller v. Field, 35 F.3d 1088 (6th Cir. 1994) (judgment for defendants reversed on grounds of erroneous admission of official report disputing alleged inmate rape of plaintiff, since report was based on inadmissible hearsay statements of the assailants and the local prosecutor).

a. Are Otherwise Inadmissible Hearsay Sources Admissible for Their Truth?

FRE803(8)(C) does not by its terms admit otherwise inadmissible hearsay sources for the truth of the matters they assert, even when they are relied on by the investigator and appear to be trustworthy. If these sources appear in the text of the public report, the jury might use them to decide what really happened, regardless of the investigator's conclusions. As you know, the Federal Rules do not trust the jury to exclude inadmissible hearsay from its decisionmaking. Thus there a conflict between admitting the investigator's entire report — including the substantive contents of all of its sources — and keeping inadmissible hearsay from the jury. A similar conflict exists when opinions of testifying expert witnesses are admitted together with all of the expert's underlying, potentially inadmissible sources, as will be discussed in Chapter Nine. FRE 703 now provides its own approach to this conflict, as we discuss on page 667, infra. It has been held that public reports that state conclusions based on scientific or technical expertise must comply with the requirements of "validity" of methodology under FRE 702. Jones v. Ford Motor Co., 320 F.Supp. 2d 440 (E.D.Va. 2004). Thus it seems possible that the balancing test provided in Rule 703 could be applied to subsection (C) reports as well. The jury would be instructed that the underlying hearsay sources are admitted not for their truth but in order for the jury to evaluate the basis for the investigation's findings. Otherwise, the hearsay sources would be redacted from the report, or application of the untrustworthiness clause of Rule 803(8) could be used to exclude the report altogether.

b. Administrative Findings

It is well established that the findings and conclusions that result from judicial proceedings do not fall within FRE 803(8)(C). Nipper v. Snipes, 7 F.3d 415, 417 (4th Cir. 1993) ("a judge in a civil trial is not an investigator"). However, agency hearings within the executive branch, even those presided over by officials called Administrative Law Judges, do qualify as investigations. In a case involving a trial-type hearing, the presentations of witnesses, cross-examination and a review of records and tests, the ALJ issued a decision with detailed factual findings concerning the airworthiness of an airplane for purposes of suspending the aircraft's National Transportation Safety Board certificate of airworthiness. These findings and decision were later admitted in a trial for breach of contract against the company that had attempted to restore the aircraft to airworthy condition. Zeus Enterprises, Inc. v. Alphin Aircraft, Inc., 190 F.3d 238 (4th Cir. 1999). Such findings are not automatically admissible, however. The trial judge has discretion pursuant to FRE 403 to assess the probative value of such reports and findings, as well as their Rule 403 dangers:

> The party against whom such a determination is admitted must attempt to expose the weaknesses of the report . . . an effort that may well confuse or mislead the jury and result in an undue waste of time. . . . We believe that the district court is in the best position to consider the quality of the report, its potential impact on the jury, and the likelihood that the trial will deteriorate into a protracted and unproductive struggle over how the evidence admitted at trial compared to the evidence considered by the agency. [Paolitto v. John Brown E.&C., Inc., 151 F.3d 60, 65 (2d Cir. 1998).]

16. Other Exceptions for Records Under FRE 803

In addition to the business and official records exceptions, FRE 803 contains a variety of exceptions for other types of records. You should read FRE 803(9), (11), (12), (13), (14), (15), (16), and (17) at least once. These exceptions for the most part are based on the notion that the records are likely to be reliable because of the nature of the entity preparing them, the routine nature of their preparation and their subject matter. The scope and operation of these exceptions should be easily discernable from the language of the rule and the Advisory Committee Notes.

FRE 803(7) and FRE 803(10) set forth hearsay exceptions for the *absence* of entries in business and public records, offered for the purpose of proving the nonoccurrence or nonexistence of a matter that probably would have been included in the particular record if the matter had occurred or existed. As the Advisory Committee noted, it is unlikely that the failure to make the entry is the result of a conscious intent to assert that an event did not occur. Thus the failure to make an entry may not constitute a hearsay "statement" in the first place. Nonetheless, there is some precedent for treating the absence of an entry as hearsay. The exceptions exist, according to the Advisory Committee, "[i]n order to set the question at rest in favor of admissibility. . . ." The search for public records must be diligent, and a showing must be made that the documents searched are proper business or public records. The results of such a search have been held *not* to be excluded in criminal cases by the exclusionary clauses of subsections (B) and (C).

KEY POINTS

1. FRE 803(8) provides for the admission of (A) records of the activities of public offices and agencies, of (B) matters observed pursuant to public duty by employees of public offices and agencies, and of (C) public investigative reports, including factual findings. The testimony of a foundation witness may be necessary, but is not required by FRE 803(8).

2. All public records are subject to exclusion by the trial court for lack of trust-worthiness.

3. In criminal cases, the prosecution may not use FRE 803(8)(B) to admit reports of matters observed by police or law enforcement officials against criminal defendants. This limitation may not apply to records of public officers not engaged in the investigation or prosecution of individual criminal cases, nor to routine and regular records kept by police.

4. Under FRE 803(8)(C), factual findings include opinions and conclusions. Investigative reports and factual findings may not be used by the prosecutor against defendants in criminal cases. Multiple hearsay contained in such reports may be used as the basis for the findings, but unless it falls within an exemption or exception, is not admitted for its truth. Courts may also exclude factual findings as lacking trustworthi-ness because of reliance on inadmissible and unreliable hearsay.

PROBLEMS

8.68. A defendant in a criminal case, charged with kidnapping and assault, has filed a Motion to Suppress statements made by him to three law enforcement officers following his indictment, arrest, and request for assistance of counsel. The defendant claims that continued questioning by the three officers violated his right to counsel under the Sixth Amendment. At the suppression hearing, the prosecution offers the report of FBI Agent Peters, who observed the defendant's arrest and questioning. The report was prepared several weeks after the defendant's Motion was filed. It includes Peters's own recollection of events, including that he, and the three other officers whom he interviewed, never heard the defendant say that he wanted to speak to an attorney.

(a) Can the prosecution secure the admission of this report under any Rule 803 hearsay exception? Could the officers use this report if the defendant were pursuing a civil rights claim against them for money damages?

(b) Could the defendant secure the admission of a written finding made by a police department review board, after a full hearing, that a year ago the same three officers had denied an arrestee the assistance of counsel by ignoring her requests for an attorney?

8.69. In the *Johnson* case, each correctional officer prepared a CDC 115 Report of his own observations of the incident involving inmate Johnson. These reports, as described on page 17, supra, may lead to officer or inmate discipline. Can the prosecution use Walker's CDC 115 Report to prove Walker's version of the incident? Could defendant Johnson offer the report in his own defense?

8.70. Return to Problem 3.2, Pedroso v. Driver, on page 129. The defendants offer a police report filed on the day of the accident by Officer Rojas who arrived at the scene five minutes after the accident. The report describes the location and position of the school bus after the impact. It states that Driver said, "Paul ran out unexpectedly." It also states "Officer Nelson arrived at the scene a few minutes after I did. She interviewed children who had witnessed the incident. She reports that several of them claimed that the boy ran in front of the bus, and that although they were very distressed, they seemed to be reliable." In the space for "Conclusions," Officer Rojas wrote "No apparent violation." How much of the police report can the defendants introduce against plaintiffs? Must Officer Rojas testify as a witness in order to secure the report's admission?

8.71. Wilson is being prosecuted for illegally shipping arms to Libya. His defense is that he had an ongoing special relationship with the CIA, and that he shipped the arms with their tacit approval. To rebut this claim, the government offers an affidavit signed by the Executive Director of the CIA stating that he had ordered a diligent search of all CIA records and that the search revealed no evidence of any special relationship with Wilson. Wilson objects to the admissibility of the affidavit on the ground of hearsay. How should the court rule?

8.72. A Liberian corporation, Bridgeton, seeks to enforce in federal court the final judgment rendered in its favor by the Supreme Court of Liberia against Citibank. Citibank is defending against the enforcement action by challenging the legitimacy of the Liberian judicial system, claiming that Liberia's courts do not constitute a system of jurisprudence likely to secure an impartial judgment, and thus Bridgeton's judgment is unenforceable in the United States. As proof of its claim, Citibank offers the U.S. State Department Country Reports for Liberia for the years 1994-1997. Country Reports are prepared annually by area specialists at the Department of State and report on human rights conditions prevailing in the subject country. Federal law requires their annual submission to Congress. In describing their preparation, the State Department says that "[w]e have given particular attention to attaining a high standard of consistency despite the multiplicity of sources and the obvious problems related to varying degrees of access to information, structural differences in political and social systems, and trends in world opinion regarding human rights practices in specific countries." Are the Country Reports admissible?

17. Interpretation and Illustration of FRE 803(22): Judgment of Previous Conviction

A judgment on the merits in a criminal or civil action is relevant to prove the actual occurrence of the facts essential to support the judgment. The judgment is hearsay evidence of those facts. Indeed, it may be multiple hearsay. A defendant's plea of guilty is itself a hearsay statement, and a judge's or a jury's conclusions about the evidence presented in a trial or summary proceeding are offered to prove the truth of those conclusions.

FRE 803(22) provides for the use of criminal felony convictions:

> (22) Judgment of previous conviction. Evidence of a final judgment, entered after a trial or upon a plea of guilty (but not upon a plea of nolo contendere), adjudging a person guilty of a crime punishable by death or imprisonment in excess of one year, to prove any fact essential to sustain the judgment, but not including, when offered by the Government in a criminal prosecution for purposes other than impeachment, judgments against persons other than the accused. The pendency of an appeal may be shown but does not affect admissibility.

a. Preliminary Factfinding

The foundational requirements for the use of a judgment are as follows:

- the judgment must follow a criminal trial or guilty plea;
- the judgment must be for a crime punishable by death or more than one year's imprisonment;
- the judgment must be offered to prove the truth of a fact essential to the judgment; and
- a judgment offered against a criminal defendant must be a judgment entered against that defendant, unless it is offered only for impeachment.

The relevance of a judgment to prove underlying events requires a determination as to what "essential" facts were necessarily decided by the judge or jury. Also keep in mind that the judgment serves only as *some evidence* of those facts. The exception does not raise issues of the possible *binding* effect of a prior judgment — a matter to be resolved under principles of collateral estoppel or issue preclusion.

b.   Justification for the Admissibility of Criminal Judgment

FRE 803(22) reflects confidence that a judgment of guilt in a criminal felony case is reliable proof of the facts essential to sustain the judgment. The high standard of proof — beyond a reasonable doubt — is probably the strongest argument in favor of reliability. The exclusion of judgments entered after a plea of nolo contendere is based on the fact that a nolo plea, which can be entered only with the leave of the court, is specifically designed to resolve a criminal matter without the expense of a trial or the defendant's acknowledgment of guilt. Judgments entered against persons other than the defendant are excluded from criminal trials, unless used for impeachment, because of concern about the defendant's right to confront and cross-examine those adverse witnesses whose testimony provided the basis for judgment. United States v. Austin, 786 F.2d 986 (10th Cir. 1986) (marijuana convictions reversed because government informed jury that 10 co-conspirators had already been convicted for participating in the same alleged conspiracy). Confidence in the reliability of judgments in civil cases is not so deeply felt. When claims involve substantial monetary damages or important principles, it is reasonable to believe that the parties will put forth their best efforts in trying to vindicate their positions. Nevertheless, the standard of persuasion — a preponderance of the evidence — is significantly lower than in criminal cases. If the stakes are small, a litigant may not have a serious interest in devoting the resources that would be necessary to vindicate the litigant's position. Even if one wanted to include judgments from major civil cases, any attempt to define the difference between major and minor cases would probably seem quite arbitrary.

c.   The Admission of Misdemeanor Convictions for Impeachment

The most frequent use of judgments is to impeach testifying witnesses pursuant to FRE 609. As we noted on page 382, supra, courts invariably admit misdemeanor convictions for *crimen falsi* to impeach witnesses pursuant to FRE 609(a)(2), even though misdemeanors are not included within FRE 803(22).

E. HEARSAY EXCEPTIONS REQUIRING THE UNAVAILABILITY OF THE DECLARANT

FRE 804 provides five categorical hearsay exceptions that may be used only when the hearsay declarant is unavailable — former testimony, dying declarations, declarations against interest, statements of personal and family history, and statements offered against a party whose wrongdoing procured the unavailability of the declarant as a witness.

Why unavailability is a requirement for only these five categorical exceptions is by no means clear. The Advisory Committee Note to FRE 803 suggests that unavailability is not required for the FRE 803 exceptions because they are reliable hearsay and, therefore, as acceptable as live testimony. By contrast, according to the Advisory Committee, hearsay falling within an FRE 804 exception "is not equal in quality to testimony of the declarant on the stand . . ." These hearsay statements are admissible only as a last resort; that is, only if the declarant is unavailable to testify in person.

We urge you to question whether there is a significant "reliability difference" between the Rule 803 and the Rule 804 exceptions. At the same time, we caution you against trying too hard to come up with an overarching theory to rationalize the existing law. The earliest common law exceptions — former testimony and dying declarations — were both premised on arguments of necessity because of death. It may be that historical precedent is the best explanation for the current state of the unavailability requirement.

1. FRE 804

RULE 804. HEARSAY EXCEPTIONS; DECLARANT UNAVAILABLE

(a) Definition of unavailability. "Unavailability as a witness" includes situations in which the declarant —

(1) is exempted by ruling of the court on the ground of privilege from testifying concerning the subject matter of the declarant's statement; or

(2) persists in refusing to testify concerning the subject matter of the declarant's statement despite an order of the court to do so; or

(3) testifies to a lack of memory of the subject matter of the declarant's statement; or

(4) is unable to be present or to testify at the hearing because of death or then existing physical or mental illness or infirmity; or

(5) is absent from the hearing and the proponent of a statement has been unable to procure the declarant's attendance (or in the case of a hearsay exception under subdivision (b)(2), (3), or (4), the declarant's attendance or testimony) by process or other reasonable means.

A declarant is not unavailable as a witness if exemption, refusal, claim of lack of memory, inability, or absence is due to the procurement or wrongdoing of the proponent of a statement for the purpose of preventing the witness from attending or testifying.

(b) Hearsay exceptions. The following are not excluded by the hearsay rule if the declarant is unavailable as a witness:

(1) Former testimony. Testimony given as a witness at another hearing of the same or a different proceeding, or in a deposition taken in compliance with law in the course of the same or another proceeding, if the party against whom the testimony is now offered, or, in a civil action or proceeding, a predecessor in interest, had an opportunity and similar motive to develop the testimony by direct, cross, or redirect examination.

(2) *Statement under belief of impending death.* In a prosecution for homicide or in a civil action or proceeding, a statement made by a declarant while believing that the declarant's death was imminent, concerning the cause or circumstances of what the declarant believed to be impending death.

(3) *Statement against interest.* A statement which was at the time of its making so far contrary to the declarant's pecuniary or proprietary interest, or so far tended to subject the declarant to civil or criminal liability, or to render invalid a claim by the declarant against another, that a reasonable person in the declarant's position would not have made the statement unless believing it to be true. A statement tending to expose the declarant to criminal liability and offered to exculpate the accused is not admissible unless corroborating circumstances clearly indicate the trustworthiness of the statement.

(4) *Statement of personal or family history.* (A) A statement concerning the declarant's own birth, adoption, marriage, divorce, legitimacy, relationship by blood, adoption, or marriage, ancestry, or other similar fact of personal or family history, even though declarant had no means of acquiring personal knowledge of the matter stated; or (B) a statement concerning the foregoing matters, and death also, of another person, if the declarant was related to the other by blood, adoption, or marriage or was so intimately associated with the other's family as to be likely to have accurate information concerning the matter declared.

(5) [Transferred to Rule 807]

(6) *Forfeiture by wrongdoing.* A statement offered against a party that has engaged or acquiesced in wrongdoing that was intended to, and did, procure the unavailability of the declarant as a witness.

(Our initial discussion focuses on FRE 804(a). We discuss the remainder of the rule later in the chapter.)

2. Interpretation and Illustration of FRE 804(a): Grounds for a Finding of Unavailability

FRE 804(a) contains a broad, reasonable definition of unavailability that applies uniformly to all of the exceptions under FRE 804(b). Before the adoption of the Federal Rules, what constituted unavailability would vary among jurisdictions and even among hearsay exceptions within a single jurisdiction. For some exceptions, a claim of privilege or absence from the jurisdiction or, occasionally, even absence from the courtroom would suffice. For dying declarations, death was the only acceptable type of unavailability. Now, any of the five subparts may be used for any of the exceptions.

a. Preliminary Factfinding

As is generally true in applying the hearsay exceptions, these preliminary questions are to be decided by the judge pursuant to FRE 104(a). Representations of counsel have been held sufficient to establish the absence or unavailability of a witness under FRE 804(a)(5), so long as good faith efforts have been made to secure the witness, including requests for voluntary attendance and subpoenas. But when the issue is a witness's claim of privilege under FRE 804(a)(1), some courts hold that statements from counsel are insufficient to show that the witness *actually* will not testify. In other words, the witness must claim the privilege in court. Invocation of FRE 804(a)(2) requires the witness's presence in court and a court order directing the witness to testify; FRE 804(a)(3) requires testimony from the witness as to failed memory but not a court order. Evidence that a mental or physical infirmity (confined to home because of heart condition, unable to walk because of back condition, incapacitated by a stroke) will continue for some length of time is usually necessary under FRE 804(a)(4); otherwise, the court may seek a continuance in order to call a witness who is merely ill, if the testimony is significant. United States v. Amaya, 533 F.2d 188 (5th Cir. 1976) (FRE 804(a) requirement of unavailability satisfied by probability that the duration of illness or loss of memory will be long enough so that the trial cannot be postponed).

b.   Preference for Former Testimony or Deposition

FRE 804(a)(5) states a preference for former testimony that applies when the declarant is absent (not deceased). The purpose of the parenthetical clause is to make clear that the proponent of an absent declarant's dying declaration, declaration against interest, or declaration of pedigree must first use the declarant's former testimony or deposition; if none exists, the proponent must make *reasonable efforts to obtain the declarant's deposition testimony* (and seek the declarant's attendance as a witness) as a precondition to the declarant being held to be unavailable. The preference for former testimony, and the requirement of an attempt to depose a declarant, may reflect even stronger suspicion about the reliability of FRE 804(b)(2), (3), and (4) exceptions. After studying these exceptions, you can decide whether this suspicion makes sense.

Unfortunately, this preference sometimes produces problematic results. Where the absent declarant has flatly denied wrongdoing in a deposition taken for a tort case, but has made inculpatory hearsay statements to various people that the defendant seeks to admit, it has been held that the deposition must be used pursuant to FRE 804(a)(5) and that the oral statements are inadmissible for their truth. Campbell v. Coleman Co., 786 F.2d 892 (8th Cir. 1986).

c.   Reasonable Means to Procure Attendance

"Reasonable means" to procure the attendance of an absent witness under FRE 804(a)(5) requires a good faith effort on the part of the proponent of hearsay, but not the doing of a futile act. In the Ninth Circuit, when the government has the name and address of a foreign witness, some effort must be made to contact that witness in the witness's native country or else a finding of unavailability will be error. United States v. Pena-Gutierrez, 222 F.3d 1080, 1086 (9th Cir. 2000). Offers from the government to pay airfare, met with refusal by the foreign witness, has been held to be a reasonable effort. United States v. Siddiqui, 253 F.3d 1318, 1323-1324 (11th Cir. 2000). A decision by the government not to personally serve subpoenas on two allegedly unavailable witnesses until after the first day of trial was found not to be "reasonable" absent further extenuating facts. United States v. Pluta, 176 F.3d 43, 48 (2d Cir. 1999); compare United States v. Olafson, 213 F.3d 435 (9th Cir. 2000) (in a criminal case, district court has broad discretion under Fed. R. Crim. P. 15(a) in deciding whether to order a deposition, and it is not unreasonable to refuse to do so when conditions in Mexico make it unsafe for American prosecutors, and there is no indication that the unavailable witnesses would cooperate).

There are also constitutional issues in criminal cases. In Barber v. Page, 390 U.S. 719 (1968), the hearsay declarant was in federal prison in another state, but there was a federal policy to honor subpoenas issued for witnesses to testify. Thus, even though the declarant was technically beyond the subpoena power of the state, it was likely that the prosecutor could have secured the declarant's attendance. The introduction of the declarant's former testimony in these circumstances, the Court held, violated the defendant's Sixth Amendment right to confront witnesses. But in Mancusi v. Stubbs, 408 U.S. 204 (1972), the hearsay declarant was out of country and, unlike the declarant in *Page*, had been extensively cross-examined at an earlier proceeding. The failure to try to contact him before the use of his former testimony was held not to violate the confrontation clause.

d.   Unavailability Caused by the Proponent

If a witness is unable to, or refuses to, testify *because of the conduct of the proponent* of the hearsay statement, FRE 804(a) directs that the witness not be found to be unavailable. Proof of threats made against a witness are not enough; there must be an actual finding of presumptive unavailability. United States v. Pizarro, 717 F.2d 336 (7th Cir. 1983). There must also be a finding of "purpose" underlying the proponent's conduct. The government's carelessness in losing custody of a witness, or an inability to keep track of a witness, may not qualify as procurement or wrongdoing that would prevent a finding of unavailability. It has also been held that the government's refusal to grant immunity to a witness who exercises a Fifth Amendment right not to testify is neither "procurement" nor "wrongdoing" and does not negate the witness's status as "unavailable" under FRE 804(a)(1), so that prior testimony may be admissible. United States v. Dolah, 245 F.3d 98, 103 (2d. Cir. 2001).

PROBLEM

8.73. Consider which of the following may be sufficient to constitute unavailability for the purposes of satisfying FRE 804(a). What other steps might the proponent have to take before unavailability is adequately proved?

(a)   A criminal defendant asserts the Fifth Amendment privilege not to testify at trial and the defense offers the defendant's own prior testimony.

(b)   A witness invokes the Fifth Amendment privilege against self-incrimination in court.

(c)   The party offering the hearsay evidence submits his or her attorney's affidavit stating that the declarant is in another state beyond the subpoena power of the court.

(d)   The party offering the hearsay evidence submits the declarant's affidavit stating that the declarant does not recall the events in question.

(e)   The hearsay declarant is on the witness stand and claims to have no current memory of the events in question, and the judge believes this testimony.

(f)   The hearsay declarant is on the witness stand and claims to have no current memory of the events in question, and the judge does not believe this testimony.

3.   Interpretation and Illustration of FRE 804(b)(1): Former Testimony

FRE 804(b)(1) states:

(1) Former testimony. Testimony given as a witness at another hearing of the same or a different proceeding, or in a deposition taken in compliance with law in the course of the same or another proceeding, if the party against whom the testimony is now offered, or, in a civil action or proceeding, a predecessor in interest, had an opportunity and similar motive to develop the testimony by direct, cross, or redirect examination.

a.   *Preliminary Factfinding*

The foundational requirements for former testimony are:
- the statement must be in the form of testimony given at a hearing or in a deposition;
- in a criminal case, the party against whom the statement is being offered must have had an opportunity and similar motive to develop the testimony at the prior hearing or deposition by direct, cross or redirect examination; and
- in a civil case, either the party against whom the statement is being offered, or a predecessor in interest to that party, must have had an opportunity and similar motive to develop the testimony at the prior hearing or deposition by direct, cross or redirect examination.

i.   Opportunity to Develop by Same Party or a Predecessor in Interest.   Former testimony of a witness who has become unavailable can be offered against a criminal defendant in the current case so long as that defendant is the one who had the earlier opportunity and similar motive to "develop" that former testimony. It does not matter whether the *former* proceeding in which the testimony was given was criminal or civil.

Where the former testimony of a now-unavailable witness is offered in a *current civil case*, the party against whom the former testimony is being offered need not be the same one who had the earlier opportunity and motive to develop the former testimony. It is permissible if a third-party "predecessor in interest" developed the former testimony. Again, that former testimony may have been given in either a civil or a criminal proceeding. Concern with a criminal defendant's personal opportunity to confront and cross-examine witnesses underlies this FRE 804(b)(1)'s differing treatment of criminal and civil cases.

ii.   Opportunity and Similar Motive.   Consider the following example:

Paula has sued Drew for personal injuries caused in an automobile accident. Wilma, a passenger in Drew's car, testifies for Paula that Drew was drunk at the time and had been driving on the wrong side of the road. There is a judgment for Paula, but the judgment is reversed on appeal because of improper jury instructions and a new trial is ordered. Wilma dies before the retrial, so Paula offers a transcript of Wilma's testimony from the first trial.

Even though Wilma's former testimony is hearsay, it will be admissible against Drew in the retrial under FRE 804(b)(1). All of the foundational requirements are satisfied. Wilma's statement was given at the first trial, obviously a *hearing*. Drew was the adverse party at that trial. Because exactly the same factual issues about which Wilma testified are disputed in the retrial, Drew's *motive* to develop the testimony fully was as great at the first trial as it is now. Moreover, Drew had an *opportunity* to develop the testimony through cross-examination. And it is clear that opportunity is enough, even if Drew did not take advantage of it. Nor is it necessary that the former testimony have been given in a trial or formal hearing: So long as the opportunity and similar motive requirements are satisfied, testimony taken in Wilma's deposition during discovery could be admitted under FRE 804(b)(1) as well.

Similar motive does not mean identical motive, thus a factual inquiry is required. Courts have identified several factors to be considered in determining whether a prior party, in a prior proceeding, had a sufficiently similar motive to develop the testimony of a witness. Most plainly, the questioner must be on the same side of the same issue at both proceedings, and must have a substantially similar interest in asserting and prevailing on the issue. United States v. DiNapoli, 8 F.3d 909, 912 (2d Cir. 1993). In addition:

> Circumstances or factors which influence motive to develop testimony include "(1) the type of proceeding in which the testimony [was] given, (2) trial strategy, (3) the potential penalties or financial stakes, and (4) the number of issues and parties." [United States v. Reed, 227 F.3d 763, 768 (7th Cir. 2000).]

Similarity between the factual issues in dispute in the first and second proceedings also influence a party's motive to develop the witness's testimony. For example, in McKnight v. Johnson Controls, Inc., 36 F.3d 1396 (8th Cir. 1994), a personal injury case against the manufacturer of a car battery that exploded, the deposition testimony from another suit against the manufacturer, given by a witness who had been injured by a similar explosion, was properly admitted under FRE 804(b)(1). In Schmidt v. Duo-Fast Corp., 1976 U.S. Dist. LEXIS 6106 (E.D. Pa. 1996), however, a witness's testimony from a prior suit against the defendant that was based on a "ricochet" accident involving defendant's pneumatic nailer machine was not admitted into a later case based on a "bumpfire" accident involving the same machine. The differing nature of the two accidents may have affected trial strategy and thus the defendant did not have a similar motive to examine that witness in the two cases.

iii.   No Opportunity.   In some proceedings where the former testimony was given, a party had no meaningful opportunity to examine the witness. In United States v. Deeb, 13 F.3d 1532 (11th Cir. 1994), defendant was a fugitive from justice, tried in absentia, and was not represented. Testimony taken against him was not admissible in a later proceeding under FRE 804(b)(1). If the former testimony is taken at a proceeding where, due to its nature or due to the conduct of the judge, a party was present but had no meaningful opportunity to develop testimony, courts have held that the prior testimony is inadmissible under FRE 804(b)(1). In re Paducah Towing Co., 692 F.2d 412 (6th Cir. 1982) (Coast Guard employee did not have necessary skills to test an expert witness's qualifications at the first hearing, and was not permitted to impeach the witness; held, no adequate opportunity to examine the witness).

iv.   No Requirement of "Offered on Same Issue."   Before FRE 804(b)(1), some cases articulated a requirement that the evidence had to be offered on the same *legal* issue. Apart from ensuring that the motive to develop the testimony is the same, however, there is no reason to insist that the legal issue be precisely the same. Assume, for example, that the judgment in our Paula v. Drew hypothetical was reversed because the jury was instructed to apply a gross negligence rather than a negligence standard to the defendant's conduct. Wilma's former testimony should not be precluded at the second trial because the issue to which the testimony relates is now somewhat different. The testimony is undoubtedly still relevant, and it is difficult to believe that the motive of the parties to develop the testimony is any different because of the different legal standard against which the defendant's culpability will be measured. Appropriately, FRE 804(b)(1) makes no reference to an "offered on same legal issue" requirement.

b. Justification for the Admissibility of Former Testimony

A principal justification for admitting former testimony under FRE 804(b)(1) is necessity. Since Wilma is dead, the choice is not between live testimony or hearsay, but rather hearsay or nothing. This all-or-nothing choice, of course, always exists when the hearsay declarant is unavailable (although there may sometimes be other relevant evidence on the same point, so the need for the hearsay will in fact vary from case to case). Although perhaps the law should be otherwise, the all-or-nothing choice is not itself enough to justify the admission of hearsay evidence. There must also be circumstantial guarantees of trustworthiness or some other reasons to justify the loss of the opportunity for cross-examination.

The *prior* opportunity and motive to develop testimony are important justifications for the lack of present cross-examination. If Drew's cross-examination of Wilma had cast any doubt on the truth of what Wilma said, Drew could introduce relevant parts of the cross-examination at the retrial. In fact, given the oath, courtroom formalities and the prior opportunity to develop testimony, prior testimony seems far closer to live testimony than any of the Rule 803 exceptions.

Yet the reason for imposing an unavailability limitation on use of former testimony is readily apparent. Without such a limitation, parties could make wholesale substitutions of former trial transcripts for live testimony in cases retried after a hung jury, mistrial, or reversal on appeal. Indeed, depositions or preliminary hearing transcripts could be substituted wholesale for live witness testimony in the initial trial. Plainly, the drafters of the rule wished to avoid such eventualities.

4. Elaboration of FRE 804(b)(1)

Variations on the Paula v. Drew lawsuit illustrate additional applications of FRE 804(b)(1).

a. The Opportunity to Develop Testimony

Although usually thought of as cross-examination, the requirement of an opportunity to develop testimony has a broader meaning:

Wilma, called as a witness by Paula at the first trial, surprised Paula by testifying on direct examination that Paula had been speeding and that Paula drove across the center line and hit Drew's car. At the second trial, Drew offers this former testimony, and Paula objects on the ground that she did not have an opportunity to cross-examine Wilma.

Under FRE 804(b)(1), it does not matter that Paula did not have an opportunity to "cross-examine" Wilma. It is sufficient, in the language of the exception, that Paula had the opportunity and similar motive "to develop the testimony by *direct*, cross, or *redirect* examination" (emphasis added). FRE 804(b)(1) specifically permits a party to impeach the credibility of any witness, including a witness called by the party, under FRE 607. And, as we discussed in Chapter Two on pages 110-111, supra, FRE 611 sets forth general guidelines for the "mode and order" of presenting evidence and provides sufficient flexibility for Paula to develop fully and to explore weaknesses in Wilma's testimony. Thus, unless the trial judge unduly restricted Paula's direct and redirect examination, she has nothing about which to complain.

b.   Identity of Parties

Returning to the original hypothetical in which Wilma testifies for Paula and adversely to Drew, what if another party, not Paula, offers Wilma's testimony against Drew at another proceeding?

> Rhoda, another passenger in Paula's car, has sued Drew for her own personal injuries. By the time Rhoda's case goes to trial, Wilma has died, and Rhoda offers Wilma's testimony from the first Paula v. Drew trial about Drew's being drunk and driving on the wrong side of the road.

Some of the older former testimony cases speak of an "identity of parties" requirement. Under FRE 804(b)(1), however, there is no requirement that the party *offering the former testimony* must have been a party to the original proceeding in which the testimony was given. Rather, it is sufficient if the party *against whom the evidence is offered* had an opportunity to develop the testimony. In our hypothetical, since Drew had an opportunity to develop the testimony, it does not matter that the person now offering the testimony is Rhoda rather than Paula as long as the "similar motive" requirement is also satisfied.

c.   Former Testimony Offered Against a Party Who Was Not a Party to the Original Action

What if Paula offers Wilma's testimony against a new party — someone who was an outsider to the original Paula v. Drew trial?

> Paula now sues Barney to recover damages for her injuries in the accident with Drew. Barney is the owner of the tavern where Drew had been drinking before the accident. Wilma has died, and Paula offers Wilma's testimony from the first Paula v. Drew trial about Drew's being drunk and driving on the wrong side of the road.

We know that in a criminal case, former testimony cannot be offered under FRE 804(b)(1) against a defendant who was not a party to the first proceeding. Offering Wilma's testimony against Barney, even in a civil case, is somewhat troublesome. Here,

Barney did not have an opportunity to develop Wilma's testimony when it was given. He was not a party to that proceeding. Of course Barney can use the prior cross-examination of Wilma from the first trial. But this is, in effect, to impose upon him Drew's selection of counsel. If Drew was represented by a mediocre attorney who did not do a good job of cross-examining Wilma, Barney would be stuck with that result even though his attorney might have done a substantially better job of discrediting Wilma. On the other hand, Drew did have the opportunity to develop the testimony and to discredit Wilma's opinion that Drew was drunk, and his motive for doing so was identical to Barney's. Given the fact that the alternative is to forego highly relevant evidence, whatever Drew's lawyer accomplished with the cross-examination of Wilma is arguably sufficient to permit admission of the evidence against Barney. Moreover, as a practical matter, Drew himself may not have been aware of the skills or able to control the actions of his attorney. Thus, while it may at first blush sound unfair to characterize use of the evidence against Barney as sticking Barney with Drew's choice of an attorney, it may be no more "unfair" to do this than to stick Drew with the choice of attorney that he initially made and that he may later regret.

i. In a Civil Case, the Party in the Former Proceeding May Also Be a Predecessor in Interest. The Federal Rules as originally promulgated by the Supreme Court permitted the use of former testimony *whenever* the party against whom the evidence is offered *or some third person with a similar motive* had the opportunity to develop the testimony. The Judiciary Committee of the House of Representatives, however, took the view that

> it is generally unfair to impose upon the party against whom the hearsay evidence is being offered responsibility for the manner in which the witness was previously handled by another party. The sole exception to this, in the Committee's view, is when a party's predecessor in interest in a civil action or proceeding had an opportunity and similar motive to examine the witness.

As a result, the existing language of Rule 804(b)(1) regarding development of testimony by a *predecessor in interest* was added.

ii. What Is a Predecessor in Interest? Is Drew a *predecessor in interest* to Barney? Cases decided soon after the enactment of FRE 804(b)(1) interpreted the statutory language and legislative history in, broadly speaking, three different ways. Some interpreted the term *predecessor in interest* narrowly, to include only relationships in which individuals stand in privity to each other in some traditional property or contract law sense. Under this view, Drew would not be a predecessor in interest to Barney. Other courts expanded the notion of privity somewhat more broadly to include, for example, subsidiary and parent corporations, or coemployees such as a district attorney and a city solicitor. More recently, courts have adopted the more liberal approach of equating *interest* with *motive*, just as the rule was originally drafted: Any party to an earlier proceeding who had a similar motive to develop the testimony fully is a predecessor in interest. Under this interpretation, since the same factual issues are in dispute in both the first and the second proceeding, and Drew and Barney are on the same side of those issues with the same interest in discrediting Wilma's opinion, Drew would have had a similar motive to develop Wilma's testimony and would be considered a predecessor in interest to Barney.

d. Lack of Similar Motive Due to Difference in Procedural Context

In some procedural contexts, parties do not have the same motive to develop a witness's testimony that they will have later at a full trial on the merits. United States v. Powell, 894 F.2d 895, (7th Cir. 1990) (no error to exclude criminal defendant's offer of former testimony given by the witness at his guilty plea hearing; the government's motive to test the voluntariness of the plea, and its factual basis, is not the same as at a trial).

In United States v. Salerno, 505 U.S. 317 (1992), the Supreme Court considered the question whether grand jury testimony could be offered *by a criminal defendant*, against the government, when grand jury witnesses were unavailable due to an assertion of privilege. The witnesses DeMatteis and Bruno had been presented to the grand jury by a member of the prosecution team. Their grand jury testimony, however, tended to exculpate the defendant. The prosecutor, presumably, then had a motive to develop their testimony — that is, to impeach or challenge it. At trial, the defendant sought to use the former testimony of DeMatteis and Bruno in his own defense. The government admitted that it was the "same party," but contended that it had not had, and would indeed never have, a "similar motive" to develop testimony at a grand jury proceeding as it would at trial: "A prosecutor . . . must maintain secrecy during the investigatory stages of the criminal process and therefore may not desire to confront grand jury witnesses with contradictory evidence. . . . [A] prosecutor may not know, prior to indictment, which issues will have importance at trial . . ." Id. at 325. The Supreme Court held that this argument had to be addressed and remanded the case to the Second Circuit.

On remand, the court held en banc that the grand jury testimony should not have been admitted under FRE 804(b)(1):

> The proper approach . . . [to similarity of motive] must consider whether the party resisting the offered testimony at a pending proceeding has at a prior proceeding an interest of substantially similar intensity to prove (or disprove) the same side of a substantially similar issue. The nature of the two proceedings — both what is at stake and the applicable burden of proof — and, to a lesser extent, the cross-examination at the prior proceeding — both what was undertaken and what was foregone — will be relevant though not conclusive on the ultimate issue of similarity of motive. [United States v. DiNapoli, 8 F.3d 909 (2d Cir. 1993).]

The Second Circuit believed that the government had no motive to press these particular witnesses at the grand jury hearing because the defendants had already been indicted. Because the grand jury was already persuaded that a conspiracy existed, the government had little incentive to attack DeMatteis's and Bruno's exculpating testimony. The prosecutor did attack them somewhat, by accusing them of lying and confronting them with contradictory evidence. The court held that this was not full-blown cross-examination, and that the questions were carefully limited to matters already publicly disclosed. Thus no secret information was used, as it might be at trial.

In light of the holdings in *Salerno* and *DiNapoli*, perhaps the admissibility of preliminary hearing testimony given by a government witness against a criminal defendant should be rethought. Traditionally, preliminary hearing testimony can be admitted under FRE 804(b)(1) against the defendant later at trial, despite the fact that the defendant had little actual motive to develop the testimony fully at the preliminary hearing. However,

> (1) the preliminary hearing is at such an early stage of the proceedings that the defendant may not have sufficient information to cross-examine the witness adequately; (2) like the prosecutor at the grand jury, the defendant at the preliminary hearing has no wish to "tip his hand" by aggressive cross-examination, and would much prefer to attack the witness at trial; and (3) because of the minimal standard of proof, it is often a foregone conclusion that the defendant will lose at the preliminary hearing, so that any attempted cross-examination or impeachment of inculpatory witnesses will be so much wasted effort at that point.... [Stephen A. Saltzburg, Michael M. Martin and Daniel J. Capra, Federal Rules of Evidence Manual 1838 (7th ed. 1998).]

These concerns about the adequacy of opportunity to cross-examine will also affect the defendant's right to confrontation under *Crawford* if preliminary hearing testimony is offered at trial. See Section G, infra.

e. Method of Introducing Former Testimony

When former testimony is admissible, any witness with present knowledge of the content of the former testimony can relate what was said. The most common method of getting former testimony before the fact finder, however, is to introduce a properly authenticated transcript of the testimony. Use of a transcript for this purpose actually involves multiple hearsay. First, there is the out-of-court statement of the now unavailable witness; second, there is the activity of the court reporter in taking down what the witness says; and third, there is the activity of the court reporter in making a transcript of the testimony. The business or official records exceptions of FRE 803(6) and (8) will generally apply to the court reporter's hearsay.

f. Objections to the Contents of the Former Testimony

Regardless of what method is used to introduce former testimony, there is a possibility that the former testimony may itself be objectionable for some reason. For example, the former testimony may have been elicited in response to a leading question; it may have contained an impermissible lay opinion; it may have been privileged; or it may recite inadmissible hearsay. In these types of situations, the question arises whether objections can be made to exclude former testimony that meets all the requirements of the former testimony exception. The Federal Rules do not address this issue. McCormick, after noting that some courts say always and other courts say never, states:

> The more widely approved view, however, is that objections which go merely to the form of the testimony — as on the ground of leading questions, unresponsiveness, or opinion — must be made at the original hearing when they can be corrected. On the other hand, objections that go to the relevancy or the competency of the evidence may be asserted for the first time when the former testimony is offered at the present trial. [McCormick on Evidence Vol. 2 §306, at 300-301 (John W. Strong, ed., 5th ed. 1999).]

KEY POINTS

1. Assuming unavailability, testimony given at a prior hearing (or deposition) may be admitted against a civil party or a criminal party if that party was present at the prior hearing, had a meaningful opportunity to examine the witness, and had the same motive to examine the witness as at the current trial.

2. The party may not have had the same motive at the prior hearing if different facts are at issue in the two proceedings, or if the procedural context in the prior hearing eliminated the party's incentive to fully examine the witness.

3. Testimony given at a prior hearing (or deposition) may also be admitted against a civil party if a predecessor in interest to that party — someone with the same motive because disputing the same factual issues — had the opportunity to examine the witness at the prior hearing.

PROBLEMS

8.74. David Bond and his parents have sued David's treating physicians and their practice group for medical malpractice in failing to diagnose David's extremely rare form of encephalitis. Defendants noticed a deposition of Plaintiffs' expert witness, Dr. Lakeman, whose test of David's cerebral spinal fluid was positive for this disease whereas Defendants' test, administered one day previously, was negative. At trial, Dr. Lakeman is unavailable and Plaintiffs seek the admission of his deposition pursuant to FRE 804(b)(1). Defendants object on the grounds that they did not have a "similar motive" to develop Lakeman's testimony because Lakeman's deposition was a "discovery" deposition. They intended to discover Lakeman's opinions and the basis for those opinions; they asked open-ended questions to produce answers to submit to their own experts for review; and they were not prepared and did not cross-examine Lakeman to challenge or discredit his opinions. What result?

8.75. Alex and Brenda Dawson are suing the Delta Insurance Company for the loss they sustained when a warehouse they jointly owned was destroyed in a fire. Delta has refused payment because a clause in the policy precludes recovery in the event that either owner is responsible for damage to the property. The insurance company claims that Alex arranged to have Eddy Hall burn the building. Eddy pleaded guilty to arson and testified against Alex at Alex's arson trial, which resulted in a hung jury. Eddy falls ill in prison and is not available to testify in the current action. Delta offers a properly authenticated transcript of Eddy's testimony at Alex's arson trial. Alex objects on the ground that he now has new evidence with which to impeach Eddy; Brenda objects on the ground that she did not have any opportunity to cross-examine Eddy. How should the court rule?

8.76. Defendant was charged with interstate transmission of child pornography via computer. At trial, after the government rested its case, defendant sought the admission of the transcript of a witness's grand jury testimony in lieu of live testimony. The court found the witness to be unavailable. In the grand jury proceeding, the following had occurred: The witness testified that she resided with defendant during the time of his alleged illegal activity, that she had access to his computer with his own password, and that she never saw any child pornography. The prosecutor had then asked about her opportunity for observing the pornography, whether she had seen a particular digital image, and then explored the witness's relationship with defendant and their living arrangements.

The government objects to the admission of the grand jury testimony on the basis of United States v. Salerno, page 556, supra. What result?

5. Interpretation and Illustration of FRE 804(b)(2): Dying Declarations

The dying declaration exception is one of the oldest common law exceptions to the rule excluding hearsay. It is also one of the most problematic in terms of the soundness of its underlying rationale. FRE 804(b)(2) provides:

> (2) Statement under belief of impending death. In a prosecution for homicide or in a civil action or proceeding, a statement made by a declarant while believing that the declarant's death was imminent, concerning the cause or circumstances of what the declarant believed to be impending death.

a. Preliminary Factfinding

The foundational requirements for dying declarations are:

- the statement concerns the cause or circumstances of what the declarant believes is impending death;
- the statement is made while the declarant believes death to be imminent; and
- the statement is offered in a homicide prosecution or a civil case.

Statements concerning the cause or circumstances of the declarant's death include identifications of the perpetrator and descriptions of accidents and of past events that led up to the mortal injury or disease. Even though the belief in imminent death may *generally* enhance a declarant's sincerity, contents other than the cause or circumstances of death are not included within the exception. Does the hearsay statement have to concern the cause of only the declarant's death, or could it extend to the cause of death of another? The language of FRE 804(b)(2) appears to be ambiguous on this point, but presumably it means the declarant's *own* death.

A belief in imminent death means the lack of hope of recovery — "a settled hopeless expectation that death is near at hand and what is said must have been spoken in the hush of its impending presence." Shepard v. United States, 290 U.S. 96, 100 (1933). This state of mind can be shown by the declarant's own statement, by circumstances such as the nature of the declarant's wound, by evidence that the declarant was told that death was imminent, or by the opinion of a physician. Vazquez v. National Car Rental System, Inc., 24 F. Supp. 2d 197 (D. Puerto Rico 1998). This preliminary question is to be decided by the judge, pursuant to FRE 104(a). Thus the jury is not instructed that it must find the declarant's belief in imminent death before it may consider the statement, but evidence that tends to show that the declarant did not have this belief may be used by the opponent to argue to the jury that the statement is not reliable.

Homicide defendants have invoked the dying declaration exception in homicide cases to show that some third person committed the murder. As a practical matter, however, it will usually be prosecutors who want to take advantage of the dying declaration exception.

b.   Justification for the Admissibility of Dying Declarations

The necessity rationale for the exception is twofold. As usual, the unavailability of the declarant means that there may not be another means of obtaining the same or similar evidence. Reliability inheres in the notion that people who realize that death is imminent will be especially likely to be sincere, since their condition obviates any motive to misstate the truth. Or, declarants may believe it is in their interest to "meet their maker" with clean hands, or least with hands that have not recently been soiled by falsehood.

However, both the necessity and reliability justifications for this exception are subject to criticism. It is not clear that the need for a dying declarant's statement about the cause or circumstances of death is any greater than the need for the statements of any unavailable witness. There may be an absence of available eyewitnesses to all sorts of events; and there may be alternative forms of evidence available to prove the cause of death in a homicide or civil case.

The notion that dying declarations are likely to be reliable is also suspect. The proposition that individuals who believe death is imminent are particularly likely to be sincere is sheer speculation. There is no requirement that dying declarants be shown to be religious, and no requirement of other circumstances that reduce a motive to misrepresent the cause of death. Furthermore, even if one assumes that dying declarants are likely to be sincere, the circumstances surrounding a dying declaration may exacerbate other hearsay dangers. If the declarant is the victim of a sudden attack, there is reason to question the accuracy of the victim's perceptions. Additionally, an individual who is suffering enough to believe that death is imminent may have somewhat reduced capacities for narration and memory.

There are additional indications of doubt about the justifications for the admission of dying declarations. In some jurisdictions the party against whom a dying declaration is admitted is entitled to a jury instruction that these statements are to be considered with caution. And the limitation to homicide cases was generated by the concern of the House Judiciary Committee: "The Committee did not consider dying declarations as among the most reliable forms of hearsay. Consequently, it amended the provision to limit their admissibility in criminal cases to homicide prosecutions, where exceptional need for the evidence is present." What this means, of course, is that we are willing to use evidence whose reliability we question in order to obtain criminal convictions that carry the most severe sanctions!

KEY POINT

Assuming unavailability, statements made by a declarant who believes that death is imminent are admissible in civil cases and in homicide cases so long as the contents of the statement concern the cause or circumstances of the declarant's impending death.

6. Interpretation and Illustration of FRE 804(b)(3): Declarations Against Interest

FRE 804(b)(3) states:

(3) Statement against interest. A statement which was at the time of its making so far contrary to the declarant's pecuniary or proprietary interest, or so far tended to subject the declarant to civil or criminal liability, or to render invalid a claim by the declarant against another, that a reasonable person in the declarant's position would not have made the statement unless believing it to be true. A statement tending to expose the declarant to criminal liability and offered to exculpate the accused is not admissible unless corroborating circumstances clearly indicate the trustworthiness of the statement.

a. Preliminary Factfinding

The foundational requirements for declarations against interest are:

- the content of the statement, at the time the statement was made, was
- against the pecuniary or proprietary interest of the declarant;
- could subject the declarant to civil or criminal liability; or
- could render invalid a claim held by the declarant;
- the statement was against any of the above interests of the declarant to an extent great enough such that a reasonable person, in declarant's position, would not have made such a statement unless it was true; and
- if the statement exposes the declarant to criminal liability and is offered to exculpate the accused, evidence of corroborating circumstances that clearly indicate the trustworthiness of the statement must be offered.

i. **Content Against Interest.** The focus of the *against interest* requirement is usually on the content of the statement. This content must be contrary to one of the specific interests of the declarant identified in the rule when the statement is made. At trial, the statement is offered to prove the truth of those facts. Assume, for example, that Mark tells a friend that he owes a lot of money to Ryan. The fact of owing money is against Mark's *pecuniary* interest. Suppose Mark told his friend that he had robbed a convenience store in order to pay the debt. This statement could subject Mark to criminal liability and thus would a be against Mark's *penal* interest. We assume that people in general have an interest in maintaining ownership of their money as well as their possessions, so Mark's statement that he owes money should qualify as contrary to his proprietary interest as well.

To be against a declarant's pecuniary, penal, or civil claim interests, a statement under FRE 804(b)(3) need not have been said in the face of immediate adverse consequences. For instance, the rule does not require that Mark's admission of robbing the store have been made to a police officer; conversely, Mark's belief that his friend would keep his statements confidential does not alter their against-interest quality. A better test is whether the statements would harm Mark's interest if disclosed publicly or to the relevant authorities.

Nevertheless, in other respects the context of the statement does matter: Sometimes a statement that on its face appears to be against interest is not in fact against the declarant's interest because of the surrounding circumstances. A statement by Mark that he owes Ryan $500 may not be against Mark's interest if Mark knows that Ryan claims that the debt is really $2,000. If the facts in the statement can no longer cause trouble for the declarant (e.g., he has been convicted of the crime whereof he speaks) then the against-interest element may not be satisfied. And as we discuss on page 563, infra, if the context within which the statement is made gives the declarant a strong self-serving motive, then the exception may not apply. On the other hand, although one might confess a crime to a spouse or close friend and expect the confession never to be disclosed, in admitting such statements courts typically focus and rely on the against-interest content of the facts disclosed.

ii.   Ascertaining the Declarant's Knowledge. The declarant's knowledge comes up in two different senses under FRE 804(b)(3). Like other FRE 803 and 804 exceptions, FRE 804(b)(3) requires a showing that the declarant (Mark) had personal knowledge of the against-interest fact when the statement was made.

In addition, FRE 804(b)(3) applies only if Mark has knows (or reasonably should know) that the fact is against his interest. If particular facts affect the declarant's assessment of what is against interest, then these facts will be taken into account. FRE 804(b)(3) calls for evaluation of the probable understanding of an individual by asking what a reasonable person in that individual's position would be thinking; and we typically apply "objective," reasonable person standards in light of the circumstances and facts known to the particular individual whose conduct or statement is at issue. In most cases, it will be relatively easy to determine that the declarant knows the statement is "against interest."

iii.   Distinct from Party Admission. It is important, as we suggested earlier, not to confuse FRE 801(d)(2)(A) admissions of a party with declarations against interest. You can see that FRE 804(b)(3) requires many more foundational requirements. It also applies to statements made by anyone, not just a party, and is typically not offered against the person who made the statement (and who is unavailable) but against someone else.

b.   Justification for the Admissibility of Declarations Against Interest

The content of Mark's statement that he owes money reflects damage to his pecuniary interest. This against-interest factor is thought to give the statement a sufficient circumstantial guarantee of trustworthiness to warrant admissibility, at least if the alternative is foregoing the evidence altogether, which it is since the exception requires unavailability. The underlying theory of human behavior is that most people generally tell the truth in the absence of a motive to lie, and motivations to lie are nearly always self-serving: statements against interest, which are the opposite of self-serving by definition, are thus seen as reflecting an absence of a motive to lie. Such a statement is therefore likely to be reliable, even though oath and cross-examination are lacking. The other types of interests that are included within the exception — not being subjected to civil and criminal liability, possessing valid claims against others — are also assumed to be important enough that people should have no reason to lie if they say something that reflects badly on such interests. Some courts speak of a requirement to show that the declarant did not have a motive to lie, but this is not an independent requirement for the exception.

7. Elaboration of FRE 804(b)(3)

a. Doubts About the Underlying Rationale for the Exception

The most serious problem with the declaration against interest exception, in our view, is its empirical assumptions. The first premise underlying the exception, with which we agree, is that people seldom intentionally state facts that truly reflect against their interest. We find troublesome, however, the next inference: that if such statements are made they would not be lies, and therefore are likely to be trustworthy. It seems much more likely that a statement that appears to be against interest is in fact not against interest, but reflects an ulterior motive that may be difficult to discern.

Most statements that are characterized as declarations against interest are likely to fall into one of two categories:

i. Mixed Motive Statements. "Mixed-motive" statements *appear* to be against interest but have a high risk of being unreliable if there was an ulterior self-interested motive for making the statement. For example, a declarant might say he owes money in order to justify asking the listener for a loan; the declarant may "admit" robbing a convenience store or dealing drugs to impress the listener. Numerous criminal cases involve statements to law enforcement officials made by declarants who both admit culpability while also blaming others in order to curry favor with the authorities, or to secure immunity from prosecution.

Sometimes, however, there may not be much available information bearing on the real motivation of the declarant and the court may fail to see that the declarant also had a self-serving reason to make the statement. Examples of cases in which conflicting motives were recognized are Donovan v. Crisostomo, 689 F.2d 869 (9th Cir. 1982) (statements of foreign employees that they did not work overtime were not declarations against their pecuniary interest, because they may have been motivated to make the statements to avoid being sent back to their country of origin), and United States v. Bobo, 994 F.2d 524 (8th Cir. 1993) (in a prosecution for possession of a firearm, no error to exclude the defendant's brother's statement that a gun was his, and not the defendant's; court distrusted the brother's motive and the timing of the statement just before trial). If courts do not discern such mixed motives, untrustworthy statements may be admitted.

ii. Statements Made with No Motive to Lie. The second type of admitted statements are reliable statements whose reliability has more to do with lack of motivation to lie and less to do with their against-interest characterization. Mark's statement that he owes money may be, to him, merely a neutral recitation of a fact The fact that the statement may be characterized as being against interest may have nothing to do with its sincerity. In this respect the statement is no different from many other hearsay statements that do not fall within the declaration against interest (or any other hearsay) exception.

b. Requirement of Corroboration for Statements Against Penal Interest Offered to Exculpate the Accused

FRE 804(b)(3) imposes special corroboration requirements on declarations against penal interest that are offered by defendants in criminal cases to exculpate themselves. In such cases, an out-of-court declarant has made a statement assuming criminal responsibility for the crime with which the defendant is charged. The requirement is framed in terms of "corroborating circumstances" that "clearly indicate the trustworthiness of the statement." See United States v. Vega, 221 F.3d 789 (5th Cir. 2000). Courts look to circumstances that corroborate either the content of the statement (other evidence that the facts that exculpate the defendant are true) or the trustworthiness of the declarant (voluntariness, lack of motive to curry favor, lack of subsequent inconsistent statements). Recantation of exculpatory statements, and assertions of the Fifth Amendment privilege, have been held to weigh against trustworthiness. United States v. Davis, 2001 WL 524374 (D.C. Cir. 2001).

The drafters of the Federal Rules were undoubtedly concerned about the fabrication of exculpatory evidence in criminal cases. Without the corroboration requirement, it could arguably be relatively easy for someone (most likely a convicted criminal) to make a false confession to the defendant's crime in order to help a friend who has not yet been convicted. Similarly, the drafters may have been concerned about the ease with which a made-up confession could be attributed to a declarant known to be unavailable — perhaps one who has absconded or died. Strictly speaking, this concern is not a hearsay problem. The witness whom the drafters fear will fabricate the against-interest statement of an unavailable declarant will himself be on the witness stand and subject to cross-examination. Nevertheless, the corroboration requirement is part of the rule.

Notwithstanding these concerns, and the corroboration requirement for the particular category of statements against interest, doubts about the credibility of the testifying witness should not be a factor in assessing the trustworthiness of the *declarant's* statement. United States v. Atkins, 558 F.2d 133 (3d Cir. 1977).

c. Statements That Inculpate Accomplices

Mixed-motive statements raise special, recurring problems in criminal cases. Consider a case in which prosecutors have charged two defendants, Worrell and Holmes, with robbing a bank. Holmes makes a written confession to the crime at the police station and in the confession names Worrell as his accomplice. At Worrell's separate trial, Holmes successfully asserts his Fifth Amendment right not to testify and is therefore unavailable. The prosecutors offer Holmes's written confession against Worrell, arguing that it is a statement against the penal interest of the declarant, Holmes under FRE 804(b)(3).

A key question presented in cases of potential statements against penal interest that inculpate the defendant in addition to the hearsay declarant will be whether the statement constitutes "testimonial" hearsay under Crawford v. Washington. If it does, then the statement is barred by the Confrontation Clause, unless the defendant had a prior opportunity to cross-examine the declarant and the declarant is currently unavailable. Inadmissibility under the Confrontation Clause cuts off any inquiry into whether the statement qualifies for admission under FRE 804(b)(3). Any statement given under police questioning at the station house, whether a written confession as in the Worrell-Holmes hypothetical or tape recorded interview, as in *Crawford* itself, plainly falls within the core application of the *Crawford* definition. But what about more casual hearsay statements? Lower courts have recently begun to struggle with the contours of the "testimonial" definition, as will be discussed in Section G, infra.

If the hearsay offered under FRE 804(b)(3) is held to be not testimonial, then it is necessary to analyze whether a mixed motive statement like Holmes's is truly against the declarant's interest. Pre-*Crawford* authorities analyzing this question in the context of statements made to law enforcement have held that FRE 804(b)(3) should not allow admission of statements that inculpate purported accomplices unless they also specifically self-inculpate the declarant as well. A broad narrative that is only generally self-inculpatory might not be found to be sufficiently against interest, while statements that intertwine self-inculpation could be genuinely against the interest of the declarant; for example, "I hid the gun in Joe's apartment" could show both self-incrimination and Joe's involvement. See Williamson v. United States, 512 U.S. 594 (1994); United States v. McClesky, 228 F.3d 640, 643 (6th Cir. 2000); United States v. Westmoreland, 240 F.3d 618, 626 (7th Cir. 2001).

d.   Should the Corroboration Requirement Apply to Inculpatory Statements Too?

Critics of the corroboration requirement in FRE 804(b)(3) contend that if penal interest statements are less reliable and require corroboration, there is no reason to limit the requirement solely to exculpatory statements. In 2001, the Advisory Committee on Evidence Rules proposed an amendment to FRE 804(b)(3) that would strike the words "and offered to exculpate the accused" from the last sentence of the rule, thus requiring corroboration for penal interest statements that inculpate and are offered by the prosecution against the accused. It is not clear whether the need, or impetus, for this amendment will continue after *Crawford*.

KEY POINTS

1. Assuming unavailability, statements that are against the declarant's pecuniary, proprietary, penal, or civil liability interest may be admissible. The statement must be so far against that interest that a reasonable person would not be lying when making that statement.

2. In order to determine whether the statement is against interest, the court should examine the situation and motives of the declarant.

3. Statements of fact that inculpate others, made in the context of a self-inculpating statement, are admissible only if each specific statement is against the declarant's interest. Courts are divided as to whether such statements, made in custody, can be admitted as against the declarant's interest.

4. Statements against penal interest offered by a criminal defendant for exoneration must be corroborated as to contents, the trustworthiness of the declarant, or both.

8.   Interpretation and Illustration of FRE 804(b)(4): Statements of Personal or Family History

FRE 804(b)(4) provides:

(4) Statement of personal or family history. (A) A statement concerning the declarant's own birth, adoption, marriage, divorce, legitimacy, relationship by blood, adoption, or

marriage, ancestry, or other similar fact of personal or family history, even though declarant had no means of acquiring personal knowledge of the matter stated; or (B) a statement concerning the foregoing matters, and death also, of another person, if the declarant was related to the other by blood, adoption, or marriage or was so intimately associated with the other's family as to be likely to have accurate information concerning the matter declared.

a.   Preliminary Factfinding

The foundational requirements for statements of personal or family history are:

- the content must concern the declarant's own personal or family history; or
- the statement concerns the personal or family history of one to whom the declarant is related or was intimately associated.

i.   Personal Knowledge of One's Own Personal and Family History.   FRE 804(b)(4)(A), like the common law pedigree exception, does not require that the declarant have personal knowledge. Obviously, a declarant has no personal recollection of birth or place of birth. United States v. Hernandez, 105 F.3d 1330, 1832 (9th Cir. 1997) (statement that declarant was born in Mexico admissible without personal knowledge). However, any declarant meeting the requirements of subsection (A) is inevitably going to have knowledge of circumstantial evidence of personal and family relationships.

ii.   Statements of Relations and Intimate Associates.   The common law also required that a declarant speaking about the pedigree of another be related by blood or marriage to the person about whom the declaration is made. FRE 804(b)(4)(B) expands the common law pedigree exception to close family members and intimate associates so long as the relationship is such that the declarant would have accurate information about the family history. Do the reasons for eliminating the personal knowledge requirement in subsection (A) also apply to the declarants listed in subsection (B)? Independent evidence may be required that the declarant was a family member or so intimately associated with a family as to be knowledgeable.

iii.   Concerning Personal History.   The exception is limited to past facts and events of an objective, rather than subjective, nature. Statements as to motives or purpose for marriage are beyond the scope of FRE 804(b)(4). United States v. Carvalho, 742 F.2d 146 (4th Cir. 1984) (statements from former spouses as to the defendants' previous motives to marry in order to obtain citizenship were admitted in error).

b.   Justification for the Admissibility of Statements of Personal or Family History

Statements about the declarant's own pedigree are assumed to be reliable enough to be admitted if the declarant is unavailable. No special assurances of reliability are required. The common law hearsay exception required that the declaration be made prior to the time of the controversy that is the subject of the litigation. The Advisory Committee Note to FRE 804(b)(4) explains the absence of this requirement on the ground that the timing of the statement has a "bearing more appropriately on weight than admissibility."

KEY POINTS

1. Assuming unavailability, a statement asserting the declarant's own family history may be admitted without a showing of personal knowledge.

2. A statement asserting the family history of another person may be admitted if the declarant had accurate knowledge as a result of being related to or intimately associated with the other person's family.

PROBLEMS

8.77. A doctor, dying from non-Hodgkins lymphoma, brought a strict product liability suit against the manufacturer of an herbicide containing 2, 4-D acid, which he alleged was the cause of his disease. After his death, the doctor's wife, as executor of his estate, was substituted as plaintiff. Eight days after filing the complaint, the doctor gave a sworn, videotaped statement to the effect that in the 1940s, when he was a teenager, he worked for a crop dusting service in Montana mixing 2, 4-D herbicide products and loading them into crop dusting aircraft. He stated that he recalled the labels on the 2, 4-D barrels and that the defendant, Dow Chemical, was the manufacturer. He also stated that his lymphoma was in "stage four," the disease's final incurable stage. Based upon his experience with patients, he stated that he might survive three months.

In fact, the doctor's condition did worsen and he died in two months. In the intervening time, he and his wife traveled to Yugoslavia on a religious pilgrimage, which he believed was the last resort to receiving healing. May his recorded statement be admitted pursuant to FRE 804(b)(2)?

8.78. Fueled by alcohol, rivalry, and the desire for the victim's new car, five men hatched a plot to carjack an acquaintance of theirs and murder him. Three of them carried out the plan. In his dying moments, the victim identified by name the three who attacked him. Unfortunately, he was wrong about two of them, which the government's own proof substantiates. The government nevertheless seeks to use the dying statement against the third attacker who, it claims, was accurately named. May this defendant prevent the admission of the dying declaration? On what grounds? May a fourth defendant, who the government claims did participate in the attack but who was not named by the victim, use the dying declaration at trial to show that he was not an attacker?

8.79. Hanna Mason has sued the Acme Rental Company for personal injuries that she sustained as a pedestrian when she was hit by an Acme truck driven by James Lowe, an Acme employee. Lowe was fired the day after the accident, and six months later moved to Acapulco. Just before leaving the country, Lowe told his friend, Andy Becker, that he had been drinking at the time of the accident and had failed to stop at a stop sign. Lowe also made the same statement in a deposition taken during the discovery phase of the current lawsuit. Lowe has refused to respond to plaintiff's letter requesting that he return to the United States to testify. At trial, Hanna calls Andy Becker to testify about Lowe's statement. Is the evidence admissible?

8.80. Cosimo Demasi sued the Whitney Trust & Savings Bank for $6,500 dollars that the plaintiff claimed the bank held in a joint savings account that he maintained with his wife. The bank defended on the ground that all but $700 had been withdrawn by the plaintiff's daughter with the consent of Mr. or Mrs. Demasi. A judgment for the defendant was reversed on appeal, and before the new trial Mrs. Demasi sought to withdraw the $700 that the bank conceded remained in the account. In order to receive the money, the bank required that Mrs. Demasi sign an affidavit indicating that she had consented to the prior withdrawals. Mrs. Demasi signed the affidavit, withdrew the $700, and died before the second trial began. At the retrial, the bank offers her affidavit. Should it be admitted?

8.81. Burton is charged with robbery and use of a firearm during a crime of violence, both in connection with the robbery of an Oriental rug store, Carpets of Asia, in Carmel, California. The government's theory is that the robbery was master-minded by Wilson, who was also charged but who remains at large. Wilson's girlfriend, Carla, was a U-Haul employee who rented out trucks illegally used by Wilson in other rug store robberies. Carla was arrested and charged with conspiracy to rob a rug store. Unbeknownst to Wilson, she then began to cooperate with the FBI once she was out on bail. Over the next six months, Carla surreptitiously tape recorded numerous conversations with Wilson. In one recording, Wilson gave a detailed account of the Carmel rug store robbery. Wilson said that he recalled how he told the others that they probably only had five minutes for the robbery due to the store alarm timer, which would probably automatically reset itself and notify the police. He recalled how Burton had shown "a lot of heart" during the robbery and had told a female customer who had wandered into the store during the robbery that the store was closed for remodeling. He told Carla that money from the robbery had been used to pay her bail. Alleging that Wilson is unavailable, the government offers Carla's tape recording in evidence against Burton. What result?

8.82. John Bowman has filed an action in probate court, claiming to be the closest kin — a nephew — of the wealthy decedent, George Bowman. George died intestate and had no children or surviving spouse. To establish his claim, John offers the affidavit of one Jacob Bowman, John's father, who John claims is brother to George. Jacob is now deceased. In this affidavit, Jacob states that he and George are brothers and that they emigrated to the United States together from Germany in 1905. John offers no other evidence of a family relationship. Another distant relative who claims the estate offers an authenticated letter from Emily Bowman, deceased wife of Jacob. The letter states that her husband, Jacob, was bribed by John to make the affidavit and that, to her knowledge, George and Jacob were not brothers. Is Jacob's affidavit admissible? Is Emily's letter admissible?

8.83. Plaintiff Maureen Sullivan has sued No-State Life Insurance Company for failure to pay benefits due upon the death of her husband, Stephen. One of the disputed issues is Stephen's age at the time of death. On direct examination of Maureen, her attorney asks her:

Q.   What is your husband's date of birth?
DEFENSE COUNSEL: Objection, hearsay. This witness has no firsthand knowledge and could only know based on what someone told her.
BY PLAINTIFF'S COUNSEL: Ms. Sullivan, did your husband ever tell you what his birthdate was?

DEFENSE COUNSEL: Hearsay, your honor. Her husband cannot possibly have remembered firsthand, as a newborn baby, the date of his own birth. He could only know this by being told.

What should plaintiff's counsel argue?

8.84. Joshua Thomas has been charged for his alleged role in arson and vandalism of an SUV dealership, destroying a number of Hummers and doing other property damage. Thomas denies any involvement in the act. A group called the Environmental Liberation Front ("ELF") claimed responsibility for the act shortly after it occurred. The city newspaper reported that an anonymous source communicated with reporter Bob Adams, the author of the news story, in three e-mails and two telephone interviews, claiming to be responsible for the arson and vandalism, while indicating that Thomas is innocent. Consider whether defense counsel for Thomas, preparing his case for trial, can introduce this information as evidence. What form would this evidence take? What witnesses would the defense need to call? What objections would the prosecution make, and how would the defense respond? What further investigation would defense counsel have to undertake in order get this evidence in admissible form?

9. Interpretation and Illustration of FRE 804(b)(6): Forfeiture by Wrongdoing

In 1997, an amendment to FRE 804(b) added a new subsection (6):

(6) Forfeiture by wrongdoing. A statement offered against a party that has engaged or acquiesced in wrongdoing that was intended to, and did, procure the unavailability of the declarant as a witness.

This new hearsay exception codified a line of cases beginning with United States v. Mastrangelo, 693 F.2d 269 (2d Cir. 1982), in which key prosecution witnesses would "suddenly" became unavailable due to violence or intimidation allegedly perpetrated against them by the defendants against whom they were to testify. Admission of the unavailable witnesses' hearsay statements was justified on a theory of waiver. *Mastrangelo* held that although a criminal defendant's Sixth Amendment right of confrontation "is an essential trial right, it may be waived by the defendant's misconduct." United States v. Dhinsa, 243 F.3d 635, 651 (2d Cir. 2001). This waiver-by-misconduct rule permitted the admission of the hearsay statements of unavailable witnesses when the defendant had "wrongfully procured the witnesses' silence through threats, actual violence or murder," id., despite the lack of confrontation. See Section G infra for discussion of this waiver rule under *Crawford v. Washington*. The waiver principle was then extended to include the hearsay rule — waiver of confrontation rights simultaneously waived "the right to object on hearsay grounds to the admission of [the] out-of-court statements." United States v. Houlihan, 92 F.3d 1271, 1281 (1st Cir. 1996). The Advisory Committee Note to FRE 804(b)(6) makes it clear that the new hearsay exception was intended to implement *Mastrangelo* and its progeny.

a.   Preliminary Factfinding.

The foundational requirements for forfeiture-by-wrongdoing statements are:

- the party engaged or acquiesced in wrongdoing
- the wrongdoing was intended to procure the unavailability of the declarant as a witness against the party
- the wrongdoing did render the declarant unavailable as a witness
- the declarant's statement is offered against the party

i.   The Declarant Was a Witness or a Potential Witness Against a Party.   It is clear from the case law that the purpose of FRE 804(b)(6) is to secure the admission at trial of hearsay statements made by unavailable declarants who were serving as witnesses against a party, for example by giving grand jury testimony or by being scheduled to appear in an upcoming trial. If there was instead only an ongoing criminal investigation, declarants are *potential* witnesses if they are assisting in this investigation. Both prior to and after FRE 804(b)(6), courts have held that the forfeiture rule applies to wrongdoing against both actual and potential witnesses. United States v. Houlihan, 92 F.3d 1271,1279 (1st Cir. 1996) ("We see no [difference] between a defendant who assassinates a witness on the eve of trial and a potential defendant who assassinates a potential witness before charges have officially been brought.")

ii.   The Party Engaged in Wrongdoing that Did Procure the Unavailability of the Declarant.   The party against whom the declarant's statements are offered must be shown to have "procured" the unavailability of the declarant by engaging in or acquiescing in "wrongdoing." The proponent of the statements must persuade the judge by a preponderance of the evidence, pursuant to FRE 104(a), that the party did so act. In general, wrongdoing is defined broadly to mean threats, intimidation, kidnapping, hiding, acts of violence and, ultimately, murder to secure the silence of the then-unavailable declarant. Engaging in wrongdoing means "he or she participated directly in planning or procuring the declarant's unavailability." United States v. Cherry, 217 F.3d 811, 820 (10th Cir. 2000) (defendant's obtaining the car used in the declarant's murder under false pretenses, and her apparent proximity to the actual murderer around the time of the murder, might be sufficient circumstantial evidence that she participated in the planning of the murder).

Evidence used to prove the party's engagement in wrongdoing may include the declarant's hearsay statements. As we know from the Supreme Court's opinion in *Bourjaily*, discussed on page 485, supra, FRE 104(a) permits the court to "bootstrap" a finding of a foundational fact by relying on the contested hearsay statement itself. Should courts impose a requirement, similar to the language in FRE 801(d)(2), that the contested hearsay statement may be used but is not sufficient to prove the party's wrongdoing?

iii.   Intent to Procure the Declarant's Unavailability as a Witness.   All courts agree that a specific finding must be made by the trial court that the party acted with the intention of making the declarant unavailable as a witness:

> [T]he government has the burden of proving by a preponderance of the evidence that...the...party against whom the out-of-court statement is offered...acted with

the intent of procuring the declarant's unavailability as an actual or potential witness. . . . The government need not, however, show that the defendant's sole motivation was to procure the declarant's absence; rather, it need only show that the defendant "was motivated *in part* by a desire to silence the witness." [United States v. Dhinsa, 243 F.3d at 652.]

As an example of proof of intent, the government produced testimony that the defendant in *Dhinsa* ordered his hit men to murder a co-conspirator who was "supposed to go see the Grand Jury . . . to prevent him from testifying against" the defendant. Id. at 656-657.

iv. **Content of Declarant's Statement.**   In the classic forfeiture by wrongdoing case, the unavailable declarant's statements pertain to past events or offenses (such as racketeering or drug sales) that the declarant could have testified about at the time the declarant was silenced by the defendant's wrongdoing. The statements are then admitted against the defendant to prove these past offenses. Increasingly, however, the government prosecutes the defendant for the act of wrongdoing — typically murder — that has made the declarant unavailable. The content of some of the declarant's hearsay statements may concern the murder itself, not the defendant's past offenses as to which the declarant would have been a witness or potential witness.

Defendants have argued that this is an improper extension of the forfeiture-by-wrongdoing principle since the declarant's status as "witness" is not related to the content of the out-of-court statements. But courts have unanimously declined to impose any limit on the application of Rule 804(b)(6), holding that its broad terminology includes within its reach the admission of statements by the declarant when the murder of the declarant is the crime charged. Dhinsa, 243 F.3d at 652. Of course, the rule still requires that the intent of the defendant be *at least in part* to prevent the declarant from testifying in some other proceeding; thus, the requirement that there be some other ongoing criminal investigation or legal dispute in which the declarant might participate must still be satisfied. United States v. Lentz, 2005 WL 2124104 *8 (E.D.Va.) (husband and wife involved in bitter custody dispute; husband charged with wife's murder motivated "at least in part" to procure her unavailability as a witness).

b. *Justification for the Admissibility of Forfeiture by Wrongdoing Statements*

The justification for the admissibility of forfeiture by wrongdoing statements is straightforward: "the law [will not] allow a person to take advantage of his own wrong." Mastrangelo, 693 F.2d at 272. An oft-quoted explication of this policy was stated in United States v. White, 116 F.3d 903, 911 (D.C. Cir. 1997):

> . . . It is hard to imagine a form of misconduct more extreme than the murder of a potential witness. Simple equity supports a forfeiture principle, as does a common sense attention to the need for fit incentives. The defendant who has removed an adverse witness is in a weak position to complain about losing the chance to cross-examine him. And where a defendant has silenced a witness through the use of threats, violence or murder, admission of the victim's prior statements at least partially offsets the perpetrator's rewards for his misconduct.

There is no reliability inquiry authorized by FRE 804(b)(6). The trial court need not look for indicia of trustworthiness under either the hearsay rule or the confrontation clause. Once the defendant has waived these rights, the court "is not required to assess independently the reliability of those statements." United States v. Dhinsa, 243 F.3d at 655.

c.   Acquiescence in Wrongdoing.

One of the principal concerns voiced to the Advisory Committee as it was considering the adoption of FRE 804(b)(6) was the breadth of the term *acquiescence in wrongdoing*. The Tenth Circuit in United States v. Cherry, supra, interpreted the new rule to permit its application to co-conspirators who did not plan or in any way participate in wrongdoing that caused the unavailability of the declarant:

> [T]he use of the words "engaged or acquiesced in wrongdoing" lends support to the government's assertion that, at least for purposes of the hearsay rules, waiver can be imputed under an agency theory of responsibility to a defendant who "acquiesced" in the wrongful procurement of a witness's unavailability but did not actually "engage" in wrongdoing apart from the conspiracy itself. [217 F.3d at 816.]

Cherry involved five defendants charged with a drug conspiracy. Much of the evidence against them came from Mr. Lurks, a cooperating witness who was murdered by one of the five prior to trial. The district court rejected the use of FRE 804(b)(6) against three of the defendants, finding that there was "absolutely no evidence" that the three "had actual knowledge of, agreed to or participated in the murder of . . . Lurks." Id. at 820. The government took an interlocutory appeal, since exclusion of Lurks's statements against the three would destroy its case.

The majority applied the principles of conspiratorial liability enunciated in Pinkerton v. United States, 328 U.S. 640 (1946) to define "acquiescence:"

> . . . A defendant may be deemed to have waived his or her Confrontation Clause rights (and, a fortiori, hearsay objections) if a preponderance of the evidence establishes . . . [that] the wrongful procurement [of the defendant's unavailability] was in furtherance, within the scope, and reasonably foreseeable as a necessary or natural consequence of an ongoing conspiracy. . . . Actual knowledge is not required for conspiratorial waiver by misconduct if the[se] elements . . . are satisfied. . . . We note that the scope of the conspiracy is not necessarily limited to a primary goal — such as bank robbery — but can also include secondary goals relevant to the evasion of apprehension and prosecution for that goal — such as escape, or, by analogy, obstruction of justice. . . . We further reiterate that . . . a defendant is not responsible for the acts of co-conspirators if that defendant meets the burden of proving he or she took affirmative steps to withdraw from the conspiracy before those acts were committed. [217 F.3d at 820.]

d.   Application of FRE 403

Admission of the unavailable declarant's statements is not automatic, however, as the court must still perform the balancing test under FRE 403. Prior to the adoption of FRE 804(b)(6), this inquiry included evaluation of the reliability of the declarant's statement to avoid the admission of "facially unreliable hearsay." Dhinsa, 243 F.3d at 655. Now that the specific exception is in place, however, it would be highly unusual for the court to exclude a statement that falls within the categorical exception on the basis "low probative value" based on the court's doubts about its reliability. However, since FRE 804(b)(6) is a categorical exception that requires absolutely no indicia of reliability, perhaps Rule 403's balancing test should take reliability into account. There also remains the danger of ambiguity, confusion, and undue prejudice from the inflammatory nature of the evidence or its context for the court to consider.

e.   Is a FRE 104(c) Hearing Required?

Several courts have ruled specifically that the district court must hold an evidentiary hearing, outside the presence of the jury, in which the government has the burden of proving by a preponderance of the evidence that the defendant did procure the unavailability of the declarant by wrongdoing, and did intend to do so to prevent the declarant from being an actual or potential witness. Dhinsa, 243 F.3d at 653. The Eighth Circuit, however, has held that the trial court can admit the hearsay evidence at trial, in the presence of the jury, "contingent upon proof of the underlying murder by a preponderance of the evidence." United States v. Emery, 186 F.3d 921, 926 (8th Cir. 1999). The court in *Emery* analogized this process to that used to admit the statements of co-conspirators pursuant to FRE 801(d)(2)(E), and noted that "the repetition necessarily inherent with a preliminary hearing would amount to a significant waste of judicial resources." Id. Consider, however, whether the jury could adhere to the admonition of the judge to ignore a contingently admitted hearsay statement of a murder victim, in a case that the judge still thinks sufficiently strong that a reasonable jury *could* find the defendant guilty of the charged act of murder beyond a reasonable doubt.

KEY POINTS

1. If a party has procured the unavailability of a hearsay declarant by wrongdoing, and intended to do so to prevent the declarant from being an actual or potential witness, then the declarant's statements are admissible against that party.

2. The party's conduct may have involved planning of, participation in, or acquiescence in the wrongdoing.

PROBLEM

8.85. Raymond Ochoa is charged with conspiracy to commit mail fraud for filing a false insurance claim on his automobile, which he falsely reported as stolen. The prosecution learned that Ochoa's former tenant, Dave McLaughlin, had put Ochoa in touch with a "chop shop" which would help him dispose of his allegedly stolen car. McLaughlin was approached by an FBI agent who told McLaughlin that he would benefit from talking to the FBI. McLaughlin made statements to the agent describing his role in the conspiracy and implicating Ochoa in the plan to dispose of the car and make the false claim. On the very next day, the FBI attempted to serve McLaughlin with a subpoena; McLaughlin's current landlord said he had left town "for Maryland" with all his belongings.

The FBI agent also visited McLaughlin's employer looking for him. He learned that McLaughlin had stopped coming to work but was owed his last paycheck. On the day after the FBI's visit, McLaughlin actually called the employer to ask for his paycheck. When he hung up, the employer used caller ID and determined that the call was made from Ochoa's home phone number. Phone records later revealed that seven phone calls were made from Ochoa's phone number to McLaughlin's employer during the next two days. McLaughlin then apparently disappeared and was never found, despite good faith efforts by the government. May the government use McLaughlin's hearsay statements against Ochoa pursuant to FRE 804(b)(6)? By what process should the foundational facts be determined?

8.86. Return to Problem 3.4, State v. Blair, at page 131. Police investigation reveals that several weeks before the attack on Norma, she filed a complaint against Jimmy for assault and battery. A police officer then interviewed both Jimmy and Norma; Norma told the officer she wanted to drop the charges. Since the attack, Norma is still unable to remember anything about what happened that night, and she says she is unwilling to testify against Jimmy. The prosecutor wants to know whether, if Norma is called to the stand as a witness, all of the entries in her diary that describe Jimmy's violent temper and his beating of her over the past three years can be admitted under FRE 804(b)(6). What issues in the application of this exception are raised in this case? What would have to happen at trial for the diary to be admitted?

F. THE RESIDUAL EXCEPTION

The Federal Rules of Evidence as originally promulgated by the Supreme Court provided a broad residual exception in both FRE 803 and FRE 804 for a "statement not specifically covered by any of the foregoing exceptions but having comparable circumstantial guarantees of trustworthiness." Effective December 1, 1997, the Rules were amended to eliminate the two subsections and to add a single, identical residual hearsay exception as FRE 807. In case law prior to 1997, remember that the residuals are FRE 803(24) and 804(b)(5).

1. FRE 807

RULE 807.   RESIDUAL EXCEPTION"

A statement not specifically covered by Rule 803 or 804 but having equivalent circumstantial guarantees of trustworthiness, is not excluded by the hearsay rule, if the court determines that (A) the statement is offered as evidence of a material fact; (B) the statement is more probative on the point for which it is offered than any other evidence that the proponent can procure through reasonable efforts; and (C) the general purposes of these rules and the interests of justice will best be served by admission of the statement into evidence. But a statement may not be admitted under this exception unless its proponent makes known to the adverse party sufficiently in advance of the trial or hearing to provide the adverse party with a fair opportunity to prepare to meet it, the proponent's intention to offer the statement and the particulars of it, including the name and address of the declarant.

2. Interpretation and Illustration of FRE 807

The foundational requirements for FRE 807 are:

- the statement must have circumstantial guarantees of trustworthiness;
- these guarantees should be "equivalent" to the exceptions in Rules 803 and 804;
- the statement is offered to prove a material fact;
- the statement is more probative on the point for which it is offered than any other evidence that can be secured through reasonable efforts;
- admission will serve the general purposes of the rules and the interests of justice; and
- notice is given to the opponent.

a. Preliminary Factfinding

The first thing to notice about FRE 807 is that it is not a categorical exception. There are no categorical requirements concerning the identity of the declarant, the content of the statement, or the circumstances in which the statement was made. There is no categorical requirement that the declarant be unavailable. Instead, the principal requirements for admission are that the statement has "circumstantial guarantees of trustworthiness" and that it is "more probative" than other reasonably available evidence — clearly individualized judgments to be made by the trial judge. These two requirements reflect the two primary justifications for admitting hearsay under the categorical system of hearsay exceptions: reliability and necessity.

The following example illustrates some of the major preliminary fact-finding issues in applying the residual exception:

> Ed Barns has sued Acme Used Cars for injuries that he sustained when he and a friend were examining a used car at the Acme lot. The car would not start, so Fred Anders, an Acme mechanic, offered his assistance. Barns was pouring gasoline from a small can into the carburetor while his companion attempted to start the engine. The engine backfired and ignited the can, and Barns suffered severe burn injuries. At trial, Barns claimed that he was acting pursuant to Fred Anders's instructions to pour the gasoline directly into the carburetor. Acme claimed that, to the contrary, Anders warned Barns to stop what he was doing.
>
> Anders died before the trial. Acme offers into evidence Exhibit B, an authenticated handwritten statement signed by Anders that describes the incident and states that he warned Barns not to pour the gasoline. Acme offers the foundational testimony of Anders's supervisor, Georgia Breen:
>
>> I learned of the accident within several hours of its occurrence. I immediately instructed Fred Anders to go into a room, not to talk to anyone else, and to write down everything that happened. Anders obeyed my instruction and came back with a handwritten statement within 30 minutes. I recognized his handwriting and he signed the document in my presence. I recognize Exhibit B as that document.

You can see that Exhibit B does not fall within any of the categorical exceptions under FRE 803 and FRE 804. Should it be admitted into evidence under FRE 807?

b.   Circumstantial Guarantees of Trustworthiness

Looking at Exhibit B, what foundation facts would you use to argue that Anders's statement bears "circumstantial guarantees of trustworthiness"? Case law has established two principal means of establishing trustworthiness.

i.   Reliability of Testimonial Qualities.   The most common means of satisfying the trustworthiness requirement is to show that one or more of Anders's testimonial qualities appears to be reliable because of the circumstances within which it was made.

> [A]ll of the traditional hearsay exceptions minimize one or more of the four hearsay risks: (1) insincerity; (2) faulty perception; (3) faulty memory; and (4) faulty narration . . . the Court must determine the relative degree to which the [proffered item] is prone to the hearsay risks, and if any of the risks are minimized by circumstantial guarantees of trustworthiness. [United States v. Southern Indiana Gas and Electric Co., 258 F.Supp. 2d 884, 890 (S.D.Ind. 2003).]

Facts relating to the identity, knowledge, qualifications, and motivation of the declarant; the content of the statement; and the circumstances in which it was made are all considered for their effect on testimonial qualities.

For example, in United States v. Tome, 61 F.3d 1446, 1453 (10th Cir.1995), the Tenth Circuit considered the admissibility under the residual exception of statements made by defendant's daughter concerning acts of alleged sexual abuse. Statements made to a social worker were considered to be trustworthy because the social worker was trained in interviewing children and used open-ended, non-leading questions (context promotes sincerity), and the declarant used childish language while describing the abuse with specificity and detail (content indicates sincerity and memory). Other circumstances, however, cast doubt on the statement's trustworthiness: The statement was not spontaneous because the declarant knew that she was taken to the social worker in order to say what the defendant had done to her (context provides opportunity for insincerity); it was made a year after the events described (context affects memory); and it was made when the declarant arguably had a motive to lie because she wanted to live with her mother, not her father (identity of declarant provides motive to lie). The court held that the statement did not qualify for the residual exception because of these equivocal circumstances.

Motive and incentive to lie commonly figure in evaluations of trustworthiness: United States v. Walker, 410 F.3d 754 (5th Cir. 2005) (facing the threat of criminal charges); United States v. Wright, 363 F.3d 237 (3d Cir. 2004) (self-serving statements made when declarant knew he was under investigation). Other courts mention factors relating to perception and memory: New Colt Holding Corp. v. RJG Holdings of Fla., Inc, 312 F.Supp.2d 195, 223 (D.Conn.2004) ("A methodologically sound survey can reduce . . . the danger of insincerity and faulty narration [and] . . . a particular memory survey which . . . relates to events that were learned by direct perception and are unlikely to be forgotten, can . . . minimize all five of the classes of risk ordinarily associated with survey evidence."); In re Columbia Securities Litigation, 155 F.R.D. 466, 475 (S.D.N.Y. 1994) ("Unless their author is available for cross-examination, newspaper stories generally will present a blank face that gives little clue as to the reliability of the reporter's perception, memory, narration, or sincerity, and in addition facts to disclose how the article was changed in the editing process").

In the hypothetical case against Acme Used Cars, what circumstances bear on the reliability of Anders's testimonial qualities? You should by now be able make arguments both for and against trustworthiness.

ii. Independent Corroboration. The second means of establishing trustworthiness is to show by way of independent corroborating evidence that the facts asserted in the particular hearsay statement are probably accurate. Larez v. City of Los Angeles, 946 F.2d 630, 643 & 643 n.6 (9th Cir. 1991) (news account of a specific quotation from the defendant met "circumstantial guarantees of trustworthiness" requirement when three independent newspapers attributed similar quotations to defendant). Testimony given before a grand jury was frequently admitted under the residual exception when its contents were corroborated. Under the Supreme Court opinion in Crawford v. Washington, however, grand jury testimony qualifies as a "testimonial" statement. Because the criminal defendant is not present during the grand jury proceeding and cannot cross-examine the witnesses there, the prosecution is prohibited from using grand jury testimony under the Confrontation Clause in criminal cases, unless the declarant also testifies. It is possible, however, that this testimony might still be admitted under the residual exception in a civil case.

How much corroborating evidence is necessary to make a hearsay statement more reliable? As an example, in United States v. Donlon, 909 F.2d 650, 654 (1st Cir. 1990), grand jury testimony concerning defendant's illegal possession of a gun at his home was corroborated by evidence that defendant did live at the pertinent address and that defendant had said he had other guns there. The court described this corroboration as "significant, but far from overwhelming. Of course, were corroborating evidence, by itself, completely convincing, there would rarely be any need to introduce the evidence that it corroborates." Is there any such corroboration of Anders's statement offered by Acme?

c. Equivalency

FRE 807 also requires that the guarantees of trustworthiness be "equivalent," presumably to the guarantees in FRE 803 and FRE 804. Since the apparent trustworthiness of the hearsay admitted under all 28 categorical exceptions varies widely in both kind and degree, it is impossible to identify a single standard, and a rigorous showing of "equivalence" is not required. But courts sometimes do analogize the hearsay sought to be admitted to the indicia of trustworthiness of some categorically admitted hearsay, such as spontaneity, against interest, or careful routine. United States v. Perez, 217 F.3d 323, 329 (5th Cir. 2000) (statements by illegal immigrants "bore . . . indicia of reliability equivalent to declarations against interest" because made to agency responsible for their deportation and possible prosecution; however, inadmissible because made not under oath and in an informal interview); Conoco, Inc. v. Department of Energy, 99 F.3d 387, 392 (Fed. Cir. 1997) (purchase summaries do not have same indicia of reliability as commercial publications).

d. Near Miss

A "near miss" occurs when a hearsay statement almost, but not quite, fits within one of the categorical hearsay exceptions and would thus be inadmissible but for the residual exception. Many courts have held that a near miss does not necessarily prevent admission under the residual exception, and that closeness to an established exception may be viewed as enhancing trustworthiness. But others have expressed concern that admitting near miss statements will undermine the categorical approach of the Federal Rules and violate the intent of the drafters that the residual exception be used sparingly. The majority of Circuits now agree that the language of FRE 807 — "not specifically covered by Rule 803 and Rule 804" — means that statements found to be inadmissible under the Rule 803 and 804 categories may still be considered under Rule 807.

e.   Offered to Prove a Material Fact

Subsection (A) requires that the proponent must show that the statement is offered as evidence of a "material" fact. Typically this term means nothing more than that the statement is relevant, but it might be argued that this requirement implements the policy of necessity in that it protects against overuse of the residual exception to prove minor points or points on which the content of the statement has low probative value. Cook v. Miss. Dep't Human Servs., 108 Fed. Appx. 852, 856 (5th Cir. 2004) (statement of belief that person was hired because of his race "not so material that it must have been admitted in the interests of justice" because it could not by itself raise a genuine issue of discrimination).

f.   More Probative on the Point Than Other Reasonably Available Evidence

Subsection (B) requires a showing that the proponent has been reasonably diligent in attempting to secure evidence — witnesses or other kinds of hearsay — that would substitute for hearsay admitted under the residual exception. Courts have required parties to produce an available hearsay declarant as a witness, In re Cypress Semiconductor Securities Litigation, 891 F. Supp. 1369, 1374 (N.D. Cal. 1995) ("the best evidence of [quotations in a news article] is not the article, but the testimony from the reporter who wrote the article"); to present the declarant through affidavits or depositions, Andrekus v. Bd. of Educ., 2004 U.S. Dist. LEXIS 19388 *28 (N.D.Ill.) (affidavits and depositions rather than hearsay note are "better evidence" for summary judgment proceedings); and to produce original records underlying secondary evidence such as summaries, Conoco Inc. v. Department of Energy, 99 F.3d 387, 393 (Fed. Cir. 1997) (original underlying records of purchases of crude oil were more probative than summaries and DOE made no showing that reasonable efforts would not produce them).

If the declarant is deceased and once had knowledge about a central fact that would be otherwise unavailable, courts weigh this need heavily in making the Rule 807 decision. Bohler-Udderholm Am., Inc., v. Ellwood Group, Inc., 247 F.3d 79 (3d Cir. 2001) (affidavit of deceased representative of plaintiff at a crucial board of directors' meeting was the only available source to contradict defendant's version of what was said at the meeting). If diligence in seeking alternative proof can be demonstrated, and nothing better is available, then the proponent has a legitimate case of need to use the residual.

g. Serve the General Purposes of the Rules and Interests of Justice

Because of the generality in which these lofty ideals are expressed in subsection (C), they are not likely to be of much assistance to the trial judge in deciding whether to admit individual items of hearsay. In re Drake, 786 F. Supp. 229, 233 (E.D.N.Y. 1992) (the third factor "is so abstruse in formulation as to constitute little guidance for the court").

h. Notice

The proponent is required to inform the opponent of the intent to use the residual exception, and of the particulars of the statement and location of the declarant. This enables the opponent to prepare in order to argue more effectively against admission. And it serves as a limit both on the last-minute creativity of lawyers and on the susceptibility of judges to accede to lawyers' last-minute protestations of need. The requirement that notice be given before trial is, however, far from absolute. Some courts have interpreted the requirement liberally, upholding admission if the hearsay statement was disclosed within sufficient time — even on the first day of trial — to permit the opponent to prepare to contest the use of the statement. A continuance may be granted to permit the opponent to meet the evidence. In United States v. Panzardi-Lespier, 918 F.2d 313, 316-318 (1st Cir. 1990), the court discussed the conflicting case law on the strict versus the flexible approach to pretrial notice. It held that even in a criminal case, notice on the first day of trial was sufficient where seven days elapsed before the statement was actually offered into evidence. There was no surprise to its content, and opposing party had ample time to review it and prepare its defense. And if the proponent could not have reasonably anticipated the need for the residual exception, the notice requirement may be excused altogether by the judge. There are limits, however, even to this flexible approach. In United States v. Coney, 51 F.3d 164 (8th Cir. 1995), it was held to be not an abuse of the trial court's discretion to refuse admission to a report offered by the defendant under the residual exception 45 minutes before she wanted to introduce it. If the opponent knows of the existence of the hearsay statement before trial, and of the proponent's intent to use it, courts have applied the notice requirement flexibly where there is no prejudice. Dal-Tile Corp. v. United States, 2004 Ct.Intl.Trade LEXIS 24, 107-109 (Ct. Int'l Trade). If notice of reliance on the residual exception was not given to admit a hearsay statement at trial, admissibility under Rule 807 cannot be argued for the first time on appeal. Rowland v. Am.Gen.Finan., Inc., 340 F.3d 187, 195 (4th Cir. 2003).

3. Elaboration of FRE 807: How Much Hearsay Is Admitted Under the Residual Exception?

The trial judge's decision whether to admit Anders's statement under FRE 807 might be influenced by the general policy underlying the residual exception. Is the residual exception — which is, after all, a radical departure from the strict categorical approach of the common law — to be used frequently or rarely? liberally or sparingly? According to the Senate Judiciary Committee:

It is intended that the residual hearsay exceptions will be used very rarely, and only in exceptional circumstances. The committee does not intend to establish a broad license for trial judges to admit hearsay statements that do not fall within one of the other exceptions contained in rules 803 and 804(b). The residual exceptions are not meant to authorize major judicial revisions of the hearsay rule, including its present exceptions. Such major revisions are best accomplished by legislative action.

There is language in appellate opinions in most of the Circuits that acknowledges the "rare and exceptional" standard in the Note. But there is concern that the residuals are not used sparingly. In a study of reported decisions from 1975 through 1991, the following kinds of statements were most frequently admitted under the residual exceptions (also called "catchall" exceptions):

> Prosecutors attempted to introduce grand jury testimony in thirty-seven cases pursuant to the 804(b)(5) catchall exception. In twenty-nine of these cases, the court admitted the hearsay. Another hidden catchall category encompasses written and oral statements made to law enforcement officials which are prior consistent or inconsistent statements [of a testifying witness] not fitting the Rule 801 criteria. A growing number of cases appear to include statements to law enforcement officials by declarants not present at trial. Such declarants have ranged from accomplices to spouses, victims, and truly disinterested individuals. [Myrna S. Raeder, Commentary: A Response to Professor Swift, 76 Minn. L. Rev. 507, 514-516 (1992).]

Professor Raeder concluded that "the catchall exceptions permit the total erosion of the hearsay rule by judicial discretion . . . appellate decisions are not offering an effective stopgap, in part, because they review the admission of such hearsay for abuse of discretion and harmless error." Id. at 517. Notice, however, that the application of the Confrontation Clause following Crawford v. Washington will change these results in criminal cases. Grand jury testimony has been held to be "testimonial," and statements made to law enforcement by accomplices, spouses, and victims may also be found to be "testimonial." These types of statements would be prohibited unless the declarant is unavailable and the defendant has had a prior opportunity to cross-examine. Crawford also permits the introduction of all prior statements of a testifying witness, because the witness-declarant would be subject to cross-examination at trial. See Section G, infra.

KEY POINTS

1. Under FRE 807, the judge has discretion to admit hearsay statements that appear to be reliable; that is, they have circumstantial guarantees of trustworthiness either because the circumstances indicate that the declarant has reliable testimonial qualities or because the contents of the statement are corroborated.

2. The statement must also be more probative than other available evidence, typically because the hearsay declarant is unavailable.

3. The proponent of the statement must also notify the opponent of the intent to invoke the residual exception, preferably before trial but not in cases of necessity.

PROBLEMS

8.87. Return to problem 8.45 at page 501. At 3:00 A.M. on January 26, Mrs. D'Onofrio was asked to complete and sign a complaint form by one of the police officers. She repeated, in writing, the statements she had made earlier concerning her husband's behavior on January 24, 25 and 26. She signed her name twice, acknowledging that the police officer was relying upon her allegations to establish probable cause to arrest Louis D'Onofrio for brandishing a weapon, and affirming that her statements were true. This form, as well as the hearsay statements in Problem 8.45, are the only proof that Louis D'Onofrio had a gun in his possession and threatened her with it. At trial, Mrs. D'Onofrio asserts her marital privilege, which prevents the government from calling her as a witness against her husband. Is the written statement admissible into evidence?

8.88. David Dixon has been charged with conspiracy to sell and with selling heroin. Two alleged co-conspirators, Brown and Green, were granted immunity and were prepared to testify against Dixon. Since Green had a long history of involvement with drugs and several drug-related convictions, the prosecution planned to make Brown the star witness. Brown, however, died of a heart attack several days before the trial. At Dixon's trial the prosecution authenticates and offers into evidence a letter from Brown to his mother, telling her that he is feeling sick, that he thinks he is about to die, and that he wants to confess to her. The letter then describes his drug dealings with Dixon. What arguments can be made for and against admission under FRE 807? How should the court rule?

8.89. Four victims of abduction and brutal torture during the reign of terror conducted by El Salvadoran Security Forces in 1979 are suing two El Salvadoran military commanders. The suit is filed in federal court in Florida, where the two defendants reside, and seeks compensatory and punitive damages pursuant to federal and state law. One element of plaintiffs' claim requires proof that the defendants had actual or constructive knowledge of ongoing criminal conduct by troops over which they had command.

To prove actual or constructive knowledge, plaintiffs seek to introduce a properly authenticated English language translation of a tape-recorded diary kept by the Archbishop of El Salvador, Oscar Adulfo Romero. Romero kept this diary from March 1978 until his assassination in 1980 while conducting a Mass. He created the diary by making notes throughout each day of events connected with his ministry, including meetings and conversations with various individuals. Later that same day he would dictate a narrative version of these notes into a portable tape recorder. These tapes (but not the notes) were preserved, copied, transcribed and translated, as can be proved by authenticating witnesses. Their contents were not made public until 1990. An early entry in the diary states that "I want this diary to be record of the chancery team and of the life of the archdiocese." Entries in the diary state that meetings were held between the archbishop and both of the defendants in 1978 and 1979. The diary states that human rights abuses, the acts of violence committed by the security forces, the need for remedial action, and even the archbishop's public denunciation of one of the defendants were discussed. Both defendants deny ever meeting with the archbishop. There is also evidence that the archbishop made statements critical of the defendants and the security forces during his "homilies" that were broadcast throughout the country. The defendants deny hearing the homilies.

Is the Romero diary admissible under FRE 807? What other hearsay exceptions might apply?

G.   HEARSAY AND THE CONFRONTATION CLAUSE

The confrontation clause in the Sixth Amendment to the United States Constitution states: "In all criminal prosecutions, the accused shall enjoy the right...to be confronted with the Witnesses against him." The meaning of this terse phrase is far from clear: There is virtually no legislative history shedding light on the Framers' intent, and the words themselves are subject to a number of possible interpretations. When the prosecution presents a *witness* at trial, the Supreme Court's most frequently cited analysis is that the clause requires

> a personal examination and cross-examination of the witness in which the accused has the opportunity, not only of testing the recollection and sifting the conscience of the witness, but of compelling him to stand face to face with the jury in order that they may look at him, and judge by his demeanor upon the stand and the manner in which he gives his testimony whether he is worthy of belief. [Mattox v. United States, 156 U.S. 237, 242-243 (1895).]

As you know, most hearsay admitted through the exceptions and exemptions does not require the presence of the hearsay declarant as a witness in court. Thus the admission of hearsay presents an immediate threat to the criminal defendant's confrontation right. A literal reading of the clause, however, might hold that it operates *only* when the prosecutor calls witnesses. *All* hearsay could be admitted without regard to confrontation rights. Or, "witnesses" might be interpreted more broadly to include all individuals who provide evidence against the defendant. *All* hearsay would then be within the reach of the clause and *no* hearsay could be admitted without confrontation and cross-examination.

In Crawford v. Washington, 541 U.S. 124 (2004), the U.S. Supreme Court provided a new interpretation of criminal defendants' confrontation right. In keeping with its own past opinions, the Court held that the confrontation clause bars the use of some, but not of all, hearsay against criminal defendants. It provided a new set of standards by which to test when the confrontation right is violated, and left open some important questions in the administration of those standards. The *Crawford* opinion will concern us throughout this section because it purports to include within its scope the two recurring situations in which the prosecution introduces hearsay against a criminal defendant: hearsay admitted under an exemption or exception, and hearsay admitted as a prior statement of a testifying witness. We begin our discussion with a brief analysis of the Court's interpretation of the confrontation clause prior to *Crawford*. The approach developed in Ohio v. Roberts, 448 U.S. 56 (1980) may continue to have some applicability post-*Crawford*, and it is important background for understanding the Court's new stance.

1.   Ohio v. Roberts

In *Roberts*, the Supreme Court had seemed to establish a two-pronged test — unavailability and reliability — for satisfying the accused's confrontation right when hearsay is admitted but the declarant does not testify:

> The Confrontation Clause operates in two separate ways to restrict the range of admissible hearsay. First, in conformity with the Framers' preference for face-to-face accusation, the Sixth Amendment establishes a rule of necessity. In the usual case (including cases where prior cross-examination has occurred), the prosecution must either produce, or demonstrate the unavailability of, the declarant whose statement it wishes to use against the defendant.... The second aspect operates once a witness is shown to be unavailable. Reflecting its underlying purpose to augment accuracy in the factfinding process by ensuring the defendant an effective means to test adverse evidence, the Clause countenances only hearsay marked with such trustworthiness that "there is no material departure from the reason of the general rule." The Court has applied this "indicia of reliability" requirement principally by concluding that certain hearsay exceptions rest upon such solid foundations that admission of virtually any evidence within them comports with the "substances of the constitutional protection." [Mattox v. United States, 156 U.S. 237, 244 (1895).]... In sum, when a hearsay declarant is not present for cross-examination at trial, the Confrontation Clause normally requires a showing that he is unavailable. Even then, his statement is admissible only if it bears adequate "indicia of reliability." Reliability can be inferred without more in a case where the evidence falls within a firmly rooted hearsay exception. In other cases, the evidence must be excluded, at least absent a showing of particularized guarantees of trustworthiness. [448 U.S. at 65-66.]

Twelve years later, the Court virtually abandoned the unavailability requirement in *White v. Illinois*, 502 U.S. 346, 354 (1992), by limiting it to statements admitted as former testimony under FRE 804(b)(1).

Thus for most hearsay, the confrontation clause under *Roberts* imposed only an inquiry whether the hearsay statement fits within a "firmly rooted" exception and, if it does not, whether there are "particularized guarantees" of the statement's trustworthiness.

a. Firmly Rooted Hearsay Exceptions

Most of the exceptions under FRE 803 and 804 were found to be "firmly rooted." In *Roberts*, the Court stated that exceptions for business records, dying declarations, and public records are firmly rooted. Co-conspirator statements were found to be firmly rooted in Bourjaily v. United States 483 U.S. 171, 182 (1987) (with vigorous dissent); and statements falling within the traditional exceptions for present sense impression, excited utterances, statements of state of mind, and past recollection recorded survived challenge under the confrontation clause. This meant that legislatively drawn categorical hearsay exceptions stood in for judicial analysis of the right to confrontation in most cases.

b. Not Firmly Rooted Exceptions Require "Particularized Guarantees of Trustworthiness"

A Supreme Court plurality in Lilly v. Virginia, 527 U.S. 116 (1999) held that statements against penal interest, admitted under FRE 804(b)(3), are not firmly rooted. The Court had previously discussed the "particularized guarantees of trustworthiness" test in Idaho v. Wright, 497 U.S. 805 (1990), when it held that the residual exception (now FRE 807) was not firmly rooted. In *Wright*, the Court characterized "particularized guarantees of trustworthiness" as the inherent trustworthiness of the declarant's statement, to be found in the circumstances that "surround the making of the statement." Id. at 821. The Court specifically prohibited the consideration of corroboration, that is, independent evidence that corroborates the contents of the statement itself. Courts had come to rely on corroboration to satisfy the residual exception's requirement of "circumstantial guarantees of trustworthiness," particularly in admitting statements of grand jury witnesses, which often bore few indicia of inherent trustworthiness. Under *Wright*, the use of corroboration was prohibited to satisfy the "particularized" trustworthiness standard for all not firmly rooted hearsay.

2. Crawford v. Washington

In Lilly v. Virginia, Justices Scalia and Thomas each wrote separately to state their views that the proper scope of the confrontation right was more limited than the Court's opinions in *Roberts*, *Wright* and *Lilly* had held. That right, they asserted, "is implicated by extra judicial statements only insofar as they are contained in formalized testimonial material, such as affidavits, depositions, prior testimony or confessions." 527 U.S. at 365. Justice Breyer wrote in his separate concurrence that *Roberts'* linkage of the confrontation right so closely to the "firmly rooted" provisions of the hearsay rule was both too broad and too narrow a standard, and that this linkage was an open question to be considered at another time. In *Crawford*, five years after *Lilly*, that time had come.

CRAWFORD v. WASHINGTON
541 U.S. 36 (2004)

Justice SCALIA delivered the opinion of the Court, in which Stevens, Kennedy, Souter, Thomas, Ginsburg, and Breyer, JJ., joined. Rehnquist, C. J., filed an opinion concurring in the judgment, in which O'Connor, J., joined.

Petitioner Michael Crawford stabbed a man who allegedly tried to rape his wife, Sylvia. At his trial, the State played for the jury Sylvia's tape-recorded statement to the police describing the stabbing, even though he had no opportunity for cross-examination. The Washington Supreme Court upheld petitioner's conviction after determining that Sylvia's statement was reliable. The question presented is whether this procedure complied with the Sixth Amendment's guarantee that, "[i]n all criminal prosecutions, the accused shall enjoy the right...to be confronted with the witnesses against him."

I

On August 5, 1999, Kenneth Lee was stabbed at his apartment. Police arrested petitioner later that night. After giving petitioner and his wife *Miranda* warnings, detectives interrogated each of them twice.[8] Petitioner eventually confessed that he

---

8. Petitioner Michael Crawford's and his wife Sylvia's interrogations were tape recorded by the Olympia Police Department. — EDS.

and Sylvia had gone in search of Lee because he was upset over an earlier incident in which Lee had tried to rape her. The two had found Lee at his apartment, and a fight ensued in which Lee was stabbed in the torso and petitioner's hand was cut.

Petitioner gave the following account of the fight:

"Q. Okay. Did you ever see anything in [Lee's] hands?
"A. I think so, but I'm not positive.
"Q. Okay, when you think so, what do you mean by that?
"A. I coulda swore I seen him goin' for somethin' before, right before everything happened. He was like reachin', fiddlin' around down here and stuff... and I just... I don't know, I think, this is just a possibility, but I think, I think that he pulled somethin' out and I grabbed for it and that's how I got cut... but I'm not positive. I, I, my mind goes blank when things like this happen. I mean, I just, I remember things wrong, I remember things that just doesn't, don't make sense to me later." (punctuation added).

Sylvia generally corroborated petitioner's story about the events leading up to the fight, but her account of the fight itself was arguably different — particularly with respect to whether Lee had drawn a weapon before petitioner assaulted him:

"Q. Did Kenny do anything to fight back from this assault?
"A. (pausing) I know he reached into his pocket... or somethin'... I don't know what.
"Q. After he was stabbed?
"A. He saw Michael coming up. He lifted his hand... his chest open, he might [have] went to go strike his hand out or something and then (inaudible).
"Q. Okay, you, you gotta speak up.
"A. Okay, he lifted his hand over his head maybe to strike Michael's hand down or something and then he put his hands in his... put his right hand in his right pocket... took a step back... Michael proceeded to stab him... then his hands were like... how do you explain this... open arms... with his hands open and he fell down... and we ran (describing subject holding hands open, palms toward assailant).
"Q. Okay, when he's standing there with his open hands, you're talking about Kenny, correct?
"A. Yeah, after, after the fact, yes.
"Q. Did you see anything in his hands at that point?
"A. (pausing) um um (no)." (punctuation added).

The State charged petitioner with assault and attempted murder. At trial, he claimed self-defense. Sylvia did not testify because of the state marital privilege, which generally bars a spouse from testifying without the other spouse's consent. In Washington, this privilege does not extend to a spouse's out-of-court statements admissible under a hearsay exception, so the State sought to introduce Sylvia's tape-recorded statements to the police as evidence that the stabbing was not in self-defense. Noting that Sylvia had admitted she led petitioner to Lee's apartment and thus had facilitated the assault, the State invoked the hearsay exception for statements against penal interest, Wash. Rule Evid. 804(b)(3) (2003).

Petitioner countered that, state law notwithstanding, admitting the evidence would violate his federal constitutional right to be "confronted with the witnesses against him." *Amdt. 6.* According to our description of that right in *Ohio v. Roberts*, 448 U.S. 56 (1980), it does not bar admission of an unavailable witness's statement against a criminal defendant if the statement bears "adequate 'indicia of reliability.'" To meet that test, evidence must either fall within a "firmly rooted hearsay exception" or bear "particularized guarantees of trustworthiness." The trial court here admitted the statement on the latter ground, offering several reasons why it was trustworthy: Sylvia was not shifting blame but rather corroborating her husband's story that he acted in self-defense or "justified reprisal;" she had direct knowledge as an eyewitness; she was describing recent events; and she was being questioned by a "neutral" law enforcement officer. The prosecution played the tape for the jury and relied on it in closing, arguing that it was "damning evidence" that "completely refutes [petitioner's] claim of self-defense." The jury convicted petitioner of assault.

The Washington Court of Appeals reversed. It applied a nine-factor test to determine whether Sylvia's statement bore particularized guarantees of trustworthiness, and noted several reasons why it did not: The statement contradicted one she had previously given; it was made in response to specific questions; and at one point she admitted she had shut her eyes during the stabbing. The court considered and rejected the State's argument that Sylvia's statement was reliable because it coincided with petitioner's to such a degree that the two "interlocked." The court determined that, although the two statements agreed about the events leading up to the stabbing, they differed on the issue crucial to petitioner's self-defense claim: "[Petitioner's] version asserts that Lee may have had something in his hand when he stabbed him; but Sylvia's version has Lee grabbing for something only after he has been stabbed."

The Washington Supreme Court reinstated the conviction, unanimously concluding that, although Sylvia's statement did not fall under a firmly rooted hearsay exception, it bore guarantees of trustworthiness: "'[W]hen a codefendant's confession is virtually identical [to, *i.e.*, interlocks with,] that of a defendant, it may be deemed reliable.'" The court explained:

"Although the Court of Appeals concluded that the statements were contradictory, upon closer inspection they appear to overlap. . . .

"[B]oth of the Crawfords' statements indicate that Lee was possibly grabbing for a weapon, but they are equally unsure when this event may have taken place. They are also equally unsure how Michael received the cut on his hand, leading the court to question when, if ever, Lee possessed a weapon. In this respect they overlap.

"[N]either Michael nor Sylvia clearly stated that Lee had a weapon in hand from which Michael was simply defending himself. And it is this omission by both that interlocks the statements and makes Sylvia's statement reliable."[9]

We granted certiorari to determine whether the State's use of Sylvia's statement violated the Confrontation Clause.

---

9.   The court rejected the State's argument that guarantees of trustworthiness were unnecessary since petitioner waived his confrontation rights by invoking the marital privilege. It reasoned that "forcing the defendant to choose between the marital privilege and confronting his spouse presents an untenable Hobson's choice." The State has not challenged this holding here. The State also has not challenged the Court of Appeals' conclusion (not reached by the State Supreme Court) that the confrontation violation, if it occurred, was not harmless. We express no opinion on these matters.

II

The Sixth Amendment's Confrontation Clause provides that, "[i]n all criminal prosecutions, the accused shall enjoy the right . . . to be confronted with the witnesses against him." We have held that this bedrock procedural guarantee applies to both federal and state prosecutions. *Pointer v. Texas, 380 U.S. 400 (1965)*. As noted above, *Roberts* says that an unavailable witness's out-of-court statement may be admitted so long as it has adequate indicia of reliability — *i.e.*, falls within a "firmly rooted hearsay exception" or bears "particularized guarantees of trustworthiness." Petitioner argues that this test strays from the original meaning of the Confrontation Clause and urges us to reconsider it.

A

The Constitution's text does not alone resolve this case. One could plausibly read "witnesses against" a defendant to mean those who actually testify at trial, those whose statements are offered at trial, see 3 J. Wigmore, Evidence §1397, p 104 (2d ed. 1923) (hereinafter Wigmore), or something in-between. We must therefore turn to the historical background of the Clause to understand its meaning.

The right to confront one's accusers is a concept that dates back to Roman times. The founding generation's immediate source of the concept, however, was the common law. English common law has long differed from continental civil law in regard to the manner in which witnesses give testimony in criminal trials. The common-law tradition is one of live testimony in court subject to adversarial testing, while the civil law condones examination in private by judicial officers. See 3 W. Blackstone, Commentaries on the Laws of England 373-374 (1768).

Nonetheless, England at times adopted elements of the civil-law practice. Justices of the peace or other officials examined suspects and witnesses before trial. These examinations were sometimes read in court in lieu of live testimony, a practice that "occasioned frequent demands by the prisoner to have his 'accusers,' *i.e.* the witnesses against him, brought before him face to face." 1 J. Stephen, History of the Criminal Law of England 326 (1883). In some cases, these demands were refused. See 9 W. Holdsworth, History of English Law 216-217, 228 (3d ed. 1944); *e.g., Raleigh's Case, 2 How. St. Tr. 1, 15-16, 24 (1603)*.

Pretrial examinations became routine under two statutes passed during the reign of Queen Mary in the 16th century. These Marian bail and committal statutes required justices of the peace to examine suspects and witnesses in felony cases and to certify the results to the court. It is doubtful that the original purpose of the examinations was to produce evidence admissible at trial. Whatever the original purpose, however, they came to be used as evidence in some cases, see M. Hale, Pleas of the Crown 284 (1736), resulting in an adoption of continental procedure.

The most notorious instances of civil-law examination occurred in the great political trials of the 16th and 17th centuries. One such was the 1603 trial of Sir Walter Raleigh for treason. Lord Cobham, Raleigh's alleged accomplice, had implicated him in an examination before the Privy Council and in a letter. At Raleigh's trial, these were read to the jury. Raleigh argued that Cobham had lied to save himself: "Cobham is absolutely in the King's mercy; to excuse me cannot avail him; by accusing me he may hope for favour." 1 D. Jardine, Criminal Trials 435 (1832). Suspecting that Cobham would recant, Raleigh demanded that the judges call him to appear, arguing that "[t]he

Proof of the Common Law is by witness and jury: let Cobham be here, let him speak it. Call my accuser before my face...." The judges refused, and, despite Raleigh's protestations that he was being tried "by the Spanish Inquisition," the jury convicted, and Raleigh was sentenced to death.

One of Raleigh's trial judges later lamented that "the justice of England has never been so degraded and injured as by the condemnation of Sir Walter Raleigh." Through a series of statutory and judicial reforms, English law developed a right of confrontation that limited these abuses. For example, treason statutes required witnesses to confront the accused "face to face" at his arraignment. Courts, meanwhile, developed relatively strict rules of unavailability, admitting examinations only if the witness was demonstrably unable to testify in person. Several authorities also stated that a suspect's confession could be admitted only against himself, and not against others he implicated.

One recurring question was whether the admissibility of an unavailable witness's pretrial examination depended on whether the defendant had had an opportunity to cross-examine him. In 1696, the Court of King's Bench answered this question in the affirmative, in the widely reported misdemeanor libel case of *King v. Paine*. The court ruled that, even though a witness was dead, his examination was not admissible where "the defendant not being present when [it was] taken before the mayor ... had lost the benefit of a cross-examination."

Paine had settled the rule requiring a prior opportunity for cross-examination as a matter of common law, but some doubts remained over whether the Marian statutes prescribed an exception to it in felony cases. The statutes did not identify the circumstances under which examinations were admissible, and some inferred that no prior opportunity for cross-examination was required....

B

Controversial examination practices were also used in the Colonies. Early in the 18th century, for example, the Virginia Council protested against the Governor for having "privately issued several commissions to examine witnesses against particular men *ex parte*," complaining that "the person accused is not admitted to be confronted with, or defend himself against his defamers." A decade before the Revolution, England gave jurisdiction over Stamp Act offenses to the admiralty courts, which followed civil-law rather than common-law procedures and thus routinely took testimony by deposition or private judicial examination. Colonial representatives protested that the Act subverted their rights "by extending the jurisdiction of the courts of admiralty beyond its ancient limits." Resolutions of the Stamp Act Congress §8th (Oct. 19, 1765). John Adams, defending a merchant in a high-profile admiralty case, argued: "Examinations of witnesses upon Interrogatories, are only by the Civil Law. Interrogatories are unknown at common Law, and Englishmen and common Lawyers have an aversion to them if not an Abhorrence of them." Draft of Argument in *Sewall v. Hancock* (1768-1769).

Many declarations of rights adopted around the time of the Revolution guaranteed a right of confrontation. The proposed Federal Constitution, however, did not. At the Massachusetts ratifying convention, Abraham Holmes objected to this omission precisely on the ground that it would lead to civil-law practices: "The mode of trial is altogether indetermined; ... whether [the defendant] is to be allowed to confront the witnesses, and have the advantage of cross-examination, we are not yet told.... [W]e shall find Congress possessed of powers enabling them to institute judicatories little less inauspicious than a certain tribunal in Spain, . . . the *Inquisition.*" 2 Debates on the Federal Constitution 110-111 (J. Elliot 2d ed. 1863). Similarly, a prominent Anti-federalist writing under the pseudonym Federal Farmer criticized the use of "written evidence" while objecting to the omission of a vicinage right: "Nothing can be more essential than the cross examining [of] witnesses, and generally before the triers of the facts in question. . . . [W]ritten evidence . . . [is] almost useless; it must be frequently taken ex parte, and but very seldom leads to the proper discovery of truth." R. Lee, Letter IV by the Federal Farmer (Oct. 15, 1787). The First Congress responded by including the Confrontation Clause in the proposal that became the Sixth Amendment. . . .

III

This history supports two inferences about the meaning of the Sixth Amendment.

A

First, the principal evil at which the Confrontation Clause was directed was the civil-law mode of criminal procedure, and particularly its use of *ex parte* examinations as evidence against the accused. It was these practices that the Crown deployed in notorious treason cases like Raleigh's; that the Marian statutes invited; that English law's assertion of a right to confrontation was meant to prohibit; and that the founding-era rhetoric decried. The Sixth Amendment must be interpreted with this focus in mind.

Accordingly, we once again reject the view that the Confrontation Clause applies of its own force only to in-court testimony, and that its application to out-of-court statements introduced at trial depends upon "the law of Evidence for the time being." 3 Wigmore §1397, at 101; accord, *Dutton v. Evans,* 400 U.S. 74, 94 (Harlan, J., concurring in result). Leaving the regulation of out-of-court statements to the law of evidence would render the Confrontation Clause powerless to prevent even the most flagrant inquisitorial practices. Raleigh was, after all, perfectly free to confront those who read Cobham's confession in court.

This focus also suggests that not all hearsay implicates the Sixth Amendment's core concerns. An off-hand, overheard remark might be unreliable evidence and thus a good candidate for exclusion under hearsay rules, but it bears little resemblance to the civil-law abuses the Confrontation Clause targeted. On the other hand, *ex parte* examinations might sometimes be admissible under modern hearsay rules, but the Framers certainly would not have condoned them.

The text of the Confrontation Clause reflects this focus. It applies to "witnesses" against the accused — in other words, those who "bear testimony." 1 N. Webster, An American Dictionary of the English Language (1828). "Testimony," in turn, is typically "[a] solemn declaration or affirmation made for the purpose of establishing or proving some fact." *Ibid.* An accuser who makes a formal statement to government officers bears testimony in a sense that a person who makes a casual remark to an acquaintance does not. The constitutional text, like the history underlying the common-law right of confrontation, thus reflects an especially acute concern with a specific type of out-of-court statement.

Various formulations of this core class of "testimonial" statements exist: "*ex parte* in-court testimony or its functional equivalent — that is, material such as affidavits, custodial examinations, prior testimony that the defendant was unable to cross-examine, or similar pretrial statements that declarants would reasonably expect to be used prosecutorially," Brief for Petitioner 23; "extrajudicial statements . . . contained in formalized testimonial materials, such as affidavits, depositions, prior testimony, or confessions," *White v. Illinois*, 502 U.S. 346 (1992) (Thomas, J., joined by Scalia, J., concurring in part and concurring in judgment); "statements that were made under circumstances which would lead an objective witness reasonably to believe that the statement would be available for use at a later trial," Brief for National Association of Criminal Defense Lawyers et al. as *Amici Curiae* 3. These formulations all share a common nucleus and then define the Clause's coverage at various levels of abstraction around it. Regardless of the precise articulation, some statements qualify under any definition — for example, *ex parte* testimony at a preliminary hearing.

Statements taken by police officers in the course of interrogations are also testimonial under even a narrow standard. Police interrogations bear a striking resemblance to examinations by justices of the peace in England. The statements are not *sworn* testimony, but the absence of oath was not dispositive. Cobham's examination was unsworn, see 1 Jardine, Criminal Trials, at 430, yet Raleigh's trial has long been thought a paradigmatic confrontation violation. Under the Marian statutes, witnesses were typically put on oath, but suspects were not. Yet Hawkins and others went out of their way to caution that such unsworn confessions were not admissible against anyone but the confessor.

That interrogators are police officers rather than magistrates does not change the picture either. Justices of the peace conducting examinations under the Marian statutes were not magistrates as we understand that office today, but had an essentially investigative and prosecutorial function. England did not have a professional police force until the 19th century, so it is not surprising that other government officers performed the investigative functions now associated primarily with the police. The involvement of government officers in the production of testimonial evidence presents the same risk, whether the officers are police or justices of the peace.

In sum, even if the Sixth Amendment is not solely concerned with testimonial hearsay, that is its primary object, and interrogations by law enforcement officers fall squarely within that class.[10]

B

The historical record also supports a second proposition: that the Framers would not have allowed admission of testimonial statements of a witness who did not appear at trial unless he was unavailable to testify, and the defendant had had a prior opportunity for cross-examination. The text of the Sixth Amendment does not suggest any open-ended exceptions from the confrontation requirement to be developed by the courts. Rather, the "right . . . to be confronted with the witnesses against him," *Amdt. 6*, is most naturally read as a reference to the right of confrontation at common law, admitting only those exceptions established at the time of the founding. As the English authorities

---

10.   We use the term "interrogation" in its colloquial, rather than any technical legal, sense. Cf. *Rhode Island v. Innis*, 446 U.S. 291, 300-301 (1980). Just as various definitions of "testimonial" exist, one can imagine various definitions of "interrogation," and we need not select among them in this case. Sylvia's recorded statement, knowingly given in response to structured police questioning, qualifies under any conceivable definition.

above reveal, the common law in 1791 conditioned admissibility of an absent witness's examination on unavailability and a prior opportunity to cross-examine. The Sixth Amendment therefore incorporates those limitations. The numerous early state decisions applying the same test confirm that these principles were received as part of the common law in this country.[11]

[This] is not to deny, as the Chief Justice notes, that "[t]here were always exceptions to the general rule of exclusion" of hearsay evidence. Several had become well established by 1791. See 3 Wigmore §1397, at 101. But there is scant evidence that exceptions were invoked to admit *testimonial* statements against the accused in a *criminal* case.[12] Most of the hearsay exceptions covered statements that by their nature were not testimonial — for example, business records or statements in furtherance of a conspiracy. We do not infer from these that the Framers thought exceptions would apply even to prior testimony. Cf. *Lilly v. Virginia*, 527 U.S. 116 (1999) (plurality opinion) ("[A]ccomplices' confessions that inculpate a criminal defendant are not within a firmly rooted exception to the hearsay rule").[13]

IV

***

Our cases have . . . remained faithful to the Framers' understanding: Testimonial statements of witnesses absent from trial have been admitted only where the declarant is unavailable, and only where the defendant has had a prior opportunity to cross-examine.[14]

V

Although the results of our decisions have generally been faithful to the original meaning of the Confrontation Clause, the same cannot be said of our rationales. *Roberts* conditions the admissibility of all hearsay evidence on whether it falls under a "firmly rooted hearsay exception" or bears "particularized guarantees of trustworthiness." 448 U.S., at 66. This test departs from the historical principles identified above in two respects. First, it is too broad: It applies the same mode of analysis whether or not the hearsay consists of *ex parte* testimony. This often results in close

11.   The Chief Justice claims that English law's treatment of testimonial statements was inconsistent at the time of the framing, but the examples he cites relate to examinations under the Marian statutes. As we have explained, to the extent Marian examinations were admissible, it was only because the statutes *derogated* from the common law[.]

12.   The one deviation we have found involves dying declarations[.] Although many dying declarations may not be testimonial, there is authority for admitting even those that clearly are. We need not decide in this case whether the Sixth Amendment incorporates an exception for testimonial dying declarations. If this exception must be accepted on historical grounds, it is *sui generis*.

13.   []Involvement of government officers in the production of testimony with an eye toward trial presents unique potential for prosecutorial abuse — a fact borne out time and again throughout a history with which the Framers were keenly familiar. This consideration does not evaporate when testimony happens to fall within some broad, modern hearsay exception, even if that exception might be justifiable in other circumstances.

14.   [W]e reiterate that, when the declarant appears for cross-examination at trial, the Confrontation Clause places no constraints at all on the use of his prior testimonial statements. See *California v. Green*, 399 U.S. 149 (1970). The Clause does not bar admission of a statement so long as the declarant is present at trial to defend or explain it. (The Clause also does not bar the use of testimonial statements for purposes other than establishing the truth of the matter asserted.)

constitutional scrutiny in cases that are far removed from the core concerns of the Clause. At the same time, however, the test is too narrow: It admits statements that *do* consist of *ex parte* testimony upon a mere finding of reliability. This malleable standard often fails to protect against paradigmatic confrontation violations.

Members of this Court and academics have suggested that we revise our doctrine to reflect more accurately the original understanding of the Clause. They offer two proposals: First, that we apply the Confrontation Clause only to testimonial statements, leaving the remainder to regulation by hearsay law — thus eliminating the overbreadth referred to above. Second, that we impose an absolute bar to statements that are testimonial, absent a prior opportunity to cross-examine — thus eliminating the excessive narrowness referred to above.

In *White*, we considered the first proposal and rejected it. Although our analysis in this case casts doubt on that holding, we need not definitively resolve whether it survives our decision today, because Sylvia Crawford's statement is testimonial under any definition. This case does, however, squarely implicate the second proposal.

A

Where testimonial statements are involved, we do not think the Framers meant to leave the Sixth Amendment's protection to the vagaries of the rules of evidence, much less to amorphous notions of "reliability." Certainly none of the authorities discussed above acknowledges any general reliability exception to the common-law rule. Admitting statements deemed reliable by a judge is fundamentally at odds with the right of confrontation. To be sure, the Clause's ultimate goal is to ensure reliability of evidence, but it is a procedural rather than a substantive guarantee. It commands, not that evidence be reliable, but that reliability be assessed in a particular manner: by testing in the crucible of cross-examination. The Clause thus reflects a judgment, not only about the desirability of reliable evidence (a point on which there could be little dissent), but about how reliability can best be determined. Cf. 3 Blackstone, Commentaries, at 373 ("This open examination of witnesses . . . is much more conducive to the clearing up of truth"); M. Hale, History and Analysis of the Common Law of England 258 (1713) (adversarial testing "beats and bolts out the Truth much better").

The *Roberts* test allows a jury to hear evidence, untested by the adversary process, based on a mere judicial determination of reliability. It thus replaces the constitutionally prescribed method of assessing reliability with a wholly foreign one. In this respect, it is very different from exceptions to the Confrontation Clause that make no claim to be a surrogate means of assessing reliability. For example, the rule of forfeiture by wrongdoing (which we accept) extinguishes confrontation claims on essentially equitable grounds; it does not purport to be an alternative means of determining reliability. See *Reynolds v. United States*, 98 U.S. 145, 158-159.

The Raleigh trial itself involved the very sorts of reliability determinations that *Roberts* authorizes. In the face of Raleigh's repeated demands for confrontation, the prosecution responded with many of the arguments a court applying *Roberts* might invoke today: that Cobham's statements were self-inculpatory, that they were not made in the heat of passion, and that they were not "extracted from [him] upon any hopes or promise of Pardon." It is not plausible that the Framers' only objection to the trial was that Raleigh's judges did not properly weigh these factors before sentencing him to death. Rather, the problem was that the judges refused to allow Raleigh to confront Cobham in court, where he could cross-examine him and try to expose his accusation as a lie.

Dispensing with confrontation because testimony is obviously reliable is akin to dispensing with jury trial because a defendant is obviously guilty. This is not what the Sixth Amendment prescribes.

B

The legacy of *Roberts* in other courts vindicates the Framers' wisdom in rejecting a general reliability exception. The framework is so unpredictable that it fails to provide meaningful protection from even core confrontation violations. Reliability is an amorphous, if not entirely subjective, concept.

* * *

The unpardonable vice of the *Roberts* test, however, is not its unpredictability, but its demonstrated capacity to admit core testimonial statements that the Confrontation Clause plainly meant to exclude. Despite the plurality's speculation in *Lilly*, 527 U.S., at 137, that it was "highly unlikely" that accomplice confessions implicating the accused could survive *Roberts*, courts continue routinely to admit them. One recent study found that, after *Lilly*, appellate courts admitted accomplice statements to the authorities in 25 out of 70 cases — more than one-third of the time. Kirst, Appellate Court Answers to the Confrontation Questions in *Lilly v. Virginia*, 53 Syracuse L. Rev. 87, 105 (2003). Courts have invoked *Roberts* to admit other sorts of plainly testimonial statements despite the absence of any opportunity to cross-examine. See [, e.g.,] *United States v. Aguilar*, 295 F.3d 1018, 1021-1023 (CA9 2002) (plea allocution showing existence of a conspiracy); *United States v. Papajohn*, 212 F.3d 1112, 1118-1120 (CA8 2000) (grand jury testimony).

To add insult to injury, some of the courts that admit untested testimonial statements find reliability in the very factors that *make* the statements testimonial. As noted earlier, one court relied on the fact that the witness's statement was made to police while in custody on pending charges — the theory being that this made the statement more clearly against penal interest and thus more reliable. Other courts routinely rely on the fact that a prior statement is given under oath in judicial proceedings, [e.g., plea allocution, grand jury testimony]. That inculpating statements are given in a testimonial setting is not an antidote to the confrontation problem, but rather the trigger that makes the Clause's demands most urgent. It is not enough to point out that most of the usual safeguards of the adversary process attend the statement, when the single safeguard missing is the one the Confrontation Clause demands.

C

Roberts' failings were on full display in the proceedings below. [The Court recounted the lower courts' reliance on conflicting factors indicating that Sylvia Crawford's recorded statement was both seemingly unreliable and reliable as an example of *Roberts*' "unpredictable and inconsistent application."]

* * *

We readily concede that we could resolve this case by simply reweighing the "reliability factors" under *Roberts* and finding that Sylvia Crawford's statement falls short. But we view this as one of those rare cases in which the result below is so improbable that it reveals a fundamental failure on our part to interpret the Constitution in a way that secures its intended constraint on judicial discretion. Moreover, to reverse the Washington Supreme Court's decision after conducting our own reliability analysis would perpetuate, not avoid, what the Sixth Amendment condemns. The Constitution prescribes a procedure for determining the reliability of testimony in criminal trials, and we, no less than the state courts, lack authority to replace it with one of our own devising.

We have no doubt that the courts below were acting in utmost good faith when they found reliability. The Framers, however, would not have been content to indulge this assumption. They knew that judges, like other government officers, could not always be trusted to safeguard the rights of the people; the likes of the dread Lord Jeffreys were not yet too distant a memory. They were loath to leave too much discretion in judicial hands. Cf. *U.S. Const., Amdt. 6* (criminal jury trial); *Amdt. 7* (civil jury trial). By replacing categorical constitutional guarantees with open-ended balancing tests, we do violence to their design. Vague standards are manipulable, and, while that might be a small concern in run-of-the-mill assault prosecutions like this one, the Framers had an eye toward politically charged cases like Raleigh's — great state trials where the impartiality of even those at the highest levels of the judiciary might not be so clear. It is difficult to imagine *Roberts'* providing any meaningful protection in those circumstances.

> * * *

Where nontestimonial hearsay is at issue, it is wholly consistent with the Framers' design to afford the States flexibility in their development of hearsay law — as does *Roberts*, and as would an approach that exempted such statements from Confrontation Clause scrutiny altogether. Where testimonial evidence is at issue, however, the Sixth Amendment demands what the common law required: unavailability and a prior opportunity for cross-examination. We leave for another day any effort to spell out a comprehensive definition of "testimonial." Whatever else the term covers, it applies at a minimum to prior testimony at a preliminary hearing, before a grand jury, or at a former trial; and to police interrogations. These are the modern practices with closest kinship to the abuses at which the Confrontation Clause was directed.

In this case, the State admitted Sylvia's testimonial statement against petitioner, despite the fact that he had no opportunity to cross-examine her. That alone is sufficient to make out a violation of the Sixth Amendment. *Roberts* notwithstanding, we decline to mine the record in search of indicia of reliability. Where testimonial statements are at issue, the only indicium of reliability sufficient to satisfy constitutional demands is the one the Constitution actually prescribes: confrontation.

The judgment of the Washington Supreme Court is reversed, and the case is remanded for further proceedings not inconsistent with this opinion.

It is so ordered.

Chief Justice REHNQUIST, with whom Justice O'CONNOR joins, concurring in the judgment.

I dissent from the Court's decision to overrule *Ohio v. Roberts* [. . .] It is a change of course not in the least necessary to reverse the judgment of the Supreme Court of Washington in this case. The result the Court reaches follows inexorably from *Roberts* and its progeny without any need for overruling that line of cases. In *Idaho v. Wright*, 497 U.S. 805, 820-824 (1990), we held that an out-of-court statement was not admissible simply because the truthfulness of that statement was corroborated by other evidence at trial. [T]he Supreme Court of Washington gave decisive weight to the "interlocking nature of the two statements." No re-weighing of the "reliability factors," which is hypothesized by the Court, is required to reverse the judgment here. A citation to *Idaho v Wright, supra*, would suffice.

NOTES AND QUESTIONS

1. The *Crawford* opinion leaves open a number of critical questions. The most important is the meaning of "testimonial." The Court cites three different doctrinal definitions of that term, from three different sources. How do they differ in content? How do you think they will differ in application? Note that one of them had been previously adopted by Justices Scalia and Thomas. Why, do you think, did the Court not settle on a single definition?

2. The definitions offer two principal concerns about testimonial statements. One concern is that such statements are produced in the context of government interrogation. Why is this a concern? What statements of this type does the Court say are definitely testimonial? A second concern is that the declarant might think that what is being said could be used at a trial. Why is this a concern? Are these both concerns about unreliability or something else?

3. Another question is whether there are circumstances in which a testimonial statement can be used by the prosecution even though the declarant is not present at trial. The majority implies that dying declarations might be an exception to the ban on testimonial statements due to their historical pedigree. Are there others?

4. The Court also indicates that certain types of hearsay are not testimonial, including business records and co-conspirators' statements. Unless "testimonial" is confined to government interrogations, this seems plainly wrong. Both types of statements could certainly fit within the "might know that the statement could be used at trial" test. Business records are often created just for that purpose, as are the declarations authorized by FRE 902 (11) and (12).

5. Another important question is whether the confrontation clause has any effect on the admission of "nontestimonial" hearsay in criminal cases. Is there anything at all left to *Ohio v. Roberts*, in other words?

6. Note that the Supreme Court did not review the holding below that Sylvia Crawford was unavailable due to the defendant's invocation of the state marital privilege. Doesn't it seem a bit peculiar to think of Mrs. Crawford as constitutionally unavailable for cross-examination by her husband when it is her husband's choice to keep her off the stand?

7. For critiques of the Supreme Court's analysis and use of English and American legal history, see articles at Symposium: Crawford and Beyond, 71 Brook. L. Rev. 35, 105, 219, 235 (2005).

3. The Definition of Testimonial Statements in the Aftermath of Crawford v. Washington

Federal and state courts throughout the United States have been applying the *testimonial* standard of the *Crawford* opinion since the case was decided. The volume of reported opinions is staggering, and the degree to which courts disagree about important questions is equally impressive. Some cases have reached federal circuit courts, and a few have reached state supreme courts. We report here on some of the more significant decisions that take a strong position on key issues regarding the kinds of statements that do, or do not, fall within the Supreme Court's definitions of *testimonial*. These positions cannot yet be said to be a "majority" view; where there is a clear dispute on an important question, we have included it. The Supreme Court has granted certiorari in two cases involving statements made to investigating police officers and 911 calls seeking emergency help.

a. Formalized Testimonial Materials

One of the definitions of testimonial offered by the Supreme Court was that proposed by Justices Scalia and Thomas in White v. Illinois — "extrajudicial statements . . . contained in formalized testimonial materials, such as affidavits, depositions, prior testimony, or confessions," 502 U.S. at 346. And in *Crawford* itself, the majority concluded its opinion by stating that, at a minimum, "testimonial" applies to "prior testimony at a preliminary hearing, before a grand jury, or at a former trial; and to police interrogations." 541 U.S. at 68. Courts have readily adopted these categories. United States v. Bruno, 383 F.3d 65, 78 (2d Cir. 2004) (plea allocution transcripts and grand jury testimony of unavailable witnesses are testimonial).

Police interrogations that are formal, recorded, consist of structured questions, and have a law enforcement purpose lie at the core of concern about a defendant's confrontation right. But there is difference of opinion as to how broadly this core concern extends. Some courts have defined *interrogation* to include most statements made in response to police questions. Commonwealth v. Gonzalves, 445 Mass. 1, 13-14 (Mass. 2005) ("questioning by law enforcement agents, whether police, prosecutors, or others acting directly on their behalf, other than to secure a volatile scene or to establish the need for or provide medical care, is interrogation in the colloquial sense."). See also United States v. Jordan, 357 F.Supp. 2d 889, 907-911 (E.D.Va. 2005) (volunteered confessional statement to police department is testimonial, and confrontation problem cannot be cured through "redaction" under *Bruton* as declarant was not a co-defendant). Other courts have held that responses to initial inquiries at a crime scene are typically not testimonial. Hammon v. State, 892 N.E. 2d 444, 456 (Ind. 2005) (testimonial statement is one "given or taken in significant part for purposes of preserving it for potential future use in legal proceedings . . . the motive of the questioner, more than that of the declarant, is determinative, but if either is principally motivated by a desire to preserve the statement it is sufficient to render the statement 'testimonial.'") Hammon's petition for certiorari was recently granted by the Supreme Court on the question of whether "an oral accusation made to an investigating officer at the scene of an alleged crime" is testimonial.

Questioning by other agents of government with a law enforcement purpose has also been held to be testimonial. United States v. Bordeaux, 400 F.3d 548, 556 (8th Cir. 2005) (child's statement about sexual abuse to a "forensic interviewer" at a child evaluation center held testimonial; two tape recordings produced, one for medical records and one for law enforcement officials). But similar information obtained by a non-government employee at a Child Assessment Center has been held to be non-testimonial. People v. Geno, 261 Mich. App. 624 (2004).

There is a split of authority as to whether routine and non-adversarial reports prepared by government officers who are not law enforcement personnel, such as blood tests and drug analyses, are non-investigative and therefore not "testimony" for trial. Commonwealth v. Verde, 827 N.E.2d 701 (Mass. 2005) (reciting split of authority while holding that public reports, if not based on opinion or discretion, are excepted from the confrontation clause).

b. Statements a Reasonable Person Would Realize Would Be Used in Investigation or Prosecution of a Crime.

An additional definition of testimonial was urged by the Petitioner in *Crawford* and mentioned by the Supreme Court — statements that declarants would reasonably expect to be used prosecutorially. 541 U.S. at 1364. This definition was developed by Professor Richard Friedman, one of the principal advocates for the testimonial standard prior to *Crawford*. See, e.g., Richard D. Friedman, Grappling with the Meaning of "Testimonial", 71 Brook. L. Rev. 241 (2005) ("testimonial" would include any statement made in circumstances in which a reasonable person would have understood that there was a significant probability that it likely would be used in investigation or prosecution of a crime). An influential Sixth Circuit opinion adopted this "reasonable person" standard and applied it to statements given by confidential informants to police that implicated others in criminal activities." United States v. Cromer, 389 F.3d 662, 674-678 (6th Cir. 2004) (testimony by police officer explicitly informed the jury that someone [the confidential informant] had implicated defendant in criminal activities). Accord, United States v. Summers, 414 F.3d 1287, 1302 (10th Cir. 2005) ("common nucleus" present in the Court's formulations of testimonial statements centers on the "reasonable expectations" of the declarant):

> It is "the reasonable expectation that a statement may be later used at trial that distinguishes the flippant remark, proffered to a casual acquaintance . . . from the true testimonial statement. Certain factual circumstances surrounding the out-of-court statement give rise to just such an expectation . . . [w]e further reject a narrow approach that would limit testimonial statements to those made by witnesses 'who testify . . . via government-prepared affidavits, depositions, videotapes, and the like.'" [Id. at 1302.]

Statements made during 911 calls to a police dispatcher are evaluated under this "reasonable expectations" standard. Several courts have concluded that such calls, if admissible under the hearsay exception for excited utterances, and made shortly after a criminal offense while under the stress of that event, are nontestimonial. Justification for this conclusion includes the assumption that such calls are made because callers want protection from immediate danger, not because they expect the report to be used later at trial; and that the cloak of anonymity of 911 calls encourages citizens to make these calls and not fear repercussion. State v. Wright, 686 N.W. 2d 295, 302 (Minn. App. 2004). Does this analysis square with your view of the "reasonable expectations" of most people who report crimes to 911 operators? Another court held excited 911 calls to be nontestimonial because they are "emotional and spontaneous rather than deliberate and calculated." United States v. Brun, 416 F.3d 703, 706 (8th Cir. 2005). Calls made to the 911 operator that are not excited have been held to be testimonial. Certiorari on the question whether a "putative victim's statements to a 911 operator naming her assailant, admitted as an excited utterance" are testimonial was recently granted in the case of Davis v. Washington,

2005 Wash. LEXIS 462 (Wash.) (911 call seeking emergency help is not "bearing witness").

When the responding authorities arrive after a 911 call, the immediate statements made to them have been held to be both testimonial and nontestimonial. In *Brun*, for example, statements made to police ten minutes after 911 call by a visibly distraught victim during an "unstructured" interaction held nontestimonial, while statements made somewhat later in response to specific questions, after the declarant had the opportunity to deliberate and reflect on what she had said previously to the officer, were testimonial. Id. at 706.

Statements about the mental condition of a criminal defendant, made by associates of the defendant to the prosecution's expert psychiatrist in an insanity defense case, have been held to be testimonial. People v. Goldstein, 843 N.E. 2d 727 (N.Y. 2005) (expert was retained by the state and all declarants should reasonably have expected their statements to be used prosecutorially). In *Goldstein*, it was therefore held to be error for the expert to relate these statements to the jury as a basis for her opinion that defendant was not legally insane. Expert witnesses' use of out of court hearsay in forming their opinions, and in testifying at trial, is subject to FRE 703, as will be discussed in Chapter Nine, infra.

Examples of statements found not to be made with the reasonable expectation that they would be used prosecutorially include statements made unwittingly to a confidential informant and secretly recorded under wiretap order, United States v. Hendricks, 395 F.3d 173, 180-82 (3d Cir. 2005), and the contents of the diary of an unavailable witness. Parle v. Runnels, 387 F.3d 1030, 1037 (9th Cir. 2004) (dictum).

c.   *Categories of Nontestimonial Statements Mentioned in Crawford*

The Supreme Court asserted in *Crawford* that there are certain types of hearsay statements, corresponding to specific hearsay exceptions, that are simply not testimonial "by their nature" and thus not within the scope of the Confrontation Clause. 541 U.S. at 1367. Courts have relied on this seeming "categorical" approach. For example, statements not intended as assertions (such as questions) may escape the definition of hearsay and thus the reach of the confrontation clause. United States v. Summers, 414 F.3d 1287 (10th Cir. 2005) (question "How did you guys [the police] find us so fast?" intended to make an inculpatory assertion and thus was hearsay and testimonial). Other such types include casual remarks to acquaintances, United States v. Lee, 374 F. 3d 637, 645 (8th Cir. 2004) (declarant's confession to his mother "do[es] not implicate the core concerns of the confrontation clause ... [and is] more like causal remarks to an acquaintance"); business records, Johnson v. Renico, 314 F.Supp. 2d 700 (E.D.Mich. 2004); party admissions, id. at 707; and co-conspirator statements in furtherance of a conspiracy, United States v. Felton, 417 F.3d 97, 103 n.2 (1st Cir. 2005).

4.   Testimonial Statements That Satisfy the Confrontation Right

Under *Crawford*, testimonial statements can satisfy the confrontation right in two ways: (1) if the declarant testifies as a witness at trial and thus is available for cross-examination by the defendant, and (2) if the declarant is unavailable at trial but the defendant has previously had the opportunity to cross-examine the declarant. Existing case law has established the parameters of these requirements, and the Court in *Crawford* gave no indication that their meaning was to change.

a.   The Declarant Testifies

The Supreme Court stated in *Crawford* that

> When the declarant appears for cross-examination at trial, the Confrontation Clause places no constraints at all on the use of his prior testimonial statements. See *California v. Green*, 399 U.S. 149 (1970). The Clause does not bar admission of a statement so long as the declarant is present at trial to defend or explain it. [541 U.S. at 59, n.9]

The prior statements must, of course, fall within a hearsay exception; the confrontation right may not coincide precisely with the hearsay rule.

The issue of the adequacy of cross-examination of the declarant, such as when the declarant is unable to recall the events that are the subject of the hearsay statement, appears to be well-settled under United States v. Owens, 484 U.S. 554 (1988), as discussed on pages 158, supra. For example, when children testify, they may be quite difficult to cross-examine. In United States v. Kappell, 418 F.3d 550 (6th Cir. 2005), the defendant in a child sexual abuse case claimed that the child witnesses were unresponsive and inarticulate, therefore "unavailable" to him to cross-examine. Citing *Owens*, the court held that the Confrontation Clause guarantees only the opportunity for cross-examination, and that testimonial infirmities revealed in court (such as Owens' amnesia) can be used by the jury in evaluating the witnesses' credibility. Id. at 555.

Victims of domestic abuse who have made "testimonial" hearsay statements may appear at trial and then refuse to testify at all, with no valid claim of privilege. Does such behavior on the witness stand satisfy the confrontation requirement, or is admission of the victim's hearsay statements in this situation a violation of the defendant's right? The refusing witness, like the amnesiac in *Owens*, is before the jury but access to meaningful cross-examination is barred. The court in Fowler v. State, 829 N.E.2d 459, 467-468 (Ind. 2005) held that in such a situation, the defendant must seek an order to compel a response and thus subject the witness to the threat of contempt in order to preserve a Confrontation Clause objection. Failure to request such an order waives the confrontation right.

b.   Unavailability and Prior Opportunity for Cross-examination

The Court in *Crawford* stated that the Framers would not have permitted the admission of testimonial statements *unless* the declarant "was unavailable to testify and the defendant had had a prior opportunity for cross-examination." 541 U.S. at 57. Prior cross-examination can thus satisfy the confrontation right, if the declarant is unavailable at trial.

i.   Unavailability.   Typically the federal or state requirements of "unavailability" under the hearsay rule, such as FRE 804(a), will be used to determine unavailability for Confrontation Clause purposes as well, with one addition. In Barber v.

Page, 390 U.S. 719 (1968), the Supreme Court held that the Sixth Amendment requires the prosecution to demonstrate in court that it had made a good faith effort to produce the hearsay declarant, even if its effort was unsuccessful. There is also Supreme Court precedent that does not permit the prosecution to offer a testimonial statement when the unavailability of the declarant was caused by the prosecution's own negligence. Motes v. United States, 178 U.S. 458, 474 (1900). The *Crawford* opinion does not mention *Barber* or *Motes*, although in the circumstances of Crawford's exercise of his spousal privilege, there was no need to do so. State courts have help that prior standards of good faith and reasonable diligence are still applicable after *Crawford*.

ii. Prior Opportunity for Cross-examination. In Ohio v. Roberts, the Supreme Court approved the admission of statements made by the declarant at a preliminary hearing when the defendant's counsel had engaged in cross-examination of the now-unavailable declarant. Such prior testimony, admitted under FRE 804(b)(1) only when the defendant had the opportunity and similar motive as at trial to develop the declarant's testimony, will presumably be admissible under *Crawford's* language as quoted above. However, as we stated on page 557, supra, a criminal defendant may lack motivation to cross-examine witnesses vigorously at preliminary hearings, due to an inability to prepare adequately and reluctance to reveal strategy. There are also states in which preliminary hearings are truncated proceedings, and cross-examination is fruitless because the court will not weigh the credibility of witnesses. *See* People v. Fry, 92 P.3d 970 (Colo. 2004). The *Roberts* court left open the question whether opportunity alone, or merely cursory questioning, would satisfy the confrontation requirement, and the Court in *Crawford* did not mention this issue.

5.   Exceptions to the Requirement of Confrontation

The *Crawford* opinion mentioned two possible exceptions to the confrontation requirement that could be used to admit testimonial hearsay statements. The first is an exception for dying declarations, grounded on the historical admission of such statements during the time when the right to confrontation was developed. 541 U.S. at 56, n.6. The second is an exception based on a defendant's "forfeiture" of the right to confrontation based on wrongful conduct that has made the declarant unavailable to testify. 541 U.S. at 62.

a.   Dying Declarations

Taking the hint dropped by the Supreme Court, several courts have held that dying declarations may be admitted as an historical exception to the Confrontation Clause. People v. Monterroso, 34 Cal. 4th 743, 765 (Calif. 2004); State v. Martin, 695 N.W.2d 578, 585 (Minn. 2005). But other courts have rejected this exception on grounds of unreliability, United States v. Mayhew, 380 F.Supp.2d 961, 966 (S.D.Ohio 2005) (rejecting dying declarations as an exception to the Confrontation Clause because not inherently reliable, although court's holding based on other grounds), and on grounds that the dying declaration exception did not in fact exist in the United States at the time of the Sixth Amendment. United States v. Jordan, 2005 WL 513501 (D.Colo. 2005).

b. *"Forfeiture-by-Wrongdoing"*

As was explained on page 569, supra, a theory of "forfeiture" of a defendant's confrontation right developed from the holding in United States v. Mastrangelo, 693 F.2d 269 (2d Cir. 1982), that this right may be waived by the defendant's misconduct in making the hearsay declarant unavailable. The Supreme Court accepted this doctrine explicitly in *Crawford*:

> The rule of forfeiture by wrongdoing (which we accept) extinguishes confrontation claims on essentially equitable grounds; it does not purport to be an alternative means of determining reliability. [541 U.S. at 62].

Under this doctrine, and similar to the hearsay exception defined in FRE 804(b)(6), a testimonial hearsay statement may be admitted against a defendant if the prosecution proves by a preponderance of the evidence, pursuant to FRE 104(a), that the defendant's wrongdoing was responsible for the unavailability of the hearsay declarant at trial.

However, it appears from recent decisions that the limiting principle of forfeiture under the hearsay rule (FRE 804(b)(6)) – that the purpose of the defendant's wrongdoing must be to prevent the declarant from testifying against the defendant – is not required to justify forfeiture of the constitutional confrontation right. Instead, courts have held that the motive for the defendant's wrongdoing is irrelevant, since "the forfeiture doctrine's equitable basis, as enunciated in Crawford, prevent[s] the defendant from benefiting in any way from his wrongdoing. . . ." United States v. Mayhew, 380 F. Supp. 2d 961, 968 (S.D. Ohio 2005) citing United States v. Garcia-Meza, 403 F.3d 364, 370-371 (6th Cir. 2005) (defendant charged with murder of his wife; court upheld admission of wife's statements to police, made after being assaulted by her husband five months previously, that he was becoming violent toward her after she had spoken to a former boyfriend). Thus, if a testimonial hearsay statement of an unavailable declarant is admissible against a defendant under any hearsay exception – for example, an excited utterance – then the defendant forfeits his Confrontation Clause rights if the court determines by a preponderance of the evidence that the declarant is unavailable because of the defendant's intentional conduct, "regardless of whether the defendant is standing trial for the identical crime that caused the declarant's unavailability." United States v. Mayhew, supra, 380 F.Supp.2d at 968. It remains to be seen what other forms of "wrongdoing" will satisfy the constitutional standard of forfeiture. For example, will defendant's threats to and intimidation of a victim of domestic violence suffice if the victim then exercises a spousal privilege?

6. Defendants' Right to Confrontation When Nontestimonial Statements Are Offered Against Them

The Supreme Court left open the question of whether the confrontation analysis under its prior opinion in Ohio v. Roberts would apply to nontestimonial statements offered against criminal defendants. Courts have since held that *Roberts* does apply, and permits the admission of hearsay under "firmly rooted" hearsay exceptions such as excited utterances, United States v. Brun, 416 F.3d 703, 707 (8th Cir. 2005), and hearsay with "particularized guarantees of trustworthiness" such as statements to a friend that are against penal interest, United States v. Franklin, 415 F.3d 537, 546 (6th Cir. 2005) ("Court frankly ridiculed *Roberts* but did not quite over-rule [it]. Consequently, with respect to non-testimonial hearsay statements, *Roberts* and its progeny remain the controlling precedents.").

NOTES AND QUESTIONS

1. In California and other states, special hearsay exceptions had been created by statute to provide for the admission of statements made by alleged victims of child abuse, domestic violence, and elder or dependent abuse. These statutes had required that victim statements bearing indicia of trustworthiness be videotaped by police or other investigative agencies. After *Crawford*, admission of such videotaped statements has been held to be testimonial and thus to violate the defendant's right to confrontation in all three types of cases. These results illustrate that *Crawford* will have a special impact on cases involving vulnerable victims who will not or cannot testify, or who cannot be effective as witnesses. Commentators believe that police practices will change to accommodate the change in law, in particular by creating more informal questioning opportunities that do not cry out "interrogation;" by creating more opportunities for pre-trial cross-examination in pre-trial hearings or depositions; and by working closely with fearful witnesses to enable them to testify. *See* Myrna Raeder, Remember the Ladies and the Children Too: Crawford's Impact on Domestic Violence and Sexual Abuse Cases, 71 Brook. L. Rev. 311 (2005); Robert P. Mosteller, Crawford v. Washington: Encouraging and Ensuring the Confrontation of Witnesses, 39 Univ. Richmond L.Rev. 511 (2005); Tom Lininger, Prosecuting Batterers After Crawford, 91 Va. Law Review 747 (2005); Celeste E. Byrom, The Use of the Excited Utterance Hearsay Exception in the Prosecution of Domestic Violence Cases After *Crawford v. Washington*, 23 Rev. of Litig. 409 (2005).

2. Child witnesses may testify by closed circuit television, pursuant to the narrow exception established in Maryland v. Craig, 497 U.S. 836 (1990) to protect the physical and psychological well-being of the child. When they do, it has been held, prior to *Crawford*, that this counts as an in-court appearance for purposes of admitting their other hearsay statements, so long as the specific finding of necessity mandated in *Craig* is satisfied. United States v. Turning Bear, 357 F.3d 730, 738 (8th Cir. 2004).

3. The new approach to confrontation announced in *Crawford* has been applied to cases currently pending in both federal and state courts. Whether *Crawford* is retroactive, meaning applicable to convictions upon habeas corpus review, is currently being litigated in federal courts. The Ninth Circuit has held that the rule in *Crawford* is new, that it is a "bedrock rule of criminal procedure," and thus is retroactive. Bockting v. Bayer, 399 F.3d 1010 (9th Cir. 2005). The Second and Tenth Circuits have disagreed and held that *Crawford* is not retroactive. Commentators have suggested that if retroactivity is established, the volume of cases from state courts may create pressure on courts both to construe the definition of "testimonial" narrowly, and perhaps to broaden the "forfeiture-by-wrongdoing" exception. Robert P. Mosteller, Crawford v. Washington: Encouraging and Ensuring the Confrontation of Witnesses,

39 Univ. Richmond L.Rev. 511 (2005); Richard D. Friedman, The Confrontation Clause Re-Rooted and Transformed, 2004 CatoSCTR 439 (2004).

4. In addition to works already cited, recent articles on the aftermath of Crawford v. Washington include: Symposium, Crawford and Beyond, 71 Brook. L. Rev. 1 (2005); Miguel A. Mendez, Crawford v. Washington: A Critique, 57 Stan.L.Rev. 569 (2004); Thomas J. Reed, Crawford v. Washington and the Irretrievable Breakdown of a Union: Separating the Confrontation Clause from the Hearsay Rule. 56 S.C.L.Rev. 185 (2004).

PROBLEMS

Throughout Chapter 8, hearsay statements offered in criminal cases against the defendant have been the subject of Problems, the answer to which required application of the hearsay rule. You can now return to those Problems and ask whether the same hearsay statements violate the Confrontation Clause as interpreted in Crawford v. Washington. Or, would they be admissible under *Crawford*, and why? See Problems 8.2; 8.3(a),(b) and (c); 8.31; 8.33; 8.34(a) and (b); 8.35; 8.36(a),(b) and (c); 8.39; 8.41; 8.43; 8.45; 8.46; 8.47; 8.54; 8.55; 8.58; 8.59; 8.60; 8.67; 8.68; 8.69; 8.71; 8.76; 8.78; 8.81; 8.85; 8.86; 8.87; 8.88.

H. REFLECTION ON THE HEARSAY RULE

Critics of the hearsay rule are plentiful. Their criticisms focus primarily on the complexity of the categorical structure of the exemptions and exceptions and on whether such an elaborate structure is necessary to fulfill hearsay policy. This, in turn, raises the deeper question of what hearsay policy should be in the context of modern litigation.

1. The Traditional Goals of Hearsay Policy

We presented the traditional formulation of the policy excluding hearsay in Section A of this chapter: A witness's oath, demeanor, and cross-examination are thought to reduce testimonial dangers and make in-court testimony *more* reliable than out-of-court statements. A somewhat stronger version of this policy would state that hearsay is inherently weak evidence, that juries cannot properly evaluate it, that verdicts should not be based on hearsay, and that excluding hearsay protects against fraudulent evidence. A thorough analysis and critique of this traditional policy can be found in Paul S. Milich, Hearsay Antinomies: The Case for Abolishing the Rule and Starting Over, 71 Ore. L. Rev. 723 (1992).

Based on this view of the weaknesses of hearsay evidence, the two primary justifications for admitting it through categorical exceptions and exemptions are *reliability* and *necessity*: The goal of traditional hearsay policy is to admit hearsay that is more reliable than run-of-the mill hearsay, or that seems necessary to the rational resolution of litigated disputes. This "reliability theory" of the hearsay exceptions presumes that reliable hearsay can be identified in advance by identifying those circumstances that may reduce some risks of insincerity, to a lesser extent risk of loss of memory, and only occasionally a risk of inaccurate perception.

2.   The Reliability Theory Does Not Work

It is easy to criticize the reliability theory of the traditional hearsay rule. We have done so implicitly throughout this chapter by pointing out where the foundational requirements of the categorical exceptions and exemptions fail to fulfill their goal. Much seemingly unreliable hearsay is admitted, and it may be that much that seems reliable is excluded. Even the Advisory Committee's Introductory Note to Article VIII of the Federal Rules of Evidence acknowledges these criticisms:

> The solution evolved by the common law has been a general rule excluding hearsay but subject to the numerous exceptions under circumstances supposed to furnish guarantees of trustworthiness. Criticisms of this scheme are that it is bulky and complex, fails to screen good from bad hearsay realistically, and inhibits the growth of the law of evidence.

A similar critique is found in Michael Seigel, Rationalizing Hearsay: A Proposal for a Best Evidence Hearsay Rule, 72 B.U. L. Rev. 893, 912-913 (1992):

> Sadly, our current system employs the *least rational* means of evaluating the reliability of hearsay evidence: preconceived categories. Each categorical exception is theoretically supported by an initial inductive hypothesis about human behavior that, if true, reduces the probability that an out-of-court statement falling within the category suffers from one of the hearsay dangers. Accordingly, any such statement is deemed reliable and, therefore, admissible. However, even assuming the accuracy of the categories' foundation hypotheses, an out-of-court statement's reliability is simply not measurable through what is, in effect, an unidimensional test. A statement may be grossly unreliable despite the fact that it falls within the bounds of a categorical exception, in light of other information in the case. This more specific information may demonstrate that the category's behavioral assumption is inapplicable to the particular statement at issue; or the statement may present a danger not accounted for by the assumption underlying the specific exception; or other more definitive evidence might make the accuracy of the hearsay suspect. At the same time, the categorical exceptions are not comprehensively inclusive; the facts surrounding excluded hearsay may indicate that it is reliable even though it fails to meet the strictures of any given exception.

The trouble is, there is not much agreement on an alternative approach to determining the reliability of the hearsay that should be admitted.

3.   A Rule of Discretion

One option is to change the rule to a Rule 403-type of balancing test, whereby the trial judge would be given discretion to admit hearsay that the judge thinks is more probative because it is more credible, and to exclude hearsay that is less probative because less credible. Under the categorical approach, the credibility of hearsay evidence is not to be weighed by the judge. The advantages of a discretionary rule were forcefully argued in Jack B. Weinstein, The Probative Force of Hearsay, 46 Iowa L. Rev. 331 (1961). A discretionary approach was also described, but rejected, in the Advisory Committee's Introductory Note:

> Admissibility would be determined by weighing the probative force of the evidence against the possibility of prejudice, waste of time, and the availability of more satisfactory evidence. The bases of the traditional hearsay exceptions would be helpful in assessing probative

force. . . . Procedural safeguards would consist of notice of intention to use hearsay, free comment by the judge on the weight of the evidence, and a greater measure of authority in both trial and appellate judges to deal with evidence on the basis of weight. The Advisory Committee has rejected this approach to hearsay as involving too great a measure of judicial discretion, minimizing the predictability of rulings, enhancing the difficulties of preparing for trial, adding a further element to the already over-complicated congeries of pretrial procedures, and requiring substantially different rules for civil and criminal cases.

According to Professor Seigel, a discretionary rule would vest considerably more authority over the outcomes of trials in the judge:

> Simply put, the power to exclude evidence is the power to determine the outcome of cases. If truly discretionary — in other words, if not subject to appellate review — this power is too great to vest in individual trial judges. Moreover, absent clear guidelines defining reliable hearsay, the exclusionary process would be akin to a game of roulette. On the other hand, imposing clear guidelines and enforcing them through appellate review would cause the standard of reliability to evolve slowly into a set of rules. The final outcome would be the recreation of what existed prior to codification of the rules of evidence: an ad hoc common law hearsay regime. [Seigel, B.U. L. Rev. at 914.]

4. Abolition

The more extreme option would be to abandon the search for reliability and abolish the rule of exclusion altogether. The admission of hearsay would be governed only by its relevance under FRE 401 and its risks of FRE 403 dangers, which should not include concerns about the credibility of the declarant. Under a truly *abolitionist* regime, exclusion would depend solely on the judge's estimation of Rule 403 dangers that might negatively affect the jury's ability to evaluate the credibility of hearsay.

What might be the consequences of an abolitionist regime? An article by Professor Eleanor Swift, Abolishing the Hearsay Rule, 75 Cal. L. Rev. 495 (1987), predicted that potentially admissible hearsay would raise three kinds of problems: (1) statements by unidentified persons about whom very little is known, so that the jury has little factual basis on which to apply its own general knowledge and experience; (2) statements that bear obvious risks, in particular a declarant's motive to misrepresent, requiring the jury to make hard choices between conflicting inferences; and (3) statements presented in documentary form without any witness to supply information about them, thus permitting the proponent to avoid presenting either the declarant or a foundation witness for cross-examination

The Advisory Committee rejected an abolitionist regime on grounds that it "has been unconvinced of the wisdom of abandoning the traditional requirement of some particular assurance of credibility as a condition precedent to admitting the hearsay declaration of an unavailable declarant."

5. Reformulating Hearsay Policy

a. *Is There a Need for a Hearsay Rule in Modern Civil Litigation?*

In his article The Evolution of the Hearsay Rule to a Rule of Admission, 76 Minn. L. Rev. 797, 797-801 (1992), Professor Ronald Allen describes why the hearsay rule of exclusion is no longer important in civil litigation due to prevalent use of discovery depositions, party admissions, and the numerous exceptions and exemptions. His concern is that its continued existence imposes too great a cost:

> My instinct is that . . . [g]iven all the inroads into the rule, it no longer can seriously be contended that the rule contributes in any robust way to substantial justice.[15] To be sure, an occasional case will turn on hearsay, and occasionally justice might be done because of exclusion for reason of hearsay, but against this must be balanced the probability that without a hearsay rule the evidence would have been excluded under some other rule, most likely relevancy. Further to be considered in the balance are cases of injustice resulting from the exclusion of hearsay as well as the astounding cost of maintaining the rule.
>
> The cost of maintaining the rule is not just a function of its contribution to justice. It also includes the time spent on litigating the rule. And of course that is not just a cost voluntarily borne by the parties, for in our system virtually all the cost of the court — salaries, administrative costs, and capital costs — are borne by the public. As expensive as litigation is for the parties, it is supported by an enormous public subsidy. Each time a hearsay question is litigated, the public pays. The rule imposes other costs as well. Enormous time is spent teaching and writing about the hearsay rule, which are both costly enterprises. In some law schools, students spend over half their time in evidence classes learning the intricacies of the hearsay rule, and . . . enormous academic resources are expended on the rule.
>
> Like other social practices, the hearsay rule should be required to pull its own freight; only if its costs are justified should it be maintained.

b. Regulation Premised on the Excesses of the Adversary System

One justification for regulating the admission of hearsay derives from the excesses of the adversary system of proof.

> Consider for instance, the possibility that a hearsay declarant might be a bad witness, or . . . might be shown incredible on cross-examination. A party might prefer to offer the [hearsay statement] rather than to call the declarant to the stand. In effect, such a choice would be a deliberate choice to mislead the factfinder, because the hearsay would not be accompanied by information that would enable the jury to evaluate the evidence properly. [Craig R. Callen, Foreword to the First Virtual Forum: Wallace Stevens, Blackbirds and the Hearsay Rule, 16 Miss. Col. L. Rev. 1, 10 (1995).]

Hearsay policy could be premised on mitigating this adversarial tactic. Professor Seigel proposes a principle for admitting hearsay only when it is the "best evidence" available from a particular declarant source. Seigel, 72 B.U. L. Rev. at 930-938. Professor Swift proposes that admission of hearsay be based on the production of a foundation witness who would be able to present information that the jury needs to evaluate the hearsay statement. Eleanor Swift, A Foundation Fact Approach to Hearsay, 75 Cal. L. Rev. 1339 (1987).

c. Notice-based Admission in Civil Cases: Reliance on the Adversary System

Several proposals have been made to admit hearsay more freely in civil cases, premised on sufficient notice to the opponent. Professor Roger Park recommends a

---

15. I put aside Confrontation Clause questions in criminal cases.

notice-based residual exception that makes no provision for reliability screening by judges in A Subject Matter Approach to Hearsay Reform, 86 Mich. L. Rev. 51 (1987). The proponent of hearsay would state whether the declarant is available or unavailable. Then, the opponent could demand that the declarant be produced and examined by the proponent and be available for cross-examination. In certain circumstances, the trial judge would be authorized to shift costs of production to the opponent. In the view of Professor Milich, all that is needed is notice of an intent to offer information from a source *not* to be called to testify at trial. The notice would include the name and location of the source so that the opponent could interview, depose, or produce the source if desired. Milich, 71 Ore. L. Rev. at 774-776.

d.   Why Hearsay Should Be Treated Differently in Criminal Cases

The confrontation clause does place a constraint on hearsay reform in criminal cases. Most legislators, courts, attorneys, and commentators agree that the criminal defendant's interest in personal liberty does weigh more heavily in favor of a requirement that the prosecution's use of hearsay be limited. Eileen A. Scallen, Constitutional Dimensions of Hearsay Reform: Toward a Three Dimensional Confrontation Clause, 76 Minn. L. Rev. 623 (1992). The approach in *Crawford* is to identify what might be thought of as the most *unreliable* categories of hearsay – testimonial statements – and to exclude them unless confrontation is or has been provided. These same risks of unreliability were identified previously by Professor Park in recommending that a categorical approach to admitting hearsay in criminal cases be maintained:

> Generally, out-of-court statements relevant to criminal cases are made, in the broadest sense, with a view to litigation, or at least with knowledge that the legal process may be brought to bear on the matter being described. . . . Moreover, many of the declarants' statements are taken by police, often under interrogation — a process essential in producing investigative leads but not calculated to elicit spontaneous statements that spring from a spirit of candor. [Park, A Subject Matter Approach to Hearsay, 86 Mich. L. Rev. at 94-97, 99.]

Under *Crawford*, prosecutors will remain constrained in their use of hearsay even should the hearsay rule itself be changed and further liberalized.

e.   Conclusion

This debate over hearsay reform should convince you of at least one thing: Hearsay evidence presents fundamental challenges to the values that underlie our system of trial proof — reliance on the inferential reasoning of lay fact finders, adversarial control of proof, and relaxed judicial control. Despite the liberalization of proof under the Federal Rules of Evidence, hearsay is treated with suspicion and remains subject to judicial regulation. None of the commentators discussed herein favors total abolition of the general rule against hearsay offered against criminal defendants.

CHAPTER NINE

LAY OPINIONS AND EXPERT WITNESSES

Recall the following portion of the *Johnson* transcript (direct examination of Officer Huston by Mr. Cummings):

Q: At some point in time it became clear to you that inmate Johnson was not going to slide the trays through the food port door.

A: No. When he picked up the trays and brought them to the food port it was not subtle, I guess. He didn't say anything, he was calm, walked up to the door and held the tray.

Q: At that point in time did somebody order the door be opened?

A: Yes. Officer Smith.

Q: And is that an appropriate method to get back the trays?

A: Yes.

MR. DEEMER: Excuse me. A, lack of qualifications; B, lack of foundation; and, C, it's leading.

THE COURT: Are you asking for an expert opinion, Mr. Cummings?

Q: BY MR. CUMMINGS: Officer Huston, you stated that you have worked as a correctional officer at Pelican Bay for six years?

A: Yes.

Q: And during those six years, did you receive special education and training for your job?

A: Yes.

Q: What was that?

A: There are training manuals, and training courses for correctional officers on-site and throughout the state that we attend.

Q: And does this training include the handling of specific problems that inmates sometimes cause?

A: Yes, it does.

Q: And based on this training, do you have an opinion on the proper means to handle situations like inmate Johnson's, that is, on whether it is appropriate to open the cell door? Just tell us whether you have an opinion.

A: Yes, I do.

MR. CUMMINGS: I would offer Officer Huston's opinion now as based on his special experiences and training at Pelican Bay.

THE COURT: You may answer.

Q: BY MR. CUMMINGS: Is opening the cell door an appropriate way to get back the food trays?

A: Yes, on the General Population side it is. If the inmates are General Population inmates so they are out of their cells a lot of the time and if they are, what we say, programmed and everything else and they seem calm and everything else, well, we — yeah, we get the trays that way, especially when they have more than two trays or have two trays with garbage on the top. . . .

Q: Was the door opened?

A: Yes, the door was opened.

Q: What happened when the door opened?

A: Inmate Johnson — when the door was opened up inmate Johnson immediately instantly dropped the food trays. He was standing just inside the door, up next to the door. Dropped the food trays immediately and bowed his head, brought up his fists and just tried to come through the door and hit Officer Walker in the chest.

Q: Where did Officer Walker make contact or where did Johnson make contact with Walker?

A: In the door. In the doorway after the door was opened. Officer Walker was on the outside of the cell. . . .

Q: What happened when Johnson charged the officers and made contact with Walker?

A: Officer Walker immediately grabbed him and pushed him inside the cell and inmate Johnson fell back up against the desk area, which is approximately three feet inside the cell.

Q: What was inmate Johnson doing at that time?

MR. DEEMER: One moment, Your Honor. I am going to object to that term. It's conclusionary.

THE COURT: Overruled.

Q: BY MR. CUMMINGS: Describe for me what you mean by "combative"?

A: Swinging his arms, not complying with orders, using his strength.

This short excerpt contains examples of two different kinds of opinions. The reference to Johnson as "combative" is a lay opinion. It relates not what the witness *observed*, but instead a *conclusion or inference* about a situation. In this case, the witness inferred from the observation of Johnson's "[s]winging his arms, not complying with orders, using his strength" that Johnson was primed for a fight and physically resisting the authority of the guards. He added to the testimony of his observations a summary of what he believed their import to be; he expressed an opinion, in other words. Witnesses are allowed, but not encouraged, to give lay opinions. Opinions always rest on underlying generalizations, and the value of the opinion is in direct proportion to the reliability of the underlying generalization. In this sense, the structure of lay opinions is identical to that of relevancy discussed in Chapter Three. It is the fact finder's task to determine the pertinent underlying generalizations and the extent to which they should be credited; it is the witness's task to provide an accurate recitation of what was observed. The lay opinion rule polices this boundary.

Often the boundary does not need formal policing. Note in the transcript that the direct examiner, Mr. Cummings, asked the witness to describe the factual basis of his conclusion, even though the judge let the witness testify in conclusory terms. This is because facts are usually more persuasive than opinions, and in this case the underlying factual predicate was not difficult to extract. In cases like this, the opinion rule is self-policing; the self-interest of the parties will generate the proper result.

Officer Huston also offered an "expert opinion" about the proper manner to retrieve trays. This opinion was based on his special training and experience as a correctional officer, which includes information not within the general run of human knowledge and experience. When such knowledge exists and would be helpful to a fact finder, it may be presented either through a description of the relevant knowledge or through the offering of expert opinions in the fashion of Officer Huston's testimony. Often experts provide information and opinions about scientific matters; but as this example demonstrates, expert testimony is not limited to science. It can extend to any knowledge that might be helpful but is not likely to be possessed by the fact finder.

In this chapter, we examine the various issues involved in the offering of opinions at trial, both lay and expert; we also examine the implications of the law's need for information from other disciplines that possess specialized knowledge. If the trial judge determines that a witness is offering a lay opinion, FRE 701 applies, as is discussed in Section A where we examine what lay opinions are and when they may be offered at trial.

If the judge determines a witness is offering an expert opinion or testifying about specialized knowledge, the remainder of Article VII, (FRE 702-706), applies. Section B examines expert testimony and the conditions under which specialized evidence may be adduced at trial. Section C addresses briefly the recurring problem of opinions being offered on ultimate issues of fact. Section D discusses the use of court appointed experts. Section E presents a number of areas involving scientific evidence and expert testimony in which there have been recent developments.

A. LAY OPINIONS

1. FRE 701

RULE 701.   OPINION TESTIMONY BY LAY WITNESSES
If the witness is not testifying as an expert, the witness' testimony in the form of opinions or inferences is limited to those opinions or inferences which are (a) rationally based on the perception of the witness, and (b) helpful to a clear understanding of the witness' testimony or the determination of a fact in issue, and (c) not based on scientific, technical or other specialized knowledge within the scope of Rule 702.

2. Interpretation and Illustration of FRE 701

FRE 701 captures the common law rule concerning lay opinions. Like its common law counterpart, the rule states a preference for witnesses not to testify in the form of opinions. In the traditional language of the common law, witnesses were to testify to what they observed (i.e., "facts") rather than to any inferences about, summaries of, or conclusions of fact, all of which together were referred to as "opinions." Notwithstanding the rule, the testimony in the form of opinions is common at trial, largely because it is common in our conventional manner of speaking. In a sexual harassment suit, for example, testimony that the defendant "winked" expresses a summary of observations in the form of a conclusion, which is to say an opinion. Consider another example: testimony concerning the speed of a car. A witness testifying that a car was going "approximately 60 miles an hour" is actually testifying about the conclusion of an unconscious calculation that computes the speed from watching the car pass a certain distance over a certain time. In the subsections below, we examine when such conclusory testimony is allowed and when it will likely be forbidden, and why.

a.   Fact versus Opinion

Some commentators believe that FRE 701 is more liberal than its common law counterparts, but generalizations are difficult because the line between "fact" and "opinion" is unclear. As early as 1878, a court commented that lay opinions were admissible on a wide variety of topics, including

> identity, handwriting, quantity, value, weight, measure, time, distance, velocity, form, size, age, strength, heat, cold, sickness, and health; questions also concerning various mental and moral aspects of humanity, such as disposition and temper, anger, fear, excitement, intoxication, veracity, general character, and particular phases of character, and other conditions and things, both moral and physical, too numerous to mention.

Hardy v. Merrill, 56 N.H. 227, 22 Am. Rep. 441 (1878).

The line between what is a fact and what is an "opinion" is unclear because the distinction is not an analytical one; it is a question of degree. All testimony involves "opinions." Consider the testimony of a witness that the blue car ran the red light. There is no scientific or analytical standard being applied here by the witness concerning what a "blue car" or a "red light" is. Rather, the witness is offering an "opinion" of what the witness thinks was observed. What this witness calls red, someone else may call green, and what this witness calls blue somebody else may call black. This may not convince you (although we think that on further reflection it will). Consider, then, that the witness will not be testifying to what happened but instead as to what the witness believes was observed. The witness's perspective may have been bad, whether known to the witness or not, and memory may have decayed. These points — observational and memory problems, whether realized or not — are unavoidable and make it clear that every word uttered at trial is an "opinion" of the person uttering the word.

If the distinction between "fact" and "opinion" is analytically untenable, you may be wondering why the rules of evidence nonetheless insist on making the distinction. Good question. The answer is that doing so pushes witnesses toward relating sensory impressions that are less rather than more thickly varnished. Testimony can be more or less loaded with opinions (inferences, summaries, and conclusions), and we prefer to have less rather than more. Even though relating sensory impressions ("I saw the blue car run the red light") involves opinions ("I *believe* I saw . . ."), the more testimony concentrates on relating sensory impressions, the easier it is for the fact finder to mediate among conflicting versions from the various witnesses, and thus to decide what actually happened almost as though the juror had access to the inner workings of the witnesses' minds. The juror is aided in this task by quite liberal rules of cross-examination that allow the cognitive and affective states of witnesses to be examined thoroughly for whatever clues they may yield as to why the witnesses testified as they did.

The question of how to distinguish between allowable and inappropriate lay opinions remains, but very little more can be suggested than a reliance on common sense, which is precisely what many common law courts appeared to do by applying an "I know it when I see it" standard for defining opinions. Thus, virtually all judges would agree that the statement "the platform was dangerous" is an opinion whereas the assertions "John shot me" or "the object is a chair" are statements of fact. The difficulty, of course, is that this does not provide much guidance for classifying statements. For example, what about a statement that the defendant was "speeding" or was driving "recklessly" or was driving "too fast given the weather conditions"? Moreover, even supposedly clear examples may be unclear in some contexts. Is the statement "John shot me" one of fact or opinion if we know that John and Jim are identical twins?

Although relying on "common sense" is often problematic, here there is no plausible alternative. The legitimate concern underlying the prohibition against lay opinions, upon which common sense will operate, is that we do not want witnesses to substitute their conclusions for facts that would be helpful to the jury. Thus, in the dangerous platform case, we would prefer to have the witness describe to the jury the condition of the platform in some detail. Without the detailed information about the condition of the platform, the jury's only choice would be whether to rely on the conclusion of the witness, and the condition of the platform most likely will not defy straightforward description. With the detailed information the jurors would be in a better position to determine for themselves whether the platform was dangerous, and this is what we want them to do. Similarly, in the identical twin case, we would prefer to have the victim describe the particular characteristics of the assailant or the prior encounters with John that led the victim to conclude that the assailant was John rather than Jim, which should be relatively easy to do. In short, in cases like these, sustaining a lay opinion objection rather obviously, "commonsensically", forces the witness to articulate the underlying details that gave rise to their "opinion" without impeding the efficient flow of the trial.

b. Rationally Based on the Perception of the Witness

Bear in mind that the lay opinion rule does not excuse or substitute for the requirement of firsthand knowledge; indeed, section (a) of FRE 701 restates the firsthand knowledge requirement. The rule merely allows firsthand knowledge to be summarized in the form of an opinion. For a good example of the import of this point, see Alexis v. McDonald's Restaurants of Mass., Inc., 67 F.3d 341 (1st Cir 1995). In *Alexis*, the plaintiff got into an argument with a McDonald's employee. The manager asked the plaintiff to leave. She refused and was arrested. Later she filed a civil rights action alleging racial discrimination. On motion for summary judgment, she offered depositions of eyewitness family members and an unrelated eyewitness that contained opinions to the effect that the plaintiff would have been treated differently had she been "a rich white woman." The only bases for these opinions were that the McDonald's staff had reacted angrily toward the plaintiff, with "a negative tone," and were generally unfriendly and impolite. As the court pointed out in affirming exclusion of the evidence, such actions may be consistent with racial discrimination, but they do not demonstrate it. The opinions to the contrary, in short, were not rationally based on firsthand knowledge.

You must bear in mind how case specific these rulings are. In Bohannon v. Pegelow, 652 F.2d 729 (7th Cir. 1981), plaintiff filed a civil rights action alleging wrongful arrest. The trial court allowed, and the Seventh Circuit affirmed, testimony from a friend of the plaintiff that the arrest was motivated by racial prejudice, despite the fact that the rest of the witness's testimony did not contain any facts indicating prejudice. The court rejected the argument that the testimony could not have been rationally based on the perception of the witness. The court said it was enough that the witness had observed the arrest: "When, as here, the witness observes first hand the altercation in question, her opinions on the feelings of the parties are based on her personal knowledge and rational perceptions and are helpful to the jury." The appellate court believed this to be similar to the cases that admitted lay opinions concerning the state of another, such as United States v. Lawson, 653 F.2d 299 (7th Cir. 1981), admitting the FBI agent's testimony that the defendant was sane. In your judgment, what is the lesson here? Is it that few generalizations will operate in this context? That the rulings will be radically case specific? That *Alexis* and *Bohanon* are inconsistent? It is impossible to say from the cold appellate record. The conclusion of a trial judge to permit opinion testimony is conditioned by all the events at trial, including behavioral cues from the witnesses that are not reflected in the record. This in turn means that trial court decisions on lay opinions are largely unreviewable. We know the proper question: Is the witness testifying rationally from firsthand knowledge? But there are virtually no standards available to systematically judge the answer given.

c.   *Helpful to a Clear Understanding of the Witness's Testimony or the Determination of a Fact in Issue*

If a judge is convinced that a witness is testifying from firsthand knowledge, even though expressed in the form of an opinion (e.g., "The defendant was belligerent"), the judge may allow the testimony if it is "helpful to a clear understanding of the witness' testimony or the determination of a fact in issue." When is that? Again, it is very difficult to say in a systematic way, which means that once more trial judges will be invested with substantial discretion. The pertinent concerns are easily identifiable, however. The purpose of the lay opinion rule is to facilitate a certain mode of proceeding at trial. The more opinions are allowed, the more the witness usurps the role of the fact finder. The fact finder is the one charged to draw inferences; the witnesses are to relate factual observations, leaving to the fact finder the inferences to be drawn from those factual observations. This point is illustrated in Lynch v. City of Boston, 180 F.3d 1, 16 (1st Cir. 1999). Helen Lynch sued the City of Boston alleging that she was wrongfully terminated from her position with the City's "Can Share" hunger program. At trial, Lynch sought admission of the testimony of one of her coworkers, Michael Devlin, on the specific question of whether her work was adequate. Specifically, Lynch sought to have Devlin answer the question: "In the time that you worked in the

Can Share program, who would you say was responsible for the success and growth the program had?" Though Devlin had years of experience working with Lynch, the trial court ruled his testimony on this question inadmissible, stating

> Even though rationally based on the witness's personal perception, lay opinion testimony will be excluded if it is not "helpful" to the trier of fact.... Lay opinions are not helpful when the jury can readily draw the necessary inferences and conclusions without the aid of the opinion.... Here, as Lynch herself points out, Devlin testified at some length concerning his personal observation of Lynch's excellent organizational skills, her proficiency at long-term program planning, her "phenomenal" ability to recruit participants from the business community, her "incredible" motivational skills, and her ability to communicate clearly. Devlin testified that Lynch's ability to recruit in the business community "brought in a lot of people to take part in the campaign fully." Contrary to Lynch's assertion that the jury could not determine "how effective plaintiff was in her job" without Devlin's lay opinion, the jury, unaided by Devlin's opinion, could readily have drawn the inference from Devlin's detailed factual account of Lynch's exceptional work at Can Share that Lynch was quite effective in her position and was responsible for the success and growth of the Can Share program during the time she and Devlin worked together.... Hence the district court may well have believed — in finding the opinion not to pertain to an appropriate subject for lay opinion testimony — that it would simply not be helpful. [citations omitted]

In a similar case, the court excluded, and its opinion was upheld on appeal, testimony from a son and former wife that a person in a photograph was the father/former husband. United States v. Dixon, 413 F.3d 540 (6th Cir. 2005). There was testimony that the defendant's physical appearance had not changed from the time of the photograph to the time of trial, the photo was of good quality, and thus the jury would not be helped by the testimony of the son and former wife.

"Helpfulness" has two sides to it. In addition to being helpful to the fact finder, presenting lay opinions can be helpful to the orderly presentation of testimony by permitting individuals to testify consistent with their normal use of language. If insisting on testimony about "facts" rather than "opinions" proves difficult if not impossible, and impedes rather than facilitates inquiry at trial, lay opinions should be allowed. In many instances, the underlying generalization or the very observations themselves defy articulation by the witness, or the elaboration of such generalizations would be a waste of time. When either is the case, the purposes of trial are advanced by allowing the "lay opinion." Earlier, we gave the statement that the defendant winked at the plaintiff as an example of an opinion testimony in a harassment suit. "Winking" is a summary of a complex physical act. A witness could be required to describe scrunching up one's nose and closing an eyelid while leaning forward with a provocative look on one's face (but what is a "provocative look"?), but no obvious benefit would come from imposing this requirement on the witness. Thus, virtually all judges would allow the lay opinion about a wink. Consider also the example of testimony about the speed of a car. Forcing witnesses to testify about such matters in a nonconclusory fashion — to make them testify about observations of distance divided by time and to forbid them from testifying that the car was going approximately 60 miles an hour — would make it virtually impossible to get useful information from them. Similarly, when a witness identifies another person with whom the witness is acquainted, the witness can just say "That's John," rather than say "John has a certain facial structure just like the person you are asking me to identify," and so on. In such cases, FRE 701 permits testimony in the form of an opinion.

Compare testimony about winking or the speed of a car to testimony that a person observed by a witness was drunk. Like testimony that a person winked at somebody, testimony that a person was drunk is a summary of observations such as lack of balance, fumbling around, slurred speech, and odor of alcohol. Unlike testimony about speed of cars or winking, these matters can be testified to fairly easily. Thus, many courts would exclude testimony that a person was "drunk," and instead insist that the witness relate the observations on which that conclusion was based.

There is a line of cases that fairly directly indicates that FRE 701 permits the trial courts to align testimony at trial with our normal conventions of both observing and relating what we observe. Appraising the state of mind of another person is something that is done constantly in life, but often is done on the basis of nonverbal cues that are difficult to describe. Think of your use of the word "impression." When you have an "impression" that someone is upset, angry, or depressed, what exactly do you mean? When you express such a view, and a friend queries you about it, do you normally respond by shrugging your shoulders and saying, "I don't know, I just had the impression that...." Not surprisingly, in similar situations courts often admit lay opinions. For example, in United States v. Garcia, 982 F. Supp. 112 (D.P.R. 1997), the court admitted lay opinion testimony that the defendant did not seem mentally retarded and that she "appeared to be logical." Though witnesses should not be forced to break their testimony into the smallest component parts, judges must be watchful and prevent witnesses from, either purposely or carelessly, drawing conclusions that they are no more qualified than the jury to reach. Witnesses were held to this standard even before the passage of the Federal Rules of Evidence. In Tyndall v. Harvey, 226 N.C. 620 (1946), the court found that the trial court had erred by allowing a nonexpert witness who had arrived at the scene in the aftermath of an accident, to testify about the speed of one of the cars involved. The witness testified about the position of the car and the skid marks left on the pavement and then deduced the car's speed. On appeal, the court explained:

> [O]ne who did not see a vehicle in motion will not be permitted to give an opinion as to its speed. The "opinion" must be a fact observed. The witness must speak of facts within his knowledge. He cannot, under the guise of an opinion, give his deductive conclusion from what he saw and knew. [Id. at 624.]

This standard did not substantially change with the adoption of the Federal Rules nor has it changed over the subsequent 30 years.

Of course, the benefits of opinion testimony must be balanced by its risks, but in general these are small. Judge Learned Hand explained why there need be no great fear about lay opinion testimony in United States v. Cotter, 60 F.2d 689, 693-694 (2d Cir. 1932):

> No rule is subject to greater abuse [than the opinion testimony rule]; it is frequently an obstacle to any intelligible account of what happens. Most witnesses will tell their story in colloquial speech which skips the foundations and runs in terms of the "ultimate facts." Ordinarily, they tell it much more plainly in this way, and the warrant for what they say can be perfectly probed by cross-examination.

d. Not Based on Scientific, Technical, or Other Specialized Knowledge Within the Scope of Rule 702

Section (c) of FRE 701 was added as an amendment in 2000. To understand fully its significance requires you to first work through the remainder of the material in this chapter. In brief, this is what you will find. The Supreme Court has interpreted FRE 702 to require trial judges to act as gatekeepers to the admissibility of expert testimony. The trial judge must be convinced that the expert is testifying on the basis of knowledge acquired in a reliable way and applied appropriately to the case at hand. The form of knowledge most likely to meet such standards is the results of controlled scientific studies, but the scope of expert testimony, as you will soon see, reaches far beyond "scientific knowledge" to "scientific, technical, or other specialized knowledge." FRE 702. The Supreme Court also instructed the lower courts that "technical or other specialized knowledge" must be justified in ways at least roughly analogous to the justifications for the admissibility of "scientific knowledge." This increased the difficulty of gaining admission of certain forms of testimony that previously had passed muster under FRE 702. In response, trial lawyers began offering such testimony as "lay opinions" under FRE 701, directly contravening the Supreme Court's interpretation of the rules. See, e.g., Asplundh Mfg. Div. v. Benton Harbor Eng'g, 57 F.3d 1190 (3d Cir. 1995) (Courts have "commonly interpreted [Rule 701] to permit individuals not qualified as experts but possessing experience or specialized knowledge about particular things, to testify about technical matters that might have been thought to lie within the exclusive province of experts."). The rule was amended to put a stop to that practice. As the Advisory Committee commented:

> Rule 701 has been amended to eliminate the risk that the reliability requirements set forth in Rule 702 will be evaded through the simple expedient of proffering an expert in lay witness clothing. Under the amendment, a witness' testimony must be scrutinized under the rules regulating expert opinion to the extent that the witness is providing testimony based on scientific, technical, or other specialized knowledge within the scope of Rule 702. By channeling testimony that is actually expert testimony to Rule 702, the amendment also ensures that a party will not evade the expert witness disclosure requirements set forth in Fed. R. Civ. P. 26 and Fed. R. Crim. P. 16.

A few trial court decisions have been reversed under Rule 701(c), but it is unlikely that such reversals will ever become common. More than as a change in the law, this amendment should be understood as an admonition to trial judges that they must conscientiously apply the rule appropriate to a situation and limit testimony to that which a witness, as designated, is qualified to offer. But see, e.g., JGR, Inc. v. Thomasville Furniture Indus., 370 F.3d 519 (6th Cir. 2004) (vacating damage award where award was based on improper admission of accountant's testimony under FRE 701 and accountant should have been classified as expert under FRE 702); Bank of China v. NBM LLC, 359 F.3d 171 (2d Cir. 2004) (ruling that admission of bank employee's testimony on bank practice, which spanned several days of trial, was erroneous under FRE 701 but might be admissible under FRE 702).

Even prior to the revision to Rule 701(c), many courts recognized a rigid division between expert and lay testimony. See, e.g., Certain Underwriter's at Lloyd's, London v. Synkovich, 232 F.3d 200 (4th Cir. 2000) ("This rule . . . generally does 'not permit a lay witness to express an opinion as to matters which are beyond the realm of common experience and which require the special skill and knowledge of an expert witness.' ") (citing Randolph v. Collectramatic, Inc., 590 F.2d 844, 846 (10th Cir. 1979). This amendment allows judges much discretion to tailor a ruling on the admissibility of testimony to the qualifications and the extent of first hand knowledge of an individual witness. See, e.g., United States v. Ayala-Pizarro, 407 F.3d 25 (1st Cir. 2005) (law enforcement agent allowed to testify about nature of drug distribution points and what occurs there without being qualified as expert, because knowledge of points was gained through firsthand observation). Rules 701 and 702 distinguish between expert and lay testimony rather than expert and lay witnesses and so it is possible for the same witness to provide both lay and expert testimony in a single case. See, e.g., United States v. Figueroa-Lopez, 125 F.3d 1241, 1246 (9th Cir. 1997) (law enforcement agents allowed to testify that the defendant was acting suspiciously, without being qualified as experts; however, the rules on experts were applicable where the agents testified on the basis of extensive experience that the defendant was using code words to refer to drug quantities and prices). This allows judges to faithfully follow the letter and spirit of Rule 702 and yet not be forced into formulaic exclusions of testimony. We are about to turn to expert testimony. When you have finished studying that material, you will be in a better position to appraise the significance of this amendment and may want to return to this section to reconsider its implications.

3.   Elaboration of FRE 701: Trial Court Discretion

As we have tried to show, FRE 701 basically stands as an admonition to the trial judge to preserve the role of the fact finder, but not to impede significantly the progress of the trial. Little more can be said about the matter, as indicated by the small number of appellate cases finding trial courts' decisions under FRE 701 to be reversible error. Because it is largely an admonition, its implementation is left largely to the discretion of the trial judges. This does not mean that the rule is of no consequence. Rather, it means that its importance lies primarily in its implications for trial preparation and strategy for the opposing attorneys.

Interestingly, there is no logical need for a special evidentiary provision dealing with lay opinions. A court could rely on FRE 402 and FRE 403 to exclude opinions or conclusions that are not helpful to the fact finder. However, the absence of a lay opinion provision in a general codification of evidentiary rules would be ambiguous. It might suggest that the common law prohibition against opinions should not be disturbed or equally plausible, that it had been rejected. Perhaps the primary utility of FRE 701 is simply to indicate that the Federal Rules maintain the common law's approach to opinions.

Although the vast run of cases indicates the breadth of discretion vested in trial courts, on occasion the failure to exclude a lay opinion will be reversible error. An example is United States v. Forrester, 60 F.3d 52 (2d Cir. 1995), holding that the trial court's allowance of a lay opinion concerning the credibility of another witness was reversible error. In *Forrester*, two men were indicted for conspiracy to distribute cocaine. At trial, an acquaintance of the two men testified that she had smuggled drugs for them and that she had so informed an FBI agent when interviewed by him. She also testified that she had identified one of the men from a photograph during that same interview. Neither of these allegations appeared in the agent's report. Later, the FBI agent was called to testify about his investigation of the case. The agent's report, made during the investigation, showed that the witness had identified one of the men, but not the other, as the only person who had asked her to smuggle drugs. The agent was then read the witness's earlier testimony, and was asked whether her testimony was in any way "inconsistent" with what she had previously told him. Over the defense's objection, the agent was allowed to testify that he "didn't find her testimony to be inconsistent." The government tried to justify the agent's testimony on the grounds that he was the only person present for both the interview and the witness's trial testimony, and thus that his testimony would be "helpful" to the jury. The trial court, while allowing the testimony, gave a special jury instruction: "In light of [the agent's] testimony regarding the testimony of another witness here today, I want to remind the members of the jury, and I instruct the members of the jury, that it is the function of the jury to determine the credibility of each witness." The judge's instruction and the government's contention were not enough in the eyes of the appellate court. The court stated that, as a matter of law, the credibility of witnesses is exclusively for the determination of the jury, and witnesses cannot express their opinion as to the credibility of other witnesses. "Far from being helpful," the court said, the agent's testimony "invaded the traditional province of the jury." The court also felt that the government was trying to "cloak" the witness's testimony with the "heightened credibility" some jurors afford testimony given by government witnesses.

Although there are cases like *Forrester* requiring the exclusion of lay opinions, courts operating under the Federal Rules have been fairly liberal in overruling objections based on FRE 701. In United States v. Skeet, 665 F.2d 983 (9th Cir. 1982), the court gave as examples of permissible lay opinions the mental or physical condition of a person, his or her character or reputation, emotions manifested by the person's acts, speed of a moving object, size, height, odor, flavor, color, and heat. However, the same court approved the trial court's refusal to permit an opinion that a shooting was accidental, indicating again the trial judge's discretion over these matters. Similarly, United States v. Lawson, 653 F.2d 299 (7th Cir. 1981), affirmed admission of the opinions of FBI agents that the defendant was "sane." Compare Gorby v. Schneider Tank Lines, 741 F.2d 1015 (7th Cir. 1984), upholding a trial court's exclusion of an opinion in a suit arising out of a collision between a truck and a semitanker that the driver of the tanker "did everything he could to avoid this accident." These cases also demonstrate how case-specific rulings on opinions are. In some instances, the underlying facts might be easy to describe, whereas in others it would be quite difficult. Trial judges have a great deal of discretion in deciding which is the case, and rarely are their determinations reversed on appeal.

An example of how case-specific rulings on lay opinions can be is a series of cases dealing with whether a police detective can testify about the identity of a person in surveillance photographs taken during robberies. Compare two, United States v. Henderson, 68 F.3d 323 (9th Cir. 1995), and United States v. Lapierre, 998 F.2d 1460 (9th Cir. 1993). In *Lapierre*, the court ruled that the officer's testimony was inadmissible because he had not known the defendant before the robbery investigation, and thus had no substantial previous contact with him. His only knowledge of the defendant's appearance came from photographs or from eyewitness descriptions. Consequently, the court concluded that his testimony would not be "helpful" to the jury, and would invade the jury's role. The court stated that there were two cases where this sort of identification would be allowed — where the identifying officer had had substantial contact with the defendant, and where the defendant's appearance had changed from the time the surveillance photographs were taken and the time the defendant was on trial.

In *Henderson*, the court allowed the officer's testimony, stating that it did "not require a showing of both sustained contact and special knowledge as prerequisites to a lay witness giving identification testimony." Even though the court held that "specialized knowledge" of the defendant was not required, in this particular case the witness had such knowledge, because he had seen the defendant wearing a heavy overcoat, of the same sort worn by the robber in the bank's photographs. The jury had not seen the defendant wearing the coat, which the court felt could lead to an incorrect conclusion regarding his "weight and bulk." The *Henderson* court also noted that the witness had known the defendant for over 15 years and was thus "more likely" than the jury to make a correct identification of him.

The common law prohibition against lay opinions was informed by one other concern, which is the desire to forbid witnesses from expressing an opinion on the ultimate issue in the case. Interestingly, even though FRE 704 has eliminated the common law prohibition of opinions on ultimate issues, it remains true that the more germane an opinion is to an ultimate issue, the more likely the courts seem to be to require a recitation of the facts underlying the opinion. As one court said, "the closer the subject of the opinion gets to critical issues, the likelier the judge is to require the witness to be more concrete." United States v. Allen, 10 F.3d 405, 414 (7th Cir. 1993). We discuss FRE 704 in Section C, infra.

KEY POINTS

1. The concern underlying the prohibition against lay opinions is that a witness's opinion (inferences, summaries, or conclusions) may sometimes deprive the jurors of important data they need to perform their fact-finding role.

2. Whether a jury is deprived of important data does not depend on an *a priori* distinction between fact and opinion. It depends instead on an assessment of what information will be optimally helpful to jurors in their fact-finding role in the context of a particular case.

3. If a summary or conclusion that foregoes underlying details will be adequate for the jury's purposes, the testimony in that form should be admissible. If, to the contrary, the jurors need underlying details and it is feasible to provide them, the witness should be required to provide those details rather than the witness's own summary or conclusion.

PROBLEMS

9.1. Defendant was driving his car, and crashed into Plaintiff's car at an intersection. Plaintiff alleges that Defendant was driving over the speed limit, was intoxicated, and ran a red light. To establish these facts, Plaintiff wants to call W_1, who was at the scene and will testify that Defendant, when he exited his car, was wobbly and looked like he was drunk, and that the smell of alcohol was detectable. W_2 will testify that he was getting his hair cut in a barber shop about a mile away from the accident and observed Defendant's car "whiz by the barber shop going about 70 miles an hour." W_3 will testify that she heard the squeal of tires that could only be made by a car greatly exceeding the speed limit trying to stop quickly, that she looked up and "thought she saw Defendant's car enter the intersection while the light was against him" but she "can't be positive that's so." W₄, also at the scene, will testify that the first thing Defendant did when he got out of his car after the wreck is walk toward Plaintiff's car, trip over a small piece of wire, get up, and say, "My God, I need another drink," although W₄ isn't absolutely sure that Defendant said "another." Can all these witnesses testify accordingly?

9.2. In his capacity as an auto parts delivery driver, Jack Miller delivered metal tubing to Prairie Center Muffler. Miller was directed to place the tubing on a storage rack inside Prairie Center. The storage rack had been constructed by Prairie Center a number of years prior and was not affixed to the wall or the floor.

Miller alleges that while loading the tubing onto the storage rack, both the metal tubing and the storage rack fell onto him, causing him to fall to the ground and be seriously injured. Miller alleges that by constructing the rack to hold metal tubing, but failing to secure the rack to the wall, Prairie Center created and maintained an unreasonably dangerous condition, which ultimately caused the rack, with the metal tubing, to fall over on him and to cause him serious injury.

Miller concedes that he did not see the rack fall because he had his back to the rack when it allegedly fell over. He would testify as follows:

> The rack had approximately six levels of support arms on which the tubing was to be stacked. The support arms were made of either metal rods or metal tubing. I placed the various diameters of tubing on the various support arms and turned my back to the rack. When I was 4 or 5 feet away from the rack, with my back to it, the rack tipped over and one of the metal support arms struck me on my left upper back/left shoulder, dug into my left upper back, left shoulder, and left arm, and threw me to the floor.
>
> I have been a weightlifter all my life and am familiar with weights and forces. I also had extensive experience handling, lifting, and carrying the tubing that I was placing on the rack. The force and weight of what hit me was such that I know it was the rack — it could not have only been the metal tubing. Had the metal tubing fallen off the rack and hit me, it would not have had the weight or the force to have dug into my back, shoulder and arm nor would it have had the weight or the force to have thrown me to the ground.
>
> Further, I know that the rack tipped over because of the distance I was from the rack when it hit me and threw me to the ground. Had the metal tubing rolled off the support arms, they would have cascaded downward like a waterfall. They would not have flown horizontally across the room, five or six feet above the ground, and struck me in the upper back and shoulder. Nor would the tubing have had the force necessary to push me to the ground. On the other hand, the rack tipping over would have reached me, where I stood, and would have had the force to have knocked me to the ground.

Should Miller's testimony be admissible lay opinion under Rule 701? Argue for and against admissibility.

9.3. Mr. Sheley regularly abused his wife, violently beating her, running her over with a car, and threatening her with a gun and other deadly weapons. Though Mrs. Sheley had never before responded with force, she killed him during one of his brutal attacks. On that occasion, Mrs. Sheley shot and killed her husband with a handgun while Mr. Sheley threatened her and her daughters with a shotgun.

Mr. Sheley had previously purchased a life insurance policy that provided for double benefits in the case of accidental death. Under Georgia law, the death of an insured spouse during a domestic dispute is considered accidental for the purposes of redeeming life insurance if the decedent reasonably believed that his wife would not respond to his aggression with force. Gail, Mrs. Sheley's daughter, testified that she believed that Mr. Sheley never thought that Mrs. Sheley would shoot him. After the jury found the death to have been accidental, the insurance company appealed. It argued that Gail's testimony should not have been admitted under Rule 701 because Gail could not have had personal knowledge of Mr. Sheley's subjective state of mind and that Gail's opinions were therefore not rationally based upon her perceptions. Should the appellate court reverse?

9.4. In a real estate deal gone sour, several hotel chains were sued for breach of contract by DIJO, Inc., the real estate developer for a project in Tunica, MI. The project never got beyond the planning stages. During the portion of the trial on lost profits, Kerry Skinner (a lay witness, representing DIJO's potential lender and otherwise uninvolved in the project) testified that "based on projected earnings of $1 million per year, the value of the Project to DIJO was $8,000,007." Skinner was a knowledgeable financial consultant, but his testimony revealed that he had little significant actual knowledge about DIJO and its operations. The jury later returned an $8 million plaintiff's verdict. Should Skinner's testimony have been permitted?

9.5. Police officers in New Bern, North Carolina, found Eddie Roberts on his kitchen floor, dead from a bullet wound to the head. At the trial of Don Duncan, a witness, Dove, testified that he saw a man fire a rifle into Roberts's kitchen. "It was dark, but the man looked to be about the same size and height of Don Duncan." The witness was familiar with Duncan's appearance because he was acquainted with Duncan and had seen him earlier on the day of the murder. Again explaining what he had witnessed, the witness stated:

> I couldn't tell what kind of clothes he had on. The rifle sounded like a .22 — in my opinion, it was a .22. I had a chance to see the man, but I couldn't tell who he was. After he shot the rifle, he climbed over the fence and crossed Broad Street. He was about the same size and height of Don. I am not willing to identify any man that I couldn't see his face. There are hundreds of people in town who are the same height and I have seen a lot of people in this town who are the same size.

Is all of Dove's testimony admissible?

9.6. On April 12, 1964, Texas Gulf Sulfur Company issued an optimistic press release about the results of its recent exploratory drilling in Timmins, Ontario. The press release led to a substantial increase in the price of the company's stock, benefiting several corporate officials who had purchased large quantities of the stock only days before. The SEC filed charges of insider trading against the corporate officials and charged the company with making a misleading statement that might make reasonable investors rely on it. The SEC introduces several investors who testified as lay witnesses that the press release created erroneous impressions. Should this testimony be allowed?

9.7. Annie Hester worked in the BIC Corporation's order-processing department for seven years before BIC merged its order-processing department with its customer service department. Beck, the manager of the new department, may have shown favoritism to those employees from the old customer service department and thus there was some tension in the new group. Despite Beck's recommendation of an employee from the old customer service department, Hester was promoted to a group leadership position for which she was well qualified. After only a few months in the new position, customers began complaining about Hester's performance and

Beck transferred her to another department. Hester sued BIC for race discrimination, alleging that Beck had given white Group Leaders additional training and feedback and had promoted a white employee with fewer qualifications than Hester to replace her. Hester called four lay witnesses who were prepared to testify to the following:

(1) Mary Ende, a white file clerk, believed that Beck treated those from the customer service department like "stepchildren." She did not know anything about Hester's performance as a Group Leader. (2) Darlene Miller, a white employee who had worked with Hester prior to the merging of the two departments, felt that Beck "was mean to everyone in order-processing, but she was more mean to Hester." Like Ende, Miller admitted that she, too, had no personal knowledge of Hester's job performance. (3) Patricia Wright, an African-American receptionist who had been fired from BIC, had had the chance to observe Beck's treatment of Hester but was more eager to testify that her own termination had been because of race and that she had received mysterious racist phone calls around the time of her dismissal. (4) Lillian Turner, an African-American employee, had observed on two or three occasions Beck treating Hester with "borderline disrespect and condescension" but had never seen Beck treating white employees in this way. Turner was herself suing BIC for racial discrimination and wished to explain that, absent any other reason, she believed she must have been treated poorly because of her race.

How, if at all, should the trial judge limit this testimony?

9.8. Two former corporate executives of Cal Micro, Henke and Douglas, were accused of being part of a false revenue reporting conspiracy that portrayed the company as a good investment option when in reality it was struggling. Proving that Henke and Douglas had knowledge of the false reporting scheme was critical to the government's case. To do this, it called Wade Meyercord, Douglas's replacement as Chairman of Cal Micro's Board of Directors, and asked him about the Board's reasons for terminating the defendants:

Q. [Prosecution]: What happened next . . . ?
A. [Meyercord]: There was another Board meeting in October of '94, so that the — later that month. I don't recall the exact date. At which time, if I recall correctly, we removed Mr. Douglas as Chairman of the company, and I was elected Chairman.
Q. Why did you remove — yeah, why did you remove Mr. Douglas?
[Defense counsel]: Objection, Your Honor.
The court: You can rephrase that, counsel.
Q. [Prosecution]: If you know, what — how did the Board reach that decision?
[Defense counsel]: Your honor, that's simply an opinion that they reached — conclusion that they reached.
The court: Well, no. I think the witness can testify as to the understanding that he has of the reason that the Board took that action. That's, I think, the appropriate question. All right? With that in mind, Mr. Meyercord, what is your understanding of the reason that the Board took the action which you did in removing Mr. Douglas as Chairman of the Board?
A. Because we felt there was — we removed Mr. Douglas as Chairman because we felt there was a high probability that he knew that the revenues had been misstated and that we could not in good conscience leave him in that position. . . .

Q. [Prosecution]:   Did Mr. Henke resign around this time period?

A. [Meyercord]:   Yes, he did.

Q. And was — were you aware of the fact that he had negotiated a severance package with Mr. Douglas?

A. I became aware later, yes.

Q. Well, Mr. Meyercord, did the Board accept this severance packet?

A. No, we did not.

Q. Why not?

[Defense counsel]:   Well, I object to it, Your Honor, on the same grounds that we've objected to the other documents, that it's prejudicial, and it's — actually this is testimony.

The court: Well, now, no speaking objections, Mr. Hallinan. What's the basis of the objection?

[Defense counsel]:   Well, first of all, under the circumstances, it's so prejudicial. That's one. Second of all, there's no basis for it, doesn't show any special knowledge. And third of all, it calls for an opinion of this witness.

The court: Overruled. The witness may testify as to his understanding of the reason that the Board took the action which it did.

[Meyercord]:   The Board — the Board did not feel that a severance package for Mr. Henke was appropriate given the evidence we had in front of us.

Q. What evidence was that?

[Defense counsel]:   Well, there, Your Honor. Object to that.

The court: Objection overruled.

A. The evidence that the revenue had been misstated.

Q. Did you have an understanding as a Board — did you learn as a Board member what Mr. Henke's role was in that?

[Defense counsel]:   Your honor, what relevance — ?

The court: Objection overruled.

Q. Did you learn in the investigation — ?

The court: What was the witness's understanding of the facts?

[Prosecution]:   Right.

Q. What was your understanding of the facts as they concerned Mr. Henke?

A. My understanding of the facts were that Mr. Henke must have known about this — about the revenue misstatements.

[Defense counsel]:   Well, I'll move to strike that. That is just an opinion, he "must have known." That shouldn't even be before the jury, Your Honor.

The court: Objection overruled.

[Prosecution]:   No further questions, Your Honor.

The defendants appealed the conviction. Should the court have excluded the opinion testimony that the defendants "must have known"?

9.9. A police officer investigating a murder found a hatchet near the scene of the crime. In the trial of the accused, should the officer be allowed to testify to his estimation of how long the hatchet had rested in that spot? Or, should the officer be required to describe that the area where he found the hatchet contained old, brown, moist grass in the late stages of decomposition, and that when he retrieved the hatchet, its face was caked with moist, decomposing grass? Or both?

B. EXPERT WITNESSES

Expert witnesses present evidence based on knowledge acquired through specialized study or unusual training and experience that permits them to generate, piece together, or interpret data in a manner that would not be readily apparent to the fact finder. Experts can be useful at every stage of the fact-finding process:

(1) Experts can generate evidentiary facts themselves. An example is a chemist who has analyzed a substance in a case in which the chemical makeup of the substance matters, such as in litigation over water pollution or a criminal drug charge. Another example is the medical worker who does blood or tissue analysis. Such individuals provide basic facts for the fact finder.

(2) Experts can educate the jury regarding specialized or scientific information that is needed to draw inferences about evidentiary facts. For example, with respect to the safety of a car's construction, an engineer may testify to the tensile strength of its component metals. Another example is a medical specialist who educates the fact finder about the implications of symptoms of disease.

(3) Most prevalent, and in our view least justifiable, experts may present inferences and conclusions to which fact finders may defer. A psychiatrist who testifies about the sanity of a criminal defendant is an example; a scientist who testifies that water pollution caused a person's health problems is another. A fact finder may have to rely on little more than a hunch when choosing to defer, and accept as accurate, the scientifically sophisticated conclusions of one of two conflicting experts.

Given the many roles they can play, it is not surprising that experts are ubiquitous in both state and federal trials today

SAMUEL GROSS, EXPERT EVIDENCE
1991 Wis. L. Rev. 1113, 1118-1120

There is next to nothing to be learned from published data on the use of experts in American litigation. A few patchy studies report that experts are used in a sizeable minority of felony prosecutions, and that they are more likely to be called by the prosecution. There are no systematic studies of the use of experts in civil cases. The data described here will begin to fill that gap. They are based on reports on 529 civil trials that led to jury verdicts in California State Superior Courts in 1985 and 1986. . . .

1. *The frequency of expert testimony.* Experts testified in 86% of these civil jury trials. Overall, there were an average of 3.3 experts per trial; in the trials in which any experts appeared, there were an average of 3.8. Most trials with experts had two, three, four or five of them. Plaintiffs called more expert witnesses than defendants — about 64% of the total.

2. *The specialties of expert witnesses.* Half of the experts in our data were medical doctors, and an additional 9% were other medical professionals — clinical psychologists, rehabilitation specialists, dentists, etc. Engineers, scientists and related experts

made up the next largest category, nearly 20% of the total. The only other sizeable categories were experts on various aspects of business and finance (11%), and experts in reconstruction and investigation (8%).

3. *The cases in which experts appear.* Over 70% of these trials concerned claims of wrongful death or personal injury. As a group, these trials involved more experts than the remainder. There were expert appearances in nearly 95% of the personal injury or death trials, an average of 3.8 witnesses per case. Looking at smaller categories, the highest rates of use were in: (i) medical malpractice cases (97% of trials, an average of five witnesses per trial), where almost all the witnesses were medical experts and (ii) products liability cases (100% of trials, an average of 4.7 witnesses per trial), where an unusually high proportion of the witnesses (1.8 per trial) were engineers, scientists and the like.

4. *Conflicts between opposing experts.* In nearly three-quarters of the trials in which experts testified (or 63% of all trials) there were experts on both sides. In two-thirds of the trials with expert testimony (57% of all trials) there were opposing experts in the same general area of expertise — most often, opposing medical experts. Similarly, for over two-thirds of the appearances by expert witnesses, there were opposing experts in the same general area. Again, such conflicts were particularly common for medical witnesses — their testimony was opposed by other medical witnesses 78% of the time. In sum, most expert witnesses were disputed by similar experts for the opposing side, and most juries had to resolve such disputes.

5. *The testimonial experience of expert witnesses.* Most expert testimony is given by repeat players. Nearly 60% of the appearances by expert witnesses in California Superior Court civil jury trials were by witnesses who testified in such cases at least two times over a six-year period. For a particular appearance before a jury, the average number of times the same expert testified over a six-year period was 9.4; the median was 2.2. It is important to note that these numbers greatly underrepresent the experts' total experience in litigation. They do not, for instance, include testimony in criminal trials or in civil trials in courts other than California State Superior Courts. More important, the numbers do not catch the many cases in which the same experts were consulted, wrote reports, or even testified in depositions, but failed to testify in court because the cases were settled or dismissed before trial.

One way to put the trial experience of witnesses in perspective is to compare it to that of trial lawyers. Judging from 1985-86 cases, when an attorney examines an expert witness in a civil jury trial in California, the expert is twice as likely to have testified in another such case in the preceding six months as the attorney is to have tried one (42% to 21%).

CAROL KRAFKA ET AL., JUDGE AND ATTORNEY EXPERIENCES, PRACTICES, AND CONCERNS REGARDING EXPERT TESTIMONY IN FEDERAL CIVIL TRIALS
Federal Judicial Center (2002)

Questions that remain about expert evidence far outnumber those that research has begun to address . . . What types of cases, for instance, are most likely to involve expert testimony? What types of experts testify, how frequently do they appear, and on whose behalf are they testifying? What issues do the experts address? . . . The research we report here involved [three] surveys of judges and attorneys. Data sources included a 1998 survey of [303 U.S. district court] judges, a 1991 survey of [335 U.S. district court] judges, and a 1999 survey of [302] attorneys [involved in district court cases presided over by the aforementioned judges]. The most frequent types of [federal] trials involving experts — 45% of the 299 trials reported — were tort cases, primarily those involving personal injury or medical malpractice. Tort cases were followed in frequency by civil rights cases (23%); contract cases (11%); intellectual property cases, primarily patent cases (10%); labor cases (2%); prisoner cases (2%); and other civil cases (8%).

To gauge whether expert testimony is differentially associated with certain case types, we compared the distribution of sample cases to the distribution of all federal civil cases terminating during or after a bench or jury trial in the year before and year of our survey. Compared to all civil trials, experts were overrepresented in tort cases (which constituted only 26% of all civil trials) and intellectual property cases (3% of all civil trials). Experts were underrepresented in contract cases (14% of all civil trials); labor cases (4% of all civil trials); general (nonprisoner) civil rights cases (31% of all civil trials); and prisoner cases, nearly all of which are civil rights actions (14% of all civil trials). In cases classified as "other" civil trials, experts were represented in equal proportion to the general case type (8%).

Ninety-two percent of reported trials involved expert testimony by plaintiffs, and 79% of trials involved expert testimony by defendants. Seventy-three percent of the trials had experts testifying for both plaintiffs and defendants. These figures are comparable to statistics from 1991, when 95% of trials involved expert testimony for the plaintiff, 81% involved expert testimony for the defendant, and 76% had experts testifying on both plaintiff and defendant side. Seventy-seven percent of the civil trials we surveyed in 1998 were conducted before juries... The jury trial rate for cases with expert evidence is somewhat higher than for cases as a whole — in 1998 jury trials accounted for 64% of all civil trials — suggesting that experts appear with somewhat disproportionate frequency in jury trials.

The average number of experts testifying for plaintiffs was 2.47, compared to 1.85 for defendants. Tort cases had the highest mean number of testifying experts — an average of 3.11 experts testified for plaintiffs, with 2.28 testifying for defendants. Civil rights cases averaged 1.81 experts for the plaintiff and 1.24 experts for the defense; case types that fell into the "other" category averaged 2.70 and 2.00 experts, respectively... The mean number of testifying experts in 1998 was 4.31 per trial. This figure is somewhat lower than in 1991, when cases averaged 4.80 experts per trial...

In both the judge and attorney surveys, respondents were asked to describe the types of experts who testified and the issues addressed by their testimony... Medical and mental health specialists were the most frequently presented category of experts, accounting for more than 40% of the experts presented overall. The medical profession, representing many types of specialists, collectively accounted for about one-third of all testifying experts. This showing is not surprising, given that 45% of the survey trials were tort cases. Specialists from business, law, and financial worlds accounted for another 25% of experts. This category includes the most frequently heard professional, the economist, representing almost 12% of all experts. Engineers and other safety, or process, specialists registered close behind experts from the business/ law/ financial sector. These professionals accounted for about 22% of all experts. Individuals representing scientific fields such as chemistry, ballistics, toxicology, and metallurgy accounted for only a small percentage, less than 8%, of testifying experts.

1. FRE 702

RULE 702.   TESTIMONY BY EXPERTS

If scientific, technical, or other specialized knowledge will assist the trier of fact to understand the evidence or to determine a fact in issue, a witness qualified as an expert by knowledge, skill, experience, training, or education, may testify thereto in the form of an opinion or otherwise, if (1) the testimony is based upon sufficient facts or data, (2) the testimony is the product of reliable principles and methods, and (3) the witness has applied the principles and methods reliably to the facts of the case.

2.   Interpretation and Illustration of FRE 702

a.   *Scientific, Technical, or Other Specialized Knowledge*

FRE 702 makes admissible a broad array of testimony from a multitude of sources covering an enormous range of affairs. It includes scientific, technical, and medical experts, but its pragmatic phrase "other specialized knowledge" extends the scope of the rule far beyond those confines. In the words of the Advisory Committee:

> The rule is broadly phrased. The fields of knowledge which may be drawn upon are not limited merely to the "scientific" and "technical" but extend to all "specialized" knowledge. Similarly, the expert is viewed, not in a narrow sense, but as a person qualified by "knowledge, skill, experience, training, or education." Thus within the scope of the rule are not only experts in the strictest sense of the word, e.g. physicians, physicists, and architects, but also the large group sometimes called "skilled" witnesses, such as bankers or landowners testifying to land values.

Consistent with the Advisory Committee's views, the cases admit a vast array of expert testimony. A person experienced in the practices of a particular business or industry can testify about those practices. Courts regularly admit ballistics and fingerprint evidence, expert testimony about valuation in a condemnation proceeding, and expert medical testimony about a criminal defendant's competence to stand trial or insanity at the time of the alleged crime. On the other hand, courts have traditionally been reluctant to admit, in the absence of prior stipulation by the parties, the results of lie detector tests, and most courts have traditionally excluded expert testimony about the vagaries of eyewitness identification. A court would almost certainly exclude an astrologer's or palm reader's "expert" testimony about an individual's violent tendencies or life expectancy. Cf. United States v. Tranowski, 659 F.2d 750 (9th Cir. 1981) (excluding testimony on photograph dating using astronomy charts).

b.   *Assist the Trier of Fact*

Any knowledge that is not likely to be possessed by the fact finder qualifies for admission under this rule, no matter how the knowledge is obtained. A person possessing a "skill" can testify to it and its implications, even if the skill was gained through experience rather than traditional formal study. Moreover, the knowledge that qualifies for admission is relative to the fact finder. If a potential witness possesses knowledge that the fact finder is not likely to possess, even though some other fact finder some-where else might, the testimony is admissible. For example, if the qualities of nitrogen fertilizer are relevant to a case in New York City, a farmer from Iowa knowledgeable of the matter through years of experience would qualify as an expert, even though the farmer had never formally studied the matter. If the trial were held in an Iowa farming community, quite possibly no expert testimony would be admissible because the fact finder's common knowledge and experience might very well extend to the relevant issues. It is these two factors — (1) specialized knowledge relative to the fact finder (2) gained by experience — that explain the court's decision in *Johnson* permitting Officer Huston to give an expert opinion about tray collection from inmates.

The helpfulness component of FRE 702 is not superfluous. Courts have been reluctant, for example, to admit expert testimony on the limits of eyewitness identifica-tions because the jury may already sufficiently understand the point. If the jurors already are appropriately skeptical of eyewitness identifications, putting an expert on the stand to discourage the jury from believing eyewitness testimony may result in an erroneous verdict through increasing the already appropriate level of skepticism of the jurors. See, e.g., United States v. Smith, 122 F.3d 1355 (11th Cir. 1997) (holding expert testimony on the reliability of eyewitness identification inadmissible, because not helpful to jury); United States v. Hall, 165 F.3d 1095 (7th Cir. 1998) ("expert testimony relating to eyewitness identification is strongly disfavored"). To be confident that such testimony is "helpful," one must know the reliability of the information presented and how it is likely to affect the fact finder, which includes knowing the baseline from which the fact finder is presently operating. This judicial attitude may be changing, however, as courts find that such evidence is admissible in certain circumstances. See, e.g., United States v. Brien, 59 F.3d 274 (1st Cir. 1995) (holding the exclusion of such evidence discretion-ary, not per se inadmissible); United States v. Smithers, 212 F.3d 306 (6th Cir. 2000) (exclusion of expert on eyewitness identification reversible error). Admissibility of such testimony is favored by some legal scholars as well. See Harvey Gee, Eyewitness Tes-timony and Cross-Racial Identification, 35 New Eng. L. Rev. 835 (2001) (reviewing Elizabeth Loftus, *Eyewitness Testimony* (1996)); Jennifer L. Devenport, Steven D. Penrod, and Brian L. Cutler, Eyewitness Identification Evidence: Evaluating Com-monsense Evaluations, 3 Psy. Pub. Pol'y & L. 338 (1997); Michael R. Leippe, The Case for Expert Testimony About Eyewitness Memory, 1 Psy. Pub. Pol'y & L. 909 (1995). In any event, the person offering an expert witness must be prepared to qualify the witness as having knowledge that the jury lacks that would be helpful to its decision.

c. A Witness Qualified as an Expert

If specialized information will assist the trier of fact, the trial judge must then determine whether the person offered to present the information is qualified to do so. As we previously indicated, the qualifications need not include formal education in the subject matter. Rather, as FRE 702 provides, one can be qualified as an expert based on "knowledge, skill, experience, [or] training," as well as education. As a result, courts admit an extremely wide variety of testimony on this basis. FBI agents have been permitted to testify to the structure of various criminal schemes based on their law enforcement experience. Farmers have testified to the likely value of their ruined crops, and so on. The crucial questions are whether the proposed witness has specialized knowledge, however obtained, and whether it would be helpful to the jury.

Qualifying an expert involves a voir dire of the witness that brings out the person's expertise. If there is no reasonable doubt about the expertise, the opposing party may try to stipulate to it. Wise counsel usually reject the stipulation because they want the fact finder to hear the credentials of the witness. The opposing party can object to qualifying the witness as an expert, and can also voir dire the witness in an effort to show that the witness is not qualified or has nothing of relevance to add to the trial. The trial judge then decides if the person qualifies as an expert pursuant to FRE 104(a).

d.   FRE 403 and Litigation Incentives

As the foregoing illustrations suggest, whether scientific or specialized evidence should be admitted turns on an evaluation of the relevance of the evidence and the countervailing FRE 403 factors. Some purportedly specialized evidence may appear to have no probative value. Evidence with slight probative value arguably should be excluded because of FRE 403 concerns: The evidence may be misleading if scientific jargon gives the evidence an aura of legitimacy that it does not deserve; the complexity of the evidence may tend to confuse rather than help jurors; and perhaps most important, the speculative nature or low probative value of some specialized evidence may not warrant spending the time, first, to demonstrate the possible relevance of the evidence and, second, to explore all of the possible weaknesses in the evidence.

Perhaps FRE 401-403 are adequate tools for dealing with the potential problems raised by scientific and specialized evidence, and perhaps courts should be especially reluctant to exclude specialized evidence pursuant to these rules, for there are at least three factors inherent in the litigation process that may inhibit parties from procuring unreliable specialized evidence.

First, the attorney will need to develop some familiarity with any specialization about which the attorney desires to interrogate a witness, and the specialist is likely to demand a fee for preparing for the litigation and testifying. These expenditures of time and money are likely to make the cost of procuring specialized evidence higher than the cost of procuring other evidence.

Second, the seemingly bizarre nature of some specialized evidence may lead jurors to reject it out of hand. Even if there appears to be an initial aura of legitimacy to the specialized evidence, opposing counsel will have the opportunity through cross-examination and rebuttal to demonstrate the irrelevance or low probative value of the evidence. In either situation, jurors' skepticism about the specialized evidence may lead them not merely to reject the specialized evidence; it may lead them to draw an inference similar to the inference that one can draw from the exposure of an attempt to bribe a witness or the knowing presentation of perjured testimony: If the party must resort to this type of unreliable evidence, the party's case must be a weak one.

Third, perhaps the nature of scientific evidence increases the possibility that unreliable evidence will be exposed on cross-examination. The probative value of specialized evidence is likely to depend in large measure on the rationality and methodology of allegedly scientific processes. These are matters that can be extensively explored during the examination of witnesses. The witnesses, of course, may be lying or may have misperceived or forgotten something that will not come to light during the examination. We can think of no reason, however, why this problem is likely to be any greater with purported specialists than with other witnesses.

Admittedly, these factors will not ensure the reliability of all specialized evidence, and quite frankly we cannot say how significant these factors are. Particularly in the context of a criminal prosecution, where discovery may not be readily available, opposing counsel may not be sufficiently knowledgeable about the specialty or adequately prepared to cross-examine specialists and offer opposing experts. Additionally, a litigant with a weak case may decide that the best chance of prevailing is through attempting to sow confusion by the presentation of unreliable or extremely complex specialized evidence, and we do not really know how effective this tactic is. Moreover, it is arguably inappropriate to place on opposing counsel the burden of having to respond to specialized evidence unless the offering party first demonstrates that it has a relatively high degree of probative value. Finally, perhaps some jurors will be impressed by even bizarre specialized evidence merely because the evidence is presented to them: They may think, *Why would the judge let us hear this evidence if it were not relevant?* Again, we do not know the extent of this phenomenon, just as we do not know the extent to which jurors reject specialized evidence because it appears to them bizarre.

There is one other factor to take into account in deciding how receptive the law should be to specialized evidence: A judge's proclivity to exclude unusual types of specialized evidence can prevent litigants from taking advantage of innovative, highly probative information and, as a result, detract from the search for truth. See, e.g., E.S. Lander and B. Budowle, DNA Fingerprinting Dispute Laid to Rest, 371 Nature 735 (1994) (discussing the initial controversy over the use of DNA fingerprinting); United States v. Martinez, 3 F.3d 1191 (8th Cir. 1993) (discussion of admissibility of DNA evidence).

e.   Summary Witnesses

Summary witnesses represent a blurring of the line between who qualifies as an "expert witness" and who remains a "lay witness". In some trials, usually those involving large amounts of evidence or extraordinarily complicated evidence, a lay witness will be permitted to testify as to what the aggregate of the evidence shows — in other words, to summarize the evidence. Because the witness is simply serving as a human "tape recorder", the witness need not be qualified as an expert to provide this summary. However, if the witness draws conclusions from this evidentiary summation for the purposes of assisting the jury, it is probable that the witness should be certified as an expert. See, e.g., United States v. Pree, 408 F.3d 855, 869 (7th Cir. 2005) (admission of summary witness testimony regarding the tax consequences of a series of complicated stock sales in a fraud case). For more on summary witnesses, see D. Michael Risinger, Preliminary Thoughts on a Functional Taxonomy of Expertise for the Post-Kumho World, 31 Seton Hall L. Rev. 508.

3.   Elaboration of "Scientific Evidence" Under FRE 702: Frye and Daubert

a.   From Frye to Daubert

You have probably noticed that we have not yet discussed subsections 1, 2, and 3 of FRE 702. They are new additions to FRE 702, added in the aftermath of the *Daubert* case, which is reproduced later in this section, and the *Kumho Tire* case, reproduced in the following section. To understand the amendments, you need to understand these two cases. To understand the cases in turn, you must understand Frye v. United States, 293 F. 1013 (D.C. Cir. 1923). In *Frye*, the federal circuit court for the District of Columbia adopted a special rule for the admissibility of scientific evidence. The defendant, Frye, sought to introduce into evidence the results of an early type of lie detection device — a systolic blood pressure test. In upholding the trial court's exclusion of the evidence the Court of Appeals stated:

> Just when a scientific principle or discovery crosses the line between the experimental and demonstrable stages is difficult to define. Somewhere in this twilight zone the evidential force of the principle must be recognized, and while courts will go a long way in admitting expert testimony deduced from well-recognized scientific principle or discovery, the thing from which the deduction is made must be sufficiently established to have gained general acceptance in the particular field in which it belongs. [Id. at 1014.]

The *Frye* opinion is unclear about whether "the thing" that must have gained "general acceptance" is the relationship between truth-telling and blood pressure, or the ability of an expert to measure and interpret the changes in blood pressure, or both. Despite this ambiguity and despite the court's failure to explain further or to cite precedent for its holding, a number of courts adopted the "general acceptance" test, commonly referred to as the "*Frye* test":

> Polygraphy, graphology, hypnotic and drug induced testimony, voice stress analysis, voice spectrograms, various forms of spectroscopy, infrared sensing of aircraft, retesting of breath samples for alcohol content, psychological profiles of battered women and child abusers, post traumatic stress disorder as indicating rape, penile plethysmography as indicating sexual deviancy, astronomical calculations, blood group typing, and DNA testing all have fallen prey to its influence. [McCormick on the Evidence §203, at 306 (John William Strong, ed., 5th ed. 1999).]

Particularly in recent years the *Frye* test has been the subject of extensive criticism, primarily because a rigorous application of the test prevents use of scientific evidence based on emerging disciplines or cross-disciplinary studies. The Federal Rules make no reference to the "general acceptance" standard. Consider again the language of FRE 702:

> If scientific, technical, or other specialized knowledge will assist the trier of fact to understand the evidence or to determine a fact in issue, a witness qualified as an expert by knowledge, skill, experience, training, or education, may testify thereto in the form of an opinion or otherwise.

On its face, the "assist the trier of fact" criterion appears to be nothing more than an incorporation of the basic relevance concepts embodied in FRE 401-403. Given the language of FRE 702, some commentators took the position that the Federal Rules rejected the *Frye* test. E.g., 3 Jack Weinstein & Margaret Berger, Weinstein's Evidence ¶702[03], at 702-716 (1982). Lower courts divided on the issue. E.g., compare United States v. Brown, 557 F.2d 541 (6th Cir. 1977) (applying *Frye*) with United States v. Williams, 583 F.2d 1194 (2d Cir. 1978). If the *Frye* test is abandoned, should there be some substitute test for the admissibility of scientific and specialized evidence that is more rigorous than the standards embodied in FRE 401-403? Less rigorous? Instead of focusing on standards of admissibility, would it be desirable for there to be some mandatory process — perhaps implemented through discovery and pretrial conferences — that would ensure that both the lawyers and the judge were sufficiently versed in the specialty to address questions of admissibility in a reasonable and helpful way? Should there be a panel of experts either to make decisions about the admissibility of specialized evidence, or perhaps even to make the ultimate factual determination of questions that turn on the evaluation of scientific evidence? The Supreme Court recently addressed a number of these issues, including the continuing viability of the *Frye* rule:

DAUBERT v. MERRELL DOW PHARMACEUTICALS, INC.

509 U.S. 579 (1993)

Justice BLACKMUN delivered the opinion of the Court.

In this case we are called upon to determine the standard for admitting expert scientific testimony in a federal trial.

I

Petitioners Jason Daubert and Eric Schuller are minor children born with serious birth defects. They and their parents sued respondent in California state court, alleging that the birth defects had been caused by the mothers' ingestion of Bendectin, a prescription anti-nausea drug marketed by respondent. Respondent removed the suits to federal court on diversity grounds.

After extensive discovery, respondent moved for summary judgment, contending that Bendectin does not cause birth defects in humans and that petitioners would be unable to come forward with any admissible evidence that it does. In support of its motion, respondent submitted an affidavit of Steven H. Lamm, physician and epidemiologist, who is a well-credentialed expert on the risks from exposure to various chemical substances.[1] Doctor Lamm stated that he had reviewed all the literature on Bendectin and human birth defects — more than 30 published studies involving over 130,000 patients. No study had found Bendectin to be a human teratogen (i.e., a substance capable of causing malformations in fetuses). On the basis of this review, Doctor Lamm concluded that maternal use of Bendectin during the first trimester of pregnancy has not been shown to be a risk factor for human birth defects.

Petitioners did not (and do not) contest this characterization of the published record regarding Bendectin. Instead, they responded to respondent's motion with the testimony of eight experts of their own, each of whom also possessed impressive credentials.[2] These experts had concluded that Bendectin can cause birth defects. Their

---

1. Doctor Lamm received his master's and doctor of medicine degrees from the University of Southern California. He has served as a consultant in birth-defect epidemiology for the National Center for Health Statistics and has published numerous articles on the magnitude of risk from exposure to various chemical and biological substances.

2. For example, Shanna Helen Swan, who received a master's degree in biostatics from Columbia University and a doctorate in statistics from the University of California at Berkeley, is chief of the section of the California Department of Health and Services that determines causes of birth defects, and has served as a consultant to the World Health Organization, the Food and Drug Administration, and the National

conclusions were based upon "in vitro" (test tube) and "in vivo" (live) animal studies that found a link between Bendectin and malformations; pharmacological studies of the chemical structure of Bendectin that purported to show similarities between the structure of the drug and that of other substances known to cause birth defects; and the "reanalysis" of previously published epidemiological (human statistical) studies.

The District Court granted respondent's motion for summary judgment. The court stated that scientific evidence is admissible only if the principle upon which it is based is "sufficiently established to have general acceptance in the field to which it belongs." The court concluded that petitioners' evidence did not meet this standard. Given the vast body of epidemiological data concerning Bendectin, the court held, expert opinion which is not based on epidemiological evidence is not admissible to establish causation. Thus, the animal-cell studies, live-animal studies, and chemical-structure analyses on which petitioners had relied could not raise by themselves a reasonably disputable jury issue regarding causation. Petitioners' epidemiological analyses, based as they were on recalculations of data in previously published studies that had found no causal link between the drug and birth defects, were ruled to be inadmissible because they had not been published or subjected to peer review.

The United States Court of Appeals for the Ninth Circuit affirmed. Citing Frye v. United States, the court stated that expert opinion based on a scientific technique is inadmissible unless the technique is "generally accepted" as reliable in the relevant scientific community. The court declared that expert opinion based on a methodology that diverges "significantly from the procedures accepted by recognized authorities in the field . . . cannot be shown to be generally accepted as a reliable technique." The court emphasized that other Courts of Appeals considering the risks of Bendectin had refused to admit reanalyses of epidemiological studies that had been neither published nor subjected to peer review. Those courts had found unpublished reanalyses "particularly problematic in light of the massive weight of the original published studies supporting [respondent's] position, all of which had undergone full scrutiny from the scientific community." Contending that reanalysis is generally accepted by the scientific community only when it is subjected to verification and scrutiny by others in the field, the Court of Appeals rejected petitioners' reanalyses as "unpublished, not subjected to the normal peer review process and generated solely for use in litigation." The court concluded that petitioners' evidence provided an insufficient foundation to allow admission of expert testimony that Bendectin caused their injuries and, accordingly, that petitioners could not satisfy their burden of proving causation at trial.

We granted certiorari in light of sharp divisions among the courts regarding the proper standard for the admission of expert testimony.

II

A

In the 70 years since its formulation in the *Frye* case, the "general acceptance" test has been the dominant standard for determining the admissibility of novel scientific

---

Institutes of Health. Stewart A. Newman, who received his master's and a doctorate in chemistry from Columbia University and the University of Chicago, respectively, is a professor at New York Medical College and has spent over a decade studying the effect of chemicals on limb development. The credentials of the others are similarly impressive.

evidence at trial. Although under increasing attack of late, the rule continues to be followed by a majority of courts, including the Ninth Circuit.

The *Frye* test has its origin in a short and citation-free 1923 decision concerning the admissibility of evidence derived from a systolic blood pressure deception test, a crude precursor to the polygraph machine. In what has become a famous (perhaps infamous) passage, the then Court of Appeals for the District of Columbia described the device and its operation and declared:

> Just when a scientific principle or discovery crosses the line between the experimental and demonstrable stages is difficult to define. Somewhere in this twilight zone the evidential force of the principle must be recognized, and while courts will go a long way in admitting expert testimony deduced from a well-recognized scientific principle or discovery, the thing from which the deduction is made must be sufficiently established to have gained general acceptance in the particular field in which it belongs.

Because the deception test had "not yet gained such standing and scientific recognition among physiological and psychological authorities as would justify the courts in admitting expert testimony deduced from the discovery, development, and experiments thus far made," evidence of its results was ruled inadmissible.

The merits of the *Frye* test have been much debated, and scholarship on its proper scope and application is legion. Petitioners' primary attack, however, is not on the content but on the continuing authority of the rule. They contend that the *Frye* test was superseded by the adoption of the Federal Rules of Evidence. We agree.

We interpret the legislatively-enacted Federal Rules of Evidence as we would any statute. Beech Aircraft Corp. v. Rainey, 488 U.S. 153, 163 (1988). Rule 402 provides the baseline: "All relevant evidence is admissible, except as otherwise provided by the Constitution of the United States, by Act of Congress, by these rules, or by other rules prescribed by the Supreme Court pursuant to statutory authority. Evidence which is not relevant is not admissible." "Relevant evidence" is defined as that which has "any tendency to make the existence of any fact that is of consequence to the determination of the action more probable or less probable than it would be without the evidence." Rule 401. The Rule's basic standard of relevance thus is a liberal one.

Frye, of course, predated the Rules by half a century. In United States v. Abel, 469 U.S. 45 (1984), we considered the pertinence of background common law in interpreting the Rules of Evidence. We noted that the Rules occupy the field, id. at 49, but, quoting Professor Cleary, the Reporter, explained that the common law nevertheless could serve as an aid to their application:

> In principle, under the Federal Rules no common law of evidence remains. "All relevant evidence is admissible, except as otherwise provided. . . . " In reality, of course, the body of common law knowledge continues to exist, though in the somewhat altered form of a source of guidance in the exercise of delegated powers.

Id., at 51-52.

We found the common-law precept at issue in the *Abel* case entirely consistent with Rule 402's general requirement of admissibility, and considered it unlikely that the drafters had intended to change the rule. In Bourjaily v. United States, 483 U.S. 171 (1987), on the other hand, the Court was unable to find a particular common-law doctrine in the Rules, and so held it superseded.

Here there is a specific Rule that speaks to the contested issue. Rule 702, governing expert testimony, provides:

> If scientific, technical, or other specialized knowledge will assist the trier of fact to understand the evidence or to determine a fact in issue, a witness qualified as an expert by knowledge, skill, experience, training, or education, may testify thereto in the form of an opinion or otherwise.

Nothing in the text of this Rule establishes "general acceptance" as an absolute prerequisite to admissibility. Nor does respondent present any clear indication that Rule 702 or the Rules as a whole were intended to incorporate a "general acceptance" standard. The drafting history makes no mention of *Frye*, and a rigid "general acceptance" requirement would be at odds with the "liberal thrust" of the Federal Rules and their "general approach of relaxing the traditional barriers to 'opinion' testimony." Beech Aircraft Corp. v. Rainey, 488 U.S. at 169 (citing Rules 701 to 705). Given the Rules' permissive backdrop and their inclusion of a specific rule on expert testimony that does not mention "general acceptance," the assertion that the Rules somehow assimilated *Frye* is unconvincing. *Frye* made "general acceptance" the exclusive test for admitting expert scientific testimony. That austere standard, absent from and incompatible with the Federal Rules of Evidence, should not be applied in federal trials.

B

That the *Frye* test was displaced by the Rules of Evidence does not mean, however, that the Rules themselves place no limits on the admissibility of purportedly scientific evidence. Nor is the trial judge disabled from screening such evidence. To the contrary, under the Rules the trial judge must ensure that any and all scientific testimony or evidence admitted is not only relevant, but reliable.

The primary locus of this obligation is Rule 702, which clearly contemplates some degree of regulation of the subjects and theories about which an expert may testify. "If scientific, technical, or other specialized knowledge will assist the trier of fact to understand the evidence or to determine a fact in issue" an expert "may testify thereto." The subject of an expert's testimony must be "scientific . . . knowledge."[3] The adjective "scientific" implies a grounding in the methods and procedures of science. Similarly, the word "knowledge" connotes more than subjective belief or unsupported speculation. The term "applies to any body of known facts or to any body of ideas inferred from such facts or accepted as truths on good grounds." Webster's Third New International Dictionary 1252 (1986). Of course, it would be unreasonable to conclude that the subject of scientific testimony must be "known" to a certainty; arguably, there are no certainties in science. But, in order to qualify as "scientific knowledge," an inference or assertion must be derived by the scientific method. Proposed testimony must be supported by appropriate validation — i.e., "good grounds," based on what is known. In short, the requirement that an expert's testimony pertain to "scientific knowledge" establishes a standard of evidentiary reliability.[4]

---

3.   Rule 702 also applies to "technical, or other specialized knowledge." Our discussion is limited to the scientific context because that is the nature of the expertise offered here.

4.   We note that scientists typically distinguish between "validity" (does the principle support what it purports to show?) and "reliability" (does application of the principle produce consistent results?). See Black, A Unified Theory of Scientific Evidence, 56 Ford. L. Rev. 595, 599 (1988). Although "the difference

Rule 702 further requires that the evidence or testimony "assist the trier of fact to understand the evidence or to determine a fact in issue." This condition goes primarily to relevance. "Expert testimony which does not relate to any issue in the case is not relevant and, ergo, non-helpful." 3 Weinstein & Berger ¶702[02], p. 702-18. See also United States v. Downing, 753 F.2d 1224, 1242 (C.A.3 1985) ("An additional consideration under Rule 702 — and another aspect of relevancy — is whether expert testimony proffered in the case is sufficiently tied to the facts of the case that it will aid the jury in resolving a factual dispute"). The consideration has been aptly described by Judge Becker as one of "fit." Ibid. "Fit" is not always obvious, and scientific validity for one purpose is not necessarily scientific validity for other, unrelated purposes. The study of the phases of the moon, for example, may provide valid scientific "knowledge" about whether a certain night was dark, and if darkness is a fact in issue, the knowledge will assist the trier of fact. However (absent creditable grounds supporting such a link), evidence that the moon was full on a certain night will not assist the trier of fact in determining whether an individual was unusually likely to have behaved irrationally on that night. Rule 702's "helpfulness" standard requires a valid scientific connection to the pertinent inquiry as a precondition to admissibility.

That these requirements are embodied in Rule 702 is not surprising. Unlike an ordinary witness, see Rule 701, an expert is permitted wide latitude to offer opinions, including those that are not based on first-hand knowledge or observation. See Rules 702 and 703. Presumably, this relaxation of the usual requirement of first-hand knowledge — a rule which represents "a 'most pervasive manifestation'" of the common law insistence upon 'the most reliable sources of information,'" Advisory Committee's Notes on Fed. Rule Evid. 602 — is premised on an assumption that the expert's opinion will have a reliable basis in the knowledge and experience of his discipline.

C

Faced with a proffer of expert scientific testimony, then, the trial judge must determine at the outset, pursuant to Rule 104(a),[5] whether the expert is proposing to testify to (1) scientific knowledge that (2) will assist the trier of fact to understand or determine a fact in issue.[6] This entails a preliminary assessment of whether the reasoning or methodology underlying the testimony is scientifically valid and of whether that reasoning or methodology properly can be applied to the facts in issue. We are confident that federal judges possess the capacity to undertake this review. Many factors will bear on the

---

between accuracy, validity, and reliability may be such that each is distinct from the other by no more than a hen's kick," Starrs, Frye v. United States Restructured and Revitalized: A Proposal to Amend Federal Evidence Rule 702, 26 Jurimetrics J. 249, 256 (1986), our reference here is to evidentiary reliability — that is, trustworthiness. Cf., e.g., Advisory Committee's Notes on Fed. Rule Evid. 602 ("'[T]he rule requiring that a witness who testifies to a fact which can be perceived by the senses must have had an opportunity to observe, and must have actually observed the fact' is a 'most pervasive manifestation' of the common law insistence upon 'the most reliable sources of information.'" (citation omitted)); Advisory Committee's Notes on Art. VIII of the Rules of Evidence (hearsay exceptions will be recognized only "under circumstances supposed to furnish guarantees of trustworthiness"). In a case involving scientific evidence, evidentiary reliability will be based upon scientific validity.

5. These matters should be established by a preponderance of proof.

6. Although the Frye decision itself focused exclusively on "novel" scientific techniques, we do not read the requirements of Rule 702 to apply specially or exclusively to unconventional evidence. Of course, well-established propositions are less likely to be challenged than those that are novel, and they are more handily defended. Indeed, theories that are so firmly established as to have attained the status of scientific law, such as the laws of thermoydnamics, properly are subject to judicial notice under Fed. Rule Evid. 201.

inquiry, and we do not presume to set out a definitive checklist or test. But some general observations are appropriate.

Ordinarily, a key question to be answered in determining whether a theory or technique is scientific knowledge that will assist the trier of fact will be whether it can be (and has been) tested. K. Popper, Conjectures and Refutations: The Growth of Scientific Knowledge 37 (5th ed. 1989) ("[T]he criterion of the scientific status of a theory is its falsifiability, or refutability, or testability").

Another pertinent consideration is whether the theory or technique has been subjected to peer review and publication. Publication (which is but one element of peer review) is not a sine qua non of admissibility; it does not necessarily correlate with reliability, see S. Jasanoff, The Fifth Branch: Science Advisors as Policymakers 61-76 (1990), and in some instances well-grounded but innovative theories will not have been published, see Horrobin, The Philosophical Basis of Peer Review and the Suppression of Innovation, 263 J. Am. Med. Assn. 1438 (1990). Some propositions, moreover, are too particular, too new, or of too limited interest to be published. But submission to the scrutiny of the scientific community is a component of "good science," in part because it increases the likelihood that substantive flaws in methodology will be detected. The fact of publication (or lack thereof) in a peer-reviewed journal thus will be a relevant, though not dispositive, consideration in assessing the scientific validity of a particular technique or methodology on which an opinion is premised.

Additionally, in the case of a particular scientific technique, the court ordinarily should consider the known or potential rate of error, and the existence and maintenance of standards controlling the technique's operation.

Finally, "general acceptance" can yet have a bearing on the inquiry. A "reliability assessment does not require, although it does permit, explicit identification of a relevant scientific community and an express determination of a particular degree of acceptance within that community." United States v. Downing, 753 F.2d, at 1238. Widespread acceptance can be an important factor in ruling particular evidence admissible, and "a known technique that has been able to attract only minimal support within the community," Downing, supra, may properly be viewed with skepticism.

The inquiry envisioned by Rule 702 is, we emphasize, a flexible one. Its overarching subject is the scientific validity — and thus the evidentiary relevance and reliability — of the principles that underlie a proposed submission. The focus, of course, must be solely on principles and methodology, not on the conclusions that they generate.

Throughout, a judge assessing a proffer of expert scientific testimony under Rule 702 should also be mindful of other applicable rules. Rule 703 provides that expert opinions based on otherwise inadmissible hearsay are to be admitted only if the facts or data are "of a type reasonably relied upon by experts in the particular field in forming opinions or inferences upon the subject." Rule 706 allows the court at its discretion to procure the assistance of an expert of its own choosing. Finally, Rule 403 permits the exclusion of relevant evidence "if its probative value is substantially outweighed by the danger of unfair prejudice, confusion of the issues, or misleading the jury...." Judge Weinstein has explained:

> Expert evidence can be both powerful and quite misleading because of the difficulty in evaluating it. Because of this risk, the judge in weighing possible prejudice against

probative force under Rule 403 of the present rules exercises more control over experts than over lay witnesses.

Weinstein, 138 F.R.D., at 632.

III

We conclude by briefly addressing what appear to be two underlying concerns of the parties and amici in this case. Respondent expresses apprehension that abandonment of "general acceptance" as the exclusive requirement for admission will result in a "free-for-all" in which befuddled juries are confounded by absurd and irrational pseudoscientific assertions. In this regard respondent seems to us to be overly pessimistic about the capabilities of the jury, and of the adversary system generally. Vigorous cross-examination, presentation of contrary evidence, and careful instruction on the burden of proof are the traditional and appropriate means of attacking shaky but admissible evidence. Additionally, in the event the trial court concludes that the scintilla of evidence presented supporting a position is insufficient to allow a reasonable juror to conclude that the position more likely than not is true, the court remains free to direct a judgment, Fed. Rule Civ. Proc. 50(a), and likewise to grant summary judgment, Fed. Rule Civ. Proc. 56. These conventional devices, rather than wholesale exclusion under an uncompromising "general acceptance" test, are the appropriate safeguards where the basis of scientific testimony meets the standards of Rule 702.

Petitioners and, to a greater extent, their amici exhibit a different concern. They suggest that recognition of a screening role for the judge that allows for the exclusion of "invalid" evidence will sanction a stifling and repressive scientific orthodoxy and will be inimical to the search for truth. It is true that open debate is an essential part of both legal and scientific analyses. Yet there are important differences between the quest for truth in the courtroom and the quest for truth in the laboratory. Scientific conclusions are subject to perpetual revision. Law, on the other hand, must resolve disputes finally and quickly. The scientific project is advanced by broad and wide-ranging consideration of a multitude of hypotheses, for those that are incorrect will eventually be shown to be so, and that in itself is an advance. Conjectures that are probably wrong are of little use, however, in the project of reaching a quick, final, and binding legal judgment — often of great consequence — about a particular set of events in the past. We recognize that in practice, a gatekeeping role for the judge, no matter how flexible, inevitably on occasion will prevent the jury from learning of authentic insights and innovations. That, nevertheless, is the balance that is struck by Rules of Evidence designed not for the exhaustive search for cosmic understanding but for the particularized resolution of legal disputes.

IV

To summarize: "general acceptance" is not a necessary precondition to the admissibility of scientific evidence under the Federal Rules of Evidence, but the Rules of Evidence — especially Rule 702 — do assign to the trial judge the task of ensuring that an expert's testimony both rests on a reliable foundation and is relevant to the task at hand. Pertinent evidence based on scientifically valid principles will satisfy those demands.

The inquiries of the District Court and the Court of Appeals focused almost exclusively on "general acceptance," as gauged by publication and the decisions of other courts. Accordingly, the judgment of the Court of Appeals is vacated and the case is remanded for further proceedings consistent with this opinion.

It is so ordered.

Chief Justice REHNQUIST, with whom Justice STEVENS joins, concurring in part and dissenting in part.

The petition for certiorari in this case presents two questions: first, whether the rule of Frye v. United States, remains good law after the enactment of the Federal Rules of Evidence; and second, if *Frye* remains valid, whether it requires expert scientific testimony to have been subjected to a peer-review process in order to be admissible. The Court concludes, correctly in my view, that the *Frye* rule did not survive the enactment of the Federal Rules of Evidence, and I therefore join Parts I and II-A of its opinion. The second question presented in the petition for certiorari necessarily is mooted by this holding, but the Court nonetheless proceeds to construe Rules 702 and 703 very much in the abstract, and then offers some "general observations." "General observations" by this Court customarily carry great weight with lower federal courts, but the ones offered here suffer from the flaw common to most such observations — they are not applied to deciding whether or not particular testimony was or was not admissible, and therefore they tend to be not only general, but vague and abstract. This is particularly unfortunate in a case such as this, where the ultimate legal question depends on an appreciation of one or more bodies of knowledge not judicially noticeable, and subject to different interpretations in the briefs of the parties and their amici. Twenty-two amicus briefs have been filed in the case, and indeed the Court's opinion contains no less than 37 citations to amicus briefs and other secondary sources.

The various briefs filed in this case are markedly different from typical briefs, in that large parts of them do not deal with decided cases or statutory language — the sort of material we customarily interpret. Instead, they deal with definitions of scientific knowledge, scientific method, scientific validity, and peer review — in short, matters far afield from the expertise of judges. This is not to say that such materials are not useful or even necessary in deciding how Rule 703 should be applied; but it is to say that the unusual subject matter should cause us to proceed with great caution in deciding more than we have to, because our reach can so easily exceed our grasp.

But even if it were desirable to make "general observations" not necessary to decide the questions presented, I cannot subscribe to some of the observations made by the Court. In Part II-B, the Court concludes that reliability and relevancy are the touchstones of the admissibility of expert testimony. Federal Rule of Evidence 402 provides, as the Court points out, that "[e]vidence which is not relevant is not admissible." But there is no similar reference in the Rule to "reliability." The Court constructs its argument by parsing the language "[i]f scientific, technical, or other specialized knowledge will assist the trier of fact to understand the evidence or to determine a fact in issue...an expert...may testify thereto...." Fed. Rule Evid. 702. It stresses that the subject of the expert's testimony must be "scientific... knowledge," and points out that "scientific" "implies a grounding in the methods and procedures of science," and that the word "knowledge" "connotes more than subjective belief or unsupported speculation." From this it concludes that "scientific knowledge" must be "derived by the scientific method." Proposed testimony, we are told, must be supported by "appropriate validation." Indeed, ... the Court decides that "[i]n a case involving scientific evidence, evidentiary reliability will be based upon scientific validity." Questions arise simply from reading this part of the Court's opinion, and countless more questions will surely arise when hundreds of district judges try to apply its teaching to particular offers of expert testimony. Does all of this dicta apply to an expert seeking to testify on the basis of "technical or other specialized knowledge" — the other types of expert knowledge to which Rule 702 applies — or are the "general observations" limited only to "scientific knowledge"? What is the difference between scientific knowledge and technical knowledge; does Rule 702 actually contemplate that the phrase "scientific, technical, or other specialized knowledge" be broken down into numerous subspecies of expertise, or did its authors simply pick general descriptive language covering the sort of expert testimony which courts have customarily received? The Court speaks of its confidence that federal judges can make a "preliminary assessment of whether the reasoning or methodology underlying the testimony is scientifically valid and of whether that reasoning or methodology properly can be applied to the facts in issue." The Court then states that a "key question" to be answered in deciding whether something is "scientific knowledge" "will be whether it can be (and has been) tested." Following this sentence [is a] quotation ... which states that "the criterion of the scientific status of a theory is its falsifiability, or refutability, or testability." I defer to no one in my confidence in federal judges; but I am at a loss to know what is meant when it is said that the scientific status of a theory depends on its "falsifiability," and I suspect some of them will be, too. I do not doubt that Rule 702 confides to the judge some gatekeeping responsibility in deciding questions of the admissibility of proffered expert testimony. But I do not think it imposes on them either the obligation or the authority to become amateur scientists in order to perform that role. I think the Court would be far better advised in this case to decide only the questions presented, and to leave the further development of this important area of the law to future cases.

NOTES AND QUESTIONS

1. The *Daubert* opinion is curious in many respects. Although the majority in *Daubert* purported to bury *Frye*, the case was not long interred; immediately following the announcement of its demise came the resurrection. To say that "scientific knowledge" that may be helpful to the trier of fact is admissible is not to say what "scientific knowledge" is. In its examination of the meaning of "scientific knowledge" and the *Frye* rule, the Court noted four factors that will help guide the lower courts in making determinations of the admissibility of proffered expert testimony. Three of them either restate or are derivative of *Frye*, and the fourth is merely a quite sensible admonition that is consistent with, even if not strictly derivable from, *Frye*.

The first factor is whether the subject matter may be tested, but attempts to falsify propositions take place virtually exclusively within normal scientific endeavors, which means within the context of generally accepted scientific canons. The Court's second factor is "whether the theory or technique has been subjected to peer review and publication." In addition to ruling out almost all legal knowledge (although perhaps it is "specialized"), this guide line again will tend to limit material to that which is generally accepted; rarely does unaccepted "science" get published. Third, in determining whether data is sufficiently reliable to be admitted, a court may also look to general acceptance. The first two standards restate general acceptance; the third adopts it explicitly. The fourth is merely that rate of error in scientific techniques is a prudential consideration to be taken into account in the admissibility determination, a factor that if not taken into account by "scientists" would seriously undermine the "general acceptance" of their work.

2. Even though *Frye* apparently lives, although in the guise of "guidelines" rather than "rule," the immediate reaction to *Daubert* was that it loosened the standards of admissibility for expert testimony through its conclusion that the *Frye* test was not a necessary condition of admissibility. Interestingly, the lower federal courts saw in *Daubert* the justification to take long, hard looks at expert witnesses being proffered, and they have increasingly declined to admit the testimony. See Section E, infra. It is not too much to say that *Daubert* has prompted a revolution in the manner in which expert testimony is being treated by the lower courts.

3. Although the lower courts have become much more active in policing the admissibility of expert testimony, and are making serious efforts to grapple with the various problems presented, the difficulty remains that the trial judges remain scientific amateurs. The deeper problem is that the Court's opinion simply ignored the issue that is presently informing the use of and fueling the controversy over expert testimony. That issue is the tension between the conventional understanding of trials that demands that fact finders be educated about the relevant facts and the use of experts that introduce a large dose of deference. The most regrettable aspect of the Court's opinion in *Daubert* is that it lost an opportunity to discuss this legal issue. Having not discussed the issue that drives contemporary problems, the Court's decision will largely leave those problems unaffected and undisturbed. We discuss the distinction between education and deference, and its implications for expert testimony, in greater detail in subsection 5, infra.

The Court did emphasize, although in difficult to follow language, that scientific evidence must be relevant, which includes a "helpfulness" component. What is "helpful" depends on the task. If the task is simply to decide a case, there need be no means of connecting scientific (or any other) evidence to the understanding of the jurors. Providing an opinion or conclusion to defer to would suffice nicely (as would providing the jurors a coin to flip). However, if the task is to decide rationally, then any scientific evidence will have to be sufficiently explained so that the jurors have a reasonable chance of understanding it. If this is what the Court meant, then *Daubert* could eventually revolutionize in a second direction the area of scientific and expert testimony by its rejection of the deference approach and its embrace of the educational model.

4. Whatever the precise standards for the admission of specialized testimony, the evidentiary principles involved in dealing with the evidence are quite simple and straightforward: They are, as we have suggested, the principles embodied in FRE 401-403 and 104. What is not simple and what is by far the most important aspect of dealing with specialized evidence is that the attorney must have a solid working grasp of the specialized or scientific principles to which the testimony relates, for it is the attorney who will be responsible for developing and refuting the information through the direct and cross-examination of witnesses. In short, the attorney must be an expert.

5. The actual holding in *Frye* excluding the result of lie detector tests became for a time the universal rule in this country. This rule began to slowly change in the mid-1990s with several decisions allowing polygraph evidence coming in the wake of

Daubert. A number of jurisdictions began admitting the evidence, probably because a per se rule of exclusion seemed contradictory to the new statement of the standard which was enunciated in *Daubert.* See, e.g., United States v. Piccinonna, 885 F.2d 1529 (11th Cir. 1989). *Piccinonna,* which was decided pre-Daubert, also held that polygraph results would be admissible to impeach or corroborate testimony if three conditions were met: (1) notice of intent to use the evidence must be given to the opposition; (2) the opposing side must be given an opportunity to administer its own test; and (3) admissibility of the evidence is to be governed by the normal rules for the admissibility of corroboration and impeachment evidence, so that, for example, corroborating evidence would not be admissible until a witness's character for truthfulness has been attacked under FRE 608. The 11th Circuit has continued to adhere to these three conditions post-Daubert. See United States v. Henderson, 409 F.3d 1293 (11th Cir. 2005) (stating that Piccinonna's ruling is still valid post-Daubert). In United States v. Posado, 57 F.3d 428 (5th. Cir. 1995), the court held that the results of polygraph examinations may be admissible in certain criminal cases regardless of stipulations (here one was offered but rejected). The court read *Daubert* as liberalizing the admission of scientific evidence, and concluded that the 70 percent to 90 percent accuracy rate now achieved with polygraphs exceeded the level of reliability of much evidence presently admitted. The court expressed concern about the prejudicial effect of such evidence, but found it not to be a problem here because the issue was who to believe, the state or the defendants, at a suppression hearing where dramatically different stories were being told and where other evidence cast doubt on the state's version of events. In any event, the evidence was not going to be heard by a jury. Admissibility was taken a step further in United States v. Galbreth, 908 F. Supp. 877 (D.N.M. 1995). *Galbreth* involved a prosecution for tax evasion. The defendant moved to admit a polygraph examination that showed that he was telling the truth in stating that he did not realize he had underreported his income. The court found the technique valid and the operator qualified, and admitted the evidence.

Despite these decisions, courts in some jurisdictions are still regularly excluding polygraph evidence. In Cervantes v. Jones, 188 F.3d 805 (7th Cir. 1999), the court stated that "due to the suspected unreliability of polygraphs, Illinois courts have created a rule that the police, grand juries, and courts may not rely on polygraph evidence in determining whether probable cause exists." The court in United States v. Prince-Oyibo, 320 F.3d 494 (4th Cir. 2003), stated that they would continue to adhere to a per se inadmissibility standard for polygraph results, despite more lenient standards in other courts. See also United States v. Thomas, 167 F.3d 299, 308 (6th Cir.1999) ("[This Court does] . . . generally disfavor admitting the results of polygraph examinations."); United States v. Benavidez-Benavidez, 217 F.3d 720 (9th Cir. 2000) (upholding the exclusion of unstipulated polygraph evidence and the conviction of the defendant).

The Supreme Court has spoken on the issue a few times in recent years, but rather than clarifying the issue, has merely reiterated the aura of skepticism that surrounds polygraph evidence. In Wood v. Bartholomew, 516 U.S. 1 (1995), the court held that the prosecutor has no constitutional duty ever to disclose to a criminal defendant the fact that a witness has "failed" a polygraph test. United States v. Scheffer, 523 U.S. 303 (1998), seems to have merely revealed the Court's hesitance about seeing polygraphs become commonplace, stating that because there is no consensus about the reliability of polygraph tests, there is no violation of rights where a per se rule against admitting polygraphs is applied. The gatekeeping role for trial judges created in *Daubert* makes it difficult on appeal to find that an exclusion of expert testimony was in error. Still, the Supreme Court's finding of "no consensus" makes it sound like a stricter test is applied to polygraph tests than to other expert evidence. It may make sense, however, that judges instinctively require a higher level of reliability for assessments of witness veracity. A judge may, in a given case, simply rely on a Rule 403 exclusion of overly prejudicial evidence if she is concerned that the jury may confuse evidence of veracity for proof of accuracy. See, e.g., United States v. Lea, 249 F.3d 632 (7th Cir. 2001) ("[A] district court need not conduct a full *Daubert* analysis in order to determine the admissibility of standard polygraph evidence, and instead may examine the evidence under a Rule 403 framework.") Still, it is not clear how polygraph tests, if found to be generally admissible, can be allowed in any fewer than all cases. Whenever there is witness testimony, the truthfulness of that witness is relevant. For a discussion of the slippery slope into the world of mandatory polygraph tests for all witnesses during the discovery stage of all civil and criminal trials, see D. Michael Risinger, Navigating Expert Reliability: Are Criminal Standards of Certainty Being Left on the Dock?, 64 Alb. L. Rev. 99 (2000). For an assessment of the present state of polygraph techniques and a précis of the scientific literature on the subject, see David C. Raskin, et al., The Scientific Status of Research on Polygraph Techniques: The Case for Polygraph Tests, 19-2.0, in 1 Modern Science Evidence: The Law and Science of Expert Testimony (David L. Faigman, David H. Kaye, Michael J. Saks, and Joseph Sanders eds., 2002 & Supp. 2003).

6. Note that in *Daubert* the Court said that in determining admissibility of expert testimony the "focus, of course, must be solely on principles and methodology, not on the conclusions that they generate." Can this distinction be maintained? Should it be maintained? What if an expert applies a reliable methodology but draws an unsupportable inference? In General Electric Co. v. Joiner, 522 U.S. 136 (1997), the Court essentially rejected this distinction. "But nothing in either *Daubert* or the Federal Rules of Evidence requires a district court to admit opinion evidence that is connected to existing data only by the *ipse dixit* of the expert. A court may conclude that there is simply too great an analytical gap between the data and the opinion proffered." The *Joiner* Court also clarified that the standard of review was abuse of discretion, thus making it difficult for courts of appeals to overturn trial court decisions either way on the admissibility of expert testimony. Under such a standard, trial courts have tremendous leeway and can in essence fashion a test more or less "austere" despite *Daubert*'s warning that the liberality of the Federal Rules of Evidence must be preserved. The result may be that each jurisdiction, or even each judge, may develop a habit, supported by growing bodies of precedent, of accepting or excluding specific types of expert testimony. The *Daubert* court would not disagree that two judges, applying substantially the same test, might reach two different decisions on admissibility without abusing their discretion. See Jerome P. Kassirer & Joe S. Cecil, Inconsistency in Evidentiary Standards for Medical Testimony, 288 JAMA 1382, 1384-85 (2002) (discussing the different admissibility standards across jurisdictions for similar medical testimony). If two judges routinely reach divergent decisions, this may lead to what is known as "forum shopping." Litigants may try to bring their suits in specific jurisdictions, or even before specific judges, in the hopes of a favorable ruling on the admissibility of expert testimony. Appellate courts have little power to create a consistent standard because of the difficulty of finding abuse of discretion.

7. On remand, the Ninth Circuit, now applying *Daubert*, reached the same conclusion it had previously that the evidence was inadmissible. Daubert v. Merrell

Dow Pharmaceuticals, Inc., 43 F.3d 1311 (9th Cir. 1995). In reaching that conclusion, however, the court also considered a number of factors in addition to the Supreme Court's list. One was whether the expert was testifying on the basis of research conducted independently of the litigation. How important is this criterion? The Ninth Circuit is concerned about the biasing effects of research conducted for hire, but how much research is now conducted for hire in one way or another?

8. *Daubert* stimulated, and continues to stimulate, an avalanche of academic writing on the topic of scientific evidence. See, e.g., Edward K. Cheng and Albert H. Yoon, Does Frye or Daubert Matter? A Study of Scientific Admissibility Standards, 91 Va. L. Rev. 471 (2005); Paul C. Giannelli, Admissibility of Scientific Evidence, 28 Okla. City U. L. Rev. 1, 11 (2003); Jennifer L. Groscup et al., The Effects of Daubert on the Admissibility of Expert Testimony in State and Federal Criminal Cases, 8 Psy. Pub. Pol'y & L. 339 (2002); Joseph Sanders et al., Legal Perceptions of Science and Expert Knowledge, 8 Psy. Pub. Pol'y & L. 139 (2002); Malcolm B. Coate and Jeffrey H. Fischer, Can Post-Chicago Economics Survive *Daubert*?, 34 Akron L. Rev. 795 (2001); Jeffrey L. Harrison, Reconceptualizing the Expert Witness: Social Cost, Current Controls and Proposed Responses, 18 Yale J. on Reg. 253 (2001); Brandon L. Jensen, Litigating the Crossroads Between Sweet Home and *Daubert*, 24 V. L. Rev. 169 (2000); Derek L. Mogck, Are We There Yet? Refining the Test for Expert Testimony Through *Daubert*, *Kumho Tire* and Proposed Federal Rule of Evidence 702, 33 Conn. L. Rev. 303 (2000); Robert J. Goodwin, The Hidden Significance of Kumho Tire Co. v. Carmichael: A Compass for Problems of Definition and Procedure Created by Daubert v. Merrell Dow Pharmaceuticals, Inc., 52 Baylor L. Rev. 603 (2000); Navigating Uncertainty: Gatekeeping in the Absence of Hard Science, 113 Harv. L. Rev. 1467 (2000); The Expert Witness Predicament: Determining "Reliable" Under the Gatekeeping Test of *Daubert*, *Kumho*, and Proposed Rule 702, 54 Miami L. Rev. 317 (2000); Symposium, At the *Daubert* Gate: Managing and Measuring Expertise in an Age of Science, Specialization, and Speculation, 57 Wash. & Lee L. Rev. 661 (2000) (with articles by David L. Faigman, David S. Caudill and Richard E. Redding, D. Michael Risinger, Roger D. Blair and Jill Boylston Herndon, Andrew I. Gavil, Michael J. Saks, John Monahan, and Christopher Slobogin); Erica Beecher-Monas, a Ray of Light for Judges Blinded by Science: Triers of Science and Intellectual Due Process, 33 Ga. L. Rev. 1047 (1999); Separating the Scientist's Wheat from the Charlatan's Chaff: Daubert's Role in Toxic Tort Litigation, vol. 28, n.6 Environmental Law Rptr. 10293 (1998); Improving Judicial Gatekeeping: Technical Advisors and Scientific Evidence, 110 Harv. L. Rev. 941 (1997); Jay P. Kesan, An Autopsy of Scientific Evidence in a Post-*Daubert* World, 84 Geo. L.J. 1985 (1996); Joe Price, Gretchen Gates Kelly, Junk Science in the Courtroom: Causes Effects and Controls, 19 Hamline L. Rev. 395 (1996); Ronald J. Allen, Expertise and the *Daubert* Decision, 84 J. Crim. L. & Crim. 1157 (1994); Burt Black et al., Science and the Law in the Wake of *Daubert*: A New Search for Scientific Knowledge, 72 Tex. L. Rev. 715 (1994); Developments in the Law, Confronting the New Challenges of Scientific Evidence, 108 Harv. L. Rev. 1481 (1995); Rochelle Dreyfuss, Is Science a Special Case: The Admissibility of Scientific Evidence After Daubert v. Merrell Dow, 73 Tex. L. Rev. 1779 (1995); David Faigman, Mapping the Labyrinth of Scientific Evidence, 46 Hast. L.J. 555 (1995); Edward J. Imwinkelried, The Meaning of "Facts or Data" in Federal Rule of Evidence 703: The Significance of the Supreme Court's Decision to Rely on Federal Rule 702 in Daubert v. Merrell Dow Pharmaceuticals, Inc., 54 Md. L. Rev. 352 (1995); Linda Sinnard and William Young, *Daubert*'s Gatekeeper: The Role of the

District Judge in Admitting Expert Testimony, 68 Tul. L. Rev. 1457 (1994); Symposium, Evidence after the Death of *Frye*, 15 Cardozo L. Rev. 1745 (1994); Symposium, Scientific and Technological Evidence, 43 Emory L.J. 853 (1994); Symposium, Behavioral Science Evidence in the Wake of *Daubert*, 13 Behav. Sci. & L. 127 (1995).

4.   Elaboration of Technical or Other Specialized Knowledge under Kumho Tire

Daubert explicitly dealt only with scientific evidence. Immediately following the case, the circuits split on how, or whether, *Daubert* applied to "technical or other specialized knowledge." The Court addressed this issue in the following case involving a tire blowout. A purported expert was willing to testify on the basis of a highly subjective methodology that the cause of the blowout was a manufacturing defect. The trial judge applied *Daubert* and excluded the evidence. The court of appeals reversed, holding that *Daubert* only applies to scientific evidence and not to "technical or otherwise specialized knowledge," which it claimed was involved in this case. The Supreme Court reversed, and also expanded on the meaning of the "abuse of discretion" standard.

<u>KUMHO TIRE COMPANY, LTD. v. CARMICHAEL</u>
<u>526 U.S. 137 (1999)</u>

JUSTICE BREYER delivered the opinion of the Court.
    ... This case requires us to decide how Daubert applies to the testimony of engineers and other experts who are not scientists. We conclude that Daubert's general holding — setting forth the trial judge's general "gate-keeping" obligation — applies not only to testimony based on "scientific" knowledge, but also to testimony based on "technical" and "other specialized" knowledge. See Fed. Rule Evid. 702. We also conclude that a trial court may consider one or more of the more specific factors that Daubert mentioned when doing so will help determine that testimony's reliability. But, as the Court stated in Daubert, the test of reliability is "flexible," and Daubert's list of specific factors neither necessarily nor exclusively applies to all experts or in every case. Rather, the law grants a district court the same broad latitude when it decides how to determine reliability as it enjoys in respect to its ultimate reliability determination. See General Electric Co. v. Joiner, 522 U.S. 136, 143 (1997) (courts of appeals are to apply "abuse of discretion" standard when reviewing district court's reliability determination). Applying these standards, we determine that the District Court's decision in this case — not to admit certain expert testimony — was within its discretion and therefore lawful. ...

II

A

    In Daubert, this Court held that Federal Rule of Evidence 702 imposes a special obligation upon a trial judge to "ensure that any and all scientific testimony ... is not only relevant, but reliable." The initial question before us is whether this basic gatekeeping obligation applies only to "scientific" testimony or to all expert testimony. We, like the parties, believe that it applies to all expert testimony. For one thing, Rule 702 itself says:

> If scientific, technical, or other specialized knowledge will assist the trier of fact to understand the evidence or to determine a fact in issue, a witness qualified as an expert by knowledge, skill, experience, training, or education, may testify thereto in the form of an opinion or otherwise.

This language makes no relevant distinction between "scientific" knowledge and "technical" or "other specialized" knowledge. It makes clear that any such knowledge might become the subject of expert testimony. In *Daubert,* the Court specified that it is the Rule's word "knowledge," not the words (like "scientific") that modify that word, that "establishes a standard of evidentiary reliability." Hence, as a matter of language, the Rule applies its reliability standard to all "scientific," "technical," or "other specialized" matters within its scope. We concede that the Court in Daubert referred only to "scientific" knowledge. But as the Court there said, it referred to "scientific" testimony "because that was the nature of the expertise" at issue.

Neither is the evidentiary rationale that underlay the Court's basic Daubert "gatekeeping" determination limited to "scientific" knowledge. Daubert pointed out that Federal Rules 702 and 703 grant expert witnesses testimonial latitude unavailable to other witnesses on the "assumption that the expert's opinion will have a reliable basis in the knowledge and experience of his discipline." 509 U.S. at 592 (pointing out that experts may testify to opinions, including those that are not based on firsthand knowledge or observation). The Rules grant that latitude to all experts, not just to "scientific" ones.

Finally, it would prove difficult, if not impossible, for judges to administer evidentiary rules under which a gatekeeping obligation depended upon a distinction between "scientific" knowledge and "technical" or "other specialized" knowledge. There is no clear line that divides the one from the others. Disciplines such as engineering rest upon scientific knowledge. Pure scientific theory itself may depend for its development upon observation and properly engineered machinery. And conceptual efforts to distinguish the two are unlikely to produce clear legal lines capable of application in particular cases. Cf. Brief for National Academy of Engineering as Amicus Curiae 9 (scientist seeks to understand nature while the engineer seeks nature's modification); Brief for Rubber Manufacturers Association as Amicus Curiae 14-16 (engineering, as an "applied science," relies on "scientific reasoning and methodology"); Brief for John Allen et al. as Amici Curiae 6 (engineering relies upon "scientific knowledge and methods").

Neither is there a convincing need to make such distinctions. Experts of all kinds tie observations to conclusions through the use of what Judge Learned Hand called "general truths derived from . . . specialized experience." Hand, Historical and Practical Considerations Regarding Expert Testimony, 15 Harv. L. Rev. 40, 54 (1901). And whether the specific expert testimony focuses upon specialized observations, the specialized translation of those observations into theory, a specialized theory itself, or the application of such a theory in a particular case, the expert's testimony often will rest "upon an experience confessedly foreign in kind to [the jury's] own." Ibid. The trial judge's effort to assure that the specialized testimony is reliable and relevant can help the jury evaluate that foreign experience, whether the testimony reflects scientific, technical, or other specialized knowledge.

We conclude that Daubert's general principles apply to the expert matters described in Rule 702. The Rule, in respect to all such matters, "establishes a standard of evidentiary reliability." 509 U.S. at 590. It "requires a valid . . . connection to the pertinent inquiry as a precondition to admissibility." 509 U.S. at 592. And where such testimony's factual basis, data, principles, methods, or their application are called sufficiently into question, the trial judge must determine whether the testimony has "a reliable basis in the knowledge and experience of [the relevant] discipline." 509 U.S. at 592.

B

The petitioners ask more specifically whether a trial judge determining the "admissibility of an engineering expert's testimony" may consider several more specific factors that Daubert said might "bear on" a judge's gate-keeping determination. These factors include:

— Whether a "theory or technique . . . can be (and has been) tested";
— Whether it "has been subjected to peer review and publication";
— Whether, in respect to a particular technique, there is a high "known or potential rate of error" and whether there are "standards controlling the technique's operation"; and
— Whether the theory or technique enjoys "general acceptance" within a "relevant scientific community." 509 U.S. at 592-594.

Emphasizing the word "may" in the question, we answer that question yes.

Engineering testimony rests upon scientific foundations, the reliability of which will be at issue in some cases. See, e.g., Brief for Stephen Bobo et al. as Amici Curiae 23 (stressing the scientific bases of engineering disciplines). In other cases, the relevant reliability concerns may focus upon personal knowledge or experience. As the Solicitor General points out, there are many different kinds of experts, and many different kinds of expertise. See Brief for United States as Amicus Curiae 18-19, and n. 5 (citing cases involving experts in drug terms, handwriting analysis, criminal modus operandi, land valuation, agricultural practices, railroad procedures, attorney's fee valuation, and others). Our emphasis on the word "may" thus reflects Daubert's description of the Rule 702 inquiry as "a flexible one." Daubert makes clear that the factors it mentions do not constitute a "definitive checklist or test." And Daubert adds that the gatekeeping inquiry must be " 'tied to the facts' " of a particular "case." We agree with the Solicitor General that "the factors identified in Daubert may or may not be pertinent in assessing reliability, depending on the nature of the issue, the expert's particular expertise, and the subject of his testimony." The conclusion, in our view, is that we can neither rule out, nor rule in, for all cases and for all time the applicability of the factors mentioned in Daubert, nor can we now do so for subsets of cases categorized by category of expert or by kind of evidence. Too much depends upon the particular circumstances of the particular case at issue.

Daubert itself is not to the contrary. It made clear that its list of factors was meant to be helpful, not definitive. Indeed, those factors do not all necessarily apply even in every instance in which the reliability of scientific testimony is challenged. It might not be surprising in a particular case, for example, that a claim made by a scientific witness has never been the subject of peer review, for the particular application at issue may never previously have interested any scientist. Nor, on the other hand, does the presence of Daubert's general acceptance factor help show that an expert's testimony is reliable where the discipline itself lacks reliability, as, for example, do theories grounded in any so-called generally accepted principles of astrology or necromancy.

At the same time, and contrary to the Court of Appeals' view, some of Daubert's questions can help to evaluate the reliability even of experience-based testimony. In certain cases, it will be appropriate for the trial judge to ask, for example, how often an engineering expert's experience-based methodology has produced erroneous results, or whether such a method is generally accepted in the relevant engineering community. Likewise, it will at times be useful to ask even of a witness whose expertise is based purely on experience, say, a perfume tester able to distinguish among 140 odors at a sniff, whether his preparation is of a kind that others in the field would recognize as acceptable.

We must therefore disagree with the Eleventh Circuit's holding that a trial judge may ask questions of the sort Daubert mentioned only where an expert "relies on the application of scientific principles," but not where an expert relies "on skill- or experience-based observation." We do not believe that Rule 702 creates a schematism that segregates expertise by type while mapping certain kinds of questions to certain kinds of experts. Life and the legal cases that it generates are too complex to warrant so definitive a match. To say this is not to deny the importance of Daubert's gatekeeping requirement. The objective of that requirement is to ensure the reliability and relevancy of expert testimony. It is to make certain that an expert, whether basing testimony upon professional studies or personal experience, employs in the courtroom the same level of intellectual rigor that characterizes the practice of an expert in the relevant field. Nor do we deny that, as stated in Daubert, the particular questions that it mentioned will often be appropriate for use in determining the reliability of challenged expert testimony. Rather, we conclude that the trial judge must have considerable leeway in deciding in a particular case how to go about determining whether particular expert testimony is reliable. That is to say, a trial court should consider the specific factors identified in Daubert where they are reasonable measures of the reliability of expert testimony.

C

The trial court must have the same kind of latitude in deciding how to test an expert's reliability, and to decide whether or when special briefing or other proceedings are needed to investigate reliability, as it enjoys when it decides whether that expert's relevant testimony is reliable. Our opinion in Joiner makes clear that a court of appeals is to apply an abuse-of-discretion standard when it "reviews a trial court's decision to admit or exclude expert testimony." 522 U.S. at 138-139. That standard applies as much to the trial court's decisions about how to determine reliability as to its ultimate conclusion. Otherwise, the trial judge would lack the discretionary authority needed both to avoid unnecessary "reliability" proceedings in ordinary cases where the reliability of an expert's methods is properly taken for granted, and to require appropriate proceedings in the less usual or more complex cases where cause for questioning the expert's reliability arises. Indeed, the Rules seek to avoid "unjustifiable expense and delay" as part of their search for "truth" and the "just determination" of proceedings. Fed. Rule Evid. 102. Thus, whether Daubert's specific factors are, or are not, reasonable measures of reliability in a particular case is a matter that the law grants the trial judge broad latitude to determine. And the Eleventh Circuit erred insofar as it held to the contrary.

III

[The Court then reviewed the basis of the expert's testimony, and decided that the District Court was acting within its discretion in excluding the testimony, and thus that the Court of Appeals erred in reversing.]

 . . . In sum, Rule 702 grants the district judge the discretionary authority, reviewable for its abuse, to determine reliability in light of the particular facts and circumstances of the particular case. The District Court did not abuse its discretionary authority in this case. Hence, the judgment of the Court of Appeals is Reversed.

NOTE

We said earlier, at page 632, that to understand the amendments to FRE 702 that added the three subsections to the rule, you have to understand *Daubert* and *Kumho Tire*. The reason for this is now obvious. The amendments requiring the testimony to be the product of reliable principles and methods and to be based upon sufficient facts and data, and requiring a showing that the witness has reliably applied the principles and methods to the facts of the case, are an effort to embody in the rule the essence of the cases.

KEY POINTS

1. FRE 702 adopts a functional approach to the meaning of "scientific," "technical," and "specialized" knowledge. If a witness possesses knowledge, however obtained, that would be helpful to the jury, the witness may testify to that knowledge.

2. The *Frye* test has been replaced with the requirement that "scientific" evidence be reliable and relevant, which essentially means scientifically valid and helpful to the jury.

3. *Kumho* extends *Daubert's* reach to technical and other specialized knowledge, and also extends *Joiner's* articulation of the discretionary authority of trial judges by emphasizing that it is up to the trial judges to decide how best to fulfill their gatekeeping function.

4. *Kumho* also modifies the central meaning of *Daubert* through its conversion of the *"Daubert* criteria" into the *Daubert* "neither necessary nor sufficient" list of possibly relevant factors.

PROBLEMS

9.10. A jury found that ABC Radio breached its contract with Children's Radio and misappropriated trade secrets. During the trial, the judge allowed economist Stephen Willis to testify that, absent ABC's damaging conduct, Children's Radio would have been valued at $30 million. On defendant's posttrial motion, the judge ruled that Willis's testimony should not have been admitted because, although he applied an "uncontroversial accounting method," his ultimate opinions were dubious. On appeal, Children's Radio argued that, under *Daubert*, a court can review only the methodology of the expert, not his or her conclusions. Is it within the trial court's discretion to exclude expert testimony on this ground?

9.11. Ms. Elcock fell and was injured while shopping in a Kmart store. In her suit against the Kmart Corporation, Dr. Copemann, a vocational rehabilitationist, testified that through his evaluation and treatment of Ms. Elcock he found her to be depressed and suffering from disorders linked to her pain and inability to adapt, and that all of her ailments were brought on by her fall at Kmart. He went on to opine that Ms. Elcock would never recover and would always be 50 percent to 60 percent vocationally disabled. Copemann testified that he valued Elcock's injuries using the Fields (comparing pre- and post-injury access to labor market) and Gamboa (more holistic approach, examining extent of injury and client's perceptions among other factors) analyses. The jury returned a verdict in favor of the plaintiff and awarded her $650,000. The Kmart Corporation appealed. In reviewing the trial record the appellate court found that Dr. Copemann was adequately qualified to testify, but it also noted that his testimony failed to meet several of the *Daubert* factors. First, the court found that Copemann had not provided "an inkling as to the standards controlling his method — i.e., how he excludes for other variables, such as Elcock's pre-existing injuries or job limitations — an expert trying to reproduce Copemann's method would be lost." Second, the plaintiff introduced evidence that both the Gamboa approach and the Fields approach to vocational rehabilitation assessments have received general acceptance in the field. Dr. Copemann, however, had testified that he used a "hybrid methodology," employing some aspects of both techniques. There was no evidence demonstrating that this "hybrid" had reached a level of general acceptance. Are these shortcomings in Dr. Copemann's testimony sufficient for a finding of abuse of discretion? How should the appellate court rule?

9.12. Rhonda Woods and Darla Burns worked as operators of a specially designed forklift called the TSP. Both Woods and Burns were injured on the job when they were struck by empty wooden pallets while driving the TSP down narrow warehouse aisles. Both sued the manufacturer of the TSP, alleging negligence in the design, maintenance, and operational warnings. Daniel Pacheco, who had a B.S. degree in mechanical engineering and had been a registered Professional Engineer for 30 years, was prepared to testify for the plaintiffs. Everyone agreed that Pacheco's credentials were adequate. In his investigation prior to trial, Pacheco read the depositions of the plaintiffs and 10 other people who had knowledge relevant to the incidents, he reviewed the defendant's manufacturing and service documents for the TSP, and he read the TSP's sales brochures, a training manual, and engineering drawings. Pacheco explained that he had seen photographs of the TSP and had read the manufacturer's literature but had never operated or observed another person operating the TSP. Despite this, he was prepared to testify that it was his opinion that an extension of the existing wire mesh guard would have prevented the plaintiffs' injuries and that an alternative warning would have been more effective to this end as well. At the time of the pretrial hearing to determine the admissibility of his testimony, he had not drafted such an alternative warning to present to the court. Should Pacheco be allowed to testify to both or either of these opinions?

9.13. Soon after Kenneth Goodwin purchased a MTD lawn mower, he suffered an eye injury while cutting the grass in front of his home. He had to undergo eye surgery for a cut in his cornea and sued MTD Products for the dangerous and defective design of its mower. During the trial, Goodwin testified that he had been mowing about five feet from his house when he felt something hit his left eye. He stated that when he later returned to the spot, he found a plastic wing nut with a slice mark in it. Goodwin proposed to the jury the theory that the mower was defective in that the motor's vibrations had loosened the wing nut, allowing it to fall into the cutting blades. The nut then shot out at about 190 mph and ricocheted off the plaintiff's house and into his left eye.

In support of this theory, lawn mower experts testified about the manufacture, design, and condition of the mower, and medical experts testified about his eye injury. To rebut this evidence, MTD called Gunter Plamper, its vice president in charge of product development and safety. Plamper explained why he felt MTD's mower was safe but when he tried to explain that it was impossible for a wing nut to cause Goodwin's eye injury, the attorney for the plaintiff objected. What were the best grounds for this objection and how should the judge rule?

Later, the defense attorney tried to elicit from Plamper his expert opinion about whether he believed Goodwin when he stated that he was in the operator's zone behind the lawn mower with the discharge chute facing down when he was injured. The plaintiff's attorney again objected. How should the court rule?

9.14. Officer Muirhead was sued for use of excessive force by Mr. Nimely, who was rendered paraplegic when Muirhead shot him after an armed chase on foot. During the trial, the plaintiff offered the testimony of several experts to the extent that Muirhead's shot was fired while Nimely was facing away from him, fleeing. The defense countered with the testimony of Dr. Stuart Dawson, a consulting expert in forensic pathology. Dawson testified that regardless of the actual course of events, Muirhead probably perceived Nimely as turning to face him as Muirhead fired; thus Muirhead's use of force would have been justified (since Nimely was armed at the time). Dawson's testimony on the "misperception" of Officer Muirhead was based in part on his review of Muirhead's pre-trial deposition, in which Muirhead related his belief that Nimely was turned to face him when the shot was fired. Dawson further testified that he based his expert opinion on his independent conclusion that Muirhead must not have been lying in his account of the course of the events leading up to the shot:

Q: Now, Doctor Dawson, did you also review the deposition testimony of Police Officers Muirhead and McCarthy?

A: Yes.

Q: Was there testimony about what Mr. Nimely was doing at the time Sergeant Muirhead thought he shot him consistent with your findings?

. . . .

A: Well, yes and no. There was testimony that Mr. Nimely was turning, but taken literally, the testimony wasn't consistent with the facts because the literal testimony was that the officer felt that he shot directly in front of the chest of Mr. Nimely but he did say that Mr. Nimely was in the process of turning, so in effect my analysis considered both of those aspects and realized they could basically be synthesized in something reasonable.

Q: In doing your analysis, in light of — what you described as the entrance and exit wound and trajectory of the bullet, did you consider that the police officer who said that he shot him straight in the chest wasn't telling the truth?

A: That certainly is one of the considerations that goes through your mind, is perhaps the officer is simply lying about the incident. I considered that possibility and — but fairly quickly rejected it as being the less likely of the things that happened.

Q: Why did you reject it? . . .

A: Well, I rejected it because, you know, in — it's generally an acceptable concept that police officers aren't going to discharge their weapons —

Mr. *Kelton:* Judge, I object to what is an acceptable concept of what police officers will do.

The court: Overruled. The witness is explaining his answer. He may complete it.

A: Thank you, Judge. What it boils down to is police officers don't discharge weapons lightly because the discharge of a weapon creates all kinds of problems . . .

The court: . . . You may continue with your answer.

A: Thank you. It causes problems of criminal litigation, civil litigation, et cetera. The other thing is, it's reasonable to infer that a police officer is going to know that whenever a discharge does occur, there is going to be a big investigation and that will include forensic examination of wounds, so it didn't make much sense to me that the police officer would say that the person was shot in the front if it would be obvious to the police officer that an investigation would be done and that would show the person was shot in the back.

The jury found for the defense. Should Dawson's testimony have been permitted?

9.15. In a personal injury suit (a "slip and fall case") against a grocery store, Maxine Black sought to introduce the testimony of Dr. Reyna, her algologist (a doctor who treats persistent pain). Ms. Black developed fibromyalgia (a non-specific, chronic-pain illness) after the accident. At trial, Dr. Reyna testified that she fully apprised herself of Ms. Black's prior medical history before the accident, that she determined that no post-accident incident was an intervening cause for the onset of Ms. Black's fibromyalgia, and that no other factors — based upon her review of tests performed prior to accepting Ms. Black as a patient, as well as those tests which Dr. Reyna, herself, directed to be made — contributed to Ms. Black's fibromyalgia. Reyna acknowledged that fibromyalgia has no known etiology (i.e., medical science does not know whether the cause of the condition is muscle, nerve, or hormone damage); but she was willing to testify that the fall contributed to the development of Ms. Black's condition. Should Dr. Reyna be allowed to testify?

9.16. The defendant, Mr. Salimonu, is being tried for conspiracy to import heroin, a federal offense. As one of the elements of the crime, the prosecution has the burden of proving that Mr. Salimonu knew, and was in contact with, another member of the conspiracy. To this end, it presented tape recordings of incriminating conversations between "Laddie" and McKinnon and between "Laddie" and Petrosino. McKinnon and Petrosino are alleged co-conspirators. A voice exemplar that contains a recording of Salimonu's voice was also played for the jury for purposes of comparison. The prosecution seeks to convince the jury that "Laddie" was in fact Mr. Salimonu.

To refute this argument, Salimonu wishes to introduce the testimony of two expert witnesses to establish that Laddie's voice and Salimonu's voice on the exemplar are different. Robert Berkovitz, the developer of a spectogram computer program that plots the frequency and magnitude of speech signals, is prepared to testify that substantial differences between the spectograms of the two voices indicate that the tapes are of two different people. Dr. Stephen Cushing, a linguist, has listened to the tapes and, based on this, is willing to testify that the two voices were different.

In the voir dire, Dr. Cushing states that he has listened to the tapes several times and has distinguished 14 differences between the two voices. Cushing admits that he has had no training or special certification in voice identification or comparison, and that he has only engaged in voice recognition procedures two or three times before. He also concedes that a person may be able to disguise his voice and that he does not know whether the voice in this exemplar is disguised. Finally, Cushing states that a layperson without training in linguistics would be able to discern the same differences that he has by listening to the tapes. Should the trial judge allow both experts to testify?

9.17. As part of a conspiracy trial, the government called a handwriting analyst to testify to the identity of persons who had addressed an envelope containing illegal drugs. The analyst, Dr. Learned, had attended courses and seminars on handwriting identification, was employed by the secret service as a handwriting expert, and had testified in over 100 court cases. Handwriting analysis essentially involves comparing a known sample of a person's writing with the writing on the document sought to be identified. The analyst compares the characteristics of the writing, including the slant of the writing, the height and shape of the letters, and the spacing between letters and words.

After the court ruled that Dr. Learned's testimony was admissible, the defense tried to call Lou Bowden, a law professor who had no formal training in handwriting analysis and who lacked practical experience in the field. Bowden nevertheless had published an article in a well-respected law review, criticizing the field of handwriting analysis and its use in litigation. Bowden's main critique of this type of analysis was that it lacked standards to guide experts in weighing the match or nonmatch of particular handwriting characteristics.

The trial court ruled Bowden's testimony inadmissible. Was the court correct?

5.   Reflection on Scientific Evidence and the Daubert Case

Trials in the Anglo-American tradition were originally the means by which conventional disputes were resolved. The original mode of trial gathered together individuals with knowledge of local affairs to decide notorious disputes. The existence of disputes was part of conventional knowledge, as was the knowledge necessary to resolve them. The local conventions determining borders or access to bodies of water or the proper maintenance of property were truly conventions, and thus known throughout the relevant community. As times changed, various forces coalesced that required modification in the self-informing aspect of juries, with the result that the knowledge of jurors was supplemented with the testimony of other members of the community, but disputes were for the most part still conventional ones requiring primarily the judgment of responsible members of the community for decision.

Over time litigated matters became more complex, and the gap of ignorance separating the fact finders from the witnesses increased. More and more frequently what witnesses said had to be explained to make it understandable. A case may depend on the conventions of a certain business or industry rather than the conventions of the society at large, and jurors will often need to be informed of those conventions. A witness may not speak English, and thus the testimony must be translated.[7] The

7.   Apparently a party can insist on its being translated. In Hernandez v. New York, 500 U.S. 352 (1991), the Supreme Court upheld the exclusion of Spanish-speaking jurors in a case in which some witnesses would testify in Spanish on the ground that the jurors might not accept the translator's rendition of the testimony.

case may involve a technical vocabulary that, like a foreign vocabulary, must be made accessible to those lacking the technical training. As such cases became more common, the traditional model of factfinding was largely adhered to. The parties were merely obligated to explain a little bit more, to put the juror in a position to understand what the witnesses were saying, and thus to decide the case in an intelligent fashion.

Are there any cases that cannot be accommodated within the traditional model? Do some cases present issues for decision that defy the ability of fact finders to understand them? Perhaps the answer to these questions is no. Perhaps with enough time and resources, jurors can be sufficiently informed so that they can decide intelligently all litigated cases. Yet now another set of questions lurks in the shadows: At what cost is this knowledge purchased, and is the bargain a wise one? Would resources be better used elsewhere? Who should decide on what "better" use of resources may be available?

The answer to the first question, whether there are cases that defy the ability of fact finders to understand them, seems clear enough upon reflection, even though it may be counterintuitive, and the answer is surely no. The deficits of juridical fact finders are not primarily cognitive; they are informational. Judges and jurors lack knowledge about various branches of human inquiry, as we all do, but there is little reason to believe that, with instruction, they could not adequately master the relevant fields. Ironically, and again counterintuitively, jurors, because they sit on juries, are possibly better able to master the relevant subjects than judges. The issue is not whether every single juror understands adequately every single issue, but whether the jury adequately understands. The question is not whether each of the jurors ends up understanding all there is to know about a field, or even knows as much as does any particular expert. The question is whether the jury collectively knows or can learn enough for rational deliberation. With the wealth of talent almost always contained in even a randomly selected group of six to 12 individuals, it would be a remarkable case that truly defied their collective cognitive abilities. Moreover, that experts like witnesses know more than they can communicate does not disprove this point. Experts may very well develop intuitive skills that could not be imparted to a jury. Still, the question is whether those skills matter for rational decision in any particular litigated case. If deciding a case actually reduced to a choice between the hunches of experts that cannot be further explained, the case most likely does not belong in the courts.

The argument that there are cases that defy the ability of fact finders to understand them may not be just counterintuitive; it may appear to be disproved by common experience. Many ideas, especially in their youth, are extremely difficult to grasp. A good example is Einsteinian relativity theory, which was understood by only a small handful of individuals for a considerable time following its creation. But we do not know of any case that required for decision an understanding of general relativity theory, nor of an analogous case, one involving string theory, for example. Perhaps there is one, but again it would be the exception that proves the rule.

General relativity theory is not the only difficult idea to grasp. Many individuals find calculus and probability theory obscure, for example, and both are often integral to trials. But many people do not find mathematics at this level obscure. In determining whether a jury possessed the necessary tools for rational decision, again the question is not whether all jurors do; it is whether the jury does. Nor is the question whether the jury already knew enough about calculus or probability; it is whether they could learn enough. Furthermore, if a case posed an issue requiring a certain technical or mathematical capacity, that capacity could be a condition of serving on the jury. This would make the seating of a jury no more difficult than doing so in a notorious case.[8] The real objection to the argument for educating juries is not that it is wrong; the real objection is that it would be too costly. No doubt educating jurors adequately to decide intelligently cases with complicated issues would be costly. In many instances, the jurors would literally have to go to school, or the school brought to them. One can easily imagine cases that would require months of evidence before jurors would be competent to decide intelligently. It is, however, much more difficult to find cases that would defy this educational process, which brings us full circle.

But the circle reveals a paradox. There are many cases that do not involve scientific or technical questions but do require months of instruction so that the jury can understand them. In these cases we do not permit juror deference to juridical outsiders such as experts; we require the parties to connect the case through evidence to the experience of the jurors. Why, then, do we flirt with, and perhaps adopt, a more deferential mode when something comes into court labeled "expert testimony"? The cognitive questions are highly similar, even if not identical, in both sets of cases. The economic questions are truly identical. In all cases, parties must take into account the costs of presenting their cases and responding to their opponents' cases in determining their optimal strategy. This variable is independent of the distinction between conventional and expert testimony. The economics of public subsidy are also highly analogous, if not identical. All trials have public subsidies, such as the cost of the courthouse and various governmental salaries. From the public point of view, a subsidy to a six-month trial that involved educating the jury about calculus is no different from the subsidy to a six-month bank fraud trial. If there is a difference, it favors the subsidy in support of the instruction in calculus, as that might lead to social benefits that are very difficult to see flowing from the educational effort directed toward the jury in a bank fraud case.

Perhaps the difference between complex conventional cases and cases that call for expert testimony is that the latter demand expertise that is missing from the former. People do possess specialized nonconventional knowledge about mathematics, economics, toxicology, oncology, and so on. Perhaps no one possesses expertise about complex conventional cases such as bank fraud or criminal conspiracies. Perhaps so, but this argues not for our current system of presenting competing versions of expertise at trial, but instead for a form of judicial notice (see FRE 201, discussed in Chapter Eleven, infra).

If expertise exists and can be identified with the certainty that the existence of Lake Michigan bordering the city of Chicago can be, trials should not pause over it. Its lessons should be taken as true, and the fact finder so constricted. Whether in any particular case there is expertise in this sense should be easy to determine by judges or

8. In some cases, this could run up against the notion that defendants must be tried by a jury of their peers. Though not explicit in the Seventh Amendment or elsewhere in the Constitution, the Supreme Court has often reiterated that the doctrine should not be abandoned in criminal cases. See, e.g., Apprendi v. New Jersey, 530 U.S. 466, 548 (2000). The requirement has also been codified in federal law. See, e.g., 28 U.S.C.S. 1861 (2001) ("It is the policy of the United States that all litigants in Federal courts entitled to trial by jury shall have the right to grand and petit juries selected at random from a fair cross section of the community in the district or division wherein the court convenes.") A jury comprised of the highly educated would neither represent a fair cross-section nor would it provide a poor defendant with a jury of his peers. If juries were to be selected by their level and area of knowledge this could be a significant concern, but the essence of this problem may already exist where juries defer to experts, allowing them to decide crucial issues. When a jury defers, an expert who is likely not the defendant's peer in several respects, essentially tries the defendants.

legislatures, and its implications mined for what they are worth. We would defer to such knowledge just as we defer to the indisputable knowledge that Lake Michigan borders Chicago. We would not litigate whether Lake Michigan does; that would simply waste resources. If expertise does exist, we waste resources each time (at least beyond the first or unless conditions have changed) that we litigate the issue.

We not only waste time when we litigate the existence of expertise; we also deliberately engage in nonsensical activity. One of the reasons to litigate the existence of expertise is to provide opinions to which jurors can defer. This is the opposite of education, of course. Jurors are not expected to understand the relevant fields of inquiry; they are simply to decide which expert to believe. How is this to be done intelligently without understanding the relevant fields? This question, which reverberates over the increasing use of expertise at trial, has no satisfactory answer, precisely because the two points cannot be reconciled. Though it is true that juries routinely evaluate the credibility of witnesses and the veracity of their statements, the senses and instincts useful in judging the testimony of an eyewitness are useless when contrasting the credentials of two experts or the scientific likelihood of the theories they propound. It is painfully obvious that jurors (and judges) who do not know enough about the relevant fields of knowledge to decide intelligently cannot decide intelligently which expert to believe among those providing competing versions of that field. Consequently, even if our view of the cognitive capacity of juries is rejected, the present system still is nonrational, and the central problem remains. Obversely, if jurors can decide intelligently about which expert to believe, they can with a little more education reason intelligently about the matters in issue, so that deference to the expert is not necessary.

Deference and education are not analytically distinct entities; they are opposite points on a spectrum. Jurors will virtually never see true "raw" data at trial. Deference occurs to some extent whenever a jury decides whether a witness has testified truthfully. Still, the extent of deference, or of education, is a variable; one can have more of one and less of the other. This is particularly obvious when one considers a case involving not just reporting of sensory experience ("the light was red") but the drawing of inferences ("in light of these studies, I am of the opinion that Bendectin causes birth defects"). In the typical case, the jury is supposed to be able to understand the reasoning process that led the witness from observation to conclusion. Understanding may bring either acceptance or rejection, of course, and the decision will be made by the jury's own lights. Often with experts there is no expectation that the reasoning process can be understood. Acceptance or rejection cannot occur by the jury's own lights, and thus we see a much larger dose of deference. How well a witness's analytical process can be understood is again clearly a variable. Some can be understood completely, some partially, and some not at all. The legal question is the significance of this variable.

Out of this cauldron of concerns emerge three competing methods of handling expert testimony, each with its own strengths and weaknesses:

The Normal, Educational Approach. Expert testimony can be treated just like any other testimony, which means for it to be relevant it must be understandable by the fact finder. To make an expert's testimony understandable will require the jury to be educated about the relevant matters, and thus the "normal approach" collapses into adopting an education model. The difficulty is cost, especially the fact that cost may skew decision toward those with greater resources. The more impecunious a party, the less able the party will be to provide the necessary educative function or to respond to an opponent's case. The latter point is another detrimental aspect of our system's failure to make parties bear the true cost of their cases, which includes the opponent's cost of responding. Without cost shifting, a wealthier party can make the cost of suit too high for the opponent. Adopting the normal approach to expert testimony would exacerbate this problem by tending to make cases involving expertise more protracted. Offsetting this factor in part is that higher costs are a laudable disincentive to sue or an equally laudable incentive to agree to resolution in other, less costly forums.

The Deference Model. Fact finders can be required to defer to established expertise, as occurs whenever experts are required to testify in hypothetical question format. The advantages are obvious. Those with the ability to decide rationally make the decision, costs are reduced, and consistency in decision is advanced. If the decisions about expertise are correct, accuracy in decision should be advanced as well. The disadvantage is the resultant extension of official orthodoxy, which removes decision from the jury and trial judge to some higher level court or legislature. Also, if the decision about expertise is incorrect, consistency of decision will remain, but the decisions will be consistently wrong.

The Adversary Model. Parties can choose either to educate the jury with the assistance of expert testimony or to convince the jury to defer to an expert's opinion. This leaves the whole matter up to the parties, save only for the admissibility decision of judges. That admissibility decision, in turn, would have to be made in anticipation of either education or a request for deference. Again, the advantages are obvious. The parties know their dispute and their resources better than anyone else, and are in the best position to make choices that optimize their interests. The difficulties are that the cost of education will tend to make deference more attractive and that deference cannot occur rationally with any great frequency. The reduction in the likelihood of rationality is at odds with the essence of the common law mode of trial, that is, the pursuit of factual accuracy through rational deliberation. Indeed, there is a high irony here. In a case in which the parties employ a deference mode, the mere admission by the trial judge of competing expert views without requiring full explanation of those views, including instruction on the underlying field of inquiry, ensures that decision will be nonrational if not irrational. Only if a juror could see clearly that one side was right and the other wrong would nonrationality be avoided; but if that were so, the judge would admit only the one version and exclude the other. If reasonable people could rationally disagree about which expert is right, they in addition would be able to understand the underlying dispute, and thus deference would not be needed. Note also what a dramatic qualification of the normal rules of relevancy deference entails. Normally a party must explain the relevance of evidence by adequately connecting the evidence to the fact finder's understanding. With experts in a deferential model, one party can shift that cost of explanation to the opponent by producing an unexplained opinion.

As this brief presentation demonstrates, the use of expert testimony poses fundamental challenges to the common law system of adjudication. Experts are often expert because of years of specialized training, and thus there often will be formidable barriers to educating the fact finder about the relevant issues at trial. Hence, pressure arises to defer to the expertise of experts as a means of keeping trials to a manageable length, but the pressure to defer constitutes a challenge to the core concept of trials, and puts into issue our basic commitment to decisions based on rational deliberation on the evidence. This explains in part the remarkable controversy over expert testimony even as expert testimony is becoming ever more prevalent at trial, for lurking here is the fundamental question of the nature of litigation: To what extent is rational deliberation the hallmark of adjudication?

The *Daubert* case presented these issues to the Court, but its opinion did not address them. The opinion offered no recognition that what was at stake was not just a technical rule of evidence but a conception of trial, and thus the implications of its decision for rational deliberation were not addressed. The Court focused on two other matters that formed the basis of the lower court's ruling in favor of the defendants: First, that the general acceptance standard of *Frye* governed the admissibility of expert testimony in federal court, and second that the standard could not be met with evidence of reanalyses of data that had not previously been published and subjected to peer review. The deep conceptual issue of the defining characteristics of litigation was overlooked in the Court's unenlightening, but thankfully not positively harmful, discussion of the general acceptance standard.

The Court's failure to deal with the core issues presented to it in *Daubert* is all the more unfortunate because still operating are the pressures that over time have resulted in modification of the litigation process to permit large amounts of deference to experts. First is the added cost of educating fact finders so that they may follow the reasoning of the expert in the same way the fact finders can follow the reasoning of a lay witness (thus essentially converting an expert into a lay witness). There is in addition the lottery effect. If reasons for opinions need not be given in detail, one has an increased chance of a lottery-effect jury verdict if the trial judge qualifies a witness as an expert. One effect of *Daubert* has been to transmute the present mechanical invocation of the *Frye* test by the trials courts into a more ostensibly subtle but in fact largely identical process of qualification of expert witnesses. What else can they do? The Supreme Court did not take its opportunity to tell trial judges to admit purported expertise only if the basis of the expertise were understandable, as it could and should have done. Trial judges will thus continue to look for a justification to defer to expertise, and they will continue to find it in the general acceptance of that expertise in generally accepted bodies of knowledge.

Telling the lower courts not to invoke mechanically "general acceptance" may prove marginally helpful, but none of the important questions in the case was addressed. In particular, the conflict between the demands of education and deference was ignored. Indeed, if anything the dichotomy between deference and education was reinforced by the Court's opinion. The list of criteria provided by the Court is only relevant to a system willing to defer; by providing the list, the Court, although surely unintentionally, gave sustenance to deference. This is also why the Court's limitation of its discussion to "scientific" evidence is not problematic. The other kinds of information listed in Rule 702 are unlikely to require deference; information of those types can be explained. A car mechanic can qualify as an expert under the rule, but few would claim that such expertise would defy the cognitive capacity of fact finders. As you saw in *Kumho*, however, the court has proved even more willing to perpetuate the tendency to allow deference than some critics initially thought.

The most regrettable aspect of *Daubert* is that the Court seemed quite unaware of the implications of admitting data without a basis for believing that the data can be understood. By doing so, it seems to be putting its stamp of approval on undeliberative and nonrational legal decisionmaking, which are the antitheses of the law's aspirations. Jurors or judges who cannot understand the reasoning of a witness can only accept or reject the witness's conclusions, but neither acceptance nor rejection will occur rationally. The choice will not be made because a fact finder understands the reasoning and sees either its cogency or its flaws; it will be made for some other reason.

And the set of "some other reasons" is, from the point of view of the law's aspirations, filled with unsavory characters.

Yet another interesting aspect of the expert evidence area that may remain undisturbed by *Daubert* is the special treatment that expert testimony gets with regard to the distinction between sufficiency and admissibility. Often trial courts seem to make a sufficiency determination in the guise of an admissibility determination. The explanation, we think, is that trial judges are admitting evidence that they know they and jurors cannot be expected to understand. Such evidence should not be admitted unless the trial judge is willing to let a verdict rest on it, and so the admissibility decision becomes a sufficiency decision. This all confirms the entrenchment of a deference mode of decision at the trial court level.

Perhaps there is no feasible alternative. Perhaps the cost of truly educating the fact finders would be too high in some cases, or perhaps our skepticism about the point does not dispose of concerns about the cognitive capacity of fact finders. If either is true, the answer again is obvious: Unless we are also wrong that the core aspiration of litigation is decision through rational deliberation, the common law form of decisionmaking should not be employed for those cases.

6.   FRE 705

RULE 705.   DISCLOSURE OF FACTS OR DATA UNDERLYING EXPERT OPINION

The expert may testify in terms of opinion or inference and give reasons therefor without first testifying to the underlying facts or data, unless the court requires otherwise. The expert may in any event be required to disclose the underlying facts or data on cross-examination.

7.   Interpretation and Illustration of FRE 705

At common law, once a witness was qualified to testify as an expert it was necessary to elicit the basis for the opinion before asking the witness about the opinion. This requirement, coupled with the requirement that opinions be based on admissible evidence, tended to force reliance on the use of hypothetical questions. Experts typically were asked long and involved questions containing the evidence as summarized by the examiner. An opinion was then offered on that basis. Use of the hypothetical question approach ensured that the premises of an opinion had been the subject of earlier testimony and that the factual basis of an opinion had been set forth before the opinion being given, but it also created a significant artificiality in trials. The most important innovation of FRE 705 is its elimination of the requirement of experts testifying in the form of a response to a hypothetical question.

FRE 705 gives the direct examiner the flexibility to elicit the opinion or conclusion before developing all the details that support it. The rule goes further, however, and permits the opinion without requiring the proponent ever to produce the underlying basis. The advantage to this approach is that it permits the proponent of the evidence to structure its case most effectively. If the proponent is concerned that the fact finders will not pay careful attention without having the summarizing opinion of the expert already before them, the opinion can be introduced early in the expert's testimony. If the proponent believes that laying the foundation first and then bringing out the opinion is optimal, that approach is permissible, also. There is one disadvantage to FRE 705's loose structuring of the evidentiary process. If there is reason to suspect that the information on which the expert bases the opinion is so unreliable that it may be appropriate to exclude the opinion altogether, the opponent will often desire to test that suspicion before rather than after the jury hears the opinion. By explicitly giving the judge authority to require that the basis for an opinion be elicited before the opinion is given, FRE 705 provides a reasonable means for solving this type of problem. See, e.g., United States v. Brien, 59 F.3d 274 (1st Cir. 1995) (holding that the defense was not entitled to offer expert testimony without disclosing the underlying data, leaving it to be developed on cross-examination; rather the data must be supplied to the judge upon demand and may be used in making a preliminary ruling on admissibility). Neither the rule nor the Advisory Committee Note suggests any criteria for the judge to apply in deciding whether to require that the basis for the opinion precede the opinion. And for good reason, this is a matter that could not easily be reduced to rules, and thus is best left to the discretion of the trial judge.

An unsubstantiated opinion is not likely to impress the jury as much as one that has a demonstrably solid basis. Thus, as a matter of strategy, the direct examiner is likely to explore the bases for an expert's opinion sometime during the direct examination. There may be times, however, when the attorney's voluntary exploration of the basis for the testimony on direct examination is less than complete or when there is no substantial basis for the opinion. Rather than ensuring in every case that direct examination will reveal the basis for an opinion, FRE 705 leaves these matters to cross-examination. See, e.g., Smith v. Ford Motor Co., 626 F.2d 784, 793 (10th Cir. 1980) (the effect of Rule 705 is to "place the full burden of exploration of the facts and assumptions underlying the testimony of an expert witness squarely on the shoulders of opposing counsel's cross-examination"). In some cases, the information revealed upon cross-examination can be quite damaging to the party that proffered the evidence, either because it weakens the expert's credibility or because it muddles the story the jury hears. In Skidmore v. Precision Printing & Packaging, Inc., 188 F.3d 606 (5th Cir. 1999), the plaintiff sued her employer for sexual harassment by a coworker that damaged her mental and physical health. The plaintiff introduced her psychiatrist who testified to his diagnosis that the plaintiff suffered from posttraumatic stress disorder and depression brought on by the coworker's conduct. When pressed, under Rule 705, to reveal the underlying facts upon which he had relied, it became clear that he had relied on facts in conflict with the plaintiff's own testimony. The jury was then free to consider the likelihood of the accuracy of the expert's diagnosis in this light.

The Advisory Committee explained the role of cross-examination as follows:

> If the objection is made that leaving it to the cross-examiner to bring out the supporting data is essentially unfair, the answer is that he is under no compulsion to bring out any facts or data except those unfavorable to the opinion. *The answer assumes that the cross-examiner has the advance knowledge which is essential for effective cross-examination.* This advance knowledge has been afforded, though imperfectly, by the traditional foundation requirement. *Rule 26(b)(4) of the Rules of Civil Procedure, as revised, provides for substantial discovery in this area, obviating in large measure the obstacles which have been raised in some instances to discovery of findings, underlying data, and even the identity of the experts.* [Emphasis added.]

The Advisory Committee's answer to bringing out supporting data may be sufficient for civil cases. In criminal cases, where discovery traditionally has been more limited, the cross-examiner may be at a serious disadvantage if the underlying facts and data are not revealed on direct examination. In such a case it would be appropriate for the trial judge to require that the bases for the opinion be elicited on direct examination.

8.   FRE 703

RULE 703.   BASES OF OPINION TESTIMONY BY EXPERTS

The facts or data in the particular case upon which an expert bases an opinion or inference may be those perceived by or made known to the expert at or before the hearing. If of a type reasonably relied upon by experts in the particular field in forming opinions or inferences upon the subject, the facts or data need not be admissible in evidence in order for the opinion or inference to be admitted. Facts or data that are otherwise inadmissible shall not be disclosed to the jury by the proponent of the opinion or inference unless the court determines that their probative value in assisting the jury to evaluate the expert's opinion substantially outweighs their prejudicial effect.

9.   Interpretation and Illustration of FRE 703

In a crucial sense, the primary point of this chapter is to examine the implications of the proposition that to decide some cases correctly requires access to specialized bodies of knowledge. The law needs the knowledge that other disciplines possess, but there is a problem. The knowledge of other disciplines — medicine is a good example — is not organized according to legal requirements. In particular, many disciplines do quite well without the hearsay rule, as when the night nurse informs the day nurse who informs the doctor that the patient vomited during the evening, and the doctor prescribes action in part on the basis of that report. Another example: The surgeon is operating to remove cancerous tissue. In order to determine whether enough tissue has been removed, samples are sent to pathology for immediate evaluation. Reports come back, and on that basis decisions are made whether to remove more tissue. In preparing for trial, an expert witness will "review the file" and formulate an opinion in part on the hearsay contained in the file.

When faced with a conflict between the legal requirements concerning evidence, such as the hearsay rule, and the conventions of other disciplines, such as the reliance on hearsay accounts in a hospital setting, the common law tended to demand that witnesses from other disciplines conform their practice to ours (although some federal circuits adopted a rule allowing physicians to testify on the basis of information from nurses, radiologists, pathologists, and the like; see the discussion in Zenith Radio Corp. v. Matsushita Elec. Indus. Co., 505 F. Supp. 1313, 1322-1323 (E.D. Pa. 1980) *rev'd on other grounds,* 723 F.2d 238 (3d Cir. 1983)). That meant that they could testify but only on the basis of admissible evidence. This, in large measure, was the point of the hypothetical question mode of proceeding. The disadvantage of requiring other disciplines to conform to the legal requirements is that it can make obtaining good and reliable evidence more difficult and costly. The drafters of the Federal Rules rejected this aspect of the common law in FRE 703, providing that experts can testify on the basis of data that would be legally inadmissible, so long as the data is "of a type reasonably relied upon by experts in the particular field." Thus under FRE 703 experts no longer must conform their practices to the law's conventions, but rather the law bends to accommodate the practices of the other disciplines. This is most significant for experts, such as medical personnel, who take action and make decisions on the basis of reliable hearsay. FRE 703 makes clear that expert testimony based on such otherwise inadmissible evidence is permissible, notwithstanding the lack of symmetry between the law's rules about evidence and medicine's practices. Thus the nurse's observations written on the patient's chart, radiological and pathological evaluations, lab reports, and so on may legitimately form the basis of an expert testifying at trial.

Though the law bends to accommodate other disciplines, judges are not obligated to bend over backward. The "reasonably relied upon" requirement is taken seriously by courts and can be a basis for finding an expert's testimony inadmissible. In Redman v. John D. Brush & Co., 111 F.3d 1174 (4th Cir. 1997), a burglary victim brought a products liability suit against the manufacturer of the safe from which his coin collection had been stolen. A metallurgic engineer testified for the plaintiff about the failure analysis he had conducted on the safe. From this analysis he had learned what materials the safe was made of and how those materials were assembled. He also reached the conclusion that the burglar broke into the safe by prying the door open. Based on his findings, he opined that, the safe was not "burglar deterrent." The expert, however, admitted that he had never before analyzed a safe, engaged in the design or manufacture of safes, received any special training in regard to safes, and was not personally familiar with the standards and rating systems used in the safe industry for burglary protection capacity. In order to reach the conclusion that the defendant's safe was not "burglar deterrent," the expert relied upon the hearsay of store personnel to ascertain the meaning of "burglar deterrent." The plaintiff did not call those employees as witnesses nor did he attempt to qualify them as witnesses. Discussing the "reasonably relied upon" requirement, the appellate court noted:

> In this case an expert in the relevant field would be familiar with the design and manufacture of safes and the industry standards regarding safes. There is no proof and no reason to believe that such an expert would rely upon conversations with store personnel to identify a standard of burglar protection capacity. Thus, [the plaintiff's] expert should not have been permitted to rely on the inadmissible hearsay of the store personnel for the purpose of establishing a purported industry standard. Ill F.3d. at 1179.

In contrast, in Sphere Drake Insurance PLC v. Trisko, 226 F.3d 951 (8th Cir. 2000), the court affirmed the lower court's admission of expert testimony that had been objected to on Rule 703 grounds. Here, a jeweler's jewelry went missing from the trunk of the car he was traveling in, although he was in the car the whole time. His insurance policy covered lost or damaged jewelry but excepted "unexplained loss" or a "mysterious disappearance." At trial, the jeweler called a police detective as an expert witness to give testimony about crime patterns in the Miami area, including the covert *modi operandi* of jewel thieves. The detective testified that two unidentified informants had reported to him that someone had paid two persons $20,000 each to steal the jewelry. Though the informants were not available for cross-examination and there was no evidence as to their credibility, the detective was permitted to opine that someone had probably stolen the jewelry and it was thus not a "mysterious disappearance." On appeal, the court held that since the detective testified that he "regularly relied on the statements of informants," he should also be allowed to do so in forming the basis of his expert opinion.

In addition to accommodating the practices of other disciplines, FRE 703 solves another problem. Latent in the common law's opposition to inadmissible evidence forming the basis of expert opinion is a subtle but important fraud. What makes an expert an expert in many instances is a heavy dose of book learning. To the extent that an expert relies on academic study (books and treatises and the like) or on conversations with others such as occur during "rounds" at teaching hospitals, the expertise is based on hearsay, much of which would be inadmissible or too costly to produce at trial. The common law courts overlooked this point. Thus, even though the common law courts "purported" to require a basis in admissible evidence for an expert's opinion, opinions remained admissible even though they relied heavily on knowledge gained through a form of inadmissible, or at least unadmitted, hearsay. Under the FRE 703, this is not a problem.

10.   Elaboration of FRE 703: Opinions Based on Otherwise Inadmissible Evidence

You may have noted a peculiarity in FRE 703 and in our discussion above. FRE 703 makes admissible an opinion based on inadmissible evidence, if it is "reasonably relied upon," but, as a consequence of the last sentence of the rule, the proponent of the opinion may not present to the jury the evidence the expert "reasonably is relying upon" unless a reverse FRE 403 standard is met ("probative value ... substantially outweighs ... prejudicial effect). Even then, the admission is limited to "assisting the jury to evaluate the expert's opinion," rather than admitted substantively for its truth. This sentence was added to the rule in the 2000 amendments to clear up a controversy over the rule's meaning. While the controversy has been resolved, there is considerable doubt whether the resolution makes any sense.

When an expert bases an opinion in whole or in part on inadmissible evidence, there is an inevitable tension between whatever rule makes the evidence inadmissible and FRE 703. As we discussed above, most often this is a tension between FRE 703 and 705 and the hearsay rule, but data on which an opinion is based may be inadmissible for other reasons as well. For example, the expert may have relied on the oral recitation of the contents of an X ray, whereas the best evidence rule would require reliance on the X ray itself; or the expert may have relied on writings that have been insufficiently authenticated. Prior to the amendment to FRE 703, this potential conflict in the rules posed an important question: Does FRE 703 operate as a rule of admission that can take precedence over various specific exclusionary rules, or does it merely permit an expert to express and explain an opinion based on inadmissible evidence? May, in other words, the fact finder rely on the data to draw inferences concerning the material propositions in the case? Or is it "admissible" only to help the fact finder understand the opinion that is based on it? And if the latter is true, to what extent can the fact finder rely on the opinion in deciding the case? Only to the extent that independent admissible evidence of the basis of the opinion is produced?

Courts had taken inconsistent approaches to the problem. Some restricted the otherwise inadmissible data to be used solely to help the fact finder appraise the opinion. Some permitted the underlying data to be used substantively. An example of the former is United States v. Madrid, 673 F.2d 1114 (10th Cir. 1982), where the jury was instructed: "I have instructed you as to opinions by experts and that they may state their reasons for such opinions. You are not to consider such evidence for any other purpose than in evaluating the expert testimony." Unfortunately, the *Madrid* court did not explain how the jurors can consider the opinion unless they consider the basis of the opinion, and it is a puzzle. The jury can consider whether the opinion makes sense in light of its basis, but only if the basis is true will an opinion relate to the case at hand. This approach to the problem of FRE 703, while the typical response of the courts, makes very little sense. For other examples of this approach, see Sphere Drake Insurance PLC v. Trisko, 226 F.3d 951 (8th Cir. 2000) (affirming the jury instruction to "give no weight to the statements of [the informants] in the consideration of the issues in this case. You are to consider that testimony only in developing what [the expert witness] did in the course of his investigation."); United States v. Affleck, 776 F.2d 1451 (10th Cir. 1985).

An example of a court seeing that the typical response to this issue makes little sense is In re Melton, 597 A.2d 892 (D.C. 1991). In *Melton*, psychiatrists offered opinions concerning whether the respondent was a danger to himself or others. The opinions were based in part on accounts of the respondent's behavior given by his mother to the psychiatrists. In an interesting passage, the court captured the dilemma we are discussing:

> We begin by noting that the testimony by Dr. Byrd and Dr. Cornet as to what they learned from others was not admitted in order to prove the truth of the matter asserted. The trial judge specifically instructed the jury that any out-of-court statements by third parties which were reported in the experts' testimony were to be considered only "for the purpose of evaluating the reasonableness and correctness of the doctors' conclusions," and not "to establish the truth of the matters asserted by [the declarants]." As the court explained in United States v. Williams, 447 F.2d 1285, 1290 (5th Cir. 1971) (en banc), *cert. denied,* 405 U.S. 954 (1972),
>
>> an expert's opinion is derived not only from records and data, but from education and from a lifetime of experience. Thus, when the expert witness has consulted numerous sources, and uses that information, together with his own professional knowledge and experience, to arrive at his opinion, that opinion is regarded as evidence in its own right and not as hearsay in disguise.
>
> The problem raised by Melton cannot, however, be avoided simply by calling the evidence expert testimony rather than hearsay. Labels cannot perform juridical alchemy. By resort to expert testimony, the District was able to bring to the jury's attention matters that could obviously prejudice Melton, including, e.g., reports that he had punched his mother, and that on an earlier occasion he had threatened his sister with a screwdriver. Melton was never able to cross-examine those who accused him of these anti-social acts. Such a procedure presents obvious problems of basic fairness. Courts are not blind to these concerns and have attempted to fashion rules which afford reasonable latitude to expert witnesses but simultaneously protect the rights of litigants against whom expert testimony has been offered. The tension between these competing interests is at the heart of this case.

The problem in *Melton* was exacerbated because the trial court gave its instruction four days after the evidence was admitted. Consequently, the appellate court treated the case as one in which no limiting instruction was given:

> Even if, as we have concluded, the psychiatric witnesses testified on the basis of the kind of data on which experts in their field reasonably rely, we have some concern for another reason about the admission and use of the evidence. If we look at the substance rather than the form of what occurred, the secondhand testimony about Melton having punched his

mother came to the jurors' attention in such a way that they might well have considered it for the truth of the out-of-court statement. This may also have occurred with respect to some other incidents.

On October 17, 1985, Dr. Byrd testified that Melton "became impulsive and lost control of his temper, which is a characteristic of a schizophrenic. And he punched his mother in the nose and became very angry with her." The trial judge gave no contemporaneous instruction as to the purpose for which this testimony was received. It was not until four days later, during his final instructions, that the judge told the jurors, with respect to testimony by Dr. Byrd and Dr. Cornet as to information given to them by other individuals, that:

> these statements are admitted only to demonstrate the information relied upon by the doctors in forming their conclusion. They are to be considered by you only for the purpose of evaluating the reasonableness and correctness of the doctors' conclusions. They are not to be considered by you as actual proof of the incidents described. They are hearsay and as such are not admissible to establish the truth of the matters asserted by them.

This court has recently noted that some students of the law of evidence consider the distinction sought to be articulated in such a "limiting" instruction as "most unlikely to be made by juries." In re Samuels, 507 A.2d 150 (D.C. 1986). As Judge Salzman aptly remarked for the court in that case, "conceptual problems are bound to arise when a judge tells a jury that the jury may consider psychiatric diagnoses based on medical records customarily relied on in professional practice, but then tells the jury that it may not consider the 'truthfulness' of those records for any other purpose." Id. With his customary eloquence, Justice Cardozo made a similar point for the Court in a somewhat different context in Shepard v. United States, 290 U.S. 96 (1933): "Discrimination so subtle is a feat beyond the compass of ordinary minds. The reverberating clang of those accusatory words would drown all weaker sounds. It is for ordinary minds, and not for psychoanalysts, that our rules of evidence are framed." The "conceptual" problems to which we referred in Samuels are especially serious with respect to a discrete dramatic act like punching one's mother on the nose. To tell the jurors that they are to consider the testimony about the punch as a basis for the expert's finding of dangerousness, but not with respect to whether Mr. Melton punched his mother, may call for mental gymnastics which only the most pristine theoretician could perform. We suspect that the reaction of that elusive individual, the reasonable person, would be that you cannot believe that the testimony about the punch tends to show that Melton is dangerous unless you first believe that he actually punched his mother. Since the expert apparently believed that he punched her, the jury was likely to believe it too. The distinction sought to be made may therefore become ephemeral.

The problem is a perplexing one, because it is difficult to articulate reasonable or workable limits on any rule which would exclude testimony of the kind here at issue and still vindicate the policies underlying Rule 703.

As the *Melton* court so aptly put it, "you cannot believe that the testimony about the punch tends to show that Melton is dangerous unless you first believe that he actually punched his mother." The restrictive approach exemplified above by the jury instruction from *Madrid* quite literally makes no sense. By contrast, permitting the admission of otherwise inadmissible evidence would not create a dangerous loophole in the rules for unreliable evidence (although there is some disagreement about this among the authors of this text). First, the admitted data would have to be data that could reasonably be relied on. If the data in question is reasonably reliable, even though it may be technically improper, accurate outcomes at trial are likely to be advanced by its admission. To admit data that is likely to advance accuracy hardly sounds like the creation of a regrettable loophole. Indeed, the kind of information that would be admitted pursuant to a liberal reading of FRE 703 is likely to be significantly more reliable than other forms of admissible evidence under the rule. Reflect on our discussion at page 537, supra, of *Beech Aircraft Corp.* v. Rainey. As you recall, *Beech Aircraft Corp.* interpreted FRE 803(8)(c), which makes admissible over a hearsay objection "reports . . . setting forth . . . factual findings resulting from an investigation made pursuant to authority granted by law, unless the sources of information or other circumstances indicate lack of trustworthiness." The Court held that the phrase "factual findings" included opinions or inferences based on observations made during the investigation. In *Beech Aircraft Corp.*, the report in question contained the assertion that "[t]he most probable cause of the accident was the pilot's failure to maintain proper interval." If FRE 803(8)(c) indicates a baseline of reliability for the admission of evidence over technical objections such as hearsay or opinion, evidence reasonably relied on by experts in other disciplines clearly meets the test for admissibility.

Also bear in mind that FRE 703 does not provide the only basis for excluding unreliable opinion testimony. FRE 702 requires that the subject matter be one that requires specialized knowledge to be understood, that the purported expert have that knowledge, and that the expert's opinion be of assistance to the fact finder. In addition, FRE 403 permits the exclusion of evidence whose probative value is substantially outweighed by various countervailing concerns of unreliability and inefficiency.

In any event, the amendment to FRE 703 resolves these matters in favor of the largely incoherent view that an opinion can be understood and credited independently of the basis for that opinion. This will leave intact the prior practice of most courts of excluding reference to the underlying data or giving juries an incomprehensible instruction concerning the use of the otherwise inadmissible evidence. It will also leave intact a practice that cannot conceivably advance the objective of rational decision making. Quite remarkably, the Advisory Committee in its note on this amendment failed even to address, let alone attempt to respond to in a coherent fashion, this fundamental point.

The amendment to FRE 703 adopts a balancing test that the proponent of the opinion (and thus the underlying facts) must meet before otherwise inadmissible facts that the expert "reasonably relied upon" may be disclosed to the jury. This amendment does not eliminate, indeed may exacerbate, the conceptual confusion at the heart of the rule. It perpetuates the myth that one can appraise the expert's opinion without regard to the truth of facts relied upon by the expert, which is plainly false (as in Melton, he either hit his Mom or he didn't). Given that the amended rule remains so confused, it is perhaps not surprising that what it might possibly mean for the "probative value" of the underlying facts to "substantially outweigh their prejudicial effect" is completely opaque. Not surprisingly, the Advisory Committee's Note to the 2000 Amendment is rather sparse in this regard, noting only that "an adversary's attack on an expert's basis will often open the door to a proponent's rebuttal," and "in some circumstances the proponent might wish to disclose information that is relied upon by the expert in order to 'remove the sting' from the opponent's anticipated inference." The amendment to the rule was not necessary to permit fair response. This suggests that the only example the Advisory Committee could come up with where the amendment to the rule would make a difference and that meets this "balancing" test is one in which the underlying facts were helpful to the opponent of the testimony. But cf., Turner v. Burlington Northern Santa Fe RR, 338 F.3d 1058, 1062 (9th Cir. 2003) (applying balancing test to exclude evidence where underlying facts helpful to proponent of testimony).

Whether there are cases where facts helpful to the proponent may be disclosed on direct, and more generally what the cases will make of this mess of a rule, remain to be seen. If, for example, this rule applied to the Melton case, we have no idea how the case would have come out. A new wrinkle may added to the implications of FRE 703 by way of *Crawford* which is reproduced at page 584. At least one case has held that statements to psychiatrists are testimonial, thus triggering the *Crawford* analysis. People v. Goldstein, 843 N.E. 2d 727 (N.Y. 2005). See page 598, supra.

KEY POINTS

1. Under FRE 702, an expert is simply a person with knowledge not likely to be possessed by the fact finder, and they may testify to basic facts, general principles, or inferences to be drawn from the basic facts.

2. The Federal Rules have eliminated the necessity, but not the possibility, of testifying in the form of an answer to a hypothetical question. Under the FRE 705, an expert may give an opinion before the basis of the opinion is offered into evidence.

3. FRE 703 allows opinions based on reasonably reliable but otherwise inadmissible data. The underlying data normally is not admitted at trial. On occasion it is admitted but only for purposes of appraising the opinion, even though the data only matters for that purpose if true.

PROBLEMS

9.18. Wally Daniels is charged with murder and arson. The prosecution's theory is that Wally killed his wife and then, at about 7:00 P.M., set fire to the house in order to make the death look like an accident. Wally claims that he was not near the house at the relevant times and that the fire was the result of bad electrical wiring. The prosecutor's expert, a fire marshal, offers to testify that in his opinion the fire was the result of arson. The fire marshal is prepared to testify about the bases for his opinion, which include, inter alia, the following:

(a) interviews with next door neighbors, John and Wilma Smith, who say they saw Wally running from the house about 7:00 P.M. shortly before they noticed the fire; (b) a written police report prepared by Officer June Adkins, stating that she was patrolling the area shortly before the fire was discovered and that she observed an adult male running from the defendant's house at about 7:00 P.M.; and (c) the fact that Wally had twice previously been convicted of arson.

Wally has objected to all of this evidence. To support the objection, he offers to prove that John Smith is an alcoholic who almost daily is in an alcohol-induced stupor from 3:00 P.M. until midnight. What result?

9.19. Waitress Tina Brennan received an electric shock from a coffee maker while working and allegedly developed fibromyalgia as a result. Ms. Brennan brought a personal injury suit against Reinhart Corp., the manufacturer and installer of the coffee maker. At trial, her vocational rehabilitation counselor Mr. Ostrander testified that in his opinion Ms. Brennan's fibromyalgia would be a permanent condition. As part of the basis for this conclusion, Ostrander stated that Ms. Brennan's rheumatologist had reported that the plaintiff had "permanent partial impairment of 11 percent of the whole person" and that her specialist in physical medicine and rehabilitation had also examined the patient and agreed with Ostrander's analysis. The defense objected to

Ostrander's use of out-of-court hearsay, pointing out that both the rheumatologist and the specialist would be unavailable for cross-examination and, although the rheumatologist had given testimony by deposition, he had not mentioned the 11 percent impairment conclusion. The jury returned a verdict for the plaintiff and the defendant appealed, maintaining that the trial court erred in allowing Ostrander to summarize the opinions of others. Should the appellate court reverse?

9.20. A year after Jimmy Boyd complained about a racial slur made by his supervisor, he received an unfavorable performance review and subsequently remained absent from work for over five weeks. He was terminated after his psychologists reported that his leave was not medically required. Boyd brought suit under the Family Medical Leave Act (FMLA).

During the initial hearing, the employer offered the depositions of Boyd's treating physicians, neither of whom supported Boyd's claim that his absence, purportedly due to the stress and anxiety of his job, constituted protected leave under the FMLA. Boyd responded with the affidavit testimony of his expert witness, Dr. Emory:

> Based upon my review of the records and my examination of Mr. Boyd, it is my professional opinion that Mr. Boyd's health condition rendered him unable to perform his job, and in fact left him disabled. Continued work would have increased his health problems and, in my professional opinion, the only solution to Mr. Boyd's medical condition would have been a leave of absence. At a minimum, Mr. Boyd required a leave of absence to obtain treatment for his condition.

The district court excluded the affidavit, finding that it was "vague and conclusory," provided no foundation for Dr. Emory's conclusions, and spoke only in general terms. On appeal, Boyd argued that Dr. Emory's affidavit should not have been excluded because Rule 705 permitted Dr. Emory to give his opinion without prior disclosure of the underlying facts and data. If allowed, Dr. Emory's statements would create a genuine issue of fact as to whether he suffered a serious health condition under FMLA. Should the court admit Dr. Emory's testimony?

9.21. David Ricci was an environmental engineer doing testing on defendant companies' biomass smoke stack when he fell to his death from a platform surrounding the stack. The platform was about 80 feet from the ground and a ladder ran up the stack's side to the platform. No eyewitnesses saw the fall but Ricci's father inferred that his son inadvertently stepped through the platform ladderway opening that admittedly was missing safety guards, and sued the stack's owner based on this theory. Defendants inferred that the fall occurred as the son descended the ladder.

A safety inspector was qualified as an expert for the plaintiff and testified at trial that it was more probable than not that Ricci had inadvertently fallen through the ladderway opening. This opinion was based in part on statements from Ricci's father and coworkers that Ricci was always careful and that it was his practice to wear gloves while climbing. The defense objected. Do you think the father's and coworkers' testimonials are of the type of data "reasonably relied upon by experts in the particular field"?

9.22. In a criminal trial, the defendant pleaded not guilty by reason of insanity. The prosecution called a psychiatrist as an expert witness to testify to an opinion that the defendant was sane at the time he committed the criminal act. During direct examination, the witness was asked how confident he was in his opinion. He responded: "Very confident. Indeed, I called Dr. Smith, the world's leading expert in this particular area. I explained the case and my diagnosis to him, and he concurred in my conclusions." The defense counsel objected and moved to strike this answer. Should it be stricken?

C.   OPINIONS ON AN ULTIMATE ISSUE

In the most radical rejection of the common law dealing with opinion testimony, the Federal Rules explicitly permit opinion on ultimate issues in all save one situation.

1.   FRE 704

RULE 704.   OPINION ON ULTIMATE ISSUE

(a) Except as provided in subdivision (b), testimony in the form of an opinion or inference otherwise admissible is not objectionable because it embraces an ultimate issue to be decided by the trier of fact.

(b) No expert witness testifying with respect to the mental state or condition of a defendant in a criminal case may state an opinion or inference as to whether the defendant did or did not have the mental state or condition constituting an element of the crime charged or of a defense thereto. Such ultimate issues are matters for the trier of fact alone.

2.   Interpretation and Illustration of FRE 704(a)

In the nineteenth and early twentieth century a number of courts adopted the rule that witnesses — lay as well as expert — could not offer opinions on an ultimate issue in a case. The typical rationale for this rule was that such an opinion would invade the province of the jury. As Wigmore pointed out, it is not clear how or why an opinion on an ultimate issue "invades the province of the jury." 7 John Henry Wigmore, Evidence §1920 at 18 (James Chadbourn rev. 1978). Indeed, it is not entirely clear what constitutes an opinion on an ultimate issue. Consider a case in which the defendant is charged with possessing drugs with the intent to sell them. Presumably it would be an opinion on an ultimate issue for a narcotics officer to testify that the amount of drugs possessed by the defendant indicated that the defendant intended to sell the drugs. But would it be an opinion on an ultimate issue for the officer (1) to testify that the amount possessed was far in excess of what one would possess for personal use or (2) to offer her opinion about how much of the particular drug a typical user or addict is likely to consume in a given period of time? If not, the prohibition against opinions on an ultimate issue would appear to be more one of form than of substance.

The foregoing example illustrates both the benefit and one of the potential problems with opinions about matters that are, or are closely related to, ultimate issues in a lawsuit. Jurors unfamiliar with the use of drugs may not know what quantities of a particular drug individuals are likely to possess for personal use. Thus the narcotics officer's testimony can be helpful — indeed, perhaps critical — to the jury's evaluation of the defendant's intent. The narcotics officer's testimony would be most helpful if the jury were assured of learning the basis for the officer's opinion, for example, how much of the particular drug a person can be expected to use in a given period of time and the habits of drug users with respect to stockpiling. Yet the prosecutor may fail to bring out all of the underlying data on direct examination for fear of running afoul of the "ultimate opinion" rule, and defense counsel may be reluctant to explore the matter on cross-examination for fear of bolstering the officer's testimony. If the subject matter of the opinion testimony is not critical to the resolution of the lawsuit, the failure to develop the underlying facts may not be a problem of major concern. It is particularly important, however, that jurors have as much detailed factual information as possible on the ultimate issues in a lawsuit, for the resolution of those issues is their primary responsibility.

There are at least two other potential problems with opinions about ultimate issues. First, even if jurors have all of the underlying facts and data and are fully capable of resolving the ultimate issues, the mere fact that they hear witnesses express opinions on those issues may mislead them into believing that they should give some special deference to the opinions. Why else would the evidence be presented to them? Second, if an opinion on an ultimate issue embraces a legal concept or conclusion, there may be uncertainty about whether the expert is using that concept in the same manner in which the law uses it.

Adequate means exist for dealing with these potential problems without altogether prohibiting opinions on an ultimate issue. The judge has the discretion to exclude opinions that are not helpful (see, e.g., FRE 701 and 702) or whose probative value is substantially outweighed by the possibility of confusing or misleading the jury (see, e.g., FRE 403). If there is a concern that the underlying facts and data may not be forthcoming, the judge can require that they be set forth before the opinion is offered (see, e.g., FRE 705); and if there is concern that the expert's use of a particular term may differ from the legal definition of a term, the judge can deal with this possibility in the instructions to the jury.

During the last several decades a number of courts have rejected an absolute prohibition against opinions on ultimate issues, but at the same time courts generally prohibit opinions on questions of law. If by "questions of law" one means questions that are for the judge rather than the jury to decide, it is obviously appropriate that jurors not hear evidence on the issue in any form. The evidence from their perspective would be irrelevant. On the other hand, if the issue is one for the jury to decide, there would appear to be no sound reason to prohibit an opinion merely because one can characterize the issue as embodying 'law' or a 'legal concept.' Indeed, to have a rule that prohibits opinions on jury issues that are characterized as questions of law — or, as some courts have said, "mixed questions of law and fact"[9] — and, at the same time, to permit opinions about ultimate issues of "fact" may lead to an abstract, meaningless debate about whether the issue is one of "fact" or "law."[10] There may, of course, be times when an opinion embracing a legal concept would be confusing (e.g., if the witness were using the term differently from the manner in which the law used it) or not

---

9. See, e.g., Grismore v. Consolidated Products Co., 232 Iowa 328, 5 N.W.2d 646 (1942) (opinions on ultimate questions of fact permissible, but opinions on questions of law or questions of mixed fact and law not permissible).

10. See, e.g., State v. Ogg, 243 N.W.2d 620 (Iowa 1976) (in prosecution for possession of LSD with intent to distribute, prosecution witness testified that in his opinion the amount of drugs possessed by defendant far exceeded the amount one would possess for personal use; majority and dissent disagree on whether witness's testimony is impermissible opinion of law, with majority labeling opinion as one of law).

very helpful (e.g., if it were a substitute for the underlying facts and data). Courts can deal adequately with these problems on a case-by-case basis, just as they can deal adequately on a case-by-case basis with opinions on ultimate issues of 'fact.' Regardless of how one characterizes the issue to which the opinion is directed, the critical question should be whether the opinion will be helpful to the jury.

3.   Interpretation and Illustration of FRE 704(b)

FRE 704, as promulgated by the Supreme Court and initially adopted by Congress, followed the lead of those courts that had rejected the prohibition against opinions on an ultimate issue. FRE 704 provided that there was no such general prohibition for opinions on an "ultimate issue to be decided by the trier of fact." According to the Advisory Committee:

> The older cases often contained strictures against allowing witnesses to express opinions upon ultimate issues. . . . The rule was unduly restrictive, difficult of application, and generally served only to deprive the trier of fact of useful information. . . . Efforts to meet the felt needs of particular situations led to odd verbal circumlocutions which were said not to violate the rule. Thus a witness could express his estimate of the criminal responsibility of an accused in terms of sanity or insanity, but not in terms of ability to tell right from wrong or other more modern standard. And in cases of medical causation, witnesses were sometimes required to couch their opinions in cautious phrases of "might or could," rather than "did," though the result was to deprive many opinions of the positiveness to which they were entitled, accompanied by the hazard of a ruling of insufficiency to support a verdict. In other instances the rule was simply disregarded, and, as concessions to need, opinions were allowed upon such matters as intoxication, speed, handwriting, and value, although more precise coincidence with an ultimate issue would scarcely be possible.

In 1984, in the aftermath of John Hinckley's acquittal on insanity grounds of the attempt to assassinate President Reagan, there was substantial public debate about and criticism of the insanity defense. Congress enacted legislation that for the first time provided a federal statutory definition for insanity and that made insanity an affirmative defense that must be proved by the defendant. As part of that legislation, Congress amended FRE 704 to add FRE 704(b).

According to the Report of the House Judiciary Committee (quoting an earlier Senate Judiciary Committee Report):

> The purpose of this amendment is to eliminate the confusing spectacle of competing expert witnesses testifying to directly contradictory conclusions as to the ultimate legal issue to be found by the trier of fact. Under this proposal, expert psychiatric testimony would be limited to presenting and explaining their diagnoses, such as whether the defendant had a severe mental disease or defect and what the characteristics of such a disease or defect, if any, may have been. . . .
>
> Moreover, the rationale for precluding ultimate opinion psychiatric testimony extends beyond the insanity defense to any ultimate mental state of the defendant that is relevant to the legal conclusion sought to be proven. The Committee has fashioned its Rule 704 provision to reach all such "ultimate" issues, e.g., premeditation in a homicide case, or lack of predisposition in entrapment.

In support of this view, the Committee quoted from the American Psychiatric Association's Statement on the Insanity Defense (1982):

> [I]t is clear that psychiatrists are experts in medicine, not the law. As such, it is clear that the psychiatrist's first obligation and expertise in the courtroom is to "do psychiatry," i.e., to present medical information and opinion about the defendant's mental state and motivation and to explain in detail the reason for his medical-psychiatric conclusions. When, however, "ultimate issue" questions are formulated by the law and put to the expert witness who must then say "yea" or "nay," then the expert witness is required to make a leap in logic. He no longer addresses himself to medical concepts but instead must infer or intuit what is in fact unspeakable, namely, the probable relationship between medical concepts and legal or moral constructs such as free will. These impermissible leaps in logic made by expert witnesses confuse the jury. Juries thus find themselves listening to conclusory psychiatric testimony that defendants are either "sane" or "insane" or that they do or do not meet the relevant legal test for insanity. This state of affairs does considerable injustice to psychiatry and, we believe, possibly to criminal defendants. In fact, in many criminal insanity trials both prosecution and defense psychiatrists do agree about the nature and even the extent of mental disorder exhibited by the defendant at the time of the act.
>
> Psychiatrists, of course, must be permitted to testify fully about the defendant's diagnosis, mental state and motivation (in clinical and common sense terms) at the time of the alleged act so as to permit the jury or judge to reach the ultimate conclusion about which they and only they are expert. Determining whether a criminal defendant was legally insane is a matter for legal fact finders, not for experts.

Do you think that jurors may sometimes have difficulty relating a psychiatrist's diagnosis to the legal standard for insanity without some expert assistance? If so, does the problem lie with the amendment to FRE 704 or with the legal definition of insanity or both?

Even if a witness cannot offer an opinion about a defendant's "sanity," "premeditation," "predisposition," or other mental state, is it likely that jurors will be unaware of what the witness feels about such an issue? If not, of what practical benefit is the amendment to FRE 704? Keeping in mind that FRE 403, 701, 702, and 705 are available to regulate opinion testimony about ultimate issues, do you believe that the amendment to FRE 704 improved the Federal Rules of Evidence?

Note again how the crucial issue is the unstated distinction between education and deference. Provisions like FRE 704(b) only matter in a system willing to defer to the opinions of experts. In a system that required the expert to play an educational role, FRE 704(b) would be superfluous. Even if an opinion were offered, the fact finder would be in a position to appraise it rather than simply defer to or reject it. Only if we fear silly or capricious opinions to which fact finders might defer because of ignorance do provisions like FRE 704(b) make sense. If that is the case, however, the problem lies in the structure of litigation that allows the responsibility for deliberate, rational decision to be transferred from the juridical fact finder, judge or jury, to third party "experts."

KEY POINT

The Federal Rules have rejected the common law limitation forbidding opinions on ultimate issues, except for opinions concerning the mental states of criminal defendants.

PROBLEMS

9.23. Reconsider the narcotics possession hypothetical set forth at page 670, supra. To what extent and in what manner does the amendment to FRE 704 restrict the ability of the narcotics officer from offering helpful evidence about the defendant's intent?

9.24. Edward Santos is being tried for threatening to kill President Bill Clinton. In its attempts to prove the mental element of the crime, the prosecution elicits testimony from a psychiatric expert that Santos's efforts to "throw people off his trail" indicate that he "knew what he was doing was wrong." As an attorney for the defense, make an objection. Do you think you will be able to persuade the judge that the statements should be stricken from the record?

9.25. Taxpayer D was accused of making erroneous deductions from his taxable income. The government claimed that he owed over $200,000. The tax court in which the case was heard excluded two letters from certified public accountants that contained analyses that lead to the conclusion that the law did not preclude Taxpayer D from making these deductions. Taxpayer D appealed, arguing that Rule 704(a) supports the admission of these reports. Did the court err?

9.26. Corey Boyd was convicted by a jury in the United States District Court for the District of Columbia for possession with intent to distribute crack cocaine. Boyd was arrested after police officers briefly spotted him on the street holding a plastic bag between himself and another individual. The officers observed the two men for only a couple of seconds, so they could not see precisely what Boyd and his compatriot were doing, nor could they tell who controlled the plastic bag that was between them. Neither Boyd nor his compatriot was heard to say anything, nor seen to do anything (other than look into the plastic bag), and no money or drug paraphernalia was seen or found. Both men ran upon being spotted by the police, Boyd with the plastic bag still in hand. While being chased, he threw the bag under a truck, and it was recovered by the police. During his trial, the government introduced the expert testimony of Officer Stroud, who testified that, on the basis of a "hypothetical situation" exactly mirroring the facts of Boyd's arrest, in his opinion, the hypothetical facts showed possession with intent to distribute. Is there a problem with, or an appropriate objection to, this testimony?

9.27. Latana Slayton worked as a corrections officer for the Ohio Department of Youth Services with her coworker Corry Appline. In a suit against her employer, Slayton alleged that the DYS maintained a hostile work environment in which she was required to endure routine sexual harassment. Appline, she claimed, encouraged the young men to drop their towels while Slayton was on shower duty, sent her to check on an inmate who he knew was masturbating at the time, and provided the inmates with sexually explicit movies and music that referred to women as "bitches." On several occasions, Slayton sought redress from her superiors, who never took any action to remedy the situation. During the jury trial, the judge permitted the lay opinions of Slayton's supervisors that the alleged conduct violated its internal sexual harassment policy. During the testimony of one of the supervisors, the judge interrupted to ask: "Hypothesize that the plaintiff's testimony is true. In your view does that constitute under the terms of your policy, the state's policy, does that constitute sexual harassment in the workplace?" The supervisor answered that it would. After a verdict for the plaintiff, the defense appealed claiming that the lay opinions of the supervisors were inadmissible because they spoke to the ultimate issue. Was the trial judge right to allow the testimony?

9.28. Joe, a United States citizen of Filipino dissent, is suing his employer for discrimination. Joe asserts that he was denied a promotion because of his national origin. His employers counter that they decided to hire from outside the company because of certain perceived dissension within the ranks of its present employees. The employers called one of their directors, Mr. Queeg, to the witness stand. Queeg had taken part in the hiring of the new employee. Defense counsel asked Queeg, "Is it true that you did not believe that Joe had been discriminated against in the interview process because of his national origin?" Over the defense's objection, Queeg was allowed to answer that counsel's statement was correct. Should Queeg's opinion testimony have been allowed before the jury?

9.29. Mark Bruck's business was failing when he purchased additional insurance to cover a building into which he moved equipment and highly flammable substances. The building burned down and Bruck was charged with arson and bank fraud. At trial, the prosecution called an expert who testified as follows:

Q: (By Asst. U.S. Attorney Kinder). Based on the training and experience you have had in arson investigations, have you learned that there's certain indicators in an arson for profit scheme that you look for?
MR. MURRAY [Defense counsel].   Objection.
THE COURT: He may testify.
A: Yes.
Q: Did you find any of those indicators for the investigation of the Advance Resins' fire?
A: Yes, I did.
Q: What were they?
A: The fire was deliberately set in multiple locations. The fire was set for economic —
MR. MURRAY: I object and move to strike. That is a conclusion left to the jury's determination, not this agent's.
THE COURT: Well, he may give his opinion based on his experience, background and training, and on the number of fires he's investigated, teaching experience and so forth. Based on that, he may give his opinion as to whether or not it was a set fire and to show how he determined it.

After his conviction, Bruck argued on appeal that the expert's testimony was inadmissible under Rule 704(b). Was it error for the court to allow the expert to testify in this way?

D.   COURT APPOINTED EXPERTS

1.   FRE 706

RULE 706. COURT APPOINTED EXPERTS

(a) Appointment. The court may on its own motion or on the motion of any party enter an order to show cause why expert witnesses should not be appointed, and may request the parties to submit nominations. The court may appoint any expert witnesses agreed upon by the parties, and may appoint expert witnesses of its own selection. An expert witness shall not be appointed by the court unless the witness consents to act. A witness so appointed shall be informed of the witness' duties by the court in writing, a copy of which shall be filed with the clerk, or at a conference in which the parties shall have opportunity to participate. A witness so appointed shall advise the parties of the witness' findings, if any; the witness' deposition may be taken by any party; and the witness may be called to testify by the court or any party. The witness shall be subject to cross-examination by each party, including a party calling the witness.

(b) Compensation. Expert witnesses so appointed are entitled to reasonable compensation in whatever sum the court may allow. The compensation thus fixed is payable from funds which may be provided by law in criminal cases and civil actions and proceedings involving just compensation under the fifth amendment. In other civil actions and proceedings the compensation shall be paid by the parties in such proportion and at such time as the court directs, and thereafter charged in like manner as other costs.

(c) Disclosure of appointment. In the exercise of its discretion, the court may authorize disclosure to the jury of the fact that the court appointed the expert witness.

(d) Parties' experts of own selection. Nothing in this rule limits the parties in calling expert witnesses of their own selection.

2.   Interpretation and Illustration of FRE 706

FRE 706 permits courts to appoint their own experts. The advantage in doing so is the securing of disinterested, objective testimony concerning the issues in the case. This can provide a fact finder with important information when the adversarial system fails to bring the two sides of an issue to light. See, e.g., Grove v. Principle Mutual Life Insurance Co., 200 F.R.D. 434 (S.D. Iowa 2001) (appointing two experts to assist the court where both parties in a class action suit supported a settlement agreement but what was missing was someone to play the "devil's advocate"). The disadvantage is that many disciplines have internal disputes so that any expert selected by the court would not be truly "objective," but instead would be testifying from the perspective of one not universally shared view of the field. A good example of this is psychiatry. Freudian psychiatrists are called as expert witnesses, yet very little within the field has been empirically verified. As a consequence, psychiatry as a field is moving away from Freudian concepts, yet Freudian concepts still have their adherents.[11] The choice of an "expert" in psychiatry must thus resolve the contested issue of the validity of these concepts. As a consequence of problems like this, courts have essentially refused to take advantage of the power given them by this rule, leaving it a functional dead letter and the parties to fight out among themselves basic disciplinary disputes when necessary for the adjudication of a case. The lawyers view this favorably, for they are disinclined to have judges interfere with their presentation of the case. Our view is that this is regrettable, and leads to such spectacles as juries rejecting the implications of DNA testing or accepting explanations of pertinent matters that are virtually without any rational support. The best that can be said to the contrary is that the refusal of judges to employ this rule reduces somewhat the tendency toward the creation of an official orthodoxy, thus leaving all factual matters constantly open for reconsideration. Such epistemological modesty has its virtues, but also its price. For a discussion of court-

---

11.   For an interesting review of the status of Freudian psychiatry, see Frederick Crews, The Memory Wars (1997).

appointed expert panels see Karen Butler Reisinger, Court-Appointed Expert Panels: A Comparison of Two Models, 32 Ind. L. Rev. 225 (1998).

Rule 706 did come into noted use in one area recently: the litigation of silicone breast implant tort claims. U.S. District Judge Robert E. Jones, while he was overseeing all federal breast implant litigation in Oregon, noted that "litigation over the ability of silicone gel breast implants to cause disease in women has been chaotic in its results" and thus appointed a panel of independent experts to review all of the scientific evidence supporting the plaintiffs' claim that breast implants have caused serious diseases in women. See Hall v. Baxter Healthcare Corp., 947 F. Supp. 1387 (1996). In this decision, however, Judge Jones made the interesting decision to appoint the panel under FRE 104 (Preliminary Questions) rather than under FRE 706. He appointed a panel of "technical advisors," representing the fields of epidemiology, rheumatology, immunology, toxicology, and polymer chemistry, but refrained from designating them as court appointed experts "[t]o keep the advisors independent of any ongoing proceedings." Faced with the daunting task of evaluating extensive scientific evidence in silicone breast implant cases, other courts followed suit. U.S. District Judges Jack Weinstein and Harold Baer Jr., who managed all breast implants cases in the U.S. District Courts for the Eastern and Southern Districts of New York respectively, came up with a similar plan but named a team of three special masters to help determine the types of expertise that would be needed in a Rule 706 panel. See Mark Hansen, Panel to Examine Implant Evidence: Unusual Move by Two New York Federal Judges Could be Copied Elsewhere, 82 June A.B.A J. 34 (June, 1996).

The most far-reaching order was issued by Judge Samuel Pointer of the U.S. District Court for the Northern District of Alabama, who was at the time coordinating about 21,000 cases on a pretrial basis. In a two-step plan, Judge Pointer appointed a "Selection Panel" whose duty it would be to recommend to the court the names of "neutral, impartial persons," qualified to sit on the "Science Panel" and "review, critique, and evaluate exiting scientific literature, research, and publications — addressing such matters as the meaning, utility, significance, and limitations of such studies — on topics as, from time to time, may be identified by the Court as relevant in breast-implant litigation, particularly on issues of 'general causation.'" Order No. 31 (May 31, 1996). As Judge Pointer envisioned it, the appointments would be made on a national basis "for potential use in all federal courts and as permitted in state courts." Though both the attorneys for the plaintiffs and for the defendants expresses some trepidation about the process, Rule 706 preserves a party's right to call its own expert witnesses and to cross-examine the court appointed experts. The four member panel of scientists eventually appointed by Judge Pointer, issued a report in December of 1998, after two years of investigation, concluding that the evidence had not yet shown that silicone breast implants caused disease, though the connection might still be established in the future. By all accounts, the report was very damaging to plaintiffs, who now found themselves in a disadvantaged position for settlement and with diminished prospects for success at trial. In the years since the report was issued, judges from many jurisdictions have cited the panel's findings as support for exclusion of expert testimony intended to prove a causal link between implants and disease. See, e.g., Pozefsky v. Baxter Healthcare Corp., 2001 U.S. Dist. LEXIS 11813 (N.D.N.Y. Aug. 16, 2001); Havard v. Baxter International Inc., 2000 U.S. Dist. LEXIS 21316 (N.D. Ohio, July 21, 2000); Toledo v. Medical Engineering Corp., 50 Pa. D. & C.4th 129 (Com. Pleas

Ct. of Phila. County, Dec. 29, 2000). Though the courts succeeded in adopting a more efficient system of hearing expert testimony, do you think that one court should be able to exercise so great an influence over the success of cases in so many jurisdictions?

E. VARIETIES OF SCIENTIFIC EVIDENCE AND EXPERT TESTIMONY

Herein we examine different kinds of scientific evidence and expert testimony that have, for one reason or another, caused difficulties for the courts. We begin with a recent development that has the potential to change dramatically the way much litigation occurs — DNA evidence.

1. DNA Profiling

In the limited space available here, it would be impossible to provide you with enough information to enable you to handle DNA evidence competently. As noted earlier, attorneys who present expert evidence or examine expert witnesses must become knowledgeable in the area of expertise. The following excerpt will provide you with only a brief overview of the science of DNA profiling. As a ubiquitous and widely accepted type of scientific evidence, it is important that you have at least a rudimentary knowledge of its mechanics.

DAVID H. KAYE & GEORGE F. SENSABAUGH JR., REFERENCE GUIDE ON DNA EVIDENCE
Federal Judicial Center, 2nd ed. (2000)

I. INTRODUCTION

Deoxyribonucleic acid, or DNA, is a molecule that encodes the genetic information in all living organisms. Its chemical structure was elucidated in 1954. More than thirty years later, samples of human DNA began to be used in the criminal justice system, primarily in cases of rape or murder. The evidence has been the subject of extensive scrutiny by lawyers, judges, and the scientific community. It is now admissible in virtually all jurisdictions, but debate lingers over the safeguards that should be required in testing samples and in presenting the evidence in court.[12] Moreover, there are many types of DNA analysis, and still more are being developed. New problems of admissibility arise as advancing methods of analysis and novel applications of established methods are introduced....

---

12.   See D. H. Kaye, DNA, NAS, NRC, DAB, RFLP, PCR, and More: An Introduction to the Symposium on the 1996 NRC Report on Forensic DNA Evidence, 37 Jurimetrics J. 395 (1997); William C. Thompson, Guide to Forensic DNA Evidence, in Expert Evidence: A Practitioner's Guide to Law, Science, and the FJC Manual 185 (Bert Black & Patrick W. Lee eds., 1997).

B.   OBJECTIONS TO DNA EVIDENCE

The usual objective of forensic DNA analysis is to detect variations in the genetic material that differentiate individuals one from another.[13] Laboratory techniques for isolating and analyzing DNA have long been used in scientific research and medicine. Applications of these techniques to forensic work usually involve comparing a DNA sample obtained from a suspect with a DNA sample obtained from the crime scene.[14] Often, a perpetrator's DNA in hair, blood, saliva, or semen can be found at a crime scene, or a victim's DNA can be found on or around the perpetrator.[15] In many cases, defendants have objected to the admission of testimony of a match or its implications. Under Daubert v. Merrell Dow Pharmaceuticals, Inc., the district court, in its role as "gatekeeper" for scientific evidence, then must ensure that the expert's methods are scientifically valid and reliable. Because the basic theory and most of the laboratory techniques of DNA profiling are so widely accepted in the scientific world, disputed issues involve features unique to their forensic applications or matters of laboratory technique. These include the extent to which standard techniques have been shown to work with crime-scene samples exposed to sunlight, heat, bacteria, and chemicals in the environment; the extent to which the specific laboratory has demonstrated its ability to follow protocols that have been validated to work for crime-scene samples; possible ambiguities that might interfere with the interpretation of test results; and the validity and possible prejudicial impact of estimates of the probability of a match between the crime-scene samples and innocent suspects.

C.   RELEVANT EXPERTISE

DNA identification can involve testimony about laboratory findings, about the statistical interpretation of these findings, and about the underlying principles of molecular biology. Consequently, expertise in several fields might be required to establish the admissibility of the evidence or to explain it adequately to the jury. The expert who is qualified to testify about laboratory techniques might not be qualified to testify about molecular biology, to make estimates of population frequencies, or to establish that an estimation procedure is valid.[16]

Trial judges ordinarily are accorded great discretion in evaluating the qualifications of proposed expert witness, and decisions depend on the background of each witness. Courts have noted the lack of familiarity of academic experts — who have done respected work in other fields — with the scientific literature of forensic DNA typing, and on the extent to which their research or teaching lies in other areas.

13.   Biologists accept as a truism the proposition that, except for identical twins, human beings are genetically unique.

14.   E.g., United States v. Beasley, 102 F.3d 1440 (8th Cir. 1996) (two hairs were found in a mask used in a bank robbery and left in the abandoned get-away car); United States v. Two Bulls, 918 F.2d 1127 (1991) (semen stain on victim's underwear).

15.   E.g., United States v. Cuff, 37 F. Supp. 2d 279 (S.D.N.Y. 1999) (scraping from defendant's fingernails); State v. Bible, 858 P.2d 1152 (Ariz. 1993) (bloodstains on defendant's shirt); People v. Castro, 545 N.Y.S.2d 985 (Bronx Co. Sup. Ct. 1989) (bloodstains on defendant's watch). . . .

16.   . . . Nevertheless, if previous cases establish that the testing and estimation procedures are legally acceptable, and if the computations are essentially mechanical, then highly specialized statistical expertise might not be essential. Reasonable estimates of DNA characteristics in major population groups can be obtained from standard references, and many quantitatively literate experts could use the appropriate formulae to compute the relevant profile frequencies or probabilities. . . . Limitations in the knowledge of a technician who applies a generally accepted statistical procedure can be explored on cross–examination. . . .

Although such concerns may give trial judges pause, they rarely result in exclusion of the testimony on the ground that the witness simply is not qualified as an expert.

The scientific and legal literature on the objections to DNA evidence is extensive. By studying the scientific publications, or perhaps by appointing a special master or expert adviser to assimilate this material, a court can ascertain where a party's experts falls into the spectrum of scientific opinion. Furthermore, an expert appointed by the court under Rule 706 could testify about the scientific literature generally or even about the strengths or weaknesses of the particular arguments advanced by the parties.

II.   OVERVIEW OF VARIATION IN DNA AND ITS DETECTION

A.   DNA, CHROMOSOMES, SEX, AND GENES

DNA is a complex molecule that contains the "genetic code" of organisms as diverse as bacteria and humans.[17] The molecule is made of subunits that include four nucleotide bases, whose names are abbreviated to A, T, G, and C.[18] . . . [F]or general purposes it suffices to say that a DNA molecule is like a long sequence of these four letters, where the chemical structure that corresponds to each letter is known as a base pair.

Most human DNA is tightly packed into structures known as chromosomes, which are located in the nuclei of most cells. If the bases are like letters, then each chromosome is like a book written in this four-letter alphabet, and the nucleus is like a bookshelf in the interior of the cell. All the cells in one individual contain copies of the same set of books. This library, so to speak, is the individual's genome.

In human beings, the process that produces billions of cells with the same genome starts with sex. Every sex cell (a sperm or ovum) contains 23 chromosomes. When a sperm and ovum combine, the resulting fertilized cell contains 23 pairs of chromosomes, or 46 in all. It is as if the father donates half of his collection of 46 books, and the mother donates a corresponding half of her collection. During pregnancy, the fertilized cell divides to form two cells, each of which has an identical copy of the 46 chromosomes. The two then divide to form four, the four form eight, and so on. As gestation proceeds, various cells specialize to form different tissues and organs. In this way, each human being has immensely many copies[19] of the original 23 pairs of chromosomes from the fertilized egg, one member of each pair having come from the mother and one from the father.

All told, the DNA in the 23 chromosomes contains over three billion letters (base pairs) of genetic "text." About 99.9% is identical between any two individuals. This similarity is not really surprising — it accounts for the common features that make humans an identifiable species. The remaining 0.1% is particular to an individual (identical twins excepted). This variation makes each person genetically unique.

A gene is a particular DNA sequence, usually from 1,000 to 10,000 base pairs long, that "codes" for an observable characteristic. For example, a tiny part of the

---

17.   Some viruses use a related nucleic acid, RNA, instead of DNA to encode genetic information.
18.   The full names are adenine, thymine, guanine, and cytosine.
19.   The number of cells in the human body has been estimated at more than 10^{15} (a million billion).

sequence that directs the production of the human group-specific complement protein (GC) is

GCAAAATTGCCTGATGCCACACCCAAGGAACTGGCA[20]

This gene always is located at the same position, or locus, on chromosome number 4. As we have seen, most individuals have two copies of each gene at a given locus — one from the father and one from the mother.

A locus where almost all humans have the same DNA sequence is called monomorphic ("of one form"). A locus at which the DNA sequence varies among individuals is called polymorphic ("of many forms"). The alternative forms are called alleles. For example, the GC protein gene sequence has three common alleles that result from single nucleotide polymorphisms (SNPs, pronounced "snips") — substitutions in the base that occur at a given point. In the scientific literature, the three alleles are designated Gc*1F, Gc*1S, and Gc*2, and the sequences at the variable sites are shown in Figure 1.

Figure 1.

The variable sequence region of the group-specific component gene. The base substitutions that define the alleles are shown in bold.

Allele*2:   GCAAAATTGCCTGATGCCACACCCAAGGAACTGGCA

Allele*1F: GCAAAATTGCCGCCTGCCACACCCACGGAACTGGCA

Allele*1S: GCAAAATTGCCTGAGGCCACACCCACGGAACTGGCA

In terms of the metaphor of DNA as text, the gene is like an important paragraph in the book; a SNP is a change in a letter somewhere within that paragraph, and the two versions of the paragraph that result from this slight change are the alleles. An individual who inherits the same allele from both parents is called a homozygote.[21] An individual with distinct alleles is termed a heterozygote.[22] Regions of DNA used for forensic analysis usually are not genes, but parts of the chromosome without a known function. The "non-coding" regions of DNA have been found to contain considerable sequence variation, which makes them particularly useful in distinguishing individuals. Although the terms "locus," "allele," "homozygous," and "heterozygous" were developed to describe genes, the nomenclature has been carried over to describe all DNA variation — coding and non-coding alike — for both types are inherited from mother and father in the same fashion.

B. Types of Polymorphisms and Methods of Detection

By determining which alleles are present at strategically chosen loci, the forensic scientist ascertains the genetic profile, or genotype, of an individual. Genotyping

---

20. The full GC gene is nearly 42,400 base pairs in length. The product of this gene is also known as vitamin D — binding protein. GC is one of the five loci included in the polymarker (PM) typing kit, which is widely used in forensic testing.

21. For example, someone with the Gc*2 allele on both number 4 chromosomes is homozygous at the GC locus. This homozygous GC genotype is designated as 2,2 (or simply 2).

22. For example, someone with the Gc*2 allele on one chromosome and the Gc*1F allele on the other is heterozygous at the GC locus. This heterozygous genotype is designated as 2,1F.

does not require "reading" the full DNA sequence; indeed, direct sequencing is technically demanding and time-consuming. Rather, most genetic typing focuses on identifying only those variations that define the alleles and does not attempt to "read out" each and every base as it appears.

For instance, simple sequence variation, such as that for the GC locus, is conveniently detected using a sequence-specific oligonucleotide (SSO) probe. With GC typing, probes for the three common alleles (which we shall call A1, A2, and A3) are attached to designated locations on a membrane. When DNA with a given allele (say, A1) comes in contact with the probe for the allele, it sticks. To get a detectable quantity of DNA to stick, many copies of the variable sequence region of the CG gene in the DNA sample have to be made.[23] All this DNA then is added to the membrane. The DNA fragments with the allele A1 in them stick to the spot with the A1 probe. To permit these fragments to be seen, a chemical "label" that catalyses a color change at the spot where the DNA binds to its probe can be attached when the copies are made. A colored spot showing that the A1 allele is present thus should appear on the membrane.

Another category of polymorphism is characterized by the insertion of a variable number of tandem repeats (VNTR) at a locus. The core unit of a VNTR is a particular short DNA sequence that is repeated many times end-to-end. This repetition gives rise to alleles with length differences; regions of DNA containing more repeats are larger than those containing fewer repeats. Genetic typing of polymorphic VNTR loci employs electrophoresis, a technique that separates DNA fragments based on size.

The first polymorphic VNTRs to be used in genetic and forensic testing had core repeat sequences of 15-35 base pairs. Alleles at VNTR loci of this sort generally are too long to be measured precisely by electrophoretic methods — alleles differing in size by only a few repeat units may not be distinguished. Although this makes for complications in deciding whether two length measurements that are close together result from the same allele, these loci are quite powerful for the genetic differentiation of individuals, for they tend to have many alleles that occur relatively rarely in the population. At a locus with only twenty such alleles (and most loci typically have many more), there are 210 possible genotypes.[24] With five such loci, the number of possible genotypes is 2105, which is more than 400 billion. Thus, VNTRs are an extremely discriminating class of DNA markers.

More recently, the attention of the genetic typing community has shifted to repetitive DNA characterized by short core repeats, two to seven base pairs in length. These non-coding DNA sequences are known as short tandem repeats (STRs). Because STR alleles are much smaller than VNTR alleles, eletrophoretic detection permits the exact number of base pairs in an STR to be determined, permitting alleles to be defined as discrete entities. Figure 2 illustrates the nature of allelic variation at a polymorphic STR locus. The first allele has nine tandem repeats, the second has ten, and the third has eleven.[25]

---

23.   The polymerase chain reaction (PCR) is used to make many copies of the DNA that is to be typed. PCR is roughly analogous to copying and pasting a section of text with a word processor....

24.   There are 20 homozygous genotypes and another $(20 \times 19)/2 \times 190$ heterozygous ones.

25.   To conserve space, the figure uses alleles that are unrealistically short. A typical STR is in the range of 50-350 base pairs in length. In contrast, typical VNTR is thousands of base pairs long.

Figure 2. Three Alleles of an STR with the Core Sequence ATTT

ATTTATTTATTTAATTTATTTATTTATTTATTTATTT

ATTTATTTATTTATTTATTTATTTATTTATTTATTTATTT

ATTTATTTATTTATTTATTTATTTATTTATTTATTTATTTATTT

Although there are fewer alleles per locus for STRs than for VNTRs, there are many STRs, and they can be analyzed simultaneously. As more STR loci are included, STR testing becomes more revealing than VNTR profiling at four or five loci.[26]

Full DNA sequencing is employed at present only for mitochondrial DNA (mtDNA).[27] Mitochondria are small structures found inside the cell. In these organelles, certain molecules are broken down to supply energy. Mitochondria have a small genome that bears no relation to the chromosomal genome in the cell nucleus. Mitochondrial DNA has three features that make it useful for forensic DNA testing. First, the typical cell, which has but one nucleus, contains hundreds of identical mitochondria. Hence, for every copy of chromosomal DNA, there are hundreds of copies of mitochondrial DNA. This means that it is possible to detect mtDNA in samples containing too little nuclear DNA for conventional typing. Second, the mtDNA contains a sequence region of about a thousand base pairs that varies greatly among individuals. Finally, mitochondria are inherited mother to child,[28] so that siblings, maternal half-siblings, and others related through maternal lineage possess the same mtDNA sequence.[29] This last feature makes mtDNA particularly useful for associating persons related through their maternal lineage — associating skeletal remains to a family, for example.[30] Just as genetic variation in mtDNA can be used to track maternal lineages, genetic variations on the Y chromosome can be used to trace paternal lineages. Y chromosomes, which contain genes that result in development as a male rather than a female, are found only in males and are inherited father to son. Markers on this chromosome include STRs and SNPs, and they have been used in cases involving semen evidence.[31] In sum, DNA contains the genetic information of an organism. In humans, most of the DNA is found in the cell nucleus, where it is organized into separate chromosomes. Each chromosome is like a book, and each cell has the same library of books of various sizes and shapes. There are two copies

26.   Usually, there are between seven and fifteen STR alleles per locus. Thirteen loci that have ten STR alleles each can give rise to 55^{13}, or 42 billion trillion, possible genotypes.

27.   The first use of this mtDNA analysis as evidence in a criminal case occurred in Tennessee in State v. Ware, No. 03C01-9705CR00164, 1999 WL 233592 (Tenn. Crim. App. Apr. 20, 1999). See Mark Curriden, A New Evidence Tool: First Use of Mitochondrial DNA Test in a U.S. Criminal Trial, A.B.A.J., Nov. 1996, at 18.

28.   Although sperm have mitochondria, these are not passed to the ovum at fertilization. Thus the only mitochondria present in the newly fertilized cell originate from the mother.

29.   Evolutionary studies suggest an average mutation rate for the mtDNA control region of one nucleotide difference every 300 generations, or one difference every 6,000 years. Consequently, one would not expect to see many examples of nucleotide differences between maternal relatives. On the other hand, differences in the bases at a specific sequence position among the copies of the mtDNA within an individual have been seen. This heteroplasmy, which is more common in hair than other tissues, counsels against declaring an exclusion on the basis of a single base pair difference between two samples.

30.   See, e.g., Peter Gill et al., Identification of the Remains of the Romanov Family by DNA Analysis, 6 Nature Genetics 130 (1994).

31.   They also were used in a family study to ascertain whether President Thomas Jefferson fathered a child of his slave, Sally Hemings. See Eugene A. Foster et al., Jefferson Fathered Slave's Last Child, 396 Nature 27 (1998); Eliot Marshall, Which Jefferson Was the Father?, 283 Science 153 (1999).

of each book of a particular size and shape, one that come from the father, the other from the mother. Thus, there are two copies of the book entitled "Chromosome One," two copies of "Chromosome Two," and so on. Genes are the most meaningful paragraphs in the books, and there are differences (polymorphisms) in the spelling of certain words in the paragraphs of different copies of each book. The different versions of the same paragraph are the alleles. Some alleles result from the substitution of one letter for another. These are SNPs. Others come about from the insertion or deletion of single letters, and still others represent a kind of stuttering repetition of a string of extra letters. These are the VNTRs and STRs. In addition to the 23 pairs of books in the cell nucleus, another page or so of text resides in each of the mitochondria, the power plants of the cell. . . .

III.   DNA PROFILING WITH LOCI HAVING DISCRETE ALLELES

Simple sequence variations and STRs occur within relatively short fragments of DNA. These polymorphisms can be analyzed with so-called PCR-based tests (PCR _ polymerase chain reaction). The three steps of PCR-based typing are (1) DNA extraction, (2) amplification, and (3) detection of genetic type using a method appropriate to the polymorphism. . . .

A.   DNA EXTRACTION AND AMPLIFICATION

DNA usually can be found in biological materials such as blood, bone, saliva, hair, semen, and urine. A combination of routine chemical and physical methods permits DNA to be extracted from cell nuclei and isolated from the other chemicals in a sample. Thus, the premise that DNA is present in many biological samples and can be removed for further analysis is firmly established.

   Just as the scientific foundations of DNA extraction are clear, the procedures for amplifying DNA sequences within the extracted DNA are well established. The first National Academy of Sciences committee on forensic DNA typing described the amplification step as "simple . . . analogous to the process by which cells replicate their DNA." . . .

   For amplification to work properly and yield copies of only the desired sequence, however, care must be taken to achieve the appropriate biochemical conditions and to avoid excessive contamination of the sample. A laboratory should be able to demonstrate that it can faithfully amplify targeted sequences with the equipment and reagents that it uses and that it has taken suitable precautions to avoid or detect handling or carryover contamination.[32]

B.   DNA ANALYSIS

To determine whether the DNA sample associated with a crime could have come from a suspect, the genetic types as determined by analysis of the DNA amplified from the crime-scene sample are compared to the genetic types as determined for the suspect.

32.   Carryover occurs when the DNA product of a previous amplification contaminates samples or reaction solutions. . . .

For example, Figure 3 shows the results of STR typing at four loci in a sexual assault case.[33]

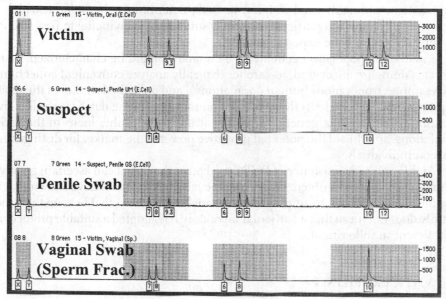

Figure 3. Sexual Assault Case (CTTA)

The peaks result from DNA fragments of different sizes.[34] The bottom row shows the profile of sperm DNA isolated from a vaginal swab. These sperm have two alleles at the first locus (indicating that both X and Y chromosomes are present),[35] two alleles at the second locus (consisting of 7 and 8 repeat units), two at the third locus (a 6 and an 8), and one (a 10 on each chromosome) at the fourth. The same profile also appears in the DNA taken from the suspect. DNA from a penile swab from the suspect is consistent with a mixture of DNA from the victim and the suspect.

Regardless of the kind of genetic system used for typing — STRs, Amp-FLPs,[36] SNPs, or still other polymorphisms — some general principles and questions can be applied to each system that is offered for courtroom use. As a beginning, the nature of the polymorphism should be well characterized. Is it a simple sequence polymorphism

---

33. The initials CTTA refer to these loci, which are known as CPO, TPO, THO, and amelogenin.
34. The height of (more, precisely, the area under) each is related to the amount of DNA in the gel.
35. The X-Y typing at the first locus is simply used to verify the sex of the source of the DNA, XY is male, and XX is female. . . . That these markers show that the victim is female and the suspect male helps demonstrate that a valid result has been obtained.
36. "Amp-FLP" is short for "Amplified Fragment Length Polymorphism." The DNA fragment is produced by amplifying a longish sequence with a PCR primer. The longer Amp-FLPs, such as D1S180, overlap the shorter VNTRs. In time, PCR methods will be capable of generating longer Amp-FLPs.

or a fragment length polymorphism? This information should be in the published literature or in archival genome databanks.

Second, the published scientific literature also can be consulted to verify claims that a particular method or analysis can produce accurate profiles under various conditions. Although such validation studies have been conducted for all the discrete-allele systems ordinarily used in forensic work, determining the point at which the empirical validation of a particular system is sufficiently convincing to pass scientific muster may well require expert assistance.

Finally, the population genetics of the marker should be characterized. As new marker systems are discovered, researchers typically analyze convenient collections of DNA samples from various human populations[37] and published studies of the relative frequencies of each allele in these population samples. These database studies give a measure of the extent of genetic variability at the polymorphic locus in the various populations, and thus of the potential probative power of the marker for distinguishing between individuals.

At this point, the existence of PCR-based procedures that can ascertain genotypes accurately cannot be doubted. Of course, the fact that scientists have shown that it is possible to extract DNA, to amplify it, and to analyze it in ways that bear on the issue of identity does not mean that a particular laboratory has adopted a suitable protocol and is proficient in following it. . . . [38]

IV. VNTR PROFILING

VNTR profiling, described in section II, was the first widely used method of forensic DNA testing. Consequently, its underlying principles, its acceptance within the scientific community, and its scientific soundness have been discussed in a great many opinions. Because so much has been written on VNTR profiling, only the basic steps of the procedure will be outlined here.

1. Like profiling by means of discrete allele systems, VNTR profiling begins with the extraction of DNA from a crime-scene sample. (Because this DNA is not amplified, however, larger quantities of higher quality DNA[39] are required.)

2. The extracted DNA is "digested" by a restriction enzyme that recognizes a particular, very short sequence; the enzyme cuts the DNA at these restriction sites. When a VNTR falls between two restriction sites, the resulting DNA fragments

---

37.   The samples come from diverse sources, such as blood banks, law enforcement personnel, paternity cases, and criminal cases. Reliable inferences probably can be drawn from these samples. . . .

38.   Some commentators have assumed or argued that some or all of these issues are aspects of admissibility under Federal Rule of Evidence 702. E.g., Edward J. Imwinkelried, The Debate in the DNA Cases over the Foundation for the Admission of Scientific Evidence: The Importance of Human Error as a Cause of Forensic Misanalysis, 69 Wash. U. L.Q. 19 (1991); Barry C. Scheck, DNA and Daubert, 15 Cardozo L. Rev., 1959, 1979-87 (1994); William C. Thompson, Accepting Lower Standards: The National Research Council's Second Report on Forensic DNA Evidence, 37 Jurimetrics J. 405, 417 (1997). This reading of Daubert is rejected in United States v. Shea, 957 F. Supp. 331, 340-41 (D.N.H. 1997), but the protocols of a specific laboratory and the proficiency of its analysts are factors that affect probative value under Federal Rule of Evidence 403. See Margaret A. Berger, Laboratory Error Seen Through the Lens of Science and Policy, 30 U.C. Davis L. Rev. 1081 (1997); Edward J. Imwinkelried, The Case Against Evidentiary Admissibility Standard that Attempt to "Freeze" the State of a Scientific Technique, 67 U. Colo. L. Rev. 887 (1996).

39.   "Quality" refers to the extent to which the original, very long strands of DNA are intact. When DNA degrades, it forms shorter fragments. RFLP testing requires fragments that are on the order at least 20,000-30,000 base pairs long.

will vary in size depending on the number of core repeat units in the VNTR region. (These VNTRs are thus referred to as a restriction fragment length polymorphism, or RFLP.)

3. The digested DNA fragments are then separated according to size by gel eletrophoresis. The digest sample is placed in a well at the end of a lane in an agarose gel, which is a gelatin-like material solidified in a slab. Digested DNA from the suspect is placed in another well on the same gel. Typically, control specimens of DNA fragments of known size, and, where appropriate, DNA specimens obtained from a victim, are run on the same gel. Mild electric current applied to the gel slowly separates the fragments in each lane by length, as shorter fragments travel farther in a fixed time than longer, heavier fragments.

4. The resulting array of fragments is transferred for manageability to a sheet of nylon by a process known as Southern blotting.[40]

5. The restriction fragments representing a particular polymorphic locus are "tagged" on the membrane using a sequence-specific probe labeled with a radioactive or chemical tag.[41]

6. The position of the specifically bound probe tag is made visible, either by autoradiography (for radioactive labels) or by a chemical reaction (for chemical labels). For autoradiography, the washed nylon membrane is placed between two sheets of photographic film. Over time, the radioactive probe material exposes the film where the biological probe has hybridized with the DNA fragments. The result is an autoradiograph, or an autorad, visual pattern of bands representing specific DNA fragments. An autorad that shows two bands in a single line indicates that the individual who is the source of the DNA is a heterozygote at that locus. If the autorad shows only one band, the person may be homozygous for the allele (that is, each parent contributed the same allele), or the second band may be present but invisible for technical reasons. The band pattern defines the person's genotype at the locus associated with the probe.

Once an appropriately exposed autorad is obtained, the probe is stripped from the membrane, and the process is repeated with a separate probe for each locus tested. Three to five probes are typically used, the number depending in part on the amount of testable DNA recovered from the crime-scene sample. The result is a set of autorads, each of which shows the results of one probe. If the crime-scene and suspect samples yield bands that are closely aligned on each autorad, the VNTR profiles from the two samples are considered to match.

A.   VALIDITY OF THE UNDERLYING SCIENTIFIC THEORY

The basic theory underlying VNTR profiling is textbook knowledge. The molecular structure of DNA, the presence of highly polymorphic VNTR loci, and the existence of methods to produce VNTR fragments and measure their lengths are not in doubt.

40.   This procedure is named after its inventor, Edwin Southern. Either before or during this transfer, the DNA is denatured ("unzipped") by alkali treatment, separating each double helix . . . into two single strands. The weak bonds that connect the two members of a base pair are easily broken by heat or chemical treatment. The bonds that hold a base to the backbone and keep the backbone intact are much stronger. Thus, the double-stranded helix separates nearly into two single strands, with one base at each position.

41.   This locus-specific probe is a single strand of DNA that binds to its complementary sequence of denatured DNA in the sample. . . . The DNA locus identified by a given probe is found by experimentation, and individual probes often are patented by their developers. Different laboratories may use different probes (i.e., they may test for alleles at different loci). Where different probes (or different restriction enzymes) are used, test results are not comparable.

Indeed, some courts have taken judicial notice of these scientific facts.[42] In short, the ability to discriminate between human DNA samples using a relatively small number of VNTR loci is widely accepted.

B. VALIDITY AND RELIABILITY OF THE LABORATORY TECHNIQUES

The basic laboratory procedures for VNTR analysis have been used in other settings for many years: "The complete process — DNA digestion, electrophoresis, membrane transfer, and hybridization — was developed by Edwin Southern in 1975.... These procedures are routinely used in molecular biology, biochemistry, genetics, and clinical DNA diagnosis...." Thus, "no scientific doubt exists that [these technologies] accurately detect genetic differences."[43]

Before concluding that a particular enzyme-probe combination produces accurate profiles as applied to crime-scene samples at a particular laboratory, however, courts may wish to consider studies concerning the effects of environmental conditions and contaminants on VNTR profiling as well as the laboratory's general experience and proficiency with these probes. And the nature of the sample and other considerations in a particular case can affect the certainty of the profiling....

Of late, PCR DNA evidence has become so ubiquitous that many jurisdictions have taken judicial notice of the general reliability of such DNA testing. See, e.g., United States v. Wright, 215 F.3d 1020, 1027 (9th Cir. 2000); United States v. Hicks, 103 F.3d 837, 846-47 (9th Cir. 1996); United States v. Beasley, 102 F.3d 1440, 1448 (8th Cir. 1996) (taking judicial notice of general reliability of PCR testing); United States v. Shea, 957 F. Supp. 331, 338-39 (D.N.H. 1997); United States v. Ewell, 252 F. Supp. 2d 104, 106 (D.N.J. 2003) (looking specifically at PCR/STR testing and listing 12 state appellate court cases finding PCR/STR DNA testing to be scientifically reliable); United States v. Cuff, 37 F. Supp. 2d 279, 282 (S.D.N.Y. 1999); United States v. Gaines, 979 F. Supp. 1429, 1433-36 (S.D.Fla. 1997) (collecting at least 20 state appellate court cases finding PCR DNA testing to be scientifically reliable); United States v. Trala, 162 F. Supp. 2d 336, 351 (D. Del., 2001) (looking specifically at PCR/STR testing); United States v. Lowe, 954 F. Supp. 401, 416-17, 420-21 (D. Mass. 1997) (collecting approximately 20 state appellate court cases finding that PCR testing methodology comports with Daubert).

In addition, the use of mtDNA testing has been deemed reliable enough under the Daubert standard to be admitted into evidence by at least one federal jurisdiction and several state jurisdictions as well. See, e.g., United States v. Beverly, 369 F.3d 516 (6th Cir. 2004), *cert. denied*, 125 S. Ct. 122 (2004) (stating that the scientific basis for

---

42.   See, e.g., State v. Fleming, 698 A.2d 503, 507 (Me. 1997) (taking judicial notice that "the overall theory and techniques of DNA profiling [are] scientifically reliable if conducted in accordance with appropriate laboratory standards and controls"); State v. Davis, 814 S.W.2d 593, 602 (Mo. 1991); People v. Castro, 545 N.Y.S.2d 985, 987 (N.Y. Sup. Ct. 1989)....

43.   Office of Tech. Assessment, Genetic Witness: Forensic Uses of DNA Tests 59 (1990). The 1992 NRC report therefore recommends that courts take judicial notice that: [t]he current laboratory procedure for detecting DNA variation (specifically, single-locus probes analyzed on Southern blots without evidence of band shifting) is fundamentally sound, although the validity of any particular implementation of the basic procedure will depend on proper characterization of the reproducibility of the system (e.g. measurement variation) and the inclusion of all necessary scientific controls.

...The 1996 report reiterates the conclusion that "[t]he techniques of DNA typing [including RFLP analysis] are fully recognized by the scientific community."...It insists that "[t]he state of the profiling technology and the methods for estimating frequencies and related statistics have progressed to the point where the admissibility of properly collected and analyzed DNA data should not be in doubt."...

such testing is well-established, no abuse of discretion by district court in admitting evidence under Daubert); State v. Underwood, 518 S.E.2d 231 (N.C. Ct. App. 1999); State v. Scott, 33 S.W.3d 746 (Tenn. 2000); State v. Council, 515 S.E.2d 508 (S.C. 1999); People v. Klinger, 713 N.Y.S. 2d 823 (N.Y. Crim. Ct. 2000); Williams v. State, 679 A.2d 1106 (Md. 1996).

Keep in mind, however, that though the science of DNA profiling may be relatively well-accepted, such evidence cannot determine precisely the probability of parenting or involvement in a crime. It can only determine the probability of obtaining this kind of blood from blood taken from an individual randomly chosen from the population at large. And even that assumes that no mistakes have been made, such as contamination of samples or laboratory errors. Suppose, for example, that sophisticated blood sampling shows that the probability of obtaining the kind of blood found at the scene of a crime, blood that matches the defendant's, from a randomly chosen individual is .0001. What exactly does this mean? It does not mean what it is often taken to mean. The "Prosecutor's Fallacy" asserts that a .0001 probability of a match means a .9999 (99.99 percent) probability of guilt. Nor does it mean what the "Defense Fallacy" asserts it means: that in a country of 280,000,000, a .0001 probability of a match means that at least 28,000 other people have this characteristic, and therefore the chances of guilt are 1 in 28,000. Both interpretations are erroneous because, at a minimum, they ignore all the other evidence. This evidence is certainly relevant, but it must be assimilated to all the other evidence in the case. It is not clear, however, how best to do this. The difficulty is that the rest of the evidence in the case will virtually always not be in statistical form, and there are no accepted algorithms for combining differing kinds (quantitative and nonquantitative) of evidence.[44]

2.   Some Recent Controversies

In part because Daubert has given trial judges such broad discretion in their role as "gatekeepers," inconsistent rulings on admissibility are not uncommon when a new type of "scientific" evidence first begins appearing in court. There is often significant disagreement even between experts within a field, thus making it almost impossible for a fact-finder using the deference model to reach a rational conclusion. We have already mentioned the ongoing debates surrounding polygraph testing, see note 5, page 642, supra, and the vagaries of eyewitness identification, see page 629, supra. The following discussion highlights a few more of these hot topics.

a.   Psychological and Behavioral Sciences

Following some widely publicized convictions based on syndrome evidence and repressed memory, courts have begun to recognize that such "scientific evidence," if

44.   The forensic laboratory of the FBI announced in 1997 that "DNA profiles can now prove with reasonable scientific certainty that DNA in an evidence stain comes from a specific person." The lab's new policy was described in 66 U.S.L.W. 2313 (11/25/1997): Under the FBI lab's new policy, once a match between the stain and the suspected source is declared, the matching profile is compared to DNA profiles collected from various population groups, and the likelihood of selecting an individual from the population who would have a similar profile is calculated. "If that number is exceedingly rare as compared to the number of people in the U.S. population, the individual is declared to be the source of the evidentiary stain," according to the laboratory. Though this changed the way FBI experts testified, criminal defendants continued to contest the evidence in court. See D. Michael Risinger, Navigating Expert Reliability: Are Criminal Standards of Certainty Being Left on the Dock?, 64 Alb. L. Rev. 99 (2000).

misused, can be a dangerous tool. "Syndromes" are collections of symptoms that occur together and characterize a particular abnormality. Experts frequently are offered at trial for information and opinions about syndromes of various kinds. In medical science, the term tends to be used to refer to a set of symptoms whose underling etiology was not fully understood at the time the syndrome was identified, as is the case, for example, with Down's Syndrome. The knowledge of experts in the relevant medical areas frequently is based on carefully controlled studies (Down's Syndrome is again a good example), and can be valuable in litigation. In a medical malpractice suit alleging a mistake involving amniocentesis leading to the birth of a seriously retarded child, medical testimony concerning Down's Syndrome and its detectability through amniocentesis will be crucial.

Over the last few decades, syndrome evidence of a different kind has emerged. Battered woman syndrome, posttraumatic stress disorder, post-Vietnam syndrome, rape trauma syndrome, and child sexual abuse accommodation syndrome, are just a few. As the diagnosis of these syndromes began producing therapeutic successes and thus respectability, experts were permitted to testify that a person has suffered some legally cognizable harm, such as child or sex abuse, based on various symptoms that the alleged victim possesses.[45] These claims were often coupled with testimony that the victim repressed memory of the traumatic event for a considerable period of time, in many instances stretching into decades.

When a therapist diagnoses a patient with a psychological syndrome, the therapist is making a decision to use certain methods of treatment that have been beneficial to patients with like symptoms. The diagnostic process may not reveal any of the causes of the patient's symptoms and a therapist's speculative opinions about such causes may be highly prejudicial. Though syndrome evidence is usually inadequate for proof of causation, it can be effectively and appropriately used as rebuttal evidence. An example is in rape prosecutions where the victim has delayed reporting the crime. The defense may present this fact as an indication of a false charge. It may be helpful to the fact finder in such a case to be educated about the frequency of delayed reports among rape victims. See, e.g., People v. Hampton, 746 P.2d 947 (Colo. 1987) (admitting such evidence). For a more detailed examination of the controversy surrounding this and other types of psychological and behavioral evidence, see Christopher Slobogin, Doubts About *Daubert*: Psychiatric Anecdata as a Case Study, 57 Wash. & Lee L. Rev. 919 (2000) (arguing that opinion testimony from psychologists and psychiatrists concerning past mental state and proffered by criminal defendants, should be admissible under *Daubert-Kumho* though it may be considered "unreliable"); Rosemary L. Flint, Child Sexual Abuse Accommodation Syndrome: Admissibility Requirements, 23 Am. J. Crim. L. 171 (1995).

b.   Toxic Tort Causation

A toxic tort . . . is a cause of action that arises when a plaintiff has developed a disease following long-term exposure to a physical agent — either a chemical or a form of energy such as electromagnetic fields (EMFs). Typically, the defendant's economic activity

---

45.   See Robert Rosenthal, *State of New Jersey v. Margaret Kelly Michaels: An Overview* 1 Psychol., Pub. Poly. & L. 246 (1995) for a description of the prosecution of Margaret Kelly Michaels for child abuse on the basis of repressed memory.

resulted in the plaintiff's exposure to the agent. Courts essentially must determine whether the plaintiff's exposure and subsequent disease are causally related, as that relationship is defined by the applicable law, or whether the exposure and disease are associated merely by chance. For example, did the asbestos inhaled by the plaintiff cause his lung cancer? Did the radar gun used by the traffic control officer cause his testicular cancer? Did the Bendectin taken by the plaintiff cause the birth defects that occurred thereafter? Traumatic injury occurs instantaneously, but disease develops over a period of time. The cause of disease, therefore, cannot be the direct object of the senses and can only be inferred. [Andrew A. Marino & Lawrence E. Marino, The Scientific Basis of Causality in Toxic Tort Cases, 21 Dayton L. Rev. 1, 2 (Fall, 1995).]

You will recall that *Daubert* addressed the admissibility of expert testimony in a case in which a family alleged that their children's birth defects had been caused by the mothers' ingestion of Bendectin during pregnancy. The defendant, Merrell Dow Pharmaceuticals, Inc., argued that the plaintiffs could not prove that the prescription antinausea drug had caused the defects.[46] It is not surprising that such a seminal case should grow out of a dispute about toxic tort causation. As a central element of all toxic tort claims and one about which most fact finders know little, proving causation can be extremely difficult and often requires the plaintiff to call numerous expert witnesses.

The expert in a toxic tort case must rationalize an assertion that the plaintiff's disease and the dosage of the toxin received were causally related and not merely a chance association. For example, in the case of a traffic control officer who used a radar gun and developed cancer, the plaintiff's exposure to electromagnetic fields and his disease occurred in the context of many factors, among others: the plaintiff ate peanuts; smoked cigarettes; wore blue socks; drove a motorcycle; lifted weights; collected coins; lived near a superhighway; and had arthritic knees. The question arises, therefore, why the expert singled out electromagnetic fields as the causative agent, as opposed to myriad other co-existing circumstances. [Andrew A. Marino & Lawrence E. Marino, The Scientific Basis of Causality in Toxic Tort Cases, 21 Dayton L. Rev. 1, 21 (Fall, 1995).]

Since it is unlikely that the mechanism by which an agent causes a disease will be known in a toxic tort case, to be able to opine that the agent "caused" the disease, the expert will have to express why this explanation is more likely than other possible explanations. It may be that this logical gap, inherent in evidence of a toxic tort, creates a certain uneasiness among trial courts and leads them to decide cases one at a time, making it difficult for observers to predict the outcomes.

In Wright v. Willamette Industries, Inc., 91 F.3d 1105 (8th Cir. 1996), the appellate court asked whether sufficient evidence had been offered at trial to support the plaintiffs' claim that the formaldehyde emitted by the defendant's fiberboard manufacturing plant had caused the plaintiffs' headaches, sore throats, watery eyes, running noses, dizziness, and shortness of breath. The jury found for the plaintiffs and awarded compensatory damages of $226,250.00. The court reversed, explaining that, although the plaintiffs had proved their exposure to the defendant's emissions, they had failed to prove that their level of exposure was hazardous and that the defendant's emissions probably caused their particular ailments. The court characterized the expert testimony that had been offered in the following way:

46. For a thorough look at the steady stream of Bendectin case that began in 1977, see Joseph Sanders, Bendectin on Trial: A Study of Mass Tort Litigation (Ann Arbor: The University of Michigan Press, 1998).

Their experts' information on this subject was simply insufficient. Dr. Fred Fowler, an industrial hygienist, and Dr. Jimmie Valentine, a pharmacologist, did offer testimony about the levels of gaseous formaldehyde that might be expected to cause symptoms like the ones that plaintiffs claim to have experienced. But the Wrights do not claim to have been injured from breathing gaseous formaldehyde, and they make no reference to any studies that reveal the levels of exposure to wood fibers impregnated with formaldehyde that are likely to produce adverse consequences. It is true that Dr. Frank Peretti, after a great deal of prodding, testified that the Wrights' complaints were more probably than not related to exposure to formaldehyde, but that opinion was not based on any knowledge about what amounts of wood fibers impregnated with formaldehyde involve an appreciable risk of harm to human beings who breathe them. The trial court should therefore have excluded Dr. Peretti's testimony, as Willamette requested it to do, because it was not based on scientific knowledge. See Daubert v. Merrell Dow Pharmaceuticals, Inc., 509 U.S. 579, 589-91 (1993); Fed. R. Evid. 702; Federal Judicial Center, Reference Manual on Scientific Evidence 47-48 (1994). Dr. Peretti's testimony regarding the probable cause of the Wrights' claimed injuries was simply speculation. [Wright v. Willamette Industries, Inc., 91 F.3d 1105, 1107-1108 (8th Cir. 1996).]

Thus, the court accepted scientific testimony that "gaseous formaldehyde" could cause the types of ailments suffered by the plaintiffs but it distrusted the experts' opinion that formaldehyde carried by particulate matter could have the same effect. For a critique of *Wright*, see Erica Beecher-Monas, The Heuristics of Intellectual Due Process: A Primer for Triers of Science, 75 N.Y.U. L. Rev. 1563 (2000).

In Zuchowicz v. United States, 140 F.3d 381 (2d Cir. 1998), the United States appealed an unfavorable decision in which the district court held that the plaintiff's wife's fatal lung condition was the result of the government's negligence in prescribing an overdose of the drug Danocrine. There was no question that the government had erred in its prescription or that the plaintiff's wife died from primary pulmonary hypertension (PPH). The only question before the trial court had been whether the one had caused the other. The trial court found that Danocrine had been extensively studied and prescribed for many years and that even though the Food and Drug Administration had approved it for use in dosages not exceeding 800 mg/ day, the plaintiff's wife was accidentally instructed to take 1600 mg/day. At the time of the trial, there had been no formal studies of effects of such high doses of Danocrine and it was thought that very few women had ever taken so much. Despite the plaintiff's inability to close this gap, his experts were permitted to testify that, although all of the other possible causes of the plaintiff's wife's PPH could not be excluded, the experts were "confident to a reasonable medical certainty that the Danocrine caused Mrs. Zuchowicz's PPH." There are many more examples of courts being more or less demanding of a plaintiff's experts in toxic tort litigation. With the great discretion accorded to trial judges within this area, it will take some time for courts to begin reaching more consistent conclusions. But cf. Plourde v. Gladstone, 190 F. Supp. 2d 708, 721 (D. Vt. 2002) (discussing some factors considered in admissibility of expert testimony in toxic tort cases).

c.   *Traditional Law Enforcement Investigative Tools*

Recently, several types of evidence that have been used for years in U.S. courtrooms have been questioned anew. The renewed scrutiny of handwriting identification, fingerprint identification, and comprehensive bullet lead analysis (CBLA) may be attributed to a belated recognition that "new" scientific techniques are not the only ones that should be subject to a Daubert analysis. As a result, the use of each of these techniques, though not novel, is less settled now than 10 or even five years ago.

According to the thorough history provided in D. Michael Risinger, Mike P. Denbeaux, and Michael J. Saks, Exorcism of Ignorance as a Proxy for Rational Knowledge: The Lessons of Handwriting Identification "Expertise," 137 U. Pa. L. Rev. 731, 762 (1988), by 1925 all but five jurisdictions in the United States had declared handwriting expertise permissible. Despite its early and continued[47] recognition, some courts can still be persuaded to exclude handwriting identification evidence. In United States v. Saelee, 162 F.Supp.2d 1097 (D.Alaska 2001), the defendant, charged with three counts of importing opium in violation of federal drug laws, sought to exclude the testimony of John W. Cawley, III, a forensic document analyst with the U.S. Postal Service. After concluding that the 2000 amendments to FRE 702 required a Daubert hearing on the admission of Mr. Cawley's testimony, as it was based on "technical or other specialized knowledge," the court concluded that testimony on handwriting identification was unreliable for several reasons:

[Reliability in this case may be determined by asking] whether the theories and techniques of handwriting comparison have been tested, whether they have been subjected to peer review, the known or potential error rate of forensic document examiners, the existence of standards in making comparisons between known writings and questioned documents, and the general acceptance by the forensic evidence community [of handwriting analysis]. [United States v. Saelee, 162 F.Supp.2d 1097, 1101 (D.Alaska 2001)]

After concluding that the field of handwriting analysis failed to meet the first four of these requirements, the court examined the fifth and ultimately excluded the evidence, stating:

Finally, the evidence does indicate that there is general acceptance of the theories and techniques involved in the field of handwriting analysis among the closed universe of forensic document examiners. This proves nothing. Testimony from these experts has, until recently, been uncritically accepted as reliable in the courts. Having previously testified somewhere as an expert document examiner was usually sufficient qualification. "Courts have long received handwriting analysis testimony as admissible evidence." United States v. Paul, 175 F.3d 906, 910 n.2 (11th Cir. 1999). However, the fact that this type of evidence has been generally accepted in the past by courts does not mean that it should be generally accepted now, after Daubert and Kumho. [United States v. Saelee, 162 F.Supp.2d 1097, 1101 (D.Alaska 2001).

47. Many courts continue to allow handwriting identification evidence. See D. Michael Risinger, Navigating Expert Reliability: Are Criminal Standards of Certainty Being Left on the Dock?, 64 Alb. L. Rev. 99, 140 n.161 (2000) for an extensive list which includes: United States v. Battle, No. 98-3246, 188 F.3d 519 (10th Cir. Aug. 6, 1999) (rejecting the defendant's challenge to the testimony of a qualified document examiner who testified that the defendant had forged the signature of another individual); United States v. Paul, 175 F.3d 906, 911 (11th Cir. 1999) (affirming the trial court's decision to allow a F.B.I. document examiner to testify that the defendant authored an extortion note); United States v. Jones, 107 F.3d 1147, 1161 (6th Cir. 1997) (upholding the admissibility of a United States Postal Service forensic document analyst's testimony that the defendant's signature was on various documents related to a stolen credit card). . . .

The court's statement to the fact that such evidence "has been generally accepted in the past . . . does not mean that it should be generally accepted now" might just as well be applied to a recent decision on fingerprint analysis, which seemed to be well-settled evidence until United States v. Plaza, 179 F. Supp. 2d 492 (D. Pa. 2002), *vacated*, 188 F. Supp. 2d 549 (D. Pa. 2002). In Plaza, the defendant moved to exclude testimony on FBI fingerprint analysis (ACE-V) for failure to meet the criteria set forth in Daubert and Kumho. After a lengthy consideration of the history of the use of fingerprint evidence in U.S. courts and the science behind such evidence, the court ruled that "no expert witness for any party will be permitted to testify that, in the opinion of the witness, a particular latent print is — or is not — the print of a particular person." *Plaza*, 179 F. Supp 2d at 518. The reasoning for the ruling was stated as follows:

> The court finds that ACE-V does not adequately satisfy the "scientific" criterion of testing (the first Daubert factor) or the "scientific" criterion of peer review (the second Daubert factor). Further, the court finds that the information of record is unpersuasive, one way or another, as to ACE-V's "scientific" rate of error (the first aspect of Daubert's third factor), and that, at the critical evaluation stage, ACE-V does not operate under uniformly accepted "scientific" standards (the second aspect of Daubert's third factor). [United States v. Plaza, 179 F.Supp.2d 492, 517 (D.Pa. 2002)]

Though the court later reversed its decision in light of new evidence on the reliability of the ACE-V methodology, the *Plaza* case marked the first time that fingerprint evidence had been rejected under a Daubert analysis. Subsequent cases have generally admitted testimony on fingerprint identification. See, e.g., United States v. Mitchell, 365 F.3d 215 (3d Cir. 2004) (admitting fingerprint identification testimony after extensive Daubert hearing); United States v. Crisp, 324 F.3d 261 (4th Cir. 2003), *cert. denied*, 124 S. Ct. 220 (2003); United States v. George, 363 F.3d 666 (7th Cir. 2004); United States v. Janis, 387 F.3d 682 (8th Cir. 2004); United States v. Abreu, 406 F.3d 1304 (11th Cir. 2005). However, after *Plaza*, exclusion of fingerprint evidence is now at the district court's discretion in at least one jurisdiction. See Jacobs v. V.I., 53 Fed. Appx. 651 (3d Cir. 2002) (affirming exclusion of fingerprint evidence as within district court's discretion).

Another previously well-settled area of expert testimony that has been called into question as of late is 'Compositional Analysis of Bullet Lead' (CABL or CBLA), a method by which bullets used in the commission of a crime are compared with bullets found in the possession of a suspect. In such an analysis, metal from the bullets at the scene is compared on a molecular level with metal from bullets possessed by the suspect; if the bullets are sufficiently similar in composition, the bullets are deemed to be from the same lot and the suspect may be charged accordingly. This method of analysis has been used by law enforcement since the 1960s.[48] CABL has traditionally been admitted by courts. However, in the wake of a number of recent reports calling into question the reliability of CABL as a methodology,[49] courts have begun to subject

48.   See Committee on Scientific Assessment of Bullet Lead Elemental Composition Comparison, National Research Council: Forensic Analysis: Weighing Bullet Lead Evidence (2004).
49.   See, e.g., Michael O. Finkelstein & Bruce Levin, Compositional Analysis of Bullet Lead As Forensic Evidence, 13 J.L. & Pol'y 119 (2005); William A. Tobin, Comparative Bullet Lead Analysis: A Case Study In Flawed Forensics, 28 Champ. 12 (July 2004); Edward J. Imwinkelried & William A. Tobin, Comparative Bullet Lead Analysis (CBLA) Evidence: Valid Inference or Ipse Dixit?, 28 Okla. City U.L. Rev. 43 (2003); William A. Tobin & Wayne Duerfeldt, How Probative Is Comparative Bullet Lead

the method to renewed scrutiny and, in some cases, exclude expert testimony on CABL for failure to meet Daubert criteria. In United States v. Mikos, 2003 U.S. Dist. LEXIS 22069 (D. Ill. 2003), the defendant moved to exclude CBLA expert testimony that a bullet recovered from the body of a murder victim matched bullets found in the defendant's possession. The reasoning of the court in that case reflects the new skepticism in CABL as a scientific technique:

> We understand that the FBI Laboratory has performed comparative bullet lead analysis (CBLA) for many years. Furthermore, we understand that persons from the FBI Laboratory . . . have for years been allowed to testify at trials as to their opinions regarding the source of tested bullets based on CBLA. In our opinion, however, the required standard of scientific reliability is met only as to the proposed opinion testimony that the elements composition of the bullets recovered from the body is indistinguishable from the composition of the bullets found in the Defendant's car. There is no body of data to corroborate the government's expert's further opinion that from this finding it follows that the bullets must or even likely came from the same batch or melt. The motion to exclude the expert testimony . . . relating to comparative bullet lead analysis is therefore granted . . .
> [United States v. Mikos, 2003 U.S. Dist. LEXIS 22069, 18 (D. Ill. 2003)]

In contrast to fingerprint evidence, which is still generally believed to be reliable despite the initial decision in *Plaza*, CABL evidence is beginning to be viewed with disfavor in many jurisdictions, to the point that some courts have reversed previous convictions that were based on CABL evidence. See, e.g, State v. Behn, 375 N.J. Super. 409 (N.J. Super. Ct. 2005) (reversing conviction and remanding for new trial where defendant was convicted on the basis of unreliable CABL testimony).

Perhaps most pertinently, at the request of the FBI, the National Academies of Science recently completed a study on the reliability of CBLA as a technique, concluding:

> The available data do not support any statement that a crime bullet came from a particular box of ammunition. In particular, references to "boxes" of ammunition in any form should be avoided as misleading under Federal Rule of Evidence 403.
>
> Compositional analysis of bullet lead data alone also does not permit any definitive statement concerning the date of bullet manufacture.
>
> Detailed patterns of the distribution of ammunition are unknown, and as a result, experts should not testify as to the probability that the crime scene bullet came from the defendant. Geographic distribution data on bullets and ammunition are needed before such testimony can be given.
>
> It is the conclusion of the committee that, in many cases, CABL is a reasonably accurate way of determining whether two bullets could have come from the same compositionally indistinguishable volume of lead. It may thus in appropriate cases provide additional evidence that ties a suspect to a crime, or in some cases evidence that tends to exonerate a suspect. CABL does not, however, have the unique specificity of techniques such as DNA typing to be used as standalone evidence. It is important that criminal justice professionals and juries understand the capabilities as well as the significant limitations of this forensic technique. [50]

Analysis?, 17 Crim. Just. 26 (2002); Robert D. Koons & Diana M. Grant, Compositional Variation in Bullet Lead Manufacture, 47 J. Foren. Sci. 950 (2002); Erik Randich et al., A Metallurgical Review of the Interpretation of Bullet Lead Compositional Analysis, 127 Foren. Sci. Int'l. 174 (2000).

50.   Supra n. 48.

QUESTION

The above discussion touches only a few of the more controversial types of scientific evidence. Debates also surround statistics, survey research, horizontal gaze nystagmus (the observation of eye tremors as a method for gauging intoxication), the estimation of economic losses in damages awards, identification through bite marks, modus operandi, and the outer reaches of medical testimony. Though each type of scientific evidence raises unique questions, can you articulate a systematic approach for determining whether a given piece of expert testimony will be admissible under the Federal Rules and *Daubert/Kumho*? Do you have a sense of the concerns, either enunciated by judges or not, that will lead courts to exclude probative evidence?

CHAPTER TEN

THE PROCESS OF PROOF IN CIVIL AND CRIMINAL CASES:
Burdens of Proof, Judicial Summary and Comment, and Presumptions

We have studied in great detail the proof process at the level of individual elements and items of evidence. We turn now to a consideration of aspects the process of proof that affect the structures of trials. The roles of the judge and the jury and their relationship to each other continue to be a central focus of our inquiry. Whereas previously we analyzed the judge-jury relationship from the perspective of individual elements, here we view that relationship from the perspective of the case as a whole.

Even if all the evidence each party wishes to produce is admitted into evidence, the role of the trial judge is not at an end. Just as the trial judge must make a preliminary determination concerning the logical force of any offered evidence, the judge must also make a preliminary determination of the overall strength of each party's case. The judge is empowered to issue preclusive rulings — rulings that terminate the litigation — at various stages in the proceedings based in large measure on the judge's assessment as to how reasonable people would analyze the evidence offered at trial. If the judge does not issue a preclusive ruling, the judge must instruct the jury about what standard of proof to apply in assessing the evidence. It is in part the rules governing this process that are the subject matter of this chapter.

We will see that in addition to determining the sufficiency of the evidence to go to the jury and instructing the jury about the standard of proof, the trial judge has various means to influence the jury's deliberations on the evidence. We have already encountered one indirect instance of such power. By ruling on the admissibility of specific proffers, the judge can dramatically influence the jury's perspective. For example, if a judge finds that a proposed witness lacks personal knowledge and thus cannot be placed on the stand, the jury will not have before it that witness's testimony. Suppose that witness would have contradicted an important witness of the adversary. By excluding the testimony, the judge affects the proof process by constraining the jury's perspective. Similarly, a judge will decide whether to admit evidence that casts doubt on the credibility of the testimony of a witness. A jury that has heard that a witness has reason to be biased against a party is likely to view the evidence that witness provides quite differently from a jury that did not have access to the impeaching testimony. Thus the judge, by deciding questions of the admissibility of evidence, has significant power to influence the deliberative process.

There are other ways in which the judge influences the jury's perspective. In some jurisdictions the judge has the power to sum up the evidence for the benefit of the jury. Subtle shifts of emphasis by the judge in summing up, even if unintended, may communicate to the jury the judge's view of aspects of the case. That, of course, may influence the jury's view, since the judge is likely to be an authority figure of some importance. In some jurisdictions the judge has the power to influence directly the jury's deliberations by expressing an opinion about the evidence by commenting on it. These processes, too, will be studied here.

We begin with a consideration of the burdens of proof — first in civil actions and then in criminal cases. We treat civil and criminal cases separately because the constitutional requirement of proof beyond reasonable doubt affects the discretion legislatures have in allocating burdens of proof in criminal cases. We then consider briefly devices for tinkering with or fine-tuning burdens of proof: (1) judicial summary and comment and (2) presumptions. We continue this theme in the next chapter where we focus on judicial notice, another device for regulating proof.

Many of the principles that we discuss here are applicable to bench trials as well as jury trials. For example, regardless of whether the ultimate decision maker is the judge or the jury, the decision maker must apply the appropriate standard of proof in evaluating the evidence. Similarly, there can be preclusive rulings that bring an early termination to the litigation in both bench trials and jury trials. Nonetheless, the rules governing the process of proof, like evidentiary exclusionary rules, have primary practical importance in the context of jury trials. Moreover, some of the rules (e.g., rules regarding comments on the evidence) are significant only in the context of jury trials. Thus the focus of our discussion will be on jury trials.

A.   THE BURDENS OF PROOF IN CIVIL CASES

A critical part of evaluating the parties' evidence, which involves both the jury and the judge, is the application of rules governing the burden of proof. There are two aspects to the burden of proof — the burden of persuasion and the burden of production, and there are rules governing both. For the burden of persuasion, there are the familiar procedural rules of decision that the *jury* must apply in evaluating the evidence. For most civil cases that rule is a "preponderance of the evidence." For example, a plaintiff in a negligence action must persuade the jury by a preponderance of the evidence that the defendant negligently injured the plaintiff. In some civil actions the standard is "clear and convincing evidence." The second aspect of the burden of proof is the production burden or the burden of producing evidence. The judge applies the burden of production rule to determine if a party has produced enough evidence to avoid a directed verdict (or some other adverse ruling that terminates the right of the party to proceed). Fed. R. Civ. P. 50 ("Judgment as Matter of Law," i.e., directed verdict); Fed. R. Civ. P. 56 ("Summary Judgment"). Because the burden of production rules have their impact earlier in time than the burden of persuasion rules, we will deal first with the burden of production.

1. The Burden of Production

a. *The Role of and Rationale for Production Burdens*

Our system of civil litigation does not give each party the automatic right to proceed through the entire trial process and have the jury resolve the case on the basis of whatever evidence the parties choose to introduce. Rather, in order to proceed to that stage a party must produce evidence that satisfies a sufficiency standard, often referred to as a burden of production.

Each issue to be litigated, whether it is an element or an affirmative defense, has a burden of production associated with it that requires one party or the other to produce evidence relevant to the particular issue (hence the name "burden of production"). If the party with a burden of production fails to produce sufficient evidence on a particular issue, the judge will not permit the issue to go to the jury. Thus the burden of production informs the parties how issues will be decided if no evidence is produced.

How, though, is one to know when a party with a burden of production has produced sufficient evidence to avoid a preclusive ruling that would decide an issue for purposes of the litigation? A burden of production should be satisfied when the underlying purpose of the requirement is met. In civil cases, the primary purpose of a burden of production is to ensure that there are issues in the case that need to be resolved by the jury. Issues need to be resolved by juries when there could be reasonable disagreement about which party should prevail. If there could be no reasonable disagreement, there is no reason to go to the expense and trouble of a trial, or to risk the possibility that the jury will render an irrational verdict. In such a case, the judge should, and will, render a verdict for the appropriate party (or otherwise dispose of the case, by dismissal, for example). Thus another implication of a burden of production is that the failure to satisfy its requirements will result in the adversary's prevailing on that particular issue. For this reason the burden of production is sometimes referred to as the *risk of nonproduction.*

b. *The Relationship Between Production Burdens and Persuasion Burdens*

To decide if there could be reasonable disagreement about which party should prevail, the judge must consider the burden of persuasion. Assume, for example, that the plaintiff must prove a particular fact by a preponderance of the evidence, a standard commonly understood to mean "more than a 50 percent chance of being true." The plaintiff will satisfy the burden of production by presenting enough evidence to create a jury issue regarding that fact. In other words, the plaintiff must produce enough evidence so that a jury could find by a greater-than-50-percent probability that the fact is likely to be true. If no reasonable person could conclude that the plaintiff has satisfied the relevant burden of persuasion, then there is no reason to prolong any judicial proceedings with further consideration of that fact. The judge should terminate the proceedings with respect to the fact in favor of the defendant. Similarly, if the plaintiff's evidence is so overwhelming that no reasonable person could find the fact to be less than 50 percent true, and if the defendant does not challenge or rebut the plaintiff's evidence, the judge should terminate the proceedings with respect to that fact in favor of the plaintiff. In short, as Professor McNaughton developed in an important article, the burden of production is a function of the burden of persuasion. John T. McNaughton, Burden of Production of Evidence: A Function of a Burden of Persuasion, 68 Harv. L. Rev. 1382 (1955). The test to determine if a burden of production has been met is whether, in light of the evidence, there could be reasonable disagreement over which party should win. If there could be such disagreement, a jury question has been generated. If not, the judge may as well dispose of the case as expeditiously as possible.

c.   The Relationship Between the Burden of Production and the Burden of Persuasion Illustrated

The relationship between burdens of production and burdens of persuasion deserves a closer look. Presumably jurors evaluate evidence by making rough estimates of the likelihood that facts are true. In other words, although jurors may not articulate or even tacitly assign specific quantified degrees of probability to their conclusions, they, like the rest of us, make factual assessments that are based on — or at least that can be explained in terms of — probabilities. Regardless of whether juries actually think in these terms, courts instruct them to apply a probabilistic concept in deciding cases whenever the standard preponderance of the evidence instruction is given. For purposes of simplicity, we will assume for now that jurors do think in roughly probabilistic terms and that a preponderance of the evidence means more than a 50 percent chance of the relevant fact being true.

Under these assumptions, one may diagram the evidentiary process in such a way as to highlight the relationship between burdens of production and burdens of persuasion. Assume that the party with a burden of production produces some evidence. That evidence will indicate that there is a certain chance that the relevant facts are true. However, the evidence is likely to be not perfectly clear as to what probability it generates. Looking at that evidence, reasonable people could disagree about the probability to which the evidence establishes some necessary fact. Does that mean that every time evidence is produced a jury issue is generated because there always will be reasonable disagreement about its implications? No; a jury issue will be generated only when there is disagreement about which party should win, and that requires referring to the burden of persuasion. Consider now the three possibilities charted in Diagram 10-1:

Diagram 10-1

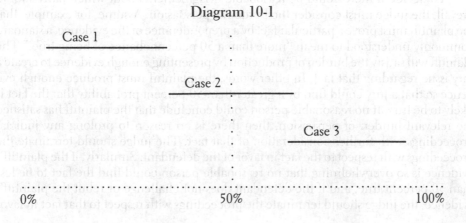

After a party produces evidence on an issue, this chart reflects the three relevant possibilities in terms of the implications of the evidence. First, the evidence produced may not be very convincing. A reasonable person looking at it may conclude that it has some persuasive force, but not very much. That possibility is represented by Case 1. It indicates that, given the evidence, the probability of the relevant fact being true ranges from about 10 to 35 percent (we could have drawn that line segment anywhere between 0 and 50 percent, just so long as it did not exceed 50 percent). In this case, the burden of production has not been satisfied. Since no reasonable person could conclude that the party producing the evidence should win, there is no reason to send this issue to the jury. In Case 2, the evidence has generated a jury issue. The evidence indicates a range of reasonable persuasiveness from about 40 to 60 percent (here we could have drawn the line segment in any fashion so long as it ranged over 50 percent). Since reasonable people could disagree about the implications of the evidence in this case, the issue will be sent to the jury. Case 3 is similar to Case 1 in that again no reasonable disagreement could exist as to the implications of the evidence. The evidence indicates somewhere between a 65 and 90 percent chance of the relevant fact being true (here the line could be drawn anywhere to the right of 50 percent).

Case 3 is different from Case 1 in one respect. We have been assuming that the party with the burden of production has produced evidence. In Case 1, the burden has not been met, and thus there is no reason to proceed further. In Case 2, the burden of production has been met, and the case will proceed. In Case 3, the burden has not only been met, but exceeded. No reasonable person could disagree about who should win. This conclusion, though, is based solely on the evidence produced by one party. Case 3 differs from Case 1 in that rather than the judge disposing of the issue, Case 3 requires that the adversary be given a chance to produce contrary evidence in order to demonstrate that there is a reasonable dispute about the relevant fact. In Case 1, there is no reason to have the adversary proceed because the party's evidence itself indicates that the relevant fact cannot be established. Having the adversary produce still more information substantiating that conclusion would be a waste of time and money. In Case 3, however, the adversary has not yet been heard and may be in possession of information that would affect the analysis of how likely the relevant fact is, given all the evidence (including the adversary's). Accordingly, in Case 3, the judge will not dispose of the relevant issue. The party with the initial burden of production cannot prevail before the adversary has an opportunity to respond.

After the adversary responds, one or both parties may once more ask the judge to test the sufficiency of the evidence. To determine how the judge ought to proceed in light of such requests, we must consider how the evidentiary process proceeds. Assume that the party with the burden of production produces sufficient evidence so that something akin to Case 2 is generated. At that point, the adversary will have the right to respond. The adversary's evidence will likely decrease the probability of the relevant fact being true, thus shifting the probability range on the chart to the left. In most jurisdictions, after the adversary has responded the party with the initial burden of production is entitled to produce "rebutting" evidence, that is evidence that responds to the evidence produced by the adversary, and typically the adversary may respond to that new offer of evidence. This process continues until neither party has anything new to offer, at which point the evidence taken as a whole will approximate one of the three cases diagrammed on the chart. If the evidence fits into Case 1, the judge should decide the issue in favor of the adversary; if the evidence fits into Case 2, the judge should give the issue to the jury; if the evidence fits into Case 3, the judge should decide the issue in favor of the party who initially bore the burden of production.

d.   Procedural Mechanisms for Enforcing Burdens of Production

The manner in which a party asks a judge to determine whether the opponent has met a production burden depends on the time at which the judge is asked to make such a ruling, and here we see the interaction between the rules of evidence and civil procedure. One possibility is that before any evidence is produced a party can move for summary judgment. Fed. R. Civ. P. 56. The judge will grant the motion if it can be determined from the pleadings and any supporting documentation that there are no issues in need of judicial resolution in the case. Such a decision, however, is equivalent to saying that either Case 1 or Case 3 in the Diagram 10-1 is present — either the party with the burden of production will not be able to meet it, or the adversary will not be able to show that the party's evidence does not justify taking the case away from a jury. If Case 2 is present, the judge will deny the motion for summary judgment (by either party) and the litigation will proceed.

Another possibility is that, if a case goes to the evidence-taking phase, the judge may be asked to test the strength of the evidence by a motion for directed verdict at the end of a party's case. Fed. R. Civ. P. 50. The analysis here is quite similar to the analysis of summary judgment motions; in fact there is only one significant difference between directed verdicts and summary judgments. After the party with the burden of production rests its case-in-chief, if Case 1 is present the court should direct a verdict for the adversary; if Case 2 is present, the trial obviously should proceed. It will also proceed if Case 3 is present because the adversary has not yet been heard from. So long as the party resisting a preclusive motion has evidence to offer that might affect the judge's analysis of the case, the judge should not grant the preclusive motion.

The important point to note with respect to both summary judgments and directed verdicts is that the judge's decision will rest on the ability of a party to meet its burden of production and the adversary's ability to respond to a party's proof with sufficient evidence to justify taking the issue to a jury. As the Supreme Court observed in Anderson v. Liberty Lobby, Inc., 477 U.S. 242, 252 (1986):

> [T]he inquiry involved in a ruling on a motion for a summary judgment . . . necessarily implicates the substantive evidence standard of proof that would apply at trial on the merits. . . . The judge's inquiry, therefore, invariably asks whether reasonable jurors could find by a preponderance of the evidence that the plaintiff is entitled to a verdict.

In short, both the burden of production and preclusive motions are functions of the burden of persuasion.

Throughout the remainder of the chapter we will use the term *directed verdict* as a shorthand for the preclusive motions that a party might make. You should keep in mind that when we use that term, we are not speaking of anything unique about the concept of directed verdict; rather, we are referring to preclusive motions generally.

e.   The Allocation of Burdens of Production

Typically the pleading or moving party bears both the burden of pleading and the burden of production. In general, then, whoever is asking the courts to modify the status quo, which is either the plaintiff or a party who has made a motion for some sort of relief, must introduce sufficient evidence of the relevant factual claims to justify a finding of fact consistent with those claims. Thus who bears the burden of production will normally be a function of the position of the parties. If X sues Y over a contract, X will bear the burden of production on most factual issues. If, by contrast, Y sues X in a declaratory judgment action, Y will bear the burden of production on most of the identical factual issues. The burden of production, in short, is primarily a rule of convenience, and in most instances there will be well-established precedent allocating the burden of production. If there is no such precedent, there is "no satisfactory test" for allocating the burden of production. Fleming James Jr., Burden of Proof, 47 Va. L. Rev. 58, 58 (1961). Moreover, since burden of production rules are primarily matters of convenience, policy reasons that may justify the allocation of persuasion burdens, see Note 4 at page 711 and Note 8 at page 712, infra, have little, if any, applicability to the question how burdens of production should be allocated.

KEY POINTS

1. Every factual element of a claim or a defense has a production burden associated with it.

2. The purpose of the production requirement is to require the party who has it to present enough evidence to create a jury question.

3. The failure to satisfy the burden of production will result in a directed verdict or other preclusive action against the party with the burden.

4. The party with the burden of pleading a matter typically has the burden of production with respect to that matter.

2. The Burden of Persuasion

The skeptic will say that we can know nothing with certainty (although one might ask how the skeptic knows that). Nonetheless, there are some matters about which many of us feel a high degree of certainty. Each of you could probably make a list of propositions that on the basis of empirical evidence or faith you regard as beyond dispute. Moreover, if you were conservative in making your list, you could probably get a large number of your classmates to agree with some of the propositions that you regard as beyond dispute. There are many things that we cannot know with certainty, however. Consider, for example, the question whether the defendant's car entered an intersection against the red light when there is conflicting eyewitness testimony; or the question whether a defendant committed an assault when the principal evidence against the defendant is DNA bloodtyping and the defendant claims that some of the blood samples have been contaminated.

For a variety of reasons jurors (or judges in bench trials) will usually be less than certain about the determinations they are called upon to make. There may be credible, conflicting accounts about what happened, as the conflicting eyewitness testimony in the red light example illustrates. There may be uncertainty about how much weight to give scientific evidence, as the DNA example illustrates. There may be conflicting views about how much weight to give a circumstantial inference. For example, in the *Johnson* case, to what extent does evidence of Officer Walker's character for violence suggest that he may have been the first aggressor? There may be uncertainty about how to evaluate the culpability of a person's conduct. For example, was the defendant's speeding down an urban street in order to get an injured child to the hospital negligent behavior? And keep in mind that because of the burden of production rules, a case will get to the jury only if reasonable people could disagree about the appropriate outcome.

a.   The Role of Rules Setting Forth Burdens of Persuasion

A burden of persuasion is a rule of decision that informs the decision maker how to decide a case in light of the uncertainties that inevitably will accompany the presentation of evidence. For example, one possible rule of decision is that a plaintiff should prevail only if the evidence establishes the plaintiff's case to a 95 percent certainty. This rule would require a verdict for the defendant if there were more than a slight doubt about the truth of the facts that the plaintiff must establish.

Such a rule may initially seem to have an intuitive appeal — people (defendants) should not be required to pay unless they have done something wrong. Notwithstanding this intuitive appeal, it is not the rule generally found in civil litigation because it would put plaintiffs at a serious disadvantage. Requiring plaintiffs to meet such a high burden, it is believed, would result in a disproportionate number of wrongful verdicts for defendants at the expense of deserving plaintiffs. The opposite rule — requiring defendants to show to a 95 percent certainty that they should not be held liable — would have the opposite effect, of course. Rather than adopt either of these two extremes, the virtually uniform practice in civil litigation is to define the burden of persuasion as a preponderance of the evidence. Plaintiffs must prove each of their necessary factual claims to a preponderance of the evidence, and defendants must establish affirmative defenses by the same standard. Accordingly, judges instruct juries in civil cases to analyze the evidence and render a verdict for the party in whose favor the evidence "preponderates." As we noted earlier, preponderance is usually defined as meaning "more than a 50 percent chance of being true." Thus the task for juries is to determine whether the evidence favors the plaintiff's story with respect to the factual elements of a cause of action and to determine whether the evidence favors the defendant's story with respect to affirmative defenses.

b.   The Premises Underlying the Preponderance Rule

The preponderance rule incorporates an underlying assumption concerning the participants in litigation: that plaintiffs as a class and defendants as a class generally ought to be treated equivalently. The reason for this assumption is that before a case is resolved, one cannot know who should win; it is as likely that the defendant should win as the plaintiff. Assume that the plaintiff is suing the defendant for $200 allegedly owed under a contract. Before the parties to this dispute produce evidence relevant to its resolution, how should we conceptualize the case — as one in which the plaintiff is trying to get $200 of the defendant's money, as a case in which the defendant is wrongfully refusing to pay, or as a case in which two individuals are contesting whose $200 it is? The last view is intuitively most compelling. Without knowing the facts, it seems just as likely that the defendant is refusing to pay what is owed as that the plaintiff is attempting to obtain an undeserved benefit.

One implication of the equivalency notion generalized in the preponderance standard is that there should be roughly the same number of errors made for plaintiffs as for defendants. The preponderance standard, however, will achieve this result only if certain conditions exist. Assume that in the set of all cases going to trial there are approximately as many deserving plaintiffs as deserving defendants. Assume further that the jury will make a rough probability assessment of the strength of each case presented by the parties. Presumably those probability assessments will range from 0.0 to 1.0. Now compare the set of cases in which plaintiffs deserve to win to the set of cases in which defendants deserve to win. It is not unreasonable to suppose that in most of the cases in which plaintiffs deserve to win the facts will support that conclusion, thus creating a probability assessment of more than 0.5, which will result in a verdict for the plaintiff. Only in those cases in which the probability assessment is 0.5 or less will there be wrongful verdicts for defendants. This supposition is equally applicable to the set of cases that defendants deserve to win: Presumably the evidence in most of these cases will demonstrate that the defendant deserves to win, thus creating a probability assessment of 0.5 or less. Only in those cases in which the probability assessment is more than 0.5 will there be wrongful verdicts for plaintiffs. If one assumes that the probability assessments for these two sets are in a normal distribution over the range of 0.0 to 1.0, then the number of errors made for plaintiffs will approximate the number of errors made for defendants, and the preponderance of the evidence standard will have done its job.

Diagram 10-2 demonstrates this proposition geometrically.[1] The horizontal axis is the probability that juries assign to cases, and the vertical axis is the number of cases assigned a particular probability. Graph I is the set of cases in which defendants deserve to win (which means if we knew all the facts to certainty, the defendant would win); graph II is the set of cases in which plaintiffs deserve to win.

Diagram 10-2

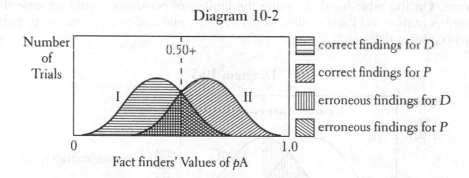

Fact finders' Values of pA

In graph I all of those cases to the right of the 0.5 level, which is the heavily shaded area, are errors. In graph II all of the cases to the left of the 0.5 level, which is again the heavily shaded area, are errors. The larger the heavily shaded areas are, the more errors there are; the smaller the heavily shaded areas are, the fewer errors there are. So long as the heavily shaded areas under the two graphs are of approximately equal size, then the preponderance standard will have done its appointed task of equalizing errors among plaintiffs and defendants. Note, however, that this equalization will occur only if the relevant areas under the two graphs are roughly the same size, which is an empirical

---

1.   We are indebted for what follows, including the graphs, to Richard S. Bell, Decision Theory and Due Process: A critique of the Supreme Court's Law making for Burdens of Proof, 78 J. Crim. L. & Criminology 557 (1987).

question. If the contours of the two graphs differ markedly from what we have presented, then the size of those areas under the graphs will change, with the result being that errors may not be allocated equally among plaintiffs and defendants. The manner in which we have drawn these graphs reflects assumptions that are pertinent to civil cases but that are dubious in criminal cases, a matter to which we will return below.

c.   Higher Burdens of Persuasion

We can use these same graphs to demonstrate why alternative, higher burdens of persuasion are occasionally relied on in civil cases. Many jurisdictions require allegations in civil cases of fraud or of activity that would be criminal to be proven by clear and convincing evidence. Because of the seriousness of such allegations, errors should favor the person against whom such allegations are made (which also explains the higher burden of persuasion in criminal cases). Making the same assumptions as we did above, we illustrate the effect of raising the burden of persuasion from a preponderance to "clear and convincing evidence" in Diagram 10-3. The shaded area again represents errors, and the effect of raising the burden of proof is obvious. Errors favoring defendants increase and errors favoring plaintiffs decrease, which is precisely the effect that the higher burden of persuasion is designed to accomplish. Again, though, bear in mind that what these graphs would look like if they reflected reality is an empirical question. Should reliable data ever be obtained on that issue, it might be justifiable to modify the burden of persuasion in light of that information. For example, we might decide after reviewing the data that too many errors favoring defendants are made when there is an allegation of fraud. Lowering the burden of persuasion may decrease those errors. On the other hand, lowering the burden of persuasion could increase the number of marginal fraud claims, which in turn could lead to more erroneous judgments against defendants.

Diagram 10-3

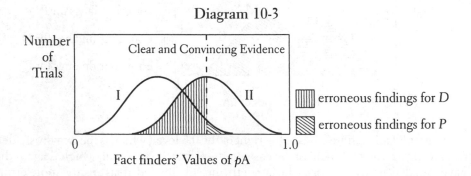

Although our primary concern here is with civil cases, note that Diagram 10-3 can also explicate the proof beyond reasonable doubt requirement in criminal cases: Assume that the horizontal and vertical axes retain the same significance and simply move somewhat to the right the vertical line representing the burden of persuasion standard. What do you think graph I — that is, the set of all innocent people who go to trial in criminal cases — would look like? If that set is quite small, and it may well be given all the diversion mechanisms in criminal cases, there may be few cases of wrongful convictions to offset whatever wrongful acquittals occur. If that is so, this empirical phenomenon may provide a basis for arguing that the burden of persuasion in criminal cases should be lower. The strength of that argument, however, would depend — as it does in considering the impact of lowering the "clear and convincing" evidence standard in civil cases — on assessing the secondary consequences of lowering the "proof beyond a reasonable doubt" standard. Presumably one factor that prosecutors take into account in deciding how far to pursue a case is the standard of proof. If it is lowered, prosecutors might bring more problematic cases to trial, which would then change the size and configuration of graph I, thus resulting in more errors of innocent individuals being convicted.

d. The Meaning of "Preponderance of the Evidence" in Practice

Burdens of persuasion, or at least the standard preponderance burden, may not operate as they are intended to. In an interesting study, Professors Rita James Simon and Linda Mahan obtained data indicating that jurors may understand "preponderance of the evidence" to mean a probability somewhere between .7 and .8, while judges consistently indicate that it means slightly more than .5. Rita James Simon and Linda Mahan, Quantifying Burdens of Proof, 5 Law & Soc. Rev. 319 (1971). In this study, jurors were asked to translate the phrase *preponderance of the evidence* into a probability assessment rather than being informed that the phrase means "50 percent plus." When so informed, there is data indicating that individuals can follow such instructions. Dorothy K. Kagehiro and W. Clark Stanton, Legal v. Quantified Definitions of Standards of Proof, 9 Law & Hum. Behav. 159 (1985). In this study, individuals were given a data set and varying instructions on the burden of persuasion; some were instructed in legal terminology such as "a preponderance of the evidence" and "clear and convincing evidence" and others in probabilities ranging from .51 to .91. The results showed that the legal definitions of burdens of persuasion did not much affect the outcome in cases, whereas the instructions in probabilistic terms did. If you were convinced that this study accurately reflected how most individuals react to such instructions, what implications does it have for the structuring of trials?

e. The Relative Nature of the Burden of Persuasion

From the standpoint of the parties to an action, any burden of persuasion is relative. If the plaintiff has a greater than 50 percent burden of persuasion, the defendant will lose unless the jury can be convinced by at least a 50 percent probability that the plaintiff's version of the facts is untrue. If the defendant does not carry that burden, the inevitable logical result will be that the jury believes that the plaintiff's version of the facts is more than 50 percent likely to be true. Thus to say that the plaintiff has a greater than 50 percent burden of persuasion is to say that the defendant has a 50 percent burden of persuasion. Similarly, to say that a plaintiff has a 70 percent burden of persuasion is to say that a defendant has a greater than 30 percent burden of persuasion.

f. The Allocation of the Burden of Persuasion

As is true of production burdens, a burden of persuasion for each necessary element of a cause of action must be allocated to one party or the other. Usually the law is clear on which party has the burden of persuasion. If the law is not clear on this issue, however, there is no very helpful formula or litmus test for determining who should have the burden. Fleming James Jr., Burden of Proof, 47 Va. L. Rev. 58-59 (1961).

The normal rule is that plaintiffs and moving parties bear the burden to prove by a preponderance all the facts necessary to justify a verdict or judgment in their behalf. There are, however, exceptions to the normal rule. On occasion, defendants are required to bear the burden of persuasion on specified factual questions that are typically referred to as "affirmative defenses." It is not unusual, for example, to find a defendant in a negligence action having the burden to prove the plaintiff's contributory negligence. There are also jurisdictions that require one party to plead an issue and the other party to bear both the burden of production and the burden of persuasion with respect to that issue. Similarly, there are situations in which one party bears the burden of production with respect to a fact, but the opposing party must disprove the fact (or prove its negation, however you want to view it) by the relevant burden of persuasion. Such cases fit no general rule, but you should be aware that they do occasionally arise. In any event, states are free to allocate burdens of proof in civil cases virtually any way they like. Lavine v. Milne, 424 U.S. 577, 585 (1976) ("Outside the criminal area, where special concerns attend, the locus of the burden of persuasion is normally not an issue of federal constitutional concern."). States on occasion exercise that power in interesting ways. Consider the following case.

SCHECHTER v. KLANFER
321 N.Y.S.2d 99, 28 N.Y.2d 228, 269 N.E.2d 812 (1971)

BREITEL, Judge.

In this negligence action for personal injuries, the issue is whether the jury should have been instructed to hold plaintiff, who had by amnesia lost his memory of the events causing his injury, to a lesser degree of proof than a plaintiff who could have testified to the events.

Upon the trial, a verdict in favor of defendants was returned. The trial court initially instructed the jury to hold plaintiff to a lesser degree of proof if it found his amnesia to be genuine. Upon defendants' objection, however, the charge was withdrawn, plaintiff taking exception.

There should be a reversal and a new trial in order that the jury may consider whether plaintiff should be held to a lesser degree of proof.

Robert Schechter and his companion, Alice Stone, were involved in a motorboat collision on the night of August 25, 1964. Both were then 14 years old. They had left a party at a lakeshore home and, with Robert operating his father's boat, had begun motoring across the lake. Alice sat in the front seat, to the left of Robert. Alice testified that the night was clear and moonlit, that the boat's lights were on, and that Robert was taking a straight course at about four miles an hour. They had not gone far, Alice continued, when she looked to her right and saw a motorboat some 50 feet distant heading towards them, its bow out of water. About one second later, she estimated, the other boat, operated by defendant Robert Klanfer, struck the Schechter boat near the driver's seat. Alice estimated that the Klanfer boat was traveling at 30 miles an hour. The nighttime speed limit on the lake was 10 miles an hour. The defendants disputed Alice's testimony as to the speed of their boat and the lighting of the Schechter boat. Robert testified but not as to the accident, claiming that, as a result of the collision, he had no memory of the events. He had sustained a fractured skull, fractured arm, fractured jaw, and other physical injuries. He had been comatose for several days. Plaintiff's medical expert testified that Robert had suffered severe emotional shock and psychiatric change, including amnesia, due to brain damage.

The rule providing when a plaintiff may prevail on a lesser degree of proof was best crystallized in Noseworthy v. City of New York, 80 N.E.2d 744. The court there held that "in a death case a plaintiff is not held to as high a degree of proof of the cause of action as where an injured plaintiff can himself describe the occurrence." Moreover, despite some contrary notions, the rule has been applied in wrongful death cases where the plaintiff has called an eyewitness. . . .

The Committee on Pattern Jury Instruction of the Association of Supreme Court Justices recommends, in a pattern instruction, that the amnesiac plaintiff be held to a lesser degree of proof if the jury is satisfied from medical and other evidence that plaintiff is suffering from loss of memory and that the injuries plaintiff incurred were a substantial factor in causing plaintiff's loss of memory (PJI 1:62).[2] In a thoughtful and well-documented comment to the instruction, the committee explains: "The limitation that the accident must have been a substantial factor in causing the loss of memory is predicated on the rationale of the Noseworthy case, which is not merely plaintiff's inability to present proof, but the unfairness of allowing the defendant, who has knowledge of the facts, to benefit by standing mute when plaintiff's inability *results from defendant's acts*." (1 N.Y. PJI 36, emphasis in original).

Of course, an amnesiac plaintiff can no more "describe the occurrence" that produced his injury than can a plaintiff's decedent, a toddler or an imbecile. Other States, faced with an analogous choice of extending to amnesiac plaintiffs a "presumption of due care" normally accorded plaintiffs' decedents, have reasoned that the amnesiac's inability to testify entitles him to the preferential rule.

The rule even as applied to amnesiacs does not, however, shift the burden of proof or eliminate the need for plaintiffs to introduce evidence of a *prima facie* case. The jury must rest its findings on some evidence to establish negligence and also the absence of contributory negligence. In this case, however, plaintiff did introduce evidence to make out a *prima facie* case, so that there was an opportunity to apply the lesser burden of persuasion. If the jury had been told to apply a lesser burden of persuasion, it could have and, therefore, might have found plaintiff free from contributory negligence. The circumstances testified to by Alice Stone that Robert drove the boat in a straight line, at a speed of four miles an hour, and with the boat lights on, were relevant on the issue of contributory negligence. It also could have found defendants negligent upon Alice's testimony of the speed and course of the Klanfer boat.

The danger is, of course, that amnesia is easily feigned. The dangers may be ameliorated. Plaintiff has the burden of proof on the issue of amnesia as on other issues. A jury should be instructed that before the lesser burden of persuasion is applied, because of the danger of shamming, they must be satisfied that the evidence of amnesia is clear and convincing, supported by the objective nature and extent of any other physical injuries sustained, and that the amnesia was clearly a result of the accident.

2. "If, however, you are satisfied from the medical and other evidence presented that plaintiff is suffering from a loss of memory that makes it impossible for him to recall events at or about the time of the accident and that the injuries plaintiff incurred in the accident were a substantial factor in causing his loss of memory, the plaintiff is not held to as high a degree of proof as would be a plaintiff who can himself describe the occurrence."

The above is undoubtedly a more severe test than that suggested by the Pattern Jury Instructions. Yet it would seem a small price to pay for a liberal rule treating amnesiac plaintiffs on a par with the representatives of decedents in death actions. The reasons for so treating amnesiacs are similar to those advanced for representatives of persons silenced in fatal accidents, but the risk and ease of shamming are measurably greater.

Accordingly, the order of the Appellate Division should be reversed and a new trial ordered, with costs to abide the event.

Order reversed, etc.

NOTES AND QUESTIONS

1. According to the *Schechter* court, the plaintiff must present a prima facie case of negligence in order to be in a position to get the benefit of the reduced burden of proof rule. What is a prima facie case? The *Schechter* court does not tell us, but usually courts use that term to describe the production burden that a party must meet. If that is what the court means here, and it seems likely that it is, the plaintiff must introduce enough evidence of the defendant's negligence to raise a jury issue. In other words, in holding that the plaintiff had presented a prima facie case, the court, in effect, was saying that the evidence of the defendant's negligence resembled Case 2 in Diagram 10-1 on page 700, supra.

2. Could or should the *Schechter* court have been more precise in articulating how amnesia could affect the plaintiff's burden of proof? The court stated that in the case of amnesia caused by the defendant the plaintiff "is not held to as a high a degree of proof as would be a plaintiff who can himself describe the occurrence," and the court also stated that "the rule even as applied to amnesiacs does not . . . shift the burden of proof." If the plaintiff's ordinary burden of persuasion is just slightly greater than 50 percent, and if that burden is lessened, how is the burden of persuasion not shifted to the defendant?

3. What justification is there for giving a reduced burden of persuasion to a plaintiff with amnesia? The *Schechter* court's answer to this question was to quote with approval a statement from the recommendations of the New York Supreme Court Justices Committee on Pattern Jury Instructions:

> The limitation that the accident must have been a substantial factor in causing the loss of memory is predicated on the rationale of the *Noseworthy* case, which is not merely plaintiff's inability to present proof, but the unfairness of allowing the defendant, who has knowledge of the facts, to benefit by standing mute when plaintiff's inability results from defendant's acts.

Consider what this statement means and what relationship it has to the facts of *Schechter*. With respect to the plaintiff's possible "inability to present proof," the plaintiff in *Schechter* produced his boating companion as an eyewitness.

What is the court's concern when it refers to the "unfairness of allowing the defendant, who has knowledge of the facts, to benefit by standing mute"? If standing mute with knowledge is "unfair," is it unfair, as the court suggests, only when the defendant is the cause of plaintiff's amnesia? In any event, the defendant in *Schechter* did not stand mute, and other defendants are not likely to stand mute — unless the plaintiff's amnesia prevents the plaintiff from meeting the initial production burden. But if the plaintiff has not met the production burden, the case will not go to the jury, so there will be no occasion to apply a reduced burden of proof!

Are there other justifications for applying a burden-of-persuasion rule favorable to a plaintiff who suffers amnesia as a result of the defendant's conduct? If so, what do you think of the requirement that the plaintiff must establish the amnesia by clear and convincing evidence?

4. What justifications are there generally for allocating burdens of persuasion to one party or another? See Fleming James Jr., Burden of Proof 47 Va. L. Rev. 51, 58-61 (1961), in which Professor James suggests several factors that may influence allocation of the burden of proof. These include (1) "readier access to knowledge," (2) "the extent to which a party's contention departs from what would be expected in light of ordinary human experience," (3) "a feeling that a charge of wrongdoing should in fairness be proven by the party making it," and (4) "real or supposed reasons of policy [for which] the law sometimes disfavors claims or defenses which it nevertheless allows." Assuming a mature discovery system is in place, of what significance is it that one party may have readier access to evidence than another? Does it make sense to handicap certain claims by allocating to their proponents the burden of persuasion either because such claims are typically unlikely to be true or because such claims are disfavored?

5. If burdens of persuasion operate as they are intended to operate, precisely what cases would come out differently under a rule that allocated the preponderance burden of persuasion to one party instead of the other? Is not the answer only those cases in which the jury is in equipoise and is unable to say whether the burden of persuasion is met or not? How large a class of cases do you think that is likely to be? Changing a burden of persuasion from preponderance to clear and convincing evidence, by contrast, is more likely to affect the results in cases, again assuming burdens of persuasion operate roughly as intended.

Of course, if juries in fact think of the preponderance standard as meaning 70 to 80 percent, as the Simon and Mahan study suggests they sometimes may, see page 707, supra, then even a shift in the preponderance standard may be significant.

Consider the implication of these observations in the context of *Schechter*. If holding the plaintiff with amnesia to a lower standard of persuasion than other plaintiffs means that the plaintiff's burden is reduced slightly from the preponderance standard, the effect is to make the plaintiff's burden something less than 50-plus percent — say, 49 percent. This is the equivalent of saying that the burden of persuasion shifts to the defendant to persuade the jury by a 51-plus percent preponderance that the defendant is not negligent. Thus, contrary to the court's assertion, the amnesia rule does shift the burden of proof to the defendant (unless, of the course, the fact finder understands preponderance to mean more than 50-plus percent). Such a shift, however, unlikely to affect many cases. The practical impact of the amnesia rule lies not in the question whether there is a shifting of the preponderance burden but rather in how much of a shift the amnesia rule creates.

6. In most instances questions about the appropriate burden of proof rule are for the judge (or legislature) and not the jury. For example, whether a clear and convincing evidence standard will apply in a particular cause of action is a legal issue that the judge resolves. *Schechter*, however, contemplates that the jury will determine what burden of proof rule to apply on the basis of its assessment of the amnesia question. Would it be preferable for the judge to make the findings about amnesia and remove from the jury any consideration of what burden of proof rule to apply?

7. There are statements in many cases, in particular the older ones, that the "burden of proof never shifts; it always rests with the party to whom it was originally allocated." For the most part this statement is true, but it is more misleading than helpful. Reconsider Diagram 10-1, page 700, supra. When a party has demonstrated such a strong case that no reasonable person could disagree that the party deserves on the evidence so far produced to win, a directed verdict will be entered unless the adversary produces more evidence that lowers the probabilities to a point where reasonable people could disagree. In such a case, the adversary bears a functional burden of production; the adversary can produce evidence or lose. In this sense, the "burden of production" can shift numerous times during the course of a trial. Typically, though, a judge would not say that an adversary who fails to produce more evidence in this circumstance has not met a burden of production. Rather, the judge would merely enter a directed verdict without referring to the idea of a burden of production. Note that regardless of what a judge would say in this situation, conceptually the adversary has failed to meet a "burden of production." Unlike burdens of production, burdens of persuasion do not tend to get shifted around even functionally during a trial. In this sense, wherever the law initially allocates a burden of persuasion is generally where it remains from beginning to end of the litigation. *Schechter* appears to be an exception to this general rule in that the burden of persuasion rule — if it is a preponderance of the evidence — seems inevitably to shift to the defendant on proof of amnesia. We will see similar exceptions when we consider presumptions in Section D, infra.

8. There are various policies that could be pursued through different choices concerning burdens of persuasion. We have mentioned some, such as error equalization over parties. Others include the reduction of erroneous determinations of liability, reduction of total dollars wrongfully allocated as a result of trial, and the minimization of large mistakes. Different burden of proof rules may serve these various policies better than others. Neil Orloff and Jery Stedinger, A Framework for Evaluating the Preponderance of the Evidence Standard, 131 U. Pa. L. Rev. 1159 (1983).

9. Not all states define the burden of persuasion in civil cases in quasi-mathematical terms. Some states, such as Kentucky, instruct jurors that they are to return a verdict for the plaintiff only if the jury "believes from the evidence" that the plaintiff's allegations are true. In such states, it is not altogether clear what the measure of "belief" is.

KEY POINTS

1. A burden of persuasion is a procedural rule of decision that requires a party to persuade the fact finder of a proposition to a specified degree of certainty.

2. The normal burden of persuasion in civil cases is a "preponderance of the evidence," which is generally understood as meaning greater than 50 percent; in civil cases in which a claim is based on activity proscribed by criminal statutes the burden of persuasion may be "clear and convincing evidence."

3. From the perspective of the parties to the action, the burden of persuasion is relative: To say that the plaintiff must prove some proposition to be true by greater than 50 percent in order to win is to say that the defendant must prove that proposition to be false by 50 percent.

4. The burden of persuasion is usually on the party who has the burden of pleading on the matter.

B. THE BURDENS OF PROOF IN CRIMINAL CASES

The process of proof in criminal cases is similar but not identical to the process of proof in civil cases. As in civil cases, the law determines what facts need to be proven in order to establish that a crime has occurred. The criminal law also possesses virtually the same rules for the allocation of burdens of proof as in civil cases. The "plaintiff," which is the state, must plead and prove the necessary elements of the crime, and in many jurisdictions there are affirmative defenses that defendants must plead and with respect to which defendants bear the burden of production or persuasion. The primary differences between the civil and criminal arenas are that the normal burden of persuasion in criminal cases is proof beyond reasonable doubt and that as a result of In re Winship, 397 U.S. 358 (1970), the state always carries that burden with respect to the necessary elements of the offense.

1. The Burden of Persuasion: In re Winship's Mandate of Proof Beyond a Reasonable Doubt

Because the proof beyond a reasonable doubt rule has been so uniformly accepted as the standard of proof for criminal cases, the Supreme Court did not have occasion specifically to address the question whether due process required that standard of proof until 1975 in In re Winship. Even then, the immediate issue for the Court was not whether a criminal defendant was entitled to have guilt proven beyond a reasonable doubt. Rather, *Winship* was a challenge to the New York rule utilizing the preponderance standard in juvenile delinquency cases. The Court affirmed its prior dictum that due process required the proof beyond a reasonable doubt standard in adult criminal prosecutions and went on to hold that due process required the same standard in delinquency adjudications based on conduct that would be criminal if committed by an adult. According to the Court:

> The requirement that guilt of a criminal charge be established beyond a reasonable doubt dates at least from our early years as a Nation. The "demand for a higher degree of persuasion in criminal cases was recurrently expressed from ancient times, [though] its crystallization into the formula 'beyond a reasonable doubt' seems to have occurred as late as 1789. It is now accepted in common law jurisdictions as the measure of persuasion by which the prosecution must convince the trier of all the essential elements of guilt." Although virtually unanimous adherence to the reasonable-doubt standard in common-law jurisdictions may not conclusively establish it as a requirement of due process, such adherence does "reflect a profound judgment about the way in which law should be enforced and justice administered." . . .
>
> The reasonable-doubt standard plays a vital role in the American scheme of criminal procedure. It is a prime instrument for reducing the risk of convictions resting on factual error. The standard provides concrete substance for the presumption of innocence — that bedrock "axiomatic and elementary" principle whose "enforcement lies at the foundation of the administration of our criminal law." . . .
>
> The requirement of proof beyond a reasonable doubt has this vital role in our criminal procedure for cogent reasons. The accused during a criminal prosecution has at stake interests of immense importance, both because of the possibility that he may lose his liberty upon conviction and because of the certainty that he would be stigmatized by the conviction. Accordingly, a society that values the good name and freedom of every

individual should not condemn a man for commission of a crime when there is reason-able doubt about his guilt. As we said in Speiser v. Randall[, 357 U.S. 513, 525-526 (1958)]: "There is always in litigation a margin of error, representing error in factfinding, which both parties must take into account. Where one party has at stake an interest of transcending value — as a criminal defendant his liberty — this margin of error is reduced as to him by the process of placing on the other party the burden of . . . persuading the factfinder at the conclusion of the trial of his guilt beyond a reasonable doubt. Due process commands that no man shall lose his liberty unless the Government has borne the burden of . . . convincing the factfinder of his guilt." To this end, the reason-able-doubt standard is indispensable, for it "impresses on the trier of fact the necessity of reaching a subjective state of certitude of the facts in issue." Dorsen & Rezneck, In Re Gault and the Future of Juvenile Law, 1 Family Law Quarterly, No. 4, pp. 1, 26 (1976).

Moreover, use of the reasonable-doubt standard is indispensable to command the respect and confidence of the community in applications of the criminal law. It is critical that the moral force of the criminal law not be diluted by a standard of proof that leaves people in doubt whether innocent men are being condemned. It is also important in our free society that every individual going about his ordinary affairs have confidence that his government cannot adjudge him guilty of a criminal offense without convincing a proper factfinder of his guilt with utmost certainty.

Lest there remain any doubt about the constitutional stature of the reasonable-doubt standard, we explicitly hold that the Due Process Clause protects the accused against conviction except upon *proof beyond a reasonable doubt of every fact necessary to constitute the crime with which he is charged.* [397 U.S. at 362-364 (emphasis added).]

NOTES AND QUESTIONS

1. Despite the wide acceptance and the familiarity of the reasonable doubt stan-dard, its precise meaning remains elusive. Although the due process clause requires courts to apply the beyond a reasonable doubt standard, "the Constitution neither prohibits trial courts from defining reasonable doubt nor requires them to do so as a matter of course." Victor v. Nebraska, 511 U.S. 1, 8 (1994). Consider the following three attempts to define proof beyond a reasonable doubt:

a. A reasonable doubt is one that is founded upon a real tangible substantial basis and not upon mere caprice and conjecture. It must be such doubt as would give rise to a grave uncertainty, raised in your mind by reasons of the unsatisfactory character of the evidence or lack thereof. A reasonable doubt is not a mere possible doubt. It is an actual substantial doubt. It is a doubt that a reasonable man can seriously entertain. What is required is not an absolute or mathematical certainty, but a moral certainty.

b. A defendant in a criminal action is presumed to be innocent until the contrary is proved, and in case of a reasonable doubt whether his guilt is satisfactorily shown, he is entitled to a verdict of not guilty. This presumption places upon the State the burden of proving him guilty beyond a reasonable doubt.

Reasonable doubt is defined as follows: It is not a mere possible doubt; because everything relating to human affairs, and depending on moral evidence, is open to some possible or imaginary doubt. It is that state of the case which, after the entire comparison and consideration of all the evidence, leaves the minds of the jurors in that condition that they cannot say they feel an abiding conviction, to a moral certainty, of the truth of the charge.

c. The burden is always on the State to prove beyond a reasonable doubt all of the material elements of the crime charged, and this burden never shifts.

"Reasonable doubt" is such a doubt as would cause a reasonable and prudent person, in one of the graver and more important transactions of life, to pause and hesitate before taking the represented facts as true and relying and acting thereon. It is such a doubt as will not permit you, after full, fair, and impartial consideration of all the evidence, to have an abiding conviction, to a moral certainty, of the guilt of the accused. At the same time, absolute or mathematical certainty is not required. You may be convinced of the truth of a fact beyond a reasonable doubt and yet be fully aware that possibly you may be mistaken. You may find an accused guilty upon the strong probabilities of the case, provided such probabilities are strong enough to exclude any doubt of his guilt that is reasonable. A reasonable doubt is an actual and substantial doubt arising from the evidence, from the facts or circumstances shown by the evidence, or from the lack of evidence on the part of the state, as distinguished from a doubt arising from mere possibility, from bare imagination or from fanciful conjecture.

In Cage v. Louisiana, 498 U.S. 39 (1990) (per curiam), the Supreme Court held that instruction (a) above violated the defendant's right to due process. The Court concluded that "a reasonable juror could have interpreted the instruction to allow a finding of guilt based on a degree of proof below that required by the Due Process Clause." Id. at 41. Instructions (b) and (c) were before the Court in Victor v. Nebraska, supra. The Victor Court distinguished Cage and held that the instructions were constitutional. What precisely is there in instructions (b) and (c) that suggests the requirement of a higher degree of proof than the first instruction? Are any of the instructions likely to be helpful to the jury? Or is that question impossible to answer until we have clearer guidance as to what the legal meaning of "beyond a reasonable doubt" in fact is?

2. Is the notion of reasonable doubt sufficiently difficult to define that we would be better off not trying to define it for jurors? No, according to Justice Ginsburg in her separate opinion in Victor:

> Because the trial judges in fact defined reasonable doubt in both jury charges we review, we need not decide whether the Constitution required them to do so. Whether or not the Constitution so requires, however, the argument for defining the concept is strong. While judges and lawyers are familiar with the reasonable doubt standard, the words "beyond a reasonable doubt" are not self-defining for jurors. Several studies of jury behavior have concluded that "jurors are often confused about the meaning of reasonable doubt," when that term is left undefined. Note, Defining Reasonable Doubt, 90 Colum. L. Rev. 1716, 1723 (1990) (citing studies). Thus, even if definitions of reasonable doubt are necessarily imperfect, the alternative — refusing to define the concept at all — is not obviously preferable. Cf. Newman, Beyond "Reasonable Doubt," 68 N.Y.U. L. Rev. 979, 984 (1993) ("I find it rather unsettling that we are using a formulation that we believe will become less clear the more we explain it.") [511 U.S. at 43.]

Justice Ginsburg then endorsed the following reasonable doubt instruction:

> The government has the burden of proving the defendant guilty beyond a reasonable doubt. Some of you may have served as jurors in civil cases, where you were told that it is only necessary to prove that a fact is more likely true than not true. In criminal cases, the

government's proof must be more powerful than that. It must be beyond a reasonable doubt.

Proof beyond a reasonable doubt is proof that leaves you firmly convinced of the defendant's guilt. There are very few things in this world that we know with absolute certainty, and in criminal cases the law does not require proof that overcomes every possible doubt. If, based on your consideration of the evidence, you are firmly convinced that the defendant is guilty of the crime charged, you must find him guilty. If on the other hand, you think there is a real possibility that he is not guilty, you must give him the benefit of the doubt and find him not guilty. [Id. at 44, quoting Federal Judicial Center, Pattern Criminal Jury Instructions 17-18 (1987) (instruction 21).]

3. Whereas *Winship* spoke of three considerations underlying the reasonable doubt rule — the defendant's liberty interest, the defendant's interest in being free from stigmatization, and community confidence in the criminal law — the Court more recently has limited its articulation of the *Winship* rationale to the defendant's liberty interest. Patterson v. New York, 432 U.S. 197 (1977). The failure to mention the stigmatization and community confidence factors, however, should not have any impact on the *Winship* rule and its place in constitutional jurisprudence. Typically, a criminal defendant's liberty interest will be at least as great as any interest in being free from unwarranted stigmatization; and the community confidence factor, to the extent that it is independent of the defendant's interest in avoiding undeserved punishment, is a concern of the states, not the federal government.

4. Although the question *what* the prosecution has to prove beyond a reasonable doubt was not specifically at issue in *Winship*, the Court characterized the requirement as applying to "every fact necessary to constitute the crime . . . charged." What is a "fact necessary" to constitute the crime? To what extent should states be free to manipulate the scope of the *Winship* requirement by the manner in which they define crimes? Does *Winship* mean only that the state must prove beyond a reasonable doubt the facts that the state chooses to articulate in defining a crime? For example, if a state defined capital murder as "causing the death of a human being," would it be sufficient for the state to prove death and causation beyond a reasonable doubt and leave all questions of mens rea, mitigation, and justification for the defendant to prove? If so, the *Winship* mandate would appear to be so hollow that it is not worth imposing on the states in the first place. If not, by what criteria can one judge whether a state has satisfied *Winship*?

KEY POINT

In a criminal prosecution, due process requires proof beyond a reasonable doubt of every fact necessary to constitute the crime charged.

2.   The Scope of Winship: Explicit Shifts in the Burden of Persuasion and Other Matters

a.   The Mullaney Decision

Mullaney v. Wilbur, 421 U.S. 684 (1975), involved a homicide defendant who claimed that he killed his victim in the heat of passion provoked by a homosexual assault.

The issue was the applicability of *Winship* to a Maine homicide statute that placed the burden of persuasion on the defendant to prove that a killing was "in the heat of passion on sudden provocation" in order to reduce the crime from murder to manslaughter. The Supreme Court affirmed the granting of a writ of habeas corpus to the defendant:

> After reading the statutory definitions of both offenses [murder and manslaughter], the court charged that "malice aforethought is an essential and indispensable element of the crime of murder," without which the homicide would be manslaughter. The jury was further instructed, however, that if the prosecution established that the homicide was both intentional and unlawful, malice aforethought was to be conclusively implied unless the defendant proved by a fair preponderance of the evidence that he acted in the heat of passion on sudden provocation. The court emphasized that "malice aforethought and heat of passion on sudden provocation are two inconsistent things"; thus, by proving the latter the defendant would negate the former and reduce the homicide from murder to manslaughter....
>
> ...Felonious homicide is punished as murder — i.e., by life imprisonment — unless the defendant proves by a fair preponderance of the evidence that it was committed in the heat of passion on sudden provocation, in which case it is punished as manslaughter — i.e., by a fine not to exceed $10,000 or by imprisonment not to exceed 20 years....
>
> [T]he fact at issue here — the presence or absence of the heat of passion on sudden provocation — has been, almost from the inception of the common law of homicide, the single most important factor in determining the degree of culpability attaching to an unlawful homicide. And ... the clear trend has been toward requiring the prosecution to bear the ultimate burden of proving this fact....
>
> Petitioners ... note that as a formal matter the absence of the heat of passion on sudden provocation is not a "fact necessary to constitute the crime" of felonious homicide in Maine. This distinction is relevant, according to petitioners, because in *Winship* the facts at issue were essential to establish criminality in the first instance.... [H]ere ..., petitioners maintain, the defendant's critical interests in liberty and reputation are no longer of paramount concern since, irrespective of the presence or absence of the heat of passion on sudden provocation, he is likely to lose his liberty and certain to be stigmatized....
>
> Maine has chosen to distinguish those who kill in the heat of passion from those who kill in the absence of this factor. Because the former are less "blameworth[y]," they are subject to substantially less severe penalties. By drawing this distinction, while refusing to require the prosecution to establish beyond a reasonable doubt the fact upon which it turns, Maine denigrates the interests found critical in *Winship*.
>
> ... [W]hen viewed in terms of the potential difference in restrictions of personal liberty attendant to each conviction, the distinction established by Maine between murder and manslaughter may be of greater importance than the difference between guilt or innocence for many lesser crimes.
>
> Moreover, if *Winship* were limited to those facts that constitute a crime as defined by state law, a State could undermine many of the interests that decision sought to protect without effecting any substantive change in its law. It would only be necessary to redefine the elements that constitute different crimes, characterizing them as factors that bear solely on the extent of punishment. [Id. at 696-698.]

Mullaney, which was a unanimous decision, generated considerable litigation challenging state rules placing burdens of persuasion on the defendant. The Court revisited the issue only two years later in Patterson v. New York, 432 U.S. 197 (1977). Although the Patterson Court purported to distinguish *Mullaney*, *Patterson* in fact overrules *Mullaney* in all but the most formalistic sense. As you will see, however, that formalistic sense appears to retain considerable importance.

b.   The Patterson Decision

Patterson was convicted of murdering the partner of his estranged wife. The killing took place after the defendant had "observed his wife through a window in a state of semiundress" with the victim. The New York homicide statute defined the elements of murder as an "intent to cause the death of another person" and "causing the death of such person." New York also recognized as an affirmative defense acting "under the influence of extreme emotional disturbance for which there was a reasonable explanation or excuse." Extreme emotional distress reduced murder to manslaughter, and the burden of persuasion with respect to this affirmative defense rested with the defendant.

In rejecting Patterson's contention that placing the burden of proof with respect to extreme emotional distress on him was unconstitutional the Court observed that

1. "dealing with crime is much more the business of the States than it is of the Federal Government";
2. the New York "extreme emotional distress" defense is "a considerably expanded version of the common-law defense of heat of passion on sudden provocation";
3. subsequent to *Mullaney* the Court in Rivera v. Delaware, 429 U.S. 877 (1976), reaffirmed that placing the burden of proof with respect to insanity on the defendant did not violate due process; and
4. states may be reluctant to create or expand defenses if they have to disprove the defenses beyond a reasonable doubt.

Mullaney, according to the Court, was not controlling for the following reasons:

The crime of murder [in New York] is defined by statute . . . as causing the death of another person with intent to do so. The death, the intent to kill, and causation are the facts that the State is required to prove beyond a reasonable doubt if a person is to be convicted of murder. No further facts are either presumed or inferred in order to constitute the crime. The statute does provide an affirmative defense [of extreme emotional disturbance] . . . which, if proved by a preponderance of the evidence would reduce the crime to manslaughter, an offense defined in a separate section of the statute. It is plain enough that if the intentional killing is shown, the State intends to deal with the defendant as a murderer unless he demonstrates the mitigating circumstances. . . .

In *Mullaney* . . . the Maine statute defined [murder] as the unlawful killing of a human being "with malice aforethought, either express or implied." The trial court instructed the jury that the words *malice aforethought* were most important because "malice aforethought is an essential and indispensable element of the crime of murder." . . . The instructions emphasized that "malice aforethought and 'heat of passion on sudden provocation are two inconsistent things.'" . . .

The Maine Supreme Judicial Court held that murder and manslaughter were varying degrees of the crime of felonious homicide and that the presumption of malice arising from the unlawful killing was a mere policy presumption operating to cast on the defendant the burden of proving provocation if he was to be found guilty of manslaughter rather than murder. . . .

This Court . . . unanimously agreed with the Court of Appeals [in *Mullaney*] that [the defendant's] due process rights had been invaded by the presumption casting upon him the burden of proving by a preponderance of the evidence that he had acted in the heat of passion upon sudden provocation.

Mullaney's holding, it is argued, is that the State may not permit the blameworthiness of an act or the severity of punishment authorized for its commission to depend on the presence or absence of an identified fact without assuming the burden of proving the presence or absence of that fact, as the case may be, beyond a reasonable doubt. In our view, the Mullaney holding should not be so broadly read. . . .

Mullaney surely held that a State must prove every ingredient of an offense beyond a reasonable doubt, and that it may not shift the burden of proof to the defendant by presuming that ingredient upon proof of the other elements of the offense. . . . Such shifting of the burden of persuasion with respect to a fact which the State deems so important that it must be either proved or presumed is impermissible under the Due Process Clause.

It was unnecessary to go further in *Mullaney*. . . . [A] killing became murder in Maine when it resulted from a deliberate, cruel act committed by one person against another, "suddenly without any, or without a considerable provocation." . . . [M]alice, in the sense of absence of provocation, was part of the definition of that crime. Yet malice, i.e., lack of provocation, was presumed and could be rebutted by the defendant only by proving by a preponderance of the evidence that he acted with heat of passion upon sudden provocation. . . .

As we have explained, nothing was presumed or implied against Patterson. [432 U.S. at 205-206, 212-216.]

c.   The Functional Equivalence of Mullaney and Patterson

Except for the fact that New York's "extreme emotional distress" defense is somewhat broader than the Maine "heat of passion" defense, *Mullaney* and *Patterson* are functionally identical. In both cases to obtain a murder conviction the state had to prove an intentional killing beyond a reasonable doubt, and in both cases proof of provocation made a killing, that would otherwise be murder, manslaughter. The only difference between the two cases is in the language that the state legislatures used to achieve this gradation in homicide crimes. Maine defined the critical element of murder as "malice aforethought," a concept that encompassed the absence of provocation. Maine then created a rule that proof of intent gave rise to a presumption or mandatory finding of malice unless the defendant proved provocation by a preponderance of the evidence. New York defined murder initially as requiring only proof that the defendant intentionally killed a person and then defined provocation as an affirmative defense for the defendant to prove by a preponderance of the evidence. Admittedly, the New York formulation is less cumbersome than the Maine formulation. As long as the formulation is not so confusing or incomprehensible to raise void-for-vagueness types of concerns, however, the language that the legislature uses to define crimes should not raise a due process issue and certainly not a *Winship* issue.

d.   Mullaney's Departure from Winship

In one respect *Mullaney* is a significant departure from *Winship*. The *Winship* Court observed that the universal acceptance of the beyond a reasonable doubt standard strongly implied the necessity of employing that standard to protect a fundamental value — preferring errors benefitting the accused over those favoring the prosecution. The Court then supplemented its analysis by articulating the interests that this value preference protects — principally the accused's liberty and good name — in order to demonstrate that they were of sufficient magnitude to justify including the procedure safeguarding them among the elements of due process. In *Mullaney*, by contrast, the Court reversed its order of reasoning, concentrating almost exclusively on the interests protected by the reasonable doubt standard rather than on whether Maine's statute was consistent — which it was — with common practices in the states.

In short, *Mullaney* invoked *Winship* to invalidate a practice long accepted throughout the country, whereas *Winship* relied on the "traditions and conscience of our people" to hold that due process required application of the proof beyond a reasonable doubt standard. Thus *Mullaney*, which purported to "apply" *Winship*, drastically altered that case from one that looks to traditional practice and prevailing usage by the states to aid in due process analysis to one that frees the federal courts to impose their own view about the appropriate use of the reasonable doubt standard on the states notwithstanding widely shared views to the contrary.

e.   Evaluating Mullaney and Patterson: The Theory that the Greater Includes the Lesser

The fact that *Mullaney* is a departure from *Winship* in the sense just described does not necessarily lead to the conclusion that *Patterson* rather than *Mullaney* is the correct decision. Whenever a defendant fails to establish an affirmative defense, the possibility is presented that, had the prosecution been required to disprove the defense beyond reasonable doubt, the trier of fact would have either convicted the defendant of a lesser offense or acquitted altogether. Such verdicts would expose the defendant to a lesser punishment or no punishment at all. Thus affirmative defenses undeniably affect the interests articulated in *Winship*. Yet one cannot jump from this fact alone to the conclusion that requiring the prosecutor to disprove affirmative defenses beyond a reasonable doubt serves the due process interest. Assuming that the punishment for the higher offense is constitutionally acceptable, *given what the prosecution must prove beyond a reasonable doubt*, the allocation of the persuasion burden of the mitigating factor has no bearing on whether the defendant suffers unconstitutional punishment.

An example may help to clarify this point. Consider a state with an intentional homicide statute that punishes every intentional homicide with 30 years of imprisonment; if the state proves that the defendant intentionally killed the victim, then a flat sentence of 30 years is imposed regardless of the presence of any mitigating factor. *Assume* that such a statute is constitutional. Now consider how the constitutionality of that statute is affected if we simply add to it a provision that no more than 20 years of imprisonment may be imposed when defendants prove by a preponderance of the evidence that they acted under the influence of extreme emotional disturbance. If the constitutional interest in the reasonable doubt standard centers on liberty deprivation, the addition of a chance to mitigate a constitutionally valid punishment cannot invalidate the statute. To put it another way, if a state may constitutionally imprison all intentional killers for 30 years by proving beyond reasonable doubt only intent and causation, then whatever liberty interest defendants constitutionally possess in the context of homicide prosecutions surely is fully accommodated by such a statute. The addition of a mitigating circumstance in the form of an affirmative defense — a factor that reduces punishment — cannot violate the already fully accommodated interest.

According to this theory — sometimes referred to as the theory that "the greater includes the lesser" — the analysis of the constitutionality of an affirmative defense must proceed to another level. One must ask whether the greater punishment — the punishment authorized in the event the defendant fails to establish the affirmative defense — is constitutional. In other words, one must ask how to give content to *Winship*'s command that the state "prove beyond a reasonable doubt every fact necessary to constitute the crime." To state the matter in terms of the issue in *Mullaney* and *Patterson*: Is it constitutionally permissible for Maine or New York to impose its penalty for nonprovoked or nonemotionally-distressed intentional killings on individuals whose killings are the result of extreme provocation or extreme emotional distress? In the next subsection we discuss several possible tests for resolving this issue.

f.   Giving Content to Winship: Tests for Assessing the Validity of Affirmative Defenses

i.   The Elements Test.   Pursuant to the elements test, the state must prove beyond reasonable doubt whatever factual issues it labels as elements of the offense. A component of this test is the "physical location" rule, a rule of statutory construction providing that a particular factual issue is an element of an offense only if it is incorporated into the text of the basic statute describing the offense.

At various points throughout the *Patterson* opinion the Court alluded to the elements test, most explicitly in the statement that the Court "will not disturb the balance struck in previous cases holding that the Due Process Clause requires the prosecution to prove beyond reasonable doubt all of the elements included in the definition of the offense of which the defendant is charged." 432 U.S. at 210. Both examples given by the Court of unconstitutional burden shifts also tend to support this view. The Court noted that the legislature cannot declare an individual guilty or presumptively guilty, nor can it declare that the finding of an indictment or proof of the identity of the accused shall create a presumption of the existence of all the facts essential to guilt. These are situations in which no elements are included within the definition of "crime," which may suggest that any affirmative defense will be sustained so long as the legislature does not drain all substantive content from a crime's definition.

It is difficult to see what constitutional interest is served by the elements test. The physical location rule is obviously an arbitrary means of determining the "definition" of an offense. The legislature may wish to "define" an offense in one way but determine the elements of the prosecution's case in another, and either could be considered the "definition" of the crime. There is no reason why the validity of a state statute placing the burden of proving provocation on the defendant should depend on whether the state "defines" murder (1) as intent, causation, and no provocation in one statute and in another places the burden of proving provocation on the defendant, or simply (2) as intent and causation with another statute authorizing provocation as an affirmative defense.

ii.   The Political Compromise Test.   A second standard that has been proposed for judging the validity of an affirmative defense, while somewhat more sophisticated than the elements test, is no more persuasive. This is the "political compromise" test, which permits affirmative defenses that result from the compromise of competing forces in the legislature. This test responds to the fear that states may be unwilling to provide certain affirmative defenses if they cannot place on the defendant the burden of proof for the factual issue created. Commentators have often pointed out that a decision like *Mullaney*, if followed, would likely inhibit experimentation with new affirmative defenses. To avoid that harsh irony, the political compromise test looks to whether the legislature would have refused to adopt the defense but for the provision imposing the burden of proof on the defendant.

The most disturbing feature of this test is its paradoxical quality. It is paradoxical in the sense that if the only justification for allowing affirmative defenses is that otherwise the legislature will be forced to choose between two diametrically opposed but constitutional alternatives, then the argument implicitly assumes the unconstitutionality of affirmative defenses. The real point, in other words, is that affirmative defenses are unconstitutional but that such a conclusion may result in an unfortunate legislative choice, and thus the better tack is to permit an unconstitutional choice as an expedient.

iii.   The Proportionality Test.   Within the last century the cruel and unusual punishment clause of the Eighth Amendment[3] has been interpreted to require a rough proportionality between the culpability of an offense and the punishment that is imposed. This requirement of proportionality provides the method of testing the constitutionality of affirmative defenses, and it also provides the means of delineating the extent of the federal interest in the reasonable doubt standard. Reconsider the intentional homicide hypothetical in subsection 2-e, supra. If the courts conclude that a given punishment (30 years in the hypothetical) is not disproportional to what the state has proved beyond reasonable doubt (intentional killing), notwithstanding the presence or absence of any mitigating factors, then a defendant's liberty interest would obviously be satisfied by a statute that required proof of only those elements and that imposed that particular punishment. Accordingly, the mere addition to that statute of an affirmative defense, which after all could constitutionally be ignored, should be equally satisfactory. The import of the proportionality principle is, then, that the state should be required to prove enough to justify the imposition of the maximum sentence permissible under the statute. Once that is accomplished, the accused has been fully protected against an unwarranted deprivation of liberty, and the state should be permitted to elaborate on the basic statute as it sees fit.

The thesis that due process requires proof beyond a reasonable doubt only with respect to those elements of the offense that are "essential" by virtue of the Eighth Amendment concretely expresses the role of the reasonable doubt standard. Due process and the Eighth Amendment protect criminal defendants from unwarranted deprivations of liberty by requiring the state to establish sufficient factual elements to justify the allotted punishment and by requiring the state, in establishing those elements, to minimize the risk of error adverse to the defendant. Once the overriding constitutional command is satisfied, however, the need for the protective procedure is likewise satisfied, and the traditional state power should reassert itself, permitting the states to allocate burdens of proof as they desire.

The theoretical appeal of the proportionality test, in our view, is compelling. Reasonable people, however, may disagree about its practical utility. The inherent vagueness of the notion of proportionality may lead an activist court to impinge too

---

3.   U.S. Const. Amend. VIII ("Excessive bail shall not be required, nor excessive fines imposed, or cruel and unusual punishment inflicted.").

much on legislative judgments about affirmative defenses. An alternative and probably more likely possibility is that the vagueness may lead courts to defer to legislative judgments except in the most extreme cases, thereby perhaps giving insufficient substance to the Winship requirement. Indeed, the Supreme Court, particularly in recent years, has upheld against proportionality challenges quite severe penalties for relatively minor misconduct. Hutto v. Davis, 454 U.S. 370 (1982) (upholding 40-year prison term for possession and distribution of approximately nine ounces of marijuana); Rummell v. Estelle, 445 U.S. 263 (1980) (upholding constitutionality of a recidivist statute under which defendant received mandatory life sentence for three crimes of fraud that netted a total sum of less than $230). But see Solem v. Helm, 463 U.S. 277 (1983) (striking down life sentence for uttering "no-account" check for less than $100).

iv. **Justice Powell's Two-part Test.** In his *Patterson* dissent, Justice Powell suggested a two-part test for determining whether it is permissible to place the burden of persuasion on the defendant. First, the facts must make "a substantial difference in punishment of the offender and in the stigma associated with the conviction." Second, in the Anglo-American legal tradition the facts must historically have had "that level of importance." If, but only if, both of these things are true — as Justice Powell argued they were with respect to extreme emotional distress, it is unconstitutional to place the burden of proof on the defendant.

If one extrapolates from the Court's recent proportionality cases, it would seem that *Patterson* was properly decided. If that conclusion is correct and if Justice Powell's conclusion that his test would require the opposite result in *Patterson* is also correct, Justice Powell's test finds a due process violation despite the absence of any infringement on the defendant's liberty interest. In many cases, however, Justice Powell's test and a proper application of the proportionality test may reach the same result. If that is the case and if, as we suggested previously, courts may err on the side of deferring to state legislatures in applying the proportionality test, one can regard Justice Powell's test as an easier to apply surrogate for the proportionality test. Viewed from this perspective, it has much to commend it.

g. Affirmative Defenses After Patterson

Patterson did not adopt either the proportionality test or Justice Powell's two-part test for determining what the state must prove beyond a reasonable doubt. *Patterson*, however, did acknowledge, as *Mullaney* pointed out earlier, that reliance solely on the elements test creates the possibility that states can undermine *Winship* by making most factors critical to the imposition or degree of punishment affirmative defenses. Moreover, the *Patterson* Court stated that "there are obviously constitutional limits beyond which the States may not go in this regard." What might those limits be?

MARTIN v. OHIO
480 U.S. 228 (1987)

Justice WHITE delivered the opinion of the Court.

The Ohio Code provides that "(e)very person accused of an offense is presumed innocent until proven guilty beyond a reasonable doubt, and the burden of proof for all elements of the offense is upon the prosecution. The burden of going forward with the evidence of an affirmative defense, and the burden of proof by a preponderance of the evidence, for an affirmative defense, is upon the accused." Ohio Rev. Code Ann. §2901.05(A) (1982). An affirmative defense is one involving "an excuse or justification peculiarly within the knowledge of the accused, on which he can fairly be required to adduce supporting evidence." Ohio Rev. Code Ann. §2901.05(C)(2) (1982). The Ohio courts have "long determined that self-defense is an affirmative defense," and that the defendant has the burden of proving it as required by §2901.05(A).

As defined by the trial court in its instructions in this case, the elements of self-defense that the defendant must prove are (1) that the defendant was not at fault in creating the situation giving rise to the argument; (2) the defendant had an honest belief that she was in imminent danger of death or great bodily harm and that her only means of escape from such danger was in the use of such force; and (3) the defendant must not have violated any duty to retreat or avoid danger. The question before us is whether the Due Process Clause of the Fourteenth Amendment forbids placing the burden of proving self-defense on the defendant when she is charged by the State of Ohio with committing the crime of aggravated murder, which, as relevant to this case, is defined by the Revised Code of Ohio as "purposely, and with prior calculation and design, caus[ing] the death of another." Ohio Rev. Code Ann. §2903.01 (1982).

The facts of the case, taken from the opinions of the courts below, may be succinctly stated. On July 21, 1983, petitioner Earline Martin and her husband, Walter Martin, argued over grocery money. Petitioner claimed that her husband struck her in the head during the argument. Petitioner's version of what then transpired was that she went upstairs, put on a robe, and later came back down with her husband's gun which she intended to dispose of. Her husband saw something in her hand and questioned her about it. He came at her, she lost her head and fired the gun at him. Five or six shots were fired, three of them striking and killing Mr. Martin. She was charged with and tried for aggravated murder. She pleaded self-defense and testified in her own defense. The judge charged the jury with respect to the elements of the crime and of self-defense and rejected petitioner's Due Process Clause challenge to the charge placing on her the burden of proving self-defense. The jury found her guilty.

Both the Ohio Court of Appeals and the Supreme Court of Ohio affirmed the conviction. . . . We granted certiorari, and affirm the decision of the Supreme Court of Ohio.

In re Winship declared that the Due Process Clause "protects the accused against conviction except upon proof beyond a reasonable doubt of every fact necessary to constitute the crime with which he is charged." A few years later, we held that Winship's mandate was fully satisfied where the State of New York had proved beyond reasonable doubt, each of the elements of murder, but placed on the defendant the burden of proving the affirmative defense of extreme emotional disturbance, which, if proved, would have reduced the crime from murder to manslaughter. Patterson v. New York[, 432 U.S. 197 (1977)]. . . . Referring to Leland v. Oregon, 343 U.S. 790, and Rivera v. Delaware, 429 U.S. 877, we added that New York "did no more than Leland and Rivera permitted it to do without violating the Due Process Clause" and declined to reconsider those cases. It was also observed that "the fact that a majority of the States have now assumed the burden of disproving affirmative defenses — for whatever reasons — [does not] mean that those States that strike a different balance are in violation of the Constitution." As in Patterson, the jury was here instructed that to convict it must find, in light of all the evidence, that each of the elements of the crime of aggravated murder must be proved by the State beyond reasonable doubt and that the burden of proof with respect to these elements did not shift. To find guilt, the jury had to be convinced that none of the evidence, whether offered by the State or by Martin in connection with her plea of self-defense, raised a reasonable doubt that Martin had killed her husband, that she had the specific purpose and intent to cause his death, or that she had done so with prior calculation and design. It was also told, however, that it could acquit if it found by a preponderance of the evidence that Martin had not precipitated the confrontation, that she had an honest belief that she was in imminent danger of death or great bodily harm, and that she had satisfied any duty to retreat or avoid danger. The jury convicted Martin.

We agree with the State and its Supreme Court that this conviction did not violate the Due Process Clause. The State did not exceed its authority in defining the crime of murder as purposely causing the death of another with prior calculation or design. It did not seek to shift to Martin the burden of proving any of those elements, and the jury's verdict reflects that none of her self-defense evidence raised a reasonable doubt about the state's proof that she purposefully killed with prior calculation and design. She nevertheless had the opportunity under state law and the instructions given to justify the killing and show herself to be blameless by proving that she acted in self-defense. The jury thought she had failed to do so, and Ohio is as entitled to punish Martin as one guilty of murder as New York was to punish Patterson.

It would be quite different if the jury had been instructed that self-defense evidence could not be considered in determining whether there was a reasonable doubt about the state's case, i.e., that self-defense evidence must be put aside for all purposes unless it satisfied the preponderance standard. Such instruction would relieve the state of its burden and plainly run afoul of *Winship*'s mandate. The instructions in this case could be clearer in this respect, but when read as a whole, we think they are adequate to convey to the jury that all of the evidence, including the evidence going to self-defense, must be considered in deciding whether there was a reasonable doubt about the sufficiency of the state's proof of the elements of the crime.

We are thus not moved by assertions that the elements of aggravated murder and self-defense overlap in the sense that evidence to prove the latter will often tend to negate the former. It may be that most encounters in which self-defense is claimed arise suddenly and involve no prior plan or specific purpose to take life. In those cases, evidence offered to support the defense may negate a purposeful killing by prior calculation and design, but Ohio does not shift to the defendant the burden of disproving any element of the state's case. When the prosecution has made out a *prima facie* case and survives a motion to acquit, the jury may nevertheless not convict if the evidence offered by the defendant raises any reasonable doubt about the existence of any fact necessary for the finding of guilt. Evidence creating a reasonable doubt could easily fall far short of proving self-defense by a preponderance of the evidence. Of course, if such doubt is not raised in the jury's mind and each juror is convinced that the defendant purposely and with prior calculation and design took life, the killing will still be excused if the elements of the defense are satisfactorily established. We note here, but need not rely on it, the observation of the Supreme Court of Ohio that "Appellant did not dispute the existence of [the elements of aggravated murder], but rather sought to justify her actions on grounds she acted in self-defense." Petitioner submits that there can be no conviction under Ohio law unless the defendant's conduct is unlawful and that because self-defense renders lawful what would otherwise be a crime, unlawfulness is an element of the offense that the state must prove by disproving self-defense. This argument founders on state law, for it has been rejected by the Ohio Supreme Court and by the Court of Appeals for the Sixth Circuit. White v. Arn, 788 F.2d 338, 346-347 (6th Cir. 1986); State v. Morris, 8 Ohio App. 3d 12, 18-19, 455 N.E.2d 1352, 1359-1360 (1982). It is true that unlawfulness is essential for conviction, but the Ohio courts hold that the unlawfulness in cases like this is the conduct satisfying the elements of aggravated murder — an interpretation of state law that we are not in a position to dispute. The same is true of the claim that it is necessary to prove a "criminal" intent to convict for serious crimes, which cannot occur if self-defense is shown: the necessary mental state for aggravated murder under Ohio law is the specific purpose to take life pursuant to prior calculation and design.

As we noted in *Patterson*, the common law rule was that affirmative defenses, including self-defense, were matters for the defendant to prove. "This was the rule when the Fifth Amendment was adopted, and it was the American rule when the Fourteenth Amendment was ratified." Indeed, well into this century, a number of States followed the common law rule and required a defendant to shoulder the burden of proving that he acted in self-defense. We are aware that all but two of the States, Ohio and South Carolina, have abandoned the common law rule and require the prosecution to prove the absence of self-defense when it is properly raised by the defendant. But the question remains whether those States are in violation of the Constitution; and, as we observed in *Patterson*, that question is not answered by cataloging the practices of other States. We are no more convinced that the Ohio practice of requiring self-defense to be proved by the defendant is unconstitutional than we are that the Constitution requires the prosecution to prove the sanity of a defendant who pleads not guilty by reason of insanity. We have had the opportunity to depart from Leland v. Oregon but have refused to do so. Rivera v. Delaware, 429 U.S. 877 (1976). These cases were important to the Patterson decision and they, along with *Patterson*, are authority for our decision today.

The judgment of the Ohio Supreme Court is accordingly affirmed.

Justice POWELL, with whom Justice BRENNAN and Justice MARSHALL join, and with whom Justice BLACKMUN joins with respect to Parts I and III, dissenting.

Today the Court holds that a defendant can be convicted of aggravated murder even though the jury may have a reasonable doubt whether the accused acted in self-defense, and thus, whether he is guilty of a crime. Because I think this decision is inconsistent with both precedent and fundamental fairness, I dissent.

I

...The Court today relies on the *Patterson* reasoning in affirming the Ohio decision. If one accepts *Patterson* as the proper method of analysis for this case, I believe that the Court's opinion ignores its central meaning.

In *Patterson*, the Court upheld a state statute that shifted the burden of proof for an affirmative defense to the accused. New York law required the prosecutor to prove all of the statutorily defined elements of murder beyond a reasonable doubt, but permitted a defendant to reduce the charge to manslaughter by showing that he acted while suffering an "extreme emotional disturbance." The Court found that this burden-shifting did not violate due process, largely because the affirmative defense did "not serve to negate any facts of the crime which the State is to prove in order to convict of murder." The clear implication of this ruling is that when an affirmative defense does negate an element of the crime, the state may not shift the burden. In such a case, In re Winship requires the state to prove the nonexistence of the defense beyond a reasonable doubt.

The reason for treating a defense that negates an element of the crime differently from other affirmative defenses is plain. If the jury is told that the prosecution has the burden of proving all the elements of a crime, but then also is instructed that the defendant has the burden of disproving one of those same elements, there is a danger that the jurors will resolve the inconsistency in a way that lessens the presumption of innocence. For example, the jury might reasonably believe that by raising the defense, the accused has assumed the ultimate burden of proving that particular element. Or, it might reconcile the instructions simply by balancing the evidence that supports the prosecutor's case against the evidence supporting the affirmative defense, and conclude that the state has satisfied its burden if the prosecution's version is more persuasive. In either case, the jury is given the unmistakable but erroneous impression that the defendant shares the risk of nonpersuasion as to a fact necessary for conviction.[4]

Given these principles, the Court's reliance on *Patterson* is puzzling. Under Ohio law, the element of "prior calculation and design" is satisfied only when the accused has engaged in a "definite process of reasoning in advance of the killing," i.e., when he has given the plan at least some "studied consideration." In contrast, when a defendant such as Martin raises a claim of self-defense, the jury also is instructed that the accused must prove that she "had an honest belief that she was in imminent danger of death or great bodily harm." In many cases, a defendant who finds himself in immediate danger and reacts with deadly force will not have formed a prior intent to kill. The Court recognizes this when it states: "It may be that most encounters in which self-defense is claimed arise suddenly and involve no prior plan or specific purpose to take life. In those cases, evidence offered to support the defense may negate a purposeful killing by prior calculation and design. . . ." Under *Patterson*, this conclusion should suggest that Ohio is precluded from shifting the burden as to self-defense. The Court nevertheless concludes that Martin was properly required to prove self-defense, simply because "Ohio does not shift to the defendant the burden of disproving any element of the state's case." The Court gives no explanation for this apparent rejection of *Patterson*. The only justification advanced for the Court's decision is that the jury could have used the evidence of self-defense to find that the state failed to carry its burden of proof. Because the jurors were free to consider both Martin's and the state's evidence, the argument goes, the verdict of guilt necessarily means that they were convinced that the defendant acted with prior calculation and design, and were unpersuaded that she acted in self-defense. The Court thus seems to conclude that as long as the jury is told that the state has the burden of proving all elements of the crime, the overlap between the offense and defense is immaterial.

4. Indeed, this type of instruction has an inherently illogical aspect. It makes no sense to say that the prosecution has the burden of proving an element beyond a reasonable doubt and that the defense has the burden of proving the contrary by a preponderance of the evidence. If the jury finds that the prosecutor has not met his burden, it of course will have no occasion to consider the affirmative defense. And if the jury finds that each element of the crime has been proved beyond a reasonable doubt, it necessarily has decided that the defendant has not disproved an element of the crime. In either situation the instructions on the affirmative defense are surplusage. Because a reasonable jury will attempt to ascribe some significance to the court's instructions, the likelihood that it will impermissibly shift the burden is increased. Of course, whether the jury will in fact improperly shift the burden away from the state is uncertain. But it is "settled law . . . that when there exists a reasonable possibility that the jury relied on an unconstitutional understanding of the law in reaching a guilty verdict, that verdict must be set aside." Francis v. Franklin, 471 U.S. 307, 323 n.8.

This reasoning is flawed in two respects. First, it simply ignores the problem that arises from inconsistent jury instructions in a criminal case. The Court's holding implicitly assumes that the jury in fact understands that the ultimate burden remains with the prosecutor at all times, despite a conflicting instruction that places the burden on the accused to disprove the same element. But as pointed out above, the *Patterson* distinction between defenses that negate an element of the crime and those that do not is based on the legitimate concern that the jury will mistakenly lower the state's burden. In short, the Court's rationale fails to explain why the overlap in this case does not create the risk that *Patterson* suggested was unacceptable.[5] Second, the Court significantly, and without explanation, extends the deference granted to state legislatures in this area. Today's decision could be read to say that virtually all state attempts to shift the burden of proof for affirmative defenses will be upheld, regardless of the relationship between the elements of the defense and the elements of the crime. As I understand it, *Patterson* allowed burden-shifting because evidence of an extreme emotional disturbance did not negate the mens rea of the underlying offense. After today's decision, however, even if proof of the defense does negate an element of the offense, burden-shifting still may be permitted because the jury can consider the defendant's evidence when reaching its verdict.

I agree, of course, that States must have substantial leeway in defining their criminal laws and administering their criminal justice systems. But none of our precedents suggests that courts must give complete deference to a State's judgment about whether a shift in the burden of proof is consistent with the presumption of innocence. In the past we have emphasized that in some circumstances it may be necessary to look beyond the text of the State's burden-shifting laws to satisfy ourselves that the requirements of *Winship* have been satisfied. In Mullaney v. Wilbur, we explicitly noted the danger of granting the State unchecked discretion to shift the burden as to any element of proof in a criminal case.[6] The Court today fails to discuss or even cite *Mullaney*, despite our unanimous agreement in that case that this danger would justify judicial intervention in some cases. Even *Patterson*, from which I dissented, recognized that "there are obviously constitutional limits beyond which the States may not go [in labeling elements of a crime as an affirmative defense]."[7] Today, however, the Court simply asserts that Ohio law properly allocates the burdens, without giving any indication of where those limits lie.

Because our precedent establishes that the burden of proof may not be shifted when the elements of the defense and the elements of the offense conflict, and because it seems clear that they do so in this case, I would reverse the decision of the Ohio Supreme Court.

5.   This risk could have been reduced — although in my view, not eliminated — if the instructions had made it clear that evidence of self-defense can create a reasonable doubt as to guilt, even if that same evidence did not rise to the level necessary to prove an affirmative defense. But the instructions gave little guidance in this respect. The trial court simply told the jury that the prosecution must prove the elements of the crime, and the defendant must prove the existence of the defense. The instructions gave no indication how the jury should evaluate evidence that affected an element of both the crime and the defense. . . .

6.   We noted, for example: "[I]f in *Winship* were limited to those facts that constitute a crime as defined by the state law, a State could undermine many of the interests that decision sought to protect without effecting any substantive change in its law. It would only be necessary to redefine the elements that constitute different crimes, characterizing them as factors that bear solely on the extent of punishment." 421 U.S. at 698.

7.   See also McMillan v. Pennsylvania, 477 U.S. 79 (1986) ([I]n certain limited circumstances *Winship's* reasonable-doubt requirement applies to facts not formally identified as elements of the offense charged.).

II

Although I believe that this case is wrongly decided even under the principles set forth in *Patterson*, my differences with the Court's approach are more fundamental. I continue to believe that the better method for deciding when a state may shift the burden of proof is outlined in the Court's opinion in *Mullaney* and in my dissenting opinion in *Patterson*. In *Mullaney*, we emphasized that the state's obligation to prove certain facts beyond a reasonable doubt was not necessarily restricted to legislative distinctions between offenses and affirmative defenses. The boundaries of the state's authority in this respect were elaborated in the *Patterson* dissent, where I proposed a two-part inquiry:

> The Due Process Clause requires that the prosecutor bear the burden of persuasion beyond a reasonable doubt only if the factor at issue makes a substantial difference in punishment and stigma. The requirement of course applies a fortiori if the factor makes the difference between guilt and innocence.... It also must be shown that in the Anglo-American legal tradition the factor in question historically has held that level of importance. If either branch of the test is not met, then the legislature retains its traditional authority over matters of proof....

There are at least two benefits to this approach. First, it ensures that the critical facts necessary to sustain a conviction will be proved by the state. Because the Court would be willing to look beyond the text of a state statute, legislatures would have no incentive to redefine essential elements of an offense to make them part of an affirmative defense, thereby shifting the burden of proof in a manner inconsistent with *Winship* and *Mullaney*. Second, it would leave the states free in all other respects to recognize new factors that may mitigate the degree of criminality or punishment, without requiring that they also bear the burden of disproving these defenses.

Under this analysis, it plainly is impermissible to require the accused to prove self defense. If petitioner could have carried her burden, the result would have been decisively different as to both guilt and punishment. There also is no dispute that self-defense historically is one of the primary justifications for otherwise unlawful conduct. Thus, while I acknowledge that the two-part test may be difficult to apply at times, it is hard to imagine a more clear-cut application than the one presented here.

III

In its willingness to defer to the State's legislative definitions of crimes and defenses, the Court apparently has failed to recognize the practical effect of its decision. Martin alleged that she was innocent because she acted in self-defense, a complete justification under Ohio law. Because she had the burden of proof on this issue, the jury could have believed that it was just as likely as not that Martin's conduct was justified, and yet still have voted to convict. In other words, even though the jury may have had a substantial doubt whether Martin committed a crime, she was found guilty under Ohio law. I do not agree that the Court's authority to review state legislative choices is so limited that it justifies increasing the risk of convicting a person who may not be blameworthy. The complexity of the inquiry as to when a state may shift the burden of proof should not lead the Court to fashion simple rules of deference that could lead to such unjust results.

NOTES AND QUESTIONS ON MARTIN

1. Consider carefully the relationship between self-defense and the "prior calculation and design" element of aggravated murder. Justice Powell argued that "prior calculation" and self-defense were mutually exclusive. Thus he regarded self-defense as negating one of the elements of murder. The defendant, however, apparently disagreed. As the majority pointed out, the defendant did not dispute the existence of the elements of aggravated murder.

To the extent that Justice Powell's characterization of the relationship between "prior calculation" and self-defense is correct, the principal problem with *Martin*, as Justice Powell pointed out in footnote 4, is a potentially confusing jury instruction: "It makes no sense to say that the prosecution has the burden of proving an element beyond a reasonable doubt and that the defense has the burden of proving the contrary by a preponderance of the evidence." On the other hand, if the mens rea for aggravated murder is not inconsistent with self-defense, *Martin* is a much more troubling decision. Assume for the sake of argument that "prior calculation and design" means no more forethought than would typically go into a decision to kill in self-defense or under extreme emotional distress. Now compare a killing allegedly committed under extreme emotional distress with a killing allegedly committed in self-defense. Reasonable people may differ about whether extreme emotional distress is sufficiently mitigating that the defendant should not be punished as a *murderer* unless the prosecution disproves the extreme emotional distress claim beyond a reasonable doubt. The defendant who kills under the influence of extreme emotional distress will be punished, however. The killing is a culpable, criminal act; the extreme emotional distress mitigates the crime but does not justify or excuse it. By contrast, the person who kills in self-defense has not committed a crime; the killing is justified. Thus, when the central issue in a case is self-defense, the entire question whether there was culpable criminal conduct turns on a resolution of that issue. To convict a person claiming self-defense of aggravated murder — a capital offense in Ohio, incidently — without requiring the prosecution to disprove self-defense beyond a reasonable doubt is to convict someone for whom there has been no proof beyond a reasonable doubt of culpable conduct!

2. Unfortunately, the broad, troublesome implications of *Martin* appear to be the correct ones. The *Martin* majority's superficial analysis did not move beyond the fact that Ohio proved beyond a reasonable doubt the elements that it had included in its murder statute. Moreover, White v. Arn, 788 F.2d 338 (6th Cir. 1986), one of the cases setting forth constitutional interpretations of Ohio law that the *Martin* majority was "not in a position to dispute," involved self-defense and nonaggravated murder. In that case, there was no plausible inconsistency between having the mental state defined in the murder statute (purposefulness) and having the mental state required for self-defense. In other words, there could be a purposeful killing in self-defense. Indeed, *White* specifically relied on this lack of inconsistency to hold that proof of self-defense does not negate purposefulness and, therefore, that it was not unconstitutional to place the burden of proof with respect to self-defense on the defendant. Id. at 346.

3. After *Martin*, is it still true, as the *Patterson* majority claimed, that "there are obviously constitutional limits beyond which the States may not go"? Reconsider Note

4 at page 716, supra, where we hypothesized a statute defining murder as "causing the death of another human being." How is that statute different from what the Court approved in *Martin*?

KEY POINTS

1. Courts interpret the *Winship* mandate as a requirement that the prosecution prove beyond a reasonable doubt each fact listed in the statutory definition of the crime.

2. It is permissible to place the burden of persuasion on the defendant with respect to affirmative defenses such as extreme emotional distress or self-defense, as long as the state categorizes them as affirmative defenses rather than elements of the crime.

3. There are some unspecified limits beyond which the states may not go in creating affirmative defenses that limit the *Winship* proof beyond a reasonable doubt mandate.

NOTES AND QUESTIONS ON THE APPLICATION OF WINSHIP IN OTHER CONTEXTS

1. *Mullaney* and *Patterson* déjà vu. Apprendi v. New Jersey, 530 U.S. 466 (2000), involved a defendant convicted of weapons offenses as a result of his shooting a gun into the home of an African-American family that had recently moved into a previously all-white neighborhood. The maximum sentence for Apprendi's offenses was 10 years, but a separate New Jersey statute — a "hate crimes" statute — permitted adding up to 10 additional years to the sentence if the judge found by a preponderance of the evidence that the crime was racially motivated. At Apprendi's sentencing, the judge made the requisite finding and sentenced Apprendi to 12 years imprisonment. The Supreme Court held that the sentencing violated Apprendi's constitutional rights. According to the Court, any fact increasing the penalty beyond the prescribed statutory maximum (here 10 years), other than the fact of a prior conviction, must be submitted to the jury and proven beyond a reasonable doubt.

Apprendi, like Mullaney v. Wilbur, page 716, supra, unleashed a flood of litigation. Would *Apprendi* apply if, for example, (a) the hate-crime provision had been part of the same statute that was the basis for Apprendi's conviction, (b) the judge did not exceed the statutory maximum but gave an unusually harsh sentence on the basis of facts found by a preponderance of the evidence at sentencing, or (c) the judge relied on sentencing guidelines to increase a defendant's sentence? In the last case, would it matter if the guidelines were mandatory or discretionary?

Patterson v. New York, page 718, supra, resolved many of the uncertainties created by *Mullaney* with its adoption of the "elements" test for determining what the prosecution must prove beyond a reasonable doubt. Similarly, United States v. Booker, 125 S.Ct. 738 (2005) appears to have resolved many of the constitutional uncertainties created by *Apprendi*.

Booker was convicted of possessing with the intent to distribute over 50 grams of cocaine. The statutory penalty for the offense was 10 years to life imprisonment. The Federal Sentencing Guidelines, however, required a sentence of between 17 and 22 years in the absence of any aggravating or mitigating factors. The sentencing judge found by a preponderance of the evidence that Booker had obstructed justice and had possessed an additional 566 grams of cocaine. With these aggravating factors, the Federal Sentencing Guidelines mandated a sentence of between 30 years and life. The judge imposed a 30-year sentence — 12 years longer than the sentence that could have been imposed on the basis of facts found by the jury beyond a reasonable doubt.

The same five-justice majority that had upheld Apprendi's claim (Stevens, Souter, Scalia, Thomas, and Ginsburg) held that *Apprendi* applied to mandatory sentencing guidelines: The judge cannot impose a sentence that exceeds the maximum authorized by the jury's finding or a guilty plea, regardless of whether the maximum is created by statute or sentencing guideline. All nine justices agreed that in the absence of statutory or guideline mandates, there would be no constitutional problem. In other words, if there had been no guidelines or only voluntary guidelines and a statutory penalty of 10 years to life, the trial judge could have given Booker any sentence within the statutory range — even if the judge chose a relatively high sentence on the basis of a preponderance finding that Booker obstructed and justice and possessed additional amounts of cocaine! In short, the *Booker* "solution" to the *Apprendi* problem is as formalistic and artificial as is the *Patterson* solution to the *Mullaney* problem. In one case it is a matter of statutory "elements," and in the other it is a matter of mandatory sentencing limits.

In one important respect, though, *Booker* is quite different from *Patterson*. *Patterson*'s elements test has the effect of deferring to legislative judgments about how to define crimes. By contrast, *Booker* interferes with legislative judgments about how to regulate sentencing: Mandatory sentencing guideline systems, which a number of jurisdictions had adopted to regulate sentencing disparity, are now unconstitutional. Unregulated sentence discretion, on the other hand, is alive and well. What values protected by the *Winship* reasonable doubt requirement and the Sixth Amendment jury trial right justify this type of interference with legislative judgments?

2. *Winship* problems that are analytically similar to the problems in the burden shifting cases may also arise when a state permits the jury to convict the defendant of a single crime without necessarily agreeing on the facts that support the conviction. See Schad v. Arizona, 501 U.S. 624 (1991) (upholding first degree murder conviction under jury instructions that did not require jury to distinguish between felony-murder and premeditated murder).

3. If a jury believes the defendant, although not guilty of the crime charged, is nonetheless guilty of *some* crime and if the court refuses to instruct the jury on an available lesser included offense, there is a risk that the jury may ignore its reasonable doubt and convict the defendant of the greater crime. To avert this possibility should the defendant have a due process right to a lesser offense instruction? The Supreme Court addressed this issue in Beck v. Alabama, 447 U.S. 625 (1980), and returned to it in *Schad*, supra, Note 1. In *Schad* the trial judge instructed the jury with respect to two theories of capital murder, felony murder and premeditated murder. The judge also instructed the jury with respect to second degree murder, a lesser included offense of premeditated murder. The judge refused, however, to instruct the jury with respect to robbery. Justice Souter, writing for the Court, rejected the defendant's contention that he was entitled to a robbery instruction:

> Petitioner's . . . contention is that under Beck v. Alabama, 447 U.S. 625 (1980), he was entitled to a jury instruction on the offense of robbery, which he characterizes as a lesser included offense of robbery/murder. *Beck* held unconstitutional an Alabama statute that

prohibited lesser included offense instructions in capital cases. Unlike the jury in *Beck*, the jury here was given the option of finding petitioner guilty of a lesser included non-capital offense, second-degree murder. While petitioner cannot, therefore, succeed under the strict holding of Beck, he contends that the due process principles underlying *Beck* require that the jury in a capital case be instructed on every lesser included non-capital offense supported by the evidence, and that robbery was such an offense in this case.

Petitioner misapprehends the conceptual underpinnings of *Beck*. Our fundamental concern in *Beck* was that a jury convinced that the defendant had committed some violent crime but not convinced that he was guilty of a capital crime might nonetheless vote for a capital conviction if the only alternative was to set the defendant free with no punishment at all. . . . We repeatedly stressed the all-or-nothing nature of the decision with which the jury was presented. As we later explained in Spaziano v. Florida, 468 U.S. 447, 455 (1984), "[t]he absence of a lesser included offense instruction increases the risk that the jury will convict . . . simply to avoid setting the defendant free. . . . The goal of the *Beck* rule, in other words, is to eliminate the distortion of the factfinding process that is created when the jury is forced into an all-or-nothing choice between capital murder and innocence." This central concern of *Beck* simply is not implicated in the present case, for petitioner's jury was not faced with an all-or-nothing choice between the offense of conviction (capital murder) and innocence.

Petitioner makes much of the fact that the theory of his defense at trial was not that he murdered Mr. Grove without premeditation (which would have supported a second-degree murder conviction), but that, despite his possession of some of Mr. Grove's property, someone else had committed the murder (which would have supported a theft or robbery conviction, but not second-degree murder). Petitioner contends that if the jurors had accepted his theory, they would have thought him guilty of robbery and innocent of murder, but would have been unable to return a verdict that expressed that view. Because *Beck* was based on this Court's concern about "rules that diminish the reliability of the guilt determination" in capital cases, the argument runs, the jurors should have been given the opportunity "to return a verdict in conformity with their reasonable view of the evidence." The dissent makes a similar argument.

The argument is unavailing, because the fact that the jury's "third option" was second-degree murder rather than robbery does not diminish the reliability of the jury's capital murder verdict. To accept the contention advanced by petitioner and the dissent, we would have to assume that a jury unconvinced that petitioner was guilty of either capital or second-degree murder, but loath to acquit him completely (because it was convinced he was guilty of robbery), might choose capital murder rather than second-degree murder as its means of keeping him off the streets. Because we can see no basis to assume such irrationality, we are satisfied that the second-degree murder instruction in this case sufficed to ensure the verdict's reliability.

That is not to suggest that *Beck* would be satisfied by instructing the jury on just any lesser included offense, even one without any support in the evidence. In the present case, however, petitioner concedes that the evidence would have supported a second-degree murder conviction, and that is adequate to indicate that the verdict of capital murder represented no impermissible choice. [Id. at 645-648.]

With its focus on the accuracy of capital verdicts, is the majority suggesting that in noncapital cases there are no due process constraints on judge's refusal to give a lesser included offense instruction? Or is the *Schad* majority simply saying that the jury's capital murder verdict, when it could have chosen second degree murder, demonstrates that the defendant was not prejudiced by the failure to give a robbery instruction? Compare Pitts v. Lockhart, 911 F.2d 109, 112 (8th Cir. 1990) (failure to give lesser included offense instruction supported by evidence in noncapital case does not raise federal constitutional issue), with Geschwendt v. Ryan, 967 F.2d 877, 884 (3d Cir. 1992) ("*Schad* teaches us that, in cases involving offenses on a ladder, if the trial court wrongfully refuses to charge the offense at the bottom rung, that error is harmless provided the jury returns a guilty verdict for an offense higher up rather than for an intermediate offense which was also charged."). For the proposition that federal defendants are entitled to lesser included offense instructions supported by the evidence, see Keeble v. United States, 412 U.S. 205 (1973); Fed. R. Crim. P. 31(c).

4. In Montana v. Egelhoff, 518 U.S. 37 (1996), a murder prosecution, the Supreme Court upheld a Montana statute that made evidence of voluntary intoxication inadmissible "in determining the existence of a mental state which was an element of the offense." According to Justice Scalia's plurality opinion, this restriction on the right to introduce evidence did not violate a "'fundamental principle of justice.'" Id. at 42.

The defendant had argued, inter alia, that the statute had the effect of reducing the state's burden of proof on the mens rea element in violation of In re Winship. The Montana Supreme Court had agreed, relying on the following passage from Martin v. Ohio:

> It would be quite different if the jury had been instructed that self-defense evidence could not be considered in determining whether there was a reasonable doubt about the State's case, i.e., that self-defense evidence must be put aside for all purposes unless it satisfied the preponderance standard. Such instruction would relieve the State of its burden and plainly run afoul of *Winship*'s mandate. The instructions in this case ... are adequate to convey to the jury that all of the evidence, including the evidence going to self-defense, must be considered in deciding whether there was a reasonable doubt about the sufficiency of the State's proof of the elements of the crime. [480 U.S. at 233-234.]

Justice Scalia's response to the *Winship-Martin* argument was as follows:

> This passage can be explained in various ways — e.g., as an assertion that the right to have a jury consider self-defense evidence (unlike the right to have a jury consider evidence of voluntary intoxication), is fundamental, a proposition that the historical record may support. But the only explanation needed for present purposes is the one given in Kokkonen v. Guardian Life Ins. Co., 511 U.S. 375, 379 (1994): "It is to the holdings of our cases, rather than dicta, that we must attend." [518 U.S. at 56.]

What do you think of the defendant's *Winship* argument? Of Justice Scalia's response?

Justice Ginsburg, concurring in the judgment, maintained that the Montana statute should be understood as redefining mens rea, not as restricting evidence:

> Beneath the labels (rule excluding evidence or redefinition of the offense) lies the essential question: Can a State, without offense to the Federal Constitution, make the judgment that two people are equally culpable where one commits an act stone sober, and the other engages in the same conduct after his voluntary intoxication has reduced his capacity for self-control? [Id. at 57.]

What do you think of Justice Ginsburg's formulation of the issue? Of her affirmative answer? See Ronald J. Allen, Forward: Montana v. Egelhoff — Reflections on the

Limits of Legislative Imagination and Judicial Authority, 87 J. Crim. L. & Criminology. 633 (1997).

KEY POINTS

1. *Winship* requires proof beyond a reasonable doubt of any fact, other than a prior conviction, that increases a defendant's penalty beyond the statutory maximum.

2. Just as *Winship*, at least in theory, places some limits on the extent to which a state can shift the burden of persuasion to the defendant, *Winship* also, at least in theory, limits the extent to which jurors can disagree about the facts giving rise to the conclusion that a defendant is guilty.

3. To help ensure the integrity of death penalty verdicts, a defendant in a capital case is entitled to a lesser included offense instruction supported by the evidence. It is not clear to what extent noncapital defendants are entitled to such an instruction.

3.   The Burden of Production in Criminal Cases

As we discussed in Section A, at pages 699-703, supra, the primary significance of a production burden is that the failure to meet it will preclude the party who has that burden from presenting the matter to the jury. The court will resolve the issue against the party with the production burden. For example, if the prosecution fails to present sufficient evidence to permit a finding beyond a reasonable doubt of each element of the crime, the court will direct a verdict of acquittal for the defendant.

It is frequently said that because of a criminal defendant's constitutional right to a jury trial, it is impermissible to direct a verdict against a criminal defendant. In fact, however, courts commonly engage in activity that is the equivalent of directing verdicts against criminal defendants. Consider, for example, the refusal of a judge to instruct the jury on a particular defense or lesser included offense on the grounds that insufficient evidence of that defense has been produced, a practice approved by the Supreme Court in United States v. Bailey, 444 U.S. 394 (1980).

Bailey involved defendants' challenges to their convictions for escaping from a federal institution. In upholding the convictions, the Court rejected claims that the trial court erred in failing to instruct the jury on the common law defenses of duress and necessity. The defendants testified that their actions were motivated by death threats, and they requested an instruction on duress or necessity. The Court concluded that even if Congress intended to allow such defenses, a point left undecided, the defendants failed to make a sufficient showing of duress or necessity to justify a jury instruction. The defendants, in other words, failed to meet a burden of production, and the district court directed a verdict on their defense by refusing to instruct on it.

NOTES AND QUESTIONS

1. What the *Bailey* Court did not do, unless it did so implicitly, was to inquire into the constitutional necessity of establishing the fact in issue — in this case, whether or not the defendants had acted under duress or necessity. Without that inquiry, the

Court's analysis is incomplete. If the fact in issue was one that must be established in order to justify the potential sanction, then permitting the district court to remove that issue from the case resulted in a conviction when one essential fact had not been proven beyond reasonable doubt to the jury's satisfaction, which is inconsistent with In re Winship.

2. If the fact in issue does not need to be established beyond a reasonable doubt, then *Bailey* provides an acceptable, if not ideal, analysis of burdens of production on nonessential elements. The analysis is not ideal because of the majority's position that personal testimony of the defendants did not justify a jury instruction. 444 U.S. at 415. The Court is playing the role of fact finder with such a test and concluding that the defendants' testimony is incredible. As a matter of policy, such questions should be left to the jury even on nonessential issues.

Analyzing burdens of production in this fashion not only tidies up the analytical scheme, but also has significant pragmatic appeal. The present rules governing the placement of burdens of production are not altogether clear. Were a court today to strike down a statute placing a burden of production on a defendant, it probably would do so on the basis of the comparative convenience and rational relationship tests, but analyzing burdens of production functionally provides a much clearer articulation of the appropriate question: whether the Constitution requires that the fact in issue be established by the state.

3. One pragmatic objection to analyzing burdens of production functionally is that the result would be too burdensome — the state would have to disprove a series of issues that quite clearly have nothing to do with the case at hand. The force of the objection, however, is considerably blunted by two factors. First, normally not that many factors are crucial to liability, and the ones that are will not create extraordinary problems of proof for the government. In *Bailey*, for example, if the government had to establish the lack of a genuine fear of death, it would have to show only that these defendants were treated no differently from other inmates, and that protective custody was available to them if requested. Second, the absence of the "unusual" exculpatory factor will frequently be inferable from the circumstances that the government has proven. Cf. Rossi v. United States, 289 U.S. 89, 91 (1933) ("The general principle, and we think the correct one . . . e.g., is that it is not incumbent on the prosecution to adduce positive evidence to support a negative averment the truth of which is fairly indicated by established circumstances."). Accordingly, defendants will be forced to introduce some evidence of an unusual exculpatory factor before it arises in the case in any real sense, although defendants should be entitled to an instruction on it (if requested), regardless of whether they have presented evidence.

KEY POINTS

1. Courts typically refuse to give instructions on defenses and lesser included offenses on the ground that the defendant has produced insufficient evidence to warrant such instructions. These rulings are the equivalent of directed verdicts against criminal defendants.

2. Although the Supreme Court has not addressed the issue, refusing to give such an instruction has the potential for undermining *Winship*.

C.   JUDICIAL SUMMARY OF AND COMMENT ON THE EVIDENCE

At common law, trial judges had the power to sum up the evidence at the close of the trial and to comment on its implications. The power to sum up the evidence allows the judge to review for the jury all the evidence that the parties presented. The value of summary is that it gives the jury an impartial review of the evidence. The power to comment on the evidence goes considerably further. It permits the court to express its own views on the implications of the evidence, thus injecting the judge's personal opinion into the litigation.

The drafters of the Federal Rules proposed the following rule:

SUMMING-UP AND COMMENT BY JUDGE

After the close of the evidence and arguments of counsel, the judge may fairly and impartially sum up the evidence and comment to the jury upon the weight of the evidence and the credibility of the witnesses, if he also instructs the jury that they are to determine for themselves the weight of the evidence and the credit to be given to the witnesses and that they are not bound by the judge's summation or comment.

According to the commentary to the proposed rule, the intent was to codify the common law in the federal courts. Congress rejected the rule on the ground that such a rule is more properly one of procedure than evidence. The intention, though, was not to affect or change the existing power of the trial judge.

Many states have rejected the common law relating to summary and comment. Indeed, some states still have constitutional or statutory provisions prohibiting summary or comment, or both. Curtis Wright Jr, Instructions to the Jury: Summary Without Comment, 1954 Wash. U. L.Q. 177; Curtis Wright Jr., The Invasion of the Jury: Temperature of the War, 27 Temple L.Q. 137 (1953).

1.   The Advantages and Disadvantages of Permitting Summary and Comment

The attractiveness of comment and summary is that it may inject into the trial process a disinterested element that is valuable to the jury in its appraisal of the evidence. To the extent one believes that there is such a thing as a "disinterested observer," and to the extent one distinguishes the "evidence" presented at trial from "inferences" one draws from the evidence, one may be convinced that summary and comment are laudable features of trials. Both of these points have another side to them, however.

Trial judges certainly are disinterested in some respects, but they, like the rest of us, have their own way of looking at things that undoubtedly affects both what they observe and retain as well as what inferences they draw from evidence. Reconsider the discussion of relevancy in Chapter Three. Fact finders evaluate evidence in the context of their belief systems — the way they look at the world. Suppose, for example, that a person returns home one night and before entering the house wonders if her husband is at home. She notices that the evening paper is not on the doorstep and that the deadbolt on the front door is unlocked. Moreover, she knows from prior experience that when her husband returns home he invariably picks up the paper and leaves the deadbolt unlocked after entering the house. She also knows that she has a reliable paper delivery service. By comparing what she observes — no newspaper and deadbolt unlocked — she can infer that her spouse has already arrived home.

Of course, the inference she has drawn may be erroneous. It is possible, for example, that the paper blew away or was not delivered that day and that she or her husband inadvertently left the deadbolt unlocked in the morning. These matters, too, might be considered in light of observations made at the time, which would also be compared to previous experience. Is it a windy day? What happens to the paper on such a day? How often is the deadbolt inadvertently unlocked? The process of inference, in short, requires that evidence be compared to previous experience. That is what jurors do when they consider evidence, and indeed it explains in large measure why we cherish the jury system. In deciding the facts of a case, we want a representative mix of the population to bring their differing views to bear on the question what inferences may be drawn from evidence.

This inevitable reliance on personal experience in factfinding explains in large measure the resistance to judicial comment on the evidence, and to some extent summary as well. Judges commenting on the implications of evidence are, in a very real sense, commenting on their previous experience, and the injection of their previous experience into the fact-finding process may have an unwarranted influence. Trial judges, like all of us, have individual biases and prejudices that may affect how they summarize or comment on the evidence. In addition, there may be a kind of group bias stemming from the common, not particularly diverse backgrounds that judges to a substantial extent share. Judges as a class tend to be well educated, educated in a similar manner, economically comfortable, and accustomed to respect in the community. In addition, judges still tend to be predominantly white and male and from middle- or upper-class backgrounds. Any small and coherent group, such as trial judges were and probably still are, tends to share beliefs and attitudes that may affect how they perceive evidence as well as what inferences they draw from that evidence. Allowing judges to summarize and comment on the evidence permits their beliefs and attitudes to creep into the fact-finding process, skewing it in favor of the interests of this particular elite group. J. Willard Hurst, The Growth of American Law: The Lawmakers, 97-98, 104, 145, 351-352 (1940).

There are other objections to judicial comment in particular, although they, like the concern with individual and group biases, are also applicable to a lesser degree to summary. Some argue that comment is unnecessary because the attorneys for the parties are in a position to provide whatever argument about the evidence that they believe would prove useful or necessary. If the parties do not wish to develop certain implications of the evidence, the trial judge should not second guess that decision. Moreover, the judge's comment or summary usually comes at the time of instructing the jury. As a result the parties typically are not able to respond to what the trial judge says. Even if there were an opportunity to respond, one can reasonably wonder whether the judge is so powerful an authority figure in many instances that nothing the parties could do in response to judicial comment would be of any consequence in the eyes of the jury.

Judicial comment, then, presents a fundamental dilemma. It is in fact a source of further "evidence," but of a very different kind than is normally produced at trial. The "evidence" comes from the bench rather than from the adversaries, and it is presented in such a way that the jury may not perceive it for what it is. On the other hand, judges presumably have substantial experience with the kinds of matters involved in the trials before them. They have observed many situations that are undoubtedly similar in nature, and quite likely they are more sophisticated in their appraisal of evidence than are most jurors. To deprive the jurors of the views of the judge may deprive the fact-finding process of an extremely valuable source of "evidence."

2. The Criteria for Evaluating Judicial Summary and Comment

In the federal judiciary, where the common law power to summarize and comment has never been called into question, courts deal with the fundamental dilemma of comment and summary with rulings that attempt to walk the fine line between the judge being helpful as compared to "intruding" too far into the jury process. Summary and comment are appropriate "to assist [the jury] in arriving at a just conclusion." Vicksburg & M.R.R. v. Putnam, 118 U.S. 545, 553 (1886). The difficulty is that the criteria for determining what properly assists a jury are not clear. For example, in Quercia v. United States, 289 U.S. 466, 468-469 (1933), a criminal case, the trial judge instructed the jury in the following manner:

> And now I am going to tell you what I think of the defendant's testimony. You may have noticed, Mr. Foreman and gentlemen, that he wiped his hands during his testimony. It is rather a curious thing, but that is almost always an indication of lying. Why it should be so we don't know, but that is the fact. I think that every single word that man said, except when he agreed with the Government's testimony, was a lie.
>
> Now, that opinion is an opinion of evidence and is not binding on you, and if you don't agree with it, it is your duty to find him not guilty.

In reversing the ensuing conviction, the Supreme Court stated:

> This privilege of the judge to comment on the facts has its inherent limitations. His discretion is not arbitrary and uncontrolled, but judicial, to be exercised in conformity with the standards governing the judicial office. In commenting upon testimony he may not assume the role of a witness. He may analyze and dissect the evidence, but he may not either distort it or add to it. His privilege of comment in order to give appropriate assistance to the jury is too important to be left without safeguards against abuses. . . .
>
> Nor do we think that the error was cured by the statement of the trial judge that his opinion of the evidence was not binding on the jury and that if they did not agree with it they should find the defendant not guilty. His definite and concrete assertion of fact, which he had made with all the persuasiveness of judicial utterance, as to the basis of his opinion, was not withdrawn. [Id. at 469, 472.]

Quercia was a criminal case, but at least ostensibly the standards are the same for comment in civil and criminal cases. Capital Traction Co. v. Hof, 174 U.S. 1 (1899). Consider Nunley v. Pettway Oil Co., 346 F.2d 95 (6th Cir. 1965), where the jury was unable to decide if the plaintiff had been an invitee or a licensee. In order to encourage the jury to break the impasse, the judge gave the jury the following instruction during a break from deliberations:

> Now, the jury of course is the sole and exclusive judge of the facts in this lawsuit. It is appropriate that the court in an effort to be possibly of some help to the jury may comment

upon the evidence. I refrain from doing that and have refrained until this time from doing it in this case. However, in an effort to be of some possible assistance to you I think that I should under these circumstances make some comment upon the evidence upon this issue of invitee-licensee. I want you to understand, however, that in making these comments that you are not in any degree, in any respect, obligated to receive or accept or agree with what I may say. It is your duty to accept what I say with regard to the law in the case, but it is not your duty to accept any comment that I may make or any evaluation that I make or conclusion that I might reach on the evidence. That is solely your responsibility and solely your duty. But, with that understanding, it is the opinion of the court in this case that, from all the evidence upon the issue of invitee or licensee, that the evidence will establish that at the time and place of the accident the plaintiff was a licensee and not an invitee. Now, I say that just for the purpose, as I say, of possibly being of some help to you, but I want you to understand that making that comment you are not obligated whatsoever to accept that comment as your comment or as your opinion in the case, because it is your job and your responsibility to resolve that issue. I only make that with the thought and the hope that it may be of some possible assistance to you. At any rate, I want to ask you once again to retire and consider your verdict and see if you cannot come to some agreement, some verdict that will reflect the views of all of the jurors. Have respect for the views of your fellow jurors. If you find there are jurors that have different views from you, don't hesitate to change your mind if you should be persuaded by reason and logic to accept a different view. Attempt if you can in good conscience to arrive at a unanimous verdict. After you have considered the views of all others you shouldn't give up a firm conviction that you have just for the purpose of arriving at a unanimous verdict, but see if you cannot resolve this issue. Make one more effort, please. [Id. at 98.]

In reversing a judgment for the defendant, the court of appeals, while recognizing the common law power to comment on the evidence, said that "the trial judge's opinion on the licensee-invitee issue was an opinion on an ultimate fact question peculiarly for jury consideration and amounted to an instructed verdict as to defendant. . . ." Id. Do you agree?

NOTES AND QUESTIONS

1. Courts regularly cite and quote from *Quercia* in both criminal and civil cases involving challenges to judicial summary and comment. In most of these cases the judge's statements to the jury are not as extreme as the remarks in *Quercia* and *Nunley*. United States v. Maguire, 918 F.2d 254, 268-269 (1st Cir. 1990) (instruction summarizing government's theory of the case proper); United States v. Paiva, 892 F.2d 148, 159 (1st Cir. 1989) (judge's explanation of what a field test for cocaine is went beyond proper bounds of judicial comment since there had not been testimony about what a field test was or involved, but error was harmless); Rocha v. Great American Ins. Co., 850 F.2d 1095, 1099-1100 (6th Cir. 1988) (judge's interrogation of and disparaging comments about expert witness were prejudicial error).

2. Is the standard implicit in *Quercia* inherently inconsistent? How can one "analyze and dissect the evidence" without "adding to it"? For a discussion, see Ronald J. Allen, More on Constitutional Process-of-Proof Problems, 94 Harv. L. Rev. 1795 (1981); and Charles R. Nesson, Rationality, Presumptions, and Judicial Comment: A Response to Professor Allen, 94 Harv. L. Rev. 1574, 1589-1590 (1981).

3. A judicial comment will either be obvious or not obvious to the jury. If it is obvious, the reiteration of the obvious by the trial judge should not be grounds for

reversal. If the judge's comment is not obvious, a critical question should be whether the comment is accurate:

> Consider a murder trial where the defendant has injected the "defense" of alibi. Assume that on the basis of the evidence adduced without judicial comment, a well-informed, rational jury would conclude that there is a 15 per cent chance that the facts of the alibi story are true. The verdict would be not guilty, since a 15 per cent chance of error surely is a "reasonable doubt." First, take the case in which the trial judge comments on the evidence tending to prove or disprove the alibi and assume that the comment is factually inaccurate. Assume further that as a result of the inaccurate comment, the same jury would conclude that there is only a very small chance that the alibi is true. The verdict, then, all other things remaining the same, would be guilty. In order to escape the guilty verdict, and the effect of the trial judge's comments, the defendant would unfairly be forced to produce stronger, more persuasive evidence of the alibi. In effect, his burden of persuasion has been increased beyond that of merely raising a reasonable doubt.
>
> Now consider the case where the judge's comments on the evidence are accurate. Assume again that the comments caused the jury to discredit the alibi sufficiently to render a guilty verdict. Once again, the defendant's burden of persuasion has been increased — he would have to present stronger evidence to gain an acquittal — but this time the defendant has no constitutional grounds to complain. By altering the jury's factual matrix to one more in accordance with reality, the judicial comment has enabled the jury to perceive that guilt was indeed proven beyond a reasonable doubt.
>
> The example illustrates that inaccurate judicial comment detrimental to the defendant, on an issue that constitutionally must be included in a state's definition of a crime, violates the mandate of In re Winship by effectively lowering the state's burden of proving guilt beyond a reasonable doubt. . . . Accurate comment, on the other hand, can prevent an erroneous verdict when the jury is unable to appreciate the implications of certain facts proven at trial. [Ronald J. Allen, Structuring Jury Decisionmaking in Criminal Cases: A Unified Constitutional Approach to Evidentiary Devices, 94 Harv. L. Rev. 321, 348-349 (1980)]

Even in situations in which *Winship* is not applicable, comments on the evidence have the same impact on the applicable burden of proof: First, as the preceding example illustrates and as we elaborate in Section 4, infra, a nonobvious comment alters the parties' relative burdens of persuasion. Second, if the comment is inaccurate, it may result in a factual finding that does not satisfy the requisite standard of proof.

4. Why do you suppose the Court did not address the factual basis of the comment in *Quercia*? Do you agree with the *Nunley* court's criticism of the comment in that case? Are there other reasons for being critical of the comment?

3. Standardized Comments

Perhaps in response to the formal and informal restraints on the power to summarize and comment there has developed a practice of providing "standardized inferences." These are instructions to the jury that inform it that proof of one fact gives rise to an inference of another fact. Such instructions come in a variety of forms, and for that reason to some extent defy generalization. For examples, see Longenecker v. General Motors, 594 F.2d 1283 (9th Cir. 1979) (inference of a defect from a product failure); Ina Aviation Corp. v. United States, 468 F. Supp. 695, (E.D.N.Y.), *aff'd*, 610 F.2d 806 (1st Cir. 1979) (inference that evidence in a party's control but not produced at trial would have been unfavorable to that party). For a discussion see 2 McCormick Evidence §342, at 434 n.9, 435-436 (John W. Strong, ed., 5th ed 1999).

The sources of a standardized inference can be statutory or common law. When the source is the common law, the standardized inference is, in essence, a summary of collected judicial wisdom with respect to a certain matter. Such a standardized inference may be preferable to a normal comment on the evidence because the personal views of the trial judge are relegated to a lesser role. The trial judge will not be commenting on the evidence from the judge's own perspective; rather, the judge will be providing a summation of the collected wisdom of the judiciary. To some extent the same is true of standardized inferences that are authorized by statute, except that the source of the inference is legislative rather than judicial wisdom. On the other hand, because instructions on standardized inferences typically do not incorporate references to specific evidence in the case and because they sometimes contain excessive legal jargon, they may not convey information to the jury as well as individualized comments. Charles T. McCormick, Charges on Presumptions and Burdens of Proof, 5 N.C. L. Rev. 291, 299-301 (1972). Consequently, a standardized instruction may tend to promote an irrational decision-making process, even though it may also enhance the probability of a more accurate result to the extent the underlying inference is valid.

4.   The Relationship Between Comments on the Evidence and the Burden of Persuasion

Despite *Quercia*'s statement that a judicial comment may not "add" to the evidence, a comment, as we suggested in our questions following *Quercia*, inevitably will have one of two consequences: Either a comment will have no impact on the jury because it reflects what the jurors are already thinking, or it will push the jurors in the direction of deciding the case in favor of one of the parties. The latter consequence, of course, is the one that the judge intends. What would be the point of merely stating the obvious?

When a comment has its intended effect, it inevitably has the consequence of shifting the relative burdens of persuasion of the parties in the case. Consider, for example, a comment that is favorable to the plaintiff, who has the persuasion burden of proving fact X by a preponderance of the evidence. If there were no comment, the plaintiff in order to prevail would have to introduce enough evidence to convince the jury that fact X is 50-plus percent likely to be true; the defendant in order to prevail would have to convince the jury that there was at least a 50-50 chance that fact X is untrue. With a comment favorable to the plaintiff, the plaintiff will have to do less to persuade the jury that fact X is true, and the defendant will have to do more to persuade the jury that fact X is untrue. For example, the plaintiff's evidence standing alone may convince the jury that there is only a 45 percent probability that X is true, but the evidence along with the comment may convince the jury by a greater than 50 percent probability that X is true. In such a case, the effect of the comment is to permit the plaintiff to prevail even though the plaintiff has introduced evidence to satisfy only a 45 percent persuasion burden. The defendant, in order to prevail in the case, would have had to introduce enough evidence to convince the jury by a 55-plus percent probability that X was untrue.

Even though a comment on the evidence shifts the relative burdens of persuasions of the parties, a comment does nothing to shift the burden of persuasion from the jury's perspective. Whether the judge comments on the evidence or not, the judge will tell the jury that it must be persuaded that fact X has a 50-plus percent probability of being true. If there is no comment, the 50-plus percent probability must come from the evidence alone. If there is a comment favorable to the plaintiff, the 50-plus percent can come from a combination of the evidence (which, standing alone, may be less than 50-plus percent convincing) and the comment.

The validity of the point in the preceding paragraphs does not depend on the particular form the jury instruction takes. Even if the instruction states that "the plaintiff must convince you" or "the plaintiff's evidence must convince you" by a preponderance of the evidence that X is true, the fact remains that the jury will be making its evaluation with the benefit of any comment that the judge has given the jury. Thus, in the preceding hypothetical, a jury without the benefit of the comment favorable to the plaintiff may believe that X is only 45 percent likely to be true, whereas a jury with the benefit of the comment may have a different view of the evidence and, as a result, regard X as being at least 50-plus percent true. In short, as long as the comment does more than merely state what the jury already regards as obvious, it will be helpful to one party and detrimental to the other. This help or detriment constitutes an inevitable shift in the relative burdens of persuasion.

KEY POINTS

1. Judicial summary of and comment on the evidence are permissible in federal courts, but many states prohibit judicial comment or summary or both.

2. If summary or comment is permissible, an important criterion for evaluating the propriety of a particular summary or comment should be its accuracy.

3. Unless a summary or comment merely states the obvious to the jury, the summary or comment will inevitably be helpful to one party and harmful to the other, thereby shifting the parties' relative burdens of persuasion.

4. An inaccurate comment may result in a factual finding that does not satisfy the requisite standard of proof. In a criminal prosecution, such a comment about an "element" of an offense should be regarded as a *Winship* violation.

NOTES AND QUESTIONS

1. Reconsider the *Schechter* case at page 708, supra. Try to formulate a comment on the evidence that would have roughly the equivalent effect of the burden-reducing amnesia instruction that the court approved.

2. Would a comment of the type contemplated in Note 1 be permissible? If the answer is yes, which device — the comment or the explicit burden-reducing instruction — is preferable? If that answer is no, why should it be permissible to reduce the plaintiff's burden of persuasion in one way but not the other?

3. The purpose of the comparison between comments on the evidence and burdens of persuasion has been to demonstrate how comments on the evidence have an impact on the burden of proof. We are *not* suggesting that comments do have or should have any impact on how persuasive a case parties actually make with their evidence. As we noted earlier, judicial comment typically occurs after the presentation of evidence, and parties may not know what the particular comment will be until that time. In any

event, the primary factors that affect the strength of a party's evidence are likely to be the incentive to prevail in the lawsuit and economic constraints that may cause a litigant to forego some forms of proof. Ultimately, litigants are likely to and should present the strongest cases that they can afford to present without regard to whether there will be a favorable or unfavorable judicial comment.

D. PRESUMPTIONS

Presumption is a term that courts and commentators use to describe rules that regulate the process of proof by creating a special *legal* relationship between one fact, A, a proven fact that gives rise to the presumption, and another fact, B, the presumed fact. For example, many jurisdictions have a rule that on proof of the fact that a person has been missing for seven years (fact A), there is a presumption that the person is dead (fact B). Typically, this rule or presumption means that proof of fact A (e.g., that a person has not been heard from in seven years) *requires* a finding of fact B (e.g., that the person is dead) unless the party against whom the presumption operates adequately rebuts fact B. Here we will deal with the nature of various relationships that presumptions create.

There almost always will be some *inferential* relationship between a presumed fact and the fact that gives rise to the presumption. For example, in the presumption of death illustration, proof of fact A (not heard from in seven years) provides some inferential support for fact B (death). Indeed, in some cases a reasonable fact finder may be warranted in finding fact B on proof only of fact A even if there were no presumption. The significance of saying that proof of fact A gives rise to a presumption of fact B is that the presumption connotes some special *legal* relationship between the two facts. There is, however, no independent substance that inheres in the concept of *presumption*. Rather, *presumption* is only a label that courts, legislatures, and commentators attach to a variety of devices that manipulate the process of proof. It would be possible to describe those manipulations specifically and directly and to eliminate the term *presumption* from legal discourse. Indeed, as the materials throughout this section imply, such a reform would be desirable.

Presumptions come in different shapes and forms. Some are irrebuttable or conclusive, and some are rebuttable. Some rebuttable presumptions affect only the burden of production, and some affect the burden of persuasion. Some rebuttable presumptions are mandatory, in the sense that they require a finding of the presumed fact in the absence of sufficient rebuttal. Other rebuttable presumptions are permissive. They permit but do not require a finding of the presumed fact even if there is no rebuttal.

After beginning with relatively straightforward examples of conclusive presumptions, production burden presumptions, persuasion burden presumptions, and permissive presumptions, we will explore some of the complexities of traditional presumption analysis. We will then consider and critique the approach to presumptions in the Federal Rules of Evidence. Finally, we will consider briefly the impact of *Winship* on presumption analysis in criminal cases.

As we begin the consideration of presumptions, you should keep in mind two issues that affect the operation of presumptions but that courts and commentators rarely address.

First, who has what burden of persuasion with respect to the facts that give rise to presumptions? In other words, in order for the aforementioned presumption of death (fact B) to come into play, who has what burden of persuasion with respect to proof that the individual has not been heard from in seven years (fact A)? The *who* part of this question is not controversial: The person who wishes to take advantage of the presumption has the burden of establishing the facts that give rise to the presumption. The answer to the *what* part of the question is likely to be a preponderance of the evidence, which is the common although seldom articulated standard of proof for most preliminary facts. There may be instances, however, in which a court sets forth a higher standard. Cf. Schechter v. Klanfer at page 708, supra (to get advantage of reduced burden of proof plaintiff must prove amnesia by clear and convincing evidence).

Second, who decides whether the party wishing to take advantage of a presumption has satisfied the appropriate burden of persuasion with respect to the facts that give rise to the presumption? Assume, for example, that a woman wishes to take advantage of the presumption of death (fact B) with respect to her husband. If there is conflicting evidence about whether he has been heard from within seven years (fact A), does the judge decide or does the jury decide that question? We will elaborate on this issue in the context of our discussion of the different types of presumptions.

1. Irrebuttable or Conclusive Presumptions Explained and Illustrated

Some presumptions are conclusive or irrebuttable. In other words, once there is proof of fact A, the fact giving rise to the presumption, fact B, the presumed fact, is conclusively established. The party against whom the presumption operates is not allowed to present evidence of non-B. The Federal Coal Mine Health and Safety Act of 1969, which entitles totally disabled coal miners to compensation creates such an irrebuttable or conclusive presumption. Upon proof by X–ray or other clinical evidence that a miner has complicated pneumoconiosis (fact A), the law conclusively presumes that the miner is totally disabled (fact B) and, therefore, entitled to compensation. 30 U.S.C. §921(c) (1994). In other words, if the miner can establish fact A, the miner is entitled to compensation; the mine owner is not permitted to try to prove that the miner may not in fact be totally disabled (fact B).

A conclusive presumption is nothing more than a somewhat awkwardly worded substantive rule of law: If the law states that a plaintiff must prove fact B to prevail and if, on proof of fact A, fact B is conclusively presumed to exist, the rule of law really is that the plaintiff will prevail by proving *either* fact A *or* fact B. Usery v. Turner Elkhorn Mining Co., 428 U.S. 1 (1976).

As long as the classification created by a conclusive presumption is not so arbitrary or irrational that it raises due process or equal protection concerns, there is no valid basis for objecting to it. For example, if, as the Court held in *Usery*, Congress could have enacted a statute specifically providing that the two categories of miners were entitled to compensation, there should be no reason to object to the statute merely because Congress utilized presumption jargon to accomplish this objective. On the other hand, if a court were to conclude that a legislative classification is so arbitrary or irrational that it is unconstitutional, the classification should be unconstitutional regardless of whether the legislature used presumption language to create the categories. In short, what should matter is not the manner in which the legislature chooses to formulate its categories, but rather whether the categories themselves present constitutional issues.

Because a conclusive presumption is nothing more than a substantive rule of law, the question whether the facts giving rise to a conclusive presumption exist is, as it should be, one for the jury to decide. To put the matter somewhat differently, a conclusive presumption is nothing more than a somewhat awkward way of stating that identical legal ramifications follow from two classifications (fact B, which may be proved without regard to the presumption, and fact A, which by virtue of the conclusive presumption is legally indistinguishable from fact B). If the jury is the decision maker with respect to fact B, the jury should also be the decision maker with respect to fact A.

KEY POINTS

1. A conclusive presumption is a somewhat awkward way of stating a substantive rule of law.

2. As long as it is constitutionally permissible to attribute the same legal consequences to the presumed fact and the fact giving rise to the conclusive presumption, there should be no reason for objecting to a conclusive presumption.

PROBLEMS

10.1. Casanova, a life beneficiary, and Linus and Lucy, two remaindermen of a testamentary trust, seek to accelerate and thereby terminate the trust. They argue that the class of remaindermen who are the issue of Casanova has been effectively closed by reason of a vasectomy performed on Casanova, which rendered him sterile. The Trustee defends on the ground that there is in this jurisdiction an irrebuttable presumption that a man or woman irrespective of his or her age or physical capacity is conclusively presumed to be capable of producing children. Moreover, the Trustee argues the vasectomy may be reversible. The Trustee moves for a directed verdict. Should it be granted?

10.2. Husband is being sued by Wife for support for a child born to Wife during the marriage to Husband. The marriage has since ended in divorce, and Husband defends on the ground that he and his wife had not had sexual relations for two years before the birth of the child. Wife asks the trial judge to instruct the jury on the irrebuttable presumption that a child born during wedlock is presumed to belong to the husband. Should such an instruction be given, assuming that the law is as Wife asserts? Would it make any difference if Husband could prove beyond any doubt, based on blood test for example, that he is not the father of the child?

2. Mandatory Rebuttable Presumptions Explained and Illustrated

Mandatory rebuttable presumptions create special burden of proof rules for designated situations. The particular rationale for a special burden of proof rule — like the rationales for general allocations of production and persuasion burdens — is often elusive. Nonetheless, it is fair to say that in general the purpose for creating special burden of proof rules is to fine-tune the process of proof in order to advance the goal of rational and accurate factfinding or other goals related to the allocation of burdens of proof. See Notes 4 and 8 at pages 711 and 712, supra. Because of the complexity and confusion in the analysis of presumptions, however, the use of presumptions often detracts from rather than advances these goals.

a.   Mandatory Production Burden Presumptions

Some presumptions create a mandatory relationship between fact A, the proved fact, and fact B, the presumed fact, that affects only the burden of producing evidence. Once a party establishes fact A, there *must* be finding of fact B unless the party against whom the presumption operates produces evidence of non-B. In other words, if the party against whom the presumption operates fails to produce evidence of the presumed fact, the party will lose on that fact. If the party meets the production burden, the presumption has no further impact on the case. Courts and commentators, following the lead of Professor Thayer, commonly refer to this type of presumption as a "bursting bubble" presumption. Once the party against whom the presumption operates produces sufficient evidence, the presumption, the bubble, disappears or bursts. See James B. Thayer, A Preliminary Treatise on Evidence at Common Law 336 337 (1898).

Consider a case in which, in the absence of any presumption, the plaintiff would have to establish that the defendant received a letter in order to prevail. Assume that there is a mandatory production burden presumption that on proof of mailing (fact A) receipt of the letter (fact B) is presumed. In re Yoder Co., 758 F.2d 1114 (6th Cir. 1985); City & County of Denver v. East Jefferson County Sanitation District, 771 P.2d 16 (Colo. App. 1988); Winkfield v. American Continental Insurance Co., 110 Ill. App. 2d 156, 249 N.E.2d 174 (1969) (all dealing with the presumption of receipt on proof of mailing). In order to take advantage of the presumption, the person in whose favor the presumption operates must establish that the facts giving rise to the presumption exist. Thus, in our example, to take advantage of the presumption the plaintiff must establish that the letter was mailed. If the plaintiff fails to do so and if there is no other evidence of receipt, the plaintiff will lose. If the plaintiff establishes that the letter was mailed (fact A) and if the defendant produces no evidence of nonreceipt (non-B), the court will direct a verdict in favor of the plaintiff on the receipt issue regardless of the strength or weakness of inference of receipt in the particular case; the presumption mandates that result. On the other hand, if the defendant meets the production burden, the presumption disappears and the case will proceed as if there had been no presumption in the first place. Typically this means that the judge will send the case to the jury with the instruction that the plaintiff, in order to prevail, must convince the jury by a preponderance of the evidence that the defendant received the letter (fact B). In any particular instance, however, whether the judge should send the matter to the jury or direct a verdict for one of the parties should depend on which Case in Diagram 10-1 at page 700, supra, accurately represents the totality of the evidence. In re Estate of Wood, 374 Mich. 278, 132 N.W.2d 35 (1965).

As the preceding discussion demonstrates, a mandatory production burden presumption is in effect a specialized directed verdict rule. As such, it has two consequences. First, establishing the facts that give rise to such a presumption will require the court to direct a verdict on the presumed fact against an opposing party who fails to meet the production burden mandated by the presumption. Second, establishing the facts that give rise to a mandatory production burden presumption protects the party in whose favor the presumption operates from a directed verdict, at least until the opposing party produces evidence: Since proof of fact A requires a finding of fact B in the absence of rebuttal, it would be improper, before rebuttal, to direct a verdict against the person invoking the presumption regardless of how weak the inference from fact A to fact B may be.

NOTES AND QUESTIONS

1. Courts rarely focus in detail on how much evidence a party must produce to burst the bubble of a mandatory production burden presumption. Courts use phrases like "some evidence" or "any evidence" or "credible evidence" to describe what the presumption demands, but whether a party's evidence meets the articulated standard is seldom an issue. Graham C. Lilly, An Introduction to the Law of Evidence 68-71 (3d ed 1996). In our view, the evidence necessary to rebut a production burden presumption should be no different from the evidence required to satisfy other production burdens. The question should be whether the party who has the production burden has produced enough evidence to create a jury issue on the nonexistence of the presumed fact. See Diagram 10-1 and accompanying discussion at pages 700-703, supra.

2. General burden of production rules serve an important role in expediting trials: They tell the parties who must proceed with evidence in order to advance the litigation. Consider, however, whether a special rule allocating the burden of production on a particular *fact* makes any sense. For example, in the mailing/receipt example, both parties as a result of discovery are likely to have access to information about whether the letter was received, and whichever party has the general production burden will have a strong incentive to present the evidence in order to avoid a directed verdict. What value is served by complicating the litigation with the production burden presumption of receipt?

3. Even if there are instances in which special production burden rules seem appropriate, it is important to note that there is no need to resort to the rhetoric of presumption to accomplish the desired end. One can simply and directly allocate the production burden.

KEY POINTS

1. A mandatory production burden presumption is the equivalent of a specialized directed verdict rule.

2. Once a party establishes facts giving rise to a mandatory production burden presumption, the presumption requires a finding of the presumed fact in the absence of any rebuttal of the presumed fact.

3. Establishing the facts that give rise to a mandatory production burden presumption also protects a party in whose favor the presumption works from an opponent's request for a directed verdict — at least before any rebuttal of the presumed fact.

b.   Mandatory Persuasion Burden Presumptions

Some mandatory rebuttable presumptions shift the burden of persuasion to the party against whom they operate. Consider, for example, a case in which the plaintiff wishes to establish that the defendant, her former husband, is the father of her child. Normally, the plaintiff as the moving party would have both the burden of introducing sufficient evidence of paternity and the burden of persuading the fact finder that the defendant was the father. Assume, though, that there is a mandatory rebuttable presumption in the jurisdiction that a child born or conceived during a valid marriage relationship is the child of the husband. Assume further that this presumption shifts the burden of persuasion to the person against whom it operates. Cal. Fam. Code §7611. To take advantage of the presumption the plaintiff will have to establish that she was legally married (fact A_1) to the defendant (fact A_2) at the time of the child's conception or birth (fact A_3). If the plaintiff can establish these facts, the fact finder must find that the defendant is the father (fact B) unless the defendant rebuts the presumption. One possible strategy for the defendant in this case is to attack one or more of the facts giving rise to the presumption, facts A_1, A_2, and A_3. If the plaintiff cannot establish by the requisite degree of proof — probably a preponderance of the evidence — that they exist, there is no presumption in the case, and the plaintiff retains the burden of persuading the fact finder that the defendant is the father of the child. (Even if there were doubts about whether the child was born or conceived during the marriage relationship, the plaintiff may be able to establish with blood test or other evidence that the defendant is probably the father.) Another, not mutually exclusive, strategy for the defendant is to attack the presumed fact, paternity, directly. For example, the defendant might present witnesses to testify that he was out of the country during the possible time of conception and, therefore, could not be the father. If the plaintiff can establish facts A_1, A_2, and A_3, the reasonable inference of paternity that one can draw from these facts is sufficiently strong, without regard to the presumption, to permit the fact finder to find paternity. Regardless of the strength of this inference, however, the mandatory persuasion burden presumption means, at a minimum, that the defendant must persuade the jury that he is not the father of the child.

A persuasion burden presumption is similar to an "affirmative defense," the term used to describe the direct placement of a persuasion burden on a defendant. Fed. R. Civ. P. 8(c) (listing a number of affirmative defenses that must be proven by defendants). Consider, for example, the persuasion burden presumption of paternity that arises on proof of conception during a valid marriage. To say that there is a "presumption of paternity that allocates or shifts the burden of persuasion" to the defendant and that there is an "affirmative defense of nonpaternity" that requires the defendant to prove the fact is to make functionally identical statements. There is nothing in the concept of a presumption that facilitates the allocation of a burden of persuasion. Rather, presumptions that shift the burden of persuasion are simply affirmative defenses created for the same reasons of policy that generally inform the decision to allocate burdens of persuasion.

NOTES AND QUESTIONS

1. What is the justification for allocating the burden of persuasion to a (former) husband in a paternity action?

2. As we pointed out in our initial discussion of burdens of persuasion, shifting the preponderance burden from one party to another may not have an impact on very many cases, at least if the jury understands preponderance to mean 50-plus percent. Jurors, however, may not understand "preponderance" as meaning only 50-plus

percent. Moreover, just as jurisdictions have the power to create higher burdens of proof directly, see page 708, supra, they may and sometimes do create higher burdens of proof with persuasion burden presumptions. For example, in our hypothetical, the defendant's burden to persuade the jury that he is not the father may be the standard of clear and convincing evidence. Cal. Fam. Code §7612 (alleged father must rebut the §7611 presumption of paternity with clear and convincing evidence).

KEY POINTS

1. A mandatory persuasion burden presumption requires the party against whom the presumption operates to carry the burden of persuasion on the issue.

2. A mandatory persuasion burden presumption is the functional equivalent of an affirmative defense.

c.   Decisionmaking with Respect to the Facts Giving Rise to Mandatory Presumptions

Despite the functional equivalence of mandatory rebuttable presumptions and direct allocations of burdens of proof, courts tend to implement the presumptions differently from the manner in which they implement direct allocations of burdens of proof. If there is a question about who has the "normal" burden of proof with respect to an issue, there is general agreement that the question is one for the court or legislature to determine. By contrast, when the burden of proof rule depends on proof of some particular fact, which is of course always the situation with presumptions, the question whether that fact exists typically is one for the jury.

Consider, for example, the preceding mailing and receipt example. If the defendant produces sufficient evidence of nonreceipt to satisfy the production burden created by the presumption, there is no need to deal further with the presumption; the bubble has burst. Indeed, it is not necessary even to consider whether the presumption arose in the first place. If the defendant produces no evidence of nonreceipt, however, it will be necessary to determine whether the plaintiff should have the benefit of the presumption. In such a situation, the jury typically decides whether the plaintiff has established the fact of mailing (fact A), which gives rise to the presumption of receipt (fact B). If there were no evidence of receipt other than the plaintiff's evidence of mailing, the court would instruct the jury that it must find for the plaintiff if it finds that the plaintiff mailed the letter.

If the evidence were more complicated — if, for example, the plaintiff had alternative theories of how the defendant may have received the letter so that findings of nonmailing and receipt were not mutually exclusive — the instruction would be considerably more complicated. It might say, for example, "if you find by a preponderance of the evidence that the plaintiff mailed the letter, you must find for the plaintiff regardless of what you believe about receipt; but if you are not convinced by a preponderance of the evidence that the plaintiff mailed the letter, you must decide for the defendant unless the plaintiff's other evidence has persuaded you by a preponderance of the evidence that the defendant received the letter." Although the jury's role in deciding whether presumptions exist is reasonably well settled, there are at least two reasons for preferring the judge as decision maker on these questions. First, it is more consistent with the traditional allocation of fact-finding responsibility between judge and jury to place facts relating to burdens of proof and directed verdicts with the judge. Like preliminary facts regarding, for example, the existence of a privilege or whether an out-of-court statement satisfies the conditions of a hearsay exception, these are typically the kinds of matters that judges decide, whereas jurors typically decide disputed facts that are essential elements of claims and defenses. Indeed, with respect to burden of production rules not described as presumptions, it is clear that the judge decides whether a party has met the burden. Second, and more important, instructing the jury about these matters can make for extremely complex instructions. Instructions that are essential to inform the jury about its traditional adjudicatory factfinding are themselves frequently complex. It is a mistake, in our view, to add a nonessential layer of complexity by instructing juries about how to apply rebuttable presumptions.

KEY POINT

Typically the jury decides whether the facts giving rise to a mandatory rebuttable presumption exist.

PROBLEMS

10.3. Plaintiff sues Defendant and one element of Plaintiff's claim is fact B. In the absence of any presumption, Plaintiff would have to prove fact B by a preponderance of the evidence. There is presumption in the jurisdiction that if fact A is proven, fact B is presumed to exist. It is a mandatory *production* burden presumption.

Assume that Plaintiff introduces no direct evidence of fact B, but that Plaintiff introduces sufficient evidence of fact A to create a jury issue over whether fact A exists. Assume further that the inference from fact A to fact B is sufficiently strong that if fact A exists, a reasonable juror could find that fact B exists. Finally, assume that there is nothing in the evidence or common experience that would permit a finding of fact B in the absence of fact A.

a. At the close of Plaintiff's case, both parties move for a directed verdict. What result?

b. Assume that there is no motion for a directed verdict at the close of Plaintiff's case and that Defendant rests without presenting any evidence. Now both parties move for a directed verdict. Should either party's motion for a directed verdict be granted? If not, what should the judge tell the jury about how to decide the case? In answering this question assume alternatively (1) that Plaintiff's evidence of fact A is so overwhelming that no reasonable person could disbelieve it and (2) that reasonable people could disagree about the existence of fact A.

c. Assume that Defendant introduces evidence of only non-A before resting and that reasonable people viewing all of the evidence could disagree about the truth of both fact A and fact B. What should the judge tell the jury about how to decide the case?

d. Assume that Defendant introduces evidence of only non-B before resting and that reasonable people could disagree about the truth of both fact A and fact B. What should the judge tell the jury about how to decide the case?

e. Assume that Defendant introduces evidence of both non-A and non-B before resting and that reasonable people could disagree about the truth of both fact A and fact B.

What should the judge tell the jury about how to decide the case?

10.4. Assume the same facts and alternative possibilities as in Problem 10.3 except now the mandatory rebuttable presumption is one that places the burden of *persuasion* on the party against whom it operates.

3.   Permissive or "Weak" Presumptions Explained and Illustrated

Sometimes the law creates a special relationship between two facts — fact A, the proven fact, and fact B — but makes that relationship permissive rather than mandatory. In other words, on proof of fact A the fact finder may but is not required to find fact B even if the opponent makes no effort to rebut fact B. Commentators refer to these permissive relationships variously as weak presumptions, permissive presumptions, or inferences. We shall use the term permissive presumption, but we have no interest in quarreling about or promoting any particular terminology. We wish only to put in perspective the nature and role of these permissive devices.

The most common permissive presumption is res ipsa loquitur. Although the content and impact of res ipsa loquitur vary somewhat among the jurisdictions, a fair statement of the doctrine is this: If the plaintiff proves that the plaintiff was injured by an act that would normally not occur without negligence (fact A_1), that the defendant was in exclusive control of the instrumentality that caused the act (fact A_2), and that the plaintiff was not contributorily negligent (fact A_3), the fact finder may (but is not required to) find that the defendant negligently caused the defendant's injury (fact B). Although facts A_1, A_2, and A_3 standing alone create a fairly strong inference of fact B without regard to the res ipsa doctrine, the significance of res ipsa is that the judge in a special instruction will commend the relationship among these facts to the jury. In other words, to say that there is a permissive presumption from fact A to fact B is to say that the judge will instruct the jury that if they find fact A to be true the law permits them to infer fact B. At the same time, the judge will tell the jury that the law does not require a finding of fact B on proof of fact A and that the jury still must be convinced by the requisite burden of persuasion that fact B exists.

Even if the term *permissive presumption* is new to you, the foregoing explanation and illustration of what constitutes a permissive presumption should sound familiar. A permissive presumption in reality is a standardized comment on the evidence. Our discussion in Section C of comments in general and standardized comments in particular is fully applicable to permissive presumptions.

KEY POINTS

1. Permissive presumptions — sometimes referred to as "weak" presumptions or inferences — are the equivalent of standardized comments on the evidence.

2. Standardized comments couched in presumption language are not likely to advance reasoned decisionmaking because such comments typically do not inform the jury of reasons why the court is commending certain facts to the jury.

4.   The Complexity of Presumptions

Despite the intricacies in the foregoing material on presumptions, the presentation thus far has to a substantial extent been a sanitized, oversimplified glimpse at the world of presumptions. The reality is considerably more complex for a variety of reasons. Sometimes the complexity is simply a function of the difficult proof problems in complex litigation, Usery v. Turner Elkhurn Mining Co., 428 U.S. 1 (1976), but presumptions can create difficult problems even in relatively simple litigation. For example, it may not be clear from the existing law what impact the presumption is supposed to have; there may sometimes be "conflicting" presumptions, see 2 McCormick on Evidence §344, at 448-449 (John W. Strong, ed., 5th ed. 1999); and there may be precedent for instructing juries that a "presumption is evidence" of the presumed fact, which is a nonsensical notion. In at least some cases, the problem seems to be that the court is grappling with a tension between its assumption that the term presumption connotes something important and the reality that a typical production burden presumption frequently has no impact on litigation or the litigants. See Note 2 at page 748, supra. The result is confusing jury instruction that attempts to transform production burden presumption rhetoric into what becomes in effect a not very comprehensible comment on the evidence. Employer's Nat. Life Ins. Co., of Dallas, Tex. V. Willits, 436 S.W.2d 918, 921 (Tex. Civ. App. 1968); Carson v. Metropolitan Life Ins. Co., 165 Ohio St. 238, 135 N.E. 2d 263 (1956).

NOTES AND QUESTIONS

1. The Supreme Court has recognized that legislatures have wide latitude in allocating burdens of proof as they like. Lavine v. Milne, 424 U.S. 577, 585 (1976) ("Outside the criminal law area, where special concerns attend, the locus of the burden of persuasion is normally not an issue of federal constitutional moment."). Thus, one would think that the use of a presumption to allocate a burden of production or burden of persuasion should give rise to no special difficulty. Nonetheless, in dealing with rebuttable presumptions, the Supreme Court has stressed the need for a rational relationship between the proven fact that gives rise to a presumption and the presumed fact. Consider, for example, Usery v. Turner Elkhorn Mining Co., 428 U.S. 1 (1976), where the Court upheld several production burden presumptions set forth in the Federal Coal Mine Health and Safety Act of 1969. One of the presumptions provided that upon proof that a coal miner with 10 years of employment in the mines had pneumoconiosis, it was presumed that the miner contracted the disease from employment. According to the Court:

> We have consistently tested presumptions arising in civil statutes such as this, involving matters of economic regulation, against the standard articulated in Mobile, J. & K.C.R. Co. v. Turnipseed, 219 U.S. 35, 43 (1910):
>
>> That a legislative presumption of one fact from evidence of another may not constitute a denial of due process of law or a denial of the equal protection of the law it is only essential that there shall be some rational connection between the fact proved and the ultimate fact presumed, and that the inference of one fact from proof of another shall not be so unreasonable as to be a purely arbitrary mandate.
>
> Moreover, as we have recognized:
>
>> The process of making the determination of rationality is, by its nature, highly empirical, and in matters not within specialized judicial competence or completely commonplace, signifi-

cant weight should be accorded the capacity of Congress to amass the stuff of actual experience and cull conclusions from it. United States v. Gainey, 380 U.S. 63, 67 (1965).

Judged by these standards the . . . [presumption is] constitutionality valid. . . . [I]t is agreed here that pneumoconiosis is caused by breathing coal dust, and that the likelihood of a miner's developing the disease rests upon both the concentration of dust to which he was exposed and the duration of his exposure. Against this scientific background, it was not beyond Congress' authority to refer to exposure factors in establishing a presumption that throws the burden of going forward on the operators. And in view of the medical evidence before Congress indicating the noticeable incidence of pneumoconiosis in cases of miners with 10 years' employment in the mines, we cannot say that it was "purely arbitrary" for Congress to select the 10-year figure as a point of reference for these presumptions. No greater mathematical precision is required. [428 U.S. at 28-29.]

Perhaps an allocation of a burden of proof — whether by way of presumption or otherwise — could be so arbitrary or unreasonable as to raise a constitutional issue. If the implications of *Lavine* are correct, however, Congress seemingly could enact — without regard to any medical evidence — a compensation scheme for coal miners that did not mention presumptions that placed on coal mine operators the burden of coming forward with evidence that a miner's pneumoconiosis was not contracted during employment. If that is correct, why is the Court concerned, as it was in *Usery*, about the empirical relationship between a proven fact and presumed fact when Congress uses presumption language to allocate a burden of production?

2. Compare *Usery* with the following passage from Lavine v. Milne, supra. In *Lavine* the Court considered the constitutionality of a statute that "deemed" persons applying for welfare within 75 days after voluntarily terminating their employment or reducing their earning capacity to have done so "for the purpose of qualifying for such assistance or a larger amount thereof, in the absence of evidence to the contrary. . . . N.Y. Soc. Serv. Law §131(11)":

Although the District Court found this [provision] to be an unconstitutional "rebuttable presumption," the sole purpose of the provision is to indicate that, as with other eligibility requirements, the applicant rather than the State must establish that he did not leave employment for the purpose of qualifying for benefits. The provision carries with it no procedural consequence; it shifts to the applicant neither the burden of going forward nor the burden of proof, for he appears to carry the burden from the outset.

The offending sentence could be interpreted as a rather circumlocutory direction to welfare authorities to employ a standardized inference that if the Home Relief applicant supplies no information on the issue, he will be presumed to have quit his job to obtain welfare benefits. However, such an instruction would be superfluous for the obvious reason that the failure of an applicant to prove an essential element of eligibility will always result in a nonsuit. The only "rebuttable presumption" — if, indeed, it can be so called — at work here is the normal assumption that an applicant is not entitled to benefits unless and until he proves his eligibility.

Despite the rebuttable presumption aura that the second sentence of §131(11) radiates, it merely makes absolutely clear the fact that the applicant bears the burden of proof on this issue, as he does on all others. And since appellees do not object to the substantive requirement that Home Relief applicants must be free of the impermissible benefit-seeking motive, their underlying complaint may be that the burden of proof on this issue has been unfairly placed on welfare applicants rather than on the State [, a complaint that the Court rejected]. [424 U.S. at 583-585.]

Note that the Court said that there was no "procedural consequence," as though it is one thing to structure burdens of proof before any evidence is heard, and another to provide for burdens of proof to shift after evidence is heard. Can you make any sense out of that distinction?

3. Compare *Usery* with United States v. Klein, 80 U.S. (13 Wall.) 128 (1872). Klein dealt with congressional statutes passed during the reconstruction era that purported to modify the effect of presidential pardons of former Southern loyalists. Congress passed a statute that in essence provided that the oath that a person to be pardoned had to take to receive the pardon was proof of disloyalty in any proceeding where the pardoned person was attempting to obtain his or her property that had fallen into the possession of the forces of the United States. The presidential pardon, by contrast, provided for the return of such property to those who had received pardons, with certain specified exceptions. As the Court said: "The substance of this enactment is that an acceptance of a pardon . . . shall be conclusive evidence of the acts pardoned, but shall be null and void as evidence of the rights conferred by it, both in the Court of Claims and in this court on appeal." Id. at 144. The Court held the statute to be unconstitutional as an attempt of Congress to provide "a rule of decision, in causes pending, prescribed by Congress." Id. at 146. In addition, the Court said, "the court is forbidden to give the effect to evidence which, in its own judgment, such evidence should have, and is directed to give to it an effect precisely contrary. We must think that Congress has inadvertently passed the limit which separates the legislative from the judicial power." Id. at 147. How is *Klein* different from *Usery*? Is a rule of evidence different from a rule of decision in causes pending? How? If there is a difference, what are or ought to be the standards that permit Congress to provide for rules of evidence, and when do factual matters come within judicial competence? If the standard actually is "matters 'not within specialized judicial competence or completely commonplace,'" how do the specific relevancy rules fare?

4. In St. Mary's Honor Center v. Hicks, 509 U.S. 502 (1993), a racial discrimination case brought under Title VII of the Federal Civil Rights Act of 1964, the Supreme Court elaborated on the nature of a rebuttable presumption that it had created to help resolve discrimination claims. The *Hicks* Court began with a description of the prior law:

> With the goal of "progressively . . . sharpening the inquiry into the elusive factual question of intentional discrimination," Texas Dept. of Community Affairs v. Burdine, 450 U.S. 248, 255 n.8 (1981), our opinion in McDonnell Douglas Corp. v. Green, 411 U.S. 792 (1973), established an allocation of the burden of production and an order for the presentation of proof in Title VII discriminatory-treatment cases. The plaintiff in such case, we said, must first establish, by a preponderance of the evidence, a "prima facie" case of racial discrimination. . . .
>
> . . . "[E]stablishment of the prima facie case in effect creates a presumption that the employer unlawfully discriminated against the employee." To establish a "presumption" is to say that a finding of the predicate fact (here, the prima facie case) produces "a required conclusion in the absence of explanation" (here, the finding of unlawful discrimination). Thus, the McDonnell Douglas presumption places upon the defendant the burden of producing an explanation to rebut the prima facie case — i.e., the burden of "producing evidence" that the adverse employment actions were taken "for a legitimate, nondiscriminatory reason." [509 U.S. at 506-507.]

There was no dispute in *Hicks* that the defendant had established a prima facie case by proving "(1) that he is black, (2) that he was qualified for the position of shift commander, (3) that he was demoted from that position and ultimately discharged, and (4) that the position remained open and was ultimately filled by a white man." Id. at 506. There was also no dispute that the upon adequate rebuttal the plaintiff retained the burden of persuasion. The issue involved the adequacy of the defendant's rebuttal:

> The District Court, acting as trier of fact in this bench trial, found that the reasons petitioners gave [severity and accumulation of rule violations] were not the real reasons for respondent's demotion and discharge. . . . It nonetheless held that respondent had failed to carry his ultimate burden of proving that his race was the determining factor in petitioners' decision first to demote and then to dismiss him. In short, the District Court concluded that "although [respondent] has proven the existence of a crusade to terminate him, he has not proven that the crusade was racially rather than personally motivated." The Court of Appeals set this determination aside on the ground that "once [respondent] proved all of [petitioners'] proffered reasons for the adverse employment actions to be pretextual, [respondent] was entitled to a judgment as a matter of law. [Id. at 508.]

A majority of the Supreme Court, in an opinion by Justice Scalia, agreed with the district court and reversed the judgment of the court of appeals. Justice Souter, in a dissent joined by Justices White, Blackmun, and Stevens, agreed with the court of appeals.

   5. Neither opinion in *Hicks* is right or wrong as far as presumptions in the abstract are concerned. *Presumption*, after all, is only a term used to describe various rules that modify or fine-tune general burden of proof rules. Once the plaintiff establishes a prima facie case, it is analytically coherent, as the majority holds, to have a burden of proof rule that merely requires the defendant to come forward with some evidence of nondiscrimination and that has no other impact on the case. Similarly, it is analytically coherent to have a burden of proof rule that, on proof of a prima facie case, treats the defendant's rejected reasons as the equivalent of failing to produce evidence. This latter approach, as the *Hicks* dissent points out, has the effect of focusing the inquiry on the legitimacy of the defendant's reasons. The plaintiff's burden of persuasion, once the primary facie case is established, is to show the falsity of the defendant's proffered reasons. The ultimate question should be which burden of proof rule better serves the objectives of Title VII of the Civil Rights Act.

   6. In defense of its position that offering disbelieved reasons was adequate to rebut the presumption in *Hicks* Justice Scalia wrote:

> We have no authority to impose liability upon an employer for alleged discriminatory employment practices unless an appropriate factfinder determines, according to proper procedures, that the employer has unlawfully discriminated. We may, according to traditional practice, establish certain modes and orders of proof, including an initial rebuttable presumption of the sort . . . [that we hold applies in this case]. But nothing in law would permit us to substitute for the required finding that the employer's action was the product of unlawful discrimination, the much different (and much lesser) finding that the employer's explanation of its action was not believable. [Id. at 514-515.]

If the Court can, as the *Hicks* majority conceded, hold the nonresponding employer liable regardless of how weakly the plaintiff's prima facie case may suggest discrimination, why should the Court not be able to require that the employer's explanation be believable? Indeed, is it not true, as the dissent maintained, that the majority's approach substantially undermines the purpose for placing a production burden on the employer in the first place?

5. The Federal Rules Approach to Presumptions

Congress attempted to deal with the problem of presumptions in FRE 301. As promulgated by Congress, FRE 301 provides that the effect of a presumption is to place a burden of production on the party against whom the presumption operates:

> In all civil actions and proceedings not otherwise provided for by Act of Congress or by these rules, a presumption imposes on the party against whom it is directed the burden of going forward with evidence to rebut or meet the presumption, but does not shift to such party the burden of proof in the sense of the risk of nonpersuasion, which remains throughout the trial upon the party on whom it was originally cast.

The exception for what is otherwise provided in "these rules" is an apparent cross-reference to FRE 302:

> In civil actions and proceedings, the effect of a presumption respecting a fact which is an element of a claim or defense as to which State law supplies the rule of decision is determined in accordance with State law.

For similar deferrals to state law, see FRE 501 (privileges) and FRE 601 (competency).

Despite the seemingly straightforward language of FRE 301, the rule is fraught with difficulties. We touch on two of them here. For a more comprehensive analysis of FRE 301's deficiencies, see Ronald J. Allen, Presumptions, Inferences and Burdens of Proof in Federal Civil Actions — An Anatomy of Unnecessary Ambiguity and a Proposal for Reform, 76 Nw. L. Rev. 892 (1982).

a. The "Not Otherwise Provided for by Act of Congress" Exception

Even if the intended effect of FRE 301 is clear, the rule nevertheless is seriously inadequate. By it own terms, it creates an exception for "actions and proceedings . . . otherwise provided for by Act of Congress." What are the criteria for determining whether a presumption fits within the "otherwise provided for" language? Nothing in the rule or its legislative history specifically addresses this question. As a result, it is not clear whether, for example, the "otherwise provided" category includes presumptions that do not directly shift the burden of persuasion but that have been interpreted as doing so. Similarly, it is not clear whether the language extends to all of the variations of language that Congress in its wisdom has chosen to employ in formulating evidentiary burdens created by statute. Poncy v. Johnson & Johnson, 460 F. Supp. 795, 803 (D.N.J. 1978) (FRE 301 applies to federal statute containing provision for a prima facie case).

If FRE 301 does not apply to a wide variety of statutes, and is limited in its applicability to those that clearly allocate burdens of production, it is, of course, superfluous. If, by contrast, it was intended to have a wider application, Congress has effected significant change in federal law in the form of a simple rule of evidence.

Not surprisingly, courts that have wanted a presumption to have a greater effect than merely shifting a production burden have not found FRE 301 to be a constraint. Hood v. Knappton Corp., 986 F.2d 329 (9th Cir. 1993); American Coal Co. Benefits Review Board, 738 F.2d 387 (10th Cir. 1984).

b.   The Relationship Between FRE 301 Presumptions and Other Means of Allocating Burdens of Production and Persuasion

FRE 301 purports to deal with presumptions without reference to a judge's authority to allocate burdens of production and persuasion, to instruct the jury on inferences, or to comment on the evidence. Yet as we have seen, the word *presumption* is merely a label applied to various manipulations of these other judicial prerogatives. To define the scope of presumptions without dealing with these related areas is thus to engage in an effort preordained to be futile at best and confusing at worst. Not surprisingly, the dominant judicial response to FRE 301 has been either to ignore it or to misapply it.

The Supreme Court has apparently (and ironically) noted the impotency of FRE 301. In National Labor Relations Board v. Transportation Management Corp., 462 U.S. 393 (1983), the Court reviewed a change in NLRB rules that required employers to bear the burden of persuasion on the issue whether discharge of an employee was for a permissible reason. The employer argued that this shift in the burden of persuasion was in contravention of FRE 301. The Court concluded to the contrary, but in such a way that demonstrates that the rule has virtually no significance. "The Rule merely defines the term 'presumption.' It in no way restricts the authority of a court or an agency to change the customary burdens of persuasion in a manner that otherwise would be permissible." Id. 403 n.7.

Examples abound of the rule's inadequacies resulting from its failure to address the relevant evidentiary areas. First, FRE 301 does not purport to limit the federal courts' power to allocate burdens of persuasion; it merely says presumptions do not have that effect. May a court allocate a burden of persuasion consistently with the allocation of a burden of production affected by FRE 301? Understandably, the answer is unclear. Some courts have suggested that FRE 301 prohibits such an allocation by implication, while others view FRE 301 either as not applicable or as impliedly authorizing such allocations. For example, in National Labor Relations Board v. Tahoe Nugget, Inc., 584 F.2d 293 (9th Cir. 1978), the court said, "Respondents contend a presumption cannot [shift a burden of persuasion] . . . under rule 301. . . . Only a superficial reading of the rule supports this contention. The courts have approved the presumption's [burden of persuasion shifting effect] . . . both before and after the adoption of the Federal Rules of Evidence." Id. at 297. Unfortunately, the court neglected to provide a more sophisticated reading of FRE 301, so its assertion is difficult to appraise. See also Bunge Corp. v. M/V Furness Bridge, 558 F.2d 790, 794-795 (5th Cir. 1977).

Perhaps in response to this ambiguity, other courts seem simply to ignore FRE 301's existence. Moreover, the effect of FRE 301 on pre-FRE 301 decisions is not clear. Compare Plough, Inc. v. The Mason & Dixon Lines, 630 F.2d 468, 471-472 (6th Cir. 1980) (rule found to have no effect since presumption used before and after rule's adoption) and *Tahoe Nugget*, supra, at 297 (same) with Legille v. Dann, 544 F.2d 1, 5-7 n.37 (D.C. Cir. 1976) (court suggests that rule's application would change decision rendered). Finally, the relationship between FRE 301 and the remaining evidentiary powers of the courts is simply unaddressed.

KEY POINTS

1. FRE 301 purports to make federal presumptions production burden presumptions unless Congress has otherwise provided.

2. Because of the uncertain scope of the "except as otherwise provided" clause and because FRE 301 fails to address devices other than presumptions that allocate burdens of proof, FRE 301 is virtually useless.

6. Presumptions in Criminal Cases: The Impact of *Winship*

Review the discussion of *Mullaney* and *Patterson* at pages 716-723, supra. A presumption that explicitly shifts the burden of persuasion to the defendant is obviously unconstitutional if the presumed fact is one that the prosecution must prove beyond a reasonable doubt. For example, the Court in *Mullaney*, beginning with the premise that the prosecution must establish malice aforethought beyond a reasonable doubt, held unconstitutional the "conclusive inference" of malice from proof of an unlawful, intentional killing. This "conclusive inference," which *Patterson* characterized as a presumption, was indeed a traditional mandatory persuasion burden presumption. See pages 747-748, supra.

Patterson, of course, called into question the underlying premise that the state had to prove malice (i.e., the absence of provocation) beyond a reasonable doubt. As we suggested in Section B, however, the Supreme Court has relied primarily on how a state chooses to define a crime as the basis for determining what the state must prove beyond a reasonable doubt. Thus *Mullaney* apparently stands for the proposition that once a state includes a fact as part of the definition of a crime, the state cannot create a presumption that shifts the burden of persuasion on that fact. Similarly, the state cannot create a conclusive or irrebuttable presumption that an element of a crime exists. Sandstrom v. Montana, 442 U.S. 510. Unless we state otherwise, we will assume in the ensuing discussion that we are dealing with facts that the state has defined as elements of offenses and that must, therefore, be proven beyond a reasonable doubt.

It is by no means clear that one can reconcile the Supreme Court's cases dealing with presumptions in criminal cases. Many commentators think that the cases are hopelessly at odds with one another. Peter Lushing, Faces Without Features: The Surface Validity of Criminal Inferences, 72 J. Crim. L. & Criminology 82 (1981). For an elaboration on many of the issues created by the Court's criminal presumption cases, see Ronald J. Allen and Lee Ann DeGrazia, The Constitutional Requirement of Proof Beyond Reasonable Doubt in Criminal Cases: A Comment Upon Incipient Chaos in the Lower Courts, 20 Am. Crim. L. Rev. 1 (1982). Here, we put those problems aside and attempt to describe the most salient features of current constitutional law regarding *Winship* and presumptions.

In order to avoid a *Mullaney*-type conflict with *Winship*, presumptions in criminal cases are typically permissive rather than mandatory: If the fact finder believes the facts giving rise to the presumption, the fact finder may but is not required to find the presumed fact. The fact finder must be convinced of the presumed fact beyond a reasonable doubt. Merely making the presumption permissive, however, does not necessarily eliminate *Winship* problems.

To determine whether a jury instruction about a presumption violates *Winship*, it is important to focus on the language of the instruction itself. If jurors could reasonably understand the instruction as permitting proof of the presumed fact by less than beyond a reasonable doubt, the instruction is unconstitutional. Sandstrom v. Montana, 442 U.S. 510 (1979) According to County Court of Ulster County v. Allen, 442 U.S. 140 (1979), a permissive presumption instruction with respect to an element of an offense is constitutional (1) if the instructions as a whole make it clear that the jury must be convinced of each element of the crime beyond a reasonable doubt and (2) if there is a "more likely than not" relationship between the proven facts and the presumed fact. In deciding whether the relationship exists, the primary focus is on the evidence in the case, not on whether the relationship exists in the abstract.

A production burden presumption — that is, a presumption informing the jury that a presumption exists with respect to some element of the crime unless the defendant produces evidence to rebut the presumed fact — may or may not be constitutional. The best guide for dealing with this type of presumption is dictum in *Ulster County*. If jurors could reasonably understand such an instruction as requiring them to find the presumed fact unless the defendant produces a certain amount of evidence, the instruction is probably unconstitutional. In essence it permits conviction because of the defendant's failure to come forward with evidence, regardless of whether the jury is convinced beyond a reasonable doubt that the fact exists. On the other hand, if the instruction makes it clear that the defendant's obligation is minimal and if the instructions as a whole stress the *Winship* beyond a reasonable doubt mandate, the instruction may be tantamount to a permissive presumption — at least if it is clear that the defendant has in fact produced some evidence. Such an instruction would apparently be constitutional if the presumption met the "more likely than not" requirement for permissive presumptions. *Ulster County*, 442 U.S. at 157 n.16.

NOTES AND QUESTIONS

1. In criminal cases prior to *Ulster County*, the Supreme Court had assessed the constitutionality of presumptions primarily in terms of the empirical relationship between the presumed facts and the facts giving rise to the presumption. The recurring issues was whether the relationship had to exist beyond a reasonable doubt or whether a more-likely-than-not relationship was sufficient. Barnes v. United States, 412 U.S. 837 (1973); Turner v. United States, 396 U.S. 398 (1970). *Ulster County* resolved the issue for permissive presumptions by settling on the more-likely-than-not standard. In addition, dictum in *Ulster County* suggests that a presumption shifting the burden of persuasion to the defendant may be constitutional if the facial (as opposed to case-specific) relationship between the proven fact and the presumed facts exists beyond a reasonable doubt. 442 U.S. at 157-159 and nn.16, 17. Sandstrom v. Montana, however, makes no reference to this dictum in holding unconstitutional a presumption instruction that could have been understood as shifting the burden of persuasion to the defendant.

2. Why should it matter what the empirical relationship is between facts that give rise to a presumption and the presumed fact? As we have pointed out, instructions on inferences and presumptions are either awkward methods of allocating burdens of proof or comments on the evidence designed to inform the jury of the inferential relationship between facts.

If an instruction allocates a burden of persuasion to the defendant, the issue should be whether *Winship* requires the fact finder to prove that fact beyond a reasonable doubt. How, if at all, is the nature of the empirical relationship between the facts that the prosecution must prove and the facts that the defendant must prove important to the resolution of the *Winship* issue?

If an instruction is a comment on the evidence, it may be a comment on an ultimate fact or it may be a comment on an evidentiary fact. It may accurately point out that one fact may be inferred from another beyond reasonable doubt or it may, just as accurately, point out that one fact may be inferred from another without meeting the reasonable doubt standard. Alternatively, a comment could be inaccurate, but in such a way as to be helpful to either the prosecution or the defense. The empirical relationship tests employed in *Ulster County* and its predecessors are inadequate to deal with these and other nuances.

To take just one example, assume that the court specifically instructs the jury that about 50 percent of the time individuals in possession of stolen treasury checks know they are stolen. Assume further that the instruction is accurate and that the jury in the absence of the instruction would have estimated that the relationship between possession and knowledge existed about a third of the time. Given these assumptions, the instruction, which favors the prosecution, meets neither the more-likely-than-not nor the beyond-a-reasonable-doubt" test. Yet the instruction gives the jury accurate information. Why should there be a *Winship* problem?

3. In Carella v. California, 491 U.S. 263 (1989), where the defendant was convicted of grand theft for failure to return a rental car, the Court disapproved of a presumption instruction that merely quoted from the statutes defining the crime. The two jury instructions at issue were:

> Intent to commit theft by fraud is presumed if one who has leased or rented the personal property of another pursuant to a written contract fails to return the personal property to its owner within 20 days after the owner has made written demand by certified or registered mail following the expiration of the lease or rental agreement for return of the property so leased or rented.
> Whenever any person who has leased or rented a vehicle wilfully and intentionally fails to return the vehicle to its owner within five days after the lease or rental agreement has expired, that person shall be presumed to have embezzled the vehicle. [Id. at 264.]

As the Supreme Court quite reasonably observed, the jurors could have understood these instructions as creating conclusive presumptions. It should not necessarily follow, however, that there was a *Winship* violation. Rather, one can view the presumptions as part of the statutory definition of the crime, which requires *either* actual intent to steal *or* (wilful) failure to return the vehicle after the specified time. Cf. discussion of conclusive presumptions at pages 745-746, supra (in Usury v. Turner Elkhorn Mining Co., Supreme Court acknowledged that conclusive presumption was merely a substantive rule of law). Nonetheless, the Supreme Court, following *Sandstrom*, held that the instructions "relieved the State of its burden of proof articulated in *Winship*, namely proving by evidence every essential element of Carella's crime beyond a reasonable doubt. The two instructions violated the Fourteenth Amendment." Id. at. 266.

4. Compare *Carella* with Warner v. Zent, 997 F.2d 116 (6th Cir. 1993). The defendant appealed his securities fraud conviction on the ground that the trial court allowed the jury to find him guilty on the basis of a conclusive presumption that he "knowingly" misrepresented facts even though the proof at trial established only that he ought to have known the facts to be false. The court acknowledged that it is

impermissible to "instruct the jury that proof of the existence of certain facts automatically establishes the element of intent where intent is an element of the charged offense." Id. at 133. The court, however, rejected the defendant's claim:

> Within constitutional limits . . . a state has discretion to determine the elements of state offenses. On habeas review, we are bound by state court interpretations of state criminal law except in extreme circumstances where it appears that the interpretation is an obvious subterfuge to evade consideration of federal issues.
>
> Ohio Revised Code §1709.29 — the statute under which the jury was instructed that Mr. Warner should be deemed to have knowledge of any fact of which he should have secured knowledge in the exercise of reasonable diligence — has a heading that reads "Presumption of Knowledge." Such headings, however, do not constitute any part of Ohio law. Resort to a title in construing a statute is unnecessary and improper. See Ohio Rev. Code. §1.01.
>
> Prior to the Ohio Supreme Court's decision in the instant case, one Ohio Court of Appeals had held that §1707.29 does not create a presumption. The Supreme Court reached the same conclusion, holding in the instant case that §1707.29 merely sets forth what the term "knowledge" encompasses for purposes of criminal liability. This interpretation is entitled to deference.
>
> . . . [W]e conclude that §1707.29 is nothing more than a definitional provision setting forth Ohio's standard of reasonable diligence for securities fraud cases. [Id.]

5. In Sullivan v. Louisiana, 508 U.S. 275 (1993), the Supreme Court held that an instruction directly misstating the reasonable doubt concept could never be subject to harmless error analysis. If a *presumption instruction* undermines the *Winship* mandate, however, it may be harmless error. Yates v. Evatt, 500 U.S. 391 (1991). Is this another example of the Court's focusing on the term *presumption* to laud form over substance?

6. For a discussion of the criteria that should be used in evaluating presumptions in criminal cases, see Ronald J. Allen, Structuring Jury Decisionmaking in Criminal Cases: A Unified Constitutional Approach to Evidentiary Devices, 94 Harv. L. Rev. 321 (1980).

KEY POINTS

1. In assessing the constitutionality of a presumption instruction, it is important to focus on precisely what the court tells the jury. If the jury could understand the instruction in a manner that violates *Winship*, the presumption is unconstitutional.

2. Presumptions that make defined elements of crimes irrebuttable are unconstitutional.

3. Presumptions that shift the burden of persuasion to the defendant with respect to elements of offenses are also unconstitutional, except perhaps in cases in which the general relationship between the proven facts and the presumed fact exists beyond a reasonable doubt.

4. Permissive presumptions are constitutional if the relationship between the proven facts and the presumed fact meets the "more likely than not" standard in light of the evidence in the case.

5. The empirical relationship between proven facts and presumed facts, despite is constitutional significance, is not relevant to the issues that *should* inform judgments about whether presumption instructions violate *Winship*.

PROBLEMS

10.5. Defendant Morgan was convicted of driving under the influence of intoxicating beverages. Some 90 minutes after Morgan drove his vehicle off the road and through a fence, an officer interviewed him at a friend's home. According to the officer Morgan appeared unsteady and smelled of alcohol, but Morgan claimed that he had not consumed any alcohol since the accident. A breathalyzer test at the time of the interview indicated that Morgan had a blood alcohol level of .14 percent. Morgan is 19 years old, 5 feet 10 inches tall, and weighs 190 pounds. In the instructions to the jury the judge stated that Morgan was to be found guilty "if, and only if, you believe from all the evidence beyond a reasonable doubt (a) that the defendant was driving a motor vehicle and (b) that while doing so he was under the influence of alcohol." The judge also read verbatim to the jury the following statutory language and told the jury to "consider this as evidence in the case":

> (a) In any criminal prosecution in which the defendant is charged with having operated a vehicle while under the influence of intoxicating beverages, the amount of alcohol in the defendant's blood as determined at the time of making an analysis of his blood, urine, breath, or other bodily substance, shall give rise to the following presumptions: (i) If there was .05 percent or less by weight of alcohol in such blood, it shall be presumed that the defendant was not under the influence of intoxicating beverages; (ii) If there was more than .05 percent but less than .10 percent by weight of alcohol in such blood, such fact shall not constitute a presumption that the defendant either was or was not under the influence of intoxicating beverages, but such fact may be considered together with other competent evidence, in determining the guilt or innocence of the defendant; (iii) If there was .10 percent or more by weight of alcohol in such blood, it shall be presumed that the defendant was under the influence of intoxicating beverages.
>
> (b) The provisions of subsection (a) of this section shall not be construed as limiting the introduction of any other competent evidence bearing on the question whether the defendant was under the influence of intoxicating beverages.

Did the instruction violate the defendant's constitutional rights?

10.6. Davis, a union official, was convicted of lying to the grand jury. The allegedly false statement was his denial that he had accepted campaign contributions from an employer. The trial judge's jury instructions included the following:

> Under federal law, it is improper for a union official to accept any union campaign contributions from any employer. Specifically, federal law provides that "no moneys of an employer shall be contributed or applied to promote the candidacy of any person in any election." This law applied even where the contribution may have been minimal.
>
> I want to caution you that the defendant is not charged in this indictment with receiving improper payments of union campaign expenses. I want to instruct you that you may only consider this instruction in determining the defendant's intent and state of mind in answering questions before the grand jury.

The purpose of the instruction, according to the prosecution, was to suggest to the jury that Davis had a motive to lie to the grand jury: Because receiving such funds is illegal and because Davis presumably knew it was illegal, he had a motive to lie about whether he had received the funds. Davis, on the other hand, points out that the only sanction for receiving such funds would have been his removal from office for the one remaining month of his term. Avoiding such a minor sanction, he suggests, is not worth the risk of a possible criminal conviction for lying to the grand jury. He claims that the instruction was unconstitutional because it created for the jury either an irrational permissive inference or a mandatory presumption. What result?

10.7. Libby was convicted of murder for stabbing his victim to death in a fight. There were no eyewitnesses to the stabbing, but witnesses did testify that Libby had been seen carrying a knife before the stabbing, that he had been seen running away from the site of the fight with blood on his clothes, that he was seen holding a knife shortly after the stabbing, that he admitted having stabbed the victim, and that he threatened anyone who might "snitch" on him. There was also testimony that he stabbed the victim because he thought the victim was about to jump him from behind and because he believed the victim was beating up a third person. The trial judge instructed the jury with respect to murder and voluntary manslaughter. The murder instruction included the following:

> Murder is the killing of a human being without legal justification or without excuse or without such extenuating circumstances as may reduce the crime to manslaughter; but with what is called in the law malice aforethought.
>
> Any intentional killing of a human being without legal justification or excuse and with no extenuating circumstances sufficient in law to reduce the crime to manslaughter is malicious.
>
> If the wicked intent to do injury to another person precedes the act by which the injury was done, it is malice aforethought. If the homicide is committed without legal justification or, that is to say, without due authority of law and not in self defense, and there is no issue here of self defense, nor in the heat of passion on great provocation, but with the specific intent to take the life of the one killed, or an unlawful act, the natural consequence of which would be to deprive another person of life, it is murder.
>
> Malice is implied in every deliberate cruel act by one against another.

The judge then gave the manslaughter instruction explaining that a killing under the influence of extreme emotional distress was manslaughter and that if there were evidence of extreme emotional distress, the jury could convict the defendant only of manslaughter unless the prosecution proved beyond a reasonable doubt that the killing was not done under the influence of extreme emotional distress. The judge told the jury to consider first whether the defendant was guilty of murder and then to consider the manslaughter charge unless the jury agreed that the defendant was guilty of murder. The judge also told the jury that to find the defendant guilty of any crime the prosecution had to prove each element beyond a reasonable doubt.

What constitutional challenges can the defendant make to these instructions?

CHAPTER ELEVEN

JUDICIAL NOTICE

Consider a case in which a large-scale livestock operation is being sued for allowing agricultural wastes to run off the animal lot into nearby waterways. Suppose the plaintiff is required to establish, as part of its case, the amount of rainfall that fell in the area during the preceding year. It seems as though there should be a clear, undisputed answer to the rainfall question; yet for the plaintiff to prove that by the introduction of the kinds of evidence you have studied thus far might be difficult or exceedingly costly. There is no percipient witness who could give precise eyewitness testimony about how many inches of rainfall occurred. The plaintiff might have to go to the trouble of retaining an expert simply to establish an undisputable fact. However, the Federal Rules provide a procedure that might simplify proof in this situation, known as "judicial notice."

The term "judicial notice" actually encompasses a range of situations in which judges take official cognizance of propositions of fact and of law. FRE 201, discussed in Section A, deals with judicial notice in the strict sense of a formal judicial determination that a particular "adjudicative" fact is "not subject to reasonable dispute." However, the term "judicial notice" is also often used more loosely to refer to other forms of judicial factfinding not addressed by the Federal Rules of Evidence at all. These are discussed in Sections B and C.

A. JUDICIAL NOTICE OF ADJUDICATIVE FACTS

1. FRE 201

RULE 201. JUDICIAL NOTICE OF ADJUDICATIVE FACTS

(a) Scope of rule. This rule governs only judicial notice of adjudicative facts.

(b) Kinds of facts. A judicially noticed fact must be one not subject to reasonable dispute in that it is either (1) generally known within the territorial jurisdiction of the trial court or (2) capable of accurate and ready determination by resort to sources whose accuracy cannot reasonably be questioned.

(c) When discretionary. A court may take judicial notice, whether requested or not.

(d) When mandatory. A court shall take judicial notice if requested by a party and supplied with the necessary information.

(e) Opportunity to be heard. A party is entitled upon timely request to an opportunity to be heard as to the propriety of taking judicial notice and the tenor of the matter noticed. In the absence of prior notification, the request may be made after judicial notice has been taken.

(f) Time of taking notice. Judicial notice may be taken at any stage of the proceeding.

(g) Instructing jury. In a civil action or proceeding, the court shall instruct the jury to accept as conclusive any fact judicially noticed. In a criminal case, the court shall instruct the jury that it may, but is not required to, accept as conclusive any fact judicially noticed.

2.   Interpretation and Illustration of FRE 201 (a) and (b)

We have already seen that trial judges have the authority to circumvent the ordinary process of proof-taking and jury decisionmaking by granting directed verdicts and summary judgments. As we discussed in Section A of Chapter 10, a judge's authority to resolve some or all of the issues in a case "as a matter of law" means that the judge will preclude jury factfinding on a claim or defense if there are no material facts in dispute or if reasonable people could not disagree about the facts necessary to establish the claim or a defense. FRE 201 gives judges a somewhat analogous authority with respect to specific facts that are parts of or relevant to disputed claims. If a fact is "not subject to reasonable dispute," the judge may instruct the jury (at least in a civil case) that it must take certain matters as true because they have been "judicially noticed" by the judge

a.   Types of Adjudicative Facts That Are Frequently Noticed

Because judicial notice could in theory apply to the entire inferential process that occurs at trial, the examples of facts that may be subject to judicial notice under FRE 201 are incredibly varied. Of course not all evidentiary facts or propositions of background knowledge could meet the high standards of certainty required by FRE 201(b). The analysis of recent cases presented in 1 Stephen A. Saltzburg, Michael M. Martin, and Daniel J. Capra, Federal Rules of Evidence Manual 132-148 (7th ed. 1998) shows that the main types of facts about which parties seek judicial notice pursuant to FRE 201, and are sometimes successful, are: business or government custom; calendar dates and time limits; product characteristics in copyright, patent, and trademark litigation; current events; general principles of economics and economic information; fees and salaries; geography; historical information; judicial records and proceedings; medical information; official records; scientific facts and principles, and performance of scientific equipment; and weather.

b.   The Scope of FRE 201(a): What Are Adjudicative Facts?

FRE 201(a) states that the rule applies only to those situations in which judges take official cognizance of "adjudicative facts," but the rule itself does not define that term. Adjudicative facts are those facts that the jury typically decides at trial. Adjudicative facts may be either the alleged facts of consequence that are the essential elements of a dispute under the substantive law or the evidentiary facts that are relevant to prove those facts of consequence. As described by the Advisory Committee Note to FRE 201(a):

> Adjudicative facts are simply the facts of the particular case. . . . [T]he adjudicative facts are those to which the law is applied in the process of adjudication. They are the facts that normally go to the jury in a jury case. They relate to the parties, their activities, their properties, their businesses. [2 Kenneth Davis, Administrative Law Treatise 353 (1958).]

And as defined by the Alaska Rules of Evidence, Rule 201(a):

> Judicial notice of a fact as used in this rule means a court's on-the-record declaration of the existence of a fact normally decided by the trier of fact, without requiring proof of that fact.

You know by now from your study of evidence how broad this concept of adjudicative facts really is — potentially any fact relevant to a dispute under FRE 401 would be an adjudicative fact and *could be* subject to FRE 201. The real limits to the scope of this rule come from FRE 201(b), which sets forth the standards of certainty to which a judicially noticed fact must conform.

c.   The Scope of FRE 201(b): The Required State of Knowledge of Adjudicative Facts That May Be Judicially Noticed

If a party requests the court to take judicial notice of an adjudicative fact pursuant to FRE 201, the party must persuade the court that the fact satisfies the standards of FRE 201(b). The fact must be indisputable as defined by the rule; it must not be subject to "reasonable dispute." That indisputability can be established through either of two means. First, the fact may be the kind of fact that is "generally known within the territorial jurisdiction of the trial court." For example, in Goldblatt v. Fed. Deposit. Ins. Corp., 105 F.3d 1325, 1329 n.3 (9th Cir. 1999), the court took judicial notice of the interest bearing nature of money market accounts. By contrast, in Carley v. Wheeled Coach, 991 F.2d 1117, 1126 (3d Cir. 1993), the appellate court concluded that the trial court had erred in taking judicial notice of the "well known rollover propensities of vehicles having a high center of gravity." According to the court, "[m]ost people probably know little, if anything, about how high centers of gravity cause vehicular accidents." The parties thus had to produce evidence on this issue, and the jury would ultimately decide it.

The second way to establish indisputability is by reference to "sources whose accuracy cannot reasonably be questioned." For example, in United States v. Pozsgai, 999 F.2d 719, 731 (3d Cir. 1993), the appellate court held that the trial court had properly taken judicial notice of the fact that the Pennsylvania Canal was or could be used in interstate commerce. The status of the Canal in interstate commerce was established by two scholarly history books and a U.S. Army Corps of Engineers report. As a result, the parties needed to produce no evidence on this issue, and the jury was instructed as to its truth. If indisputability cannot be established under either of these standards, the factual issue is subject to proof at trial.

3.   Elaboration of FRE 201(a) and (b)

a.   *Further illustration of 201(b) standards*

IN RE THIRTYACRE
154 B.R. 497 (Bankr. C.D. Ill. 1993)

WILLIAM V. ALTENBERGER, Bankruptcy Judge.

[In a bench trial, a judgment creditor sought a finding from the Bankruptcy Court that the debt was nondischargeable as a willful and malicious injury, because it was based on a state court judgment that the debtor Thirtyacre had assaulted the creditor. The debtor Thirtyacre's defense was that his mental capacity to form an intent to act in a willful and malicious manner was impaired because he had been taking the drug Pamelor and drinking alcohol at the time of the assault. Thirtyacre asked the court to take judicial notice of the effects of Pamelor.] . . .

The first evidentiary issue is whether this Court should take judicial notice of the drug manufacturer's pamphlet for the drug Pamelor. This pamphlet contains sections entitled: Description, Actions, Indications, Contraindications, Warnings, Precautions, Adverse Reactions, Dosage and Administration, and How Supplied. The Defendant [Mr. Thirtyacre] asked this Court to take judicial notice of the definition of Pamelor. In effect he was asking this Court to take judicial notice of the matters in the pamphlet, including that the drug when taken with an excessive consumption of alcohol may have adverse consequences.

Rule 201 of the Federal Rules of Evidence governs judicial notice of adjudicative facts. . . .

Clearly the pamphlet does not fall within the scope of the rule. . . . It cannot be said that the effects of Pamelor when taken with an excessive consumption of alcohol are generally known within the jurisdiction of this Court. As stated in McCormick on Evidence:

> [T]he more reflective opinions speak in terms of the knowledge of "most men," or of "what well-informed persons generally know," or "the knowledge that every intelligent person has."

The information contained in the pamphlet does not fall within those standards.

Nor can it be said that the effect of the drug when taken with an excessive consumption of alcohol can be accurately or readily determined by resorting to the pamphlet. It is appropriate to take judicial notice of a proposition of science, but the Defendant's request does not fall within that category. Rather, the Defendant asks this Court to take judicial notice from the pamphlet of the effect on the Defendant of his using the drug while drinking. It does not follow from the pamphlet what the specific effect of the Defendant's use while drinking might be.

As the court stated in Clark v. South Central Bell Tel. Co. . . . :

> F.R.E. 201 states that facts may be noticed if they are "capable of accurate and ready determination by resort to sources whose accuracy cannot reasonably be questioned." For a Court to notice facts judicially, if they are not matters of general knowledge, the sources of those facts must be placed before the Court. If a party places the source before the

Court and requests judicial notice, the Court must take it if the facts are susceptible of judicial notice.

This standard of "indisputability" was discussed in Louisell & Mueller, Federal Evidence, §57, Rule 201, p.437:

Facts may be indisputable within the meaning of Rule 201 because (even though not generally known) they can be verified by resort to sources whose accuracy cannot reasonably be questioned. At one time courts indulged in the obvious fiction of consulting sources to refresh recollection, but it is clear enough that courts in reality simply inform themselves of facts which nobody is likely to carry around in his head from whatever sources the trial judge deems to be unquestionably accurate. Almanacs, encyclopedias, calendars, historical works and charts tabulating information deduced from the application of the laws of physics form only a part of what must be a list too long to be worth enumerating of sources to which a court may in proper circumstances resort for the purpose of deriving judicially noticeable information.

If the Defendant had submitted information regarding Pamelor that had been obtained from the FDA or a medical dictionary (as he represented it was), then perhaps it would have been admissible. But for this Court to find that the manufacturer's own representations regarding the drug are "sources whose accuracy cannot reasonably be questioned" within the meaning of FRE 201(b) goes far beyond any reported application of that rule. There is no element of objectivity with such an application. In United States v. Houston, . . . the court held that judicial notice could be taken of a two-page publication setting out information pertaining to the background, pharmacological information, pattern of use, and subjective effects of the drug phencyclidine, finding that the information was factual and could be readily obtained from the National Institute of Drug Abuse. The court in that case was willing to go beyond the record and do its own independent verification. In this Court's view, the burden is on the party seeking to have the court take judicial notice of the fact to put the sources before the court and establish their complete accuracy.

NOTES AND QUESTIONS

1. As Thirtyacre's lawyer, how would you state the proposition of fact that you would ask the court to judicially notice? Why is this an adjudicative fact?

2. If you sought judicial notice of this fact on behalf of Thirtyacre, what kind of information might you have attempted to present to satisfy FRE 201(b)? What kind of instruction, in a jury trial, would you request from the court if you were able to satisfy FRE 201? And what would you do if the court refused to take judicial notice of this fact?

b. Sources of Information Under FRE 201

The *Thirtyacre* opinion lists the kinds of sources of information that judges typically use to satisfy the "general knowledge" and "accurate and ready determination" standards of FRE 201(b). The more specifically the facts concern the individual litigant, the more difficult it is to satisfy these standards. Storm Plastics, Inc. v. United States, 770 F.2d

148, 155 (10th Cir. 1985) (trial judge improperly took judicial notice of the quality of plaintiff's fishing lures, as this fact was not generally known in the community nor one capable of accurate determination by plainly accurate sources). If sources are used to establish propositions of generalized background knowledge, then they must be well recognized. United States v. Simon, 842 F.2d 552, 555 (1st Cir. 1988) (trial judge not required to take judicial notice of the fact that Rastafarians use marijuana as part of their religion because this fact is not generally known and the offered sources — a 1967 dissertation and a 1960 research paper — were "hardly sources whose accuracy cannot reasonably be questioned"). And if judges take judicial notice of adjudicative facts on the basis of their own personal experience, they are likely to be reversed. United States v. Lewis, 833 F.2d 1380, 1384 (9th Cir. 1987) (judge erred in finding a confession to be involuntary by taking judicial notice of the effects of general anesthetic following an operation, relying on his own personal experience).

4.   Interpretation and Illustration of FRE 201(c), (d), and (e)

Subsection (c) of FRE 201 provides that a court *may* take judicial notice of a fact on its own initiative; the court may determine that a fact should be noticed, and it may obtain information from its own investigation to determine whether the standards of FRE 201(b) are met. The judge in *Thirtyacre* refused to engage in his own search for information concerning the indisputability of the Pamelor pamphlet. He held instead that "the burden is on the party seeking to have the court take judicial notice of the fact to put the sources before the court and establish their complete accuracy." This holding is consistent with FRE 201(c). Nothing in Rule 201 requires a court to take judicial notice by its own independent action. Under subsection (d), the court *must* take judicial notice of an adjudicative fact *only* when the party seeking notice has provided the information necessary to satisfy FRE 201(b). (The word "information" in FRE 201(d) is obviously just another way of saying evidence or sources of knowledge.) As the court points out in the *Thirtyacre* opinion, the defendant failed to do this. Under FRE 201(c) and (d), it is well within the power of the court to strictly enforce the moving party's burdens of production and persuasion.

FRE 201 contains only minimal direction for the court on the process to be followed before notice of an adjudicative fact is taken. Because of the close connection of these facts to the matters in dispute, they will usually have an immediate impact on the litigants' case. Therefore FRE 201(e) provides that a party, upon timely request, has the right to be heard on the "propriety of taking judicial notice and the tenor of the matter noticed." For example, if defendant Thirtyacre had produced scientific literature concerning the effects of taking Pamelor with alcohol, the plaintiff could have requested the opportunity to attack the accuracy of defendant's sources or to produce other contradictory information. This opportunity must be given upon the party's request whether the judge is operating under subsection (c) or (d) of the rule. Typically, however, a court will notify the parties that judicial notice may be taken and will set a date for objections to be filed. The "opportunity to be heard" does not necessarily mean the right to a formal hearing, particularly for the party urging the court to take judicial notice. American Stores v. Commission of Internal Revenue Service, 170 F.3d 1267 (10th Cir. 1999) (last sentence of FRE 201(e) implies special concern with right to *object* to the taking of judicial notice; proponent of judicial notice has no right to formal hearing; to the extent that proponent of judicial notice has right to be heard, trial court honored that right by considering proponent's briefs).

5.   Interpretation and Illustration of FRE 201(f) and (g)

a.   *Judicial Notice of Adjudicative Facts in Civil Cases: Mini Directed Verdicts*

Judicial notice of adjudicative facts has two major effects on the civil trial process: (1) It simplifies the jury's fact-finding role because it removes a fact from dispute and (2) it relieves a party both from the burden of producing evidence of the noticed fact to the jury and from the threat of having the jury hear contradictory evidence from the opponent. Remember that the party must present evidence *to the judge* that satisfies the standards of FRE 201(b). Once the judge decides that these standards are satisfied, the jury will be instructed that it must accept the noticed fact. The party's evidence need not be presented to the jury; the opponent may present no contradictory evidence; no closing argument need be made in support of the fact; and no argument can be made against it. In effect, the court is directing a verdict on the judicially noticed fact.

b.   *Judicial Notice of Adjudicative Facts in Criminal Cases: Judicial Comments*

As is evident in FRE 201(g), judicial notice in criminal cases poses somewhat different problems from judicial notice in civil cases. FRE 201(g) provides that "[i]n a criminal case, the court shall instruct the jury that it may, but is not required to, accept as conclusive any fact judicially noticed." It may seem contradictory to tell the jury that it "may" accept a fact that has been judicially noticed. After all, judicial notice is supposed to dispose of issues. The explanation for this apparent incongruity is that juries are given greater deference in criminal cases than in civil. Indeed, it is frequently said that there are no directed verdicts against criminal defendants, and as we have just observed, to take binding judicial notice of a fact is to direct a verdict on that fact. Thus treating judicial notice as binding would seem to conflict with the conventional view of the role of jurors in criminal cases. United States v. Mentz, 840 F.2d 315, 318 (6th Cir. 1988) (a conclusive instruction to the jury on a noticed fact in a criminal case is an error of constitutional magnitude).

FRE 201(g) responds to this concern about the role of juries by making judicial notice nonbinding in criminal cases. While this response may appear to be inconsistent with traditional notions of judicial notice, it is not an incoherent response. Rather, what FRE 201(g) does is to create an opportunity for judicial comment. See Chapter 10, Section C, supra. If the judge takes judicial notice in a criminal case, the judge will call the noticed fact to the jury's attention and instruct the jury that it *may* accept the noticed fact if it chooses to do so. For example, in United States v. Chapel, 41 F.3d 1338, 1339 (9th Cir. 1994), the trial judge took judicial notice that a bank's deposits were insured by the Federal Deposit Insurance Corporation. The appellate court approved of the instruction that was given:

> You may accept the court's declaration as evidence and regard as proved the fact or event which has been judicially noticed. You are not required to do so, however, since you are the sole judges of the facts.

Such an instruction allows the judge to comment on the obvious, the generally known, or the indisputable. And remember that under FRE 201(c) the court may take judicial notice on its own, subject of course to the opponent's right to be heard under FRE 201(e). In short, FRE 201 merely authorizes judges to comment on the obvious in criminal cases. There is nothing particularly mysterious about the last sentence of FRE 201(g) except its placement and its consequent peculiar wording. Instead of being part of a rule on judicial notice, perhaps it should be in a rule that deals with judicial comments.

At least two states treat judicial notice as nonbinding and, therefore, as a judicial comment even in civil cases. Conn. R. Evid. 201(e); Pa. R. Evid. 201(g).

c.   Timing of Judicial Notice

Pursuant to FRE 201(f), judicial notice may be taken at any time in the proceeding. This means that adjudicative facts may be noticed during pretrial proceedings, such as in a motion to narrow the scope of discovery or in a motion for directed verdict. In a jury trial, facts are usually noticed before the court gives its instructions so that the proper instructions may be given. In a bench trial, notice can be taken or refused at any time during the judge's deliberations, as was done in the *Thirtyacre* case.

   i.   Judicial Notice to Preserve Civil Verdicts.   At least in civil cases, courts may also take judicial notice after a case has been submitted to the jury, after the jury's verdict has been rendered, or on appeal, even if not requested during the trial. When there is a gap in a winning party's proof, judicial notice of that fact could be taken by either the trial court or the appellate court in order to protect the jury's verdict.

What should a judge do in such cases? If the gap in proof is discovered before the jury's verdict is rendered, the most attractive solution would be to open up the evidentiary process for evidence on that point. On occasion that course might be unavailable, however. For example, the gap may not become apparent until a party moves for a directed verdict after the jury has begun to deliberate. In addition, some states have rules forbidding the reopening of a case after a side has rested. In such cases, the trial judge must either grant the motion for a directed verdict or take judicial notice of the relevant fact.

If the jury's verdict has been rendered, the trial and appellate courts face a similar dilemma. Under the terms of FRE 201(f), it would seem that a court could notice such facts as long as the other criteria for judicial notice are satisfied. For example, in Gustafson v. Cornelius Co., 724 F.2d 75, 79 (8th Cir. 1983), the appellate court took judicial notice of an unfair labor practice charge for the purpose of determining the date at which a cause of action accrued; and in Havens Steel Co., v. Randolph Engin. Co., 813 F.2d 186 (8th Cir. 1987), the appellate court took judicial notice of the average annual prime interest rate in rejecting the defendant's claim that the proof of damages at trial had been too imprecise. But cf. Colonial Leasing Co. v. Logistics Control Group Int'l, 762 F.2d 454, 461, *modified*, 770 F.2d 479 (5th Cir. 1985) (where defendant relied on plaintiff's lapse of proof of its status as a creditor, and thus its failure to make a prima facie case, taking judicial notice after trial would raise due process concerns).

   ii.   Judicial Notice to Preserve Criminal Verdicts.   Some courts have taken the same verdict-saving approach in criminal cases in which prosecutors have failed to prove the facts necessary for federal jurisdiction. United States v. Lavender, 602 F.2d 639 (4th Cir. 1979) (court took judicial notice that the Blue Ridge Parkway was located in federal territory); United States v. Piggie, 622 F.2d 486, 487-488 (10th Cir. 1980). This approach is sound, it is argued, because it is consistent with the spirit of judicial notice to promote judicial efficiency by obviating the need for evidentiary proof of irrefutable facts.

But some courts have refused to take judicial notice in such circumstances and have rendered or upheld judgments of acquittal, on the grounds that FRE 201(g) plainly reflects Congress's intent to have the jury decide all issues of fact in criminal cases. See United States v. Jones, 580 F.2d 219 (6th Cir. 1978. In United States v. Dior, 671 F.2d 351, 358 n.11 (9th Cir. 1982), the prosecution failed to prove an essential element, that the goods had a value of $5,000 or more, because the evidence showed the value of the goods in Canadian dollars without any evidence of the U.S.-Canadian exchange rate., The appellate court refused to take judicial notice of the exchange rate in order to uphold the conviction:

> For a court, however, to take judicial notice of an adjudicative fact after a jury's discharge in a criminal case would cast the court in the role of a fact-finder and violate defendant's Sixth Amendment right to trial by jury. . . .
>
> Indeed, for a trial court (in a post-verdict motion) or an appellate court to take judicial notice of an adjudicative fact in a criminal case would frustrate the policies Congress sought to achieve in providing in F. R. Evid. 201(g) that a jury is not required to accept as conclusive a judicially noticed fact. These policies are to preserve the jury's traditional prerogative, in a criminal case, to ignore even uncontroverted facts in reaching a verdict and to prevent the trial court from violating the spirit of the Sixth Amendment right to counsel by directing a partial verdict as to facts. United States v. Jones, 580 F.2d at 223-224; . . . Another point: just because a fact may be generally known does not mean that the need to introduce evidence of that fact, or to request that it be judicially noticed, is dispensed with automatically. As Mr. Dooley once said: "Nuth'n walks itself into evidence."

It appears, therefore, that federal courts are somewhat ambivalent about the value of the constraints that FRE 201(g) appears to place on taking judicial notice of clearly indisputable facts in criminal cases. Several states with evidentiary codes based on the Federal Rules have rejected the last sentence of subsection (g) and provide for conclusive judicial notice in criminal cases. Ark. R. Evid. 201(g); Maine R. Evid. 201(g). It remains unclear, however, to what extent federal or state constitutional jury trial provisions may prohibit binding judicial notice that adversely affects a criminal defendant.

KEY POINTS

1. FRE 201 provides that courts may take judicial notice of adjudicative facts. Adjudicative facts are those facts that are usually decided by the jury.

2. Facts judicially noticed pursuant to FRE 201(b) must be established as certain beyond reasonable dispute, and this standard of certainty must be satisfied on the basis of general knowledge within the jurisdiction or from sources whose accuracy cannot reasonably be questioned.

3. In civil cases, the judge will instruct the jury that it must accept a judicially noticed fact as true. In criminal cases, the judge will instruct the jury that it may, but need not, accept the noticed fact as true.

4. Facts may be judicially noticed at any time, but if the winning party has failed to prove an essential element at trial, the taking of judicial notice to preserve the winning party's jury verdict may violate the constitutional rights of the opponent in both criminal and civil cases.

NOTES AND QUESTIONS

1. Although the second sentence of FRE 201(g) applies to criminal cases generally, the underlying concern is the supposed tension between binding judicial notice and a *criminal defendant's* right to jury trial. Compare FRE 201(g) with Md. R. Evid. 5-201(g), which makes judicial notice nonbinding only when the noticed fact is "adverse to the defendant."

2. Particularly in light of the fact that courts regularly direct verdicts against criminal defendants by not instructing juries on defenses for which there is insufficient evidence, why is it arguably unconstitutional for courts to take binding judicial notice in criminal cases? Should it matter whether the noticed fact is a jurisdictional matter (e.g., the location of the crime) or a substantive element (e.g., the value of stolen goods)?

3. Even if binding judicial notice adverse to criminal defendants is not unconstitutional, one may for prudential reasons want to avoid restricting the scope of the jury's fact finding role. If so, would it be preferable to ban any form of "judicial notice" that is adverse to criminal defendants? Consider whether a nonbinding judicial notice instruction like the one quoted at page 773, supra, is likely to contribute to the jury's rational decisionmaking.

4. Since the last sentence of FRE 201(g) calls for what is in effect judicial comment, does FRE 201 imply that all judicial comment in criminal prosecutions must satisfy the certainty requirements of FRE 201(b)?

PROBLEMS

11.1. Review the agricultural waste runoff hypothetical at the beginning of this chapter. What sources might the plaintiff rely upon to request that the court take judicial notice of the amount of rainfall that occurred in the region the year preceding the runoff event? Can the defendant object to judicial notice without having a reasonable basis to dispute the amount of rainfall asserted in plaintiff's request for judicial notice?

11.2. The ship S.S. *Norton* broke from its moorings and ran aground, releasing 200,000 barrels of crude oil into the ocean near Guam. The owner, Kramden, sued the captain and the charterers for negligence, arguing that mooring the ship in Guam during the month of November — the peak of the typhoon season — posed a great danger to both the cargo of oil and the environment. At trial, the judge is asked to take notice that Guam is seriously vulnerable to typhoons, and that the month of November is the peak of the typhoon season. Objection? What kind of sources might be found that would satisfy FRE 201(b)?

11.3. In imposing sanctions against an extremely litigious inmate and issuing an injunction against further filings without paying full filing fees, the trial judge made a finding of fact that the inmate had access to considerable sums of money. That finding was based in part on the judge's judicial notice of a local newspaper article describing the inmate as extremely wealthy and quoting him as saying that he had made thousands of dollars from his extortion activities in prison. Was taking judicial notice proper?

11.4. In an age discrimination suit against Acme Aircraft Corp., defendant claims that the reason plaintiff lost his job was inadequate performance and reduction in the workforce. To support the latter claim, the defendant presents the court with a newspaper article describing widespread layoffs at Acme and asks the court to take judicial notice of the contents of the article. What result?

11.5. In a suit against tobacco companies for injuries related to smoking, the defendants request that the court take judicial notice that since the late-1960s (when plaintiffs began smoking) the health hazards and the addictive nature of smoking have been common knowledge. Are these proper matters for judicial notice?

11.6. The United States brought a civil action against Dr. Jones to recover federal student loans that Jones had received from the National Health Service Corps. Dr. Jones allegedly breached his mandatory four-year contract of employment with a community health center. The issue at trial was whether Dr. Jones left the health center because of a salary dispute or whether he was terminated because of attendance and other problems, which would trigger an obligation to pay back his loans. The district court granted summary judgment in favor of the government by taking judicial notice of factual findings that Jones was terminated for attendance and other problems. These findings had been made in an order entered by another district court in a suit by Jones against the health center. Dr. Jones contests this result on appeal. What result?

11.7. Defendant is charged with assault within federal territory. After proof at trial that Raybrook Federal Prison was owned by the federal government, the district court gave the following instruction that removed the federal jurisdictional element from defendant's assault charge:

> The Government must prove the alleged assault took place within the special maritime and territorial jurisdiction of the United States. This simply means that the alleged assault must have occurred in any lands reserved or acquired for the use of the United States and under the exclusive or concurrent jurisdiction thereof. I charge you now that [Raybrook] is a place that falls within the territorial jurisdiction of the United States. Therefore, if you find beyond a reasonable doubt that the acted [sic] alleged occurred at [Raybrook], the sixth element of the offense has been met.

On appeal, defendant contends that this instruction violated FRE 201(g) and his constitutional right to be convicted by the jury on proof beyond a reasonable doubt. What result?

11.8. Plaintiff has sued defendants alleging that they participated in a scheme to defraud him through the fictitious sale of Nigerian crude oil. Plaintiff asks the trial court to take judicial notice of the following: (1) that at all times pertinent to the law suit, there were Nigerian fraud scams perpetrated on people in the United States and other countries in the world, and (2) that the fraud scams involved, among other things, oil deals that never materialized. To support this request for judicial notice plaintiff has provided the trial judge with a congressional report dated December 12, 1995, a Senate committee report, at least two newspaper articles, a videotape from the television news magazine "20/20," a videotape from the television news magazine "60 Minutes," and a videotape from the British Broadcasting Corporation. What result?

B. JUDICIAL NOTICE AS PART OF JUDICIAL DECISIONMAKING

In performing their judicial function, judges must take official account of propositions of law, of generalized knowledge, and of specific facts in many different contexts. Although the types of propositions, the sources from which they are established, and the uses to which they are put in judicial decisionmaking vary enormously, all of these judicial behaviors are sometimes called "taking judicial notice," even though FRE 201 does not — and often, as a practical matter, could not — apply. For example, if preliminary facts necessary to make admissibility decisions had to meet the certainty standard of FRE 201(b), much currently admissible evidence would be inadmissible. Similarly, if the factual premises underlying a court's interpretation of law had to meet the FRE 201(b) standard, it would be virtually impossible for courts to engage in the process of law interpretation. This section briefly discusses some of the contexts in which judges take official account of facts and of law — sometimes, but not always, under the guise of taking "judicial notice" — without the necessity of complying with FRE 201. As you can imagine, this loose and inconsistent usage of the term "judicial notice" occasionally creates confusion.

A caveat is in order about the materials that follow. Outside the area of adjudicative facts, the term *judicial notice* is most commonly associated with "legislative facts," which we discuss in subsection 2, infra. Keep in mind, though, that (1) there is nothing analytically significant about the use of the term judicial notice for any of the fact finding that we discuss here and (2) there is nothing analytically significant about the distinct categories of judicial fact finding that we describe here. Rather, the controlling and only analytically significant issue should be whether the judge is making a factual finding that would normally be made by a jury or whether the judge is making the finding for some other purpose. In the former situation FRE 201 applies; in the latter, it does not. If there is uncertainty about whether the finding is an adjudicative fact — that is, a "jury issue" — the uncertainty has nothing to do with judicial notice. Rather, the uncertainty is about application of the criteria for allocating fact finding generally between judge and jury.

For the leading scholarly critique of the limited scope of FRE 201 in light of these broader notions of "judicial notice," see Kenneth C. Davis, Judicial Notice, 1969 Law & the Soc. Order 513 (1969), and Dennis J. Turner, Judicial Notice and Federal Rule of Evidence 201 — A Rule Ready for Change, 45 U. Pitt. L. Rev. 181 (1983).

1. Judicial Cognizance of Common Knowledge Without Formal Judicial Notice

a. The Jury's General Background Knowledge

We know that when juries decide questions of fact they must rely on their own generalized knowledge and experience to make the inferences necessary to jury reasoning. The jury's background knowledge and experience are largely unexamined by the judicial system. In a few contexts, however, judges do consider what common generalized knowledge the jury can be assumed to have. This is sometimes called taking judicial notice of such common knowledge, although FRE 201 does not apply and the propositions relied on could not possibly satisfy the rule's standards of certainty. For example, when judges rule on questions of relevance in admitting evidence, they will occasionally articulate the generalized background knowledge that they assume the jurors can use to make the necessary inferences. And when there is a gap in proof to sustain a verdict, the court may find that, based on all the evidence, the jury's background knowledge could fill the gap. In United States v. Luckenbill, 421 F.2d 849 (9th Cir. 1970), the defendant was charged with forcing an accomplice to forge an endorsement on a government check in Spokane, Washington. No evidence was presented that the crime occurred in Spokane, which was necessary for venue. However, references in testimony to areas called "Nine Mile" and "Seven Mile" (areas known to be close to Spokane) were sufficient, the court held, to justify the jury in finding that the crime took place in Spokane.

b. Judges' Own Background Knowledge

When judges decide questions of fact, they must draw inferences on the basis of their own generalized knowledge and experience. Commentators sometimes refer to the process of using such background knowledge and experience as judicial notice:

> When the judge or jury use their pre-existing knowledge, they are said to be taking "judicial notice" of the facts thus utilized. Probably 99% of the judicial notice taken could be called "tacit" or "unconscious" judicial notice; that is, the process goes on without anyone being aware that reliance is being placed on extra-record facts. [21 Charles A. Wright and Kenneth W. Graham Jr., Federal Practice and Procedure §5102, at 460 (1990).]

As the Advisory Committee Note to FRE 201(a) makes clear, the rigors of FRE 201 do not apply: "It is apparent that this use of nonevidence facts in evaluating the adjudicative facts of the case is not an appropriate subject for a formalized judicial notice treatment." Unlike juries, however, judges must account for their decisions. Frequently, judges will articulate in their judicial opinions the background generalizations that they have used in their factfinding. Since FRE 201 does not apply, these generalizations are reviewed on appeal for their reasonableness. If reasonable, appellate courts will defer to the trial court's use of them under the deferential standard of "abuse of discretion." But what if a judge's background or experience is relatively unusual, giving the judge a unique factual perspective on the case? Should it be sufficient that the judge's fact finding is reasonable, or should any unique factual assumptions have to satisfy the certainty criteria of FRE 201(b)? Consider the analogous situation of a jurors' reliance on unique personal knowledge or their independent investigatory information. If the content of such knowledge or investigation is discovered and examined by the judge, it can lead to a mistrial or overturning of a verdict. If such independently obtained information is not general or common enough for the judge to assume that reasonable jurors already share it, then its injection into the jury room may violate the principles of public, adversarial proof-taking. In the now famous case of Thomas v. Kansas Power & Light Co., 340 P.2d 379 (Kan. 1959), for example, the court granted a new trial when it discovered that a juror had borrowed a book on electricity and had shared information on the arcing characteristics of electricity with other jurors.

2. Judicial Cognizance of Legislative Facts

Courts must make factual assumptions to decide law. Thus, judges take cognizance of propositions of fact when they interpret statutes (facts about legislative history or policy, or about how the statute affects the population) and when they develop principles of common law (facts about changed societal or economic conditions that justify a new legal rule). As an example, the Advisory Committee Note to FRE 201(a) cites the Supreme Court case of Hawkins v. United States, 358 U.S. 74 (1958), in which the Court relied on the following proposition to uphold the spousal testimonial privilege: If spouses testify against each other this would "be likely to destroy almost any marriage." Id. at 78. Another frequently cited example is the social science research, showing that segregation creates a feeling of inferiority, relied on in Brown v. Board of Education, 347 U.S. 483, 494 n.11 (1954), to hold that segregated schools are inherently unequal. These propositions are rarely indisputable, and they are necessary for judges to make sense of most questions of legal policy. It is clear from the text of the rule, and from the Advisory Committee Note, that FRE 201 does not apply to judges' use of such facts; and even the rules of evidence do not limit the materials that courts can use to resolve disputed issues of legislative fact.

Judges obtain information about these empirical propositions from their own research and from the parties, either at trial or in briefs to the court. Thus the parties often do have the opportunity to debate the propriety of the court's reliance on certain legislative facts. However, not all facts necessary to creating law or policy can be put "into a party-prepared record of evidence. Judges . . . cannot confine their thoughts to facts that parties have prepared in a formal record. . . ." 2 Kenneth C. Davis and Richard J. Pierce Jr., Administrative Law Treatise §10.5, at 142 (3d ed. 1994). When judicial use of disputable legislative facts is based on the judges' own independent research, the parties may be excluded from the decision-making process. Some commentators have found this to be troublesome:

> We do not claim that Judges cannot rely on a broad range of facts to force the law forward. We suggest only that the parties should be permitted to participate in the march. . . . If a fact or set of facts is likely to be critical to a decision on the law to be applied to parties, there is every reason to want the parties to be heard on the factual question. Evidence need not always be taken. Briefs may work better in many situations. But some chance for the parties to be heard on decisive legislative facts is desirable. [1 Stephen A. Saltzberg, Michael M. Martin, and Daniel J. Capra, Federal Rules of Evidence Manual 125 (7th ed. 1998).]

Although the Federal Rules do not expressly authorize judicial notice of legislative facts, the reality that courts must make factual assumptions to decide legal questions — under the rubric of "legislative fact" — has been recognized in numerous judicial decisions. Therefore the distinction between "adjudicative" and "legislative" facts can have significant practical impact on whether and how a party meets its burden of proof. Consider United States v. Gould, 536 F.2d 216 (8th Cir. 1976), in which the prosecution's expert failed to provide testimony that the cocaine hydrochloride found in defendants' possession was a derivative of coca leaves, as required to establish a violation of the drug laws then in force. The appellate court affirmed the conviction on the ground that the trial judge had permissibly taken judicial notice of a legislative fact. Not only did this obviate the need for expert testimony linking cocaine hydrochloride to cocaine, but the court could simply issue a jury instruction permitting the jury to so find without going through the formalities of FRE 201, which apply only to adjudicative facts:

> The precise line of demarcation between adjudicative facts and legislative facts is not always easily identified[.] "Legislative facts . . . do not relate specifically to the activities or characteristics of the litigants . . . ." Legislative facts are established truths, facts or pronouncements that do not change from case to case but apply universally, while adjudicative facts are those developed in a particular case.
>
> . . . . When a court attempts to ascertain the governing law in a case for the purpose of instructing the jury, it must necessarily rely upon facts which are unrelated to the activities of the immediate parties. These extraneous, yet necessary, facts fit within the definition of legislative facts and are an indispensable tool used by judges when discerning the applicable law through interpretation. The District Court, therefore, was judicially noticing such a legislative fact when it recognized that cocaine hydrochloride is derived from coca leaves. . . . [536 F.2d at 219-220.]

NOTES AND QUESTIONS

1. Was the result in *Gould* correct, or was the court struggling to resolve the tension created when indisputable facts are essential elements in criminal cases? How does one determine whether a fact is legislative or adjudicative? Should the result in *Gould* depend upon the generality or universality of the fact that cocaine hydrochloride is a derivative of coca leaves, the incongruity of giving a nonbinding judicial notice instruction, the intent of congress, or something else?

2. Reconsider the instruction given in Problem 11.7 at page 775. Is this instruction a violation of FRE 201(g)? Is the federal status of Raybrook prison an adjudicative or a legislative fact?

3. Consider again the case of United States v. Dior, discussed at page 773, supra. Could the American-Canadian exchange rate be classified as a legislative fact under *Gould*? If not, then could the jurors be permitted to find that the illegally imported goods (worth $13,690 in Canadian dollars) were worth $5,000 or more in U.S. currency, based on their own generalized knowledge? The dissent in *Dior* suggested they could:

> [T]he only issue is whether the jurors could find beyond a reasonable doubt that $13,690 Canadian dollars equaled $5,000 American dollars at the time of the theft.
>
> Seattle, the place of trial, is approximately 100 miles from the long Canadian border. The two countries share a long history of cultural, personal and trade relations sustained and encouraged by easy and warm reciprocal travel on many levels. They interconnect by multi-lane superhighways. Out of this proximity and close relationship the jurors, as people of both countries everywhere, could easily have possessed the elementary and practical knowledge of the worth of Canadian currency. [671 F.2d at 359.]

4. What if a frustrated juror deciding the *Dior* case looked up the American-Canadian exchange rate for the date of the alleged crime and reported this fact to the rest of the jury during deliberations? If Dior is convicted, is the juror's conduct grounds for a new trial? Would your answer be the same if the trial judge in a bench trial had looked up the exchange rate?

3.   Judicial Notice of Substantive Law

A court may "judicially notice," or is "presumed to know," the law of its own jurisdiction, which governs the cases before it. Obviously the judge investigates such law through traditional legal research. Questions of sister state and foreign law, however, have proved more troublesome. Common law rules required parties to plead and prove the content of such law. This requirement has been eliminated in the federal courts by Fed. R. Civ. P. 44.1 and Fed. R. Crim. P. 26.1, which commit the question of foreign law to the judge, whose "determination shall be treated as a ruling on a question of law," but many states still possess the common law rule.

KEY POINT

Courts use propositions of generalized knowledge in their own factfinding. Courts also use propositions of specific or general fact when interpreting legal standards and applying and developing rules of law. FRE 201 does not apply to judicial use of facts in these contexts.

C.   REFLECTION ON JUDICIAL NOTICE: CAN THE APPROPRIATE BOUNDS OF JUDICIAL NOTICE BE SPECIFIED WITH ANY CLARITY?

FRE 201's very high standards of certainty apply only to "adjudicative" facts. When the term "judicial notice" is used in other contexts, it is important to differentiate those contexts from adjudicative facts because FRE 201 need not be applied. Yet, as you will see in reading the following material, such differentiation is not always easy.

1.   Judicial Use of Background Knowledge

IN RE MARRIAGE OF TRESNAK
297 N.W.2d 109 (Iowa 1980)

McCORMICK, Justice.

This appeal involves a parental dispute over custody of two sons, Rick, age eleven, and Ryan, age nine. The parents are Emil James Tresnak (Jim) and Linda Lou Tresnak (Linda) who were married in 1965. In the August 1979 decree dissolving the marriage, the trial court awarded custody of the children to Jim. Linda appeals. We reverse and remand. . . .

In awarding custody of the children to Jim, the trial court said:

> The Petitioner at this time in life now desires to continue her education by attending law school at the University of Iowa. Although this is commendable insofar as her ambition for a career is concerned, in the opinion of the Court, it is not necessarily for the best

interest and welfare of her minor children, who are now ten and eight years of age. Anyone who has attained a legal education can well appreciate the time that studies consume. Although the Petitioner, during her undergraduate work, was able to care for the children while attending the Northeast Missouri University at Kirksville by studying after the children were placed in bed, the study of law is somewhat different in that it usually requires library study, where reference material is required. Also, other than time in class during the day, there will be study periods during the day in the library necessary, as well as in the evening, and which would necessarily require the children being in the hands of a babysitter for many hours a day when not attending school. The weekends are usually occupied by study periods, and although the Petitioner has a high academic ability, she will find that by reason thereof there will be additional activities bestowed upon her, such as becoming a member of a law review, which is time-consuming. Although the Petitioner may believe that she would not have to engage in such, she by not doing so would be interfering with her own achievements for her own benefit and welfare in future years.

The Respondent father has a stable position in the Chariton school system, president of the teachers' association, and, so far as known now, can remain in the Chariton schools for many years in the future. The Respondent's salary, though not exceptionally high, is adequate to maintain the children properly, and give them all the necessities of life. The Respondent father will be able to engage in various activities with the boys, such as athletic events, fishing, hunting, mechanical training, and other activities that boys are interested in. It would also be a benefit to the children if they were allowed to remain in the Chariton school system where they have attended school and have many friends and acquaintances. Placing custody with the Petitioner would require the children to be placed in the Iowa City school system for only a temporary time of three years, and again undoubtedly removed and placed in another system where the Petitioner would locate to practice her profession. . . .

I. THE TRIAL COURT'S ANALYSIS

In challenging the trial court's reasoning, Linda contends no evidentiary support existed for the court's assumptions about law school and the children's activities. She also contends the assumed facts are not a proper subject of judicial notice.

A. THE DEMANDS OF LAW SCHOOL

The only evidence about the demands of law school appeared in Linda's testimony. She acknowledged on cross-examination that law school would require many hours of study. However, she also said she did not expect to leave the children with babysitters often, she would take them to the library with her if necessary, and she did not believe her studies would interfere with her care of the children. Thus, while the record supports the trial court's inference that law school studies would occupy much of Linda's time, it does not lend much support to the court's statements about the necessity of library work away from the children, the likelihood of her involvement in extracurricular activities, or the effect of such factors on her care of the children.

Nor are these matters subject to judicial notice. "To be capable of being judicially noticed a matter must be of common knowledge or capable of certain verification." Motor Club of Iowa v. Department of Transportation, 251 N.W.2d 510, 517 (Iowa 1977). Courts are permitted to dispense with formal proof of matters which everyone knows. In this case, in overruling Linda's motion for new trial, the trial court defended its findings by asserting a "personal acquaintanceship with the studies of law school."

However, judicial notice "is limited to what a judge may properly know in his judicial capacity, and he is not authorized to make his (personal) knowledge of a fact not generally or professionally known the basis of his action." Bervid v. Iowa State Tax Commission, 78 N.W.2d 812, 816 (1956). It is common knowledge in the legal profession that law school studies are demanding and time-consuming, but the requirements of a specific law school curriculum are not generally or professionally known.

The trial court's statements about the necessity of extensive library study and likelihood of Linda's work on the law review at the University of Iowa law school are not matters of common knowledge or capable of certain verification within the meaning of the judicial notice principle. Because the statements have only tenuous support in the evidence, they are entitled to little weight in evaluating the merits of the custody dispute. In saying this, however, we do not suggest the court could not consider the demands of law school which were shown in the evidence. . . .

II. THE MERITS OF THE CUSTODY AWARD

Our review of the record is de novo. Although we give weight to the court's findings, we are not bound by them.

Because either parent would be a good custodian of the children, the decision on the merits is difficult. Linda and Jim are stable and responsible persons who love their children and are capable of giving them adequate care. . . .

The trial court believed Linda's pursuit of a legal education would be detrimental to the children's interests. We do not think the record bears out this concern. She very capably cared for the children during her undergraduate studies. During that time Jim did not complain of her ability to do so. Moreover, the children did not suffer when, by agreement of the parties, they lived with Linda and attended the Kirksville schools in the 1978-79 school year. No question existed about their moving again. The only issue was whether they would return to Chariton or accompany Linda to Iowa City.

Furthermore, no basis exists for characterizing Linda's law school years as unstable. She has demonstrated she can control the time she spends on her studies as well as Jim can control the time he spends on his work. Although she may move again when she finishes law school, this prospect differs little from Jim's readiness to move to a junior college teaching position if an opportunity arises.

It is common knowledge that in many homes today both parents have demanding out-of-home activities, whether in employment, school or community affairs. Neither should necessarily be penalized in child custody cases for engaging in such activities. In this case, Linda seeks a legal education for self-fulfillment and as a means of achieving financial independence. These goals are not inimical to the children's best interests. Because the record shows she is capable of continuing to provide the children with the same high quality of care she has given them in the past, her attendance at law school should not disqualify her from having their custody. We perceive no reason for believing she will not give the children excellent care during her law school years and thereafter.

. . . We believe the long-range best interests of the children will be better served if Linda has their custody. Therefore we reverse the trial court and remand to permit the court to enter appropriate orders relating to child support and visitation.

Reversed and remanded.

NOTES AND QUESTIONS

The appellate court's reliance in *Tresnak* on "common knowledge" seems somewhat ironic, given its discussion of the trial court's decision. What kind of facts had the trial court judicially noticed? Can you tell, based on the appellate opinion, whether FRE 201 should have applied if the action were in federal court? Or was the court taking cognizance of propositions of fact that were not adjudicative facts? Would you say that the real lesson of cases like *Tresnak* is that trial judges should not explain the basis of their reasoning if they wish to avoid being reversed? Is that a disturbing commentary on the legal system?

PROBLEMS

11.9. To establish the unavailability for the purpose of offering testimony pursuant to the declaration against interest exception to the hearsay rule, the defendant offers affidavits of several individuals who state that the declarant is living someplace in Milan. In ruling that the hearsay testimony is admissible the trial judge states, "On the basis of the uncontested affidavits I find that the declarant is living in Milan, and I take judicial notice of the fact that Milan is in Italy, far beyond the jurisdiction of this court." Following a verdict for the defendant, the plaintiff appeals on the ground that the trial judge's taking of judicial notice was improper. According to the plaintiff, the declar-ant's unavailability is subject to reasonable dispute because "Milan" could refer to the small farming community of Milan (pronounced MY-lan), which is only several miles away. Assuming that the hearsay testimony is critical to the defendant's defense, what result?

11.10. The local M&P Grocery Store has sued Harold Hays for food purchased on credit by his estranged wife, Stella. M&P bases its claim on a state statute that makes husbands liable for all "necessaries" purchased by their wives. It is clear from the statute that food falls within the category of necessaries. At trial M&P establishes that Stella did in fact make the purchases and that she was married to Harold at the time. Harold establishes that he did not authorize or benefit from any of the purchases. The judge takes the matter under advisement and eventually issues the following opinion:

> The statute was enacted at a time when husbands were the primary breadwinners; its purpose was to ensure that merchants would not deny wives the necessities of life. Today, we live in a much different world. I take judicial notice that the statute in question actually perpetuates the stereotypical notions of women as second class citizens. As a result I declare the statute unconstitutional under the state constitution's due process and equal protection provisions.

On appeal the plaintiff claims that the judicial notice was improper because the matter noticed does satisfy the certainty criteria in FRE 201(b). Plaintiff further claims that because there was no mention of the statute's possible unconstitutionality or the judicially notice fact at trial, plaintiff was denied the FRE 201(e) opportunity to be heard. What result?

11.11. Reconsider Problem 11.8 at page 775, where the plaintiff asked the court to take judicial notice of Nigerian fraud scams throughout the world. The problem is based on Qualley v. Clo-Tex Int'l, Inc., 212 F.3d 1123 (8th Cir. 2000). The trial judge granted the judicial notice request, and the jury returned a verdict for the plaintiff. The court of appeals, relying on *Gould* and quoting a portion of the excerpted passage, supra, held that the facts were legislative facts:

> The facts of which the trial court took judicial notice did not specifically concern the parties before the court. The trial court acknowledged that the evidence underlying the noticed facts "[had] to do with the pretty much universal publicity that was out about what Nigeria was doing...." The videotapes contained nothing involving anyone with whom [plaintiff] had communicated. Nor were the other exhibits considered "specific to... others [involved in the scheme...]."...Thus...[the facts] were "legislative" rather than "adjudicative," and were therefore outside the scope of [FRE 201]. [212 F.3d at 1128.]

The court of appeals then concluded that the trial judge's action was prejudicial error:

> [B]oth during the trial and in the final instructions, the trial court instructed the jury pursuant to Federal Rule of Evidence 201(g) that it must accept the judicially noticed facts as proven.3 Thus, the trial court injected legislative facts — facts not within the jury's fact-finding province — into the jury's deliberations by telling the jury that they must treat those facts as conclusively proven. [Id. at 1132.]

What do you think of the court's reasoning? the result?

11.12. Perez, an illegal alien, is seeking review of his denial of political asylum. The asylum request is based on his claim that if he is returned to his native country, he will be persecuted because of his religious affiliation. He claims to be a Jehovah's Witness. The immigration judge rejected Perez's asylum request on the ground that Perez had failed to establish the sincerity of his claim to religion and membership in the Jehovah's Witnesses. The judge's decision rested in part on the following: "In this proceeding Perez took the standard oath to testify truthfully. I take judicial notice that Jehovah's Witnesses are prohibited from swearing under oath." The judge went on to explain that "many Jehovah's Witnesses who have appeared before this court have declined to take the oath and have indicated that it is prohibited by their religion to swear under God or swear under oath." Was the judge's action proper?

11.13. In United States v. Jakobetz, 955 F.2d 786, 799-800 (2d Cir. 1992), the district court had conducted an extended hearing on the admissibility of DNA evidence against the defendant. The court heard nine experts, five for the government and four for the defense. The appellate court held:

> Given the findings made by the district court, and after careful consideration and review by this court, it appears that in future cases with a similar evidentiary issue, a court could properly take judicial notice of the general acceptability of the general theory and the use of these specific [laboratory] techniques....Beyond such judicial notice, the threshold for admissibility should require only a preliminary showing of reliability of the particular data to be offered....

Is this a proper application of FRE 201? Is the "general acceptance" (under *Frye*) or the "validity" (under *Daubert*) of the basic scientific theory and techniques underlying DNA profiling an adjudicative fact?

11.13. Lewis was convicted of carjacking in the Virgin Islands. The statute is applicable only to motor vehicles that have been "transported, shipped, or received in interstate or foreign commerce." To establish this element the prosecution relied on the testimony of Edgar Ames. Ames described himself as a police officer and lifelong resident of the Virgin Islands. He testified that no motor vehicles are manufactured in the Virgin Islands that all motor vehicles have to be shipped to the islands. On appeal Lewis claims that there is insufficient evidence of interstate or foreign commerce. He argues that Ames was not qualified to testify to this element merely because he was a lifelong resident of the Virgin Islands and that no foundation was laid for his testimony. In affirming the conviction, the court of appeals stated:

> We take judicial notice of the fact that the United States Virgin Islands consist of three main islands, which are closely grouped and have an area of only 136 square miles. We further take judicial notice of the fact that a police officer and life long resident of a place of this size has a sufficient basis to testify as to whether any motor vehicle manufacturing facilities are located there.

Was the court's action proper?

CHAPTER TWELVE

PRIVILEGES

A. *THE LAW OF PRIVILEGE*

1. A General Introduction

Most rules of evidence are designed to facilitate the fact-finding process, but rules creating evidentiary privilege are different. For the most part, they exclude relevant evidence in order to promote extrinsic policies unrelated to accurate factfinding. Their primary aim is to protect certain relationships and interests in the world outside the courtroom that are deemed of sufficient importance to justify the costs imposed on the judicial process through the loss of useful evidence.

The scope of privilege law is quite broad. Some privileges have a direct constitutional basis; examples are the Fifth Amendment privilege against self-incrimination (the Fourth Amendment exclusionary rule for evidence obtained as the result of an illegal search and seizure has aspects of a privilege) and the executive privilege claimed by various presidents of the United States. These rules typically are considered in criminal procedure and constitutional law courses and they will be addressed in this chapter only where they intersect with nonconstitutional privileges. Our main focus will be on evidentiary privileges with common law or statutory origins. Many of these privileges are designed to protect confidential communications, thereby encouraging the free flow of information in certain relationships. This group includes the most prevalent privileges: the attorney-client, physician-patient, priest-penitent, and marital communications privilege. Still other privileges are intended to prevent interference with certain favored relationships, such as the marital testimonial privilege. Finally, privileges also exist to protect against the disclosure of specific types of information, such as privileges for the identity of news reporters' sources, diplomatic secrets, and other sensitive government information (the identity of informants is an example).

The traditional justification for rules of privilege is the utilitarian argument espoused by Dean Wigmore. This argument has been most commonly advanced in support of the confidential communication privileges. It is based on an underlying, untested empirical assumption: The benefit derived from recognizing a privilege — such as open communication between attorney and client or between spouses — outweighs the cost of barring relevant evidence. The argument rests on an empirical assumption about how the existence of the privilege affects individual behavior. Without the protection of the privilege, Wigmore argued, communication will be impeded and certain relationships, such as attorney-client and physician-patient, will be jeopardized. This justification has been widely accepted by the courts and has greatly influenced the development of the law of privilege. Wigmore's conditions for the establishment of a privilege flow directly from his justification for privileges: (1) the communications must originate in a *confidence* that they will not be disclosed; (2) the element of *confidentiality must be essential* to the full and satisfactory maintenance of the relation between the parties; (3) the *relation* must be one that in the opinion of the community ought to be *sedulously fostered*; and (4) the injury that would inure to the relation by the disclosure of the communications must be *greater than the benefit* thereby gained for the correct disposal of the litigation. 8 John Henry Wigmore, Evidence §2285, at 527 (John T. McNaughton rev. 1961).

In recent years, a distinct privacy-based rationale has emerged for certain privileges. Rather than focus on the inducement of conduct in certain relationships, the privacy argument emphasizes the protection that privileges afford to individual privacy. According to this rationale, the confidentiality of communications is a privacy interest that itself acts as a legitimate constraint on the truth-finding function of trial. An advocate of the privacy rationale would argue, for example, that the existence of a marital communications privilege may have little if any impact on the extent to which spouses engage in confidential communications; nonetheless, the privilege is desirable because it provides some recognition of and protection for the privacy of intimate aspects of the marital relationship. For an argument reconciling the traditional utilitarian justification and the privacy rationale, see Developments in the Law — Privileged Communications, 98 Harv. L. Rev. 1450, 1481-1486 (1985).[1] The existence and scope of privileges vary from jurisdiction to jurisdiction. Under FRE 501 (reproduced in subsection 3, infra), federal common law governs the privileges applicable in federal question and criminal cases, while state law determines the privileges applicable in diversity actions. In state courts and in federal cases applying state law, the law of privilege is a varied collection of rules, created mostly by the state legislatures.

2. The Unique Operation of Privilege Rules

Regardless of the particular justification, rules of privilege operate differently from other rules of evidence in at least two and sometimes three respects. First, since the objective of the privilege would be frustrated by forced disclosure of privileged information at any time, the rules of privilege apply to all stages of judicial proceedings. Other rules of evidence are designed primarily to enhance the accuracy of factfinding, particularly in jury trials, and they therefore do not apply to various preliminary or relatively informal aspects of the adjudicatory process. For example, FRE 1101 provides that the rules of evidence, other than those relating to privileges, do not apply to

---

1.   In Chapter Four we noted that similar utilitarian and nonutilitarian justifications provide partial support for some of the relevance rules. See page 233-235, supra.

FRE 104(a) preliminary fact determinations, grand jury proceedings, and other specified, relatively informal proceedings.

Second, the person who can claim or invoke a rule of privilege to exclude evidence will not necessarily be one of the litigants. Because the rules of evidence other than the rules of privilege are designed to enhance the fact-finding process, they exist for the benefit of and may be invoked only by the parties to the dispute. By contrast, rules of privilege exist for the benefit of the persons whose communications or actions are covered by a privilege. Only these intended beneficiaries of a privilege (or persons acting on their behalf), who need not be parties to the action, can claim or forego a privilege.

The third way in which rules of privilege sometimes differ — and perhaps should always differ — from other evidentiary rules relates to the impact on appeal of an erroneous trial court decision regarding admissibility of allegedly privileged information. If the trial judge erroneously excludes the evidence, the party who would have benefited from the evidence will be able to raise the improper exclusion on appeal. As is true whenever a judge erroneously excludes relevant evidence, the exclusion deprives the fact finder of information that would have enhanced the likelihood of a factually accurate result; this type of error, if serious enough, can be cured on appeal by reversal and retrial. And if a trial judge erroneously admits evidence, inflammatory character evidence for example, the result often is to interject prejudicial or misleading information into the trial.

By contrast, a trial judge's erroneous admission of privileged information results in the jurors having before them more relevant, helpful information than they would otherwise have had. The only impact of such an error is to enhance the likelihood of a factually accurate result. Thus, even if the person entitled to invoke the privilege happens to be one of the litigants, the injury from the erroneous admission of the evidence does not adversely affect the person's legitimate interests *as a litigant*. Moreover, the injury caused by the wrongful denial of the privilege is complete at the time the privileged information is presented to the fact finder. Reversal on appeal cannot unring the bell. Unless there is reason to believe that the possibility of reversal on appeal is a desirable way to make litigants and trial judges more sensitive to and more prone to accept claims of privilege, the error should not be grounds for reversal. And if the erroneous denial of a privilege claim is recognized as a possible ground for reversal on appeal, it should make no difference whether the person entitled to claim the privilege happens to be one of the litigants. Nonetheless, appellate courts on occasion entertain such grounds for reversal, particularly in situations in which the appellant is also the primary beneficiary of the privilege, but they typically do not analyze carefully what interests are being vindicated.

3. Historical Background and Current Status of Privilege Rules

The earliest recognized privileges, the attorney-client and marital privileges, were judge-made.[2] The attorney-client privilege, which has Roman law roots, finds its first expressions in the common law in the sixteenth century. The privilege of a witness

---

2. For a more comprehensive historical analysis, see 21 Charles A. Wright and Kenneth W. Graham Jr., Federal Practice and Procedure: Evidence §5001-5005 (1977 & Supp. 2001), and Lawrence Meir Friedman, A History of American Law 134-137 (1973).

spouse not to testify against a party spouse, which we will refer to as the marital testimonial privilege, also dates back to the sixteenth century. The origins of this privilege are obscure, although the privilege is frequently associated with the general common law rule of competency that prevented interested parties from testifying as witnesses. By contrast, the privilege for confidential communications between spouses received wide recognition in the latter part of the nineteenth century, and it is frequently said to have common law origins. The privilege, however, received substantial support and recognition through legislative action both in this country and in England. We discuss these two privileges in Section D, infra.

During the last half of the nineteenth century, courts became increasingly reluctant to expand existing privileges or to create new ones. Since that time the fashioning of privileges has become primarily — but not exclusively — a legislative matter. For example, both the physician-patient and the priest-penitent privileges are creatures of the legislature, not the common law. As a result of such statutory revision of evidence law, privilege law varies widely from state to state.

Significantly, a detailed law of privileges has not been codified by the Federal Rules of Evidence. As drafted by the Advisory Committee and proposed by the Supreme Court, the Proposed Federal Rules of Evidence set forth nine discrete privileges governing: i) required reports; ii) attorney-client confidential communications; iii) psychotherapist-patient confidential communications; iv) prevention of spousal testimony; v) clergy-communicant confidential communications; vi) political vote; vii) trade secrets; viii) state secrets and other official information; and ix) the identity of an informer.[3] Noticeably absent were the physician-patient, marital confidential communication, and journalist's privileges. Moreover, Proposed FRE 501 made it clear that, in the absence of a constitutional mandate, courts were not at liberty to alter the list.

Once submitted to Congress, the proposed rules excited considerable controversy and criticism, culminating in a congressional decision to delete the proposed rules relating to privilege. In its place, Congress enacted one general privilege rule, FRE 501:

> Except as otherwise required by the Constitution of the United States or provided by Act of Congress or in rules prescribed by the Supreme Court pursuant to statutory authority, the privilege of a witness, person, government, State, or political subdivision thereof shall be governed by the principles of the common law as they may be interpreted by the courts of the United States in the light of reason and experience. However, in civil actions and proceedings, with respect to an element of a claim or defense as to which state law supplies the rule of decision, the privilege of a witness, person, government, State, or political subdivision thereof shall be determined in accordance with state law.

At the same time, Congress revoked the Supreme Court's rule-making power with respect to rules of privilege. This new Enabling Act stated that "[a]ny . . . amendment creating, abolishing, or modifying a privilege shall have no force or effect unless it shall be approved by act of Congress." 28 U.S.C. §2076 (1976). Thus FRE 501 created a bifurcated system of privilege rules. In the situations in which state law supplies the rule of decision, such as diversity cases, state rules of privilege apply even though the case is in federal district court. In the situations in which federal law governs, the common law determines the applicable rules of privilege.

---

3. See Proposed FRE 502-510 and Advisory Committee Notes, 51 F.R.D. 260-280 (1971).

This system is designed to protect state policies concerning privilege, but it does so only to a degree. If a case is not based on state law, state privileges do not apply, and information that a state would immunize from disclosure will be disclosed unless there is a corresponding federal privilege (which often times there is not). For an example, see United States v. Schenheinz, 548 F.2d 1389 (9th Cir. 1977). Cases involving supplemental jurisdiction (pendent and ancillary jurisdiction) can pose particular problems, because the same case will have both federal and state claims. The typical resolution is to apply federal privilege law to all claims. See Hancock v. Hobbs, 967 F.2d 462 (11th Cir. 1992).

In contrast to the proposed rules, FRE 501 provides for fluidity in the federal law of privilege. FRE 501's reference to "principles of the common law ... interpreted ... in light of reason and experience" grants courts discretion both to modify common law privileges and to create new ones:

> In rejecting the proposed rules and enacting Rule 501, Congress manifested an affirmative intention not to freeze the law of privilege. Its purpose rather was to "provide the courts with the flexibility to develop rules of privilege on a case-by-case basis" and to leave the door open to change. [Trammel v. United States, 445 U.S. 40, 47 (1980), quoting Statement by Representative Hungate, 120 Cong. Rec. 40,891 (1974).]

In accordance with this mandate the Supreme Court, as we shall see shortly, has substantially narrowed the scope of one common law privilege,[4] and the Supreme Court and lower courts have recognized new privileges.[5] Although courts have referred to the proposed rules in deciding privilege questions, such rules have not controlled the development of the federal law of privileges.

Although well over half of the states, 41 to date, have adopted rules of evidence modeled after the Federal Rules, the failure of Congress to enact specific rules of privilege has contributed to less uniformity among the states in this area of evidence law. Approximately one-third of the states that have promulgated rules of evidence since the adoption of the Federal Rules have followed their lead and omitted specific privilege provisions. In these states the preexisting statutory and common law rules of privilege govern. Most of the remaining states have tended to use as models the Proposed Federal Rules relating to privilege or the privilege provisions in the Revised Uniform Rules of Evidence (1974). The Revised Uniform Rules are themselves based on the Proposed Federal Rules, but the Revised Uniform Rules differ in some important respects.[6] States using either model have not been reluctant to deviate from it.[7] Within the fluid, bifurcated system of privilege rules, new privileges can spread among jurisdictions, gradually gaining or losing recognition over time. An interesting example of a privilege not recognized at common law but slowing gaining acceptance is the

---

4. See Trammel v. United States, page 848, infra.
5. See, e.g., Jaffee v. Redmond, 518 U.S. 1 (1996) (recognizing psychotherapist-patient privilege — *Jaffee* is reproduced at page 857, infra); In re Grand Jury Investigation, 918 F.2d 374 (3d Cir. 1990) (recognizing clergy-communicant privilege; In re Microsoft Corporation, 162 F.3d 708 (1998) (acknowledging similarity of academic research and work product of journalists, thus recognizing limited scholar's privilege); In re Zuniga, 714 F.2d 632 (6th Cir.) (acknowledging but not applying psychotherapist-patient privilege); In re Agosto, 553 F. Supp. 1298 (D. Nev. 1983) (recognizing parent-child privilege).
6. See generally 3 Jack B. Weinstein and Margaret A. Berger, Weinstein's Federal Evidence §§501.02-501.04 (Joseph M. McLaughlin, ed., Matthew Bender, 2d ed. 1997).
7. See generally 1 Gregory P. Joseph and Stephen A. Saltzburg, Evidence in America: The Federal Rules in the States ch. 23-24 (1987).

parent-child privilege. Under Wigmore's utilitarian test and the privacy-based rationale discussed above, this privilege has obvious appeal. There is currently no federal
parent-child privilege but a few states recognize some form of the privilege and it seems
to be gaining support with federal legislators. See Section G of this chapter, infra, for a
discussion of the evolution of the parent-child privilege.

B. GENERAL STRUCTURE OF PRIVILEGES

1. Holder of the Privilege

A critically important concept in dealing with rules of privilege is that of "holder"
of a privilege. The holder is the person to whom in a sense the privilege "belongs."
Since the attorney-client relationship exists for the benefit of the client, for example,
the client is the holder of the privilege. The holder is entitled to claim the privilege and
only the holder may waive a privilege. Once the holder has waived a privilege, no other
person can invoke it.

The person who holds a privilege will not necessarily be one of the litigants.
Nonparty witnesses may hold privileges that allow them to withhold evidence. Jurisdictions sometimes differ as to who holds a given privilege. Within the marital privilege, for example, the holder may be the spouses jointly, the communicating spouse,
the witness spouse, or the party spouse. Section D, infra, discusses some of the reasons
behind, and the implications of, locating the marital privilege with one or both
spouses.

2. Invocation

A person other than the holder may be able to invoke the privilege on the holder's
behalf. For example, a nonparty eyewitness to the event that is the subject of litigation
may have made a confidential communication to his or her attorney for the purpose of
obtaining legal advice about the event. The out-of-court communication of some
historical fact, of course, is hearsay, but the communication may fall within a hearsay
exception. Assume, for example, that the declaration is an excited utterance, or that the
declarant is presently unavailable and the communication is a declaration against
interest. The nonparty declarant may invoke the privilege; and in the absence of the
declarant, the declarant's attorney may invoke the privilege *on behalf of* the declarant.
If the declarant has expressed a desire not to claim the privilege, however, nobody can
invoke the privilege.

Typically, if the holder of a privilege is unavailable to claim the privilege, individuals acting on behalf of the holder or the holder's estate, such as the holder's
conservator or guardian, may claim the privilege. In the case of privileges covering
conversations between a patient or client and a professional, the professional may
claim the privilege on behalf of the patient or client. For example, in the physician-
patient relationship, if the patient-holder has not specifically waived the privilege, the
doctor may be able to claim the privilege on the patient's behalf. In some instances, as
in the attorney-client relationship, the professional is obligated by rules of professional
conduct to maintain confidentiality where the client has not expressed an intent to

waive his privilege. In addition, there is precedent permitting the trial judge to invoke a privilege on behalf of an absent holder.[8] Interesting questions sometimes arise when the holder of the privilege is an entity, such as a corporation or governmental agency, rather than an individual. In Nixon v. Administrator of General Services, 433 U.S. 425 (1977), the former President sought to invoke the executive privilege "against the very Executive Branch in whose name the privilege is invoked." The Presidential Recordings and Materials Preservation Act required the former President to deliver presidential papers and tape recordings to an archivist of the Executive Branch to be screened and cataloged. Nixon resisted turning the materials over and invoked the presidential privilege. The Supreme Court held that the "privilege survives the individual President's tenure" but that the expectation of the confidentiality of executive communications is "subject to erosion over time after an administration leaves office." Though the Court allowed Nixon to invoke the privilege on behalf of the government, it upheld the act as facially constitutional because the screening by the archivist would be but a "limited intrusion by personnel in the Executive Branch sensitive to executive concerns." It is unclear whether the former President would have been allowed to invoke the privilege if the Office of the President had attempted to waive it.

In the corporate setting, some courts have struggled with whether an attorney may invoke the attorney-client privilege on behalf of the client-corporation when shareholders seek disclosure of communications between corporate officers and corporate attorneys. In Fausek v. White, 965 F.2d 126 (6th Cir. 1992), the defendant and majority shareholder of the corporation, Robert E. White, appealed from a district court judgment denying his claim of attorney-client privilege in an action alleging securities violations. The plaintiffs, former shareholders, brought suit against White alleging that he had abused his position to their financial detriment. The plaintiffs subpoenaed the corporation's attorney to testify about communications he had had with White but the attorney resisted, asserting the attorney-client privilege on behalf of the corporation. The appellate court affirmed the lower court, holding that the corporation could not claim the attorney-client privilege because it owed fiduciary duties to the plaintiffs and the latter had shown "good cause" for not permitting defendant to rely on the privilege.

The court provided a long list of factors for determining whether there is "good cause" to recognize an exception to the attorney-client privilege, including the

> number of shareholders and the percentage of stock they represent; . . . the nature of the shareholders' claim and whether it is obviously colorable; the apparent necessity or desirability of the shareholders having the information and the availability of it from other sources; . . . the extent to which the communication is identified versus the extent to which the shareholders are blindly fishing; the risk of revelation of trade secrets or other information in whose confidentiality the corporation has an interest for independent reasons.

The Fifth Circuit took a similar approach in Garner v. Wolfinbarger, 430 F.2d 1093 (5th Cir. 1970), and Ward v. Succession of Freeman, 854 F.2d 780 (5th Cir. 1988), but the Ninth Circuit refused to recognize the exception in Weil v. Investment/

---

8.   See, e.g., Coles v. Harsch, 129 Or. 11, 30-31, 276 P.2d 248, 255 (1929). Judge Weinstein and Professor Berger have suggested that this is an inherent judicial power that is not abrogated by the failure of a rule specifically to mention the authority of the judge to act on the holder's behalf. 3 Jack B. Weinstein and Margaret A. Berger, Weinstein's Federal Evidence §503.20[3] (Joseph M. McLaughlin, ed., Matthew Bender 2d ed. 1997).

Indicators, Research & Management, 647 F.2d 18 (9th Cir. 1981). For further discussion, see Keith W. Johnson, Fausek v. White: The Sixth Circuit Garners Support for a Good Cause Exception to the Attorney-Client Privilege, 18 Dayton L. Rev. 313 (1993).

Another related subtlety of privileges is the ability of third parties to invoke them after the holder's death. Though confidential communications privileges are generally thought to survive the death of a holder, they may not always be invoked. The personal representative of the deceased, for example, may choose not to invoke the privilege; or an attorney may be deprived of the opportunity to invoke a privilege by the commonly recognized exception to the attorney-client privilege for communications "relevant to an issue between parties who claim through the same deceased client." Proposed FRE 503(d)(3).

The Supreme Court acknowledged the importance of maintaining the attorney-client privilege after a client's death in Swidler & Berlin v. United States, 524 U.S. 399 (1998). The Court allowed Deputy White House Counsel Vince Foster's attorney to invoke the attorney-client privilege on Foster's behalf after Foster committed suicide. The government sought to obtain notes from Foster's attorney that were taken in a meeting between the two, nine days before Foster's death. The Court held that an attorney's notes from his meeting with his client are privileged and immune to a federal grand jury subpoena. The dissent agreed that attorney-client privilege ordinarily survives the death of the client, but emphasized that the common law also dictates that privileges should be construed narrowly. In this criminal investigation into wrongdoings in the White House, the dissent stated, the "paramount value" of our criminal justice system — the protection of an innocent defendant — should "outweigh a deceased client's interest in preserving confidence." For further discussion of the case see Michael Stokes Plausen, Dead Man's Privilege: Vince Foster and the Demise of Legal Ethics, 68 Fordham L. Rev. 807 (1999) (arguing that the Supreme Court ignored the complexity of the case and instituted a broader rule than is supported by policy or precedent).

3. Scope and Limits

Each privilege has a particularized scope; it covers some things but not others. The confidential communications privileges, for example, extend only to confidential communications. If an unnecessary third party is present during a conversation between lawyer and client or husband and wife, the conversation will not be privileged. Another example: The attorney-client privilege extends only to communications for purposes of obtaining legal advice. If a person who happens to be, or who becomes, a client communicates with a lawyer for some other purpose, the communication is not privileged. Similarly, conversations between clergy and their flock are only privileged if in a confessional, or perhaps counseling, situation.

Privileges may also be limited by the potential benefit and harm to the litigants. While most of the confidential communications privileges are immune to claims of need by the opposing party, privileges to protect disclosure of specific types of information are often less secure. When considering whether to protect the identity of an informant, for example, a court may balance the importance to the defendant of the informant's testimony against the government's interest in resisting disclosure. See United States v. Fischer 531 F.2d 783 (5th Cir. 1976). Similarly, scholars enjoy a privilege limited by a party's nonfrivolous claim of need and inability to otherwise obtain the information. See In re: Microsoft Corporation, 162 F.3d 708 (1st Cir. 1998).[9]

4. Waiver

The holder of a privilege may waive the privilege in at least four different ways. First, the holder may indicate through words or conduct a desire to forego the privilege. Second, if the holder refrains from invoking the privilege, the failure to assert the privilege typically will be regarded as a waiver. Third, the voluntary disclosure of the confidential communication, such as a client discussing legal advice he received from his attorney with a third person, will constitute a waiver. Voluntary disclosure of a confidential communication in the context of another privileged communication will not result in waiver. For instance, if a person, in the presence of his spouse, made a confidential statement to his attorney that was covered under the attorney-client privilege, the marital communication privilege would preclude the waiver of the attorney-client privilege. Proposed FRE 511 captured well this aspect of the common law:

> A person upon whom these rules confer a privilege against disclosure of the confidential matter or communication waives the privilege if he or his predecessor while holder of the privilege voluntarily discloses or consents to disclosure of any significant part of the matter or communication. This rule does not apply if the disclosure is itself a privileged communication.

With respect to waiver by disclosure, it is important to note that the voluntary disclosure must be a disclosure of *the confidential communication itself.* A voluntary statement — either as a witness or in a casual conversation — of facts that were the subject of the communication is not a waiver of the privilege. The privilege protects solely the confidential communication, not the facts. For example, if a patient discussed a crime that she had committed in a confidential session with her psychotherapist, but she later voluntarily confessed the facts of the crime to a third party, the communication with the psychotherapist would still be privileged, as long as she did not disclose what she had actually communicated to the therapist.

Fourth, waiver may also occur through asserting a claim based on privileged information. "Waiver by claim assertion" of privileged materials has been generally recognized as requiring disclosure when a party "asserts a claim that in fairness requires examination of protected communications." United States v. Bilzerian, 926 F.2d 1285, 1292 (2d Cir. 1991). For example, in In re Grand Jury Proceedings, 350 F.3d 299, 305 (2d Cir. 2003), the Second Circuit held that where a letter was sent by a corporation to a U.S. attorney explaining that it had been told by federal agents that its actions were legal, there was no unfairness to the government and thus the company did not waive its privilege as a result of placing its claims at issue. In contrast, a party who asserts that action was taken on the advice of counsel waives the attorney-client privilege with respect to those communications. For example, in U.S. v. Cohn, 303 F. Supp. 2d 672,

---

9.   See also Nixon v. United States, 418 U.S. 683 (1974) (claim of absolute executive privilege for presidential communications will not prevail over demonstrated need for particular evidence); Dellwood Farms v. Cargill, Inc., 128 F.3d 1122 (7th Cir. 1997) (law enforcement investigatory privilege not absolute, rather surmountable by strong showing of need).

681 (D. Md. 2003), the court held that an investment company indicted for mail and wire fraud waived its attorney-client privilege after its general counsel raised an advice of counsel defense in his opening statement at trial.

5.   Exceptions

Each privilege has a set of exceptions that are derived from the underlying policies the particular privilege is created to serve. For example, the attorney-client privilege does not extend to communications in furtherance of a crime or fraud. The purpose of the privilege is to facilitate the giving of legal advice with respect to presently existing legal problems and to assist a client in conforming to the dictates of the law; its purpose is not to facilitate transgressions of the law. Similarly, the marital privileges do not apply in cases of alleged spousal abuse and the priest-penitent privilege does not apply when child abuse has been alleged. Again, these privileges are designed to preserve relationships, not to encourage assaultive behavior.

6.   Drawing Adverse Inferences from Invoking a Privilege

In Griffin v. California, 380 U.S. 609 (1965), the Supreme Court held that allowing comment on the defendant's decision not to testify violated his Fifth Amendment privilege against self-incrimination "by making its assertion costly." Proposed FRE 513 applied the *Griffin* rationale to the law of privileges generally:

(a) Comment or inference not permitted. The claim of a privilege, whether in the present proceeding or upon a prior occasion, is not a proper subject of comment by judge or counsel. No inference may be drawn therefrom.

(b) Claiming privilege without knowledge of jury. In jury cases, proceedings shall be conducted, to the extent practicable, so as to facilitate the making of claims of privilege without knowledge of the jury.

(c) Jury instructions. Upon request, any party against whom the jury might draw an adverse inference from a claim of privilege is entitled to an instruction that no inference may be drawn therefrom.

Presently, there appears to be no general *constitutional* rule barring comment on a party's invocation of a confidential communications privilege, and the case law is divided[10] as to the propriety of comment about invoking privileges outside the *Griffin* context.[11] Cases allowing comment frequently draw an analogy to the long-established practice of permitting comments on and drawing adverse inferences from the destruction of evidence or the failure to produce available witnesses or documents. In contrast, cases barring comment echo *Griffin's* concern that comment or adverse inferences undermine the privilege.

---

10.   See 3 Jack B. Weinstein and Margaret A. Berger, Weinstein's Federal Evidence §513.04 (Joseph M. McLaughlin, ed., Matthew Bender 2d ed. 1997).

11.   *Griffin* itself applies only to comments regarding a criminal defendant's invocation of the privilege in a criminal prosecution. See Baxter v. Palmigiano, 425 U.S. 308 (1976); Brink's, Inc. v. City of New York, 717 F.2d 700 (2d Cir. 1983).

7. Constitutional Limitations on Privilege

The Sixth Amendment creates constitutional limits on privileges in criminal prosecutions. If a privilege is claimed by a witness from whom a criminal defendant seeks to elicit testimony, the privilege directly conflicts with the defendant's rights under the Compulsory Process and Confrontation Clauses. Various Supreme Court decisions have explored whether a claim of privilege must yield when a defendant either needs to present the privileged evidence in his defense or needs to introduce the privileged evidence to impeach the government's testimony; other opinions have explored the limits of privilege, such as the executive privilege, when opposed to a legitimate governmental investigation.[12] Privileges that impede a defendant's rights or governmental investigation may be unconstitutional, in violation of the Sixth Amendment or the due process clause of the Fourteenth Amendment,[13] or not recognized as a matter of the common law development of privileges.

C. THE ATTORNEY-CLIENT PRIVILEGE

1. Elements of the Privilege

A good statement of the modern attorney-client privilege is contained in Proposed FRE 503:

(a) Definitions. As used in this rule:

(1) A "client" is a person, public officer, or corporation, association, or other organization or entity, either public or private, who is rendered professional legal services by a lawyer, or who consults a lawyer with a view to obtaining professional legal services from him.

(2) A "lawyer" is a person authorized, or reasonably believed by the client to be authorized, to practice law in any state or nation.

(3) A "representative of the lawyer" is one employed to assist the lawyer in the rendition of professional legal services.

(4) A communication is "confidential" if not intended to be disclosed to third persons other than those to whom disclosure is in furtherance of the rendition of professional legal services to the client or those reasonably necessary for the transmission of the communication.

(b) General Rule of Privilege. A client has a privilege to refuse to disclose and to prevent any other person from disclosing confidential communications made for the

---

12. See Nixon v. United States, 418 U.S. 683 (1974) (claim of absolute executive privilege for general presidential communications will not prevail over demonstrated need for specific evidence); Nixon v. Administrator of General Services, 433 U.S. 425 (1977) (former President directed to deliver presidential papers and tape recordings to an official of the Executive Branch for the creation of public access under the Presidential Recordings and Materials Preservation Act, held to be facially constitutional and not violative of the residential privilege doctrine); Davis v. Alaska, 415 U.S. 308 (1974) (defendant's right to confront and cross-examine key prosecution witness includes right to bring out witness's juvenile record despite state statute privileging those records); Washington v. Texas, 388 U.S. 14 (1967) (state statute prohibiting individuals charged with participating in same crime from testifying for one another violates right to compulsory process).

13. See Pennsylvania v. Ritchie, 480 U.S. 39 (1987).

purpose of facilitating the rendition of professional legal services to the client,

(1) between himself or his representative and his lawyer or his lawyer's representative, or

(2) between his lawyer and the lawyer's representative, or

(3) by him or his lawyer to a lawyer representing another in a matter of common interest, or

(4) between representatives of the client or between the client and a representative of the client, or

(5) between lawyers representing the client.

(c) Who May Claim the Privilege. The privilege may be claimed by the client, his guardian or conservator, the personal representative of a deceased client, or the successor, trustee, or similar representative of a corporation, association, or other organization, whether or not in existence. The person who was the lawyer at the time of the communication may claim the privilege but only on behalf of the client. His authority to do so is presumed in the absence of evidence to the contrary.

(d) Exceptions. There is no privilege under this rule:

(1) Furtherance of crime or fraud. If the services of the lawyer were sought or obtained to enable or aid anyone to commit or plan to commit what the client knew or reasonably should have known to be a crime or fraud; or

(2) Claimants through same deceased client. As to a communication relevant to an issue between parties who claim through the same deceased client, regardless of whether the claims are by testate or intestate succession or by *inter vivos* transaction; or

(3) Breach of duty by lawyer or client. As to a communication relevant to an issue of breach of duty by the lawyer to his client or by the client to his lawyer; or

(4) Document attested by lawyer. As to a communication relevant to an issue concerning an attested document to which the lawyer is an attesting witness; or

(5) Joint clients. As to a communication relevant to a matter of common interest between two or more clients if the communication was made by any of them to a lawyer retained or consulted in common, when offered in an action between any of the clients.

As Proposed FRE 503 suggests, much of the law governing the attorney-client privilege is quite straightforward. The attorney-client privilege originally was based on the theory that it would be unprofessional for the lawyer to reveal confidential communications from the client. Thus the lawyer was the holder of the privilege. Today, jurisdictions uniformly recognize that the attorney-client privilege exists for the benefit of the client, who is thus now the holder of the privilege. The privilege may be claimed on the client's behalf by various individuals representing the client. If the client waives the privilege, the attorney cannot refuse to reveal the confidential communications. Although Proposed FRE 503 does not treat the matter, the client alone may waive the privilege by disclosing the information, and Proposed FRE 503(d) lists the standard exceptions to the attorney-client privilege.

The primary difficulty is determining the scope of the privilege. The following sections discuss which communications are and which are not covered by the privilege.

a. Communications with a Lawyer or Representative of a Lawyer

The attorney-client privilege applies to any communication between client and lawyer made for the purpose of securing legal advice. If a person approaches someone reasonably believed to be an attorney for the purpose of obtaining legal advice, confidential communications between the two are privileged even if the person is mistaken in the belief, unless one of the exceptions applies. The privilege also attaches to preliminary discussions with an attorney, even if the attorney is not ultimately retained. Moreover, the presence of third parties who are necessary or useful to the objective of rendering legal advice, such as translators, does not destroy confidentiality. The attorney-client privilege applies not only to communications between the attorney and the client but also to communications between the client and a representative of the attorney, which is defined as a person who is "employed to assist the lawyer in the rendition of professional services." Proposed FRE 503(a)(3). But how far does the privilege extend over employees of a law firm who are not attorneys? In United States v. Kovel, 296 F.2d 918 (2d Cir. 1961), Judge Friendly wrote an influential opinion discussing the issue. In *Kovel*, an accountant was employed by a law firm specializing in tax law. Id. at 919. Although Kovel was not an attorney, he met with clients to discuss complex tax issues. Id. The suit involved Kovel's refusal to reveal communications with one of his clients when subpoenaed by a grand jury, invoking the attorney-client privilege. Id. The court held that the attorney-client privilege extends to nonlawyer employees of a law firm so long as the communications relate to legal advice. Id. at 922. The court justified extending the privilege as follows:

> [T]he complexities of modern existence prevent attorneys from effectively handling clients' affairs without the help of others . . . 'The assistance of these agents being indispensable to his work and the communications of the client being often necessarily committed to them by the attorney or by the client himself, the privilege must include all the persons who act as the attorney's agents.' 8 Wigmore, Evidence, §2301. [Id. at 921].

The court in *Kovel* further stated that the privilege exists if the lawyer has directed the client to tell his story to an accountant in order to provide better advice. Id. at 922.

The notorious prosecution of Martha Stewart for obstructing justice raised an interesting twist on the *Kovel* situation. *In re Grand Jury Subpoenas Dated March 24, 2003, 265 F. Supp.2d 321*, dealt with "the troublesome question whether and to what extent the attorney-client privilege and the protection afforded to work product extend to communications between and among a prospective defendant in a criminal case, her lawyers, and a public relations firm hired by the lawyers to aid in avoiding an indictment." Martha Stewart and her lawyers had hired a public relations firm, and the grand jury subpoenaed communications between Stewart, the lawyers, and the firm. Discovery was resisted on the ground that the public relations firm had been hired as part of Stewart's legal defense. In particular, Stewart claimed that the "unbalanced and often inaccurate press reports about Target created a clear risk that the prosecutors and regulators conducting the various investigations would feel public pressure to bring some kind of charge against her," and the public relations firm was hired to help redress the purported imbalance in the media. In an interesting opinion that relied heavily on *Kovel*, the court concluded that:

> This Court is persuaded that the ability of lawyers to perform some of their most fundamental client functions — such as (a) advising the client of the legal risks of speaking publicly and of the likely legal impact of possible alternative expressions, (b) seeking to avoid or narrow charges brought against the client, and (c) zealously seeking acquittal or vindication — would be undermined seriously if lawyers were not able to engage in frank discussions of facts and strategies with the lawyers' public relations consultants. For example, lawyers may need skilled advice as to whether and how possible statements to the press—ranging from "no comment" to detailed factual presentations—likely would be reported in order to advise a client as to whether the making of particular statements would be in the client's legal interest. And there simply is no practical way for such

discussions to occur with the public relations consultants if the lawyers were not able to inform the consultants of at least some non-public facts, as well as the lawyers' defense strategies and tactics, free of the fear that the consultants could be forced to disclose those discussions. In consequence, this Court holds that (1) confidential communications (2) between lawyers and public relations consultants (3) hired by the lawyers to assist them in dealing with the media in cases such as this (4) that are made for the purpose of giving or receiving advice (5) directed at handling the client's legal problems are protected by the attorney-client privilege.

The court did note that, notwithstanding the formalism of it all, had Stewart hired the public relations firm herself, the privilege would not apply, and further that any communications for purposes other than legal advice would not be covered by the privilege. For a critical appraisal of the case, see Ann M. Murphy, Spin Control and then High-Profile Client — Should the Attorney-Client privilege Extend to Communications With Public Relations Consultants?, 55 Syracuse L. Rev. 545 (2005).

A difficult question is whether the privilege covers communications between a criminal defendant and psychiatric experts retained by defense counsel, where the defendant asserts an insanity defense. The rule noted above that the attorney-client privilege applies to communications between a client and agents retained by defense council usually is extended to include psychiatrists. See Ballew v. State, 640 S.W.2d 237 (Tex. Crim. App. 1982); United States v. Talley, 790 F.2d 1468, 1470-71 (9th Cir. 1986) (recognizing "attorney-psychotherapist-client privilege" based in common law); but see Colo. Rev. Stat. §13-90-107(3) (scope of attorney-client privilege does not cover communications between a psychiatrist and a criminal defendant who asserts an insanity defense). However, some jurisdictions consider an insanity defense a waiver of the privilege through the assertion of a claim based on privileged information. This "waiver by claim assertion" of privileged materials has been generally recognized as requiring disclosure when a party "asserts a claim that in fairness requires examination of protected communications." United States v. Bilzerian, 926 F.2d 1285, 1292 (2d Cir. 1991). Compare Gray v. District Court, 884 P.2d 286, 292 (Colo. 1994) (holding that a defendant waives the right to claim the attorney-client and psychiatrist-patient privileges if mental condition is an issue), with People v. Knuckles, 165 Ill. 2d 125, 140, 650 N.E.2d 974, 981 (1995) (holding that there was no waiver of the attorney-client privilege with respect to communications between a defendant who raises an insanity defense and a psychiatrist employed by defense counsel to aid in the preparation of the defense). Also, Sixth Amendment challenges may arise from a state's limiting of the scope of the attorney-client privilege with respect to defense psychiatrists. However, the majority rule is that the Sixth Amendment is not violated by denying the privilege. See, e.g., Lange v. Young, 869 F.2d 1008, 1013 (7th Cir. 1989), aff'g State v. Lange, 126 Wis. 2d 513, 376 N.W.2d 868 (1985).

b.   Communications for the Purpose of Legal Service

The person invoking the privilege bears the burden of proof to show that the attorney was contacted for a legal professional purpose. If the attorney was contacted for some other purpose, the privilege does not apply. For example, if the client solicits business or financial advice, or sees a lawyer about an accounting issue rather than legal matters, any communications between them are not protected by the privilege. See, e.g., In re Grand Jury Testimony of Attorney X, 621 F. Supp. 590, 592 (E.D.N.Y. 1985) (where attorney is a "mere conduit" the client may not invoke the privilege); United States v. Woodruff, 383 F. Supp. 696, 698 (E.D. Pa. 1974) (attorney-client communication regarding time of trial not privileged). It can be a challenge to distinguish a "legal" purpose from another purpose, such as business or financial advice. In Georgia-Pacific Corp v. GAF Roofing Manufacturing Corp., 1996 U.S. Dist. LEXIS 671 (S.D.N.Y. 1996), GAF's in-house council, Scott, was asked to review certain environmental provisions of a proposed asset purchase agreement. He then negotiated the provisions of the agreement, and after execution of the agreement, he negotiated related matters. After the agreement was terminated, his testimony was needed to determine whether GAF agreed to assume certain environmental risks. Scott asserted the attorney-client privilege to avoid disclosure, stating that he had merely provided legal advice to management. The court held that, as a negotiator for GAF, Scott was acting in a business capacity, and with no litigation in sight, he was not giving legal advice. Therefore, no attorney-client privilege applied.

Proposed FRE 503(d)(5) implies that in a joint client situation, communications between an attorney and either of his joint clients are privileged against outsiders, which is the standard rule. Where two different parties have different representation, courts typically extend the privilege to cover what is called "common interest" or "joint defense" situations, as again Proposed FRE 503(b)(3) indicates. United States v. Schwimmer, 892 F.2d 237 (2d Cir. 1989). Problems arise when the joint defense breaks down and the previous cooperating parties become adversaries. Some courts take the position that in such circumstances a lawyer may not use against the now adverse party any confidences disclosed while the parties were cooperating, at least if their agreement so specifies. See, e.g., United States v. Anderson, 790 F. Supp. 231 (W.D. Wash. 1992).

c. The Scope of Confidential Communications Included in Privilege

Confidential conversations between an attorney and client are covered, so long as the conversations relate to legal advice. However, what about non verbal communications, or documents exchanged between an attorney and client? In In Re Navarro, 93 Cal. App. 3d. 325, 155 Cal. Rptr. 522 (1979), the court considered whether an attorney's act of handing a police report to his client was a "communication" within the attorney-client privilege. In *Navarro*, an attorney was subpoenaed and refused to answer whether or not she showed a police report to her client, invoking the privilege. The court stated that the privilege covers "information transmitted between a client and his lawyer," and thus even turning over to the client a public document, such as the police report in question, if given as part of her legal advice or strategy, is covered by the privilege. Id. at 327.

Some courts have extended the privilege beyond mere communications. In State v. Meeks, 666 N.W.2d 859 (Wis. 2003), the Wisconsin Supreme Court held that an attorney's opinions and impressions of a former client's competence were protected by the attorney-client privilege. Although the attorney's opinion is not a communication, the court stated that "a lawyer's opinion about a client's competence or state of mind is inextricably mixed with the client's private communications", Id. at 870. However, a majority of courts have held that the attorney-client privilege does not protect an attorney's perceptions of a former client's mental competency unless the relating the perceptions would reveal the substance of a confidential communication. See Darrow v. Gunn, 594 F.2d 767 (9th Cir. 1979).

For the privilege to attach, not only must the communication be confidential, but also clients must take "reasonable precautions" to ensure confidentiality. 3 Jack B. Weinstein and Margaret A. Berger, Weinstein's Federal Evidence, §503.15[3] (Joseph M. McLaughlin, ed., Matthew Bender 2d ed. 1997). See Suburban Sew 'N Sweep v. Swiss-Bernina, 91 F.R.D. 254 (N.D. Ill. 1981) (client who placed confidential documents in trash Dumpster failed to take adequate precautions and lost protection of the privilege). Eavesdroppers present special problems for the privilege. The modern trend is to allow the claim of privilege to prevent testimony by the eavesdropper as long as the setting of the conversation suggests that the speakers intended the conversation to be confidential. Communicating in a public setting, for example, would tend to negate the claim that the participants intended the conversation to be confidential. Still, location is not dispositive. If the parties were speaking in hushed tones and thus not likely to be overheard, that their meeting took place in a public place would not automatically negate a claim of confidentiality. See e.g. In re Sealed Case, 737 F.2d 94, 101-102 (D.C. Cir. 1984).

What if confidential material is inadvertently disclosed, perhaps as a result of a clerical error during discovery? Most courts provide some protection where inadvertent waivers have occurred in modern, document-intensive litigation if the party holding the privilege can show that it has not been careless with the privileged materials. See, e.g., Gray v. Bicknell, 86 F.3d 1472, 1484 (8th Cir. 1996). Some courts, however, still strictly find waiver in cases of inadvertent disclosure. See, e.g., Wichita Land & Cattle Co. v. American Federal Bank, F.S.B., 148 F.R.D. 456 (D.D.C. 1992) ("Disclosure of otherwise-privileged materials, even where the disclosure was inadvertent, serves as waiver of the privilege."). For a discussion, see Roberta M. Harding, Waiver: A Comprehensive Analysis of a Consequence of Inadvertently Producing Documents Protected by the Attorney-Client Privilege, 42 Cath. U. L. Rev. 465 (1993). Does it make a difference who discloses the information? What about situations in which an attorney, rather than a client, mistakenly reveals communications, perhaps due to misunderstanding the scope of the privilege? Is protection given against the derivative use of such information? "The near universal answer is that there is no protection given to the indirect or derivative use . . . when only an evidentiary privilege is involved," although concerns about unfairness may alter the result. Robert P. Mosteller, Admissibility of Fruits of Breached Evidentiary Privileges: The Importance of Adversarial Fairness, Party Culpability, and Fear of Immunity, 81 Wash. U. L.Q. 962 (2003).

Inadvertent waiver can be particularly harsh when conjoined with what is sometimes called subject matter waiver. Some courts have held that disclosure of any aspect of privileged material results in a waiver of all privileged material related to the topic. For an excellent discussion of the general area of waiver, see Richard L. Marcus, The Perils of Privilege: Waiver and the Litigator, 84 Mich. L. Rev. 1605 (1986).

KEY POINTS

1. The attorney-client privilege extends to confidential communications between an attorney and client made for the purpose of obtaining legal advice. The privilege does not cover communications made to a lawyer for the purpose of obtaining any

other kind of advice, such as business or tax advice. Determining which is which is not always easy.

2. The client is the holder of the privilege, but the privilege may be claimed on behalf of the client by the attorney and other individuals responsible for the client's interests.

3. The privilege extends over communications between joint clients and their attorney, and also covers "common interest" or "joint defense" cases, in which multiple parties and multiple attorneys are involved.

4. A communication does not necessarily have to be verbal. However, reasonable precautions must be taken by the parties to ensure confidentialily for the privilege to attach.

PROBLEMS

12.1. Brent Carson and Gloria Green were charged with importing cocaine, and retained separate counsel. At a meeting involving Brent, Gloria, and Gloria's attorney, Gloria supposedly said that Brent did not know anything about the plan to import cocaine. Gloria subsequently fled the jurisdiction, and Brent is now on trial. He calls Gloria's attorney to testify about her statement that he was not involved in the cocaine scheme. The prosecutor has objected to this testimony and asserted the attorney-client privilege on behalf of Gloria. How should the court rule?

12.2. Metro Display Advertising, Inc. (MDA) was in the business of buying and selling advertising space on bus stop shelters before it was forced to declare bankruptcy in the aftermath of an S.E.C. investigation. The government has charged Munoz, one of MDA's independent sales agents, with mail fraud and has subpoenaed Sherron to testify against him. Sherron was once Munoz's attorney in an unrelated matter prior to either's employment with MDA. Subsequently Sherron was retained by MDA. Munoz communicated to Sherron about the current charges against him, mistakenly believing that Sherron was representing him as well as MDA. Munoz now seeks to prevent Sherron from testifying about his damaging statements by invoking his attorney-client privilege. Should the court allow Sherron's testimony?

12.3. Ed Brown has been charged with assault. At a pretrial hearing to determine Brown's competence to stand trial, the attorney called himself as a witness for the purpose of explaining how difficult it was to communicate with Brown. The attorney's testimony included the details of three quite different stories that Brown had told at various times about the incident in question. The court found Brown competent to stand trial. At trial, where Brown was represented by a different attorney, the prosecutor called the former attorney to testify about Brown's earlier inconsistent statements regarding the crime. Brown has objected on the ground that his statements are protected by the attorney-client privilege. What result?

12.4. Dunlap was the director of the Lincoln Challenge Project, a betterment program for teenaged high school dropouts. In 1994 he hired Peters to teach in the program, requiring him to consent to criminal and educational background checks as a condition of his employment. When Peters sought to have his contract renewed in 1996, Dunlap informed him that he would be required to sign a much broader release consenting to, among other things, the full and complete disclosure of the records of attorneys, whether representing him or another person, in any case in which Peters has had an interest. Peters refused to sign the release and his employment contract was not renewed. Peters sued Dunlap. Can an employer require an employee to waive all attorney-client privileges as a condition of employment? Could any constitutional argument(s) be made by Peters to protect the privileged information?

12.5. Suburban Sew 'N Sweep is a retail store selling sewing machines manufactured and distributed by Fritz, Inc. A few years ago Suburban began suspecting that Fritz was engaging in unlawful price discrimination and conspiring to restrain trade in violation of the Clayton Act and the Sherman Antitrust Act. To confirm its suspicions, Suburban began regularly searching the Dumpster behind Fritz's office. Over the course of two years, Suburban found hundreds of relevant documents, many of which were confidential correspondences between Fritz's officers and Fritz's corporate counsel. It is uncontested that the documents were intended to be confidential and would be protected by attorney-client privilege if they had not been discovered by Suburban. Are these documents privileged?

12.6. Connolly was laid off as a part of a reduction in workforce by his employer, Athens Enterprises. He sued the company, alleging that it discriminated against him on the basis of race, in violation of federal and state law. Connolly, who is white, offered evidence that the company considered federal Equal Employment Opportunity reasons when it reduced its workforce, specifically that it targeted white employees for elimination while keeping less qualified minorities. Davis, an in-house attorney for Athens, advised the company regarding the layoffs. He prepared a memo from the law department on proposed guidelines for implementing the cutbacks. In addition, he advised the company regarding possible legal problems with the lists of employees the company proposed to fire. Connolly moved to compel the production of these documents, arguing that they were not privileged because they were prepared in the ordinary course of business, and not for the purpose of giving legal advice. Should the documents be produced? With regard to the lists, would it make a difference if they were prepared at the request of the law department?

12.7. Habs Brewing Company brought suit against Blue Jay Importers, alleging patent and trademark infringement resulting from Blue Jay's marketing of "dry" beer. Blue Jay motioned the court to compel production of certain documents, which Habs claims are protected by the attorney-client privilege. The 15 documents for which the plaintiffs are asserting the privilege were initiated by or received by Beardsley. Beardsley is a member of the legal department of Habs, and serves as their Intellectual Property Officer. Although not an attorney, Beardsley is registered as a patent agent before the U.S. Patent and Trademark Office. The Patent office allows nonlawyer patent agents to perform certain legal tasks before it, such as giving patent advice and preparing patent applications. Patent agents do not have any corresponding authorization to practice trademark law. Can Habs successfully assert the attorney-client privilege with respect to the communications by and to Beardsley? Does it make a difference whether such communications involved patent or trademark law?

NOTE ON THE ATTORNEY-CLIENT PRIVILEGE, THE WORK-PRODUCT DOCTRINE, AND THE ETHICAL DUTY OF CONFIDENTIALITY

Three sources protect confidentiality in the attorney-client relationship: the attorney-client privilege, the work-product doctrine, and the ethical duty of confidentiality.

While the attorney-client privilege and work-product doctrine find their source in the law of evidence, the duty of confidentiality is grounded in the code of professional ethics.

The work-product doctrine often overlaps or supplements the attorney-client privilege. Protection for the "work product" of an attorney or party has been codified under Fed. R. Civ. P. 26(b)(3). Under Rule 26(b)(3), a party may obtain discovery of documents and tangible things prepared "in anticipation of litigation" by an attorney or representative of the opposing party only on a showing of "substantial need" and on a showing that the party seeking discovery is unable, without undue hardship, to obtain the substantial equivalent from alternative means. Furthermore, even if the required showing is put forth, the court must protect against disclosure of "the mental impressions, conclusions, opinions, or legal theories of an attorney or other representative of a party concerning the litigation." While both the attorney-client privilege and work-product doctrine act as a bar to discovery, there exist some crucial distinctions between the two. First, the work-product doctrine recognizes a qualified privilege, while the attorney-client privilege is usually considered absolute, although this is slowly beginning to change. See, for example, Greater Newburyport Clamshell Alliance v. Public Service Co. of N.H., 838 F.2d 13, 19 (1st Cir. 1988) (in civil damages action, "fairness requires that the privilege holder surrender the privilege to the extent that it will weaken, in a meaningful way, the defendant's ability to defend"); In re Grand Jury Proc., Des Moines, Iowa, 568 F.2d 555, 557 (8th Cir. 1977) (opponent's need relevant to a determination of privilege). At least with respect to discovery of "documents and tangible things" as opposed to "mental impressions, conclusions, opinions, or legal theories of an attorney," work product protection is subject to a substantial need test. By contrast, if the attorney-client privilege is applicable, a showing of need will typically not overcome the privilege.

Second, whereas the work-product doctrine applies only to information prepared "in anticipation of litigation," the attorney-client privilege protects confidential communications, regardless of whether litigation is expected. Although the scope of work product protection may seem unduly limited by the litigation requirement, in reality the work-product doctrine covers a much larger category of material than the attorney-client privilege. The work-product doctrine applies to all information collected by the attorney or the agent of the client insofar as it is gathered in anticipation of litigation. Thus it applies not only to information passing from client to attorney, but to information from outside sources as well, such as a statement of a nonparty witness to an attorney as well as work compiled by an investigator, without the attorney's participation. In contrast, the attorney-client privilege applies solely to confidential communications between attorney and client, or representatives on either party's behalf.

A third source for the protection of confidentiality in attorney-client relations is the ethical duty of a lawyer to keep confidential matters about a client's affairs. The American Bar Association's Model Rules of Professional Conduct set forth this obligation in Rule 1.6, which as amended in 2005 now states:

> (a) A lawyer shall not reveal information relating to the representation of a client unless the client gives informed consent, the disclosure is impliedly authorized in order to carry out the representation or the disclosure is permitted by paragraph (b).
> (b) A lawyer may reveal information relating to the representation of a client to the extent the lawyer reasonably believes necessary:

(1) to prevent reasonably certain death or substantial bodily harm;

(2) to prevent the client from committing a crime or fraud that is reasonably certain to result in substantial injury to the financial interests or property of another and in furtherance of which the client has used or is using the lawyer's services

(3) to prevent, mitigate or rectify substantial injury to the financial interests or property of another that is reasonably certain to result or has resulted from the client's commission of a crime or fraud in furtherance of which the client has used the lawyer's services;

(4) to secure legal advice about the lawyer's compliance with these Rules;

(5) to establish a claim or defense on behalf of the lawyer in a controversy between the lawyer and the client, to establish a defense to a criminal charge or civil claim against the lawyer based upon conduct in which the client was involved, or to respond to allegations in any proceeding concerning the lawyer's representation of the client; or

(6) to comply with other law or a court order.

Comment Two accompanying Model Rule 1.6 provides the rationale behind the ethical obligation.

> A fundamental principle in the client-lawyer relationship is that, in the absence of the client's informed consent, the lawyer must not reveal information relating to the representation . . . This contributes to the trust that is the hallmark of the client-lawyer relationship. The client is thereby encouraged to seek legal assistance and to communicate fully and frankly with the lawyer even as to embarrassing or legally damaging subject matter. The lawyer needs this information to represent the client effectively and, if necessary, to advise the client to refrain from wrongful conduct. . . .

The duty of confidentiality is an important mechanism by which the rules of ethics protect these interests. The Rule was relaxed slightly in the 2005 update, now allowing the lawyer to breach confidentiality to prevent any reasonably certain bodily harm, no longer limited to harm caused by a client's criminal act. Further, in the wake of recent financial scandals, such as Enron, the updated Rule allows for a breach of confidentiality where a client has used the lawyer's services to prevent a client's crime or fraud from causing harm to financial interests or property. Despite these few exceptions, the ethical duty of confidentiality remains essential to the protection of the client-lawyer relationship. Violation of Rule 1.6 may lead to professional censure and possible suspension or loss of license.

Comment Three to Rule 1.6 clarifies the distinction between evidentiary privileges and the ethical duty of confidentiality:

> The principle of client-lawyer confidentiality is given effect by related bodies of law: the attorney-client privilege, the work product doctrine and the rule of confidentiality established in professional ethics. The attorney-client privilege and work-product doctrine apply in judicial and other proceedings in which a lawyer may be called as a witness or otherwise required to produce evidence concerning a client. The rule of client-lawyer confidentiality applies in situations other than those where evidence is sought from the lawyer through compulsion of law. The confidentiality rule, for example, applies not only to matters communicated in confidence by the client but also to all information relating to the representation, whatever its source. A lawyer may not disclose such information except as authorized or required by the Rules of Professional Conduct or other law. . . .

The duty of confidentiality covers much more than the privilege — it covers all communications between a client and an attorney, including those that are not specifically tied to seeking legal advice, and those that are not meant to be confidential.

The duty of confidentiality also covers more than just verbal communications, unlike the attorney-client privilege. However, a lawyer can still be called on to testify regarding these communications, so the protection afforded by the duty of confidentiality may not be as great as that afforded by the privilege.

An interesting empirical question is whether the lawyer's ethical obligation to maintain confidentiality is sufficiently analogous to the privilege to encourage communications between client and attorney. If clients can be encouraged by the attorney's ethical obligation to disclose information, then the attorney-client privilege may not be needed. See, in this regard, ABA Code of Professional Responsibility, Ethical Consideration 4-1:

> A lawyer should be fully informed of all the facts of the matter he is handling in order for his client to obtain the full advantage of our legal system. It is for the lawyer in the exercise of his independent professional judgment to separate the relevant and important from the irrelevant and unimportant. The observance of the ethical obligation of a lawyer to hold inviolate the confidences and secrets of his client not only facilitates the full development of facts essential to proper representation of the client but also encourages laymen to seek early legal assistance.

NOTES AND QUESTIONS

1. How absolute should the protection be for a client's confidential communications or a lawyer's thought processes and other creative efforts? Even if the existence of rules of confidentiality produce benefits, isn't it conceivable in a particular case that their costs would exceed their benefits? What should happen in such cases? In thinking about this issue, do not neglect the costs of deciding on a case-by-case basis if the costs of confidentiality exceed the benefits. If a witness uses a document protected by the attorney-client privilege or the work-product doctrine to refresh the witness's memory before testifying, should the judge be able to order production of the document pursuant to FRE 612?

2. The American Bar Association's Model Code of Professional Responsibility, the predecessor to the Model Rules of Professional Conduct, included a similar confidentiality provision. ABA Model Code of Professional Responsibility Disciplinary Rule 4-101. The exception for contemplated criminal conduct by a client, however, extended to *all* crimes, and there was also an exception permitting a lawyer to reveal confidences "when required by law or court order." With respect to the omission of this latter exception in the Model Rules, the Comment accompanying Rule 1.6 states: "Whether another provision of law supersedes Rule 1.6 is a matter of interpretation beyond the scope of these Rules, but a presumption should exist against such a supersession." How compelling a case for confidentiality does the Comment to Rule 1.6 make? Do the rule and commentary deal adequately with the relationship between the ethical obligation of confidentiality and the attorney-client privilege? Is Rule 1.6's permission for a lawyer to disclose a client's contemplated criminal conduct too narrow? Why should there be a "presumption" that provisions of law mandating disclosure do not supersede Rule 1.6's obligation of confidentiality?

3. There is one situation in which the Model Rules of Professional Conduct specifically provide that the rule of confidentiality is superseded. See Model Rule 3.3:

    (a) A lawyer shall not knowingly:
        (1) make a false statement of material fact or law to a tribunal;
        (2) fail to disclose a material fact to a tribunal when disclosure is necessary to
avoid assisting a criminal or fraudulent act by the client;
        (3) fail to disclose to the tribunal legal authority in the controlling jurisdiction
known to the lawyer to be directly adverse to the position of the client and not disclosed by
opposing counsel; or
        (4) offer evidence that the lawyer knows to be false. If a lawyer has offered
material evidence and comes to know of its falsity, the lawyer shall take reasonable
remedial measures.
    (b) The duties stated in paragraph (a) continue to the conclusion of the proceeding,
and apply even if compliance requires disclosure of information otherwise protected by
Rule 1.6.
    (c) A lawyer may refuse to offer evidence that the lawyer reasonably believes is false.

    4. For further discussion of the relation between the attorney-client privilege and
the ethical rules of confidentiality, see Harry Schaffner, Reconciling Attorney-Client
Privilege with the Rules of Professional Conduct, 81 Ill. B.J. 410 (1993); see also Fred
C. Zacharias, Harmonizing Privilege and Confidentiality, 41 S.Tex. L. Rev. 69 (1999).

PROBLEMS

    12.8. Al Driver, who is suspected of bank robbery, tells his attorney, George
Shippers, where to locate the mask and gun used in the robbery. Shippers retrieves
the mask and gun and places them in the office safe. Has Shippers acted unethically?
What disclosures about the gun and mask is he now permitted or required to make?
    What if it had been Shippers's secretary who had, without Shippers's permission,
retrieved the mask and gun? In either case, should it matter (a) whether the police or
some third person would have been likely to find the mask and gun or (b) whether the
initial information about the mask and gun came from some person other than the client?
    After Shippers first learned about the mask and gun, what would have been the
appropriate course of action for him to take?
    12.9. Sarah Johnson, an attorney, represents Oscar Rivers, who has been charged
with murder. Rivers and his girlfriend, Elsie Lewis, are both prepared to testify that they
were together at Elsie's apartment at the time of the killing. Oscar has consistently told
Sarah this alibi story; Elsie, however, has confided in Sarah that she was not with Oscar
at the time of the killing and that Oscar admitted to her that he was the murderer. The
only eyewitness to the killing, Elvira Dugan, is an elderly woman with failing eyesight.
    What should Sarah do if both Oscar and Elsie are adamant about testifying that
they were together at Elsie's apartment when the murder was committed? Does your
answer depend on whether Sarah believes Oscar or Elsie?
    Sarah is convinced that she can neutralize Elvira Dugan's eyewitness testimony
during cross-examination. Is there any problem with her doing so if she is convinced
that Oscar is guilty and that Elvira's identification is in fact accurate?

2.   The Corporate Client

    The attorney-client privilege extends not only to individual clients but also to cor-
porate and other organizational clients. Application of the privilege in this context has

proved troublesome because an organization can make confidential communications only through individual members. Thus the question necessarily arises: Who can speak for the organization for the purposes of the attorney-client privilege? Or to phrase the issue in terms of the language of Proposed FRE 503: Who is a "representative of the client"?

Courts are divided as to the extent of the privilege in the corporate context. As the law has evolved on the subject, three approaches can be discerned. Under the early decisions, any officer, employee, or member of an organization was a representative of the organization. See, e.g., United States v. United Shoe Mach. Corp., 89 F. Supp. 357 (D. Mass. 1950). Although this definition had the advantage of ease in application, it was widely criticized for being too broad.

A second approach to defining representative of the client was the "control group" test. See City of Philadelphia v. Westinghouse Elec. Corp., 210 F. Supp. 483 (E.D. Pa. 1962). According to this test an employee's communication is privileged only if the employee "is in a position to control or even to take a substantial part in a decision about any action which the corporation may take upon the advice of the attorney." Although widely adopted, the control group test was subject to criticism on two grounds. First, it was unclear precisely to whom the privilege would apply, and this lack of certainty would inhibit candid communication. Second, because the control group test tended to limit the attorney-client privilege to communications by upper level management, the test did not go far enough in protecting communications of employees who might have information that would be critical in order for the attorney to give sound legal advice to the organization.

A third approach to defining representative of the client was the "subject matter" test. See Harper & Row Publishers, Inc. v. Decker, 423 F.2d 487 (7th Cir. 1970), aff'd mem., 400 U.S. 955 (1971). Under this test an employee's communication is privileged if the employee "makes the communication at the direction of his superiors" and the subject matter of the communication "is the performance by the employee of the duties of his employment." This test avoids both the problem of bringing within the scope of the privilege communications by any and all employees and the problem of limiting the privilege to communications from members of the control group. But is the subject matter test itself too broad? Would the first prong of the test be satisfied if every employee were routinely directed to channel all business reports through corporate counsel? See Note, Evidence — Privileged Communications — The Attorney-Client Privilege in the Corporate Setting: A Suggested Approach, 69 Mich. L. Rev. 360 (1970). Would the first prong be satisfied if any superior for any reason directed the employee to communicate with the attorney?

The drafters of the Federal Rules chose not to define "representative of the client." Without elaboration, the Advisory Committee concluded that the matter was "too hot to handle" and "better left to resolution on a case-by-case basis."[14] The Supreme Court addressed the issue in Upjohn.

---

14. See Hearings on Proposed Rules of Evidence Before the Special Subcommittee on Reform of Federal Criminal Laws of the House Committee on the Judiciary, 93d Cong., 1st Sess. 524 (1973) (testimony by Professor Cleary). In earlier drafts the Advisory Committee had included a version of the control group test in the definition section of Proposed FRE 503. Prior to the final draft, however, the Supreme Court affirmed by an equally divided vote the decision that had announced the subject matter test. Harper and Row Publishers v. Decker, 400 U.S. 348 (1970). As Weinstein and Berger noted: The Advisory Committee recognized that lack of consensus in the Supreme Court precluded the possibility of drafting a rule satisfactory to a majority of the justices. Consequently, the Committee eliminated the definition of "representative of the client" in subdivision (a) of the rule. [3 Jack B. Weinstein and Margaret A. Berger, Weinstein's Federal Evidence §503App.01[2] (Joseph M. McLaughlin, ed., Matthew Bender 2d ed. 1997).]

UPJOHN CO. v. UNITED STATES
449 U.S. 383 (1981)

Justice REHNQUIST delivered the opinion of the Court.

We granted certiorari in this case to address important questions concerning the scope of the attorney-client privilege in the corporate context and the applicability of the work-product doctrine in proceedings to enforce tax summonses.... We...conclude that the attorney-client privilege protects the communications involved in this case from compelled disclosure and that the work-product doctrine does apply in tax summons enforcement proceedings.

I

Petitioner Upjohn Co. manufactures and sells pharmaceuticals here and abroad. In January 1976 independent accountants conducting an audit of one of Upjohn's foreign subsidiaries discovered that the subsidiary made payments to or for the benefit of foreign government officials in order to secure government business. The accountants so informed petitioner Mr. Gerard Thomas, Upjohn's Vice President, Secretary, and General Counsel. Thomas is a member of the Michigan and New York Bars, and has been Upjohn's General Counsel for 20 years. He consulted with outside counsel and R. T. Parfet, Jr., Upjohn's Chairman of the Board. It was decided that the company would conduct an internal investigation of what were termed "questionable payments." As part of this investigation the attorneys prepared a letter containing a questionnaire which was sent to "All Foreign General and Area Managers" over the Chairman's signature. The letter began by noting recent disclosures that several American companies made "possibly illegal" payments to foreign government officials and emphasized that the management needed full information concerning any such payments made by Upjohn. The letter indicated that the Chairman had asked Thomas, identified as "the company's General Counsel," "to conduct an investigation for the purpose of determining the nature and magnitude of any payments made by the Upjohn Company or any of its subsidiaries to any employee or official of a foreign government." The questionnaire sought detailed information concerning such payments. Managers were instructed to treat the investigation as "highly confidential" and not to discuss it with anyone other than Upjohn employees who might be helpful in providing the requested information. Responses were to be sent directly to Thomas. Thomas and outside counsel also interviewed the recipients of the questionnaire and some 33 other Upjohn officers or employees as part of the investigation.

On March 26, 1976, the company voluntarily submitted a preliminary report to the Securities and Exchange Commission on Form 8-K disclosing certain questionable payments. A copy of the report was simultaneously submitted to the Internal Revenue Service, which immediately began an investigation to determine the tax consequences of the payments. Special agents conducting the investigation were given lists by Upjohn of all those interviewed and all who had responded to the questionnaire. On November 23, 1976, the Service issued a summons pursuant to 26 U.S.C. sec. 7602 demanding production of:

All files relative to the investigation conducted under the supervision of Gerard Thomas to identify payments to employees of foreign governments and any political contributions made by the Upjohn Company or any of its affiliates since January 1, 1971 and to determine whether any funds of the Upjohn Company had been improperly accounted for on the corporate books during the same period.

The records should include but not be limited to written questionnaires sent to managers of the Upjohn Company's foreign affiliates, and memorandums or notes of the interviews conducted in the United States and abroad with officers and employees of the Upjohn Company and its subsidiaries....

The company declined to produce the documents specified in the second paragraph on the grounds that they were protected from disclosure by the attorney-client privilege and constituted the work product of attorneys prepared in anticipation of litigation.... [T]he United States filed a petition seeking enforcement of the summons... in the United States District Court for the Western District of Michigan. That court adopted the recommendation of a Magistrate who concluded that the summons should be enforced. Petitioners appealed to the Court of Appeals for the Sixth Circuit which rejected the Magistrate's finding of a waiver of the attorney-client privilege, ... but agreed that the privilege did not apply "[t]o the extent that the communications were made by officers and agents not responsible for directing Upjohn's actions in response to legal advice ... for the simple reason that the communications were not the client's." ... The court reasoned that accepting petitioners' claim for a broader application of the privilege would encourage upper-echelon management to ignore unpleasant facts and create too broad a "zone of silence." Noting that Upjohn's counsel had interviewed officials such as the Chairman and President, the Court of Appeals remanded to the District Court so that a determination of who was within the "control group" could be made. In a concluding footnote the court stated that the work-product doctrine "is not applicable to administrative summonses issued under 26 U.S.C. sec. 7602." ...

II

... The attorney-client privilege is the oldest of the privileges for confidential communications known to the common law.... Its purpose is to encourage full and frank communication between attorneys and their clients and thereby promote broader public interests in the observance of law and administration of justice. The privilege recognizes that sound legal advice or advocacy serves public ends and that such advice or advocacy depends upon the lawyer's being fully informed by the client. [I]n Fisher v. United States, 425 U.S. 391, 403 (1976), we recognized the purpose of the privilege to be "to encourage clients to make full disclosure to their attorneys." This rationale for the privilege has long been recognized by the Court.... Admittedly complications in the application of the privilege arise when the client is a corporation, which in theory is an artificial creature of the law, and not an individual; but this Court has assumed that the privilege applies when the client is a corporation, ... and the Government does not contest the general proposition.

The Court of Appeals, however, considered the application of the privilege in the corporate context to present a "different problem," since the client was an inanimate entity and "only the senior management, guiding and integrating the several operations, ... can be said to possess an identity analogous to the corporation as a whole." ... The first case to articulate the so-called "control group test" adopted by the court below, Philadelphia v. Westinghouse Electric Corp., 210 F. Supp. 483, 485 (ED Pa.), *petition for mandamus and prohibition denied sub nom.* General Electric Co. v. Kirkpatrick, 312 F.2d 742 (CA3 1962), *cert. denied*, 372 U.S. 943 (1963), reflected a similar conceptual approach:

> Keeping in mind that the question is, Is it the corporation which is seeking the lawyer's advice when the asserted privileged communication is made?, the most satisfactory solution, I think, is that if the employee making the communication, of whatever rank he may be, is in a position to control or even to take a substantial part in a decision about any action which the corporation may take upon the advice of the attorney, . . . then, in effect, *he is (or personifies) the corporation* when he makes his disclosure to the lawyer and the privilege would apply. (Emphasis supplied [by the Court].)

Such a view, we think, overlooks the fact that the privilege exists to protect not only the giving of professional advice to those who can act on it but also the giving of information to the lawyer to enable them to give sound and informed advice. The first step in the resolution of any legal problem is ascertaining the factual background and sifting through the facts with an eye to the legally relevant. See ABA Code of Professional Responsibility, Ethical Consideration 4-1:

> A lawyer should be fully informed of all the facts of the matter he is handling in order for his client to obtain the full advantage of our legal system. It is for the lawyer in the exercise of his independent professional judgment to separate the relevant and important from the irrelevant and unimportant. The observance of the ethical obligation of a lawyer to hold inviolate the confidences and secrets of his client not only facilitates the full development of facts essential to proper representation of the client but also encourages laymen to seek early legal assistance.

. . . In the case of the individual client the provider of information and the person who acts on the lawyer's advice are one and the same. In the corporate context, however, it will frequently be employees beyond the control group as defined by the court below — "officers and agents . . . responsible for directing [the company's] actions in response to legal advice" — who will possess the information needed by the corporation's lawyers. Middle-level — and indeed lower-level — employees can, by actions within the scope of their employment, embroil the corporation in serious legal difficulties, and it is only natural that these employees would have the relevant information needed by corporate counsel if he is adequately to advise the client with respect to such actual or potential difficulties. . . .

The control group test adopted by the court below thus frustrates the very purpose of the privilege by discouraging the communication of relevant information by employees of the client to attorneys seeking to render legal advice to the client corporation. The attorney's advice will also frequently be more significant to noncontrol group members than to those who officially sanction the advice, and the control group test makes it more difficult to convey full and frank legal advice to the employees who will put into effect the client corporation's policy. See, e.g., Duplan Corp. v. Deering Milliken, Inc., 397 F. Supp. 1146, 1164 (S.C. 1974) ("After the lawyer forms his or her opinion, it is of no immediate benefit to the Chairman of the Board or the President. It must be given to the corporate personnel who will apply it").

The narrow scope given the attorney-client privilege by the court below not only makes it difficult for corporate attorneys to formulate sound advice when their client is faced with a specific legal problem but also threatens to limit the valuable efforts of corporate counsel to ensure their client's compliance with the law. In light of the vast and complicated array of regulatory legislation confronting the modern corporation, corporations, unlike most individuals, "constantly go to lawyers to find out how to obey the law," Burnham, The Attorney-Client Privilege in the Corporate Arena, 24 Bus. Law. 901, 913 (1969), particularly since compliance with the law in this area is hardly an instinctive matter, see, e.g., United States v. United States Gypsum Co., 438 U.S. 422, 440-441 (1978) ("the behavior proscribed by the [Sherman] Act is often difficult to distinguish from the gray zone of socially acceptable and economically justifiable business conduct").[15] The test adopted by the court below is difficult to apply in practice, though no abstractly formulated and unvarying "test" will necessarily enable courts to decide questions such as this with mathematical precision. But if the purpose of the attorney-client privilege is to be served, the attorney and client must be able to predict with some degree of certainty whether particular discussions will be protected. An uncertain privilege, or one which purports to be certain but results in widely varying applications by the courts, is little better than no privilege at all. The very terms of the test adopted by the court below suggest the unpredictability of its application. The test restricts the availability of the privilege to those officers who play a "substantial role" in deciding and directing a corporation's legal response. Disparate decisions in cases applying this test illustrate its unpredictability. Compare, e.g., Hogan v. Zletz, 43 F.R.D. 308, 315-316 (ND Okla. 1967), aff'd in part sub nom. Natta v. Hogan, 392 F.2d 686 (CA10 1968) (control group includes managers and assistant managers of patent division and research and development department), with Congoleum Industries, Inc. v. GAF Corp., 49 F.R.D. 82, 83-85 (E.D. Pa. 1969), aff'd, 478 F.2d 1398 (CA3 1973) (control group includes only division and corporate vice presidents, and not two directors of research and vice president for production and research).

The communications at issue were made by Upjohn employees[16] to counsel for Upjohn acting as such, at the direction of corporate superiors in order to secure legal advice from counsel. As the Magistrate found, "Mr. Thomas consulted with the Chairman of the Board and outside counsel and thereafter conducted a factual investigation to determine the nature and extent of the questionable payments *and to be in a position to give legal advice to the company with respect to the payments.*" (Emphasis supplied [by the Court].). . . . Information, not available from upper-echelon management, was needed to supply a basis for legal advice concerning compliance with securities and tax laws, foreign laws, currency regulations, duties to shareholders, and potential litigation in each of these areas. The communications concerned matters within the scope of the employees' corporate duties, and the employees themselves were sufficiently aware that they were being questioned in order that the corporation could obtain legal advice.

---

15. The Government argues that the risk of civil or criminal liability suffices to ensure that corporations will seek legal advice in the absence of the protection of the privilege. This response ignores the fact that the depth and quality of any investigations to ensure compliance with the law would suffer, even were they undertaken. The response also proves too much, since it applies to all communications covered by the privilege: an individual trying to comply with the law or faced with a legal problem also has strong incentive to disclose information to his lawyer, yet the common law has recognized the value of the privilege in further facilitating communications.

16. Seven of the eighty-six employees interviewed by counsel had terminated their employment with Upjohn at the time of the interview. . . . Petitioners argue that the privilege should nonetheless apply to communications by these former employees concerning activities during their period of employment. Neither the District Court nor the Court of Appeals had occasion to address this issue, and we decline to decide it without the benefit of treatment below.

The questionnaire identified Thomas as "the company's General Counsel" and referred in its opening sentence to the possible illegality of payments such as the ones on which information was sought. . . . A statement of policy accompanying the questionnaire clearly indicated the legal implications of the investigation. The policy statement was issued "in order that there be no uncertainty in the future as to the policy with respect to the practices which are the subject of this investigation." It began "Upjohn will comply with all laws and regulations," and stated that commissions or payments "will not be used as a subterfuge for bribes or illegal payments" and that all payments must be "proper and legal." Any future agreements with foreign distributors or agents were to be approved "by a company attorney" and any questions concerning the policy were to be referred "to the company's general Counsel." . . . This statement was issued to Upjohn employees worldwide, so that even those interviewees not receiving a questionnaire were aware of the legal implications of the interviews. Pursuant to explicit instructions from the Chairman of the Board, the communications were considered "highly confidential" when made, . . . and have been kept confidential by the company. Consistent with the underlying purposes of the attorney-client privilege, these communications must be protected against compelled disclosure.

The Court of Appeals declined to extend the attorney-client privilege beyond the limits of the control group test for fear that doing so would entail severe burdens on discovery and create a broad "zone of silence" over corporate affairs. Application of the attorney-client privilege to communications such as those involved here, however, puts the adversary in no worse position than if the communications had never taken place. The privilege only protects disclosure of communications; it does not protect disclosure of the underlying facts by those who communicated with the attorney. . . . Here the Government was free to question the employees who communicated with Thomas and outside counsel. Upjohn has provided the IRS with a list of such employees, and the IRS has already interviewed some 25 of them. While it would probably be more convenient for the Government to secure the results of petitioner's internal investigation by simply subpoenaing the questionnaires and notes taken by petitioner's attorneys, such considerations of convenience do not overcome the policies served by the attorney-client privilege. . . .

Needless to say, we decide only the case before us, and do not undertake to draft a set of rules which should govern challenge to investigatory subpoenas. Any such approach would violate the spirit of Federal Rule of Evidence 501. See S. Rep. No. 93-1277, p.13 (1974) ("the recognition of a privilege based on a confidential relationship . . . should be determined on a case-by-case basis"). . . . While such a "case-by-case" basis may to some slight extent undermine desirable certainty in the boundaries of the attorney-client privilege, it obeys the spirit of the Rules. At the same time we conclude that the narrow "control group test" sanctioned by the Court of Appeals in this case cannot, consistent with "the principles of the common law as . . . interpreted . . . in the light of reason and experience," Fed. Rule Evid. 501, govern the development of the law in this area.

III

Our decision that the communications by Upjohn employees to counsel are covered by the attorney-client privilege disposes of the case so far as the responses to the questionnaires and any notes reflecting responses to interview questions are concerned. The summons reaches further, however, and Thomas has testified that his notes and memoranda of interviews go beyond recording responses to his questions. . . . To the extent that the material subject to the summons is not protected by the attorney-client privilege as disclosing communications between an employee and counsel, we must reach the ruling by the Court of Appeals that the work-product doctrine does not apply to summonses issued under 26 U.S.C. sec. 7602.[17] The Government concedes, wisely, that the Court of Appeals erred and that the work-product doctrine does apply to IRS summonses. . . . This doctrine was announced by the Court over 30 years ago in Hickman v. Taylor, 329 U.S. 495 (1947). In that case the Court rejected "an attempt, without purported necessity or justification, to secure written statements, private memoranda and personal recollections prepared or formed by an adverse party's counsel in the course of his legal duties." Id., at 510. The Court noted that "it is essential that a lawyer work with a certain degree of privacy" and reasoned that if discovery of the material sought were permitted

> much of what is now put down in writing would remain unwritten. An attorney's thoughts, heretofore inviolate, would not be his own. Inefficiency, unfairness and sharp practices would inevitably develop in the giving of legal advice and in the preparation of cases for trial. The effect on the legal profession would be demoralizing. And the interests of the clients and the cause of justice would be poorly served. [Id., at 511.]

The "strong public policy" underlying the work-product doctrine was reaffirmed recently in United States v. Nobles, 422 U.S. 225, 236-240 (1975), and has been substantially incorporated in Federal Rule of Civil Procedure 26(b)(3).[18]

. . . While conceding the applicability of the work-product doctrine, the Government asserts that it has made a sufficient showing of necessity to overcome its protections. The Magistrate apparently so found. . . . The Government relies on the following language in *Hickman*:

> We do not mean to say that all written materials obtained or prepared by an adversary's counsel with an eye toward litigation are necessarily free from discovery in all cases. Where relevant and nonprivileged facts remain hidden in an attorney's file and where production of those facts is essential to the preparation of one's case, discovery may properly be had. . . . And production might be justified where the witnesses are no longer available or can be reached only with difficulty. [*Hickman*, 329 U.S., at 511.]

The Government stresses that interviewees are scattered across the globe and that Upjohn has forbidden its employees to answer questions it considers irrelevant. The

---

17. The following discussion will also be relevant to counsel's notes and memoranda of interviews with the seven former employees should it be determined that the attorney-client privilege does not apply to them. See n.[16], supra.

18. This provides, in pertinent part:

[A] party may obtain discovery of documents and tangible things otherwise discoverable under subdivision (b)(1) of this rule and prepared in anticipation of litigation or for trial by or for another party or by or for that other party's representative (including his attorney, consultant, surety, indemnitor, insurer, or agent) only upon a showing that the party seeking discovery has substantial need of the materials in the preparation of his case and that he is unable without undue hardship to obtain the substantial equivalent of the materials by other means. In ordering discovery of such materials when the required showing has been made, the court shall protect against disclosure of the mental impressions, conclusions, opinions, or legal theories of an attorney or other representative of a party concerning the litigation.

above-quoted language from *Hickman,* however, did not apply to "oral statements made by witnesses . . . whether presently in the form of [the attorney's] mental impressions or memoranda." Id., at 512. As to such material the Court did "not believe that any showing of necessity can be made under the circumstances of this case so as to justify production. . . . If there should be a rare situation justifying production of these matters, petitioner's case is not of that type." Id., at 512-513. . . . Forcing an attorney to disclose notes and memoranda of witnesses' oral statements is particularly disfavored because it tends to reveal the attorney's mental processes, 329 U.S., at 513 ("what he saw fit to write down regarding witnesses' remarks"); id., at 516-517 ("the statement would be his [the attorney's] language, permeated with his inferences") (Jackson, J., concurring).[19] Rule 26 accords special protection to work product revealing the attorney's mental processes. The Rule permits disclosure of documents and tangible things constituting attorney work product upon a showing of substantial need and inability to obtain the equivalent without undue hardship. This was the standard applied by the Magistrate. . . . Rule 26 goes on, however, to state that "[i]n ordering discovery of such materials when the required showing has been made, the court shall protect against disclosure of the mental impressions, conclusions, opinions or legal theories of an attorney or other representative of a party concerning the litigation." Although this language does not specifically refer to memoranda based on oral statements of witnesses the *Hickman* court stressed the danger that compelled disclosure of such memoranda would reveal the attorney's mental processes. It is clear that this is the sort of material the draftsmen of the Rule had in mind as deserving special protection. See Notes of Advisory Committee on 1970 Amendment to Rules, 28, U.S.C. App., p.442 ("The subdivision . . . goes on to protect against disclosure the mental impressions, conclusions, opinions, or legal theories . . . of an attorney or other representative of a party. The *Hickman* opinion drew special attention to the need for protecting an attorney against discovery of memoranda prepared from recollection of oral interviews. The courts have steadfastly safeguarded against disclosure of lawyers' mental impressions and legal theories. . . . ").

Based on the foregoing, some courts have concluded that *no* showing of necessity can overcome protection of work product which is based on oral statements from witnesses. . . . Those courts declining to adopt an absolute rule have nonetheless recognized that such material is entitled to special protection. . . .

We do not decide the issue at this time. It is clear that the Magistrate applied the wrong standard when he concluded that the Government had made a sufficient showing of necessity to overcome the protections of the work-product doctrine. The Magistrate applied the "substantial need" and "without undue hardship" standard articulated in the first part of Rule 26(b)(3). The notes and memoranda sought by the Government here, however, are work product based on oral statements. If they reveal communications, they are, in this case, protected by the attorney-client privilege. To the extent they do not reveal communications, they reveal the attorneys' mental processes in evaluating the communications. As Rule 26 and *Hickman* make clear, such work product cannot be disclosed simply on a showing of substantial need and inability to obtain the equivalent without undue hardship.

19.   Thomas described his notes of the interviews as containing "what I considered to be the important questions, the substance of the responses to them, my beliefs, as to the importance of these, my beliefs as to how they related to the inquiry, my thoughts as to how they related to other questions. In some instances they might even suggest other questions that I would have to ask or things that I needed to find elsewhere." . . .

While we are not prepared at this juncture to say that such material is always protected by the work-product rule, we think a far stronger showing of necessity and unavailability by other means than was made by the Government or applied by the Magistrate in this case would be necessary to compel disclosure.... [W]e ... reverse the judgment of the Court of Appeals for the Sixth Circuit and remand the case to it for such further proceedings in connection with the work-product claim as are consistent with this opinion....

Chief Justice BURGER, concurring in part and concurring in the judgment.

I join in Parts I and III of the opinion of the Court and in the judgment. As to Part II, I agree fully with the Court's rejection of the so-called "control group" test, its reasons for doing so, and its ultimate holding that the communications at issue are privileged. As the Court states, however, "if the purpose of the attorney-client privilege is to be served, the attorney and client must be able to predict with some degree of certainty whether particular discussions will be protected." ... For this very reason, I believe that we should articulate a standard that will govern similar cases and afford guidance to corporations, counsel advising them, and federal courts.

The Court properly relies on a variety of factors in concluding that the communications now before us are privileged.... Because of the great importance of the issue, in my view the Court should make clear now that, as a general rule, a communication is privileged at least when, as here, an employee or former employee speaks at the direction of the management with an attorney regarding conduct or proposed conduct within the scope of employment. The attorney must be one authorized by the management to inquire into the subject and must be seeking information to assist counsel in performing any of the following functions: (a) evaluating whether the employee's conduct has bound or would bind the corporation; (b) assessing the legal consequences, if any, of that conduct; or (c) formulating appropriate legal responses to actions that have been or may be taken by others with regard to that conduct.... Other communications between employees and corporate counsel may indeed be privileged ... but the need for certainty does not compel us now to prescribe all the details of the privilege in this case.

Nevertheless, to say we should not reach all facets of the privilege does not mean that we should neglect our duty to provide guidance in a case that squarely presents the question in a traditional adversary context. Indeed, because Federal Rule of Evidence 501 provides that the law of privileges "shall be governed by the principles of the common law as they may be interpreted by the courts of the United States in the light of reason and experience," this Court has a special duty to clarify aspects of the law of privileges properly before us. Simply asserting that this failure "may to some slight extent undermine desirable certainty" ... neither minimizes the consequences of continuing uncertainty and confusion nor harmonizes the inherent dissonance of acknowledging that uncertainty while declining to clarify it within the frame of issues presented.

KEY POINTS

1. The attorney-client privilege extends to corporations, but there is not a simple test to determine whether a communication is covered by the privilege. If an employee makes a communication to a lawyer at the direction of a superior for the purpose of

obtaining legal advice for the corporation about a matter relevant to the scope of the employee's corporate duties, the communication is likely to be privileged.

2. Privileging the communication to the attorney does not privilege the underlying facts. The employee may be deposed and must answer truthfully and fully about the relevant matter, but may not be asked "What did you say to corporate counsel?"

NOTES AND QUESTIONS

1. *Upjohn* involved application of the work-product doctrine in addition to the attorney-client privilege. The Supreme Court initially announced the doctrine, now codified in Fed. R. Civ. P. 26(b)(3), in Hickman v. Taylor, 329 U.S. 495, 511 (1947):

> Proper preparation of a client's case demands that [the lawyer] assemble information, sift what he considers to be the relevant from the irrelevant facts, prepare his legal theories and plan his strategy without undue and needless interference. . . .
> . . . This work is reflected, of course, in interviews, statements, memoranda, correspondence, briefs, mental impressions, personal beliefs, and the countless other tangible and intangible ways — aptly though roughly termed by the Circuit Court of Appeals in this case as the "work product of the lawyer." Were such materials open to opposing counsel on mere demand, much of what is now put down in writing would remain unwritten. An attorney's thought, heretofore inviolate, would not be his own. Inefficiency, unfairness and sharp practices would inevitably develop in the giving of legal advice and in preparation of cases for trial. The effect on the legal profession would be demoralizing. And the interests of the clients and the cause of justice would be poorly served.

Although the Court's rhetoric may be a bit extreme, this language suggests a rationale for the work-product doctrine that is similar to that often suggested for the attorney-client privilege.

2. Should corporations possess an attorney-client privilege? How do they differ in relevant respects from individuals? In thinking about this, is it pertinent that corporations cannot claim the Fifth Amendment privilege against self-incrimination? Is it sensible to speak of a corporation's "expectation of privacy"?

3. What are the consequences of permitting assertion of the privilege in *Upjohn*? What would have been the consequences of forbidding it? How costly would discovery have been? How costly do you think the litigation trying to avoid discovery was? How do these costs relate to the policies of the privilege?

4. Where does the law stand in the aftermath of *Upjohn*? The Court rejected the control group test, but refused to replace it with a new test, electing instead to determine on a case-by-case basis whether the privilege exists. See page 814, supra. How clear is the Court's opinion? Could it have been clearer? Should it have been? Where does the subject matter test stand in the wake of *Upjohn*?

5. When new management take over a corporation, they, not the previous management, are the holders of the corporation's privilege, and may decide whether to assert or waive it, even with respect to statements made by previous management. Commodity Futures Trading Commn. v. Weintraub, 470 U.S. 1026 (1985).

6. One issue that often arises is whether a corporation waives its attorney client privilege when it conducts an internal investigation of corporate wrongdoing. In In re Woolworth Corp. Securities Class Action Litig., 1996 U.S. Dist. LEXIS 7773 (S.D.N.Y. June 6, 1996), the court held that an internal investigative report prepared

jointly by attorneys and accountants was protected by the attorney-client privilege. Relying on *Upjohn*, the court stated that where counsel had been retained by upper management to conduct an internal investigation, notes and memoranda reflecting communications between a corporation's employees and counsel were protected by the attorney-client privilege. The court also stated that strong public policy considerations militated against a broad finding of waiver with regard to the investigator's underlying notes and memoranda, when the investigative report was given to the SEC and released to the public: "A finding that publication of an internal investigative report constitutes waiver might well discourage corporations from taking the responsible step of employing outside counsel to conduct an investigation when wrongdoing is suspected." In contrast, in In re Kidder Peabody Securities Litigation, 168 F.R.D. 459 (S.D.N.Y. 1996), the court held that a securities firm waived the attorney-client privilege by publicly releasing an internal investigative report and by attempting to use the favorable report as a "sword" in litigation. The securities firm had invoked the privilege with respect to notes from interviews of individuals who were employed by the firm at the time of the interview. Relying on In re von Bulow, 828 F.2d 94, 100-103 (2d Cir. 1987), the court said that the scope of any waiver by virtue of disclosure was to be defined by the so-called "fairness doctrine," which turns on the circumstances of the disclosure. The court said that disclosure in a "judicial" setting does trigger a waiver by implication for related and otherwise privileged materials. It held that, under the particular facts of the case, Kidder had waived its privilege by repeated injection of the substance of the investigative report into "this and other litigations" and into related litigative contexts. The offer of the Kidder report to the SEC was said to represent Kidder's continuing effort to influence the outcome of pending or anticipated litigations and agency investigations.

7. Some critics express concern that privilege challenges and crime-fraud proceedings are undermining the ability of corporate defendants to protect legitimate claims of privilege, especially in highly regulated industries where product liability litigation has been significant. In one example, the State of Minnesota and Blue Cross and Blue Shield of Minnesota brought suit against 11 tobacco manufacturers for reimbursement of Medicaid costs related to the treatment of smoking related illnesses in State by Humphrey v. Philip Morris, Inc., 1998 Minn. App. LEXIS 431 (Minn. Ct. App. Mar. 17, 1998), stay denied 523 U.S. 1056 (1998). The plaintiffs used broad allegations of fraud and conspiracy in its production requests, which ultimately resulted in the production of more than 33 million pages and privilege logs identifying more than 200,000 privileged documents. The Minnesota district court found that an *in camera* review of the privileged documents was required after the plaintiff's prima facie showing of crime-fraud.

To facilitate the massive task of reviewing the documents, the court instituted a system of random review or spot checking. The defendants were ordered to separate the privileged documents into 16 categories. To determine where there was privilege, the special master reviewed documents from each category. He eventually reviewed approximately 800 of the 200,000 documents and made his recommendation based on this "illustrative" sample. The court held that four categories of documents were not privileged, releasing approximately 39,000 documents to the plaintiffs. Privilege challenges, it has been argued, are becoming a more common trial strategy for plaintiffs who are unburdened by massive production requests that drain the resources of corporate defendants. For an in depth discussion of the problem, see John J. Mulderig, Leslie Wharton, and Cynthia S. Cecil, Tobacco Cases May Be Only the Tip of the

Iceberg for Assaults on Privilege, 67 Def. Counsel J. 16 (2000); David J. Fried, Too High a Price for Truth: The Exception to the Attorney-Client Privilege for Contemplated Crimes and Frauds, 64 N.C. L. Rev. 443 (1986). The privilege as it relates to crime-fraud proceedings is discussed more fully in the section "Exceptions to the Privilege", beginning on page 822, infra. It is mentioned here to sensitize you to one of the problems with the attorney-client privilege that occurs within the corporate context.

PROBLEMS

12.10. Defendant Admiral Insurance Co. has filed a petition for writ of mandamus directing the district court to vacate its order compelling production of communications secured by Admiral's counsel in anticipation of a securities fraud suit. In June 1987, counsel for Admiral had interviewed the two Admiral executives who were most informed about Admiral's allegedly fraudulent transactions in Arizona properties. The two executives resigned soon after the interviews. When plaintiffs, individuals injured by the transactions, scheduled the former executives for deposition, counsel for the two executives responded that they would invoke the Fifth Amendment. Plaintiff seeks production of the statements on the basis that the information is unavailable from any other source. Admiral argues that these statements are protected from disclosure by the attorney-corporate client privilege. How should the court rule?

12.11. Plaintiffs have moved to compel the production of a diary written by Jeanette Curry while she was an employee of defendant Dayco Corporation. Jeanette compiled the diary at the direction of outside counsel to her employer. The diary chronicled events that form the basis for part of the present securities litigation. Plaintiffs contend that any privilege that might protect the contents of the diary has been waived since a newspaper reporter obtained a copy of the diary from an unidentified source. The defendants (Dayco and Jeanette) argue that the contents are protected by the attorney-corporate client privilege and work-product doctrine. They argue that since Jeanette did not authorize disclosure, there has been no waiver. What result?

12.12. Employees of several Chemical Bank branches under the supervision of Demauro were investigated for violation of the Bank Secrecy Act, which makes 'laundering' money (exchanging large denomination bills for small ones) illegal. Demauro gave false testimony to a grand jury about his knowledge of the violations and has been charged with perjury. To establish that he knowingly made false statements to the grand jury, the prosecution seeks to introduce the testimony of Chemical Bank's attorney, Martin. When Chemical Bank became aware of the criminal investigation, it asked Martin to conduct an internal investigation into employee wrongdoing. In the course of the investigation, Martin interviewed Demauro in his capacity as Vice President in charge of 23 branches. Demauro insists that his communications with Martin are protected by attorney-client privilege. Should the judge allow Martin's testimony?

12.13. Chicago Police Officer Rehling was injured and had part of one leg amputated after an automobile ran him down several years ago. Rehling finished a long period of medical leave and then requested reassignment on a limited duty basis to District 16, his former assignment. He worked for a few months processing citations at District 16 before he was transferred to the Alternative Response Unit, where officers handle incoming requests for the dispatch of squad cars. Rehling was unhappy with the transfer and sued the city under the American's with Disabilities Act, claiming discrimination against him due to his disability and failure to provide him with a reasonable accommodation. The City made a motion *in limine* to bar the testimony of Zoufal, General Counsel to the Superintendent of Police, based on their attorney-client privilege. Zoufal had allegedly stated that the Chicago Police Department could not have a "cripple" in a position where he would interact with the public because of the likelihood of the negative reaction it would draw. Rehling has argued that Zoufal, in his "business capacity as a decision-maker," decided to have him transferred out of District 16. The city has countered by asserting that Zoufal was giving legal advice when he encouraged ranking members of the Police Department to order the transfer. Is Zoufal's testimony privileged?

3. The Government Client

The attorney-client privilege extends to entity clients other than corporations. Federal courts generally agree that the government, as client, should be afforded the protection of the attorney-client privilege. Some of the same difficulties that arise in regards to corporate clients are also present when the client is the government: Who exactly is the client? Who may invoke and waive the privilege? What is required to maintain a privilege's requirement of confidentiality? And, what constitutes a waiver? Since there has been no equivalent to *Upjohn* to define the parameters of the governmental attorney-client privilege, courts have tended to follow the law of corporate privilege. See, e.g., Galarza v. United States, 179 F.R.D. 291 (S.D. Ca. 1998).

In In re: Grand Jury Subpeona Duces Tecum, 112 F.3d. 910 (8th Cir. 1997), cert. denied sub. nom. Office of the President v. Office of the Independent Counsel, 521 U.S. 1105 (1997), the court held that the White House may not use a governmental attorney-client privilege to withhold potentially relevant information from a federal grand jury. The strong public interest in honest government and in exposing wrongdoing by public officials, it said, would be ill-served by the use of a governmental attorney-client privilege in criminal proceedings.

In so deciding, the court highlighted two important distinctions between corporate and governmental clients. The White House, unlike private corporations, is not subject to any criminal liability and all government agents have a public duty to report wrongdoing. There seems to be an intuitive problem, the court said, with allowing the government to conceal evidence from a court, especially in criminal cases.

Only a year later, the Independent Counsel moved to compel the grand jury testimony of Deputy White House Counsel Bruce Lindsey after he declined to answer certain questions based on the governmental attorney-client privilege in In re Lindsey (Grand Jury Testimony), 158 F.3d 1263 (D.C. Cir. 1998). Like the Eighth Circuit, the court abrogated the governmental attorney-client privilege in criminal grand jury proceedings. Both cases clearly rejected the privilege in criminal proceedings only, leaving the governmental attorney-client privilege intact in civil cases. The Seventh Circuit also has rejected the privilege. In re Witness Before the Special Grand Jury 2000-2, 288 F.3d 289 (7th Cir. 2002) (holding that no attorney-client privilege existed between a state officer and government lawyer in context of federal criminal investigation).

However, the Second Circuit recently declined to follow *Lindsey*, in In re Grand Jury Investigation, 399 F.3d 527 (2d Cir. 2005), holding that the privilege exists and is enforceable in criminal proceedings as well. The court held that the Connecticut governor's office could invoke the attorney-client privilege against federal grand jury inquiries into conversations with former legal counsel, which were sought in connection with a federal bribery investigation. Id. at 536. The court reasoned that "[u]pholding the privilege furthers a culture in which consultation with government lawyers is accepted as a normal, desirable, and even indispensable part of conducting public business." Id. at 534. Although federal law applied in the case, the court gave weight to the fact that Connecticut had enacted a statute granting the privilege, noting that "the people of Connecticut, acting through their representatives, concluded that the public interest is advanced by upholding a governmental privilege even in the face of a criminal investigation." Id. For further discussion see Bryan S. Gowdy, Note: Should the Federal Government Have an Attorney-Client Privilege?, 51 Fla. L. Rev. 695 (1999).

4. Exceptions to the Privilege

There are four main exceptions to the attorney-client privilege:

a. Breach of Duty by a Lawyer or Client

The first exception applies to controversy between attorney and client. If a client sues for damages for the attorney's negligence or the attorney sues for fees due, the client may not invoke the privilege to bar admission of relevant evidence. Though the attorney-client communications remain protected against disclosure to outsiders, as between attorney and client the privilege is inapplicable. McCormick argues that the exception is premised on the "practical necessity that if effective legal service is to be encouraged the privilege must not stand in the way of the lawyer's just enforcement of his rights to be paid a fee and to protect his reputation." Kenneth S. Broun et al., McCormick on Evidence §91, at 143 (5th ed. 1999). Is that persuasive to you? Why is "encouraging effective legal service" important enough to pierce the veil of confidentiality, but determining, say, who committed a murder is not?

b. Document Attested by a Lawyer

A second exception concerns the attorney who acts as attesting witness on a document executed by the client. The exception is most commonly applied in will contests between the heirs or personal representatives of the deceased client. Although the privilege generally survives the death of a client, if an attorney acts as attesting witness to his client's will, the attorney is permitted to testify regarding the validity or interpretation of the will.

c. Identity of Client, Fee Information, and Related Matters

The third exception, which is the subject of increasing controversy in the courts, denies the privilege for certain fundamental information about the attorney-client relationship, such as the identity of the client, the client's address and occupation, and the attorney's fee arrangement. The exception is supported by some courts on the ground that such information does not involve a confidential communication. See In the Matter of Witnesses Before the Special March 1980 Grand Jury Appeal of United States, 729 F.2d 489 (7th Cir. 1984). Other courts have argued that such matters are not privileged because they are "preliminary, by their nature, establishing only the existence of the relation between client and counsel." In re Grand Jury Subpoenas (United States v. Hirsch), 803 F.2d 493, 496 (9th Cir. 1986).

Notwithstanding such arguments, courts have created three exceptions to the traditional rule that attorney's fees and client identity are not privileged. The first exception, known as the "legal advice" exception, holds that such information is protected by the privilege where there is a strong likelihood that disclosure would implicate the client in the very matter for which legal advice was sought. See In re Grand Jury Proceedings (Twist), 689 F.2d 1351, 1352 (11th Cir. 1982). The second exception, known as the "communication rationale" exception, holds that identity and fee information are privileged if disclosure would connect the client with a previously disclosed and independently privileged communication. See In re Shargel, 742 F.2d 61, 64 (2d Cir. 1984). The third exception privileges identity and fee information if it provides the "last link" in a chain of incriminating evidence that could result in criminal prosecution of the client. See In re Grand Jury Proceedings (Pavlick), 680 F.2d 1026, 1027 (5th Cir. 1982) (en banc), rev'g 663 F.2d 1057 (5th Cir. 1981); Baird v. Koerner, 279 F.2d 623, 633 (9th Cir. 1960) (attorney made payment to IRS of back taxes for client but refused to reveal name of client). These exceptions have not been uniformly approved by the courts. In fact, after a small burst of enthusiasm for them following the seminal decision in Baird v. Koerner, the courts have become disenchanted. For example, the Ninth Circuit, which decided Baird, now takes the position that only the "confidential communications" exception remains good law. Tornay v. United States, 840 F.2d 1424 (9th Cir. 1988). Much more typical of the current judicial attitude toward these matters is In re Grand Jury Investigation 83-2-35 (Durant), 723 F.2d 447 (6th Cir. 1983). In Durant, checks had been stolen from IBM and deposited in various bank accounts. Durant, an attorney, had been paid for legal services out of one of these accounts. Thus identifying the client who had paid him would probably identify a person involved with the thefts. Durant was required to disclose that information. For an argument that exceptions to the privilege should focus exclusively on the client's intent, see Developments in the Law — Privileged Communications, 98 Harv. L. Rev. 1501 (1985).

d. Communication in Furtherance of a Crime or Fraud

Though communications regarding a past crime or fraud are privileged, communications in furtherance of an ongoing or future illegality are not. The rationale behind the exception is that where a client seeks advice to aid a crime or fraud, the client does not retain an attorney in his professional capacity. In order to defeat the privilege, the party seeking disclosure bears the burden of bringing the communication within the crime-fraud exception.

In applying the crime-fraud exception, many courts follow the intent-based test announced in Clark v. United States, 289 U.S. 1 (1933). Under this test, the party invoking the exception must make a prima facie showing that the attorney-client communications were made for the purpose of furthering the commission of a future or present crime or fraud. The test focuses strictly on the client's intent. Thus, even if the attorney acted in good faith and was unaware of the wrongdoing, the privilege may be lost. For an example, see In re Grand Jury Proceedings No. 96-55344, 87 F.3d 377 (9th Cir. 1996). The Second Circuit has referred to the burden in terms of a probable cause showing to believe that the client consulted the attorney for the purpose of furthering wrongful conduct. See In re Grand Jury Subpoena Duces Tecum Dated Sept. 15, 1983, 731 F.2d 1032, 1039 (2d. Cir. 1984). Other courts have defined the evidentiary standard differently. For example, in In re Grand Jury Investigation, 842 F.2d 1223 (11th Cir. 1987), the court used a two part test to decide whether the crime-fraud exception applied an attorney-client communication, not only requiring the prima facie showing of crime-fraud purpose, but also "showing that the attorney's assistance was obtained in furtherance of the criminal or fraudulent activity or was closely related to it." Id. at 1226. The correct answer should be that the finding is governed by FRE 104(a), and thus that its necessary conditions must be found by a preponderance of the evidence.

Remember that privileges do apply in preliminary factfinding. Under what circumstances, then, may allegedly privileged material be consulted to determine if it is privileged? This was the question facing the Court in United States v. Zolin, 491 U.S. 554 (1989). The Court held that before engaging in in camera review of the allegedly privileged material to decide the privilege question, the trial court "should require a factual basis adequate to support a good faith belief by a reasonable person" that in camera review would establish that the crime-fraud exception applies and that the communication would be admitted. Id. at 572. The court concluded that the evidentiary threshold could be satisfied by any relevant evidence, whether or not it was independent of the allegedly privileged communication. Id. at 574. For further discussion of the effect of Zolin on the crime-fraud exception, see Christopher Paul Galanek, Note, The Impact of the Zolin Decision on the Crime-Fraud Exception to the Attorney-Client Privilege, 24 Ga. L. Rev. 1115 (1990).

The crime-fraud exception applies both to the attorney-client privilege and to the attorney's ethical duty of confidentiality. See Rules 1.2(d) and 1.6(b) in the ABA's Model Rules of Professional Conduct (2005) for provisions dealing with a client's illegal conduct. Is an attorney ethically obligated to report future crimes on the part of a client? What about past crimes? Compare ABA Model Rules of Professional Conduct, Rule 1.6(b), with ABA Model Code of Professional Responsibility, DR 4-101(C).

The crime-fraud exception has also been applied to the work-product privilege. In In re Murphy, 560 F.2d 326, 328 (8th Cir. 1977), the court applied a two-part test to determine which work-product documents would be admitted into evidence. Under the test, the party must (1) make a prima facie showing of crime or fraud; and (2) show a relationship between the illegal conduct and the attorney's work product. This test has been criticized on the ground that it disregards the client's intent. See, e.g., In re International Sys. & Controls Corp Sec. Litig., 693 F.2d 1235, 1243 (5th Cir. 1982).

For further discussion of the crime-fraud exception, see generally David J. Fried, Too High a Price for Truth: The Exception to the Attorney-Client Privilege for Contemplated Crimes and Frauds, 64 N.C. L. Rev. 443 (1986); Ann M. St. Peter-Griffith, Abusing the Privilege: The Crime-Fraud Exception to Rule 501 of the Federal Rules of Evidence, 48 U. Miami L. Rev. 259 (1993).

PROBLEMS

12.14. A federal grand jury indicted Edwin Lewis and three others with conspiring to violate federal immigration laws. The indictment alleged that Lewis had falsely held himself out to be an attorney, and had filed fraudulent amnesty applications with the Immigration and Naturalization Service (INS) on behalf of over 100 clients. A search warrant allowed the government to seize client files from Lewis's office. The files contained four types of documents: (1) completed INS forms; (2) forms prepared in house by the law firm (forms designed to elicit information for the applications); (3) materials designed to corroborate the information contained in the INS forms; and (4) notes apparently prepared by agents of the law firm. Some of the other items seized from the offices included blank boarding passes; blank stationery from airlines and blank stationery from various Consulates General, presumably used to create false evidence of foreign travel; and blank pay receipts from various businesses, presumably used to create false evidence of employment.

Some of Lewis's clients had filed for amnesty with the INS, while others had sought his legal advice regarding amnesty but had not filed applications at the time Lewis was arrested. The only way the government can find out the identity of these latter clients is by looking at Lewis's files. What arguments can the government make that they are entitled to all of the evidence seized from Lewis's office? Are there any special problems they might run into regarding the anonymous clients?

12.15. The government obtained a warrant and seized files and materials from a law firm that is the subject of a criminal proceeding. The files are currently sealed by court order, pending a decision as to whether the files should be protected by the attorney-client privilege. The government concedes that the firm has the right to invoke the privilege on behalf of its clients but contends that the crime-fraud exception removes these materials from the scope of the privilege. Should the crime-fraud exception apply where the alleged criminality being investigated is solely that of the law firm? If so, the government will be given access to the confidential files of innocent clients. If not, the law firm will be able to hinder an investigation of its own alleged criminal conduct by asserting a privilege designed to protect clients. Should the court allow the files to be unsealed?

12.16. Ralls was paid by a client/fee-payer to defend Bonnette against criminal charges connected to Bonnette's attempt to transport 300 pounds of cocaine from Arizona to California. The government sought to discover the name of the person who hired Ralls and the amount and method of payment. Ralls moved to quash the government's grand jury subpoena on the basis of attorney-client privilege. The district court ordered Ralls to testify as to the client's identity and the fee arrangements but held that the conversations between Ralls and the client were privileged. Should an appellate court affirm this decision?

12.17. Elsa and Arlen were in the midst of a messy divorce. During a custody fight over their two sons, Lars and Herbie, Elsa met with her attorney, Friedman. Elsa was convinced that Arlen had been sexually abusing the children. Friedman invited Elsa's friend, Margie, to be present in order to have a "cool head" in the room. While in front of Friedman, Elsa and Margie began discussing ways of killing Arlen or hurting the children and framing Arlen for it. Friedman, afraid that Elsa and Margie might be serious, informed a judge. The judge announced the substance of Friedman's disclosure at the custody hearing, and Arlen was granted custody, while Friedman's appearance as Elsa's counsel was stricken. Margie later broke into Arlen's house carrying a gun, found him asleep in his bed, and fired two shots, hitting him once in the leg. Margie was arrested and pled guilty to a serious of assault related crimes. Elsa is now on trial for conspiracy to commit murder and conspiracy to commit assault. The prosecution has called Friedman to testify to the conspiracy related communications that he witnessed between Elsa and Margie in his office, but Elsa has asserted the attorney-client privilege to bar his testimony. What result?

5. Reflection on the Attorney-Client Privilege

The attorney-client privilege is the oldest of the confidential communication privileges. Still, debate has continued over why the privilege should exist. Such debate has often focused on the costs that the privilege entails. One argument, employing a microeconomic perspective, has been made that the attorney-client privilege has benefits that justify its costs. The following excerpt discusses these and other related matters:

RONALD J. ALLEN, MARK F. GRADY, DANIEL D. POLSBY, AND MICHAEL S. YASHKO, A POSITIVE THEORY OF THE ATTORNEY-CLIENT PRIVILEGE AND THE WORK PRODUCT DOCTRINE

19 J. Legal Stud. 359 (1990)

I. INTRODUCTION

Protecting the confidentiality of legal information is an odd goal in a judicial system that values openness as highly as ours does. In some litigation settings we make a fetish out of free access to all information. Modern discovery rules can require parties to exchange boxcars of records with one another, and attorneys are under an obligation to disclose cases that run against the arguments that they make. The argument for openness is in principle strong. When there are no surprises at trial, the parties more likely will join issue on the real questions of fact and law — those that properly should determine case outcomes.

Why, then, do the confidentiality doctrines remain? The conventional response quickly runs up against an insoluble dilemma. It accepts the aspirations of modern discovery systems, including the one forbidding counsel from participating in perjurious efforts; it posits costless rules of confidentiality that have no effect on the opponent's ability to obtain information; and then it asserts that these supposedly costless rules nonetheless create incentives for clients to disclose information to counsel.[20] How can this be? If confidentiality rules do not increase the cost of obtaining information once it is in the lawyer's possession, and if the lawyer must rigorously police the client's responses to the opponent to ensure no prevarication or sleight of hand, then the client will have no incentive to disclose unfavorable information to the lawyer.

---

20. See for example Stephen A. Saltzburg, Corporate and Related Attorney-Client Privilege Claims: A Suggested Approach, 12 Hofstra L. Rev. 279, 283-284 (1984).

Because of the tension between the conventional view of the confidentiality rules and their purported consequences, some scholars have recognized that the justifications for the rules are insubstantial,[21] but they have not examined the assumption that confidentiality rules are costless.[22] This failure may be a testament to the strength of the commitment to openness in the legal process. To admit that the rules of confidentiality are costly requires one to recognize that they do indeed constrain openness. If confidentiality rules impose costs, and we assert that they do, the effect is to increase the cost to the opponent of securing the relevant information, whatever it may be. Because of the confidentiality rules, for example, rather than simply asking the attorney to turn over the entire case file, the opponent must secure that information in other ways, such as deposing the client. That in itself may increase costs, and in addition the client will have the aid of counsel before and at the deposition, which may make the opponent's task of extracting the information more difficult and thus more costly still. After all, merely having to ask two questions instead of one to get the requested information increases costs. Under our theory, however, the costs of confidentiality are not regrettable; rather, they are the conditions that create incentives to disclose to the lawyer: the more costly an opponent's efforts to obtain information disclosed to the lawyer, the less likely the opponent will secure that information, and the greater the corresponding incentive to disclose it to the lawyer. Once the information is in the lawyer's possession, the lawyer may guide the litigation in directions unanticipated by the client, and here lie the benefits of the confidentiality rules that justify their costs.

We develop these points here and propose a positive theory that explains the confidentiality rules. Two doctrines authorize or mandate lawyers to preserve the confidentiality of their clients' legal affairs. The attorney-client privilege exempts from discovery and production at trial confidential communications from client to lawyer, and confidential communications from lawyer to client that may expose a client's confidential communication, if made for the purpose of securing legal advice.[23] The work product doctrine exempts from production material generated by the attorney in anticipation of litigation.[24] These doctrines affect decision making on two margins. The expectation of confidentiality can affect a client's decision concerning how much unfavorable information to divulge to a lawyer and, at a limit, whether to go to a lawyer at all. Without legal protection, a client might otherwise anticipate that divulging information to a lawyer would reduce an opponent's cost of acquiring it. Thus, contrary to the conventional theory of the privilege, one of effects of the privilege must be to raise — or at least not lower — the cost of obtaining useful information once it is in the hands of the attorney. Confidentiality can also affect the amount of information produced by the lawyer. When lawyers cannot produce favorable information without also producing unfavorable information, lack of confidentiality would reduce the amount of favorable information that

---

21.   It is this recognition that makes explaining such matters as waiver under the privilege so difficult. See, for example, Richard Marcus, The Perils of Privilege: Waiver and the Litigator, 84 Mich. L. Rev. 1605, 1619-1622 (1986).

22.   Yet other scholars, convinced that the rules of confidentiality impose greater costs than they secure benefits, argue for eliminating some or all of the rules. See, for example, Marvin Frankel, Partisan Justice (1980). For a discussion, see Albert Alschuler, The Preservation of a Client's Confidences: One Value Among Many or a Categorical Imperative?, 52 Colo. L. Rev. 349 (1981).

23.   John Henry Wigmore, 4 Evidence §§2285-2292 (1905). We are relying on the 1905 edition of Wigmore because we are more interested in his views than his subsequent compilers. See also Developments in the Law: Privileged Communications, 98 Harv. L. Rev. 1450, 1501 (1985).

24.   Hickman v. Taylor, 329 U.S. 495 (1947); Fed. Rule Civil Proc. 26(b)(3).

lawyers would produce.[25] In brief, our argument is that the attorney-client privilege and the work product doctrine offer two perspectives on a larger goal, which is to increase the amount of information available to courts about disputes and to work against the disincentives to the production of that information which would otherwise exist. In our legal system, lawyers are both conduits of information from their clients to the courts and independent producers of information for the same audience. The attorney-client privilege takes the client's perspective and establishes the level of confidentiality needed to get the client to consult a lawyer and to divulge the optimum amount of information to him. The work product doctrine then takes the attorney's perspective and provides the level of confidentiality needed to induce the attorney to perform the optimal amount of legal investigation. . . .

II.   THE ATTORNEY-CLIENT PRIVILEGE AND THE CONTINGENT CLAIM THEORY . . .

A.   Theories About The Attorney-Client Theory

1.   The Contingent Claim Theory

In contrast to some contemporary theories of the privilege, ours assumes that it must impose some costs upon the adversary. If a person believes that disclosure of an unfavorable fact to an attorney could reduce the other side's costs to discover it, this belief may deter the party from divulging the fact to his lawyer. And without a privilege, a party may very well believe that disclosure to an attorney would reduce his opponent's cost of discovery. The attorney is a repeat player in the legal system, and so is likely to co-operate with other repeat players. Moreover, the attorney is ethically bound to respect the system's rules. Accordingly, a client reasonably could believe that in the absence of a privilege an attorney would truthfully answer the question: "What has your client told you?" A client left entirely to his own, by contrast, may feel that he has more room to maneuver. Thus, one might expect a client to conclude that, absent a privilege, divulging information to a lawyer will reduce his opponent's costs of discovering information.

The existence of a privilege changes things. The privilege at a minimum does not decrease the adversary's costs in obtaining information, and in fact it may increase them. There is no decrease because the adversary must still obtain information from the client, just as he would have been required to do had the client never consulted an attorney. Costs may increase because the lawyer may give the client guidance in how to respond honestly but craftily to an interrogatory, thus making the adversary's task of obtaining complete information more difficult. In any event, if the privilege does not increase the other side's discovery costs, there is no conceivable reason for it, a point

25.   Ethical rules also comprise a form of legally mandated confidentiality. The lawyer's ethical obligations pose the problem of how to prevent the agent from expropriating the principal — the lawyer could threaten to inform on his client and thereby get a payment from him. The other two rules — the attorney-client privilege and the work product doctrine — address a different problem: how much information about legal disputes will clients and lawyers produce. Accordingly, the ethical obligations of lawyers are beyond the scope of this Article. . . .

We also put aside the question of the implications of the privilege for nonlitigation oriented activity. The problem there, again, does not center on the production of legal information. Instead, it centers on providing the optimum incentives to ensure compliance with the law. For a preliminary exploration of that issue, see Ronald J. Allen and Cynthia M. Hazelwood, Preserving the Confidentiality of Internal Corporate Investigations, 12 J. Corp. L. 355 (1987).

that Kaplow and Shavell have made before us.[26] Moreover, there is evidence suggesting that the privilege does increase discovery costs. The most telling datum may be the continuing existence of attorney-client privilege cases. If opponents could acquire information just as cheaply by alternative means, there would be little reason for them to litigate whether that same information is protected by the privilege. In addition, studies indicate that lawyers often assert after trial that the other side did not acquire all the relevant unfavorable facts. Some of these unfavorable facts must be privileged under the current rules, which is one reason they never see the light.

Moreover, notwithstanding the ostensible dedication of the legal system to open discovery, the attorney is not in fact expected to act as a policeman regulating in detail the forthrightness of the client's responses to an opponent. Perjury is a limit, but there is a large gap between absolute candor and perjury. As the activity of the client moves towards the perjurious pole, the chances increase that a court will hold there to be no privilege, but there nonetheless remains a large area within which clients and attorneys may maneuver while blanketed with the protections of the privilege.[27] It is here that the actual incentives created by the privilege become clear, and they entail the possibility that the privilege will detract from, rather than just be neutral with respect to, the objective of openness in the system.

Given that the privilege must entail costs — and the enormous volume of litigation over the privilege could hardly be explained unless it were pretty clear that the privilege did impede full discovery — it is necessary to understand the benefits it provides. Existing theories of the privilege do not answer this question. In fact, two benefits result. First, the privilege facilitates the examination of contingent claims and in so doing furthers the values served by those claims. Second, it reduces perjury in the system as a whole. We discuss these points in turn.

Many legal claims depend on facts that may appear to the lay person as unfavorable to the party asserting the legal claim. For example, a party's defense of contributory negligence often entails the concession of his own negligence. Similarly, for a party to claim that he was incompetent to enter a contract often involves conceding that an agreement was reached.

This contingent structure of the law may be the most visible remnant of the old system of special pleading.[28] Under common law pleading requirements, the parties pleaded against each other until they joined issue on a question of law or fact. Each time one party pleaded, the other would have an opportunity either to demur, or to deny the truth of his opponent's allegations, or to introduce new matter and thus to confess and avoid it.[29] In the earliest days of the common law, unlike our modern era,

---

26. Louis Kaplow and Steven Shavell, Legal Advice About Information to Present in Litigation: Its Effects and Social Desirability, 102 Harv. L. Rev. 565, 570 (1989).

27. The formal rules of confidentiality actually protect a certain amount of evasion by the attorney. For example, the Model Rules of Professional Conduct, in a Comment to rules on "Candor Toward the Tribunal," state that "An advocate . . . is usually not required to have personal knowledge of matters asserted in [pleadings and other litigation documents], for litigation documents ordinarily present assertions by the client, or by someone on the client's behalf, and not assertions by the lawyer." Rule 3.3, Comment, Representations by a Lawyer [2] (1984). Creating a distinction between the client's and the lawyer's knowledge encourages lawyers to learn of the client's information without fully "knowing" it for purposes of the ethical rules.

28. See Richard A. Epstein, A Theory of Strict Liability, 2 J. Legal Stud. 151 (1973); Richard A. Epstein, Defenses and Subsequent Pleas in a System of Strict Liability, 3 J. Legal Stud. 165 (1974).

29. See Thomas Chitty, Treatise on Pleading with Precedents and Forms (13th ed. 1859); James Fitzjames Stephen, A Treatise on the Principles of Pleading in Civil Actions (Tyler ed. 1882); Joseph H. Koffler and Alison Reppy, Common Law Pleading 433-531 (1969); Richard A. Epstein, Pleadings and Presumptions, 40 U. Chi. L. Rev. 556 (1973).

the two were strict alternatives. The common law's nurturance of special pleas made contingent claims common. Parties could and frequently did confess and avoid the pleas of their opponents. Thus, if a party pleaded the making of a contract, his opponent could specially plead that he was incompetent to contract because of age or some other reason. If a party pleaded that the defendant struck him, his opponent could specially plead that he was acting in self defense. A special plea (confession and avoidance) by the defendant would open the door to further special pleading by the plaintiff, for instance, that the defendant used more force than was necessary to defend himself. Ultimately special pleading made lawsuits depend on narrow issues of fact or law, a result that seems alien to our civil procedure. Nonetheless, the hierarchical imprint and doctrinal structure both remain.

Our theory proceeds on the assumption that a modern litigant, like his common law ancestors, still has two main strategies for defeating an adverse claim. He can deny the claim in its own terms or defeat it with an affirmative defense, or some similar contingent claim. In the driver-pedestrian example, the driver can deny he was negligent or prove that the pedestrian was contributorily negligent. However, and this is the heart of the matter, a potential client ignorant of the law has one option and not two. He must deny the claim against him in its own terms. Of course if potential clients were always honest, they would never deceitfully deny claims. We assume that individuals will sometimes be dishonest in pursuit of their self-interest. However — and this is the second crucial component of our argument — a legal regime that reduces the costs of information about contingent claims should facilitate their examination and consequently reduce the amount of perjury. Reducing the cost of litigating contingent claims gives potential clients an incentive to substitute away from dishonest denials. Even a client inclined to commit perjury about whether he was in the intersection against the light will have less reason to do so if he can easily learn from his lawyer that the plaintiff's claim can be defeated honestly — by proving that the plaintiff was contributorily negligent in jumping out into the intersection so soon after the light changed, and without looking for opposing traffic.

In sum, by increasing the adversary's costs of obtaining information about communications between lawyers and clients, the privilege facilitates inquiry into legal claims beyond the ken of lay persons. By doing so, the values that underlie contingent claims are furthered, and contingent claims, no less than others, produce real benefits. For instance, if contributory negligence were less often interposed as a defense, it would reduce the incentives of potential victims to use the proper amount of precaution.[30] This praiseworthy result is also accompanied by a decrease in fraud in the system, which occurs each time an individual who otherwise would have committed fraud in litigation is channeled to litigate a truthful contingent claim. Under our theory, then, the ultimate justification for the privilege lies in the improvements in behavior that result from the increased availability of contingent claims.

The foregoing discussion has emphasized how "No, I didn't" and "Yes, but" can be substituting strategies for defendants. What about plaintiffs' claims, though? A plaintiff's original claim may appear to be uncontingent, depending only on facts favorable to it, but even plaintiffs' claims can become contingent when defendants oppose them. For instance, a plaintiff's claim that he lent the defendant money, which

---

30.   See for example Richard Posner, A Theory of Negligence, 1 J. Legal Stud. 29 (1973); John Prather Brown, Toward An Economic Theory of Liability, 2 J. Legal Stud. 323 (1973); Mark Grady, Common Law Control of Strategic Behavior: Railroad Sparks and the Farmer, 17 J. Legal Stud. 15 (1988).

the defendant never repaid, begins life in an entirely uncontingent form, as every prima facie showing does. Nonetheless, if the defendant maintains that he was underage at the time he borrowed, the plaintiff's claim changes character, because it can then depend on whether he made the loan so that the defendant could purchase "necessities." Similarly a plaintiff who originally pleads that the defendant was negligent may find that his ultimate claim depends on whether he or the defendant had the last clear chance.

Contingent claims are not strictly affirmative defenses. Suppose that someone has promised that he will put X's first born daughter through college. Making his communication with his lawyer confidential would increase the odds that he would truthfully claim that there was no consideration and reduce the odds that he would falsely claim that he never said it. So long as there is any set of facts more favorable to the party than those which a typical lay person would think necessary to secure a claim or defense, the contingent claim theory would predict a privilege. To give a different example, a plaintiff in a contracts case may think that all contracts have to be in writing to be enforceable, and thus is willing to assert falsely that a writing has been destroyed in order to win a case in which there was an oral promise in front of a witness. Encouraging the plaintiff to be truthful with the lawyer will lead the lawyer to direct the litigation toward the enforceable oral contract. Similarly, if a plaintiff is unaware of the nature of executory contracts, he may falsely assert reliance; but if he fully discloses to counsel, the litigation can be channeled in the proper direction.

Because both plaintiffs' and defendants' claims are or can become contingent in the litigation process, we would expect that the privilege would apply to both types. If by contrast defendants simply denied claims made against them in precisely the same form originally used by plaintiffs, or if plaintiffs' claims were not or could not become contingent, we would not predict a privilege, even though we would predict that clients would still hire lawyers. . . .

The legal system might, but does not, make confidentiality depend on whether the client's communication actually bore on a denial or a contingent claim. It would be difficult, even after litigation, to sort communications so strictly; so much more while litigation is still in progress. Moreover, a strict privilege would neglect the fact that the critical incentives must exist at a time when the reluctant client is still ill-informed about the law. Thus, if a hypothetical client would assess some nontrivial probability that a communication would be helpful in devising a contingent claim, we would expect that the communication would be privileged (unless the opponent's costs of self-production by other means are very high). If the privilege were narrower, some contingent claims would be lost. Our theory thus predicts a broad privilege, but not an unlimited one. When the lawyer could not possibly use information to develop a contingent claim, and even a relatively ignorant client would know it, our theory predicts that the client's communication would not be privileged. Many cases bear out this hypothesis.

Our theory also predicts that the privilege does not reduce the cost of making a dishonest contingent claim.[31] We will return to this point when we examine the cases, because it is critical to our theory. Nonetheless, even if the privilege did to some extent reduce the cost of dishonest contingent claims, there would still be the question of

---

31. This prediction is confirmed in cases such as Nix v. Whiteside, [475] U.S. [157] (1986), in which the Supreme Court held that the attorney acted properly in refusing to permit the client to testify falsely about a claim of self-defense.

which effect dominates: whether the privilege prevents more dishonest denials or induces more dishonest contingent claims.

In sum, the real question raised by the attorney-client privilege is virtually the opposite of the one posed by the many scholars who have criticized it. The question is not whether the privilege increases perjury, but whether the increased costs created by the privilege can be justified by the *reduced* perjury that the privilege brings about and the greater number of contingent claims that it allows to be litigated, with their beneficial real-world effects.

This perspective also provides a powerful ordering principle for the privilege. As a result of failing properly to perceive the incentive structure that underlies the privilege, traditional theorists such as Wigmore have promulgated a general "absolute" rule followed by a welter of apparently ad hoc case law exceptions. Under our theory, the appropriate question would always remain the same: Would providing a privilege advance the exploration of contingent claims at trial? Cases finding no privilege can best be understood as expressing conclusions to the contrary.[32]

Numerous critics have charged that the attorney-client privilege encourages perjury and reduces the deterrent power of the law. We think these theories are wrong, and examine the best known ones here.

2.   The Morgan Theory

Edmund Morgan's argument against the privilege was that its only practical consequence is to protect perjurers. Morgan thought that the complexity of modern law cases oblige lay persons to seek legal counsel.[33] Such persons could choose either to reveal all their facts to their lawyer or to suppress some. Called as a witness at the subsequent trial, the client would be positioned thus:

> If he told his lawyer the truth, he must now tell the same thing from the witness box. If he told his lawyer a lie and sticks to it, he will tell the same story at the trial or hearing. If he told his lawyer the truth and now tells a lie, why should he be protected from exposure? Is the privilege retained in order to protect perjurers? How can that either directly or indirectly further the administration of justice?[34]

Morgan's primary error was to use the average case to discredit the marginal one. When the marginal case is considered, it becomes evident that instead of increasing perjury, the attorney-client privilege reduces it. Typically, a client will be motivated to commit perjury when someone has made a claim against him. Even if Morgan was

---

32.   The prediction of the contingent claim theory that the privilege is best understood as a qualified rather than an absolute bar to discovery is beginning to be explicitly expressed in the cases. See, for example, Greater Newburyport Clamshell Alliance et al. v. Public Service Co. of N.H., 838 F.2d 13, 19 (1st Cir. 1988); In re Grand Jury Proc., Des Moines, Iowa, 568 F.2d 555, 557 (8th Cir. 1977) (opponent's need relevant to a determination of privilege).

33.   Edmund M. Morgan, Forward to the American Law Institute's Model Code of Evidence 25 (1942).

34.   Id. at 26-27. Morgan's theory was foreshadowed by Whiting v. Barney, 30 N.Y. 330, 332 (1864), in which Judge Selden stated that the original purpose of the privilege came from the ancient rule of procedure that parties could not be compelled to testify. As the rules of litigation became more complex, lawyers became necessary, but "as parties were not then obliged to testify in their own cases, and could not be compelled to disclose facts known only to themselves, they would hesitate to employ professional men, and make the necessary disclosures to them, if the facts thus communicated were thus within the reach of their opponent." Id. at 333. Judge Selden then wondered whether legislation placing parties under obligations to testify had removed the reason for the privilege. Id. at 342.

correct that people with legal problems will usually consult lawyers, it does not follow that therefore a client will necessarily disclose to his lawyer all unfavorable facts about himself. On the margin, he will be less likely to do so as the costs associated with disclosure increase. The defendant who is unaware of the defense of contributory negligence is that much less likely to admit his own negligence.

Morgan thought, mistakenly, that the law can reduce perjury only by using sticks; he did not think of carrots. But it makes perfect sense to conceive of confidentiality as a carrot to induce people to refrain from lying; when the attorney-client privilege reduces the cost of contingent claims, it should also reduce the amount of perjury.

3. *The Bentham-Kaplow-Shavell Theory*

Jeremy Bentham's argument against the attorney client privilege has recently been taken up and extended by Professors Louis Kaplow and Steven Shavell. According to Bentham, the attorney-client privilege reduces the deterrent effect of the law by giving lawbreakers the hope that the unfavorable information that they reveal to their attorneys would never be presented against them in a court of law. With his characteristic flair, he wrote,

> "A counselor, solicitor, or attorney, cannot conduct the cause of his client," (it has been observed) "if he is not fully instructed in the circumstances attending it; but the client" (it is added) "could not give the instructions with safety, if the facts confided to his advocate were to be disclosed." Not with safety? So much the better. To what object is the whole system of penal law directed, if it be not that no man shall have it in his power to flatter himself with the hope of safety, in the event of his engaging in the commission of an act which the law, on account of its supposed mischievousness, has thought fit to prohibit? The argument employed as a reason against the compelling such disclosure, is the very argument that pleads in favour of it. . . .
>
> [T]o the man who, having no guilt to disclose, has disclosed none to his lawyer, nothing could be of greater advantage than that this should appear; as it naturally would if the lawyer were subject to examination.[35]

Kaplow and Shavell make the same point, albeit with a much more elaborate model.[36] Kaplow and Shavell posit that lawyers act as filters for the information that triers of fact ultimately receive. When the lawyer is effective, the trier of fact receives less unfavorable information and more favorable information about the client and so is more likely to decide in his favor. According to this theory, the primary effect of the privilege is to reduce the expected sanction that a party faces for a possibly unlawful act. Hence, the privilege ought to be regarded as counterproductive whenever the client is factually liable, excepting only the case where the sanctions for the individual's act are too high. Deterrence would therefore increase, and that would be undesirable only in cases in which the law had established excessive sanctions in the first place. In such a case, the proper reform would be to correct the sanction rather than extend a privilege to suppress evidence.

Although superficially attractive, the Bentham-Kaplow-Shavell theory proves too much. By the same reasoning, for example, people should not be allowed to have

35. Jeremy Bentham, 7 The Rationale of Evidence, b. 9, 4, ch. 5 at 474 et. seq. (Bowring ed. 1827).
36. Kaplow and Shavell, supra [note 26]. The basic model employed by Kaplow and Shavell in large measure is an elaboration of a model first proposed by B. Peter Pashigian, Regulation, Preventive Law, and the Duties of Attorneys, 21-25, in William J. Carney, ed., The Changing Role of the Corporate Attorney (1982).

lawyers at all. Kaplow and Shavell give no account of the good that the privilege might do, other than acknowledging that the privilege makes it easier for the innocent to escape liability. Under a normative interpretation of their theory, the privilege should be available only to individuals who have been mistakenly (or maliciously) accused of wrongdoing; or, put differently, that people charged with wrongdoing should not be able to consult lawyers unless they are in fact innocent. But of course if we could tell how cases ought to be decided dehors the legal process there would be little reason to have a legal process, or indeed to have lawyers.[37] Kaplow and Shavell's argument fails because it ignores the useful role lawyers play in helping clients to develop contingent claims. To recur to our example, the absence of the attorney-client privilege would make some pedestrians a little more eager to step out into traffic without looking, even though the average pedestrian would not be affected. When clients are deterred from asserting contingent claims, because they are reluctant to reveal the bad facts upon which such claims may depend, society loses the benefit of whatever interest the contingent claim is supposed to serve. Kaplow-Shavell miss this effect, as did Bentham before them.

4.   The Wigmore Theory

John Henry Wigmore defended the theory of the privilege against Bentham's attack, declaring: "In order to promote freedom of consultation of legal advisers by clients, the apprehension of compelled disclosure by the legal advisers must be removed; and hence the law must prohibit such disclosure by the legal advisers except on the client's consent.[38] Bentham's argument was that the privilege operates as a mere filter that would encourage unlawful acts. As Wigmore pointed out, this argument erroneously assumed that "all the acts and facts on one side have been wholly right and lawful and all of those on the other wholly wrong and unlawful."[39] But in a large proportion of cases, each party would have something to fear. Without a privilege, "a person who has a partly good cause would often be deterred from consultation by virtue of the bad part or of the part that might possibly (to his notion) be bad."[40] Wigmore's idea that the privilege is needed to ensure full disclosure — still the dominant theme in the literature — adumbrates the contingent claim theory by recognizing that the facts and law will not uniformly favor either party. Nevertheless, this idea is too simple to explain the cases. This is particularly evident in the famous Wigmore gloss upon the privilege. According to Wigmore, the conditions for the privilege are:

> Where legal advice of any kind is sought (2) from a professional legal adviser in his capacity as such, (3) the communications relevant to that purpose, (4) made in confidence (5) by the client, (6) are at his instance permanently protected (7) from disclosure by himself or by the legal adviser, (8) except the client waives the protection.[41]

The critical ingredient missing from his exegesis, which has exposed it to the contemporary attack, is any recognition of the relevance of behavioral incentives.

37.   It is unclear precisely of what the Kaplow/Shavell theory of the attorney-client privilege consists. Theories are generally tested by their predictive power. The only prediction that seems to emerge from the Kaplow/Shavell theory is that lawyers should only be provided for innocent individuals, if sanctions are set at the appropriate levels. This prediction is falsified by the facts.
38.   Wigmore, supra note [23], §2991, at 3196.
39.   Id. at 3202.
40.   Id.
41.   Wigmore, supra note [23], §2292, at 3204.

Even if each of Wigmore's conditions is met, it would be senseless to provide confidentiality if the privilege would not advance the exploration of contingent claims. Courts have intuited this point, and have often refused to recognize a privilege, even when the Wigmore conditions have clearly been met, where doing so would not advance the exploration of contingent claims. Of course, courts have not formulated the issue in this way, but have simply engrafted upon Wigmore a long list of ad hoc exceptions. The contingent claim theory explains the cases more parsimoniously than Wig-more's ideas do because it focuses explicitly on the relevant incentives, and it gives a more satisfactory account of the beneficial purposes that the privilege seeks to advance.

5. Rights-Based Theories

Several commentators have proposed that under some circumstances it would be wrong — immoral — for the legal system to force the disclosure of attorney-client communications. David Louisell, for example, has urged that respect for privacy could adequately explain the privilege.[42] Charles Fried, on another tack, has defended the privilege as necessary to allow people in legal scrapes to discover what their rights are.[43] Neither of these theories adequately explains the privilege.

(a) Privacy

Louisell's notion that the privilege is founded on privacy leaves one to ponder: what is privacy founded upon? The legal system has routinely sacrificed the privacy of litigants to the interests of justice. A litigant can be obliged to reveal the most sordid and intimate details of his marriage or even to pull his pants down in front of the jury. Of course one could say that the system respects privacy, not absolutely, but only to the extent that it respects privacy. Surely a useful theory requires a deeper tread.

(b) Adjective Right

According to Fried, the attorney-client privilege is rooted in the sense of personal autonomy that legal systems must respect.[44] "[I]t is immoral for society to limit [a person's] liberty other than according to the rule of law," and is therefore "immoral for society to constrain anyone from discovering what the limits of its power over him are." Similarly, it is "immoral for society to constrain anyone from informing another [about] those limits. . . ."[45] Supposing that certain attorney-client communications would be less likely to occur in the absence of the privilege, Fried must explain why refusing to recognize the privilege ought to count as a morally unacceptable "constraint." Not every change in the world that makes a certain end state more or less likely qualifies as a "constraint." When government subsidizes a certain activity (or refuses to subsidize it) it makes the activity more or less likely to occur without "constraining" that result. But even if denial of the privilege is a constraint, the question of

---

42.   Louisell has written:

[T]here are things more important to human liberty than accurate adjudication. One of them is the right to be left by the state unmolested in certain human relations. . . . It is the historic judgment of the common law . . . that whatever handicapping of the adjudicatory process is caused by recognition of the privilege, it is not too great a price to pay for secrecy in certain communicative relations. . . .

David Louisell, Confidentiality, Conformity and Confusion: Privileges in Federal Court Today, 31 Tul. L. Rev. 101, 110 (1956).

43.   Charles Fried, Correspondence, 86 Yale L.J. 573, 586 (1977).
44.   Id. at 586.
45.   Id.

justification must be addressed by more than mere assertion. Again some inquiry into the particular consequences and their desirability is required.[46] . . .

III. THE WORK PRODUCT DOCTRINE AND THE JOINT PRODUCTION THEORY

A. INTRODUCTION

The work product doctrine has proven to be as puzzling as the attorney-client privilege. The doctrine was first articulated in 1947, in Hickman v. Taylor,[47] where the Supreme Court held that there is a qualified immunity from discovery for attorney work product prepared in anticipation of litigation. The plaintiff had brought suit to recover for the death of a seaman in the sinking of the defendants' tug. The defendants' attorney had interviewed all of the survivors of the sinking and taken statements from them. The plaintiff sought copies of these statements in discovery, and the district court held the attorney in contempt for failing to provide them. The Supreme Court reversed, holding that the statements that the plaintiff sought were protected from discovery as attorney's work product. In so holding, the Court did not rely upon the Federal Rules of Civil Procedure — though after the Hickman case an explicit work product provision was added[48] — but instead found an analogy in the English practice of protecting from discovery "all documents prepared by or for counsel with a view to litigation." Two opinions were filed in the case, that of the Court, authored by Justice Murphy, and a concurring opinion by Justice Jackson (in which Justice Frankfurter joined). The Murphy opinion stressed that the plaintiff's attorney could have acquired similar statements directly from the witnesses themselves, since they were all still alive, and asserted that the purpose of the doctrine is to protect the privacy of the lawyer's thoughts. He worried that, if the plaintiff won, lawyers would be deterred from writing down their thoughts. He also predicted that "Inefficiency, unfairness and sharp practices would inevitably develop in the giving of legal advice and in the preparation of cases for trial," presumably because in the absence of a work product doctrine lawyers would seek other ways to keep the relevant material out of the hands of their opponents.[49] The Jackson approach had a different emphasis: that discovery of work product would be inconsistent with the adversary system and would allow a lawyer to live on "wits borrowed from the adversary."[50] Modern scholars have disagreed on both the

---

46.   Some commentators have justified the privilege on the grounds that individuals in trouble with the law are in need of a friend. Albert Alschuler, The Preservation of a Client's Confidences: One Value Among Many or a Categorical Imperative?, 52 Colo. L. Rev. 349 (1981). The cases do not support such a theory. See for example U.S. v. Tedder, 801 F.2d 1437 (4th Cir. 1986). Indeed, in Morris v. Slappy, 461 U.S. 1 (1983), the Supreme Court held that the sixth amendment does not guarantee a "meaningful relationship" between attorney and client. Nor are people in trouble with the law the only ones in need of friends. The point, in short, has little explanatory power.

47.   329 U.S. 495 (1947).

48.   See Fed. Rule Civil Proc. 26.

49.   Hickman, 329 U.S. at 511. Murphy wrote: "[T]he general policy against invading the privacy of an attorney's course of preparation is so well recognized and so essential to an orderly working of our system of legal procedure that a burden rests on the one who would invade that privacy to establish adequate reasons to justify production through a subpoena or court order." Hickman, 329 U.S. at 512.

50.   Id. at 516. Jackson also worried that a contrary decision would allow witnesses to be impeached with opposing counsel's summaries of their pre-trial statements and that in many cases opposing counsel himself would have to be called as a witness.

merits of the doctrine and its justification.[51] The best explanatory account now available is Judge Easterbrook's. He argues that the work product doctrine operates in much the same way as other rights restricting the use of intellectual property.[52] Just as too few songs would be written if there were no copyrights, too little legal information would be produced in the absence of the work product doctrine.[53] Although we rely on Easterbrook's argument that the work product doctrine is essentially a property-right system in some ways similar to copyright,[54] we think he missed the essential idea that makes it important for the law to enforce these property rights. Easterbrook suggests that the doctrine protects and nurtures lawyer creativity; we think that it mainly protects and encourages something different but just as important — lawyer perseverance.

B.   THEORIES ABOUT THE WORK PRODUCT DOCTRINE

1.   *The Joint Production Theory*

Most litigation activity involves a form of "joint production," whereby the lawyer cannot get information helpful to his side of the case without also producing information helpful to the other side. In order to get helpful information (of which more is preferred to less), he has to take harmful information (of which less is preferred to more). Both a trial lawyer's factual investigations and the resulting legal theorizing are subject to joint production. It is difficult to generate helpful legal theories and useful "facts" without also generating theories and facts more helpful to the other side. In many factual investigations, the same conditions apply. It is often impossible to interview witnesses to find facts helpful to one's own side without discovering facts helpful to the other side.[55] A lawyer will normally want to consider carefully the strongest positions that could be asserted by an opponent, and this may oblige an attorney to think about a case from the opponent's point of view.

As Gordon Tullock has pointed out, the private and social value of the investment in lawyering activity may be significantly out of line with each other.[56] Tullock hypothesized that the net benefits from litigation would often appear higher to private litigants than they would to society, giving private parties an incentive to overinvest. In

---

51.   As even those who provide the justifications acknowledge. See, for example, Kevin Clermont, Surveying Work Product, 68 Corn. L. Rev. 755 (1983): "As proof of [the] difficulty [of the work product doctrine], I note — without insult by citation — the serious shortcomings of almost all of that commentary."

52.   Frank Easterbrook, Insider Trading, Secret Agents, Evidentiary Privileges, and the Production of Information, 1981 Sup. Ct. Rev. 309. See also Richard Posner, The Economics of Justice 244 (1983) ("the attorney-work product doctrine is, I think, best understood as the use of secrecy to protect the lawyer's (and hence client's) investment in research and analysis of a case").

53.   See generally Edmund Kitch, The Law and Economics of Rights in Valuable Information, 9 J. Legal Stud. 683 (1980); Edmund Kitch, The Nature and Function of the Patent System, 20 J. L. and Econ. 265 (1977).

54.   The first suggestion of this idea in the literature is in Richard Posner, Privacy, Secrecy, and Reputation, 28 Buff. L. Rev. 1, 11 (1979), although the idea is not developed.

55.   Wigmore writes, "Men do not gather grapes of thorns, nor figs of thistles; yet they may enter one and the same field and find diverse fruits." Wigmore, supra note [23], §2295, at 3212. He makes little of this insight however.

It should be noted that whether evidence is helpful or not is a function of at least two variables: its absolute value, that is, does it tend to confirm or deny the party's allegations, and its relative value, that is, its value given the evidence already known. Indeed, there are further complexities, for the attorney must make at least two different assessments: 1. what probability range will the jury assign to the evidence; 2. what is the probability that further investigation will turn up information that will affect the probability range the jury would assign. These matters are beyond the scope of the present article.

56.   Gordon Tullock, Trial on Trial: The Pure Theory of Legal Procedure 154-158 (1980).

the context of much of lawyering activity, however, the reverse may be true. If a legal investigation is subject to joint production, it can be quite easy for the expected private value of the information generated to be zero, even when its expected social value is large. In such a case, there would be inadequate private incentive to undertake such investigations even when they are socially valuable. To the extent this is true, the concern is the opposite of Tullock's; it is not that too much will be invested in the resolution of "private" disputes but rather too little. The work product rule is a solution to this problem. Under this doctrine, attorneys are allowed to hold the detrimental results of their joint production investigations in confidence from the other side, thus lowering the private costs of the lawyering effort.[57] This strategy has social costs, however, which we predict are reflected in the rules themselves. The principal one is the duplication of production. An optimal rule of confidentiality would seek to maximize the private incentive to undertake socially valuable joint production investigation subject to the constraint of duplication. Formally stated, a party should be able to suppress disclosure up to the point where the value of the increased information produced is equal to the increased cost of duplicative effort. In addition, under our theory no valuable incentive is lost by requiring a party to disclose information favorable to his case, so we would expect that such information would be discoverable even when it was produced under conditions of joint production. It is coerced disclosure of unfavorable information and ambiguously favorable information (for example, early drafts of legal briefs) that would reduce the private incentive for joint production, so it is here that the courts should be especially protective if they are deciding cases in a way explained by our theory.

We do not claim that courts have adopted the joint production theory in their opinions, but only that this theory gives a better account of their actual results in work product cases than their stated theories. The privacy theory that Murphy emphasized in Hickman is both too broad and too narrow when measured against the subsequent case results that define the doctrine, including the Court's own. Nonetheless, it is probably no accident that the Court found the Hickman facts to be an especially appealing basis for the doctrine. In terms of our theory, the documents that the plaintiff sought were the quintessential result of joint production. When the defendants' attorney interviewed the accident survivors, no one knew the cause of the tug's sinking. Ex ante, the lawyer would have predicted that the interviews would reveal both favorable and unfavorable information about why the tug sank. In this situation, if the defendants' lawyer knew that he would have to disclose to his opponent all the information that he acquired, he would have less incentive to conduct the interviews in the first place. The consequence would be a reduction in the amount and quality of information available at trial.

Indeed, Murphy's opinion may be read to suggest the joint production theory, although one almost needs a microscope to find it. Recall that Murphy predicted that without the doctrine lawyers would not write things down and "inefficiency, unfairness

---

57. The typical criticism of the work product doctrine is to the effect that lawyers will investigate and prepare their cases even in the absence of the doctrine. See for example Kathleen Waits, Work Product Protection for Witness Statements: Time for Abolition, 1985 Wisc. L. Rev. 305, 331 ("Because preparation increases the chances of a favorable outcome, it is its own reward. This remains true even if some of the preparatory documents must be shared with the other side. We therefore should not fear that abolition of work product would cause parties to abandon all investigative efforts."). This is another lump-up argument. The concern is not whether all investigative efforts will be abandoned but rather with the scale of the efforts that are undertaken. Disincentives to such efforts are likely to reduce their scale.

and sharp practices" would result. Perhaps what he meant was that in the absence of the work product doctrine lawyers would still be reluctant to disclose the unfavorable information yielded by their joint production activities. Hence, lawyers would be reluctant to record this unfavorable information, because this would make it more accessible to their opponents. By extension, if lawyers had to constantly cull their records to ensure that they contained nothing unfavorable to their side, it would certainly be inefficient, and for lawyers to suppress unfavorable information (in the absence of the doctrine's protection) may be the sharp practice that Murphy envisioned. Hence, what the Court wrote in Hickman is consistent with the joint production theory.

2. The Easterbrook Theory

Frank Easterbrook stresses that our legal system relies on the attorney's self-interest to stimulate the production of legal goods or "lawyering." If such goods are to be produced, it will be necessary to allow the producer to profit from the production or otherwise to subsidize the production of such goods. If producers cannot derive any special benefits from their creation, if nonproducers are welcome to use them without having to pay for or contribute to their creation, there is a substantial risk that not enough of the good will be produced. Under Easterbrook's theory, the work product doctrine is analogous to copyright protection. Just as the creative efforts of artists must be protected in order to induce the optimal scale of them, so must be the creative efforts of lawyers.

The copyright theory of the work product doctrine places the wrong stress on the legal production process. The work product doctrine protects not so much legal inspiration, but legal perspiration. Thomas Edison would maintain that the two are related, and so do we. Nonetheless, instead of merely protecting the lawyer's creative inspirations as such, the work product doctrine protects a broader class of information: the results of investigations that can yield both favorable and unfavorable information. Of course, even legal inspiration may be produced under joint production conditions. In simply thinking about the theory of a case, a lawyer may produce insights more helpful to the other side than to his own. In this situation, both our theory and Easterbrook's predict that the unfavorable insight would be protected by the work product doctrine.

The joint production theory includes legal creativity as a subset. When lawyer-produced information involves no legal creativity, we would predict that the work product doctrine would nonetheless protect it if the information is produced under joint conditions. Thus, interviewing witnesses in an accident case certainly involves little legal creativity — indeed, the lawyer may often delegate the task to an investigator for this reason — but the results of the interviews should nonetheless be protected, at least if courts accept the joint production theory. The reason is simple: interviewing witnesses can just as easily yield unfavorable as favorable information.

We have one further disagreement with Judge Easterbrook's analysis. Easterbrook, elaborating on a model first suggested by Tullock, suggests that litigation is often a "fight over spilt milk" where the outcome of the case may have little influence on how the parties behave in the future. If litigation has only a stakes dividing function, it is socially desirable to restrict as much as possible the expenditure of resources resolving the dispute. Thus, any incentives to expend resources on such an effort — such as those created by the work product doctrine — would be, as Tullock points out, socially perverse. The error in this argument is that it overlooks the intimate relation-ship between accurate stakes dividing and rule enforcement. If cases are not accurately decided, the underlying rules will not be implemented, with a corresponding loss in the deterrent function of those rules. Thus by offsetting disincentives to the production of legal information, the work product doctrine advances rather than retards the social interest, which explains its persistence in the cases.

In any event, whether the better account of the doctrine is Easterbrook's theory or our own is something that ultimately must be determined by looking at the cases.

NOTES AND QUESTIONS

1. One of the many interesting facets of the attorney-client privilege is that even its friends have serious doubts about it. Among the strongest advocates of the privilege, Dean Wigmore stated:

> [T]he privilege remains an exception to the general duty to disclose. Its benefits are all indirect and speculative; its obstruction is plain and concrete. . . . It is worth preserving for the sake of a general policy, but is nonetheless an obstacle to the investigation of the truth. It ought to be strictly confined within the narrowest possible limits consistent with the logic of its principle. [8 John Henry Wigmore, Evidence §2291, at 554 (1905).]

Similarly, in United States v. Nixon, 418 U.S. 683 (1974), the Supreme Court addressed the scope of privileges generally, specifically referring to the attorney-client privilege:

> [T]he public . . . has a right to every man's evidence, except for those persons protected by a constitutional, common-law, or statutory privilege, [citing precedents]. . . . And, gen-erally, an attorney . . . may not be required to disclose what has been revealed in profes-sional confidence. . . . [P]rivileges against forced disclosure . . . [a]s exceptions to the demand for every man's evidence are not lightly created nor expansively construed, for they are in derogation of the search for truth. [Id. at 709-710.]

Thus the Supreme Court seems to be in accord with the view that the privilege should be narrowly construed. The reason for this is that the costs of privilege are obvious, while the benefits obscure. Do the contingent claim and joint production theories redress this imbalance? Are they persuasive? Plausible?

2. Recall that the Supreme Court in *Upjohn* took a somewhat different view of the privilege than that expressed in *Nixon*. There the Court said: "Application of the attorney-client privilege to communications such as those involved here, however, puts the adversary in no worse position than if the communication had never taken place. The privilege only protects disclosure of communications; it does not protect disclosure of the underlying facts by those who communicated with the attorney." Is this correct? In large measure it depends on what the baseline is, doesn't it? If the baseline is the cost of securing information from the opposing client, the Court might be right, but why is that the correct baseline? Why isn't it instead the cheapest cost of obtaining the information, which obviously is from the attorney, once the attorney is in possession of the relevant information? Rather than depose the client, the adversary need merely ask the attorney for copies of the attorney's files. So, we are back to the

same question: What justifies the increased cost of obtaining the relevant information? In addition, do you believe that putting the information in the hands of the attorney will not increase the adversary's costs of obtaining that information from the client? Isn't it obvious that part of what counsel will do is advise how to answer discovery requests in a legal, but as unhelpful as possible, manner?

Last, don't arguments like the Court's in *Upjohn* suggest that counsel will not engage in behavior that raises the costs of their adversary? But what exactly does that mean? Suppose a client says X to its lawyer, but Y at a deposition. Must the lawyer correct this misimpression? If so, as the conventional arguments for the privilege implicitly suggest, isn't it obvious that the privilege provides no incentive to disclose? Isn't it thus obvious that we do not expect attorneys to police their clients in this fashion? Isn't it thus obvious that one thing that must be explained is why such tactics are tolerated, and that naive statements such as the Court's in *Upjohn* dramatically miss the point of what is going on? Again, how do the contingent claim and joint production theories measure up here?

3. In thinking about the contingent claim theory, remember that its predictions and Wigmore's are largely consistent. The difference lies in Wigmore's need to create numerous ad hoc exceptions. The central argument of the contingent claim theory is that it captures the essence of what the cases do without the need for exceptions.

4. In the Allen et al. article from which the preceding excerpt is taken, the authors proceed to discuss numerous cases in an effort to show that their theories better explain the cases than any of the alternatives. We cannot reproduce the detailed arguments here, but urge you to consult that discussion. To whet your appetite, consider two matters:

(a) The contingent claim theory predicts that the privilege will become qualified rather than absolute. This is a somewhat bold prediction, but in fact cases are beginning to adopt this view. See, e.g., Greater Newburyport Clamshell Alliance et al. v. Public Service Co. of N.H., 838 F.2d 13, 20 (1st Cir. 1988) (in civil damages action, "fairness requires that the privilege holder surrender the privilege to the extent that it will weaken, in a meaningful way, the defendant's ability to defend"); In re Grand Jury Proceedings, Des Moines, Iowa, 568 F.2d 555, 557 (8th Cir. 1977) (opponent's need relevant to a determination of privilege).

(b) Also, consider the following from the same article:

> The theory has a number of other predictions that are borne out by the cases. First, when a client consults a lawyer to perform some function that could not possibly lead to a contingent claim, the client's communications ought not to be privileged. In this type of case, the client's expectation that he would be conveying unfavorable information to the lawyer could not deter him from obtaining the lawyer's advice about a contingent claim, since that is not his purpose. Accordingly, we find in the cases that the privilege does not apply when the attorney has been retained as an agent to procure a loan, when the attorney is asked to witness a deposit, and in similar cases.
>
> Our core proposition is that the purpose of the privilege is to encourage clients to divulge unfavorable information to their attorneys upon which contingent claims might rest. It follows that there is no need for the privilege when a regulatory agency or some other binding authority has obliged the client to hire an attorney and divulge unfavorable information to him. The cases bear out this prediction.
>
> A recent case in the Eighth Circuit, Simon v. G.D. Searle & Co., 816 F. 2d 397 (8th Cir. 1987), provides yet another demonstration of the explanatory power of the contingent claim theory. The case involved litigation over Searle's intrauterine contraceptive device. During discovery, Searle refused to turn over certain documents prepared by its risk

management department. This department monitors the company's products liability litigation and analyzes its litigation reserves. In doing so, the department utilizes individual case reserves determined by the assessment of the company's legal staff. Relying on various arguments of Wigmore, the court held that the attorney-client privilege did not protect the documents prepared by the risk management department. The court asserted that these documents did not embody communications relevant to obtaining legal advice and that the documents related to business rather than legal matters.

In dissent, Judge Gibson politely noted the court's opinion verged on the incoherent: "Only by concluding that Searle is in the business of litigation can the court convert these litigation-oriented documents into business planning documents." Judge Gibson's lament is correct, but so too is the majority's result. No contingent claim could conceivably rest upon the information collected and utilized by the risk management department and the company's lawyers. The result reached, then, is perfectly in accord with the predictions of the contingent claim theory, even though, as Judge Gibson rightly says, the court's opinion is virtual nonsense if analyzed from the perspective of the conventional explanations of the privilege. [Allen et al. supra, 19 J. Legal Stud. at 382-383.]

D. THE MARITAL PRIVILEGES

There are two distinct marital privileges, the marital communications privilege and the marital testimonial privilege: The *marital communications privilege* protects confidential communications between spouses; the *marital testimonial privilege* (usually applicable only in all phases of criminal prosecutions) prevents a witness spouse from testifying against the party spouse. A particular jurisdiction may have either or both privileges. Prior to the adoption of the Federal Rules of Evidence, federal courts recognized both privileges. In drafting the Proposed Federal Rules on privilege, the Advisory Committee included only the marital testimonial privilege. Subsequently, the Supreme Court in Trammel v. United States, 445 U.S. 40, 51 (1980), indicated in dictum that it would continue to apply the marital confidential communications privilege as well. *Trammel* is reproduced in subsection 2, infra.

1. The Marital Communications Privilege

a. Elements of the Privilege and Its Justifications

The marital communications privilege has three requirements: (1) the privilege extends only to words or acts that are communications to the other spouse, (2) the communication must have been made during a valid marriage, and (3) the communication must have been made with the intent that it remain confidential. See United States v. Marashi, 913 F.2d 724, 729 (9th Cir. 1990). The party asserting the privilege has the burden of proving that disclosure would reveal words or acts "intended as communications." The party also has the burden of proving that the communication was made during a valid marriage. If these two elements are established, then the final element of confidentiality is presumed. See United States v. Hamilton, 19 F.3d 350, 354 (7th Cir. 1994). The party opposing the privilege can overcome this presumption by showing that the communication in question was not intended to be confidential.

Similar to the justifications that have been offered for the attorney-client privilege, two justifications are commonly offered for the marital communication privilege: (1) to encourage open and frank discussions between spouses and (2) regardless of the privilege's encouraging effect, to protect the privacy of intimate spousal communications. Consistent with both these rationales, the marital communications privilege applies to communications that take place during the marriage relationship, and the privilege does not end with the termination of the marriage.

b. Holder

Jurisdictions differ as to who holds this privilege. The holder may be the spouses jointly, the communicating spouse, the witness spouse who heard the communication, or the spouse who is also a party. Most federal courts have held that the privilege is held by both spouses and that each can invoke the privilege to prevent the other from testifying about spousal communications. See United States v. 281 Syosset Woodbury Rd., 71 F.3d 1067 (2d Cir. 1995). In criminal cases, some courts have held that the exclusive holder of the privilege is the defendant. See, e.g., United States v. Acker, 52 F.3d 509 (4th Cir. 1995). This permits the defendant to compel the spouse to testify about spousal communications, if such evidence can exculpate the defendant. In cases where both spouses are holders of the privilege, one but not the other may have waived it. Can a nonwaiving witness or party subsequently claim the privilege? The cases have been split on this issue.

c. Scope of the Privilege

As with all privileges, the marital communications privilege is limited by judicial interpretation of its requirements.

    i. Valid Marriage. The party who asserts the privilege must prove that a valid marriage existed at the time the communication was made. If the parties were separated, the privilege technically still applies, but many courts refuse to uphold the privilege in such circumstances. Some courts adopt a categorical rule rejecting the privilege in such circumstances. United States v. Fulk, 816 F.2d 1202 (7th Cir. 1987). More commonly, courts use a balancing test to determining whether upholding the privilege will serve the purpose of promoting full communication between spouses. In United States v. Roberson, 859 F.2d 1376 (9th Cir. 1988), the court upheld the district court's ruling that the privilege did not apply because the couple was "irreconcilably" separated at the time of their confidential communications. In future cases, the court said, judges should consider whether, at the time of the communication, a divorce action had been filed, as well as other relevant evidence: for example, whether there were statements by either party regarding irreconcilability; or whether there were allegations of gross misconduct or grievances stretching back over a period of years. Such evidence "may distinguish the failed marriage from the occasional disharmony that sometimes accompanies these relationships." Id. at 1380. How well suited do you think courts are to make these kinds of determinations? The Roberson court also said that the inquiry should address the interest society has in preserving the confidentiality of marriages generally, not the confidentiality of the couple before the court. Does a categorical rule better achieve this purpose?

For the most part, courts construe the marriage requirement very narrowly. For instance, neither federal nor state courts have extended the protection of the privilege to unmarried opposite-sex couples who cohabitate. United States v. Acker, 52 F.3d 509 (4th Cir. 1995) (finding no valid marriage where the heterosexual couple involved had been living together for 25 years in two states that did not recognize common law marriage). But see In re Grand Jury Proceedings Witness Ms. X, 562 F. Supp. 486 (N.D. Cal. 1983) (stating in dicta that it might be appropriate to allow unmarried opposite-sex partners to invoke the marital communication privilege). The reason for this refusal to recognize unmarried partnerships rests on two grounds. First, courts point to the benefits of a bright-line rule that does not require an inquiry into the details of the relationship. United States v. Acker, 52 F.3d at 515 (discussing the administrative difficulty of determining what relationships would qualify as "de facto" marriages). Second, some courts also have stated that the privilege should not extend to unmarried cohabitants because they have not assumed the responsibilities of marriage. Id.

In the case of same-sex couples, the idea that couples are intentionally avoiding the responsibilities of marriage does not hold true, as until recently such individuals were legally prevented from obtaining valid marriages in every state. However, in a landmark 1999 case, the Supreme Court of Vermont held that excluding same-sex couples from the benefits and protections incident to marriage violated the State Constitution. Baker v. State, 744 A.2d 864, 886 (Vt. 1999). This ruling paved the way for Vermont's statute recognizing same-sex civil unions. Vt. Stat. Ann. Tit. 15, §1201 (2002). The statute provides parties to a civil union with "immunity from compelled testimony and the marital communication privilege." Id. at §1204(e)(15). See also N.J. Stat. Ann. §26:8A (West Supp. 2005) (recognizing domestic partnerships between same-sex couples). Massachusetts became the first state to allow same-sex marriage, when the Supreme Judicial Court of Massachusetts held that denying same-sex couples the right to marriage was a violation of the state's constitution. Goodridge v. Dept. of Pub. Health, 798 N.E.2d 941 (Mass. 2003). As Massachusetts now allows same-sex marriage, the marriage communication privileges should be applicable to married same-sex couples in the state. Although a few states have granted marriage benefits to same-sex couples, the majority of states remain opposed to the idea, and several states have even passed constitutional amendments banning same-sex marriage. Nonetheless, the issue of same-sex marriage and the application of the spousal communication privilege to such relationships remain open questions, as a recent decision by the U.S. District Court for the District of Nebraska highlights. In Citizens for Equal Protection, Inc. v. Bruning, 368 F. Supp.2d 950 (D.Neb. 2005), the court held that the state's ban on same-sex marriage violated Equal Protection and the First Amendment. See Developments in the Law — Privileged Communications, 98 Harv. L. Rev. 1563, 1589 (1985), for argument that same-sex relationships should have the benefit of the "marital" communication privilege.

ii. Confidentiality. It is a near universal rule that all marital communications will be treated as confidential unless the party seeking to introduce the evidence shows that the communication was not intended to be, or should not be, considered confidential. The presence of third persons is an almost certain indication that the requisite intent of confidentiality is lacking. Wolfle v. United States, 291 U.S. 7, 16 (1934) (use of stenographer destroyed the privilege). If a child is old enough to comprehend what is being said, spousal statements made in the presence of the child — at the dinner table, for example, or on a drive in the family automobile — will typically not be privileged. Chamberlain v. State, 348 P.2d 280, 286 (Wyo. 1960). Sometimes courts will find that a third party is constructively present if the spouse made the same communication to a third party on another occasion. People v. Burton, 286 N.E.2d 792, 798 (Ill. Ct. App. 1972). The location in which the communication is made also is probative as to whether the spouse intended a confidential communication. State of Maine v. Smith, 384 A.2d 687, 691 (1978) (finding that communicating in a public location does not necessarily mean that the communication was not confidential; rather, the inquiry should focus on the spouse's reasonable expectation of confidentiality).

iii. What Is a "Communication"?

An issue that often arises in cases involving the marital communications privilege is whether conduct — acts and gestures — is protected by the privilege. Courts are required to distinguish between noncommunicative behavior and conduct that has communicative content. For example, testimony from a wife identifying a pair of pants as being the style and size worn by her husband was admitted as involving no communication at all. United States v. Bolzer, 556 F.2d 948 (9th Cir. 1977); similarly, in United States v. Lefkowitz, 618 F.2d 1313 (9th Cir. 1980), testimony concerning the fraudulent nature of documents turned over to the IRS, and the location of other records, was found to be based on the personal observations of the wife, not on any communicative conduct of the husband. Other acts observed by spouses, however, have been found by some courts to be communicative and thus privileged:

> [W]hen the defendant revealed the stolen objects [a gun and camera] to his wife he was imparting a confidence as clearly as if he had told his wife, "I have stolen a gun and a camera" . . . Where as here conduct by a spouse can be reasonably interpreted as intending to convey a message to the other spouse, a marital communication has occurred. [State v. Smith, 384 A.2d 687, 690 (Me. 1978).]

The "intent to communicate" test as to whether spousal conduct should be privileged replicates the test provided under FRE 801(a)(2) to determine whether conduct is hearsay or not. Some courts, however, adopt a broader test. In People v. Daghita, 299 N.Y. 194, 86 N.E.2d 172 (N.Y. 1949), the court held that it was a violation of the confidential communications privilege to admit a wife's testimony that her husband hid proceeds of a theft under the bed:

> [T]he term communication . . . includes knowledge derived from the observance of disclosive acts done in the presence or view of one spouse . . . because of the confidence existing between them by reason of the marital relation. . . . [The husband] was, in a word, confiding in her the information disclosed by his conduct. [Id. at 198-199.]

Contrast Daghita with the holding in United States v. Estes, 793 F.2d 465, 467 (2d Cir. 1986), that "counting, hiding and laundering of the money conveyed no confidential message. . . . Acts do not become privileged communications simply because they are performed in the presence of the actor's spouse." Which do you think is the better result?

d. Exceptions

Like the attorney-client privilege, there is an exception to the marital communications privilege that permits the admission — by a willing spousal witness — of statements made in the course of, or concerning, ongoing criminal activity between the spouses. In *Estes*, the first communications from the husband to the wife that first disclosed his crime to her were privileged; only those communications made after she became an accessory were excepted from the privilege. Id. at 466.

At common law, the privilege did not apply to spousal communications in specific kinds of litigation. Although there is variation from state to state, the privilege is most frequently inapplicable in prosecutions for crimes committed by one spouse against the other or against children of either, and in actions by one spouse against the other, typically divorce. McCormick on Evidence, vol. 1, §84, 131 (5th ed. 1999).

The Supreme Court of Pennsylvania recently held that a defendant's communications to his spouse were not subject to the spousal communication privilege where the statements were intended to create or further marital discord. Commonwealth v. Spetzer, 572 Pa. 17, 813 A.2 707 (Pa. 2002). In *Spetzer*, the defendant admitted to his wife that he had raped his stepdaughter, detailed plans for future abuse, and attempted to intimidate his wife. 572 Pa. at 39. The court noted that the communications were not of the 'marital harmony-inspiring' type envisioned by the common law or the Pennsylvania General Assembly:

> Certainly the persistent and sadistic statements at issue here, concerning a husband's actual and contemplated crimes against his wife and her children, cannot rationally be excluded on the pretext that 'considerations of domestic peace and harmony of the marital relation forbid their disclosure.' *Seitz*. It would be perverse, indeed, to indulge a fiction of marital harmony to shield statements which prove the declarant spouse's utter contempt for, and abuse of, the marital union. Accordingly, we hold that here, as in Seitz, the challenged communications 'did not arise from the confidence existing between the parties, but from the want of it,' *id.*, and, as such, the communications were admissible. [*Spetzer*, 572 Pa. at 40.]

PROBLEMS

12.18. Randy Dwayne Hurley was charged and convicted of armed robbery, felony murder, and first degree murder. On appeal, the defendant objects to the trial court's admission of letters containing incriminating information that were written from him to his wife on the ground that the letters should have been protected by the marital confidential communications privilege. Hurley, who had married his wife after the arrest but prior to trial, had written the letters to his wife from jail. At the time of the trial, however, the two were separated. The wife was a willing witness. What result?

12.19. Jim Montague and his sister Mary O'Connell are charged with conspiracy to commit mail fraud and several counts of mail fraud for mishandling reservations of rentals by their property management company and sidetracking money from the owners of the units by not reporting reservations. Jim's wife, Louise, also was an owner but agreed to cooperate with the government and to testify against Jim and Mary. The prosecution is seeking to present as evidence a letter that Louise wrote Jim and left for him on the kitchen counter in their home. The letter discussed Mary's fraudulent activities and stated that Louise wanted Jim to confront Mary. Louise testified that she did not intend the information in the letter to remain private, as she hoped that Jim would communicate it to Mary. Jim and Louise had children residing in the house at the time the letter was left on the kitchen counter. Jim has asserted the spousal communication privilege to prevent the letter, or testimony about its contents, from being used in the trial. Was the communication privileged? If so, can Mary waive the privilege?

12.20. Craig Klaxon is charged with mail fraud and wire fraud for filing a fraudulent insurance claim for a $4,000 silver tray that he listed as having been stolen. Klaxon's wife, Connie, is prepared to testify that she and her husband never owned a silver tray and that she refused, when her husband had asked her (when both Klaxon and the insurance agent were on the phone) to sign the insurance claim. Would this testimony be excluded by the marital communications privilege?

12.21. Chester Newman is being prosecuted for arson, burglary, and theft. An investigation had uncovered that a fire at the Good Times Club was a result of arson and that stereo equipment owned by the club was missing. Defendant's wife, Catherine Newman, is prepared to testify about certain events involving her husband on the night of the fire. Catherine will testify that on the night in question her husband returned home from the Good Times Club with a set of expensive stereo equipment. She then accompanied her husband to sell the stereo equipment to John Palmer, a potential purchaser. Communications concerning the source of the equipment — that it had been "snatched" from the Club — took place during the negotiation and sale of the equipment. Defendant filed a motion to suppress his wife's testimony on the ground that such conversations constituted privileged confidential communications. Should this testimony be admissible over Chester's objection?

12.22. Arlene is suing the Major League Broadcasting Corp. (MLBC) for employment discrimination. She alleges violations of the Equal Pay and Fair Labor Standards Act and of Title VII. MLBC has subpoenaed Arlene's husband, Fred, to give deposition testimony that might involve conversations he had with the plaintiff. Specifically, MLBC wants to ask Fred about the following: (1) Fred's assistance with his wife's job search following her departure from MLBC; (2) his observation of injuries suffered by his wife in an automobile accident that may bear on injuries allegedly suffered in this case, (3) Fred's conversations with his wife concerning incidents of harassment allegedly occurring at MLBC; (4) miscellaneous areas including his knowledge of Arlene's work habits, what her last evaluation at MLBC was before she lost her job, and her claim against MLBC; and (5) his knowledge of Arlene's confrontation with her supervisor at her new job. Can Fred claim marital communications privilege?

Prior to her husband's deposition, Arlene asserts the marital communications privilege to block his testimony regarding these conversations. Should the court uphold the privilege as to each of the areas MLBC wants to discover?

2. The Marital Testimonial Privilege

a. *Elements of the Privilege and Its Justifications*

The modern justification for the marital testimonial privilege is that it exists to promote harmony in an on-going marriage relationship; without the privilege, one spouse could be required to testify against the other in a criminal proceeding, bringing disharmony to the marriage. Consistent with this rationale, the privilege is not limited to testimony about confidential communications, and for the privilege to apply the witness and the party must be married at the time the privilege is invoked. See United States v. Bolzer, 556 F.2d 948 (9th Cir. 1977).

In contrast to the marital communications privilege, the marital testimonial privilege generally applies only in criminal actions. In federal courts, it is now well-established that the testifying spouse holds the privilege and may waive it in order to testify. The Supreme Court addressed this issue, and the scope of the privilege, in the following case:

TRAMMEL v. UNITED STATES
445 U.S. 40 (1980)

Mr. Chief Justice BURGER delivered the opinion of the Court....

I

On March 10, 1976, petitioner Otis Trammel was indicted with two others, Edwin Lee Roberts and Joseph Freeman, for importing heroin into the United States from Thailand and the Philippine Islands and for conspiracy to import heroin in violation of 21 U.S.C. sec. 952(a), 962(a), and 963. The indictment also named six unindicted co-conspirators, including petitioner's wife Elizabeth Ann Trammel.

According to the indictment, petitioner and his wife flew from the Philippines to California in August 1975, carrying with them a quantity of heroin. Freeman and Roberts assisted them in its distribution. Elizabeth Trammel then traveled to Thailand where she purchased another supply of the drug. On November 3, 1975, with four ounces of heroin on her person, she boarded a plane for the United States. During a routine customs search in Hawaii, she was searched, the heroin was discovered, and she was arrested. After discussions with Drug Enforcement Administration agents, she agreed to cooperate with the Government.

Prior to trial on this indictment, petitioner moved to sever his case from that of Roberts and Freeman. He advised the court that the Government intended to call his wife as an adverse witness and asserted his claim to a privilege to prevent her from testifying against him. At a hearing on the motion, Mrs. Trammel was called as a Government witness under a grant of use immunity. She testified that she and petitioner were married in May 1975 and that they remained married.[58] She explained that her cooperation with the Government was based on assurances that she would be given lenient treatment.[59] She then described, in considerable detail, her role and that of her husband in the heroin distribution conspiracy.

After hearing this testimony, the District Court ruled that Mrs. Trammel could testify in support of the Government's case to any act she observed during the marriage and to any communication "made in the presence of a third person"; however, confidential communications between petitioner and his wife were held to be privileged and inadmissible. The motion to sever was denied.

At trial, Elizabeth Trammel testified within the limits of the court's pretrial ruling; her testimony, as the Government concedes, constituted virtually its entire case against

---

58. In response to the question whether divorce was contemplated, Mrs. Trammel testified that her husband had said that "I would go my way and he would go his."

59. The Government represents to the Court that Elizabeth Trammel has not been prosecuted for her role in the conspiracy.

petitioner. He was found guilty on both the substantive and conspiracy charges and sentenced to an indeterminate term of years pursuant to the Federal Youth Corrections Act, 18 U.S.C. sec. 5010(b). . . . [The Court of Appeals affirmed the conviction.]

II

The privilege claimed by petitioner has ancient roots. Writing in 1628, Lord Coke observed that "it hath been resolved by the Justices that a wife cannot be produced either against or for her husband." 1 E. Coke, A Commentarie upon Littleton 6b (1628). See, generally, 8 J. Wigmore, Evidence sec. 2227 (McNaughton rev. 1961). This spousal disqualification sprang from two canons of medieval jurisprudence: first, the rule that an accused was not permitted to testify in his own behalf because of his interest in the proceeding; second, the concept that husband and wife were one, and that since the woman had no recognized separate legal existence, the husband was that one. From those two now long-abandoned doctrines, it followed that what was inadmissible from the lips of the defendant-husband was also inadmissible from his wife.

Despite its medieval origins, this rule of spousal disqualification remained intact in most common-law jurisdictions well into the 19th century. . . . Indeed, it was not until 1933, in Funk v. United States, 290 U.S. 371, that this Court abolished the testimonial disqualification in the federal courts, so as to permit the spouse of a defendant to testify in the defendant's behalf. *Funk*, however, left undisturbed the rule that either spouse could prevent the other from giving adverse testimony. Id., at 373. The rule thus evolved into one of privilege rather than one of absolute disqualification. . . .

The modern justification for this privilege against adverse spousal testimony is its perceived role in fostering the harmony and sanctity of the marriage relationship. Notwithstanding this benign purpose, the rule was sharply criticized. Professor Wigmore termed it "the merest anachronism in legal theory and an indefensible obstruction to truth in practice." 8 Wigmore sec. 2228, at 221. The Committee on Improvements in the Law of Evidence of the American Bar Association called for its abolition. 63 American Bar Association Reports 594-595 (1938). In its place, Wigmore and others suggested a privilege protecting only private marital communications, modeled on the privilege between priest and penitent, attorney and client, and physician and patient. See 8 Wigmore sec. 2332 et seq.[60] . . .

In Hawkins v. United States, 358 U.S. 74 (1958), this Court considered the continued vitality of the privilege against adverse spousal testimony in the federal courts. There the District Court had permitted petitioner's wife, over his objection, to testify against him. With one questioning concurring opinion, the Court held the wife's testimony inadmissible; it took note of the critical comments that the common-law rule had engendered, . . . but chose not to abandon it. Also rejected was the Government's suggestion that the Court modify the privilege by vesting it in the witness-spouse, with freedom to testify or not independent of the defendant's control. The Court viewed this proposed modification as antithetical to the widespread belief, evidenced in the rules then in effect in a majority of the States and in England,

---

60. This Court recognized just such a confidential marital communications privilege in Wolfle v. United States, 291 U.S. 7 (1934), and in Blau v. United States, 340 U.S. 332 (1951). In neither case, however, did the Court adopt the Wigmore view that the communications privilege be substituted *in place of* the privilege against adverse spousal testimony. The privilege as to confidential marital communications is not at issue in the instant case; accordingly, our holding today does not disturb *Wolfle* and *Blau*.

"that the law should not force or encourage testimony which might alienate husband and wife, or further inflame existing domestic differences." Id., at 79.

Hawkins, then, left the federal privilege for adverse spousal testimony where it found it, continuing "a rule which bars the testimony of one spouse against the other unless both consent." Id., at 78. . . . However, in so doing, the Court made clear that its decision was not meant to "foreclose whatever changes in the rule may eventually be dictated by 'reason and experience'." [Id.], at 79.

III

. . . The Federal Rules of Evidence acknowledge the authority of the federal courts to continue the evolutionary development of testimonial privileges in federal criminal trials "governed by the principles of the common law as they may be interpreted . . . in the light of reason and experience." Fed. Rule Evid. 501. . . .

Although Rule 501 confirms the authority of the federal courts to reconsider the continued validity of the *Hawkins* rule, the long history of the privilege suggests that it ought not to be casually cast aside. That the privilege is one affecting marriage, home, and family relationships — already subject to much erosion in our day — also counsels caution. At the same time, we cannot escape the reality that the law on occasion adheres to doctrinal concepts long after experience suggests the need for change. . . .

Since 1958, when *Hawkins* was decided, support for the privilege against adverse spousal testimony has been eroded further. Thirty-one jurisdictions, including Alaska and Hawaii, then allowed an accused a privilege to prevent adverse spousal testimony. . . . The number has now declined to 24. In 1974, the National Conference on Uniform State Laws revised its Uniform Rules of Evidence, but again rejected the *Hawkins* rule in favor of a limited privilege for confidential communications. See Uniform Rules of Evidence, Rule 504. That proposed rule has been enacted in Arkansas, North Dakota, and Oklahoma — each of which in 1958 permitted an accused to exclude adverse spousal testimony.[61] The trend in state law toward divesting the accused of the privilege to bar adverse spousal testimony has special relevance because the laws of marriage and domestic relations are concerns traditionally reserved to the states. . . .

Testimonial exclusionary rules and privileges contravene the fundamental principle that "'the public . . . has a right to every man's evidence.'" United States v. Bryan, 339 U.S. 323, 331 (1950). As such, they must be strictly construed and accepted "only to the very limited extent that permitting a refusal to testify or excluding relevant evidence has a public good transcending the normally predominant principle of

---

61. In 1965, California took the privilege from the defendant-spouse and vested it in the witness-spouse, accepting a study commission recommendation that the "latter [was] more likely than the former to determine whether or not to claim the privilege on the basis of the probable effect on the marital relationship." See Cal. Evid. Code Ann. sec. 970-973 (West 1966 and Supp. 1979) and 1 California Law Revision Commission, Recommendation and Study relating to The Marital "For and Against" Testimonial Privilege, at F-5 (1956). See also 6 California Law Revision Commission, Tentative Privileges Recommendation — Rule 27.5, pp.243-244 (1964).

Support for the common-law rule has also diminished in England. In 1972, a study group there proposed giving the privilege to the witness-spouse, on the ground that "if [the wife] is willing to give evidence . . . the law would be showing excessive concern for the preservation of marital harmony if it were to say that she must not do so." Criminal Law Revision Committee, Eleventh Report, Evidence (General) 93.

utilizing all rational means for ascertaining truth." Elkins v. United States, 364 U.S. 206, 234 (1960) (Frankfurter, J., dissenting)....Here we must decide whether the privilege against adverse spousal testimony promotes sufficiently important interests to outweigh the need for probative evidence in the administration of criminal justice.

It is essential to remember that the *Hawkins* privilege is not needed to protect information privately disclosed between husband and wife in the confidence of the marital relationship.... Those confidences are privileged under the independent rule protecting confidential marital communications.... The *Hawkins* privilege is invoked, not to exclude private marital communications, but rather to exclude evidence of criminal acts and of communications made in the presence of third persons.

No other testimonial privilege sweeps so broadly. The privileges between priest and penitent, attorney and client, and physician and patient limit protection to private communications. These privileges are rooted in the imperative need for confidence and trust. The priest-penitent privilege recognizes the human need to disclose to a spiritual counselor, in total and absolute confidence, what are believed to be flawed acts or thoughts and to receive priestly consolation and guidance in return. The lawyer-client privilege rests on the need for the advocate and counselor to know all that relates to the client's reasons for seeking representation if the professional mission is to be carried out. Similarly, the physician must know all that a patient can articulate in order to identify and to treat disease; barriers to full disclosure would impair diagnosis and treatment.

The *Hawkins* rule stands in marked contrast to these three privileges. Its protection is not limited to confidential communications; rather it permits an accused to exclude all adverse spousal testimony. As Jeremy Bentham observed more than a century and a half ago, such a privilege goes far beyond making "every man's house his castle," and permits a person to convert his house into "a den of thieves." 5 Rationale of Judicial Evidence 340 (1827). It "secures, to every man, one safe and unquestionable and ever ready accomplice for every imaginable crime." Id., at 338.

The ancient foundations for so sweeping a privilege have long since disappeared. Nowhere in the common-law world — indeed in any modern society — is a woman regarded as chattel or demeaned by denial of a separate legal identity and the dignity associated with recognition as a whole human being. Chip by chip, over the years those archaic notions have been cast aside so that "[n]o longer is the female destined solely for the home and the rearing of the family, and only the male for the marketplace and the world of ideas." Stanton v. Stanton, 421 U.S. 7, 14-15 (1975).

The contemporary justification for affording an accused such a privilege is also unpersuasive. When one spouse is willing to testify against the other in a criminal proceeding — whatever the motivation — their relationship is almost certainly in disrepair; there is probably little in the way of marital harmony for the privilege to preserve. In these circumstances, a rule of evidence that permits an accused to prevent adverse spousal testimony seems far more likely to frustrate justice than to foster family peace.[62] Indeed, there is reason to believe that vesting the privilege in the accused could actually undermine the marital relationship. For example, in a case such as this, the Government is unlikely to offer a wife immunity and lenient treatment if it knows

---

62. It is argued that abolishing the privilege will permit the Government to come between husband and wife, pitting one against the other. That, too, misses the mark. Neither *Hawkins* nor any other privilege prevents the Government from enlisting one spouse to give information concerning the other to aid in the other's apprehension. It is only the spouse's testimony in the courtroom that is prohibited.

that her husband can prevent her from giving adverse testimony. If the Government is dissuaded from making such an offer, the privilege can have the untoward effect of permitting one spouse to escape justice at the expense of the other. It hardly seems conducive to the preservation of the marital relation to place a wife in jeopardy solely by virtue of her husband's control over her testimony.

IV

Our consideration of the foundations for the privilege and its history satisfy us that "reason and experience" no longer justify so sweeping a rule as that found acceptable by the Court in *Hawkins*. Accordingly, we conclude that the existing rule should be modified so that the witness-spouse alone has a privilege to refuse to testify adversely; the witness may be neither compelled to testify nor foreclosed from testifying. This modification — vesting the privilege in the witness-spouse — furthers the important public interest in marital harmony without unduly burdening legitimate law enforcement needs.

Here, petitioner's spouse chose to testify against him. That she did so after a grant of immunity and assurances of lenient treatment does not render her testimony involuntary.... Accordingly, the District Court and the Court of Appeals were correct in rejecting petitioner's claim of privilege, and the judgment of the Court of Appeals is affirmed.

[The concurring opinion of Justice Stewart is omitted.]

NOTES AND QUESTIONS

1. Consider carefully the last footnote in *Trammel*. As the Court acknowledged early in its opinion, Mrs. Trammel was heavily involved in drug trafficking and thus faced the possibility of serious criminal penalties. Thus, the government's offer of immunity to her was a substantial incentive for her to testify against her husband. Perhaps the Trammels' marriage was likely to end regardless of the immunity, and perhaps she would have been willing to testify against her husband in any event. If it were clear that she would have testified without a grant of immunity, however, it seems unlikely that the prosecutor would have offered her immunity. In any event, if we are serious about trying to preserve marital harmony — as recognizing the testimonial privilege suggests we are — why should we formulate the privilege in a way that encourages prosecutors to pressure one spouse into testifying against the other? If the accused spouse could claim the privilege, the government, as the Court recognized, would have no incentive to try to drive a wedge between the husband and wife with an offer of leniency or immunity in cases where the spouses were cohorts in crime or by trying to pit an innocent spouse against the charged spouse. On the other hand, in states where the accused spouse holds the privilege, prosecutors may not be able to compel testimony from the victim spouse in domestic violence cases. Malinda L. Seymore, Isn't It a Crime: Feminist Perspectives on Spousal Immunity and Spousal Violence, 90 N.W. L. Rev. 1032, 1036 (1996).

2. The privilege may not apply if the marriage relationship is no longer viable at the time the testimony is sought. Should courts focus on whether the marriage is in a

state of "disrepair" when the testimonial privilege is claimed? In United States v. Brown, 605 F.2d 389 (8th Cir. 1979), the Eighth Circuit reversed its prior approach and premised its rejection of the privilege primarily upon its opinion of the health of the marriage. Noting that the husband and wife had not seen each other for eight months, the court stated that is was "difficult to visualize" how protection of the marital bond "would have required the total exclusion of Mrs. Clincy from the witness stand." Should courts have the discretion to make such judgments? Some don't think so. See United States v. Lilley, 581 F.2d 182 (8th Cir. 1978).

3. Like the marital communications privilege, the testimonial privilege is construed narrowly to prevent fraud. Courts are reluctant to apply the privilege when it appears that the marriage was entered into solely for the purpose of preventing testimony. As stated by the Supreme Court in Lutwak v. United States, 344 U.S. 604, 614-615 (1953):

> When the good faith of the marital relation is pertinent and it is made to appear . . . that the relationship was entered into with no intention of the parties to live together as husband and wife but only for the purpose of using the marriage ceremony in a scheme to defraud, the ostensible spouses are competent to testify against each other.

However, the "sham marriage" doctrine is not easy of application. See, for example, In re Grand Jury Subpoena, 884 F. Supp. 188 (D. Md. 1995) (holding that, while the marriage may have been primarily intended to prevent adverse testimony from one spouse against the other, there was evidence to suggest the marriage was in fact genuine); and Glover v. State, 816 N.E.2d 1197 (Ind. App. 2004) (refusing to recognize fraudulent marriage exception, as state's statutory scheme does not permit the exception).

Most courts hold that the privilege applies only to testimony by the spouse and does not block admission of out-of-court statements when such statements are admissible under the hearsay rule. In United States v. Chapman, 866 F.2d 1326 (11th Cir. 1986), a bank robbery case, the out-of-court statements made by the defendant's spouse were held to be admissible hearsay. The requirement of unavailability was met because the out-of-court declarant was unavailable in that she refused, on the basis of her marital privilege, to give any substantive testimony. The court also held that the out-of-court statements bore sufficient indicia of reliability to be admissible. In holding the marital testimonial privilege to be inapplicable, the court relied on the Supreme Court's statement in *Trammel* that nothing in the law of privileges "prevents the Government from enlisting one spouse to give information concerning the other or to aid in the other's apprehension. It is only the spouse's testimony in the courtroom that is prohibited." Id. At 1333. In United States v. James, 128 F. Supp. 2d 291 (D. Md. 2001), the district court upheld the admissibility of the defendant's wife's call to the 911 operator, stating that her husband had assaulted her, as an excited utterance.

4. The marital privileges may attach to common-law marriages, provided that the law of the domicile state recognizes them and that the marriage itself is legally valid under state law. See United States v. Lustig, 555 F.2d 737, 747-748 (9th Cir. 1978), (both of the marital privileges were lost because Alaska did not recognize common-law marriages).

However, neither federal nor state courts have extended the protection of the privilege to unmarried cohabitants. See, e.g., United States v. Acker, 52 F.3d 509 (4th Cir. 1995) (finding no valid marriage where the heterosexual couple involved had been living together for 25 years in states that do not recognize common law marriage).

5. As with the marital communications privilege, the marital testimonial privilege, as applied to same-sex couples, now exists in a few states. As discussed on page 844, supra, recent developments in state law, such as the creation of same-sex civil unions in Vermont and the acceptance of same-sex marriage by Massachusetts courts, require that same-sex couples be given the same benefits and privileges as other married couples. However, most states do not recognize same-sex unions of any kind, and thus provide no marital testimonial privileges to such individuals.

6. For further discussion on the marital privileges generally, see Regan, Spousal Privilege and the Meanings of Marriage, 81 Va. L. Rev. 2045 (1995).

b. *Exceptions*

It is well-established that the marital testimonial privilege does not apply when one spouse is prosecuted for a crime against the person or property of the other. Some states extend this exception to charges of crimes committed against family members or cohabitants. For example, Cal. Evid. Code §972(e)(1) (West 1995) provides:

> A married person does not have a privilege under this article in: (e) A criminal proceeding in which one spouse is charged with: (1) A crime against the person or property of the other spouse or of a child, parent, relative, or cohabitant of either, whether committed before or during marriage.

In People v. Bogle, 41 Cal. App. 4th 770, 782 (1995), the court said that "cohabitant" should be interpreted broadly, because "individuals are uniquely vulnerable in their domestic environment." In *Bogle*, the court applied this exception to the privilege and upheld the wife's ability to testify against her husband in his trial for murder of the wealthy couple with whom he lived as a boarder, even though he was not related to them. More commonly, of course, the exception is applied where the defendant is charged with a crime against his spouse or against their children. If the crime is one of domestic violence, then the witness spouse can be compelled to testify despite her assertion of the privilege. But even where this exception exists, "married women [are left] unprotected by the legal system because of very narrow and uninformed views of what constitutes spousal violence." Malinda L. Seymore, Isn't It a Crime: Feminist Perspectives on Spousal Immunity and Spousal Violence, 90 N.W. L. Rev. 1032, 1036 (1996).

There is a split among federal circuits as to whether there is a "joint participants in crime" exception to the testimonial privilege. Some courts require the witness spouse to testify when the spouses have engaged in joint illegal behavior. United States v. Clark, 712 F.2d 299 (7th Cir. 1983). Others still apply the privilege, reasoning that the policy of *Trammel* to protect the marriage is not outweighed and that compelled testimony would "undermine the marriage precisely in the manner that the privilege is designed to prevent." Appeal of Malfitano, 633 F.2d 276, 279 (3d Cir. 1980).

The marital testimonial privilege also does not apply to prosecutions under the Mann Act, where a wife is transported across state lines by her husband for the purpose of prostitution. Wyatt v. United States, 362 U.S. 525, 530 (1960).

KEY POINTS

1. Two privileges relate to the marital relationship. One immunizes confidential communications made during the marriage from disclosure; it applies in civil and criminal cases. The other permits a spouse not to testify (or permits the accused spouse from stopping the other spouse from testifying) against the accused spouse in a criminal case.

2. The confidential communications privilege survives the marriage; the testimonial privilege does not.

3. Neither privilege applies in litigation between the spouses, or involving accusations of criminal acts of one spouse against the other.

PROBLEMS

12.23. Ellen Graves has been subpoenaed to provide a handwriting exemplar and fingerprints to the grand jury, which is investigating the filing of false joint income tax returns by Ms. Graves and her husband. Ms. Graves moves to quash the subpoena on the ground that compliance would violate her privilege not to testify against her husband. What result?

12.24. Ms. Witness's husband is the target of a grand jury investigation into illegal drug trafficking. Ms. Witness has been summoned to appear before the grand jury to testify about her own bank accounts and financial history both before and after the marriage. The government's purpose is to determine whether her accounts were used for money laundering from illegal drug sales. Ms. Witness refuses to testify and seeks to invoke the marital testimonial privilege. Should she be compelled to testify? What if the government asserts that since ts questions are about her personal financial history, they should be asked, answered, and examined on a question-by-question basis to determine whether the information elicited is "adverse" to the husband?

E.   THE PHYSICIAN-PATIENT AND PSYCHOTHERAPIST-PATIENT PRIVILEGES

Neither the physician-patient privilege nor the psychotherapist-patient privilege existed at common law. The physician-patient privilege was first recognized in the United States by an 1828 New York statute that granted a testimonial privilege to physician-patient communications. In contrast, the psychotherapeutic privileges did not gain approval until the 1950s, when the fields of psychology and psychotherapy were first accorded professional recognition. The traditional justification for both privileges is the standard utilitarian argument that the privilege is necessary to encourage the patient to disclose information for the proper diagnosis and treatment of illness. By protecting the patient from the disclosure of potentially incriminating or liability-related information in court, the privilege helps to ensure the provision of effective medical or therapeutic treatment.

The utilitarian justification for the physician-patient privilege has been roundly criticized on the ground that patients will communicate all information that may aid in proper diagnosis and treatment whether or not a privilege exists. In contrast, the psychotherapist-patient privilege has received approval by both courts and commentators. Advocates argue that some form of protection is necessary in the psychotherapist-patient context because the communications usually involve matters that a patient regards as extremely personal.

We examine these two privileges in the next two subsections.

1.   The Physician-Patient Privilege

The Proposed Federal Rules of Evidence did not recognize a physician-patient privilege. The Advisory Committee's Note to Proposed FRE 504 observed:

> While many states have by statute created the [physician-patient] privilege, the exceptions which have been found necessary in order to obtain information required by the public interest or to avoid fraud are so numerous as to leave little if any basis for the privilege. . . . California, for example, excepts cases in which the patient puts his condition in issue, all criminal proceedings, will and similar contests, malpractice cases, and disciplinary proceedings. . . . [Cal. Evid. Code §§990-1007.]

To this should be added the point noted above that the behavioral incentives typically are not needed in this context. For both reasons, most federal courts have rejected a physician-patient privilege. See United States v. Bercier, 848 F.2d 917, 920 (8th Cir. 1988) ("[b]ecause no physician privilege existed at common law . . . federal courts do not recognize the physician-patient privilege under federal common law); Patterson v. Caterpillar, 70 F.3d 503, 506 (7th Cir. 1995) (stating unequivocally that federal common law does not recognize this privilege).

Over three-quarters of the states have enacted statutes recognizing a physician-patient privilege. Most state statutes refer generally to "physicians" or "physicians or surgeons" to denote the type of health care providers covered by the statute. The Arizona physician-patient privilege statute is typical:

> In a civil action a physician or surgeon shall not, without the consent of his patient . . . be examined as to any communication made by his patient with reference to any physical or mental disease or disorder . . . or as to any such knowledge obtained by personal examination of the patient. [Ariz. Rev. Stat. Ann. sec. 12-2235 (West 2003).]

Some state statutes, however, are more expansive, such as the Minnesota privilege statute which includes "dentists, chiropractors, and registered nurses" within the protection of the privilege. Minn. Stat. Ann. §§595.02(1)(d), (g) (West 2000).

Typically the patient is the holder, and the privilege covers confidential communications made for the purpose of, or in connection with, obtaining medical assistance or advice. Such information could be obtained through conversation with the patient or through the physician's physical examination. The privilege is also sometimes extended to "[a] record of identity, diagnosis, evaluation, or treatment of a patient by a physician that is created or maintained by a physician." Tex. Occ. Code §159.002(b) (Vernon 2004). Similar to the attorney-client privilege, the facts that a patient has consulted a physician, has been treated by him, and the number and dates of the visits, are not covered by the privilege. In some states, the physician-patient privilege applies only to judicial proceedings and does not prohibit defense counsel from engaging in ex parte communications with plaintiff's physicians. Steinberg v. Jensen, 534 N.W.2d 361, 370 (Wis. 1995).

Waiver occurs in the normal manner through disclosure or putting physical condition into issue in litigation. Carson v. Fine, 867 P.2d 610 (Wash. 1994) (privilege waived as to fact and opinion information held by all physicians when plaintiff filed malpractice action). A patient may expressly waive his privilege by authorizing the release of medical information. A patient may also impliedly waive the privilege by either voluntarily disclosing such medical information to an outside party or through partial disclosure in a judicial proceeding. In Ziegler v. Department of Fire, 426 So. 2d 311, 313 (La. Ct. App. 1983), a patient's failure to assert the privilege in objection to a physician's testimony at trial resulted in a waiver for all later trials.

The presence of third persons may destroy the required confidentiality of a physician-patient communication. However, if the third person is a necessary participant to the consultation, such as a nurse acting under the direction of the physician, the privilege may remain intact. Sims v. Charlotte Liberty Mut. Ins. Co., 125 S.E.2d 326, 331 (N.C. 1962) (records made by "nurses, technicians, and others" may be included under the privilege statute if they are acting under a physician or surgeon).

In addition, state statutes commonly require physicians to report certain information related to public health and safety, such as information regarding child abuse, venereal disease, and gunshot injury. In the absence of the statutes, this information would generally be protected by the privilege. In most instances, the reporting systems expressly prohibit public release of the information obtained.

2.   The Psychotherapist-Patient Privilege

a.   Jaffee v. Redmond

In 1996, the U.S. Supreme Court established the psychotherapist-patient privilege under FRE 501 in the case of Jaffee v. Redmond, 518 U.S.1 (1996). This privilege had been included as Rule 504 in the Proposed Federal Rules of Evidence, and each state has a version of the privilege. The existence of this privilege is thus well established, but it is by no means free from controversy; nor is its scope entirely clear. Our study of this privilege begins with *Jaffee*, which thoroughly canvasses the then-existing law and the relevant policy justifications.

JAFFEE v. REDMOND
518 U.S. 1 (1996)

Justice STEVENS delivered the opinion of the Court.

After a traumatic incident in which she shot and killed a man, a police officer received extensive counseling from a licensed clinical social worker. The question we address is whether statements the officer made to her therapist during the counseling sessions are protected from compelled disclosure in a federal civil action brought by the family of the deceased. Stated otherwise, the question is whether it is appropriate for federal courts to recognize a "psychotherapist privilege" under Rule 501 of the Federal Rules of Evidence.

I

Petitioner is the administrator of the estate of Ricky Allen. Respondents are Mary Lu Redmond, a former police officer, and the Village of Hoffman Estates, Illinois, her employer during the time that she served on the police force. Petitioner commenced this action against respondents after Redmond shot and killed Allen while on patrol duty. On June 27, 1991, Redmond was the first officer to respond to a "fight in progress" call at an apartment complex. As she arrived at the scene, two of Allen's sisters ran toward her squad car, waving their arms and shouting that there had been a stabbing in one of the apartments. Redmond testified at trial that she relayed this information to her dispatcher and requested an ambulance. She then exited her car and walked toward the apartment building. Before Redmond reached the building, several men ran out, one waving a pipe. When the men ignored her order to get on the ground, Redmond drew her service revolver. Two other men then burst out of the building, one, Ricky Allen, chasing the other. According to Redmond, Allen was brandishing a butcher knife and disregarded her repeated commands to drop the weapon. Redmond shot Allen when she believed he was about to stab the man he was chasing. Allen died at the scene. Redmond testified that before other officers arrived to provide support, "people came pouring out of the buildings," and a threatening confrontation between her and the crowd ensued.

Petitioner filed suit in Federal District Court alleging that Redmond had violated Allen's constitutional rights by using excessive force during the encounter at the apartment complex. At trial, petitioner presented testimony from members of Allen's family that conflicted with Redmond's version of the incident in several important respects. They testified, for example, that Redmond drew her gun before exiting her squad car and that Allen was unarmed when he emerged from the apartment building. During pretrial discovery petitioner learned that after the shooting Redmond had participated in about 50 counseling sessions with Karen Beyer, a clinical social worker licensed by the State of Illinois and employed at that time by the Village of Hoffman Estates. Petitioner sought access to Beyer's notes concerning the sessions for use in cross-examining Redmond. Respondents vigorously resisted the discovery. They asserted that the contents of the conversations between Beyer and Redmond were protected against involuntary disclosure by a psychotherapist-patient privilege. The district judge rejected this argument. Neither Beyer nor Redmond, however, complied with his order to disclose the contents of Beyer's notes. At depositions and on the witness stand both either refused to answer certain questions or professed an inability to recall details of their conversations. In his instructions at the end of the trial, the judge advised the jury that the refusal to turn over Beyer's notes had no "legal justification" and that the jury could therefore presume that the contents of the notes would have been unfavorable to respondents. The jury awarded petitioner $45,000 on the federal claim and $500,000 on her state-law claim. The Court of Appeals for the Seventh Circuit reversed and remanded for a new trial. Addressing the issue for the first time, the court concluded that "reason and experience," the touchstones for acceptance of a privilege under Rule 501 of the Federal Rules of Evidence, compelled recognition of a psychotherapist-patient privileg. . . .

The Court of Appeals qualified its recognition of the privilege by stating that it would not apply if "in the interests of justice, the evidentiary need for the disclosure of

the contents of a patient's counseling sessions outweighs that patient's privacy interests." . . . [T]he court concluded that the trial court had erred by refusing to afford
protection to the confidential communications between Redmond and Beyer.

The United States courts of appeals do not uniformly agree that the federal courts
should recognize a psychotherapist privilege under Rule 501.

II

. . . The common-law principles underlying the recognition of testimonial privileges
can be stated simply. "'For more than three centuries it has now been recognized as a
fundamental maxim that the public . . . has a right to every man's evidence. When we
come to examine the various claims of exemption, we start with the primary assumption that there is a general duty to give what testimony one is capable of giving, and that
any exemptions which may exist are distinctly exceptional, being so many derogations
from a positive general rule.'" United States v. Bryan, 339 U. S. 323, 331 (1950)
(quoting 8 J. Wigmore, Evidence §2192, p. 64 (3d ed. 1940)).[63] See also United States
v. Nixon, 418 U. S. 683, 709 (1974). Exceptions from the general rule disfavoring
testimonial privileges may be justified, however, by a "'public good transcending the
normally predominant principle of utilizing all rational means for ascertaining the
truth.'" Trammel, 445 U.S., at 50.

Guided by these principles, the question we address today is whether a privilege
protecting confidential communications between a psychotherapist and her patient
"promotes sufficiently important interests to outweigh the need for probative
evidence. . . ." Both "reason and experience" persuade us that it does.

III

Like the spousal and attorney-client privileges, the psychotherapist-patient privilege is
"rooted in the imperative need for confidence and trust." Trammel, 445 U.S., at 51.
Treatment by a physician for physical ailments can often proceed successfully on the
basis of a physical examination, objective information supplied by the patient, and the
results of diagnostic tests. Effective psychotherapy, by contrast, depends upon an atmosphere of confidence and trust in which the patient is willing to make a frank and
complete disclosure of facts, emotions, memories, and fears. Because of the sensitive
nature of the problems for which individuals consult psychotherapists, disclosure of
confidential communications made during counseling sessions may cause embarrassment or disgrace. For this reason, the mere possibility of disclosure may impede
development of the confidential relationship necessary for successful treatment.[64]
As the Judicial Conference Advisory Committee observed in 1972 when it recommended that Congress recognize a psychotherapist privilege as part of the Proposed

---

63. The familiar expression "every man's evidence" was a well-known phrase as early as the mid-
18th century. Both the Duke of Argyll and Lord Chancellor Hardwicke invoked the maxim during the May
25, 1742, debate in the House of Lords concerning a bill to grant immunity to witnesses who would give
evidence against Sir Robert Walpole, first Earl of Orford. 12 T. Hansard, Parliamentary History of England
643, 675, 693, 697 (1812). The bill was defeated soundly. Id., at 711.

64. See studies and authorities cited in the Brief for American Psychiatric Association et al. as Amici
Curiae 14-17, and the Brief for American Psychological Association as Amicus Curiae 12-17.

Federal Rules of Evidence, a psychiatrist's ability to help her patients:

> "is completely dependent upon [the patients'] willingness and ability to talk freely. This makes it difficult if not impossible for [a psychiatrist] to function without being able to assure ... patients of confidentiality and, indeed, privileged communication. Where there may be exceptions to this general rule ..., there is wide agreement that confidentiality is a sine qua non for successful psychiatric treatment." Advisory Committee's Notes to Proposed Rules, 56 F.R.D. 183, 242 (1972) (quoting Group for Advancement of Psychiatry, Report No. 45, Confidentiality and Privileged Communication in the Practice of Psychiatry 92 (June 1960)).

By protecting confidential communications between a psychotherapist and her patient from involuntary disclosure, the proposed privilege thus serves important private interests.

Our cases make clear that an asserted privilege must also "serve public ends." ... The psychotherapist privilege serves the public interest by facilitating the provision of appropriate treatment for individuals suffering the effects of a mental or emotional problem. The mental health of our citizenry, no less than its physical health, is a public good of transcendent importance.[65] In contrast to the significant public and private interests supporting recognition of the privilege, the likely evidentiary benefit that would result from the denial of the privilege is modest. If the privilege were rejected, confidential conversations between psychotherapists and their patients would surely be chilled, particularly when it is obvious that the circumstances that give rise to the need for treatment will probably result in litigation. Without a privilege, much of the desirable evidence to which litigants such as petitioner seek access — for example, admissions against interest by a party — is unlikely to come into being. This unspoken "evidence" will therefore serve no greater truth-seeking function than if it had been spoken and privileged.

That it is appropriate for the federal courts to recognize a psychotherapist privilege under Rule 501 is confirmed by the fact that all 50 States and the District of Columbia have enacted into law some form of psychotherapist privilege. We have previously observed that the policy decisions of the States bear on the question whether federal courts should recognize a new privilege or amend the coverage of an existing one. See Trammel, 445 U.S., at 48-50.... Because state legislatures are fully aware of the need to protect the integrity of the fact-finding functions of their courts, the existence of a consensus among the States indicates that "reason and experience" support recognition of the privilege. In addition, given the importance of the patient's understanding that her communications with her therapist will not be publicly disclosed, any State's promise of confidentiality would have little value if the patient were aware that the privilege would not be honored in a federal court.[66] Denial of the federal privilege therefore would frustrate the purposes of the state legislation that was enacted to foster these confidential communications.

65. This case amply demonstrates the importance of allowing individuals to receive confidential counseling. Police officers engaged in the dangerous and difficult tasks associated with protecting the safety of our communities not only confront the risk of physical harm but also face stressful circumstances that may give rise to anxiety, depression, fear, or anger. The entire community may suffer if police officers are not able to receive effective counseling and treatment after traumatic incidents, either because trained officers leave the profession prematurely or because those in need of treatment remain on the job.

66. At the outset of their relationship, the ethical therapist must disclose to the patient "the relevant limits on confidentiality." See American Psychological Association, Ethical Principles of Psychologists and Code of Conduct, Standard 5.01 (Dec. 1992). See also National Federation of Societies for Clinical Social Work, Code of Ethics V(a) (May 1988); American Counseling Association, Code of Ethics and Standards of Practice a.3.a (effective July 1995).

It is of no consequence that recognition of the privilege in the vast majority of States is the product of legislative action rather than judicial decision. Although common-law rulings may once have been the primary source of new developments in federal privilege law, that is no longer the case. In Funk v. United States, 290 U.S. 371 (1933), we recognized that it is appropriate to treat a consistent body of policy determinations by state legislatures as reflecting both "reason" and "experience." That rule is properly respectful of the States and at the same time reflects the fact that once a state legislature has enacted a privilege there is no longer an opportunity for common-law creation of the protection. . . . [67] The uniform judgment of the States is reinforced by the fact that a psychotherapist privilege was among the nine specific privileges recommended by the Advisory Committee in its proposed privilege rules. . . . In rejecting the proposed draft that had specifically identified each privilege rule and substituting the present more open-ended Rule 501, the Senate Judiciary Committee explicitly stated that its action "should not be understood as disapproving any recognition of a psychiatrist-patient- . . . privilege contained in the [proposed] rules." Because we agree with the judgment of the state legislatures and the Advisory Committee that a psychotherapist-patient privilege will serve a "public good transcending the normally predominant principle of utilizing all rational means for ascertaining truth," Trammel, 445 U.S., at 50, we hold that confidential communications between a licensed psychotherapist and her patients in the course of diagnosis or treatment are protected from compelled disclosure under Rule 501 of the Federal Rules of Evidence.[68]

IV

All agree that a psychotherapist privilege covers confidential communications made to licensed psychiatrists and psychologists. We have no hesitation in concluding in this case that the federal privilege should also extend to confidential communications made to licensed social workers in the course of psychotherapy. The reasons for recognizing a privilege for treatment by psychiatrists and psychologists apply with equal force to treatment by a clinical social worker such as Karen Beyer.[69] Today, social workers provide a significant amount of mental health treatment. Their clients often

67. Petitioner acknowledges that all 50 state legislatures favor a psychotherapist privilege. She nevertheless discounts the relevance of the state privilege statutes by pointing to divergence among the States concerning the types of therapy relationships protected and the exceptions recognized, a small number of state statutes, for example, grant the privilege only to psychiatrists and psychologists, while most apply the protection more broadly. Compare Haw. Rules Evid. 504, 504.1 and N. Rule Evid. 503 (privilege extends to physicians and psychotherapists), with Ariz. Rev. Stat. Ann. §32-3283 (1992) (privilege covers "behavioral health professionals"); Tex. Rule Civ. Evid. 510(a)(1) (privilege extends to persons "licensed or certified by the State of Texas in the diagnosis, evaluation or treatment of any mental or emotional disorder" or "involved in the treatment or examination of drug abusers"); Utah Rule Evid. 506 (privilege protects confidential communications made to marriage and family therapists, professional counselors, and psychiatric mental health nurse specialists). The range of exceptions recognized by the States is similarly varied. Compare Ark. Code Ann. §17-46-107 (1987) (narrow exceptions); Haw. Rules Evid. 504, 504.1 (same), with Cal. Evid. Code Ann. §§1016-1027 (West 1995) (broad exceptions); R.I. Gen. Laws §5-37.3-4 (1956) (same). These variations in the scope of the protection are too limited to undermine the force of the States' unanimous judgment that some form of psychotherapist privilege is appropriate.

68. Like other testimonial privileges, the patient may of course waive the protection.

69. If petitioner had filed her complaint in an Illinois state court, respondents' claim of privilege would surely have been upheld, at least with respect to the state wrongful death action. An Illinois statute provides that conversations between a therapist and her patients are privileged from compelled disclosure in any civil or criminal proceeding. Ill. Comp. Stat., ch. 740, §110/10 (1994). The term "therapist" is broadly defined to encompass a number of licensed professionals including social workers. Ch. 740, §110/2. Karen Beyer, having satisfied the strict standards for licensure, qualifies as a clinical social worker in Illinois. . . .

include the poor and those of modest means who could not afford the assistance of a
psychiatrist or psychologist, but whose counseling sessions serve the same public goals.
Perhaps in recognition of these circumstances, the vast majority of States explicitly
extend a testimonial privilege to licensed social workers. We therefore agree with the
Court of Appeals that "drawing a distinction between the counseling provided by costly
psychotherapists and the counseling provided by more readily accessible social workers
serves no discernible public purpose." We part company with the Court of Appeals on
a separate point. We reject the balancing component of the privilege implemented by
that court and a small number of States. Making the promise of confidentiality contingent upon a trial judge's later evaluation of the relative importance of the patient's
interest in privacy and the evidentiary need for disclosure would eviscerate the effectiveness of the privilege. As we explained in *Upjohn*, if the purpose of the privilege is to
be served, the participants in the confidential conversation "must be able to predict
with some degree of certainty whether particular discussions will be protected. An
uncertain privilege, or one which purports to be certain but results in widely varying
applications by the courts, is little better than no privilege at all." These considerations
are all that is necessary for decision of this case. A rule that authorizes the recognition of
new privileges on a case-by-case basis makes it appropriate to define the details of new
privileges in a like manner. Because this is the first case in which we have recognized a
psychotherapist privilege, it is neither necessary nor feasible to delineate its full contours in a way that would "govern all conceivable future questions in this area."[70]

V

The conversations between Officer Redmond and Karen Beyer and the notes taken
during their counseling sessions are protected from compelled disclosure under Rule
501 of the Federal Rules of Evidence. The judgment of the Court of Appeals is
affirmed.

It is so ordered.

JUSTICE SCALIA, with whom THE CHIEF JUSTICE joins as to Part III, dissenting.

The Court has discussed at some length the benefit that will be purchased by
creation of the evidentiary privilege in this case: the encouragement of psychoanalytic
counseling. It has not mentioned the purchase price: occasional injustice. That is the
cost of every rule which excludes reliable and probative evidence — or at least every
one categorical enough to achieve its announced policy objective. In the case of some
of these rules, such as the one excluding confessions that have not been properly
"Mirandized," see Miranda v. Arizona, 384 U.S. 436 (1966), the victim of the injustice
is always the impersonal State or the faceless "public at large." For the rule proposed
here, the victim is more likely to be some individual who is prevented from proving a
valid claim — or (worse still) prevented from establishing a valid defense. The latter is
particularly unpalatable for those who love justice, because it causes the courts of law
not merely to let stand a wrong, but to become themselves the instruments of wrong.

---

70. Although it would be premature to speculate about most future developments in the federal
psychotherapist privilege, we do not doubt that there are situations in which the privilege must give way, for
example, if a serious threat of harm to the patient or to others can be averted only by means of a disclosure
by the therapist.

In the past, this Court has well understood that the particular value the courts are distinctively charged with preserving — justice — is severely harmed by contravention of "the fundamental principle that "the public . . . has a right to every man's evidence." . . . The Court today ignores this traditional judicial preference for the truth, and ends up creating a privilege that is new, vast, and ill-defined. I respectfully dissent.

I

The case before us involves confidential communications made by a police officer to a state-licensed clinical social worker in the course of psychotherapeutic counseling. Before proceeding to a legal analysis of the case, I must observe that the Court makes its task deceptively simple by the manner in which it proceeds. It begins by characterizing the issue as "whether it is appropriate for federal courts to recognize a 'psychotherapist privilege,'" and devotes almost all of its opinion to that question. Having answered that question (to its satisfaction) in the affirmative, it then devotes less than a page of text to answering in the affirmative the small remaining question whether "the federal privilege should also extend to confidential communications made to licensed social workers in the course of psychotherapy." Of course the prototypical evidentiary privilege analogous to the one asserted here — the lawyer-client privilege — is not identified by the broad area of advice-giving practiced by the person to whom the privileged communication is given, but rather by the professional status of that person. Hence, it seems a long step from a lawyer-client privilege to a tax advisor-client or accountant-client privilege. But if one recharacterizes it as a "legal advisor" privilege, the extension seems like the most natural thing in the world. That is the illusion the Court has produced here: It first frames an overly general question ("Should there be a psychotherapist privilege?") that can be answered in the negative only by excluding from protection office consultations with professional psychiatrists (i.e., doctors) and clinical psychologists. And then, having answered that in the affirmative, it comes to the only question that the facts of this case present ("Should there be a social worker-client privilege with regard to psychotherapeutic counseling?") with the answer seemingly a foregone conclusion. At that point, to conclude against the privilege one must subscribe to the difficult proposition, "Yes, there is a psychotherapist privilege, but not if the psychotherapist is a social worker." Relegating the question actually posed by this case to an afterthought makes the impossible possible in a number of wonderful ways. For example, it enables the Court to treat the Proposed Federal Rules of Evidence developed in 1972 by the Judicial Conference Advisory Committee as strong support for its holding, whereas they in fact counsel clearly and directly against it. The Committee did indeed recommend a "psychotherapist privilege" of sorts; but more precisely, and more relevantly, it recommended a privilege for psychotherapy conducted by "a person authorized to practice medicine" or "a person licensed or certified as a psychologist," Proposed Rule of Evidence 504, 56 F.R.D. 183, 240 (1972), which is to say that it recommended against the privilege at issue here. That condemnation is obscured, and even converted into an endorsement, by pushing a "psychotherapist privilege" into the center ring. The Proposed Rule figures prominently in the Court's explanation of why that privilege deserves recognition, and is ignored in the single page devoted to the sideshow which happens to be the issue presented for decision.

This is the most egregious and readily explainable example of how the Court's misdirection of its analysis makes the difficult seem easy; others will become apparent when I give the social-worker question the fuller consideration it deserves. My initial point, however, is that the Court's very methodology — giving serious consideration only to the more general, and much easier, question — is in violation of our duty to proceed cautiously when erecting barriers between us and the truth.

II

To say that the Court devotes the bulk of its opinion to the much easier question of psychotherapist-patient privilege is not to say that its answer to that question is convincing. At bottom, the Court's decision to recognize such a privilege is based on its view that "successful [psychotherapeutic] treatment" serves "important private interests" (namely those of patients undergoing psychotherapy) as well as the "public good" of "the mental health of our citizenry." I have no quarrel with these premises. Effective psychotherapy undoubtedly is beneficial to individuals with mental problems, and surely serves some larger social interest in maintaining a mentally stable society. But merely mentioning these values does not answer the critical question: are they of such importance, and is the contribution of psychotherapy to them so distinctive, and is the application of normal evidentiary rules so destructive to psychotherapy, as to justify making our federal courts occasional instruments of injustice? On that central question I find the Court's analysis insufficiently convincing to satisfy the high standard we have set for rules that are in derogation of the search for truth.

When is it, one must wonder, that the psychotherapist came to play such an indispensable role in the maintenance of the citizenry's mental health? For most of history, men and women have worked out their difficulties by talking to, inter alios, parents, siblings, best friends and bartenders — none of whom was awarded a privilege against testifying in court. Ask the average citizen: Would your mental health be more significantly impaired by preventing you from seeing a psychotherapist, or by preventing you from getting advice from your mom? I have little doubt what the answer would be. Yet there is no mother-child privilege. How likely is it that a person will be deterred from seeking psychological counseling, or from being completely truthful in the course of such counseling, because of fear of later disclosure in litigation? And even more pertinent to today's decision, to what extent will the evidentiary privilege reduce that deterrent? The Court does not try to answer the first of these questions; and it cannot possibly have any notion of what the answer is to the second, since that depends entirely upon the scope of the privilege, which the Court amazingly finds it "neither necessary nor feasible to delineate." If, for example, the psychotherapist can give the patient no more assurance than "a court will not be able to make me disclose what you tell me, unless you tell me about a harmful act," I doubt whether there would be much benefit from the privilege at all. That is not a fanciful example, at least with respect to extension of the psychotherapist privilege to social workers.

Even where it is certain that absence of the psychotherapist privilege will inhibit disclosure of the information, it is not clear to me that that is an unacceptable state of affairs. Let us assume the very worst in the circumstances of the present case: that to be truthful about what was troubling her, the police officer who sought counseling would have to confess that she shot without reason, and wounded an innocent man. If (again to assume the worst) such an act constituted the crime of negligent wounding under Illinois law, the officer would of course have the absolute right not to admit that she shot without reason in criminal court. But I see no reason why she should be enabled both not to admit it in criminal court (as a good citizen should), and to get the benefits of psychotherapy by admitting it to a therapist who cannot tell anyone else. And even less reason why she should be enabled to deny her guilt in the criminal trial — or in a civil trial for negligence — while yet obtaining the benefits of psychotherapy by confessing guilt to a social worker who cannot testify. It seems to me entirely fair to say that if she wishes the benefits of telling the truth she must also accept the adverse consequences. To be sure, in most cases the statements to the psychotherapist will be only marginally relevant, and one of the purposes of the privilege (though not one relied upon by the Court) may be simply to spare patients needless intrusion upon their privacy, and to spare psychotherapists needless expenditure of their time in deposition and trial. But surely this can be achieved by means short of excluding even evidence that is of the most direct and conclusive effect....

The Court suggests one last policy justification: since psychotherapist privilege statutes exist in all the States, the failure to recognize a privilege in federal courts "would frustrate the purposes of the state legislation that was enacted to foster these confidential communications." ... Since, as I shall discuss, state policies regarding the psychotherapist privilege vary considerably from State to State, no uniform federal policy can possibly honor most of them. If furtherance of state policies is the name of the game, rules of privilege in federal courts should vary from State to State, a la *Erie*.

The Court's failure to put forward a convincing justification of its own could perhaps be excused if it were relying upon the unanimous conclusion of state courts in the reasoned development of their common law. It cannot do that, since no State has such a privilege apart from legislation.... The Court concedes that there is "divergence among the States concerning the types of therapy relationships protected and the exceptions recognized." To rest a newly announced federal common-law psychotherapist privilege, assertable from this day forward in all federal courts, upon "the States' unanimous judgment that some form of psychotherapist privilege is appropriate," is rather like announcing a new, immediately applicable, federal common law of torts, based upon the States' "unanimous judgment" that some form of tort law is appropriate. In the one case as in the other, the state laws vary to such a degree that the parties and lower federal judges confronted by the new "common law" have barely a clue as to what its content might be.

III

Turning from the general question that was not involved in this case to the specific one that is: The Court's conclusion that a social-worker psychotherapeutic privilege deserves recognition is even less persuasive. In approaching this question, the fact that five of the state legislatures that have seen fit to enact "some form" of psychotherapist privilege have elected not to extend any form of privilege to social workers, ought to give one pause. So should the fact that the Judicial Conference Advisory Committee was similarly discriminating in its conferral of the proposed Rule 504 privilege. The Court, however, has "no hesitation in concluding ... that the federal privilege should also extend" to social workers — and goes on to prove that by polishing off the reasoned analysis with a topic sentence and two sentences of discussion, as follows (omitting citations and nongermane footnote):

> "The reasons for recognizing a privilege for treatment by psychiatrists and psychologists apply with equal force to treatment by a clinical social worker such as Karen Beyer. Today,

social workers provide a significant amount of mental health treatment. Their clients often include the poor and those of modest means who could not afford the assistance of a psychiatrist or psychologist, but whose counseling sessions serve the same public goals."

So much for the rule that privileges are to be narrowly construed.

Of course this brief analysis — like the earlier, more extensive, discussion of the general psychotherapist privilege — contains no explanation of why the psychotherapy provided by social workers is a public good of such transcendent importance as to be purchased at the price of occasional injustice. Moreover, it considers only the respects in which social workers providing therapeutic services are similar to licensed psychiatrists and psychologists; not a word about the respects in which they are different. A licensed psychiatrist or psychologist is an expert in psychotherapy — and that may suffice (though I think it not so clear that this Court should make the judgment) to justify the use of extraordinary means to encourage counseling with him, as opposed to counseling with one's rabbi, minister, family or friends. One must presume that a social worker does not bring this greatly heightened degree of skill to bear, which is alone a reason for not encouraging that consultation as generously. Does a social worker bring to bear at least a significantly heightened degree of skill — more than a minister or rabbi, for example? I have no idea, and neither does the Court. The social worker in the present case, Karen Beyer, was a "licensed clinical social worker" in Illinois, a job title whose training requirements consist of "master's degree in social work from an approved program," and "3,000 hours of satisfactory, supervised clinical professional experience." . . . But the rule the Court announces today — like the Illinois evidentiary privilege which that rule purports to respect, — is not limited to "licensed clinical social workers," but includes all "licensed social workers." "Licensed social workers" may also provide "mental health services" as described in §20/3(5), so long as it is done under supervision of a licensed clinical social worker. And the training requirement for a "licensed social worker" consists of either (a) "a degree from a graduate program of social work" approved by the State, or (b) "a degree in social work from an undergraduate program" approved by the State, plus "3 years of supervised professional experience." With due respect, it does not seem to me that any of this training is comparable in its rigor (or indeed in the precision of its subject) to the training of the other experts (lawyers) to whom this Court has accorded a privilege, or even of the experts (psychiatrists and psychologists) to whom the Advisory Committee and this Court proposed extension of a privilege in 1972. Of course these are only Illinois' requirements for "social workers." Those of other States, for all we know, may be even less demanding. Indeed, I am not even sure there is a nationally accepted definition of "social worker," as there is of psychiatrist and psychologist. It seems to me quite irresponsible to extend the so-called "psychotherapist privilege" to all licensed social workers, nationwide, without exploring these issues.

Another critical distinction between psychiatrists and psychologists, on the one hand, and social workers, on the other, is that the former professionals, in their consultations with patients, do nothing but psychotherapy. Social workers, on the other hand, interview people for a multitude of reasons. The Illinois definition of "licensed social worker," for example, is as follows:

"Licensed social worker" means a person who holds a license authorizing the practice of social work, which includes social services to individuals, groups or communities in any one

> or more of the fields of social casework, social group work, community organization for social welfare, social work research, social welfare administration or social work education."

Thus, in applying the "social worker" variant of the "psychotherapist" privilege, it will be necessary to determine whether the information provided to the social worker was provided to him in his capacity as a psychotherapist, or in his capacity as an administrator of social welfare, a community organizer, etc. Worse still, if the privilege is to have its desired effect (and is not to mislead the client), it will presumably be necessary for the social caseworker to advise, as the conversation with his welfare client proceeds, which portions are privileged and which are not.

Having concluded its three sentences of reasoned analysis, the Court then invokes, as it did when considering the psychotherapist privilege, the "experience" of the States — once again an experience I consider irrelevant (if not counter-indicative) because it consists entirely of legislation rather than common-law decision. It says that "the vast majority of States explicitly extend a testimonial privilege to licensed social workers." There are two elements of this impressive statistic, however, that the Court does not reveal.

First — and utterly conclusive of the irrelevance of this supposed consensus to the question before us — the majority of the States that accord a privilege to social workers do not do so as a subpart of a "psychotherapist" privilege. The privilege applies to all confidences imparted to social workers, and not just those provided in the course of psychotherapy....

Second, the Court does not reveal the enormous degree of disagreement among the States as to the scope of the privilege.... In Illinois and Wisconsin, the social-worker privilege does not apply when the confidential information pertains to homicide, and in the District of Columbia when it pertains to any crime "inflicting injuries" upon persons. In Missouri, the privilege is suspended as to information that pertains to a criminal act, and in Texas when the information is sought in any criminal prosecution. In Kansas and Oklahoma, the privilege yields when the information pertains to "violations of any law," in Indiana, when it reveals a "serious harmful act," and in Delaware and Idaho, when it pertains to any "harmful act." In Oregon, a state-employed social worker like Karen Beyer loses the privilege where her supervisor determines that her testimony "is necessary in the performance of the duty of the social worker as a public employee." In South Carolina, a social worker is forced to disclose confidences "when required by statutory law or by court order for good cause shown to the extent that the patient's care and treatment or the nature and extent of his mental illness or emotional condition are reasonably at issue in a proceeding." The majority of social-worker-privilege States declare the privilege inapplicable to information relating to child abuse. And the States that do not fall into any of the above categories provide exceptions for commitment proceedings, for proceedings in which the patient relies on his mental or emotional condition as an element of his claim or defense, or for communications made in the course of a court-ordered examination of the mental or emotional condition of the patient.

Thus, although the Court is technically correct that "the vast majority of States explicitly extend a testimonial privilege to licensed social workers," that uniformity exists only at the most superficial level. No State has adopted the privilege without restriction; the nature of the restrictions varies enormously from jurisdiction to jurisdiction; and 10 States, I reiterate, effectively reject the privilege entirely. It is fair to say that there is scant national consensus even as to the propriety of a social-worker psychotherapist privilege, and none whatever as to its appropriate scope. In other words, the state laws to which the Court appeals for support demonstrate most convincingly that adoption of a social-worker psychotherapist privilege is a job for Congress. . . .

The question before us today is not whether there should be an evidentiary privilege for social workers providing therapeutic services. Perhaps there should. But the question before us is whether (1) the need for that privilege is so clear, and (2) the desirable contours of that privilege are so evident, that it is appropriate for this Court to craft it in common-law fashion, under Rule 501. Even if we were writing on a clean slate, I think the answer to that question would be clear. But given our extensive precedent to the effect that new privileges "in derogation of the search for truth" "are not lightly created," United States v. Nixon, 418 U.S., at 710, the answer the Court gives today is inexplicable.

In its consideration of this case, the Court was the beneficiary of no fewer than 14 amicus briefs supporting respondents, most of which came from such organizations as the American Psychiatric Association, the American Psychoanalytic Association, the American Association of State Social Work Boards, the Employee Assistance Professionals Association, Inc., the American Counseling Association, and the National Association of Social Workers. Not a single amicus brief was filed in support of petitioner. That is no surprise. There is no self-interested organization out there devoted to pursuit of the truth in the federal courts. The expectation is, however, that this Court will have that interest prominently — indeed, primarily — in mind. Today we have failed that expectation, and that responsibility. It is no small matter to say that, in some cases, our federal courts will be the tools of injustice rather than unearth the truth where it is available to be found. The common law has identified a few instances where that is tolerable. Perhaps Congress may conclude that it is also tolerable for the purpose of encouraging psychotherapy by social workers. But that conclusion assuredly does not burst upon the mind with such clarity that a judgment in favor of suppressing the truth ought to be pronounced by this honorable Court. I respectfully dissent.

NOTES AND QUESTIONS

1. Who has the better of the argument, the majority or the dissent? Could you have written a more persuasive majority opinion? Could you have responded more effectively to the dissent?

2. One of the concerns is that embarrassing revelations are frequently made in therapeutic sessions, and the Court is certainly correct that the possibility of exposing such matters will be a disincentive to their creation. Still, is the patient's knowledge that there is a privilege necessary to effective mental health counseling? To support the argument of necessity, the majority relied heavily on amicus briefs filed by various organizations that promote psychotherapy. Careful analysis of the studies relied on in these briefs, however, shows that they "do not substantiate the empirical claim that the typical patient is so concerned about the prospect of litigation that the . . . privilege will significantly affect his or her willingness to seek treatment or make necessary revelations to a therapist." Edward Imwinkelried, The Rivalry Between Truth and Privilege: The Weakness of the Supreme Court's Reasoning in Jaffee v. Redmond, 518 U.S. 1 (1996), 49 Hastings L.J. 969, 980 (1998). Should courts require that the utilitarian justification for privileges be empirically valid? How can courts, as opposed to legislatures, obtain empirical data?

3. Is that majority's policy analysis satisfactory? Reflect back on the contingent claim theory about the attorney-client privilege. Like there, isn't the question here the marginal gains and losses under two different regimes: one with a privilege and one without a privilege? And if that data is not available in some form (including judicial experience), should a court create a privilege? In this respect, is the legislative process fundamentally different from the judicial process?

4. The majority purports to establish an absolute privilege in *Jaffee*; that is, it rejected the balancing component that the Seventh Circuit Court of Appeals believed necessary to evaluate the patient's interest in autonomy and privacy versus the evidentiary need for disclosure. Yet, in its final footnote, the majority acknowledges that "there are situations in which the privilege must give way" and cites as an example the situation in which disclosure is the only means to protect the patient or others from the serious threat of harm by the patient. See page 862, n.70, supra. We discuss below the circumstances under which federal courts have found that the privilege must "give way." See generally Christopher B. Mueller, The Federal Psychotherapist-Patient Privilege After *Jaffee*: Truth and Other Values in a Therapeutic Age, 49 Hastings L.J. 945 (1998).

b.   Scope of the Privilege After Jaffe

In the years since *Jaffe* was decided, the scope of the psychotherapist privilege has been tested in federal litigation. The privilege has developed on a case-by-case basis, since the Court did not spell out its full contours.

i.   Who Is a Psychotherapist?   The psychotherapist-patient privilege in Proposed FRE 504 includes "a person authorized to practice medicine" — in other words, all physicians — and "a person licensed or certified as a psychologist" within the definition of psychotherapist. Since *Jaffe*, courts have also included licensed social workers and other mental health workers within the privilege. For example, rape crisis counselors who are not licensed but who have undergone special training and work under the direct control and supervision of social workers or psychotherapists were included in United States v. Lowe, 948 F. Supp. 97, 99 (D. Mass. 1996), citing the fact that a majority of states have a privilege for rape counselling communications. But see Jane Student 1 v. Williams, 206 F.R.D. 306 (S.D. Ala. 2002) (holding that the psychotherapist-patient privilege does not extend to unlicensed professional counselors).

In Oleszko v. State Compensation Insurance Fund, 243 F.3d 1154, 1158, (9th Cir. 2001), the Ninth Circuit extended the privilege to unlicensed counselors employed by an Employee Assistance Program, which provides worksite assistance, including mental health counseling. The court cited *Jaffe* in noting:

> the provision of mental health services has significantly changed in the last quarter century. EAPs embody what may be viewed as a team approach to providing mental health services. Thus, although EAP personnel do not engage in psychotherapy themselves, they serve as a primary link between the troubled employee and psychotherapeutic treatment. [Id.]

Some courts are also willing to consider licensed Marriage, Family and Child Counselors as within the privilege. Speaker v. County of San Bernadino, 82 F. Supp. 2d

1105, 1109 (C.D. Cal. 2000). In Carman v. McDonnell Douglas Corp., 114 F.3d 790, 793 (8th Cir. 1997), however, the Eighth Circuit held that communications to an ombudsman employed to resolve workplace disputes without litigation were not protected by the psychotherapist privilege because the assistance was limited to dealing with workplace disputes, not mental health problems.

 ii. Communications. Communications falling within the privilege must be made in the course of or for the purpose of obtaining mental health services. For example, Proposed FRE 504 limits the psychotherapist-patient privilege to confidential communications "made [by the patient] for the purpose of diagnosis or treatment of his mental or emotional condition, including drug addiction." See Doe v. Ensey, 220 F.R.D. 422, 425 (M.D. Pa. 2004). California's psychotherapist-patient privilege is unusual in that it extends the privilege to communications made "for the purpose of scientific research on mental or emotional problems." Cal. Evid. Code §1011. Information that does not reveal the client's confidential communications — such as identity of therapist and client, occurrence of psychotherapy and dates of treatment — are not privileged. See, e.g., Vinson v. Humana, Inc., 190 F.R.D. 624, 626-27 (M.D. Fla. 1999); and Merrill v. Waffle House, Inc., 2005 WL 928602 (N.D. Tex. 2005).

 In situations where employees, such as police officers, are required to undergo psychological evaluations regarding fitness for duty and the results are disclosed to employers, it has been held that a psychotherapist privilege is not established because there is no treatment involved and there is no expectation of confidentiality. Kemper v. Gray, 182 F.R.D. 597, 599 (E.D. Mo. 1998). But where only a general conclusion is disclosed to the employer and the employee has been assured of confidentiality, the privilege has attached and prevents disclosure. See, e.g., Caver v. City of Trenton, 192 F.R.D.154, 162 (D.N.J. 2000).

 iii. Waiver. As with the physician-patient privilege, the patient is the holder of the psychotherapist-patient privilege. Thus, the privilege may be waived only by the patient or an authorized representative on the patient's behalf. Parents can assert or waive the privilege on behalf of their minor children. But courts may find that invocation of the privilege may not be in the "best interests" of the child, for example in custody disputes where there are allegations of child abuse. Ellison v. Ellison, 919 P.2d 1, 8 (Okla. 1996).

 Taking a broad view of waiver, some courts have held that a patient impliedly waives the psychotherapist privilege by raising the patient's mental condition as an element of the claim or defense; generally, by making any claims for mental and emotional distress. See, e.g., Vann v. Lone Star Steakhouse & Saloon of Springfield, Inc., 967 F. Supp. 346, 349-350 (C.D. Ill. 1997) (claims of sexual harassment and emotional injury placed mental condition at issue). A more restrictive view of waiver, however, has been taken by other courts. This narrower view requires that the privilege holder make an affirmative use of the privileged material by calling the therapist as a witness or putting specific communications at issue. See, e.g., Vanderbilt v. Town of Chilmark, 174 F.R.D. 225, 230 (D. Mass. 1997); United States v. Sturman, 1998 U.S. Dist. LEXIS 3488 (S.D.N.Y. 1998) (a criminal defendant's intention to use psychiatric testimony to negate the government's proof of specific intent does not waive the privilege prior to trial; defendant bears no burden on the issue of intent and does not put his mental condition "at issue" until he uses the testimony at trial).

A useful summary of this split in federal court opinions is contained in Fritsch v. City of Chula Vista, 187 F.R.D. 614 (S.D. Cal. 1999). The Supreme Court in *Jaffe* gave no guidance on this point. Indeed, the Supreme Court rejected the balancing test proposed by the Seventh Circuit Court of Appeals, but acknowledged that there would be circumstances in which the privilege must give way. See page 862, n.70, supra. Thus, both sides of this split of opinion are able to rely on policies discussed in *Jaffe* to justify their positions. The narrow view, requiring what amounts to actual waiver, protects the patient's imperative need for confidentiality and prevents post hoc balancing of the importance of privacy versus the evidentiary need for disclosure. Id. at 630. The broader view has been justified by the need for a fair discovery process when a patient "desires the jury to compensate for damage to her emotional condition . . . defendant is entitled to explore the circumstance [that] caused that injury." Id. at 569. See generally Melissa Nelkin, The Limits of the Privilege: The Developing Scope of Federal Psychotherapist-Patient Privilege Law, 20 Rev. Litig. 1 (2000).

Many decisions regarding the waiver of the privilege are made during the discovery phase of trial when one party seeks to compel production of medical records or to depose a psychotherapist. Some courts require the party seeking discovery to show cause why the "intrusion into the therapeutic relationship is the only possible means to obtain relevant information" and to narrowly tailor discovery requests to information directly relevant to the lawsuit. Vasconcellos v. Cybex International, Inc., 962 F. Supp. 701, 709 (D. Md. 1997).

Due to the prevalence of group counseling sessions, several courts have held that the psychotherapist-patient privilege is not waived when statements are made by patients in the presence of others in the group. The rationale is that the joint therapy comprises part of the treatment. See, e.g., State v. Andring, 342 N.W.2d 128, 133-134 (Minn. 1984). However, the statements are not privileged in joint litigation between the patients. Redding v. Virginia Mason Medical Ctr., 878 P.2d 483 (Wash. Ct. App. 1994).

c.   Exceptions to the Privilege

Although the Court in *Jaffee* rejected an outright balancing test, there are several exceptions to the privilege where the need for probative evidence is great or the interests underlying the privilege are nonexistent.

i.   Constitutional limits.   Doe v. Diamond, 964 F.2d 1325 (2d Cir. 1992), decided prior to *Jaffe*, involved a criminal defendant's request for the psychiatric records of a victim, Doe, who had initiated the criminal charges, and who would be a witness against him. Consider the following excerpt from the opinion, and pay close attention to the significance of the Confrontation Clause to the analysis. The Confrontation Clause may often mandate discovery regardless of the parameters of a privilege:

> Although appellant's [Doe's] psychiatric files do contain material that squarely implicates his privacy interests, the balance in this case weighs overwhelmingly in favor of allowing an inquiry into his history of mental illness. Appellant is not only the person who initiated the criminal investigation against Diamond [the criminal defendant] but also a witness whose credibility will be the central issue at trial. He has a long history of

emotional illness, and there is expert psychiatric opinion in the record that this history is relevant to his credibility. That opinion includes the observation that appellant's "interpretation of reality" might have been affected during times in which he was undergoing psychiatric treatment, as he was at the time of the events about which he is to testify. We agree with Chief Judge Platt that a preclusion of any inquiry into appellant's psychiatric history would violate the Confrontation Clause and vitiate any resulting conviction of Diamond.

Appellant poses for us various hypotheticals concerning the disclosure of communications made to psychotherapists thirty years ago, destruction of the privacy interests of a third party, and the violation of the professional obligations of the psychotherapists involved. These matters are not before us, however. The questions that appellant declined to answer concerned times at which he received psychiatric treatment and the names of particular psychotherapists. They also concerned his refusal to consent to those psychotherapists being interviewed by counsel under the protective order. The hearing held by Chief Judge Platt was in camera, and appellant's answers to the questions and counsel's interviews of appellant's psychotherapists would have been subject to a protective order sufficient to prevent public revelation of confidential matters. His answers to the questions and consenting to the interests as an important factor to be weighed in the interviews would not, therefore, have resulted in the public disclosure of confidential matters. [Id. at 1329.]

In cases since *Jaffee*, courts have adhered to the reasoning in Doe and have held that a criminal defendant's Sixth Amendment rights to information that establishes an element of defense or impeaches a witness can justify discovery of a victim and/or witness's mental health records. United States v. Alperin, 128 F. Supp. 2d 1251, 1254 (N.D. Cal. 2001). But see United States v. Doyle, 1 F. Supp. 2d 1187 (D. Oregon 1999) (victim's mental health records, relevant only to sentencing enhancement, need not be disclosed to already convicted defendant).

The psychotherapist-patient privilege can arise in criminal cases involving alleged child sexual abuse. If the child accuser confides his or her memories of abuse with a psychiatrist, the child may then assert the privilege when the accused attempts to discover the communications. See, e.g., Goldsmith v. State, 651 A.2d 866 (Md.1995); State v. Speese, 545 N.W.2d 510 (Wis. 1996). The majority of courts hold that the defendant can have access to the psychiatric records of his accuser if the psychiatrist testifies at trial. Other concerns raised by these cases are whether courts should appoint counsel or guardians ad litem to assist minors in determining whether to assert or waive the privilege, whether the privilege should apply during discovery, and whether a person's refusal to waive the privilege should preclude that person from testifying at trial. Id. at 517.

ii.   Compelled Disclosures.   Statutory law typically abolishes the psychotherapist-patient privilege in proceedings to hospitalize the patient for mental illness, if the psychotherapist has determined that the patient is in need of hospitalization. And if a judge orders an examination of the mental or emotional condition of the patient, communications made in the course of the examination are not privileged with respect to the particular purpose for which the examination is ordered unless the judge orders otherwise. In many states, mental health professionals are also required to report their reasonable suspicions that children whom they treat have been abused, and some states create an exception to the privilege where child abuse is known or suspected. Note, Overriding the Psychologist-Patient Privilege in Child Custody Disputes: Are Anyone's

Best Interests Being Served?, 68 U.M. (K.C.) L. Rev. 169 (1999) (critiquing the application of this exception in divorce and child custody cases where the use of psychotherapy records become a tool between battling parents).

    iii. Dangerous Patient. In its concluding footnote, the majority opinion in *Jaffee* noted that "there are situations in which the privilege must give way, for example, if a serious threat of harm to the patient or to others can be averted only by means of a disclosure by the therapist." See page 862, n.70, supra. This footnote has generated some case law on whether threats made during therapy sessions can form the basis of prosecutions for violation of federal laws that define such threats as criminal conduct. In such instances, the therapist's testimony about the threats — in violation of the psychotherapist privilege — is the only evidence that the prosecutor has. Thus, the government has sought judicial recognition of a so-called "dangerous patient" exception. So far, federal courts have split on the question of whether the exception exists. The Sixth and Ninth Circuits have declined to adopt the dangerous patient exception. See United States v. Hayes, 227 F.3d 578 (6th Cir. 2000); and United States v. Chase, 340 F.3d 978 (9th Cir. 2003). Recognizing that psychotherapists have professional and ethical duties to protect potential victims when threats are made during therapy, the court in *Hayes* stated that these duties "may require, among other things, disclosure to third parties or testimony at an involuntary hospitalization proceeding." Hayes, 227 F.3d at 585. The court held, however, that "compliance with the professional duty to protect does not imply a duty to testify against a patient in criminal proceedings or in civil proceedings other than directly related to the patient's involuntary hospitalization, and such testimony is privileged and inadmissible if a patient properly asserts the psychotherapist/patient privilege." Id. The court reasoned that once the appropriate warning had been given, or proceedings initiated, it would be highly unlikely that the therapist's testimony in a criminal prosecution would be the only means of avoiding harm to others, which was the standard adverted to in *Jaffee*. Thus, the court in *Hayes* construed the *Jaffee* footnote was no more than an aside

> to the effect that the federal psychotherapist/patient privilege will not operate to impede a psychotherapist's compliance with the professional duty to protect identifiable third parties from serious threats of harm. We think the *Jaffee* footnote was referring to the fact that psychotherapists will sometimes need to testify in court proceedings, such as those for the involuntary commitment of a patient, to comply with their "duty to protect" the patient or identifiable third parties. [Id. at 584.]

However, in United States v. Glass, 133 F.3d 1356, 1360 (10th Cir. 1998), the Tenth Circuit stated that if the threat of harm was serious and could be averted only by disclosure, compelled disclosure may be warranted. For further discussion, see George C. Harris, The Dangerous Patient Exception to the Psychotherapist-Patient Privilege: The Tarasoff Duty and the Jaffee Footnote, 74 Wash. L. Rev. 33 (1999).

    iv. Crime-Fraud Exception. In re Grand Jury Proceedings (Gregory P. Violette), 183 F.3d 71 (1st Cir. 1999) held that a "crime-fraud exception" applies to the psychotherapist patient privilege. The defendant was the target of a federal grand jury investigation focused on possible bank fraud crimes involving false claims of his disabilities. By analogy to the attorney-client privilege, the court found that the rationale for the privilege diminishes when communications made in therapy are in furtherance of crime. The exception will only apply, however, when the patient's purpose in making a communication is not therapy, but to promote a particular crime or fraud. It would not apply, for example, to a career criminal's confessions to his therapist even though the therapy may generally increase the patient's professional productivity. When the evidence indicates that defendant's communications to the therapists were made as part of a scheme to defraud lenders and/or disability insurers, the key ingredients of the crime-fraud exception are established.

KEY POINTS

1. Federal law recognizes a psychotherapist-patient privilege but not a physician-patient privilege. Most states recognize both privileges.

2. The federal psychotherapist-patient privilege has been extended to all physicians, psychologists, licensed social workers, and a variety of other mental health workers, when communications for the purpose of diagnosis or treatment of a mental or emotional condition are made with the reasonable expectation of confidence.

3. The privilege may not apply if disclosure of the communication is necessary to protect the Sixth Amendment rights of criminal defendants, if the patient has placed the patient's emotional or mental condition at issue in litigation, or if the communications are intended to promote a crime or fraud.

4. The courts are in disagreement over the existence of a dangerous patient exception.

PROBLEMS

12.25. At Alice Draper's prosecution for murder of a federal official, the prosecution offers to introduce the following evidence. Shortly after the victim's death, an individual called an Alcoholics Anonymous hotline manned by volunteers and asked to speak with a doctor. When the volunteer who had answered the phone asked what the problem was, the caller responded, "Murder. I just killed a man. I need help." Another volunteer called the police, and the police traced the telephone call to a telephone booth, where they found and arrested Draper. Draper has objected to evidence of what she said to the AA volunteer on the ground that her statements fall within the psychotherapist-patient privilege. What result? What additional facts might affect the outcome?

12.26. Plaintiff Peters brought an action in federal court against his employer for unlawful discrimination and violation of the Family Medical Leave Act due to his termination from employment on the basis of his mental illness. The defendant employer seeks discovery of a journal that Peters started keeping after losing his job, but which he has not shown to the doctor who is providing psychological counseling. The journal concerns the events that surrounded Peters's termination. Peters claims that the journal should be protected pursuant to the psychotherapist-patient privilege because he started keeping the journal when his doctor suggested that "writing down what happened can help you understand some of the situation." Is the journal privileged?

12.27. Plaintiff Salter has filed an action under the American with Disabilities Act (ADA) against her employer for unlawful discharge and failure to make reasonable accommodation for her clinical depression, which, she claims, required medication that caused her difficulty in waking up and chronic tardiness at work. The ADA requires the plaintiff to make a prima facie case of discrimination, which includes that she is a member of a protected category, which means a person with physical or mental impairment; a person with a record of such impairment; or a person being regarded as having such impairment. May plaintiff protect the release of her medical records of her treating psychiatrist pursuant to the psychotherapist-patient privilege?

12.28. Walter and Sarah Wong have sued Walter's tax preparer H & R Block, Inc. for breach of contract for its unauthorized disclosure in 1998 of Walter's tax return information, a disclosure that led to a criminal investigation and civil audits by the IRS. Plaintiffs allege that they incurred actual damages in the form of legal fees and "severe emotional distress, including physical mental suffering, shame, and humiliation." In 1998, prior to their marriage but after the conduct alleged in this suit, Walter and Sarah attended joint counseling sessions with a licensed social worker to help with the health of their relationship. In 1999, Sarah went for an initial consultation to a licensed psychologist. Defendant H & R Block has filed notices of taking depositions of both the social worker and psychologist. Defendant asserts that any psychotherapist-patient privilege was waived (1) by plaintiffs alleging serious claims for emotional distress and (2) through the revelation in their own depositions of the identities of their mental health providers, as well as the dates and costs of the sessions, and the purpose of the visits to the social worker. Plaintiffs contend that they have not waived the privilege because they have not alleged psychic injury or disease nor psychiatric injury or disease or disorder, and that no psychological testimony will be offered at trial. What result?

F. THE CLERGY-COMMUNICANT PRIVILEGE

The priest-penitent privilege — now more commonly referred to as the clergy communicant privilege — was not recognized at common law, largely because of the hostile climate in England toward the Roman Catholic Church during the Reformation. Today, however, its legitimacy is accepted by scholars and courts, at least to some degree. Indeed, every state has legislatively enacted some version of this privilege, and Proposed Federal Rule 506 specifically recognized a privilege protecting "confidential communication[s] by [a] person to a clergyman in his professional character as spiritual advisor." Pursuant to FRE 501, federal courts have recognized the existence of a clergy-communicant privilege as a matter of federal common law. See In re Grand Jury Investigation, 918 F.2d 374 (3d Cir. 1990); United States v. Dube, 820 F.2d 886 (7th Cir. 1987); United States v. Gordon, 655 F.2d 478 (2d Cir. 1981). See generally Whitaker, The Priest-Penitent Privilege: Its Constitutionality and Doctrine, 13 Regent U. L. Rev. 145 (2000-2001). The privilege is accepted in some form by all 50 states, but in the wake of the many high-profile cases involving child sexual abuse by clergy members in recent years, 40 states now require clergy members to report instances of child abuse as part of those states' mandatory reporting statutes, although many of those states provide exceptions for communications within the scope of the privilege. 1 David M. Greenwald et al., Testimonial Privileges §6:14 (Trial Practice Series, 3d ed. 2005).

1. The Privilege and Its Justifications

The clergy-communicant privilege generally applies "to protect communications made (1) to a clergy person (2) in his or her spiritual and professional capacity (3) with a reasonable expectation of confidentiality." In re Grand Jury Investigation, 918 F.2d 374, 384 (3d Cir. 1990). The privilege has been justified in four ways: (1) The traditional utilitarian justification, that the privilege is necessary to preserve the confidential relationship between clergy person and communicant, is often given. In this respect the privilege is similar to the attorney-client, physician-patient, psychotherapist-patient, and marital communications privileges.

(2) Another justification is constitutional in origin, based upon the free exercise clause of the First Amendment. According to this argument, the clause prevents courts from compelling a priest to reveal confidential communications, where such disclosure would contradict their religious practice. Although the privilege is probably not mandated by the Constitution, the principle of religious freedom has historically offered compelling support for the privilege.

(3) The privacy rationale, emphasizing the private nature of religious worship, is occasionally invoked. By creating a zone of privacy and protecting spiritual counseling from disclosure, the privilege accords respect for the intimacy of the communicant's relationship to clergy. According to this rationale, confidentiality is a privacy interest that itself acts as a legitimate constraint on the truth-finding function of trial. This may be no more persuasive here than in the attorney-client context.

(4) Last, the privilege is said to protect the credibility of our judicial system by preventing controversial clashes between court and clergy. Advocates of this rationale contend that "the spectacle of courts imprisoning members of the clergy for refusing to violate confidences entrusted to them might tend to subvert public faith in the judicial process." Developments in the Law — Privileged Communications, 98 Harv. L. Rev. 1450, 1562 (1985). In this sense, the privilege accords respect to the separation between church and state.

2. Scope of the Privilege

The most important issues in the interpretation of the clergy-communicant privilege are who counts as a clergy person, what kinds of communications are protected, and when does the presence of third persons waive the privilege. In most jurisdictions the holder of the privilege is the communicant, but a small minority of states grant the privilege and the decision to disclose communications to the clergy. Most state statutes, however, explicitly prohibit clergy from disclosing confidential communications without the communicant's consent. In a well-publicized case in New York, a priest revealed the confessional statement of a deceased parishioner, made 11 or 12 years earlier, that helped to exculpate two men wrongly convicted of the murder to which the deceased parishioner confessed. Such brief of confidence was proper, according to the priest and the Archdiocese of New York, because the confessional statement was not a formal confession within Catholic practice. Had the confession been formal, the priest would never have been able to reveal it, even after the parishioner's death. Morales v. Portuondo, 154 F. Supp.2d 706, 714 (S.D.N.Y. 2001).

Even if the clergy person does not hold the privilege, the clergy have their own interests in protecting the privacy of their religious counseling. In Mockaitis v. Harcleroad, 104 F.3d 1522 (9th Cir. 1997), the court held that a tape-recorded conversation between a priest and a jail inmate — which the inmate knew was being taped by the state — was not privileged, but that disclosure would violate the priest's Fourth Amendment expectation of privacy and the federal Religious Freedom Restoration Act.

a. Definition of Clergy

Proposed FRE 506(a)(1) defined a member of the clergy as "a minister, priest, rabbi, or other similar functionary of a religious organization, or an individual reasonably believed so to be by the person consulting him." This definition was adopted by the Third Circuit in In re Grand Jury Investigation, 918 F.2d 374, 384-385 (3d Cir. 1990). The "reasonably believed to be" a clergy person clause serves to protect the reasonable expectations of the individual. Some state statutes fail to provide a any definition other than "clergyman or priest," while others provide very broad language in defining the individuals covered. See, e.g., 735 Ill. Comp. Stat. 5/8-803 (2002) (referring to "a clergyman or practitioner of any religious denomination accredited by the religious body to which he or she belongs") Georgia explicitly delineates which members of the clergy are included, confining the privilege to "any Protestant minister of the Gospel, and any priest of the Roman Catholic faith, any priest of the Greek Orthodox Catholic faith, any Jewish rabbi, or to any Christian or Jewish minister, by whatever name called." Ga. Code Ann. §24-9-22 (West 2003).

One issue that often arises is whether the privilege extends to situations in which communicants receive spiritual advice from individuals who are not officially ordained members of the clergy. The Third Circuit foresaw this problem and stated, in dicta, that its adoption of the broad definition of clergy in Proposed Rule 506 did not imply "that the privilege should be interpreted to comprehend communications to and among members of sects that denominate each and every member as clergy." In re Grand Jury Investigation, 918 F.2d at 384, n. 13. The burden is on the party asserting the privilege to show that the person to whom communications were made is regularly engaged in activities which conform generally to the conduct of Catholic priests, Jewish rabbis, or Protestant ministers. United States v. Napolean, 46 M.J. 279, 284-285 (Ct. App. A.F. 1997) (citing 2 S. Saltzburg and M. Martin, Federal Rules of Evidence Manual 601-602 (5th ed. 1990)). In In re Verplank, 329 F. Supp 433, 435-436 (C.D. Cal. 1971), the court protected confidential communications made to non-ordained counselors from disclosure, because the counselors' services sufficiently resembled acts performed by the ordained minister who supervised them. The complexity of this issue can be seen in Cox v. Miller, 154 F. Supp. 2d 787 (S.D.N.Y. 2001), where the district court dramatically expanded the privilege to include statements made at Alcoholics Anonymous (AA) meetings. In Cox, the defendant's confession to two murders, made to his fellow AA members, were covered by the privilege, as the court noted that the Second Circuit had held that AA *was a religion*, by reason of the religious nature of its "Twelve Steps of Recovery". Although the decision was subsequently reversed by the Second Circuit in Cox v. Miller, 296 F.3d 89 (2d Cir. 2002), the case indicates how the clergy-communicant privilege can be susceptible to a quite broad interpretation.

b.   Nature of the Communication

The clergy-communicant privilege applies only to communications made to a clergy person in that person's spiritual or professional capacity. Courts have interpreted this to mean that the communication is "related to a religious function.... [T]he communication must be essentially for an ecclesiastical and religious purpose." Ellis v. United States, 922 F. Supp. 539, 542 (D. Utah 1996). Such communications are to be distinguished from communications that simply advise clergy about events, as in *Ellis* (witness to a tragic accident at a church-sponsored outing informed church officials about the event for secular purposes), or that are made for emotional support and consolation rather than guidance and forgiveness as a formal act of religion or as a matter of conscience. United States v. Napolean, 46 M.J. at 285. A narrower view of the privilege — to apply only to acts of "confession" — could raise serious first amendment and equal protection concerns by limiting the privilege to certain religions.

c.   Expectation of Confidentiality

As is the case with the attorney-client privilege, the presence of third parties, if essential to and in furtherance of the communication, should not void the privilege. For example, transmission of the communications within a church hierarchy may remain privileged. In Scott v. Hammock, 133 F.R.D. 610 (D. Utah 1990), the court applied Utah law to hold that communications from the communicant to a clergy person, and then passed vertically from one religious authority up to another within the church hierarchy, were privileged because such communication was necessary to the carrying out of church discipline. If communications among the church officers themselves could be discovered, then the privilege would be destroyed and the communicant's confidence abridged.

In In re Grand Jury Investigation, the government sought to compel the disclosure of communications among several family members and their pastor on the grounds that a nonfamily member had also been present. The Third Circuit reasoned as follows:

> In essence, the government claims that persons who are not related by blood or by marriage cannot, under federal law, engage together in protected communications with a member of the clergy acting in a spiritual or professional capacity....
>
> The government is correct in observing that the traditional clergy-communicant privilege protected a penitential relationship in which a person privately confessed his or her sins to a priest, in order to receive some form of church sanctioned discipline or absolution. Neither family nor other types of group counseling fit neatly within this "one-to-one" model of the privilege. We have explained, however, that the modern view of the privilege is more expansive than the traditional one. We discern nothing in modern clergy-communicant privilege doctrine, as it finds expression in either proposed Rule 506 or the cases recognizing the privilege, that would limit the privilege's application solely to group discussions involving family members related by blood or marriage. Modern clergy-communicant privilege doctrine focuses, rather, on whether the presence of a third party is essential to or in furtherance of a communication to a member of the clergy. We think, consistent with the general constructional rule that evidentiary privileges should be narrowly construed, that recognition of the clergy-communicant privilege in this circumstance depends upon whether the third party's presence is essential to and in furtherance of a communication to a member of the clergy. As is the case with

consultations between attorneys and clients, the presence of multiple parties, unrelated by blood or marriage, during discussions with a member of the clergy may, but will not necessarily, defeat the condition that communications be made with a reasonable expectation of confidentiality in order for the privilege to attach. [918 F.2d at 386.]

However, the appellate court also found that the district court had not developed adequate facts upon which to make the necessary finding that the family members reasonably expected that their communications to their pastor were confidential. It remanded the case to the district court "to determine whether the [family members] communicated with Pastor Knoche in his spiritual or professional capacity and with a reasonable expectation of confidentiality. . . ." Id. at 387. This might require an inquiry "into the nature of the communicants' relationship as well as the pastoral counseling practices of the relevant synod of the Lutheran church . . . whether the parties shared a commonality of interest at the time of the communication and, if so, in what respect . . . [and] a fuller record . . . as to [the third person's] role in the counseling session. In order to ascertain whether her presence worked to vitiate or to waive the privilege, the court will have to inquire into whether the other group members, who apparently are subjects of the grand jury investigation, reasonably required her presence at the counseling session, either in furtherance of their communications to the pastor or to protect their interests." Id. at 387-388. And the appellate court was well aware that such an inquiry might require some degree of disclosure from the pastor as to what was discussed in the group meeting. It left to the discretion of the district court how to ascertain this information; whether to use in camera hearings; whether or not parties and/or counsel should be present; and how to accommodate "delicate first amendment issues." Id. at 388.

d. Exceptions

The main exception to the clergy-communicant privilege in state statutes involves a clash between the privilege and state mandatory reporting statutes in the area of child abuse. Due to clergy child sex abuse scandals in recent years, public outrage has spurred state legislatures to act. "Every state has passed a statute requiring mandatory reporting of child abuse." 1 Greenwald et al., Testimonial Privileges §6:14. In recent years, some states have amended these mandatory reporting statutes by including clergy members in the list of groups required to report instances of child abuse. See, e.g., Mass. Gen. Laws Ann. ch. 119, §51A (West 2002); Ala. Code §26-14-3 (1992 & Supp. 2004). Currently, the mandatory reporting statutes of approximately 40 states require clergy to disclose known or suspected incidents of child abuse, either by specifically listing clergy members within the list of applicable groups, or by the use of a catchall phrase, such as "any person". Greenwald, et al. §6:4. However, the majority of the states that require clergy to report child abuse still maintain an exception in the case of the clergy-communicant privilege, protecting such communications from the mandatory reporting requirements. Id. For example, although Massachusetts has amended its mandatory reporting statute to include clergy members, the statute still provides the following exception:

> [A] . . . clergy member . . . shall report all cases of abuse under this section, but need not report information solely gained in a confession or similarly confidential communication

in other religious faiths. Nothing in the general laws shall modify or limit the duty of a ... clergy member ... to report a reasonable cause that a child is being injured as set forth in this section when the ... clergy member ... is acting in some other capacity that would otherwise make him a reporter. [Mass. Ann. Laws ch. 119 §51A].

Essentially, this means that, in many states, a clergy member is required to report suspected or known child abuse so long as doing so would not reveal the substance of a confession or an otherwise confidential communication with a penitent. A few states do the opposite, by specifically denying the privilege in their mandatory reporting statutes, see, e.g., Tex. Fam. Code Ann. §261.101 (Vernon 2002); N.H. Rev. Stat. Ann. §169-C:29 (2001), while others that require mandatory reporting do not mention its effect on the privilege. See, e.g., Ind. Code Ann. §31-33-5-1 (West 1999). For further discussion, see Norman Abrams, Addressing the Tension between the Clergy-Communicant Privilege and the Duty to Report Child Abuse in State Statutes, 44 B.C. L. Rev. 1127 (2003); Christopher R. Pudelski, The Constitutional Fate of Mandatory Reporting Statutes and the Clergy-Penitent Privilege in a Post-Smith World, 98 Nw. U. L. Rev. 703, 706-07.

KEY POINTS

1. A clergy-communicant privilege has been recognized under federal law and in all state jurisdictions, though exceptions exist in several states for mandatory reporting of known or suspected child abuse.

2. Courts extend the privilege to communications made to ordained clergy or to people performing the same activities. The communications must be relevant to a religious function.

3. Communications made in the presence of third persons can be privileged if the third person's presence was essential to and in furtherance of the communication to the clergy.

PROBLEMS

12.29. Darlene is being tried for the crime of making threats through the U.S. mail. Darlene raises an insanity defense. The clergy person who leads Darlene's religious congregation testifies that during the time of Darlene's conduct, Darlene did "know right from wrong." The clergy person further states that this opinion is based on knowing Darlene, on observations of Darlene, and on speaking with Darlene during this period. Does this testimony violate the clergy-communicant privilege?

12.30. Jim Jones joined a mail order church for a fee of $100, which entitled him to the status of lay minister. The tenets of the church included a vow of poverty and the belief that personal income of ministers was not taxable by the federal government. Jones stopped paying income taxes and is now prosecuted for failure to file income tax returns from 1996-2000. In 1999, Jones also joined an established church and had several conversations with the minister concerning his beliefs about taxation. The government plans to call the minister who would testify that he advised Jones that his income was not exempt from taxation. Can Jones enforce the clergy-communicant privilege?

12.31. Sam Evans is being prosecuted for sexually assaulting his 12-year-old step-daughter. Shortly after the incident that is the subject of the prosecution, Sam and his wife were separated. Sam began seeing his minister for spiritual guidance. At one session, which concerned marriage counseling, Sam's wife was also present. At this session, Sam admitted that he had sexually assaulted the stepdaughter, and he said that he had told his wife this the night before. The prosecution plans to call Sam's wife, who is willing to testify about both of Sam's admissions. The prosecution also plans to call the minister and ask him about what Sam said at the counseling session. The minister, however, has expressed an unwillingness to testify about these matters, and the minister is disturbed that Sam's wife is willing to testify. Does the minister have any personal right not to testify or to prevent Sam's wife from testifying? What objections can Sam make to the testimony of his wife and the minister? What additional facts might be needed to answer these questions? How would they be determined?

G.   OTHER PRIVILEGES

1.   Other Professional-Client Relationships

Privileges are occasionally recognized for confidential communications to other professionals, such as accountants, teachers, family and marriage counselors, social workers, lay advocates, and private detectives who counsel, advise, or act on behalf of their clients. Statutes enacting such privileges have been passed in a minority of states. For example, an accountant-client privilege exists in approximately one-third of the states. One interesting issue relating to the accountant-client privilege is whether the privilege is waived for the underlying information that is used to develop a publicly disclosed financial report, such as an Annual Report prepared by independent auditors that is required by the SEC for public companies. If a state's law does not create an exception for the privilege in such a situation, then it is likely that the privilege will still be available for the underlying information. See, e.g., In re Hillsborough Holdings Corp., 176 B.R. 223, 237 (M.D. Fla. 1994). However, until recently there was neither a privilege nor work-product protection for accountants in federal court. See United States v. Arthur Young & Co., 465 U.S. 805 (1984); Couch v. United States, 409 U.S. 322 (1973). In 1998, 26 U.S.C. §7525 extended the attorney-client privilege to "a federally authorized tax practitioner," who is a non-lawyer authorized to practice before the Internal Revenue Service. Though work product is still not protected, the new privilege provides that "the same common law protections of confidentiality which apply to a communication between a tax-payer and an attorney shall also apply to a communication between a taxpayer and a federally authorized tax practitioner to the extent the communications would be considered a privileged communication if it were between a taxpayer and an attor-ney." §7525(a)(1).

Another example is that privileges for various counseling professionals may be recognized under a state's psychotherapist-patient privilege. *Psychotherapist* may be defined to include professionals other than psychiatrists, psychologists, and psy-chotherapists, such as social workers; psychiatric nurses; counselors of rape victims, battered women, and drug and alcohol abusers; as well as school, family, and marriage counselors whose functions are analogous to those of a psychotherapist. See Catharina J. H. Dubbleday, Comment, The Psychotherapist-Client Testimonial Privilege: Defining the Professional Involved, 34 Emory L.J. 777 (1985). Another "counseling privilege" that some states recognize is a sexual assault victim-counselor privilege. See, e.g., Cal. Evid. Code §1035-1036.2 (West 1995 & Supp. 2005); 735 Ill. Comp. Stat. 5/8-802.1 (2002); 42 Pa. Cons. Stat. Ann. §5945.1(b) (West 2000 & Supp. 2005) ("[n]o sexual assault counselor may, without the written consent of the victim, disclose the victim's confidential oral or written communications to the counselor nor consent to be examined in any court or criminal proceeding"). Some states, such as Massachusetts, provide for an absolute privilege, while others, such as California, have enacted a qualified privilege permitting disclosure under certain circumstances. For further discussion, see Euphemia B. Warren, She's Gotta Have It Now: A Qualified Rape Crisis Counselor-Victim Privilege, 17 Cardozo L. Rev. 141 (1995).

2. Parent-Child Privilege

A privilege for parent-child communications was not recognized at common law. Presently, five states, Colorado, Idaho, Massachusetts, Minnesota, and Washington, have enacted legislation adopting a parent-child confidential communications privilege, although in Colorado and Washington the privilege is limited to communications made to an attorney by a child while in the presence of a parent. In contrast, the majority of states have refused to adopt the privilege. See, e.g., People v. Dixon, 161 Mich. App. 388, 393, 411 N.W.2d 760, 763 (1987); In re Gail D., 217 N.J. Super. 226, 232, 525 A.2d 337, 340 (1987). A New York court recognized a parent-child privilege based on the constitutional right to privacy. People v. Fitzgerald, 101 Misc. 2d 712, 422 N.Y.S.2d 309 (Westchester County Ct. 1979). However, Fitzgerald has not been followed by any New York court decision, and has since been limited by People v. Harrell, 87 A.D.2d 21, 450 N.Y.S.2d 501, 504 (1982) and criticized in People v. Hilligas, 175 Misc. 2d 842, 670 N.Y.S.2d 744 (Erie County Ct. 1998) for its inappropriate extension of the privilege to adult children.

Prior to the passage of Washington's parent-child privilege statute, the Washington Supreme Court refused to adopt a general privilege. State v. Maxon, 110 Wash. 2d 564, 574, 756 P.2d 1297, 1302 (1988). As noted above, the Washington statute creates only a limited privilege, and as such the decision denying a general parent-child privilege in Maxon remains in effect, narrowing the scope of the privilege in Washington. Addressing the constitutional claim for the privilege, the Washington Supreme Court stated:

> The Constitution does not mandate recognition of a parent-child privilege. The right of privacy line of cases gives no indication that the interest in confidential communications between parent and child qualifies as a fundamental right for the purpose of substantive due process analysis. Any infringement of this interest caused by nonrecognition of a parent-child privilege is indirect and incidental.

Maxon, supra, 756 P.2d at 1301 (quoting Donald Cofer, Comment, Parent-Child Privilege: Constitutional Right or Specious Analogy?, 3 U. Puget Sound L. Rev. 177, 210-211 (1079)).

In the absence of congressional action, federal courts have generally refused to recognize a parent-child privilege. Almost every circuit has ruled against such a privilege[71] but four of these courts noted in dicta that cases of adult and minor children are distinguishable and that they might be willing to recognize a parent-child privilege where an unemancipated minor confided in a parent.[72] Only a few federal district courts have recognized any form of the privilege. See In re Grand Jury Proceedings, Unemancipated Minor Child, 949 F. Supp. 1487 (E.D. Wash. 1996). In re Agosto, 553 F. Supp. 1298, 1325 (D. Nev. 1983); In re Greenburg, 11 Fed. R. Evid. Serv. 579, 582-584 (D. Conn. 1982). The *Agosto* court granted both parent and child the right to claim the privilege, in order to "protect communications made within an indissoluble family unit, bonded by blood, affection, loyalty and tradition." Courts that have rejected the privilege have found no "systematic regulation" of protected family interests that might give rise to a constitutional claim of privacy. United States v. Davies, 768 F.2d 893, 899-90 (7th Cir. 1985); see also In re Inquest Proceedings, 676 A.2d 790 (Vt. 1996).

An interesting issue raised by many courts presented with a claim of the privilege has been whether the privilege would apply solely to communications from child to parent or to communications from parent to child as well. Commentators argue that the privilege should apply solely to conversations from child to parent since the policy behind the privilege is to encourage the child to confide in the parent.

Though parent-child privileges have not gained widespread acceptance, their supporters often refer to what has been called the "cruel trilemma" that witnesses face. The first option for a testifying parent or child is to choose to commit perjury in order to protect a family member. Rather than implicate his father, a son in *United States v. Ismail*, 756 F.2d 1253 (6th Cir. 1985), perjured himself at a grand jury hearing. The son later broke down on the witness stand, admitting that he had lied to the grand jury and had considered suicide to avoid testifying against his father. The second option for a witness in this position is to tell the truth and face what damage may be done to the relationship and the guilt that will come from having hurt a loved one. Terry Nichols was convicted for his involvement in the 1995 Oklahoma City bombing after his son Josh, 13, was forced to testify before a grand jury. Josh's mother told reporters that her son suffered from nightmares as a result of testifying.[73] The third option is to refuse to testify and be found in contempt of court. In *State v. DeLong*, 456 A.2d 877 (Me. 1983), a 15-year-old girl who had been sexually abused by her adoptive father was sentenced to jail for refusing to testify against him.

Because of the difficulty of choosing to testify truthfully against a family member, many judges and prosecutors worry about the veracity of a parent's or child's testimony. Furthermore, the appeal of family privacy can make the support of a parent-child privilege politically attractive. The issue came under national scrutiny in February 1998 when Independent Counsel Kenneth Starr subpoenaed Marcia Lewis, mother of Monica Lewinsky, to testify before a grand jury about her daughter's relationship with President Clinton. In the 1998 and 1999 congressional sessions, the spectacle inspired

---

71.   See, e.g., In re Grand Jury Proceedings of John Doe, 842 F.2d 244, 248 (10th Cir. 1988); United States v. Ismail, 756 F.2d 1253 (6th Cir. 1985); In re Santerelli, 740 F.2d 816 (11th Cir. 1984)

72.   See In re Erato, 2 F.3d 11, 16 (2d Cir. 1993); Port v. Heard, 764 F.2d 423, 430 (5th Cir. 1985); United States v. Ismail, 756 F.2d 1253, 1258 (6th Cir. 1985); United States v. Jones, 683 F.2d 817, 819 (4th Cir. 1982).

73.   See Lance Gay, Lewinsky's Mother Torn Between Law and Loyalty, *Times Union*, Feb. 14, 1998, at A1.

three bills in the U.S. House of Representatives and one in the Senate,[74] each of which proposed the creation of a federal parent-child privilege. The "Confidence in the Family Act," 105 H.R. 3577 (1998), was rejected by the House Judiciary Committee for many reasons, including concern that the broad scope of the bill might cover natural parents as well a stepparents and grandparents, adult as well as minor children, and criminal as well as civil cases.[75] The three remaining bills did not emerge from the House and Senate Judiciary Committees. Representative Andrews, a Democrat from New Jersey, has repeatedly attempted to obtain legislative approval for a parent-child privilege statute, most recently introducing the Parent-Child Privilege Act of 2003, 108 H.R. 538 (2003), though each attempt has been unsuccessful.

For further discussion, see generally Shonah P. Jefferson, The Statutory Development of the Parent-Child Privilege: Congress Responds to Kenneth Starr's Tactics, 16 Ga. St. U. L. Rev. 429 (1999); Yolanda L. Ayala and Thomas C. Martyn, To Tell or Not To Tell? An Analysis of Testimonial Privileges: The Parent-Child and Reporter's Privileges, 9 St. John's J. Legal Comment. 163 (1993); Note, Parent-Child Loyalty and Testimonial Privilege, 100 Harv. L. Rev. 910 (1987); Developments in the Law — Privileged Communications, 98 Harv. L. Rev. 1450, 1575 (1985).

3. Communications Made in Settlement Negotiations

One emerging area of privilege law is that of settlement negotiations. As discussed in Chapter Six, FRE 408 precludes communications made in settlement negotiations from being used at trial as evidence of liability. However, Rule 408 "does not require exclusion when the evidence is offered for another purpose, such as proving bias or prejudice of a witness, negativing a contention of undue delay, or proving an effort to obstruct a criminal investigation or prosecution." Fed. R. Evid. 408. A question remains as to whether FRE 408 applies only to admissibility of evidence at trial, or whether it implies that a privilege should exist to protect settlement communications from discovery. The primary justification for the privilege is the desire to promote settlements and the need for open discussion in settlement negotiations, including adopting hypothetical positions that may not be entirely self-interested in order to compromise effectively. If the statements made in settlement negotiations are not privileged, despite FRE 408 as a barrier to the use of the communications as evidence at trial, the statements could be subject to discovery, which could create a disincentive to open discussions during settlement negotiations.

The Six Circuit Court of Appeals recently held that a privilege does exist for communications made in furtherance of settlement negotiations, protecting them from third-party discovery. Goodyear Tire & Rubber Co. v. Chiles Power Supply, Inc., 332 F.3d 976 (6th Cir. 2003). In *Goodyear*, after the case was concluded, Chiles gave an interview in which settlement communications were improperly disclosed. Id at 978. After learning about the communications, the plaintiffs in a separate lawsuit

---

74.   See Confidence in the Family Act, 105 H.R. 3577 (1998) (amending Federal Rules of Evidence to include parent-child adverse testimonial privilege and confidential communications privilege in federal civil and criminal proceedings); Parent-Child Privilege Acts of 1998 and 1999, 105 H.R. 4286 (1998), 106 H.R. 522 (1999) (amending Federal Rules of Evidence establishing a parent-child privilege); Attorney General Guidelines for Familial Privacy, 105 S. 1721 (directing the Attorney General of the United States to develop guidelines for Federal prosecutors to protect familial privacy and communications between parents and children).

75.   The bill was ultimately rejected by a vote of 162 to 256. See 144 Cong. Rec. H2278 (daily ed. Apr. 23, 1998).

against both Goodyear and Chiles joined the suit and petitioned the district court to permit discovery of statements made in settlement negotiations. Id. at 979.

The Sixth Circuit relied heavily on the Supreme Court's decision in Jaffee v. Redmond, 518 U.S. 1 (1996), in discussing the parameters of a privilege. Id. at 979-80. The Sixth Circuit found a strong public policy interest in recognizing the privilege, as well as noting the tradition of confidentiality in settlement communications. Id. at 980. The court further concluded that information discovered from settlement negotiations was unlikely to be relevant:

> There exists a strong public interest in favor of secrecy of matters discussed by parties during settlement negotiations. This is true whether settlement negotiations are done under the auspices of the court or informally between the parties. The ability to negotiate and settle a case without trial fosters a more efficient, more cost-effective, and significantly less burdened judicial system. In order for settlement talks to be effective, parties must feel uninhibited in their communications. Parties are unlikely to propose the types of compromises that most effectively lead to settlement unless they are confident that their proposed solutions cannot be used on cross examination, under the ruse of "impeachment evidence," by some future third party. Parties must be able to abandon their adversarial tendencies to some degree. They must be able to make hypothetical concessions, offer creative quid pro quos, and generally make statements that would otherwise belie their litigation efforts. Without a privilege, parties would more often forego negotiations for the relative formality of trial. Then, the entire negotiation process collapses upon itself, and the judicial efficiency it fosters is lost. [Id. at 980].

Although the Sixth Circuit has adopted the privilege, the issue has not yet been decided in other circuits. However, at least one district court has declined to follow the Sixth Circuit. In In re Subpoena Issued to Commodity Futures Trading Commission, 370 F. Supp. 2d 201 (D.D.C. 2005), the District Court for the District of Columbia held that it would not recognize a new settlement privilege to protect documents from third-party discovery. The court discussed several factors that the Supreme Court considers in assessing a potential privilege in reaching its decision. Id. at 208. The court noted that there is no broad consensus in federal courts, as few federal courts recognize the privilege, nor is there a consensus in state law supporting the privilege. Id. at 208-09. The court also reasoned that by enacting FRE 408, Congress chose to limit the admissibility of settlement matter rather than discoverability. Id. Last, the court opined that the proponents of the privilege had not made an adequate showing that the privilege would effectively advance a public good. Id. at 212.

For further discussion of see Jeffrey J. Lauderdale, A New Trend in the Law of Privilege: The Federal Settlement Privilege and the Proper Use of Federal Rule of Evidence 501 for the Recognition of New Privileges, 35 U. Mem. L. Rev. 255 (2005).

Another similar privilege is the mediation communications privilege. The mediation privilege protects from discovery communication and documentation related to mediation negotiations between parties. The mediation privilege was not recognized in Common Law, but every state has enacted some statutory form of the privilege. By passing the Alternative Dispute Resolution (ADR) Act in 1998, 28 U.S.C. §651, Congress requires federal district courts to authorize by local rule ADR programs for all civil litigation. The ADR Act requires ADR proceedings to be confidential and requires district courts to develop safeguards to protect the confidentiality of communications within these ADR proceedings. Id. at §652(d). Although the ADR Act did not actually create a privilege, some federal courts have adopted the privilege to protect the confidentiality of such mediation communications. See, e.g., Folb v. Motion Picture Industry Pension & Health Plans, 16 F. Supp. 2d 1164 (C.D. Cal. 1998); Sheldone v. Pennsylvania Turnpike Commission 104 F. Supp. 2d 511 (W.D. Pa. 2000). However, other federal courts have declined to adopt such a privilege without a clearer mandate from Congress. See F.D.I.C. v. White, 76 F. Supp. 2d 736, 738 (N.D. Tex. 1999) ("[t]he [c]ourt does not read the ADR [Act] or its sparse legislative history as creating an evidentiary privilege"). For further discussion of the mediation privilege, see Ellen E. Deason, Predictable Mediation Confidentiality in the U.S. Federal System, 17 Ohio St. J. on Disp. Resol. 239 (2002).

4. Privileges Protecting Outside Sources of Information

A unique category of privileges exists to protect confidential sources of information. Three privileges of this type are the government informant's privilege, the journalist's privilege, and the scholar's privilege. These privileges can be distinguished from the confidential communications privileges, for rather than focusing on the communication's content, these privileges mainly focus on the protection of the source's identity. The common justification is that absent protection, the mere possibility of disclosure would disrupt the future flow of information and thereby "harm the public by impeding law enforcement efforts, the dissemination of news, or the advancement of knowledge." Developments in the Law — Privileged Communications, 98 Harv. L. Rev. 1592, 1594 (1985).

a. Government Informant's Privilege

The government informant's privilege protects the identities of individuals who provide the government with information regarding crimes or other suspect activity. Though the privilege was once recognized as absolute, it has been qualified due to concern for the constitutional rights of criminal defendants. In Roviaro v. United States, 353 U.S. 53, 62 (1957), the Supreme Court announced a test that "balanc[ed] the public interest in protecting the flow of information against the individual's right to prepare his defense." The informant's privilege arises most frequently in cases where a criminal defendant alleges that an informant's testimony is critical to his defense. In such circumstances, courts freely conduct in camera hearings with an informant to determine how the Roviaro balance should be struck. See, e.g., United States v. Anderson, 509 F.2d 724, 730 (9th Cir. 1974); United States v. Fischer, 531 F.2d 783 (5th Cir. 1976). The privilege is also frequently invoked in the context of a defendant's challenge to a search in which the government claims that the informant provided the basis for probable cause. The privilege has been applied in civil cases as well. In applying the Roviaro balancing test, some civil courts maintain that the "strength of the privilege is greater in civil litigation than in criminal," In re United States, 565 F.2d 19, 22 (2d Cir. 1978), while others adhere to the standard used in criminal cases, see, e.g., Hodgson v. Charles Martin Inspector of Petroleum, Inc., 459 F.2d 303, 305 (5th Cir. 1972).

b. Journalist's Privilege

A privilege to protect journalists against the disclosure of the identities of their news sources has been consistently advocated by members of media organizations.

Proponents assert a twofold justification for the privilege: (1) the privilege is necessary to encourage the flow of confidential information from external sources; and (2) the privilege protects the First Amendment guarantee of a free press. The constitutional argument was rejected by the Supreme Court in the 5 to 4 decision of Branzburg v. Hayes, 408 U.S. 665 (1972), which analyzed the privilege claim in the grand jury setting. Noting "the limited nature of the Court's holding," Justice Powell in his concurrence proposed a balancing test to determine journalist privilege claims. In line with Justice Powell's concurrence, many lower federal courts have recognized a qualified journalist's privilege based on the First Amendment. See, e.g., Continental Cablevision, Inc. v. Stores Broadcasting Co., 583 F. Supp. 427 (E.D. Mo. 1984); United States v. Burke, 700 F.2d 70 (2d Cir. 1983). But see Herbert v. Lando, 441 U.S. 153 (1979) (declining to recognize an editorial process privilege). In a recent decision, the D.C. Circuit reiterated *Branzburg* in rejecting a First Amendment challenge to a federal grand jury subpoena. In re Grand Jury Subpoena, Judith Miller, 397 F.3d 964 (D.C. Cir. 2005). In *Miller*, two reporters and Time, Inc., the parent company of Time Magazine, were subpoenaed to testify about sources used in their articles to a federal grand jury investigating the alleged leak of a CIA agent's identity by government officials. Id. at 966-68. The court held that the First Amendment does not grant journalists a right to refuse to divulge information about sources in the context of a grand jury subpoena, and further held that, even if there is a common law journalist privilege, which was not determined, the privilege would be qualified, and the government overcame any qualification. Id. at 972-73.

At least one federal court has specifically held that the reporter's privilege does not apply in grand jury proceedings. In re Grand Jury Proceedings (Scarce), 5 F.3d 397, 403 (9th Cir. 1993).

Efforts to enact a federal statutory privilege have not succeeded. However, most states have enacted shield laws that vary in levels of protection. When a reporter's sources are confidential, normally the plaintiff must make a more substantial showing of need in order to overcome the privilege. Mark v. Shoen, 48 F.3d 412 (9th Cir. 1995). New York law states that in order to overcome the privilege, the party seeking disclosure must make "a clear and specific showing that the news: (i) is highly material and relevant; (ii) is critical or necessary to the maintenance of a party's claim, defense or proof of an issue material thereto; and (iii) is not obtainable from any alternative source." N.Y. Civ. Rights Law §79-h(c) (McKinney 1992). See also In re Application to Quash Subpoena to National Broadcasting Co., Inc., 79 F.3d 346, 351 (2d Cir. 1996), where the court held that in order to find unpublished news to be critical or necessary, there must be a finding that the claim for which the information is to be used "virtually rises or falls with the admission or exclusion of the proffered evidence." In contrast, the test is much less stringent where the material is not confidential:

> [W]here information sought is not confidential, a civil litigant is entitled to requested discovery notwithstanding a valid assertion of the journalist's privilege by a nonparty only upon a showing the requested material is: (1) unavailable despite reasonable alternative sources; (2) noncumulative; and (3) clearly relevant to an important issue in the case. [Mark v. Shoen, 48 F.3d at 416.]

For further discussion of state press shield laws, see Theodore Campagnolo, The Conflict Between State Press Shield Laws and Federal Criminal Proceedings: the Rule 501 Blues, 38 Gonz. L. Rev. 445 (2002/03).

The application of this privilege in libel and slander cases has been limited. In Desai v. Hersh, 954 F.2d 1408 (7th Cir. 1992), the court held that the privilege could not be invoked by a libel defendant, because the plaintiff had the burden of proving actual malice on the part of the reporter. Proof of actual malice under New York Times v. Sullivan, 376 U.S. 254 (1964), depends on knowing the identity of a reporter's source, since a libel plaintiff needs to demonstrate that the source was unreliable or that the reporter failed to take sufficient steps to verify the factual accuracy of the story. Because of this, the general rule is that in defamation actions in which a plaintiff must establish actual malice the reporter's privilege must give way to disclosure. Miller v. Transamerican Press, Inc., 621 F.2d 721, 725-726 (5th Cir. 1980). But see Condit v. National Enquirer, Inc., 289 F. Supp. 2d 1175 (E.D. Cal. 2003) (wife of former Congressman Gary Condit sued tabloid for libel; court upheld privilege protecting confidential source, concluding that plaintiff did not investigate all reasonable alternative information sources).

c. Scholar's (Academic Researcher's) Privilege

Academic researchers have advocated a privilege to protect the confidentiality of their research and the identity of their research subjects. Proponents advance two arguments to support their claim of the privilege. First, the scholar's privilege can arguably fall within the ambit of the more widely recognized journalist's privilege, particularly if the scholarly research is to result in publication. Second, proponents argue that academic freedom is a special concern of the First Amendment and that the privilege is necessary to protect the research process and encourage the flow of information from research subjects. In In re: Microsoft Corporation, 162 F.3d 708 (1st Cir. 1998), the court considered whether academic researchers who had interviewed over 40 current and former Netscape employees in preparation for a book could maintain the confidentiality of the interview notes, tapes, transcripts, and recordings. Microsoft moved to compel the surrender of the research materials after the researchers resisted a subpoena. The court held that academic researchers are analogous to journalists and that the First Amendment interest of preventing the "chilling effect on speech" mandates the protection of the scholar's sources as well as the journalist's. Without such a privilege, the court wrote, "an academician, stripped of sources, would be able to provide fewer, less cogent analyses" and thus would be less able to disseminate information to the public. The court found that Microsoft's need was not compelling when balanced against the First Amendment protection.

Other asserted bases for the privilege are that interference with ongoing research, especially scientific research, could occur if data were forced to be disclosed, and the potential for publishing research in peer reviewed or other scholarly publications could be harmed. This last asserted rationale has met with little success in the courts. See Burka v. United States Department of Health and Human Services, 87 F.3d 508 (D.C. Cir. 1996) (stating that there is not an established or well-settled practice of protecting research data on the ground that disclosure would harm a researcher's publication prospects).

Several federal and state statutes protect research and sources of academic researchers, although in limited areas, such as drug research. See, e.g., 21 U.S.C. §872(c) (2000) (drug research); Cal. Health & Safety Code §11603 (West 1991) (drug research); N.Y. Pub. Health Law §3371 (McKinney 2002, Supp. 2005) (drug research). Courts have generally been reluctant to recognize a scholar's privilege. See In re Grand Jury Subpoena, 750 F.2d 223 (2d Cir. 1984) (refusing to recognize scholar's privilege); In re Grand Jury Proceedings (Scarce), 5 F.3d 397 (9th Cir. 1993); United States v. Doe, 460 F.2d 328 (1st Cir. 1972). But see Richards of Rockford, Inc. v. Pacific Gas and Elec. Co., 71 F.R.D. 388 (N.D. Cal. 1976). For further discussion, see Howard Gray Curtis, Comment, Academic Researchers and the First Amendment: Constitutional Protection for Their Confidential Sources?, 14 San Diego L. Rev. 876 (1977); David A. Kaplan and Brian M. Cogan, The Case Against Recognition of a General Academic Privilege, 60 U. Det. J. Urb. L. 205 (1983).

5. Peer Review Privilege

A peer review privilege has been claimed by both academic institutions and hospitals to protect the confidentiality of the peer review process, a process that ultimately determines which candidates receive academic tenure and hospital privileges. The justification for the privilege is the standard argument that compelled disclosure of peer review evaluations would obstruct the free flow of information that is essential to the integrity of the peer review process. Without protection against disclosure, the quality of the critiques would decline and less qualified candidates would be promoted, with a resultant impact on the quality of our universities and hospitals.

Notwithstanding such arguments, in University of Pennsylvania v. E.E.O.C., 493 U.S. 182 (1990), the Supreme Court refused to recognize a federal privilege protecting the confidentiality of academic peer review materials from disclosure. The claim arose out of a race and sex discrimination suit brought by an associate professor of the University of Pennsylvania. The Court held that the privilege would not be recognized under either common law or First Amendment grounds. The Court was "especially reluctant to recognize a [common law] privilege" in an area where Congress, under Title VII, has balanced the problem of "invidious" discrimination in educational institutions against the interest of academic autonomy "but has not provided the privilege itself." The Court refused to expand the protection of the First Amendment right of academic freedom to embrace confidential peer review materials. Before the decision, a majority of federal courts of appeals had recognized a qualified peer review privilege in the academic setting.

In the hospital setting, federal and state courts have generally rejected claims of a peer review privilege. See Memorial Hosp. v. Shadur, 664 F.2d 1058 (7th Cir. 1981); Robinson v. Magovern, 83 F.R.D. 79 (W.D. Pa. 1979). Several states have enacted statutes that accord protection to the hospital peer review process. See, e.g., Mich. Comp. Laws Ann. §333.21515 (West 2001). Some states have included an exception to provide for disclosure in the area of discrimination suits. See, e.g., Cal. Evid. Code §1157(c) (West 1995). Even though some courts recognize the privilege, it has been narrowly construed to allow plaintiffs to uncover evidence of wrongdoing. In Moretti v. Lowe, 592 A.2d 855, 857 (R.I. 1991), the court held that while the internal communications and deliberative processes of a peer review committee were privileged, the effect of those proceedings was not. Thus the plaintiff in a medical malpractice action could discover whether a particular nurse had been disciplined by her hospital review committee. The court in Moretti also said that the privilege did not protect the identity of persons who might serve on peer review committees or who have given information to such committees.

The privilege also does not protect pre-existing documents that have been turned over to the peer-review committee. Roach v. Springfield Clinic, 157 Ill. 2d 29, 40-42, 623 N.E.2d 246, 251 (1993). In *Roach*, the court stated:

> If the simple act of furnishing a committee with earlier acquired information were suffi-cient to cloak that information with the statutory privilege, a hospital could effectively insulate from disclosure virtually all adverse facts known to its medical staff, with the exception of those matters actually contained in a patient's records.

For a decision upholding the privilege under difficult circumstances, see Jackson v. Scott, 667 A.2d 1365 (D.C. Ct. App. 1995). In this case, the defendant hospital's review of deaths during cardiac surgery revealed evidence of gross negligence. A confidential informant, who "had to [have been] in the operating room" during the surgery per-formed on the plaintiff's wife, revealed that the surgery was "very mismanaged," result-ing in the patient's death. The court upheld the hospital's claim of privilege regarding its internal investigation of the death. Relying on the District of Columbia's Health Care Peer Review Act of 1992, D.C. Code §§32-501 et seq., the court stated that the privilege was unqualified. Defense witnesses testified, without mentioning the internal report, that the hospital was not negligent in the patient's death. The court nevertheless held that, under a plain reading of the statute, the report could not be used for impeach-ment purposes.

For further analysis of the peer review privilege, see David McMillin, University of Pennsylvania v. E.E.O.C. and Dixon v. Rutgers: Two Supreme Courts Speak on the Academic Freedom Privilege, 42 Rutgers L. Rev. 1089 (1990); Don Mark North, University of Pennsylvania v. E.E.O.C.: The Denial of an Academic Freedom Privi-lege, 18 Pepp. L. Rev. 213 (1990); Susan O. Scheutzow and Sylvia Lynn Gillis, Con-fidentiality and Privilege of Peer Review Information: More Imagined Than Real, 7 J.L. & Health 169 (1992/ 1993).

6.   Self-evaluative Privilege

A privilege similar to the peer review privilege, the "self-critical analysis privilege" has been asserted in the corporate context. The privilege is often asserted by companies with affirmative action policies, to protect against disclosure of intracorporate com-munications made during the employee review process and against disclosure of com-pliance investigations done by the corporation. The asserted justification for the privilege is that forcing disclosure of these communications will have a chilling effect on compliance with equal employment opportunity laws. In Aramburu v. Boeing Co., 885 F. Supp. 1434 (D. Kan. 1995), the court refused to recognize the privilege in a Title VII case. Relying on University of Pennsylvania v. E.E.O.C., the court stated that it was reluctant to recognize such a privilege when it appeared that Congress had considered the issue but had failed to provide for the privilege. 885 F. Supp. at 1440. Similarly, the court in Roberts v. Hunt, 187 F.R.D. 71 (W.D.N.Y. 1999), found that the Supreme Court, in rejecting a "peer review" privilege in *University of Pennsylvania*, implicitly rejected the rationale for a self-evaluation privilege and thus left the privilege unavailable under federal law. However, some lower federal courts have recognized this privilege. See, e.g., Troupin v. Metropolitan Life Insurance Company, 169 F.R.D. 546 (S.D.N.Y. 1996) (recognizing the privilege where "an intrusion into the self-evaluative analyses of an institution would have an adverse effect on the [evaluative] process, with a net detriment to a cognizable public interest"); Reichhold Chemicals, Inc. v. Textron, Inc., 157 F.R.D. 522 (N.D. Fla. 1994) (collecting cases recognizing self-critical analysis privilege); Banks v. Lockheed-Georgia Co., 53 F.R.D. 283 (N.D. Ga. 1971) (recognizing privilege in employment discrimination case). For a discussion see Ronald J. Allen and Cynthia M. Hazelwood, Preserving the Confidentiality of Internal Corporate Investigations, 12 J. Corp. L. 355 (1987).

Congress has created a privilege for state and local governments, similar to the self-evaluative privilege, in the context of highway safety. In order to promote highway safety, in 1973 Congress created a hazard elimination program for public roadways, providing federal funds for states to identify, study, and eliminate hazardous conditions on the nation's roads. 23 U.S.C. §152. The program required the states to conduct surveys and collect data on accident statistics in order to identify potentially hazardous sites. Id. Although the program provided a mechanism to enhance highway safety, the information collected by the states became a potential liability, due to the threat of discovery in lawsuits against the states. In response to these threats and in the interest of obtaining the best possible information from the states to enhance highway safety, Congress enacted a statutory privilege similar to the self-evaluative privilege, protecting information collected by states for enhancing safety and improving hazardous roadways. 23 U.S.C. §409 (1995). The statute provides as follows:

> [R]eports, surveys, schedules, lists, or data compiled or collected for the purpose of identifying evaluating, or planning the safety enhancement of potential accident sites, hazardous roadway conditions, or railway-highway crossings, pursuant to sections 130, 144, and 152 of this title [23 USCS §130, 144, and 152] or for the purpose of developing any highway safety construction improvement project which may be implemented utilizing Federal-aid highway funds shall not be subject to discovery or admitted into evidence in a Federal or State court proceeding or considered for other purposes in any action for damages arising from any occurrence at a location mentioned or addressed in such reports, surveys, schedules, lists, or data. [23 U.S.C. §409.]

Although the statute establishes a federal privilege, the statute was challenged in the case of Pierce County v. Guillen. 537 U.S. 129 (2003). In Guillen, a widower engaged in a negligence suit against a county government sought discovery of information obtained by the county relating to the intersection where his wife had been in an automobile accident. Id. The Supreme Court held that the statute was within the scope of Congress's power under the Commerce Clause, and that "§409 protects all . . . data actually compiled or collected for §152 purposes, but does not protect information that was originally compiled or collected for purposes unrelated to §152 and that is currently held by the agencies that compiled or collected it, even if the information was at some point 'collected' by another agency for §152 purposes." Id. at 144. "Under this interpretation, an accident report collected only for law enforcement purposes and held by the county sheriff would not be protected under §409 in the hands of the county sheriff, even though that same report would be protected in the hands of the Public Works Department, so long as the department first obtained the report for §152 purposes. Id.

Although the development of a general self-evaluative privilege in the cases has been spotty, numerous statutes protecting discrete interests have been passed, particularly in the states. A good example is Oregon's environmental audit privilege for reports prepared as a result of voluntary environmental audits designed to assure compliance with the state's environmental laws. The privilege is thorough, protecting virtually all materials created for and during the audit, with no distinction between objective and subjective material. It protects the information from both private and governmental parties, even when filing a report is mandatory, and courts may not make case-by-case determinations whether disclosure would best serve the public interest. For a discussion, see Peter Gish, The Self-critical Analysis Privilege and Environmental Audit Reports, 25 Envtl. L. 73 (1995).

7.   Government Privileges — Executive Privilege

The Executive Branch has been the focus of most of the discussion of whether evidentiary privileges should be created to protect confidential communications within the government. But see United States v. Gillock, 445 U.S. 360 (1980) (holding that there is no privilege for state legislator in federal prosecution). The term *executive privilege* includes several different categories of privileges for governmental secrets. First, the state secrets privilege protects military, diplomatic, or sensitive national security secrets. Second, the qualified presidential communications privilege protects confidential conversations between the president and the president's advisers (e.g., the members of the cabinet). Last, there are privileges to protect a wide range of official information, such as law enforcement files and governmental agency deliberations.

a.   State Secrets Privilege

The state secrets privilege protects against the disclosure of highly secret military and diplomatic information. Here the concern is that the release of such information might endanger the public or harm the nation. The privilege has protected such information as FBI activities, see In re United States, 872 F.2d 472 (D.C. Cir.), *cert. dismissed sub nom.* United States v. Albertson, 493 U.S. 960 (1989), missile technology, see Bentzlin v. Hughes Aircraft Co., 833 F. Supp. 1486 (C.D. Cal. 1993), radar system capabilities, see Zuckerbraun v. General Dynamics Corp., 935 F.2d 544 (2d Cir. 1991), and diplomatic conversations, see Attorney Gen. v. Irish People, Inc., 502 F. Supp. 63, 64-65 (D.D.C. 1980).

In United States v. Reynolds, 345 U.S. 1 (1953), the Supreme Court provided a thorough examination of the state secrets privilege. According to the court, the government is the exclusive holder of the privilege. The privilege must be formally invoked by the head of the government department concerned, after "actual personal consideration" by that executive official. In deciding on a claim of the privilege, the standard to be applied is whether there is a reasonable danger that disclosure will harm national security. If the reasonable danger standard is met, the privilege is absolute. The court noted that "even the most compelling necessity cannot overcome the claim of privilege if the court is ultimately satisfied that military secrets are at stake." In Black v. United States, 62 F.3d 1115 (8th Cir. 1995), the court dismissed a harassment suit against federal intelligence agencies where litigation would necessarily breach the state secrets privilege. Black was an electrical engineer who had government security clearance to work on defense projects with various contractors. After a Soviet mathematician at a lecture in Zurich allegedly asked him suspiciously intrusive questions, Black reported the contact to the U.S. Consulate and soon thereafter his security clearance was "unplugged." He claimed that he was the victim of harassment and psychological attack and sued the United States for the actions of the CIA, FBI, and Department of State. R. James Woolsey, Director of the CIA, formally invoked the state secret privilege and asserted that litigation of the claim would result in the disclosure of highly sensitive names, dates, and locations of U.S. counterintelligence operations. The lower court reviewed the documents *in camera* and dismissed all of the claims. The Court of Appeals affirmed the decision, according the "utmost deference" to the executive's determination of the impact of disclosure.

Whether the privilege is claimed in a criminal or civil proceeding, the denial of discovery will dramatically affect the opposing party's preparation of the case. In both criminal and civil proceedings, the court may order dismissal as it did in *Black* or other less drastic relief, such as striking particular testimony of a witness or finding against the government on a particular issue.

The Classified Information Procedures Act (CIPA), 18 U.S.C.A. App. 3, §§1 et seq. (West 2001), grants statutory recognition to the state secrets privilege in the area of criminal proceedings. The act sets forth detailed procedures governing a criminal defendant's efforts to reveal or to obtain discovery of classified information and was passed by Congress in 1980 to address the defense tactic known as "graymail." The defendant who threatens to disclose classified information creates a dilemma for the government. It must either dismiss the charges against the defendant or allow the disclosure of sensitive information. The goal of CIPA is to provide pretrial procedures for the resolution of discovery and admissibility issues.

CIPA primarily functions in two ways. Section 5 requires defendants to notify the government of its intention to disclose classified information in the course of presenting a defense. Pretrial hearings on discovery and admissibility of evidence are governed by §§4 and 6. Section 4 expands on Federal Rule of Criminal Procedure 16 and permits courts to authorize the United States to delete specific classified information from documents, to substitute a summary of the information, or to substitute a statement admitting relevant facts that the classified information would tend to prove. Section 6 provides a pretrial hearing to determine relevance, §6(a), and a pretrial hearing to determine whether the substitutions offered in lieu of the classified documents provide the defendant with "substantially the same ability to make his defense as would disclosure of the specific classified information," §6(c).

"Graymail" may not be just a sneaky defense tactic but may be the result of legitimate efforts to prepare a criminal defense. In recent years, several high-profile defendants have raised the question of the constitutionality of CIPA because of the limitations it places on defendants' ability to launch effective defenses. In United States v. North, 708 F. Supp. 399 (D.C. Dist. 1988), the defendant, Oliver North, filed a written statement of relevant and material testimony he expected to disclose during the course of the trial for the court to consider in a pretrial hearing. North later objected to the fulfillment of the CIPA provision requiring the disclosure of the statement to the Independent Counsel on the grounds that it would violate his Fifth and Sixth Amendment rights. The court held that the Fifth Amendment due process claim was meritless because modern litigation involves extensive pretrial discovery and additionally, North had been given access to much of the government's information and witnesses. Similarly, the Sixth Amendment right to effective assistance of counsel argument was found by the court to be unpersuasive because North would still be able to call or not to call witnesses, and the tactical disadvantage of minimizing surprise would be "slight." The court held CIPA to be facially constitutional.

Since *North*, courts have consistently upheld the constitutionality of CIPA against arguments asserting the violation of due process, the Fifth Amendment privilege against self-incrimination and the right to remain silent unless and until one decides to testify, the Fifth and Sixth Amendment rights to testify in one's own defense, and the Sixth Amendment right to cross-examine witnesses. See United States v. McVeigh, 923 F. Supp. 1310 (D. Colo. 1996) (finding it unnecessary to reach the issue of the constitutionality of CIPA); United States v. Wen Ho Lee, 90 F. Supp. 2d 1324 (D. N.M. 2000) (denying the defendant's motion to find §§5 and 6 of CIPA unconstitutional); United States v. Bin Laden, 2001 U.S. Dist. LEXIS 719 (S.D.N.Y. 2001) (denying the defendant's motion to find CIPA unconstitutional as it applies to him).

For further discussion of CIPA, see Tamanaha, a Critical Review of the Classified Information Procedures Act, 13 Am. J. Crim. L. 227 (1986); Salgado, Note, Government Secrets, Fair Trails, and the Classified Information Procedures Act, 98 Yale L.J. 427 (1988). For further discussion of the state secrets privilege generally, see J. Steven Gardner, The State Secret Privilege Invoked in Civil Litigation: a Proposal for Statutory Relief, 29 Wake Forest L. Rev. 567 (1994).

b.   *Presidential Communications Privilege*

President Jefferson first sought to maintain the confidentiality of presidential communications in United States v. Burr, 25 F. Cas. 187 (C.C. Dist. Va. 1807) when Chief Justice Marshall issued two subpoenas for letters written by General Wilkinson to the President. Jefferson asserted an exclusive right to the papers and resisted the subpoenas. Since that time, several presidents have invoked the privilege but United States v. Nixon provided the first clear description of its parameters.

In United States v. Nixon, 418 U.S. 683 (1974), the Supreme Court addressed whether a privilege exists to protect confidential communications between the president and the president's close advisors. President Nixon raised three claims: that the separation of powers doctrine precludes judicial review of a President's claim of privilege; that the Constitution provides an absolute privilege of confidentiality for all presidential communications; and alternatively, that the "presumptive" privilege for presidential communications should prevail over the subpoena in question. The Court, quoting Marbury v. Madison, reaffirmed that "it is the providence of this Court 'to say what the law is' with respect to the claim of privilege presented in this case," thus asserting the appropriateness of judicial review. The Court went on to recognize a constitutionally based privilege derived from the separation of powers, but noted that the presidential communications privilege is a qualified one. The Court stated that the privilege "must yield to the demonstrated, specific, need for evidence in a pending criminal trial."[76] In recognizing the qualified privilege, the Court noted that the presidential need for confidentiality justified a presumptive

---

76.   Three years later the Court again declined to permit the executive privilege to prevent the release of information where an ex-president sought to invoke the privilege "against the very Executive Branch in whose name the privilege is invoked." Nixon v. Administrator of General Services, 433 U.S. 425 (1977) (former president directed to deliver presidential papers and tape recordings to an official of the Executive Branch for the creation of public access under the Presidential Recordings and Materials Preservation Act, held to be facially constitutional and not violative of the presidential privilege doctrine).

privilege for presidential communications. The burden rests with the person seeking discovery of the information to rebut the presumption of privilege. Moreover, in conducting an in camera inspection, the trial court must use "scrupulous protection" to ensure that presidential communications that are not relevant or admissible are not disclosed. The privilege may be stronger in civil proceedings. In Cheney v. U.S. Dist. Court for Dist. of Columbia, 124 S.Ct. 2576 (2004), a case involving the assertion of executive privilege to prevent disclosure of the names of certain de facto members of the National Energy Policy Development Group, the court stated that "[t]he need for information for use in civil cases, while far from negligible, does not share the urgency or significance of the criminal subpoena requests in Nixon." Id. at 2589. For further discussion, see K. A. McNeely-Johnson, Comment, United States v. Nixon, Twenty Years After: The Good, the Bad and the Ugly — An Exploration of Executive Privilege, 14 N. Ill. U. L. Rev. 251 (1993). See also Mark J. Rozell, Symposium: Executive Privilege and the Clinton Presidency, 8 Wm. & Mary Bill of Rts. J. 541 (2000) (arguing that presidents should use the power only for the most compelling reasons and not to protect information that is merely embarrassing or politically damaging, and proposing that each administration adopt guidelines for its members with formal procedures for handling and resolving executive privilege issues).

In re Sealed Case, 121 F.3d 729 (D.C. Cir. 1997) provided the District of Columbia Court of Appeals with the opportunity to determine how far beyond direct communications with the President the presidential communications privilege might reach. As part of a grand jury investigation of former Secretary of Agriculture Mike Espy, the Office of the Independent Counsel tried to compel performance of a subpoena *duces tecum* issued by the grand jury and served on the Counsel to the President. The White House provided many of the requested documents but withheld 84 as privileged. The court held that the presidential privilege extends "down the line" from the President to his aides and advisors whenever they are in the "course of preparing advice" for the President even when they are not communicating directly with the President. The court found that all of the 84 documents — authored by White House Counsel, Deputy and Associate White House Counsel, legal externs to the White House Counsel's office, the Chief of Staff, the Press Secretary, and even three "no authored" documents — were privileged. The Office of the Independent Counsel, however, was given the opportunity on remand to demonstrate "sufficient need" in order to overcome the presidential communications privilege. The court sought to strike the "appropriate balance between openness and informed presidential deliberation."[77] In In re Sealed Case, 148 F.3d 1073 (D.C. Cir. 1998), cert. denied sub. nom. Rubin v. United States, 119 S. Ct. 461 (1998), the Government sought to extend the executive privilege to create a "protective function privilege" that would shield Secret Service agents from testifying. The Secret Service resisted the Independent Counsel's subpoena of 33 Secret Service officers to testify to about their knowledge of President Clinton's affair with White House intern Monica Lewinsky. The Secret Service proposed an "absolute privilege that would preclude the OIC from compelling any testimony regarding information learned by Secret Service agents and officers while performing protective functions in physical proximity to

---

77.   See Recent Case, 111 Harv. L. Rev. 861 (1998) (arguing that the court failed to recognize the difference in the privilege for the President and his advisors and disregarded other protections, such as the deliberative process privilege and statutory exceptions to the Freedom of Information Act, which would preserve the effectiveness of the executive branch).

the President where the information would tend to reveal the President's contemporaneous activities."[78] The court considered the three factors detailed by the Supreme Court in *Jaffe* (page 860-861, supra). It found that the privilege is not based in federal law[79] and Secret Service officers have testified previously;[80] the privilege is not supported by state precedents though the same need would presumably exist for state governors; and while there is a strong public policy interest in ensuring the safety of the President, the President will not resist the closeness of his protectors because of his own interest in his safety and because he is required by law to accept protection.[81] The court held that the absence of federal and state precedents and the Secret Service's failure to establish the need for the protective function privilege prevented its creation by the judiciary at this time. For further discussion of the case and an the argument that the D.C. Court of Appeals inappropriately relaxed the Supreme Court's standard that required more than a compelling public interest, see T. Spencer Crowley, Case Comment: Evidence: The Clinton Administration's Battle to Gain Evidentiary Privilege for Secret Service Agents — Another Tainted Legacy?, 51 Fla. L. Rev. 743 (1999).

c. *Official Information (Deliberative Process) Privilege*

The official information privilege exists to protect government deliberative processes and provides a limited executive privilege for executive officers other than the President. Not surprisingly, the rationale is that compelled disclosure of such communications would inhibit the exchange of opinions and advice among executive officials, and thereby impair the decision-making process. A related justification for the privilege is that the judiciary is not authorized to probe the mental processes of an executive or administrative officer. In re Franklin National Bank Securities Litig., 478 F. Supp. 577, 580-581 (E.D.N.Y. 1979). The privilege is the government's. Examples are government agency policy deliberations and law enforcement investigatory files. Both Proposed FRE 509 and the exemption provisions of the Freedom of Information Act, 5 U.S.C. §552 (1994), address the need for protection of such official information.

A qualified privilege protecting official information has been widely accepted by the federal courts. See, e.g., Kelly v. City of San Jose, 114 F.R.D. 653 (N.D. Cal. 1987); United States v. Board of Educ. of City of Chicago, 610 F. Supp. 695 (N.D. Ill 1985); Kinoy v. Mitchell, 67 F.R.D. 1 (S.D.N.Y. 1975). In In re "Agent Orange" Product Liability Litig., 97 F.R.D. 427, 434 (E.D.N.Y. 1983), the court described the limited scope of the privilege:

[The privilege] applies only to material reflecting [the] deliberative process — evaluations, expressions of opinions, and recommendations on policy matters.... Raw data and

---

78. In re Grand Jury Proceedings, 1998 WL 272884 (D.D.C. May 22, 1998).
79. There has been discussion in the Judiciary Committees of both the United States House of Representatives and the Senate about a potential protective function privilege. Senator Leahy introduced the Secret Service Protective Privilege Act of 1999, 106 S. 1360, which would prohibit testimony by Secret Service personnel or former personnel that was acquired during the performance of the protective function in physical proximity to the protectee. It was referred to the Senate Committee on the Judiciary but a report has not yet been issued.
80. See In re Grand Jury Proceedings, 1998 WL 272884 at *3 (D.D.C. May 22, 1998) discussing President Nixon's taping system and John Hinckley's attempted assassination of President Reagan where the Secret Service did not assert a protective function privilege.
81. 18 U.S.C. 3056 (a) mandates the protection of the President.

factual findings do not fall within the scope of the privilege because disclosures of facts, as opposed to opinions, would not hinder candor among government officials.

The D.C. Court of Appeals in In re: Sealed Case, 121 F.3d 729 (1997) reiterated this requirement that the material be "deliberative" and not merely factual and also emphasized that it must be "predecisional." Furthermore, the court noted that the privilege is not absolute and may be overcome by a showing that the need for evidence in the specific case outweighs the harm that would result from disclosure. Quoting In re Subpoena Served Upon the Comptroller of the Currency, 967 F.2d 630 (D.C. Cir. 1992), the court described the appropriate test:

> "Each time [the deliberative process privilege] is asserted the district court must undertake a fresh balancing of the competing interests," taking into account factors such as "the relevance of the evidence," "the availability of other evidence," "the seriousness of the litigation," "the role of the government," and the "possibility of future timidity by government employees."

In Dellwood Farms v. Cargill, Inc., 128 F.3d 1122 (7th Cir. 1997), private civil plaintiffs sought materials gathered by the Department of Justice for use in criminal investigations. The FBI had been investigating charges of price fixing by Archer Daniels Midland and other agricultural producers. The FBI recorded more than 150 hours of conversations within ADM and between ADM and its competitors. The government, without seeking any confidentiality agreement, played some of the recordings to the law firm representing ADM's outside directors to induce ADM to plead guilty to the criminal antitrust offenses. The plaintiffs in this civil case subpoenaed the tapes in the hope that they contained evidence of illegal conspiracy. The Department of Justice attempted to block the subpoena with the law enforcement investigatory privilege. The court held that the subpoena should be quashed because, though the privilege is not absolute and can be overridden though a showing of need, there ought to be a "pretty strong presumption" against lifting the privilege. It reasoned that crime investigation is the duty of the Executive Branch and it is inappropriate for the courts to be "thrust too deeply" into the process. Since the Freedom of Information Act would make the information available after the criminal trial is over, the court said, the civil suit could be postponed to await its release.

The plaintiffs additionally raised the issue of waiver since the Department of Justice had voluntarily played the recordings for ADM's lawyers. The court found that there had been a mere "selective waiver," described as the situation where, "having voluntarily disclosed privileged information to one person, the party who made the disclosure asserts the privilege against another person who wants the information." The court acknowledged that the government should have been more careful and obtained a protective order against further disclosure, as is normally required in selective disclosure cases. This error, however, the court said, should not be punished too harshly because there was no deliberate waiver of the privilege to withhold the tapes from the plaintiffs and interference with criminal investigation would be an "excessive punishment."

The Supreme Court finally addressed the relationship between the official government information privilege and the Freedom of Information Act in United States v. Weber Aircraft Corp., 465 U.S. 792 (1984). The engine of an Air Force aircraft had failed, and the pilot was severely injured when he was ejected from the plane. He sued several entities responsible for the design and manufacture of his plane's ejection equipment. After the crash, the Air Force conducted both a "collateral investigation," designed to preserve evidence for use in whatever claims may ensue and a "safety investigation," designed solely to permit corrective action to be taken in order to reduce the risk of similar occurrences. During safety investigations, witnesses are not sworn and are promised complete confidentiality. Lower courts had previously held the results of such investigations to be privileged from discovery, a holding the Supreme Court embraced. The plaintiff thus attempted to obtain the same information through a FOIA request, to which the Court responded:

> [R]espondents' contention that they can obtain through the FOIA material that is normally privileged would create an anomaly in that the FOIA could be used to supplement civil discovery. We have consistently rejected such a construction of the FOIA. We do not think that Congress could have intended that the weighty policies underlying discovery privileges could be so easily circumvented. [Id. at 801-802.]

After the passage of the Freedom of Information Act in 1967, many private litigants sought to use the new act rather than the normal rules of discovery to obtain information from the government in judicial proceedings. In NLRB v. Sears, Roebuck & Co., 421 U.S. 132 (1975), however, the Court examined the relationship between Exemption 5 of the FOIA and governmental privileges. The Court expressly found that Exception 5 contains a deliberative process privilege and a work product privilege and implied that a governmental attorney-client privilege should be recognized as well.

The Freedom of Information Act lists what each governmental agency must make available to the public and how the information is to be made accessible. There are several exceptions that allow agencies to maintain the confidentiality of some materials including those containing: matters of national defense or foreign policy, internal personnel rules, privileged or confidential trade secrets or financial information, geological or geophysical information and data concerning wells, and records or information compiled for law enforcement purposes to the extent that disclosure would interfere with enforcement, deprive a person of the right to a fair trial, constitute an unwarranted invasion of personal privacy, reveal the identity of a confidential source, endanger the life or physical safety of any individual, or disclose techniques and procedures for law enforcement investigations or prosecutions.

Exception 5 to the FOIA, which excludes inter-agency or intra-agency communications, has allowed agencies to resist disclosure of information by claiming the deliberative process privilege. The Supreme Court defined the deliberative process as covering documents "reflecting advisory opinions, recommendations and deliberations comprising part of a process by which governmental decisions and policies are formulated." NLRB v. Sears, Roebuck & Co., 421 U.S. 132, 150 (1975) (quoting Carl Zeiss Stiftung v. V.E.B. Carl Zeiss, Jena, 40 F.R.D. 318, 324 (D.C. 1966)).

In Department of the Interior and Bureau of Indian Affairs v. Klamath Water Users Protective Association, 532 U.S. 1 (2001), the Supreme Court addressed for the first time the question of whether the deliberative process privilege could be extended to cover communications between government agencies and "outsiders." The Klamath Water Users, an association of water users in the Klamath River Basin, filed requests under the FOIA for communications between the Bureau of Indian Affairs and the Native American Tribes of the area, regarding the allocation of water. The Bureau had consulted with the Tribes on the proposed Klamath Project Operation

Plan in efforts to assess the likely impact of the plan. The Bureau sought to invoke the deliberative process privilege of Exception 5 to resist the plaintiffs' request for information. The Court acknowledged that courts have extended the privilege to communications between governmental agencies and outside consultants[82] but rejected the Bureau's portrayal of the Tribes as filling this sort of role. The Tribes, the Court found, had communicated with the Bureau with their own interests in mind and had acted as "self-advocates at the expense of others seeking benefits inadequate to satisfy everyone." The Court thus rejected the intra-agency nature of the communications and held that they could not be exempted from discovery under Exception 5.

In the states, the extent of the protection afforded depends on the type of official information at issue. For example, in the context of government agency deliberations, a majority of states have recognized a qualified privilege based on the federal rule. In the context of law enforcement records, some states have enacted statutory privileges to protect the information, while others have conferred some level of protection through the more general "classified" official information statutes. Where a disclosure statute such as a state Freedom of Information Act is in effect, the statute takes precedence in determining the scope of protection. For further discussion of the various classes of official information, see 3 Jack B. Weinstein and Margaret A. Berger, Weinstein's Evidence §§509.20-509.24 (Joseph M. McLaughlin, ed., Matthew Bender 2d ed. 1997).

In order to prevail on a claim of the official information privilege, the agency official asserting the privilege typically must specifically identify what government interest or privacy interest would be threatened by disclosure and describe how disclosure, even if made under a protective order, would create a substantial risk of harm. Chism v. County of San Bernadino, 159 F.R.D. 531, 534 (C.D. Cal. 1994). In *Chism,* the court held that a deputy sheriff's declaration failed to show that documents produced during an internal review of an allegedly unjustified shooting were protected by the official information privilege. The court said that a general assertion that the police department's internal investigatory system would be harmed by disclosure of its documents was insufficient. This information was presumptively discoverable because information in police files is often developed closer in time to the events in question, and therefore substantially comparable evidence is not available from other sources.

The official information privilege often arises in cases involving alleged violations of civil rights by police officers under 42 U.S.C. §1983 where plaintiffs want to discover the personnel records of police officer defendants. Despite the fact that many states have statutes protecting the confidentiality of these records, see, e.g., Kansas Open Records Act, Kan. Stat. Ann. §45-221(4) (2000); Cal. Penal Code §§832.7, 832.8 (Supp. 2005), and despite the fact that there are comparable confidentiality provisions for federal officers, 5 U.S.C. §552(b)(6) and (b)(7)(c), federal courts have been reluctant to recognize a privilege for police officer personnel records in §1983 cases. See, e.g., Mason v. Stock, 869 F. Supp. 828 (D. Kan. 1994); see also Welsh v. City and County of San Francisco, 887 F. Supp. 1293 (N.D. Cal. 1995).

---

82. See e.g., Hoover v. Dept. of Interior, 611 F.2d 1132, 1138 (5th Cir. 1980) ("the government may deem it necessary to seek the objective opinion of outside experts rather than rely solely on the opinions of government appraisers"); Lead Industries Assn. v. OSHA, 610 F.2d 70, 83 (2d Cir. 1979) (applying Exemption 5 to cover draft reports "prepared by outside consultants who had testified on behalf of the agency rather than agency staff"); Government Land Bank v. GSA, 671 F.2d 663, 665 (5th Cir. 1982) ("Both parties agree that a property appraisal, performed under contract by an independent professional, is an 'intra-agency' document for purposes of the exemption").

PROBLEMS

12.32. Michael McKinley is being prosecuted in Ireland for directing terrorism. He has asked the district court for an order to produce a tape recording that he believes will help him in cross examining David Rogers, a key prosecution witness. The tape recordings are held by journalists who conducted interviews with Rogers for a contracted biography that they are writing. Rogers has not objected to the discovery, but the journalists have challenged, asserting the journalist's privilege. What result?

12.33. Ryan has lived with his grandmother for 15 years, all but a few months of his life, and she has always supported him financially and otherwise. Ryan has been charged with a crime and the prosecution is seeking to elicit the testimony of his grandmother about his statements to her following the alleged crime. Ryan's defense attorney objects on the ground that such statements were confidential and should be protected from disclosure under the parent-child privilege that is recognized in the state. Should the court permit testimony relative to statements made by Ryan to his grandmother?

12.34. All 230 persons aboard TWA flight 800 were killed when it exploded over the Atlantic Ocean on July 17th, 1996. The United States salvaged much of the wreckage and secured it in a building in Calverton, New York, to be used in the investigation of the accident. Sanders, an investigative journalist, pursued the hypothesis that a missile had caused the explosion and spoke with Captain Terrell, a senior 747 pilot with TWA who was involved in the investigation. Captain Terrell told Sanders that a "reddish" substance had been found on some of the seats that might be residue from an explosive. He later provided Sanders with a small portion of the substance that had been removed from the wreckage. Sanders wrote a book entitled The Downing of TWA Flight 800 in which he reported that this "reddish" substance tested consistent with the presence of solid rocket fuel. The FBI began investigating Sanders for violation of 49 U.S.C. §1155(b), which bans the unauthorized removal of "a part of a civilian aircraft involved in an accident." The government offered Sanders a nonprosecution agreement in exchange for the name of his confidential source but Sanders refused. After the government discovered his identity through other sources, Captain Stacey testified against Sanders in return for a reduction of his offense to a misdemeanor. Sanders argues that the journalist's privilege bars government coercion to disclose news sources and thus urges the court to use a balancing test weighing "the governmental interest served by prosecution" against "the detrimental impact of permitting such a prosecution to be used as a means of coercing disclosure of a journalist's source." Should the court hold that the journalist's privilege prevents prosecution from being used in this way?

12.35. Dr. Tambone has filed a complaint against Memorial Hospital for restraint of trade in violation of federal and state antitrust laws. He alleges that the physicians of Memorial Hospital have used the peer review and disciplinary process to exclude him from its medical staff, effectively destroying his practice. Dr. Tambone claims that he was the victim of a sham disciplinary proceeding that was used as a means of implementing the alleged restraint of trade. To prove this allegation he has sought discovery regarding the hospital's treatment of other doctors in comparable disciplinary proceedings. Can the hospital resist disclosure of the information under a peer review privilege?

12.36. The Federal Death Penalty Act of 1994 authorizes the death penalty for more than 40 crimes and sets the procedure for seeking the death penalty in federal cases. An Attorney General's Death Penalty Committee (DPC) reviews each case and conducts a meeting where the defendant's attorney may try to persuade the government not to seek the death penalty. The DPC then assists in advising the Attorney General as to the ultimate decision whether to pursue the death penalty. Defendant Jacobo is considered by the government to be a member of the "Mexican Mafia" and has been charged with murder in the furtherance of racketeering, an offence covered by the Federal Death Penalty Act. Jacobo has sought to discover information that might tend to mitigate the sentence in his case, including information from the DPC meetings and its completed "death penalty evaluation form." The government objects to the discovery request based on the deliberative process privilege. Should the court allow it to withhold this information from Jocobo?

12.37. USAID is a federal agency that oversees development projects under the government's foreign assistance program. USAID was involved in building a water treatment facility in Egypt, financing the project to be carried out by an Egyptian government agency. USAID hired a U.S. engineering firm, CDM, to design the project, while the construction contract was awarded to a joint venture (JV) between two companies. Under the contract, the builders deal directly with the host country, but USAID retains approval rights for significant changes and additional compensation.

The JV requested additional funds, but USAID refused after CDM assessed that the request should be much lower, and the parties have not been able to agree. USAID urged CDM to hire a consultant to evaluate the challenges to settlement. CDM hired Richard J. Roy, providing that a report of his findings was to be given only to USAID and the Egyptian government agency, without disclosure to other parties.

A Freedom of Information Act (FOIA) request was filed with USAID on behalf of the JV members for documents related to the dispute, including the Roy Report, which USAID refused to provide, arguing that the report was attorney work-product and was privileged under the attorney-client privilege. An FOIA lawsuit was filed in federal court alleging that USAID unlawfully withheld the report. What result?

Table of Cases

Principal cases are in italics.

Abel; United States v., 399, 400, 401
Abreu; United States v., 180, 694
Acevedo; United States v., 302
Acker; United States v., 843, 844, 853
Adair; United States v., 285, 287
Adams; United States v., 400
Ad-Vantage Tel. Directory Consultants,
  Inc. v. GTE Directories Corp., 366
Affleck; United States v., 665
Agne; United States v., 481
Agosto, In re, 791
AgriBioTech, Inc. v. Thomas, 527
Air Crash Disaster, In re, 325
Air Disaster at Lockerbie Scotland on December 21
  1988, In re, 541
Alarcon-Simi; United States v., 499
Albertson; United States v., 892
Alcade; People v., 508
Alexander; United States v., 375, 498
Alexis v. McDonald's Rest. of Mass., Inc., 613
All Am. Life & Cas. Co. v. Oceanic Trade Alliance
  Council Int'l, Inc., 349
Allen; United States v., 620
Allen J.; United States v., 170
Alperin; United States v., 872
Alvarez; United States v., 285, 287
Amachia; United States v., 381
Amaya; United States v., 549
American Coal Co. v. Benefits Review Bd., 758
American Stores v. Commission of Internal Revenue
  Serv., 770
Ammar; United States v., 486
Anderson v. Liberty Lobby, Inc., 702
Anderson v. Malloy, 326
Anderson; United States v., 509 F.2d 724, 886
Anderson; United States v., 933 F.2d 1261, 219
Anderson; United States v., 790 F. Supp. 231, 801
Andrekus v. Board of Educ., 578

Andring; State v., 871
Angelilli; United States v., 264
Ansaldi; United States v., 221
Appeal of. *See name of party*
Application of. *See name of party*
Apprendi v. New Jersey, 656, 731, 732
Aramburu v. Boeing Co., 890
Ariza v. City of N.Y., 538
Arthur Young & Co.; United States v., 881
Asplundh Mfg. Div. v. Benton Harbor Eng'g, 617
Athey v. Farmers Ins. Exch., 331
Atkins; United States v., 564
Attorney Gen. v. Irish People, Inc., 892
Austin v. Hopper, 270
Austin; United States v., 546
Awkard; United States v., 356
Ayala-Pizarro; United States v., 618

Badgett v. Rent-Way, Inc., 207
Bailey; United States v., 333, 735, 736
Baird v. Koerner, 823
Baker v. State, 521, 844
Bakshinian; United States v., 482
Ballew v. State, 800
Ballis; United States v., 429
Ballou v. Henri Studios, Inc., 136
Bank of China v. NBM LLC, 617
Barber v. Page, 550, 599
Barnes v. United States, 760
Barnes; United States v., 377
Batson v. Kentucky, 81
Battle; United States v., 693
Baxter v. Palmigiano, 796
BE&K Constr. Co. v. Will & Grundy Bldg. & Trades
  Council, AFL-CIO, 138
Beard v. Mitchell, 360
Beck v. Alabama, 732, 733

Beech Aircraft Corp. v. Rainey, 537, 541, 667
Behn; State v., 695
Bell; United States v., 527
Benavidez-Benavidez; United States v., 643
Bensimon; United States v., 378
Bentzlin v. Hughes Aircraft Co., 892
Bercier; United States v., 856
Betts; United States v., 400
Bigham; United States v., 460
Big O Tire Dealers, Inc. v. Goodyear Tire &
   Rubber Co., 332, 333
Bilderbeck; United States v., 247
Bilzerian; United States v., 795, 800
Bisbee; United States v., 197
Bitterman; United States v., 407
Bizzle v. McKesson Corp., 322
Black v. M & W Gear Co., 121
Black v. United States, 892
Blackburn v. Foltz, 357
Black; Commonwealth v., 316
Blair; State v., 194, 235, 421, 516
Blake v. Pellegrino, 134, 151
Blu-J, Inc. v. Kemper C.P.A. Group, 333
Bobo; United States v., 563
Bockting v. Bayer, 602
Bogle; People v., 854
Bogosian v. Mercedes-Benz, Inc., 325
Bohanon v. Pegelow, 614
Bohler-Udderholm Am., Inc. v. Ellwood
   Group, Inc., 578
Bokshoven; United States v., 182
Bolick; United States v., 356
Bolzer; United States v., 845, 847
Booker; United States v., 731, 732
Bordeaux; United States v., 596
Boucher v. Grant, 495
Bourjaily v. United States, 215, 485, 570, 583
Bowie; United States v., 245
Branzburg v. Hayes, 887
Bray; United States v., 207, 208
Bridges; United States v., 346
Brien; United States v., 629, 661
Brink; United States v., 465
Brink's, Inc. v. City of N.Y., 796
Briscoe; United States v., 202
Brocklesby v. United States, 331
Brooks v. Chrysler Corp., 269
Brooks; United States v., 245
Brown v. Board of Educ., 778
Brown; United States v., 557 F.2d 541, 632
Brown; United States v., 605 F.2d 389, 853
Brown; United States v., 254 F.3d 454, 499, 500
Brumley; United States v., 345
Brun; United States v., 597, 601
Bruno; United States v., 596
Bruton v. United States, 475, 476
Bucci v. Essex Ins. Co., 513
Buchanan; United States v., 135
Buck; United States v., 207
Bulaich v. AT&T Info. Sys., 334
Bunge Corp. v. M/V Furness Bridge, 758
Burch; United States v., 346
Burka v. United States Dep't of Health &
   Human Servs., 888
Burke; United States v., 700 F.2d 70, 887

Burr; State v.; United States v., 894
Burston; United States v., 381
Burton; People v., 845

Cage v. Louisiana, 715
Cagle v. State, 221
California v. Green, 90, 598
Californian & Hawaiian Sugar Co. v. Kansas City
   Terminal Warehouse Co., 331
Call; United States v., 140
Campbell v. Coleman Co., 549
Campbell; United States v., 462, 497
Candelaria-Silva; United States v., 144
C & H Commercial Contractors v. United States, 482
Capelton; United States v., 486
Capital Traction Co. v. Hof, 739
Carella v. California, 761
Carley v. Wheeled Coach, 767
Carman v. McDonnell Douglas Corp., 870
Carmichael; United States v., 456
Carson v. Fine, 857
Carson v. Metropolitan Life Ins. Co., 753
Carter v. University of Toledo, 480
Carvalho; United States v., 566
Cash; United States v., 517, 518
Cassidy; United States v., 170
Castillo; United States v., 297, 362
Caver v. City of Trenton, 870
Certain Underwriters at Lloyd's, London v.
   Sinkovich, 529, 617
Cervantes v. Jones, 643
Chamberlain v. State, 844
Chambers v. Mississippi, 313, 316, 318
Chapel; United States v., 771
Chapman; United States v., 853
Charmley v. Lewis, 259, 261
Chase v. General Motors Corp., 324, 325
Chase; United States v., 873
Chemtool, Inc. v. Lubrication Techs., Inc., 479
Cherry; United States v., 570, 572
Citizens for Equal Prot., Inc. v. Bruning, 844
City & County of Denver v. East Jefferson County
   Sanitation Dist., 747
City of. *See specific city*
Clark v. United States, 823
Clark; United States v., 854
Cleveland v. KFC Nat'l Mgmt. Co., 302, 304
Cohen; United States v., 508
Cohn; United States v., 795
Coles v. Harsch, 793
Coles v. Jenkins, 141
Collins v. Kibort, 518
Collins; United States v., 288
Colon; United States v., 246
Colonial Leasing Co. v. Logistics Control Group
   Int'l, 772
Columbia Sec. Litig., In re, 576
Commodity Futures Trading Comm'n v. Weintraub,
   818
Commonwealth v. *See name of opposing party*
Conde v. Starlight I, Inc., 338
Condit v. National Enquirer, Inc., 888
Coney; United States v., 579
Conoco, Inc. v. Department of Energy, 577, 578

Continental Cablevision, Inc. v. Stores Broad. Co., 887
Cook v. Mississippi Dep't of Human Servs., 578
Cornett; United States v., 484
Cotter; United States v., 616
Couch v. United States, 881
County Court of Ulster County v. Allen, 760, 761
Cox v. Miller, 877
Cox v. State, 316
Crawford v. Washington, 455, 540, 564, 565, 569, 582, 584, 584, 595, 597, 598, 599, 600, 602
Cree v. Hatcher, 376, 377
Crisp; United States v., 201, 694
Croce v. Bromley Corp., 349
Cromer; United States v., 597
Crosby; United States v., 139, 150
Cross v. United States, 201
Crowder; United States v., 159, 246, 247
Cruz; United States v., 356, 498
Cruz-Garcia; United States v., 151
Cypress Semiconductor Sec. Litig., In re, 578

Daghita; People v., 845
Dakota; United States v., 527
Dal-Tile Corp. v. United States, 579
Daly; State v., 383
Darrow v. Gunn, 802
Datz; United States v., 477
Daubert v. Merrell Dow Pharm., Inc., 509 U.S. 579, 631–632, 633, 641, 642, 643, 644, 645, 650, 651, 659, 660, 689, 690, 691, 692, 694, 696, 784
Daubert v. Merrell Dow Pharm., Inc., 43 F.3d 1311, 644–645
Davies; United States v., 883
Davis; United States v., 136, 564
Davis v. Alaska, 314, 316, 318, 797
Davis v. State, 163
Davis v. Washington, 597
DeBoer; United States v., 207
Dedman; State v., 596
Deeb; United States v., 552
DeGeratto; United States v., 366, 367
Dellwood Farms v. Cargill, Inc., 795
DeLong; State v., 883
Demarey; United States v., 182
Demjanjuk; United States v., 192
Dennis, Ex parte, 316
Dennis; United States v., 460
Denton; United States v., 395
Desai v. Hersh, 888
Desrosiers v. Flight Int'l of Fla., Inc., 538
Devin; United States v., 170
Dhinsa; United States v., 569, 571, 572, 573
Diamond; Doe v., 871
Diehl v. Blaw-Knox, 341
DiMaria; United States v., 496, 504
DiNapoli; United States v., 552, 556
Dior; United States v., 773, 779
DiPaola; United States v., 404
DirecTV v. Murray, 533
Dixon v. International Harvester Co., 326
Dixon; People v., 882
Dixon; United States v., 368, 615
Doe v. See name of opposing party

Doe; United States v., 460 F.2d 328, 889
Doe; United States v., 655 F.2d 920, 345
Dolah; United States v., 550
Donlon; United States v., 577
Donovan v. Crisostomo, 563
Doyle; United States v., 872
Drake, In re, 579
Dring; United States v., 366
Dube; United States v., 875
Dullard; State v., 441, 442, 443, 444, 447, 448, 449

Eagle; United States v., 300
Edward J.; United States v., 515
EEOC v. See name of opposing party
E.I. DuPont de Nemours & Co.; EEOC v., 193
Ellis v. United States, 878
Ellis; United States v., 395
Ellison v. Ellison, 870
Emery; United States v., 573
Employer's Nat'l Life Ins. Co. of Dallas, Tex. v. Willits, 753
Enjady; United States v., 297
Ensey; Doe v., 870
Erato, In re, 883
Estate of. See specific party
Estes; United States v., 845
Evans; United States v., 419, 482
Ewoldt; People v., 247

Fasanaro v. Mooney Aircraft Corp., 324
Fausek v. White, 793
F.D.I.C. v. White, 886
Felton; United States v., 598
Ferber; United States v., 498, 533
Ferreira; United States v., 123
Field v. Trigg County Hosp., Inc., 513
Figueroa-Lopez; United States v., 618
First Sec. Bank v. Union Pac. R. Co., 269, 324
Fischer; United States v., 794, 886
Fitzgerald; People v., 882
Flaminio v. Honda Motor Co., 324
Folb v. Motion Picture Indus. Pension & Health Plans, 886
Footman; United States v., 380
Ford v. Schmidt, 324
Forrester; United States v., 618, 619
Four Corners Helicopters, Inc. v. Turbomeca, 269
Fowler v. State, 599
Frank v. County of Hudson, 137, 300
Frank; United States v., 345
Franklin; United States v., 601
Fritsch v. City of Chula Vista, 871
Fry; People v., 600
Frye v. United States, 632, 641, 642
Fuentes v. Thomas, 222
Fulk; United States v., 843

Gabe; United States v., 300, 301
Gail D., In re, 882
Gainey; United States v., 754
Gajo; United States v., 460, 484
Galarnyk v. Hostmart Mgmt., 336

Galarza v. United States, 821
Galbreth; United States v., 643
Gamerdinger v. Schaefer, 261
Garcia; United States v., 616
Garcia-Meza; United States v., 601
Garcia-Rosa; United States v., 144
Garcia-Torres; United States v., 483
Garner; People v., 239
Garner v. Wolfinbarger, 793
Gaskell; United States v., 185
Gear Petroleum, Inc.; EEOC v., 331
General Elec. Co. v. Joiner, 644
General Signal Corp. v. MCI Telecomm. Corp., 141
General Wood Preserving Co., NLRB v., 191
Geno; People v., 596
George; United States v., 694
Georgia-Pacific Corp. v. GAF Roofing Mfg. Corp., 801
Geschwendt v. Ryan, 734
Geston; United States v., 365
Gilbert v. California, 466
Gilbert; United States v., 374
Gillock; United States v., 892
Glass; United States v., 873
Glover v. State, 853
Goichman; United States v., 177
Goldblatt v. Federal Deposit Ins. Corp., 767
Goldsmith v. State, 872
Gomez v. Rodriguez, 479
Gonzalez v. Digital Equip. Corp., 144, 189
Gonzalez-Maldonado; United States v., 191
Gonzalves; Commonwealth v., 596
Goodridge v. Department of Pub. Health, 844
Goodyear Tire & Rubber Co. v. Chiles Power Supply, Inc., 884
Gorby v. Schneider Tank Lines, 619
Gordon; United States v., 875
Gould; United States v., 778, 779, 784
Government of. See specific government
Grady; United States v., 288
Grand Jury Investigation, In re, 842 F.2d 1223, 824
Grand Jury Investigation, In re, 918 F.2d 374, 791, 875, 876, 877, 878
Grand Jury Investigation, In re, 399 F.3d 527, 821
Grand Jury Investigation (Durant), In re, 823
Grand Jury Proceedings, In re, 795
Grand Jury Proceedings (Des Moines, Iowa), In re, 805, 841
Grand Jury Proceedings (Gregory P. Violette), In re, 873
Grand Jury Proceedings (John Doe), In re, 883
Grand Jury Proceedings (Pavlick), In re, 823
Grand Jury Proceedings (Scarce), In re, 887, 889
Grand Jury Proceedings (Twist), In re, 823
Grand Jury Proceedings No. 96-55344, In re, 824
Grand Jury Proceedings Unemancipated Minor Child, In re, 883
Grand Jury Proceedings Witness Ms. X, In re, 844
Grand Jury Subpoena, In re, 750 F.2d 223, 889
Grand Jury Subpoena, In re, 884 F. Supp. 188, 853
Grand Jury Subpoena Dated March 24, 2003, In re, 799
Grand Jury Subpoena Duces Tecum, In re, 821
Grand Jury Subpoena Duces Tecum Dated Sept. 15, 1983, In re, 824

Grand Jury Subpoena, Judith Miller, In re, 887
Grand Jury Subpoenas (U.S. v. Hirsch), In re, 823
Grand Jury Testimony of Attorney X, In re, 801
Grant; United States v., 181
Gray v. Bicknell, 802
Gray v. District Court, 800
Gray v. Maryland, 476
Great Atl. & Pac. Tea Co. v. Custin, 336
Great Coastal Express, Inc. v. Atlanta Mut. Cos., 336
Greater Newburyport Clamshell Alliance v. Public Serv. Co. of N.H., 805, 841
Green; United States v., 498, 518, 520
Greenburg, In re, 883
Greer v. Hoffman-LaRoche, Inc., 341
Griffin v. California, 796
Grismore v. Consolidated Prods. Co., 671
Grooms; United States v., 391, 407
Grove v. Principal Mut. Life Ins. Co., 676
Guardia; United States v., 297, 300
Guillermety v. Secretary of Educ., 527
Gustafson v. Cornelius Co., 772
Gutierrez-Rodriguez v. Cartagena, 427

Hale; State v., 221
Hall v. Baxter Healthcare Corp., 677
Hall; United States v., 159, 629
Halvorsen v. Baird, 139
Hamilton; United States v., 842
Hammon v. State, 596
Hampton; People v., 690
Hancock v. Hobbs, 791
Handlin; United States v., 483
Hardy v. Merrill, 612
Harper & Row Publishers, Inc. v. Decker, 809
Harrell; People v., 882
Harrell v. State, 239
Harris; United States v., 158
Hart; United States v., 208
Hauert; United States v., 331
Havard v. Baxter Int'l Inc., 677
Havens Steel Co. v. Randolph Eng'g Co., 772
Hawkins v. United States, 778
Hayes; United States v., 873
Haywood; United States v., 137, 138, 144, 240
Henderson; United States v., 619, 620, 643
Hendricks; United States v., 598
Herbert v. Lando, 887
Hernandez v. New York, 654
Hernandez; United States v., 566
Hernandez-Herrera; United States v., 192
Hickman v. Taylor, 818, 836
Hickson Corp. v. Norfolk S. Ry. Co., 538, 541, 542
Higa; United States v., 392
Hill; United States v., 247
Hilligas; People v., 882
Hillsborough Holdings Corp., In re, 881
Hilton; United States v., 356
Hinkle v. City of Clarksburg, 186
Hitt; United States v., 107, 151, 187, 235
Hodgson v. Charles Martin Inspector of Petroleum, Inc., 886
Homestore.Com, Sec. Litig., In re, 193
Hood v. Knappton Corp., 758
Houlihan; United States v., 569, 570

Howard; United States v., 953 F.2d 610, 206
Howard; United States v., 51 Fed. Appx. 118, 185
Howard-Arias; United States v., 181
Huddleston v. United States, 172, 222, 239, 248, 298
Hughes Capital Corp.; SEC v., 530
Hull v. Chevron U.S.A., Inc., 324, 326
Humphrey v. Philip Morris, Inc., 819
Hunziker v. Scheidemantle, 337
Hutto v. Davis, 723

Idaho v. Wright, 583, 584
Ina Aviation Corp. v. United States, 741
Inquest Proceedings, In re, 883
Insaulgarat; United States v., 537
International Sys. & Controls Corp. Sec. Litig., In re, 824
Ismail; United States v., 883

Jackson v. Crews, 206
Jackson v. Scott, 890
Jacobs v. Virgin Islands, 694
Jacques; State v., 316
Jaffee v. Redmond, 791, 857, 857, 869, 871, 872, 873, 885
Jakobetz; United States v., 784
James; United States v., 853
Jane Student 1 v. Williams, 869
Janis; United States v., 694
Jasin; United States v., 459
J.E.B. v. Alabama ex rel. T.B., 81
Jefferson; United States v., 484
Jenkins; United States v., 246
Jensen; United States v., 365
Jenson v. Eveleth Taconite Co., 317
Jewell v. CSX Transp., Inc., 471
JGR, Inc. v. Thomasville Furniture Indus., 617
Jinadu; United States v., 476
Jinro Am. Inc. v. Secure Invs., Inc., 123
Johnson v. Lutz, 532
Johnson; People v., 1, 2, 77, 79, 82, 83, 85, 90, 91, 101, 104, 106, 110, 112, 113, 114, 119, 120, 122, 128, 129, 133, 138, 169, 173, 184, 187, 192, 197, 206, 218, 232, 233, 270, 274, 275, 276, 281, 283, 359, 360, 369, 382, 384, 393, 544, 609, 629
Johnson v. Renico, 598
Johnson; State v., 255
Johnson; United States v., 509
Joint Asbestos Litig., In re, 324
Jones v. Ford Motor Co., 139, 542
Jones v. Southern Pac. R.R. Co., 261
Jones; United States v., 191, 693, 773, 883
Joon Kyu Kim; State v., 140
Jordan; United States v., 288, 596, 600
Joshi; United States v., 477

Kappell; United States v., 599
Kaquatosh; United States v., 465
Karmer; United States v., 376
Kassel v. Gannet Co., 527
Kately; State v., 262
Katona v. Federal Express Corp., 497
Keeble v. United States, 734

Keeter; United States v., 458, 460
Kelly v. Crown Equip. Co., 325
Kemper v. Gray, 870
Keogh v. IRS, 525
Kidder Peabody Sec. Litig., In re, 819
Klein; United States v., 755
Klinzing; United States v., 528
Knapp v. State, 127
Knight v. Otis Elevator Co., 324
Knuckles; People v., 800
Koch, United States ex rel. v. Koch Indus., 258
Kokkonen v. Guardian Life Ins. Co., 734
Koontz; United States v., 221
Kovacs v. Chesapeake & Ohio Ry., 259
Kovel; United States v., 799
Kraus v. Sobel Corrugated Containers, Inc., 180
Krilich; United States v., 346
Kumho Tire Co. v. Carmichael, 632, 646, 650, 659, 690, 694, 696

LaClair; State v., 316
Ladd; United States v., 181, 182
Lange; State v., 800
Lange v. Young, 800
Lannan v. State, 299
Lapierre; United States v., 619
Larez v. City of Los Angeles, 577
Larson; United States v., 300
Las Vegas, City of v. Walsh, 596
Lavender; United States v., 772
Lavine v. Milne, 708, 753, 754
Lawson; United States v., 614, 619
Lea; United States v., 644
LeCompte; United States v., 300, 301
Lee v. E.I. Dupont, 326
Lee; United States v., 484, 598
Lefkowitz; United States v., 845
Legille v. Dann, 758
Lentz; United States v., 571
Levin v. United States, 261
Levine; United States v., 205
Lewis; United States v., 833 F.2d 1380, 770
Lewis; United States v., 954 F.2d 1386, 518
Lightly; United States v., 170
Lilley; United States v., 853
Lilly v. Virginia, 583, 584
Lindemann; United States v., 359
Lindsey (Grand Jury Testimony), In re, 821
Logan; United States v., 333, 391
Long; United States v., 446
Longenecker v. General Motors, 741
Lopez; United States v., 365–366, 465
Lopez-Lopez; United States v., 457
Lossiah; United States v., 498
Loughan v. Firestone Tire & Rubber Co., 262
Lowe; United States v., 869
Lowry's Reports, Inc. v. Legg Mason, Inc., 212
Loyola-Dominguez; United States v., 538
Lucas; United States v., 150
Luce v. United States, 383, 384
Luckenbill; United States v., 777
Lustig; United States v., 853
Lutwak v. United States, 853
Lynch v. City of Boston, 614

Mackaitis v. Harcleroad, 877
Maddox v. Los Angeles, 324
Madrid v. Gomez, 2, 76, 270
Madrid; United States v., 664, 666
Maguire; United States v., 740
Maine, State of v. Smith, 845
Malfitano, Appeal of, 854
Mancusi v. Stubbs, 550
Mandel; United States v., 507
Manfre; United States v., 497
Manson v. Brathwaite, 464, 466
Marashi; United States v., 842
Marbury v. Madison, 894
Mark v. Shoen, 887
Marriage of. See name of party
Martin v. Ohio, 723, 730, 734
Martin; State v., 600
Martinez; United States v., 631
Maryland v. Craig, 602
Mastrangelo; United States v., 569, 571, 600
Mateo-Sanchez; United States v., 367
Matter of. See name of party
Mattox v. United States, 582, 583
Maxon; State v., 882
Mayhew; United States v., 600, 601
McClesky; United States v., 565
McCollum v. McDaniel, 514
McDonnell Douglas Corp. v. Green, 755
McEachron v. Glans, 184
McGinnis; State v., 239
McKnight v. Johnson Controls, Inc., 552
McNaboe v. NVF Co., 428
McQueeney v. Wilmington Trust Co., 146, 151
McVeigh; United States v., 126, 145, 159, 894
MDU Res. Group v. W.R. Grace & Co., 220, 222
Meacham; United States v., 300
Medical Therapy Sci., Inc.; United States v., 359, 360
Meeks; State v., 801
Mehojah v. Drummond, 341
Mejia-Alarcon; United States v., 376
Melia; United States v., 368
Melton, In re, 665, 666
Memorial Hosp. v. Shadur, 889
Mentz; United States v., 771
Mercado v. City of Orlando, 480
Merino-Balderrama; United States v., 159
Merrill v. Waffle House, Inc., 870
Mezzanatto; United States v., 346
Michelson v. United States, 284, 287, 288
Microsoft Corp., In re, 791, 795, 888
Middleton v. Harris Press & Shear, Inc., 341
Midwest Fireworks Mfg. Co.; United States v., 538
Mikos; United States v., 695
Millard; United States v., 345
Miller v. Crown Amusements, Inc., 500
Miller v. Field, 542
Miller v. Keating, 500
Miller v. Transamerican Press, Inc., 888
Miller; United States v., 363, 395
Milton; United States v., 458
Mitchell; United States v., 500, 694
Mobile, J. & K.C.R. Co. v. Turnipseed, 753
Modena; United States v., 202
Molina; United States v., 476
Monell v. New York City Dep't of Soc. Servs., 270

Monotype Corp. PLC v. International Typeface Corp., 527
Montana v. Egelhoff, 734
Montana; United States v., 428
Montero-Camargo; United States v., 500
Monterroso; People v., 600
Moore; State v., 255
Moore; United States v., 149 F.3d 773, 388
Morales; People v., 505
Morales v. Portuondo, 876
Morales-Evans v. Administrative Office of the Courts, 310
Moreland, Estate of v. Dieter, 150
Moretti v. Lowe, 889
Morgan; United States v., 345
Morris v. Slappy, 836
Morrison; United States v., 188
Morrow; United States v., 376
Morton v. Zidell Explorations, Inc., 337
Motes v. United States, 599
Mullaney v. Wilbur, 716, 717, 718, 719, 720, 721, 722, 723, 731, 732, 759
Munoz; United States v., 366
Murphy, In re, 824
Murphy Auto Parts Co. v. Ball, 499
Mutual Life Ins. Co. of New York v. Hillmon, 507, 509

Napolean; United States v., 877, 878
Napolitano v. Compania Sud Americana De Vapores, 150
National Broad. Co., In re Application to Quash Subpoena to, 887
Navarro, In re, 801
New Colt Holding Corp. v. RJG Holdings of Fla., Inc., 576
Newell v. Harold Shaffer Leasing Co., 337
New York Times v. Sullivan, 888
Nipper v. Snipes, 542
Nixon v. Administrator of Gen. Servs., 793, 797, 894
Nixon v. United States, 795, 797
Nixon; United States v., 840, 894
NLRB v. See name of opposing party
North; United States v., 893, 894
Nunley v. Pettway Oil Co., 739, 740, 741

Oates; United States v., 539, 540
Obayagbona; United States v., 496, 497
Obrey v. Johnson, 141
Office of the President v. Office of the Indep. Counsel, 821
Ogg; State v., 671
Ohio v. Roberts, 582, 583, 584, 599, 600, 601
Ohler v. United States, 383, 384
Olafson; United States v., 549
Old Chief v. United States, 154, 158, 159
Olden v. Kentucky, 315, 316, 318
Oleszko v. State Comp. Ins. Fund, 869
Olsen v. Class, 514
Olsen v. Correiro, 344
Orozco; United States v., 540
Ortiz; United States v., 537
Osorio-Soto; United States v., 483
Owens; United States v., 457, 458, 459, 599

Pace v. Insurance Co. of N. Am., 428
Pacheco; United States v., 514
Paducah Towing Co., In re, 552
Pageau; United States v., 188
Paiva; United States v., 740
Palmer v. Hoffman, 529, 533
Pandozzi; United States v., 381
Panzardi-Lespier; United States v., 579
Paoli R.R. Yard PCB Litig., In re, 140
Paolitto v. John Brown E.&C., Inc., 543
Park v. Huff, 445
Parle v. Runnels, 598
Passman v. Blackburn, 357
Patrick; United States v., 532
Patterson v. Caterpillar, 856
Patterson v. New York, 716, 717, 718, 719, 720, 721,
   723, 730, 731, 732, 759
Pau v. Yosemite Park & Curry Co., 341
Paul; United States v., 693
Payne; United States v., 395
Peat, Inc. v. Vanguard Research, Inc., 202
Pedroso v. Driver, 194, 208, 421, 431, 516, 544
Pena-Gutierrez; United States v., 541, 549
Pennsylvania v. Ritchie, 797
Perez; United States v., 870 F.2d 1222, 460
Perez; United States v., 217 F.3d 323, 577
Perkins; United States v., 496
Perry; United States v., 643 F.2d 38, 345
Perzinski v. Chevron Chem. Co., 332
Peters; SEC v., 151
Pheaster; United States v., 508
Philadelphia, City of v. Westinghouse Elec. Corp.,
   809
Piccinonna; United States v., 643
Pierce v. F.R. Tripler & Co., 334
Pierce; United States v., 139
Pierce County v. Guillen, 891
Piggie; United States v., 773
Pillsbury Co. v. Cleaver-Brooks Div. of Aqua-Chem,
   Inc., 477
Pinkerton v. United States, 572
Pintar; United States v., 366
Pitts v. Lockhart, 733
Pizarro; United States v., 550
Platero; United States v., 316
Plaza; United States v., 694, 695
Plough, Inc. v. The Mason & Dixon Lines, 758
Plourde v. Gladstone, 692
Pluta; United States v., 197, 549
Poncy v. Johnson & Johnson, 757
Pope; United States v., 378
Port v. Heard, 883
Posado; United States v., 643
Potamkin Cadillac Corp. v. B.R.I. Coverage Corp.,
   533
Powell; United States v., 556
Pozefsky v. Baxter Healthcare Corp., 677
Pozsgai; United States v., 767
Pree; United States v., 631
Pregeant v. Pan Am World Airways, 123
Prentiss & Carlisle v. Koehring-Waterous, 322
Prewitt; United States v., 333
Prieto; United States v., 463
Prince-Oyibo; United States v., 643
Pryce; United States v., 404

Pulido-Jacobo; United States v., 476
Puryear v. State, 465

Qualley v. Clo-Tex Int'l, Inc., 486, 783
Queen Caroline's Case, 387
Quercia v. United States, 739, 740, 741, 742
Quinto; United States v., 395

Racz v. R.T. Merryman Trucking, Inc., 186
Ramada Dev. Co. v. Rauch, 331
Rambus, Inc. v. Infineon Techs. Ag., 197
Ramirez; United States v., 871 F.2d 582, 169
Randolph v. Collectramatic, Inc., 618
R&R Assoc., Inc. v. Visual Scene, Inc., 205
Rangel-Arreola; United States v., 258
Ray; United States v., 131, 148, 194, 224, 235, 242,
   264, 421, 431, 468, 488
Raysor v. Port Auth. of N.Y. & N.J., 356
Redding v. Virginia Mason Med. Ctr., 871
Redman v. John D. Brush & Co., 663
Reed v. Thalacker, 498
Reed; United States v., 552
Reese; United States v., 287, 369
Regina v. Kearley, 449
Reichhold Chems., Inc. v. Textron, Inc., 891
Remtech, Inc., United States ex rel. v. National
   Union Fire Ins. Co., 506
Reyes; United States v., 506
Reynolds; United States v., 892
Rhodes; United States v., 128
Richards of Rockford, Inc. v. Pacific Gas & Elec. Co.,
   889
Richardson v. Marsh, 143, 476
Rivera v. Delaware, 718
Roach v. Springfield Clinic, 890
Roach v. United States, 487
Roberson; United States v., 843
Roberts v. Hollocher, 404
Roberts v. Hunt, 890
Robinson v. Magovern, 889
Robinson; United States v., 483
Robinson v. Watts Detective Agency, Inc., 368
Rocha v. Great Am. Ins. Co., 740
Rocky Mountain Helicopters, Inc. v. Bell Helicopters,
   324
Rodriguez v. Woodall, 375
Roland v. Johnson, 428
Rosa; United States v., 891 F.2d 1063, 365
Rosa; United States v., 11 F.3d 315, 540
Ross; United States v., 201
Rossi v. United States, 736
Roulette; United States v., 541
Roviaro v. United States, 886
Rowland v. American Gen. Fin., Inc., 579
Ruberto v. Commissioner, 201
Rummell v. Estelle, 723

Saddey; United States v., 191
Saelee; United States v., 693
St. Clair v. Johnny's Oyster & Shrimp, Inc., 193
St. Mary's Honor Ctr. v. Hicks, 755, 756
Salerno; United States v., 556

Samaniego; United States v., 207
Sampson; United States v., 145
Sanchez v. Zabihi, 317
Sandstrom v. Montana, 759, 760, 761
Saneaux; United States v., 487
Sanitary Grocery Co. v. Snead, 499
Santerelli, In re, 883
Santobello v. New York, 345
Savoie v. Otto Candies, Inc., 336
Sawyer; United States v., 208, 541
Sayakhom; United States v., 346
Schad v. Arizona, 732, 733
Schechter v. Klanfer, 708, 710, 711, 712, 743, 745
Scheffer; United States v., 643
Schenheinz; United States v., 791
Schmidt v. Duo-Fast Corp., 552
Scholl; United States v., 289, 526
Scholle; United States v., 533
Schreck; People v., 596
Schultz; United States v., 177
Schwimmer; United States v., 801
Scott v. Hammock, 878
Scott; United States v., 365
Sealed Case, In re, 802
SEC v. *See name of opposing party*
Secor; United States v., 504
Segura-Gallegos; United States v., 483
Seifert; United States v., 200
Seiler v. Lucasfilm, Ltd., 202, 212
Shafer, Estate of v. Commissioner, 471
Shargel, In re, 823
Shaw; United States v., 180
Sheffield v. Hilltop Sand & Gravel Co., 310
Sheldone v. Pennsylvania Tpk. Comm'n, 886
Shepard v. United States, 559
Sheppard v. Union Pac. R.R. Co., 172
Sherrod v. Berry, 270
Shonubi; United States v., 124
Shores; United States v., 201
Siddiqui; United States v., 193, 549
Simon v. G.D. Searle & Co., 841
Simon; United States v., 770
Simplex, Inc. v. Diversified Energy Sys., Inc., 261
Simpson; United States v., 193
Sims v. Charlotte Liberty Mut. Ins. Co., 857
Sinclair; United States v., 201
Sivils; United States v., 188
Skeddle; United States v., 526
Skeet; United States v., 619
Skidmore v. Precision Printing & Packaging, Inc., 661
Skipper; United States v., 175
Sliker; United States v., 206
Slovinski; People v., 316
Smith v. Ford Motor Co., 661
Smith v. Isuzu Motors Ltd., 537
Smith; State v., 845
Smith; United States v., 122 F.3d 1355, 629
Smith; United States v., 131 F.3d 685, 381
Smithers; United States v., 629
Socks-Brunot v. Hirschvogel Inc., 310
Sokolow; United States v., 532
Solem v. Helm, 723
Southern Ind. Gas & Elec. Co.; United States v., 576
Spaziano v. Florida, 733

Speaker v. County of San Bernadino, 869
Specht v. Jensen, 324
Special Fed. Grand Jury Empanelled Oct. 31, 1985 Impounded, In re, 471
Speese; State v., 872
Speiser v. Randall, 714
Spell v. McDaniel, 331
Sperling; United States v., 509
Spetzer; Commonwealth v., 846
Sphere Drake Ins. PLC v. Trisko, 663, 665
Spurlock v. Commissioner, 527
State v. *See name of opposing party*
Stein; United States v., 345
Steinberg v. Jensen, 857
Stephens v. Miller, 317
Stephens; United States v., 188
Stern; United States v., 345
Storm Plastics, Inc. v. United States, 769
Stotts; United States v., 486
Stuart v. Unum Life Ins. Co., 429
Sturman; United States v., 870
Subpoena Issued to Commodity Futures Trading Comm'n, In re, 885
Suburban Sew 'N Sweep v. Swiss-Bernina, 802, 804
Sullivan v. Louisiana, 762
Summers; United States v., 597, 598
Sumner; United States v., 300
Sutton; United States v., 390
Swidler & Berlin v. United States, 794

Tabaja; United States v., 498
Tahoe Nugget, Inc.; NLRB v., 758
Talley; United States v., 800
Tank; United States v., 193
Tarantino; United States v., 391
Taylor; United States v., 208
Tedder; United States v., 836
Texas Dep't of Cmty. Affairs v. Burdine, 755
Thirtyacre, In re, 768, 769, 770, 772
Thomas v. Kansas Power & Light Co., 777
Thomas; United States v., 768 F.2d 611, 360
Thomas; United States v., 167 F.3d 299, 643
Thomas; United States v., 321 F.3d 627, 249
Thompson; United States v., 189, 460
Threadgill v. Armstrong World Indus., Inc., 192
Toledo v. Medical Eng'g Corp., 677
Tollardo; State v., 185
Tome v. United States, 513 U.S. 150, 394, 462, 463
Tome; United States v., 61 F.3d 1446, 514, 576
Tornay v. United States, 823
Tracinda Corp. v. DaimlerChrysler AG, 205
Tracy; United States v., 216
Trammel v. United States, 791, 842, 848, 852, 853, 854
Tranowski; United States v., 628
Transportation Mgmt. Corp.; NLRB v., 758
Travelers Ins. Co. v. United States, 206
Tresnak, In re Marriage of, 780, 783
Troupin v. Metropolitan Life Ins. Co., 890
Trujillo; United States v., 463
Trull v. Volkswagen of Am., Inc., 325, 471
Turner v. Burlington N. Santa Fe R.R., 667
Turner v. United States, 760
Turning Bear; United States v., 151, 602

281 Syosset Woodbury Rd.; United States v., 843
Tyndall v. Harvey, 616

United Shoe Mach. Corp.; United States v., 809
United States v. *See name of opposing party*
United States, In re, 565 F.2d 19, 886
United States, In re, 872 F.2d 472, 892
University of Pa. v. EEOC, 889, 890
Upjohn Co. v. United States, 809, 810, 818, 819, 821, 840
Urbanik; United States v., 484
Urrego-Linares; United States v., 484
Usery v. Turner Elkhorn Mining Co., 745, 753, 755, 761

Vallejo; United States v., 159
Van der AA v. Commissioner, 530
Vanderbilt v. Town of Chilmark, 870
Vann v. Lone Star Steakhouse & Saloon of Springfield, Inc., 870
Vasconcellos v. Cybex Int'l, Inc., 871
Vaska v. State, 458
Vazquez v. National Car Rental Sys., Inc., 559
Vega; United States v., 564
Velez; United States v., 346
Verplank, In re, 877
Vicksburg & M.R.R. v. Putnam, 739
Victor v. Nebraska, 714, 715
Vining, Vining ex rel. v. Enterprise Fin. Group, 258
Vinson v. Humana, Inc., 870
Virgin Islands, Government of v. Albert, 189
von Bulow, In re, 819

Wagner v. Firestone Tire & Rubber Co., 376
Wagstaff v. Protective Apparel Corp., 477
Walker v. Horn, 376
Walker; United States v., 170, 576
Wall; Commonwealth v., 316
Ward v. Succession of Freeman, 793
Ward; United States v., 477
Warner v. Zent, 761
Washington v. Texas, 797
Watson; United States v., 284
Weaver; United States v., 477
Weil v. Investment/Indicators, Researchers & Mgmt., 793–794
Weil v. Seltzer, 261
Weinstock; United States v., 138
Welch; United States v., 188
Weller; United States v., 522
Wellons; United States v., 288
Wen Ho Lee; United States v., 894
Wesley; United States v., 381
West; United States v., 140
Westerbrook; United States v., 286
Westfield Ins. Co. v. Harris, 249
Westmoreland; United States v., 565
Weston-Smith v. Cooley Dickinson Hosp., Inc., 478
Wheeler v. John Deere Co., 269
Whitaker; United States v., 192
White v. Arn, 730
White v. Honeywell, Inc., 146

White v. Illinois, 583, 596
White; United States v., 571
Whitehead; United States v., 365
Whitmore; United States v., 365
Whitted v. General Motors Corp., 197
Wichita Land & Cattle Co. v. American Fed. Bank, F.S.B., 802
Wilkinson v. Carnival Cruise Lines, 480
Williams; United States v., 583 F.2d 1194, 632
Williams; United States v., 238 F.3d 871, 247
Williams; United States v., 85 Fed. Appx. 341, 180
Williams v. Virgin Islands, 513
Williamson v. United States, 565
Willingham v. Crooke, 514
Wilson v. City of Chicago, 381
Wilson; United States v., 344 F.2d 1208, 365
Wilson; United States v., 985 F.2d 348, 365, 376
Wilson v. Zapata Off-Shore Co., 513
Wimberly; United States v., 518
Winkfield v. American Cont'l Ins. Co., 747
Winship, In re, 713, 716, 717, 719, 720, 721, 723, 731, 732, 734, 735, 736, 741, 743, 744, 759, 760, 761, 762
Winters; United States v., 498
Witness Before the Special Grand Jury 2000-2, In re, 821
Witnesses Before the Special March 1980 Grand Jury Appeal of U.S., In re, 823
Wolak v. Spucci, 310
Wolfle v. United States, 844
Wood, In re Estate of, 747
Wood v. Bartholomew, 643
Woodruff; United States v., 801
Woolworth Corp. Sec. Class Action Litig., In re, 818
WorldCom, Inc. Sec. Litig., In re, 526, 527, 530
Wright; State v., 597
Wright v. Tatham, 443, 449, 450
Wright; United States v., 932 F.2d 868, 187
Wright; United States v., 363 F.3d 237, 576
Wright v. Willamette Indus., Inc., 691, 692
Wyatt v. United States, 851
Wynn v. State, 249

Yahweh; United States v., 144, 185
Yates v. Evatt, 762
Yazzie; United States v., 514
Yellow; United States v., 299
Yildiz; United States v., 482
Yoder Co., In re, 747
York; United States v., 247, 249
Young; United States v., 101, 391

Zackowitz; People v., 234, 244
Zackson; United States v., 245
Zenith Radio Corp. v. Matsushita Elec. Indus. Co., 662
Zenni; United States v., 445
Zeus Enters., Inc. v. Alphin Aircraft, Inc., 543
Ziegler v. Department of Fire, 857
Zolin; United States v., 824
Zuchowicz v. United States, 692
Zuckerbraun v. General Dynamics Corp., 892
Zuniga, In re, 791

Table of Authorities

Principal authorities are in italics.

Abrams, Addressing the Tension between the Clergy-Communicant Privilege and the Duty to Report Child Abuse in State Statutes, 44 B.C. L. Rev. 1127 (2003), 880

Aiken, Sexual Character Evidence in Civil Actions: Refining the Propensity Rule, 1997 Wis. L. Rev. 1221, 302, 305

Allen, The Evolution of the Hearsay Rule to a Rule of Admission, 76 Minn. L. Rev. 797 (1992), 605

————, Expertise and the *Daubert* Decision, 84 J. Crim. L. & Criminology 1157 (1994), 645

————, Factual Ambiguity and a Theory of Evidence, 88 Nw. U.L. Rev. 604 (1994), 161

————, Forward: *Montana v. Egelhoff* — Reflections on the Limits of Legislative Imagination and Judicial Authority, 87 J. Crim. L. & Criminology 633 (1997), 734–735

————, More on Constitutional Process-of-Proof Problems, 94 Harv. L. Rev. 1795 (1981), 740

————, The Myth of Conditional Relevancy, 25 Loy. L.A. L. Rev. 871 (1992), 221, 223

————, Presumptions, Inferences and Burden of Proof in Federal Civil Actions — An Anatomy of Unnecessary Ambiguity and a Proposal for Reform, 76 Nw. U.L. Rev. 892 (1982), 757

————, Structuring Jury Decisionmaking in Criminal Cases: A Unified Constitutional Approach to Evidentiary Devices, 94 Harv. L. Rev. 321 (1980), 741, 762

Allen & DeGrazia, The Constitutional Requirement of Proof Beyond Reasonable Doubt in Criminal Cases: A Comment Upon Incipient Chaos in Lower Courts, 20 Am. Crim. L. Rev. 1 (1982), 759

Allen & Hazelwood, Preserving the Confidentiality of Internal Corporate Investigations, 12 J. Corp. L. 355 (1987), 891

Allen et al., A Positive Theory of the Attorney-Client Privilege and the Work Product Doctrine, 19 J. Legal Stud. 359 (1990), 826, 842

Allen et al., The German Advantage in Civil Procedure: A Plea for More Details and Fewer Generalities in Comparative Scholarship, 82 Nw. U.L. Rev. 705 (1988), 78

American Psychiatric Association's Statement on the Insanity Defense (1982), 673

Andrews, The Admissibility of Other-Crimes Evidence in Acquaintance-Rape Prosecutions, 17 S. Ill. U.L.J. 341 (1993), 302, 303, 304

Annotation, Admissibility, in Negligence Action, of Absence of Other Accidents or Injuries, 10 A.L.R. 5th 371 (1993), 270

Ayala & Martyn, To Tell or Not To Tell? An Analysis of Testimonial Privileges: The Parent-Child and Reporter's Privileges, 9 St. John's J. Legal Comment 163 (1993), 884

Ball, The Moment of Truth: Probability Theory and Standards of Proof, 14 Vand. L. Rev. 807 (1961), 161

_____, The Myth of Conditional Relevancy, 14 Ga. L. Rev. 435 (1980), 124, 221

Beale, Prior Similar Acts in Prosecutions for Rape and Child Sex Abuse, 4 Crim. L.F. 307 (1993), 302

Beecher-Monas, The Heuristics of Intellectual Due Process: A Primer for Triers of Science, 75 N.Y.U. L. Rev. 1563 (2000), 692

_____, A Ray of Light for Judges Blinded by Science: Triers of Science and Intellectual Due Process, 33 Ga. L. Rev. 1047 (1999), 645

Bell, Decision Theory and Due Process: A Critique of the Supreme Court's Lawmaking for Burdens of Proof, 78 J. Crim. L. & Criminology 557 (1987), 705

Bergman & Moore, Mistrial by Likelihood Ratio: Bayesian Analysis Meets the F-Word, 13 Cardozo L. Rev. 589 (1991), 161–162

Binder, D.A., & Bergman, P., Fact Investigation (1984), 121

Bingham, C., & Gansler, L.L., Class Action: The Story of Lois Jenson and the Landmark Case That Changed Sexual Harassment Law (2002), 317

Black, A Unified Theory of Scientific Evidence, 56 Ford. L. Rev. 595 (1988), 636

Black et al., Science and the Law in the Wake of *Daubert*: A New Search for Scientific Knowledge, 72 Tex. L. Rev. 715 (1994), 645

Blackstone, Commentaries on the Laws of England (1768), 587

Blakely, Article IV: Relevancy and Its Limits, 30 Hous. L. Rev. 281 (1993), 142

Brownmiller, S., Against Our Will: Men, Women and Rape (1976), 312

Bryden & Lengnick, Rape in the Criminal Justice System, 87 J. Crim. L. & Criminology 1194 (1997), 304, 312

Bryden & Park, "Other Crimes" Evidence in Sex Offense Cases, 78 Minn. L. Rev. 529 (1992), 301, 304, 303

Bryom, The Use of the Excited Utterance Hearsay Exception in the Prosecution of Domestic Violence Cases After *Crawford v. Washington*, 23 Rev. of Litig. 209 (2005), 602

Callen, Foreword to the First Virtual Forum: Wallace Stevens, Blackbirds and the Hearsay Rule, 16 Miss. Col. L. Rev. 1 (1995), 606

_____, Hearsay and Informal Reasoning, 47 Vand. L. Rev. 43 (1994), 448, 449

_____, Notes on a Grand Illusion: Some Limits on the Use of Bayesian Theory in Evidence Law, 57 Ind. L.J. 1 (1982), 162

_____, Rationality and Relevance: Conditional Relevancy and Constrained Resources, 2003 Mich. St. L. Rev. 1243, 220, 223

Cammack, Using the Doctrine of Chances to Prove Actus Reus in Child Abuse and Acquaintance Rape: *People v. Ewoldt* Reconsidered, 29 U.C. Davis L. Rev. 355 (1996), 247

Campagnolo, The Conflict Between State Press Shield Laws and Federal Criminal Proceedings: the Rule 501 Blues, 38 Gonz. L. Rev. 445 (2002/03), 887

Carraway, Violence Against Women of Color, 43 Stan. L. Rev. 1301 (1991), 303, 312

Chayes, The Role of the Judge in Public Law Litigation, 89 Harv. L. Rev. 1281 (1976), 108

Cheng & Yoon, Does *Frye* or *Daubert* Matter? A Study of Scientific Admissibility Standards, 91 Va. L. Rev. 471 (2005), 645

Coate & Fischer, Can Post-Chicago Economics Survive *Daubert*?, 34 Akron L. Rev. 795 (2001), 645

Cohen, J.L., Freedom of Proof, in Facts in Law (Twining ed., 1983), 117

———, The Probable and the Provable (1977), 161

Comment, 78 Tul. L. Rev. 911 (2004), 509

Comment, Academic Researchers and the First Amendment: Constitutional Protection for Their Confidential Sources?, 14 San Diego L. Rev. 876 (1977), 889

Comment, Defining Standards for Determining the Admissibility of Evidence of Other Sex Offenses, 25 UCLA L. Rev. 261 (1977), 299

Comment, Parent-Child Privilege: Constitutional Right or Specious Analogy?, 3 U. Puget Sound L. Rev. 177 (1979), 882

Comment, The Psychotherapist-Client Testimonial Privilege: Defining the Professional Involved, 34 Emory L.J. 777 (1985), 882

Cordray, Evidence Rule 806 and the Problem of Impeaching the Nontestifying Declarant, 56 Ohio St. L.J. 495 (1995), 491

Crenshaw, Mapping the Margins: Intersectionality, Identity Politics, and Violence Against Women of Color, 43 Stan. L. Rev. 1241 (1991), 303, 312

Crews, The Memory Wars (1997), 676

Damaska, M., The Death of Legal Torture, 87 Yale L.J. 860 (1978), 117

———, Evidence Law Adrift (1997), 78

———, Evidentiary Barriers to Conviction and Two Models of Criminal Procedure, 121 U. Pa. L. Rev. 506 (1973), 78

———, The Faces of Justice and State Authority (1986), 78

Davis, K.C., Administrative Law Treatise (1958), 767

———, Judicial Notice, 1969 Law & The Soc. Order 513 (1969), 776

Davis, K.C., & Pierce, K., Jr., Administrative Law Treatise (3d ed. 1994), 778

Deason, Predictable Mediation Confidentiality in the U.S. Federal System 17 Ohio St. J. on Disp. Resol. 239 (2002), 886

Developments in the Law — Confronting the New Challenges of Scientific Evidence, 108 Harv. L. Rev. 1481 (1995), 645

Developments in the Law — Privileged Communications, 98 Harv. L. Rev. 1450 (1985), 788, 823, 844, 876, 884, 886

Devenport & Cutler, Eyewitness Identification Evidence: Evaluating Commonsense Evaluations, 3 Psy. Publ. Pol'y & L. 338 (1997), 629

Dodson, What Went Wrong with Federal Rule of Evidence 609: A Look at How Jurors Really Misuse Prior Conviction Evidence, 48 Drake L. Rev. 1 (1999), 382

Doob & Kirshenbaum, Some Empirical Evidence on the Effect of Sec. 12 of the Canada Evidence Act Upon the Accused, 15 Crim. L.Q. 88 (1972-1973), 382

Dorsen & Rezneck, *In Re Gault* and the Future of Juvenile Law, 1 Family Law Quarterly, No. 4 (1976), 714

Dreyfuss, Is Science a Special Case: The Admissibility of Scientific Evidence After *Daubert v. Merrell Dow*, 73 Tex. L. Rev. 1779 (1995), 645

Ellsworth, Are 12 Heads Better Than 1?, 38 Law Quadrangle Notes 56 (1995), 111

The Expert Witness Predicament: Determining "Reliable" Under the Gatekeeping Test of *Daubert, Kumho*, and Proposed Rule 702, 54 Miami L. Rev. 317 (2000), 645

Faigman, Mapping the Labyrinth of Scientific Evidence, 46 Hast. L.J. 555 (1995), 645

Finkelstein & Levin, Compositional Analysis of Bullet Lead As Forensic Evidence, 13 J.L. & Pol'y 119 (2005), 694

Finman, Implied Assertions as Hearsay: Some Criticisms of the Uniform Rules of Evidence, 14 Stan. L. Rev. 682 (1962), 438

Flint, Child Sexual Abuse Accommodation Syndrome: Admissibility Requirements, 23 Am. J. Crim. L. 171 (1995), 690

Fried, Too High a Price for Truth: The Exception to the Attorney-Client Privilege for Contemplated Crimes and Frauds, 64 N.C. L. Rev. 443 (1986), 820, 824

Friedman, Conditional Probative Value: Neoclassicism Without Myth, 93 Mich. L. Rev. 439 (1994), 221, 223

_____, The Confrontation Clause Re-Rooted and Transformed, 2004 CatoSCTR 439 (2004), 602

_____, A History of American Law (1973), 789

_____, Infinite Strands, Infinitesimally Thin: Storytelling, Bayesianism, Hearsay, and Other Evidence, 14 Cardozo L. Rev. 79 (1992), 162

_____, Route Analysis of Credibility and Hearsay, 96 Yale L.J. 667 (1987), 127

Friedman & McCormack, Dial-In Testimony, 150 U. Pa. L. Rev. 1171 (2002), 597

Galanek, The Impact of the *Zolin* Decision on the Crime-Fraud Exception to the Attorney-Client Privilege, 24 Ga. L. Rev. 1115 (1990), 824

Gardner, The State Secret Privilege Invoked in Civil Litigation: A Proposal for Statutory Relief, 29 Wake Forest L. Rev. 567 (1994), 894

Garland & Schmitz, Of Judges and Juries: A Proposed Revision of Federal Rule of Evidence 104, 23 U.C. Davis L. Rev. 77 (1989), 217, 475

Gee, Eyewitness Testimony and Cross-Racial Identification, 35 New Eng. L. Rev. 835 (2001), 629

Gianelli, Admissibility of Scientific Evidence, 28 Okla. City U. L. Rev. 1 (2003), 645

Gish, The Self-Critical Analysis Privilege and Environmental Audit Reports, 25 Envtl. L. 73 (1995), 892

Goodwin, The Hidden Significance of *Kumho Tire Co. v. Carmichael*: A Compass for Problems of Definition and Procedure Created by *Daubert v. Merrell Dow Pharmaceuticals, Inc.*, 52 Baylor L. Rev. 603 (2000), 645

Graham, "Stickperson Hearsay": A Simplified Approach to Understanding the Rule Against Hearsay, 1982 U. Ill. L. Rev. 887 (1982), 451

_____, There'll Always Be an England: The Instrumental Ideology of Evidence, 85 Mich. L. Rev. 1204 (1987), 133

Green, Deceit and Classification of Crimes: Federal Rule of Evidence 609(a)(2) and the Origins of Crimen Falsi, 90 J. Crim. L. & Criminology 1087 (2000), 376, 377

Greenwald et al., Testimonial Privileges (Trial Practice Series, 3d ed. 2005), 875, 879

Groscup et al., The Effects of *Daubert* on the Admissibility of Expert Testimony in State and Federal Criminal Cases, 8 Psychol. Pub. Pol'y & L. 339 (2002), 645

Gross, Expert Evidence, 1991 Wis. L. Rev. 1113, 625

_____, Make-Believe: The Rules Excluding Evidence of Character and Liability Insurance, 49 Hastings L.J. 843 (1998), 257

Groth et al., Undetected Recidivism Among Rapists and Child Molesters, 28 Crime & Delinq. 450 (1982), 303

Hale, M., History and Analysis of the Common Law of England (1713), 592

_____, Pleas of the Crown (1736), 587

Hand, Historical and Practical Considerations Regarding Expert Testimony, 15 Harv. L. Rev. 40 (1901), 647

Harding, Waiver: A Comprehensive Analysis of a Consequence of Inadvertently Producing Documents Protected by the Attorney-Client Privilege, 42 Cath. U. L. Rev. 465 (1993), 802

Harris, The Dangerous Patient Exception to the Psychotherapist-Patient Privilege: The Tarasoff Duty and the Jaffee Footnote, 74 Wash. L. Rev. 33 (1999), 873

Harrison, Reconceptualizing the Expert Witness: Social Cost, Current Controls and Proposed Responses, 18 Yale J. on Reg. 253 (2001), 645

Hart & McNaughton, Evidence and Inference in the Law, 87 Daedalus 40 (Fall 1958), 161

Hearings on Proposed Rules of Evidence Before the Special Subcommittee on Reform of Federal Criminal Laws of the House Committee on the Judiciary, 93d Cong. 1st Sess. 524 (1973), 809

Holdsworth, W., History of English Law (3d ed. 1944), 587

Horney & Spohn, Rape Law Reform and Instrumental Change in Six Urban Jurisdictions, 25 Law & Soc. Rev. 117 (1991), 303

Horrobin, The Philosophical Basis of Peer Review and the Suppression of Innovation, 263 J. Am. Med. Assn. 1438 (1990), 638

Hunter, Gender in Evidence, Masculine Norms vs. Feminist Reforms, 19 Harv. Women's L.J. 127 (1996), 133

Hurst, The Growth of American Law: The Lawmakers (1940), 738

Hutchins & Slesinger, Some Observations on the Law of Evidence: Spontaneous Exclamations, 28 Colum. L. Rev. 432 (1928), 496

Improving Judicial Gatekeeping: Technical Advisors and Scientific Evidence, 110 Harv. L. Rev. 941 (1997), 645

Imwinkelreid, E., Jr., Evidentiary Foundations (4th ed. 1998), 188

_____, Evidentiary Foundations (5th ed. 2002), 177

_____, The Meaning of "Facts or Data" in Federal Rule of Evidence 703: The Significance of the Supreme Court's Decision to Rely on Federal Rule 702 in *Daubert v. Merrell Dow Pharmaceuticals, Inc.*, 54 Md. L. Rev. 352 (1995), 645

_____, The Rivalry Between Truth and Privilege: The Weakness of the Supreme Court's
    Reasoning in *Jaffee v. Redmond*, 518 U.S. 1 (1996), 49 Hastings L.J. 969 (1998), 868
_____, A Small Contribution to the Debate Over the Proposed Legislation Abolishing the
    Character Evidence Prohibition in Sex Offense Prosecutions, 44 Syracuse L. Rev.
    1125 (1993), 295
_____, The Use of Evidence of an Accused's Uncharged Misconduct to Prove Mens Rea:
    The Doctrines that Threaten to Engulf the Character Evidence Prohibition, 130 Mil.
    L. Rev. 41 (1990), 247–248
Imwinkelried & Tobin, Comparative Bullet Lead Analysis (CBLA) Evidence: Valid
    Inference or Ipse Dixit?, 28 Okla. City U.L. Rev. 43 (2003), 694

James, F., Jr., Burden of Proof, 47 Va. L. Rev. 51 (1961), 703, 708, 711
James, et al., Civil Procedure (5th ed. 2001), 172
James, G.F., Relevancy, Probability and the Law, 29 Cal. L. Rev. 689 (1941), 128
Jardine, D., Criminal Trials (1832), 587
Jasanof, S., The Fifth Branch: Science Advisors as Policymakers (1990), 638
Jefferson, The Statutory Development of the Parent-Child Privilege: Congress Responds to
    Kenneth Starr's Tactics, 16 Ga. St. U. L. Rev. 429 (1999), 884
Jensen, Litigating the Crossroads Between Sweet Home and *Daubert*, 24 V. L. Rev. 169
    (2000), 645
Johnson, *Fausek v. White*: The Sixth Circuit Garners Support for a Good Cause Exception
    to the Attorney-Client Privilege, 18 Dayton L. Rev. 313 (1993), 794
Joseph, G.P., & Saltzburg, S.A., Evidence in America: The Federal Rules in the States
    (1987), 791
Joseph, A Simplified Approach to Computer-Generated Evidence and Animations, 43
    N.Y.L. Sch. L. Rev. 875 (1999-2000), 186

Kagehiro & Stanton, Legal v. Quantified Definitions of Standards of Proof, 9 Law & Hum.
    Behav. 159 (1985), 707
Kalven, H., Jr., & Zeisel, H., The American Jury (1966), 312, 382
Kaplan, Decision Theory and the Factfinding Process, 20 Stan. L. Rev. 1065 (1968), 161, 164
_____, Of Mabrus and Zorgs — An Essay in Honor of David Louisell, 66 Cal. L. Rev. 987
    (1978), 217
Kaplan & Cogan, The Case Against Recognition of a General Academic Privilege, 60 U.
    Det. J. Urb. L. 205 (1983), 889
Karp, Evidence of Propensity and Probability in Sex Offense Cases and Other Cases, 70
    Chi.-Kent L. Rev. 15 (1995), 297
Kassirer & Cecil, Inconsistency in Evidentiary Standards for Medical Testimony, 288
    JAMA 1382 (2002), 644
Kaye, Naked Statistical Evidence, 89 Yale L.J. 601 (1980), 162
*Kaye, D.H. & Sensabaugh, G.F., Jr., Reference Guide on DNA Evidence, Federal Judicial
    Center (2d ed. 2000)*, 678
Kedigh, Spoliation: To the Careless Go the Spoils, 67 U. Mo. (K.C.) L. Rev. 597 (1999),
    145
Kesan, An Autopsy of Scientific Evidence in a Post-*Daubert* World, 84 Geo. L.J. 1985
    (1996), 645
Kinports, Evidence Engendered, 1991 U. Ill. L. Rev. 413, 133

Kirst, Appellate Court Answers to the Confrontation Questions in *Lillvy v. Virginia*, 53 Syracuse L. Rev. 87 (2003), 593

Koons & Grant, Compositional Variation in Bullet Lead Manufacture, 47 J. Foren. Sci. 950 (2002), 695

Krafka, C. et al., Judge and Attorney Experiences, Practices, and Concerns Regarding Expert Testimony in Federal Civil Trials, Federal Judicial Center (2002), 626

Kuhns, The Propensity to Misunderstand the Character of Specific Acts Evidence, 66 Iowa L. Rev. 777 (1981), 253

Ladd, Techniques and Theory of Character Testimony, 24 Iowa L. Rev. 498 (1939), 284

LaFree, G.D., Rape and Criminal Justice: The Social Construction of Sexual Assault (1989), 303, 312

Lander & Budowle, DNA Fingerprinting Dispute Laid to Rest, 371 Nature 735 (1994), 631

Langbein, J., The German Advantage in Civil Procedure, 52 U. Chi. L. Rev. 823 (1985), 78

———, Torture and the Law of Proof: Europe and England in the Ancien Régime (1977), 117

Lauderdale, A New Trend in the Law of Privilege: The Federal Settlement Privilege and the Proper Use of Federal Rule of Evidence 501 for the Recognition of New Privileges, 35 U. Mem. L. Rev. 255 (2005), 885

Lee, R., Letter IV by the Federal Farmer (Oct. 15, 1787), 589

Leippe, The Case for Expert Testimony About Eyewitness Memory, 1 Psychol. Pub. Pol'y & L. 909 (1995), 629

Lempert, Modeling Relevance, 75 Mich. L. Rev. 1021 (1977), 161

Lempert, R.O. et al., A Modern Approach to Evidence (3d ed. 2000), 473–474

Leonard, Appellate Review of Evidentiary Rulings, 70 N.C. L. Rev. 1155 (1992), 367

———, Selected Rules of Limited Admissibility, The New Wigmore (1996), 341, 342

———, The Use of Character to Prove Conduct: Rationality and Catharsis in Evidence Law, 58 U. Colo. L. Rev. 1 (1987), 232 233

Lieberman & Arndt, Understanding the Limits of Limiting Instructions, 6 Psychol. Pub. Pol'y & L. 677 (2000), 143

Lilly, G.C., An Introduction to the Law of Evidence (3d ed. 1996), 748

Lininger, Prosecuting Batterers After *Crawford*, 91 Va. Law Review 747 (2005), 602

Loftus, E., Eyewitness Testimony (1996), 629

Lushing, Faces Without Features: The Surface Validity of Criminal Inference, 72 J. Crim. L. & Criminology 82 (1981), 759

Maguire & Epstein, Preliminary Questions of Fact in Determining the Admissibility of Evidence, 40 Harv. L. Rev. 392 (1927), 216

Marcus, The Perils of Privilege: Waiver and the Litigator, 84 Mich. L. Rev. 1605 (1986), 802

Marino & Marino, The Scientific Basis of Causality in Toxic Tort Cases, 21 Dayton L. Rev. 1 (Fall 1995), 691

McCormick, The Borderland of Hearsay, 39 Yale L.J. 489 (1930), 438

———, Charges on Presumptions and Burdens of Proof, 5 N.C. L. Rev. 291 (1972), 742

McCormick on Evidence (Broun et al., 5th ed. 1999), 822

McCormick on Evidence (Strong ed., 5th ed. 1999), 267, 299, 349, 379, 472, 520, 530, 557, 742, 753, 846

McCormick's Handbook on the Law of Evidence (Cleary ed., 3d ed. 1984), 407

McMillin, *University of Pennsylvania v. E.E.O.C.* and *Dixon v. Rutgers*: Two Supreme Courts Speak on the Academic Freedom Privilege, 42 Rutgers L. Rev. 1089 (1990), 890

McNaughton, Burden of Production of Evidence: A Function of a Burden of Persuasion, 68 Harv. L. Rev. 1382 (1955), 700

Mendez, *Crawford v. Washington*: A Critique, 57 Stan. L. Rev. 511 (2005), 602

_____, Essay: The Law of Evidence and the Search for Stable Personality, 45 Emory L.J. 221 (1996), 233

Milich, Hearsay Antinomies: The Case for Abolishing the Rule and Starting Over, 71 Ore. L. Rev. 723 (1992), 603, 606

_____, Re-Examining Hearsay Under the Federal Rules: Some Method for the Madness, 39 Kan. L. Rev. 893 (1991), 449, 451

Mogck, Are We There Yet? Refining the Test for Expert Testimony Through *Daubert*, *Kumho Tire* and Proposed Federal Rule of Evidence 702, 33 Conn. L. Rev. 303 (2000), 645

Morgan, Hearsay Dangers and the Application of the Hearsay Concept, 62 Harv. L. Rev. 177 (1957), 423, 438

Mosteller, Admissibility of Fruits of Breached Evidentiary Privileges: The Importance of Adversarial Fairness, Party Culpability, and Fear of Immunity, 81 Wash. U. L.Q. 962 (2003), 802

_____, Child Sexual Abuse and Statements for the Purpose of Medical Diagnosis or Treatment, 67 N.C. L. Rev. 257 (1989), 515

_____, *Crawford v. Washington*: Encouraging and Ensuring the Confrontation of Witnesses, 39 Univ. Richmond L. Rev. 511 (2005), 602

Mueller, C.B., & Kirkpatrick, L.C., Evidence (2d ed. 1999), 429

_____, Federal Evidence (2d ed. 1994), 326

Muldering, Wharton, Cecil, Tobacco Cases May Be Only the Tip of the Iceberg for Assaults on Privilege, 67 Def. Counsel J. 16 (2000), 819–820

Murphy, Spin Control and then High-Profile Client — Should the Attorney-Client privilege Extend to Communications with Public Relations Consultants?, 55 Syracuse L. Rev. 545 (2005), 800

Nance, Conditional Relevance Reinterpreted, 70 B.U. L. Rev. 447 (1990), 221

_____, Forward: Do We Really Want to Know the Defendant?, 70 Chi.-Kent L. Rev. 3 (1994), 297

Navigating Uncertainty: Gatekeeping in the Absence of Hard Science, 113 Harv. L. Rev. 1467 (2000), 645

Nesson, Rationality, Presumptions, and Judicial Comment: A Response to Professor Allen, 94 Harv. L. Rev. 1574 (1981), 740

North, *University of Pennsylvania v. E.E.O.C.*: The Denial of an Academic Freedom Privilege, 18 Pepp. L. Rev. 213 (1990), 890

Note, Did Your Eyes Deceive You? Expert Psychological Testimony on the Unreliability of Eyewitness Identification, 29 Stan. L. Rev. 969 (1977), 496

Note, Evidence — Privileged Communications — The Attorney-Client Privilege in the Corporate Setting: A Suggested Approach, 69 Mich. L. Rev. 360 (1970), 809

Note, Government Secret, Fair Trials, and the Classified Information Procedures Act, 98 Yale L.J. 427 (1988), 894

Note, Overriding the Psychologist-Patient Privilege in Child Custody Disputes: Are Anyone's Best Interest Being Served, 68 U.M. (K.C.) L. Rev. 169 (1999), 872–873

Note, Parent-Child Loyalty and Testimonial Privilege, 100 Harv. L. Rev. 910 (1987), 884

Note, Rule by Myth: The Social and Legal Dynamics Governing Alcohol-Related Acquaintance Rapes, 47 Stan. L. Rev. 115 (1994), 304

Note: Should the Federal Government Have an Attorney-Client Privilege?, 51 Fla. L. Rev. 695 (1999), 822

Note, To Take the Stand or Not to Take the Stand: The Dilemma of the Defendant with a Criminal Record, 4 Colum. J.L. & Soc. Probs. 215 (1968), 382

Office of Tech. Assessment, Genetic Witness: Forensic Uses of DNA Tests 59 (1990), 688

Orenstein, No Bad Men!: A Feminist Analysis of Character Evidence in Rape Trials, 49 Hastings L.J. 663 (1998), 304, 312

Orloff & Stedinger, A Framework for Evaluating the Preponderance of the Evidence Standard, 131 U. Pa. L. Rev. 1159 (1983), 712

Park, Character at the Crossroads, 49 Hast. L.J. 717 (1998), 303

_____, "I Didn't Tell Them Anything About You": Implied Assertions as Hearsay Under the Federal Rules of Evidence, 74 Minn. L. Rev. 783 (1990), 446, 449, 451

_____, McCormick on Evidence and the Concept of Hearsay: A Critical Analysis Followed by Suggestions to Law Teachers, 65 Minn. L. Rev. 423 (1981), 444

_____, A Subject Matter Approach to Hearsay Reform, 86 Mich. L. Rev. 51 (1987), 606, 607

Pennington & Hastie, A Cognitive Theory of Juror Decision Making: The Story Model, 13 Cardozo L. Rev. 519 (1991), 162

_____, Juror Decision-Making Models: The Generalization Gap, 89 Psychol. Bull. 246 (1981), 112

Pennod & Heuer, Tweaking Commonsense: Assessing Aids to Jury Decision Making, 3 Psychol. Pub. Pol'y & L. 259 (1997), 110

Perspectives on the Proposed Federal Rules of Evidence 413-415, 22 Ford. Urban L.J. 265 (1995), 295

Pineau, Date Rape: A Feminist Analysis, 8 Law & Phil. 217 (1989), 304, 312

Plausen, Dead Man's Privilege, Vince Foster and the Demise of Legal Ethics, 68 Fordham L. Rev. 807 (1999), 794

Popper, K., Conjectures and Refutations: The Growth of Scientific Knowledge (5th ed. 1989), 638

Price & Kelly, Junk Science in the Courtroom: Causes Effects and Controls, 19 Hamline L. Rev. 395 (1996), 645

Pudelski, The Constitutional Fate of Mandatory Reporting Statutes and the Clergy-Penitent Privilege in a Post-Smith World, 98 Nw. U. L. Rev. 703, 880

Raeder, Commentary: A Response to Professor Swift, 76 Minn. L. Rev. 507 (1992), 580

Randich et al., A Metallurgical Review of the Interpretation of Bullet Lead Compositional Analysis, 127 Foren. Sci. Int'l 174 (2000), 695

Rasking, D.C. et al., Modern Science Evidence: The Law and Science of Expert Testimony (Faigman, et al. eds., 2002 & Supp. 2003), 644

Reed, *Crawford v. Washington* and the Irretrievable Breakdown of a Union: Separating the Confrontation Clause from the Hearsay Rule, 56 S.C.L.Rev. 185 (2004), 602

Regan, Spousal Privilege and the Meaning of Marriage, 81 Va. L. Rev. 2045 (1995), 854

Reisinger, Court-Appointed Expert Panels: A Comparison of Two Models, 32 Ind. L. Rev. 225 (1998), 677

Risinger, Navigating Expert Reliability: Are Criminal Standards of Certainty Being Left on the Dock?, 64 Alb. L. Rev. 99 (2000), 689, 693

_____, Preliminary Thoughts on a Functional Taxonomy of Expertise for the Post-Kumho World, 31 Seton Hall L. Rev. 508 (2000), 631

Risinger et al., Exorcism of Ignorance as a Proxy for Rational Knowledge: The Lessons of Handwriting Identification "Expertise," 137 U. Pa. L. Rev. 731 (1988), 693

Roberts, Rape, Violence, and Women's Autonomy, 69 Chi.-Kent L. Rev. 359 (1993), 303, 313

Robertson & Vignaux, Probability — The Logic of Law, 13 Oxford J. of Legal Stud. 457 (1993), 162

Robins, Evidence at the Electronic Frontier: Introducing E-Mail at Trial in Commercial Litigation, 29 Rutgers Computer & Tech. L.J. 219 (2003), 193

Rosenthal, *State of New Jersey v. Margaret Kelly Michaels*: An Overview, 1 Psychol., Pub. Poly. & L. 246 (1995), 690

Ross, Does Diversity in Legal Scholarship Make a Difference?: A Look at the Laws of Rape, 100 Dick. L. Rev. 795 (1966), 312

St. Peter-Griffith, Abusing the Privilege: The Crime-Fraud Exception to Rule 501 of the Federal Rules of Evidence, 48 U. Miami L. Rev. 259 (1993), 824

Saks & Kidd, Human Information Processing and Adjudication: Trial by Heuristics, 15 Law & Socy. Rev. 123 (1980-1981), 133

Saltzburg, Standards of Proof and Preliminary Questions of Fact, 27 Stan. L. Rev. 271 (1975), 217

Saltzburg, S.A., Martin, M.M., & Capra, D.J., Federal Rules of Evidence Manual (5th ed. 1990), 877

_____, Federal Rules of Evidence Manual (7th ed. 1998), 211, 447, 448, 557, 766, 778

Sanders et al., Legal Perceptions of Science and Expert Knowledge, 8 Psychol. Pub. Pol'y & L. 139 (2002), 645

Sanders, J., Bendectin on Trial: A Study of Mass Tort Litigation (1998), 691

Scallen, Constitutional Dimensions of Hearsay Reform: Toward a Three-Dimensional Confrontation Clause, 76 Minn. L. Rev. 623 (1992), 607

Schaffner, Reconciling Attorney-Client Privilege with the Rules of Professional Conduct, 81 Ill. B.J. 410 (1993), 808

Scheutzow & Gillis, Confidentiality and Privilege of Peer Review Information: More Imagined Than Real, 7 J.L. & Health 169 (1992/1993), 890

Seidelson, Implied Assertions and Federal Rule of Evidence 801: A Quandry For Federal Courts, 24 Duq. L. Rev. 741 (1986), 449

Seigel, A Pragmatic Critique of Modern Evidence Scholarship, 88 Nw. U.L. Rev. 995 (1994), 133

_____, Rationalizing Hearsay: A Proposal for a Best Evidence Hearsay Rule, 72 B.U. L. Rev. 893 (1992), 603–604

Separating the Scientist's Wheat from the Charlatan's Chaff: Daubert's Role in Toxic Tort Litigation, Vol. 28, n.6 Environmental Law Rptr. 10293 (1998), 645

Seymore, Isn't It a Crime: Feminist Perspectives on Spousal Immunity and Spousal Violence, 90 N.W. L. Rev. 1032 (1996), 852, 854

Simon & Mahan, Quantifying Burdens of Proof, 5 Law & Soc. Rev. 319 (1971), 707

Sinnard & Young, Daubert's Gatekeeper: The Role of the District Judge in Admitting Expert Testimony, 68 Tul. L. Rev. 1457 (1994), 645–646

Slobogin, Doubts About Daubert: Psychiatric Anecdata as a Case Study, 57 Wash. & Lee L. Rev. 919 (2000), 690

Starrs, Frye v. United States Restructured and Revitalized: A Proposal to Amend Federal Evidence Rule 702, 26 Jurimetrics J. 249 (1986), 637

Stephen, J., History of the Criminal Law of England (1883), 587

Strier, The Road to Reform: Judges on Juries and Attorneys, 30 Loy. L.A. L. Rev. 1249 (1997), 110

Swift, Abolishing the Hearsay Rule, 75 Cal. L. Rev. 495 (1987), 605

———, A Foundation Fact Approach to Hearsay, 75 Cal. L. Rev. 1339 (1987), 606

Symposium, At the Daubert Gate: Managing and Measuring Expertise in an Age of Science, Specialization, and Speculation, 57 Wash. & Lee L. Rev. 661 (2000), 645

Symposium, Behavioral Science Evidence in the Wake of Daubert, 13 Behav. Sci. & L. 127 (1995), 646

Symposium, Crawford and Beyond, 70 Brooklyn L. Rev. 1 (2005), 602

Symposium, Evidence after the Death of Frye, 15 Cardozo L. Rev. 1745 (1994), 646

Symposium on Hearsay and Implied Assertions: How Would (or Should) the Supreme Court Decide the Kearley Case?, 16 Miss. Col. L. Rev. 1 (1995), 449

Symposium, Scientific and Technological Evidence, 43 Emory L.J. 853 (1994), 646

Tamanaha, A Critical Review of the Classified Information Procedures Act, 13 Am. J. Crim. L. 277 (1986), 894

Thayer, J.B., A Preliminary Treatise on Evidence at Common Law (1898), 118, 413, 747

Tiersma, Reforming the Language of Jury Instruction, 22 Hofstra L. Rev. 37 (1993), 143

Tobin, Comparative Bullet Lead Analysis: A Case Study In Flawed Forensics, 28 Champ. 12 (July 2004), 694

Tobin & Duerfeldt, How Probative Is Comparative Bullet Lead Analysis?, 17 Crim. Just. 26 (2002), 694–695

Torrey, When Will We Be Believed? Rape Myths and the Idea of a Fair Trial in Rape Prosecutions, 24 U.C. Davis L. Rev. 1013 (1991), 312

Trautman, Logical or Legal Relevancy — A Conflict in Theory, 5 Vand. L. Rev. 385 (1952), 128

Turner, Judicial Notice and Federal Rule of Evidence 201 — A Rule Ready for Change, 45 U. Pitt. L. Rev. 181 (1983), 776

Tversky & Kahneman, Judgment Under Uncertainty: Heuristics and Biases, 185 Science 1124 (1974), 133

Twining & Stein, Evidence and Proof, The International Library of Essays in Law and Legal Theory (1992), 161

Ward, C.A., Attitudes Toward Rape: Feminist and Social Psychological Perspectives (1995), 312

Warren, She's Gotta Have It Now: A Qualified Rape Crisis Counselor-Victim Privilege, 17
    Cardozo L. Rev. 141 (1995), 882
Weinstein, The Probative Force of Hearsay, 46 Iowa L. Rev. 331 (1961), 604
Weinstein, J.B., & Berger, M.A., Weinstein's Evidence (1982), 632
_____, Weinstein's Federal Evidence (McLaughlin ed., 2d ed. 1997), 791, 793, 796, 802,
    809
_____, Weinstein's Federal Evidence (McLaughlin ed., 2d ed. 2001), 122, 128
_____, Weinstein's Federal Evidence (McLaughlin ed., 2d ed. 2003), 448
_____, Weinstein's Federal Evidence (McLaughlin ed., 2d ed. 2005), 298
Wellborn, The Definition of Hearsay in the Federal Rules of Evidence, 61 Tex. L. Rev. 49
    (1982), 449
_____, Demeanor, 76 Cornell L. Rev. 1075 (1991), 419
Wells, & Motley, Reinforcing the Myth of the Crazed Rapist: A Feminist Critique of
    Recent Rape Legislation, 81 B.U. L. Rev. 127 (2001), 301, 304
Whitaker, The Priest-Penitent Privilege: Its Constitutionality and Doctrine, 13 Regent U.
    L. Rev. 145 (2000-2001), 875
Wigmore, J.H., Code of Evidence (3d ed. 1942), 138
_____, Evidence (1905), 840
_____, Evidence (2d ed. 1923), 587, 589, 591
_____, Evidence (Chadbourn rev., 1970), 95, 399, 401, 406
_____, Evidence (Chadbourn rev., 1978), 670
_____, Evidence (McNaughton rev., 1961), 788
_____, Evidence (Tillers rev., 1983), 122, 128
_____, Evidence in Trials at Common Law (3d ed. 1940), 122, 128
_____, Evidence in Trials at Common Law (Chadbourn ed., 1974), 419
_____, Evidence in Trials at Common Law (Tillers rev., 1983), 261
_____, A Treatise on the System of Evidence in Trials at Common Law 1697 (1904), 90
Wright, Instructions to the Jury: Summary Without Comment, 1954 Wash. U. L.Q. 177,
    737
Wright, C.A., & Graham, K.W., Jr., Federal Practice and Procedure (1980), 307
_____, Federal Practice and Procedure (1990), 777
_____, Federal Practice and Procedure (Supp. 2001), 295, 304, 307, 789
_____, Federal Practice and Procedure: Evidence (1977), 137, 789
_____, The Invasion of the Jury: Temperature of the War, 27 Temple L.Q. 137 (1953),
    737

Zacharias, Harmonizing Privilege and Confidentiality, 41 S. Tex. L. Rev. 69 (1999), 808

Index

A

Abuse of discretion, 149–151
Academic researcher's privilege, 888–889
Accomplices, corroboration requirement for
    statements inculpating, 565
Adjudicative facts, judicial notice
    defined, 766–767
    types of facts subject to judicial notice, 766
Admissibility. *See specific topic concerned*
Admissions by parties. *See* Party admissions, hearsay
    exemption
Adoptive admissions, hearsay exemption, 476–478
    preliminary fact-finding, 476–477
    rationale, 477
    silence, by, 477–478
Adversary system
    hearsay, regulation premised on excesses of
        adversary system, 606
    natural reasoning, 107–116
    reconsideration, 107–108
Adverse witnesses, direct examination of, 94–95
Advocates. *See* Attorneys
Affirmative defenses, burden of persuasion, 721–731
    after *Patterson*, 723–731
    elements test, 721
    political compromise test, 721–722
    Powell two-part test, 723
    proportionality test, 722–723
Agents, hearsay exemption for admissions. *See* Party
    admissions, hearsay exemption
Amnesia, burden of persuasion in civil cases, 710–711
Ancient documents, 192
Animations, authentication of exhibits by, 185–186
Appellate review, preservation of error for
    FRE 103, 98
        elaboration, 104–107
        interpretation and illustration, 98–99
    general rule, 98
    making record for, 105–106
        appeal of evidentiary rulings, 106
    standards of review, 106–107
Arrests
    examination of character witnesses regarding, 288
    examination of character witness regarding
        impeachment of witness by questions about
        arrests, charges, and findings, 365–366
    hearsay, 437–438
Assertive conduct. *See* Hearsay
Attorney-client privilege, 797–842
    Bentham-Kaplow-Shavell theory, 833–834
    communications
        attorney or representative, with, 798–800
        legal services, for purposes of, 800–801
    contingent claim theory, 828–832
    corporate clients, 808–821
        investigations of wrongdoing, 818–820
        Upjohn case, 810–817
    duty of confidentiality, 804–807
    Easterbrook theory, 839–840
    elements, 797–808
    exceptions, 822–826
        breach of duty, 822
        crime or fraud, communications in furtherance
        of, 819–820, 823–824
        document attested by attorney, 822
        fee information, 822–823
        identity of client, 822–823
    government clients, 821–822
    joint production theory, 837–839
    Model Rules of Professional Conduct, under, 805–
        806, 807–808
    Morgan theory, 832–833
    proposed Rule, 797–798
    reflection on, 826–840
    rights-based theories, 835–836
    scope, 801–802
    waiver of, 802, 818–819
    Wigmore theory, 834–835
    work product doctrine, 804–807, 818, 826–840
Attorneys
    attorney-client privilege. *See* Attorney-client privilege

role of, 79
work product doctrine, 804–807, 818, 826–840
Authentication, 173–198
    ancient documents, 192
    animations, by, 185–186
    chain of custody, 180–182
    computer-generated and recorded evidence,
        185–187
    demonstrative exhibits, 184–185
        assisting trier of fact, 184
        FRE 403 balancing test, applicability, 184–185
    electronic data, 192–193
    FRE 901, 173–174
        elaboration, 178–195
        flexibility of, 195
        interpretation and illustration, 174–178
    general rule, 173–174
    in-court demonstrations and experiments, by, 185
    judicial determination of sufficiency of evidence to
        support finding, 176–177
    laying foundation, 177–178
    production of sufficient evidence to support
        finding, 175–176
    readily identifiable characteristic for identification,
        179–180
    real evidence, 179–184
    reconstructions of events, by, 185–186
    recordings, 187–191
        FRE 403 balancing test, applicability, 189
        percipient witnesses, 187–188
        "silent" witnesses, 188–189
    reenactments, by, 185–186
    self-authentication, 195–198
        FRE 902, 195–196
        general rule, 195–196
        interpretation and illustration, 197–198
    simulations to establish, 185–186
    sufficient evidence to support finding, 175–177
    what exhibit is claimed to be, 174–175
    written documents, 191–195
        ancient documents, 192
        contents, 191–192
        electronic writings, 192–193
        signatures, 191

B

Bad acts evidence. *See* Specific acts evidence
Bayes' Theorem, 161–164
Behavioral sciences, expert witnesses, 689–690
Bench trials, 79
Best evidence rule, 198–213
    defamation actions, 204
    definitions, 198–199
    duplicates, 199
    FRE 1001, 198–199
    FRE 1002, 199
        elaboration, 205–206
        interpretation and illustration, 200
    FRE 1003, 199
        interpretation and illustration, 200–201
    FRE 1004, 199
        interpretation and illustration, 201–202
    FRE 1005, 199
    FRE 1006, 199–200

elaboration, 207–208
    interpretation and illustration, 202
FRE 1007, 200
FRE 1008, 210
    interpretation and illustration, 210–213
general rule, 199
other evidence of contents, 199
public records, 199
role of court and jury, 210
Seiler case, 202–204
summaries, 199–200, 207–208
    analytic summaries, 207–208
    illustrative aids, 207
    voluminous documents underlying summaries,
        207
testimony, 200
underlying policies, 202–205
writing offered to prove its own content, 205–206
written admissions, 200
Bias and prejudice
character evidence
    distinguished, 400–401
    prohibition on use of to prove conduct on
        particular occasion, 233–234
child molestation evidence, 302
conviction of crime, impeachment of witnesses by,
    380
    balancing tests, 374
extrinsic evidence, 399–400
impeachment of witnesses by. *See* Impeachment of
    witnesses
probative value, 138–139
sexual assault evidence, 302
specific acts evidence
    prohibition on use of to prove conduct on
        particular occasion, 233–234
    relevant acts with no character inference,
        admissibility, 240–241
stereotypes, 123
Bifurcated trials, 81
Burden of persuasion
affirmative defenses in criminal cases, 721–731
    after *Patterson*, 723–731
    elements test, 721
    political compromise test, 721–722
    Powell two-part test, 723
    proportionality test, 722–723
allocation in civil cases, 707–710, 711–712
amnesia, 710–711
burden of production, relationship with, 699–701
business records, exclusion for untrustworthiness,
    529
civil cases, 703–712
clear and convincing evidence standard in civil
    cases, 698, 704
criminal cases, 713–735
explicit shifts in criminal cases, 716–735
"extreme emotional distress" defense in criminal
    cases, 718–719
"heat of passion" defense in criminal cases,
    716–717
higher burdens in civil cases, 706–707
judicial summary and comment on evidence,
    relationship with, 742–743
jury instructions, 85–86

manslaughter, 719
mitigating factors in criminal cases, 720–721
Mullaney case, 716–717
Patterson case, 718–719
    affirmative defenses after, 723–731
preponderance of evidence standard in civil cases, 698, 704–706, 707, 711
presumptions, 745
reasonable doubt, proof beyond in criminal cases, 713–716
    defined, 714–715
    Due Process, 714, 719–720
    jury instructions, 715–716
relative nature of in civil cases, 707
role of in civil cases, 704
Winship rule, 713–716
    application in other contexts, 731–735
Burden of production
    allocation in civil cases, 702–703
    burden of persuasion, relationship with, 699–701
    civil cases, 699–703
    criminal cases, 735–736
    procedural mechanisms for enforcement in civil cases, 702
    rationale, 699
    role of in civil cases, 699
Burden of proof
    burden of persuasion. *See* Burden of persuasion
    burden of production. *See* Burden of production
Business records, hearsay exception, 524–535
    business duty, made pursuant to, 526–527
    computer documents, 532–533
    custodians, 527–528
    diagnoses, 530
    electronic data, 532–533
    FRE 803, 524–525
        elaboration, 528–533
        interpretation and illustration, 524–528
    general rule, 524–525
    multiple hearsay, 531–532
        sources of information with no business duty, 531–532
        use of multiple exemptions and exceptions, 532
    near contemporaneity requirement, 526
    opinions, 530
    personal knowledge requirement, 526
    preliminary fact-finding, 525–528
    qualified witnesses, 527–528
    rationale, 528
    untrustworthiness, exclusion for, 529–530
        burden of persuasion, 529
        circumstances indicating, 529–530
    what constitutes business record, 525–526

C

Character evidence, 227–320. *See also* Reputation evidence
    arrests, examination of character witnesses regarding, 288
    child molestation evidence. *See* Child molestation evidence
    cross-examination of character witnesses. *See* Cross-examination
    defined, 228
    distinction between prohibited and permissible evidence, 251–254
    essential element of claim or defense, character as, 291–295
        defamation actions, 293–294
        general rule, 292–293
    exceptions to prohibition on use of to prove conduct on particular occasion, 234, 273–291
        civil cases, 279–280
        conduct of victim, attacks on, 274–275
        defendant "opening the door" to character evidence, 273–274
        pertinence requirement, 275
        prosecution response, 274
        rationale, 276–279
        relevancy, 276
        witnesses, character of, 275–276
    FRE 404, 230
        elaboration, 232–235
        exceptions to prohibition on use of to prove conduct on particular occasion, 273–276, 276–280
        interpretation and illustration, 230–232
        methods of proving, 280–281, 283–290
    FRE 405, 230
        elaboration, 292–294
        interpretation and illustration, 292
        methods of proving, 280–281, 283–290
    general rule, 230
    habit evidence. *See* Habit evidence
    impeachment of witnesses by. *See* Impeachment of witnesses
    inherent weakness of, 289
    limitations on use, 289–290
    methods of proving, 230, 283–290
        opinion evidence, probative value, 283–284
        opinion evidence and reputation evidence distinguished, 284–285
        reputation evidence, probative value, 283–284
        specific acts, prohibition on use, 283
    past sexual behavior evidence. *See* Past sexual behavior evidence
    potential unfairness, 289–290
    prohibition on use of to prove conduct on particular occasion, 230–236
        diversion from main issues, 233
        general rule, 230
        low probative value, 233
        prejudice, 233–234
        rationale, 232–234
        weakness of propensity inference, 232–233
    reflection on, 251–257
    relevancy, 227–229
        exceptions to prohibition on use of to prove conduct on particular occasion, 276
    routine practice evidence. *See* Routine practice evidence
    sexual assault evidence. *See* Sexual assault evidence
    similar happenings evidence. *See* Similar happenings evidence
    specific acts evidence
        prohibition on use of to prove character, 283
        relevance to cross-examination of character witnesses, 285–286

Child abuse
    hearsay and Confrontation Clause, 601–602
Child molestation evidence, 295–306
    character evidence, 296–297, 299–302
    closing arguments, 299
    federal litigation, significance to, 304–305
    FRE 403 balancing test, applicability, 297,
        299–302
    FRE 413 to 415, 296
        elaboration, 299–305
        interpretation and illustration, 296–299
    general rules, 296
    limiting instructions, 299
    other Federal Rules of Evidence, 297–298
    preliminary fact-finding, 298
    probative value, 302–304
    rationale, 302–304
    recidivism, 302–303
    unfair prejudice, 302
Circumstantial evidence distinguished from direct
        evidence, 124–126
Civil cases
    burden of persuasion. See Burden of persuasion
    burden of production. See Burden of production
    hearsay
        need for, 605–606
        notice-based admission, proposal for, 606
    judicial notice
        mini-directed verdicts, 771
        verdicts, to preserve, 772
Clear and convincing evidence standard, 698,
        704
Clergy-communicant privilege, 875–881
    exceptions, 879–880
    expectation of confidentiality, 878–879
    holders, 877
    nature of communications, 878
    rationale, 876
    scope, 876–877
Closing arguments
    child molestation evidence, 299
    sample case, 65–75
    sexual assault evidence, 299
    specific acts evidence, 256–257
Co-conspirators, hearsay exemption for, 482–487
Communications privileges. See Privileges
Competency of witnesses, 168–173
    FRE 601, 168
        elaboration, 169–171
        interpretation and illustration, 168–169
    FRE 602, 171
        interpretation and illustration, 171–172
    general rule, 168
    mental competency, 169–171
    personal knowledge requirement, 171
    sufficient evidence to support finding, 171–172
Compromise, admissibility of offers, 329–335
    attempt to resolve disputed claim requirement,
        332–333
    criminal cases, 333–334
    discovery, 332
    exclusionary mandate, 330–331, 341–342
    FRE 403 balancing test, applicability, 330–331
    FRE 408, 329–330
        elaboration, 335

    interpretation and illustration, 330–335
    general rule, 329–330
    negotiations, conduct or statements made during,
        331–332
    party's own offer, 334
    permissible uses of, 330–331
    reflections on, 342–343
    third persons, by, 334–335
Computer documents and business records
        exception, 532–533
Computer-generated and recorded evidence,
        authentication, 185–187
Conclusive presumptions, 745–746
Conditional admissibility, 218–225
    application to conditional facts, 223
    FRE 104
        elaboration, 221–222
        interpretation and illustration, 218–219
Conditional relevancy, 218–225
    application to conditional facts, 223
    FRE 104, elaboration, 221–222
    "sufficiency" standard, 219–221
Confidential information. See Privileges
Confrontation Clause
    hearsay, 582–603
        child abuse, 601–602
        child witnesses, 602
        Crawford case, 584–595
        domestic violence, 601–602
        dying declarations, 600
        exceptions, 600–601
        exemptions and exceptions, 454–455
        firmly rooted exceptions, 583
        "forfeiture by wrongdoing," 600–601
        non-firmly rooted exceptions, 583–584
        non-testimonial statements, 598, 601
        Roberts case, 582–584
    past sexual behavior evidence, 313–316
    privileges, 797
    testimonial statements
        declarant testifying, 598–599
        defined, 595–598
        formalized testimonial material, 596
        prior opportunity for cross-examination,
            599–600
        reasonable person realizing used in investigation
            or prosecution of crime, 597–598
        satisfying confrontation right, 598–600
        unavailability, 599
Confusion of issues, probative value, 139
Constitutional rights
    Confrontation Clause. See Confrontation Clause
    cross-examination, past sexual behavior evidence,
        313–316
    Due Process, proof beyond reasonable doubt in
        criminal cases, 714, 719–720
    Fifth Amendment
        impeachment of witnesses by character
            evidence, waiver of Fifth Amendment rights,
            363–364
        party admissions, Constitutional concerns with,
            473
    hearsay exemption for prior statements of
        identification, Constitutional concerns with,
        466–467

presenting evidence, past sexual behavior evidence, 313–316

self-incrimination, Constitutional concerns with party admissions, 473

Contingent claim theory, attorney-client privilege, 828–832

Contradiction, impeachment of witnesses by. *See* Impeachment of witnesses

Convictions

    impeachment of witnesses by. *See* Impeachment of witnesses

    judgments of previous convictions, hearsay exception. *See* Judgments of previous convictions, hearsay exception

    probative value of prior felonies, 158

Corporate clients

    attorney-client privilege, 808–821

    investigations of wrongdoing, 818–820

Corroboration

    residual hearsay exception, independent corroboration, 577

    statements against interest exception, required for, 563–565

    statements inculpating accomplices, 565

Counsel. *See* Attorneys

    attorney-client privilege. *See* Attorney-client privilege

Court-appointed experts, 675–678

    FRE 706, 675–676

        interpretation and illustration, 676–678

    general rule, 675–676

Criminal cases

    burden of persuasion. *See* Burden of persuasion

    burden of production, 735–736

    guilty pleas, admissibility of withdrawal. *See* Withdrawn pleas, admissibility

    hearsay, different treatment of, 607

    judicial notice, 772–774

    no contest pleas, admissibility of withdrawal. *See* Withdrawn pleas, admissibility

    offers of compromise, 333–334

    "other sexual behavior," admissibility, 311–312

    presumptions, 759–762

    reasonable doubt standard. *See* Burden of persuasion

    "sexual predisposition," admissibility, 311–312

Cross-examination

    character witnesses, 285–289

        acts, arrests, and convictions, 288

        form of questions, 288–289

        likely knowledge of specific act, 287

        prejudicial impact of specific acts inquiries, 286

        reasonable belief that act occurred, 287–288

        relationship between character and specific acts inquiries, 286

        relevance of specific acts inquiries, 285–286

    expert witnesses, 660–662

    FRE 611

        elaboration, 92–94

        interpretation of, 90–91

    goals, 93

    hearsay exemptions, witnesses subject to cross-examination, 456–459

        denial of prior statement, 457

        inability to remember prior statement, 457

        inability to remember underlying events, 457–458

        personal knowledge requirement, 459

        preliminary fact-finding, 456–459

        statement, examination concerning, 456–457

        testimony by declarant, 456

    impeachment of witnesses by specific instances of conduct, 368

    leading questions. *See* Leading questions

    nonassertive conduct, importance to, 436–437

    past sexual behavior evidence and Constitutional right to, 313–316

    prior inconsistent statements. *See* Prior inconsistent statements, hearsay exemption

    recross-examination

        FRE 611, 91

        sample case, 30–31

    rehabilitation by, 394–396, 459

    sample case, 15–19, 23–25, 28–29, 34–35, 43–47, 49–50, 55–57, 60–61

    scope, 90–91

    strategy, 93

    techniques, 93–94

Culpability

    liability insurance. *See* Liability insurance, inadmissibility to prove negligence

    offers of compromise. *See* Compromise, admissibility of offers

    payment of medical expenses. *See* Medical expenses, admissibility of payment

    subsequent remedial measures. *See* Subsequent remedial measures, admissibility

Cumulative evidence, probative value, 140–141

Curative admissibility doctrine, 348–351

D

Declarants. *See* Hearsay

Declarations against interest. *See* Statements against interest, hearsay exception

Defamation actions

    best evidence rule, 204

    character as essential element of claim or defense, 293–294

Deliberative process privilege, 896–899

Demonstrative evidence, probative value, 144–145

Demonstrative exhibits, authentication, 184–185

    assisting trier of fact, 184

    FRE 403 balancing test, applicability, 184–185

Directed verdicts, 83

Direct evidence distinguished from circumstantial evidence, 124–126

Direct examination

    adverse witnesses, 94–95

    FRE 611

        elaboration, 91–92

        interpretation and illustration, 89–90

    hostile witnesses, 94–95

    redirect examination

        FRE 611, 91

        sample case, 19–20, 29–30, 50, 57–58

    sample case, 7–15, 20–23, 25–28, 31–34, 35–36, 40–43, 47–49, 51–54

Discretion of court. *See* Judicial discretion

Dismissal motions, 83

    sample case, 37–38

DNA profiling, expert witnesses, 678–689
Domestic violence, hearsay and Confrontation
    Clause, 601–602
Drinking
    habit evidence, 262
    lay opinion, 612
Due Process, proof beyond reasonable doubt in
    criminal cases, 714, 719–720
Duplicates, best evidence rule, 199
Dying declarations, hearsay exception, 559–560
    Confrontation Clause, 600
    FRE 804, 559
        interpretation and illustration, 559–560
    general rule, 559
    preliminary fact-finding, 559–560
    rationale, 560

E

Electronic data
    authentication, 192–193
    business records exception, 532–533
Employees, hearsay exemption for. See Party
    admissions, hearsay exemption
Examination of witnesses, 88–97
    breadth of court's power, 89
    cross-examination. See Cross-examination
    direct examination. See Direct examination
    FRE 611, 89
        elaboration, 91–95
        interpretation and illustration, 89–91
    leading questions. See Leading questions
    recross-examination. See Recross-examination
    redirect examination. See Redirect examination
Exceptions to hearsay rule. See specific exception
    concerned
Excited utterances, hearsay exception, 494–502
    categorical approach, 496–500
        categories determining admissibility, 496–497
        judicial interpretation, 497–499
        preliminary fact-finding, 499–500
        proof of personal knowledge, 500
    FRE 803, 494
        elaboration, 496–500
        interpretation and illustration, 494–496
    general rule, 494
    preliminary fact-finding, 495
        categorical approach, 499–500
    rationale, 495–496
Exclusionary rule, 160–161
Executive privilege, 892–899
Exhibits
    authentication. See Authentication
    defined, 173
Expert witnesses, 625–696
    assisting trier of fact, 628–629
    basis of opinion testimony, 662–670
        general rule, 662
        otherwise inadmissible evidence, 664–668
    behavioral sciences, 689–690
    cases in which used, 626
    conflicts between, 626
    court-appointed experts, 675–678
        FRE 706, 675–676
        general rule, 675–676

cross-examination, 660–662
disclosure of facts underlying opinion, 660–662
    general rule, 660
DNA profiling, 678–689
FRE 403 balancing test, applicability, 630–631
FRE 702, 628
    elaboration, 631–654
    interpretation and illustration, 628–631
FRE 703, 662
    elaboration, 664–668
    interpretation and illustration, 662–664
FRE 705, 660
    interpretation and illustration, 660–662
frequency of use, 625
general rule, 628
law enforcement investigative tools, 692–695
learned treatises, use of, 664
litigation incentives, 630–631
patients' statements as basis of expert opinion, 515–
    516
psychological sciences, 689–690
qualification, 629–630
scientific, technical, or other specialized
    knowledge. See also Scientific evidence and
    expert witnesses
    Daubert case, 633–646, 654–660
    Frye case, 631–633
    general rule, 628
    Kumho Tire case, 646–650
specialties, 625–626
summary witnesses, 631
syndrome evidence, 689–690
testimonial experience, 626
toxic tort causation, 690–692
translations, 654
treatises, use of, 664
ultimate issue, opinion on, 670–675
    FRE 704, 670
    general rule, 670
"Extreme emotional distress" defense, burden of
    persuasion, 718–719
Extrinsic evidence
    prejudice, 399–400
Extrinsic evidence, impeachment of witnesses by. See
    Impeachment of witnesses

F

Fact-finding
    judicial fact-finding. See Judicial fact-finding
    juries. See Juries
    preliminary fact-finding. See Preliminary fact-
        finding
Family history, hearsay exception for. See Personal or
    family history, hearsay exception for
    statements of
Federal Rules of Evidence (FRE). See also specific
    topic concerned
    rationale, 109–110
Fifth Amendment
    impeachment of witnesses by character evidence,
        waiver of rights, 363–364
    party admissions, constitutional concerns with, 473
"Fighting fire with fire" doctrine, 348–351
Firsthand knowledge rule, 423–424

"Forfeiture by wrongdoing," 569–574
  acquiescence in wrongdoing, 572
  Confrontation Clause and, 600–601
  content of statement, 571
  declarant as witness, 570
  FRE 403 balancing test, applicability, 572–573
  FRE 804, 569
  general rule, 569
  hearing requirement, 573
  intent to procure unavailability of declarant, 570–571
  preliminary fact-finding, 570–571
  procuring unavailability of declarant, 570
  rationale, 571–572
Former testimony, hearsay exception, 551–559
  FRE 804, 551
    elaboration, 553–557
    interpretation and illustration, 551–553
  general rule, 551
  identity of parties, 554
  method of introducing, 557
  not party to original action, offered against, 554–555
  objections, 557
  "offered on same issue" requirement, 552–553
  opportunity to develop testimony, 553–554
    no opportunity, 552
    same party or predecessor in interest, 551
    similar motive, 551–552
  predecessors in interest
    defined, 555
    opportunity to develop testimony, 551
  preliminary fact-finding, 551
  rationale, 553
  similar motive
    lack of due to difference in procedural context, 556–557
    opportunity to develop testimony, 551–552
Foundation for proof
  authentication. *See* Authentication
  best evidence rule. *See* Best evidence rule
  competency. *See* Competency of witnesses
  conditional admissibility. *See* Conditional admissibility
  conditional relevancy. *See* Conditional relevancy
  judicial fact-finding. *See* Judicial fact-finding
  witnesses. *See* Competency of witnesses
Fraud exception to attorney-client privilege, 819–820, 823–824

G

Government clients and attorney-client privilege, 821–822
Government informant's privilege, 886
Government privileges, 892–899
Guilty pleas, admissibility of withdrawal. *See* Withdrawn pleas, admissibility

H

Habit evidence, 257–266
  character distinguished, 259
    application of distinction, 262
    drinking, 262
    strategy, 261–262

  defined, 229
  FRE 406, 257
    elaboration, 260–264
    interpretation and illustration, 257–260
  general rule, 257
  importance, 258
  judicial fact-finding, 260
  methods of proving, 258–259
  organizational behavior, 262–264
  rationale, 260–261
  similar happenings distinguished, 267–268
Harmless error, 106–107, 158, 161
Hearsay, 413–607
  abolition, proposal for, 605
  accomplices, corroboration requirement for statements inculpating, 565
  acknowledgment of fault as, 341
  adoptive admissions exemption, 476–478
    preliminary fact-finding, 476–477
    rationale, 477
    silence, by, 477–478
  agents, exemption for admissions. *See* Party admissions, hearsay exemption
  arrests, 437–438
  assertive vs. nonassertive conduct, 434–440
    ambiguity, danger of, 436
    cross-examination, importance of, 436–437
    difficulty of classification, 436
    disguised assertions, 437–438
    exclusion of nonassertive conduct, 436–437
    lack of hearsay dangers, 434–435
    necessity, 435–436
    nonverbal conduct, 433–434
  business records exception. *See* Business records, hearsay exception
  civil cases
    need for, 605–606
    notice-based admission, proposal for, 606
  co-conspirators, exemption for admissions. *See* Party admissions, hearsay exemption
  Confrontation Clause. *See* Confrontation Clause
  criminal cases, different treatment in, 607
  criticisms of rule, 603–607
  cross-examination, witnesses subject to. *See* Cross-examination
  declarants, witnesses distinguished, 418–420
  defined, 414
  dying declarations exception. *See* Dying declarations, hearsay exception
  employees, exemption for admissions. *See* Party admissions, hearsay exemption
  exceptions. *See also specific exception concerned*
    approach to admissibility under, 452–455
    categorical approach, 453
    Confrontation Clause, 454–455
    foundational requirements, 453–454
    multiple exemptions and exceptions, 454
    process of admission, 453
    rationale, 452–453
  excesses of adversary system, regulation premised on, 606
  excited utterances exception. *See* Excited utterances, hearsay exception
  exemptions, 455–490. *See also* specific exemption concerned

approach to admissibility under, 452–455
categorical approach, 453
Confrontation Clause, 454–455
cross-examination, witnesses subject to. *See*
    Cross-examination
foundational requirements, 453–454
FRE 801, 455–456
multiple exemptions and exceptions, 454
process of admission, 453
rationale, 452–453, 459
family history, exception for statements of. *See*
    Personal or family history, hearsay exception
    for statements of
firsthand knowledge rule, 423–424
"forfeiture by wrongdoing." *See* "Forfeiture by
    wrongdoing"
former testimony exception. *See* Former testimony,
    hearsay exception
FRE 801, 414
    assertive vs. nonassertive conduct, 434–438
    elaboration, 421–424
    intent test, 445–448
    interpretation and illustration, 414–420
    nonhearsay statements, 425–430
    nonverbal conduct, 432–434
    revision, proposal for, 450–452
FRE 802, 414
    elaboration, 421–424
    interpretation and illustration, 414–420
general rule, 414
identification, exemption for prior statements of.
    See Identification, hearsay exemption for prior
    statements of
impeachment of witnesses by conviction of crime,
    381–382
implications, 421–424
intent test, 445–450
    burden of proof, 447–448
    common law approach, continued adherence to,
        448
    factual uncertainty, 447
    literal approach, rejection, 445–448
    nonverbal conduct, 434
    sincerity risk, identifying, 446–448
    unstated beliefs, intent to assert, 445–446
    what kind of intent, 446–447
against interest. *See* Statements against interest,
    hearsay exception
interest, exception for statements against. *See*
    Statements against interest, hearsay
    exception
judgments of previous convictions exception. *See*
    Judgments of previous convictions, hearsay
    exception
judicial discretion, proposal for, 604–605
lay opinion, 423–424
learned treatises, 493
medical diagnosis or treatment, exception for
    statements made for. *See* Medical diagnosis or
    treatment, hearsay exception for statements
    made for
multiple hearsay. *See* Multiple hearsay
nonhearsay statements, 425–432
    effect on listener, 427–428
    identifying nonhearsay uses, 429

legally operative facts, 428–429
    statements relevant for both hearsay and
        nonhearsay uses, 429–430
    uses of, 425–429
nonverbal conduct, 432–434
    assertive conduct, 433
    intent test, 434
    nonassertive conduct, 433–434
    relevancy, 432–433
out-of-court statements, testimony about, 423
party admissions exemption. *See* Party admissions,
    hearsay exemption
past recollections recorded exception. *See* Past
    recollections recorded, hearsay exception
personal or family history, exception for statements
    of. *See* Personal or family history, hearsay
    exception for statements of
present recollections refreshed, 521–523
    FRE 612, 522–523
present sense impressions exception. *See* Present
    sense impressions, hearsay exception
prior consistent statements exemption. *See* Prior
    consistent statements, hearsay exemption
prior inconsistent statements exemption. *See* Prior
    inconsistent statements, hearsay exemption
public records and reports exception. *See* Public
    records and reports, hearsay exception
rationale, 603
reflection on, 450–452, 603–607
reformulation of policy, proposal for, 605–607
relevancy, 415, 417–418
reliability, criticism of as rationale, 603–604
residual exception. *See* Residual hearsay exception
servants, exemption for admissions. *See* Party
    admissions, hearsay exemption
statements against interest exception. *See*
    Statements against interest, hearsay exception
state-of-mind declarations exception. *See* State-of-
    mind declarations, hearsay exception
testimonial dangers, 415–417
truth that statement is offered to prove, 421–423
unavailability of declarant
    caused by proponent, 550
    exceptions not requiring, 490–546. *See also*
        specific exception concerned
    exceptions requiring, 547–574. *See also* specific
        exception concerned
    FRE 803, 491–493
    FRE 804, 547–548
    grounds for finding, 548–553
    other exceptions, 543
    preference for former testimony or deposition,
        549
    preliminary fact-finding, 548–549
    reasonable means to procure attendance,
        549–550
unstated beliefs, 440–445
    common law approach, 443–445, 448
    intent to assert, 445–446
    literal approach, 442–443, 445–448
    relevancy and, 440–442
witnesses, declarants distinguished, 418–420
"Heat of passion" defense, burden of persuasion,
    716–717
Hostile witnesses, direct examination of, 94–95

Hostile work environment cases, past sexual behavior
    evidence, 310–311
Hypothetical questions, 515, 660–662

I

Identification, hearsay exemption for prior statements
    of, 464–469
    Constitutional concerns, 466–467
    FRE 801, 459
        interpretation and illustration, 464–467
    general rule, 459
    made after perceiving person, 464–465
    person, identification of, 465
    preliminary fact-finding, 464–465
    rationale, 465–466
Identification of exhibits. *See* Authentication
Impeachment of witnesses, 351–411
    bias, by, 399–403
        character evidence distinguished, 400–401
        extrinsic evidence, 399–400
        relevancy, 399
        Wigmore on, 399
    bolstering credibility, 356–357
    character evidence, by, 357–386
        bias distinguished, 400–401
        clarifying amendment, 362–363
        cross-examination, 368
        extrinsic evidence, prohibition against use, 362,
          364
        Fifth Amendment waiver, 363–364
        FRE 403 balancing test, applicability, 366
        FRE 608, 358
        FRE 609, 372–373
        good faith requirement, 367
        judicial discretion, 366–367
        limited scope of inquiry, 363, 364–366
        opinion evidence of truthfulness, 358–362
        questions about arrests, charges, and findings,
          365–366
        reputation evidence of truthfulness, 358–362
        specific instances of conduct, 362–369
        truthfulness, showing good character for, 367–368
        untruthfulness, meaning of, 364–365
    contradiction, by, 364–365, 405–409
        extrinsic evidence, 406
        "no extrinsic evidence to impeach on a collateral
          matter" doctrine, 407–408
        relevancy, 405–406
        Wigmore on, 406
    conviction of crime, by, 372–386
        balancing tests, 373–375
        criminal defendants, reverse balancing test for,
          374–375, 378
        dishonesty or false statement convictions,
          automatic admissibility, 375–378
        extrinsic evidence, 380–381
        factual details of conviction, 375, 381
        hearsay evidence, 381–382
        misdemeanor convictions, by, 546
        other witnesses, 375
        practical considerations, 382–384
        prejudice, 380
        probative value, 374

        rationale, 379–380
        unfair prejudice, 374
    extrinsic evidence, 355–356
        bias, by, 399–400
        contradiction, by, 406
        conviction of crime, by, 380–381
        mental or sensory incapacity, by, 404
        prior statements of witness, by, 388–390
    impeachment evidence
        substantive evidence distinguished, 353–355
        types of, 353
    inconsistent statements, 410
    inferential process, 351–355
        testimonial inferences, 351–353
    learned treatises, by, 393–394
    mental or sensory incapacity, by, 403–405
        bar to testimony, 404
        extrinsic evidence, 404
        relevancy, 403–404
    misdemeanor convictions, by, 546
    "no extrinsic evidence to impeach on a collateral
        matter" doctrine
        directly relevant evidence, 407
        evidence impeaching apart from contradiction,
          407–408
        logically undermining witness's story, 408
        test for "collateralness," 408
        what is not collateral, 407
    perjury and, 410
    prior statements of witness, by, 386–398
        collateral matters, inconsistent statements about,
          391–392
        consistent statements in other contexts, 395–396
        elaboration, 388–393
        examination of witnesses, 387–388
        experts, statements in treatises, 393–394
        extrinsic evidence, 388–390, 396
        FRE 613, 387
        interpretation and illustration, 387–388
        loss of memory and inconsistency, 391
        prior consistent statements, 394–396
        probative value, 390–392
        putting inconsistent statements in context, 395
        rehabilitation, admissibility for, 394–396
        risk of improper substantive use, 390–391
        truth, admissibility for, 394
    reflection on, 410–411
    truthfulness defined, 357
Inconsistent statements, impeachment of witnesses,
    410
In-court demonstrations and experiments,
    authentication by, 185
Inferences
    impeachment of witnesses, testimonial inferences,
        351–353
    privileges, drawing adverse inferences from, 796
    probative value, strength of underlying inferences,
        135–136
    subsequent remedial measures, inference of
        negligence or culpability, 322
Insanity defense, 800
Instructions to jury. *See* Jury instructions
Insurance, inadmissibility to prove negligence. *See*
    Liability insurance, inadmissibility to prove
    negligence

Intent
  hearsay, intent test. *See* Hearsay
  specific acts evidence, problems in proving,
    245–247
    exclusion, argument for, 246
    Old Chief case, 246–247
    where intent not disputed, 245–247
Interest, statements against. *See* Statements against
    interest, hearsay exception
Intoxication
  habit evidence, 262
  lay opinion, 612
Investigative reports, hearsay exception, 537–538
Irrebuttable presumptions, 745–746

J

JNOV, 83, 87–88
Journalist's privilege, 886–888
Judges
  background knowledge, judicial notice of, 777
  role of, 79
Judgments notwithstanding the verdict (JNOV), 83,
    87–88
Judgments of previous convictions, hearsay exception,
    545–546
  FRE 803, 545
    interpretation and illustration, 545–546
  general rule, 545
  impeachment by misdemeanor convictions, 546
  preliminary fact-finding, 545–546
  rationale, 546
Judicial discretion
  abuse of discretion, 149–151
  hearsay, proposal regarding, 604–605
  lay opinion, 618–620
  probative value
    appellate review, 149–160
    reflection on, 160–161
Judicial fact-finding, 213–217
  admissibility, 214–215
  burden of persuasion, 215–216
  FRE 104, 214
    interpretation and illustration, 214–216
  general rule, 214
  habit evidence, 260
  process of decision, 216
  standard of proof, 215–216
Judicial notice, 765–785
  adjudicative facts
    defined, 766–767
    types of facts subject to judicial notice, 766
  appropriate bounds of, specifying, 780–785
  background knowledge, use, 780–785
    judge, knowledge of, 777
    jury, knowledge of, 776–777
  civil cases
    mini-directed verdicts, 771
    verdicts, to preserve, 772
  common knowledge, cognizance of without
    judicial notice, 776–777
    judge, general background knowledge of, 777
    jury, general background knowledge of, 776–777
  criminal cases
    binding notice, 774

  judicial comments, 771–772
  verdicts, to preserve, 772–773
  decisionmaking, as part of, 776–780
  FRE 201, 765–766
    elaboration, 768–770
    interpretation and illustration, 766–767,
      770–774
    scope, 766–767
  general rule, 765–766
  judicial comments, 771–772
  legislative facts, cognizance, 778–779
  mini-directed verdicts, 771
  sources of information, 769–770
  standards, 768–769
  state of knowledge required, 767
  substantive law, cognizance, 780
  Thirtyacre case, 768–769
  timing, 772–773
  Tresnak case, 780–782
Judicial summary and comment on evidence,
    737–744
  accuracy, 740–741
  advantages, 737–739
  burden of persuasion, relationship with, 742–743
  criteria for evaluating, 739–740
  disadvantages, 737–739
  proposed Rule, 737
  standardized comments, 741–742
Juries
  background knowledge, judicial notice, 776–777
  deliberations, 86–87
  instructions. *See* Jury instructions
  natural reasoning and behavior of fact finders,
    113–115
  past recollections recorded, reading to jury, 519
  peremptory challenges, 81
  probative value and danger of misleading jury,
    139–140
  role of, 78–79
  selection, 80–81
  venire, 80
  voir dire, 80–81
Jury instructions
  burden of persuasion, 85–86
  child molestation evidence, limiting instructions,
    299
  preliminary jury instructions, 81
  reasonable doubt, proof beyond, 715–716
  sample case, 3–5, 61–65, 75
  sexual assault evidence, limiting instructions, 299
  specific acts evidence, limiting instructions,
    256–257

K

Knowledge
  business records exception, personal knowledge
    requirement, 526
  competency of witnesses, personal knowledge
    requirement, 171
  cross-examination
    character witnesses, likely knowledge of specific
      act, 287
    hearsay exemptions, personal knowledge
      requirement, 459

excited utterances exception, proof of personal
    knowledge, 500
hearsay, firsthand knowledge rule, 423–424
judges, judicial notice of background knowledge
    of, 777
juries, judicial notice of background knowledge of,
    776–777
lay opinion not based on scientific, technical or
    other specialized knowledge, 617–618
party admissions exemption, personal knowledge
    requirement
    agents, servants and employees, 481–482
    party's own statement, 472
past recollections recorded exception
    correct reflection of witness's knowledge, 519
    personal knowledge, statement made with,
        518–519
personal or family history exception, personal
    knowledge requirement, 566
present sense impressions exception, proof of
    personal knowledge, 500
probability of fact of consequence determined from
    knowledge and experience, 121–122
statements against interest exception, ascertaining
    declarant's knowledge, 562

L

Law enforcement personnel
    investigative tools, expert witnesses, 692–695
    public records and reports exception, 539–541
        Oates case, 539
        prosecutorial function, 539–540
        relationship with other exceptions, 540–541
        routine and regular activities, 540
Lay opinion, 611–624
    fact vs. opinion, 612–613
    FRE 701, 611
        elaboration, 618–620
        interpretation and illustration, 611–618
        general rule, 611
    hearsay, 423–424
    helpful to clear understanding of testimony or
        determination of fact in issue, 614–616
    intoxication, 612
    judicial discretion, 618–620
    not based on scientific, technical or other
        specialized knowledge, 617–618
    party admissions
        agents, servants and employees, 481–482
        party's own statement, 472
    rationally based on perception of witness, 613–614
Leading questions, 95–97
    defined, 95–97
    FRE 611
        elaboration, 95–97
        interpretation and illustration, 95
    tactical considerations, 97
Learned treatises
    expert witnesses using, 664
    hearsay, 493
    impeachment or rehabilitation of witnesses by,
        393–394
Liability
    offers of compromise, admissibility. See

Compromise, admissibility of offers
    payment of medical expenses, admissibility. See
        Medical expenses, admissibility of payment
    subsequent remedial measures, admissibility. See
        Subsequent remedial measures, admissibility
Liability insurance, inadmissibility to prove
    negligence, 337–338
    exclusionary mandate, 337, 341–342
    FRE 411, 337
        interpretation and illustration, 337–338
    general rule, 337
    permissible uses of evidence, 337–338
    reflections on, 342–343
Libel actions
    best evidence rule, 204
    character as essential element of claim or defense,
        293–294
Limited admissibility. See Jury instructions

M

Mandatory rebuttable presumptions. See
    Presumptions
Manslaughter, burden of persuasion, 719
Marital privileges, 842–855
    communications privilege, 842–847
        exceptions, 845–846
        rationale, 842–843
    testimonial privilege, 847–854
        exceptions, 854
    valid marriage requirement, 843–844
Materiality. See Relevancy
McCormick, Charles
    curative admissibility doctrine, 349
    "fighting fire with fire" doctrine, 349
Medical diagnosis or treatment, hearsay exception for
        statements made for, 512–517
    diagnostic evaluations for litigation, 515
    FRE 803, 512
        elaboration, 515–516
        interpretation and illustration, 512–515
    general rule, 512
    patients' statements as basis of expert opinion,
        515–516
    pertinence requirement, 513–514
    preliminary fact-finding, 512–513
    proof of medical purpose, 514–515
    rationale, 513
Medical expenses, admissibility of payment, 335–337
    admissibility of statements made in conjunction
        with, 336
    exclusionary mandate, 335–336, 341–342
    FRE 409, 335
        interpretation and illustration, 335–337
    general rule, 335
    permissible uses of evidence, 336
    reflections on, 342–343
    "similar" expenses, what constitutes, 336–337
Mental incapacity, impeachment of witnesses by,
        403–405
    bar to testimony, 404
    extrinsic evidence, 404
    relevancy, 403–404
Mini-directed verdicts, judicial notice, 771
Misleading jury, probative value, 139–140

Model Rules of Professional Conduct, attorney-client privilege under, 805–806, 807–808
Molestation evidence. *See* Child molestation evidence
Motions
dismissal motions, 83
sample case, 37–38
in limine, 80
post-trial motions, 87–88
pretrial motions, 80
Motive, specific acts evidence used to prove, 238
Multiple hearsay
business records exception, 531–532
sources of information with no business duty, 531–532
use of multiple exemptions and exceptions, 532
past recollections recorded exception, 521
public records and reports exception, 541–543
administrative findings, 542–543
admissibility of otherwise inadmissible sources, 542

N

Natural reasoning
adversary system, 107–117
behavior of fact finders, 113–115
trials, 110–113
Negligence
liability insurance, inadmissibility to prove. *See* Liability insurance, inadmissibility to prove negligence
offers of compromise, admissibility. *See* Compromise, admissibility of offers
payment of medical expenses, admissibility. *See* Medical expenses, admissibility of payment
subsequent remedial measures, admissibility. *See* Subsequent remedial measures, admissibility
Negotiations, privilege for communications made in, 884–886
New trials, 88
No contest pleas, admissibility of withdrawal. *See* Withdrawn pleas, admissibility
Nonassertive conduct. *See* Hearsay
Nonhearsay statements. *See* Hearsay
Nonverbal conduct. *See* Hearsay
Notice
judicial notice. *See* Judicial notice
past sexual behavior evidence, notice requirement, 312
residual hearsay exception, 579

O

Objections, 97–107
admissibility of answer, 99–101
"cheat sheet," 115–117
former testimony, admissibility, 557
FRE 103, 98
elaboration, 99–104
interpretation and illustration, 98–99
general rule, 98
improper form of question, 99–101
stating, 103–104
tactical considerations, 104
timing, 101–103

types of, 99–101
Offers of compromise, admissibility. *See* Compromise, admissibility of offers
Offers of proof, 98–99
Opening statements
sample case, 5–7, 39–40
Opinion testimony. *See also* Expert witnesses; Lay opinion
basis of testimony, 662–670
general rule, 662
otherwise inadmissible evidence, 664–668
Opportunity, specific acts evidence used to prove, 238
Other crimes. *See* Specific acts evidence
Out-of-court statements, testimony about, 423

P

Parent-child privilege, 882–884
Party admissions, hearsay exemption, 469–488
adoptive admissions, 476–478
preliminary fact-finding, 476–477
rationale, 477
silence, by, 477–478
agents, servants and employees, 478–482
attorneys, 479
government employees, 482
lay opinion, 481–482
matter within scope of agent's employment, statement regarding, 479–480
personal knowledge, 481–482
preliminary fact-finding, 478–480
rationale, 480–481
specially authorized statements, 479
Bruton case, 475–476
co-conspirators, 482–487
additional evidence requirement, 486
Bourjaily case, 485
during course of conspiracy, 483–484
in furtherance of conspiracy, 484
preliminary fact-finding, 482–484
process for admission, 486–487
proof of co-membership, 483
rationale, 484
FRE 801, 470
adoptive admissions, 476–478
agents, servants and employees, 478–482
co-conspirators, 482–484, 485–487
elaboration, 472–476
party's own statement, 470–472
general rule, 470
multiparty cases, 475–476
party's own statement, 470–472
individual capacity, 471–472
lay opinion, 472
personal knowledge, 472
preliminary fact-finding, 470–471
representative capacity, 471–472
preliminary fact-finding
adoptive admissions, 476–477
agents, servants and employees, 478–480
coconspirators, 482–484
identity of declarant, 474–475
party's own statement, 470–471
rationale, 472–474

fairness, 473–474
  Fifth Amendment concerns, 473
  moral responsibility for own statements, 473–474
  opportunity to explain, 473
  statements against interest distinguished, 562
Past recollections recorded, hearsay exception, 517–524
  contents of statement, 517–518
  correct reflection of witness's knowledge, 519
  failed memory requirement, 518
  FRE 803, 517
    elaboration, 520–523
    interpretation and illustration, 517–520
  fresh memory, statement made with, 518–519
  general rule, 517
  multiple declarants, created by, 520
  multiple hearsay, 521
  personal knowledge, statement made with, 518–519
  preliminary fact-finding, 517–519
  present recollections refreshed, 521–523
    FRE 612, 521–523
  rationale, 519–520
  record read to jury, 519
Past sexual behavior evidence, 306–320
  applicability in other contexts, 310
  Chambers case, 313–314, 316
  Confrontation Clause, 313–316
  cross-examination right, 313–316
  Davis case, 314–315, 316
  defendant's right to testify, 317
  discovery, 317–318
  FRE 412, 307
    elaboration, 312–318
    interpretation and illustration, 307–312
    scope, 309–312
  general rule, 307
  hostile work environment cases, 310–311
  notice requirement, 312
  Olden case, 315–316
  "other sexual behavior"
    approaches to exclusion, 316–317
    civil cases, admissibility in, 311
    construed, 309
    criminal cases, admissibility in, 311–312
  particular occasion, behavior on, 309
  presentation of evidence right, 313–316
  rape shield laws, 316–317
  rationale for exclusion, 312–313
  relevancy, 308
  "sexual predisposition"
    approaches to exclusion, 316–317
    civil cases, admissibility in, 311
    construed, 309
    criminal cases, admissibility in, 311–312
  underlying propensity theory, 308–309
Payment of medical expenses, admissibility. See Medical expenses, admissibility of payment
Peer review privilege, 889–890
Peremptory challenges, 81
Perjury and impeachment of witnesses, 410
Permissive presumptions, 752
Personal knowledge. See Knowledge
Personal or family history, hearsay exception for statements of, 565–569

FRE 804, 565–566
  general rule, 565–566
  personal history, 566
  personal knowledge, 566
  preliminary fact-finding, 566
  rationale, 566–567
  relations and intimate associates, statements of, 566
Photographs, probative value, 144–145, 154, 159
Physician-patient privilege, 856–857
Plan, specific acts evidence used to prove, 238
Pleas, admissibility of withdrawal. See Withdrawn pleas, admissibility
Post-evidence matters, 84–85
Post-trial motions, 87–88
Prejudice. See Bias and prejudice
Preliminary fact-finding
  business records, 525–528
  child molestation evidence, 298
  dying declarations, 559–560
  excited utterances, 495
    categorical approach, 499–500
  "forfeiture by wrongdoing," 570–571
  former testimony, 551
  identification, prior statements of, 464–465
  judgments of previous convictions, 545–546
  medical diagnosis or treatment, statements made for, 512–513
  party admissions
    adoptive admissions, 476–477
    agents, servants and employees, 478–480
    co-conspirators, 482–484
    identity of declarant, 474–475
    party's own statement, 470–471
  personal or family history, statements of, 566
  present sense impressions, 494
    categorical approach, 499–500
  prior consistent statements, 461–463
  prior inconsistent statements, 459–461
  public records and reports, 536–538
  residual hearsay exception, 575–576
  sexual assault evidence, 298
  specific acts, 239–240
  statements against interest, 561–562
  state-of-mind declarations, 502–503
  unavailability of declarant, 548–549
Preliminary jury instructions, 81
Preparation, specific acts evidence used to prove, 238
Preponderance of evidence standard, 698, 704–706, 707, 711
Presentation of evidence
  order of presentation, 82–83
  past sexual behavior evidence and Constitutional right to, 313–316
Present recollections refreshed, 521–523
  FRE 612, 521–523
Present sense impressions, hearsay exception, 493–494
  categorical approach, 496–500
    categories determining admissibility, 496–497
    judicial interpretation, 497–499
    preliminary fact-finding, 499–500
    proof of personal knowledge, 500
  FRE 803, 493
    elaboration, 496–500

interpretation and illustration, 493–494
general rule, 493
preliminary fact-finding, 494
    categorical approach, 499–500
rationale, 494
Preservation of error for appellate review. *See*
        Appellate review, preservation of error for
Presidential communications privilege, 894–896
Presumptions, 744–764
    burden of persuasion, 745
    complexity, 752–757
    conclusive presumptions, 745–746
    criminal cases, 759–762
    defined, 744
    FRE 301, 757
        "not otherwise provided for by act of Congress"
            exception, 757–758
        other means of allocating burdens of
            production and persuasion, relationship
            with, 758–759
    irrebuttable presumptions, 745–746
    mandatory rebuttable presumptions, 746–752
        decisionmaking, 750–751
        mandatory persuasion burden presumptions,
            748–750
        mandatory production burden presumptions,
            747–748
    permissive presumptions, 752
    "weak" presumptions, 752
    Winship rule, 759–762
Pretrial motions, 80
Prior arrests, examination of character witnesses
        regarding, 288
Prior consistent statements, hearsay exemption,
        461–464
    FRE 801, 459
        statements outside scope of, 464
    general rule, 459
    improper influence or motive, charge of, 462
        rebutting, 462–463
    preliminary fact-finding, 461–463
    rationale, 463
    recent fabrication, charge of, 462
        rebutting, 462–463
Prior identification. *See* Identification, hearsay
        exemption for prior statements of
Prior inconsistent statements, hearsay exemption,
        459–461
    evasion, inconsistency due to, 460
    FRE 801, 459
        interpretation and illustration, 459–461
        statements outside scope of, 461
    general rule, 459
    inconsistency, 459–460
    under oath or at proceeding, 460–461
    preliminary fact-finding, 459–461
    rationale, 461
Prior statements, impeachment of witnesses by. *See*
        Impeachment of witnesses
Privileges, 787–901
    academic researcher's privilege, 888–889
    attorney-client privilege. *See* Attorney-client
        privilege
    clergy-communicant privilege. *See* Clergy-
        communicant privilege

Confrontation Clause, 797
current status of law, 789–792
deliberative process privilege, 896–899
drawing adverse inferences from, 796
exceptions, 796
executive privilege, 892–899
FRE 501, 790
general rule, 790
general structure, 792–797
government informant's privilege, 886
government privileges, 892–899
historical background, 789–792
holders, 792
invocation, 792–794
journalist's privilege, 886–888
limitations, 794–795
    Constitutional limitations, 797
marital privileges. *See* Marital privileges
outside sources of information, protecting,
        886–889
parent-child privilege, 882–884
peer review privilege, 889–890
physician-patient privilege, 856–857
Presidential communications privilege, 894–896
professional-client privileges, 881–882
psychotherapist-patient privilege. *See*
        Psychotherapist-patient privilege
scope, 794–795
self-evaluation privilege, 890–892
settlement negotiations, communications made in,
        884–886
state secrets privilege, 892–894
unique operation of privilege rules, 788–789
waiver, 795–796
White House counsel, 794
Probative value, 133–161
    authentication of exhibits
        demonstrative evidence, 184–185
        recordings, 189
    balancing test, 133–144
    Bayes' Theorem, 161–164
    certainty of starting point, 136
    child molestation evidence, 297, 299–302
    confusion of issues, danger of, 139
    cumulative evidence, danger of, 140–141
    defined, 135
    demonstrative evidence, 144–145
    expert witnesses, 630–631
    "forfeiture by wrongdoing," 572–573
    FRE 403, 134
        dangers of, 137–141
        elaboration, 149–160
        interpretation and illustration, 134–149
    general rule, 134
    Hitt case, 151–154
    impeachment of witnesses
        specific instances of conduct, 366
    judicial discretion
        appellate review, 149–160
        reflection on, 160–161
    misleading jury, danger of, 139–140
    need, 136–137
    offers of compromise, 330–331
    Old Chief case, 154–158
    photographs, 144–145, 154, 159

prior felonies, 158
probability, 161–166
sexual assault evidence, 297, 299–302
similar happenings evidence, 269
"smoking guns," 146–147
spoliation of evidence, 145–146
statistics, 161–166
strength of underlying inferences, 135–136
subsequent remedial measures, 327
substantially outweighed by dangers of FRE 403, 141–144
  defined, 141–142
  limiting instructions, effect of, 142–144
  undue delay, danger of, 140–141
  unfair prejudice, danger of, 138–139
  victims' statements, 145
  waste of time, danger of, 140–141
Products liability actions, subsequent remedial measures in, 322–324
Professional-client privileges, 881–882
Propensity evidence
  defined, 228, 251
  past sexual behavior evidence, underlying propensity theory, 308–309
  reflection on, 251–257
Psychological sciences, expert witnesses, 689–690
Psychotherapist-patient privilege, 857–875
  exceptions, 871–874
    compelled disclosures, 872–873
    Constitutional limitations on, 871–872
    crime-fraud exception, 873–874
    dangerous patients, 873
  holders, 869–870
  Jaffee case, 857–869
  nature of communications, 870
  scope, 869–871
  waiver, 870–871
Public records and reports, hearsay exception, 535–543
  activities of office or agency, 536
  duty imposed by law, matters observed and recorded pursuant to, 536–537
  FRE 803, 535
    elaboration, 539–543
    interpretation and illustration, 535–538
  general rule, 535
  investigative reports, 537–538
  law enforcement personnel, 539–541
    Oates case, 539
    prosecutorial function, 539–540
    relationship with other exceptions, 540–541
    routine and regular activities, 540
  multiple hearsay, 541–543
    administrative findings, 542–543
    admissibility of otherwise inadmissible sources, 542
  preliminary fact-finding, 536–538
  rationale, 538
  untrustworthiness, exclusion for, 538

Q

Qualification as expert witnesses, 629–630

R

Rape
  rape shield laws, 316–317. *See also* Past sexual behavior evidence
  sexual assault evidence, 301–302
Real evidence, authentication, 179–184
Reasonable doubt standard. *See* Burden of persuasion
Rebuttal examination, sample case, 58–60
Reconstructions of events, authentication of exhibits by, 185–186
Recordings, authentication of. *See* Authentication
Recross-examination
  FRE 611, 91
  sample case, 30–31
Redirect examination
  FRE 611, 91
  sample case, 19–20, 29–30, 50, 57–58
Reenactments, authentication of exhibits by, 185–186
Refreshing memory, 521–523
  FRE 612, 521–523
Rehabilitation of witnesses. *See* Impeachment of witnesses
Relevancy, 117–133
  background information, 126
  chain of reasoning, 128
  character evidence, 227–229
    exceptions to prohibition on use of to prove conduct on particular occasion, 276
  circumstantial vs. direct evidence, 124–126
  conditional relevancy. *See* Conditional relevancy
  defined, 118
  direct vs. circumstantial evidence, 124–126
  FRE 401, 118
    elaboration, 127–132
    interpretation and illustration, 118–126
  FRE 402, 118
    elaboration, 127–132
    interpretation and illustration, 118–126
  general rule, 118
  hearsay, 415, 417–418
  impeachment of witnesses
    bias, by, 399
    contradiction, by, 405–406
    mental or sensory incapacity, by, 403–404
  materiality, 119–121
  nonverbal conduct, 432–433
  offer for proof of fact of consequence, 119–121
  past sexual behavior evidence, 308
  probability of fact of consequence, 121–124
    "any tendency" standard, 123–124
    knowledge and experience, determined from, 121–122
    reasonable generalizations, 122–123
  reflections on
    concept of relevancy, 161–166
    requirement of relevancy, 132–133
  specific relevant acts with no character inference, admissibility. *See* Specific acts evidence
  sufficiency distinguished, 126
  unstated beliefs, 440–442
  Wigmore on, 117, 128–129
Remedial measures, admissibility. *See* Subsequent remedial measures, admissibility
Reputation evidence

impeachment of witness and reputation evidence
  of truthfulness, 358–362
opinion evidence distinguished, 284–285
probative value, 283–284
Res gestae, 244–245
Residual hearsay exception, 574–582
  circumstantial guarantees of trustworthiness,
    576–577
  equivalency, 577
  FRE 807, 574–575
    elaboration, 579–580
    interpretation and illustration, 575–579
  general rule, 574–575
  how much hearsay admitted, 579–580
  independent corroboration, 577
  material fact, offered to prove, 578
  more probative than other available evidence,
    578
  "near miss," 577–578
  notice, 579
  preliminary fact-finding, 575–576
  serving general purposes of justice, 579
  testimonial qualities, reliability, 576–577
Rights-based theories, attorney-client privilege,
  835–836
Routine practice evidence, 257–266
  FRE 406, 257
    elaboration, 260–264
    interpretation and illustration, 257–260
  general rule, 257
  importance, 258
  methods of proving, 258–259
  organizational behavior, 262–264
  rationale, 260–261
Rules of Evidence. *See also* specific topic concerned
  rationale, 109–110

S

Scientific evidence and expert witnesses, 678–696
  adversary model, 658
  behavioral sciences, 689–690
  Daubert case, 633–646, 654–660
  deference model, 658
  DNA profiling, 678–689
  Frye case, 631–633
  Kumho Tire case, 646–650
  law enforcement investigative tools, 692–695
  normal educational approach, 657–658
  psychological sciences, 689–690
  toxic tort causation, 690–692
Self-authentication, 195–198
  FRE 902, 195–196
    interpretation and illustration, 197–198
    general rule, 195–196
Self-evaluation privilege, 890–892
Self-incrimination and party admissions, 473
Sensory incapacity, impeachment of witnesses by,
  403–405
  bar to testimony, 404
  extrinsic evidence, 404
  relevancy, 403–404
Servants, hearsay exemption for. *See* Party admissions,
  hearsay exemption
Settlements

negotiations, privilege for communications made
  in, 884–886
offers of compromise admissibility. *See*
  Compromise, admissibility of offers
Sex offenses
  child molestation evidence. *See* Child molestation
    evidence
  past sexual behavior evidence. *See* Past sexual
    behavior evidence
  sexual assault evidence. *See* Sexual assault
    evidence
Sexual assault evidence, 295–306
  acquaintance rape, 301–302
  character evidence, 296–297, 299–302
  closing arguments, 299
  federal litigation, significance to, 304–305
  FRE 403 balancing test, applicability, 297, 299–
    302
  FRE 413 to 415, 296
    elaboration, 299–305
    interpretation and illustration, 296–299
  general rules, 296
  limiting instructions, 299
  "offense of sexual assault" construed, 298
  other Federal Rules of Evidence, 297–298
  preliminary fact-finding, 298
  probative value, 302–304
  rationale, 302–304
  recidivism, 302–303
  sexual harassment, 301–302
  stranger rape, 301–302
  unfair prejudice, 302
  "without consent" construed, 298–299
Signatures, 191
Similar happenings evidence, 266–273
  approach to admissibility, 268–269
  character distinguished, 267–268
  characteristics of objects, 266–267
  FRE 403 balancing test, applicability, 269
  habit distinguished, 267–268
  institutional policy or practice use of to prove, 270
  lack of Federal Rules governing, 267
  nonhappenings, evidence of, 270
  organizational liability, 266
  organizational propensity, 266
Simulations, authentication of exhibits by, 185–186
Slander actions
  best evidence rule, 204
  character as essential element of claim or defense,
    293–294
Specific acts evidence, 227–320
  approaches to admissibility, 254–256
  character. prohibition on use of to prove, 283
  child molestation evidence. *See* Child molestation
    evidence
  closing arguments, 256–257
  cross-examination of character witnesses. *See*
    Cross-examination
  defined, 228–229
  distinction between prohibited and permissible
    evidence, 251–254
  exceptions to prohibition to prove conduct on
    particular occasion, 234
  FRE 404, 230, 236
    prohibition on use of to prove conduct on

particular occasion, 230–235
relevant acts with no character inference.
    admissibility, 236–250
FRE 405, 230
general rule, 230
habit evidence. *See* Habit evidence
limiting instructions, 256–257
motive, to prove, 238
opportunity, to prove, 238
past sexual behavior evidence. *See* Past sexual
    behavior evidence
plan, to prove, 238
preparation, to prove, 238
prohibition on use of to prove conduct on
    particular occasion, 230–236
    diversion from main issues, 233
    general rule, 230
    low probative value, 233
    prejudice, 233–234
    rationale, 232–234
    weakness of propensity inference, 232–233
reflection on, 251–257
relevant acts with no character inference,
    admissibility, 236–251
    anticoincidence theory, 247–249
    exclusion, argument for, 246
    general rule, 236
    identity, evidence showing, 239
    intent, problems in proving, 245–247
    modus operandi and character inference,
        249–250
    narrative of proponent's case, evidence
        completing, 238
    Old Chief case, 246–247
    permissible uses, 237–239
    prejudice, 240–241
    preliminary fact-finding, 239–240
    probative value, 240–241
    relevant states of mind, evidence showing,
        238–239
    res gestae problem, 244–245
    where intent not disputed, 245–247
routine practice evidence. *See* Routine practice
    evidence
sexual assault evidence. *See* Sexual assault
    evidence
similar happenings evidence. *See* Similar
    happenings evidence
Spoliation of evidence, 145–146
Spousal privileges. *See* Marital privileges
Statements against interest, hearsay exception,
    561–565
ascertaining declarant's knowledge, 562
content against interest, 561–562
corroboration requirement, 563–565
    statements inculpating accomplices, 565
FRE 804, 561
    elaboration, 563–565
    interpretation and illustration, 561–562
general rule, 561
mixed motive statements, 563
party admission distinguished, 562
preliminary fact-finding, 561–562
rationale, 562
    doubts regarding, 563

statements inculpating accomplices, 564–565
    corroboration requirement, 565
statements made with no motive to lie, 563
State-of-mind declarations, hearsay exception,
    502–512
circumstantial statements, 504–505
direct statements, 504–505
evidence used to prove facts, 506–507
FRE 803, 502
    elaboration, 505–509
    interpretation and illustration, 502–505
future conduct, 506, 508
future state of mind, 505–506
general rule, 502
Hillmon case, 507–509
past state of mind, 505–506
preliminary fact-finding, 502–503
rationale, 503–504
State secrets privilege, 892–894
Statistics, probative value, 161–166
Stereotypes, 123
Stipulations, 158–159
Subsequent remedial measures, admissibility,
    322–329
activities deemed to be, 324
discouraging desirable conduct, policy against,
    327–328
effectiveness of, 324
exclusionary mandate, 322–325, 341–342
FRE 403 balancing test, applicability, 327
FRE 407, 322
    elaboration, 327–328
    interpretation and illustration, 322–326
general rule, 322
"if controverted" requirement, 326
inference of negligence or culpability, 322
low probative value, 327
permissible uses of evidence, 325–326
prior to plaintiff's injury, 325
products liability actions, 322–324
punishing desirable conduct, policy against, 328
rationale for general rule of exclusion, 327–328
reflections on, 342–343
third persons, by, 328, 340–341
timing, 324–325
Substantive rules of law. *See* Presumptions
Sufficiency
authentication of exhibits, 175–177
relevancy distinguished, 126
Summaries, best evidence rule, 199–200, 207–208
analytic summaries, 207–208
illustrative aids, 207
voluminous documents underlying summaries,
    207
Summary expert witnesses, 631
Summing up and comment by judge. *See* Judicial
    summary and comment on evidence
Syndrome evidence, expert witnesses, 689–690

T

Testimonial privilege. *See* Marital privileges
Testimony. *See specific topic concerned*
Toxic tort causation, expert witnesses, 690–692
Transcript of sample case, 2–75

Translations, expert witnesses, 654
Treatises
    expert witnesses, 664
    hearsay, 493
    impeachment or rehabilitation of witnesses by,
        393–394
Trials
    bench trials, 79
    bifurcated trials, 81
    burden of persuasion, 85–86
    burden of production, 83–84
    closing arguments, 85
    jury deliberations, 86–87
    jury instructions, 85–86
    jury selection, 80–81
    natural reasoning, 110–113
    new trials, 88
    opening statements, 81–82
    post-evidence matters, 84–85
    post-trial motions, 87–88
    preliminary jury instructions, 81
    presentation of evidence, 82–84
        order of presentation, 82–83
    pretrial motions, 80
    roles of trial participants, 78–79
    sample transcript, 2–75
    structure, 80–88
    trifurcated trials, 81
    verdicts, 86–87
Trifurcated trials, 81

                            U

Ultimate issue, expert opinion on, 670–675
    FRE 704, 670
        interpretation and illustration, 670–673
    general rule, 670
Unavailability of declarant. See Hearsay
Underlying propensity theory and past sexual
        behavior evidence, 308–309
Undue delay and probative value, 140–141
Unstated beliefs. See Hearsay
Untrustworthiness
    business records, exclusion, 529–530
        burden of persuasion, 529
        circumstances indicating, 529–530
    public records and reports, exclusion of, 538

                            V

Verdicts
    directed verdicts, 83
    judgments notwithstanding the verdict, 83,
        87–88
    judicial notice to preserve
        civil cases, 772
        criminal cases, 772–773
Victims' statements, probative value, 145

Violent Crime Control and Enforcement Act of
        1994, 295
Voir dire, 80–81

                            W

Waiver
    of attorney-client privilege, 802, 818–819
    of Fifth Amendment rights for impeachment of
        witnesses by character evidence, 363–364
    of privileges, 795–796
    of psychotherapist-patient privilege, 870–871
    of withdrawn pleas, admissibility under FRE 410,
        346
Waste of time, probative value, 140–141
"Weak" presumptions, 752
White House counsel privilege, 794
Wigmore, John Henry
    attorney-client privilege, 834–835
    impeachment of witnesses
        bias, by, 399
        contradiction, by, 406
    relevancy, 117, 128–129
Winship rule
    burden of persuasion in criminal cases, 713–716
        application in other contexts, 731–735
    presumptions, 759–762
Withdrawn pleas, admissibility, 343–348
    FRE 410, 343
        exceptions, 346
        interpretation and illustration, 343–346
        scope, 345–346
        waiver, 346
    general rule, 343
    guilty pleas, 343–344
    no contest pleas, 344
    nolo contendere pleas, 344
    statements made in conjunction with pleas, 344–
        345
Witnesses
    adverse witnesses. See Adverse witnesses
    character. See Character evidence
    competency. See Competency of witnesses
    confrontation of witnesses. See Confrontation
        Clause
    cross-examination. See Cross-examination
    examination. See Examination of witnesses
    expert. See Expert witnesses
    hearsay. See Hearsay
    hostile witnesses. See Hostile witnesses
    impeachment. See Impeachment of witnesses
    lay opinion. See Lay opinion
    rehabilitation of. See Impeachment of witnesses
Work product doctrine, 804–807, 818, 826–840
Writings
    authentication. See Authentication
    best evidence rule. See Best evidence rule
    signatures, 191